ENERGY TECHNOLOGY XV

"Repowering America"

Proceedings of the

Energy Technology Conference
February 17-19, 1988
Washington, D.C.

PUBLISHER'S NOTE

Government Institutes is indebted to many individuals and organizations for the preparation and publication of this most timely contribution to the field of energy technology. We would like to express our gratitude to all the authors who contributed to these proceedings and made the extra effort to meet our December deadline. Our appreciation for their efforts will be shared by the thousands who will read and use the information contained in these proceedings.

The views and opinions of the authors expressed herein do not necessarily state or reflect those of Government Institutes, Inc.

February 1988

966 Hungerford Drive, #24, Rockville, Maryland 20850
United States of America

Library of Congress Catalog Card Number 80-66431
ISBN: 0-86587-428-X
ISSN: 0161-6048

Printed and bound in the United States of America

PROGRAM ADVISORY COMMITTEE
for the
1988 ENERGY TECHNOLOGY CONFERENCE

Louis Abernethy
IBM, Real Estate &
Construction Division

W. Bradford Ashton
Battelle Memorial Institute
Pacific Northwest
Laboratories

Phil D. Baumann
TU Electric

Millard Carr
U.S. Department of
Defense

Peyton Collie
National Rural Electric
Cooperative Association

Keith Davidson
American Cogeneration
Association

Bill Elder
Tennessee Valley Authority

Leonard W. Fish
American Gas Association

Martin Gutstein
Industrial Fuel Cell
Association

William C. Hall, Jr.
Dominion Energy, Inc.
Dominion Resources, Inc.

Nicholas Hanks
Washington Gas Light
Company

Richard F. Hill
Great Oaks Research
Corporation

Richard L. Hobson, Sr.
Baltimore Gas and Electric
Company

Sally Hooks
Edison Electric Institute

Dorsey Jacobs
West Virginia University

Larry M. Joseph
U.S. Department of Energy

Robert Kennel
National Wood Energy
Association

Milton Klein
Electric Power Research
Institute

Russell Mosher
American Boiler
Manufacturers Association

Joseph Mullan
National Coal Association

E. D. Neuberger
Westinghouse Electric
Corporation

Flemming L. Nielsen
Lockheed Missiles & Space
Corporation

Donald S. Parry
Architect of the Capitol

Frederick J. Pearson
Henry Adams, Inc.

Jerry Pell
Clean Coal Technology
Office, U.S. Department
of Energy

Bill Prindle
National Association
of Energy Service
Companies

J. Terry Radigan
Federal Energy Management Program, U.S.
Department of Energy

Robert Rosenberg
Gas Research Institute

Claire Sink
Office of Energy
Research, U.S.
Department of Energy

Jack E. Smith
Energy, Mines &
Resources (Canada)

James F. Strother
Institute of Electrical and Electronic
Engineers

Thomas F. P. Sullivan
Government Institutes,
Inc.

Robert I. Taylor
Turbo Systems, Inc.

Michael Tinkleman
Electric Power Research
Institute

Herbert S. Wheary
Virginia Power Company

Tyler E. Williams, Jr.
Naval Designers &
Planners

Fred Zerkel
Institute of Gas
Technology

Michael J. Zimmer
Cogeneration Coalition
of America, Inc.

TABLE OF CONTENTS

STATE OF ENERGY

COGENERATION

TABLE OF CONTENTS

TABLE OF CONTENTS

ENERGY MANAGEMENT

TABLE OF CONTENTS

TABLE OF CONTENTS

TABLE OF CONTENTS

TABLE OF CONTENTS

TABLE OF CONTENTS

STATE OF ENERGY

STATE OF ENERGY ADDRESS

BY WILLIAM W. BERRY
CHAIRMAN AND CHIEF EXECUTIVE OFFICER
DOMINION RESOURCES, INC.

The State of Energy Address by Mr. Berry will be provided at the Energy Technology Conference and Exposition.

Mr. Berry will review energy developments in 1987. Noting the strong continuing trends toward greater use of energy in the form of electricity, he will examine the problems and prospects of the U. S. electric power industry. The industry has already been greatly altered by economic, technological and regulatory changes that have made the addition of traditional types of electric generation capacity unattractive and have left the traditional system for developing new capacity in disarray. At the same time, the electric utility industry has become subject to increasing competition and pressures for competition, often on terms inconsistent with economic efficiency and reliable electric service.

The challenge for the United States is to adopt sound new policies that will provide for adequate, efficient and reliable electric service in a more competitive, market-oriented era. Meeting this challenge will require wise and constructive action by regulators and legislators at both the Federal and state levels and by electric utilities. Mr. Berry will set forth his views of the policies which can and should be adopted to foster economically efficient competition in the supply of incremental generating capacity. He will review the proposed actions of the Federal Energy Regulatory Commission to provide increased opportunities for competition and the need for follow up actions by FERC, Congress and state authorities. He will examine the impacts of competition on the structure of the electric power industry and on electricity consumers.

COGENERATION

TECHNOLOGY ISSUES AND CONTRAINTS IN A TRANSITION TO COMPETITIVE BULK POWER MARKETS[1]

Peter D. Blair, Manager
Energy and Materials Program
Office of Technology Assessment
U.S. Congress
Washington, DC

INTRODUCTION

A wide variety of proposals to increase competition in the electric power industry have been promoted by utilities, regulators, non-utility power producers, consumers and other interested parties. Initiatives by utilities and others to construct generating facilities outside the regulatory purview of local public utility commissions as well as the growing amount of non-utility self generation, cogeneration and small power generation, prompted in part by the Public Utilities Regulatory Policies Act (PURPA) of 1978, are examples of increasing competition in power generation. Many proposals seek to improve economic efficiency by providing increased access to a power transmission facilities by a wider range of electricity suppliers and consumers, including other utilities, non-utility power producers or, in some cases, retail customers.

Proponents of increased competition view mechanisms for increasing access to transmission service as essential to achieving a more economically efficient electric power supply system. Opponents to increased access argue that the present voluntary system of permitting access on a case-by-case basis has worked well, and that due to technological constraints, some proposals are unworkable or could reduce system reliability. Use of the existing transmission system has intensified in the last decade as utilities reduced operating costs through economy energy exchanges with other utilities. As a result, transmission capacity is constrained in some areas, and technological complexity in coordinating transactions has increased.

A current study at the Office of Technology Assessment focuses on the technological factors constraining as well as encouraging competition, particularly the technical ability to provide the increased transmission access and capacity desired by some utilities, non-utility power producers and consumers. These factors include the

---

1. This paper is drawn from past and on-going work at the Office of the Technology Assessment. The views expressed are those of the author's and not of OTA or the Technology Assessment Board.

capacity of the existing transmission system and the technology available to increase capacity; the demand for transmission by utilities, consumers and non-utility power producers; the ability to determine the cost of transmission services and the reliability impacts of additional use; and the impact of dispersed non-utility generation on system operation, control and planning. The technical ability to implement alternative regulatory options and the resulting economic efficiency and reliability impacts will be examined. This paper reviews the scope of the OTA assessment, the economic and regulatory scenarios toward which the electric power industry may evolve, and, finally, the range of technologies that would influence the feasibility of pursuing each scenario.

ALTERNATIVE SCENARIOS FOR INCREASED COMPETITION

In the course of the OTA assessment, a number of alternative economic-regulatory scenarios were defined to capture the range of possible futures toward which the electric power industry might evolve, each of which has very different implications as far as future planning and operations of the U.S. electric power supply is concerned. The following are summaries of these scenarios.[2]

Scenario 1: Strengthening the Existing Regulatory-Utility Bargain

Scenario 1 continues the existing regulatory framework and electric power industry structure and reaffirms the regulatory-utility bargain with minor modifications of regulatory rules and procedures to improve the ability of utilities to attract capital for construction of new facilities and to assure a reasonable return to investors (e.g., "rolling prudence reviews"). Modifications of PURPA rules to correct perceived imbalances in avoided cost pricing rules for power from qualifying facilites under PURPA (QFs) would also be allowed. Many utilities will continue to rely on QFs and independent power producers (IPPs) for a portion of new power needs. Transmission access would remain on a voluntary basis to be negotiated between the participants. The Federal Energy Regulatory Comission (FERC) would retain its authority over transmission rates and wholesale power sales.

Industry structure: A mix of vertically-integrated utilities, investor-owned utilities, public power, cooperatives, and Federal power authorities, self-generators, QFs, and IPPs. Trends of internal realignments, restructuring initiatives, and mergers and acquisitions continue within limits of existing laws.

Regulatory structure: Existing Federal and State regulatory scheme. No changes in PURPA, the Federal Power Act (FPA), the Public Utility Holding Company Act (PUHCA). Minor modifications or adjustments to rules as noted above.

Transmission Access: Utilities may provide access voluntarily for wholesale and retail customers. No new Nuclear Regulatory Commission (NRC) wheeling orders as part of new nuclear plant approvals are likely - no new nuclear plants; stringent standards for FERC wheeling orders also likely to preclude mandatory wheeling; States have limited jurisdiction.

---

2. The scenarios are defined as discussed in more detail in U.S. Congress, Office of Technology Assessment, "Alternative Scenarios for Increasing Competition in the Electric Power Industry" (unpublished working paper), September 1987.

System Operation:

System reliability and coordination is maintained by the local utility control center. For non-utility power supplies, operational responsibilities are based on contract terms with the local utility.

Dispatch (maintenance, unit loading) is determined by the local utility (perhaps under a power pool agreement) for utility owned or leased units. For QFs and IPPs, dispatch depends on contract terms with local utility.

Emergency curtailments are allocated according to state regulated curtailment policies.

Planning and Developing Resource Additions:

Generating capacity: Utilities develop capacity expansion plans with state regulatory oversight. QFs are assured market for their power under the state's implementation of PURPA and are a component of the expansion plan. IPPs may be included in the expansion plan as determined by the utility and state regulators. QFs, IPPs and self-generators plan and build capacity based on their own perceptions of need and profitability.

Transmission additions are developed by local utilities subject to regulatory approval. Some non-utility entities may build private transmission lines, but have no eminent domain authority and uncertain regulatory status.

Distribution additions are the responsibility of local utilities with regulatory approval.

Conservation and load management programs are developed by local utilities with regulatory approval.

Pricing:

Prices are set by utilities in regulatory proceedings. Most retail services are bundled, but states allow utilities to offer special rates based on different reliablility levels and services to large retail customers in response to competitive pressures. Transmission prices are regulated by FERC. States have limited jurisdiction over transmission.

Scenario 2: Expanding Transmission Access in the Existing Institutional Structure

Scenario 2 is intended to increase both the number of bulk power sellers and the number of potential bulk power buyers by 1) removing some of the size, technology, fuel, and ownership limitations for QFs through legislative modifications to PURPA and the PUHCA; and 2) changing the mandatory transmission access provisions of the FPA to a broader public interest standard to make utilities and large retail customers eligible to apply for mandatory wheeling orders. Policies intended to encourage bulk power sales and wheeling are continued and expanded.

Industry structure: Existing mix of utilities, self-generators, co-generators, independent power producers; unregulated utility subsidaries/affiliates will increase participation in bulk power supply; current trends of restructuring, mergers and acquisitions continue.

Regulatory structure: Existing Federal-State regulatory scheme with wider eligibility for QFs under PURPA and broader FERC authority for issuing mandatory wheeling orders for utilities and large retail customers.

Transmission access: Utilities and large retail customers can petition FERC for mandatory wheeling orders to nonlocal generators based on a new public interest standard.

System Operation:

System reliability and coordination is maintained as in Scenario 1.

Dispatch (maintenance, unit loading) are the same as in Scenario 1, with the following exception. For transmission facilities users not subject to utility control, loading and dispatchability are determined by contracts between generator and consumer.

Emergency curtailments are allocated according to state regulated curtailment policies. (Same as in scenario 1). For outages of nonutility wheeled power, curtailment and backup power are based on standby service contract with local utility.

Planning and Developing Resource Additions:

Generating capacity: Same as in Scenario 1, with one addition. IPPs (as well as QFs) are assured a market for their power under the state's implementation of PURPA and are a component of the utility capacity expansion plan.

Transmission additions: Same as in Scenario 1, with the following exception. States may require that utilities include provisions for adequate transmission capacity for wheeling services in system planning.

Distribution additions: Same as in Scenario 1.

Conservation and load management: Same as Scenario 1.

Pricing:

The existing structure of price and service regulation is largely left undisturbed. Prices paid to power suppliers under PURPA are based on States' avoided cost rules (includes use of bidding systems by some states). Transmission services and the pricing of those services are established by contract negotiation under FERC jurisdiction.

Scenario 3: Competition for New Bulk Power Supplies

Scenario 3 establishes an institutional structure to allow all source competition for new bulk power supplies with market based pricing. Transmission access is included as a prerequisite for participation in the competitive system. Mandatory transmission access under the public interest standard of Scenario 2 is also available for bulk power transactions by utilities. Provision of wheeling services to retail customers remains voluntary. Utilities are able to participate in "bidding" for new capacity within their own service territories and those of other utilities with appropriate safeguards to limit problems of self-dealing, conflict of interest, etc.

Scenario 3 creates a two-tiered bulk power supply system: new power supplies under a minimally regulated, "workably competitive" market; and existing generation remaining under current state-federal scheme of regulated entry and pricing. The electric power supply industry will gradually evolve to an all competitive generating sector as existing plants are replaced. Transmission and distribution services remain highly regulated.

Industry structure: Existing mix of utilities, self-generators, co-generators, independent power producers is expanded by entry of unregulated utility subsidiaries, divisions, or spinoffs created to build and operate new generating facilities and to sell power in competitive market and other new entrants made eligible by modification of PURPA QF requirements and changes to PUHCA.

Regulatory structure: Underlying Federal-State public utility regulatory scheme is maintained but entry and pricing regulation for new power supplies is replaced by all source competition. The generating sector gradually is transformed to an all competitive system as existing capacity is phased out. Transmission and distribution remain highly regulated.

Transmission access: Three mechanisms exist for provision of transmission services: 1) voluntary transmission agreements for utilities and retail customers; 2) transmission access for new power supplies is assured as a precondition for utility participation in the competitive "bidding" system; and 3) mandatory "public interest" transmission orders are available from FERC for utilities, but not for retail customers.

System Operation:

System reliability and coordination is maintained as in Scenarios 1 and 2.

Dispatch (maintenance, unit loading) is the same as in Scenario 2.

Emergency curtailments are the same as in Scenario 2.

Planning and Developing Resource Additions:

Generating capacity: Same as in Scenario 2 with the following exception. The states' are required to use competitive bidding including consideration of non-price factors in selecting new power supplies.

Transmission additions: Similar to Scenario 2, the public utility transmission company/division plans and constructs transmission capacity with review and approval of regulatory authorities. State rules may require utilities to plan for adequate capacity for instate wheeling of new power supplies and to consider regional transmission needs.

Distribution additions: Same as in Scenario 2.

Conservation and load management: Same as in Scenarios 1 and 2.

Pricing:

"Old" power supplies remain under existing price regulation. Prices for new power supplies are market based - set by competitive auction or negotiation. New power supply prices can reflect level of service and other non-price factors. Greater reliance on transmission services may increase pressure for transmission pricing based on actual cost of service with allowances for non-price factors. Transmission prices are regulated by FERC.

Scenario 4: All Source Competition for All Bulk Power Supplies with Generation Segregated from Transmission and Distribution Services

Scenario 4 would create a competitive system for electric power supplies. Existing and new sources would compete to sell power to regulated transmission and/or distribution companies. Integrated utilities would be required to segregate generation activities both institutionally and operationally from transmission and distribution - through creation of separate divisions, subsidiaries or spinoffs. Transmission and distribution activities would be heavily regulated. Modifications to PURPA QF requirements and PUHCA restrictions allow broad participation in generation markets. Local distribution companies would be primarily responsible for securing adequate power supplies from competing suppliers. Transmission divisions or subsidiary companies would provide wheeling services for utilities under regulated rate schedules and could also act as power brokers linking local distribution companies with power suppliers. Distribution companies could obtain mandatory transmission orders could be obtained from FERC on a public interest standard. There would be no mandatory wheeling for retail customers, however it is expected that generators and transmission companies would engage in direct sales to large retail customers on a voluntary basis with bypass or standby payments to local distribution companies.

Industry structure: Vertical integration of industry is reduced by separation of utility generating segments from transmission and distribution segments. Segregated utility generators, QFs, and IPPs compete to provide power supplies to transmission - distribution and local distribution companies. Some transmission companies also act as power brokers. Industry structure is similar to that of natural gas industry.

Regulatory structure: Price and entry regulation for electric power supply is replaced with competitive market. State regulation of distribution companies and retail sales. Mixed federal-state regulation of transmission capacity and services. Under this scenario there is the potential for increased Federal regulation and oversight of power sales and formerly intrasystem transmission arrangements, however, implementing legislation could provide for a more balanced Federal-State division of regulatory authority to give states greater control over intrastate activities.

Transmission access: With FERC endorsement, States condition nondiscriminatory access to transmission services as precondition for existing regulated generation, transmission, and distribution companies to participate in new competitive system. FERC has authority to order wheeling for customer utilities on a public interest standard. Transmission access for retail customers is provided on a voluntary basis.

System Operation:

System reliabilty and coordination is maintained by the regulated transmission company or transmission-distribution company. Operational responsibilities of power suppliers and the local distribution companies are specified in contracts.

Dispatch (maintenance, unit loading) is determined by various contracts between power suppliers and either: 1) the regulated transmission companies; 2) the regulated distribution companies; or 3) retail customers.

Emergency curtailments for retail customers served by local distribution companies are allocated according to state regulated curtailment policies. For other customers, curtailments are specified in contracts with the transmission and generation suppliers.

Planning and Developing Resource Additions:

Generating capacity: Electric supply requirements are determined through local distribution company planning processes with state oversight. Competition for supply contracts is open to all generating sources, as in Scenario 3. Transmission utilities may contract for generating capacity to allow them to serve as power brokers subject to state and federal regulation.

Transmission additions: The regulated transmission or transmission-distribution companies have the obligation to provide transmission capacity necessary to support wheeling needs for instate utilities. States may require transmission capacity planning to include consideration and coordination of regional transmission system needs.

Distribution additions: Same as in Scenario 3.

Conservation and load management: Conservation and load management programs are provided by local distribution companies, possibly in conjunction with transmission companies.

Pricing:

Bulk power sales are set through competitive markets. Transmission services are regulated by state and federal authorities. Power purchases by distribution companies and retail rates are regulated as now by state authorities.

Scenario 5: Common Carrier Transmission Services in a Disaggregated, Market-Oriented Electric Power Industry.

The electric power industry is divided into institutionally separate generation, transmission, and retail distribution segments. The major difference between this scenario and scenario 4 is that separate transmission companies would explicitly be required to provide transmission services as a common carrier - i.e. non-discriminatory service based on approved wheeling tariffs - to all parties requesting service. The transmission company would have an obligation to provide adequate transmission capacity. Retail customers would have access to transmission services. Distribution and transmission services would remain tightly regulated, but in the electric generation segment, market entry and bulk power pricing would primarily be left to market forces. Federal and state policies might encourage greater aggregation in transmission services to create coordinated large regional transmission systems - either through mergers and acquisitions or through operational agreements among neighboring systems.

Industry structure: Competitive generation segment includes formerly regulated utility generation operations, QFs, and IPPs. Regulated transmission systems are operated as common carriers. Regulated local distribution companies provide retail services.

Regulatory structure: Generation segment subject to minimal regulation to assure existence of workably competitive markets. Transmission segment regulated as a common carrier by Federal and State governments. Local distribution companies regulated by state authorities.

Transmission access: Common carrier transmission access - services available on non-discriminatory basis to wholesale and retail customers. Wheeling customers could contract for different levels of service.

System Operation:

System reliability and coordination is maintained by the separate, regulated transmission company. Operational responsibilities of power suppliers and the local distribution are specified by contracts between them and the transmission company.

Dispatch (maintenance, unit loading) is determined as in Scenario 4.

Emergency curtailments is allocated as in Scenario 4.

Planning and Developing Resource Additions:

Generating capacity: Same as in Scenario 4.

Transmission additions: The transmission utility has an obligation to provide an adequate and reliable transmission capacity necessary to supply the wheeling needs of anticipated customers. (Regulatory authorities may require consideration and/or coordination of regional transmission capacity needs.)

Distribution additions: Same as in Scenario 4.

Conservation and load management: Same as in Scenario 4.

Pricing:

Bulk power sales are set through competitive markets. Transmission services are regulated by state and federal authorities on common carrier basis. Transmission rates include adequate signals to assure construction of new transmission facilities. Power purchases by distribution companies and retail rates are regulated as now by state authorities.

TECHNOLOGY ISSUES

Technology Impediments to Increased Intersystem Wheeling

Many of the arguments voiced most strongly against increased intersystem wheeling are technology-based rather than economic. In assuring reliable system operation, a utility must maintain control of its transmission and distribution network. In addition to reliability concerns, utilities may experience operational difficulties in scheduling bulk power transfers. In particular, the reliability and operating constraints limiting increased wheeling and the extent to which the existing U.S. transmission system could accommodate various degrees of increased wheeling must be addressed before economic debates can be productively entered.

Even under current circumstances, the level of intersystem bulk power transfers in the U.S. has increased dramatically in the past decade as utilities attempt to reduce operating costs through transfers of power between utilities on a day-to-day basis to take advantage of the most efficient generating equipment available, even if the equipment is operated by another utility -- so called economy energy exchanges or coordination transactions (see Table 1). The level of increased power transfers through such transactions has resulted in a much heavier loading of existing transmission systems, leading to, in many instances, increased technological complexity in control of such transfers. The control problems have resulted from the wider effects of inter-system transfers on system operating characteristics leading in turn to a need for more coordination among systems in order to maintain control. Concern over increasing inter-system effects led in part to the establishment of the North American Electric Reliability Council (NERC) in 1968 and continues today in the industry. These effects would, of course, be exacerbated with further increased wheeling, whether voluntarily initiated or mandated.

In many regions existing capabilities are being nearly fully utilized with transmission utilization over 95 percent in some regions.[3] As a result most opportunities for increased wheeling would require increasing the transfer capabilities between regions either through reinforcement of existing facilities or adding new transmission lines and related facilities. In many cases, however, determining the lowest cost method for increasing transfer capabilities is not a straightforward analysis and may require extensive system studies. The physical transfer capacity limits may be due to current flow limits, voltage gradient concerns, or phase angle criteria.[4] Table 2 shows a summary of the technologies currently under consideration. The following are examples of technical concerns associated with increased wheeling that are addressed by the technologies listed in the table:

Transmission Line Voltage Drop. Long power transmission lines experience voltage drops that increase with increased line loading. As a result, with increased line loading the rest of the power system must be able to compensate for this voltage drop in order to maintain constant system voltage.

Parallel Path Flows. Since much of the U.S. transmission system is a highly interconnected network, electricity flows from point to point in the grid through many parallel paths simultaneously. As a result, limitations to the flow could occur in portions of the grid controlled neither by the purchasing utility or the selling utility in a wheeling transaction. Such a situation raises issues of cost reimbursement to the third utility and regulatory jurisdiction over the transaction.

Operating Limits. The level of intersystem transfers is limited by the system operating constraints as well as the limits of individual components of the generation/transmission system. Such constraints include minimum output re-

---

3. See, for example, North American Electric Reliability Council, "ECAR/MAAC Interregional Power Transfer Analysis," (Princeton, NJ: NERC), ECAR/MAAC Coordinating Group, Prepared for the U.S. Department of Energy, June 1985.

4. American Public Power Association, "Report of the APPA Transmission Task Force," Feb. 8, 1984.

quirements for generators, system spinning reserve requirements, and operation within capacity limits of substation buses, switches, circuit breakers, and other components.

Losses. Transmission system losses vary with the square of the current carried by the system. As a result, incremental line losses associated with wheeling transactions on an already heavily load system could be very high as a percentage of the transaction being made, much more than the average losses on the system. This presents both an accounting and efficiency problem to the power system.

Maintenance. All transmission lines and terminal equipment must be taken out of service periodically for maintenance. Removal of a major line from service reduces the ability to effect transfers. Moreover, if the transmission system is nearly fully loaded due to an increased level of transfers, it is more difficult to reconfigure the transmission system to operate without the line(s) being maintained.

Reliability Limits. A fundamental task in transmission planning is providing mechanisms for reacting to abnormal conditions. For example, an adequate provision of redistribution of power in the event of a generator or transmission line outage is very important and becomes more difficult if lines are nearly fully loaded.

Reactive Power Control. The problem of controlling reactive power flows, caused by inductive loads such as motors as well as transmission lines themselves, is exacerbated with increased intersystem power flows. The cost, effectiveness, and flexibility of technology for maintaining reactive power control under conditions of increased power flows, such as additional transformers, series reactors, and shunt capacitors, need to be more clearly determined.

Technology Issues Affecting Non-Utility Transmission Access

As the level of so called off-system electricity purchases (involving power production neither owned or operated by a local utility) increases the utility's ability to respond to hour-by-hour load flucuations becomes more difficult, particularly if such transactions still require use of the transmission system. Moreover, the existing transmission system was designed for one-way power flows so that more complicated two-way power flow patterns associated with dispersed sources of generation are more difficult to accommodate. In particular, the concern is the effect on stability measured by area control error[5] (ACE). High ACE results from fast-changing, unpredictable conditions including a drop in power coming from an off-system generating source or from a neighboring utility over a high voltage line.

---

5. In an interconnected power system in which two or more subsystems or "areas" are linked by a power exchange tie line, the change required required in each area's generation to restore the frequency and net power interchange values to their desired levels is referred to as the area control error.

The Prospects for Resolution of Technology Issues

Many of the technology issues associated with increased wheeling and transmission access will need technology solutions and that depend on future developments in transmission coordination and distribution automation, system control under abnormal conditions, and transmission technology, all of which are likely to play pivotal roles in balancing the risk versus return of increased wheeling. Future trends in decentralized generation technologies will play an important role in the future of wheeling. In theory, a highly decentralized generation system is more reliable. In that case the principal source of potential forced outages would become the transmission system and, as a result, the need for more coordination of and control over transmission facilities becomes even greater.

Superconductivity: A Long Term Opportunity

An area of high commercial potential for the recently discovered high-temperature superconducting materials is in electricity generation, transmission, and storage. Highly efficient transmission, perhaps even at low DC voltages, could be possible with substantial savings. With pressures to increase utilization of existing transmission corridors and environmental concerns over high voltage power lines, superconducting transmission may be very important in the long term. In addition, the prospects of increasing generator efficiency and developing high capacity storage devices, could substantially transform the way we generate and use electricity. Development of these technologies, however, is likely to take a long time. In the shorter term, other applications of superconductors may also have a substantial impact on the industry, e.g., development of computers with substantially higher speed and simpler designs could be very important to advanced electric power communications and control systems. Ultimately, the most important impact on superconductors may be in modifying demand, e.g., new motor designs, magnetic levitation of trains, and electric energy storage.

CONCLUSIONS

Resolution of the wheeling issue may well be the linchpin to broader structural reform in the electric power industry, whether that reform evolves in the direction of reregulation or deregulation. It is clear that however the industry evolves, increased demands on existing and future transmission systems are certain.

Some scientists have argued that space vehicles only became useful after computers and control systems of sufficient power and speed were available to control them. The Nation's transmission and distribution grid may only be amenable to more extensive use with a control system adequate to maintain system integrity under a much wider variety of circumstances than we currently experience. While a variety of mechanisms for promoting increased wheeling on the Nation's power grid show great promise for increased economic efficiency, the capabilities of existing control mechanisms as well as the likely availability of new technology to better accommodate increased wheeling must be assessed before the economic costs and benefits of alternative mechanisms can be productively assessed.

* * *

Table 1
U.S. Generation, Sales, and Bulk Power Transactions
(Billions of Kilowatthours)

Year	Generation	Wheeling Deliveries	Purchases	Sales for Resale	Interchanges In	Out
1975	1,493	67	230	261	282	255
1976	1,571	71	251	291	305	281
1977	1,684	74	237	292	321	305
1978	1,722	93	261	307	324	293
1979	1,756	95	257	294	366	333
1980	1,785	114	280	321	375	341
1981	1,771	119	292	341	396	352
1982	1,690	124	310	330	398	345
1983	1,739	129	324	325	379	331
1984	1,814	171	337	336	399	342

Table 2
Technologies for Expanding
Bulk Power Transfer Capabilities

TRANSMISSION LINE LIMITATIONS

Voltage Uprating

Tower Extensions
Improved Insulators
Non-standard Voltages

Current uprating

Dynamic Conductor Rating
Sag Assessment and Monitoring
Restringing (live line restringing)

Tower design

Conversion to Multiple Circuit Towers
High Voltage Direct Current Lines
Multiple Phase Lines
Live Line Construction Methods

Table 2 (Cont'd)
Technologies for Expanding
Bulk Power Transfer Capabilities

TERMINAL EQUIPMENT LIMITATIONS

New Transformer Design
Circuit Breaker Design
Effects of Equipment Aging
Relay Design
Overvoltage Protection

SYSTEM OPERATIONS LIMITATIONS

Control of Loop Flows
Phase Angle Regulators
Series Reactance or Capacitance
System Reconfiguration
HVDC Control Features
Redispatch of Generation
Reactive Power Management Techniques
Shunt Capacitors
Series Capacitors
Static VAR Compensators (SVCs)
Synchronous Condensors
Generators as a VAR Source

TRANSIENT AND DYNAMIC STABILITY LIMITS

Reducing Clearing Time
Series Capacitors
Rapid Adjustment of Network Impedence
Generator Tripping and Fast Runback
Fast Valving
Braking Resistors and Load Switching
High-speed Reclosing
Advanced Excitation Systems and Stabilizers
Transient excitation Boost
Rast Acting Phase Angle Regulators
Generator Reactors
SVCs and Synchronous Condensors
Adding Switching Stations (sectionalizing)

Source: Casazza, Schultz, and Associates, Inc., Contract Progress Report, November 11, 1987.

Figure 1
U.S. Utility Purchases and Wheeling

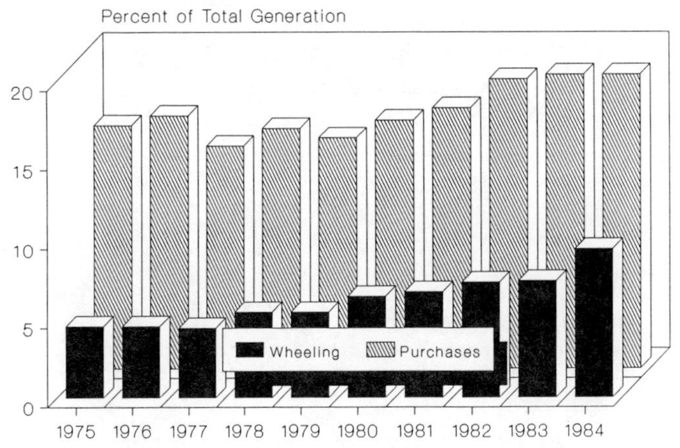

Source: Energy Information Admin.

COGENERATORS AS COMPETITORS TO PROVIDE NEW ELECTRIC GENERATION

Edward A. Myers, Jr.
President and CEO
Mission Energy Company

It is a distinct privilege to address this knowledgeable audience on my personal views of the problems and opportunities for cogenerators competing in the rapidly emerging business of alternative independent power production.

Power production, by other than utilities, is now a significant and real business, which promises to grow at an accelerated rate. It is a potential resource which a utility industry in transition from regulated status to regulated deregulation must learn to live with, accommodate, and even rely upon -- all in the interest of electric consumers.

The future of the independent power producer is foretold in the experience of other industries which have agonized through the trauma of leaving the fur lined fox hole of regulation to plow the battlefield of "open markets." For many decades the public just didn't give a damn about its electric service -- prices came down, lights stayed on, and personal budgets for utility service were tolerable. Shareholders received a competitive return on investments in utilities, vendors performed the necessary research and development and received construction contracts for ever larger projects, fuel suppliers received long term contracts and regulation substituted for competition.

It wasn't until prices were perceived to be too high for consumers that this historical tranquility was breached. There were abundant good reasons for the price rises -- but when the 2 cents kwhr became the over 10 cents kwhr the public was incensed and legislated alternatives became attractive. Independent power producers as QF's received great incentives and protection to pioneer a new era of energy supply under early PURPA sales contracts. After that early honeymoon increasing competition, utility recalcitrance, and opening markets seem to be rapidly overwhelming the fledgling industry. A recent wave of acquisitions, the falling value of public offerings, the failure to produce profits in line with pro-formas, the abandoned projects, the cancelled power purchase agreements; these are all symptoms of big trouble in the power business.

More tightly run, more efficient operators are already emerging. Such fine tuned survivors should be highly competitive for the future generation dollar. This current chaos of deregulation impacts utilities too. Mergers, lease backs, spinoffs, municipalizations, and threatened bankruptcies give loud warnings that <u>all</u> factors in this business are entering into an era of "survival of the fittest."

Sophisticated customers are already exploiting new found bargaining power. They confront utilities with demands for price reductions, or else -- the else being a cogeneration plant today -- or perhaps a wheeling contract from a lower cost off-system service tomorrow.

From now 'til the mid-nineties, the shake out of the power producers should go on. Predictably there will be fewer utilities and fewer independents when today's surplus capacities are absorbed. And when our nation re-emerges into a period of energy need the open power market could rival any other commodity exchange in its deregulated "wheeling and dealing."

The deregulation promise is that of greater efficiencies, higher risks, newer technologies, and lower costs to the consumer. Of course, similar promises were tendered about telephones, airlines, etc. -- the confusion in those lucky industries is certainly being felt, while few of the promised cost and other benefits are as yet realized.

The independent power business has matured and is now coalescing under the benign umbrella of the federal and state "deregulators." As business units became stronger they have united to form a stronger voice to influence federal energy regulatory commission policy. Note, here I say FERC, because congress appears no longer interested in any "energy crisis" -- congressmen are not expected to impose any legislative changes on the energy marketplace -- certainly not now, and maybe at the next inevitable energy crisis it will be too late. FERC is the lone force which seeks to expand the nation's power supply by opening up the energy marketplace. FERC's own interpretations of existing PURPA law will probably prevail in straightening out past PURPA errors, and in introducing new players into the monopoly game. All of this activity presents a problem with an opportunity for alert cogenerators.

Any commentary on the competitive future of cogeneration merits a brief overview of history, as a precursor of cogeneration as it will probably evolve over the next few years. In light of the current problems which threaten the orderly expansion of QF's, we will try to put a time perspective on the marketplace for power, and suggest where cogenerators should be heading to assure themselves a major role as a power seller to the nation's energy grid.

Historically, throughout many years as a utility vice president, my range of responsibilities allowed me to follow the evolution of the energy entrepreneur, as we dealt with the reliability, cost, and operating impacts of non-utility generation on the electric system and on rate paying customers. In the sixties, we had built cogeneration plants at customer sites because it was in the customers best interest to do so. In the seventies, we had pioneered sunshine and wind power, and experimented in geothermal installation because we wanted to reference data base to help developers of alternative energy do their job better. In the early eighties, under rigid prodding from regulators, we educated ourselves as to how to deal with questions of pricing, interconnections, standby service, etc., as a plethora of new independent power producers began to clamor for a place in our generating resource plan.

In May 1986, I became a power entrepreneur. My company, Mission Energy, is proud of its role as a producer of alternative energy for sale to industries and utilities, despite its short history. We are a wholly owned, unregulated subsidiary of an investor owned utility operating under the federal PURPA rules. Technically, we are not exactly "independent," but we have endured the wide range of problems associated with pioneering in this business -- in fact, due to an absolute policy of arms length dealing - we may be having a more intense exposure to utility hassles than some of our good truly independent colleagues.

From such a deep background one could reasonably observe that utilities in general had decried the passage of the public utility regulatory policy act of 1978 (PURPA) which sought to open up a new marketplace -- utilities were ambivalent about turning any part of their power production responsibilities to selected aspiring power producers who could build "qualifying facilities." And truly there are problems with the implementation of PURPA. Today those problems are categorized as: 1) compelling an often unwilling buyer to buy sometimes unneeded power at a price controlled by regulatory fiat,

2) providing unfair tax breaks and operating cost advantages for the QF which seemed designed to make sales under PURPA profitable only to the QF to the detriment of the ratepayer, and 3) imposing no obligation on the QF for reliability of service to the end user. Utilities claimed the social compact which undergirded the traditional conduct of a regulated monopoly in utility operations was breached. In any event, the independent power producer re-emerged from a half century of hibernation to again participate as a competitive force in the energy marketplace.

With the advent of PURPA, conducting "business as usual" was no longer a sound utility management decision. But that conclusion had already been stimulated by the energy crises factors of the seventies, thus the need for some drastic changes in the conduct of the enterprise was not totally unanticipated. By the early eighties, more than a few enlightened utilities had concluded that their responsibility to meet future generating needs might best be met by using smaller, decentralized, modular, easily licensed, and quickly built production facilities. That description does closely fit a typical cogeneration system -- and at first, utilities were disposed to tolerate small cogenerators.

The activities of true small independent power entrepreneurs were of marginal concern to utilities. Impact on traditional utility resource planning appeared very light. In hindsight the behavior of the marketplace is usually underestimated -- and the marketplace predictably behaved unpredictably in this instance. Large industrial customers, well-financed and eager for the operating cost savings and the apparently risk free, above average returns on equity available through state implementation of PURPA in states like Texas and California, entered the independent power production marketplace with huge cogeneration facilities. Most often these industrial giants utilized combustion turbines, then a restricted option for utilities under the fuel use act, and their multi-hundred megawatt installations precipitately ate up utility planners projected capacity needs for years to come.

Beginning about a year ago, a new term crept into the utility lexicon -- "QF bashing." Believe it or not, in many major markets, cogenerators are unloved.

Although certain utilities were overwhelmed by a seeming frankenstein monster of new entrepreneurial generating capacity, this abundance proved the imagination and "can do" spirit of the independent power producer -- and caused regional reactions ranging from the incorporation of this reality in new "scenario resource planning" to the extremes of QF bashing in the press and high pitched lobbying battles in legislative halls today. Lessons can be gleaned from these historical observations.

The most important lesson is that we entrepreneurs must never forget that an open market in energy supply was brought about by consumer dissatisfaction with their utility which induced an attempted solution through legislation, thus the market is artificial. Eventually this PURPA legislated marketing opportunity will have to be earned by providing the ultimate electric consumer a perceived value in lower costs through higher efficiency, competitive reliability, and/or tailored benefits for specific customers. The energy playing field is being levelled; the cogenerator's job is not to be levelled as well.

At this writing there are over 45,000 MW of FERC approved QF's. Of this, about 35,000 MW are known "active projects" of over 50 MW size nation wide, some 20,000 MW of which are over 100 MW. About 40% of these larger projects are along the Atlantic Seaboard, 30% in the Texas area and 20% in the far west -- over half are gas/oil fired.

Such an anticipated performance from independents seem to represent at least 10% of the nation's planned capacity additions. It is obvious that there is a minimum need for at least 50,000 MW of new power from somebody by the year 2000. Yet, there is evidence that fewer than 10,000 MW of non-utility produced power can be identified in the filed resource plans of the nation's utilities.

It seems likely, within today's proven accomplishments, that independent producers would be able to move the fastest and at the lowest cost to meet a major part of this particular generation gap if given any reasonable opportunity -- but it doesn't appear that cogenerators, large and small, can cover the entire need.

Although Mission Energy's 1500 MW QF fleet of operating joint ventures and projects under construction consist largely of cogeneration installations over 100 MW in size, we foresee that sites where major corporations act as steam out-takers, are very limited. Like hydro projects, there is a finite limit on industrial sites where QF standards can be met.

This reality alone would seem to presage that relying only on PURPA QF's as potential suppliers of major new blocks of power could soon be history. While some utilities and independents are now ferociously battling to save or kill PURPA, the real concentration of cogenerators should be focused on broadening the competitive arena through eliminations of "QF's only." Fortunately, there are further changes in the legal and regulatory structure governing the electric utility business which are looming large on the horizon. Changes in laws, regulations, and circumstances will indeed introduce ever more intensive competition to the entire spectrum of electric utility operations, not limited as today just to one controlled segment of the generating resource mix being fought over by militant QF's.

Recent pronouncements from key FERC people indicate an impetus to create a new wide open market auction system which is expected to fulfill <u>all</u> future utility generating capacity needs. FERC is expected to try to open up the energy supply world to QF's and IPP's, and whomever, bidding for future energy supply needs. The responsible serving utility may even be relegated to the ignominious role of builder of last resort in its own service territory.

Of course, adoption of this FERC philosophy would be touted as voluntary to the states, but the FERC dream clearly is to establish a nation wide marketplace -- utilizing expanded access to transmission corridors to wheel power across state lines and through utility grids to reach the consumer with the lowest cost service.

"Where competition is possible, competition is the best way to allocate resources and protect customers." This revived faith in competition, as fostered by FERC and tolerated by a seemingly uncaring body of consumers, will continue to offer unprecedented opportunities for aggressive independent power entrepreneurs to occupy a significant niche and perhaps eventually dominate the electric power market for new generation. But it will take patience, staying power, prompt employment of technological innovations, efficient application of appropriate resources, and a large measure of visceral fortitude. And the cogenerator, as an advocate of "once is not enough" in the energy business, should be able to gain a competitive advantage through energy efficiencies alone.

In reality, such an increasing dependence on raw market forces cannot, in the best interest of <u>all</u> consumers, long neglect the historical regulatory goal of maintaining the viability of integrated utility systems. After all, the public has a huge investment in existing utilities -- and that interest must be protected. Hence, the levelling of the playing field must consider that it may not be to the advantage of the vast bulk of consumers to force a separation of the generated commodity from the widespread distribution obligations heretofore assured by the strong arm of regulation -- it certainly is not to the advantage of independent generators to have to assume any part of an unmitigated "obligation to serve" at the retail level.

That fact suggests that utilities and independents must learn to live together seeking synergy for ratepayer benefit instead of conflict to ratepayer detriment. Although utilities in many states are now talking tough and bashing QF's, it is from the temporary security of seeming over capacity. Rapport is possible at some point in time, given even nominal growth plus wear and tear on existing plants -- every utility will need new capacity -- and at that point they may or may not have the choice of building capacity themselves. If traditional rate making persists, a utility would seem to be advantaged by a do-it-yourself-add-to-the-rate-base approach, but having been hoist with the petard of regulatory hindsight imposing substantial disallowances on major investments in generating plants -- a better deal from an independent producer may be the most prudent utility management decision in the future.

What all of the foregoing indicates is that in order for there to be an orderly transition to a national power auction, all independents should be pushing for the widest ability to participate -- as cogenerator, power producer, or whatever.

This means that the rules should be clear, concise, and universally applied, including provisions for allowing utilities to meet their sunk costs and to upgrade their existing facilities where economically advantageous. Thus, bidding rules should be limited to incremental future capacity needs, and allow for select non-price criteria (fuel mix, reliability, dispatch, etc.), which provides compatibility with utility system operations. The widest possible range of independent bidders should seek continuing regulatory oversight of the bidding process, fair pricing on transmission access, and continued support of the role of responsible, reliable power entrepreneurs.

In the hallowed halls of utility headquarters buildings, utility resource planners are even now re-examining their future options, and incorporating flexible action plans to cover a panoply of scenarios. Their current alternatives for future power supply surely encompass:

1. A rework of existing power plants to extend useful life.

2. A plan to upgrade and transform existing base load units to intermediate or peaking use.

3. The use of transmission networks to tap any surplus which a neighbor may offer.

4. The offer of price incentives to the lowest cost independent power producers to match variable utility system operating needs.

5. The continued promotion of energy management options, both customer actions with proper incentive motivation as well as installed load shifting devices (thermal storage, batteries, etc.)

6. To build modular new resources as the utility itself, in conjunction with other utilities, or as a partner in an independent power production facility.

There is obviously a major role in future power supply which can and should be played by those who would be the surviving cogenerators of the future. Under any reasonable scenario, a properly located, designed, constructed and financed cogeneration project, with balance between electric and thermal outputs, with access to a well priced, long term fuel supply should be competitive with most other resource planning options available to a utility now and in the future. When the decision comes down to submit bids to a utility with a need for power, one obvious economic choice could well be a firm bid from a responsible independent cogenerator featuring reliability standards and operating philosophies compatible with efficient service through the utility to the end user. Such an independent credible bid moves the construction and operating risks from the rate payer to the independent. Consumers want power to be there when they want it -- at a cost they perceive to be reasonable -- independents can do that well; cogenerators can probably do it better.

The surviving cogenerators will be those who, in consideration of the electric consumer, maintain an efficient, reliable, synergism with the utilities or industries they supply. Mission Energy intends to be such a survivor and we hope you will be too.

I wish you every success in being a profitable player in a powerful future.

Encouraging Competitive Bidding for Electric Capacity - The Case for Removing the Regulatory Albatross From the Neck of the Emerging Independent Power Producers

John D. Kuhns, President and Chief Executive Officer
Catalyst Energy Corporation

Energy Technology Conference & Exposition
Washington, D.C.*

My name is John D. Kuhns and I am the President and Chief Executive Officer of Catalyst Energy Corporation. Catalyst Energy is an independent power producer which sells electricity and steam in a largely non-regulated environment. We produce our power and steam from generation resources of all sizes and fuel types located around the country. I want to take this opportunity to thank the members and participants of the Energy Technology Conference & Exposition and, in particular, Keith P. Kroell for this opportunity to appear as a speaker today and to express my views on the need for new policies toward the independent power industry, and the much broader question of seeking to encourage competition within that industry in light of current laws and regulations.

In a general sense, I stand here before you today because of the widespread success of the Public Utility Regulatory Policies Act of 1978 ("PURPA") which is the primary force behind the emergence of the independent power industry. "Independent power producer" best characterizes a non-regulated organization selling power produced at utility-grade generating plants to the wholesale power market.

Catalyst Energy, is a good example of what one industry participant has been able to accomplish. Formed in 1982, Catalyst Energy went public in 1984 with revenues of $10 million and assets of $8 million. Today we have assets in excess of $1 billion and 1987 revenues are expected to be approximately $425 million. In Inc. magazine's list of 1987's fastest growing small public companies, Catalyst Energy was ranked number one with a compound annual sales growth rate over five years of 579%.

---

* Please note that the text of Mr. Kuhns' comments was prepared on December 1, 1987 and that any changes in the status of certain transactions discussed herein will be reflected in his remarks on February 17, 1988.

Catalyst owns and operates a diversified mix of generation assets with 30 facilities in operation or under construction in over 20 states including conventional coal-fired plants, hydro-electric plants, cogeneration plants, district steam heating and cooling systems, alternative fuel plants and waste-to-energy plants. As an entity operating in roughly half of the regions in the country, we are geographically diversified. We are also diversified in terms of the type of customer we serve. We sell a large portion of our energy output at wholesale directly to utilities. However, we also sell a significant portion of the company's output, primarily steam, at retail to non-utility "direct" users, whether they be industrial, commercial or high density residential customers. With over 750 megawatts of capacity on line and another 250 megawatts under construction as well as over 15 billion pounds of steam capacity, Catalyst is the largest independent power producer in the country and the nation's second largest steam producer.

Catalyst Thermal Energy Corporation which owns the Company's steam system assets and recently completed an initial public offering represents Catalyst Energy's ability to invest in and make profitable utility assets which had been neglected and underutilized by the utilities. Catalyst is currently negotiating and expects to close before year end the purchase of the Cleveland Steam System. The Cleveland purchase will bring the number of large urban steam systems owned by Catalyst Thermal to six. These include Boston, Philadelphia, Baltimore, St. Louis and Youngstown. This reflects Catalyst Energy's ongoing commitment to "least cost" power generation and serves as an example of that spirit within the competitive power industry.

While galvanized by PURPA, the growth of our industry has, ironically, really been fueled by the regulated electric utilities themselves. The early days of PURPA were also days when, coincidentally, certain utilities in key power sectors like California, Texas and the northeast were facing dwindling capacity, escalating rates and deteriorating financial conditions. As the utilities with foresight realized that an independent power producer could solve many of their problems, they began to encourage such developers by offering attractive rates, terms, and, above all, readily available power purchase contracts. California is an excellent example of a state where independent power has provided almost all of the state's planned generation capacity since the enactment of PURPA.

In late 1985 and early 1986 the benign environment for our industry changed. The electric utilities realized that they did not need the independent power producers in the same way that they did a few years ago. They have had many of their problems solved, thanks in large part to our fledgling industry responding and doing its job. Because of us, they are the recipients of the output of thousands of megawatts of cheap, long-term capacity that they did not have to build or finance and that does not burn oil or nuclear fuel rods. In the same connection, their balance sheets, financial performance and credit ratings have improved as a result of the reliability of efficient independent power producers. The reliability of hydroelectric facilities built and operated by Catalyst Energy, for example, exceeds 95%. Financially stable and flush with cash and capacity, the utilities now can afford to dispense with us. They have started to suspend entrance into future contracts, to hold up those contracts in negotiation and have even threatened to cancel existing agreements. Such contracts are obviously the key to financing the construction of any new generation facilities.

In 1990 or shortly thereafter, the utilities will be forced to make tough decisions concerning new capacity additions. There is currently little or no construction of new generating capacity by the utilities. It is clear that, in choosing between building a plant themselves or getting a better deal from an independent power producer, few utilities will choose and few state PUC's will permit, the old way of developing and owning generation. This will provide a real opportunity for the utility subsidiaries and independent power producers who comprise the competitive power industry, to either make available existing capacity or develop new facilities.

Today there is no reason for the large number of vertically integrated utilities that are in existence; nor is there a reason for them not to be more specialized. The party that pays the additional costs inherent in this inefficient structure is the ratepayer. Each time a utility decides to build its one additional plant, the ratepayers bear the cost of bringing what is frequently a distribution company up to speed on the current innovations in construction, operation and management. This is inefficient, costly and potentially disasterous. Shoreham, Diablo Canyon and Seabrook are only a few examples where the real losers will be the ratepayers. Over the past two decades, ratepayer costs have been trending up and can be expected to continue to do so whenever new plant additions are made by utilities. As the Office of Economic Policy at FERC recently noted(1), electric rates have more than tripled since 1970, and after adjusting for inflation have increased by 27%. Therefore, we are confident that the next generation of plant additions, because they will force even higher rates, will be the "last straw" leading to deregulation of the electric utility industry. The key, however, is action by Congress, the Federal Energy Regulatory Commission ("FERC") and the Securities and Exchange Commission ("SEC") to anticipate such results now and to resolve the potential problems of the future before they occur. FERC must be careful to set in place an equitable bidding structure and should along with the SEC encourage action by Congress to remove the antiquated and weighty albatross embodied in the Public Utility Holding Company Act of 1935 ("PUHCA") from the shoulders of the independent power producers.

I would now like to address my comments to three specific areas affecting the independent power producers in the future. I will briefly touch upon the competitive bidding issue, dwell at length upon the problems that I see with PUHCA and finally cite certain issues relating to the Federal Power Act that merit discussion.

I. COMPETITIVE BIDDING

We at Catalyst feel that competition is laudable and a necessary step in the maturation of the independent power industry. However, the bidding rules which replace avoided cost determinations as the primary method of calculating compensation for independent power producers must take into account at a minimum the following factors:

---

1 In its October 13 report: "Regulatory Independent Power Producers: A Policy Analysis", at page 14.

(1) technological diversity,

(2) a reasonable mix of renewable and fossil fueled generation,

(3) the fact that an independent power producer and its shareholders, rather than the ratepayers, bear the risk of the fixed price construction, technological integrity, performance and financing of a facility,

(4) energy-related safety and environmental goals,

(5) protection against self-dealing by the utilities both within and outside of geographic and economic spheres of influence,

(6) access to transmission and non-discriminatory wheeling rates,

(7) protection against short-term foreign dumping of cheap power.

The goal of any bidding system should be to provide the ratepayers with the lowest cost, the least risk and the most efficient energy production possible while encouraging broader markets and greater transmission capacity for energy within regional markets. In any such scheme, the host utility should be the bidder of last resort and be held to a fixed-price for construction. This fixed-price, set by the utility, would be the price against which the independents would bid. If the independent power producers are unable to meet or beat that bid, then the host utility, itself could construct the facility. The regulations should, however, safeguard against the host utility trying to "low-ball" the independent power producers by forcing the utility to be fiscally responsible and prohibiting it from passing any cost increases, above this fixed price, on to the shoulders of its ratepayers.

The risks to be assumed by the consumers should be the major criteria of any bidding system. Providers of electric generation in the future, like independent power producers do now, should provide electric generation capacity while assuming the risks of construction, completion, technology, performance and financing. As long as the provider of electric generation assumes these risks, the consumer will pay a comparatively lower pre-set, pre-negotiated price for electricity when it is delivered -- clearly a benefit to our nation's ratepayers.

Bidding is, however, a complex subject and I would also like to focus upon the problems which PUHCA and the Federal Power Act present to the independent power industry and the implementation of a truly competitive bidding program.

II. PUHCA IMPEDIMENTS TO THE COMPETITIVE POWER INDUSTRY

The single greatest barrier to competition and to the logical development and maturation of the competitive power industry is PUHCA. While PUHCA may have been needed when it was passed in the 1930's, improvements in communications, accounting standards and integrated disclosure laws administered by the SEC have rendered it anachronistic. Today the economic costs of its cumbersome procedures, the inflexibility of interpretation by the

SEC staff, and draconian consequences for actions in violation of PUHCA far outweigh its intended protections against the practices which it identifies as injurious to investors, consumers and the general public -- all of which are currently either outlawed by other means or outmoded by current business practice.

A. PUHCA Discourages Investment in New Generating Capacity

Almost no investor is willing to become subject to SEC regulation under PUHCA as a holding company (even an exempt one) in order to invest in a non-QF generating plant. According to the language of PUHCA _any_ company that "owns, holds or controls with power to vote" ten percent or more of an electric utility's or a holding company's voting securities is automatically a holding company. This makes it virtually impossible for an independent power producer to find investors to take a large share of voting stock in a generating plant project.

Further, entities owning _less_ than ten percent of a utility's voting securities may nevertheless be declared to be a holding company if the SEC finds that they control or have "an arrangement" with others to control an electric utility or holding company. This makes it difficult to put together a group of investors or to find a general partner for a partnership to finance a generation project. Worst of all, the SEC staff has refused in at least two cases to agree that limited partners, with _no_ voting rights, would _not_ be declared to be holding companies. Thus, even passive investors in generation projects are not assured that they will not be regulated.

The potential for becoming a holding company, therefore, severely limits the types of investors and the choice of financing vehicles available to independent power producers. Independent power producers may not only have to pass up the least-cost financing, such as master limited partnerships, but may also be unable to obtain sufficient financing at any acceptable cost because of PUHCA.

B. The Agency Charged With Enforcement Has Called for the Repeal of PUHCA

Independent power producers are not the only ones calling for a roll-back of PUHCA jurisdiction, the SEC itself has called for the repeal of PUHCA. In a letter to the General Accounting Office, Daniel L. Goelzer, General Counsel to the SEC, questioned whether such regulation was desirable or even necessary at the federal level when he set forth the SEC's position regarding PUHCA(2). He stated:

> "Registered public utility systems are the only entities over which the Commission has such authority; the Commission has no such comprehensive authority over other types of utility or non-utility holding company systems or

2 Letter dated April 29, 1983 and incorporated as Appendix III to the GAO's Analysis of the SEC's Recommendation to repeal PUHCA dated August 30, 1983.

over the approximately ninety holding company systems exempted from the 1935 Act pursuant to Section 3(a) thereunder. The development of the securities registration and corporate disclosure requirements under the Securities Act of 1933 and the Securities Exchange Act of 1934, the evolution of the federal securities laws relating to fraud, and the increased sophistication of the accounting profession have significantly increased the level of investor protection beyond that existing in 1935. Accordingly, the Commission believes that the Act does little to safeguard investors and the public interest from the risks of improper sales practices and abusive corporate management and control in utility holding companies. Moreover, in the event the 1935 Act is repealed, securities issuances, utility acquisitions, and affiliate transactions by companies engaged in wholesale sales of electric energy in interstate commerce would be subject to regulatory scrutiny by the Federal Energy Regulatory Commission...or by state [PUC's]."

C. Narrow Exemptions From Registration Inhibit Independent Power Producer Operations

If an independent power producer itself must become a holding company in order to own and operate a generating plant, it must either obtain an exemption under Section 3(a)(1) of PUHCA pursuant to which it must be organized and substantially operating in a single state or become regulated by the SEC in almost all aspects of its business as a registered holding company. Without another available exemption, this restriction makes it impossible for an independent power producer to use its expertise in financing and constructing numerous geographically diverse generating plants and to own such plants wherever they are most needed and can most feasibly be bought or built.

A case in point is Catalyst Energy's 192 megawatt hydroelectric project located near Vidalia, Louisiana. Catalyst has entered into an agreement with Dominion Capital to jointly own and permanently finance this facility. PUHCA barriers, however, almost prevented this initially advantageous transaction from occuring. Catalyst has decided to migrate to the state of Louisiana and thus avail itself and the transaction of the 3(a)(1) exemption. This is a ridiculous outcome and a clear example of excessive government regulation truly run amuck. While the substance of the transaction is unchanged, the additional burden and expenses of sending a proxy statement to shareholders and calling a Special Meeting of Shareholders to approve the migration along with the uncertainties of uncharted legal issues in Louisiana and the costs of additional local counsel for all future transactions have unnecessarily burdened Catalyst and have imposed additional time delays and money to the costs of the Vidalia transaction itself. The SEC estimated in 1983 that, exclusive of costs attributable to SEC staff delays, PUHCA annually cost the twelve registered holding companies over $3 million. A greater cost, yet more difficult to estimate, relates to the foregone business opportunities and financings due to the smothering effect of PUHCA upon the competitive power industry. Indeed, regulated utilities which wish to join with independent power producers in power plant projects are equally limited by the geographical restraints and the delay problems resulting from PUHCA regulation of generating plants. Thus, utilities are ironically forced to invest more in airplanes and boxcars than in the utility business they know best and which would profit from their expertise. These restrictions, costs and delays adversely affect registered utilities, independent power producers and passive investors and are clearly unconscionable.

D. Acquisition of a Second Plant Must be Approved by SEC Under Restrictive Rules

If an independent power producer wishes to expand and buy a second power plant, PUHCA's "two-bite" rule will probably control and may well prevent the acquisition. Section 9(a) requires any person to obtain SEC approval to buy 5% or more of the voting stock of a second utility if the person owns 5% or more of the voting stock of another utility or holding company. The real catch is that, under Section 10, the SEC will not approve the acquisition unless it finds (among other things) that the acquisition tends toward the development of an "integrated public-utility system." Such a requirement, like the 3(a)(1) geographic restrictions, discourages or prohibits the development of numerous power plants by the competitive power industry wherever they can best be built since they would presumably not be part of an "integrated" system.

E. Delay May Scuttle Acquisition

In addition to the "integrated system" restriction, Section 10 proceedings are notoriously slow. The friendly Centerior merger took the SEC one year to approve and the approval of the American Electric Power/Columbus and Southern Ohio Company transaction required more than ten years. Such glacial movement makes an unfriendly takeover of a poorly managed utility by an independent power producer unlikely, and might make even a friendly acquisition impractical due to, among other factors, the vagaries of the capital markets.

F. Staffing at SEC Exacerbates PUHCA Problems

The many restrictions imposed by PUHCA are exacerbated by the small staff at the SEC which currently handles all PUHCA exemption questions. The staff lacks the time and resources, as well as apparent guidance from the Commission itself, to study new ideas or to initiate interpretations of PUHCA that would more accurately apply the intent of its drafters to today's evolving utility industry. Thus, any discretion which Congress gave to the SEC to relax PUHCA constraints in certain areas is not being exercised.

G. Suggestions for the Removal of PUHCA Impediments Through Legislation

1. Amend PUHCA Definition of "Electric Utility"

The most straight-forward approach to removing PUHCA impediments to the competitive power industry would be to conform the PUHCA definition of "electric utility" to that of a "gas utility" under PUHCA and limit it to facilities used for the distribution of electric energy at retail. If the electric transmission grid is thought to be fundamentally different from the nation's natural gas pipeline system, PUHCA "electric utilities" could include transmission as well as distribution facilities. However, as in the case of gas producers, competitive independent power producers should be relatively free to explore new opportunities and technologies and should be encouraged to compete and expand their facilities -- to the benefit of ratepayers and shareholders alike.

Alternatively, the PUHCA definition of "electric utility" could be amended to specifically exempt generation facilities owned and operated by independent power producers with no transmission or distribution systems. In the interest of fairness, this exception should include generation facilities owned or partially owned by utilities or utility holding companies outside their franchise areas or, to use FERC's term, "zones of influence". Such an exemption would leave intact the current registered holding company systems, but would free the competitive power industry from the geographic and other restraints of PUHCA which were never intended for them.

2. Amend PURPA to Permit FERC to Exempt Independent Power Producers Without Distribution Systems From PUHCA

The independent power industry grew out of and continues to advance the original goal of PURPA, which was to provide the nation with a reliable, independent source of electric generating capacity that didn't exclusively use foreign oil. In recognition of this, PURPA could be amended to permit FERC to exempt competitive power producers in addition to qualifying facilities from PUHCA.

Competitive power producers need no other PURPA benefits, such as forced purchases or avoided cost pricing, and would not receive them under this amendment. Nor should independent power producers be exempted from state laws or from FERC regulation where applicable. However, the competitive power industry should be freed from restrictive and burdensome PUHCA regulations which were not designed with them in mind.

3. Add PUHCA Exemption For Independent Power Producers

A specific exemption from registered holding company status could be crafted to include in Section 3 of PUHCA independent power producers and utilities owning generating plants outside their zones of influence. However, such exempt holding companies would remain subject to the "two-bite" rule of Sections 9(a)(2), so, unless othersie cured, this would be only a partial and less favorable solution.

III. THE FEDERAL POWER ACT'S BARRIERS TO COMPETITION

FERC has already shown that it can be innovative in its interpretation of the Federal Power Act (the "FPA") and that it recognizes that market forces are effective regulators. FERC's competitive bidding proposals are one example of its commitment to competition within the industry. Catalyst along with the competitive power industry applauds these recent developments.

Unfortunately, the FERC has also attempted to expand its jurisdiction under Section 203 to include changes in ownership of utility securities. We hope that the FERC will reconsider its jurisdictional interpretations in this area, since they appear ill-founded and could have a serious chilling effect on potential reorganizations in the utility industry that would enhance bulk power supply competition. At a minimum, if the FERC's expansion of jurisdiction over restructurings is upheld, the Commission should request legislation granting it exclusivity in reviewing such transactions and it should be prepared to move quickly so that market realities and sound economics, rather than regulatory delay, will determine the outcome of restructuring proposals.

In Section 201(b) of the FPA, FERC jurisdiction is explicitly stated to exclude generating facilities as well as local distribution. Section 204 gives the FERC jurisdiction over the issuance of securities by a utility if no state commission has jurisdiction. In recent orders (such as Catalyst Energy's Alamito transaction) FERC held that a generation company which owned no transmission facilities was subject to Section 203 when it merged into a company that was previously not a utility and that securities issued by that company prior to the merger were in effect issued by the utility and therefore an application should have been filed. While the Section 203 portion is being challenged, this expansion of FERC jurisdiction if permitted to stand will chill the potential reorganization of the utility industry. The redundancy caused by PUHCA and FPA regulations only create a climate of stagnation and uncertainty for our industry.

CONCLUSION

I hope that the thoughts which I have submitted to you today have conveyed Catalyst Energy's conviction that the independent power industry is both a vital and positive force which is critical to our nation's energy future; but that care must be taken to safeguard the industry from the anticompetitive proclivities of certain utilities and to encourage its growth and expansion by the removal of certain statutory and regulatory restraints from both independent power producers and the electric generation subsidiaries of regulated utilities.

Most importantly, and possibly the key to the growth of the competitive power industry, Catalyst has called upon FERC and the SEC to recommend to Congress legislation which would embrace those independent power producers, who desire to efficiently construct and operate larger power plants and to permit them to do so without the encumbrances which, as I have previously cited, are placed upon them by PUHCA and the FPA.

The competitive power industry is in the best position and truly has the greatest incentive to embrace new technology and new financing techniques. This clearly benefits our entire nation. We have the <u>synergies</u> which come from a diverse network of energy producing facilities located across the country, both large and small, and the <u>reliability</u> and <u>expertise</u> which is derived from the construction, financing, operation and management of such facilities. We are willing to bear the risks and reap the rewards that come with such a role. An individual utility which builds one or two facilities every other decade does not have either the synergies or the expertise that would reside in an independent power producer. In order to permit us to thrive in a competitive and profitable environment, the antiquated legal restraints, such as those embodied in PUHCA, must be summarily done away with. This will benefit the independent power producers and their stockholders, will permit those utilities who so choose to create competitive generating subsidiaries and otherwise to concentrate on the distribution and transmission of power and will ultimately result in greater reliability and a significant economic benefit to our nation's ratepayers - both large and small.

DAIRY PRODUCT COGENERATION FACILITY - A MULTI-NATIONAL PROJECT DEVELOPMENT

KEYS A. CURRY, JR.

PRESIDENT AND CHIEF OPERATING OFFICER

PSE INC.

INTRODUCTION

In December 1985, PSE Inc. received a Letter of Intent from Integrated Protein Technology that gave PSE the exclusive right to develop a cogeneration project at the IPT cheese products production plant in Southern California. Subsequent to receiving the Letter of Intent, PSE Inc. designed the plant, obtained all the permits, specified and procured the equipment, arranged for project financing, negotiated all necessary contracts, including arranging for certain long-term fuel supply and gas transportation contracts for the project. The cogeneration facility project, currently under construction, and the cheese plant project, which came on-line in late 1985, have proven to be a landmark cooperative effort between several national and international corporations and major financial institutions. The cogeneration facility developed by PSE and the cheese processing plant developed by Integrated Protein Technology were a very complex financial transaction in that there are two separate project financings involved and certain common facilities support the financing basis for both projects. The two projects literally combined the efforts of technical, business, legal and financial people from over the world and represent a significant international achievement. This paper describes the cogeneration project and the key components that enabled the two projects with separate financing sources to achieve a common goal and provide benefits for both projects.

THE COGENERATION APPLICATION

On October 1, 1985, Integrated Protein Technology of California began operating the world's largest cheese producing plant in the heart of the most intense dairy production area in the world, the Chino Valley, just east of Los Angeles, California. The milk intake of the plant is 800 million pounds of milk per year, which is approximately 4-5% of total California milk production. Plant receiving capacity is 2.3 million lbs. of milk per day or approximately 50 tank-truck loads of about 54,000 lbs. The plant output is about 80 million pounds of cheese per year, which is approximately 13% of the total cheese consumed in California annually.

The 165,000 sq. ft. plant operates 24 hours per day, 7 days per week, producing 80 million lbs. of cheddar, colby or monterrey jack cheese for consumers, about 5 million lbs. of whey protein concentrate of 50-75% protein, 2.2 million lbs. of whey butter, and 2.2 million gallons of ethanol.

The cheese plant employs about 166 people and represents the most highly automated plant of its type in the world. The plant's continuous cheese production technology is the first U.S. installation of a system developed in New Zealand and used by another cheese producer at plants in England and Ireland. Whey processing at the plant is based on ultra-filtration and reverse osmosis systems developed by Pasilac A/S of Denmark. Design of the alcohol plant is based on a proven whey-alcohol process developed and utilized in Ireland. The plant thus represents a scale-up from proven technology utilized in several parts of the world. Prior to startup of the cogeneration facility, plant and process heat at the cheese plant is provided by two gas-fired boilers, each capable of generating 30,000 pounds of steam per hour at 250 psi. In addition, the plant contains three conventional Freon-cooled chillers which are used for air conditioning and to refrigerate storage areas for both cheese and butter.

COGENERATION FACILITY DESCRIPTION

The Corona Cogen Facility (Figure 1) is a topping cycle cogeneration plant using one natural gas-fueled General Electric Model LM5000 packaged gas turbine generator unit, exhausting into a heat recovery boiler. The LM5000 unit will drive a generator producing 13.8 KV, 60 Hertz electric power with plant surplus power being transformed to 66 KV and delivered into the Southern California Edison grid through an

CORONA
COGENERATION FACILITY
PSE

interconnection facility. Process steam, produced from the gas turbine hot exhaust gases, will be delivered to IPT for use in their milk processing operations.

The LM5000 gas turbine generator will produce 48,810 gross kilowatts of electrical power based on the 63 degree Fahrenheit annual average temperature for the Corona area. Under normal conditions, approximately 2000 kilowatts of power will be used by the cogeneration plant auxilliary equipment, 6000 kilowatts will be delivered to the cheese plant for use in their plant and the balance will be delivered into the SCE electrical grid.

The waste heat boiler will produce a total of 141,740 pounds per hour of steam with approximately 30,000 pounds per hour normally being delivered to the plant as process steam. The balance of the steam produced will be injected into the gas turbine for NOX control and for power augmentation. At times of high steam demand by the cheese plant, the injection steam can be decreased to the gas turbine and process steam flow may be increased to meet peak load requirements.

COMBUSTION GAS TURBINE GENERATOR

The combustion gas turbine generator is a shop-assembled, skid-mounted packaged power unit manufactured by the General Electric Company. The components comprising this unit include the gas turbine, electric generator, exciter, inlet air filter, evaporative cooler, mechanical and electrical accessory skids and complete control and monitoring systems for the unit. The gas turbine components will be enclosed in a weatherproof housing insulated for sound attenuation. The housing will be cooled and pressurized by a forced air ventilation system. The LM5000 is a high efficiency aircraft derivative type, three shaft gas turbine with a 30/1 compression ratio and a direct drive electric generator.

HEAT RECOVERY BOILER

The gas turbine hot exhaust gases, at approximately 771 degrees Fahrenheit will be ducted to the heat recovery boiler. The boiler is a three pressure level, finned tube heat recovery unit. At design conditions, it will produce 72,900 pounds per hour of 630 psig, 550 degree steam; 52,810 pounds per hour of 270 psig, 450 degree steam and 16,040 pounds per hours of 112 psig, 346 degree Fahrenheit steam. The low pressure steam produced will be used for deaerating and heating the boiler feedwater.

SELECTIVE CATALYTIC REDUCTION SYSTEM

A Mitsubishi Heavy Industries catalytic converter for NOX control will be installed in the boiler to reduce NOX emissions. An Englehard catalytic converter for CO reduction will be installed in the boiler to reduce CO emissions.

BOILER WATER TREATMENT SYSTEM

Makeup water for the boiler will be supplied from the City of Corona Municipal System. A two-stage reverse electro-dialysis demineralizer water treatment system will be provided to treat the makeup water and return condensate for use in the boiler.

PLANT CONTROL SYSTEM

The plant control system will be located in a power control building. A single operator will be able to monitor and control the plant on the night shift. The gas turbine will be controlled from a GE Mark IV cabinet in the control room which is electronically tied to sensors, switches and devices in the gas turbine enclosure. The remainder of the plant equipment will be controlled through a Westinghouse distributive control system cabinet located in the control room which is electronically tied to sensors, switches and devices on the balance of equipment.

Data will be recorded and stored on microprocessor systems and displayed on CRT monitors in the control room. The operator will have the capability to start, load, unload, shutdown and monitor all equipment. Remote ties from the control room to SCE dispatchers will be through telephone and data transmission circuits.

ENERGY BALANCE

The cogeneration facility energy balance is depicted in Figure 2.

SITE PLAN

The plant site plan is shown in Figure 3.

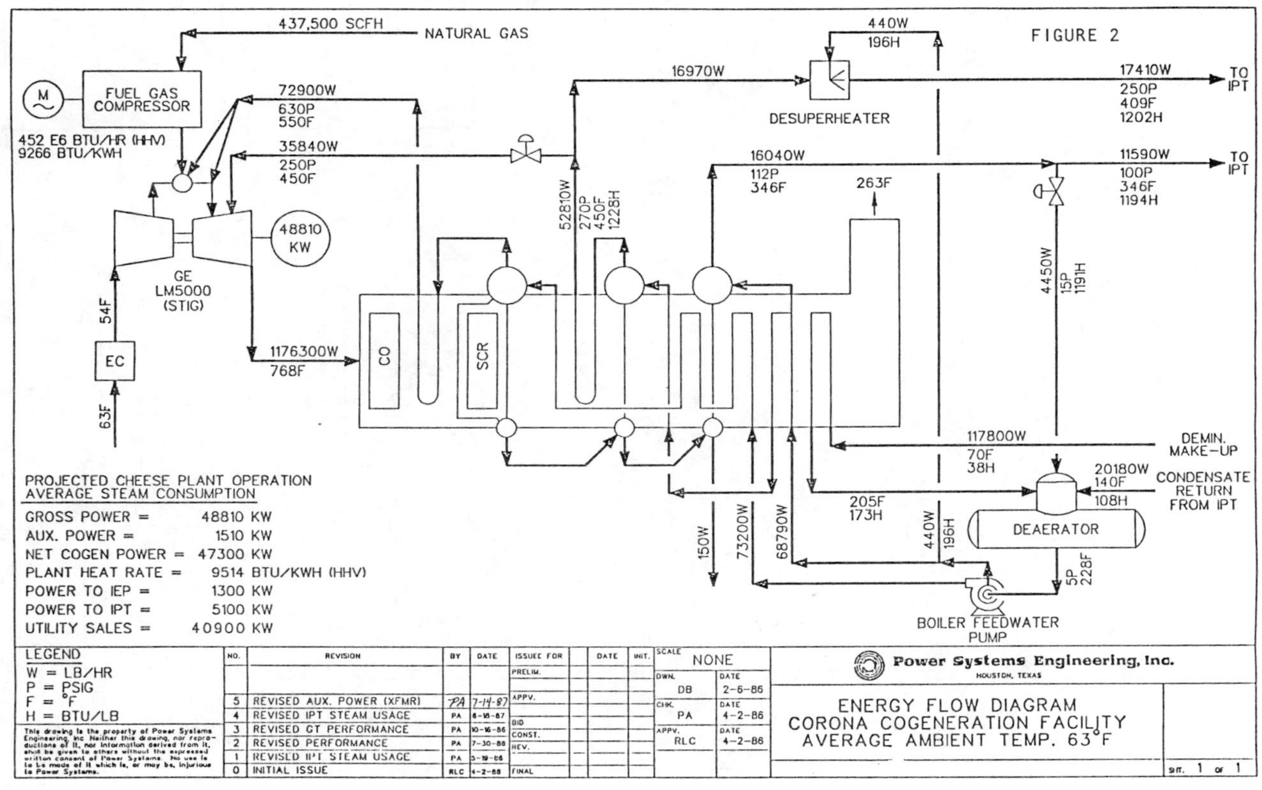
FIGURE 2
437,500 SCFH
NATURAL GAS
M
FUEL GAS COMPRESSOR
452 E6 BTU/HR (HHV)
9266 BTU/KWH
72900W
630P
550F
35840W
250P
450F
48810 KW
GE
LM5000
(STIG)
54F
EC
63F
1176300W
768F
CO
SCR
52810W
270P
450F
1228H
16970W
440W
196H
DESUPERHEATER
17410W
250P
409F
1202H
TO IPT
16040W
112P
346F
263F
11590W
100P
346F
1194H
TO IPT
4450W
15P
1191H
117800W
70F
38H
DEMIN. MAKE-UP
20180W
140F
108H
CONDENSATE RETURN FROM IPT
205F
173H
DEAERATOR
150W
73200W
68790W
440W
196H
5P
228F
BOILER FEEDWATER PUMP
PROJECTED CHEESE PLANT OPERATION
AVERAGE STEAM CONSUMPTION
GROSS POWER = 48810 KW
AUX. POWER = 1510 KW
NET COGEN POWER = 47300 KW
PLANT HEAT RATE = 9514 BTU/KWH (HHV)
POWER TO IEP = 1300 KW
POWER TO IPT = 5100 KW
UTILITY SALES = 40900 KW
LEGEND
W = LB/HR
P = PSIG
F = °F
H = BTU/LB
This drawing is the property of Power Systems Engineering, Inc. Neither this drawing, nor reproductions of it, nor information derived from it, shall be given to others without the expressed written consent of Power Systems. No use is to be made of it which is, or may be, injurious to Power Systems.
NO. REVISION BY DATE ISSUED FOR DATE INIT.
5 REVISED AUX. POWER (XFMR) PA 7-14-87
4 REVISED IPT STEAM USAGE PA 6-15-87
3 REVISED GT PERFORMANCE PA 10-16-86
2 REVISED PERFORMANCE PA 7-30-86
1 REVISED IPT STEAM USAGE PA 5-19-86
0 INITIAL ISSUE RLC 4-2-86
PRELIM.
APPV.
BID
CONST.
REV.
FINAL
SCALE NONE
DWN. DB DATE 2-6-86
CHK. PA DATE 4-2-86
APPV. RLC DATE 4-2-86
Power Systems Engineering, Inc.
HOUSTON, TEXAS
ENERGY FLOW DIAGRAM
CORONA COGENERATION FACILITY
AVERAGE AMBIENT TEMP. 63°F
SHT. 1 OF 1

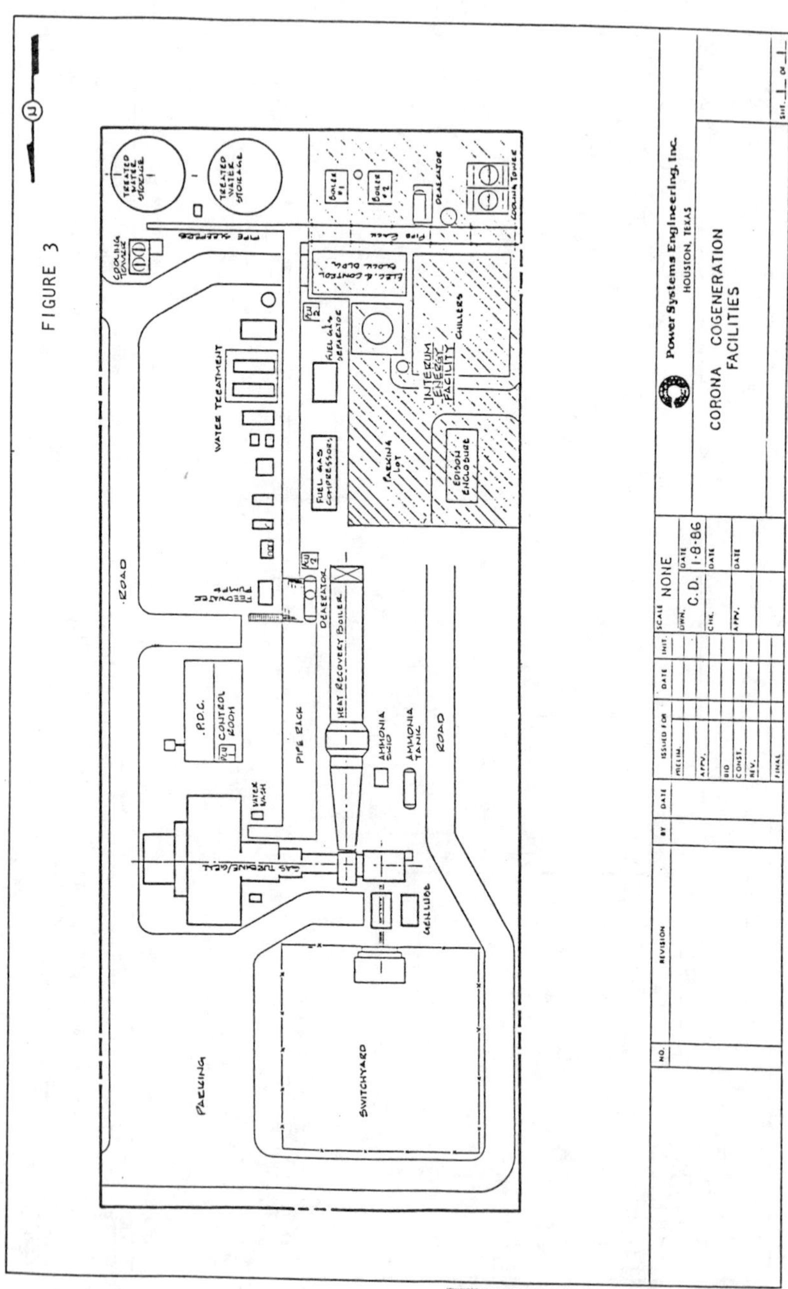
TREATED WATER STORAGE
TREATED WATER STORAGE
COOLING TOWER
PIPE SLEEPERS
BOILER #1
BOILER #2
DEAERATOR
COOLING TOWER
PIPE RACK
ELEC. & CONTROL BLDG.
FUEL GAS SEPARATOR
INTERIM ENERGY FACILITY
CHILLERS
WATER TREATMENT
FUEL GAS COMPRESSORS
PARKING LOT
EDISON ENCLOSURE
ROAD
FEEDWATER PUMPS
DEAERATOR
HEAT RECOVERY BOILER
P.D.C.
CONTROL ROOM
PIPE RACK
AMMONIA SKID
AMMONIA TANK
ROAD
WATER WASH
GAS TURBINE/GEN.
GEN LUBE
SWITCHYARD
PARKING
Power Systems Engineering, Inc.
HOUSTON, TEXAS
CORONA COGENERATION FACILITIES
SCALE NONE
DWN. C.D.
DATE 1-8-86
CHK.
APPV.
NO.
REVISION
BY
DATE
ISSUED FOR
PRELIM.
APPV.
BID
CONST.
REV.
FINAL
INIT.
SHT. 1 OF 1

FIGURE 3

PROJECT PARTICIPANTS

The combined cheese plant and cogeneration facility projects resulted in a truly international venture with project participants from over the world. A listing of project participants by project is detailed below:

The Cheese Production Facility:

Developer and Owner

Integrated Protein Technology, Corona, California

The equity ownership of IPT is held by Griswold Controls, K/S Difko XXXVI and Difko Dairy A/S. Griswold Controls is a United States corporation and the two Difko entities are Danish investment companies formed for the purpose of investing in the project.

Plant Operator

Integrated Protein Technology

The operating staff assembled by IPT consists of many workers who relocated from England and Ireland.

Financing

Lease financing was organized by Dansk Investeringsfond (a Danish investment foundation), Copenhagen, with loans provided in the U.S. by a syndicate of banks led by Lloyds International Corporation.

Project Engineering

Pettit Projects Inc., Corona, California, a subsidiary of E. G. Pettit and Company in Cork, Ireland.

Process Engineering

Pasilac A/S Silkeborg, Denmark, a member of the DDS (Danish Sugar Factories) Group

Milk Supplier

Mulligan Sales, which manages State Dairy Association, one of California's largest dairy cooperatives.

The Cogeneration Project:

Developer and Owner

Corona Energy Partners, Ltd., a Texas limited partnership with Corona Energy Corporation, a wholly-owned subsidiary of PSE Inc., Spectrum Corona, Inc., a wholly-owned subsidiary of Spectrum Capital, Ltd. and Diamond Corona, Inc., a wholly-owned subsidiary of Mitsubishi International Corporation, as its General Partner.

Plant Operator

Power Operating Company, a wholly-owned subsidiary of PSE Inc., Houston, Texas

Financing

Partnership financing was arranged by Spectrum Capital, Ltd. with a Construction Loan furnished by Mitsubishi Trust and Banking Corporation, Tokyo, Japan with the construction financing to roll into a term loan provided to the project by Mitsubishi Trust and Banking Corporation.

Project Engineering and Construction Management

Power Systems Engineering, Inc., Houston, Texas, a subsidiary of PSE Inc.

In addition to the above, there were several special purpose corporations or partnerships that were formed in order to provide the legal framework for carrying out obligations of the guarantors and contracting parties under the Qualifying Steam Agreement and the Energy Supply Agreement.

PROJECT LEGAL AND FINANCIAL STRUCTURE

Financing for the cogeneration facility was arranged by Spectrum Capital, Ltd. of New York. A limited partnership was selected as the legal entity that would be the owner/developer of the project since this best fit the equity ownership desires of the conceptual project developer, PSE Inc. of Houston and the financing plan developed by Spectrum Capital.

The project financing is based on certain key or cornerstone contracts that contain the legal obligations and guarantees of the parties to those agreements that cover the financial project risks perceived by the lenders and equity partners. The key contracts are discussed below.

THE ENERGY SUPPLY AGREEMENT

The commercial relationship between the cheese plant and the cogeneration development is defined in an Energy Supply Agreement which was prepared in response to requirements of the cogeneration developer, the cheese plant owners, the cogeneration equity partners and the cogeneration plant project lenders. The Energy Supply Agreement establishes a relationship of Seller and Buyer between Integrated Protein Technology and Corona Energy Partners, Ltd., a limited partnership which is jointly owned by subsidiaries of PSE Inc., Spectrum Capital and Mitsubishi International Corporation. The Energy Supply Agreement provides that Corona Energy Partners, Ltd. has an obligation to supply and IPT has an obligation to purchase all of the energy requirements of the cheese plant for steam, chilled water and electricity. The Energy Supply Agreement sets forth (i) the obligation for supply of these energy products, (ii) specifications of the energy products to be delivered, and (iii) the prices applicable to the purchase of these energy products. The Energy Supply Agreement also makes provisions for energy product measurement and calibration of measurement instruments, for insurance, for the liabilities of the respective parties for construction of the energy interface and for commencement of service after completion. IPT has agreed to make land available to Corona Energy Partners, Ltd. at fair market value on a long-term lease with a purchase option. Provisions for damages and other remedies in the event of failure of performance by either Seller or Buyer are also included. The Energy Supply Agreement sets forth the commercial terms that have been agreed to among all the parties and which provide the basis for financial projections that were prepared by the project developer and submitted to the project lender and their financial advisor. The financial projections examined a range of sensitivities in probable risk areas. Expected and worst case scenarios were established and used as the basis for project financing.

THE QUALIFYING STEAM AGREEMENT

The framework of the Energy Supply Agreement assumes normal and continuous operation of the complete integrated milk processing facility. The cheese plant owner has a contractual obligation to purchase all requirements for energy from Corona Energy Partners, Ltd., but if IPT does not have requirements for steam and electricity, then under the Energy Supply Agreement, IPT does not have an obligation to purchase energy from Corona Energy Partners, Ltd. However, in order to comply with Qualifying Facility requirements of the FERC implementing PURPA and in order to comply with the terms and conditions of the contract for the sale of electric power by Corona Energy Partners, Ltd. to Southern California Edison, Corona Energy Partners, Ltd. must nearly continuously produce and sell electrical and thermal energy, so that there must be a customer which will take and use at least a certain specified minimum annual average quantity of thermal energy each year the cogeneration plant is in operation. In order to satisfy these requirements, positive assurances were necessary to provide that a specified minimum quantity of steam will continuously be taken and used for commercial purposes other than the production of electricity.

Two different approaches were taken to provide the necessary positive assurance of continuous take of minimum steam. On one level, IPT has been asked to arrange for a separate qualifying facility status undertaking, so that irrespective of the requirements of the integrated milk processing facility, minimum quantities of steam to assure the maintenance of qualifying facility status will be taken and used for commercial purposes. The second approach was to create a legal and economic framework for a feasible alternate steam use. The alternate use proposed for the cheese plant is the operation of the alcohol facility as a stand-alone economic operation using a feedstock which does not depend on the operation of the milk processing facility and which has a technical capacity to continuously use at least the required minimum quantities of steam.

ALTERNATE STEAM USE

Approximately one-half of the steam normally consumed by the cheese plant is used in the alcohol facility which processes whey permeate into alcohol. From the inception of the proposal for cogeneration, IPT and PSE recommended that the best protection for assurance of the minimum take of steam was the ability, as an alternate use of steam, to operate the alcohol facility as a stand-alone plant capable of processing readily available commodity feedstocks into alcohol. Even if there is a catastrophic interruption in the supply of milk to the plant or, if for any other reason, continuing operations with milk should be suspended for a significant time, the alcohol facility can operate as an alternate steam user.

The alcohol facility is a stand-alone facility, fully capable of being operated independently of the main plant. In fact, it is not only physically separate, but also has its own office, laboratory and independent computerized control system. The alcohol facility was built as a separate facility to minimize cross-contamination with the main plant. Under the project financing agreement, the alcohol facility is made subject to a stand-by sub-lease from IPT to a Difko controlled entity for a nominal rental per annum. This sub-lease would come into effect only in the event that IPT was in default under either the Energy Supply Agreement or the Qualifying Steam Agreement. In this event, Difko would have an obligation to perform on a separate guarantee of the minimum steam take. Under the sub-lease, Difko would have the legal right to use and operate the alcohol facility during any period of IPT default. This right would survive and override the security interest of the cheese plant project's lenders in the alcohol facility. Corona Energy Partners, Ltd., under a separate agreement, agreed to provide steam and electricity to the alcohol facility as long as DIFKO is performing its obligation as guarantor of the Qualifying Steam Agreement. Taken together, the sub-lease and the assurance of the energy supply permits DIFKO to operate the alcohol facility as a stand-alone facility with only a nominal cost for production facilities. From the technical perspective, two questions were analyzed to confirm the feasibility of the alternate steam use. These issues were analyzed and reported on in a feasibility study prepared by an independent company with extensive business experience in the design, engineering and operation of alcohol production from whey permeate, molasses, grain and other products. The same company that provided the alcohol facility feasibility study also acted as engineer for the lenders for the Corona cheese plant so that it was already intimately familiar with the design and operations of all components of the milk processing facility, including the alcohol production unit.

THE POWER PURCHASE AGREEMENT

PSE Inc. acted as a consultant to Corona Energy Corporation which entered into an SCE Standard Agreement Firm Power Purchase Agreement. The particular contract was a Southern California Edison Standard Offer No. 2, Firm Capacity Option 2, Net Energy Output Option for a total term of thirty years. The Power Purchase Agreement was subsequently assigned to Corona Energy Partners, Ltd. This type of contract calls for a dollar per KW-year capacity purchase price based upon a specified capacity payment schedule for the time period beginning on the date of firm operations of the cogeneration facility and ending on the date of termination or reduction of contract capacity which can occur under certain operating conditions. The contract requires that the cogeneration facility be a facility and equipment which sequentially generates thermal and electrical energy as defined in Title 18, Code of Federal Regulations (CFR), Section 292.202. The contract further requires that the cogeneration facility remain a Qualifying Facility that meets the criteria as defined in Title 18, Code of Federal Regulations (CFR), Section 292.201 through 292.207.

Firm operation under the Power Purchase Agreement is defined as the date mutually agreed upon between the parties on which each generating unit of Seller's generating facility is determined to be a reliable source of generation and on which such unit can be reasonably expected to operate continuously at its effective rating (expressed in KW). In addition to the price paid for capacity from the cogeneration facility, the Power Purchase Agreement calls for a bonus to be paid during peak months, when the on-peak availability of the plant exceeds 85% and a bonus to be paid during non-peak months when the on-peak availability was at least 85% for each of the year's peak months and the on-peak availability exceeds 85%.

Certain penalties are provided for in the event that the cogeneration facility does not meet minimum performance requirements as outlined in the Power Purchase Agreement. In addition, the contract calls for substantial penalties to the cogenerator for failing to meet the obligation to provide power for the full thirty year term of the contract.

FIGURE 4

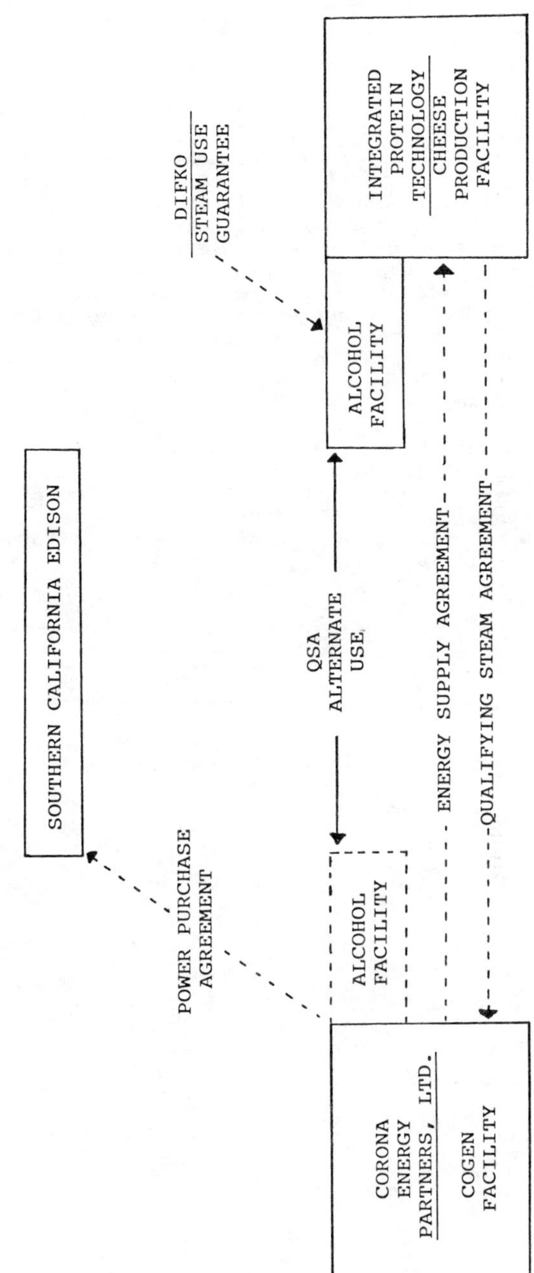
SOUTHERN CALIFORNIA EDISON
POWER PURCHASE AGREEMENT
CORONA ENERGY PARTNERS, LTD.
COGEN FACILITY
ALCOHOL FACILITY
QSA ALTERNATE USE
ALCOHOL FACILITY
DIFKO STEAM USE GUARANTEE
INTEGRATED PROTEIN TECHNOLOGY
CHEESE PRODUCTION FACILITY
ENERGY SUPPLY AGREEMENT
QUALIFYING STEAM AGREEMENT

CORNERSTONE DEVELOPMENT REQUIREMENTS

The Energy Agreement, the Qualifying Steam Agreement and the Power Purchase Agreement provided a sound legal and economic foundation for the financing of a cogeneration facility to serve the cheese plant energy requirements and sell excess electrical energy into the Southern California Edison system. Continuity of steam usage is assured by legal undertakings, by the dependency of the cheese plant on its energy supply and by the availability of a feasible alternate steam use with corporate guarantees to operate the alcohol plant alone, if necessary. Figure 4 illustrates the key components described above.

CURRENT PROJECT STATUS

Cogeneration plant construction began in early October 1987. Significant progress has been made in the past several months. Commercial Operation of the plant is scheduled for May 1988 in time to meet the peak season power requirements of Southern California Edison on June 1, 1988.

CHESTERFIELD 7

AN EFFICIENT COMBINED CYCLE

J. L. Catina, P.E.
Virginia Power Company

ABSTRACT

In every electric utility there are two major elements which influence the generation expansion process: load growth, or demand side; and supply side options.

Virginia Power has actively pursued load management techniques and is still experiencing extraordinary growth.

This paper addresses one result of Virginia Power's efforts in the supply side arena. The results of our studies have led to the conclusion that an appropriate supply side option is the repowering of two retired coal units with two 200 megawatt combined cycle units using "advanced" combustion turbines, with provisions for future coal gasification.

INTRODUCTION

Virginia Power (the company) is the principal subsidiary of Dominion Resources and provides electricity to nearly 1.6 million customers throughout a 30,350 square mile territory that serves parts of two states. The company presently has a system generating capacity of 12,489 megawatts.

The company's generating capacity is approximately 41% nuclear, 44% coal, 5% oil, 4% hydro, and 5.5% other sources.

ALTERNATIVE GENERATING TECHNOLOGIES

Beginning in 1981, the company began studying non-conventional means of meeting our power supply requirements. Some of the new technologies studied were solar photovoltaic cells, coal gasification combined cycle units, fuel cells and wind turbines. The results of this study determined that these new technologies offer some attractive options when compared to conventional large central generating units. They allow capacity to be added in small increments and involve substantial factory fabrication, thereby reducing field work. They are flexible in their use of fuels and involve modest capital investment.

In the uncertain climate of today the ability to reduce demand related risk, financing, construction and operation burdens and keep a good match between capacity and demand is crucial. These technologies allow this flexibility.

Nevertheless, the study concluded that none of these technologies had yet matured to the point of acceptable commercial status. However, phased development of combined cycle-coal gasification could provide the benefits of this technology, in stages, as the technology matures. The utility industry already has significant, positive experience with combined cycle units. They are suitable for the future addition of coal gasification, which is not yet cost effective in utility scale. But as this technology matures, the addition to an already existing combined cycle is relatively straightforward, provided certain provisions are made. In the meantime, the unit can use gas or oil while the prices of these fuels remain favorable; as it resolves its performance and cost uncertainties, coal gasification can be added for tomorrow's fuel uncertainties.

Concurrent with the company's investigation of combined cycle units, conventional coal, fluidized bed coal and simple cycle combustion turbine units were considered.

The company concluded that a conventional coal unit should be ruled out due to long lead times, large capital requirements, operational complexities of flue gas scrubbers and the inability of large coal units to allow a close match between demand and capacity.

Fluidized bed coal units were not selected since the sizes we would require had not been sufficiently proven. In addition, the ability to accurately determine their construction and operation cost is not predictable enough.

Simple cycle combustion turbines are economically feasible only as peaking units and as our demand continues to grow, the need for intermediate and baseload capacity increases. Combustion turbines are unsuited for this role.

ALTERNATIVE SUPPLY

In addition to the aforementioned self-generation options, the company investigated alternative sources of supply, namely cogeneration and purchased power.

The company has actively pursued all purchase power which has been available at favorable terms, it has also encouraged cogeneration, but again at favorable terms.

As a result of these efforts, the company has identified a significant cogeneration potential. However, due to the considerable uncertainity as to how much of this cogeneration would materialize by 1990 and beyond, it was only prudent that the company pursue all options in parallel.

CHESTERFIELD REPOWERING STUDY

In early 1985 the company began a detailed study of the repowering of two retired pulverized coal units at the Chesterfield Station with 300 to 400 MW of combined cycle units.

The Chesterfield Station is located 12 miles south of Richmond, Virginia on the James River. It consists of four active pulverized coal (PC) units, Nos. 3, 4, 5 and 6 whose total generating capacity is 1250 MW; and two inactive PC units, Nos. 1 and 2 of approximately 65 MW each. The latter two units, originally constructed in 1944 and 1945 and retired in 1981, were proposed for combined cycle repowering. The site is bounded by the river on the north, the administration building on the east and Unit 3 on the West as shown in Figure 1.

Repowering appeared preferable to new construction. A chief concern was the lack of suitably developed sites for new construction. The use of an existing site solved the anticipated environmental permitting lead time required for a new site. The potential savings in the reuse of existing equipment was also a strong motivating factor.

The Chesterfield site provides several advantages for repowering because of the extant fuel oil unloading and storage facilities, switchyard, circulating water intake and discharge system, steam turbine building, and administrative facilities to operate and maintain the new units. Significant licensing advantages could be realized if thermal rejection for the new unit could be maintained within existing permits. Also, if the existing circulating water system could be reused, a Corps of Engineers permit could be eliminated.

The general plan was to locate the combustion turbines in the remnants of the units 1 and 2 boilers, with the HRSG's toward the river, and reuse the existing steam turbines and turbine hall.

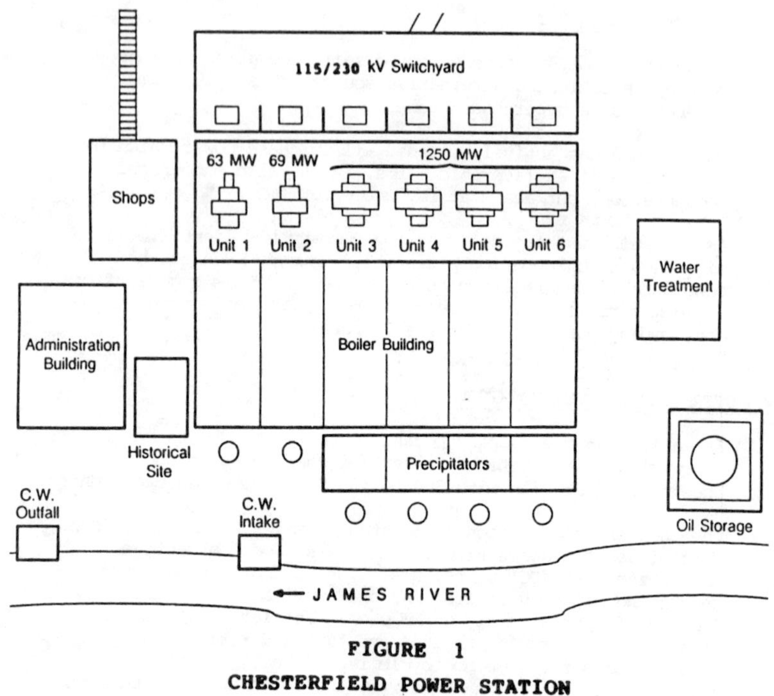

FIGURE 1

CHESTERFIELD POWER STATION

TABLE 1

REPOWERING OPTIONS

	CONVENTIONAL CYCLE	COMBINED CYCLE
Station Output	130 MW(1)	400 MW(2)
Station Auxiliary Load	15%	5%
Station Heat Rate	10,800 Btu/kWh	7,500 Btu/kWh
Capital Cost (3)	1,600 kW	$500 kW
Availability	85%	92%
Construction Duration	48 Mos.	24 Mos.
Peaking Capability	Fair	Good
Reuse of Existing Equipment	Limited	Limited
Reuse of Existing Structures	Limited	Good
Use of Available Space	Marginal	Good
Cost of Fuel (4)	Low	Intermediate

(1) Thermal Discharge Limit
(2) Includes 130 MW Steam Cycle
(3) 1985 Dollars
(4) No. 2 Fuel Oil Reference

COMBINED CYCLE VS PULVERIZED COAL

To take advantage of the existing site, the new units would have to fit into the space occupied by the retired Units 1 and 2, not exceed thermal emissions limits of the original units and have an insignificant air quality impact.

In addition, the unit would have to be capable of initial intermediate operation, later shifting to base load.

Table 1 provides a comparison between the expected performance of a typical combined cycle unit and conventional PC repowering. The following is a summary of the performance parameters listed.

Station Output - A significantly higher station output, 400 MW versus 130 MW, can be achieved by the combined cycle units for the same amount of condenser thermal discharge as compared with the conventional coal fired unit.

Station Auxiliary Load - A combined cycle requires approximately 5 percent of its output for auxiliary power (and losses) compared to approximately 15 percent for a coal-fired unit.

Station Heat Rate - Because of the inherently higher efficiently of the Brayton-Rankine cycle over the Rankine cycle alone (45 percent vs. 31 percent) and the lower station auxiliary load, the combined cycle exhibits about a 30 percent advantage in net heat rate.

Life Cycle Costs - The life cycle cost for a combined cycle is significantly less than for an equivalent pulverized coal plant. The results of the Fuel Use Act cost test calculations demonstrated a $177 million advantage over a comparable pulverized coal fired unit.

Availability - Combined cycles historically provide a higher availability than conventional coal fired units because of the reduced outage durations required for maintenance and the shorter downtime and restart time required for unscheduled outages.

Procurement and Construction Duration - Combined cycle equipment, including heat recovery boilers, in this size range can be fabricated, installed and operational in about three years.

Intermediate Capability - The starting and loading characteristics of the combined cycle make it superior to a coal fired unit for cycling duty.

COMBUSTION TURBINE MARKET SURVEY

A survey of both foreign and domestic manufacturers of combustion turbines was conducted to determine the equipment available for repowering and particular design characteristics.

The size of the units was established such that the existing units' thermal heat rejection rate requirements would not be exceeded. Therefore the total steam turbine output could not exceed 140MW. In a combined cycle the Rankine cycle constitutes one-third of the output; therefore, the combined combustion turbine output could be approximately 270 MW without exceeding the heat rejection rate limits. The existing space at Chesterfield can accommodate up to three combustion turbines so only combustion turbines 90 MW and larger were considered acceptable.

In 1985 there were two existing, conventional machines and one advanced high temperature unit, under development, which met our requirements.

CYCLE VARIATIONS

Now that there was a general idea of what size and type combustion turbines could be accommodated, it was appropriate to study the various cycle options.

The first variable studied was steam pressure. The gas turbines would accommodate a range from 1800 psig to 850 psi, the pressure of the existing turbines. As seen in Table 2 the 850 psi cycle was extremely inefficient as compared to higher pressure induction or reheat turbines. This fact, combined with our analysis that the cost refurbishment of the existing turbines would approximate that of new turbines, ruled out the 850 psi cycle.

The operating problems, combined with the lack of industry experience with 1800 psi Heat Recovery Steam Generator's (HRSG's), ruled out the 1800 psi option.

To achieve the optimum heat recovery from the gas turbine exhaust, a multiple pressure HRSG is usually required. The additional heat removal sections permit the lowering of the stack (exit) temperature from about 400°F to 300°F and below. A low pressure evaporator and economizer is also necessary for deaerator steam and feedwater heating. Therefore, at least two pressures are recommended. A third, intermediate, pressure may be required if there is a significant difference between the high and low pressure ratings. The disadvantage is in the added complexity of the feedwater circuit, including pump and level control systems. For peaking duty, a single pressure HRSG is quicker starting and simpler to maintain in hot standby condition. For both base load and intermediate duty, a dual pressure unit was most appropriate.

TABLE 2

CASE SUMMARY

CASE NO.	DESCRIPTION	No. Cts	HP	RH	IP	LP	Percent SF	Output MW	Heat Rate Btu/kWH
1A	Existing Turbines	2	800	--	--	35	0	301	Base
1B	Existing Turbines	2	800	--	--	35	25	340	+664
2	Intermediate Pressure Turbines	2	1450	--	600	35	0	301	- 50
3	Intermediate Pressure Turbines	3	1450	--	600	35	0	452	- 50
4	High Pressure Turbines with Reheat	2	1800	800	600	35	0	301	-338

A reheat combined cycle provides the optimum in cycle efficiency. When compared against non-reheat cycles the efficiency improvements can be as much as 100 Btu/KWH. The advantage of an advanced combustion turbine with reheat steam over a conventional CT with non-reheat is closer to 230 Btu/KWH.

Supplemental firing is used to raise temperature and increase the steam production of smaller units. It involves injecting and burning fuel in the exhaust of the gas turbine before it enters the HRSG. It is made possible by the approximately 400 percent excess air in the turbine exhaust. Since the exhaust is already at 1000 F, its temperature can be raised to 1400°F or 1600°F and higher without significant losses, except for minor moisture and radiation. Although not as efficient as the combined cycle itself, it is, nevertheless, a very efficient method for extending the HRSG performance.

A deaerator was desirable in the cycle because the company's experience is that condenser inleakage cannot be effectively controlled to the level that would permit proper deaeration in the condenser.

Diverter dampers were ruled out after extensive discussion with other users, a review of the availability of units without diverters and the expected dispatch modes. The availability difference was very small, and since we were not anticipating much simple cycle operation, the additional maintenance and performance penalties were best avoided.

After settling on 1450 psi and replacement of existing steam turbines, further options were investigated.

When all of the above considerations were combined, an "optimum" cycle for Chesterfield resulted and is shown in Figure 2.

FUELS

The primary fuel was designated as natural gas. However, for added protection against service interruptions, the unit was designed for distillate oil backup. As a further fuel flexibility, the unit was to be capable of burning medium-Btu coal gas from a number of acceptable processes similar to Figure 3.

Since the distillate will have a sufficient sulfur content to create acid condensation problems cause corrosion in the low temperature section of the HRSG, provisions for raising the stack temperature when burning distillate were to be provided.

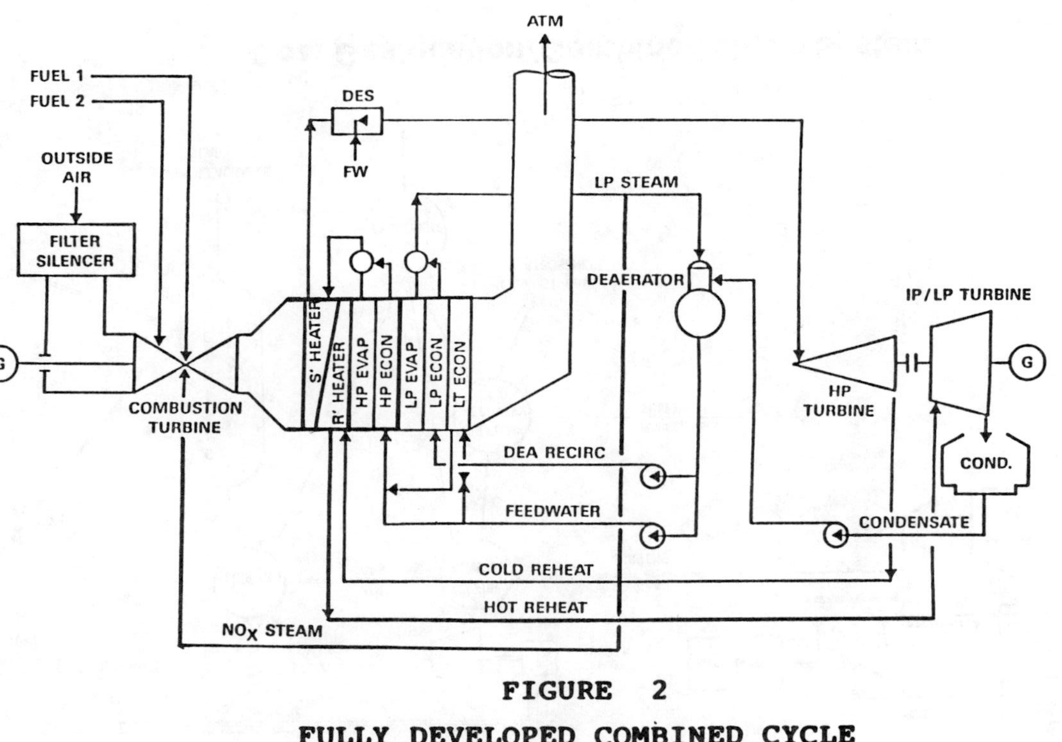

FIGURE 2

FULLY DEVELOPED COMBINED CYCLE

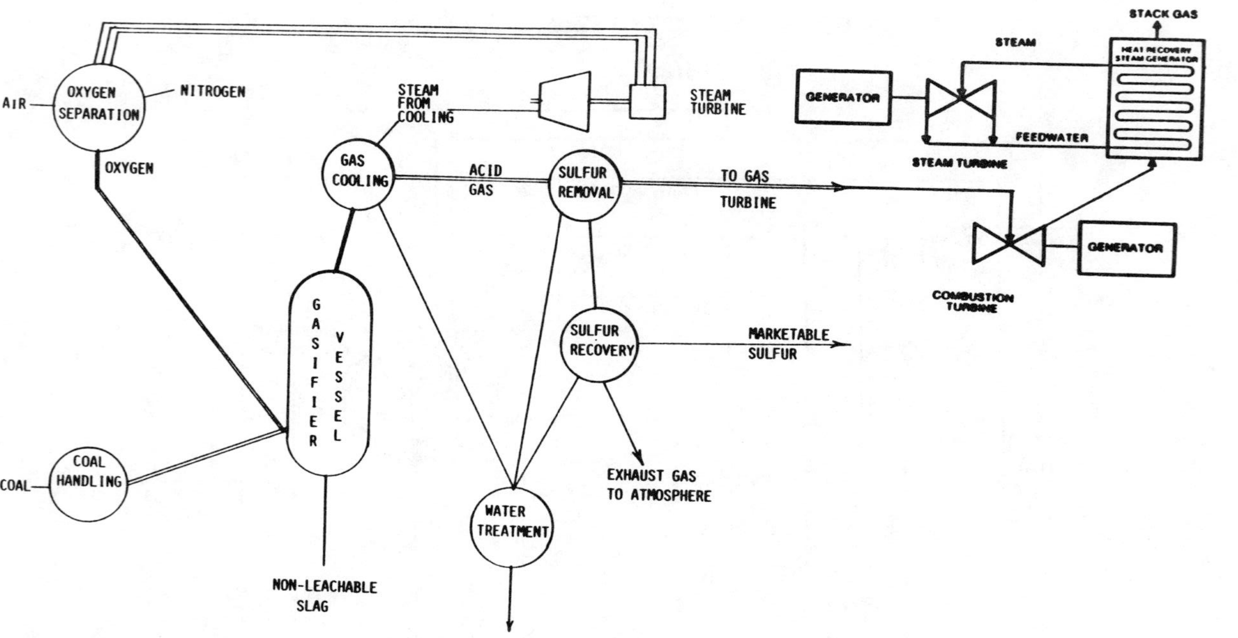

FIGURE 3
Coal Gasification/Combined Cycle System

PHYSICAL ARRANGEMENT

Now that a preliminary cycle had been developed, fitting it to the site remained.

Figure 4-1 illustrates the use of a single HRSG serving two (or three) combustion turbines. The chief advantage of this scheme is economy. The chief drawback is that the entire plant is down when the HRSG is down. If an HRSG diverter is installed, two-thirds of the power would be available from the unit. The steam turbine efficiency is also reduced when only one combustion turbine is generating.

Figure 4-2 illustrates the multitrain arrangement consisting of two trains of combustion turbines, HRSGs, and steam turbines. This arrangement provides for the greatest degree of flexibility, especially when main steam lines are interconnected, and the heat rate is not affected when one unit or component is down. Interconnection of reheat units is not recommended due to steam distribution control problems. A single turbine can also be used in this arrangement with some loss of flexibility and a higher heat rate when one HRSG or combustion turbine is down. Of course, both trains are down when the steam turbine is down.

Figure 4-3 illustrates an arrangement with three combustion turbines, three HRSGs and two steam turbines. It can also be configured with a single turbine; however, this arrangement improves system availability by not having the entire output dependent on the operation of a single steam turbine. Part load operation (when one combustion turbine or HRSG is down) is more likely to occur with this arrangement because of the high number of components and higher likelihood that one will be down. This arrangement, however, presents problems in staged construction and may only be appropriate for a unit constructed in one stage.

As previously discussed, two steam turbine pedestals are already in place at Chesterfield. These, along with major components of the circulating water system which can be salvaged, indicate that an arrangement of two steam turbines is the most economical.

The layouts for the arrangement of three combustion turbines in the space available at Chesterfield were extremely crowded. Because the physical limitations may create construction and/or maintenance problems, that plan was deemed to be less desirable than the plan utilizing two combustion turbines.

Also, phased construction would be easier if the complex were divisible into two separable units.

Based upon the above, the two-train concept was decided upon.

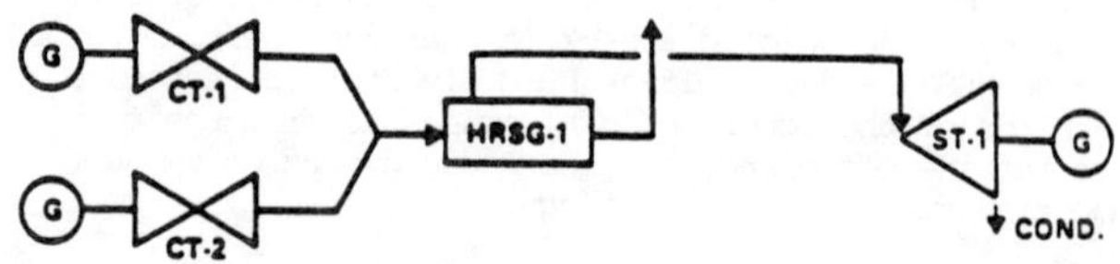

2 COMBUSTION TURBINES / 1 HRSG / 1 OR 2 STEAM TURBINES

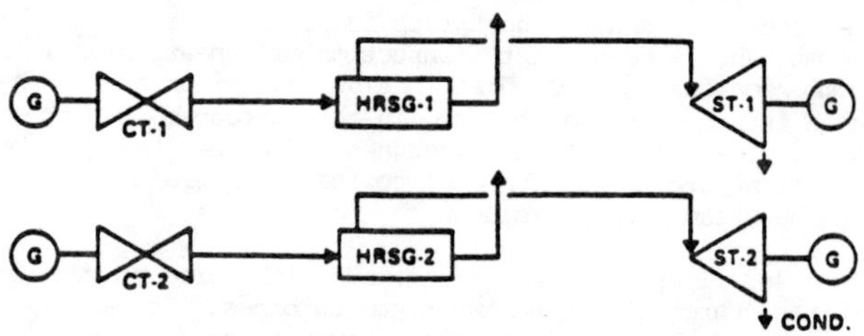

2 COMBUSTION TURBINES / 2 HRSGs / 1 OR 2 STEAM TURBINES

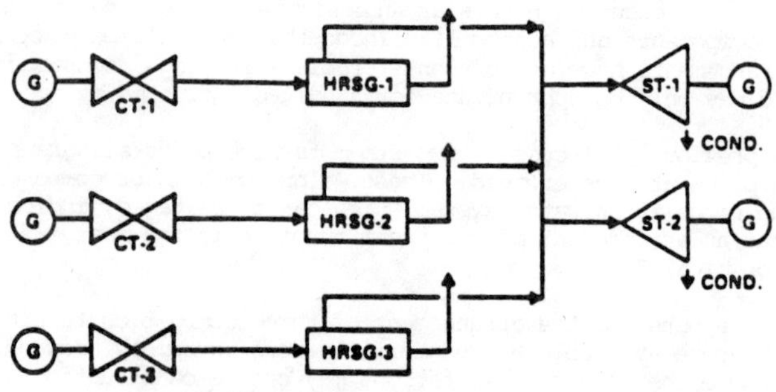

3 COMBUSTION TURBINES / 3 HRSGs / 1 OR 2 STEAM TURBINES

FIGURE 4

RECOMMENDED DESIGN

Having a preferred physical arrangement, and a concept for an "optimum" cycle, it was now time to finalize the options.

Since 300 to 400 MW was the goal for the site, and the two train arrangement was preferred, there were three final designs. Two designs involved two conventional CTs, with supplementary fired HRSGs and two steam turbines. Supplementary firing was required to make maximum use of the heat rejection permit. The third design was two advanced CTs with two unfired reheat HRSGs and two reheat steam turbines. The reheat cycle was chosen because at that time it was the only cycle available from an advanced turbine manufacturer.

Representative study performance data are shown in Table 3, which clearly demonstrates the performance advantage of an advanced CT-based combined cycle unit.

TABLE 3
COMBINED CYCLE PERFORMANCE

CONVENTIONAL	SUPPLEMENTAL FIRING	ESTIMATED OUTPUT (MW-ISO)	ESTIMATED HEAT RATE (BTU/KWH-HHV)
W501D	Y	180.5	8500
KWU-V84	Y	166.5	8400
Advanced			
GE7F	N	200	7700

FINAL DECISION

Shortly after the conclusion of the study, GE submitted a proposal for an advanced combined cycle unit which was very similar to that in the study. This proposal offered a turnkey contract at a very low cost per KW and included warrantees and assurance of timely completion. At this time, the GE unit was the only advanced unit available to meet our schedule.

Therefore, on the basis of capital cost, lead time, operating efficiency and life cycle cost, and after state regulatory approval, the Company executed a contract with GE for the installation their 210 MW unit. Approximately modified to the Company's requirements, this unit has been designated Chesterfield 7. Plans are still active for the possible construction of a second similar unit - Chesterfield 8.

UNIT DESIGN HIGHLIGHTS

Highlights of the unit design are shown in Table 4.

Plan and elevation of unit 7 and the proposed unit 8 are shown in Figures 5 and 6.

TABLE 4

Power Output (ISO, NET, MW)	210
Heat Rate (Btu/KWH, HHV)	7500
C.T. Power (Approx., MW)	140
S.T. Power (Approx., MW)	70
Arrangement	Axial, inline
HRSG	Two pressure, reheat, integral deaerator vertical tube, unfired
Steam Pressure (PSI-Main, Reheat, IP)	1450/300/300
Steam Temperature (˜F-Main/Reheat/IP)	950/950/500
Steam Turbine	Straight condensing, Reheat - No extraction
NO_x Control	Steam Injection
Fuels	Nat'l Gas, No. 2, MBTU Coal Gas w/Mods.
Availability	95%
Starting Reliability	98%
Instrumentation	Redundant, Fault tolerant
Accessories	Electric Motor Driven Skid Mounted
Authorized Project ($\$ \times 10^6$) Cost	$116.5

FIGURE 5

PROPOSED PLANT LAYOUT

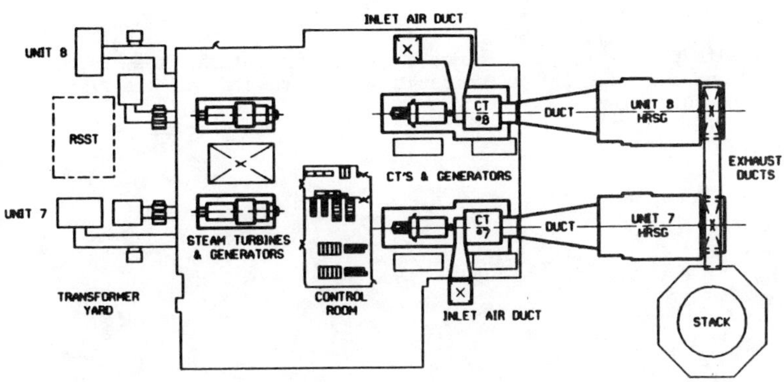

FIGURE 6

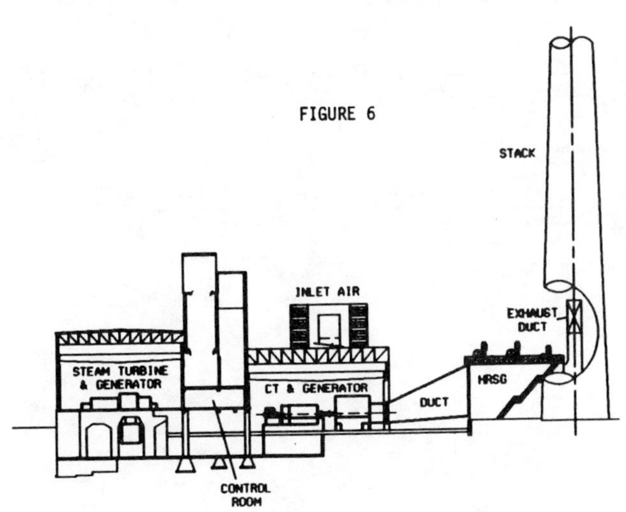

THE FUTURE

The performance, reliability, maintainability and operability of the newest generation of combined cycle units holds significant promise. It remains to be seen if these promises are realized. The advanced combustion turbine for Chesterfield 7 is currently being factory-tested and is scheduled for operation in combined cycle by June, 1990.

Already, several other manufacturers have begun their work on similar machines, which would reach the market in the early '90s.

With the further development of coal gasification, these units have the potential to dominate power production into the 21st century.

REFERENCE LISTING

1. Repowering Chesterfield 1 and 2 with Combined Cycle, J. L. Catina, H. J. Fortune, Jr., G. E. Soroka, ASME Gas Turbine Conference, 1987.

2. Petition and Supplemental Testimony and Exhibits of Virginia Electric and Power Company before the State Corporation of Virginia, March, 1987.

3. 1986 Annual Report, Dominion Resources, Inc.; Richmond, VA.

4. Combined Cycle Repowering at Chesterfield Power Station, J. L. Catina, R. W. Olney, EEI Conference, May, 1987.

REGENERATION THROUGH COGENERATION: THE MIDLAND COGENERATION VENTURE

John W. Clark, Senior Vice President - Communications
Consumers Power Company
Jackson, Michigan

Consumers Power has experienced a dramatic turnaround, literally climbing from the brink of bankruptcy two years ago. Our recovery was so dramatic that Electric Light & Power magazine crowned us "Utility of the Year" in 1987, and Forbes magazine named us the most improved U.S. utility of 1986.

Then again, being "Most Improved" is perhaps not that great a feat given the simple fact that we had nowhere to go but up.

The key to this dramatic turnaround is, appropriately, our Midland facility, which was crucified as a nuclear plant, then resurrected as a gas-fueled, combined-cycle cogeneration plant.

It's appropriate that Midland was our salvation, because it was also the cause of our downfall. It was started in Midland, Michigan twenty years ago as a nuclear plant. For a combination of reasons, the nuclear plant's cost ballooned to over $4 billion and the construction schedule stretched across two decades.

During that time, the damage we had done to ourselves was far greater than just financial. In the communications area, for example, in what was no small accomplishment, we had managed to alienate almost every important constituency in the state of Michigan. Over $4 billion and twenty years' effort had generated nothing but controversy.

Our customers, alarmed by the potential rate consequences of a $4 billion plant, were up in arms. That, in turn, worried politicians, who relied on the votes of the six million people we serve to stay in office. The few politicians who stood by us found their support becoming a volatile campaign issue against them. Our largest industrial customers and the state's most liberal politicians joined to lead a coalition against completing the plant. One of those major customers, Dow Chemical, was squared off against us in a major lawsuit over Midland. And if we felt we were the Christians in that fight, everyone in the coliseum was rooting for the lions.

As you might imagine, the media seemed united against us, fueled by a growing anti-nuclear sentiment following Three Mile Island and what they saw as a serious lack of honesty on our part regarding Midland. Eventually, in 1984, when we could no longer raise needed funds in capital markets, we were forced to shut down the project.

Our employees were severely demoralized by this seemingly unanimous public hostility, and by the years of budget restrictions from diverting needed operating dollars to what looked like a fruitless effort to complete Midland. Employees were discouraged not to see the company fighting back and failing to make its case to counter all this criticism, and shareholders were outraged when the company was forced to suspend common stock dividends to stave off bankruptcy.

With that backdrop, it is easy to understand how our board reached out for the new management and elected Bill McCormick chairman and CEO in November 1985.

Since the over $4 billion the company had spent on Midland represented some 40 percent of our total assets, it didn't take us long to figure out that the key to our success was putting that investment to work and putting to rest the controversy surrounding it. Doing this would require overcoming both engineering and communications challenges.

The entire Midland issue had been so ferociously politicized that McCormick was heavily criticized for even <u>proposing</u> to study what, if anything, could be done with the plant. The new management set the tone for what was to come by confronting the controversy squarely and backing down those opponents who were trying to keep us from even <u>examining</u> Midland's future.

The engineering challenges were addressed in a comprehensive options study to identify how best to use Midland to stave off the company's impending shortage of generating capacity -- the whole reason Midland was built in the first place.

The basic options were either abandoning the facility altogether and purchasing electricity from other utilities, or putting it to work by either <u>completing</u> it as a nuclear plant or <u>converting</u> it to either coal or gas.

As you know, we ultimately concluded that natural gas had a number of advantages. It required the least capital investment and had the shortest construction time. It provided the potential of having the highest availability and efficiency. It was proven technology. Gas-market conditions were favorable. And natural gas has the least environmental impact on the project, so the company could get its environmental permits in short order.

Subsequent agreements with Dow Chemical -- with whom we'd been in court for two years -- have enabled us to bring the additional benefits of cogeneration to Midland.

The communications challenge was as formidable as the engineering challenge, and we had to address both at the same time.

A big part of our communications challenge stemmed from the fact that the company had never really made the case that Michigan needed the power Midland could provide. We then had to show the benefits of making this power in Michigan at Midland, versus trying to either buy it outside the state or starting all over to build a new plant somewhere else in Michigan.

We had to remind the state that its future economic growth depended on the ability of Consumers Power -- Michigan's largest utility serving 6 of the state's 9 million residents in 67 of 68 Lower Peninsula counties -- to do its job of powering the state's progress.

As 1986 began, our new Communications Department developed the company's first-ever strategic communications plan. The immediate goal was to build a base of public understanding and support for the company's proposal to put Midland to work that would be announced later in the year.

The assessment of our resources was not what most political strategists would call ideal. The hour was late. There was neither the time nor money to enlist and educate sophisticated outside communications experts. It would also have been politically inappropriate -- not to mention financially out of reach -- to run a slick advertising campaign. In the end, we had to develop a home-grown, grass-roots campaign that utilized the only real resources we had available to use -- our over 10,000 employees and over 100,000 Michigan shareholders.

Strategically, these resources were well-positioned, since they lived and worked throughout Michigan in virtually every Lower Peninsula legislative district. We also found that our shareholders were the very people we needed to reach -- business and civic leaders and others in influential positions. Many of our employees had their own strong, individual ties to key politicians and community leaders. They were a largely untapped resource, since we never before had made such a concentrated effort to reach, inform, motivate and support them to help the company solve its communications problems.

The new communications initiative was kicked off with a videotape which was shown to all employees. It was a pep talk to motivate them into action. It also crystallized the messages we wanted them to carry and demonstrated tools we had produced for them to use.

We better focused our employee communications program by consolidating seven different publications into two - a monthly magazine called Progress and a weekly newspaper called CPWeekly. Progress is mailed to employees at home so we can reach their families; we also send it to all retirees and 30,000 shareholders who have indicated a willingness to be active on our behalf. CPWeekly is distributed at work.

The campaign itself was led by the CEO and other senior officers who briefed state government officials, beginning with the governor and including every Michigan legislator in both Lansing and Washington. We briefed our major customers and labor leaders. We also briefed every major media outlet in Michigan at least once and had follow-up sessions with most of them.

We actively solicited supportive editorials from the media for the general proposition of putting Midland to work rather than simply walking away from it. We encouraged business, labor and civic leaders to write supportive letters to the state's political leaders on this same point. Management led the charge at the national and state levels, while employees took the lead at the regional and local levels. Again, the basic idea was to lay the groundwork for whatever specific Midland proposal we'd make in the spring following the options study.

As a constant reminder to employees and the public of the key role the company plays in our state's economic growth, the phrase "Powering Michigan's Progress" was added to our logo. The slogan is our job description and underscores the partnership we have with the state as its largest utility. It was incorporated on all new and existing signage throughout the company.

Simultaneously, we greatly expanded the use of press releases stressing Michigan's need for the power that Midland could provide. The company issued a press release the equivalent of every business day in 1986 and handled about 4,000 telephone inquiries from the media.

The results of our activities were immediate and rewarding. News stories explaining our side of the issue began appearing. Our key audiences began to respond to arguments from us which they'd not heard before. Throughout Michigan, there was genuine appreciation for our efforts to open a dialogue on how best to use Midland to make the power Michigan required.

A major milestone in the Midland story developed late in 1986, when Consumers Power and Dow Chemical announced an agreement to form a partnership that would complete, own and operate Midland as a cogeneration plant. Dow and CPCo had originally been partners in Midland's nuclear construction phase, but, as I've said, that original relationship had dissolved into bitter lawsuits in the last several years.

Dow's support represented another dramatic "turnaround" example of a former adversary's conversion for Midland's own conversion.

A firm consensus of support now exists for putting Midland to work as we've proposed. It is evidenced by letters of support signed by the bipartisan leadership of Michigan's House and Senate, both U.S. senators and 17 of Michigan's 18 congressmen.

All in all, over 500 resolutions and letters of support were forthcoming from key governmental, business, labor and civic leaders throughout Michigan.

Our work has generated more than 150 supportive editorials -- including several in every important newspaper in Michigan -- supporting the company's conversion effort.

This very visible communications effort has contributed a great deal to our success. But it obviously hasn't been the only factor. A great deal of behind-the-scenes work has been needed to make the Midland Cogeneration Venture a reality.

First and foremost was structuring the project in a way that made it affordable for Consumers Power, yet still attractive to other investors. Since we were in such poor shape financially, we needed to develop a project structure that required a minimum of cash from the company. Our strategy was to attract equity partners who would have a vested interest in Midland. We felt that their dual interests in construction obligations and potential return on their investment in a successful project would make for a very strong consortium.

In every phase of our project, we had people bid against each other for different parts. We had Dow and Fluor bid against each other on contracting and constructing the project. Brown Boveri, GE and Westinghouse were competing for the turbines. Combustion Engineering was competing with four other manufacturers for the waste steam recovery system. Panhandle and Coastal, the two major pipelines that supply the State of Michigan, were competing against each other for the new business in this plant, which will utilize 80 bcf of gas a year.

For every partner we've gotten into this project, we have negotiated with anywhere from two to four parties simultaneously. Each of the parties knew that the terms and conditions, as well as the size of the equity investment, would affect our decision on the successful bidders. As a result, the partnership has seven multi-billion-dollar corporations, supplying $360 million of cash equity so far.

The partners are subsidiaries of Brown Boveri, CMS Energy, The Coastal Corporation, Combustion Engineering, The Dow Chemical Company, Fluor Corporation and Panhandle Eastern Corporation.

The capital structure of the project is also unique, since you're starting with Consumers having $1.5 billion of usable assets already on the site. We're contributing between $300 to $400 million of those assets to the partnership for our 49% equity ownership in the partnership. The remaining $1.2 billion of assets will be sold to the partnership in exchange for market-type notes that Consumers Power Company will own. The other investors are contributing a portion of their cash equity, with the balance due upon operation.

There's also a construction loan. We have commitments from a group of four banks, led by First Chicago, for funding to complete the project. We anticipate refinancing those notes once the project starts operating.

What you're looking at, when the plant goes into operation, is a capital structure that totals about $2.5 billion, of which 40% will be equity, and 60% debt. Consumers will hold $1.5 billion of that debt. The reason that the value of our notes goes from the $1.2 billion in contributed assets to $1.5 billion is that we're accruing interest between now and the date the plant goes into operation.

Within the first two years of operation, it is anticipated that Consumers will remarket its notes into the marketplace and be able to cash them out and hold $1.5 billion of cash at the end of the second year of operation.

We also needed a supply of gas with a predictable price - preferably long-term contracts with some kind of controlled escalation tied to coal prices. The project needs 200 million cubic feet of gas per day. This equates to about 80 bcf per year. The gas supplies we're looking at are in both Canada and the U.S. We're very fortunate that with Panhandle, ANR, and ANR's subsidiary, Great Lakes Gas Transmission Company, we have access to all the major producing areas in the U.S. and Canada. So far we've signed up about 60 million bcf a day, or about a third of our total requirements. Forty million bcf a day will come out of Canada, and the other 20 million bcf will come from U.S. suppliers.

We're offering producers an economic package that we think is attractive over 10 to 12 years. And we're willing to be flexible in meeting the objectives of the producer. If he wants a higher price escalation on the front end and slower escalation on the back end, that's fine. If he wants it fast on the back end - that's OK. So are reopeners, with some kind of caps on them. We're quite confident that what we're offering is within market prices.

The cogeneration rates that will be charged to Consumers Power Company are based on avoided costs, as most of you know. So far, the Michigan Public Service Commission has approved two cogeneration contracts - one with a capacity cost of about 4.9 cents per kilowatt-hour and the other one at about 4 cents. The rate that we're seeking in the purchased power contract between the MCV and Consumers Power is slightly less than the lowest end of that range when it is escalated to 1990. The impact on Consumers' rates are minimal. The MCV will have a rate impact in 1990 of about 14% higher than today's rates, which are currently lower in nominal terms than our electric rates were in 1984. In today's marketplace, our electric rates are about 18% lower than Michigan's other major electric utility. We believe that gap will widen because of new power plants coming on line in Michigan. When you look at the change in electric rates between now and 1991, we're really looking at an annual compound growth of 3%, which is less than the rate of inflation.

Our strategy here is not to go after the rates that we think we're entitled to. We're trying to find a formula that's acceptable in the marketplace and which can create a win-win scenario between ratepayers, cogenerators and Consumers Power Company.

From a technical standpoint, we really have upside potential in this project. We're only using the smaller of the two steam turbine generators remaining from the old nuclear plant. We have the opportunity to convert the second nuclear turbine, which is about 880 megawatts, with the addition of about 16 more gas turbines, to generate an additional 2,000 megawatts of power. That's available when and if the market needs it.

Also, all of our gas turbine units can be retrofitted for coal gasification if the gas market isn't there - either at the end of our gas contracts or when the opportunity for the second unit exists. That's kind of our insurance policy in this project. If gas prices get too high, there would be the opportunity to switch to low-Btu coal gasification. And Dow Chemical happens to possess some of the best technology in that area today.

This project, by itself, is pretty nice. We also think the conversion of Midland to the MCV represents a major step in trying to maximize our shareholders' value. This project has given us the ability to take $1.5 billion of nonproductive assets and put them to use.

We have the immediate earnings impact from this project, and we're generating about $88 million a year in interest income. We have the potential equity of those notes, to be able to sell them into the marketplace, and to cash out for about $1.5 billion. After doing that, we still own 49% equity in the partnership, which is eligible for a five-year accelerated Cost Recovery System depreciation and Investment Tax Credits. All in all, I think we will have done a pretty good job here for our shareholders when we get this project to the goal line.

I would really like to take this opportunity to get up on my soap box and do a little bit of preaching about where the electric industry is going. Our industry is changing dramatically. There are regulated prudency reviews and disallowances, the advent of cogeneration in this industry, competition that may be coming about from what we believe is an independent bulk power producing industry, and also industrial customers and their ability to build cogenerating facilities.

I think there are tremendous opportunities in this industry for companies that are innovative and decisive. Cogeneration represents one of those opportunities. As the Midland Cogeneration Venture demonstrates, this can be an exciting time for all of us.

COGENERATION IN THE MINERALS INDUSTRY

Greg Connors, P.E., Director-Cogeneration
Atlanta Gas Light Company
Atlanta, Georgia

The driving force behind the decision to cogenerate is usually the need to control and reduce electric energy costs. In parts of the country where the concept of on-site generation of power is popular, high electric rates usually predominate. Cogeneration can give the industrial energy user a cost-effective alternative to purchased power while in certain instances also increasing the reliability of power delivery.

But while the desire to control electric costs are of primary importance to a potential cogenerator, of likewise importance is the need for the thermal energy which a cogeneration system will provide. Because cogeneration by definition is the simultaneous production and use of electricity and thermal energy, it is obvious that the successful cogenerators are those making efficient use of the two forms of energy produced.

In looking at the recent rapid growth in cogeneration, the prime movers of choice appear to be the reciprocating engine and the combustion turbine. The majority of all cogeneration systems installed to date rely on natural gas to fuel their prime movers. Reciprocating engines, representing either the Diesel or Otto cycle, are the more popular prime mover in the one megawatt and under range. For larger systems found in industrial applications, the gas turbine (Brayton cycle) predominates as the preferred prime mover.

In the case of the reciprocating engine, useful waste heat can generally be recovered to produce hot water or low pressure steam when heat from both the jacket water and exhaust heat are recovered. In certain cases, the exhaust heat can be used separately to produce higher pressure (i.e., 100 psig) stream. Gas turbines by design do not have a hot water coolant cycle. Instead, cooling is done by the air stream used in the turbine itself. As much as four-fifths of the air entering a turbine is used for turbine blade cooling, and not combustion. The significance of this from the cogenerators point of view is that with a turbine, the sole source of recoverable waste heat will be the turbine's exhaust, typically at 900-1,100 degrees Fahrenheit. This exhaust stream is suitable either for recovery in a heat recovery steam generator for the production of high pressure steam, or to be used in a direct-exhaust application for purposes such as drying.

It is this latter approach that can be used in such markets as the minerals industry where the turbine's hot exhaust can be used to dry a mineral product after processing. This paper will discuss a cogeneration installation at a kaolin processing plant.

THE KAOLIN INDUSTRY

Kaolin is an aluminum silicate clay mineral found in a few parts of the world, the end result of weatherization, alteration and relocation of certain rock materials found in the earth's crust. The greatest concentration of kaolin found in the United States is located in an area in central Georgia known as the "Fall Line," which was at one time an ancient ocean front (see Figure 1). This process took place over millions of years during which time clay particles deposited in pockets along the Fall-Line carried by rivers and streams. Georgia produces about 95% of the nation's and 60% of the world's kaolin, which is used in a variety of applications ranging from paints and paper to rubber, adhesives and pharmaceuticals.

The procedure used in processing kaolin can be broken down into six steps. First, the ore is mined in an open-pit method. It is then mixed with water to form a slurry to be piped to the processing plant. A de-griting process and separation process then follow, to remove impurities and achieve a stable brightness and viscosity. Finally, the slurry is filtered and dried. Drying is done either in a rotary dryer or "dry" process, or spray dryer, known as the "wet" process in which the kaolin slurry is sprayed into a dryer through which pass hot exhaust gases. The latter case is when product brightness is of particular importance, such as for the paper industry where kaolin is used both as a filler and to put a glossy finish on paper.

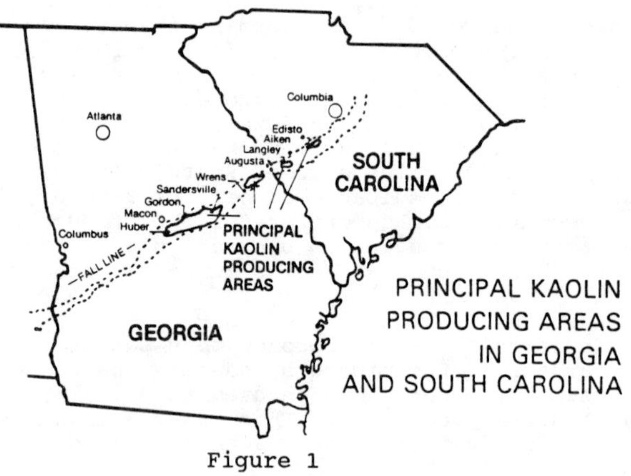

Figure 1

MATCHING THE ELECTRIC DEMAND

J. M. Huber Corporation, a large kaolin producer in Georgia, utilizes both processes. In late 1985, the company began to evaluate the possibility of using gas turbines to reduce their cost of purchased power. The company has a kaolin operation in Wrens, Georgia, as well as a location near Macon, Georgia. While the Macon plant is somewhat larger in size, both plants had an electric demand of roughly 7,000-8,000 kilowatts and both were served by Georgia Power's PL-6 Power and Light rate schedule.

It would be beneficial at this time to outline the structure of the PL-6 rate because Huber's strategy in cogenerating was to attack the most expensive on-peak segments of the rate and still benefit from the lower cost base-load charges. While the rate is a traditional stepped rate, with lower costs for greater consumption, charges can nevertheless be broken down into two components -- demand and consumption -- to more accurately reflect the cost of purchased power. In the particular load factor in which both Huber plants fall, demand charges are roughly \$9 per kilowatt per month, while the consumption charges averages 2.5 cents per kilowatt-hour (kwh). When the two charges are combined, the average cost of power comes out to be roughly 4.5 cents per kwh. Additionally, there is a billing demand period which distinguishes on-peak and off-peak times of the year. During the utility's on-peak period of June thru September, the billing demand is the highest of the following:

1) the current actual demand
2) 95% of the highest actual demand occurring in any previous summer month, or
3) 60% of the highest actual demand occurring in any previous applicable winter month (October-May).

The billing demand period considers the current month as well as the preceding eleven months. During the off-peak period, the billing demand is determined by the greater of either item two or three as outlined above. In essence, what this means is that the summer billing demand ratchet of 95% will usually determine what the billing demand is in any given month. Because of this and the demand charge previously discussed, Huber considered operating the cogeneration system in the June thru September timeframe to reduce the impact of high demand charges. In so doing, they would be able to achieve a savings in demand charges alone of roughly $100,000 per megawatt per year of power generated under the PL-6 rate.

This manner of cogeneration whereby such a system operates only in the summer months benefits not only the customer by lowering production costs but also benefits the electric utility because by having customers shed peak summer electric load, the utility foregoes the need to operate more costly peaking plants, and achieves a better year-round load factor. Some utilities such as Georgia Power have recognized the positive impact customer load shedding during on-peak periods can have for the utility itself by structuring rates to encourage such practices.

Since the cost savings mentioned above equates in essence to a savings of $100 per kw per year, it is clear that the traditional manner of installing new equipment at $800-$1,000 per kw would not be feasible because this would result in a 8-10 year simple payback. Instead Huber turned its attention to used gas turbines. In the fall of 1985, the company located four Ruston TA 1500 gas turbines which were at that time for sale after having operated at the corporate headquarters of Atlanta Gas

Light Company for some twenty years. Not only were the turbines available at an attractive price, but as will be discussed below, their thermal output was well matched to the heating requirements of Huber's spray dryers.

THE THERMAL MATCH

As shown in the schematic diagram (figure 2), a spray dryer is the apparatus in which the kaolin slurry is atomized and mixed with hot air at roughly 1,100 degrees Fahrenheit coming from the gas burner. The product is dried as it falls from the top of the spray dryer and drops out as dry kaolin, ready for packaging and shipping. The cogeneration system is fitted into the existing arrangement as shown. Huber installed two turbines at its Macon site and one at its Wrens location, with each individual turbine paired to an individual spray dryer. An additional turbine was purchased to serve as a source of spare parts. The Ruston produces approximately 47,000 cubic feet per minute of exhaust gases at roughly 915 degrees F, which is boosted to the desired drying temperature with the existing burner. The spray dryer's requirements for air are greater than that which the turbine will produce, so at all times the turbine's exhaust is utilized as opposed to being diverted to the atmosphere. This is an efficient as well as cost-effective method of heat recovery because there is no need for heat exchangers or heat recovery boilers, and this lowers the installed cost of the cogeneration system as well as eliminates the need to derate thermal output caused by heat transfer inefficiencies.

Because, as mentioned previously, the gas turbine operates on large volumes of air, it is sensitive to ambient conditions such as elevation and entering air temperature. As ambient temperatures rise, air becomes less dense, causing the turbine's output to drop. In the case of the Ruston TA 1500, (assuming 1,000 feet elevation and 92% generator efficiency) power output is rated at 1056 kw at 60 degrees ambient, and drops to 836 kw output at 100 degrees Fahrenheit, as shown in Figure 3. In other words,the turbine's power output goes down in the summer, which is when Huber needed power to be the greatest in order to maximize electric demand savings. One common method of counteracting this derating effect is to install evaporative coolers at the turbine's air inlet, although Huber chose not to take this route. In spite of this rather dramatic drop in power output, however, the turbine's mechanical efficiency does not suffer as much,

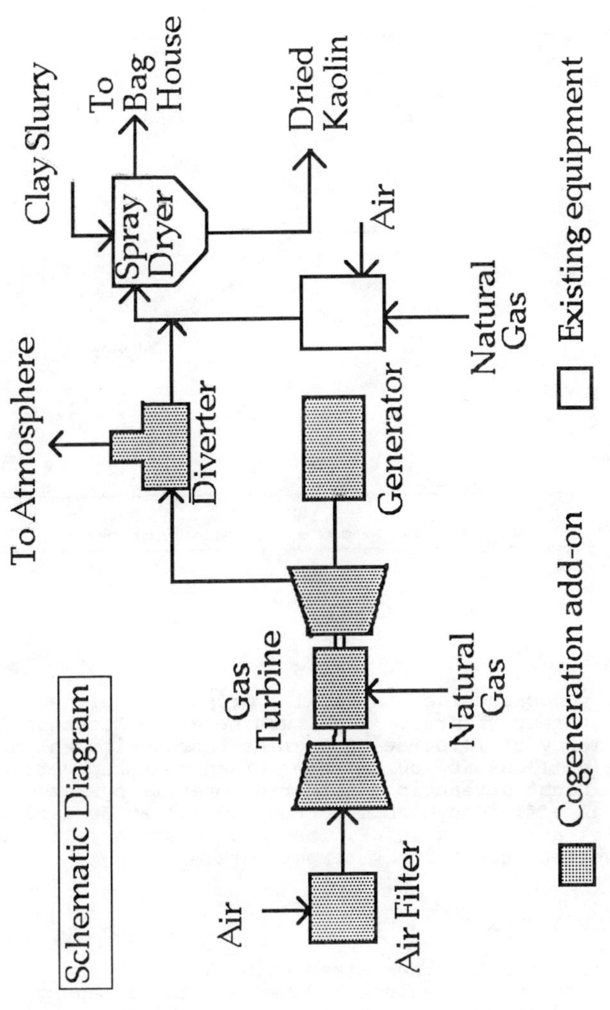
Schematic Diagram
Air
Air Filter
Gas Turbine
Natural Gas
Generator
To Atmosphere
Diverter
Natural Gas
Air
Spray Dryer
Clay Slurry
To Bag House
Dried Kaolin
Cogeneration add-on
Existing equipment

Figure 2

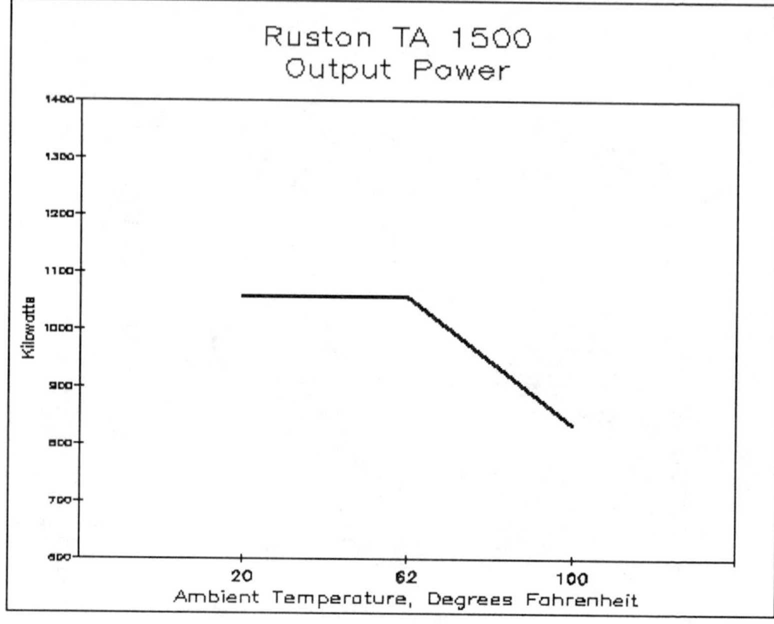

Figure 3

largely because fuel input also drops with higher ambient temperatures. Each turbine has a mechanical efficiency of 14.6% at 60 degrees Fahrenheit, which drops at 13.5% at 100 degrees. When heat recovery of the exhaust stream is considered, overall system thermal efficiency jumps to roughly 74% at 60 degrees and 65% at 100 degrees F. These numbers assume a 300 degree Fahrenheit stack temperature.

RESULTS AND EXPERIENCES

With the turbines sized both thermally and electrically to complement Huber's internal energy needs and priced attractively, the turbines were purchased at the end of 1985 with the intent of having them operational at both plants by the end of May, 1986, when the summer on-peak billing period came into effect. In the interim, the turbines were dismantled, inspected and installed, with much of the existing controls and exhaust ducts, as well as the generators, being utilized at the new sites. No overhaul was required, although Huber did eventually buy an additional turbine as a source of spare parts. The cogeneration plant went in without the need for gas compressors because the 150 PSIG gas pressure required by the turbines was provided by the local gas utility. Additional digital controls and sensors were added to provide for better control over the turbine's thermal output. In both installations, a step-up transformer was installed to boost voltage from the 480 volts produced by the turbine's generator to 4,160 volts as presently used throughout both plants. Power is used internally for loads such as pumps, electric filtration drums and magnetic separators. Although production is continuous, the turbines operated on week days (24 hours per day) at the Macon plant, while at the smaller Wrens plant they operated continuously throughout the four summer months.

Huber personnel designed the interfacing between cogeneration and existing equipment, and contracted for the actual turbine installation as well as the installation of the exhaust heat ducts. To minimize the intake of particulate matter in what is normally a dusty environment a dry regenerative-type air filtration system was installed. Operator training was carried out by the turbine installers as well as personnel from Atlanta Gas Light Company who had previously operated and maintained the equipment.

Huber utilized existing personnel for the turbine operation, which was largely a stand-alone operation, and found that while the system was new for the operators, they became familiar with its operation in a short period of time. The actual turbine start-up procedure which the Macon plant went through at the start of every Monday morning took on the order of five minutes.

At the time the turbines were installed, there was no back-up power rate in effect other than a "Limited Standby Service Rider " which provided for sales of standby power at roughly 9.0 cents per kwh. If one or both of the turbines were to have become inoperable, supplemental power could be purchased at 9.0 cents per kwh without incurring a new demand charge. As it turned out, Huber did not have to buy standby power because both cogeneration sites remained on-line when needed. This demonstrates the reliability of properly maintained gas turbines, even ones that are twenty years old. This rate did not provide for firm back-up service and so was not satisfying the requirements of the Public Utilities Regulatory Policy Act. In October, 1987, a new

"Back-Up rider" providing for both firm and interruptible power was put into effect as part of a rate hike settlement. The rate increase itself also impacted cogeneration in a positive way. In the case of J.M. Huber, demand charges increased from $9 to $10.58 per kilowatt per month. Thus, the same nominal 1000 kw of power produced by each gas turbine system now saves close to $125,000 per year in demand charges alone, an increase of 25%.

CIRCULATING FLUIDIZED BED COMBUSTION TECHNOLOGY ACHIEVES COMMERCIAL STATUS - COLORADO-UTE AND MT. POSO COGENERATION COMPANY

E. J. Oakes, President - Pyropower Corporation

K. F. Swartz, Business Development Manager - Pyropower Corporation

ABSTRACT

Though titled a "demonstration project", Colorado-Ute Electric Association's retrofit of its Nucla Station with a 925,000 lb/hr AHLSTROM PYROFLOW® CFB boiler represents significant commercial guarantees on the part of the equipment suppliers and commitments by the customer and the private and research groups involved. The purpose of the project is to demonstrate the commercial as well as the technical status of CFB technology. This plant also represents the first utility-scale CFB project, as well as the largest CFB boiler in operation in the world to date.

The Mt. Poso Cogeneration Company project successfully closed financing in June of 1987. The plant will be built, owned and operated by Pyropower Corporation and other investment partners. The steam will be used for thermally enhanced heavy oil recovery from an adjacent oil field and for generating 49.5 $MW_{(e)}$ net which will be sold to the local utility. The third-party-ownership option represents a significant share of the energy business today. Third party plant ownership and operation entails extensive contractual and financing expertise to obtain project financing, as well as demonstrated technological know-how on the part of companies emerging from the role of traditional equipment design and supply.

The Colorado-Ute Electric Association's Nucla Demonstration Project and the Mt. Poso Cogeneration Company represent both the technical and commercial status of Circulating Fluidized Bed (CFB) combustion technology today either for typical equipment supply or on a project financed basis.

SUMMARY

Since the first circulating fluidized bed combustion boiler came on line in the U.S. in 1981, the size of units in operation has grown rapidly from 50,000 lb/hr of steam output to over 900,000 lb/hr in 1987. This increase in nearly all cases has been supported by the manufacturers' confidence in the technology in the form of commercial guarantees and not by government or institutionally funded projects. Two projects which are among the leaders in certain areas of commercialization are the Colorado-Ute Electric Association 110 $MW_{(e)}$ CFB plant at Nucla, Colorado, which is the first utility CFB boiler, and the Mt. Poso cogeneration project in Bakersfield, California; a $50MW_{(e)}$ project financed plant.

At Nucla, the commercial guarantees required to reduce the risk to the customer are in the form of 100% boiler construction financing provided by the seller, with payment due only upon demonstration of 100% output capability. The Mt. Poso project required strong total schedule and performance guarantees by the turnkey supplier, Bechtel Corporation and major subcontractors to the satisfaction of the financing bank, Irving Trust.

The fact that the Nucla plant is now completed and the Mt. Poso project is fully financed and under construction is proof that CFB boilers up to around 1,000,000 lb/hr of steam have achieved commercial status in the U.S. over the past seven years with little financial support from the government.

EARLY INTRODUCTION OF THE TECHNOLOGY

Initial introduction of CFB boilers in the U.S. was promoted in areas where the fuel flexibility of fluidized bed combustion was required along with improved emission control over and above that demonstrated by bubbling fluidized bed boilers at that time. Both of these first units were 50,000 lb/hr steam generators for enhanced oil recovery designed to burn coal and/or petroleum coke with strict emission standards. **Figure 1** shows the design emission levels for the 50,000 lb/hr AHLSTROM PYROFLOW® boiler in Bakersfield, California, which started up in 1983, and the actual levels demonstrated by that facility.

Unfortunately, because of the drop in oil prices, both of these facilities were shut down in 1984. However, the experience gained here coupled with that of units overseas gave sufficient confidence for commercial sales to proceed in sizes up to 300,000 lb/hr.

FIGURE 1

DESIGN EMISSION LEVELS FOR THE 50,000 LB/HR ALHSTROM PYROFLOW® BOILER

Bakersfield, California

SO_x	5.5 lb/hr	41 ppm
NO_x (as NO_2)	17.9 lb/hr	187 ppm
CO	16.7 lb/hr	286 ppm
Particulate	3.3 lb/hr	0.019 gr/ACF

ACTUAL EMISSION AND PERFORMANCE LEVELS

SO_x (as SO_2)	2.4 lb/hr	20 ppm
NO_x (as NO_2)	12.9 lb/hr	148 ppm
CO	0.10 lb/hr	2 ppm
Particulate	0.56 lb/hr	0.0037 gr/ACF

The longest continuously operated CFB plant in the U.S. is the Calmat plant in Colton, California. This plant started up in 1985 burning Utah coal, **figure 2**. The plant is a 197,000 lb/hr unit producing steam at 825°F and 650 psig which, when coupled with steam from two waste heat boilers at the exhaust of the cement kilns, cogenerates 26 $MW_{(e)}$ for the facility. The plant's emissions have met the required permitted levels under all normal operating conditions since its commissioning, fig. 3. The plant has also demonstrated availability levels of 97.7% in 1986 and 97.3 in 1987 (exclusive of planned outages). This record has proven that CFB boilers burning coal with limestone for sulfur retention have met the same high availability levels in the U.S. as the early units in Europe and Scandinavia burning biomass and/or coal.

The experience gained from these early projects provided the basis and confidence for suppliers such as Pyropower to offer guarantees and commercial conditions such as those required by Colorado-Ute for their Nucla Demonstration Project.

COLORADO-UTE NUCLA CFB DEMONSTRATION PROJECT

Colorado-Ute decided in 1983 to modernize the Nucla plant with a CFB plant to increase its output and meet increasing emission control limits when burning coal.

The Nucla CFB project is a commitment by Colorado-Ute, Pyropower Corporation, the Electric Power Research Institute (EPRI), United Engineers and Constructors (formerly Stearn's Catalytic) Bechtel Company, Westinghouse and the Technical Advisory Group (TAG), among others, to demonstrate the feasibility of circulating fluidized bed technology on a utility scale. The project entailed retrofitting Colorado-Ute's 36 $MW_{(e)}$ Nucla Station in western Colorado with a PYROFLOW® CFB steam generator and an additional 75 $MW_{(e)}$ turbine-generator. The three existing 12 $MW_{(e)}$ turbine-generators were retained, powered by bleed steam from the new turbine.

A key aspect of the project is to evaluate the suitability of CFB technology for cost-effective life extension of the 25-year-old generating station. Nucla now has a net capacity of about 100 $MW_{(e)}$ after the retrofit of the CFB.

The demonstration aspect of this project includes an extensive 2-year utility-oriented test phase to establish operating parameters for CFB boilers for utility applications and to evaluate operating costs and fuel flexibility and efficiency. The suitability of a wide variety of coals, including those high in sulfur content will be investigated as will the effectiveness of CFB combustion to limit emissions of SO_x, NO_x and CO in power generation plants. EPRI is sponsoring and leading this program. TAG membership was solicited among interested utilities and other groups who wished to closely follow the progress of CFB in commercial applications. Membership fees have gone to support the project and the EPRI test program.

FIGURE 2

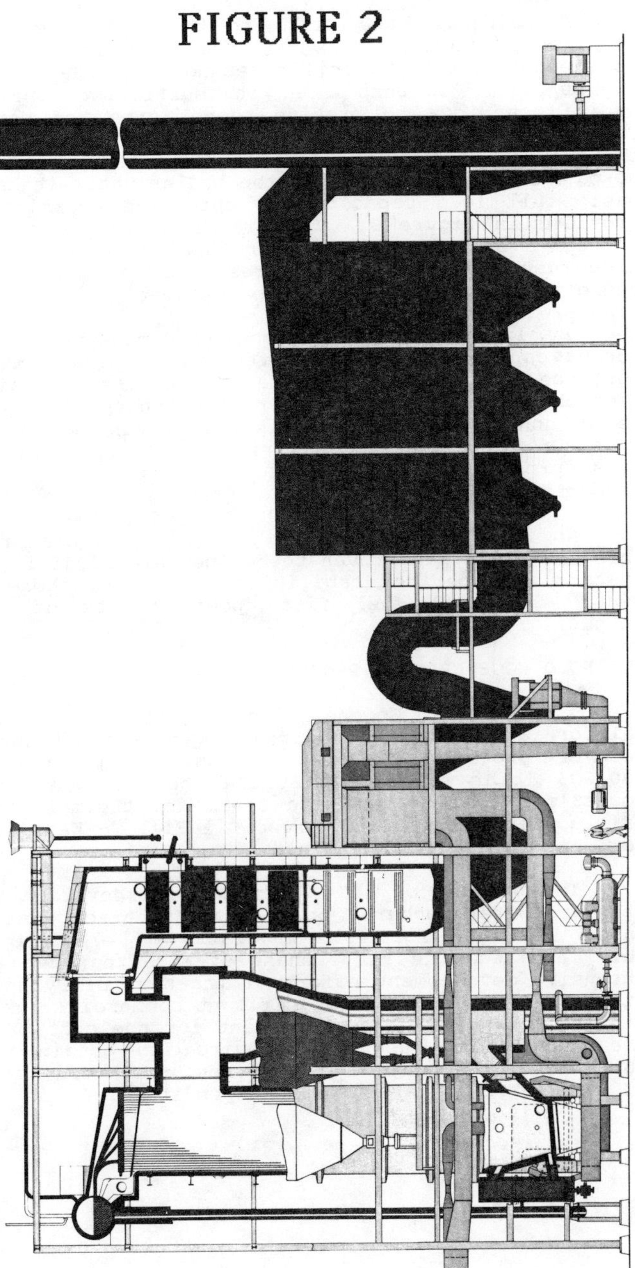

PYROFLOW® CIRCULATING FLUIDIZED BED BOILER
190,000 lb/hr, 650 psig, 825°F

CALIFORNIA PORTLAND CEMENT CO., USA

To minimize the risks to themselves, Colorado-Ute required demanding terms and conditions for the supplier to support their CFB boiler technology. There were only two suppliers at that time with sufficient confidence in their technology to provide these terms and conditions. Pyropower was one of them and was awarded the contract in the fall of 1984. The basic terms of the supply are that no payment will be made for the boiler until it has proven basic full load capacity and specified emissions levels provided in **figure 3**. This resulted in the plant going through a startup program where the suppliers took extensive responsibilities which resulted in considerable expense to the suppliers and the customer.

By late 1987, the plant had demonstrated over 60% output capability and predicted values of all major performance parameters had been met. The use of dual combustion chambers at the time of bidding the project proved to me an unnecessary conservatism, requiring extra controls to ensure that unbalanced firing by the operator does not cause problems similar to those experienced in late September of 1987.

Now that these start-up problems have been resolved, this large CFB has proven to be operable requiring control systems and operator cabilities similar to those of conventional fossil fuel fired power plants of the same output.

MT. POSO COGENERATION PROJECT

The Mt. Poso Cogeneration project in Kern County is California's first coal-fired cogeneration/enhanced oil recovery project. The $125 million power plant includes a 500,000 lb/hr AHLSTROM PYROFLOW® boiler that will burn low-sulfur coal to generate steam for thermally enhanced oil recovery from the Mt. Poso Oil Field - West Area, and for generating 49.5 $MW_{(e)}$ net.

In November of 1984, Pyropower Corporation signed a Standard Offer Number 4 power sales contract with Pacific Gas & Electric for 49.5 megawatts of electric supply. This initiated the first phase of more than two years of intensive development effort of the part of Pyropower and others. Pyropower took significant commercial risks after signing the power sales agreement for the cost of most of the development resources required to obtain financial support for the project. These resources were substantial in terms of both manhours and expenditure.

FIGURE 3

PEFORMANCE GUARANTEES FOR COLORADO-UTE NUCLA STATION-AHLSTROM PYROFLOW®

Superheater outlet steam flow, lb/hr	925,000
Temperature of steam leaving superheater, ºF	1,005±10ºF
Efficiency %:	87.5
Ca/S ration (Ca in limestone only)	1.5

Boiler Emission Levels at MCR (MCR=925,000 lb/hr)

Particulate emission shall not exceed 0.03 lb/10^6 Btu heat input at indicated steam flow.

NO_x emission shall not exceed 0.5 lb/10^6 Btu/heat input at indicated steam flow.

SO_2 emission shall not exceed 0.4 lb/10^6 Btu at indicated steam flow.

Dust loading at I.D. fan inlet duct with two compartments of the combined system in cleaning mode, and two compartments of the combined system out for maintenance shall not exceed 0.03/106 Btu at indicated steam flow.

The permitting process was critical to the success of the Mt. Poso project. Pyropower bore the brunt of the necessary expenditure to successfully satisfy permitting requirements. Included in this expenditure were options on approximately $4 million in SO_x and NO_x emission offsets. The project has had to meet U.S. EPA, and California State and local emission standards utilizing commercially available fluidized bed technology. This technology is now recognized by many state and local environmental authorities as the "Best Available Control Technology" (BACT), **figure 4**.

Pyropower entered into negotiations with several banks in April of 1987 to obtain financing for this project. By this time, strong partners which brought the necessary resources and expertise had been found who, together with Pyropower, would constitute a viable and financable project partnership. These other partners were subsidiaries of Bechtel Corporation as engineering, procurement and construction contractor, Pacific Power & Light (On-Site Energy) as the operations and maintenance contractor to the Mt. Poso Cogeneration Company and Macpherson Oil Company, who contributed the oil field leases and will operate the oil field.

In June, Irving Trust Company was selected as the agent bank for the project financing and negotiations with them were successfully concluded June of 1987. Irving required stringent performance guarantees from the project suppliers in order to support the long-term and construction debt. As is typical of third-party, non-recourse equity commitments, a bonus/penalty arrangement for both the construction and operations and maintenance contractors was required to close financing.

Bechtel and Pyropower supplied the necessary guarantees on the construction contract to ensure construction funding. On-Site Energy and Pyropower provided the necessary guarantees for the operations and maintenance contract.

Instrumental in financial closing was the confidence inspired in the project by having Pyropower and the other key contractors act both as owners of the project and supply the necessary guarantees and equity funding to a CFB project.

Suppliers such as Pyropower have had to acquire the requisite expertise and be willing to apply the necessary resources and commercial market commitments to enter into third party financed projects. Pyropower is participating with ownership of more than $500 million worth of projects in the United States at present. We are actively pursuing more business of this type with partners who bring their expertise and resources to the table and are prepared to invest in commercial CFB projects.

FIGURE 4

PYROFLOW® TECHNOLOGY HAS BEEN RECOGNIZED AS THE BEST AVAILABLE CONTROL TECHNOLOGY (BACT) BY THE FOLLOWING STATE AND LOCAL AUTHORITIES:

- **Maine State Department of Environmental Protection**
- **Kern County, California**
  Air Pollution Control District
- **Riverside County, California**
  South Coast Air Quality Management District
- **San Bernadino County, California**
- **San Joaquin County, California**
  San Joaquin Air Quality Management District
- **California Energy Commission**
  (indirectly through the BACT requirement for CEC permitting)

CONCLUSIONS

Companies formerly involved only in traditional architect/engineering services and/or equipment supply for fluid bed projects now have sufficient operating experience and confidence in the technology to offer commercial terms and conditions for financial institutions to fund CFB projects on a third party non-recourse basis. This confidence is further shown by our desire to own and operate projects which feature PYROFLOW® technology. Exacting terms and conditions are required for financing sources to support non-recourse project financing. However, offering satisfactory terms with corporate backing alone is not always sufficient for the financiers. They often employ independent technical consultants to evaluate the CFB technology being proposed for the project. In the past, it has proven very useful to have a similar CFB unit in operation with satisfactory performance demonstrated to that being proposed. Demonstrated performance on a similar scale acts to convince these technical experts that CFB technology is sufficiently commercial to recommend project financing to be committed to the proposed project.

We have found, because of our experience in developing, financing, owning and operating projects featuring PYROFLOW® CFB technology, that the financial markets are willing to offer more advantageous terms that may be otherwise expected, due to less perceived risk on their part.

It is for the above reasons that the Nucla and Mt. Poso projects have become major milestones in showing that CFB technology has achieved commercial acceptance in North America in sizes up to 100 MW_e.

CLEAN COAL

POTENTIAL APPLICATIONS OF SLAGGING COMBUSTION SYSTEMS

A. E. Margulies, T. A. Vivenzio, B. E. Feldmann, and E. R. Zabolotny

Stone & Webster Engineering Corporation
Boston, Massachusetts

INTRODUCTION

Advanced slagging combustion systems are one class of the emerging clean coal technologies being developed to improve the quality of the nation's air, while increasing the use of America's most abundant fossil energy resource, coal. Two of the projects selected by the U.S. Department of Energy (DOE) for funding under the Clean Coal Technology Program are for demonstrating slagging combustors in retrofits of boilers to coal - one project for an industrial boiler and one for a utility boiler. In these retrofits the slagging combustors will replace the existing burners mounted on the outside of the boilers. These boiler retrofits of combustors will provide NO_x, SO_2, and ash control.

These advanced slagging combustion systems are derived from past combustor development for application to magnetohydrodynamic (MHD) power generation technology. Although there is a diversity of technical approaches among slagging combustor developers, all aim at compactness by burning pulverized coal in a high intensity combustion chamber. All operate sub-stoichiometrically (fuel-rich) to suppress NO_x formation. The hot gaseous combustion products formed are ducted into the retrofitted boiler, where sufficient air is added to complete combustion of these gases. All remove most of the coal ash as liquid slag, thus reducing the fly ash loading of the boiler and avoiding capacity derating of oil/gas design boilers. Also all capture sulfur with varying degrees of success by injecting sorbents either directly into the combustor or into the combustor exit gases in the boiler, and thereby avoid the need for a flue gas scrubber.

Potential applications for these advanced slagging coal combustors include:

- Retrofit of existing industrial and utility boilers designed for burning oil and gas
- Retrofit of existing coal burning boilers that are required to meet reduced NO_x and SO_2 emissions limits
- Incorporation into the design of new coal fired boilers
- Direct and indirect coal fired gas turbine power plants

Potential performance and economics of these applications will be discussed later in the section entitled, "Slagging Combustor Applications."

The next section, will describe the design features and development status of four advanced slagging combustors currently being developed.

DESCRIPTION AND DEVELOPMENT STATUS

The four advanced slagging combustors that were selected for review are being developed by TRW, Coal Tech Corporation, TransAlta Resources Corporation, and AVCO Research Laboratory The TRW and Coal Tech slagging combustors will be demonstrated in boiler retrofits in the Clean Coal Technology Demonstration Program.

Because it is considered to be closest to readiness for commercial application, the following more detailed information is presented for the TRW slagging combustion system: system description, R&D testing, completed industrial boiler retrofit demonstration, and planned utility boiler retrofit demonstration. Following this is a brief description of the slagging combustors being developed by the other three developers.

TRW Slagging Combustor

1. System Description

The TRW slagging combustion system is shown on Figure 1. The combustor is an atmospheric pressure adaptation of Federally-sponsored MHD (pressurized) combustor development. Its major characteristics are summarized in Table 1.

Generically, the slagging combustion system consists of a small surge bin with integral dense phase feed components, a compact slagging stage combustor, a precombustor for boosting inlet air temperature, a water filled slag tank, a short connecting duct, associated controls, and a sorbent injection system.

The system can be integrated with conventional coal and ash handling systems and retrofitted to existing boilers designed for oil/gas firing. Thus, by the addition of one or more relatively small slagging combustion systems, coupled with conventional solids handling equipment and a boiler sorbent injection system, an oil/gas design boiler can be converted to coal firing.

The heart of the system is the main slagging stage. It consists of a water-cooled cylinder with a tangential air inlet and a baffle located about two-thirds of the way down the combustor axis. The air inlet and baffle combination promotes efficient mixing/combustion reactions and internal slag flow patterns. Pulverized coal is transported in a dense-phase fluidized condition to the injector located on the axis in the head end of the combustor. The coal is injected conically into the combustor, entrained by the swirling air flows, and burned sub-stoichiometrically in flight. Alternatively, coal-water mixtures (70 percent coal, 30 percent water) can also be used in the combustor by substituting an air-atomized slurry injector for the powdered coal injector.

Ash contained in the coal is released in drops of molten slag as the coal particles burn in flight. The accumulation of these drops develops a layer of slag on the water-cooled walls as a result of centrifugation from the swirling gas flow. At equilibrium, which is quickly reached, the slag is solid at the wall and liquid on the side facing the combustion. Once on the wall, the molten slag is driven to the baffle by a combination of aerodynamic and gravity forces. It is constrained by the baffle to flow through the key slot and into the slag tap located just beyond the baffle. The molten slag stream then drops into the water filled slag tank. In this manner, up to 94 percent of the ash in the coal is removed as molten slag. The water tank quenches the slag and forms a seal which prevents the escape of combustion gases through the slag tap.

Since the combustor is operated fuel-rich (air to fuel ratios of 0.7 to 0.9), the swirling hot gas is rich in CO and H_2. It is ducted into the retrofitted boiler where sufficient air is added to complete the combustion of the gases. This staged combustion process acts to minimize NO_x formation. Sufficient temperature and heat flux are generated within the coal combustor volume to achieve liquid slag flow conditions, but the classical high NO_x formation regime is avoided by the combination of temperature and gas composition control.

SO_2 emissions can be reduced by 50 to 70 percent for low sulfur coals and 80 to 90 percent for high sulfur coals by injection of sorbent materials, such as limestone, dolomite, etc, into the combustor exit gases as they pass into or through the boiler furnace volume. The combination of temperature and gas composition tends to favor formation of nongaseous sulfur compounds, mainly $CaSO_4$. Fine particulates of ash and sorbent proceed through the boiler with additional sulfur capture occurring. The particulates are then removed from the flue gas as solid material in a baghouse or precipitator.

2. Research and Development Testing

During the past 10 years, TRW performed over 1200 tests on development combustors ranging in size from 1 to 170 MMBtu/hr. About half of these have been performed with one-atmosphere test units sized at nominal 10 MMBtu/hr and 40 MMBtu/hr using 15 pulverized coals and coal-water slurries (70 percent coal, 30 percent water). The majority of tests have used the 10 MMBtu/hr, combustor and pulverized coals from Utah, Wyoming, Montana, Illinois, Pennsylvania, Kentucky, West Virginia, and Ohio.

Initial testing concentrated on combustion efficiency (carbon burnout) and flame stability at substoichiometric conditions. Next, slag removal and NO_x reduction testing was accomplished. The primary purpose of these tests was to develop the hardware geometry and operating conditions leading to 80 to 90 percent removal of the inert ash in the coal as molten slag while, at the same time, maintaining low NO_x emissions and good combustion efficiency. Finally, SO_x reduction and configuration optimization testing was accomplished, primarily at the larger 40 MMBtu/hr combustor size.

3. Industrial Boiler Retrofit Demonstration Test

The TRW Industrial Boiler Demonstration Test was initiated in January 1984. A 30,000 lb/hr industrial boiler, originally designed for Stoker coal firing and subsequently converted to gas/oil, was selected as the host unit. This boiler was located in TRW's manufacturing facility in Cleveland, Ohio. A single 40 MMBtu/hr combustor designed and constructed to commercial standards was retrofitted to the boiler. Plant modifications also included coal handling, pulverizer, slag handling, and baghouse equipment.

The primary purpose of the Industrial Boiler Demonstration was to run a 4000-hour endurance test to obtain key information on the durability, maintenance, and long duration operation of the retrofit combustor system under actual industrial plant conditions.

Test results of the demonstration confirmed earlier test performance of the TRW slagging combustor. The plant performance exceeded expectations in that steam output was increased by as much as 25 percent - up to 35,000 lb/hr. This was achieved by operating the boiler at full load (28,000 lb/hr), and by circulating the combustor wall cooling water to a flash tank to produce an additional 7200 lb/hr of steam. The resultant steam augmented boiler output. Carbon conversion rates were in excess of 99.5 percent. Slag recovery was in the 82 to 85 percent range. NO_x emissions at 3 percent excess O_2 ranged from 250 to 450 ppm, without the use of over-fire air. Further reductions to 180 ppm are considered possible with over-fire air in more conventional boilers.

Although SO_2 tests were not part of the 4000-hour test in Cleveland, pilot testing of the same combustor model on a boiler simulator at TRW's test facilities in Capistrano, California, has shown sulfur capture rates of 70 percent to 90 percent at a calcium-to-sulfur ratio of 3.0 or less for representative eastern and western coals.

In the Cleveland test, sootblowing needs in the convection section to remove a light ash were normally one cycle per shift. Furnace surface ash accumulations were removed at infrequent intervals. Turndown demonstrated during the 4000-hour test was 3 to 1.

The entire dense phase fuel feed and combustor system availability at the conclusion of testing was 83.3 percent. Availability of the combustor itself was 94.6 percent, with dense phase coal feed, flame management, and the control system at 87.7 percent, 99.9 percent, and 99.8 percent availability, respectively.

During the 4000-hour test, combustor maintenance was minimal. It involved coal injector adjustments and water tube flushing because of water quality upsets. Combustor water walls showed excellent durability and slag coverage with ultrasonic testing revealing almost no erosive tube wear.

Following the test the boiler showed no indication of any change. Water walls and convection tubes remained leak tight, and the refractory floor and lower walls were still in good condition.

4. Utility Boiler Retrofit Demonstration Test

Retrofit of TRW slagging combustors is planned in the Orange & Rockland Utilities' 69 MW Lovett - Unit 3. The retrofit scope, predicted performance, and estimated costs are discussed in a later section entitled, "Retrofit of Slagging Combustors in Coal Design Boilers."

Coal Tech Slagging Combustor

This combustor is also an outgrowth of MHD combustor development. It is a high temperature device in which a high velocity swirling gas is used to burn pulverized coal. The ash is separated from the coal in liquid form on the cyclone combustor walls, from which it flows by gravity toward a port at the downstream end of the device.

As shown in Figure 2, a gas burner, located at the center of the closed end of the unit, is used to preheat the ceramic lined combustor wall and to start coal combustion. Pulverized coal transported by primary air is injected into the combustor through tubes in an annular region enclosing the gas burner.

Secondary air is used to adjust the combustor stoichiometry. The key novel feature of this element is use of secondary air to cool the ceramic liner and maintain it at a temperature high enough to keep the slag in a liquid free flowing state. Secondary air tangential injection velocity and coal pulverization allow combustion of much of the coal particles in suspension near the combustor wall. Slag retention values in excess of 90% were achieved.

To control nitrogen oxide emissions the combustor is operated fuel-rich. It was shown in a 1 MMBtu/hr pilot combustor that minimum NO_x emissions were obtained at a stoichiometric ratio of 0.7. This result was confirmed in a 7 MMBtu/hr combustor.

Control of sulfur emissions is achieved by limestone injection (adjacent to the coal injection ports) into the fuel rich stage of the combustor.

A scaled-up 30 MMBtu/hr combustor was fabricated and installed and tested with a coal-water slurry fuel on a 23 MMBtu/hr boiler. The combustor operated as designed, especially the air cooling and slag tap features which are the novel and previously untested concepts.

This facility is currently being modified for operation for up to 900 hours with dry pulverized coal under the Clean Coal Technology Demonstration Program sponsorship. Performance goals to be demonstrated are: up to 90 percent reduction of SO_2 emissions, 70 to 80 percent reduction of NO_x emissions, retention of 90 percent of the ash, operation over a turndown factor of 3 to 1, and applicability for retrofit to an oil design boiler

TransAlta Slagging Combustor

This combustor is also an outgrowth of the MHD development experience. TransAlta Resources Corporation recently acquired this combustor technology from Rockwell International.

In this technology, coal from the pulverizer is transported directly with pulverization air and mixed with sorbent and with air from the air preheater in a rocket-type nozzle at the inlet of a relatively long, refractory-lined cylindrical combustor. Reductions of both NO_x and SO_2 emissions can be achieved by fuel-rich combustion and sorbent injection into the combustor. Figure 3 shows the configuration in the slagging combustor retrofit of a coal design boiler. In the retrofit of an oil/gas design boiler, the use of a fly ash separator (water cooled slag screen shown on Figure 4) can remove about 80 percent of the fly ash mass.

Subscale R&D testing of this combustor concept performed at the 17 MMBtu/hr firing level achieved the targeted NO_x and SO_2 control. Sulfur removal of 90 percent was achieved for both sub-bitumious and bitumimous coal. The sub-bituminous coal required no sorbent injection. Table 2 summarizes these test results. This testing was conducted at six atmospheres pressure in the combustor because that hardware was readily available at the time. In subsequent pilot-scale development testing with a 25 MMBtu/hr combustor operating at atmospheric pressure, the best sulfur capture was only 72 percent. Techniques such as finer grinding of the coal are currently being tested to improve the sulfur capture. Nonetheless, the excellent performance results obtained by operating the combustor at elevated pressure are promising for direct firing of a gas turbine.

The next development steps planned include a long term demonstration of a single commercial size (100 MMBtu/hr) slagging combustor installed in the boiler of the 66 MWe TransAlta Wabamum plant. This will followed by a second phase with two additional combustors. These two phases are scheduled to be performed over a 3-ear period. Figure 5 shows the arrangement of the combustors retrofit for the Wabamum plant demonstration.

Avco Slagging Combustor

Figure 6 shows the concept of the AVCO slagging coal combustor retrofit on a boiler as a replacement for each oil burner. The retrofit combustor is attached directly to the wind box and provides a stream of clean combustion products. These enter the boiler fire box volume where they are mixed with secondary air to complete combustion. This AVCO vortex combustor concept is based on the formation of a torroidal vortex. The vortex flow pattern results in a compact design for which the surface-to-volume ratio decreases with size so that heat losses will decrease with increasing combustor size. AVCO's retrofit combustor design approach is based on previous development work in the areas of combustion and slag management in the MHD coal combustor technology program.

The AVCO combustor development testing was performed in the modified MHD combustor and in the 25 MMBtu/hr development test combustor. The existing MHD coal combustion test apparatus at the AVCO/Haverhill facility was reactivated and the modified combustor assembly with a new exhaust/after burner system was installed. About 40 tests were conducted with the modified MHD combustor using standard power plant grind of Eastern bituminous coal to obtain data for the design of the development test combustor. The best combustion performance, using the standard power plant grind, was obtained with an air injection velocity of about 250 ft/sec at an angle of 55 degrees in the thermal input range of 8 to 18 MMBtu/hr. Tests were also performed with finer grind coal (90 percent -200 mesh). The best combustor performance was achieved using the finer grind coal, and carbon utilization of greater than 0.95 was obtained. The air-to-fuel ratio (Ø) was controlled at two levels; 1.0 and 0.85. Good flame stability was achieved without air preheat.

The design and fabrication of a 25 MMBtu/hr developmental test combustor (see Figure 7) was based on the results obtained from preliminary combustion testing, flow modeling tests, and analytical modeling of the combustor flow. The combustor walls are water cooled. High heat flux zones, such as the combustor dome, combustion chamber, and exit nozzles are cooled by forced connection, and the cooling water exits into the water pool surrounding the combustor. Gas side surfaces of the combustor are grooved to retain a layer of slag.

More than 100 brief tests have been conducted with the development test combustor in the thermal input range of 9 to 28 MMBtu/hr using primarily Eastern bituminous coal, as well as Illinois No. 6 coal and North Dakota Zap lignite. Stable coal combustion and good fuel utilization has been achieved in the combustor, with air preheat temperatures from 200° to 650°F even at turndown ratios of more than 3:1 without transient combustor behavior. Carbon conversion of $\geq$ 0.90 percent was obtained by using standard power plant grind coal and operating the combustor at an air-to-fuel ratio of 1.0. Tests have also been performed using finer grind coal (70 percent -325 mesh), achieving carbon utilization larger than $\geq$ 0.95 at Ø = 1.0.

The slag/ash rejection achieved by the collector, and in the exhaust duct, was in the range of 50 to 70 percent, depending on the coal type used and the level of the thermal throughput. The measured slag rejection level was limited by the space/dimensional constraints in placing the slag collector in the combustor exhaust housing and the large exhaust velocities present in the relatively small size exit duct. Higher slag rejection levels are projected for a modified design in which the design of the slag collector and, consequently, the amount of slag collected can be optimized.

Although SO_2 control tests have not yet been performed, preliminary designs have been developed for the combustor sorbent injection/slag removal features. Testing is planned with the Westinghouse gas turbine application discussed later.

The scaling design studies for the Phase II combustor system having a thermal input of 50 MMBtu/hr have been done as the initial step in the preliminary design of the Phase II combustor.

SLAGGING COMBUSTOR APPLICATIONS

Potential applications for advanced slagging coal combustors include:

- Retrofit of existing boilers designed for burning oil and gas
- Retrofit of existing coal burning boilers that are required to meet reduced NO_x and SO_2 emissions limits
- Incorporation into the design of new coal fired boilers
- Direct and indirect coal fired gas turbine power plants

Conversion of oil/gas design boilers to burn pulverized coal using conventional burners would present major difficulties because of design differences between such boilers and those designed for coal burning. Typical design differences and their effect on combustion performance are presented below, followed by a discussion of how slagging combustors can alleviate many of these difficulties.

Boiler Characteristics

The overall dimensions of an oil design boiler are considerably smaller than a coal boiler of comparable capacity. Heat release rates for oil boilers may be as high as 35,000 Btu per cubic foot compared to 20,000 or less for a coal fired boiler. This difference is reflected in a smaller furnace volume. Furthermore, gas temperatures leaving the furnace can be much higher when a boiler is designed for oil. In a coal design boiler, the upper portion of the furnace must provide sufficient radiant heat transfer surface to reduce gas temperatures to as low as 2000°F. The value is determined for each case by the fusion temperature of the ash. High flue gas temperatures will allow carryover of molten ash, which is then deposited on relatively cool boiler tubes or walls. Because oil contains minimal quantities of ash, much higher furnace exit gas temperatures can be accommodated and oil firing boilers are designed accordingly.

The configuration of the furnace bottom is also important. Stoker fired boilers include the means for introducing combustion air and for removing the unburned ash. Pulverized coal boilers typically have a deep hopper formed by the water walls of the boiler and a wet bottom ash removal system. Oil fired boilers may have a flat or shallow sloped bottom with no provision for continuous removal of ash. Ash can be removed only during a boiler shutdown. The boiler may be installed with limited head room between the flat bottom and the boiler house floor, making modification difficult or impossible.

Another major difference relates to the configuration of superheater and economizer tubes in the convection passes of the boiler. Typically, coal fired tubes are arranged to minimize the possibility of ash deposition or bridging of ash deposits between tubes. Tube spacing may be as large as 18 inches in the first bank of superheater tubes. In successive sections, the spacing can be reduced as the flue gases are cooled and deposition problems are minimized. However, in an oil design boiler, these superheater tubes may be spaced at 6 inches or less. Furthermore, a staggered arrangement of tubes may be used to improve the contact of flue gases with tube surfaces. Also, finned tubes may be used in economizer sections.

Gas velocities through the convection sections may be significantly different. For a coal fired boiler, it is common to limit velocities to 60 ft/sec or less to minimize erosion by hard, refractory-like particles of ash. In an oil fired boiler, velocities of 100 ft/sec or more can be encountered.

A final point relates to space restrictions for balance-of-plant equipment. In all cases, particulate collection equipment is required at the back end of a coal fired boiler. Fans may be larger than those required for an oil fired boiler due to excess air requirements. Ash removal systems occupy valuable space around the boiler. Coal unloading and storage facilities for a coal fired boiler occupy significantly more land area than equivalent oil tankage and transfer facilities. Coal bunkers, pulverizers, and pneumatic transport systems are bulkier than their oil-handling counterparts. Oil fired boilers are often "shoehorned" into plant arrangements, allowing little flexibility for future alterations.

Impacts of Using Pulverized Coal in Oil/Gas Design Boilers

The design differences between coal and oil/gas design boilers can result in significant impacts when they are converted to coal. The important impacts include:

- Tube Bank Erosion - Combustion of conventional pulverized coal results in a large increase in ash loading in the flue gases. Due to their relatively large sizes, ash particles separate from the flue gas when an obstruction such as convection section tube is encountered. At the high velocities found in oil/gas design boilers, erosion of the tubes will occur.

- Inadequate Furnace Residence Time - Pulverized coal burns more slowly than either oil or gas and, therefore, cannot attain complete carbon burnout before it passes into the section. Furthermore, the flame can impinge on the tubes, increasing the potential for slag deposition and more frequent tube maintenance.

- NO_x, SO_2, and Particulate Emissions Control - NO_x suppression could be done by use of "reburning" technology. SO_2 reduction could be done by use of in-boiler sorbents or scrubbers. Particulate control could be done with electrostatic precipitator or baghouse equipment.

- Insufficient Radiant Heat Transfer - Because the oil/gas design furnace is smaller than that required for coal, there is insufficient radiant heat transfer surface. This may result in reduced steam generating capacity.

- Ash Removal Problems - The flat or shallow sloped bottom does not allow large ash particles or slag deposits that fall from the tubes to be easily removed. Extensive modifications may be necessary to remove bottom ash. Furthermore, wall deslaggers may be required to control deposits on the furnace walls, and sootblowers for deposits on connection section tubes.

- Inadequate Space - Auxiliary systems for coal storage and handling and for ash removal can occupy large amounts of real estate. Boilers not designed for coal firing may not have the space necessary for conversion to coal.

These impacts of converting oil/gas boilers to coal firing with conventional burners could result in three types of problems. In some cases, the conversion may be simply infeasible; for example, lack of space may preclude conversion. In other cases, the problems may be technically solvable, but the solution is uneconomical. Finally, it may be necessary to significantly derate the boiler capacity (up to 50 percent) to reduce gas temperatures and velocities and/or allow more complete combustion within the smaller furnace.

However, use of slagging combustors is expected to overcome or reduce many of the problems associated with converting oil/gas design boilers to coal firing. All slagging combustors being developed will provide NO_x control, some provide varying degrees of SO_2 control, and all produce and inject into the boiler gasified coal fuel containing sufficiently small size ash particulates to avoid or minimize boiler superheater tube deposition and erosion problems. This last feature results in avoiding or minimizing the need for boiler capacity derating when converting to coal fuel.

Retrofit of Slagging Combustors in Oil Design Boilers

A conceptual design and cost estimate was developed for conversion of Florida Power & Light Company's Sanford Station Unit No. 4. This 400 MW unit has a Foster Wheeler front fired oil design boiler. The scope of work for retrofit to slagging coal combustors (based on the TRW slagging combustion system) would include:

- Replacement of the existing 18 oil/gas burners with 16 to 250 MMBtu/hr slagging combustors

- Addition of coal receiving, storage, handling and pulverization systems (based on unit train delivery)

- Addition of limestone receiving, storage, handling, grinding and injection facilities

- Addition of combustor slag handling, storage and loading facilities

- Addition of a new set of sootblowers for the boiler

- Addition of a new electrostatic precipitator and flyash collection/handling equipment

- Addition of pumps, piping, isolation valves and a heat exchanger to utilize combustor shell cooling requirements for feedwater heating

- Elimination of existing four high pressure feedwater heaters and associated extractions

- Modification of the boiler balanced draft system heater including addition of two forced draft fans; two Ljungstrom regenerative air heaters, two steam coil air heaters for low temperature corrosion protection at low load operation, two forced draft fans and ducting system with control dampers for combustor air supply. Existing flue gas ductwork will be replaced.

It is estimated that a as result of the conversion, the unit's output would be reduced by about 2 percent. Table 3 provides a capital cost breakdown for the retrofit. The estimated capital cost is $362/kW.

Retrofit of Slagging Combustors in Coal Design Boilers

Retrofit of slagging combustors in existing coal burning boilers is an application that permits meeting reduced NO_x and SO_2 emission limits. The retrofit of TRW slagging combustors in the Orange & Rockland Utilities' 69 MW Lovett Station - Unit 3 (under the Clean Coal Technologies Program sponsorship) will be the first utility scale demonstration for slagging combustion technology. The scope, predicted performance, and estimated costs for this Lovett retrofit are discussed below.

The Lovett retrofit scope includes:

- Addition of four slagging coal combustors including pulverized coal surge tanks, dense phase feed system, slag discharge system, dense phase feed system, slag discharge system, combustor water cooling system, and air, flame, combustion controls

- Using existing pulverizers add cyclones, exhaust fans, lock valves, etc., for indirect coal pulverization

- Addition of limestone handling and feed system

- Addition of baghouse

- Addition of pneumatic system to transport fly ash from baghouse to existing plant ash removal system

- Addition of two forced draft booster fans

- Addition of natural gas fuel for precombustor ignition

- Extend existing instrument and service air systems

- Interface with existing building facilities, e.g., domestic/service water, drainage, fire protection, heating, ventilation

- Extend existing plant electrical distribution system
- Add microprocessor based control system and integrate with existing and new instruments and controls
- Modify front and side boiler wall tube panels to permit installation of the slagging combustion
- Reduce boiler economizer surface
- Addition of protective enclosures to shield existing oil and gas burners in order to retain oil/gas firing capability and protect oil/gas burners during slagging combustor firing
- Refurbish existing fly ash removal equipment, sootblowers
- Integrate slagging combustor shell cooling with existing feedwater heating

The current heat rate of the Lovett unit on coal is 9514 Btu/kWh. Subsequent to the addition of the slagging combustors, the net heat rate is predicted to be 10,164 Btu/kWh. The increase is due to heat losses associated with slag removal and inefficiencies and increased auxiliary power associated with limestone injection and particulate collection.

Table 3 provides a cost breakdown for the Lovett unit retrofit. The total cost is estimated at $308/kW.

For comparison, costs are also given in Table 3 for the fluid bed retrofit of the Northern States Power Company's Black Dog unit (a 110 MW coal design unit). The cost for the Black Dog fluid bed retrofit is $485/kW, which is more than 50 percent higher than the estimated cost for the Lovett slagging combustor retrofit. Costs for the Black Dog unit do not include costs for steam turbine modification which increased the capacity of the unit from 110 to 125 MW.

New Boiler Application

Cost and performance were developed for a new 250 MW power plant using slagging combustors. Similar information was developed for a 250 MW circulating fluid bed boiler unit for comparison. Table 4 compares the design basis for the two cases. For the slagging combustor case, the boiler is assumed to be the size of a 250 MW oil design unit. For the fluidized bed case, the design is two 125 MW circulating bed boilers with a common steam turbine.

Table 4 also compares the performance for the two cases. The boiler efficiency for the slagging combustor case is lower than for fluidized bed due to the increased heat losses resulting from removal of the high temperature slag at the combustor and the higher limestone usage required by the slagging combustor system for sulfur capture. The slagging combustor system also has a higher auxiliary power requirement than fluidized bed due to the need to pulverize the coal and the increased materials handling. The result is that the slagging combustor net heat rate is 9922 Btu/kWh compared to 9690 Btu/kWh for the fluidized bed unit.

Table 4 also compares the capital costs of the two cases. Note that the boiler plant costs are significantly lower for the slagging combustor unit, while the materials handling costs are slightly higher. The net result is that the slagging combustor total cost is $286 million compared to $311 million for the fluid bed combustor case, a decrease of $100/kW.

Two additional potential applications of slagging combustors that will be discussed are in advanced coal-fueled gas turbine power plants. They are:

- Indirect fired gas-turbine combined cycle plant (also referred to as externally fired gas-turbine (EFGT) combined cycle power plants

- Direct coal fired, gas-turbine combined cycle power plant

<u>Externally Fired Gas Turbine (EFGT) Combined Cycle Plant</u>

The EFGT cycle is one of many variations of the Brayton cycle which have been proposed over the past few decades. A schematic of the EFGT cycle is shown in Figure 8 Atmospheric air enters the gas turbine compressor and is pressurized and delivered to a high temperature heat exchanger. Heat energy from the combustion process is absorbed by the working fluid (air) through the ceramic tubes, raising the air to turbine inlet temperatures (1750° to 2350°F). The working fluid is expanded through the turbine, providing power to drive the compressor and generator. The turbine exhaust air is routed to the external combustor, providing low pressure and generator. The turbine exhaust air is routed to the external combustor, providing low pressure high temperature combustion air to burn the ash-bearing fuel. The hot products of combustion from the combustor pass over the exterior surface of the heat exchanger tubes transferring energy through the tube walls to the high pressure working fluid within the tubes. The combustion flue gas from the ceramic heat exchanger passes through a heat recovery boiler to generate steam for process use or additional electric power generation. The gases then pass through conventional pollution control equipment and exit to atmosphere.

The high efficiency and simplicity of the EFGT cycle are its principal attributes. Moreover, commercially available gas turbines can be employed with relatively minor modifications to accommodate the heat exchanger in lieu of the gas turbine combustion system. The combustion system required for the EFGT is comparable to that used for conventional steam generators employing "off-spec" fuels. When desirable, waterwall circuits can be used to prolong the life of the furnace/combustor walls.

Although the cycle could accommodate a wide variety of conventional fuel burners, application of the advanced slagging combustors would enhance the overall performance and economics. Slagging combustor technology offers the ability to remove high percentages of sulfur and ash from the fuel in the form of molten slag, thus alleviating the ash burden on the heat exchanger and the duty of the gas cleanup equipment. Successful demonstration of slagging combustors could significantly reduce the emissions control equipment performance requirements and overall construction costs.

Preliminary cost assessments of the EFGT cycle as prepared by Hague International, using a GE MS6001 gas turbine, project a capital cost in the range of $1400 to $1800/kW for 55 MW commercial scale plant having a projected heat rate of under 9000 Btu/kWh.

More recently comparative economics for 250 MW plant designs were prepared to compare Pulverized Coal (PC), Circulating Fluidized Bed (CFB), Integrated Gasification Combined Cycle (IGCC), and the Externally Fired Gas Turbine (EFGT) Combined Cycle shown on Figure 9. Process contingencies were utilized in an attempt to compensate for the differences in commercial development and/or operating experience. The estimated capital, and operating and maintenance costs for each technology are compared in Tables 5 and 6, respectively. In each table EFGT shows a potential savings of more than 10 percent over the next best alternative. Note that the IGCC and EFGT costs are estimates and are not based on actual operating experience.

Because of the importance to utilities of least-cost generation planning, the EFGT system would be of particular interest in those circumstance where the progressive generation concept is of value. Addition of coal capability to a natural gas fired combined cycle plant, initially designed to accommodate such a transition, would require coal storage and handling, coal combustion with in situ sulfur removal, a furnace cavity, ceramic heat exchanger and baghouse. The projected cost of these components is equivalent to the cost of the initial natural gas fired combined cycle plant.

The EFGT concept will accommodate new gas turbines projected for the 1990s. As turbine pressure ratios and inlet temperatures increase, the ability to separate the combustion gas stream from the turbine gas path, particularly when ash bearing fuels are involved, will have increasing value. Also, STIG gas turbines can be accommodated by the EFGT concept. When steam is used to improve the turbine cycle; the increase in mass flow and specific heat of the gas streams on both sides of the heat exchanger are also enhanced thereby similarly improving the performance of the heat exchanger. The EFSTIG (externally fired STIG cycle) is currently under evaluation at Hague International with the collaboration of Stone & Webster Engineering Corporation.

Direct Fired Gas Turbine Combined Cycle Plant

In 1986, DOE awarded four contracts totalling $45 million in pursuit of advancing direct firing of coal in engines and combustion turbines. The awards were made to Solar Turbines Allison Gas Turbine, General Electric, and Westinghouse Electric. Each of these programs utilizes variations of slagging combustors.

The direct fired system under investigation by Westinghouse is shown in Figure 10. The system is designed to burn utility grade coal prepared as coal/water slurry. The slurry fuel is burned in an AVCO external slagging combustor utilizing pressurized air from the air compressor of the gas turbine. The combustion gases are then sent through the combustion turbine. The turbine exhaust heat is utilized by means of a heat recovery steam generator and associated bottoming cycle. The net power generation and net heat rate are proejcted to be 207 MW and 8,683 Btu/kWh, respectively.

An economic assessment has been prepared by Westinghouse for an "nth" generation 207 MW net generation plant in constant 1983 dollars and is included in Tables 7 and 8.

REFERENCES

1. Coal Combustion Research Report. TRW Energy Products Group, October 1986.

2. Results of the 4000 Hour Endurance Test of TRW's Entrained Combustor. TRW Energy Products Group, May 1987.

3. B. Zauderer and E. Fleming. "Test of an Advanced Cyclone Coal Combustor." Pittsburgh Coal Conference, 1987.

4. B. Zauderer and E. Fleming. "Design, Fabrication and Testing of an Advanced Cyclone Coal Combustor." DOE-PETC Contractor's Review Meeting, July 1987.

5. D. W. Dykema and W. L. Fraser. "Development and Commercialization of a Low NO_x/SO_x Burner." American Power Conference, 1987.

6. A. Mattson and J. Stankevics. "Development of Retrofit External Slagging Combustor System." Pittsburgh Coal Conference, 1985.

7. Advanced Coal-Fired Gas Turbine Systems. Westinghouse Electric Corporation for Morgantown Energy Technology Center, December, 1986.

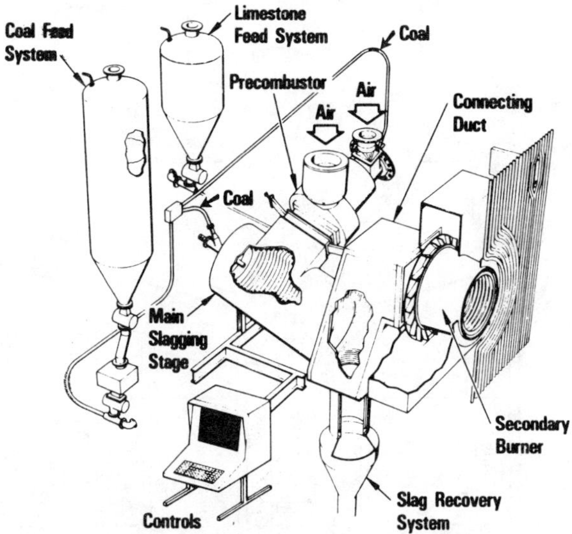

Figure 1. TRW slagging combustion system

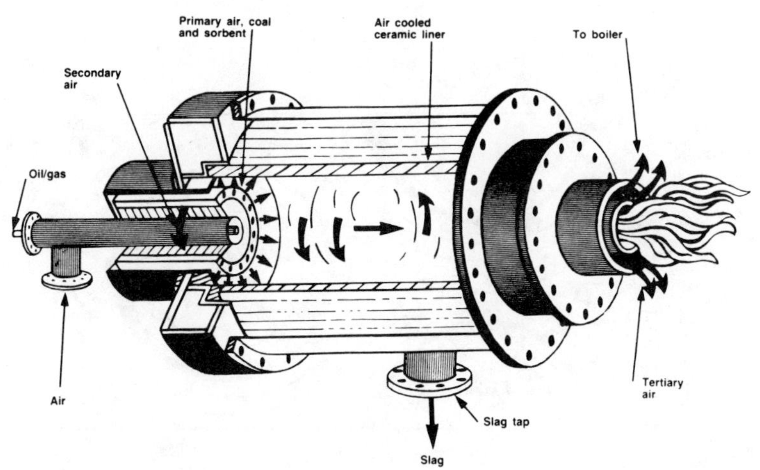

Figure 2. Coal Tech slagging combustor

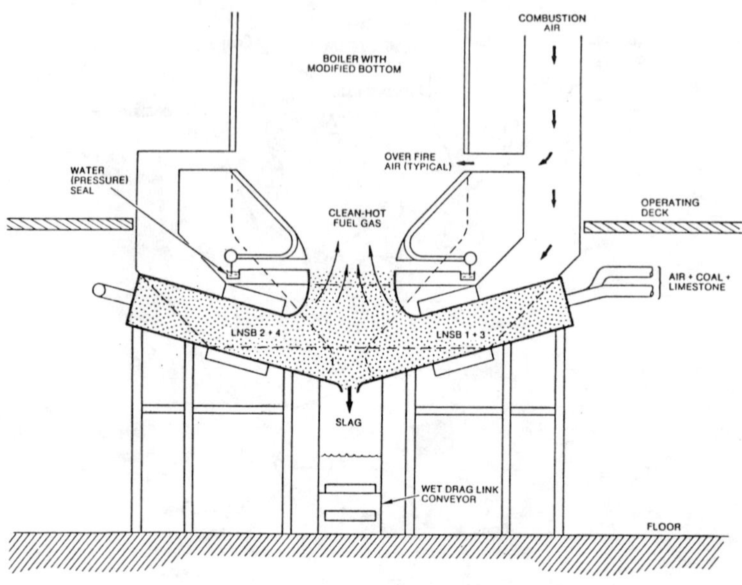

Figure 3. TransAlta slagging combustor retrofit

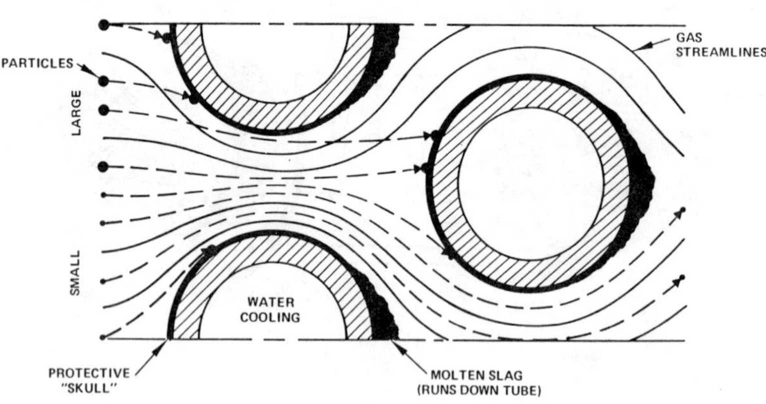

Figure 4. Particle (fly ash/slag) separator

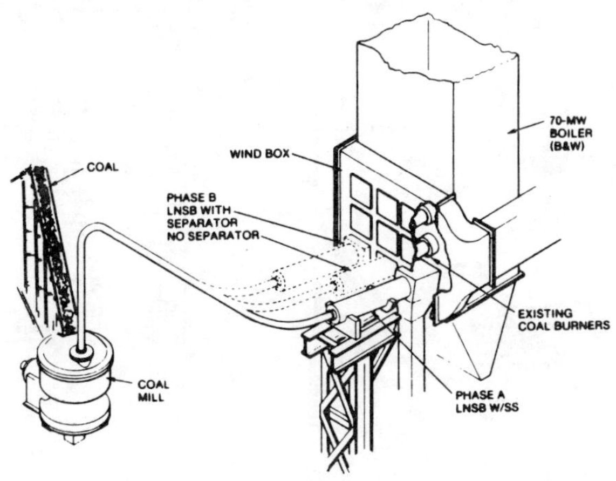

Figure 5. TransAlta slagging combustor retrofit for Wabamum Plant Demonstration

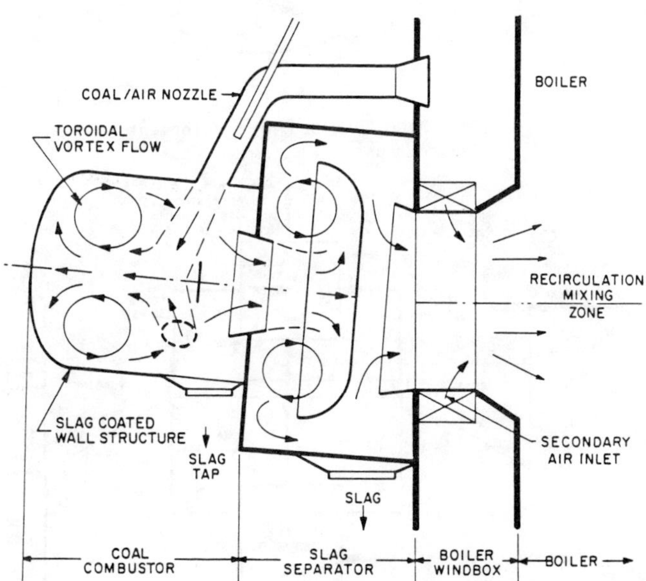

Figure 6. Boiler retrofit of AVCO combustor

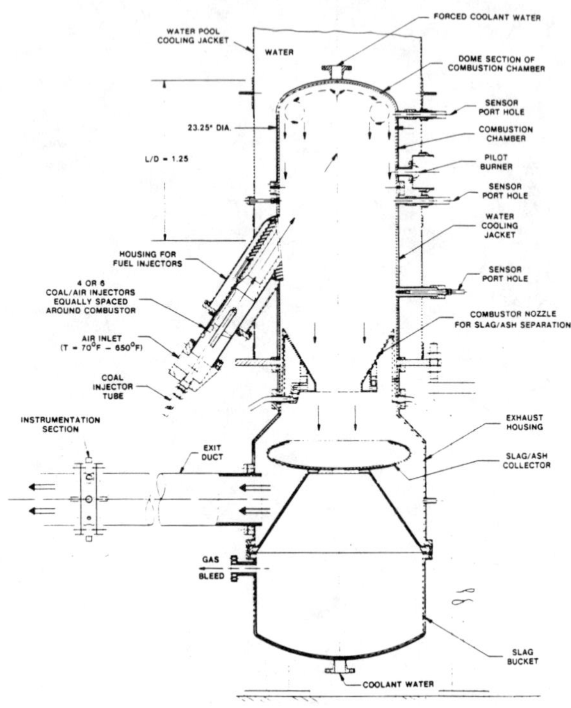

Figure 7. AVCO 25MM Btu/hr development test combustor

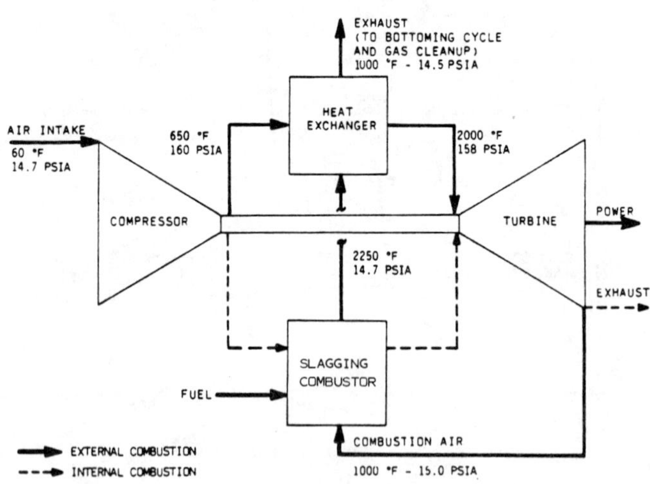

Figure 8. Externally fired gas turbine (EFGT) cycle

TABLE 1

CHARACTERISTICS OF TRW COMBUSTOR

Size	3 ft D x 5 ft L - 6 ft D x 9 ft L (40-160 MMBtu/hr)
Configuration	Cylinder, water cooled
Slag on wall	~1/2 in. slag on wall (no refractory liner)
Slag removal	80-94%
Carbon burnout	>99.5%
NO_x emission	230-450 ppm
Reduced SO_2 emission	50-90%*
Flexible device	Adjustable air and coal feed
Previous R&D tests	Short duration
State of development	Industrial boiler demonstration completed Utility plant demonstration planned for Clean Coal Technology Program

*Depends on sulfur content of the coal. SO_2 reductions achieved by injection of sorbents into combustor exit gases in the boiler furnace

TABLE 2

TRANSALTA COMBUSTOR R&D TESTING PROGRAM
SUMMARY OF TECHNICAL STATUS

Function	Combustor Pressure (atm)	Achieved: Low-Sulfur Western	Achieved: High-Sulfur Eastern	Goal
Sulfur capture (%)	6*	95	90	NSPS (70/90)
	1	70	70**	NSPS (70/90)
Retention of captured sulfur through to stack(%)	6	100	100	100
	1	100	60-70***	100
NO_x control in burner (NO_x out of burner, ppm)	6	0	0	<80
	1	50-100	30-80	<80
NO_x control through to stack (NO_x out the stack, ppm)	6	Not Tested	Not Tested	100
	1	100-150	80-140	100

*Important for direct coal-fired gas turbine/combined cycle units
**Proposed program
***Program underway

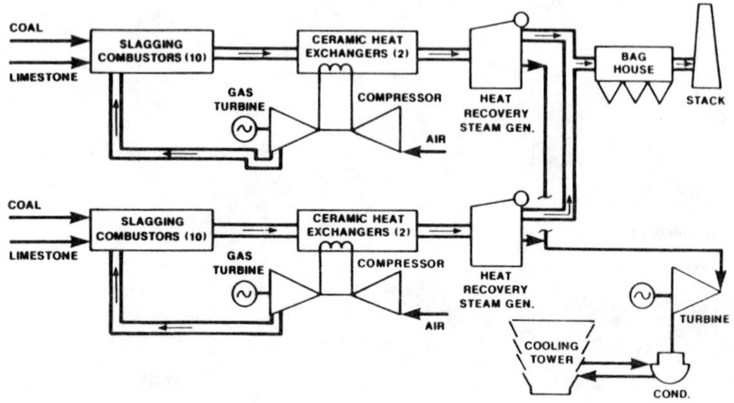

Figure 9. Externally fired gas turbine (EFGT) combined cycle 250 MW generating unit

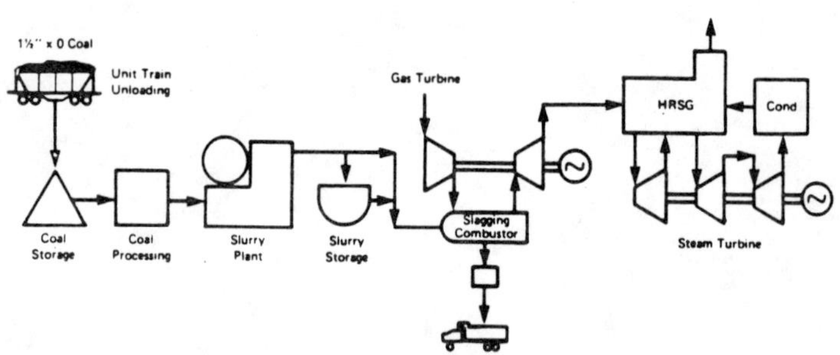

Figure 10. Direct fired combined cycle plant

TABLE 3

CAPITAL COST ESTIMATES FOR UTILITY RETROFITS
($ x 10^6)

	Coal Design Boilers		Oil Design Boilers
	FBC Retrofit	Slagging Combustor Retrofit	Slagging Combustor Retrofit
	110 MW Black Dog, Unit 2	69 MW Lovett, Unit 3	400 MW Sanford, Unit 4
Boiler & accessories	$24.80	$ 9.24	$ 53.44
Precipitator/baghouse	1.80	0.87	28.06
Materials handling	1.40	1.36	13.69
Balance of plant	5.50	5.17	8.50
Demolition & removal	1.70	0.35	0.00
Installation contracts	7.40	0.00	12.11
Total Direct Cost	$42.60	$16.99	$115.80
Indirects	10.65	4.28	28.95
Total Capital Cost	$53.25	$21.26	$144.75
$/kW	485	308	362

TABLE 4

COMPARISON OF NEW 250 MW PLANTS
SLAGGING COMBUSTION TECHNOLOGY VS FLUIDIZED BED COMBUSTION

Parameter	Hypothetical Slagging Combustor	Fluidized Bed
Design basis	Single 250 MW Boiler (oil design size) with slagging combustors	Two 125 MW CFB systems
Fuel	Illinois No. 6 coal	Illinois No. 6 coal
Cycle conditions	2400 psig/1000F/1000F	2400 psig/1000F/1000F
Boiler envelope		
Plan area, ft	110 x 110	160 x 120 (wide)
Height, ft	150	160
Fuel feed points	10 to 12	4 to 6
SO_2 capture, %	90	90
Ca:S ratio	3:1	1.5:1
Boiler efficiency, %	86.4	88.1
Auxiliary load, % of gross generation	7.2	6.8
Net heat rate, Btu/kWh	9922	9690
Capital cost ($x1000)		
Boiler plant	$82,300	$103,058
Materials handling	19,137	18,921
Turbine plant	25,606	25,606
Balance of plant	98,235	98,235
Total direct cost	$225,286	$245,820
Indirects and distributables (10%)	22,529	24,582
Contingency (15%)	37,772	40,852
Total estimate	$285,586	$311,254
$/kW	1,142	1,245

TABLE 5

ESTIMATED CAPITAL COSTS COMPARISON
($x1000)

	PC	AFB	IGCC	EFGT
Total Direct Cost	$286,800	$238,600	$314,000	$201,200
Indirect Costs	32,500	26,100	31,300	24,200
Project Contingency	47,900	39,700	51,800	33,800
Process Contingency	9,600	26,500	34,500	31,100
Total Present Day Cost	$376,800	$330,900	$431,600	$290,300
AFUDC	16,500	14,600	19,000	12,800
Total Plant Investment	$393,300	$345,500	$450,600	$303,100
$/kW	1,570	1,380	1,800	1,210

TABLE 6

ESTIMATED OPERATING AND MAINTENANCE COSTS
(Mills/kWh)

	PC	AFB	IGCC	EFGT
Fixed O & M	6.052	4.945	6.400	4.468
Variable O & M	2.594	2.119	2.743	1.915
Consumables	2.399	3.859	1.300	2.002
Fuel	15.779	15.469	15.175	13.730
Total O & M Costs	26.824	26.392	25.618	22.115

TABLE 7

ESTIMATED CAPITAL COSTS FOR
207 MW DIRECT FIRED GAS TURBINE COMBINED CYCLE PLANT
($x1000)

Total Direct Cost	$162,600
Indirect Costs	17,900
Project Contingency	16,300
Process Contingency	--
Total Present Day	$196,800
AFUDC	10,300
Total Plant Investment	$207,100
$/kW	1,000

TABLE 8

ESTIMATED OPERATING AND MAINTENANCE COSTS FOR
207 MW DIRECT FIRED GAS TURBINE COMBINED CYCLE PLANT
(Mills/kWh)

Fixed O&M (First Year)	4.573
Variable O&M (First Year)	1.960
Consumables	5.710
Fuel	15.620
Total O&M Costs	27.863

A COMPARISON OF BUBBLING AND CIRCULATING FLUID BED TECHNOLOGIES

By: Jeff Quitno

Product Manager,

Combustion Engineering

Introduction

In the early 1970's the requirement for SO_2 removal on a continuous basis for both utility and large industrial plants was formally legislated. Wet scrubbers were developed to meet this need, including numerous modifications to the original technology to enhance performance, cost, and reliability. In the late 70's, dry scrubbing using a rotary atomizer and lime slurry was introduced into the marketplace. The relative simplicity of this dry scrubbing, coupled with the reduced water requirements and ease of disposal, quickly propelled this technology into a competitive position. However, dry scrubbing was, and still is, limited to fuels with sulfur contents of about 2 1/2% maximum, and also suffers from the need to use lime at \$70/ton as opposed to limestone in the wet system at \$10-12/ton typically.

During this same period of time the concept of SO_2 removal in the combustion chamber itself began to emerge. The basic process concept is shown in Figure 1. By maintaining the combustion process between 1400°F and 1700°F (1560°F optimum), and providing sufficient limestone and adequate gas retention time, 90% or more of the SO_2 generated could be removed in the process. The elimination of the backend scrubbing equipment, the production of a dry ash, the use of inexpensive limestone, and the elimination of any water requirements were driving forces of such magnitude that the emergence of the fluidized bed concept was virtually inevitable.

Predicted Sulfur Capture

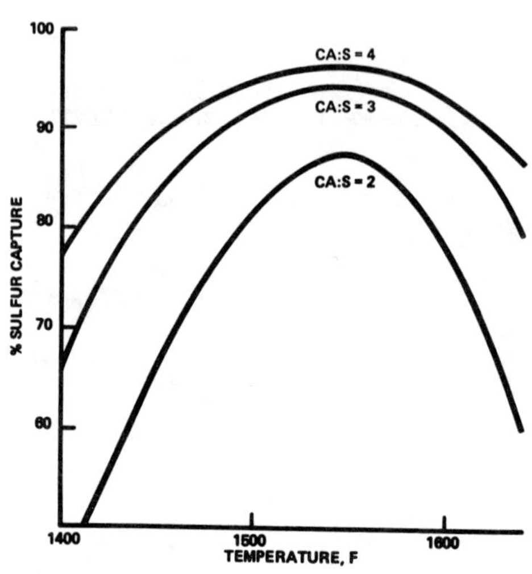

FIGURE 1

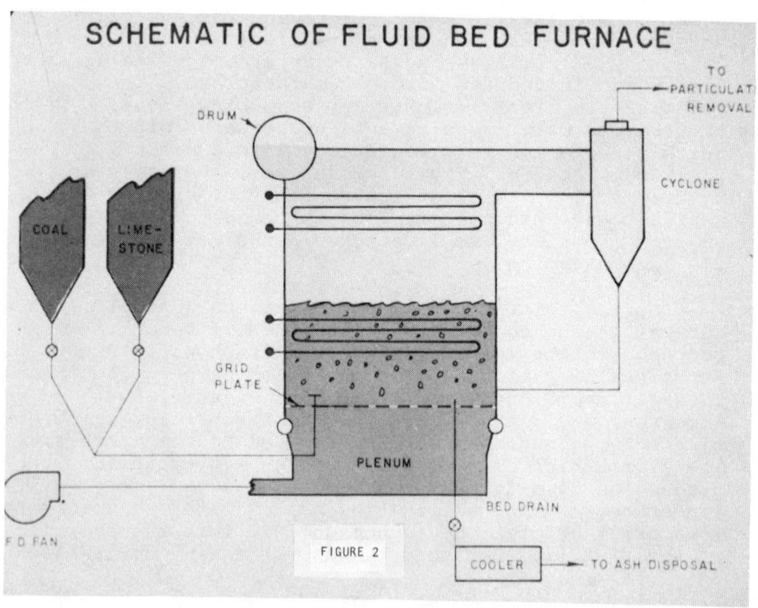

FIGURE 2

History

The initial approach taken in the U.S. on fluidized bed development involved a bubbling bed reactor as shown in Figure 2. By operating with fuel and limestone with a particle size of 1/4" to 1" typical, gas velocities of 6-10'/sec., and a bed depth of 3-4', a relatively defined bed could be achieved with very little elutriation of bed material into the upper freeboard section of the combustor. SO_2 removal of 90% and greater could be achieved, albeit with limestone requirements 3 to 5 times the stoichiometric requirements. One disadvantage of the bubbling bed was the need to insert heat transfer surface into the potentially erosive and corrosive environment of the bed to maintain the bed temperature at the desired 1560°F. Nevertheless, the process did work, and a number of small 5,000 #/hr to 200,000#/hr bubbling beds were built using this concept. Combustion Engineering was intimately involved in this conceptual phase with the development of the 50,000 #/hr bubbling bed shown in Figure 3 for the Great Lakes Naval Station near Chicago, Illinois under a grant from the DOE. C-E is also supplying a 160 M.W. Unit to TVA's Shawnee Plant in Paducah, Kentucky.

In the same time frame, however, the European community was pursuing the fluidized bed concept from a somewhat different approach. In the mid 1960's Lurgi GmbH of West Germany had developed a new concept for calcining aluminum hydroxide involving a circulating solids system (see Figure 4). This concept was able to produce alumina at much higher purity than previously achievable. It involved the injection of raw aluminum hydroxide into a fluidized chamber operating at about 22'/sec velocity and maintained at about 2000F by combustion of natural gas. The calcining operation is an endothermic process, hence the need to inject a clean fuel to provide the heat input to maintain reaction temperature. To achieve the complete reaction and uniform temperatures necessary to produce a pure product, the fluidized bed particles leaving the top of the chamber are collected in a cyclone and returned via a seal pot to the reaction chamber. A continuous stream of reacted product is withdrawn from the recirculation loop through a large plug valve and cooled in an external fluidized bed circuit using low air velocities for optimum heat transfer. Flue gas leaving the cyclone is typically cooled in a conventional steam generation circuit.

As the European community evolved strict legislation in the 1970s for SO_2 and other emissions, the applicability of using this circulating particle concept for combustion become apparent. By simply substituting coal for natural gas, and circulating the

PHOTO OF GREAT LAKES 50,000 #/HR 'A' TYPE BUBBLING BED READY FOR SHIPMENT ON SCHNABEL CAR

FIGURE 3

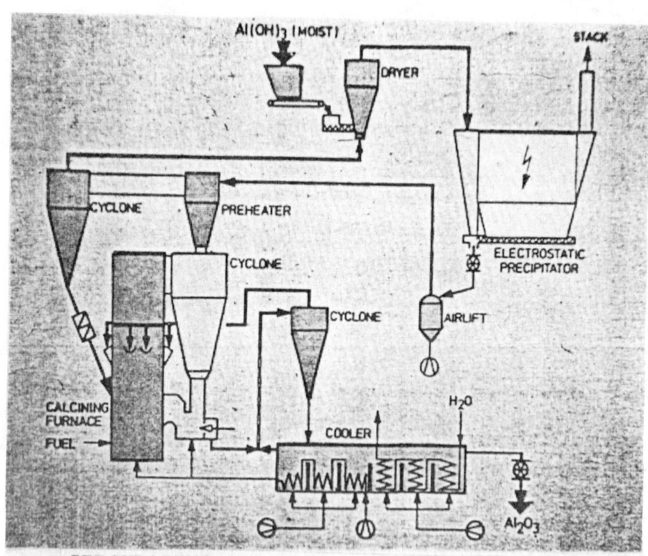

CIRCULATING FLUID BED CALCINING PLANT

FIGURE 4

coal ash and limestone instead of reacted alumina product, an innovative approach to combustion and SO_2 removal could be achieved. The concept of circulating fluid bed combustion was born.

Process Comparison

The basic process differences between the bubbling and circulating bed technologies are shown in Figure 5. This graph plots bed gas velocity on the ordinate versus bed expansion on the abscissa. The bubbling bed typically operates at about 8'/sec. At this velocity, and with bed particles at about 1000 micron mean size, the bed particles essentially remain in a defined region 4-5' high. Since the gas has a velocity of 8'/sec, and the mean bed particle has no appreciable absolute upward velocity, the differential velocity between gas and solid particle (called slip velocity) is about 8'/sec.

In the circulating bed, the gas velocity is usually 18-20'/sec. as shown. The bed particles, however, are much smaller at about 150-350 micron mean size (1/8" equals 3000 microns), and significant quantities of these particles are carried up in the gas stream into the upper area of the combustion chamber. The dynamics of the system show particles that are swept up the center of the combustor and cascade down along the walls. Some small fraction of the particles are also swept near the top of the combustor into the cyclone, are collected, and recirculated back to the bottom of the combustor. If, however, one were to calculate an average upward velocity of all particles in the combustor, that average would still be only about 3-4'/sec. Thus, the differential slip velocity between particle and gas in the circulating system is approximately 16'/sec (20'/sec minus 4'/sec).

As particle size is decreased further, and gas velocity is increased to 30-35'/sec, the particles eventually are entrained in the gas stream. The differential slip velocity decreases to zero, and we have evolved to the transport mode utilized in a traditional pulverized coal unit.

Slip velocity is an important factor in the fluidized bed process, because combustion and SO_2 removal are chemical reactions involving the migration of oxygen into a coal particle or SO_2 into a lime particle, reaction in the particle, and migration of CO_2 out of the coal and limestone particle. The greater the slip velocity, the faster and more complete the reaction. In addition, by fluidizing the particles throughout the combustion chamber instead of in a defined 4' bed, the residence time for reaction of SO_2 is increased. The SO_2 molecule released from the fuel at the bottom of the combustor in a circulating bed has

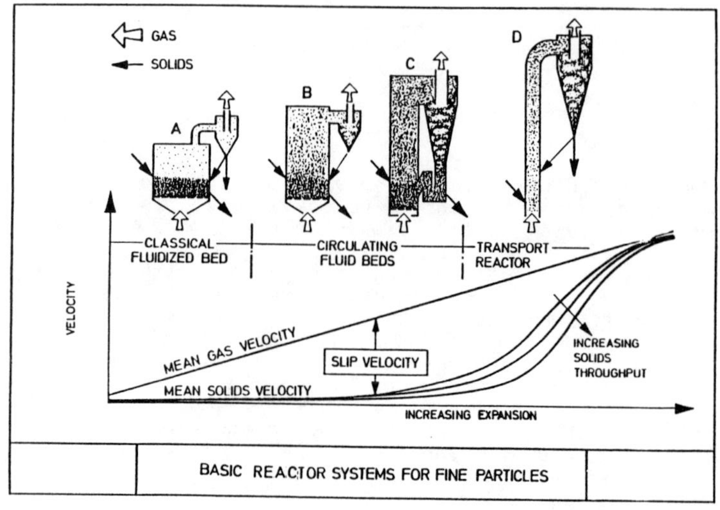

BASIC REACTOR SYSTEMS FOR FINE PARTICLES

FIGURE 5

about 6 seconds of travel time through a heavy concentration of fine calcined lime particles to find a site for reaction. In the bubbling bed, even with coal injected at the bottom of the bed, the reaction time in the bed is only about 1/2 sec, albeit in a denser concentration of particles. The same principle applies to the reaction of the oxygen with the fuel particle. The finer size of the CFB particles as compared to BFB also affects the reaction, as well as particle retention time in the system . CFB particles can be retained for as long as 2 hours in the circulating loop; BFB particles remain in the bed for a shorter period of time before being withdrawn from the bed drain.

The net effect of these differences can be significant. Carbon burnout for a bituminous coal is typically 93-96% for a bubbling bed with overbed fuel injection, 96-98% for a bubbling bed with underbed fuel injection, and 99+% for a circulating bed. Limestone usage as a ratio of stoichiometric requirements at 90% SO_2 removal on a 3% sulfur fuel is typically 4/1 with overbed injection, 3/1 with underbed, and 2/1 with the circulating bed. (It should be noted that multiclone recycle used with the larger bubbling beds has narrowed the gap between CFB's and BFB's. Ca/S ratios have been reduced to 2.3 to 2.5 and carbon burnout increased to 98.5%.)

Equipment Discussion

So why, with the apparent process advantage of the CFB, should one consider the bubbling bed? Because, for certain sizes and applications, it is considerably less expensive.

However, to understand the advantages and limitations of each type of system, it is first necessary to review the possible design variations within the bubbling and circulating systems. For the bubbling bed system, the major decision that must be made is how and where to feed the fuel. The simplest system is shown in Figure 6, and involves feeding the fuel via spreader feeders over the top of the bed. The advantage of this system is that the feed system is relatively inexpensive and that fuel preparation can be minimized, since optimum fuel sizing is 1 1/2 x 1/4". The disadvantage is that uniform fuel distribution over the entire bed is difficult. Any fines (smaller than 1000 microns) generated during the crushing process are immediately entained by the gas leaving the bed. These fines burn above the bed generating high temperatures and releasing SO_2 in the process. Since calcined lime is not present in any significance in this region of the boiler, and temperatures for that reaction are now not optimum, significant extra limestone must be used to achieve the required outlet emissions.

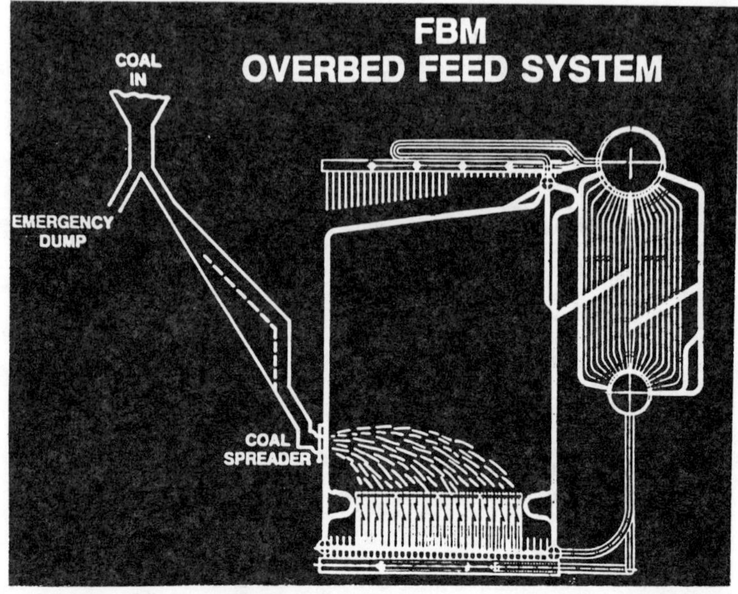

FIGURE 6

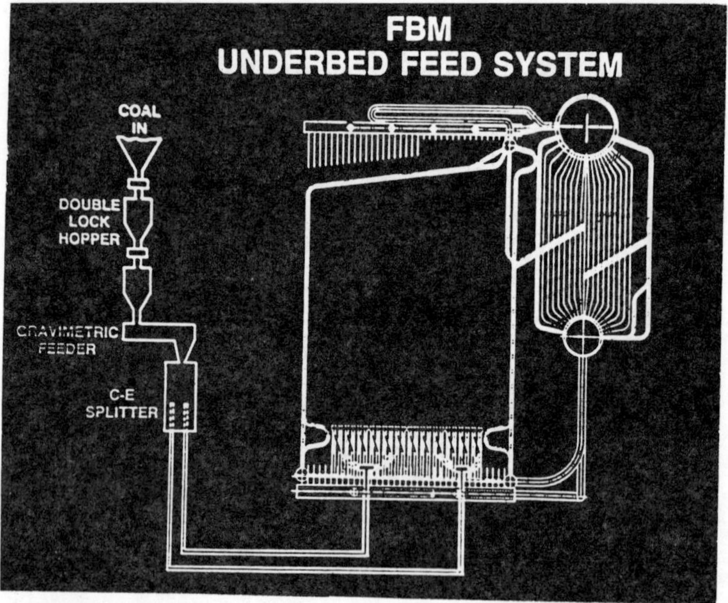

FIGURE 7

Furthermore, unevenness of fuel size distribution in the bed (the spreader tends to throw the larger particles further than the fine particles), often results in hot spots in the bed and occasional slagging.

On the other hand, for highly reactive, low sulfur fuels which burn quickly due to high inherent oxygen and do not generate excessive fines, the spreader may well be the optimum design.

All of the above deficiencies are overcome if fuel is fed into the boiler from underneath just above the air grate as shown in Figure 7. The difficulty, however, with underbed feed is that the coal must be crushed to 1/4" x 0", and it must not contain more than about 6-7% surface moisture if one is to avoid plugging of the fuel lines. Since most fuels are delivered to the plant in open trucks or railcars, the surface moisture is often excessive, and a system of crushing, drying, and classification must be provided. The complexity of this system for the 160 M.W. TVA bubbling bed design is shown in Figure 8. Fuel is first crushed in a hot flue gas-swept mill to 1/4" x 0". The resulting stream is next classified in cyclones, and the remaining fine fuel particles are collected in a baghouse. The cyclone and baghouse fuel discharges are combined and sent to the fuel day silos for injection under the boiler through 120 fuel injection points. The splitting of the fuel from the silo to the boiler is accomplished through the 12 patented bottle feeders shown in Figure 9 using fluidizing air in a circle-ten standpipe design in each bottle to achieve uniform splitting of the fuel.

This system has worked well in tests at the 20 M.W. TVA demonstration unit, but it is disproportionately expensive in smaller sizes. Even in the larger sizes, the cost of this drying system is great enough that the potential capital cost advantages of the bubbling bed design are, in large part, be negated.

There is, however, extensive work that has recently been completed at the 20 M.W. TVA pilot unit involving the mixing of the crushed coal with ash collected in the multiclone following the boiler. To achieve better carbon burnout and to lower limestone usage, most bubbling beds incorporate a multiclone at the outlet of the boiler to catch particles that escape the bed that are larger than about 20 microns; these fines are reinjected under the bed. The multiclone typically collects a quantity of fines equal to about 2 or 3 times the quantity of fuel injected. In this new concept, shown in Figure 10, about 1/3 of these fines are redirected to the fuel side and combined with the fuel in a mixing chamber following the crushers. The sensible heat in the ash at 500°F, combined with the

COAL FEED SYSTEM
TVA 160 MW UNIT

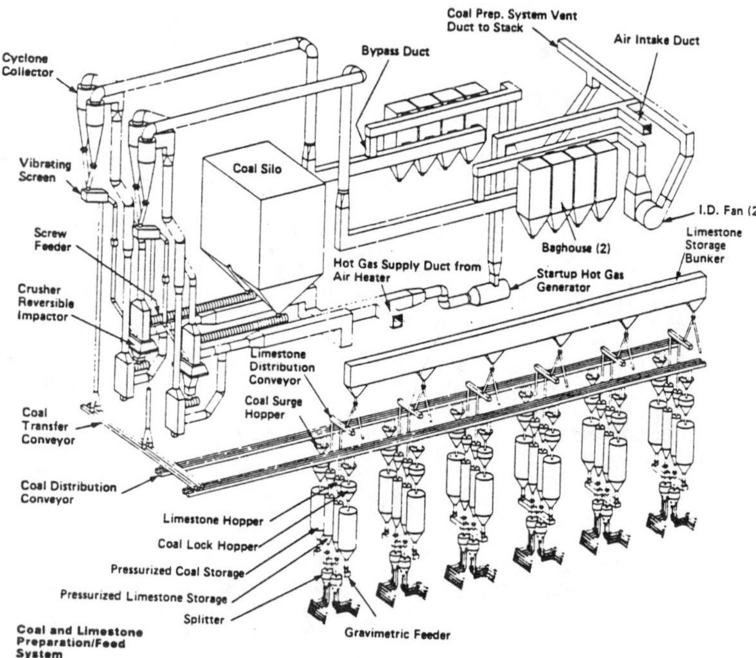

FIGURE 8

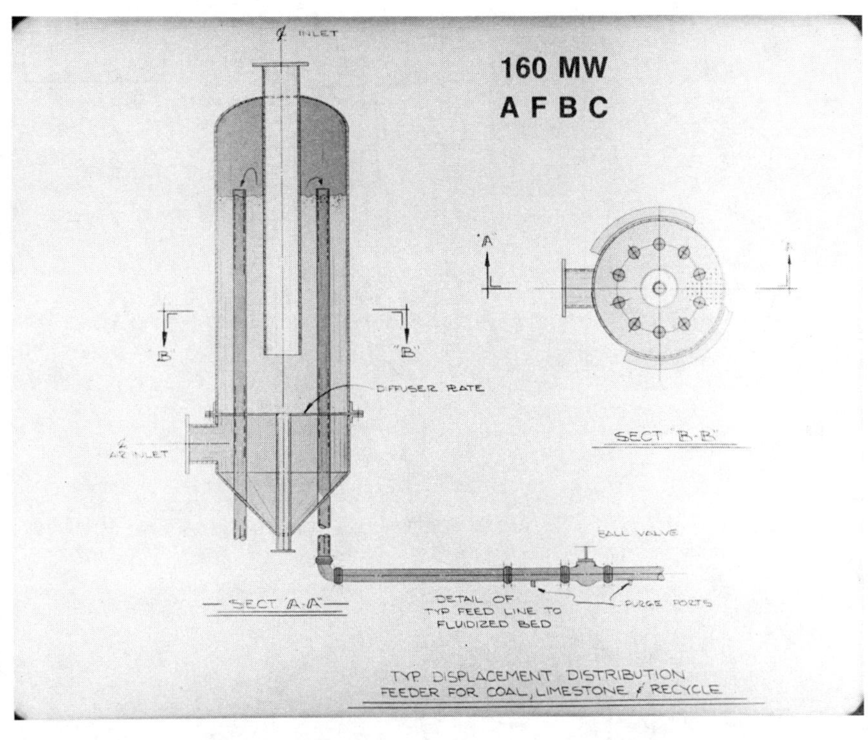

PATENTED CE FLUIDIZER FOR FUEL INJECTION IN UNDERBED SYSTEM. FUEL ENTERS FROM LOCKHOPPER LOCATED ABOVE CENTERLINE OF UNIT AND DROPS DOWN DIP LEG IN FLUIDIZER. AIR ENTERING UNDER DIFFUSER PLATE FLUIDIZES FUEL, WHICH FLOWS OVER TOP OF AND INTO MULTIPLE FEEDER LINES FOR DISTRIBUTION TO BED.

FIGURE 9

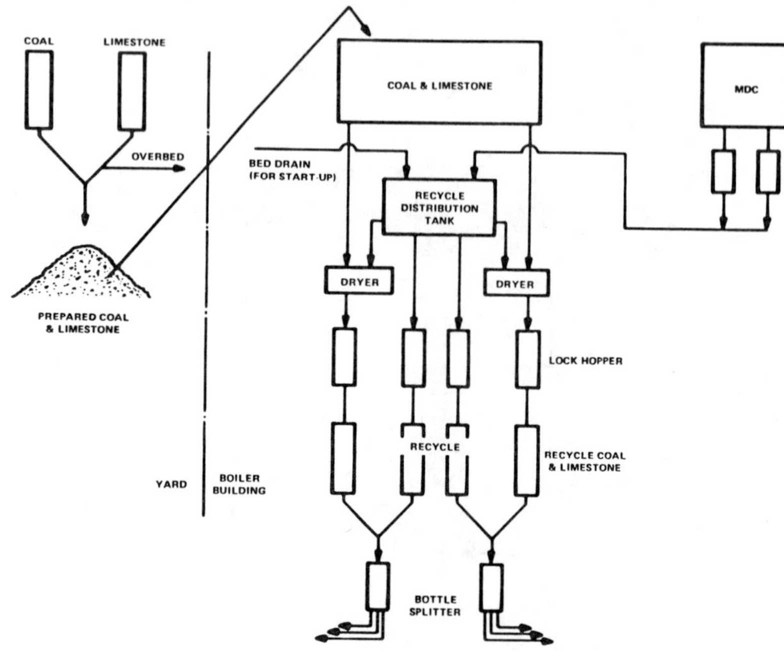

160 MW AFBC Demo Coal Recycle System FIGURE 10

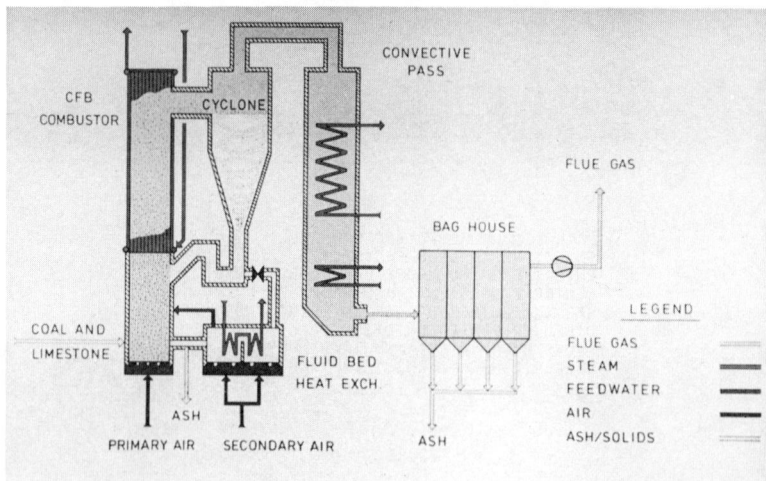

TYPICAL FLOW SHEET
FOR CIRCULATING FLUID BED BOILER SYSTEM FIGURE 11

reaction of the lime and gypsum which are hydrophilic, removes most of the surface moisture. A dry, free-flowing fuel/ash mixture results, which can then be injected into the boiler through the bottle feeders. Some technical problems related to steam evolution and condensation remain to be resolved before the concept is commercial. However, if this concept proves feasible, it could significantly affect the attitude toward the application of the bubbling bed on a wider range of fuels.

The general design of the circulating bed is depicted in Figure 11. One major deviation of the circulating bed from the bubbling bed is the absence of in-bed tubes in the CFB. Because the bed is highly expanded, bed temperature control in the CFB can be achieved for steam capacities up to about 400,000 #/hr with only the wall surface. This eliminates one of the major concerns with bubbling beds, namely, erosion of in-bed tubes, which has plagued the bubbling bed concept since its inception. The CFB wall concept, however, does not mean that erosion concerns can be totally ignored. Dust particle mass concentrations in the CFB chamber are still 500-1000 times higher than in a pulverized coal unit. However, operating experience of up to five years in a CFB shows that general wall erosion is very low, provided that the design avoids areas of turbulence or change of dust direction anywhere on the wall.

One major area of departure between circulating bed suppliers involves the fluid bed heat exchanger (FBHE). If the steam requirements of the system exceed about 400,000 #/hr, or if reheat is required, it becomes impossible to extract the required heat with only a waterwall combustor and backpass. In the combustor in particular, because height is limited by process considerations, wall surface cannot increase in proportion to gas volume. When the situation occurs where the wall surface is insufficient to extract the required heat, either extended surface must be added in the combustor or additional heat must be extracted outside of the combustor loop. C-E/Lurgi has provided systems with extended surface in the combustor with mixed results as related to erosion. The severity of the environment in this upper region continues to be a major concern; none of the operating CFB units with extended surface have sufficient operating time to provide confidence in predicting long-term erosion in this area.

An alternate approach is shown in Figure 12 involving an external heat removal technique. A portion of the dust collected by the cyclones is directed to an external heat exchanger, where some combination of superheat, reheat, and evaporative surface is placed.

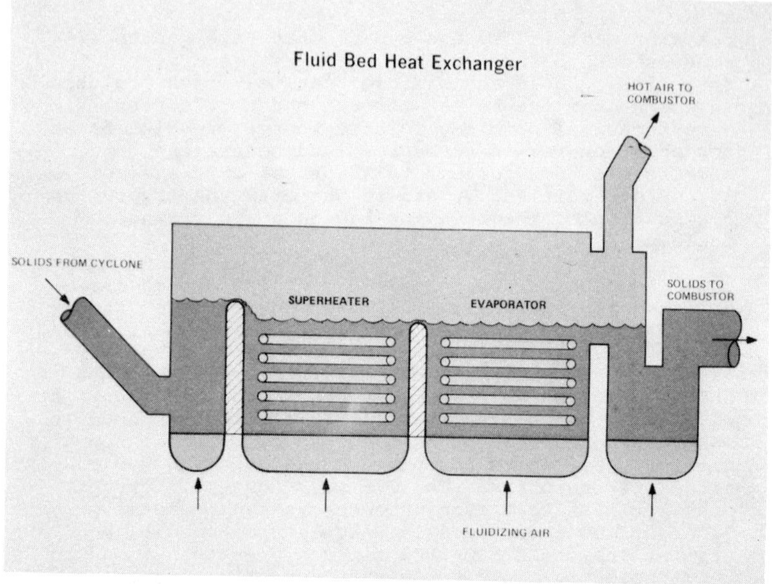

FIGURE 12

Potential Application Areas

Bubbling Fluidized Beds

- Steam Flows Below 300,000 #/hr
- Where Initial Installed Cost is Overriding Factor
- Inexpensive Fuels
- Low Sulfur Content Fuels
- Reactive Fuels
- Where Plant Height Restrictions Apply
- Large Utility Applications

FIGURE 13

The ash is cooled from the 1500-1600°F operating temperature to 1000 - 1100°F before being injected back into the boiler. The huge quantities of dust collected in the cyclones permits this concept to extend single combustor designs up to 250 M.W. at present.

It should also be noted that the large bubbling bed units, such as TVA, do involve heat transfer surface placed above the freeboard area, but the dust concentrations are low enough in this region of the bubbling bed that erosion is not a major concern with proper design considerations.

System Application

With the above understanding of system technical and process concepts in mind, it is useful to attempt to summarize the general areas of application of bubbling and circulating beds. Figure 13 highlights the areas of application that may be potentially advantageous for a bubbling bed. For steam flows of 150,000 #/hr - 350,000 #/hr the bubbling bed can be shop assembled in 2 to 4 pieces for inexpensive field erection. The low velocity provides a configuration that is compact. The circulating bed in these small sizes, due to the need to main higher velocities, becomes very tall and small in plan area, requiring excessive structural steel, expensive building enclosures, etc. In addition, particularly for the smaller sizes, the circulating bed system with its rather massive refractory-lined cyclones, seal pots, and blowers cannot be fabricated as inexpensively as the simpler bubbling bed design.

Process economics may also be a major consideration. If fuel is inexpensive, or sulfur in the fuel is low (thereby reducing limestone requirements), the extra fuel and limestone costs of the bubbling bed may be insignificant when compared to the reduced capital costs. This is particularly significant in the smaller sizes, where capital costs become disportionately high compared to operating costs.

Plant height restrictions also can come into play. A 300,000 #/hr bubbling bed has a typical total height from grade to top of steel of only 60 ft. A circulating bed is typically 140 ft. high.

Another area of potential application of bubbling beds is large utility designs. Circulating beds become quite complex with numerous cyclones, large external heat exchangers, and somewhat complex water/steam circuits in large utility sizes. Also, bubbling beds, because they contain in-bed surface as opposed to wall heating surface only, can be theoretically expanded to 500 M.W. sizes without any significant departure from the basic concept used in smaller sizes. In-bed tube erosion/corrosion continues to be a concern for the bubbling bed, but advances in controlling erosion, such as studding and hard-facing, are being aggressively pursued. The fuel feed complexity of the present bubbling bed system in large sizes is also a reliability concern as discussed earlier, but concepts in achieving better reliability are developing rapidly.

One final area of potential advantage for the bubbling bed has been n the retrofit area. By cutting off the bottom of a conventional pulverized coal boiler, and providing a flaired out bottom to achieve the required 10'/sec. fluidization velocities, a fluidized bed system can be provided economically in certain instances. The other modifications necessary to convert the entire system, such as relocation of heating surface, replacement of air heaters due to the higher differential pressure, larger I.D. fans, modification of the particulate control system, etc. frequently make the retrofit concept impractical, especially in light of the extensive outage time required to convert. In fact, a recent study completed on a major utility project comparing CFB and BFB retrofit costs suggested no particular economic advantage for either system, except that the CFB needed more plan area due to the cyclone addition. Nevertheless in certain specific cases such as the Northern States Power, Blackdog unit, and the Montana-Dakota, Heskett #2 Unit, BFB retrofits have found a definite niche.

The most obvious design for a pulverized coal retrofit to fluidized bed would be one in which no flairing out of the boiler would be required. However, this would result in a bed velocity of about 14-15'/sec., which would necessitate some type of solids recycle system. C-E is developing a unique recycle system that may allow this recycle within the confines of the p.c. envelope; if successful, this concept may alter the economics of retrofit applications for p.c. units as well as gas and oil-fired units.

The potential application areas of the CFB are highlighted in Figure 14. Between 150,000 #/hr and 300,000#/hr, the circulating bed, though more expensive on an installed basis, has generally been selected over the bubbling bed due to the perceived simplicity, flexibility, and reliability of the system. The operating difficulties with bubbling beds have tended to swing the user in favor of the CFB. Early operating experience in these smaller CFB's has generally been good, since the two major problems of BFB's, namely, tube erosion and fuel feed problems, are virtually eliminated.

Potential Application Areas

Circulating Fluidized Beds

- Steam Flows from 150,000 #/hr to 250 Mw
- Expensive Fuels
- High Sulfur Applications
- Where a Wide Range of Fuels is Expected
- Low NOx Applications (Less than .3#/10^6 Btu)
- Low SOx Applications
- Unreactive Fuels (Petroleum Coke, Anthracite Culm, Oil Shale)
- Erosive Fuels
- High-chloride Fuels

FIGURE 14

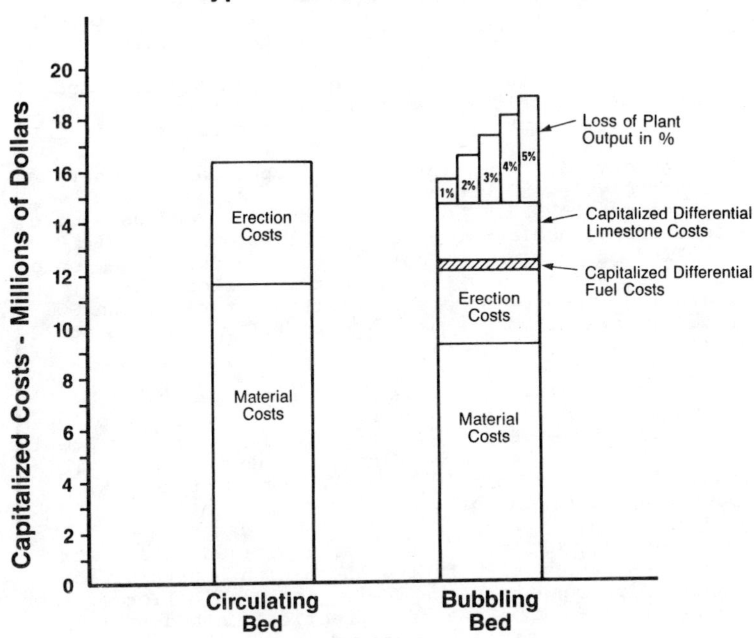

FIGURE 15

Between 300,000 #/hr and 150 mw the circulating bed has dominated. CFB's become very cost competitive in this range, and, coupled with the process advantages, evaluate favorably. In addition, the better performance of the CFB dictates its use where expensive fuels or high sulfur are encountered. The simplicity of the fuel feed system, and the perceived tolerance of the CFB to accept fuel variations, also dictate its use in applications where multiple fuels are expected. It should be noted here that the recent, more thorough understanding of the factors that govern CFB operation, such as optimum particle sizing required for heat transfer and variations in decrepitation rates, have cast some doubt in the user's mind on whether the CFB is really as versatile as previously thought. However, C-E believes that, if the system is properly designed with adequate consideration given to how to control these factors under varying fuel conditions, the CFB does, indeed, allow this flexibility. In combination with the FBHE concept, a single CFB system can be designed to handle a range of fuels from anthracite culm to petroleum coke and #6 fuel oil or natural gas.

Applications requiring unusually low NO_x emissions have also been particularly suitable for CFB's. Because the CFB is operated in a mode of staged combustion, i.e., the combustion air is introduced at various elevations in the combustor, NO_x emissions are typically 1/3 to 1/2 of the bubbling bed. In high density population areas or in pristine locations, local environmental requirements have occasionally dictated the CFB as the only system capable of achieving these NO_x levels without special $DeNO_x$ equipment.

We have also run into several applications where excessively low SO_x requirements have pushed the application to CFB. Because the bubbling bed uses more limestone to achieve the same level of SO_2 removal, the bubbling bed may not be able to achieve the SO_2 emission level without choking the bed with limestone, or operating expenses become exhorbitant at very high SO_2 removal levels. CFB's have successfully operated at SO_2 removal rates of up to 98%.

Due to the long solids retention times in the combustor loop (up to 2 hours) and the excellent process dynamics of the CFB, fuels that are unreactive or low in volatility are also particularly suited to CFB's. This includes anthracite culm with ash levels up to 70%, petroleum coke, and oil shale to mention a few.

Finally, CFB's may have particular advantage for erosive and corrosive fuels. Where high quartz silica content is present in the fuels, the elimination of the in-bed tubes may be the only practical method of preventing excessive erosion. In addition, the use of the external exchanger may be particularly suited to higher chloride fuels, since the high temperature superheat and reheat surface can be located in the FBHE, where it is out of the potentially corrosive gas stream.

Economics

It is worthwhile to review briefly the economics of bubbling and circulating beds. In particular, the capital and operating cost comparison of a typical 300,000 #/hr steam requirement is useful, since it tends to be in that grey area of selection between CFB and BFB. Figure 15 shows comparative operating and capital costs for such a system burning a 3% sulfur fuel, 11,000 Btu/#, with 90% SO_2 removal requirements. All equipment from the fuel feed inlet to the ID fan outlet is included. Limestone at $12/ton is assumed with the CFB operating at a 2/1 Ca/S molar ratio and the BFB at 3/1. Yearly operating expenses are capitalized at a 5 year payback. The CFB is assumed to achieve 99.2% carbon burnout, the BFB 98.0% with underbed feed. Fuel is assumed to cost $1.80 per million Btu's, and is also capitalized on a 5 year payback. Auxiliary power is not considered, since the differential between CFB and BFB has not proven to be significant; although the CFB operates at a higher primary air pressure (typically 60") than the bubbling bed (40"-45"), the secondary air in the CFB (usually 50% of total) is at a much lower pressure (typically 30-35"). Thus, the total power input is almost a tradeoff. Induced-draft fan power is also usually equivalent, since pressure drop in the backpass (superheat, reheat, multiclone, airheater, and baghouse) tends to be about the same. For simplicity, only capitalized <u>differentials</u> for fuel costs, limestone costs, and reliability are shown.

The graph clearly shows the cost advantage of bubbling over circulating beds when only the installed costs are evaluated. The bubbling bed material costs are only about 80% of the circulating bed costs, and erection costs are only about 60% of CFB costs due to the modularized BFB concept involved. However, when fuel and limestone capitalized cost differentials are factored in, the bubbling bed approaches 90% of the CFB on an evaluated basis. This analysis also does <u>not</u> account for any evaluation of ash disposal differences; based on the conditions detailed above, the bubbling bed would typically produce about 22% more ash than the CFB, due primarily to the higher limestone requirement. For a typical 3% sulfur fuel, this would equate to over 5000 tons/yr of extra ash. At a conservative disposal cost of $5/ton, and a 5 year payback to capitalize, ash disposal would add another $200,000 to the capital cost differential.

Nevertheless, even considering all of the above, the bubbling bed still evaluates better than the circulating bed. Why, then, has the marketplace generally swung so heavily in favor of circulating beds? The answer is shown by the impact of perceived reliability differences. If this 300,000 #/hr boiler were producing power, for example, at 6¢/Kwhr, the total net plant output of about 33,333 Kw/hr would generate revenues of about $15.8 million per year at a 90% capacity factor. Loss of 1% in output due to boiler unreliability would equate to an annual loss of $158,000, which, when capitalized at a 5 year payback, equates to about $790,000 in extra capital cost justification. The impact on the evaluation is shown graphically in Figure 15 as a cost adder to the bubbling bed evaluation. At just under 2% loss of reliability or output, the CFB is more cost effective than the bubbling bed.

Obviously, variations in boiler size, fuel costs, sulfur content in the fuel, and payback parameters will alter the final evaluation. For very small plants, (under 100,000 #/hr) the capital costs for material and erection become dominant. Reliability may also be less of a factor for some small plant operations, or may be less critical if other boilers in the system can pick up the slack. Also, the CFB is a newer concept on the American scene, and all of the factors that can cause forced shutdowns or affect long term reliability (such as refractory deterioration and localized tube erosion) may not be totally understood.

Nevertheless, the perception of the public at present from observations of both bubbling and circulating bed system operational performance is that CFB's are more reliable. And it this perception that is drawing the marketplace so heavily to the CFB concept.

Summary

Circulating fluidized beds will probably continue to dominate the marketplace for steam requirements between 300,000 #/hr and 1,000,000 #/hr, due to the performance advantages of CFB's in this size range. Below 300,000 #/hr, the choice will depend on factors related to fuel characteristics, limestone costs, environmental constraints, perceived reliability differences, and capital constraints.

For sizes over 1,000,000 #/hr (150 MW), the final picture is still somewhat unclear. The success of the TVA 160 MW bubbling bed unit scheduled for startup in 1988 may well alter the attitude of the user toward the bubbling bed system in this size range. Advances in bubbling bed technology may also reduce capital costs enough to swing the user in some instances to the bubbling bed. CFB designs in this size range are also, however, in transition with potential for cost reduction. It would, therefore, be imprudent at this time to make a final judgment on the marketplace preference in this size range. We at C-E are pursuing both technologies with a determination to make either system as reliable and as cost-effective as possible.

IMPACT OF ENERGY USE ON GLOBAL CLIMATE CHANGE

Gordon J. MacDonald, Vice President/Chief Scientist

The MITRE Corporation, McLean, Virginia

Solar radiation brings heat from the sun to the earth's surface, but without the atmosphere most of this heat would be lost and the earth would be an inhospitable 68°F colder than today. The atmosphere, through the action of small amounts of carbon dioxide, ozone and water vapor, traps part of the radiation emitted by the earth that otherwise would flow into the cold of outer space. The capacity of the earth's atmosphere to conserve solar radiation is popularly known as the "greenhouse effect." In 1861, Tyndale[1] recognized that slight changes in atmospheric composition could bring about variations in climate. By 1938, Callendar[2] had shown that man, by burning fossil fuels, was changing the composition of the atmosphere and thus could bring about shifts in global climate.

The last three decades have brought major advances in understanding the links between the atmosphere and climate. Detailed measurements of atmospheric carbon dioxide show an exponential increase that matches the rate at which carbon is placed in the atmosphere by the burning of fossil fuels. Various models of the atmosphere, which greatly differ in complexity, predict that the carbon released over the past century will generate an increase in average global temperature of about 1°F. Laborious analyses of past temperature measurements show that an average temperature increase of about 1°F has, in fact, occurred. A number of gases whose concentration depend on man's activities--ozone, methane, nitrous oxide and the chlorofluorocarbons--also contribute to the greenhouse effect. Expected future increases of these trace gases will double the warming that is anticipated from carbon dioxide alone. Measurements of ancient air trapped in glaciers indicate that the carbon dioxide concentration of the atmosphere was low during glacial periods and high during inter-glacial epochs.

These findings provide irrefutable evidence of the link between atmospheric composition and global climate. With these scientific advances has come a growing public awareness that future climate change could have adverse affects on society. In the following, I discuss how changes in atmospheric composition and in climate are linked to energy use.

Changes in Atmospheric Composition

Modern observations of atmospheric carbon dioxide began in 1958 with the measurements taken by Keeling[3] at a remote site in Hawaii. Keeling's observations show an exponential growth in carbon dioxide (see Fig. 1) on which a periodic seasonal variation is superimposed. The seasonal variation follows the biospheric uptake of carbon dioxide during the growing season and its discharge during the winter. Keeling also established and maintained an observational regime at the South Pole. The Antarctic records show a similar exponential growth in carbon dioxide concentration, but a greatly diminished seasonal variation. Because the atmosphere at the South Pole is well removed from biological activity, the smaller seasonal fluctuations are expected. Keeling's observations have been duplicated at other stations in various parts of the world over shorter time intervals. During the 1958 to 1987 period, the average carbon dioxide content of the atmosphere increased from 315 parts per million by volume (ppmv) to 349 ppmv. Measured in terms of metric tons of carbon, 72.4 billion tons (Gt) of carbon have been added to the atmosphere from 1958 to the present.

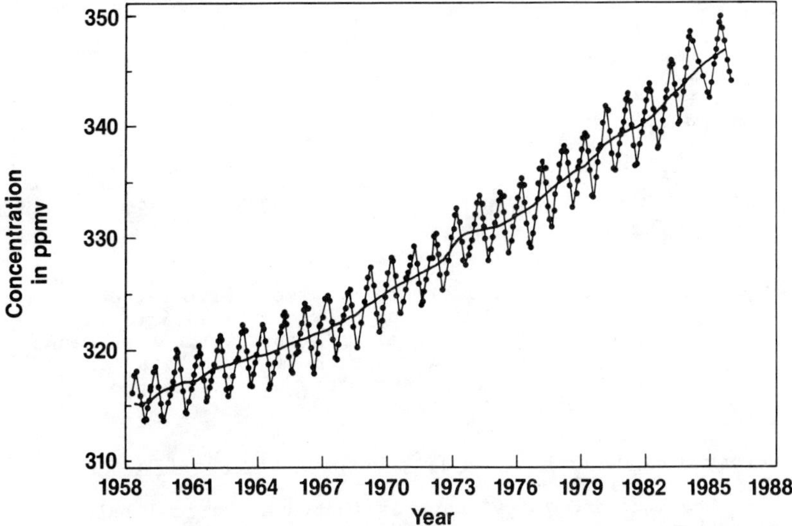

Figure 1. Atmospheric carbon dioxide concentration in parts per million by volume at Mauna Loa Observatory, Hawaii (after Keeling[4]).

The difficulty of obtaining air samples uncontaminated by local sources of CO_2, such as the observer's breath, lessens the value of carbon dioxide measurements made prior to 1958. Fortunately, during the transformation of snow into ice in glacial regions, air is trapped in the intergrain spaces of the ice. When samples of this ice are crushed, the old air is released, and its carbon dioxide concentration can be determined. The age of the ice itself can be fixed by counting the seasonal layers in a manner similar to counting tree rings. In this fashion, the carbon dioxide content of the atmosphere in historical times can be measured. Figure 2 shows the variation of CO_2 concentration over the past 250 years; data prior to 1958 are taken from ice core determinations.[6] The rise in CO_2 concentration from about 290 to 349 ppmv over the last 100 years corresponds to the addition of 126 billion tons of carbon to the atmosphere. Prior to the beginning of the industrial revolution in the early 1800s, the concentration of CO_2 remained approximately constant, with values of 275 to 285 ppmv.

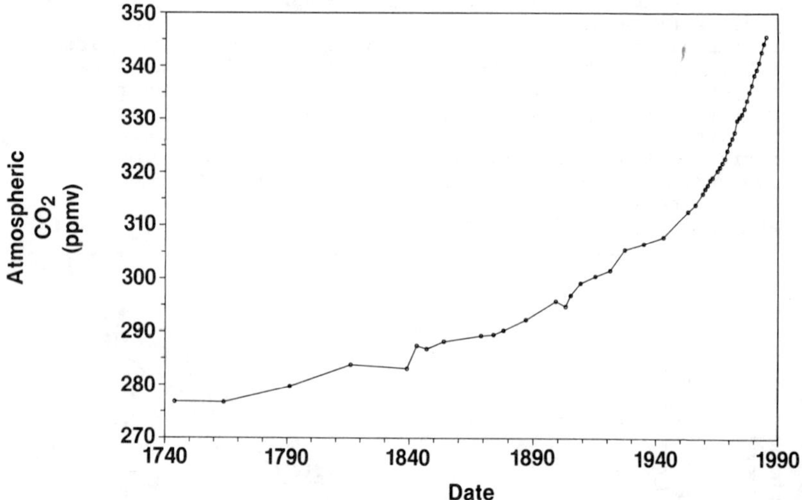

Figure 2. Historical variations in atmospheric carbon dioxide concentration. Data from 1958 to the present are from Keeling's observations at Mauna Loa, Hawaii.[5] Data for the 1740 to 1956 period are taken from measurements of air trapped in glacial ice sheets.[6]

Carbon Dioxide Production from Burning of Fossil Fuels

Keeling[7] and Rotty[8] have estimated historical releases of carbon from data accumulated by the United Nations. The accuracy of data on fossil fuel emissions depends on the reliability of information in three areas: quantities of fuel used, the carbon content of the fuel and the fraction of the fuel that is burned. The reliability of relevant data improved significantly as interest in energy heightened after the oil crisis of 1973. Energy information became, and has remained, an important item in managing world affairs. Analysis of past energy consumption patterns has assisted in improving earlier estimates. Despite these advances, uncertainties on the order of tens of percent exist in earlier values.

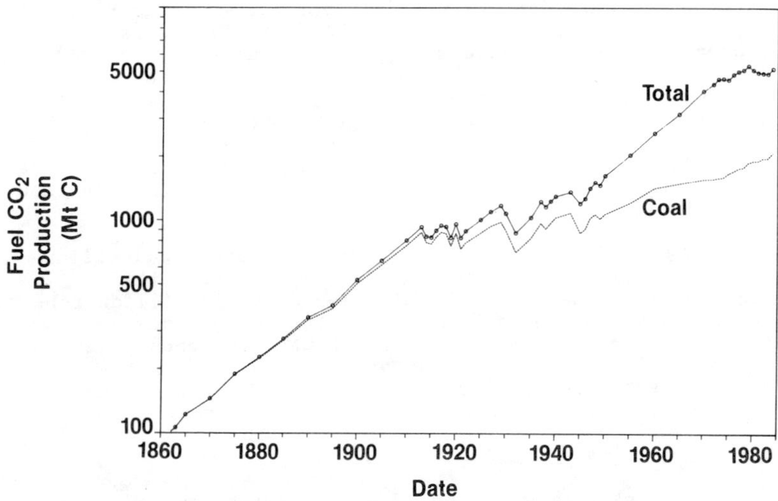

Figure 3. Historical variations in carbon dioxide emission from the burning of fossil fuels (data from Rotty[9] and Keeling[10]).

Figure 3 illustrates historical variations in the addition of carbon to the atmosphere through the burning of fossil fuels. The last 120 years of fuel combustion can be separated into four major periods, each with a distinct rate of exponential growth (see Table 1). Between the

Table 1

Historical Rates of Exponential Growth of Fossil Fuel Use (%/year)

Fuel/Period	1860-1913	1913-1950	1950-1973	1973-1984
All fuels	4.31	1.53	4.52	1.15
Coal	4.21	0.55	1.78	2.36
Oil	-	-	7.25	0.11
Gas	-	-	7.98	2.31

beginning of the data sets for 1860 and 1913, the world's consumption of fossil fuel and the emission of carbon increased at an average exponential rate of 4.31% per year. Coal was the dominant fuel throughout this span of time. The advent of World War I, the world turbulence of the 1920s, the depression of the 1930s and World War II led to a marked slow-down in the rate of growth of energy use to 1.53% per year, but then oil began to make a major contribution to the overall energy picture. For the twenty-three-year period beginning in 1950, world energy consumption grew at a 4.52% per year rate of growth. This rate, which exceeded the pre-1913 period, was primarily caused by a rapid increase in the use of oil and gas, an increase in use far exceeding that of coal (see Table 1). The oil price shock of 1973 began what appears to be another extended period of low rates of growth for fossil energy use. The 1.15% per year growth rate for carbon emissions was lower than the rate which prevailed during the 1913-1950 interval of war and depression. In 1973, the use of coal once again began to grow at a greater rate than that of oil, reversing a fifty year trend.

From 1860 to 1984, fossil fuels released 184 billion tons of carbon; during this same time interval, the atmospheric burden of carbon increased by 113 billion tons. The increase in the carbon dioxide content of the atmosphere corresponds to 61% of the total carbon released. The bulk of the remaining carbon has dissolved in the ocean, but the total carbon budget is dependent on the biosphere,[11] whose exact role is as yet uncertain.

Long-Term Climate Changes

The link between carbon dioxide variations and climate change has been greatly strengthened by the discovery that during the last glacial period, the carbon dioxide content of the atmosphere was only about 60% of recent values.[12] Figure 4 shows the variation with time of the carbon dioxide concentration of the atmosphere, as determined from air trapped within the two-kilometer-long Vostok ice core taken in Antarctica.[13] After displaying values consistent with those of the past 200 years, the samples show a sharp plunge in CO_2 concentration beginning about 9,000 years ago. Variations in CO_2 content displayed by the ice core samples closely match the period of glaciation between 12,000 and 120,000 years ago, the interglacial period between 120,000 and 135,000 years ago and the preceding glacial period. The close concordance between glacial epochs and changes in atmospheric composition demonstrates the link between long-term changes in carbon dioxide and major global shifts in climate.

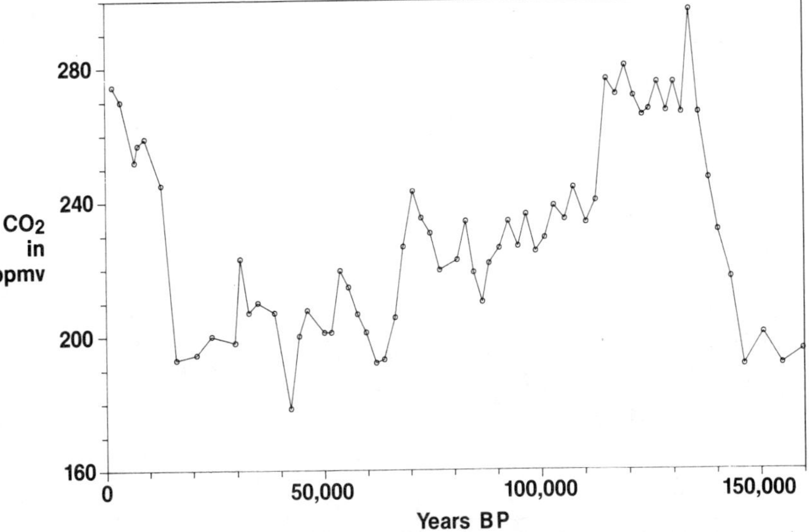

Figure 4. Variation of past concentrations of atmospheric carbon dioxide, as determined by measurements of air trapped in the Vostok ice core from East Antarctica (after Barnola et al.[14]).

Temperature Changes Associated with Changes in Atmospheric Composition

The increase in carbon dioxide concentration from 290 ppmv 100 years ago to the present value of about 350 ppmv should be reflected in an increase in surface temperature. While instrumental records of temperature exist over this time interval in most land areas, the analysis of past temperature shifts is extremely difficult. The basic problem is that of detecting a slow, long-term trend in a record made noisy by the continuous fluctuations of short-term weather. A further complication is due to past samplings of temperature that are strongly biased toward land areas. Despite these impediments, the analysis of some 63 million observations over land and sea reveals a distinct warming trend over the past century.[15] As indicated in Figure 5, the increase has been irregular, but the global average warming equals about 1°F. The three warmest years have been 1980, 1981 and 1983. Further, five of the nine warmest years occurred after 1978. Confirmatory evidence of the warming comes from measurements of variations of temperature with depth in permafrost regions of the Arctic.[17] Because of the low thermal diffusivity of rock, temperatures beneath the ground surface represent a systematic running mean of the recent temperature history of the surface; low thermal diffusivity damps out the high frequency variation in air temperature. Permafrost prevents circulating ground waters from perturbing the regime of thermal conductivity. The temperature record contained in the permafrost reveals that surface air temperature has risen 4 to 8°F over the last century. Because the increase at high latitudes is predicted to be 4 to 6 times the global average,[18] the 4 to 8°F Arctic value is in accordance with a global average temperature increase of 1°F.

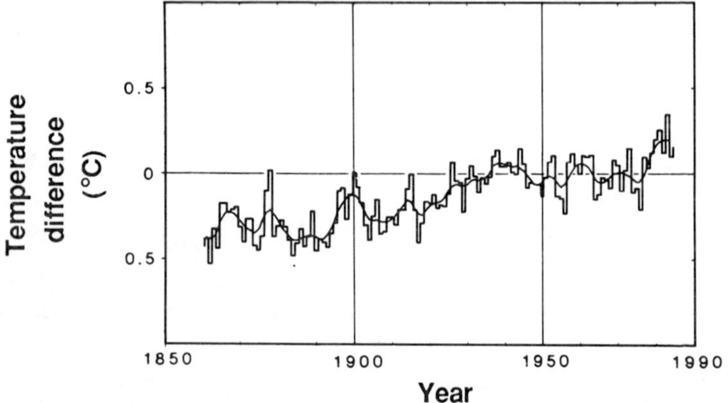

Figure 5. Annual variation of global mean temperature from 1861 to the present (after Jones, Wigley and Wright[16]).

The warming of the atmosphere due to the radiative absorption of heat by carbon dioxide is well understood. Knowledge of the warming mechanism allows changes in CO_2 concentration to be translated into changes in average global temperature due solely to CO_2, ΔT_{CO_2}. The actual temperature change ΔT will depend on various feedback processes stimulated by warming, such as alterations in cloudiness and water vapor content of the atmosphere. The actual temperature change associated with a change in CO_2 concentration can be written as

$$\Delta T = f(\Delta T_{CO_2})\ \Delta T_{CO_2},$$

where $f(\Delta T_{CO_2})$ is the unknown feedback function. Assuming a linear feedback over small temperature changes, f is constant and can be estimated from the 1°F change in temperature observed between 1880 and 1980 and the corresponding increase in CO_2 concentration from 290 to 340 ppmv. The resulting value, $f = 1.92$, is consistent with, but somewhat lower than, the value obtained by Hansen et al.[19] from analysis of computer models of climate change. Figure 6 shows the temperature change computed by using the Vostok ice core CO_2 records (from Fig. 4) together with more recent measurements of CO_2 (see Fig. 2). These calculations indicate that the total change in temperature that accompanies a shift from the cold of a glacial epoch to the warmth of an interglacial period is about 1.5°C or 3°F.

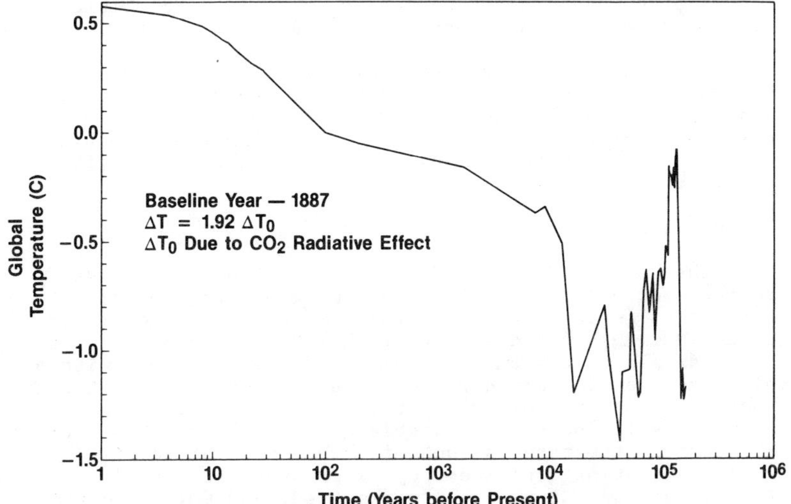

Figure 6. Calculated change in temperature resulting solely from changes in carbon dioxide concentration.

Climate Impact of Trace Gases Other Than Carbon Dioxide

Ozone (O_3), methane (CH_4), nitrous oxide (N_2O) and chlorofluorocarbons all possess strong absorption bands in the infrared window of the atmosphere and can contribute to green-house warming. Historical trends in the concentration of these gases are less well-known than those of carbon dioxide, because recognition of their significance to climate change has come only in the last decade. Over the past century, the contribution of these gases to global warming has been minor in comparison with carbon dioxide, but their effects will be of future importance because of the rapid rate at which they are accumulating.

Atmospheric methane is increasing at a rate of 1 to 2% per year.[21] The principal sources of methane are biological in nature; wetlands, rice paddies and ruminant animals all produce it. The increase of methane, however, is fuel-related. In the atmosphere, methane is oxidized to carbon dioxide through reaction with hydroxyl radical, HO. Hydroxyl is an important reactive constituent of the atmosphere, and is formed through the interaction of ultraviolet radiation and water vapor. The concentration of hydroxyl, and the degree to which it acts as a sink for methane, depend on the abundance of carbon monoxide. As fossil fuel combustion has increased, carbon monoxide concentra-tion has risen. Carbon monoxide reacts more rapidly with CO than does methane, causing a drop in background hydroxyl concentration and, consequently, a rise in methane.

The abundance of tropospheric ozone is also critically dependent on lower-atmosphere chemical reactions that involve the products of fuel combustion. High levels of ozone are associated with volatile organic compounds released by the combustion of gasoline and diesel fuels. Nitrous oxide is released during the combustion of coal containing nitrogen compounds. Of the infrared-absorbing trace gases, only the freons are unrelated to fossil fuel combustion.

Trends in Fuel Use

The amount of carbon dioxide generated by fuel use depends not only on the total energy consumed, but also on the mix of fuels. The amount of carbon dioxide generated in delivering a fixed amount of thermal energy depends on the hydrogen-to-carbon ratio of the fuel. Methane, with a high hydrogen-to-carbon ratio, releases less carbon dioxide than does coal in delivering the same amount of thermal energy, as is indicated in Table 2. When "synthetic" fuels are burned, the total amount of carbon dioxide released while generating useful energy is greater than for fossil fuels, because energy is also expended, and CO_2 released, in the initial process of making the synthetic fuel.

Table 2

Carbon Dioxide Emissions from Direct Combustion of Various Fuels

Fuel	CO_2 Emission Rate (pounds per million Btu)	Ratio Relative to Methane
Methane	28.2	1
Ethane	32.4	1.15
Propane	34.1	1.21
Butane	35.1	1.24
Gasoline	39.5	1.40
Diesel Oil	41.2	1.46
No. 6 Fuel Oil	41.8	1.48
Bituminous Coal	49.7	1.73
Subbituminous Coal	52.9	1.87

Worldwide, the patterns of energy use have changed over the years. As indicated in Figure 3, prior to 1913, the burning of coal provided the bulk of the world's energy and was the principal source of carbon dioxide fuel emissions. By 1950, the percent of energy derived from coal was down to 59%, but coal was responsible for 67% of the CO_2 emissions. Between 1950 and 1973, oil became the dominant fuel and carbon dioxide emitter (see Fig. 7). These trends underwent a major shift during the 1970s, as the sharp rise in the price of petroleum prompted a more rapid growth in coal use than in the use of oil (see Table 1). In 1980, coal produced 30% of the world's energy and 40% of the carbon dioxide. By 1984, coal's fraction of energy production had risen to 32%, and coal was responsible for 42% of the CO_2 emissions.

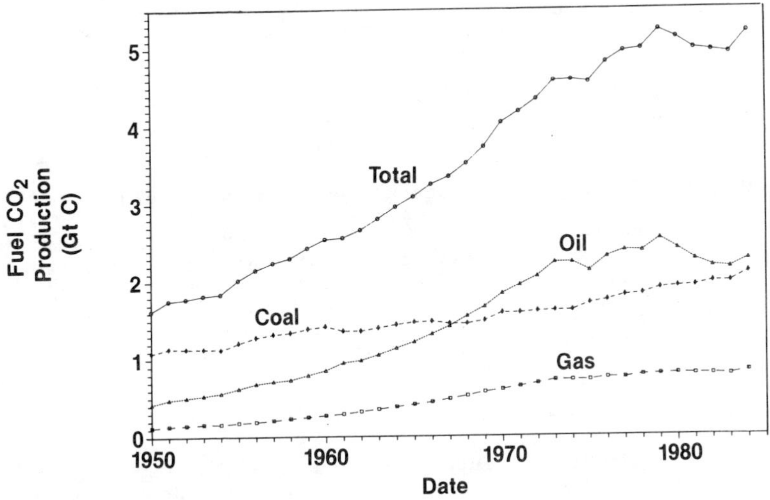

Figure 7. Variations in the contribution of various fuels to global carbon dioxide emissions. The natural gas curve includes contributions from gas that is flared at the well. The amount of flared gas has decreased with time so that the amount of gas used for energy has increased at a greater rate than the figure indicates. Data are based on Rotty's analysis of United Nation data compilations.[20]

Alterations in fuel mix have produced major shifts in the regional emission of carbon dioxide. In 1950, North America was responsible for 45% of carbon dioxide emissions, the developing world only 6%. By 1984, North America's share had dropped to 25%, with the developing world emitting 15%, as is illustrated in Figure 8.

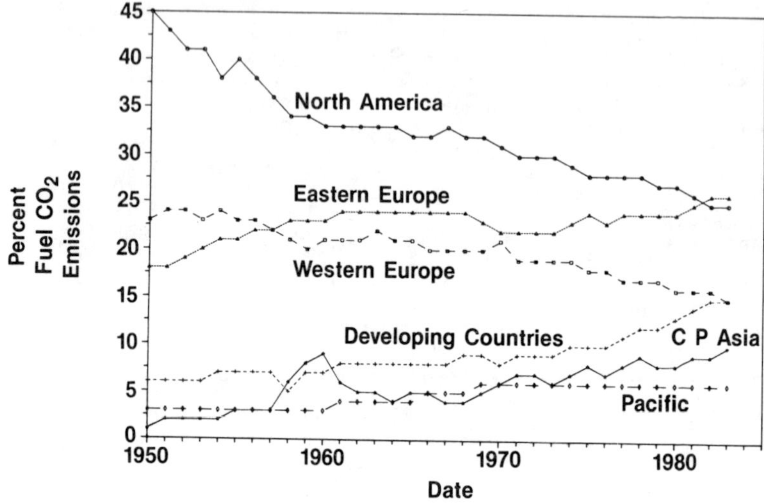

Figure 8. Changes in fractional contribution to global CO_2 emissions by major regions of the world. Eastern Europe refers to the centrally planned economies of eastern Europe, including all of the Soviet Union. C P Asia includes the centrally planned economies of Asia, China, North Korea, Mongolia, North Vietnam, etc. Japan, Australia and New Zealand comprise the Pacific region.

Future Temperature Trends

The estimation of future changes in global temperature requires several assumptions: how carbon dioxide emissions are divided among the atmosphere, oceans and biosphere; estimates of fuel use and fuel mix; and a computational methodology. Given these assumptions, any projection is bound to be uncertain. Figure 9 provides such an illustrative forecast using the same methodology employed in constructing Figure 6. The present partition of CO_2 emission among the major reservoirs is assumed to hold into the future. The rate of exponential growth for CO_2 emissions is taken to be 2.3% per year. This rate is double the rate that has held since 1973, but is half that which prevailed during periods of high growth in fossil fuel usage (see Table 1). With these assumptions, the global average temperature change resulting solely from the addition of combustion--generated carbon dioxide will equal the temperature change of a glacial to interglacial shift in the next forty years. If the present rate of fossil fuel use is maintained, the 3°F change in temperature will be postponed for 25 years.

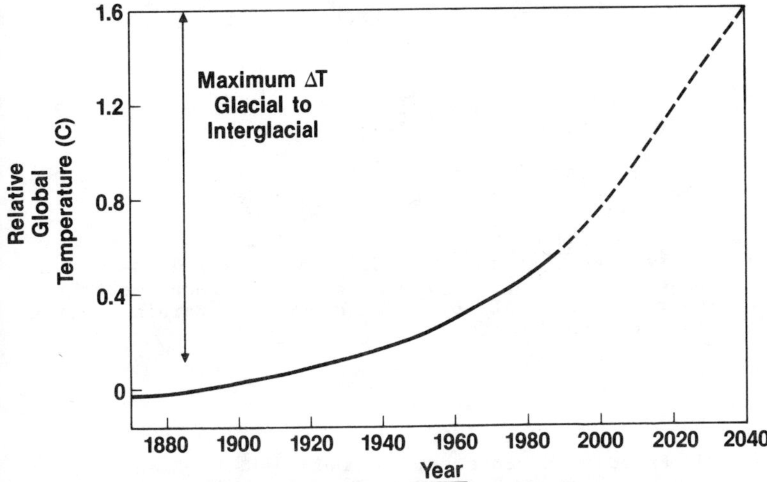

Figure 9. Past and future changes in global mean temperature from addition of carbon dioxide to the atmosphere. Other greenhouse gases will lead to further temperature increases in the future.

The temperature change illustrated in Figure 9 refers only to changes induced by carbon dioxide. The warming due to other trace gases should also be included in any estimate of future temperature. Since far less data are available on the trace gases, calculating their future climatic effects is more uncertain. However, calculations[22] suggest that the total global warming in the next forty years will be about 5 to 7°F, an increase significantly greater than that due to CO_2 alone, and also greater than the increase that accompanied glacial to interglacial transitions.

Conclusions

The burning of fossil fuels changes the composition of the atmosphere. These changes have brought about a warming that is barely perceptible, even when millions of observations are analyzed using sophisticated data reduction techniques. Warming over the next few decades will be significantly greater, and with this warming will come other changes in climate. Attempts to slow climate change must be global in nature; all countries using fossil fuels are contributing to climate alteration. Measures to reduce carbon emissions would include raising energy efficiency and promoting the use of all energy sources that do not contribute to the carbon dioxide burden of the atmosphere, such as nuclear, solar and hydropower. Of the fossil fuels, natural gas releases the least amount of carbon dioxide per unit of energy delivered; coal produces the most. The use of synthetic fuels would hasten climate change since both the production and use of synthetics contribute carbon dioxide to the atmosphere.

REFERENCES

1. J. Tyndale, "Philadelphia Magazine," J. of Sci., **22** (1861), pp. 169-194, 273-285.

2. G. Callendar, "Temperature Fluctuation and Trends Over the Earth," Quart. J. Royal Meteor. Soc., **87** (1961), pp. 1-12.

3. C. Keeling, "Atmospheric CO_2 Concentration, Mauna Loa Observatory, Hawaii, 1958-1983," U.S. Department of Energy Report NDP-001 (Oak Ridge, TN: Carbon Dioxide Information Center, 1984).

4. Ibid.

5. Ibid.

6. H. Friedli, H. Lötscher, H. Oeschger, U. Siegenthaler and B. Stauffer, "Ice Core Record of the $^{13}C/^{12}C$ Ratio of Atmospheric CO_2 in the Past Two Centuries," Nature, **324** (1986), pp. 237-238.

7. C. Keeling, "Industrial Production of Carbon Dioxide from Fossil Fuels and Limestone," Tellus, **25** (1973), pp. 174-198.

8. R. Rotty, "A Look at 1983 CO_2 Emissions from Fossil Fuels (with Preliminary Data for 1984), Tellus, **39B** (1987), pp. 203-208; G. Marland and R. Rotty, "Carbon Dioxide Emissions from Fossil Fuels: A Procedure for Estimation and Results for 1950-1982," Tellus, **36B** (1984), pp. 232-261.

9. Ibid.

10. Keeling, op. cit., 1973.

11. G. MacDonald, The Long-Term Impacts of Increasing Atmospheric Carbon Dioxide Levels (Cambridge, Mass.: Ballinger, 1982).

12. R. Delmas, J. Ascencio and M. Legrand, "Polar Ice Evidence that Atmospheric CO_2 20,000 Yr BP was 50% of Present," Nature, **284** (1980), pp. 155-157; W. Berner, H. Oeschger and B. Stauffer, "Information on the CO_2 Cycle from Ice Core Studies" in M. Stuiver and R. Kra, eds, International ^{14}C Conference, Radiocarbon, **22**, pp. 227-235.

13. J. Jouzel, C. Lorius, J. Petit, C. Genthon, N. Barkov, V. Kotlyakov and V. Petrov, "Vostok Ice Core: A Continuous Isotope Temperature Record over the Last Climatic Cycle (160,000 Years)," Nature, **329** (1987), pp. 403-408; C. Genthon, J. Barnola, D. Raynaud, C. C. Lorius, J. Jouzel, N. Barkov, Y. Korotkevich and V. Kotlyakov, "Vostok Ice Core: Climatic Response to CO_2 and Orbital Forcing Changes over the Last Climatic Cycle," Nature, **329** (1987), pp. 414-418; J. Barnola, D. Raynaud, Y. Korotkevich and C. Lorius, "Vostok Ice Core Provides 160,000-Year Record of Atmospheric CO_2," Nature, **329** (1987), pp. 408-414.

14. Barnola, et al., op. cit.

15. C. Folland, D. Parker, and F. Kates, "Worldwide Marine Temperature Fluctuation 1856-1981," Nature, **310** (1984), pp. 670-673; P. Jones, T. Wigley, and P. Wright, "Global Temperature Variation Between 1861 and 1984," Nature, **322** (1986b), pp. 430-434.

16. Jones, et al., op. cit.

17. A. Lachenbruch and V. Marshall, "Changing Climate: Geothermal Evidence from Permafrost in the Alaskan Arctic," Science, **234** (1986), pp. 689-696.

18. MacDonald, op. cit.

19. J. Hansen, G. Russell, A. Lacis, I. Fung, D. Rind and P. Stone, "Climate Response Times: Dependence on Climate Sensitivity and Ocean Mixing," Science, **229** (1985), pp. 857-859.

20. Rotty, op. cit.

21. M. Khalil and R. Rasmussen, "Sources, Sinks, and Seasonal Cycles of Atmospheric Methane," J. Geophys. Res., **88** (1983), pp. 5131-5141; M. Khalil and R. Rasmussen, "Causes of Increasing Atmospheric Methane: Depletion of Hydroxyl Radical and the Rise of Emissions," Atmos. Environ., **19** (1985), pp. 397-407.

22. V. Ramanathan, "Greenhouse Effect due to Chlorofluorocarbons: Climate Implications," Science, **190** (1975), pp. 50-51; J. Chamberlain, H. Foley, G. MacDonald, and M. Ruderman, "Climate Effects of Minor Atmospheric Constituents," in Carbon Dioxide Review: 1982 (W. Clarke, ed.), (Oxford University Press, 1982), pp. 255-277; V. Ramanathan, R. Cicerone, H. Singh, and J. Kiehl, "Trace Gas Trends and Their Potential Role in Climate Change," J. Geophys. Res., **90** (1985), pp. 5547-5566.

THE POTENTIAL IMPACTS OF CLIMATE CHANGE ON ELECTRIC UTILITIES: PROJECT SUMMARY

Kenneth P. Linder and Michael J. Gibbs

ICF Incorporated

Project Overview

This paper summarizes the analytic approach and preliminary findings of a study jointly sponsored by the Edison Electric Institute, the Electric Power Research Institute, the New York State Energy Research and Development Authority, and the U.S. Environmental Protection Agency. The project examines the potential impacts of greenhouse-gas-induced climate change on the demand for electricity and electric utility planning and operations in two case studies.

The National Academy of Sciences reports that a change in the radiative properties of the Earth's atmosphere associated with a doubling of the concentration of atmospheric carbon dioxide (CO_2) will raise the Earth's temperature by 1.5°C to 4.5°C.[1] Increases in the atmospheric concentrations of CO_2 and other greenhouse gases (such as methane, chlorofluorocarbons, and nitrous oxide) have been measured,[2] and one recent estimate of the potential rate of warming that may result from these increased concentrations is a 1°C (1.8°F) increase in global temperature by 2000.[3]

---

1 J. Charney, Chairman, Climate Research Board, Carbon Dioxide and Climate: A Scientific Assessment, Washington, D.C., National Academy of Sciences Press, 1979.

2 Atmospheric Ozone, WMO Global Ozone Research and Monitoring Project, Report No. 16, Geneva, Switzerland, 1986.

3 J. Hansen, et al., "The Greenhouse Effect: Projections of Global Climate Change," in Effects of Changes in Stratospheric

Although the potential magnitude and rate of climate change remain uncertain, a recent meeting of scientists and policy makers in Villach, Austria, recommended that analyses of the potential implications of alternative climate change possibilities be undertaken in order to begin to assess the importance of climate change for man's activities.[4] This study of the potential implications of climate change for electric utility planning and operations is one such study.

Analysis of electric utility planning and operations is relevant for two reasons:

- The demand for and supply of electricity is sensitive to local weather conditions. Utility studies of customer demands have shown that daily and seasonal peak electric demands are determined in large part by demands for services provided by weather-sensitive appliances and equipment, principally heating and air conditioning equipment. Further, a substantial portion of seasonal and annual electric sales for many utilities also are determined by the use of such equipment. On the supply side, the operating efficiency of electric generation, transmission, and distribution equipment is affected directly by temperature and other weather variables. Also, stream flow (driven by precipitation and runoff into streams and lakes and evaporation from streams and lakes) affects the availability of hydropower which is an important source of electricity in certain regions of the U.S.

- The industry is very capital-intensive and has a long planning horizon, so that uncertainty in future demand and supply associated with potential changes in climate may pose substantial economic risks.

These two characteristics of electric utilities indicate that changes in climate may have an important influence on supply and demand for electricity within the time horizon considered for current investment decisions.

Ozone and Global Climate, J.G. Titus ed., U.S. EPA and UNEP, Washington, D.C., August 1986.

4 Report of the International Conference on the Assessment of the Role of Carbon Dioxide and of Other Greenhouse Gases in Climate Variations and Associated Impacts, WMO-No. 661, Villach, Austria, 9-15 October 1985.

A case study approach was used to assess the potential impacts of climate change on utility planning and operations. Case study utility systems were selected in the Southeastern U.S. and New York State. By evaluating two diverse utility systems in detail, the relative importance of various climate change scenarios and different planning factors could be assessed. The experience gained from these detailed case studies is instructive for performing aggregate analyses of groups of geographically dispersed utilities.

The study focuses on the period 1986 to 2015. This 30-year period was chosen as representative of the time horizon of current utility planning decisions.

The approach used to perform the case studies is illustrated in Exhibit 1. The initial steps in the analysis are to (1) develop alternate climate change scenarios (i.e., changes in average seasonal temperatures for a particular area of the U.S. over time); and (2) estimate the sensitivity of electricity demand and supply to changes in weather conditions. This information is used to evaluate the potential implications of climate change for the future demand for and supply of electricity.

This demand and supply assessment is used with a set of utility planning assumptions as inputs to a utility planning model. This model is used to evaluate the implications of climate change for generating capacity requirements, fuel utilization, electricity production costs, and other utility planning factors. Climate change impacts are evaluated by comparing these planning model outputs (assuming climate change) with base case model outputs (assuming no climate change).

The utility planning assumptions were also varied to evaluate the economic risks associated with alternate planning decisions. Given that the extent and timing of future changes in climate are uncertain, utilities must make decisions today with imperfect climate-related information. The standard planning assumption implicitly employed today is that the future climate will be the same as the past climate. If the climate does change significantly within the time horizon of decisions that are based on this assumption, costly responses to changing conditions may be required in the future. By varying the planning assumptions, the potential costs and benefits of long-term planning for various amounts of climate change were evaluated.

SUMMARY OF CASE STUDY RESULTS

Exhibit 2 presents estimates of the changes in peak demand and total energy estimated for the Southeastern utility and for Upstate and Downstate New York utilities under "high" climate change assumptions, designated "temperature scenario C".[1] The table

---

1 Because of important uncertainties in modeling climate change, three alternate temperature change scenarios were developed for

EXHIBIT 1

ANALYTIC APPROACH

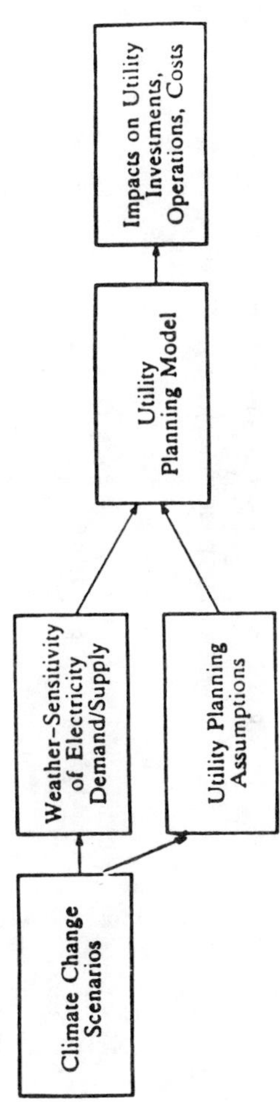

EXHIBIT 2

COMPARISON OF NEW YORK AND SOUTHEASTERN UTILITY CASE STUDIES: DEMAND SENSITIVITY (TEMPERATURE SCENARIO C)

New York	Change in Summer Temp. (°F)	Peak Sensitivity (%/°F)	Change in Peak Demand (%)	Change in Total Energy (%)
Upstate	1.46	0.66 to 1.47	0.96 to 2.14	-0.27 to -0.21
Downstate	1.46	1.51 to 2.77	2.20 to 4.04	0.49 to 1.04
System	1.46	1.19 to 2.27	1.74 to 3.32	0.13 to 0.45
Southeastern Utility	1.87	3.76	7.04	3.40

indicates that the estimated percent change in peak demand and electric energy requirements is greater for the Southeastern utility than for New York. This result is a product of: (1) higher estimated summer temperature changes in the Southeastern utility case study (1.87°F versus 1.46°F in New York); and (2) higher estimated weather-sensitivity coefficients (1.19 to 2.27 for New York versus 3.76 for the Southeastern utility). The estimates for Upstate and Downstate New York show the range of results obtained from two different modeling approaches (statistical and structural) used to estimate the weather-sensitivity of demand in the New York case studies. The two approaches differ in the data and level of detail used to estimate weather-sensitivity of demand.

It should be noted that the estimated sensitivity of peak demand to changes in temperature in Downstate New York is nearly as large as the peak-sensitivity estimated for the Southeastern utility. Given the same change in summer temperature, there would be similar estimates of percent change in peak demand in the two regions. Also, the substantially larger percentage change in total energy consumption for the Southeastern utility (3.4 percent versus 0.13 to 0.45 percent for New York) is related in large degree to the importance of air conditioning loads in all seasons for that utility. In New York air conditioning is almost exclusively a summertime use of electricity. In fact in Upstate New York, total energy requirements fall in response to the temperature increase (due to reduced winter heating loads).

Exhibit 3 indicates the estimated increase in generating capacity required by 2015 to maintain system reliability for the case study utilities. The "base requirements" shown in the table assume no climate change occurs. Increases in capacity requirements due to climate change are similar in the two regions. The range of additional capacity induced by climate change in New York is 746-1429 MW and is 1417 MW for the Southeastern utility, both under temperature scenario C assumptions. The percentage increases compared with base case additions during the period range from 10-19% in New York and is estimated as 21% for the Southeastern utility.

The potential impact of climate change on annual electricity production costs (annualized capital costs and annual fuel costs) for the case studies are summarized in Exhibit 4. Costs in New York range from $48 million to $241 million in 2015 (1985 dollars), depending upon the approach used to estimate weather-sensitivity of demand and upon the assumed impact of stream flow changes on the

---

each case study region. These scenarios are designated as "A", "B", and "C", with temperature scenario "A" showing the smallest increase in average temperatures by 2015 and scenario "C" showing the largest increase. Similarly, in analyzing the potential impacts of climate change on stream flow in the Great Lakes Basin and, therefore, on hydroelectric generation in New York State, three alternate stream flow scenarios were developed. These are designated "X", "Y", and "Z", with "X" showing the smallest changes and "Z" showing the largest.

EXHIBIT 3

COMPARISON OF NEW YORK AND SOUTHEASTERN UTILITY CASE STUDIES: GENERATING CAPACITY REQUIREMENTS (TEMPERATURE SCENARIO C)

New York	Base Requirements (MW)	Additional Requirements Induced by Climate Change (MW, %)
Upstate	160	155 - 349
Downstate	7331	591 - 1080
System	7491	746 - 1429 (10%-19%)
Southeastern Utility	6749	1417 (21%)

EXHIBIT 4

COMPARISON OF NEW YORK AND SOUTHEASTERN UTILITY CASE STUDIES: IMPACT ON TOTAL ELECTRICITY PRODUCTION COSTS IN 2015* (TEMPERATURE SCENARIO C)

New York	Fuel Cost	Capital Cost	Total Cost
Upstate	-22 to +79	+5 to +12	-17 to +91
Downstate	+44 to +112	+21 to +38	+65 to +150
System	+22 to +191	+26 to +50	+48 to +241
Southeastern Utility	+217	+50	+267

* Millions of 1985 $

availability of hydroelectric generation. The cost implications of climate change impacts on hydro generation are significant in New York. The high case costs in 2015 for the Southeastern utility are similar in magnitude, $267 million (in 1985 dollars).

IMPLICATIONS OF FINDINGS

There are many uncertainties associated with developing estimates of potential climate change impacts. In the project we have addressed uncertainties in:

- climate modeling,
- weather-sensitivity modeling, and
- other economic, technological, and behavioral conditions.

Because these uncertainties make it difficult to predict the future with precision, the results are driven by assumptions about these factors.

The relative contributions of key assumptions to the results are illustrated in Exhibit 5 for the New York State "High Impact" case. This case assumes:

- temperature scenario C (high),
- stream flow scenario Z (greatest change),
- weather-sensitivity estimated using the structural approach, and
- an increase in the saturation of residential air conditioning in response to climate change.

Regarding the estimates of additional capacity requirements (left-hand bar), use of the data and assumptions in the statistical approach to modeling the weather-sensitivity of demand results in an estimate of 746 MW by 2015. Alternatively, use of the structural approach and assumptions of a constant saturation of air conditioning equipment results in an estimate of 1158 MW. The additional assumption that air conditioning saturation increases over time pushes the estimate to 1429 MW.

The right-hand bar illustrates the impact of these factors on total annual electricity production costs. This bar emphasizes the importance of the estimated effects of stream flow reduction on hydro generation, and the assumptions regarding the utilities' response to these changes. The substitution of oil generation and off-system electricity purchases for the reduction in hydropower availability accounts for over half (52%) of the estimated total cost impact of $241 million (in 1985$). Smaller <u>increments</u> are attributed to the statistical approach to demand response ($48 million), the structural approach to demand response ($39 million), and the assumption of increased air conditioning saturation ($28 million).

Although the results are sensitive to the assumptions about these factors, this situation is little different than forecasting demand, technological change, and customer response to utility

EXHIBIT 5

NEW YORK STATE
RELATIVE CONTRIBUTION OF KEY ASSUMPTIONS TO
"HIGH IMPACT" RESULTS
(2015)

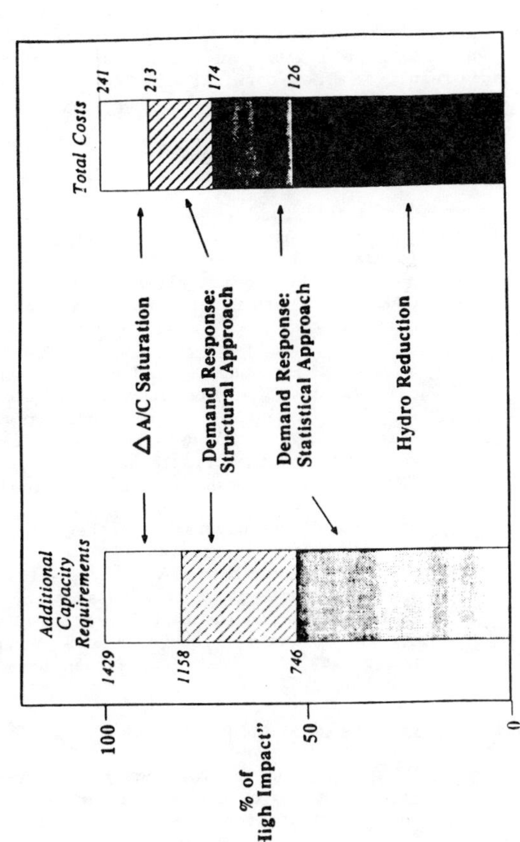

conservation or marketing programs. These types of analyses, commonly conducted by utility planners, also involve substantial uncertainties and require many assumptions. Although not precise, the estimated impacts are judged to be reasonable. The findings indicate that the potential impacts of climate change on electric utilities are not insignificant and that these impacts may start to occur within the typical time frame of current utility planning studies and decisions.

Although the case studies have been conducted on different types of utility systems in different regions of the U.S., it is difficult to generalize to regions or the nation as a whole based solely on these results (e.g., consider the different results obtained for Upstate and Downstate New York). However, the analyses suggest the following general conclusions:

Climate Change

- The temperature change scenarios developed for the two case studies indicate that current general circulation model (GCM) estimates of potential regional climate change due to a doubling of atmospheric concentration of CO_2 are quite diverse.

- Climate model outputs indicate that the rate of climate change may be uneven over time, and may vary substantially from one location to another. This result is consistent with expectations regarding how the climate system would respond to increased greenhouse gas concentrations.

- In light of the diversity of the GCM results, and the relative inexperience of using GCMs to perform transient analyses, the climate change scenarios must not be considered to be forecasts. Although the scenarios reflect the diversity of current estimates, future climate change outside the range of estimates presented here cannot be ruled out.

Utility Impacts

- It appears that climate change will have greater direct impacts on the demand for electricity than on characteristics of the supply of electricity for most utility systems:

  -- The impacts resulting from demand response to climate change are more likely to be significant for utilities with large, summer, weather-sensitive (air conditioning) loads. This is true for regions in the southern U.S. where air conditioning saturation and utilization is high, and for urban areas in northern climate zones where the potential for increased air conditioning saturation is high. Because of the nature and patterns of these weather-sensitive loads, response to climate change is likely to have greater impacts on peak demand (capacity requirements) than on energy consumption (generation requirements).

-- The order of magnitude of temperature changes examined here is unlikely to have significant impacts on the effective capacity or operating efficiency of thermal generating units. However, there can be significant implications for utilities where hydro is an important source of generation. As indicated by the New York case studies, hydro generation is critical for some utilities, and the potential planning uncertainties associated with possible climate change-induced stream flow changes are large.

- We have found that the utility capacity and cost implications of climate change potentially are significant. In the two case study analyses (1) generating capacity additions induced by climate change are on the order of 10-20% of base case (i.e., no climate change) additions through 2015 under scenario C temperature change assumptions (the highest case examined), and (2) annualized capital costs and annual fuel and O&M costs induced by climate change exceed $200 million (1985 dollars) in 2015. Because of long lead-times and the capital intensity of the most efficient electric generating units, there are economic benefits associated with being able to anticipate climate change correctly. The magnitude of the potential cost savings depends on the base case planning assumptions, and in these two case studies may be as high as $50 million per year (1985 dollars) by 2015.

- Utility planners should start now to consider climate change as a factor affecting their planning analyses and decisions. Large impacts are not imminent, but the importance of climate change impacts for utility planning is likely to increase over time. Climate change is likely to increase the uncertainties utility planners must face and to interact with other issues they must address, including:

-- the level and patterns of future electric demands,

- -- the availability and mix of future generating resources, and
- -- investment and financial planning.

TROUBLESHOOTING UTILITY FGD CHEMICAL PROCESS PROBLEMS

R. E. Moser, Project Manager
Electric Power Research Institute
Palo Alto, California

J. D. Colley, Senior Staff Engineer
A. F. Jones, Staff Engineer
Radian Corporation
Austin, Texas

Since their first commercial application in the U.S. over 15 years ago, FGD system designs have been modified and improved in an effort to achieve acceptable levels of reliability at reasonable costs. The key to successful operation of these systems is to recognize that an FGD system is a chemical process which must be monitored and controlled within the mechanical constraints of the system design. EPRI's research in FGD process chemistry began nearly 10 years ago, with the intent of thoroughly characterizing lime/limestone wet FGD chemistry in order to assist utilities in better understanding and operating these systems. In addition to laboratory bench-scale and pilot plant research, an important element of the program has been in field applications, working directly with utilities in troubleshooting problems with FGD systems. This paper will summarize the types of problems encountered and the methodology used in troubleshooting. An overview of results and a specific example will be detailed. Finally, a review of the types of operating tools which EPRI has produced to assist utilities in operating FGD systems will be presented.

TYPES OF PROBLEMS

Problems with FGD system performance are often expensive and a source of inconvenience for many utilities. Poor performance and reliability of the FGD system leads to excessive operating and maintenance costs and, in some instances, to unit derating. Many of the problems associated with wet lime/limestone FGD systems are related to the complex nature of the process chemistry. Common problems include the following:

- Insufficient SO_2 removal;
- Poor reagent utilization;
- Mist eliminator scaling and pluggage;
- Scaling of the packing;
- Poor solids dewatering;
- Positive water balance; and
- H_2S formation.

Insufficient SO_2 removal can be caused by low liquid phase alkalinity, low mass transfer surface area, and/or inadequate contact time between the flue gas and the scrubbing slurry. Poor reagent utilization can be caused by inadequate pH measurement and control systems, poor limestone particle size distribution (grind), SO_3 blinding, and/or aluminum/fluoride inhibition of limestone dissolution.

Mist eliminator scaling and pluggage and scaling of the packing can be caused by either chemical or mechanical problems, or a combination of the two. The chemical problems which can cause the mist eliminators to scale include disentraining mist with a high gypsum relative saturation, washing the mist eliminators with water that has a high gypsum relative saturation, and maintaining poor limestone utilization. Mechanically, pluggage and/or scaling of the mist eliminators can be caused by infrequent washing of the mist eliminators or a low intensity wash. Scaling of the packing can be caused by localized areas of high gypsum relative saturation (chemical problem) or by poor distribution of the slurry over the surface of the packing (mechanical problem).

Slurry dewatering problems can occur in the thickener or during filtering. Potential thickener problems include: cloudy thickener overflow, low underflow density, or high underflow density (high rake torque or unpumpable underflow). Filter problems include: blinding of the filter cloth, filter cake discharge problems, filter cake moisture too high, and cloudy filtrate.

A positive water balance results when makeup water brought in from outside the FGD system exceeds the sum of the water lost through evaporation into the flue gas plus the water leaving the system with the filter cake. Excessive makeup water can enter the FGD system in several ways: grinding limestone with makeup water, high seal water use in the recycle pumps and agitators, and excessive fresh water use for mist eliminator washing. These are usually the primary causes of a positive water balance. However, other factors (e.g., bypassing flue gas, insufficient surge capacity in the FGD system, etc.) can contribute.

The formation of H_2S generally occurs in the thickener or other areas where solids from the FGD system remain undisturbed for long periods of time. The H_2S is produced by sulfur-reducing bacteria which thrive under warm, anaerobic conditions.

PROGRAM APPROACH

Even though the problems experienced at each utility FGD system are different, the initial approach taken under EPRI's Chemical Process Problem Research Project is generally the same. The first step is an initial site visit during which process samples and design/operating data are collected. Analytical results and the design/operating data collected on site are evaluated to determine the cause of the problem(s). Potential alternatives for improved operation are developed based on past experience at other FGD systems. The alternatives are evaluated based on their effects on different parts of the system and ranked in order of maximum benefit for minimum capital expenditure. Depending on the nature of the proposed solutions, EPRI could sponsor laboratory tests or further on-site work to assist the utility in implementing the recommended changes.

The process samples collected during the initial site visit usually include liquid, solid, and slurry samples from one or more reaction tanks. Depending on the nature of the problem at the system under investigation, samples of the makeup water, mist eliminator washwater, thickener (feed, overflow, and/or underflow), reagent slurry, and filter cake could also be collected. The reaction tank samples are reactive and will change after collection. Therefore, special collection methods, which were developed under EPRI sponsorship, are used to preserve the samples prior to analysis. Analytical methods were also developed under EPRI sponsorship to address the special requirements of FGD samples. Some parameters such as pH, temperature, and liquid phase sulfite are measured at the time of sample collection.

The pH, temperature, and weight percent solids are usually determined on site for the slurry samples. If the problems involve dewatering, the appropriate slurry samples will also be subjected to settling and/or filter leaf tests to determine their dewatering characteristics. Liquid phase analyses generally include the following: calcium, magnesium, sodium, chloride, carbonate, sulfite, and sulfate. With the assistance of EPRI's FGDLIQEQ program (described later), the relative saturation of several species (including gypsum and calcium sulfite), along with other information (e.g., SO_2 alkalinity, SO_2 back-pressure, ionic charge balance, etc.), can be determined from the liquid phase analysis. Solid samples are analyzed for calcium, magnesium, carbonate, sulfite, sulfate, and inerts. The reagent utilization and sulfite oxidation can be determined from the solid phase analyses.

The design and operating data collected during the initial site visit will depend on the problems being experienced with the FGD system. The data collected could include operating and control guidelines, specific types of equipment in use, design mass and material balances, spray nozzle type and layout, mist eliminator wash system design, or other related information.

Potential solutions to the problems are identified based on the analytical results, the design/operating data, and past experience at other FGD systems. The solutions are evaluated for the effect they will have on other parts of the system, as well as their ability to solve the problem. For example, an increase in the pH setpoint may be recommended to increase SO_2 removal. However, the effect of the increased pH on limestone utilization is taken into account in ranking the solutions. These solutions are evaluated in conjunction with the utility to determine which are most cost-effective. Many times, additional testing is sponsored by EPRI on the laboratory- or full-scale to further evaluate potential solutions. Examples of testing which performed in the past include testing of several different types of organic acid to enhance SO_2 removal in EPRI's bench-scale scrubber and full-scale testing of dibasic acid (an organic acid) to determine the degradation rate. Assistance with implementing recommended solutions has also been provided by EPRI in some instances.

OVERVIEW OF RESULTS

Over 20 plants have been assisted with FGD problems under EPRI's Chemical Process Problems Research Project. Table 1 presents an overview of the problems experienced at each plant. Over half of the plants had more than one problem, and several plants experienced severe difficulties with operation and maintenance due to multiple problems. The most common problem experienced was scaling of the mist eliminators.

Table 2 presents a brief summary of the objectives identified during investigations made at three of the plants, along with a description of the benefits which resulted from implementing the recommended changes. The recommendations and benefits for these three plants are representative of the assistance provided as a part of this program. In most cases, significant savings have resulted from implementation of the recommendations.

CASE HISTORY - TEXAS UTILITIES ELECTRIC COMPANY'S MARTIN LAKE GENERATING STATION

The problems experienced with the FGD system at Texas Utilities Electric Company's Martin Lake Generating Station were investigated in depth as a part of EPRI's Chemical Process Problems program. The problems, the changes implemented, and benefits achieved are discussed below.

TABLE 1. LIST OF PLANTS ASSISTED AND THEIR PROBLEMS

Plant	Problems							
	SO_2 Removal	ME Scaling	Packing Scaling	Water Balance	Limestone Utilization	Solids Dewatering	H_2S Formation	Other
AECI Thomas Hill	X	X		X	X	X		
Allegheny Power Mitchell							X	
APS Cholla			X					
APS Four Corners		X						
CILCo Duck Creek	X	X		X	X			
City of Lakeland McIntosh 3		X		X			X	
CLECo Dolet Hills					X			
Colorado Ute Craig						X		
CWL&P Dallman		X	X	X				
Duquesne Elrama		X						X[a]
Duquesne Phillips		X						X[a]
HL&P Limestone	X							
HL&P Parrish							X	
IP&L Petersburg 3	X	X			X	X		
IP&L Petersburg 4			X	X				X[a]
KCPL LaCygne		X		X	X			
LG&E Mill Creek					X			
Minnesota Power Clay Boswell 3			X					
NYSEG Somerset		X				X		
Ohio Edison Bruce Mansfield						X		

(Continued)

TABLE 1. (Continued)

Plant	Problems							
	SO_2 Removal	ME Scaling	Packing Scaling	Water Balance	Limestone Utilization	Solids Dewatering	H_2S Formation	Other
PSI Gibson 5								X[d]
SWEPCo Pirkey		X						X[b]
TECo Big Bend 4								X[c]
TU Electric Martin Lake			X	X	X	X		
UP&L Hunter		X		X				

[a]Thiosulfate utilization

[b]Trap out tray scaling.

[c]Support NH_3 injection program.

[d]Thiosulfate from sulfur injection.

TABLE 2. EXAMPLES OF INVESTIGATION OBJECTIVES AND BENEFITS

Plant	Objectives	Benefits
CILCo Duck Creek	Improve SO_2 removal	Through the use of an organic acid (DBA), SO_2 removal now meets emission limits.
	Reduce mist eliminator scaling	Changing the mist eliminator wash intensity and source and increasing limestone utilization resulted in almost total elimination of scaling. Scrubber availability has been greater than 98% over the last 5 years.
	Improve limestone utilization	Operating the reaction tank at the optimum pH and improving the limestone grind resulted in a limestone utilization consistently over 90%. This reduced annual limestone consumption by over 20,000 tons and will reduce the FGD wastes by 20% over the life of the plant.
	Improve water balance	Installation of mechanical seals on the recycle pumps, along with changes in the mist eliminator wash duration/frequency, eliminated the positive water balance.
IP&L Petersburg 3	Reduce mist eliminator scaling and solids carryover to the downstream ductwork	Conversion to fresh water wash, modifications to wash system, and improved limestone utilization significantly reduced scaling and eliminated solids carryover.

(Continued)

TABLE 2. (Continued)

Plant	Objectives	Benefits
IP&L Petersburg 3 (Continued)	Improve limestone utilization	Improving the limestone grind, increasing the organic acid concentration, and reducing the pH setpoint in the reaction tanks resulted in a limestone utilization consistently greater than 90%.
	Eliminate thickener pluggage after startup	Modifications to the thickener operating guidelines and the polymer addition system and the addition of a flush line to the thickener underflow line eliminated costly thickener plugging episodes which were occurring after startup.
UP&L Hunter	Reduce mist eliminator scaling and solids carryover	Changing the wash frequency/duration, washwater source, and washwater pressure significantly reduced mist eliminator scaling and solids carryover.
	Eliminate positive water balance	Changing the operating guidelines with respect to the number of towers in service at various loads and controlling the lime slaking density allowed the system to operate with zero discharge as designed.

The Martin Lake Generating Station consists of three 750 MW base-loaded units which fire a lignite fuel. The flue gas from each of the three units is treated in a dual-loop limestone FGD system supplied by Research-Cottrell. From startup, the reliability of the three FGD systems was limited by scaling and pluggage of the packing and mist eliminators. The result of the scaling and pluggage was a decrease in the ability of individual FGD system towers to treat flue gas and an increase in system pressure drop. The utility was using a crew of about 80 men to clean a tower once it had scaled to the point that it could no longer treat flue gas. Typically, a tower could effectively treat flue gas for only 30 to 45 days before it required cleaning. The annual labor and material costs directly associated with scale formation in the packing and mist eliminators totaled $3,900,000 in 1983.

In addition to the severe scaling problems, the FGD systems at Martin Lake also operated with a positive water balance and had poor overall limestone utilization. In order to deal with the water balance problems, Martin Lake had to maintain a large pond capacity and operate a wastewater treatment system which included a 600-gpm brine concentrator. The brine concentrator alone consumed 3.4 MW of power.

A short characterization test was conducted on one of the FGD systems to gather information on the design, operation, and chemistry of the FGD system. Design and operating data were collected as well as samples from the FGD system. Evaluation of the data and analytical results and comparison to past experiences with limestone scrubbers identified several possibilities for the problems. Possible reasons for the scaling and pluggage of the packing and mist eliminators included: poor limestone utilization in the upper loop (30% to 70%), high local gypsum relative saturations in the absorber slurry, inadequate control of limestone addition to the scrubbers, poor quality mist eliminator washwater (gypsum relative saturation of 0.99), and low mist eliminator specific wash rate (0.4 gpm/ft^2). All of these factors have been shown to contribute to scaling. The potential reasons for the poor overall limestone utilization included a coarse limestone grind (less than 80% passing a 325 mesh sieve) and inadequate control of limestone addition to the scrubbers. The major contributors to the positive water balance were the seal water for the recycle pumps and agitators, the mist eliminator washwater, and the fresh water used for limestone grinding.

As a result of the characterization test, several changes were made to the FGD systems to alleviate the scaling and limestone utilization problems. Split limestone feed, in which limestone is fed to the quencher as well as the absorber feed tank (AFT), was installed. Feedback control based on pH was installed to control limestone addition to both the quencher and AFT (in place of the original feedforward system). Split limestone feed and pH feedback control maintained good limestone utilization in both loops while allowing the FGD system to respond rapidly to changes in inlet conditions (flue gas flow rate and SO_2 concentration). The limestone utilization was also helped by improving the limestone grind.

A small stream of slurry was also taken from each quencher recycle loop and fed to the AFT. Recycling slurry from the quencher to the AFT increased the gypsum crystal concentration in the AFT, providing a greater number of crystallization sites for the calcium sulfate formed in the towers. With increased precipitation sites, dissolved gypsum in the upper loop will tend to precipitate on existing crystals rather than on tower internals such as packing.

To decrease mist eliminator scaling, the mist eliminator washwater was switched from water nearly saturated with gypsum to lake water. The lower mist eliminator wash nozzles were also replaced with nozzles allowing a higher flow, and the wash pressure was increased. This increased the specific wash rate. The overall wash time was reduced, which decreased the wash water consumption.

The positive water balance was reduced by the changes in the mist eliminator wash system, as well as by installing mechanical seals on the recycle pumps and agitators and switching the source of limestone grinding water to thickener overflow.

As a result of the changes implemented at the Martin Lake FGD systems, scaling of the packing has essentially been eliminated, as has scaling of the mist eliminators. Limestone utilizations now average above 90% in both loops, and pH control is no longer a problem. The water balance is now negative, although the water treatment plant is still operated periodically to remove chlorides from the system. It has been estimated by Texas Utilities that over $4,000,000 per year in savings has been achieved by implementation of the above described process modifications and improvements.

TOOLS DEVELOPED TO ASSIST WITH FGD SYSTEM OPERATION AND EVALUATION

EPRI has developed several tools to assist with the operation and evaluation of FGD systems. Several more tools are currently being developed. The tools which are currently available include a handbook of chemistry and analytical methods, with an FGD process chemistry computer program designated by EPRI as FGDLIQEQ. The first three videotapes in a planned series of 15 to 20 FGD educational tapes have also been completed. In addition to the remaining videotapes, an FGD process simulation model is under development, as well as a program designed to assist

FGD operators with managing and evaluating data associated with an FGD system.

The FGD chemistry and analytical handbook consists of three volumes. The first volume explains the chemistry of commercial FGD systems (limestone, dual alkali, Wellman-Lord, magnesia, and lime wet scrubbing and spray drying). Major chemical and operating variables and the analytical determinations needed to monitor these indicators are discussed. Information on designing, equipping, and operating a laboratory for FGD analyses is also presented. A detailed procedure for acquiring and handling the various FGD samples is included.

Volume 2 of the report gives detailed procedures for 21 physical property methods for reagents and slurries and 32 chemical species determinations. Where two or more methods for a given chemical constituent are presented, a comparison of the methods in accuracy, precision, time and labor, and other important factors is made. These methods are currently being revised and expanded. A revised edition of Volume 2 will be released in 1988.

The process chemistry computer program, FGDLIQEQ, is the subject of Volume 3 of the chemistry and analytical methods handbook. The program (which operates on an IBM PC) is a liquid equilibrium model which uses analytical results for a given stream to calculate driving forces for important chemical reactions, such as SO_2 absorption and calcium sulfite and sulfate precipitation. The program also calculates a charge balance, which provides information regarding the accuracy of the analytical data.

Two of the videotapes which have been completed cover basic FGD process chemistry for limestone and magnesium-enhanced lime wet FGD systems. An overview of the process unit operations is included. The third tape is a sampling tape which shows how to take liquid, slurry, and solid samples from a limestone FGD system. A fourth tape, which is currently being produced, will cover limestone FGD performance indicators (SO_2 removal and limestone utilization). The remaining tapes will cover topics such as additional performance indicators, troubleshooting, and FGD-related computer programs.

The process simulation model, which is currently under development, will perform detailed equilibrium and mass transfer calculations around key units within an FGD system. The effects of operating and design variables (e.g., inlet SO_2 concentration, reaction tank pH setpoint, liquid-to-gas ratio, reaction tank residence time, and the use of a chemical buffer) can be determined on the FGD system's performance (e.g., SO_2 removal and limestone utilization).

The FGD Information Resource Manager (FGDIRM) is a computer program designed to manage analytical and process data to assist with monitoring the performance of an FGD system. The program consists of four parts: laboratory data manager, process data manager, mass balancer, and data presentation. The laboratory data manager will set up sampling and analytical schedules, reduce analytical data from procedures in the ERPI handbook, calculate analytical performance indicators, perform equilibrium calculations using FGDLIQEQ, provide QA/QC information, and store the analytical data in a historical database. The process data manager portion of the program is used to organize and store process data in a historical database. The mass balancer ties together the process and analytical data and performs mass balance calculations. Reports and trend plots are prepared from the analytical and process data with the data presentation part of FGDIRM. The program can be configured to match any FGD system's flowsheet.

In conclusion, we firmly believe that while FGD is a complicated chemical process, reliable operation can be attained by understanding the process, monitoring key performance indicators, and controlling the system chemistry.

JAPANESE ACTIVITIES IN SO_2 AND NO_x CONTROL

Charles B. Sedman
U.S. Environmental Protection Agency
Air and Energy Engineering Research Laboratory
Research Triangle Park, NC 27711
and
Jumpei Ando
Chuo University
Tokyo, Japan

From 1970 to 1985, energy use in Japan increased by 25% and annual coal consumption rose from virtually nothing to 20 million tonnes, yet emissions of SO_2 declined by 75% and NO_x by 40%. While increases in hydro and nuclear energy sources and use of lower sulfur fuel oil have contributed to the emissions reduction, the most prominent technological achievements have occurred in the successful implementation of SO_2 and NO_x controls. Since 1968, nearly 1600 flue gas desulfurization (FGD) systems and 250 selective catalytic reduction (SCR) units have been constructed. Recent and current activities include simplified FGD operations, SCR experience in coal-fired systems, and transfer of control technology to waste-to-energy plants.

FLUE GAS DESULFURIZATION [1, 2, 3]

Initially the FGD market in Japan was dominated by sodium scrubbing plants which produced by-product sodium sulfite used by paper mills. This demand was quickly met, resulting in the installation of gypsum-producing FGD processes in the early 1970s. Except for one brief period in 1974-76, the demand for gypsum has exceeded the supply in Japan, hence the recent and current dominance of lime/limestone FGD systems in Japan continues.

Table 1 shows wet FGD plants by major constructors in Japan. Nearly all coal-fired boilers and most larger plants, whether oil or coal, use wet-limestone-gypsum processes. About 55% of total FGD capacity, or 130 plants totaling 24,000 MWe equivalent capacity, use wet limestone with forced oxidation. Another 72 plants use indirect and/or modified lime/limestone-gypsum (double alkali) processes. Many of the double alkali systems were constructed in the earlier

TABLE 1. WET FGD PLANTS BUILT BY MAJOR CONSTRUCTORS
(Operational by the end of 1987)

Plant Constructor	Number (Capacity, 1000 Nm^3/h)				Total
	Wet lime/ limestone	Indirect/modified lime/limestone	H_2SO_4, S $(NH_4)_2SO_4$	Na_2SO_3, Na_2SO_4, $MgSO_4$	
Mitsubishi Heavy Industries (MHI)	47(35,254)	--	--	3(292)	50(35,546)
Ishikawajima-Harima H.I. (IHI)	24(12,719)	--	--	26(3,240)	50(15,959)
Hitachi Ltd./Babcock Hitachi	22(14,167)	--	2(590)	19(843)	43(15,600)
Kawasaki Heavy Industries (KHI)	2(174)	12(8,376)	--	7(256)	21(8,806)
Mitsubishi Kakoki (MKK)	5(506)	--	13(6,606)	5(1,165)	23(8,277)
Chiyoda Chemical Eng. Construc.	5(2,436)	13(4,375)	--	--	18(6,811)
Fujikasui Engineering	7(4,144)	--	--	22(2,405)	29(6,549)
Oji Engineering	--	--	--	32(6,239)	32(6,239)
Kurabo Engineering	--	5(558)	1(18)	105(4,249)	111(4,825)
Mitsui Miike Engineering	6(3,653)	--	3(760)	--	9(4,413)
Tsukishima Kikai (TSK)	1(80)	4(430)	2(325)	31(3,533)	38(4,368)
Ebara Corporation	1(26)	11(1,520)	--	10(2,006)	22(3,552)
Nippon Kokan (NKK)	3(197)	1(150)	2(1,990)	--	6(2,337)
Kobe Steel	--	6(1,925)	--	--	6(1,925)
Kureha Chemical	--	1(40)	--	7(1,380)	8(1,420)
Dowa Engineering	--	16(1,408)	--	--	16(1,408)
Shoden Engineering	--	3(1,002)	--	2(370)	5(1,372)
Mitsui Metal Engineering	4(1,006)	--	2(130)	--	6(1,136)
Ube Industries	--	--	2(210)	1(600)	3(810)
Sumitomo Chemical Engineering	--	--	5(748)	--	5(748)
Niigata Iron Works	2(265)	--	--	2(220)	4(485)
JGC Corporation	1(330)	--	1(125)	--	2(455)
Total	130(74,957)	72(19,784)	33(11,502)	272(26,798)	507(133,041)

period of FGD development, 1972-76, when scaling problems were not uncommon with lime/limestone FGD. As the reliability and economic advantages of lime/limestone FGD have improved, the recent construction of double alkali systems has diminished.

Table 1 also shows 33 regenerable process FGD systems, of which 20 produce sulfuric acid, 5 produce ammonium sulfate, and the remainder generate elemental sulfur. The sulfur producing systems are located at oil refineries where existing sulfur recovery facilities economically favor FGD sulfur production.

Numerically the dominant FGD system in Japan is sodium scrubbing, since many smaller and older FGD units in Japan still use clear liquor systems which produce sodium sulfite for paper mills, sodium sulfate for the glass industry, or waste sodium sulfate liquor. In addition to the plants listed in Table 1, nearly 1000 additional sodium systems operate in Japan on smaller commercial and industrial fossil-fuel combustors with an average unit capacity of 3.3 MWe equivalent. Lately about 20 magnesium-based FGD units have been constructed where sodium scrubbing would have normally been chosen, due to the lower cost of magnesium hydroxide reagent compared to sodium hydroxide or sodium carbonate.

RECENT FGD TRENDS IN COAL-FIRED UTILITY BOILERS [1, 2, 3]

To illustrate the types of FGD systems currently considered for utility application in Japan a classification system has been prepared by author Ando, as shown as Table 2 and illustrated as Figure 1. In this scheme, FGD processes are divided into nine major types according to by-product produced, absorbent, additive, use of prescrubbers, and use of sulfuric acid for pH control. Type I is the most popular system in the United States, but has been limited to one installation in Japan due to a lack of space for sludge disposal. Type II systems use an extra scrubber to lower the pH by further SO_2 absorption and add sodium hydroxide or sulfate to promote SO_2 absorption and oxidation. Three plants currently use Type II FGD systems.

TABLE 2. CLASSIFICATION OF WET LIME/LIMESTONE PROCESSES

Type	By-Product	Absorbent	Additive	Prescrubber[a]	Sulfuric acid[b]
I	Sludge	$Ca(OH)_2$	None	No	No
II	Gypsum	$CaCO_3$	Sodium	No	No
III, VII	Gypsum	$CaCO_3$	Sodium	No	Yes
IV	Gypsum	$CaCO_3$	None	Yes	Yes
V	Gypsum	$CaCO_3$	None	Possible	No
VI	Gypsum	$Ca(OH)_2$	MgO[c]	Possible	No
VIII	Gypsum	$CaCO_3$	None	Yes	No
IX	Gypsum	$CaCO_3$	Probable	No	No

[a]In a separate liquor loop; some waste liquor and sludge likely with prescrubber.
[b]To promote oxidation.
[c]No need when lime contains over 1% MgO.

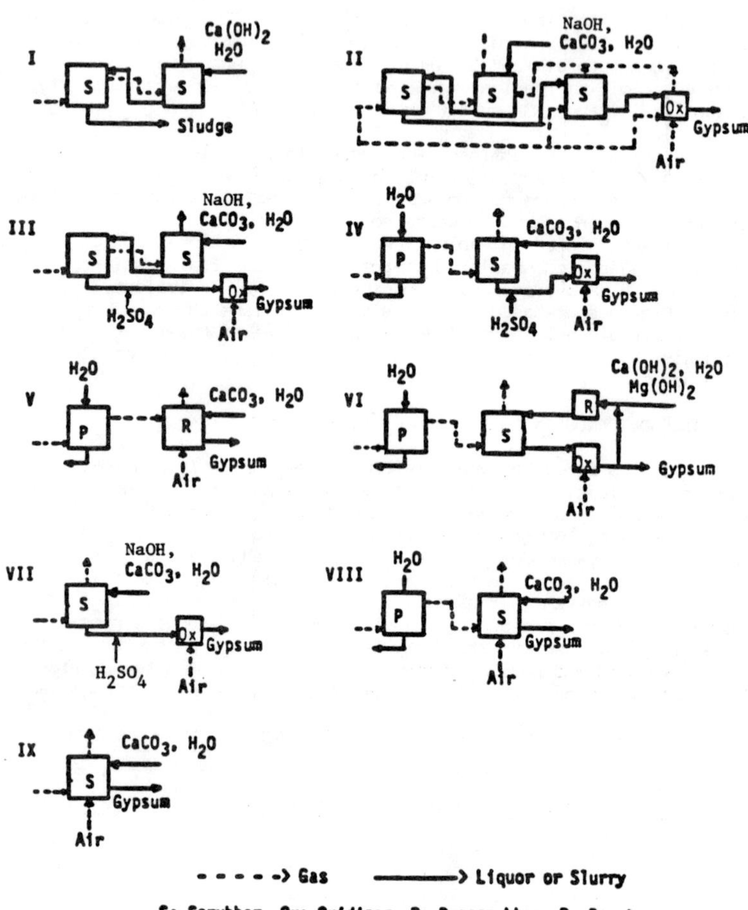

Figure 1. Wet lime/limestone process classifications.

In Type III FGD systems, the slurry pH is lowered by sulfuric acid addition and often uses a sodium promoter as do Type II systems. Four Type III plants are in operation.

Type IV, developed by Mitsubishi, is the most popular system, utilizing a prescrubber with the following functions: (1) removal of fluorides and chlorides which adversely affect FGD chemistry and materials, (2) dust removal (hence increased purity of by-product gypsum), and (3) cooling of gas and prevention of scaling. However, the prescrubber does add to system cost and produces waste liquor and sludge. Type V represents the jet bubbling reactor developed by Chiyoda, while Type VI by Kawasaki Heavy Industries uses a lime-magnesium system. Types V and VI do not use sulfuric acid. Type VII is a simplification of Type III, developed by Mitsui Miike Engineering. Types VIII and IX are new simplified concepts featuring lower power requirements and are more suited for lower sulfur fuels.

Table 3 lists FGD units constructed since 1977. All plants have electrostatic precipitators (ESPs) to remove 97-99.6% of particles and wet lime/limestone gypsum FGD units to remove 90-98% SO_2 and an additional 70-90% of particulate matter. Of the most recently installed units (1985-87), four of the seven units shown were Type IV FGD systems. A few Type IX plants are currently under construction.

NO_x CONTROL [1, 2, 3]

The vast majority of NO_x emitters in Japan meet current regulations by combustion modification techniques. However, essentially all new coal-fired utility boilers in Japan will be required to install post-combustion NO_x controls due to local agreements and recently tightened Federal (Central Government) NO_x emission standards. Combustion modifications such as flue gas recirculation (FGR), two-stage combustion (TSC), and low-NO_x burners are currently used singly and in combination to allow less strenuous operation of post-combustion NO_x controls; therefore, in the ensuing discussions the reader should keep in mind that flue gas NO_x levels are already reduced by 50-70% over uncontrolled levels.

The most advanced flue gas treatment process is selective catalytic reduction (SCR). In this technique NO_x is reduced to elemental nitrogen, N_2, and water vapor by ammonia (NH_3) injection in the presence of a catalyst. SCR usually removes 60-85% of NO_x using 0.6-0.9 moles NH_3 per mole NO_x and leaves 1-5 ppmv unreacted NH_3. The optimum flue gas temperature for SCR is 300-400°C; therefore, SCR is usually applied upstream of FGD at the boiler economizer outlet.

In the earlier stages of development, SCR had several problems:

- o catalyst poisoning by SO_x
- o plugging of catalyst by fly ash
- o ammonium bisulfate deposition on SCR catalyst (below 300°C)
- o ammonium bisulfite deposition in air preheaters (below 250°C)
- o oxidation of SO_2 to SO_3
- o errosion of catalyst by fly ash

TABLE 3. FGD AND SCR UNITS COMPLETED SINCE 1977 FOR COAL-FIRED UTILITY BOILERS

Owner	Station name	Boiler (MW)	FGD Constructor	FGD completion	FGD Type	SCR Constructor	SCR completion	SCR Type
EPDC	Takehara	250	BHK[a]	1977	III	BHK, KHI[b]	1980	L[c]
Chugoku Elec.	Shimonoseki	175	MHI[d]	1979	IV	MHI	1980	H[e]
Hokkaido Elec.	Tomato	350[f]	BHK	1980	IV	BHK	1980	L
EPDC	Matsushima	500x2[g]	BHK, IHI[h]	1981	IV	-	-	-
Chugoku Elec.	Shin-Ube	75x2	MHI	1982	IV	MHI	1982	H
Chugoku Elec.	Shin-Ube	156	MHI	1982	IV	MHI	1982	H
Kyushu Elec.	Omura	156	MHI	1982	IV	-	-	-
EPDC	Takehara	700	IHI	1983	III	BHK	1983	L
Joban Joint	Nakoso	600[i]	MHI	1983	IV	MHI	1983	H
Joban Joint	Nakoso	600[i]	MHI	1983	IV	IHI	1983	H
Kyushu Elec.	Minato	156	MME[j]	1983	VII	MHI	1983	H
Shikoku Elec.	Saijo	156	KHI	1983	VI	MHI	1983	H
Tohoku Elec.	Sendai	175x2	BHK	1983	IV	BHK	1983	H
Shikoku Elec.	Saijo	250	KHI	1984	VI	IHI	1984	H
Chugoku Elec.	Mizushima	125 & 156	BHK	1984	IV	BHK	1984	H
Sakata Joint	Sakata	350	MHI	1984	IV	MHI	1984	H
Toyama Joint	Toyama	200x2	Chiyoda	1984	V	BHK	1984	H
Tokyo Elec.	Yokosuka[k]	265	MHI	1984	IV	MHI	1984	H
Tokyo Elec.	Yokosuka[k]	265	BHK	1985	IV	MHI	1985	H
Hokkaido Elec.	Tomato	600	MHI	1985	IV	-	-	-
Chugoku Elec.	Shin-Onoda	500	IHI	1986	IV	IHI	1986	H
EPDC	Ishikawa	125	IHI	1986	III	-	-	-
Chugoku Elec.	Shin-Onoda	500	IHI	1987	IV	IHI	1987	H
EPDC	Ishikawa	125	IHI	1987	VII	-	-	-
Kyushu Elec.	Matsuura	700	MHI	1987	VIII	MHI	1987	H

[a]Babcock Hitachi K.K.
[b]Kawasaki Heavy Industries
[c]Low-dust system
[d]Mitsubishi Heavy Industries
[e]High-dust system
[f]Subjecting 50% of gas to FGD and 25% of gas to SCR
[g]Subjecting 75% of gas to FGD
[h]Ishikawajima-Harima Heavy Industries
[i]Burns both coal and oil
[j]Mitsui Miike Engineering (former Mitsui Miike Machinery)
[k]Burns a coal/oil mixture

The following countermeasures were developed and have generally proven successful:

- o use of base metal catalysts with TiO_2 instead of Al_2O_3 or Fe_2O_3 substrates
- o use of parallel-flow catalysts such as honeycomb, plate, and tube catalysts
- o use of an economizer bypass to ensure operation above 330°C
- o maintaining unreacted NH_3 below 3 ppmv
- o use of a low-oxidation catalyst
- o employing erosion mitigation measures consisting of reduced gas velocities, harder catalysts, and dummy spacers

Major SCR plant constructors and the number and capacity of the plants constructed by them are shown in Table 4. Nearly all of the plants for utility boilers have been constructed since 1979, while virtually all the industrial plants were constructed before 1978. Some of the older plants experienced the problems described previously; however, nearly all plants constructed since 1979 have operated without problems in an automatic control mode.

SCR FOR UTILITY BOILERS [1, 2, 3]

Table 5 shows SCR performance for 13 major utility boilers in Japan. Coal-fired systems typically are parallel-flow catalysts with a space velocity (SV) of 2000-4000 h^{-1} to remove 60-80% of NO_x; those with low-sulfur oil-firing typically use parallel-flow catalysts with SV higher than 5000 h^{-1} to remove 80% NO_x. The lower SV for coal results from the higher inlet NO_x and SO_2 concentrations which mandate less reactive, lower oxidation catalysts. SCR plants for gas-fired boilers use pellet catalysts having an SV of 20,000 h^{-1}.

Between 1983 and 1987, 32 new SCR plants were constructed on utility boilers, 15 new and 17 retrofit.

Performance for a utility boiler SCR unit includes the following considerations:

(1) During boiler load swings, the NO_x removal usually is inversely proportional to load, due to the smaller space velocity or longer reaction times at lower loads.

(2) Lower loads usually mean lower flue gas temperatures which may increase deposits of ammonium bisulfate on the catalyst. Economizer bypass may be used to maintain higher temperature in the catalyst bed. When bypass is used less heat is recovered by the economizer, but is compensated by increased heat recovery in the air preheater downstream.

(3) The concentration of unreacted NH_3 is held below 3 ppmv to minimize bisulfate problems.

(4) Low-dust systems (downstream of hot-side ESP) encounter less catalyst erosion by dust but may be penalized by higher ESP costs and more deposits in the air preheater. The system is suited for low-sulfur coals.

TABLE 4. NUMBER AND CAPACITY OF SCR PLANTS BY JAPANESE MAKERS
(Completed by end of 1986)

Maker	For utility (Capacity in MWe)			Industry (1000 Nm^3/h)		In foreign countries (MWe)	Total (MWe) equivalent[a]
	For coal	For oil	For gas	Boiler	Others		
Mitsubishi Heavy Industries	12 (3233)	26 (8641)	11 (3421)	20 (2080)	1 (227)	9 (1277)	79 (17341)
Babcock Hitachi K.K.	9 (1944)	18 (5059)	3 (2100)	5 (101)	6 (586)	4 (822)	45 (10154)
Ishikawajima-Harima H.I.	4 (816)	14 (5818)	1 (700)	3 (764)	0	9 (682)	31 (8271)
Hitachi Zosen	0	0	7 (1000)	3 (940)	7 (951)	0	17 (1630)
Sumitomo Chemical Eng.	0	0	0	3 (640)	13 (1035)	0	16 (558)
Mitsui Eng. & Shipbuilding	0	0	0	4 (566)	13 (1019)	0	17 (528)
Kawasaki Heavy Industries	1 (125)	0	1 (156)	4 (131)	2 (12)	3 (122)	11 (451)
Nippon Kokan	0	0	0	0	1 (1320)	0	1 (440)
Techno Universe[b]	0	0	0	4 (332)	4 (615)	5 (117)	13 (433)
Ube Industries	0	0	0	3 (548)	1 (75)	0	4 (208)
Mitsubishi Kokoki	0	0	0	2 (114)	7 (222)	0	9 (112)
JGC Corp.	0	0	0	2 (120)	1 (152)	0	3 (91)
Kobe Steel	0	0	0	0	1 (100)	0	1 (33)
Total	26 (6118)	58 (19518)	23 (7377)	53 (6336)	57 (6314)	30 (3020)	247 (40250)

[a]Calculated at 1 MWe = 3000 Nm^3/h
[b]Jointly with Mitsui Toatsu Chemical

TABLE 5. PERFORMANCE OF MAJOR SCR UNITS ON UTILITY BOILERS

Fuel	Plant owner	Plant site	Boiler No.	Boiler MW	SCR mfr	Catalyst type	Pitch (mm)	SV (h^{-1})	NO_x conc (ppmv) In	NO_x conc (ppmv) Out	$DeNO_x$ (%)	Unreacted NH_3 (ppm)	Start-up year
COAL	EPDC	Takehara	1	250x1/2	BHK[a]	Plate	10	2300	350	67	81	4	1981
	EPDC	Takehara	2	250x1/2	KHI[b]	Tube	-	2000	350	67	81	4	1981
	EPDC	Takehara	3	700	BHK	Plate	10	2370	250	48	81	2	1983
	Chugoku	Shimonoseki	1	175	MHI[c]	Honeycomb	10	3000	420	180	57	1	1980
	Chugoku	Shin-Ube	3	156	MHI	Honeycomb	7	4000	400	140	65	2	1981
	Chugoku	Mizushima	2	156	BHK	Plate	6	2200	350	120	65	2	1984
	Shikoku	Saijo	1	156	MHI	Honeycomb	7	4000	380	130	65	1	1983
	Shikoku	Saijo	2	250	IHI[d]	Honeycomb	7.5	-	330	90	70	1	1983
OIL	Chugoku	Kudamatsu	2	375	IHI	Honeycomb	-	5500	150	28	81	5	1979
(Low	Chugoku	Kudamatsu	3	700	IHI	Honeycomb	-	5500	110	21	81	6	1979
S)	Chubu	Chita	4	700	MHI	Honeycomb	8	5430	100	18	82	2	1979
GAS	Chubu	Chita	5,6	700	BHK	Pellet	5	20000	40	8	80	4	1975
	Chubu	Chita II	1	700	BHK	Pellet	5	20000	50	10	80	4	1983

[a] Babcock Hitachi K.K.
[b] Kawasaki Heavy Industries
[c] Mitsubishi Heavy Industries
[d] Ishikawajima-Harima Heavy Industries

(5) High-dust systems (upstream of ESP) encounter more dust errosion but have less reactor and air preheater deposits and lower ESP costs. This system is better suited for medium- to high-sulfur coal, and is more common in Japan than the low-dust system.

OTHER PROCESSES FOR SO_x and NO_x ABATEMENT [2, 3]

Between 1972 and 1978, approximately 30 pilot- or small-scale wet process NO_x or simultaneous SO_x/NO_x removal units were constructed. Due to high costs and or relatively low NO_x removal efficiencies, recent development has focused on dry processes as shown in Table 6.

TABLE 6. DRY PROCESSES FOR NO_x AND SO_x/NO_x ABATEMENT (Other than SCR)

Process	Developers
NO_x control only	
Selective noncatalytic reduction (SNR or Thermal $DeNO_x$)	Exxon, Mitsubishi Chemical, Mitsubishi Heavy Industries, Mitsubishi Kakoki
In-furnace NO_x reduction (IFR or Reburning)	Mitsubishi Heavy Industries, Hitachi Zosen
Molecular sieve adsorption	Union Carbide-Nissan Chemical
Simultaneous SO_x/NO_x removal	
Activated carbon adsorption	Unitika, Electric Power Federation Electric Power Development Co., Sumitomo Heavy Industries, Mitsui Mining-Bergbau Forschung
Electron beam irradiation	Ebara Corp.
Copper oxide	Shell
Fluidized bed combustion	Electric Power Development Co., Kawasaki Heavy Industries, Mitsubishi Heavy Industries

For NO_x removal only, selective noncatalytic reduction (SNR, or Thermal $DeNO_x$) has been applied to smaller furnaces and boilers firing natural gas and low-sulfur oil to remove 30-40% of NO_x at a 1:1 NH_3/NO_x molar ratio. Recent applications of SNR to refuse incinerators have been made to remove 50-60% NO_x at 1.5-2 moles NH_3 to 1 mole NO_x. In-furnace reburning (IFR) has been applied commercially in Japan to coal- and oil-fired boilers at up to 50% additional NO_x removal over levels achieved by combustion modification (staged combustion) techniques alone. Molecular sieve adsorption of NO_x has been operated at a nitric acid plant since 1976 for 90% NO_x removal. Adverse effects of SO_2 have precluded any application to boilers.

For simultaneous dry SO_x/NO_x removal, two demonstration plants -- EPDC at 95 MWe and Mitsui Mining at 10 MWe -- have been operated using activated coke as the adsorbent to produce elemental sulfur by-product. The EPDC plant removes 30% NO_x and 95+% SO_2, while the Mitsui plant removes 60-80% NO_x and 98% SO_2. Mitsui Mining recently completed a commercial plant, 75 MWe, for Idemitsu Kosan at the Aichi Refinery.

Other combined processes for SO_x/NO_x removal include the Copper Oxide process which operated for several years on an oil-fired boiler but was aborted due to high cost, and the Electron Beam process which has been operated on a pilot plant basis.

Finally, fluidized bed combustion (FBC) has been applied to about 20 small boilers (20,000-320,000 lbs/hr steam capacity) since 1980. However, the prognosis for FBC is not good in the utility sector due to (1) stringent SO_2 and NO_x regulation, (2) generation of a lime-rich waste disposal problem, and (3) limitations of FBC for intermittent operations with load swings and frequent start-up/shut-down cycles.

WASTE-TO-ENERGY PLANTS [4]

Municipal solid waste is generated in Japan at about 120,000 tonnes per day, with 70% burned in mass-burn or fluidized bed waste-to-energy plants. Energy recovered is used to meet all or part of the electrical demand and heating/cooling requirements of the plant and nearby municipal facilities. In general, no energy is transferred outside the local service area.

ACID GAS/SO_2 CONTROL [4]

SO_2 control is not critical as the concentration from waste combustion is typically 60 ppmv (12% O_2 basis). However, hydrochloric acid (HCl) vapor is typically 700 ppmv and requires control by addition of alkali to the furnace or flue gas, hence SO_2 control is achieved concurrently. Limestone injection into the furnace zone is reported to reduce HCl by 25-40% at a $CaCO_3$/HCl molar ratio of 1:1 and by 80-85% at a ratio of 4:1. Since many local agreements require HCl reduction to less than 50 ppmv, several combinations of dry injection, humidification, and wet scrubbers are used in Japan. Figures 2 and 3 show two types of scrubbing systems currently in use.

Wet scrubber systems (Fig. 2) generally use sodium hydroxide for HCl/SO_2 control and can add an oxidizing agent such as sodium chlorite ($NaClO_2$) to remove NO_2 as well. Where stringent heavy metals control and moderate (30-50%) NO_x removal is warranted, wet systems have economic advantages over dry systems; however, the complexity of operation is significantly increased. Semi-dry or dry injection with humidification systems, such as in Figure 3, use hydrated lime, $Ca(OH)_2$, and is the dominant control system in Japan for waste firing. As indicated in Figure 3, virtually all HCl and 85% SO_2 removal can be typically achieved.

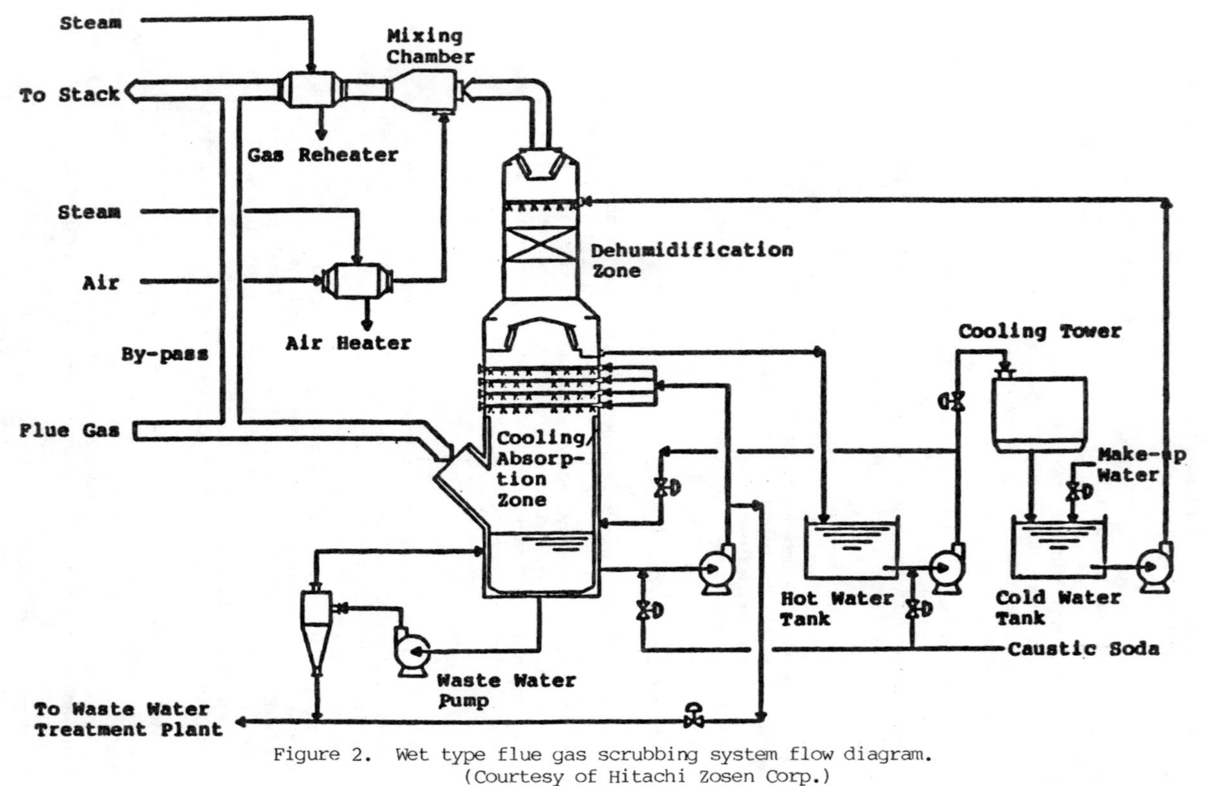

Figure 2. Wet type flue gas scrubbing system flow diagram. (Courtesy of Hitachi Zosen Corp.)

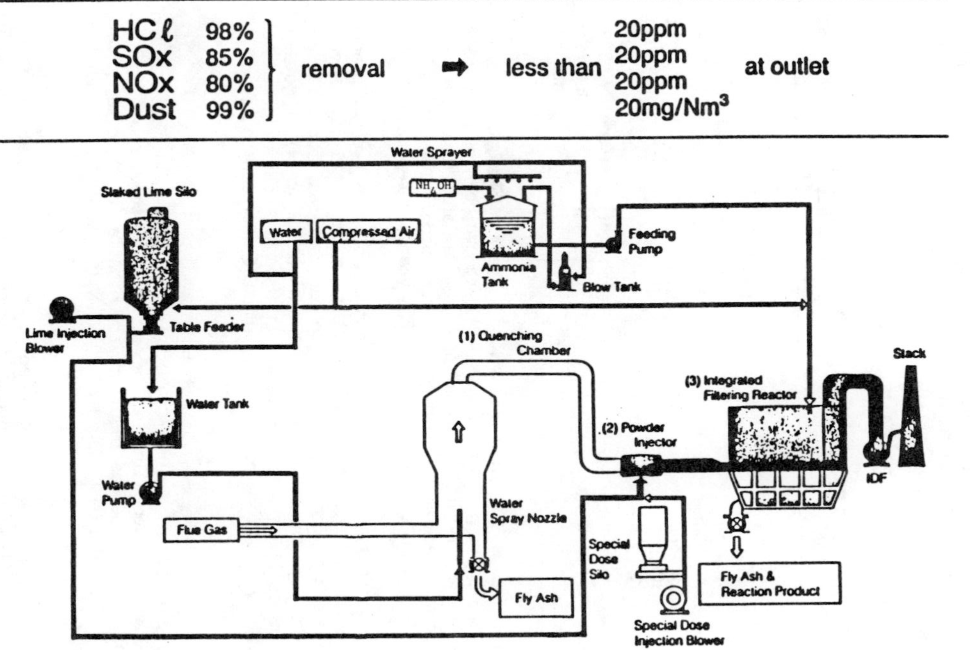

Figure 3. Integrated flue gas treatment system with pollutant removal capabilities. (Courtesy of Mitsubishi Heavy Industries, Ltd)

NO_x CONTROL [4]

Dry NO_x control is achieved in waste-to-energy plants by either in-furnace, selective noncatalytic reduction (SNR) or post-combustion selective catalytic reduction (SCR). Table 7 shows a sampling of plants using SNR, where typically 30-60% NO_x removal is achieved at 2-3.5 molar ratios of NH_3 to NO_x. The plants use aqueous ammonia (to prevent thermal damage to injection nozzles) sprayed into the furnace at about 900°C.

TABLE 7. SNR PLANTS BY MHI FOR REFUSE INCINERATORS

Location (city)	Unit Capacity Nm^3/h	Number of units	NO_x (ppm, 12% O_2) Inlet	Outlet	Completion year
Toyohaski	24,500	2	150	60	1980
Kamakura	32,000	2	175	100	1982
Kawasaki	48,540	3	200	(800 g/ton)[a]	1982
Kobe	45,000	3	180	130	1984
Yokohama	136,680	3	150	100	1984
Nagoya	47,000	3	150	80	1985
Kawasaki	70,310	2	150	(800 g/ton)[a]	1986
Kawasaki	47,000	3	200	(800 g/ton)[a]	1986
Hiroshima	38,740	2	150	100	Under construction

[a] About 100 ppm

Table 8 shows SCR units applied to 15 sewage sludge incinerators by Mitsui Engineering. Generally 90% NO_x removal can be achieved at 1:1 molar NH_3/NO_x ratio. Upstream dust removal and HCl reduction to below 20 ppmv is accomplished by sodium scrubbing. The gas is heated to 350-400°C for SCR. Catalyst life of 6 years is reported.

More recently, Mitsubishi (MHI) has constructed two SCR plants using a lower temperature (~200°C), HCl resistant catalyst. Advantages include significant savings in reheat costs and the ability to place the flue gas scrubber upstream (as in Figure 4) or downstream (wet scrubber) with little effect upon NO_x control costs or FGD operation. NO_x removal of 70% or greater has been achieved.

REFERENCES

1. Ando, Jumpei and Sedman, C.B., "Status of Acid Rain and SO_2 and NO_x Abatement Technology in Japan. In: Proceedings: Tenth Symposium on Flue Gas Desulfurization, Atlanta, Georgia, November 1986. Volume 1, EPA-600/9-87-004a (NTIS PB87-166609), February 1987.

2. Ando, Jumpei, Recent Development in SO_2 and NO_x Abatement Technology for Stationary Sources in Japan, EPA-600/7-85-040 (NTIS PB86-110186), September 1985.

3. Ando, Jumpei and Sedman, C.B., "FGD, SCR Gain Coal-fired-boiler Experience in Japan," Power, 131:2, February 1987, pp. 33-36.

4. Brna, T.G., "Pollutant Control from Municipal Waste Combustion in Japan," Trip Report, AEERL, U.S. EPA, October 5, 1987.

TABLE 8. SCR PLANTS FOR INCINERATORS CONSTRUCTED BY MITSUI ENGINEERING

Plant name	City	Gas flow (Nm^3/h)	Inlet (ppm) NO_x	Inlet (ppm) SO_x	Temp. (°C)	NH_3/NO_x	NO_x removal (%)	Completion
Sunamachi	Tokyo	108,000	100	5	350	1.0	90	1979[a]
Nanbu No. 1	Tokyo	36,000	100	5	350	1.0	90	1983
Nanbu No. 2	Tokyo	36,000	100	5	350	1.0	90	1983
Kasia	Tokyo	9,700	100	5	350	1.0	90	1983
Hirano	Osaka	24,000	130	20	400	1.0	90	1983
Hoshutsu	Osaka	47,000	130	20	400	1.0	90	1983
Shingashi	Tokyo	22,100	100	5	400	1.0	90	1983
Shingashi	Tokyo	33,100	100	5	400	1.0	90	1983
Senda	Hiroshima	2,515 x 2	130	20	400	1.0	90	1984
Sunamachi	Tokyo	108,000	100	10	350	1.0	90	1985
Kosuge	Tokyo	9,550	400[b]	30	400	1.0>	90	1985
Tsumori	Osaka	40,000	150	50	400	1.0>	80	1985
Konan	Biwako	2,700	135	25	400	1.0>	90	1985
Hojin	Nagoya	27,000	130	20	350	1.0>	80	1986

[a]Catalyst was replaced in 1986, after 6 years operation.
[b]NO_x is high (odor is less) because of the use of fluidized bed incinerator, while other incinerators are multi-stage type.

EUROPEAN ACTIVITIES IN SO2 AND NOX EMISSION CONTROL

William Ellison PE
Ellison Consultants
Monrovia, Maryland

ABSTRACT

This paper presents updated details of major flue gas desulfurization (FGD) and deNOx installations in West Germany for coal-fired boilers. The paper reviews applicable government regulations limiting stack emissions, provides an understanding of the principal types of control system designs that have been applied, outlines technological advancements that have been achieved, and reviews experience gained to date in recent expanded use of FGD and NOx control facilities in Europe. Significant differences from FGD service and practice in U.S.A. and Japan are described and specific information that may serve to help improve design, operation and reliability of new and retrofit FGD installations in U.S.A. is offered.

INTRODUCTION

As a result of significant forest damage an unprecedented program of retrofitting of SO2 and NOx emission controls on coal-fired boilers is being carried out in West Germany and is leading to substantial steps to achieve reductions in SO2 and NOx emissions in other European countries. This major, continent-wide endeavor may ultimately be expected to significantly impact future programs in North America for control of acid precipitation effects.

GOVERNMENT REGULATIONS

West German regulations issued in 1983 and 1984 impose stringent SO2 and NOx controls on all boilers above approximately 110 MW(e) and include requirements for retrofitting of flue gas desulfurization (FGD) on units as small as 35 MW(e). SO2 and NOx control compliance is stringently tied to half-hour mean values of emissions;[1] leading to purchase of gas cleaning systems with design emission levels substantially lower than the regulatory emission-limit values. In a 1986 Clean Air Act (TA Luft) stringent SO2 and NOx emission limits have been imposed for comparatively small industrial sources, existing and new.

SO2 EMISSION CONTROL

The GFAVO[2] federal regulation of 1983 requires that coal or oil firedunits larger than approximately 110 MW(e) comprising 50,000 MW(e) capacity, achieve 85% SO2 removal or an SO2 emission level of 400 mg/Nm³ (approximately 0.3 lb/MM Btu), whichever is more stringent, by July 1, 1988. However, based on other provisions of this national directive, boiler owners have designated specific units comprising 12,000 MW(e) for retirement by 1993 after no more than 30,000 additional hours of operation at an SO2 emission rate not to exceed 2,500 mg/Nm³ (2.0 lb/MM Btu). Units in the range of 35 to 110 MW(e) are specified for 60% removal or 2,000 mg/Nm³ (1.6 lb/MM Btu) by April 1, 1993. Units from 18 to 35 MW(e) are required to meet 2000 mg/Nm³ by April 1, 1993. A comprehensive Clean Air Act was put in force in West Germany in 1986 containing comprehensive SO2 emissions regulations for a wide variety of industrial sources including boilers smaller than 18 MW(e) requiring cleanup of existing discharges over an eight year compliance period.

NOX EMISSION CONTROL

A 1984 accord among federal and provincial environmental ministers in West Germany requires that existing coal fired units larger than 110 MW(e) reduce NOx emissions to 200 mg NO2/Nm³, approximately 100 ppm (vol.) Units in the range of 18 to 110 MW(e) are specified for 650 mg/Nm³ for dry bottom types, and 1,300 mg/Nm³ for wet bottom (slag tap) types. All existing boilers on a retirement schedule are allowed 650 mg/Nm³ for dry bottom and 1,300 mg/Nm³ for wet bottom. Compliance deadlines, set by individual state governments, generally specify 1989 for dry bottom boilers and 1990 for wet bottom. Emission limits are substantially lower for oil and gas firing. The 1986 West German Clean Air Act contains comprehensive NOx emission regulations for a wide variety of industrial sources including boilers smaller than 18 MW(e) requiring cleanup of existing discharges over an eight year compliance period.

OTHER EUROPEAN LEGISLATION

By influence of West Germany significant SO2 and NOx control legislation has been enacted or proposed in Austria, Switzerland, Italy, The Netherlands, Denmark, Sweden, Finland and the European Economic Community. See Table I displaying the NOx emission management objectives proposed by governing officials of EEC,[3] revised in 1985 to call for emission rates throughout Europe after 1995 comparable to current retrofit requirements in West Germany.

PRINCIPAL TYPES OF CONTROL SYSTEMS

Usable by-product yielding, wet FGD systems and selective catalytic reduction NOx removal systems are the principal technologies being utilized to control emissions from large existing electric utility plants.

SO2 EMISSION CONTROL

Wet Scrubbing

Lime/Limestone scrubbing is the principal FGD method being used. The very large market captured by this technology, (approximately 93% of all capacity sold in West Germany), has been shared by six diverse, principal system suppliers, which represent a mix of Japanese, U.S. and German design technologies.[4]

TABLE I
EFFECT OF AMENDED EUROPEAN COMMUNITY DIRECTIVE

Proposed Directive, 1983	Emission Limits (mg NO2/Nm³) Coal	Oil	Gas
All Plants over 50 MW(t): ***			
to 1995:	800*	450	350
after 1995:	400**	220	180
Amended Directive, 1985			
to 1995:			
over 50 MW(t)		450	350
50-100 MW(t)	800*		
100-300 MW(t)	800		
over 300 MW(t)	650		
after 1995:			
over 50 MW(t)		150	100
50-100 MW(t)	400**		
over 100 MW(t)	200		

* 1300 mg/Nm³ for slag tap furnaces
** 800 mg/Nm³ for slag tap furnaces
*** Note that 100 MW(t) equals approximately 37 MW(e).

A typical FGD system arrangement that is being extensively applied in European electric-utility applications incorporates the following features that are similar to those of many systems installed in U.S.A. in the 1980s:

- Lime or limestone reagent use, with limestone generally preferred

- o Spray-tower type wet absorber design, rubber-lined
- o In-situ forced oxidation facilities installed in the sump of the absorber without use of sulfuric acid reagent for pH depression/adjustment
- o Primary dewatering of gypsum slurry by liquid cyclones, with final dewatering by centrifuge or horizontal vacuum filter
- o Production of a throwaway or usable grade of gypsum
- o Single-loop wet-scrubbing system operation that omits low-pH pre-scrubbing used extensively in Japan and in many early German installations for segregated removal of hydrogen chloride and other minor raw-gas components.

Dry Scrubbing

A considerable number of small and large boilers, a substantial number in West Germany, are being equipped with conventional throwaway-waste dry scrubbing systems using spray dryers. And in instances where suitable solid waste management schemes are made available, this technique may be expected to be applied to additional existing West German boilers of size 110 MW(e) and less by a 1993 FGD startup deadline. In FGD-using European countries other than West Germany, including Denmark, Austria, and Italy, conventional dry scrubbers are being applied in recent years at substantially higher inlet flue-gas concentrations (as high as 7000 mg $SO2/Nm^3$), i.e. 5.6 lb/MM Btu, than earlier applications worldwide. In some locations, particularly Sweden, conventional dry scrubbers are being installed downstream of high-efficiency fly ash collection equipment to more readily permit the FGD solid waste to be converted to a generally usable by-product. A commercial circulating-fluid-bed dry scrubber is being applied with semi-dry operation similar to that of spray dryers at inlet flue-gas SO2 concentration as high as 13,000 mg $SO2/Nm^3$ (10.4 lb/MM Btu).[5]

NOX EMISSION CONTROL

The emission limit, (200 mg/Nm^3), set in 1984 for West German boilers above 110 MW(e) is well beyond the capabilities of combustion modification techniques and requires the use of flue gas cleaning processes to remove NOx from the flue gas. Despite the apparent attractiveness of gas cleaning processes that would simultaneously remove both SO2 and NOx, and because of imminence of compliance deadlines, the commercially developed and applied selective catalytic reduction (SCR) process (for removal of NOx alone) is being most broadly assessed, adapted and utilized. More than 10,000 MW(e) of SCR capacity has been purchased in West Germany by 1987. This process uses ammonia feed upstream of a catalytic reactor operating at approximately 300 to 400°C (570 to 750°F). A considerable number of selective noncatalytic reduction (SNCR) installations aggregating approximately 1000 MW(e) and operating at 800 to 1000°C (1470 to 1830°F), are also being carried out.

COMPARISON WITH U.S.A. AND JAPAN

SO2 EMISSION CONTROL

As in Japan, most of the wet FGD installations are in low/medium sulfur fuel service and, similarly, are designed to employ forced oxidation to yield a commercially usable by-product gypsum and to thus avoid the substantial cost and complexity in West Germany of alternative throwaway management of solid waste. At the same time, application of wet FGD in West Germany differs significantly from that in U.S.A. in some major respects:

- With typically low fuel sulfur level, e.g. flue-gas SO2 concentration of approximately 2000 mg/Nm^3, it has been possible to establish high (95%) availability system design without use of spare wet scrubber modules.
- As a nationwide energy conservation measure to avoid the use of fuel required to calcine limestone to lime, FGD installations now under construction have been generally dedicated to use of limestone reagent, and as much as 80% of wet-FGD installation capacity to date uses limestone.
- Limestone reagent supply is generally ground at the mine source rather than at the boiler site.
- Due to comparatively high energy cost in Europe, gas reheat is by scavenging of heat from the FGD inlet gas. Rotary and tubular regenerative heat exchanger systems are being commonly employed in West Germany (without need to use augmental energy supply) for the purpose of meeting a mandatory 72°C (162°F) minimum stack outlet temperature requirement.
- Due to conservative FGD-buyer policy and the unusual stringency of stack emission control regulations tied to monitoring and limiting of half-hour mean values of emission rate, systems are frequently specified by the owner for a substantially lower stack emission rate than the GFAVO emission-limit value.

NOX EMISSION CONTROL

Due to concerns about applicability at existing electric utility plants in West Germany of extensive commercial SCR experience in comparatively new, based-loaded coal-fired boilers in Japan, approximately 50 SCR pilot-plant trains have been installed and tested to assess catalyst performance and characteristics. This testing has included conventional SCR application upstream of the air preheater (high-dust), as well as use of SCR downstream of FGD (cold-side) after flue-gas heating, including 11 with activated carbon. Extensive high-dust SCR field pilot-scale investigation has taken place because German boilers to be retrofitted with SCR are considered to have a more variable load pattern (more frequent load swings) than those in Japan that have been equipped and operated with SCR, and could cause thermal shock of the catalyst structure. In addition, possible unique effects of fly ash from German boilers has been of concern and pilot plant results have indicated that catalyst poisoning is a major problem in application of high-dust SCR to wet bottom boilers. Although avoided in Japanese practice and of concern because of ammonia-slippage problems leading to fouling of the boiler air preheater, design NOx removal efficiency substantially above 80% is specified for a number of the German retrofit SCR applications.

DESIGN AND OPERATING EXPERIENCE

SO2 EMISSION CONTROL

In keeping with the 1988 target compliance-date for SO2 emission reductions, more than 100 flue gas desulfurization (FGD) installations, primarily commercial-gypsum-producing types, comprising more than 35,000 MW(e) are being erected. Approximately 50,000 MW(e) of FGD is expected to be in place by the early 1990s. Comparatively few boilers under 100 MW(e) have been retrofitted with FGD to date since the compliance deadline for these is 1993. It is understood that even in the size range of 35 to 110 MW(e), for which a specified SO2 removal efficiency is mandated, many industrial boiler owners will expect to achieve 1993 compliance by conversion to natural gas fuel as available.

Many FGD facilities already in service in West Germany are the result of a comparatively modest control program that began prior to 1983 under the jurisdiction of individual provincial governments, which led to approximately twenty FGD applications. Thus, although widespread application of flue gas desulfurization in the Federal Republic of Germany (West Germany) is comparatively recent, as of the end of 1984 almost 3000 MW(e) of lime/limestone scrubbing systems were in operation, all of single-module slip-stream design to meet requirements of pre-1983 legislation. These FGD system installations are reported to have provided acceptable reliability and performance. However, German electric utility specialists note that with only partial scrubbing of plant flue gas output these earliest installations have not been subjected to typical full-scale electric-utility-industry operating conditions requiring high availability at sustained high/variable load. Additional FGD capacity of more than 5000 MW(e) originating from the 1983 legislation has now come on line, but is in an early stage of sustained operation without a lengthy period of experience. However, based on a recent overview, system availability of 90 to 95% is being achieved after twelve months of initial operation. Substantial debugging problems/efforts have typically been encountered during the initial operations, and primarily with the gypsum solids processing equipment, i.e., centrifuges, thickeners, filters, dryers and storage facilities, and solids loading and unloading. Operating with characteristically low or moderate coal sulfur level, and applying commercially demonstrated and conservatively designed forced-oxidation systems, no critical technical problems have been experienced or forecast at the present time. Moreover, because of the comparatively low coal sulfur level, availability concerns have not required the use of spare scrubbing modules. Feasibility of regenerative flue-gas reheat using rotary regenerative heat exchangers has been effectively demonstrated. FGD retrofitting has not presented insurmountable problems.

Influenced by this new control activity in Germany, approximately 2000 MW(e) of usable-gypsum-producing FGD systems are being installed in The Netherlands, and a major FGD installation program is under way in Austria on utility boilers. Other European countries including Sweden, Denmark, Italy and England have also become major markets for FGD with many installations under construction or planned.

NOX EMISSION CONTROL

More than 10,000 MW(e) of SCR capacity has been purchased as of 1987 and more than 30,000 MW(e) of capacity is expected to be in place by 1990. The earliest major SCR facility has been installed on a 460 MW(e) bituminous-coal-fired, dry bottom boiler and commenced operation in 1986. Another early installation of 160 MW(e) capacity on a bituminous-coal-fired, wet bottom boiler will achieve close to 90% NOx removal. Early operations of these facilities indicate that catalyst poisoning by arsenic may occur in wet bottom (slag tap) applications.

PRINCIPAL TECHNOLOGICAL ADVANCEMENTS

Notable commercial developments in Europe that may be of significant value in stack gas cleaning applications in U.S.A. include the following:

HIGH SULFUR COAL APPLICATIONS

European high-sulfur coal applications of dry scrubbers of both the spray dryer and circulating fluid bed type extend the electric utility use of these semi-dry FGD processes to coal sulfur levels substantially above those of present U.S. installations. The circulating fluid bed type already has had significant European operating experience in high-sulfur coal service, and a substantial basis appears to now exist for broader use of semi-dry scrubbing in U.S.A.

REGENERATIVE REHEAT

Energy economics in West Germany has provided strong motivation for commercial application of regenerative reheat means in high capacity-factor applications. Rotary air heaters, similar to those commonly used for regenerative combustion-air preheating in large boilers, have been extensively used for this purpose with more than forty purchased, many of which are in operation. Reliable operation of these heat exchangers has followed from application of suitable materials of construction, favorable continuous performance of electrostatic precipitators dedusting the hot inlet gas, and use of high-efficiency horizontal-gas-flow type mist eliminators limiting carryover of FGD scrubbing slurry. On-line, intermittent, high-pressure water washing means have effectively prevented exchanger gas pressure drop (the sum of pressure drop across both sides) from exceeding a nominal 125% of the design value for clean conditions. Due to the inherent design of the rotary exchanger, 3-5% of design gas flow leaks from the high pressure side to the low pressure side. When, typically, the FGD booster fan is positioned on the hot dirty gas side a substantial decrease in SO2 removal occurs. However, a low-leakage design has been developed for this system arrangement that has commercially demonstrated a leakage rate of no more than 0.5%.

A comparatively simple, tubular-heat-exchanger type, regenerative reheat system requiring no added flue gas ductwork is also gaining commercial use in Germany after long-term field testing in a lignite FGD installation, and may have applicability in U.S.A. Tubes exposed to scrubbed gas are supplied in non-metallic construction and circulating water is the heat transfer medium. Four such systems of an aggregate FGD capacity of 1,200 MW(e) have been installed.

In one case in Germany the wet FGD system is sited inside a hyperbolic cooling tower serving the power plant, the FGD outlet gas intermixing with a stream of air flow approximately twenty five times greater. Because of good atmospheric dispersion assured through discharge of the FGD exhaust combined with this substantial air flow the FGD system is exempted from normal FGD stack exit temperature regulations. For corrosion control a double coating of epoxy is applied to the internal surface of the concrete casing of the cooling tower. The capital cost is reported to be only 20% of that which would otherwise be required for a rotary heat exchanger system for regenerative heat. As a result of this initial demonstration of use of the cooling tower stack for flue gas discharge, fifteen additional cooling towers, all but one previously existing, are being adapted to receive the water-saturated flue gas discharge from wet FGD systems currently under construction.

FGD WASTEWATER TREATMENT

The application of usable-byproduct-forming, wet FGD systems, common in Germany, results in a significant discharge of brackish/saline wastewater. With typically high chloride levels (0.1 to 0.2%) in German bituminous coal, FGD wastewater management is a substantial problem as would be the case at comparable inland sites in U.S.A. producing usable by-product. When discharge to receiving streams is not completely prohibited, the rate of FGD liquor outfall is usually limited to the equivalent of 25 U.S. gpm per 100 MW(e). When such saline liquor discharge is allowed, trace metal concentrations, dissolved sulfate, and suspended solids must be reduced to specified levels.

Through wastewater purge treatment carried out in the presence of gypsum precipitation from CaSO4-supersaturated liquid, very low trace metal concentrations are achieved prior to outfall discharge.[6] A typical wastewater treatment system to accomplish this includes two stages of neutralization, flocculation and sedimentation, the first stage operating at pH 9-10 to remove components such as cadmium and manganese, the second stage operating at a pH of 8.5 to remove other components such as zinc and aluminum. An additive in the form of an organic sulfur compound serves as a special precipitation agent to remove mercury. A facility to dewater sludge formed in wastewater treatment is also needed.

YIELD OF HIGH VALUE GYPSUM PRODUCT FORMS

It can be anticipated that West Germany will become a proving ground for gaining the broadest and most diverse use/recovery of FGD by-product solids. Commercially usable FGD gypsum production in West Germany is expected to be applied to convert significant amounts of FGD gypsum by-product to the more valuable forms of anhydrite (anhydrous calcium sulfate) and alpha hemihydrate (of calcium sulfate) to help ensure fullest utilization of FGD gypsum by-product. Commercial technology is now available to supply plants to process 100,000 metric tons per year of FGD gypsum yielding highly valued, alpha hemihydrate at a cost as low as 50 DM per metric ton.[7]

COLD SIDE SCR

As a result of observed significant, adverse effects of flue gas trace elements on SCR catalyst in high-dust service on wet bottom boilers, important alternative methods such as cold side SCR for high-efficiency NOx removal are likely to be broadly used and demonstrated in Germany. The anticipated 1990 deadline for efficient NOx control compliance by electric utility wet bottom boilers can however be expected to be substantially delayed.

A great many SCR installations that will commence operations by 1990 are being appled downstream of FGD to limit catalyst poisoning and impact on unit availability, and to some extent because of inadequate plot space to permit normal tie in of the SCR reactor upstream of the air preheater. This activity in Germany may be expected to provide experience needed to optimize design of SCR facilities for difficult services such as wet bottom boilers, particularly where it is coordinated with the installation of FGD. In the cold-side SCR service, activated carbon (coke) may be of considerable use despite its flamability since its catalysis is effective at a comparatively low temperature, i.e. as low as 90°C, (194°F) and less reheating of the water saturated gas is thereby required.

INTEGRATED AIR-PREHEATER/SCR-REACTOR DESIGN

Other potentially important developments for NOx removal include sustained pilot and field test programs in West Germany seeking to adapt existing rotary regenerative air preheaters to incorporate catalyst-coated plates, permitting these facilities to also serve as SCR reactors. Only moderate removal efficiencies are anticipated since catalyst temperature in this economically attractive, integrated arrangement for high-dust service varies within the heat exchanger from 150°C to less than 350°C (302°F to less than 662°F), whereas an SCR reactor typically positioned upstream of the air preheater ideally operates at approximately 350°C (662°F). Long awaited reports that would indicate conclusive, large-scale test results have not yet been published.

CONCLUSIONS

West German influence among the European countries and its projected capital expenditures for stationary source SO2 and NOx control aggregating well in excess of 40 billion West German marks (approximately U.S. $20 billion) by the early 1990s has brought about a new and extraordinary, continent-wide effort to accomplish substantial abatement of acid precipitation effects through major and widespread reductions in SO2 and NOx emission inventories.

As a result of enactment in West Germany in 1983 of a comprehensive acid rain control law more than 40,000 MW(e) aggregate FGD capacity has been purchased in West Germany alone, more than 93% of it of the form of usable-gypsum-producing wet lime/limestone scrubbing comparable to many such facilities in Japan and to a number of such flue gas cleaning systems installed in the U.S.A. beginning in the late 1970s. Other important FGD technologies are also being utilized in Europe, some of them of potential value in any future retrofit high-sulfur FGD applications in the U.S.A.

Very stringent nitrogen oxides (NOx) limits imposed in West Germany in 1984 call for emission of no more than 200 mg NOx, measured as nitrogen dioxide, NO2, per Nm^3, approximately 0.16 lb NO2 per million Btu heat input, for existing and new boilers greater than 110 MW(e), size. As of 1986 approximately 50 high-efficiency commercial systems aggregating more than 10,000 MW(e) capacity, most for retrofit addition, have been purchased in West Germany alone, and approximately 30,000 MW(e) of additional NOx removal capacity will be rquired to be retrofitted by deadlines during the period 1988 to 1990. Systems applied to date primarily use selective catalytic reduction (SCR) technology, which employs ammonia reagent to chemically convert nitrogen oxides to normal atmospheric nitrogen. A number of adaptations of typical SCR technology as previously utilized in Japan for base-loaded coal-fired boilers are being applied and evaluated in West Germany for use in peaking-boiler service. Such new process designs, some of which offer potential for significantly reducing the cost of retrofit SCR technology, may prove to be of significant value for possible application in low or high-sulfur deNOx service in the U.S.A.

REFERENCES

1. Leutzke, K., and Stahl, H., "Continuous emission monitoring for SO2 and NOx in the Federal Republic of Germany". Paper presented at the Fourth Seminar on the Control of Sulphur and Nitrogen Oxides from Stationary Sources, Graz, Austria, May, 1986.

2. Federal Republic of Germany, Thirteenth order implementing the federal emission control act (large furnaces order) - 13th BImSchV, cabinet decision of June 14, 1983 (German language).
3. Amended proposal for a council directive on limitation of pollutants from large combustion plants. COM (85) 47 final. Brussels: European Commission, February, 1985.
4. Der stand der nachruestung bei der rauchgasentschwefelung, Elektrizitaetswirtschaft, Jg 85 (1986), Heft 5, pp 170-174 (German language).

5. Schmole, C., and Dietl R., "Experience in the operation of a dry/semi-dry flue gas desulfurization plant (FGD) according to the Lurgi Circulating Fluid Bed Absorption Process (CFB) in the Schwandorf Power Station of Bayernwerk AG". Paper presented at the Third Annual Convention of the VDI-Gesellschaft Energietechnik, Darmstadt, West Germany, February, 1986.
6. Forck, B. "Flue gas desulfurization and NOx reduction". Paper presented at a technical conference, Malmo, Sweden, November 6, 1985.
7. Kappe, J., and Ellison, W., "Utilization of residuals from flue gas desulfurization". Paper presented at the Annual Meeting, American Institute of Chemical Engineers, Chicago, Illinois, November, 1985.

DEVELOPMENTS IN LIMB TECHNOLOGY

Dennis C. Drehmel
Air and Energy Engineering Research Laboratory
U.S. Environmental Protection Agency

INTRODUCTION

During the past several years, the EPA has sponsored control technology development work with the intent of providing abatement options for potential acid rain precursors. Some of these come with curious acronyms such as ADVACATE (advanced silicate low temperature dry injection), E-SO_x (electrostatic precipitator modifications to allow dry scrubbing for sulfur oxides), and LIMB (limestone injection, multistage burners). The objective of all these processes is to capture at least 50% of the sulfur dioxide (SO_2) in a flue gas stream at a cost in terms of \$/ton SO_2 removed which is competitive with wet or dry flue gas desulfurization (FGD). In addition, LIMB is to lower emissions of nitrogen oxides (NO_x) by 50% with low NO_x technology such as multistage burners.

While ADVACATE and E-SO_x are still being studied at the pilot scale, LIMB has progressed to full-scale demonstration. Advancement to demonstration has come as the result of many years of EPA sponsored R&D including tests at large pilot and prototype facilities. The LIMB program has consisted of five activity areas; namely, fundamentals, pilot and prototype scale tests, modelling, cost analysis, and demonstration. Fundamentals have focused on the kinetics of potential LIMB reactions (e.g., calcination and sulfation) and on properties of limestone and limestone products to identify and optimize properties providing high reactivity for SO_x capture. Pilot and prototype scale tests have provided information on the effect of the furnace conditions on LIMB, on the effect of LIMB on furnace operations, and on the operation of the extant particulate collection device which is almost always an electrostatic precipitator (ESP). Modelling is obviously used to analyze and extrapolate test data and to provide input to the fourth area (cost analysis) which compares LIMB to alternatives. Finally, demonstration provides the data necessary for generalization of the technology to the private sector.

The LIMB program calls for demonstration at two sites. One of these sites is a wall-fired power plant, and the other is a tangentially fired (T-fired) power plant. The wall-fired plant is the subject of this paper and is described below. The T-fired plant is a nominal 180 MWe constructed by Combustion Engineering and is located in Yorktown, Virginia. Because of the difference in firing systems, the flow patterns in wall- and T-fired boilers are significantly different. The flow pattern affects the mixing and the temperature history of injected sorbent particles. Thus, it is essential to test LIMB with these two types of firing systems which are the only two major types of firing systems for large scale utility boilers.

It is the purpose of this paper to describe the most recent results from the LIMB program which are the results from the wall-fired demonstration. However, these results are preliminary and not optimized. Consequently, it is important to bear in mind important conclusions from the other parts of the LIMB program which will aid in interpretation of the demonstration results. These conclusions are provided below in the background section. Following that is an experimental section describing the system at the LIMB demonstration. Finally, there are results and discussion of results sections.

BACKGROUND

Each of the LIMB activity areas has contributed important conclusions which explain decisions in the formulation of the LIMB demonstration and which may be useful in understanding early results recently obtained. Conclusions from the fundamentals area are as follows:

1) Both calcium carbonate ($CaCO_3$) and calcium hydroxide [$Ca(OH)_2$] convert rapidly to calcium oxide (CaO) at furnace conditions; SO_2 capture is determined by reactivity of the CaO produced.

2) The reactivity of CaO is determined by its surface area, particle size, and pore size distribution; CaO produced from $Ca(OH)_2$ has the more favorable surface area and pore size distribution for SO_2 capture.

3) Loss of surface area of CaO, called sintering, renders high surface precalcines less effective than high surface area CaO formed from $Ca(OH)_2$ in the furnace.

4) The reactivity of CaO may be enhanced by the addition of certain metal ions or surfactants; the mechanism for the metals is uncertain, but recent information shows that surfactants incorporated into the water of hydration for $Ca(OH)_2$ decrease the sintering rate of the CaO formed in the furnace after injection.

The first conclusion from pilot and prototype testing is in agreement with the results from fundamentals. The first and rest of these conclusions are as follows:

1) $Ca(OH)_2$ is a superior SO_2 sorbent to either $CaCO_3$ (limestone) or CaO; the performance of $Ca(OH)_2$ can be enhanced by the addition of calcium lignosulfonate (a surfactant).

2) The optimum injection temperature into a typical boiler furnace for $Ca(OH)_2$ is 2300°F (1250°C); incorporation of calcium lignosulfonate allows injection at slightly higher temperatures without adverse effects.

3) Deposits formed in the furnace in high temperature zones as a result of sorbent injection are soft and should be removable with normal or increased sootblowing typical of a power boiler furnace.

4) Injection of $Ca(OH)_2$ increases the resistivity of the fly ash and decreases the efficiency of an ESP; the resistivity and efficiency can be restored by humidification which will also reactivate unused CaO for further SO_2 capture at low temperatures.

5) The reactivity of commercial $Ca(OH)_2$ varies enough to affect attainment of SO_2 capture objectives; the most reactive $Ca(OH)_2$ in the area of the LIMB demonstration was found to be that supplied by Marblehead Lime Co.

Conclusions from the modeling and cost areas are as follows:

1) Heat transfer and mixing models are effective in predicting the location of optimum injection; the mixing model shows that poor injection is avoided only with great care and that poor mixing can cut overall SO_2 capture in half.

2) The sulfation model shows that the good capture resulting from high surface area sorbents is available only at small particle sizes; large particle sizes increase pore diffusion and mask differences in basic reactivity.

3) Because $Ca(OH)_2$ naturally has a much smaller particle size than $CaCO_3$, the cost to grind $CaCO_3$ to the same size would make it more expensive than $Ca(OH)_2$.

4) Because LIMB is more operating cost and less capital cost intensive than wet or even dry FGD, LIMB competes well in older boilers or those with lower load factors.

EXPERIMENTAL

The site for the wall-fired LIMB demonstration is the Edgewater unit 4 of Ohio Edison Company, in Lorain, Ohio. The boiler is a nominal 105 MWe made by Babcock & Wilcox. It is a radiant, wall-fired, Carolina boiler burning eastern bituminous coal. It has been in operation since June 1, 1957. The boiler has 12 burners fired from a single wall in a 3 column by 4 row array. The burners were B&W circular burners, recently changed to B&W XCL low NO_x burners for the "MB" (multistage burner) part of the LIMB program. Particulates are collected by a 6-field Lodge Cottrell ESP which is only 4 years old. With respect to the "LI" (limestone injection) part of LIMB, the system for injection delivers sorbent to three levels in the boiler. These levels are elevations 181, 187, and 191 which have eight nozzles each in the front wall. In addition, there are two nozzles on each side wall at elevation 187, and 3 ft (90 cm) from the front wall. Elevation 181 is slightly below and elevation 187 is slightly above the "nose" of the boiler. It is in this regime that the average injection temperature of 2300°F (1250°C) is available. Obviously, the temperature varies across a horizontal cross section of the boiler because of heat transfer to the water cooled walls. In order to provide sorbent at these elevations, there are two air conveying systems consisting of Acrison feeders which drop sorbent to a star valve and down to the transport air jet. The Acrison feeders are supplied by a small hopper or "day silo" inside the boiler house, and that hopper is in turn supplied by an external silo filled directly by truck.

Accurate determination of LIMB effectiveness is dependent on measurements of sorbent feed rate, outlet SO_2 concentration, and inlet SO_2 concentration as determined by coal feed rate and coal sulfur content. Sorbent feed rate was measured by the Acrison feeders noted above by virtue of their being differential weight loss feeders. Also, the inside hopper which feeds the Acrisons is equiped with load cells for an independent check on sorbent feed rate. For the outlet SO_2 concentration, a continuous emission monitor analyzes the flue gas between the stack and the induced draft fan after the ESP. In this monitor, gas is extracted through a filter in the stack and another filter in a heated box before being drawn to a UV analyzer. Both filters are hot (approximately 300°F -- 150°C) to avoid reactions of unused sorbent on the filter, and contamination is slight because the boiler's upstream (ESP) is highly efficient. The coal feed rate is determined by computation from the boiler heat rate, using equations for the design of the Edgewater boiler which B&W considers proprietary. The coal sulfur content is determined by sampling of the coal just before injection into the furnace. As noted above, coal feed rate and coal sulfur concentration are used to compute the inlet SO_2 concentration which is verified by the outlet monitor during periods without sorbent injection and well after any periods of sorbent injection.

RESULTS

Test periods at Edgewater were as follows:

1) Low NO_x burner characterization without limestone injection during early July 1987.

2) Shakedown of the system (primarily the feed system) from late July to late August 1987.

3) SO_2 removal tests with commercial $Ca(OH)_2$ during September 1987; the commercial sorbent was supplied by Marblehead Lime Co. and injection was primarily at elevation 181.

4) SO_2 removal tests with calcium lignosulfonate-modified $Ca(OH)_2$ during the last week of September 1987 before a regularly scheduled outage. The modified sorbent was prepared by Marblehead Lime Co. from the same CaO used to make their normal commercial $Ca(OH)_2$. Injection was at elevation 181. Unlike previous tests in which all injections were with no tilt to the nozzle, the last test with the modified sorbent was with the nozzles tilted 15 degrees down.

All the elevation 181 capture data taken are shown in Figure 1 versus the calcium to sulfur molar ratio. By dividing the SO_2 capture by the calcium to sulfur ratio, the utilization of CaO is obtained and is plotted in Figure 2. Note that utilization decreases slightly with increasing calcium to sulfur ratio in approximately a linear fashion. Figure 3 shows the data for the Marblehead commercial sorbent only, and Figure 4 the data for sorbent modified with calcium lignosulfonate. These two figures present both the SO_2 capture and the CaO utilization as a function of the calcium to sulfur ratio.

DISCUSSION OF RESULTS

Statistical analysis of the data provides a useful interpretation of the results of the Edgewater demonstration to date. Figures 5 and 6 show the predicted SO_2 captures for untreated and treated sorbents, respectively. The middle line is the average prediction, and the outside

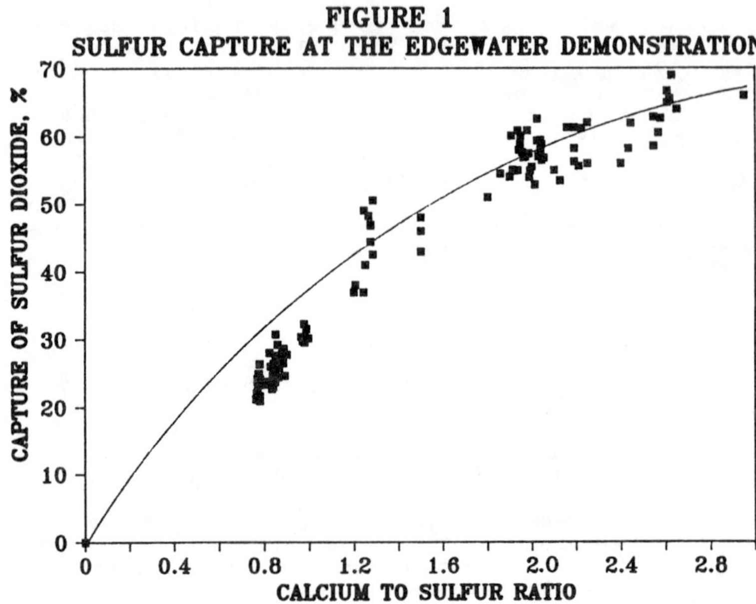
FIGURE 1
SULFUR CAPTURE AT THE EDGEWATER DEMONSTRATION
CAPTURE OF SULFUR DIOXIDE, %
0
10
20
30
40
50
60
70
0
0.4
0.8
1.2
1.6
2.0
2.4
2.8
CALCIUM TO SULFUR RATIO

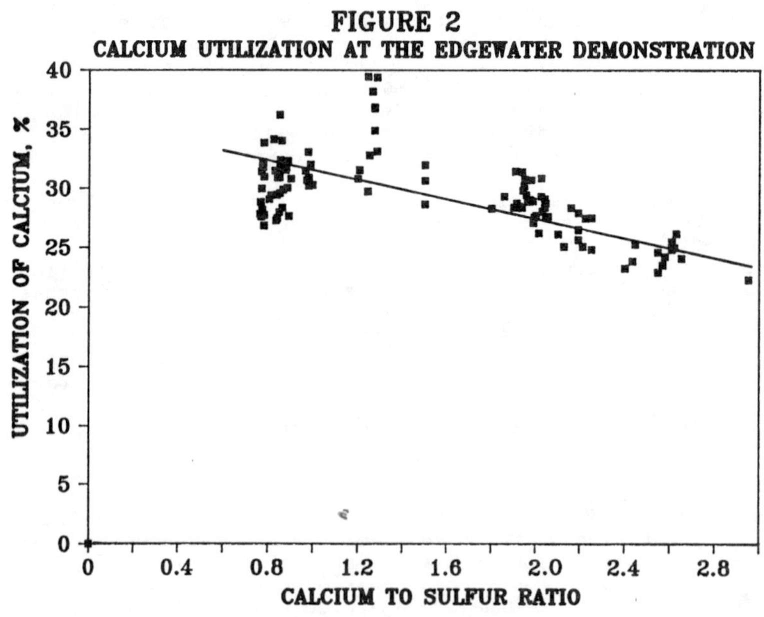
FIGURE 2
CALCIUM UTILIZATION AT THE EDGEWATER DEMONSTRATION
UTILIZATION OF CALCIUM, %
0
5
10
15
20
25
30
35
40
0
0.4
0.8
1.2
1.6
2.0
2.4
2.8
CALCIUM TO SULFUR RATIO

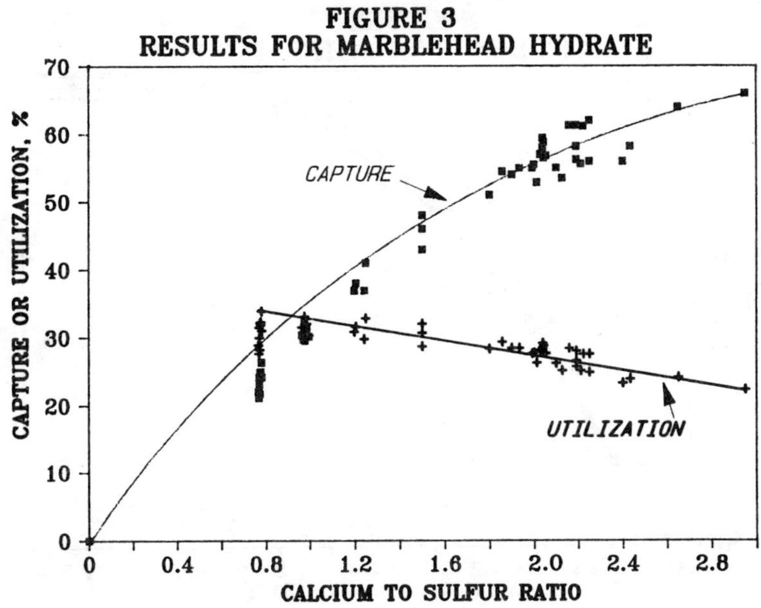
FIGURE 3
RESULTS FOR MARBLEHEAD HYDRATE
CAPTURE OR UTILIZATION, %
CAPTURE
UTILIZATION
CALCIUM TO SULFUR RATIO
0
10
20
30
40
50
60
70
0
0.4
0.8
1.2
1.6
2.0
2.4
2.8

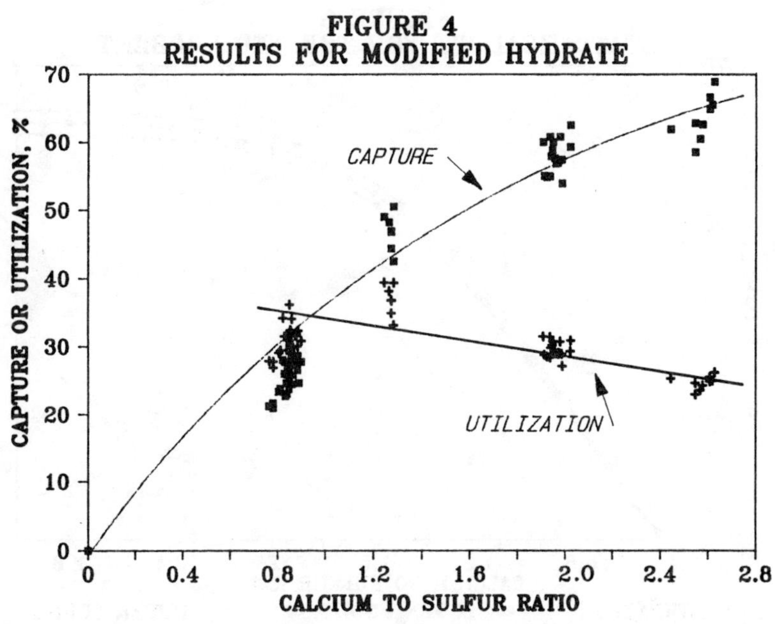
FIGURE 4
RESULTS FOR MODIFIED HYDRATE
CAPTURE OR UTILIZATION, %
CAPTURE
UTILIZATION
CALCIUM TO SULFUR RATIO
0
10
20
30
40
50
60
70
0
0.4
0.8
1.2
1.6
2.0
2.4
2.8

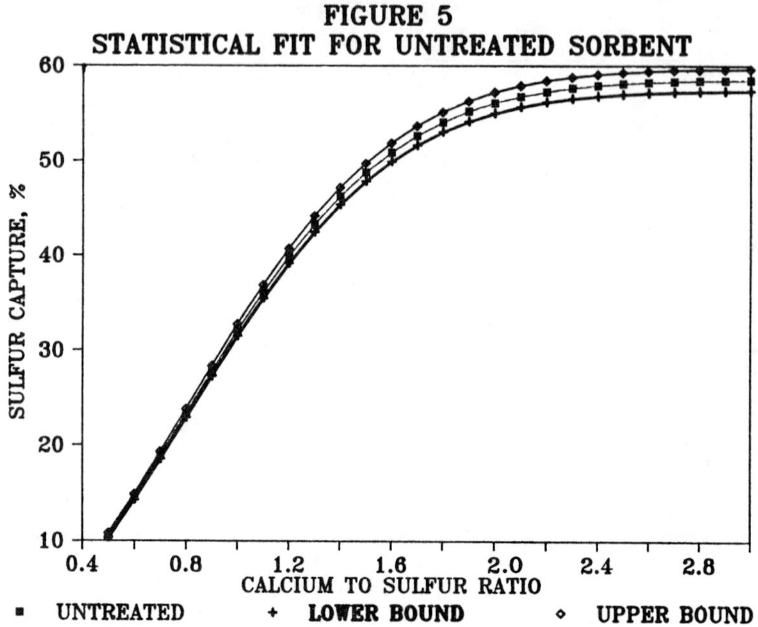
FIGURE 5
STATISTICAL FIT FOR UNTREATED SORBENT
SULFUR CAPTURE, %
60
50
40
30
20
10
0.4
0.8
1.2
1.6
2.0
2.4
2.8
CALCIUM TO SULFUR RATIO
UNTREATED
LOWER BOUND
UPPER BOUND

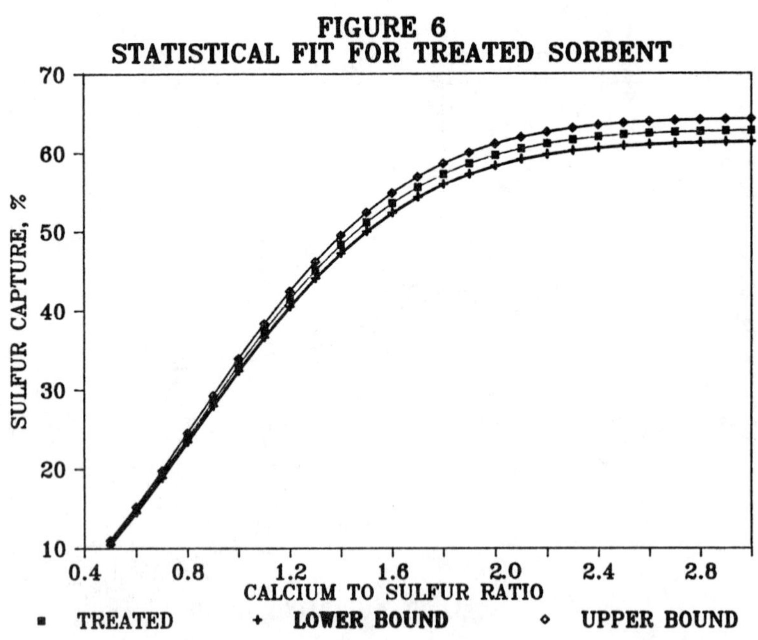
FIGURE 6
STATISTICAL FIT FOR TREATED SORBENT
SULFUR CAPTURE, %
70
60
50
40
30
20
10
0.4
0.8
1.2
1.6
2.0
2.4
2.8
CALCIUM TO SULFUR RATIO
TREATED
LOWER BOUND
UPPER BOUND

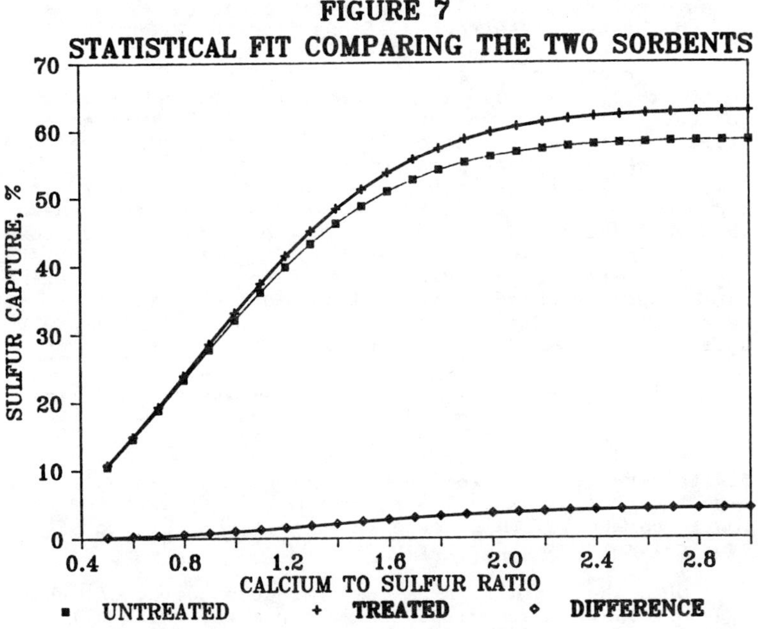
FIGURE 7
STATISTICAL FIT COMPARING THE TWO SORBENTS
SULFUR CAPTURE, %
70
60
50
40
30
20
10
0
0.4
0.8
1.2
1.6
2.0
2.4
2.8
CALCIUM TO SULFUR RATIO
UNTREATED
TREATED
DIFFERENCE

lines show the prediction for upper and lower bounds as defined by two standard deviations from the average. These figures show that LIMB easily meets its objective of 50% sulfur capture at a calcium to sulfur ratio of 2.0 or less. The average lines for both untreated and treated sorbents are shown together in Figure 7. The sorbent treated with calcium lignosulfonate is more effective than the untreated sorbent although the difference is small. Comparison of the lower bound of the treated sorbent with the upper bound of the untreated sorbent shows that there is a positive difference at calcium to sulfur ratios above 1.5. Unfortunately, there was insufficient time for testing before the scheduled outage to even begin optimization for either untreated or treated sorbent; consequently, it is too early to draw any conclusions about the ultimate difference between these two sorbents.

After the scheduled outage, a full scale humidifier will be brought on line. As noted above, the humidifier lowers the resistivity of the fly ash to the benefit of the ESP and reactivates unused lime for further SO_2 capture at low temperatures. Based on pilot plant experience, it is expected that an extra 10-15% of SO_2 will be captured at low temperature. This would raise total capture to 65-70% at a calcium to sulfur ratio of 2.0.

Once the humidifier is in continuous operation, the system will be tested in a parametric array which will identify optimum conditions for capture with and without treatment of the $Ca(OH)_2$ with calcium lignosulfonate. During this period, the ultimate comparison between treated and untreated sorbents will be determined. Also decided will be the optimum injection elevation, angle, and velocity. Once these have been established, the injection system can begin long-term testing to determine the effect of injection on boiler operation. Meanwhile, conditions for humidification will be varied to optimize the low temperature SO_2 capture. Eventually, all systems will be configured at their optimum operation for SO_2 capture to establish reliability of the LIMB-with-humidification process.

FIELD EVALUATION OF GAS REBURNING-SORBENT INJECTION TECHNOLOGY FOR NO_x AND SO_x EMISSION CONTROL FOR COAL FIRED UTILITY BOILERS

B. A. Folsom, W. Bartok, R. Payne and D. Moyeda
Energy and Environmental Research Corporation
Irvine, California 92718

ABSTRACT

Emissions of oxides of sulfur and nitrogen are thought to be responsible for acid rain deposition. A large number of existing pre-NSPS electric utility boilers fired with Midwestern and Eastern coals would be affected if acid rain control legislation is promulgated. To allow such boilers to meet potential emissions regulations with fuel flexibility and good operability, cost effective retrofit emission control technology is required. Gas Reburning-Sorbent Injection (GR-SI), a combination control technology that could be retrofitted to coal fired utility boilers, could reduce NO_x and SO_2 emissions by 60% and 50%, respectively.

A field test project has been initiated as part of the DOE's Clean Coal Technology program to demonstrate GR-SI on three pre-NSPS coal fired utility boilers in Illinois. The Gas Research Institute and the State of Illinois are the other participants in this project. The boilers selected are representative of pre-NSPS design types: one each of tangentially, wall, and cyclone fired units will be tested. Gas reburning consists of the staged introduction of fuel, with coal fired in the main heat release zone, and 15-20% of the heat input added as natural gas in the downstream reburn zone. This is followed by the burn-out zone where a dry, calcium based sorbent can also be injected for SO_2 pick-up. Alternatively, the sorbent may be injected further downstream in the boiler, or into the flue gas duct between the air heater and the precipitator. Following baseline and optimization testing, the GR-SI technology will be demonstrated in one-year field tests at each host site for a total project duration of fifty-four months.

INTRODUCTION

The cost of power generation from existing pulverized coal fired steam generating plants is strongly dependent upon coal quality and the requirements for environmental controls. Coal is not a pure hydrocarbon, it contains mineral matter, sulfur and nitrogen. Some impurities can cause operational problems due to slagging, fouling, erosion and corrosion which affect the availability and maintainability of the plant and consequently the cost of power. The impurities found in coal are converted to atmospheric pollutants during combustion. Mineral matter forms fly ash, sulfur is oxidized to sulfur dioxide and organically bound nitrogen is converted in part to nitric oxides. Acid precipitation in certain parts of the United States and Canada has been attributed to emissions of sulfur dioxide and nitric oxide from coal fired power plants. Proposed legislation to reduce the emission of these acid rain precursors would:

- Increase the cost of power due to the addition of air pollution control devices.
- Increase the use of low sulfur coals, thereby reducing the demand for high and medium sulfur content coals.

Consequently, there is a need for a low cost, retrofit acid rain precursor control technology which will provide the electric utility industry with the option to use local coals. Gas Reburning-Sorbent Injection is one such technology.

GAS REBURNING-SORBENT INJECTION TECHNOLOGY

Gas Reburning-Sorbent Injection (GR-SI) is an integration of two developmental technologies: reburning for NO_x control in conjunction with sorbent injection for SO_x control. GR-SI is a retrofit technology with applicability to all types of coal fired boilers. A schematic showing the application of GR-SI to a wall fired boiler is illustrated in Figure 1. Gas reburning involves the injection of natural gas above the main heat release zone to reduce the nitric oxide formed to molecular nitrogen. Low cost calcium based sorbents can be injected at one or more locations as the combustion gases pass from the radiant furnace, through the convective passes to the air heater.

The specific design of the GR-SI System depends on the boiler design, especially the firing configuration. For example, in a corner fired unit, the gas and sorbent injectors would be positioned at different locations in the upper furnace and in a cyclone fired boiler the gas and overfire air would be injected into the secondary furnace downstream of the cyclones with sorbent injected into the low temperature convective sections or into the duct downstream of the air heater.

REBURNING

The concept of NO reduction by flames has been recognized for over a decade. A flue gas incinerator was developed by the John Zink Company [(1)], and Sternling, Wendt and Mattovich[(2)] found that NO could be reduced in laboratory flat flames by injecting methane into

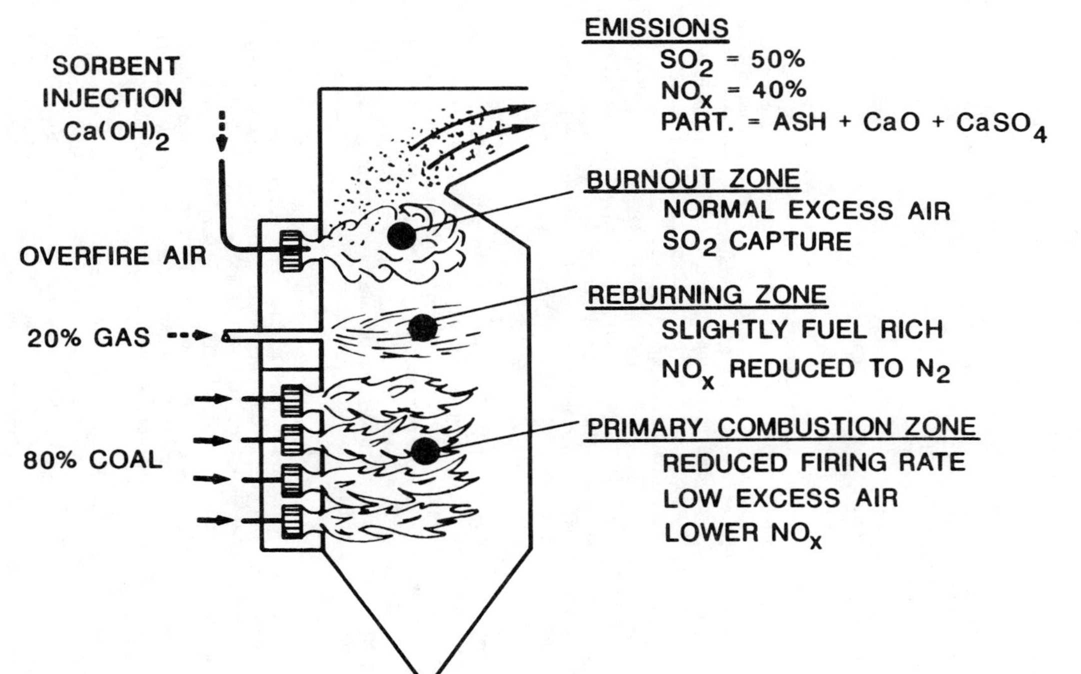

Figure 1. Gas reburning-sorbent injection technology applied to a wall fired boiler.

the combustion products. Reburning for in-furnace NO_x control has been applied to boilers in Japan [3,4] and work is being supported in the United States by EPA and EPRI as well as GRI [5,6,7]. Reburning denotes a process in which a fraction of the fuel bypasses the main heat release zone and is injected above the main burners to provide the fuel for reburning. The overall process can be divided into three zones:

1. Primary Combustion Zone: Approximately 80-85 percent of the heat is released in this zone under fuel lean conditions producing nitric oxide together with products of combustion which form the input to the reburning zone. In addition, if sufficient residence time is not provided in the main heat release zone, unburned fuel fragments may leave this zone and enter the reburning zone.

2. Reburning Zone: The reburning fuel (normally 15 to 20 percent of the total heat input to the boiler) is injected downstream of the primary zone to create a fuel rich, NO_x reduction zone. Nitric oxide formed in the main heat release zone reacts with the hydrocarbon fragments formed during the oxidation of the reburning fuel, primarily CH species, to produce intermediate species such as HCN and NH_3, and the nonpollutant species, N_2.

3. Burnout Zone: In the third and final zone, air is added to produce overall lean conditions and to oxidize all remaining fuel fragments. The remaining reduced nitrogen species (NH_3 + HCN) will either be oxidized to NO or reduced to molecular nitrogen.

Energy and Environmental Research Corporation (EER) has conducted extensive bench and pilot scale tests to evaluate the effects of process variables, establish design criteria and determine the NO_x emission control potential (8). The tests included evaluation of natural gas and coal as reburning fuels. Figure 2 compares the results obtained with these two reburning fuels in a pilot scale test facility. A high sulfur Illinois bituminous coal was fired in the primary zone. The reburning fuel (coal or gas) was injected downstream of the primary zone and burnout air was injected at 1622K (2460°F). The NO_x and CO emissions and ash were sampled from the exhaust. NO_x emissions decreased rapidly as the reburning fuel was increased from zero. Natural gas was more effective than coal, probably due to the bound nitrogen content of the coal which contributed additional NO_x. Natural gas reburning also provides distinct advantages in terms of CO emissions and carbon in ash. For gas reburning of 20%, CO emissions are actually less than for normal coal combustion.

The high CO emissions and carbon in ash for coal reburning are symptoms of insufficient residence time for burnout of the coal particles. This is a significant problem limiting the application of coal reburning in pre-NSPS utility boilers where available residence time is limited.

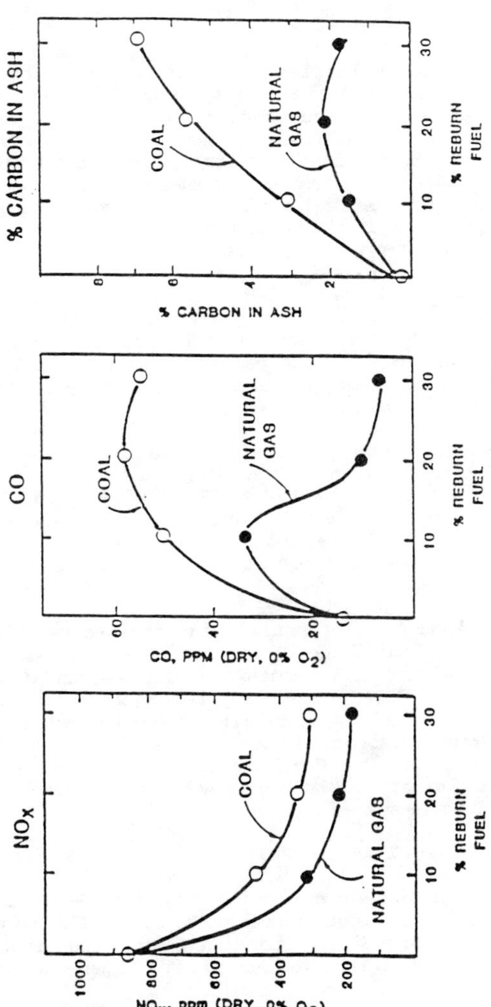

Figure 2. Benefits of natural gas reburning when applied to coal fired furnaces.

SORBENT INJECTION

As shown in Figure 1, the reburning process can be combined with sorbent injection for SO_2 control. The burnout airstream can be used as a carrier for the sorbent medium for both reburning and sorbent injection. It is important to mix the burnout air and the sorbent as quickly and effectively as possible. The design requirements of both processes are similar.

The use of calcium-based sorbents with furnace injection for SO_2 control has been studied extensively. The process involves calcination of a calcium-based sorbent, which may be either a carbonate or hydrate, producing calcium oxide. This calcium oxide reacts with SO_2 and oxygen in the sulfation zone to produce solid calcium sulfate which can be removed together with the flyash in an electrostatic precipitator or bag filter. Two major parameters control the utilization of the calcium in the sorbent and thus the cost effectiveness of the process. These are:

- The reactivity of the calcium oxide formed by calcination. This is strongly dependent upon the surface area of the calcine which is a function of the sorbent type and the thermal history of the calcine. Reactivity tends to decrease as the sorbent particle temperature is increased due to grain growth.

- The residence time of the calcine under conditions conducive to sulfation. Significant sulfation cannot occur above approximately 1500K (2250°F) and the rate of sulfation becomes negligible below approximately 1140K (1600°F). Thus, the residence time of the active particle within this temperature window is important in the sulfur capture process.

Figure 3 summarizes pilot scale data obtained by EER, which illustrate the potential of GR-SI for combined NO_x/SO_x control. These data indicate that 60 percent NO_x reductions can be achieved from typical pre-NSPS NO_x levels. SO_2 reductions in excess of 50 percent can be achieved by combining reburning with sorbent injection, if a hydrated sorbent is used. These data are typical of those obtained with optimized Gas Reburning-Sorbent Injection for a wide spectrum of primary fuels and they appear to be generally achievable in full scale systems.

OVERVIEW OF GR-SI FIELD EVALUATION PROJECT

EER is conducting a field evaluation project to demonstrate the technical feasibility and cost effectiveness of GR-SI. The project is funded jointly by the U.S. Department of Energy, The Gas Research Institute and the State of Illinois Department of Energy and Natural Resources.

The demonstration of GR-SI is not intended as the first generation of a specific technology, but rather it will build upon the results of several individual technology demonstrations now being conducted by the EPA and others. The focus of this program is to

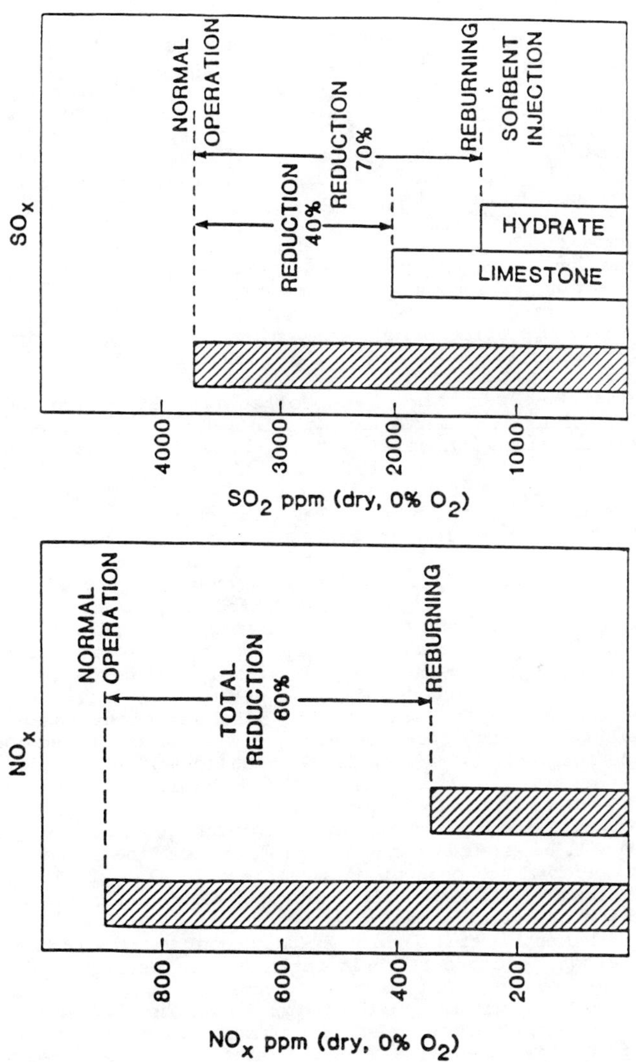

Figure 3. Pilot scale results on NO_x/SO_x reduction by GR-SI.

demonstrate the application and performance of a combined technology which will allow cost effective control of acid rain precursors.

The project was initiated in June 1987 and will be completed in 54 months. The project includes the following three phases:

- Phase 1 - Design and Permitting. This initial phase will culminate in the detailed design of gas reburning and sorbent injection systems for each of three host sites. A program plan will be prepared for equipment construction and demonstration testing. An industry panel will be established to initiate technology transfer. The gas reburning-sorbent injection system designs will be presented to the industry panel.

- Phase 2 - Construction and Startup. Following approval by the funding participants and the utility hosts, the gas reburning and sorbent injection equipment will be installed and checked out at each host site. Plans for optimizing boiler operating parameters consistent with the emission targets will be presented to the industry panel.

- Phase 3 - Operation, Data Collection, Reporting and Disposition. Each host unit will be tested over a range of conditions with several U.S. coals, culminating in approximately one-year long-term evaluations. The results will be compiled in guideline manuals which will be made available to industry. The project results will be presented to the industry panel.

A major feature of the program is that GR-SI will be demonstrated on all three types of coal fired boilers which are typical of pre-NSPS designs (i.e., wall, corner, and cyclone fired units). Each host site is being considered separately, based on its unique design parameters, operating history and performance requirements. These factors are being evaluated by reviewing historical operating and performance data and plant design specifications. At each site, field tests will be conducted to quantify performance and emissions over the normal duty cycle. Several alternative and complimentary technologies will be considered: gas reburning for NO_x control, a range of approaches to sorbent injection for SO_2 control, and coal cleaning. A technology combination will be selected for each site which meets the emissions control and performance objectives at minimum total cost. This process definition will include specification of all major components and projection of performance for each host site. EER will also prepare detailed engineering designs including complete construction plans, drawings, equipment specifications, cost estimates and construction schedules. All necessary permits will be obtained. Phase 1 will culminate in the preparation of a comprehensive program plan. It will detail the design and performance projections for the equipment to be installed at each of the three host sites, present construction plans and propose a demonstration plan for quantifying the performance at each host site. This plan will be carried out in Phases 2 and 3.

Table 1 summarizes the characteristics of each unit and presents the preliminary approach to optimization of the GR-SI technology. The three host sites selected are relatively small utility boilers now in commercial operation in the State of Illinois. All of them fire Midwest bituminous coals and are equipped with cold side electrostatic precipitators for particulate emission control. These units differ in several significant respects:

- o Firing configuration and capacity.
- o Electrostatic precipitator size.
- o Fuel characteristics.
- o Emission constraints.

The tangential and cyclone fired units fire high sulfur Illinois coals. The emission control goals for these units are reductions in NO_x and SO_2 emissions of 5Ø and 6Ø% respectively. These reductions are not required to meet existing regulations; however they could be used to meet acid rain control regulations when (and if) they are promulgated.

The wall fired unit has no NO_x emission limit but blends high sulfur Illinois coal with a low sulfur Kentucky coal to meet an SO_2 emission limit. The SO_2 emission control goal for this unit is to increase the fraction of high sulfur coal fired from 15 to above 5Ø% while maintaining SO_2 emissions in compliance. NO_x emissions will be reduced 6Ø% as in the other two units.

STATUS

Phase 1 - Design and Permitting is now in progress. Initial efforts have focused on review of the host unit design and operating data and initial evaluations of alternate approaches to applying GR-SI. Figure 4 shows the preliminary approach for the wall-fired host unit. The upper row of burners would be converted to dual purpose coal burners/gas injectors. During normal operation, the burners would fire only coal. For GR-SI, gas would be injected without combustion air to form the reburning zone. The burnout air would be injected in the upper furnace above the burners along the front wall between water wall platens. Air injection from the rear wall is also being considered. In this unit, the optimum temperature for sorbent injection (225Ø°F) occurs near the nose and above the burnout air injectors. Therefore, separate sorbent injection ports will be required.

EER has evaluated the NO_x and SO_2 control potential for this GR-SI configuration using process models developed under EPA and GRI programs. The results are illustrated in Figure 5. NO_x control of 67% is predicted (which exceeds the project goal of 6Ø%). SO_2 control of 5Ø% is predicted for sorbent injection alone at a calcium/sulfur molar ratio of 2.Ø. Including the additional SO_2 control due to the gas reburning results in 7Ø% control (which exceeds the project goal of 5Ø%). The net effect is that the unit can fire a significantly greater fraction of high sulfur coal and still meet existing emission restrictions.

TABLE 1. HOST SITE CHARACTERISTICS

GENERAL UTIITY STATION, UNIT LOCATION: STATE CAPACITY (MW)	ILLINOIS POWER HENNEPIN, 1 ILLINOIS 80	CILCO EDWARDS, 1 ILLINOIS 117	CWLP LAKESIDE, 7 ILLINOIS 40
BOILER FIRING CONFIGURATION CAPACITY (10^3 lb/hr) MANUFACTURER	TANGENTIAL 585 CE	FRONT WALL 850 RILEY	CYCLONE 320 B & W
PRECIPITATOR LOCATION SIZE (SCA) MANUFACTURER	COLD SIDE 223 BUELL	COLD SIDE 137 AMERICAN STANDARD	COLD SIDE 333-1000 SMIDTH
FUEL COAL TYPE SULFUR (%) GAS AVAILABILITY	ILLINOIS, BIT 3.8 YES, 100%	BLEND ILLINOIS, BIT KENTUCKY, BIT 1.0 0.7 MILE	ILLINOIS, BIT 3.6 0.5 MILE
EMISSIONS CONTROL APPROACH NO_x APPROACH CONTROL (%) SO_2 APPROACH CONTROL (%) ESP ENHANCEMENT	GAS REBURNING 60 UPPER FURNACE INJECTION 50 HUMIDIFICATION	GAS REBURNING 60 UPPER FURNACE INJECTION 0 HUMIDIFICATION SO_3 INJECTION	GAS REBURNING 60 DUCT INJECTION 50 NONE

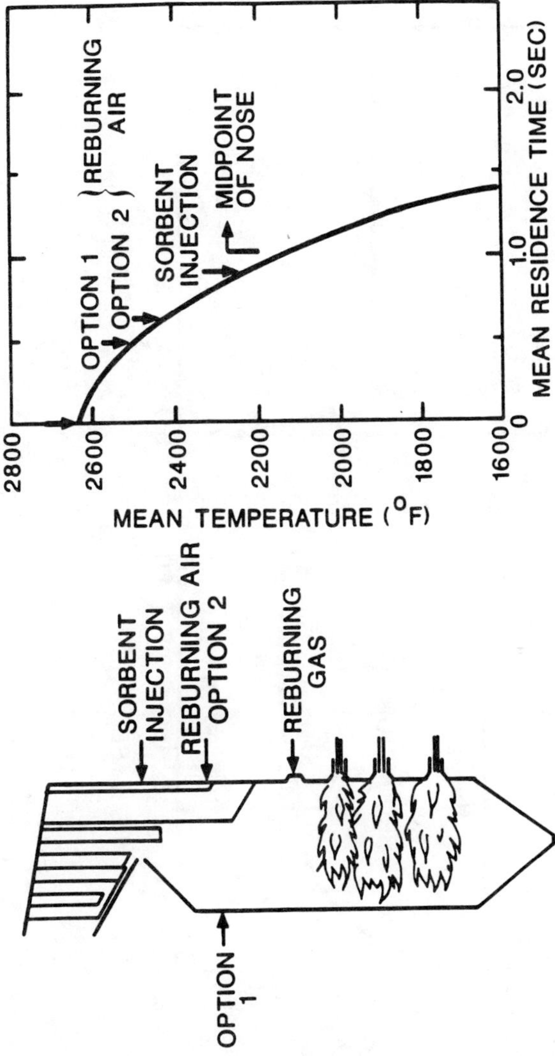

Figure 4. GR-SI process concept for wall fired host unit.

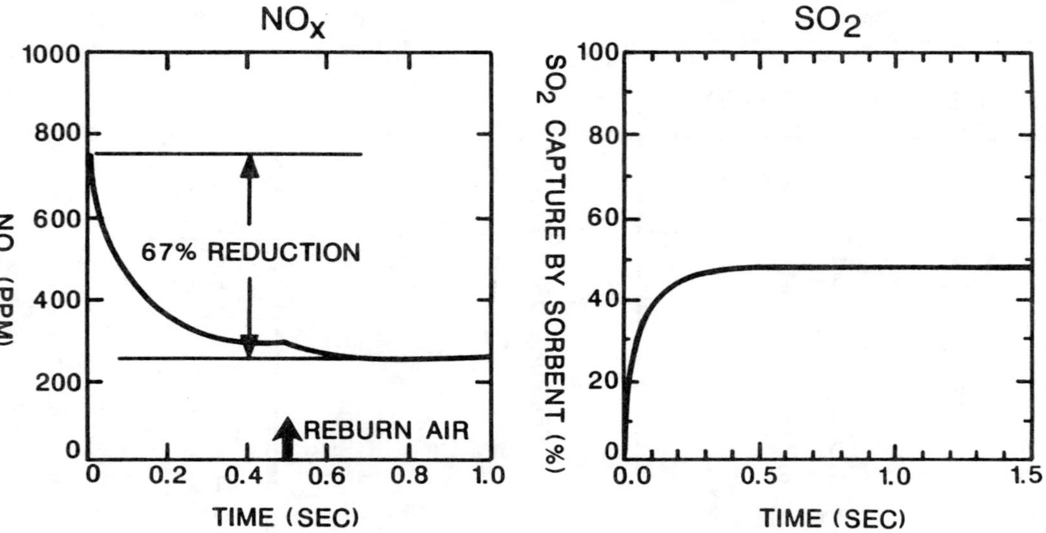

Figure 5. Predicted performance for GR-SI on the wall fired host unit.

Similar evaluations have been conducted for the tangential and cyclone fired host units. All three units have the potential for meeting the NO_x and SO_2 goals.

Current efforts are focusing on more extensive evaluations of these units. This includes construction of scale models of the three units with isothermal flow tests and mixing studies. These results will be used in three dimensional furnace heat transfer modeling. Baseline field test of each unit will be conducted early in 1988 and the Phase 1 design is expected to be complete by Fall 1988.

SUMMARY

In summary a successfully complete demonstration project will establish the following benefits of GR-SI technology:

- NO_x emissions can be reduced by 60 percent. This can be achieved without the need for modifications to the original firing equipment, thus eliminating problems associated with retrofitting low NO_x burners. Gas is ideal as a reburning fuel because it can be distributed evenly, it is more effective in reducing NO_x than coal and requires less residence time in the reburning zone.
- SO_x emissions can be reduced by 50 percent, and because the two technologies are combined the burnout air may be used as a sorbent transport medium.
- The sorbent requirements to provide a given reduction in SO_2 emissions are reduced in direct proportion to the amount of gas co-firing. This reduces the load on the particulate control devices.
- Gas reburning can be applied in conjunction with various sorbent injection technologies such as in-furnace or duct injection as well as with coal cleaning.
- GR-SI provides electric utilities with flexibility in coal selection to meet acid rain control legislation.
- GR-SI has the potential to improve the operability of some pulverized coal fired boilers, particularly to reduce problems of fouling and slagging.
- GR-SI is retrofit technology which can be applied to pre-NSPS wall, corner, and cyclone fired boilers. These units produce 12 million tons of SO_2 per year in the U.S., a significant fraction of the total manmade emissions.

ACKNOWLEDGEMENTS

The information presented in this paper is related to work funded by the U.S. Department of Energy, Pittsburgh Energy Technology Center, through Cooperative Agreement No. DE-FC-22-87PC79796; the Gas Research Institute through Contract No. 5087-254-1494; and the State of Illinois, Department of Energy and Natural Resources, through a Coal and Energy Development Agreement.

REFERENCES

1. Reed, R. D. Process for the Disposal of Nitrogen Oxide. John Zinc Company, U.S. Patent 1,274,637, 1969.

2. Sternling, C. V., J. O. L. Wendt, and M. A. Mattovich, Fourteenth Symposium (International) on Combustion, p. 897, The Combustion Institute, p. 897, 1973.

3. Takahashi, Y., et al. Development of Mitsubishi "MACT" In-Furnace NO_x Removal Process. Presented at U.S.-Japan NO_x Information Exchange, Tokyo, Japan, May 25-30, 1981.

4. Okigami, N., et al. Multistage Combustion Method for Inhibiting Formation of Nitrogen Oxides. U.S. Patent 4,395,223, 1983.

5. Greene, S. B., S. L. Chen, W. D. Clark, M. P. Heap, D. W. Pershing, and W. R. Seeker. "Bench-Scale Process Evaluation of Reburning and Sorbent Injection for In-Furnace NO_x/SO_x Reduction." EPA-600/7-85-012, March, 1985.

6. Greene, S. B., S. L. Chen, D. W. Pershing, M. P. Heap, and W. R. Seeker. "Bench-Scale Process Evaluation of Reburning for In-Furnace NO_x Reduction." ASME Paper No. 84-JPGC-APC-9, 1984.

7. Seeker, W. R., et al. "Controlling Pollutant Emissions from Coal and Oil Combustors Through the Supplemental Use of Natural Gas." Final Report, GRI 5083-251-0905, 1985.

8. Bartok, W. and B. A. Folsom. "Control of NO_x and SO_2 Emissions By Gas Reburning-Sorbent Injection." American Institute of Chemical Engineers Annual Meeting. New York, November, 1987.

OVERVIEW OF COMMERCIAL GASIFICATION PROSPECTS

Dr. James C. Selover
Vice President and Manager, Research Programs

Jimmie R. Bowden
Manager, Development Programs

Jon Pietruszkiewicz
Advanced Fossil Power Manager

Bechtel National, Inc.

Although public interest in coal gasification has greatly diminished in the last five years, significant technical and commercial progress has been made. A large number of operating hours have been accumulated making electricity, high-Btu gas, and chemicals in large scale commercial and demonstration coal gasification facilities. The technical feasibility of gasifying U. S. coals is now accepted and improvement in the operation of existing plants is producing the cost reductions expected. Further, technology under development will lead to additional reductions in production costs. Even so, adequate supplies of reasonably priced crude oil and natural gas have slowed the commercial application of coal gasification and widespread adoption of the technology is not expected in the next several years. Full scale commercial applications are expected, however, as fuel prices rise over the next decade. The first such applications are likely to be in the electric utility industry. A number of natural gas fired combined cycle systems will be installed soon with design considerations built in to accomodate future addition of gasification.

During the past decade, the electric utility industry has passed through a period of dramatic change and uncertainty which has significantly altered its needs. There is now a need for smaller, low cost, fuel-flexible, clean, and reliable plants for both new electric generating capacity and emissions retrofit situations. Coal gasification has demonstrated its flexibility to meet this challenge. This paper will discuss: the factors that will determine the timing and rate at which coal gasification will enter American industry; potential utility applications, and; the current status of the technology. It will focus on coal gasification to produce fuels since the ultimate market for chemicals from coal is a much smaller one.

MARKET ENTRY[1]

The two most prominent commercial scale applications of coal gasification in the U. S. are the Great Plains high-Btu gas plant using the Lurgi gasification technology and the Cool Water gasification combined cycle power plant using the Texaco gasification technology. Both are an outstanding technical success and reliable production has been achieved for a number of years. However, the commercial future of each is clouded by the current low price of natural gas. Even though both plants can be replicated with lower capital and operating costs because of the knowledge gained in the two pioneer plants, this won't happen until natural gas prices increase considerably or there is a return to some form of subsidized production such as that which assisted in the creation of the plants originally.

Technical progress continues in all three principal categories of coal gasification technology; entrained, fluidized and moving bed gasifiers. Process development is also continuing in very important areas of downstream gas processing and utilization of partially gasified coal or partially purified gas. Several advances at laboratory and larger scale offer the potential for improved operation and reduction of both capital and operating cost when commercialized. None, however, appear to be significant enough to vastly impact the timing of commercialization about to be discussed.

High-Btu Gas

Although the Great Plains plant is performing at or above design outputs and production costs continue to decline, it is not competitive with current natural gas prices. Operating costs (exclusive of the original capital investment) are $2.70/10^6 Btu, with a goal of being able to achieve $2.50/10^6 Btu by mid-1989[2]. While it may be possible to keep the plant operating after current government subsidies expire, it is unlikely that investment of capital in new unsubsidized high-Btu gasification plants can be justified until natural gas and oil prices rise significantly; say over $40 per barrel of crude oil.

Economics for high-Btu plants are poor because:

- High-Btu gas must compete with natural gas at field price levels.

- The regulatory climate for natural gas pricing has changed radically in the last five years.

- There is a significant additional capital and operating cost associated with converting clean, medium-Btu gas from the coal gasifier to the high-Btu gas required for commingling with natural gas in gas transmission systems.

It is unlikely that enough improvements in economics can be made to make high-Btu gas from coal competitive for widespread use until after the year 2000, when it is expected that crude oil prices will begin rising rapidly.

Medium-Btu Gas For Power Generation

The prospects for the production of electric power with coal gasification are somewhat better since low- or medium-Btu gas can be used to directly fuel electric generating units. Thus, the methanation step required for high-Btu gas production and its attendant capital and operating cost is not necessary. And, as a result, the relative economics of coal derived gas versus natural gas are significantly improved for electric power generation.

While it is true that like the Great Plains high-Btu coal gasification plant the Cool Water gasification combined cycle demonstration plant is not projected to be economic to run without government subsidy, a study of the actual Cool Water costs recently released by the Cool Water Program[3] indicates that commercial scale facilities will have much lower capital and operating costs. The demonstration aspects of the Cool Water project have contributed to higher capital costs, higher costs for coal and oxygen supply, and higher operating staff requirements than would be required in a subsequent commercial facility.

There are a number of factors other than cost that also support a belief that widespread gasification for power generation will appear before high-Btu gasification, and possibly in the next decade.

- Electric utilities have a better regulatory climate than gas transmission companies to blend higher cost power from new sources with lower cost supplies, even though that capability has been eroded over time because of nuclear plant difficulties
- Advanced gas turbines which are especially effective with coal sourced gas are being readied for production.
- Conventional gas turbine combined cycles can be designed and built to be easily retrofitted by the addition of a coal gasifier. Plant investments can be made in stages, thus improving cash flow and reducing risk.
- Tight emission standards are more easily met with gasification systems than direct coal combustion technologies.
- Technical developments in most types of gasifiers apply as well to gasification combined cycle plants as to high-Btu plants.
- Technical developments in hot gas cleanup apply more readily to gasification combined cycle plants than to high-Btu plants.

Above all, there is a genuine interest within the utility industry in eventually installing phased gasification combined cycle units. In phased construction, a gasification combined cycle plant can be implemented in stages: first, one or more gas turbines supply peaking power, followed by the addition of a bottoming cycle for intermediate duty, and finally, addition of the gasification plant to convert to coal-firing when fuel economics dictate. The phasing schedule may be advanced or delayed to closely match load growth. This will be a very important factor for the next generation of utility plants. There may also be in some extreme cases, a need for utilities to retrofit existing boilers or turbines in repowering schemes to gain incremental power or to solve a stringent environmental requirement.

UTILITY APPLICATIONS FOR COAL GASIFICATION

During the past two decades, coal gasification for electric power generation has been studied extensively for a broad range of new and retrofit plant applications.

New Plants

In the case of new generation facilities, studies have evaluated gasification in combination both with conventional steam cycles and with gas turbine combined cycle configurations. In addition, coal gasification facilities have also been examined for fueling fuel cell power plants and compressed air energy storage plants (called G-CAES plants).

Gasification applications of particular interest for new facilities include:

- Phased construction of a combined cycle plant initially fueled with natural gas or distillate followed by a later addition of a coal gasification plant
- Integrated gasification combined cycle (GCC) plants
- A stand-alone gasification plant supplying one or more power generating plants

In the near term, it can be anticipated that combined cycles will comprise a major share of new generation capacity. They are efficient, can be installed cheaply in small modules, and have short lead times. When used in conjunction with phased addition of coal gasification, they provide a high degree of planning flexibility. They can take advantage of low premium fuel prices now available, but convert to coal later.

The focus in the past has been on gasification combined cycle plants with high thermal integration between the gasification plant and the combined cycle steam system. This approach can result in excellent overall plant heat rates. However, most fully-integrated designs are not as amenable to phased construction. They require significant capital preinvestment in the combined cycle phase, such as an oversized steam turbine, in order to afford the integration efficiency after the addition of gasification. Current studies are now developing concepts which achieve the same high plant efficiencies, yet do not require unnecessary capital preinvestment.

A stand-alone gasification plant supplying one or more power generating plants may be an attractive alternative in areas where it is difficult to site coal-fired facilities. A number of medium-Btu retrofitted combined cycle units could be connected by pipeline to a centrally located, remote gasification plant.

Compared to conventional coal-fired power plants, gasification combined cycles exhibit:

- Higher fuel efficiency and equivalent availability
- Reduced solid wastes
- Lower SO_2, NO_x and particulate emissions with existing technology
- Reduced land requirements
- Lower water consumption
- No requirement for SO_2 sorbent or other raw materials

Bechtel work has shown that on a generic basis GCC plants are economically competitive with conventional coal fired plants, with their competitive position improving in applications which include:

- Strict environmental standards
- Availability of low cost, high sulfur coal
- Uncertainty regarding load growth, and prices and availability of premium fuels - thus leading to phased construction

Table 1 provides a comparison of the characteristics for two GCC plant designs with those of a conventional pulverized coal-fired plant. In general, GCC plants have competitive heat rates and are generally lower in environmental intrusions and resource requirements.

The table also compares the performance of a GCC plant using current cold gas cleanup technology with that of an advanced concept using hot gas cleanup. Current sulfur removal processes require that the hot gas exiting the gasifier be cooled prior to sulfur removal. The gas is then reheated before gas turbine-firing to improve turbine efficiency. Cooling the gas requires rather expensive heat exchangers and also introduces a cycle efficiency penalty. In the hot gas cleanup design, the gas exiting the gasifiers is scrubbed of sulfur and other contaminants at or near gasifier temperatures, followed by direct combustion in the gas turbine. A Bechtel in-house study predicts that hot gas cleanup may improve overall heat rate by about 5% and reduce capital cost by as much as 20%.

Hot gas cleanup and other advanced concepts promise to simplify gasification plants, reducing both capital and operating costs. Because gasification is a competitive, relatively young technology, it can be expected that this development will occur in rather significant increments, in contrast to the smaller increments experienced by mature technologies such as pulverized coal-fired plants. For this reason, gasification should become increasingly attractive compared to alternative, traditional technologies.

Retrofit Applications

Examples of retrofit applications which have received utility attention are:

- Refueling of existing oil- and gas-fired boilers to burn coal-derived gas. These applications were generally evaluated in anticipation of high differential fuel prices between the premium fuels and coal.

- Refueling of existing coal-fired boilers to burn coal-derived gas. The motivation here has generally been anticipation of strict environmental requirements for retrofit of a given unit or group of units.

- Retrofit of power plants originally designed to burn coal, but later converted to oil to meet requirements of clean-air laws. These applications were again generally assessed in response to high and uncertain differentials in prices between premium fuels and coal.

- Repowering of existing power plants with gas turbines firing coal-derived gas. Needs for new capacity, fuel price differentials, and environmental constraints have all served as a stimulus for these analyses.

For these retrofit applications, medium-Btu gas is more applicable than low-Btu gas because it can be more readily used in existing equipment without significant modification. Generally, medium-Btu gas can be fired in gas or oil-fired boilers, gas turbines, and process furnaces with little or no derating required.(4) Medium-Btu gas can also be transported economically over greater distances than low-Btu gas (typically 100 vs 30 miles).

CURRENT STATUS OF COAL GASIFICATION TECHNOLOGY

The last several years have seen a dramatic increase in the number of gasification processes entering large-scale demonstration and commercialization. Developers of these projects, recognizing the important role gasification will play in the utility industry, are also more closely gearing them to utility applications, rather than to the industrial focus of the past.

Gasification processes can be roughly classified into the following three types:

- Entrained-flow: These gasifiers typically produce crude gas at a temperature of approximately 2,000°F to 2,800°F and produce gases high in hydrogen and CO. The Texaco and Shell processes are typical entrained flow gasifiers. The Dow gasifier is a two stage entrained flow gasifier that provides a lower temperature gas, closer in temperature to the fluidized bed gasifiers.

- Fluidized-bed: These gasifiers yield crude gas at temperatures typically in the 1,600°F to 1,800°F range. The Kellogg Rust-Westinghouse (KRW), High-Temperature Winkler (HTW) and U-Gas gasifiers are the more advanced concepts in this category.

- Moving-bed: Moving-bed gasifiers produce crude gas at lower temperatures (1,000°F) and typically yield some methane and small amounts of higher hydrocarbons and combustible tars in addition to hydrogen and CO. The British Gas Lurgi and KILnGAS gasifiers are of this type.

Each type of gasifier offers certain advantages and disadvantages over the others. Proper selection of a process for a specific application depends on a number of factors including:

- Range of properties and costs of coal feedstocks available

- Tradeoff between plant efficiency, dispatchability, and capital cost

- Design flexibility to allow variable degree of thermal integration between the steam cycle and the gasification plant

- Turndown and cycling requirements

- Oxygen vs. air-blown capabilities

Table 2 provides an indication of the development scale of a number of the more advanced gasification systems available for electric utility applications. Brief descriptions of these systems and their development status are indicated below.

Texaco Coal Gasification Process (TGCP)[5,6]

The Texaco gasifier is a pressurized, slurry-fed, entrained flow, slagging gasifier. Feed coal is ground and mixed with water to form a coal slurry which is pumped into the gasifier burner where it reacts with oxygen. The gasification reactions take place at temperatures between 2,300°F and 2,800°F. A gas high in hydrogen and carbon monoxide is formed with no liquid hydrocarbon production. The crude gas leaving the gasifier contains a small amount of unburned carbon and molten slag. Depending on the plant design, this gas stream is either directly quenched in water or cooled in radiant and convective boilers for sensible heat recovery prior to particulate water scrubbing. The molten slag is quenched in a water pool at the bottom of the gasifier.

Initial development of the TGCP was conducted in the 1940's. Since the 1970's work has continued at Texaco's Montebello pilot plant facility. In 1977, Ruhrkohle A.G./Ruhrchemie started up a 165 tpd Texaco coal gasification pilot plant at Oberhausen-Holten, West Germany. This pilot plant has now been replaced by a 750 tpd commercial plant providing syngas for oxo-chemical production. Three other commercial scale applications of the TGCP exist; a 900 tpd unit at the Tennessee Eastman chemicals-from-coal plant, the 100 MW (net), 1,000 tpd Cool Water gasification combined cycle project, and the 1600 tpd (total) UBE Ammonia Coal Gasification Plant in Japan.

The Cool Water Coal Gasification Program is of the most significance to the electric power industry. This 100 MWe IGCC power plant, the first such plant in the U.S., is providing invaluable information to the utility industry, with specific program objectives in each of the following areas:

- Evaluate system performance at commercial scale and under actual utility operating conditions.
- Verify gas quality and environmental performance.
- Assess integrated system controllability at full load, part load, and during load following.
- Maintain complete records for equipment reliability and system availability determinations.
- Demonstrate feedstock flexibility using a variety of coals.
- Establish operating, maintenance, safety and training procedures for future plants.
- Develop a comprehensive technical and economic data base to support system scale-up to large commercial plant size.

The project has been highly successful, meeting or exceeding target performance objectives. Cool Water program sponsors are Texaco Inc., Southern California Edison Co., the Electric Power Research Institute, Bechtel Power Corp., General Electric, and Japan Cool Water Program partnership.

Dow Gasification Process[7,8,9]

The Dow Gasification Process uses a pressurized, entrained flow, slagging, slurry-fed gasifier with a continuous slag removal system. Gasification occurs in a two stage reactor which provides for efficient heat recovery and, according to Dow, high efficiency on low rank coals. The overall process is described by Dow as follows.

The coal slurry is fed at multiple points within the reactor and mixed with oxygen in the burner nozzles. The feed rate of oxygen is controlled to maintain the reactor temperature above the ash fusion point to insure slag removal. Under these conditions, high carbon conversion is achieved by partial combustion to produce synthetic gas consisting principally of hydrogen, carbon monoxide, carbon dioxide, and water. The sulfur is converted almost totally to hydrogen sulfide with small amounts of carbonyl sulfide. The gasifier system operates in such a manner that essentially no tars, oils, or phenols are produced. The ash is fused in the flame, direct quenched in a water bath and removed from the bottom of the reactor as a slurry through a special pressure reducing system. The slag is dewatered and stored.

The gas exiting the gasifier system is further cooled by a conventional heat recovery boiler to near its saturation temperature. The high pressure superheated steam produced can be used for power generation via steam turbines or to drive the compressors in the air separation plant. Particulate removal is achieved by water scrubbing the partially cooled gas. All particulates removed are recycled to the gasifier. The scrubbed gas is then cooled through a series of heat exchangers before entering the acid gas removal process. The amount of low level heat recovery is economically balanced with the heat requirements of both the gasifier and the acid gas removal process.

The Dow gasifier was first tested in 1979 in a 12 tpd pilot plant and later in a 400 tpd semi-plant, both air blown. The pilot plant was upgraded to a 36 tpd unit and both plants were converted to oxygen-blown designs. A 1600 tpd capacity semi-plant was constructed incorporating the improved Dow process. The gas from the semi-plant was used to fuel a 15 MW gas turbine. Over 15,000 hours of operation was conducted before the plant was shut down.

The Dow Syngas Project, which started up in April 1987 is Dow's first commercial-scale unit and the largest single train gasifier in the world. Its capacity is 2400 tpd on Western coal or 2900 tpd on lignite. The gasification plant output is used to fuel 5-year old Westinghouse W-501D5 gas turbines modified to burn medium-Btu gas. Dow has thus far fired the gas turbines at 75% load with coal-derived gas but is currently limited by fuel nozzle restrictions. Through October 17, 1752 hours of operation had been accumulated on the gasifier and the availability averaged 42%. Dow Chemical Company is the sole sponsor of the project with a price guarantee commitment provided by the U.S. Synthetic Fuels Corporation.

Shell Coal Gasification Process (SCGP)[10,11,12]

The Shell gasification process incorporates a dry feed, pressurized, entrained flow, slagging gasifier. The feed coal is pulverized and dried (typically to about 7-9% moisture) and then pressurized in lock hoppers. It is fed into the gasifier by dense phase conveying with nitrogen. The coal reacts with oxygen (and steam, if required) at temperatures of 2500°F - 3000°F. Most of the slag is quenched. The gas contains a small quantity of unburned carbon and a fraction of molten ash. To make the ash non-sticky, the hot gas leaving the reactor is quenched with cold recycled gas. Further cooling takes place in the waste heat recovery section, consisting of radiant and convective cells, where high-pressure superheated steam is generated. Alternatively, the hot gas can be quenched with water to cool the gas and remove solidified particles. The gas is passed through a system of cyclones and water scrubbers to remove the fly slag and particulates. The system is normally designed to be self-sustaining in water requirements, requiring only loss make-up, and thus minimizing the volume of undesirable wastewater effluent.

The gasifier is relatively insensitive to coal properties, such as size, caking tendency, moisture, sulfur, oxygen, ash, etc. The gas produced is essentially hydrogen and carbon monoxide.

Shell Internationale Petroleum Maatschappij (SIPM) B.V. began work on coal gasification in 1972. A pressurized entrained-flow slagging coal gasifier was built at Shell's Amsterdam laboratories. This six tpd process development unit has been operating since 1976. A larger 150 tpd pilot plant was built at the Shell Harburg Refinery near Hamburg, West Germany. This larger unit has been operating successfully since 1978. Both facilities have demonstrated the technical feasibility of the process through more than 5500 hours of operation in which more than 27,000 tons of coal were gasified. A wide variety of coal feedstocks were tested, including bituminous, subbituminous and lignite. U.S. coals tested in the pilot plant include Pittsburgh and Illinois bituminous coals, Wyoming subbituminous, and Texas lignite.

In April, Shell announced the completion of construction of a SCGP demonstration plant at Deer Park, Texas. Shell later stated that the plant reached full design capacity after two days of operation. The plant includes coal receiving and preparation facilities, a high pressure gasifier with high temperature heat recovery, solids removal, and gas and water treating to provide clean medium-Btu gas and high value steam to be consumed within Shell's adjacent manufacturing complex. Shell Internationale Petroleum, Shell International Research, Deutsche Shell, Shell Oil and Shell Development, EPRI, and Combustion Engineering's Lummus Crest subsidiary are jointly participating in the project.

The plant is designed to run a wide range of feeds from bituminous, at a rate of about 250 tpd (as received) to high ash lignites at a rate of about 400 tpd (as received). The plant objective is to confirm equipment life and scale-up information necessary for commercial design of the process.

PRENFLO(13,14,15)

The PRENFLO (PRessurized ENtrained FLOw) process is a dry feed, pressurized, entrained flow gasifier. Finely ground and dried coal enters the gasifier through a lockhopper system using a conveyor gas (N_2, CO_2, or possibly raw fuel gas). High purity oxygen reacts with the coal to form a medium-Btu gas. Part of the coal ash melts, leaving the reactor as a fluid at the bottom tap. The remainder of the ash is entrained with the raw gas. A recycle gas quench section then cools and solidifies the ash particles to avoid fouling in the downstream heat recovery steam generator which produces high pressure, superheated steam. Cyclone separation then removes 95% of the fly ash, followed by more heat exchange and finally a wet, two-stage venturi scrubber system to remove the rest of the fly ash.

The process has been developed by Gesellschaft fur Kohle-Technologie mbH (GKT), a subsidiary of Krupp Koppers GmbH. Both the PRENFLO and the Shell process have evolved from the Koppers-Totzek (KT) process developed in the 1940's. Between 1976 and 1981, GKT and Shell cooperated on the development of a 150 tpd gasification test facility. After that joint effort, each continued development separately, resulting in the SCGP and PRENFLO processes.

GKT commissioned a 50 tpd demonstration gasifier in Furstenhausen, West Germany in August 1986. Over a three year period, they intend to test and evaluate performance and reliability of the design. Along with other special component testing, they plan to run an installation for turbine blade testing. This will be done in cooperation with Kraftwerk Union.

The test unit results will also be used for engineering work now under way for a 1000 metric ton per day PRENFLO module, designed specifically for IGCC application. Krupp Koppers and Kraftwerk Union are working together to develop this 150 MW design.

High Temperature Winkler (HTW)[16,17]

The High-Temperature Winkler gasifier is a pressurized, non-slagging, fluidized bed gasifier. The feed coal is dried, crushed to less than 0.25 inches, then pressurized in lock hoppers. It is fed into the gasifier by screw feeders. The coal reacts with air or oxygen and steam at temperatures between 1600°F and 1900°F. Approximately, 3 to 6 percent of the carbon remains unburned. Most of the char is drawn off as an agglomerate from the bottom of the gasifier. The remaining char is entrained in the gas leaving the gasifier. Some of the oxidant is fed above the fluidized bed to burn up residual hydrocarbons. The emerging hot raw gas passes through a series of cyclones to remove most of the entrained char. Solids removed in the first cyclone are recycled to the gasifier. Solids removed from the second cyclone are depressurized and discharged by screw feeders. Hot gas from the cyclones passes into a convective cooler in which heat is extracted from the gas to generate steam. The cooled gas is scrubbed with water to remove residual particulates. The scrubbed gas then enters a low level cooling system to be cooled to the temperature required by the acid gas removal system.

The gasifier can accept all types of nonswelling coals, although the developers believe the gasifier operates to best advantage with lower rank coals. Acceptable carbon conversion is obtained with higher rank coals by operating at the upper end of the gasifier temperature range. Bechtel has suggested combusting the unburned char carbon with gasifier feed air as a means of preheating the feed air. Such a scheme would relieve the requirement to reach high carbon conversion in the gasifier proper. Bechtel has also suggested development of a slurry feed system to permit use of swelling and caking bituminous coals. The gas produced by air blown gasification contains 35 percent carbon monoxide and hydrogen, 2 percent methane, 15 percent carbon dioxide and water vapor, and 48 percent nitrogen.

Rheinische Braunkohlenwerke AG (Rheinbraun) of Cologne, and Uhde GmbH of Dortmund, West Germany, have been cooperating since 1975 in the development of the HTW pressurized gasification process, drawing on proven features of the atmospheric pressure Winkler process which has been commercial since 1927. In the development of the HTW system, preliminary bench scale tests were first conducted in the University of Aachen. Then a 48 tpd 10-atmosphere pilot plant was constructed in Cologne and was commissioned in the summer of 1978. By the end of 1984, the HTW pilot plant had processed 18,300 tons of lignite and 220 tons of peat in a total operating time of 35,000 hours. Tests were also performed with subbituminous coals.

A 600 ton per day 10-atmosphere commercial demonstration plant was constructed in Cologne between 1980 and 1985 for producing synthesis gas for methanol manufacture from a Rheinbraun lignite feedstock. In late 1985, the plant started up and during subsequent operation has consistently met or exceeded design goals such as those for carbon conversion (96%), sulfur removal (to less than one ppmv), and particulate removal (5 mglm^3). Over 5,500 hours of operation had been achieved through October 1987.

KRW[18]

The KRW gasifier is a pressurized, dry feed, ash agglomerating, fluidized bed gasifier that operates at temperatures ranging from 1550°F to 1900°F. Sized run-of-mine coal is surface dried, pressurized in lockhoppers, and injected concentrically into a high energy oxidizing jet located in the combustion zone. The coal is rapidly devolatilized and decaked, and residual char is gasified by steam in the upper region of the fluidized bed. Low carbon-containing ash agglomerates are separated from the char in a fluidized bed separator located in the bottom section of the gasifier, they are cooled with recycle gas, and are extracted by means of a rotary feeder and depressurizing lockhoppers. Fines are elutriated from the gasifier and captured in an external cyclone and recycled directly to the gasifier.

The gasifier may be operated with in-bed desulfurization using limestone or dolomite as a sorbent. Hydrogen sulfide gas produced during the gasification process, reacts with the calcium oxide forming calcium sulfide. This calcium sulfide is either oxidized by air injected into the lower section of the gasifier or it is removed as CaS with the ash and is oxidized in an external sulfator.

Over 11,000 hours of operation have been accumulated on the 25 tpd process development unit at Madison, Pennsylvania since it began operating in 1974. The pilot plant development program was initially funded by Westinghouse, the Gas Research Institute, and the Department of Energy (DOE). Kellogg-Rust purchased the majority interest in the technology and continues development with the DOE.

A KRW gasifier hot gas cleanup IGCC demonstration project was selected in the first round of the DOE Clean Coal Technology program. The 60 MW Appalachian Project will gasify 485 tons/day of coal to produce a low-Btu gas for firing in a gas turbine-based combined cycle unit. Key features of this design include:

- Over 90% in-bed sulfur reduction using limestone as the sorbent
- Hot gas cleanup, including a hot particulate filter, followed

by a zinc ferrite external-bed desulfurizer

- Gas turbine modifications to fire 1000°F, 160 Btu/scf fuel gas

Construction is scheduled to startup in late 1989. M. W. Kellogg and Bechtel are the project sponsors.

U-Gas(19)

The U-Gas gasifier is a single-stage, fluidized bed gasification process with coal decaking, devolatization and gasification, and with ash agglomeration and separation from the reacting char similar to the KRW gasifier. Coal fines elutriated from the gasifier are captured in two external cyclones. Fines from the first cyclone are returned to the bed; fines from the second cyclone are returned to the ash agglomerating zone, where they are gasified and ash is agglomerated. The raw gas is virtually free of tar and oils. A variety of feedstocks including high caking, high-sulfur, and high-ash coals can be utilized.

Most of the U-Gas process development work has been accomplished on a pilot plant put into operation in 1974 at the Institute of Gas Technology's test facility in southwest Chicago. Approximately 10,000 hours of operating time have been logged on this 30 tpd pilot unit. A U-Gas demonstration plant project has been selected for negotiation in the DOE Clean Coal Technology program.

British Gas Lurgi(20,21)

The British Gas Lurgi (BGL) gasifier is a dry feed, pressurized, moving bed, slagging gasifier. The sized coal is fed dry to the gasifier and reacted with oxygen and steam in a moving-bed, counter current, gasification process. The raw gas leaves the gasifiers containing significant amounts of tars, oils, and phenols. The raw gas is first quenched to condense the hydrocarbon byproducts, which are then treated in a series of processes to separate out the hydrocarbons and to dispose of the final effluent water stream. The quenched gas stream then passes through an acid gas removal unit for H_2S removal. All heat removal from the raw gas and the condensate from the quench generates low pressure steam since the nature of these fluid streams makes it impractical to generate high pressure steam. A wide range of coal types can be gasified, including caking coals which require a stirrer. There is a limit as to the amount of coal fines which can be utilized economically in the gasifier.

Initial development of the BGL slagging gasifier was conducted by Lurgi and Ruhrgas at Holten, West Germany in the early 1950's. In 1974, British Gas converted a conventional Lurgi dry ash gasifier at Westfield, Scotland into a slagging gasifier system. This six-foot diameter pilot plant has successfully processed a wide variety of coals at feed rates of about 300 tpd in about 8,000 hours of operation. In 1984, a larger eight-foot diameter demonstration unit began operation at Westfield with the capability of gasifying 600-700 tpd. Gas from both the six-foot and eight-foot diameter gasifiers has been successfully fired in a modified Rolls-Royce SK-30 gas turbine. It has operated for about 1000 hours to date and is currently being used to test pelletized fines, briquetts, and hydrocarbon recycle.

KILnGAS[22,23]

The KILnGAS gasification process is an air-blown, moderate pressure, dry feed, moving bed gasifier. The system is unique in that it is based on a tumbling coal bed (rotary kiln) reactor. Coal is delivered to the reactor by a pressurized feed system. Air/steam ports are located in the kiln shell pass beneath the coal bed, for air and steam injection up into the coal. The coal traveling through the kiln is subjected to four process steps: preheating and drying, devolatilization, gasification and combustion. Approximately two-thirds of the gases flow countercurrent to the coal movement and exit the unit at the feed end of the kiln. The remaining third of the gases flow out the ash discharge end of the kiln and are essentially hydrocarbon free. The feed-end gases pass through a mechanical cyclone which removes entrained particulates. These particulates are returned to the gasifier with the coal feed. Subsequent to particulate removal, the feed-end gases are quenched and scrubbed to condense and remove the tars which were volatilized in the gasifier. The collected tars are also returned to the gasifier with the coal feed. The discharge end gases also pass through a cyclone for mechanical separation of entrained particulates. These particulates contain relatively little carbon, however, and are disposed of with the ash residue. The discharge-end gases then pass through a heat recovery steam generator where the majority of the sensible energy is extracted. After being cooled, the two streams are combined and further cooled prior to removal of sulfur compounds.

The KILnGAS gasification process is being demonstrated in a 600 ton per day full-scale demonstration plant at Illinois Power Company's Wood River Station. This plant consists of a KILnGAS gasifier, Stretford sulfur removal system, and related auxiliaries which provide clean low-Btu gas to the existing Illinois Power Company Wood River No. 3 boiler. The plant has been in operation since 1984. This was preceded by a ten year development program managed by Allis-Chalmers and supported by sixteen investor-owned electric utilities.

CONCLUSION

Substantial progress has been made in coal gasification technology in recent years. Current and near-term gasification demonstration projects should continue to validate the benefits of coal gasification. The first commercial generation of gasification plants will probably be gasification combined cycle plants which will be economical in site specific situations during the next decade. High-Btu gas from coal will probably not be of commercial significance until after the year 2000.

Process improvements and simplification can be expected to improve the technology's cost and performance. These cost reductions and the inevitable increase in natural gas prices ensure a sound future for coal gasification.

Table 1

Comparison of Characteristics of 400MW to 600 MW Pulverized Coal Fired and Gasification Combined Cycle Power Plants Burning 4% Sulfur Coal

	GCC w/ Cold Gas Cleanup(1)	GCC w/ Hot Gas Cleanup(2)	Conventional Pulverized Coal-fired Plant (3)
Plant Performance			
Heat rate, Btu/kWh	8,600-10,000	7,850-8,500	9,700
Equivalent plant availability, %	73-85	Unknown	73
Environmental Intrusions			
Solid waste, lb/kWh	0.2	0.3	0.5
SO_2 emissions, lb/MWh	0.6-7.7	4.3	7.7
NO_x emissions, lb/MWh	0.9-5.2	4.6	5.8
Particulates, lb/MWh	0.01	0.3	0.3
Resource Requirements			
Land, acres/MW(4)	0.8-1.0	0.9	1.2
Water, gal/kWh	0.45-0.60	0.4	0.66
Coal, lb/kWh	0.85-1.0	0.6	0.96
SO_2 sorbent, lb/kWh	--	0.12	0.13

---

(1) Based upon a number of studies performed by Bechtel for utility clients.

(2) Based upon confidential in-house work by Bechtel for GCC power plants utilizing a High Temperature Winkler gasifier and a near-commercial limestone-fed moving bed desulfurizer.

(3) Based upon characteristics presented in Reference 24 for a pulverized coal fired power plant with a wet-limestone flue gas desulfurization system meeting NSPS requirements.

(4) Includes plant area and off-site disposal land requirements.

Table 2

Status of Gasification Processes

Gasifier Type	Development Scale, Tons per Day	Pilot Demo, or Commercial
Entrained-flow		
Texaco	1200	Commercial
Dow	2400	Commercial
Shell	400	Demonstration
PRENFLO	50	Demonstration
Fluidized-bed		
High Temperature Winkler	1000	Demonstration
Kellogg Rust Westinghouse	40	Pilot
U-Gas	30	Pilot
Moving-bed		
British Gas Lurgi	600	Demonstration
KILnGAS	600	Demonstration

References

(1) Bowden, J.R., "The Future For Coal Gasification", AMC Mining Convention '87, September 16, 1987

(2) Mujadin, M. J. and Weinreich, G.N., "The Great Plains Success Story, Seventh Annual EPRI Coal Gasification Contractor's Conference, October 28-29,1987.

(3) Watts, D. et. al., "Cool Water IGCC- Economic Electric Power from Clean Syngas", Seventh Annual EPRI Coal Gasification Contractor's Conference, October 28-29,1987.

(4) Pietruszkiewicz, J., Advanced Combustion Technology, Bechtel Group, Inc. In-House Report, January 1981.

(5) Pohani, et al, "Optimum Design of Coal Gasification Plants," 1982 Industrial Energy Conservation Technology Conference, April 4-7, 1982.

(6) Clark, W. and Shorter, V., "The Future of Integrated Gasification Combined Cycle (IGCC) Electrical Power Production," Fifth Annual EPRI Contractors' Conference, October 30-31, 1985.

(7) Bornemann, G. A. and Sundstrom, D. G., Commercialization of the Dow Gasification Process, Dow Chemical Company.

(8) Fisackerly, R. H., and Sundstrom, D. G., "The Dow Syngas Project - Project Overview and Status Report", Sixth Annual EPRI Coal Gasification Contractor's Conference, October 15-16, 1986.

(9) Webb, R..M. and Sundstrum, D.G., "The Dow Syngas Project Startup and Initial Operations", Seventh Annual EPRI Coal Gasification Contractor's Conference, October 28-29,1987.

(10) Perry, R. T. and Nager, M., "Status of the Shell Coal Gasification Process," Sixth Annual EPRI Contractors' Conference, October 15-16, 1986.

(11) Krewinghaus, A.B. and Nager, M., "Startup and Operating Experience with the Shell Coal Gasification Demonstration Plant", Seventh Annual EPRI Coal Gasification Contractor's Conference, October 28-29,1987.

(12) Coal Gasification Systems: A Guide to Status, Applications, and Economics, Palo Alto, California; Electric Power Research Institute, June, 1983, AP-3109.

(13) Pohl, H. C., and Rohm, H. J., "Pressurized Entrained Flow Gasification and its Application to Combined Cycle Power Plants", Coal Gasification and Synthetic Fuels for Power Generation Conference, April, 1985.

<u>References</u> (Continued)

(14) Pohl, H. C., "Commissioning of the PRENFLO Test Unit", Sixth EPRI Gasification Contractors' Conference, October, 1986.

(15) Buskies, U., "PRENFLO-The European Approach for IGCC", Seventh Annual EPRI Coal Gasification Contractor's Conference, October 28-29, 1987.

(16) Engelhard, J., et al, "The Rheinbraun High-Temperature Winkler (HTW) Demonstration Plant for Synthesis Gas Production: Construction and Start-up", Sixth EPRI Gasification Contractors' Conference, October, 1986.

(17) Engelhard, J., et al, "Status of the High Temperature Winkler (HTW) Coal Gasification Process", Seventh Annual EPRI Coal Gasification Contractor's Conference, October 28-29, 1987.

(18) Lewandowski, D. A., et al, "Application of the KRW Coal Gasification Hot Gas Cleanup Technology to Combined Cycle Electric Power Generation," American Institute of Chemical Engineers Boston National Meeting, August 1986.

(19) Jones, F. L. and Patel, J. G., "Performance of Utah Bituminous Coal in the U-Gas Gasifier," Fifth Annual EPRI Contractors' Conference, October 30-31, 1985.

(20) Thompson, B. H., et al, "Conversion of Coal to Electricity by Gasification Combined Cycle Systems," American Institute of Chemical Engineers Annual Meeting, August 1986.

(21) Lacey, J. A., et. al., "The BGL Gasifier, Status and Application for IGCC",Seventh Annual EPRI Coal Gasification Contractor's Conference, October 28-29, 1987.

(22) Peterson, G. T., "The KILnGAS Coal Gasification Process - Status," Coal Gasification and Synthetic Fuels for Power Generation Conference, April 14-18, 1985.

(23) Peterson, G. T., <u>The KILnGAS Demonstration Program - An Overview and Status Report</u>, Allis-Chalmers Corporation.

(24) Bomkamp, D. H., Bezella, W. D., Smith, R. S., Pietruszkiewicz, J., <u>Overview of Design of Advanced Fossil Fuel Systems (DAFFS) Study</u>, 1984.

TEXACO COAL GASIFICATION PROCESS: AN ELECTRICAL GENERATION OPTION

Vernon R. Shorter/Madeleine R. Marchese

Texaco Syngas Inc.

White Plains, New York

INTRODUCTION

The Texaco Coal Gasification Process (TCGP) is a continuous, entrained flow, pressurized, noncatalytic partial oxidation process in which carbonaceous solids react with oxygen, oxygen enriched air or air.

The feed may be wet-ground in conventional grinding mills and slurried with oil or water to concentrations typically greater than 60 weight percent. Wet grinding eliminates costly dust control systems and insures safe, reliable operations. The slurry is fed to the gasifier through a burner, simultaneously with oxygen or air. In the water slurry case, the water serves as a reactant transport medium and reactor temperature moderator. In the oil slurry case, steam or another temperature moderator is added to the burner streams. Alternatively, certain coal liquefaction residues may be fed in molten form, eliminating the grinding/slurrying step.

The gasifier is a refractory lined pressure vessel with no moving parts. It is operated at a temperature above the ash fluid temperature usually 2200-2800°F, (1200-1500°C).

Several process configuration options are available for cooling the effluent gas. For hydrogen production, the direct quench mode is preferred for raw gas cooling. The hot gas exits the gasifier and directly contacts the quench water, to cool and saturate the synthesis gas. The sensible heat in the hot gas generates internal process steam for use in a downstream catalytic shift conversion step to increase hydrogen production. No import steam is require for shifting.

BACKGROUND

There are four commercial Texaco Coal Gasification Process plants in operation:

Tennessee Eastman, a subsidiary of Eastman Kodak, has operated a 900 ton per day (TPD) gasifier at Kingsport, Tennessee since 1983 producing methanol and acetic anhydride. Performance has been excellent with an on-stream factor of approximately 98% in 1986[3].

Ube Ammonia Industry Co., Inc. owns and operates a 1,650 TPD gasification plant in Ube City, Japan, for the production of ammonia. The facility began operations in 1984 and has been on-stream over 90% of the time since startup. Ube has run on petroleum coke and has gasified a variety of coals, including some from South Africa, Australia and Canada[5].

The Synthesegas Anlage Ruhr (SAR) plant in Oberhausen, West Germany is an 800 TPD plant producing syngas for oxo-chemical manufacture. SAR, the newest of the TCGP plants, has only recently come on-line, but its management indicates that has been operating extremely well[4].

The Cool Water Coal Gasification Program's plant in Southern California came on-stream in May, 1984 and has been an outstanding technical success. The plant has successfully converted differing coal feedstocks to a clean synthesis gas for power generation. Emissions from the Cool Water plant have averaged approximately 10% of allowables under the Environmental Protection Agencies Federal New Source Performance Standards. Plant reliability has been exceptional; the capacity factor for a recent quarter (3rd quarter '87) being 90.2%.

The operational experiences from these four commercial plants will ensure reduced capital outlays and even greater reliability for future Texaco gasification plants. Presently, two other plants are under license in China: a coal to ammonia retrofit and a new plant to produce fuel gas and electrical power for a steel complex. These projects are presently in the engineering - procurement stage and should be started up within the next 2-3 years. Several evaluation studies are under way in Europe for the use of this process and it is possible that the next commercial IGCC plant will be constructed on that continent.

COOL WATER BACKGROUND

Cool Water is the only commercial-scale Texaco IGCC plant yet constructed. It represents the 1980 version of this technology. We will later explore some of the many improvements that will be incorporated in future plants.

The Cool Water Program is an unincorporated California association of six participant companies who have successfully shown that the integration of gasification with combined-cycle power production is commercially viable, environmentally superior, and competitive with other coal-burning technologies.

The six participants are Texaco, Southern California Edison (SCE), the Electric Power Research Institute (EPRI), General Electric (GE), Bechtel, and the Japan Cool Water Partnership (JCWP). Also contributing to the Program are the Empire State Electric Energy Research Company (ESEERCO) and the Sohio Alternate Energy Development Company. Cool Water was constructed under budget and ahead of schedule at a total cost of $263 million during a 28 month construction period.

The 120 nominal gross megawatt Cool Water plant is located adjacent to SCE's existing Cool Water Generating Station in the Mojave Desert, approximately mid-way between Los Angeles and Las Vegas. The location gives the Program an excellent opportunity to prove an environmentally superior process for utilizing coal in a state with some of the most stringent environmental regulations.

The Program began a five-year demonstration phase of commercial production on behalf of its joint owners in June, 1984. At this point in time, after more than three years of commercial production, the Program has successfully demonstrated IGCC on a commercial scale and has resolved many of the uncertainties previously associated with the technology. The plant has accumulated over 18,700 hours of gasifier operation, gasified over 760,000 tons of coal and produced approximately 1.85 billion kWh of gross electrical power through October, 1987.

COOL WATER PLANT PROCESS DESCRIPTION

The plant utilizes an entrained, oxygen-blown Texaco gasifier to convert 1,000 tons of coal per day to medium-Btu synthesis gas. After particulate and sulfur removal, the gas is combusted in a gas turbine to produce electricity. In addition, steam is produced by recovering heat from the hot product gas in syngas coolers and from gas turbine exhaust gas in the heat recovery steam generator (HRSG). Steam from both sources is combined and superheated in the HRSG and then utilized in a steam turbine for production of additional electricity. A simplified block flow diagram of the Cool Water design is shown in Figure 1.

COAL HANDLING

Coal is received at the plant in 84 car unit trains, bottom dumped in a specially designed enclosure which contains dust collection and suppression equipment and conveyed to two coal storage silos with 6,000 tons capacity each. From the storage silos, the coal is conveyed to the grinding section. The grinding trains produce a nominal 60% coal/40% water slurry, which is transferred to run tanks containing agitators to keep the solids suspended. The slurry is then pumped to the gasifier.

FIGURE 1

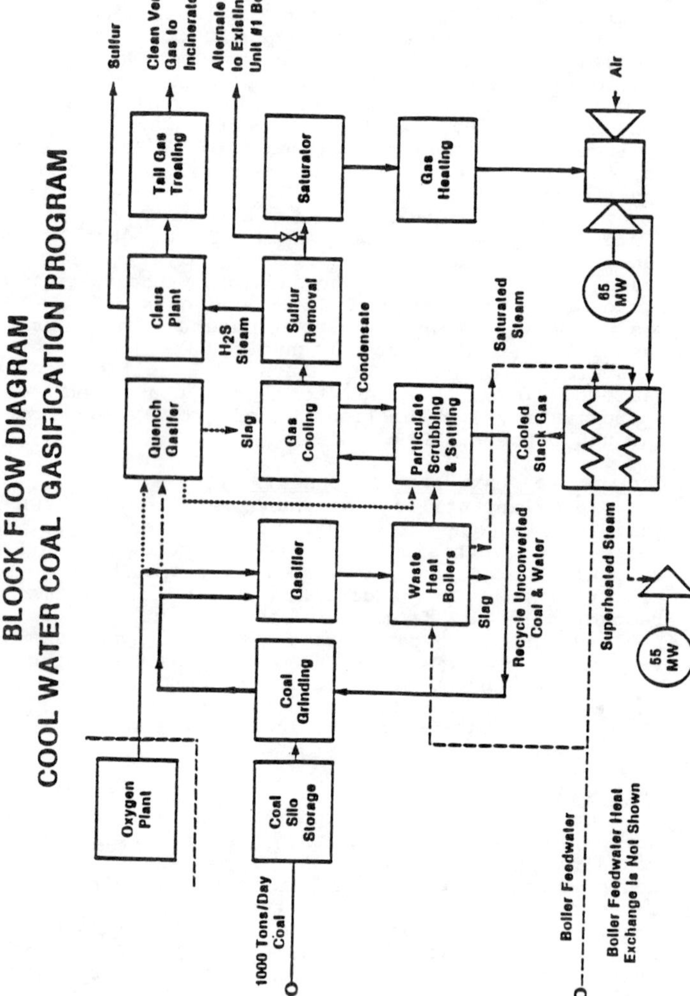
BLOCK FLOW DIAGRAM
COOL WATER COAL GASIFICATION PROGRAM
Oxygen Plant
Coal Silo Storage
1000 Tons/Day Coal
Coal Grinding
Gasifier
Quench Gasifier
Waste Heat Boilers
Slag
Gas Cooling
Particulate Scrubbing & Settling
Recycle Unconverted Coal & Water
Sulfur Removal
Condensate
H_2S Steam
Claus Plant
Sulfur
Tail Gas Treating
Clean Vent Gas to Incinerator
Alternate to Existing Unit #1 Boiler
Saturator
Gas Heating
Air
65 MW
Saturated Steam
Cooled Stack Gas
Superheated Steam
55 MW
Boiler Feedwater
Boiler Feedwater Heat Exchange Is Not Shown

GASIFICATION/SYNGAS COOLERS

At the gasifier, which is a refractory-line vessel mounted at the top of the radiant syngas cooler, the coal-water slurry is combined with 1,000 tons per day of oxygen supplied from an adjacent air-separation plant as an over-the-fence purchase. Mixed in a specially designed burner, partial oxidation reactions take place at 600 PSIG and 2,000°F-plus temperatures to produce a medium Btu syngas (approximately 300 Btu/SCF dry basis) consisting mainly of CO, H_2, CO_2 and steam. Most of the sulfur from the coal is converted to H_2S, with a smaller amount of COS formed. The hot syngas and slag from the gasifier reactor discharge into the radiant cooler below, which generates 1,600 PSIG saturated steam. The slag drops into a water pool at the bottom of the radiant cooler and is removed through a lockhopper system. The syngas proceeds into a convection cooler where additional 1,600 PSIG saturated steam is generated.

From the convection cooler, the gas enters a carbon scrubber, where essentially all of the fine particulates are removed. After further cooling, the syngas proceeds to the Selexol unit, which removes 97% of the sulfur by design. The clean, dry syngas from the Selexol unit is then contacted with water in a saturator prior to firing in the gas turbine. The water provides moisture addition that is needed to control nitrogen oxide (NO_x) emissions from the gas turbine. Alternatively, NO_x emissions can be controlled equally well by the direct injection of steam at the gas turbine. However, experience at Cool Water has shown the saturator to be a more economical method for controlling NO_x emissions since the high quality steam can be used for additional power production in the steam turbine.

POWER PRODUCTION

The major components of the power plant are a gas turbine/electric generator (65 nominal MW gross), a heat recovery steam generator (HRSG) and a steam turbine/electric generator (55 nominal MW gross). The hot exhaust from the gas turbine is used in the HRSG to produce additional steam. This steam combined with the steam from the syngas coolers is superheated in the HRSG and used to drive the 55-MW steam turbine generator. The plant nominal gross electrical generation is 120 MW at 13.8 kV before deducting the power requirements for the air separation plant and internal plant consumption. The air separation plant utilizes 17 MW and the internal plant consumption is 7 MW.

Cool Water has been the most extensively tested and monitored power plant with over 86,000 analyses, 67,650 man-hours and 43 major reports generated to date in verifying its outstanding environmental performance. In light of current environmental issues such as acid rain and air toxics, the record for IGCC is exemplary. Stringent emission limitations at Cool Water are being met. Table 1 shows plant permit limits in comparison to actual performance test results and comparable U.S. EPA New Source Performance Standards. Typical emissions from Cool Water for criteria pollutants such as SO_2, NO_x, CO and particulate matter have been shown to be 10 to 20% of allowable limits as established by U.S. EPA New Source Performance Standards.

In general, sulfur removal by the Selexol process utilized by Cool Water, has ranged between 97 and 99%. The Claus/SCOT unit efficiency is 99% resulting in an overall sulfur recovery from raw syngas of 96% typically. NO_x control using waste heat in a saturator to add water to the syngas is very effective.

COOL WATER ECONOMICS

Unique first-of-a-kind engineering costs to build the Cool Water plant, which was designed only to demonstrate the technology, presented a significant hurdle given the price volatility for competing fuels. At the time of project financing, the Partners made a decision to reduce front-end capital costs recognizing that it would be at the expense of operating efficiency and electrical production costs. Cool Water does not, for example, use a reheat steam turbine. Such a unit was not shelf-available for a 100 MW facility. The benefits, however, of such a reheat cycle can be easily extrapolated.

A recent cost study: "A Reconciliation of the Cool Water IGCC Plant Performance and Cost Data with Equivalent Projections for a Mature 360 MW Commercial IGCC Facility"[7] was completed for the Cool Water Participants in October, 1987 by EPRI and Cool Water Program management members. The major conclusions of that report are copied below:

ooo Cool Water operating data indicates that a 360 MW Texaco-based (radiant plus convective cooling configuration) IGCC plant firing bituminous coal and employing a 2300°F combustion turbine would be expected to have a net heat rate below 9,100 Btu/kWh.

ooo A mature, 360 MW, Cool Water-type IGCC power plant could be expected to be built for a total capital expenditure (including land, start-up costs, working capital, spare parts inventories and AFUDC) of less than $1,600/kW based on the plant rating at an ambient temperature of 88°F. This total capital requirement would drop to $1,400/kW if the plant were rates at ISO conditions of 59°F.

ooo A mature, 360 MW Cool Water-type IGCC power plant burning high-sulfur bituminous coal costing \$1.62/10 Btu and operating at an annual capacity factor of 65% would be expected to cost 2.5¢/kWh to operate. This includes all operating labor, materials and fuel.

Such a plant would represent a very competitive unit, utilizing a conservative cost/benefit analysis.

THE FUTURE OF TEXACO IGCC

Texaco studies indicate that such an IGCC plant could be constructed having an 8900 Btu/kWh heat rate, significantly reducing capital costs per kW of capacity when compared with the \$1400-1600/kW projection by Cool Water. Given the inherent flexibility of the technology, it is quite possible that some future plants will be cogenerators with several outputs with the ability to switch production loads among electricity, steam, carbon monoxide, hydrogen, methanol, etc. This provides impetus for economics dispatch of the unit and the earnings benefits associated with greater use of installed plant capacity[6].

The Texaco Coal Gasification Process has been proven to be suitable for commercial service in electric power production. This technology will offer an economically and environmentally superior option for the utility industry in the 1990's and beyond.

TABLE 1

HRSG Stack Emissions - lb/MM Btu

	Permit Limit(1)	SUFCo 1985 EPA Test	Ill.#6 EPA Test	Pitts.#8 Source	Federal NSPS(2)
SO_2 High S	0.16	NA	0.068	0.122	0.6
Low S	0.033	0.018	NA	NA	0.24(3)
NO_x	0.13	0.07	0.097	0.066	0.6
CO	0.07	0.004	0.004	<0.002	NS
Part. Matter	0.01	0.001	0.009	0.009	0.03

(1) Permit and Regulatory limit.
(2) New Source Performance Standards for a coal-fire power plant burning equivalent coal as CWCGP.
(3) 0.8 lb/MM Btu uncontrolled emissions X 0.30 controlled emissions

NA = Not Applicable,
NS = No Standard

LITERATURE CITED

1) Watts, Donald H., Dinkel, Paul W., and McDaniel, John E., "Cool Water IGCC Performance to Date and Its Future in the Electric utility Industry, Texaco Utilities Symposium, Palm Springs, California, October, 1987.

2) Clark, Wayne N., and Shorter, Vernon R., "Cool Water: Economically competitive and Environmentally Superior Electrical Power Production", Benelux Association of Energy Economists, The Hague, Netherlands, April, 1987.

3) Windle, John B., "Tennessee Eastman Company Gasification Plant Operational Summary for Texaco Utilities Symposium", Texaco Utilities Symposium, Palm Springs, California, October, 1987.

4) Hibbel, J., Ruhrchemie Plant Operations Experience, Texaco Utilities Symposium, Palm Springs, California, October, 1987.

5) Sueyama, T., "Ube Ammonia Industry Co., Ltd. Plant Operations", Texaco Utilities Symposium, Palm Springs, California, October, 1987.

6) Curran, Paul F., "Clean Power at Cool Water", Mechanical Engineering, August, 1987 issue.

7) Gluckman, Michael J., Spencer, Dwain F., Watts, Donald H., Shorter, Vernon R., "A reconciliation of the Cool Water IGCC Plant Performance and Cost Data with Equivalent Projections for a Mature 360 MW Commercial IGCC Facility, October, 1987.

COAL GASIFICATION AND THE COMBINED CYCLE--A UTILITY PERSPECTIVE

JOHN W. WADDILL
CORPORATE TECHNICAL ASSESSMENT
VIRGINIA POWER

INTRODUCTION

The Virginia Electric and Power Company is the principal subsidiary of Dominion Resources Incorporated. Operating in Virginia as Virginia Power and in North Carolina as North Carolina Power, the Power Company provides electricity to 1.6 million customers in a 32,000 square mile territory.

In the mid to late 1960's, Virginia Power, along with most of the utility industry, was experiencing rapid load growth approaching 10 to 11 percent per year. In 1969, Virginia Power was building two fossil units, six nuclear units, and a pumped storage facility, for a total of over 7,000 megawatts under construction.

In the fall of 1973, the first oil embargo hit. With unpredictable future world energy prices and rapidly declining local and national economies, Virginia Power faced a major turnaround in its future generation needs and thus in its construction program.

In early 1977, Virginia Power announced the cancellation of the Surry 3 and Surry 4 nuclear units, which were then scheduled for completion in 1986 and 1987. In 1980 the North Anna nuclear unit 4 was cancelled, followed thereafter by the cancellation of the North Anna unit 3 as load growth continued to deteriorate very rapidly.

By the early 80's, it appeared that the best available forecasts for long term energy demand had settled on a load growth between 2 and 3 percent a year on an annual basis. This radical change from the greater than percent a year of the previous decade, along with increasingly complex regulatory and environmental considerations, necessitated an equally radical change in the process of planning for future generation capacity additions.

In 1981, Virginia Power began a major study of conventional and alternative energy sources potentially capable of meeting future growth in demand in a cost effective manner. Demand side options such as conservation, load management, and cogeneration were evaluated as means of delaying or eliminating the need for the construction of additional power plants. On the supply side, small-scale hydro, alternative fuels, and advanced generation technologies were evaluated as a means of providing the generation needed to match the new low load growth forecast.

Current forecasts continue to lead Virginia Power to expect load growth in the range of 2 to 3 percent per year through the end of this century.

FUTURE GENERATING CAPACITY OPTIONS

Even at this low load growth, there will come a time when expected load will exceed expected available capacity. Some generating capacity must then be built or purchased to satisfy this load, or the load must be voluntarily managed or involuntarily curtailed.

Large conventional pulverized coal units are one supply side option currently available, but these units have important disadvantages for low load growths, mainly the potentially large financial impacts from delays or cancellation. In addition, large coal units have long licensing, engineering, and construction periods, they have large committed capital investments, and they threaten "rate shock" to customers. Utilities are, therefore, intensely interested in technologies which allow new capacity to be put in place quickly, in small increments, with relatively modest investments, and with fast payback. Shorter lead times and smaller units allow a better match between capacity additions and demand growth, thereby reducing financial risks when demand growth turns out to be more or less than expected. With the prospects of a highly competitive and uncertain future, the ability to limit risk and retain flexibility is a most attractive combination for today's utility. Virginia Power is especially attracted to two new smaller size technologies that look very promising as generating alternatives to provide the flexibility we need for the 1990's - Atmospheric Fluidized Bed Combustion and Coal Gasification Combined Cycle.

The Coal Gasification Combined Cycle alternative is tailor made for the utility future as it appears today. Many utilities have existing sites with generating units that are old or otherwise ready for retirement. These sites are valuable for Coal Gasification Combined Cycle facilities. In most cases, water intake structures exist, environmental licenses are current, the site already has rail, barge, or pipeline fuel capability and transmission rights-of-way, and the area has been and is acceptable as a power station site. In addition, it is usually possible to increase the capacity of the site by using the Combined Cycle concept (Exhibit 1). The combustion turbine produces about 2/3 of the power of the combined cycle unit without the need of cooling water and only 1/3 of the capacity (the steam generator) needs condenser cooling water. Take, for example, a site with two 60 MW coal units ready for retirement. This site has 120 MW using condenser cooling, which now represents only 1/3 of the power potential of that site. The total space for the old units could thus allow approximately 360 MW of generating capacity to be established. This represents a net gain of 240 MW of generating capacity without creating any additional impact on water resources.

While the Fuel Use Act considerations indicated some potential obstacles and impediments to combined cycle generation, the environmental considerations of combined cycle offer some very attractive advantages compared to construction of conventional pulverized coal generation. Conventional coal fired plants, because of stringent regulatory requirements relative to emissions of SO_x and NO_x, are burdened with the prospect of low-sulfur compliance coal or of some sort of flue gas scrubber (with all its attendant expenses, operational problems, and waste disposal considerations). Environmental air emission compliance can be achieved with combined cycle generation, using natural gas and distillate fuels. The emissions from coal gasification processes are inherently cleaner than those from coal combustion in either conventional pulverized coal units or in fluidized bed boilers.

The Fuel Use Act required that an exemption be obtained from the U. S. Department of Energy. At the same time, the projected costs of natural gas, light oil and heavy oil, and coal gas from any of the numerous gasification processes then being developed by

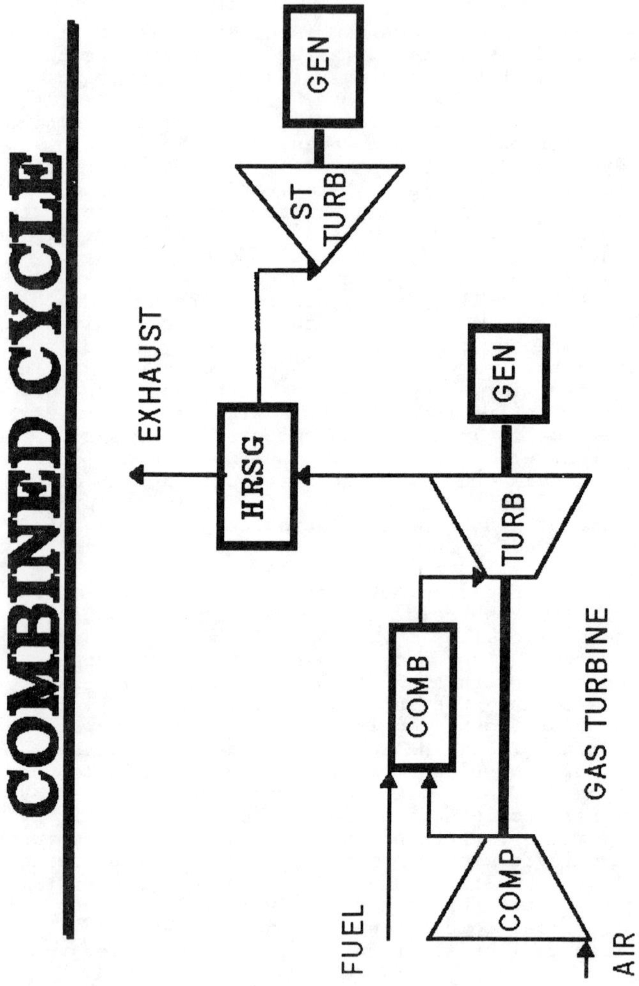

COMBINED CYCLE

EXHAUST

HRSG

ST TURB

GEN

FUEL

COMB

COMP

TURB

GEN

AIR

GAS TURBINE

Exhibit 1

the various system manufacturers were quite uncertain. Even the near-to mid-term pricing of these competing fuels was highly variable and remains so still. As long as these circumstances exist, it is extremely important that fuel flexibility be achieved and that conversion from natural gas to light or heavy oil, or even to coal gas, be possible with minimum expense and disruption to commercial operation.

This planned approach to fuel flexibility allows a utility to respond to the customer's needs in minimum time. When considering the time value of money, rapid response capability is advantageous to the Company's customers and to its shareholders. Under this approach, the utility can plan other power supply alternatives (such as long term power purchases, cogeneration, load management, longer lead time alternatives) and still retain an acceptable cost effective alternative for meeting customer demands.

COMBINED CYCLE AND PHASED CONSTRUCTION

Combined cycle generation lends itself to "Phased Construction." Phased construction is a process where the utility installs a Gas Turbine as the first phase (Exhibit 2). Phase 1 can be completed in 18 months to 2 years from decision to commercial operation. One minor difficulty in "Phased Construction" of coal gasification combined cycle (CGCC) facilities is that environmental licensing should be approached at the same time for the entire package. Combustion turbines are usually accepted by most environmental regulatory agencies if "State of the Art" such as steam injection for NO_x control are employed.

The addition of Phase II (HRSG Steam Turbine), the utilization of the waste heat from the gas turbine exhaust to make steam to operate a conventional steam cycle requires water quality licensing considerations. This phase of the licensing process could take as much as two or three years to complete if it involves a new water intake structure. However, as discussed earlier, re-use of existing sites can lessen these licensing requirements.

Finally, the addition of Phase III, the coal gasification process, if and when the economics dictate this choice, will require licensing mainly of airborne emissions. This should take a minimal amount of time since coal gasification plants have very low emissions and are well below current and projected EPA New Source Performance Standards.

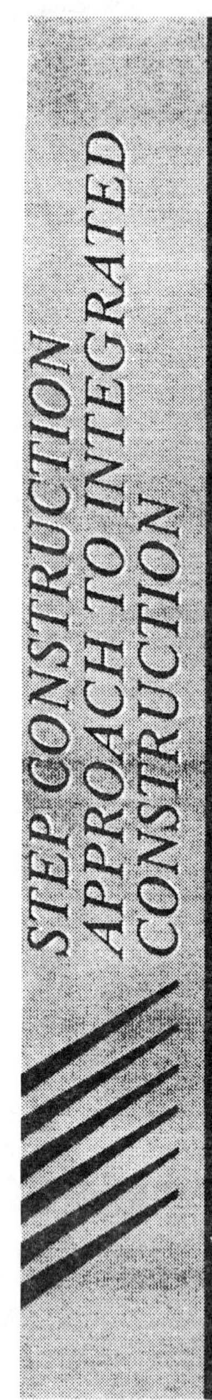

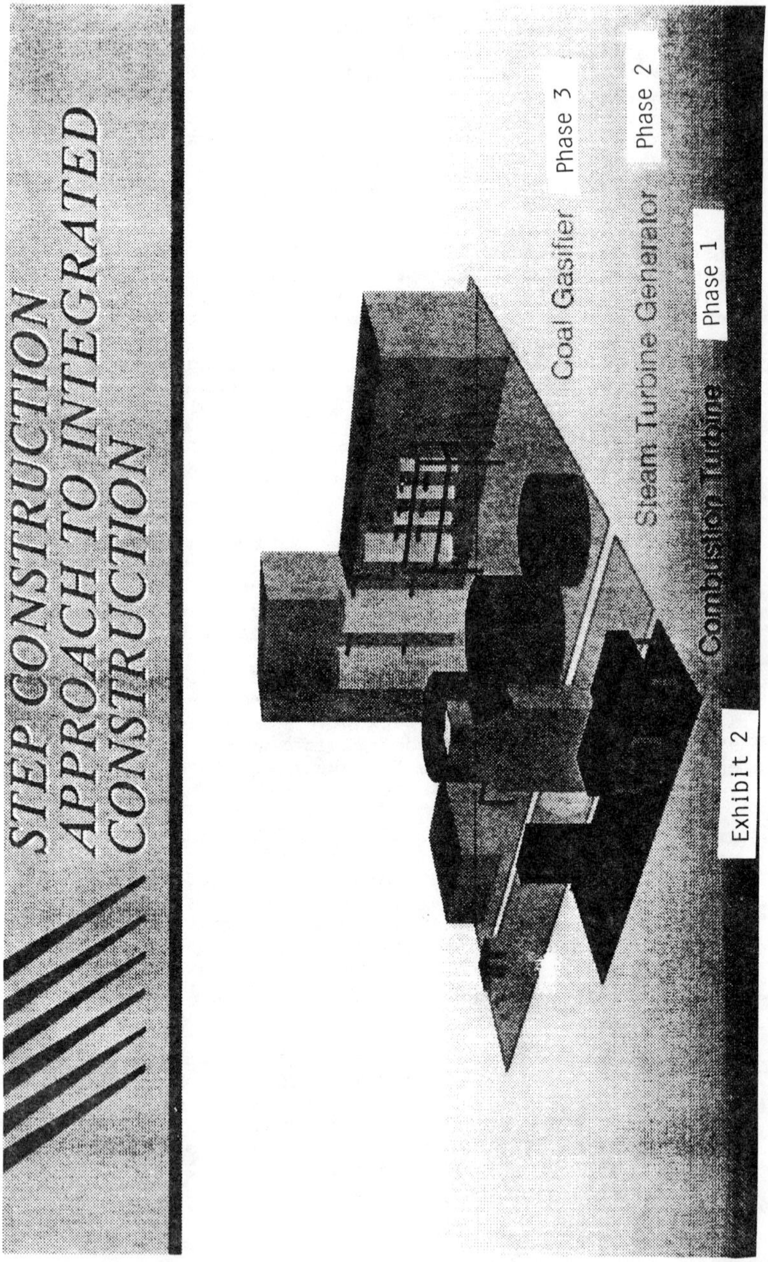

STEP CONSTRUCTION
APPROACH TO INTEGRATED
CONSTRUCTION
Coal Gasifier
Phase 3
Steam Turbine Generator
Phase 2
Combustion Turbine
Phase 1
Exhibit 2

The licensing time for all three phases could be consolidated into a three year period. This could be done well before the plant is needed. In Virginia, for example, a site license can be retained for a period of about three years, and can be renewed.

SITING THE COMBINED CYCLE UNIT

Virginia Power's Chesterfield Power Station met the host site criteria of the combined cycle concept. Virginia Power applied for and received permanent exemption from the Power Plant and Industrial Fuel Use Act of 1978 for two 210 MW combined cycle generating units to be built at its Chesterfield Power Station in Virginia. These units are designated Chesterfield Units 7 and 8 and are to be constructed in the space previously occupied by retired Units 1 and 2.

To accommodate the primary fuel source for the combined cycle units, a new 16 mile natural gas supply pipeline is planned. Certificates of convenience and necessity have been obtained from the Virginia State Corporation Commission for the combustion turbines and steam unit associated with Chesterfield 7, with the provision for a similar unit at a future date.

BUILDING THE COAL GASIFIER

The construction of a coal gasification facility at the Chesterfield site depends upon its economic and technical justification. The Cool Water demonstration project, as well as other existing commercial and demonstration applications of the various coal gasification processes, led Virginia Power to believe that coal can be gasified in the quantities, reliability, and costs needed to supply units of the size as Chesterfield Unit 7. For a given coal type, selection of a particular coal gasifier technology appears, in the general sense, to be rapidly becoming a question of vendor selection rather than a selection among risky technologies. This reduces the question of the timing of the commercial operation of a gasifier for a combined cycle unit to one of straightforward economic trade-offs between the cost of natural gas (and backup fuel oil) and the capital, operating, and fuel costs for the gasifier.

For this reason, the analysis which follows is a simple comparison of the economic value of a gasifier (defined as the present value of operating cost savings) with the capital construction cost of a gasifier (defined as the installed cost of the coal gasification facility). For simplicity, the analysis presented here is done in constant 1987 dollars, so that the clouding effects of projections of the rate of general inflation do not make the analysis and discussion needlessly more difficult.

The final category of costs incurred by a gasifier that are not experienced with a natural gas fired unit are the capital carrying costs associated with the financial resources devoted to the construction of the gasifier. These costs are determined by the interest rate and the life of the gasifier. Lets assume a real interest rate (i.e., net of inflation) of six percent for use in this analysis, and an operating life for the gasifier of fifteen years. A longer operating life of 20 to 30 years is certainly possible, and alternative real interest rates are also possible.

With these factors in mind, a very basic calculation for the operating cost savings can now be reviewed. Fuel costs burning natural gas are the product of the net heat rate and the price per Btu of natural gas. Multiplying this by the number of hours in a year gives the gas fuel cost per year in dollars per kW/yr. A similar calculation for coal gives the fuel cost per year when burning coal. Note that the net heat rates will be different for the two technologies. The difference between the results of these two calculations is the fuel maximum cost savings which would be achieved if the unit ran continuously. Multiply the fuel cost savings by the capacity factor to obtain an estimate of the anticipated fuel-only cost savings. From the fuel-only savings we subtract the operating and maintenance costs for the gasifier. The result is the sum of fuel and operating and maintenance cost savings resulting from the use of coal and the gasifier to supply the unit rather than natural gas. If this value were negative, then there would be a cost from using coal as a substitute for natural gas.

The basic economic assumptions used in the analysis are shown in Exhibit 3. Since the calculation of the net present value of operating cost savings is one of two prime elements in the comparison, the net heat rate (Btu's per kilowatt hour) of the two alternative fuels is a major assumption. The expectation for Chesterfield Unit 7 is that it will achieve a net heat rate of about 7500 Btu's per kilowatt hour. A gasifier uses heat in the gasification process, so the net heat rate using coal as a fuel will be somewhat higher than the net heat rate of the combined cycle operating alone. For the purposes of this paper, use a net heat rate on coal of 10,000 Btu's per kilowatt hour (a conservatively high estimate).

ASSUMPTIONS FOR ECONOMIC STUDY

HEAT RATE WHEN BURNING NATURAL GAS	7,500	BTU/KWH
HEAT RATE WHEN BURNING COAL	10,000	BTU/KWH
REAL DISCOUNT RATE	6	PERCENT
OPERATING AND MAINTENANCE EXPENSE	$30.00	PER KW/YEAR
CAPACITY FACTOR	70	PERCENT
REAL COAL PRICE ESCALATION	0	PERCENT

Exhibit 3

The coal gasifier incurs several costs that are not borne by a natural gas fired unit. Therefore, the coal handling, coal storage, ash disposal, and other operating and maintenance costs for the coal gasifier must be deducted from the straight fuel cost savings to obtain a realistic estimate of the operating savings expected from the gasification process. Thirty dollars per year per kilowatt of capacity are deducted for these costs.

Now repeat this cost savings calculation for each year into the future. Multiplying the result by a present value factor gives the value today of a savings to be realized in the future. Summing these anticipated present values of future savings over the expected life of the installation yields equivalent cost savings of the gasifier.

As the life of the gasifier is extended, the stream of expected future savings increases, and the cost savings from the gasifier increases. As the interest rate used in the calculation increases, the present value of a future savings decreases, and the value of the gasifier decreases. Similar sensitivities could be examined for fuel prices, the anticipated net heat rates and capacity factor, and the operating and maintenance costs of the gasifier.

The principal uncertainties which should influence planning have been determined to be the future prices of coal and natural gas cost of capital which is tied to inflation, and the installed cost of a gasifier. The other factors are assuredly not known with certainty, but they are much better understood and more certain than the prices of natural gas, coal, and gasifiers.

THE COAL GASIFICATION IMPLEMENTATION WINDOW

Exhibit 4 summarized the major forces at work in helping to determine the fuel source for new combined cycle installations over the next few years. The two horizontal lines represent the high and low estimates of the constant dollar (1989 dollars) cost of building a coal gasification facility. These estimates were obtained from a range of cost estimates developed by the Electric Power Research Institute (EPRI). The two sloping lines are derived using the formulas discussed earlier. These two lines represent the present values of future cost savings calculated using natural gas price forecast and two different baseline coal price scenarios. The value shown for a particular year is the net present value for the life of gasifiers going commercial in that year.

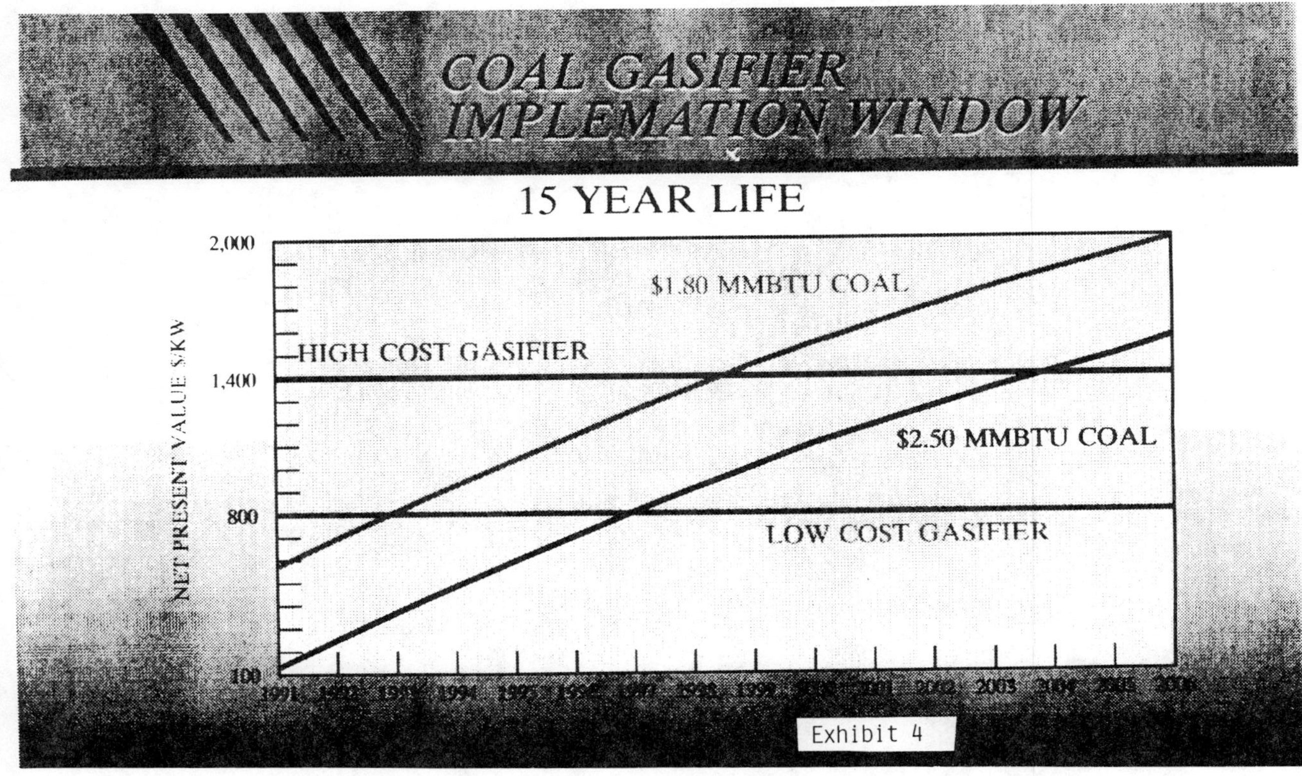
COAL GASIFIER
IMPLEMATION WINDOW
15 YEAR LIFE
$1.80 MMBTU COAL
HIGH COST GASIFIER
$2.50 MMBTU COAL
LOW COST GASIFIER
NET PRESENT VALUE $/KW
2,000
1,400
800
100
1991
1994
1995
1999
2001
2002
2003
2005
Exhibit 4

The natural gas price forecast is from the American Gas Association (TERA Base Case 1987-J, Scenario DM8704J). The rate of real price escalation for coal is representative of the projections which the National Coal Association presented to the Department of Energy as a part of their initial filing with respect to the Virginia Power application for a permanent exemption from the then existing prohibitions against using natural gas as a primary energy source for Chesterfield Units 7 and 8. Basically, the National Coal Association anticipates no real increase in freight rates for coal transportation, and anticipates that the real price of coal will fall. In this analysis the real price of coal, delivered to power stations, has been held constant.

The two scenarios are for (1.) low priced coal, such as that delivered to Chesterfield Power Station, and for (2.) a much higher priced coal, i.e., one that is roughly forty percent more expensive. You may assume that this higher priced coal represents coal that has been moved a much longer distance, or has unique properties beneficial to gasification, or you may assume that there has been a significant increase in the real cost of coal due to more stringent mining regulation.

As seen from the intersection of the four lines, there is a "window" of implementation dates for gasification processes. The earliest date is that associated with low capital costs for the gasification process and low coal prices. This is to be expected since this situation allows low priced coal to be converted to gas using a low cost gasifier. The latest date at which coal gasification becomes economically attractive is that associated with high cost gasification processes and high priced coal. The other pair of situations (high gasifier cost with low coal price and low gasifier cost with high coal price) which define the window result in implementation dates which are intermediate to the dates for the extreme combinations. In all likelihood, the actual combination of gasifier cost and coal price will fall somewhere within the window, although it is not now known with certainty where that combination will fall. The window does, however, bracket the likely range of outcomes for future gasifier costs and coal prices, and thus can be used to illustrate the likely date when combined cycle units may be built and economically fired with coal-derived gas.

The real implementation window does not have the sharp edges shown in the graph. Higher or lower real interest rates could push the window to the upper right or lower left respectively. A lower capacity factor for the combined cycle unit could push the window to the right. A better coal-gas-fired net heat rate could push the window to the left. Other combinations of events could also push the corners of the windows in various directions by large or small amounts. Each organization considering coal gasification will use the parameter values appropriate to its own situation, and hence each could be looking at a different, or rather its own unique, window.

The conclusion which can be derived from this window is clear, despite the qualifications which have been made about the assumptions used to produce it. That conclusion is: while natural gas is currently the better choice as the primary fuel for the combined cycle technology, it remains so only as long as the economics of the relative prices of natural gas, delivered coal, and gasification processes maintain their current relationship. The natural gas price forecast provided by the American Gas Association, when incorporated into an economic analysis which includes National Coal Association-based projections of real coal prices and Electric Power Research Institute estimates of gasifier costs, encourages the perception that natural gas is only an interim fuel for combined cycle applications. Natural gas, if it becomes a premium fuel, is likely to be too expensive for use as a primary fuel in combined cycle generating units.

VIRGINIA POWER PHOTOVOLTAIC FIELD TEST EXPERIENCE

J. Chuck Greene
Virginia Power
Corporate Technical Assessment Department
Richmond, Virginia

INTRODUCTION

The results of the first year of tests at the 75 kWp Virginia Integrated Solar Test Arrays (VISTA) facility provide meaningful system-scale comparisons between polycrystal and single crystal silicon photovoltaic (PV) arrays and between tracking and fixed operation in an east coast location. Virginia Power, an investor-owned utility, owns and operates the unique VISTA facility which is comprised of three autonomous 25 kWp DC arrays (or subfields) as illustrated in Figure 1. The first subfield is operated in 2-axis tracking mode and contains 200 polycrystal modules. The second subfield contains 200 fixed polycrystal modules and the third subfield contains 576 fixed single crystal modules.

Each subfield feeds its own inverter which converts the DC energy from the subfield into AC energy. The AC energy is measured and recorded and stepped up to 34.5 kV where it is injected into the Virginia Power utility grid. The AC rating of each subfield due to wiring losses and inverter inefficiencies is estimated to be 20 kWp AC or 60 kWp AC for the entire VISTA facility. Each VISTA subfield is a system in and of itself and is metered separately.

This paper presents the results of Virginia Power's first year of operation at the VISTA facility in Central Virginia. Evaluations of Virginia's solar resource are made, along with comparisons between tracking and fixed operating modes. Comparisons between single and polycrystal PV technologies are also drawn.

Various operating parameters were analyzed during the first test year including energy output (kWhrs), efficiency, and capacity factor. Initial results indicate that for two identically rated (kWp) arrays, one single crystal and one polycrystal, the polycrystal array is likely to produce more energy (kWhrs) given the insolation conditions at this site. The possible reasons for this surprising result are discussed along with other results of the data analysis.

FIGURE 1:

VIRGINIA POWER'S VISTA SOLAR FACILITY ONE LINE DIAGRAM

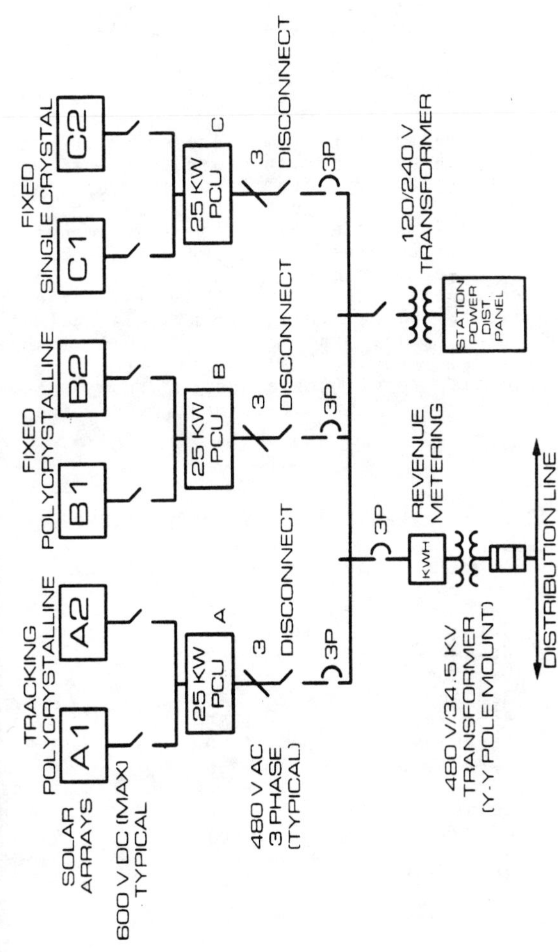

SOLAR RESOURCE EVALUATION

One of the objectives of operating the VISTA test facility is to quantify and evaluate the solar resource in the Virginia area. This information is intended to indicate how much energy is available from the sun in this area and to determine the best method of extracting the energy. This involves a detailed characterization of the quality of the solar resource.

Several different measurements are taken at the VISTA solar facility in order to quantify the amount of available energy from the sun at that location. Insolation, the measurement of available sun energy, is measured in kWhr/m^2-day and the amount of incoming insolation depends on the angle that the PV array makes with the incoming sun rays. The insolation measurements taken at the VISTA facility include horizontal plane (HI), array plane (API), tracking global (TGI), and direct normal insolation (DNI) readings. An evaluation of the solar resource available to Virginia Power from October, 1986 to September, 1987 produced the figures given in Table 1.

TABLE 1: AVERAGE MONTHLY INSOLATION (kWhrs/m^2-day)

	TGI	API	HI
October	6.03	4.98	3.97
November	3.22	2.81	1.83
December	4.29	3.49	2.14
January	2.99	2.70	1.79
February	5.85	4.49	3.36
March	7.50	5.91	4.51
April	5.55	4.24	4.06
May	7.09	5.04	5.21
June	7.66	5.40	5.96
July	8.04	5.88	6.29
August	7.20	5.50	5.50
September	5.53	4.73	4.05
Average day	5.91	4.60	4.01
Annually	2158.03	1677.84	1465.17
%Difference	28.62	14.52	-12.68
% of API	129	100	87

Table 1 shows the monthly and annual average insolation readings taken during the test period. Percent difference is taken with respect to the API averages. Based on the annual averages during the test period TGI exceeded API by 28.62% and API exceeded the available HI by 14.5%. For comparison the Electric Power Research Institute (EPRI) reported that the 1985 annual average HI at the Hesperia PV facility northeast of Los Angeles, California was approximately 5.97 kWh/m^2-day[(1)]. This insolation figure exceeds the annual average VISTA HI by nearly 50%.

The 28.62% TGI-API difference is somewhat lower than the figures reported for the Southwestern United States but still high enough to consider maximizing this extra energy. Based on PV computer simulations a single axis tracking system (which is less expensive than a two-axis system) can produce up to 86% of the energy that a two-axis flatplate system can produce[(2)]. A field test comparing single axis and two axis operations is planned for the VISTA facilty in 1989.

The HI resource equalled or exceeded the API resource for 4 of the 12 test months. This reflects the hazy skies and high humidity levels which are typical in Virginia.

The insolation data given in Table 1 matches well with typical meteorological year (TMY) data taken in previous years. The VISTA average daily TGI figure is approximately 9.7% higher than the equivalent Richmond TMY figure and the VISTA API figure is approximately 8.7% higher than the TMY figure. This indicates that the data taken during this VISTA test year reflects an above average solar resource.

A tracking system has advantages over a fixed system that a utility must take into consideration including improved capacity factor. This is due to the TGI solar resource profile as shown in Figure 2. This figure is representative of the average insolation readings taken during a typical July day at the VISTA facility. The TGI advantage over API is mainly seen in the morning and afternoon as the TGI surface faces the sun directly and the sun strikes the fixed API surface at an angle. This effect translates directly into extra PV kWhrs and improved capacity factors as is discussed in the following sections. This figure also shows the larger amount of HI present in the month of July.

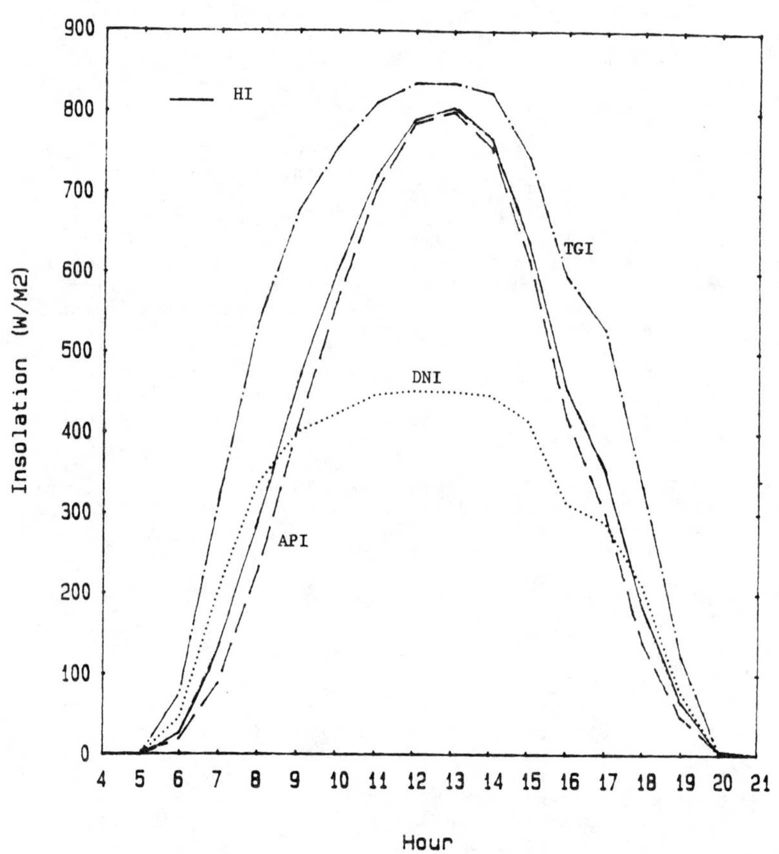

Figure 2 : Daily average insolation profile for July

COMPARATIVE PARAMETERS

Several parameters are used in comparing subfield performance at the VISTA facility including availability, capacity factor, normalized energy density, and normalized merit figure. Plant downtime includes any time during plant operation when a loss of energy occurred due to system maintenance or repairs. The capacity factor is defined as the ratio of the actual subfield AC energy output to the energy output the subfield would have produced operating at rated power during a given time period.

Subfield availability is defined as the ratio of the actual hours the subfield produced AC energy to the actual hours when sunlight was available. Available sun hours in Richmond, Virginia were provided by the National Weather Service (3). Availability differences are factored out of subfield comparisons by normalization. Normalized figures are therefore theoretical numbers based on field test data which can be used to rate the technological advantages of one subfield over another.

A normalized figure of Merit (M) is used to compare the three subfields of the VISTA facility along with a normalized energy density figure (D). M is obtained by dividing the actual normalized AC kWhr output by the system peak DC kW rating (kWhr AC/kWp DC). D is obtained by dividing the normalized actual AC kWhr output by the PV surface area of the PV array in square meters (kWhr AC/m^2). Use of these measurements provides more accurate comparisons of subfield performance than a simple measurement of the output energy or system efficiency since M is normalized to subfield installed capacity and D is normalized to subfield area.

The figure of merit is similar to a capacity factor but can be used to estimate monthly energy output for a given technology in the central Virginia area. This is useful for array sizing and costing for future PV installations. Energy density is similarly useful for array sizing and costing when array area is a consideration.

The rated installed capacities (kWp-DC) of the three VISTA subfields are modified from the original 25 kWp DC nominal ratings. Based on field data taken by the New Mexico Solar Energy Institute (4) and modified to reflect subsequent module replacements the subfield ratings (at 1000 w/m^2 and 28°C) have been revised as follows:

Subfield A: Tracking polycrystal 24.998 kWp DC
Subfield B: Fixed polycrystal 23.706 kWp DC
Subfield C: Fixed single crystal 23.095 kWp DC

Subfield B is taken as the control variable in the following VISTA data analysis. Reported percent differences for subfields A and C are with respect to subfield B. Percent differences for subfield B are with respect to subfield C.

OPERATING MODE COMPARISON

In order to evaluate various modes of PV operation at the VISTA solar facility subfields A and B are compared. Subfield A consists of 200 polycrystalline modules on eight two-axis trackers while subfield B consists of 200 polycrystalline modules mounted at a fixed angle of approximately 37.5°. This provides a direct comparison of the performance of a fixed PV system versus a two-axis tracking system in the Virginia Power service area.

The solar resource available to each of these systems is quantified in Table 1. Subfield A receives the 29% more energy intensive TGI solar resource while subfields B and C receive the API resource. Table 2 gives the monthly accumulated energy output in kWhrs from each of the three VISTA subfields along with availability and normalization figures. The actual kilowatt hour data given in Table 2 was gathered from a Virginia Power standard utility kWhr meter at the VISTA facility.

The tracking polycrystal subfield's rated installed capacity is 5.45% higher than that of the fixed polycrystal subfield. Assuming uniform current-voltage characteristics for the two subfields the tracking subfield even if it were fixed would produce 5.45% more energy than the fixed polycrystal subfield (4). Therefore, only 8.54% (20.17% after normalization) of the 13.99% additional annual energy produced by the tracking subfield can be attributed to the tracking operation (see Table 2).

Based on computer estimates (under TMY conditions) the tracking subfield should have produced 27.4% more energy than the fixed polycrystal field (2). This differs by only 1.69 percentage points with the normalized field data figure of 25.71% which reflects availability considerations. The small difference between modeled and normalized field data percent difference may then be due to the difference between actual solar resource (as shown in Table 1) and modeled solar resource. Richmond, Virginia typical meteorological year (TMY) data is used in the model.

TABLE 2: VISTA SUBFIELD PERFORMANCE

	Actual Kilowatt Hours				Availability (%)			Normalized kWhrs		
	A	B	C	Total	A	B	C	A	B	C
October	2379	2409	2111	6899	66.1	100	84.3	3600	2409	2505
November	2506	2241	2061	6808	98.4	98.4	85.6	2547	2277	2408
December	2438	2148	1733	6520	92.5	100	82.0	2635	2149	2114
January	1818	1805	1450	5073	83.7	100	97.7	2171	1805	1484
February	2082	2510	2458	7050	74.7	93.8	90.0	2788	2676	2732
March	3707	3325	3492	10524	78.7	89.3	99.8	4709	3725	3498
April	3141	2450	2355	7986	91.4	86.4	92.5	3438	2836	2546
May	3411	3062	2585	9058	95	99.4	93.4	3590	3082	2768
June	4452	3037	2718	10207	99.7	96.2	89.2	4465	3158	3046
July	4328	3307	3135	10770	94.8	99.2	99.4	4564	3335	3153
August	3376	2870	2639	8885	81	83.7	83.7	4169	3429	3153
September	3745	2752	2466	7963	75	98.5	94.1	3658	2793	2620
Average	3032	2660	2434	8124	85.9	95.4	91.0	3528	2806	2669
Total	36383	31917	29203	97483				42334	33674	32027
% Difference	13.99	9.37	-8.57					25.71	5.14	-4.89

Key: A - Tracking Polycrystal, B - Fixed Polycrystal, C - Fixed Single Crystal

The 8.54% extra energy produced by the tracking system is generated in the mornings and afternoons as shown in Figure 3. This results in a capacity factor (CF) of 16.60% (19.31% after normalization) for tracking operation as compared with 15.35% (16.20% after normalization) for fixed operation. This CF is obtained by dividing the actual kWhrs by the revised subfield kWp rating times the number of hours in the test period. For comparison, the Hesperia, California two axis tracking facility operated at a 35% capacity factor in 1985 and 22.8% in 1986[5]. These figures are higher than the VISTA capacity factor primarily because of the excellent insolation conditions in California.

FIGURE 3: DAILY AVERAGE OUTPUT PROFILE

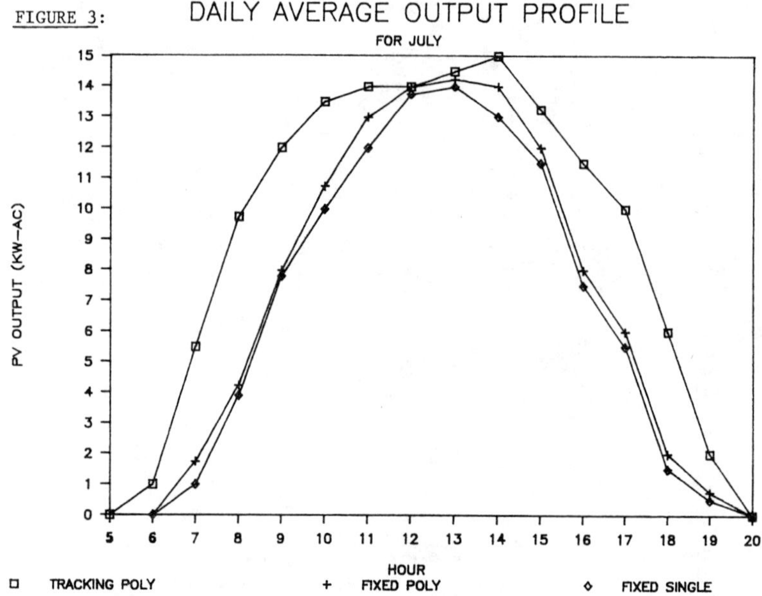

A higher level of operations and maintenance time was required for the tracking system than for the fixed system due to unplanned outages resulting in a lower annual average availability of 85.90% versus 95.40% for fixed operation. The additional downtime is partially due to failure of the Tracking Control System (TCS) computer which was brought on by poor utility voltage regulation. Poor voltage regulation frequently caused computer failures which kept the trackers in a stow position facing away from the sun.

Additional tracker downtime maintenance was due to periodic open circuiting of the DC source circuits brought on by snagging of the source circuit wiring on tracker junction boxes. Since the trackers are moving all day to track the sun additional slack is required in the tracker wiring to account for the movement. This slack wiring tends to get caught on the tracker base and pulls loose at the connection points causing an open circuit. At least one half of the output from the tracking subfield is lost each time this occurs.

One notable event occurred in late January, 1987 and lasted through mid-February, 1987. Three of the eight trackers in Subfield A failed due to unusually heavy snow (drifting up to three feet). Two trackers stalled (i.e. ceased tracking) while the third fell completely off of its pedestal after shearing all of its baseplate bolts. The pedestal and bolts were repaired and the tracker lifted back in place by North Anna construction personnel. Two PV modules were destroyed in the fall and subsequently replaced. This accounts for the low output of subfield A in January and February, 1987.

This unusual occurrence demonstrates the important differences which can be observed between the VISTA facility and other PV facilities elsewhere in the world. The seasonal Virginia climate and changing meteorological conditions may significantly affect the operation of PV systems in the service area. The VISTA test facility is designed to investigate these differences. It is anticipated that the availability of the tracking subfield will increase in subsequent test years due to planned changes in the TCS and subfield wiring.

Calculated normalized performance parameters (M and D values) for each subfield are plotted in Figures 4 and 5. The relative value of these measures generally follows the relative value of the input insolation as previously given in Table 1. The tracking subfield outperformed the fixed subfield for both the annual average Merit figure (11.2% difference) and the annual average Energy Density figure (17.3% difference) as was expected. The VISTA subfield energy densities compare well with the 132 to 178 AC kWh/m^2 figures of PV facilities in the southwest[(5)].

TECHNOLOGY COMPARISON

VISTA subfields B and C are used to compare fixed polycrystal with fixed single crystal performance. This is accomplished by comparing normalized figures as was done in comparing tracking operation with fixed operation.

FIGURE 4:

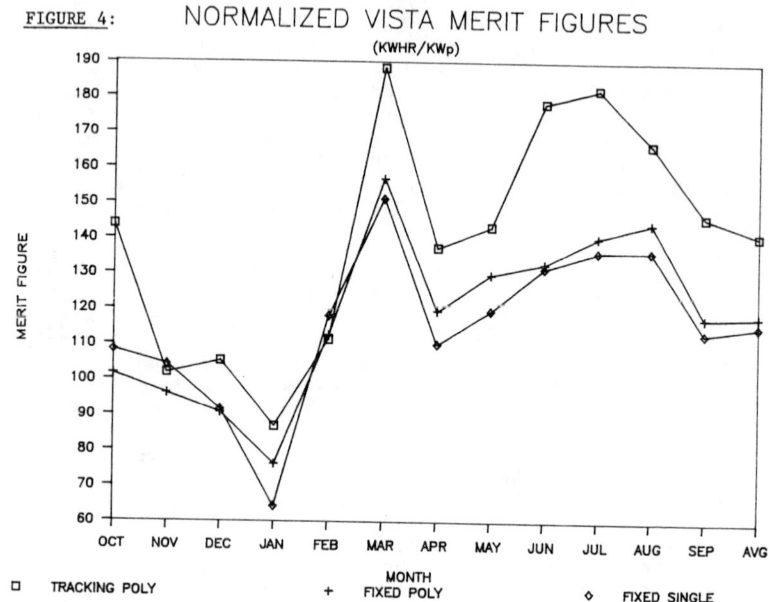

FIGURE 5:

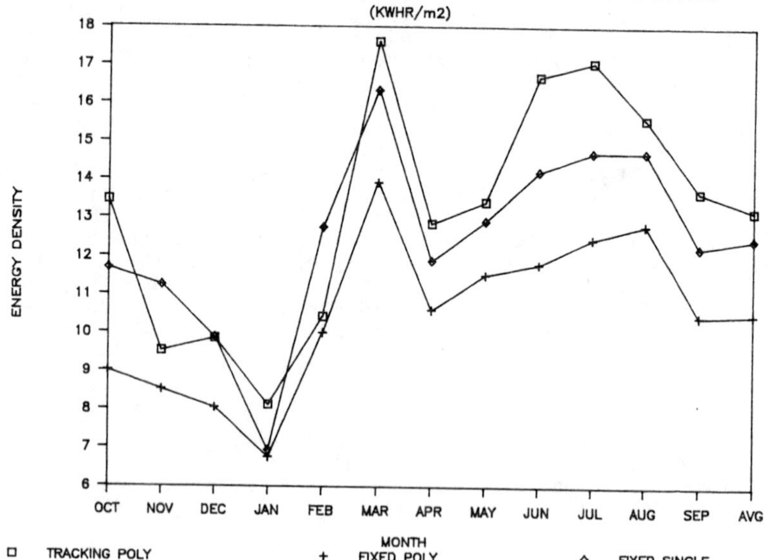

As shown previously, the fixed polycrystal subfield is rated (kWp) 2.64% higher than the fixed single crystal subfield. Table 2 shows that the polycrystal subfield generated 9.37% (5.14% after normalization) more energy than the single crystal subfield. Assuming uniform current-voltage characteristics for the two subfields (4) the polycrystal subfield produced 6.73% (2.5% after normalization) more energy than the single crystal subfield after accounting for the difference in installed rated capacity.

Although a 2.5% difference may be considered to be within experimental error, VISTA data was analyzed in order to explain this difference in subfield performance. Maximum power tracking operations of the two inverters was verified and the difference in wire losses was calculated to be less than 0.1% (6). Interarray shading was also eliminated as a possible cause of energy loss.

Under field test conditions, the polycrystal technology appears to perform closer to its rated efficiency than the single crystal technology especially during the early morning and late afternoon hours. The two technologies are standardized at rated (peak) conditions under full sun (1000 W/m^2) with efficiencies of 8.87% (polycrystal) and 10.79% (single crystal)(4). This represents a 17.79% difference in rated efficiency. When these conditions are varied (i.e. hazy cloudy skies, high humidity, or morning and afternoon sun conditions) this percent difference decreases.

By using annual average VISTA data the decreasing percent difference in efficiencies can be quantified. The VISTA annual average efficiencies of 7.79% (polycrystal) and 8.74% (single crystal) demonstrate a 10.86% difference indicating that under average field test conditions the polycrystal subfield performs better (when compared with rated conditions) than the single crystal subfield[(6)].Under average conditions in central Virginia the polycrystal subfield appears to perform 6.83% closer to its rated efficiency than the single crystal subfield. This result is to be verified in future field tests at the VISTA facility.

These efficiency derating effects may not have been as pronounced in other PV tests at other locations since most of the other side by side tests are conducted in locations where PV rated conditions (1000 W/m^2, 20°C) are more prominent than in Virginia. The fact that the VISTA test is being conducted in central Virginia's solar resource which contains more dispersed sunlight may explain the relatively strong efficiency derating effect. One technology may outperform another in this type of solar resource due to differing types of antireflective coating (a coating used to capture dispersed insolation) used among manufacturers or perhaps one technology's insolation frequency response is more sensitive to the wavelengths which are dominant in this solar resource.

A comparison of morning and afternoon VISTA PV efficiencies with similar efficiencies near solar noon shows that the angle that the sun makes with the array plane affects PV efficiency[(6)]. Also the foregoing analysis indicates that the high content of dispersed insolation in central Virginia may effect PV efficiency. The polycrystal technology appears to be able to capture more of this oblique/dispersed insolation. This performance could be due to better light trapping of the polycrystalline silicon atomic structure or due to a superior antireflective coating used by the polycrystal PV manufacturer or due to better light trapping techniques utilized by the polycrystal manufacturer.

One conclusion which could be drawn from this finding is that in comparing PV technologies, a simple kWp or efficiency rating at standard conditions is not a completely adequate measure since relative performance (energy output) could vary considerably at other than rated conditions.

CONCLUSIONS

Solar insolation for the first year of VISTA tests exceeded the TMY insolation figures by approximately 9.7% for TGI and 8.7% for API with average daily insolation of 5.91 (TGI), 4.60 (API), and 4.01 (HI) kWhrs/m^2-day. Horizontal insolation met or exceeded API for four out of the twelve test months which indicates diffuse insolation (hazy sky) conditions.

The tracking subfield produced almost 14% more energy than the fixed polycrystal subfield (36383 versus 31917 kWhrs) which produced over 9% more energy than the fixed single crystal subfield (29203 kWhrs). Annual average availabilities were 85.9%, 95.4% and 91.0% for the tracking, fixed polycrystal, and fixed single crystal subfields respectively. VISTA data indicates that, after normalizing for availability and subfield size, a tracking subfield could have produced over 20% more energy than an equally rated fixed polycrystal subfield which could have produced approximately 2.5% more energy than an equally rated fixed single crystal subfield.

The annual performance of each subfield after normalization is as expected except for the 2.5% difference between the energy generation of the single crystal subfield and the polycrystal subfield. Given the annual average insolation conditions present at the VISTA facility during the test year, the polycrystal subfield efficiency appears to remain 6.83% closer to the rated subfield efficiency than the single crystal subfield. The annual average polycrystal efficiency decreased by 12.17% while the annual average single crystal efficiency decreased by 19.00% from rated efficiency. Additional tests are to be conducted to verify these findings.

This result indicates that a simple kWp or efficiency rating at standard conditions is not a completely adequate measure of performance since relative performance (energy output) could vary considerably at other than rated conditions.

The unique design and location of the VISTA facility is providing useful information which is otherwise unavailable. This data can be used in evaluating emerging PV technologies and in estimating the performance and cost effectiveness of PV installations near the east coast.

REFERENCES

1) "Hesperia PV Power Plant: 1985 Performance Assessment," New Mexico Solar Energy Institute for the Electric Power Research Institute, (AP-5229, 1607-6), July 1987.

2) "PVFORM Version 3.2," Computer Simulations, Sandia National Labs and New Mexico Engineering Research Institute, February, 1987.

3) "Local Climatological Data Monthly Summary," National Weather Service, U. S. Dept. of Commerce, Richmond, Virginia, October 1986 - September 1987.

4) "Virginia Integrated Solar Test Arrays," New Mexico Solar Energy Institute, November 1986.

5) Draft "1986 PV Performance Evaluation Report," New Mexico Solar Energy Institute for the Electric Power Research Institute, (RP 1607-06), November 1987.

6) Draft "VISTA Solar Facility: First Annual Report," Virginia Power, Richmond, Virginia, November 1987.

STATUS OF PHOTOVOLTAICS FOR COMMERCIAL POWER GENERATION

John C. Schaefer
Electric Power Research Institute
Palo Alto, California

INTRODUCTION

Photovoltaic power generation is perhaps the simplest and most elegant mechanism known for generating electricity. The process generates direct current from sunlight, using cells that consist of a chemically treated semiconductor material--usually silicon. Each cell typically provides less than a volt and less than one ampere so they are wired in series to get more voltage and in parallel to get more current. Manufacturers produce modules ranging in size up to 20 square feet. Sunlight is a very diffuse source of energy--only about a kilowatt per square meter is available on a bright, sunny day--so large collector areas are required to generate commercially useful quantities of electricity. This fact has important implications for photovoltaics' applications, and because it would not be cost effective to repair large area systems it also places severe requirements on the reliability of the cells and interconnections in a photovoltaic (PV) system.

Experience over the past 10 years demonstrates that these systems have become extremely reliable, which is one reason for the great interest shown not only by individuals but also by institutions such as electric utilities.

COMMERCIAL APPLICATIONS

The other and perhaps more important reason for the widespread interest in PV is that it has virtually no adverse effect on the environment: no air pollution, no water pollution, no heating of rivers or lakes, no consumption of water, no consumption of expensive fuel (or any fuel), and no toxic or radioactive danger to surrounding communities.

These advantages are offset for the production of commercial electric power by one major disadvantage, high cost. The investment costs for PV systems must be reduced by a factor of at least three before PV becomes cost effective for bulk electric power. But for a wide variety of more specialized applications, PV is already cost effective: remote radio repeaters, navigational aids, small water pumping systems, highway lighting, small domestic lighting systems, cathodic protection and portable devices like radios, watches, and calculators.

Thousands of such installations exist in locations far removed from utilities' power lines. Besides remoteness of their locations, these applications are typically characterized by the need for small amounts of d.c. (a few kW or less) and high reliability. Privacy and independence are sometimes the desired characteristics; homeowners in all parts of the country have installed PV-battery-inverter systems that literally replace utility power.

EPRI believes that PV shows great promise for generating commercial grade power in the 1990's and beyond. And realizing that there is no substitute for experience with an emerging technology, an increasing number of electric utilities have installed or are evaluating line-connected systems on a test basis, with the anticipation that costs will drop within the next decade to a level that will make PV competitive with other sources of electricity. Figure 1 shows that these utilities are located in most regions of the U.S.

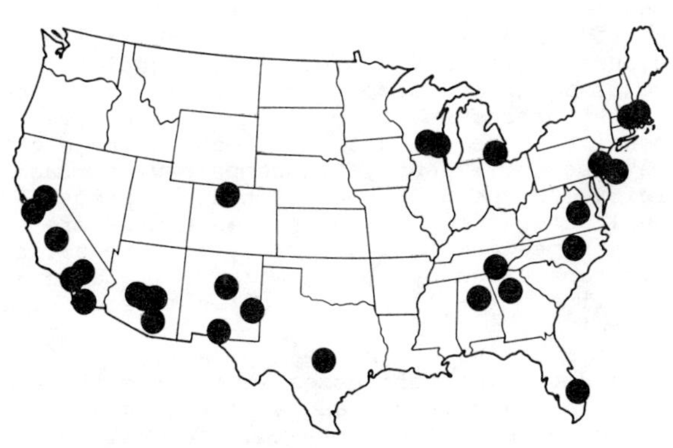

Figure 1
Utilities' Line-Connected PV Projects

REDUCING FUTURE PV COSTS FOR CANDIDATE TECHNOLOGIES

Fundamentally, two related issues determine whether a PV technology will be commercially viable for utility-scale power generation: efficiency and cost. Table 1 shows EPRI's current assessment of the industry's status and prospects for the improvements necessary to bring each of the four major technologies to commercial readiness for power generation. [1]

Table 1

Prospects for Utility-Scale Power Generation

Technology	Present Efficiency	Prospects to Increase Efficiency	Present Cost	Prospects to Reduce Cost
Flat plate crystalline	high	fair	high	fair
Flat plate polycrystalline	medium	fair	high	fair
Flat plate thin film tandem	low	good	low	good
Concentrator	medium	good	high	good

Crystalline silicon cells have been used since the beginning of PV. In such single crystal cells, all the silicon atoms are arranged in a regular lattice structure and, because it is easy to measure and analyze, the performance of a variety of cell designs is well understood. Most processes for creating single crystal cells are expensive, however, and as a result single crystal PV may always be too expensive to compete with traditional electricity sources. In the Czochralski process, the individual wafers from which cells are made are sawed from a bologna-shaped ingot of solid crystalline silicon, which itself is fabricated by slowly withdrawing a rotating seed of crystalline material from a molten mass of silicon.

Polycrystalline cells are typically cast from molten silicon, and for most processes sawed from the solid block of silicon in the same way as are single crystal cells; the difference is that polycrystalline cells consist of a collection of interlocking pieces, each of which is crystalline, whereas with single crystal cells, the whole cell is a single crystal. Polycrystalline cells are almost as efficient as single crystal, but probably not enough cheaper to make them cost effective.

Several new processes for creating crystalline and polycrystalline cells directly from molten silicon show promise for major cost reductions. In the Westinghouse dendritic web process, two dendrites or threads of crystalline silicon are placed in a molten mass of silicon and then slowly withdrawn. Under carefully controlled conditions, a web or ribbon of crystalline silicon forms between the dendrites. High efficiency cells are produced in this process, and with an approximate doubling of production rate, the cost of electricity from these cells is expected to be competitive with more conventional electricity sources.

Other processes based on a variety of ribbon growth technologies are under investigation in the U.S. and in Europe. [2]

The flat plate technology with the greatest potential for cost reduction is that based on thin film materials. Of these the best known is amorphous silicon, which is commonly employed for consumer items like calculators and watches. Because cells are formed by chemical deposition on glass or other material, the mass production costs are likely to be quite low. The materials so deposited, however, are not at all crystalline in structure, and as a result, they have properties unlike crystalline materials. One is that much less material is required to intercept the light energy, and the cells can therefore be thinner. This in turns means tandem structures can be constructed--one cell stacked on top of another--in which each layer is most responsive to a different portion of the spectrum. It is this characteristic that offers the greatest promise for thin film devices.

Other materials also show promise for PV applications: copper indium diselenide, gallium arsenide, cadmium telluride, and alloys of silicon and germanium.

Amorphous silicon modules now under test show some undesired electrical characteristics. One of these is the tendency to degrade in efficiency after exposure to light (the Staebler-Wronski effect), and another is vulnerability to electrochemical corrosion. Both of these effects are under intense investigation at this time.

The fourth major technology is based on concentrators, with which a square meter of sunlight can be collected with much less than a square meter of silicon. This saves on the amount of expensive silicon necessary (replacing it for example with acrylic fresnel lenses), and has the added benefit that at higher concentration, the cells themselves are more efficient. [3] There are some disadvantages, however. Concentrators use only the energy directly from the sun--direct or beam it is called, of which there is only about 850 watts per square meter in bright sunlight--and they require a tracking device so that the modules can be pointed directly at the sun at all times.

Here more than with any other technology high efficiency is the key to success, and development has progressed to the point where cells with 28 per cent efficiency have been built, [4] and even higher efficiency cells are possible.

With all of these different technologies as candidates it would be convenient if one or another were a clear winner. The fact that this is not the case can be viewed either as bad news or good news: the bad news is that no technology yet is a clear winner, but the good news is that all technologies are potential winners. From a strategic research and development point of view, this means research and development must proceed on all these technologies.

With respect to efficiencies, it is important to note that cells and modules form only a part of an entire system for generating a.c. Because of electrical and optical losses in a concentrator module, for example, 28 per cent cells might result in 22 per cent modules. Other wiring and inverter losses would bring total system efficiency to about 20 per cent.

The same is true of costs. In addition to modules the system consists of wiring, switchgear, inverters, and a.c. equipment, all of which could add a dollar per watt to the system costs.

FIELD TEST RESULTS

Since 1979, dozens of PV systems have been installed that now provide electricity to utilities' a.c. grids. The larger systems and the ones with more experimental technologies are described in Table 2. A quick glance at the table reveals that most are composed of single crystal modules, and only a few are amorphous or concentrators. For practical purposes, the polycrystalline systems perform like crystalline systems, and it is with these two that most systems experience has been attained. What has been learned from these line-connected systems is the following:

- Almost universally, observed outputs have fallen short of manufacturers' predictions. [5], [6], [7]
- The newer single crystal and polycrystalline cells and modules are highly reliable. [8]
- Module interconnections, blocking diodes and switches were troublesome early on, but with careful design and quality control are no longer a problem. [8], [9], [10]
- Some fires have been initiated by ground faults, and system protection issues must be carefully considered. [11]

Table 2
Line Connected PV Systems in the U.S.

Location	Date On line	Type	Manuf. Rating (kW)	Tracking	Problems
Mt. Laguna, CA	8/79	crys & poly	60	fixed	out of service
Natural Br., UT	6/80	crystalline	97	fixed	modules
Newman P.S., TX	1/81	crystalline	18	fixed	
Beverly, MA	2/81	crystalline	100	fixed	inverter problems
Lovington, NM	3/81	crystalline	100	fixed	inverter problems
Blytheville, AR	10/81	concentrator	240	1 axis	out of service (parabolic)
McClelland AFB, CA		crystalline	40	fixed	
San Bernardino, CA	1/82	polycrystalline	35	fixed	
Kauai, HI	1/82	concentrator	35	1 axis	out of service (parabolic)
Oklahoma City, OK	2/82	polycrystalline	135	fixed	
Albuquerque, NM	4/82	concentrator	47	1 axis	out of service (parabolic)
Phoenix, AZ	5/82	concentrator	225	2 axis	ground faults
Dallas FW, TX	5/82	concentrator	27	2 axis	inverter problems
Hesperia, CA	12/82	crystalline	1000	2 axis	tracker problems
Georgetown, DC	9/84	polycrystalline	300	fixed	electric & inverter problems
Carrisa 1A, CA	11/83	crystalline	5750	2 axis	
SMUD PV1, CA	8/84	crystalline	1000	1 axis	inverter fire
Carrisa 1B, CA	8/85	crystalline	750	2 axis	
SMUD PV2, CA	11/85	crys & poly	1000	1 axis	
John Long, AZ	11/85	crystalline	192	fixed	
Virginia Power	1/86	polycrystalline	25	fixed	
Virginia Power	1/86	polycrystalline	25	2 axis	snow
Virginia Power	2/86	crystalline	25	fixed	
Philadelphia Elec., PA	8/86	amorphous	4	fixed	bar graph corrosion
Alabama Power	9/86	amorphous	100	fixed	ground faults
Austin, TX	2/87	crystalline	300	1 axis	
Detroit Edison	5/87	amorphous	4	fixed	
Madison, WI	3/87	amorphous	2	fixed	

- For some western utilities at least, there is a high correspondence between system peak loads and PV output. [12], [13]

- Large scale PV plants can be designed and built in less than a year. [13]

- PV plants are generally reliable; equipment availabilities for Hesperia were 96 per cent and 97 per cent in 1985 and 1986. [6], [14]

- Operating and maintenance costs for flat plate systems are well below one cent per kWh. [6], [14]

PV systems' failure to produce the outputs predicted is due partly to manufacturers' use of rating conditions different from those encountered in the field. PV module efficiency decreases with higher temperature, and manufacturers often rate modules at 25°C module temperature or cell temperature. However, modules in the field typically operate at 45°C or higher. For purposes of evaluation, regression analysis can be used to calculate what the output would be at 25°C module temperature or at another widely used condition, 20°C ambient temperature. For the 1000 kW Hesperia plant, these calculated ratings based on measured data are 793 kW and 728 kW, respectively, for 25°C module and 20°C ambient. This considerable difference is a source of some concern, and has encouraged purchasers to specify acceptance test conditions carefully in recent purchases.

For utility applications the potential cost reductions with amorphous silicon (and eventually other thin-film materials) have encouraged utilities to install the four amorphous silicon systems shown in Table 2. Results from these systems show the following:

- Performance degradation has occurred as expected in varying amounts and over periods of time up to several months.

- Delamination of the amorphous silicon material from the glass superstrate has been observed with some modules, probably as a result of electrochemical corrosion.

- Ground faults have occurred with some developmental modules, probably also a result of electrochemical corrosion.

Discouraging though these problems may appear to be, they reflect in a general way the same kind of problems seen in some of the early crystalline modules. For example, at Natural Bridges, Utah, the modules discolored severely and the encapsulant actually leaked out, but the system continued to operate. At Mt. Laguna, California, the modules gradually failed over a period of several years. At both of these early sites, the original efficiencies in 1980 ranged from 3 to 6 per cent, just about the same range as is now seen in the commercially available amorphous silicon modules. In the intervening eight years, crystalline technology has now advanced to the point where commercial modules approach 14 per cent in efficiency.

There is no guarantee that amorphous silicon will progress along the same eight-year path that single crystal development has taken, but if it does, amorphous silicon modules of roughly 15 per cent efficiency will be on the market by the mid 1990's, and will probably be more cost effective than those of single crystal. It is this promise that has attracted researchers from all around the world to work on amorphous silicon development.

The fourth major technology noted in Table 1 now shows potential for the earliest cost effective commercialization. Although only five concentrator systems appear in Table 2, their experience plus the recent, significant breakthroughs in cell design have yielded a high probability of success; test cell efficiencies in the high 20's translate to module efficiencies over 20 per cent. There are no scientific breakthroughs known to be necessary, although a considerable amount of engineering development and testing is required in the areas of cell processing, cell mount design, optical design, module development, and tracker improvements.

Both EPRI and Sandia National Laboratories have development work under way on the newest generation of concentrator modules.

UTILITY INTEREST

About two dozen utilities are now involved in PV test programs of their own, which range in size from less than a kW to 1,000 kW. This interest stems from their belief that PV will play some role in future power generation. In the West, interest tends to focus on large-scale technology such as concentrators which can be applied in the large, open desert spaces, whereas in the East more interest centers on systems that can be mounted on rooftops or smaller land areas.

The business interest varies also. Some utilities view PV as a business opportunity in an unregulated area; at least one utility is now expanding this interest into a manufacturing partnership. Many others are sponsoring research and demonstration programs to expand their own and the industry's understanding of the technology.

INDUSTRY OUTLOOK FOR PV SUPPLY

The U.S. industry supplying capital equipment, cells, modules, inverters, and engineering services has experienced a consolidation process over the past several years, with some firms disappearing, others in Chapter 11, and almost all refocusing their efforts on new areas.

While this sounds unsettling, in fact it reflects the changes necessary to assure a healthy industry, as the technology evolves.

The U.S. industry structure now consists of very large firms like Westinghouse, Arco, and Mobil, as well as a number of very small ones; this too reflects the dynamic nature of the industry and hopefully its ability as a whole to compete in world markets.

Like many industries, PV is definitely going multinational; in fact, Japanese firms now supply about half of the world's PV capacity, up markedly from a few years ago. This can be viewed either as a threat--which it is for firms without a world view--or as confirmation of PV's bright future as seen from a worldwide perspective.

In conclusion, the industry has demonstrated the technological feasibility of PV for utility applications, and there is at this point a good likelihood that its economic feasibility for large scale applications is just as promising.

REFERENCES

[1] Edgar A. DeMeo and Roger W. Taylor, "Solar Photovoltaic Power Systems: An Electric Utility Perspective," Science, 20 April 1984.

[2] Proceedings of the Nineteenth IEEE Photovoltaic Specialists Conference, New Orleans, May, 1987 provides a wealth of detail on these and other emerging technologies.

[3] Taylor Moore, "Opening the Door for Utility Photovoltaics," EPRI Journal, January/February, 1987.

[4] R. A. Sinton and R. M. Swanson, "An Optimization Study of Si Point Contact Concentrator Solar Cells," Nineteenth IEEE Photovoltaic Specialists Conference, New Orleans, May, 1987.

[5] Boeing Computer Services, Photovoltaic Field Test Performance Assessment, EPRI Report AP4466, March, 1986.

[6] New Mexico Solar Energy Institute, Hesperia Photovoltaic Power Plant: 1985 Performance Assessment, EPRI Report AP5229, July, 1987.

[7] Pacific Gas and Electric Company, PG&E Photovoltaic Module Performance Assessment, EPRI Report AP4464, March, 1986.

[8] V. Vernon Risser and John C. Schaefer, "PV System Failures, Test Techniques, and Analysis," Seventh European Community Photovoltaic Solar Energy Conference, Sevilla, October, 1986.

[9] New Mexico Solar Energy Institute, Reports on site visits to Newman Power Station Photovoltaic System in January, September, and October, 1985.

[10] New Mexico Solar Energy Institute, Report on site visits to Lovington Square Shopping Center Photovoltaic System in Lovington, NM, in February, 1985 and August, 1987.

[11] Tom Lepley, "Report on the Array Fire at the Sky Harbor Airport Photovoltaic Concentrator Project," Arizona Public Service Company, January 18, 1985.

[12] N. W. Patapoff and D. R. Mattijetz, "Utility Interconnection Experience with an Operating Central Station MW-Sized Photovoltaic Plant," IEEE Power Engineering Society Winter Meeting, February, 1985.

[13] Tom Hoff and Gary Shushnar, "Two Years of Performance Data for the World's Largest Photovoltaic Power Plant," IEEE Transactions on Energy Conversion, June, 1987.

[14] New Mexico Solar Energy Institute, 1986 Performance Evaluation of the Hesperia, SMUD, and Phoenix Photovoltaic Power Plants, Forthcoming EPRI report.

CRYSTALLINE PHOTOVOLTAIC CELL TECHNOLOGY: PRESENT AND FUTURE*

Dan E. Arvizu, Supervisor
Photovoltaic Cell Research Division
Sandia National Laboratories
Albuquerque, New Mexico 87185

ABSTRACT

This paper will summarize the status of crystalline cell research in the program managed by Sandia National Laboratories and sponsored by the U.S. Department of Energy (DOE). Recent advances in high efficiency and program direction will be discussed for each of the three program elements which include one-sun crystalline silicon, concentrator silicon, and concentrator III-V material cells.

Introduction

The promise of photovoltaic technology to be a significant contributor in supplying the future world demand for energy is well established. It is the intent of the U.S. Department of Energy (DOE) to pursue and expedite this promise for several reasons. The desire to be energy self-sufficient, the environmental concerns with conventional fossil fuels or nuclear options, and the energy security offered by a distributed energy system are just a few of the reasons photovoltaic technology is such an attractive energy option. Recently, the U.S. DOE published its newly revised Five Year Research Plan for photovoltaics (1). In this plan the general philosophy for

---

* This work supported by the U.S. Department of Energy, Photovoltaic Energy Technology Division

conducting research is stated by the DOE. This philosophy is "to sponsor research and development in photovoltaic energy technology that will result in a technology base from which private industry can choose options for further development and competitive application in U.S. utility markets". Sandia National Laboratories, manager of the one-sun crystalline silicon and concentrator cell DOE program tasks, has fashioned its Cell Research Project consistent with this philosophy. This paper will first introduce the economic factors driving cell research, and then discuss the research status in the three primary areas of crystalline cell technology. These areas are one-sun silicon, concentrator silicon, and concentrator III-V material cells. The motivating technical issues and research directions of each will also be discussed.

Economics

The current technological status of photovoltaics can briefly be summarized by saying that utility experience with grid-connected crystalline silicon based systems has been very favorable as evidenced by continued utility interest in the advancing photovoltaic technology. The remaining obstacle for full utility acceptance is cost. Today, a commercial photovoltaic system for utility-scale application will have a levelized energy cost (LEC) in the range of \$0.30 - \$0.40/kWh (2). (The economic assumptions and the calculation procedure for LEC are given in reference 1). While at present, several economic analyses predict that system costs must be in the \$0.06 - \$0.12/kWh range to be competitive with conventional energy sources available to utilities, there remains considerable uncertainty on how the energy climate will change in the future. Furthermore, because of the variability in U.S. utilities, it appears reasonable that there is no single threshold cost that will make or break the technology. It is more feasible that as prices are reduced greater penetration into various sectors of the utility markets will occur. For these reasons it is useful to plan research programs with these economic uncertainties in mind. Specifically, it is beneficial to parametrically view the cost/performance matrix on the various technology options, so that when improvements are made, the influence on total system cost-effectiveness can be accurately assessed.

Figures 1 and 2 portray a Sandia analysis on the cell cost versus cell peak efficiency tradeoff for flat plate and concentrator applications, respectively. The analysis is an updated adaptation of previous work (3,4) and describes how cell cost (in $\$/cm^2$) and cell efficiency are interrelated with the overall system LEC. For this analysis it is assumed that system indirect charges are 25%, the systems are located in the sunny U.S. Southwest or equivalent location, and the balance of system costs are what is projected for the mid-1990s. Also, for the flat plate case it is assumed that the cell cost is roughly one-half the overall module cost. (Note Figure 1 also has axes labelled for module cost and performance which make it also more generally applicable to all flat plate modules including thin-film approaches.) Finally, in the concentrator case the data of Figure 2 assumes the cell cost is one-fourth of the total module cost (5), a 300x geometric concentration ratio, and a cell area based on die size where the cell die area to cell active area ratio is 1.5. (As in the case of Figure 1, Figure 2 has axes labelled with module cost and performance so that comparisons can be made independent of concentration ratio and percentage of the module cost that the cell represents.)

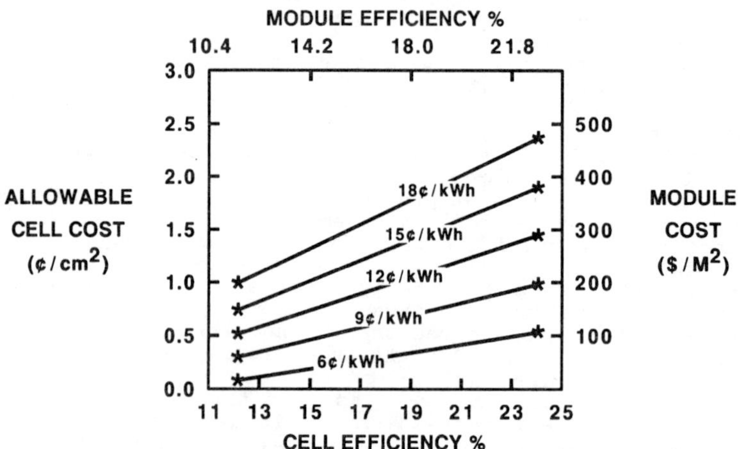

Figure 1. Fixed flat plate cell cost versus peak performance for various system levelized energy costs. See assumptions in text.

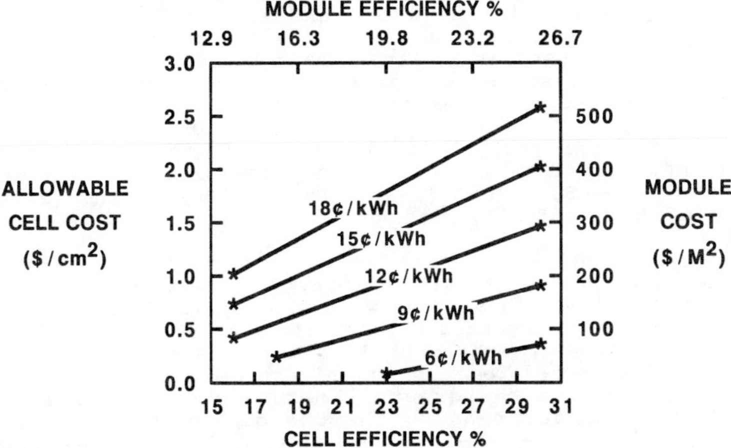

Figure 2. Concentrator cell cost versus peak performance for various system levelized energy costs. See assumptions in text.

The primary message to be extracted from Figures 1 and 2 is that to insure utility scale application of photovoltaic technology the challenges are great. From a cell research perspective the challenges are even more pronounced since it appears that cell improvements must come simultaneously in cost and performance. In the following sections the research progress and the promise of the future are indicated.

Cell Performance Status

A more extensive review of crystalline cell research status than is possible here is given in reference 6; however, special emphasis is given to recent performance demonstrations and these are included in this paper.

One-sun Crystalline Silicon

Presently, several manufacturers world-wide market flat plate crystalline silicon modules. The technologies being used can be divided into three general categories; (1) ingot or wafer-based cells that use single or polycrystalline silicon, (2) ribbon-based cells from single or polycrystalline silicon, and (3) cells from thin, polycrystalline, silicon film deposited on an inexpensive substrate. Associated with each of these is a unique set of technical issues in addition to a more generic set of issues related to fundamental understanding common to all. From Figure 1 it is apparent that regardless of the specific approach, the goals to penetrate U.S. utility markets for crystalline silicon cells are; (1) to reach costs below $0.01/cm^2$ (equivalently $100/m^2$) and (2) to achieve cell efficiencies approaching 20%.

Although the U.S. one-sun silicon research effort is modest in funding relative to previous years, the goals of the program are consistent with those needed for utility application. Program goals are aimed at first addressing the more generic fundamental technical issues primarily through sponsored research at universities. These generic issues include the growth kinetics for high quality material, understanding the charge carrier lifetime limiting mechanisms, and the requirements for high efficiency cells. As program resources permit, more specific technological issues will also be addressed.

Today ingot or wafer based modules cost about $5/W, and although current research promises to lower costs to near $2.0/W (7), this module approach is given little chance of meeting utility scale goals because of the high cost of wafer production and handling. Nonetheless, this approach enjoys an advantage in that interim markets may be pursued, and systems experience gained, as the research necessary to meet utility markets is conducted. The silicon ribbon approach has more promise because of its more effective material utilization. Today, two major ribbon approaches remain from a field of more than a dozen. These are the Westinghouse dendritic web and the Mobil edge-supported film-fed growth (EFG). Both are still in an R&D mode and face significant challenges related to reducing costs associated with silicon growth rate while maintaining high quality material. However, both have also shown significant progress in the last year, and with continued progress, there are now projections for module costs in the next few years of $1.50/W. Note both have demonstrated pilot line cell efficiencies in the 14 to 15% range (7) while continuing to improve area throughput. Noteable progress in applying high efficiency techniques to web material has been made by Westinghouse as demonstrated by a 16.6% dendritic web cell (1.0 cm^2) as measured at Sandia (AM1.5 global spectrum).

The silicon film on inexpensive substrate approach has recently achieved a significant milestone. Astropower has fabricated several 1.0 cm^2 cells over 12% efficient with the highest reported at 12.6% efficiency (as measured at Sandia for a AM1.5 global spectrum). The projection of module costs produced in a 1 MW production facility is \$1.37/W in the near term and \$0.83 in the longer term with an advanced process (7).

In one-sun high efficiency research both Stanford and the University of New South Wales (UNSW) have demonstrated the potential of silicon with research cells near 22%. More recently, UNSW has demonstrated a 19.8%, 10 Ω-cm FZ, 13 cm^2 laser-groove cell using no photo-lithography (8) which compares well with the 47 cm^2 cell in CZ at 18.9% reported by UNSW last year. In other work UNSW also has fabricated 16.6% polycrystalline silicon cells (1.0 cm^2) also measured at Sandia. Furthermore, the latest modelling results using PC1-D (9) indicate production environment efficiencies for silicon materials with greater than 10 μs carrier lifetime can be as high as 20% with light trapping and surface passivation (10).

Concentrator Silicon

Concentrator technology was originally pursued as a way to circumvent the high cost of cells in flat plate approaches. As the various photovoltaic options have evolved, concentrator approaches have come to the forefront in the race to become the most cost-effective option for utility applications. This status has been achieved primarily on the strength of the rapid progress demonstrated in high efficiency silicon cells. However, as Figure 2 indicates, cell cost, even in concentrator applications, cannot be ignored. There is a distinct tradeoff to be made when cell cost versus efficiency is considered. Clearly, increased concentration relaxes the cell cost requirement; however, current technology indicates that cell costs also increase with optimized higher concentration cells. (Also note that the best performance demonstrated to date with high efficiency silicon cells has been in the 100 to 300 suns range.) The Sandia concentrator silicon research effort is primarily aimed at continuing to understand the requirements for high efficiency and applying this understanding in the design of cells that can cost-effectively be used in commercial modules.

The best performance concentrator cells have been demonstrated in the past two years at Stanford in high resistivity silicon (11) with near 28% at 140X and at UNSW in low resistivity silicon (12) with near 25% at 110X. These results, and especially the Stanford results, have provided a new understanding in high efficiency silicon research. They have demonstrated that all of the dominant carrier recombination mechanisms can be simultaneously minimized and that light trapping can be achieved in practice. Continued work to improve these cells (modeling codes such as PC1-D predict over 30% is available) and to find inexpensive ways to fabricate cells ready for advanced concentrating modules is underway with Sandia sponsored research at Stanford, UNSW, Spire, Solarex, SERA Solar, and MA-COM/PHI. To date, UNSW has demonstrated the best module ready cells with 23% at 150X that are designed for use with Sandia's 200X Experimental Module (13). In a similar effort at Stanford, progress on module ready cells has produced several new high efficiency point contact cells with a double layer back metal. The most promising results include a cell mounted to a metallized substrate which is currently undergoing qualification testing at Sandia. Efficiency numbers will be reported at the conclusion of these tests. Some work is also underway to support the low concentration module option under development at ENTECH (currently the lowest price photovoltaic system option advertised on the market at \$3 to \$4/W_{pac}) using their novel optical prism cover and low cost one-sun technology cells. This prism cover also opens up new possibilities for advanced high concentration cells as demonstrated by new cells fabricated by UNSW with ENTECH applied prism covers that are 22.5% at 200 suns concentration despite 50% metal grid coverage.

III-V Material Concentrator Cells

It has been well established that very high efficiency can be obtained by multijunction cell approaches. In the context of concentrator technology this very high efficiency can provide significant cost leverage and could eventually be the optimum path to cost-effectiveness. However, the materials required for fabricating these multijunction cells, the III-V materials, are not well understood and large resources are required to grow and work with these materials. Although the terrestrial photovoltaic program cannot provide all the needed support, progress continues because there is strong interest in III-V's, primarily in the space applications community. The best single junction GaAs cell was demonstrated by Varian several years ago with 26.0% at 700X concentration. Since that time several groups have reported efficiencies over 25% and one sun efficiencies have recently been increased to 23.7% by Spire Corporation (7). Also, a Varian/ENTECH cell developed for NASA's Cassegrainian concentrator for space with a prism cover has recently been measured at Sandia with 26.4% efficiency at 100X AM1.5. These advances represent significant progress in the fabrication of III-V cells.

In multijunction related technology, several new advances have been made in the last year. Improvements in AlGaAs, GaAsP, InP, and InGaAs have been reported by several DOE contractors (7). In multijunction devices, Sandia has assembled a mechanically stacked GaAs (Varian) on silicon (Applied Solar Energy Corporation) cell with 26.6% efficiency at 300X. In other work Varian and Chevron have demonstrated a 26.1% GaAs on Ge mechanically stacked cell at 285X. Most recently, SERI sponsored work at Varian has produced the highest efficiency monolithic multijunction stacked cell with an AlGaAs on GaAs cell measured at one sun with over 23% efficiency in a 3-terminal configuration and 22% in a 2-terminal configuration. Varian has also made progress in high bandgap cells to be used as a top cell in a multijunction stack. Two AlGaAs cells have been measured under an AM1.5 direct spectrum at SERI with 16.8% efficiency at 1.75 eV and 14.9% efficiency at 1.93 eV. These advances are positive evidence that we are on the path to the predicted 30 to 35% multijunction cells.

Summary

Crystalline cell technology continues to make significant progress on several fronts. (See Table 1.) Our programmatic perspective is that the various competing options are in different states of maturity and all seem to provide enough promise that our research program will remain balanced. Continued progress is expected and we remain optimistic that one or more of the present crystalline cell options will meet the challenge required for utility scale applications.

CRYSTALLINE CELL RESEARCH STATUS AND PROJECTIONS

	TODAY (%)	FUTURE (%)
ONE SUN SILICON		
FLOAT ZONE	21	25
CZOCHRALSKI	19	23
POLYCRYSTALLINE	16	20
CONCENTRATOR SILICON		
HIGH RESISTIVITY	28	32
LOW RESISTIVITY	25	30
MODULE READY - 200X	23	28
MODULE READY - 20X	19	24
CONCENTRATOR III-V		
GaAs	26	34
MULTIJUNCTION - MECH STK	27	38
MULTIJUNCTION - MONO STK	24	40

Table 1.

References

[1] U.S. Dept. of Energy, Five Year Research Plan 1987-1991, National Photovoltaic Program, April 1987, DOE/CH10093-7.

[2] H. Post and M. Thomas, "Photovoltaic Systems for Current and Future Applications", Solar 87 ASES Proceedings, July 1987.

[3] H. Post, D. Arvizu, and M. Thomas, "A Comparison of Photovoltaic System Options for Today's and Tomorrow's Technology", 18th IEEE-PVSC Proceedings, October 1985, p.1353.

[4] D. Arvizu, "Photovoltaic Concentrator Research Progress", 18th IEEE-PVSC Proceedings, October 1985.

[5] E. Boes and A. Maish, "Advances in Concentrator Technololgy", 19th IEEE-PVSC Proceedings, May 1987.

[6] D. King and D. Arvizu, "Crystalline Cell Research: Today and Tomorrow", 19th IEEE-PVSC Proceedings, May 1987.

[7] Sandia National Laboratories, C. Chiang - Editor, Proceedings of the Joint Crystalline Cell Research and Concentrating Collector Projects Review, August 1987, SAND87-1750.

[8] Private communication - M. Green, UNSW and D King, Sandia, work performed on Sandia contract 06-2755.

[9] D. Rover, P. Basore, and G. Thorson, "Solar Cell Modeling on Personal Computers", 18th IEEE-PVSC Proceedings, October 1985, p.703.

[10] P. Basore, "Production Efficiency Goals for Silicon Solar Cells", 19th IEEE-PVSC Proceedings, May 1987.

[11] R. Sinton, et.al., "27.5% Silicon Concentrator Solar Cells", IEEE Electron Device Letters, Volume EDL-7, Number 10, October 1986.

[12] M. Green, "25% Efficient Low-Resistivity Silicon Concentrator Solar Cells", IEEE Electron Device Letters, Volume EDL-7, Number 10, October 1986.

[13] D. Arvizu, "Development of the Sandia 200X Experimental Silicon Module", 17th IEEE-PVSC Proceedings, May 1984.

GEOTHERMAL ENERGY -- A SECURE, COST-COMPETITIVE ENERGY SOURCE FOR THE U.S.

Dr. John E. Mock, Director
Geothermal Technology Division, Department of Energy

Gene V. Beeland, Meridian Corporation

A geothermal session on the agenda of the Energy Technology Conference is an important indicator of the widening interest and confidence in this alternative source of energy. I am pleased to represent the Geothermal Technology Division of the U.S. Department of Energy on the panel and to participate in the session with colleagues from the geothermal community.

My role in the discussion will be to set the stage for the presentations of the other geothermal speakers with a broad brush description of geothermal energy, its value, size, and technological requirements and limitations, as well as to provide a report on the current status of selected technology developments within the Geothermal Technology Division.

But, first, I would like to congratulate the U.S. geothermal industry on remaining "bullish" on geothermal energy, to quote an industry spokesman, despite the uncertainties that persist in the energy supply and cost arena that are no doubt the subject of many discussions here at the Conference.

The industry has developed or is developing 20 liquid-dominated, or hot water, reservoirs in six states for power generation. The use of this form of the resource is inherently more risky and costly than the use of the rare dry steam at The Geysers field in California, the most familiar form of geothermal energy to most people. While there are still technological limitations on hot water development in many areas, the industry is moving ahead with development at the more favorable reservoirs, primarily with small "ice-breaker" plants to test the producibility and longevity of the reservoirs at a time of very low demand for their product. This development is occurring despite conditions that could be expected to exert a very depressing effect upon an infant industry, and it demonstrates the industry's foresight in being prepared for increased power demand. When there are markets for the output of large plants, the industry will have learned enough about the reservoirs to select optimum sites for building them.

Another indication of industry's increasing confidence in the hot water resource, which has been a primary focus of DOE's technology development program from its inception, is the number of developers who are expanding their geothermal interests from The Geysers to hot water fields. The significance of this is that production of dry steam, either for sale to utilities or for the developer's own use, has been an established, very profitable enterprise for some years. On the other hand, hot water power development only began in this country seven years ago, and, until 1985, operating experience was exceedingly limited and the economics very uncertain. Yet the economics are already sufficiently attractive <u>in some areas</u> to induce Geysers' developers into expanding into more difficult and less certain hot water ventures.

The rapid pace at which hot water power development has become competitive has also impacted the overall nature of the geothermal industry. In the beginning, it was, to a large degree, a mixture of extremes in size and financial resources from major oil companies to what has been called "seat-of-the-pants" entrepreneurs. Now, while the number of major oil company participants has declined somewhat, other very substantial members of the industrial community have been attracted to the industry. The major business interests of these firms include chemical manufacture, pulp, paper, and forest products, mining and other mineral interests, architecture and engineering, and energy conversion equipment manufacture. Major firms in the financial community have also become key players in the geothermal industry. In addition, some companies that began life as small entrepreneurial firms formed solely for the exploitation of geothermal energy have become highly successful big business. In sum, while the developer arm of the industry is not large in total numbers, the industry has matured and settled in for long-term development.

<u>TYPES OF GEOTHERMAL ENERGY</u>

Perhaps I should refer to this industry more precisely as the U.S. <u>hydrothermal</u> industry because hydrothermal fluids are the only form of the geothermal resource under commercial development today. These fluids -- water and/or steam recovered from fractured or porous rocks -- are attainable at higher temperatures in shallower wells at less cost than can be achieved in other types of systems. However, within the hydrothermal category, there are wide variations in resource characteristics, technological requirements, and cost which I feel sure Dr. Otte will address.

Geopressured geothermal energy is a more complex hot fluid resource, confined under higher than normal pressures in sedimentary rocks and saturated with methane, or natural gas. The largest identified deposits lie along the Gulf Coast in Louisiana and Texas.

Igneous related geothermal systems are those containing both solidified magma, or hot dry rock as it is commonly called, and unsolidified magma, or molten rock. The technology for recovering heat from hot dry rock is to inject water into one wellbore, circulate it through a man-made, hydraulically-fractured reservoir to absorb the subsurface heat, and bring it to the surface through a second wellbore. This technology has been proven on a limited scale.

Of all geothermal categories, magma contains the most stored heat per unit volume of mass; however, the technological problems of utilizing this heat are obviously the most difficult. The accessible depths are currently believed to be between 10,000 and 30,000 feet, and temperatures are estimated to range from 850-1200°C or 1560-2200°F.

VALUE OF GEOTHERMAL ENERGY

Contribution to the National Interest

Geothermal energy in all of these forms is an extremely valuable asset to the nation. First, it contributes to both national security and energy stability -- inseparable features of the national interest-- in several ways. It provides the only viable commercially available base load alternative to fossil-fired and nuclear power plants; the short lead times for project completion would permit expeditious gear-up in an energy emergency; our vulnerability to interruptions in worldwide energy supply is reduced; and the military has another option for use on its installations, particularly in remote locations where geothermal energy is available. Geothermal energy also enhances the Nation's energy strength through its contribution to a balanced and diversified energy mix which fosters open market choices, through its capability for multiple uses, and through the modular mode of construction available. Modular construction means that power units can be delivered and installed economically, even in the remote mountainous regions where geothermal resources are often located. These units can be maintained with "off-the-shelf" components, and they can be transported for use in another area in case of early reservoir failure.

Size of the Geothermal Resource in the U.S.

As shown in Exhibit 1, geothermal energy is a large potential source of energy. A panel of geothermal experts meeting at Los Alamos, New Mexico, in October 1986, equated the U.S. total of 1.2 x 10^{6} quads to 2000 trillion barrels of oil as raw energy in the ground. But, the question is asked, how much of this energy is obtainable? In other words, after taking energy recoverability into account, is there still a large resource? By all estimates so far, there is a large source of recoverable, usable energy.

As seen in Exhibit 2, the highest quality hydrothermal reservoirs, those with temperatures in excess of 150°C (300°F), both vapor- and liquid-dominated, to a depth of 3 km, account for 4800 quads. According to USGS estimates, about 25 percent, or 1200 quads, of this accessible resource base may be extracted economically with current technology (1). In addition, another 1200 quads are available in the temperature range of 90-150°C (194-300°F) "under reasonable assumptions of technological improvement and economic favorability."

The total hydrothermal resource -- all fluids with temperatures above 90°C (194°F) -- are estimated by USGS to be capable of providing from 95,000 to 150,000 MW of electricity for 30 years, or up to the capacity of 150 large coal-fired or nuclear plants. In addition, the low-temperature portion of this resource could provide about eight

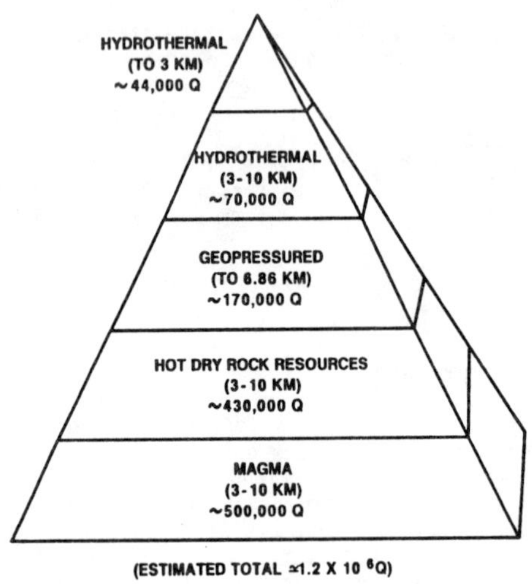

EXHIBIT 1

GEOTHERMAL IS A LARGE POTENTIAL SOURCE OF ENERGY

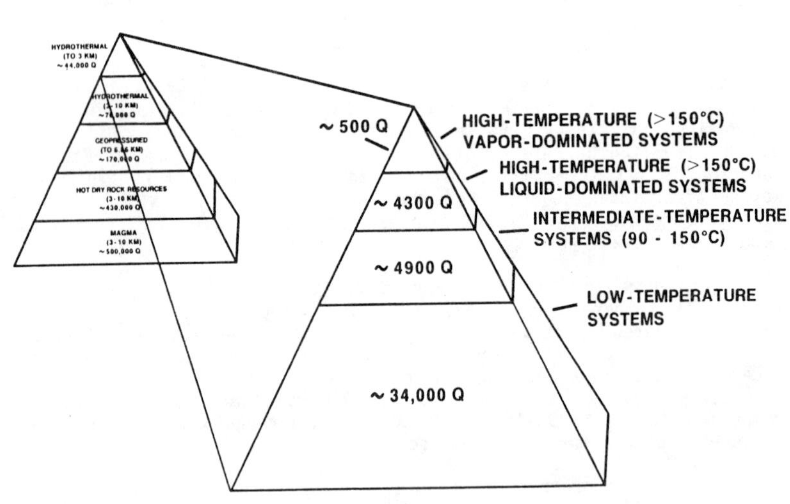

EXHIBIT 2

HYDROTHERMAL RESOURCES

quads of useful heat per year for 30 years (1).

The hydrothermal estimates could increase as more information on fluid temperatures in the Cascades Range of the Pacific Northwest is developed. Since the temperatures of these reservoirs are thought to be masked by cool groundwater, the current hydrothermal figures may be grossly underestimated.

USGS has made an estimate of the recoverability of energy in geopressured brines according to mode of production -- i.e., wellhead pressure to limit subsidence vs. unrestricted wellhead pressure. In the first case, the recoverability estimate is 0.5 percent, or 430 quads, and in the latter, 3.3 percent, or 4,400 quads (1). No subsidence attributable to geopressured long-term well tests has yet been detected even though a well was produced at a maximum rate to stress the reservoir for experimental purposes.

At the lower number, assuming a conversion efficiency of eight percent, the thermal energy in geopressured brines would provide 23,000 MWe for 30 years; at the higher number, the potential capacity would be 240,000 MWe for 30 years. These figures do not include methane since USGS did not consider it to be used locally (1). Thus, if the results of a hybrid power generation experiment set to begin next year using both the thermal energy and methane in the same operation proves to be successful the geopressured estimates will go higher, especially since such a system can produce over 15 percent more electricity than the same amount of fuel and geothermal fluids in separate power plants.

While the USGS has not published recoverability estimates for hot dry rock, the National Research Council (NRC) addressed this factor in 1979 (2). Pointing out that although information on hot dry rock was fragmentary, an assumed recovery factor of only one percent, according to its calculations, would indicate 1235 quads of producible energy at depths less than 6 km.

The NRC estimate for magma is out-of-date since it was based on the conclusion that "some" Alaskan volcanoes are the only accessible magma bodies within the U.S. (2). Using information developed since that time, the geothermal program at Stanford University is developing new estimates. Due to the high heat content of magma, the energy recoverability factor may be somewhat higher than for the other advanced systems.

Widespread Location

Geothermal energy is available to a number of states. As can be seen in Exhibit 3, the prime hydrothermal reservoirs in the U.S. capable of power generation with current or foreseeable technologies are located in the far western states. All of these states are taking geothermal energy into account in their energy planning, although the pace of development may be dictated more by factors other than the quality of the resource itself, such as the availability of enormous quantities of relatively cheap hydropower in the Pacific Northwest.

Power generated by geothermal energy currently accounts for about seven percent of the electricity used in California, and Nevada can foresee a large geothermal industry to export power to other more

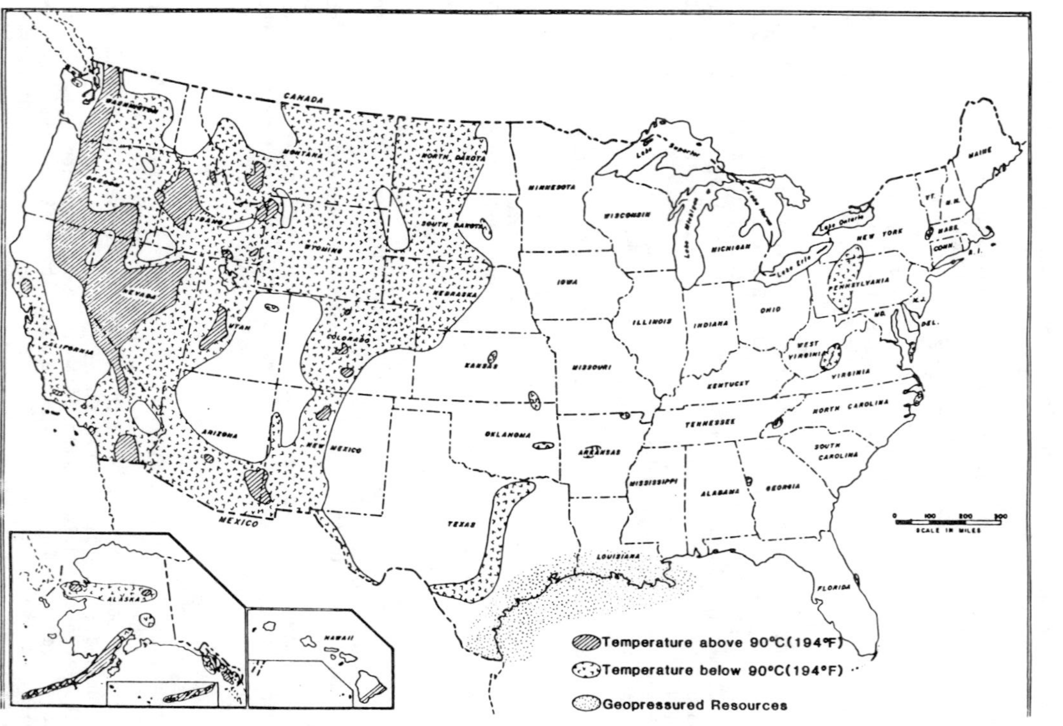

EXHIBIT 3
KNOWN AND POTENTIAL GEOTHERMAL RESOURCES

populous states. In Hawaii, if efforts to install an underwater transmission line from the Island of Hawaii, which is endowed with very hot fluids, to Oahu, the state's population center, are successful, it can be expected that geothermal energy will be used to provide a very large percentage of the power needed in that state in future years. In Oregon and Washington, the Bonneville Power Administration is taking steps to characterize their geothermal potential so that this source of energy will be included in plans for the future when additional power capacity is needed. Commercial utilization is underway in Utah with three operating plants, and small binary units have been operated in Oregon and New Mexico. Alaska appears to be on threshold of geothermal power development.

All of these states, as well as others in the west and some in the central and eastern sections of the country, have low-temperature reservoirs which are not suitable for power generation, but are attractive for direct uses. Dr. Bloomquist will discuss this potential.

Greater Reliability than Competing Fuels

Availability data on specific U.S. geothermal power plants as well as plants in Italy, Japan, Mexico, New Zealand, and El Salvador show a consistent performance above 90 percent, with the majority over 95 percent. New plants at The Geysers are approaching 100 percent, a performance achieved by two Japanese plants in 1984. A small demonstration wellhead flash plant in Hawaii is regularly available for service 98 percent of the time (3).

By comparison, according to data released by the Atomic Energy Industrial Forum, the weighted availability averages for competing fuels for 1985 were as follows (4):

Nuclear	Coal	Oil
68.4%	82.6%	79.0%

A high availability is especially important to the economics of base load plants with their high capital costs and low operating costs. When they are out of service, power from plants, which are more costly to operate, must be substituted. Thus, in areas where geothermal power is an option, it would be economic to displace some less reliable base load capacity, leaving the latter to meet peak loads.

Environmentally Preferable

Geothermal power plants generally enjoy an environmental advantage over coal-fired and nuclear plants. The geothermal plants fall into three general environmental categories:

- closed binary systems which are environmentally benign
- hot water plants using a benign resource which can comply with environmental regulations without abatement measures (e.g., a 50 MWe plant at Dixie Valley, Nevada, where the hydrogen sulfide (H_2S) and solids loads require no added controls)

- dry steam or hot water plants that employ effective abatement measures to control environmental problems.

The last category includes plants at The Geysers that use steam heavily laden with H_2S, but where all plants are in compliance with stringent California air pollution control regulations, and plants at the Salton Sea where the fluid salinity is eight times that of sea water. These are both "worst case" situations.

The substantial progress in abating H_2S emissions at The Geysers was acknowledged by Dr. Hamilton Hess, spokesman for the Sierra Club National Energy Committee and other environmental groups, speaking to a National Academy of Sciences Geothermal Workshop in February 1987. Dr. Hess reported that in 1974 at 631 MWe capacity on line, 24 tons of H_2S were emitted per day. In 1986, at approximately 1800 MWe on line, emissions had been reduced to about 4.5 tons per day. He attributed the improvement to management control at the wellheads and to abatement control equipment on the power plants. PG&E has also stated that while the quantity of steam entering its Geysers units increased about 115 percent from 1982 to 1986, the quantity of H_2S emitted to the atmosphere decreased about 78 percent (5).

The Salton Sea plants are operating successfully with the hypersaline brines through the use of a crystallizer/clarifier system. The crystallizer/clarifier controls most scaling and fouling of surface equipment, and prevents the plugging of injection formations. With this process, shown in Exhibit 4, relatively clean water is injected.

Economic Direct Uses

While DOE has contributed significantly to the refinement of direct use technologies, the Department no longer directly supports R&D on these mature technologies. However, it continues to monitor the progress of these diverse applications and the cost savings frequently involved and to provide support for direct use technology transfer. Such uses include space heating and cooling, district heating systems, agriculture, aquaculture, and industrial process heat.

A recent survey by the Geo-Heat Center at the Oregon Institute of Technology indicated a 34 percent growth in the installed capacity of direct heat geothermal projects from September 1985 to September 1986. Excluding 66 resorts, which are estimated to account for 75 billion Btu/year of energy use, the increase brought the annual use in 213 installed projects to 2081 billion Btu/year, equal to 520,000 barrels of oil.

In order to place the word "project" in the appropriate perspective, it should be remembered that in this usage, one "project" may embrace the 570 homes in Klamath Falls, Oregon, that are heated by individual wells; large multi-structure district heating systems; a heating/cooling system for an entire university -- or, conversely, one "project" may mean one residence or greenhouse. Thus, if each individual building served in some way by geothermal energy were counted as a separate project, the total would be on the order of 2000, rather than 200.

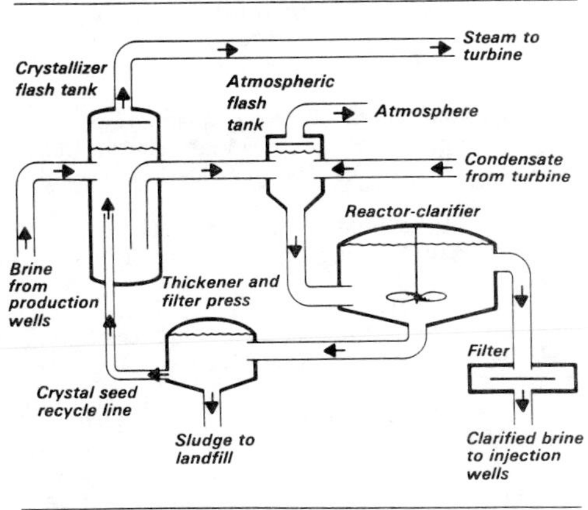

EXHIBIT 4

CRYSTALLIZER/CLARIFIER

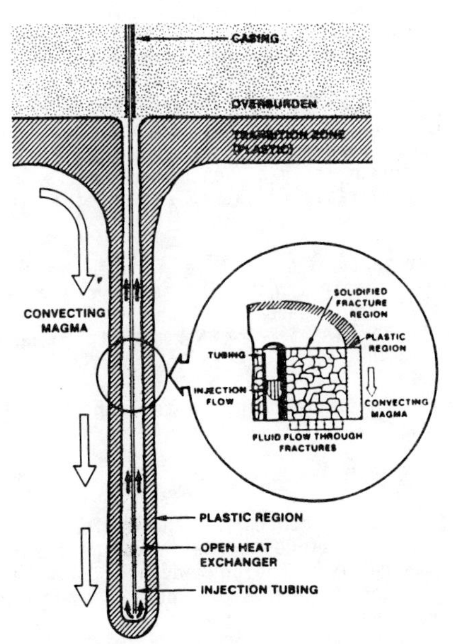

EXHIBIT 5

CONCEPTUAL REPRESENTATION OF OPEN HEAT EXCHANGER WITH FLUID FLOW THROUGH FRACTURED, SOLIDIFIED MAGMA

The most recent Geo-Heat Center listing of direct use projects indicates that 17 district heating systems are in operation, three new systems or expansions are under construction, and 11 new systems or expansions are planned. A few examples of cost savings are as follows:

- Boise Geothermal guarantees a 30 percent savings over the price of natural gas if the customer removes enough heat per gallon used to reduce the temperature by 50°F.
- Elko Heat Co., a private venture, charges its customers about 50 percent of the price of natural gas.
- First year data collected at Pagosa Springs, Colorado, indicated cost savings to individual users of 43 percent of the price of natural gas.

Greenhouse operators in Southern Idaho credit the use of geothermal energy for their success, with a consensus among them that using this heat source in the greenhouse industry is both economical and efficient. New Mexico State University has built experimental geothermal greenhouses for lease to private enterprise in order to promote expansion of the industry in that state. The Utah Rose greenhouse facility at Crystal Hot Springs in Utah initially achieved a simple pay-back of less than one year when it was constructed in 1979. It has recently been expanded to increase its cost savings in natural gas from $110,000 to $169,000 per year.

While fish and shellfish farming have long been associated with geothermal use, an unusual enterprise for Nevada has been announced--a lobster production facility south of Carson City. The owners of a number of geothermal aquaculture facilities note that without geothermal heat, their successful ventures would not have been possible.

Industrial uses of geothermal fluids are to date limited to vegetable dehydration, milk pasteurization, mushroom cultivation, commercial laundering, copper processing, and sewage digestion. Several industrial parks designed to use geothermal wells are in various planning stages and may increase industrial/commercial use very quickly.

While most direct use projects are to date located in western states, direct applications are beginning to emerge in the east. A DOE-supported heating system for two schools in Auburn, New York, is now fully operational, and the National Park Service is planning a geothermal system at Hot Springs National Park in Arkansas.

Dr. Bloomquist will provide more technical detail on direct uses and their potential in the U.S.

DOE GEOTHERMAL TECHNOLOGY DEVELOPMENT

If anyone here were hearing about geothermal energy for the first time, his logical question would be: If geothermal power generation is already so successful, why do we need technology advances? The answer is, as I have stated, that the only form of geothermal energy under commercial development is hydrothermal, and the use of hydrothermal fluids is technologically limited to the reservoirs with the most favorable combination of characteristics. Current state-of-the-art technologies do not provide the tools necessary for economic exploitation of less technically attractive resources -- i.e., poorer quality hydrothermal, geopressured, hot dry rock, and magma. Thus, without further R&D developments, the industry, and the Nation, will be limited to the use of only a fraction of our total geothermal resources.

Typically, at this point in my presentation I would discuss the status of the technologies for all four forms of geothermal energy and the Division's related R&D activities. However, today you have the opportunity to hear the hydrothermal story from Dr. Otte and the hot dry rock story from Dr. Whetten, and I shall be happy to defer to these experts for the discussions on their respective specialities and concentrate my remaining time on the status of technologies applicable to geopressured brines and magma heat extraction.

I want to add, however, that I believe it is safe to say that DOE's hydrothermal R&D activities address the problems confronting the industry since the industry participates very closely in establishing our hydrothermal R&D priorities. The industry also has a splendid record of cooperation in implementing the program, for which I extend thanks to Dr. Otte for his leadership role. If it were not for limitations on time, it would be a pleasure to describe in detail the formal and informal interaction between the industry and our R&D program. It is an exemplary record, perhaps unique, in industry/government cooperation.

Industry participation in geopressured R&D, particularly in the absence of a geopressured industry, is also very substantial. I will discuss this cooperation in connection with the geopressured R&D activities below.

Geopressured Geothermal Technology

Geopressured aquifers are underground reservoirs of hot, pressurized waters that contain methane in solution. While such reservoirs occur in several areas of the U.S., Gulf Coast sites were chosen in the early 1970's for federal experiments because of the large size of the reservoirs located there and the potential relative ease of recovery of the thermal and hydraulic energy, plus the large data base available from oil and gas exploration in the area.

Our geopressured program has tested two types of geopressured wells -- dry or abandoned oil and gas wells (Wells of Opportunity) and wells drilled specifically for production of geopressured brines (Design Wells). It is believed that geopressured wells exploited commercially before the year 2000 may fall in the former category due to the costs of drilling to depths needed for brine recovery. Some of the 6000 oil and gas wells, which were abandoned after penetrating geopressured formations in the Gulf Coast area, may be potential targets for exploiting geopressured fluids.

Considerable progress has been made over the last decade in understanding the geopressured resource. We believe we have now accurately estimated the size and magnitude of geopressured reservoirs although long-term production tests have showed that the geopressured reservoir will produce more brine than conventional methods of characterizing geothermal reservoirs had led us to believe. While this is promising on one hand, it raises questions on the ultimate effect that larger than expected flows may have on long-term production. In tests to date, sustained rates of over 30,000 barrels per day have been maintained. Questions also remain on whether variations in brine characteristics will make long-term production of methane uncertain. Thus, to provide industry with the knowledge that will permit timely and informed investment decisions on geopressured exploitation, our current objectives in this R&D area are to develop:

- a test procedure with sufficient accuracy to verify the capability of a reservoir to be produced for a 10-year period
- a theoretical model for geopressured formations which permits verification of brine temperature and gas, oil, and condensate production over the 10-year period of operation.

These objectives may be supported by tests of a far deeper geopressured well than has been flow tested previously. This is the Willis Hulin well in Louisiana, a former gas well which is over 21,000 feet deep and penetrates several high quality geopressured zones. Offered by the Mobil Oil Corp., the well may be recompleted as a geopressured producing well, serving as a means to verify the technology developed in all prior well testing and from supporting research. The ability to predict gas yields, reservoir flow, and drawdown as well as the performance of the automated surface facilities would provide a measure of the technology developed by the Geopressured Geothermal Program.

Beginning next year, DOE and the Electric Power Research Institute will cooperate in a power generation experiment at the Pleasant Bayou geopressured well near Houston, Texas. A hybrid cycle will be used which incorporates both a gas engine to use the produced methane and a geothermal binary cycle to use the heat of the brines. This will be the first use of geopressured brines for power generation anywhere in the world.

Other industry participation in the geopressured program includes support of a Rock Resistivity Laboratory which has been established in the Petroleum Engineering Department of the University of Texas at Austin. In addition to the Gas Research Institute, several major companies including Exxon, Mobil, Sun, Tenneco, and Schlumberger, Inc. are participating.

Magma Energy Extraction Technology

An earlier seven-year study of magma energy extraction, which was funded by DOE's Office of Basic Energy Sciences, demonstrated that there are no insurmountable theoretical or physical barriers to accessing and tapping magma energy. The experiments were carried out at the Kilauea Iki Crater, a prehistoric pit in the Hawaii Volcanoes National Park that was half-filled with molten lava during an eruption in 1959. Although not a true magma deposit, the only significant differences between this ponded lava flow and that of a magma body is size, gas content, and depth. Geophysical surveys and experimental drilling at the site confirmed the scientific feasibility of using this resource. Once this was established, a program was undertaken by GTD to determine the engineering feasibility. Fundamental technologies required for locating magma bodies at accessible depths, drilling in extreme temperatures, materials that will survive in the magma environment, and energy extraction techniques are areas in development. Industry will make the final assessment of commercial feasibility.

The previous heat extraction research indicated that energy extraction rates from magma systems should be comparable to or better than those in conventional geothermal fields. The high temperature of the magma and correspondingly high temperatures of the heat-transfer working fluid lead to efficient, conventional techniques for generating electricity. Chemical processes are available for using this high quality energy to generate transportable fuels in addition to electricity.

The present magma R&D program is focused on silicic magma systems which are most representative of magma bodies expected at most U.S. sites in the far west, the location of all known shallow magma bodies in the contiguous states. The optimum technology appears to be use of an open heat exchanger (shown in Exhibit 5) which uses direct working fluid/magma contact. Analyses have shown that thermal stresses created in magma solidifying around a cooled borehole will be sufficient to cause fracturing. By circulating a heat transfer fluid through the solidified and fractured magma, greatly increased surface area and energy extraction rates can be achieved. The concept was tested in the 1981 Kilauea Iki experiments.

After evaluation of over 20 potential magma sites, Long Valley, California, has been selected for drilling into an active crustal magma body. This is the most studied caldera system in the U.S. and the site of current hydrothermal industry drilling. A consortium of institutions, including Sandia National Laboratories, USGS, University of California/Santa Barbara, Lawrence Berkeley Laboratory, the University of Wyoming, and the University of Southern California/Los Angeles conducted seismic experiments in the Valley in 1985. The data from this series of experiments combined with earlier seismic data resulted in a preliminary composite view of the magma chamber underlying the Long Valley Caldera. The inferred chamber appears to be large, with dimensions on the order of the Caldera diameter of 20 km with two cupolas extending toward the surface at depths of approximately 7 and 5 km.

Plans are to design the first generation technology needed for drilling and heat extraction by 1992 and to begin drilling in the 1992-1995 timeframe. If successful, this effort will consitute a tremendous scientific and engineering achievement.

CONCLUSION

Where is geothermal energy today? Hydrothermal costs, as shown in Exhibit 6, are competitive with conventional fuels. The cost shown here is based on the costs experienced at the 45 MWe proof-of-concept binary plant at Heber, California, less R&D-related expenses which industry would probably forego if the plant were replicated at the same reservoir. Binary technology of this type is likely to be state-of-the-art technology at a number of other reservoirs similar in character to Heber. Costs for flash steam plants at the less numerous higher

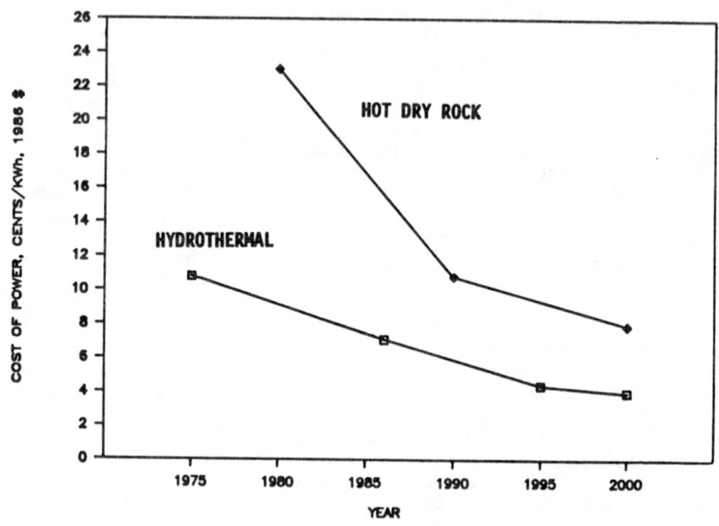

EXHIBIT 6

GEOTHERMAL ELECTRICITY COST

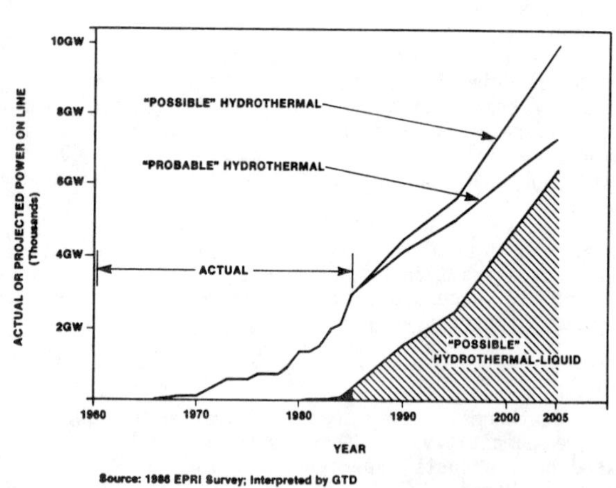

EXHIBIT 7

PROJECTED GEOTHERMAL CAPACITY GROWTH

temperature reservoirs are somewhat lower those that shown in Exhibit 6, and they are fully competitive with conventional fuels.

Thus, an acceleration in the growth of geothermal power capacity over the next 10-20 years is foreseen as indicated in Exhibit 7. The graph shows the "possible" and "probable" growth scenarios for all hydrothermal development, as projected by the Electric Power Research Institute, and the estimated possible growth in hot water capacity alone. The hot water industry grew from 20 MWe in 1980 to over 200 MWe in 1985 and is expected to top 1,000 MWe by 1990.

Exhibit 6 also shows projected costs for power generation with energy recovered from hot dry rock which indicates that competitive costs may be reached in the late 1990's.

We also look to competitive geopressured costs in the 1990's. The greatest remaining uncertainty in this technology is variation in the recoverable volume and rate of recovery from the producing reservoir; efforts have been initiated to develop accurate prediction methodology. It is estimated that if volumes and rates are large, electricity could be produced for about 6 cents/kWh in systems that convert all of the energy in the fluid (methane, thermal, and hydraulic) to electricity.

The technology for producing magma energy and its potential economic feasibility are not yet known. However, due to the fact that the high quality energy should result in high efficiencies, preliminary cost analyses indicate energy costs for magma energy systems within the range of current energy prices.

In summary, hydrothermal energy is already contributing to the current energy mix; geopressured and hot dry rock are poised to contribute in the next decade; and magma is waiting in the wings with a fascinating potential for the next century and beyond.

References Cited

1. U.S. Geological Survey, *Assessment of Geothermal Resources of the United States - 1978*, Circular No. 790/979.

2. National Research Council, National Academy of Sciences, *Energy in Transition 1985-2010*, Final Report of the Committee on Nuclear and Alternative Energy Systems, 1979.

3. U.S. Department of Energy, *Geothermal Progress Monitor*, Issue No. 10 Geothermal Technology Division, July 1987.

4. Atomic Energy Industrial Forum, U.S. Average Electrical Generating Costs and Power Plant Performance, 1985.

5. Williams, R.D., "Geothermal Operations at The Geysers -- 1986 Performance Perspective," Electric Power Research Institute Annual Geothermal Conference, June 1986.

DIRECT APPLICATION - INCREASED USE OVER THE PAST DECADE AND THE U.S. RESOURCE POTENTIAL

R. Gordon Bloomquist, Ph.D.
Washington State Energy Office
Olympia, Washington

INTRODUCTION

The direct utilization of geothermal resources dates back to early Roman times when the Etruscans extracted boric acid from fumeroles at what is now known as the Larderello Geothermal Field and hot springs were used to provide an early form of district heating in Pompeii. By 1893, geothermal wells were being used to supply the heating needs of the Warm Springs district heating system in Boise, Idaho, and by the early 1900s, individual wells were being utilized in Klamath Falls, Oregon, to provide space heating to homes and businesses. In 1930, the first district heating system was constructed in Reykjavik, Iceland, and 15 liters/second of 80°-90°C water was piped 2.8 km to heat an indoor swimming pool, a school, a hospital, and approximately 70 residences (Gudmundsson and Palmason, 1986). However, from these early endeavors to capture the natural heat of the earth until the oil crises of 1973, geothermal remained little more than a curiosity; the only exception being its popularity in the form of hot spring resorts. The oil crisis of the 1970s, however, focused attention upon an array of alternative energy sources and at the present time over 7,000 MW of geothermal energy are being utilized worldwide to meet the energy needs of major segments of the residential, commercial, and industrial sector as well as becoming ever more important in agriculture and aquaculture (Figure 1).

DIRECT UTILIZATION

Geothermal resources, as can be seen in Figure 1, can meet thermal energy needs throughout the temperature spectrum and although direct applications are often referred to in the literature as low to moderate temperature uses, many high temperature industrial process requirements, primarily in drying and dehydration, can be met through the use of geothermal energy. For example, in Iceland high temperature steam is used in the Namafjall diatomite drying facility and in New Zealand, Italy, and the United States temperatures in excess of 120°C are used to meet industrial process requirements in the pulp, chemical, and agriculture sectors. Other uses include evaporization, refrigeration, and washing (Gudmundsson, 1985).

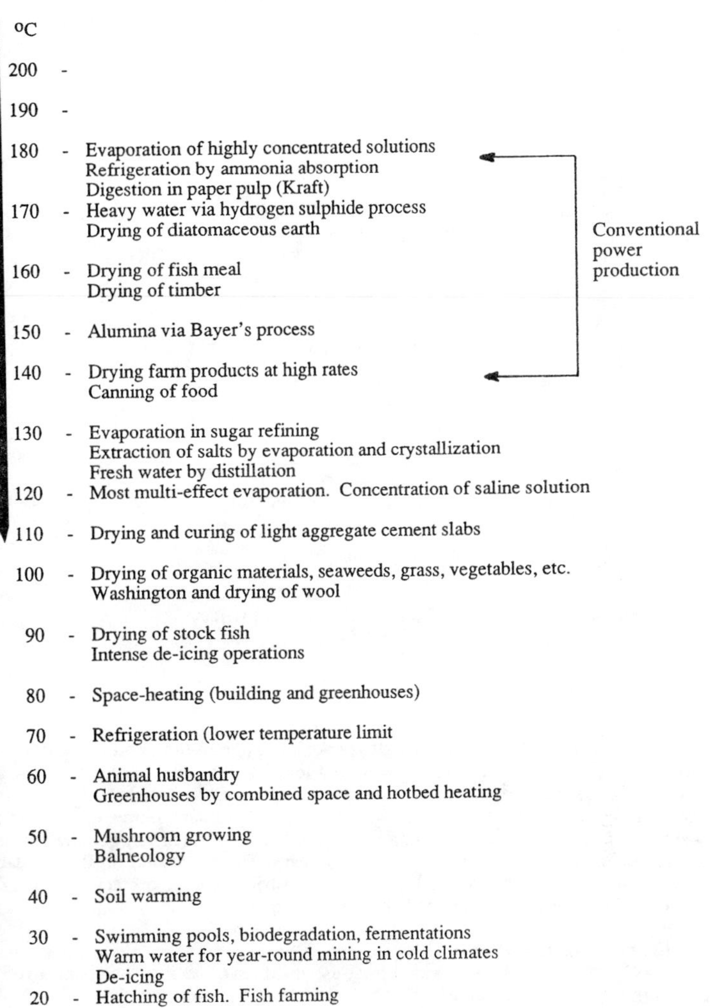

FIGURE 1
The Lindal Diagram

At the other end of the temperature spectrum, temperatures as low as 10° to 30°C are successfully meeting the ongoing requirements of aquaculture and greenhouse operation and, when coupled to water source heat pumps, the same low temperature resource can supply the space heating as well as the cooling requirements of most residential and commercial buildings (Figure 2). For example, a 30°C well in Ephrata, Washington, is providing the space conditioning for the entire Grant County Court House and annex through the use of a 1 MW heat pump. The system has resulted in energy savings of nearly 80 percent in comparison to the oil fired boiler system which was replaced and has reduced the county's utility bill from $20,000/year to $2,000 per year.

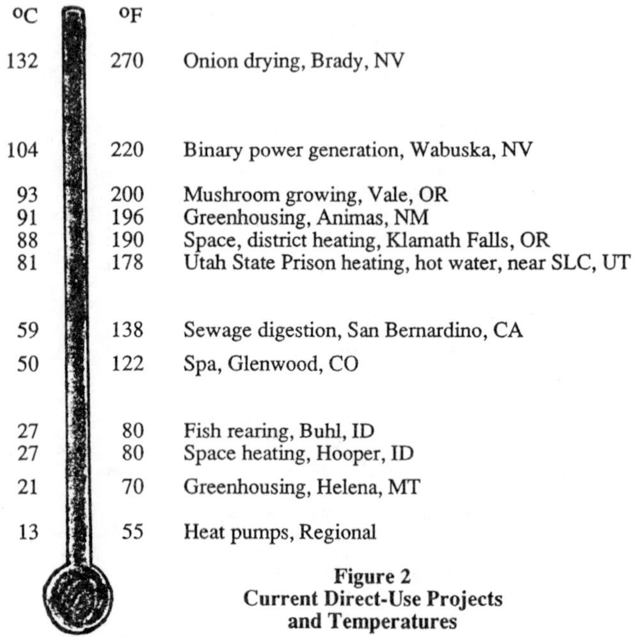

Figure 2
Current Direct-Use Projects and Temperatures

Despite the strong emergence of aquaculture, agriculture, and industrial uses of geothermal energy, district heating and, to a lesser extent, district cooling remain the largest use of direct geothermal energy in the world. District heating is the distribution of heat (hot water or steam) from a central source to two or more customers through a network of pipes. As was mentioned earlier, geothermal district heating began in the United States with the Warm Springs system in Boise, Idaho, in 1893. Today there are over 20 geothermal district heating projects on-line in the United States with another 18 projects being planned.

A DECADE OF GROWTH

In 1975, the total worldwide direct use installed capacity was about 3,100 MW consisting of 500 MW for greenhouses, 200 MW for industrial uses, 400 MW for district heating, and 2,000 MW (mostly in Japan) for bathing. By 1985, the total worldwide installed capacity had increased to over 7,000 MW (Table 1) or an annual growth of approximately 8.5 percent (Gudmundsson, 1985). If the 2,000 MW for bathing is removed from the totals, a growth of nearly 4,000 MW occurred over that 10 year period or nearly a 400 percent increase in uses which directly reduced dependence on conventional fuels.

TABLE 1
Worldwide Uses

Country	Flow Rate kg/s	Power MW	Energy GWh	Load %
China	3,540	393	1,945	56
France	2,340	300	788	30
Hungary	9,533	1,001	2,615	30
Iceland	4,578	889	5,517	71
Italy	1,745	288	1,365	54
Japan	26,101	2,686	6,805	29
New Zealand	559	215	1,484	79
Romania	1,380	251	987	45
Soviet Union	2,735	402	1,056	30
Turkey	1,355	166	423	29
United States	1,971	339	390	13
Other	1,965	142	582	47
Total	57,803	7,072	23,957	39*

*Based on total thermal power and energy
(Gundmundsson, 1985)

In the United States, the growth of the direct use geothermal industry has matched or exceeded the worldwide expansion and from a total of less than 100 projects in 1973 (Figure 3) (of which approximately 75 were hot spring resorts) there were 213 geothermal direct use projects located in the 11 western states by 1986 (Figure 4, Table 2 and 3). These 213 projects supply approximately 2,081 x 10^9 Btu/year while projects under construction or expansion were expected to account for another 236 billion Btu annually. Planned projects (Table 4) could account for nearly 1,700 x 10^9 Btu/year (Kenkeremath, et al., 1985; Lienau, 1986; Lunis, 1987).

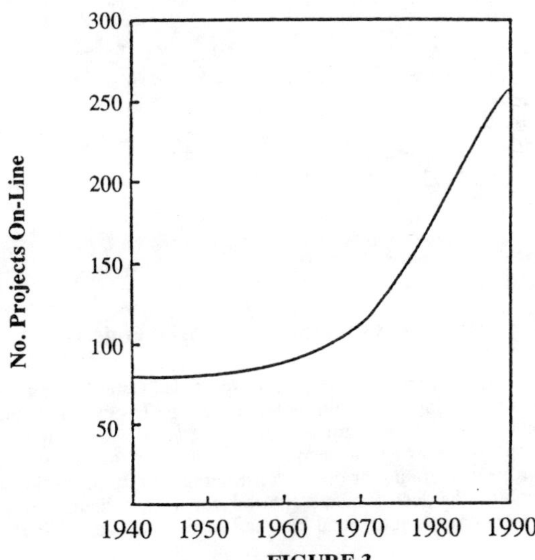

(after, Lienau, 1986)

FIGURE 3
Direct Heat Project Activity in Eleven Western States

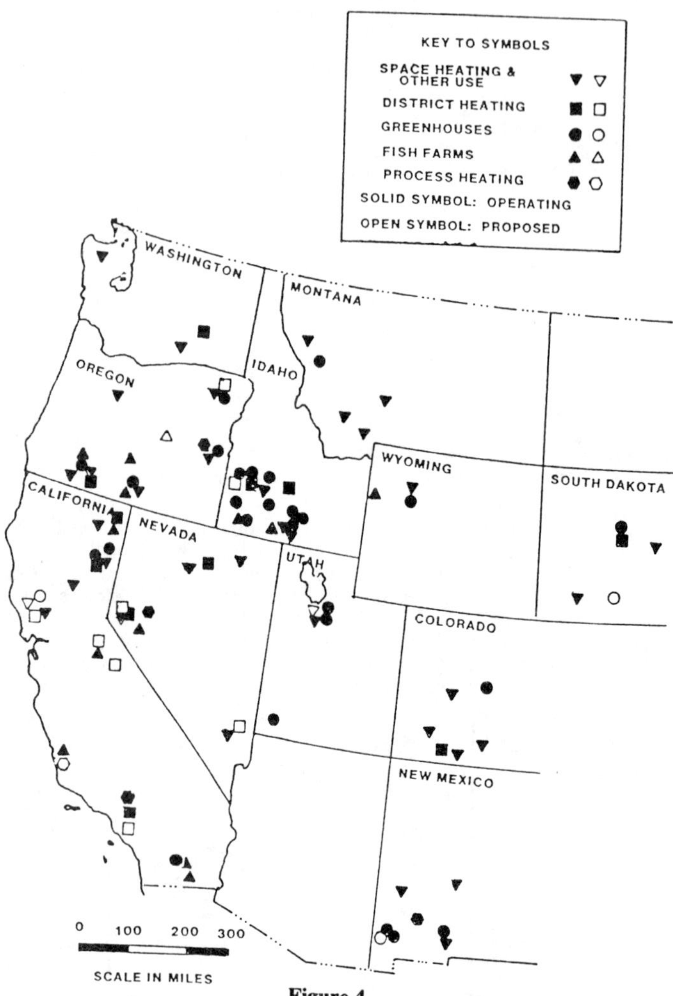

Figure 4
Location of Geothermal Direct Heat Projects
(after, Lienau, 1986)

Of the total capacity of the projects on line, space and water heating accounts for 33 percent, district heating for 28 percent, greenhouses for 21 percent, aquaculture for 12 percent, and industrial processing for 6 percent (Lienau, 1986). The total capacity does not include 66 resorts which are estimated to account for 75 billion Btu/year. Development of projects operating or under construction during the period September 1985-September 1986 (the last available period for which figures are available) represents a 34 percent growth in the total installed capacity (Lienau, 1986).

Much of the growth which has occurred since the oil crises of 1973 can be attributed to a number of federal and state tax incentives and an aggressive, well balanced DOE program.

TABLE 2
Direct-Use Project Summary

	Operataing 10^9 Btu/Yr	Planned 10^9 Btu/Yr	Total 10^9 Btu/Yr
California	278	372	650
Colorado	109	8	117
Idaho	638	155	793
Montana	75	-	75
Nevada	229	985	1,214
New Mexico	77	20	97
Oregon	309	90	97
South Dakota	150	43	193
Utah	87	2	89
Washington	37	-	37
Wyoming	33	10	43
Others	38	5	43
TOTAL	2,060	1,690	3,750

(after, Lunis, 1987)

TABLE 3
Principle Direct-Use Projects

		10^9 Btu/Yr
Greenhouses		
- Animas, New Mexico		72
- Buhl, Idaho		60
- Sandy, Utah		45
- Helena, Montana		24
District Heating Systems		
- Boise, Idaho		184
- Susanville/Litchfield, California		88
- Pagosa Springs, Colorado		55
- Reno, Nevada		49
Aquaculture Projects		
- Buhl, Idaho	Catfish	294
- Mecca, California	Prawns	71
- Wabuska, Nevada	Catfish/tropicals	13
- Ft. Bidwell, California	Catfish	11
- Paso Robles, California	Catfish	11
Industrial Projects		
- Brady, Nevada	Onion drying	86
- San Bernadino, California	Sewage treatment	29
- Vale, Oregon	Mushroom growing	16

(after, Lunis, 1987)

TABLE 4
Planned Projects

- o 8% Annual increase overall
- o 26 Projects could use 1,500-1,700 x 10^9 Btu/y
- o District heating
  - 17 projects: CA (9), OR (3), NV (2), ID, SD, CO (1 each)
- o Greenhousing
  - 6 projects: CA (2), CO, OR, SD, NM (1 each)
- o Other
  - Hawaii - glass, dyeing, drying
  - Casper, WY - penicillin culturing
  - Carson City, NV - lobster production

(after, Lunis, 1987)

Probably of greatest importance were the tax provisions of the Energy Tax Act of 1978 (Public Law 95-618) and the 1980 Windfall Profit Tax Act (Public Law 96-223) which provided a tax credit of 40 percent of the first 10,000 or a maximum of $4,000 (Bloomquist, 1986).

Several of DOE's programs have also proven to be extremely beneficial. One of the most successful and widely used of the DOE programs has been the Technical Assistance Grant Program which was originally available through John Hopkins University, the University of Utah Research Institute, EG and G Idaho, and the Oregon Institute of Technology Geo-Heat Center. Of the original technical assistance centers, only the Geo-Heat Center continues to provide technical assistance. Through 1986, the Geo-Heat Center had processed 1,644 requests for information and 64 technical association grants were provided. The 64 grants resulted in 40 on-line projects (Lienau, 1986). Also of significance were the Program Research and Development Announcements (PRDA), Program Opportunity Notices (PON), the Loan Guarantee Program, and the various state and industry coupled programs. A majority of these programs have been terminated and the federal tax credits are due to expire at the end of 1988.

Although it is impossible to attribute the growth of the direct use industry to any one incentive or program, it is safe to say that the various incentives and programs have worked very well collectively. The elimination of the geothermal tax credit and the surplus of conventional fuels throughout much of the west could be expected to have a negative effect on near term future growth; however, a desire for long term price and supply stability, fuel flexibility, and economic stability and growth appears to be providing adequate incentives to continue the growth which we have seen over the past 10 years.

LONG TERM POTENTIAL

The long term prognoses for expanding the utilization of geothermal resource in the areas of direct utilization appears to be very good. Over 60 countries worldwide are known to have geothermal resources within their boarders and this includes countries in North, Central, and South America, Europe, Asia, the Indian subcontinent, and throughout many of the island chains of both the Atlantic and Pacific oceans.

In the United States, the greatest potential is located in the 11 western states (Figure 4); however, several east and Gulf Coast states also have significant potential from radiogeneric and geopressure resources and several midwestern states have abundant sources of low temperature geothermal water associated with stratigraphic aquifers (Figure 5).

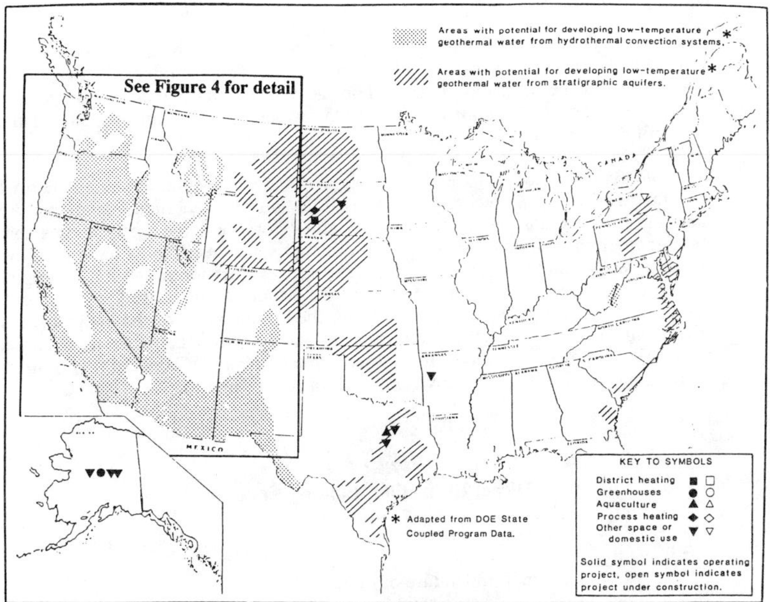

FIGURE 5
Locations of Geothermal Direct Use Projects in the United States

The United States Geological Survey (USGS) places the total U.S. geothermal potential at 139,000 MWt with 98,000 MWt being associated with resources above 90°C and 41,000 MWt being below 90°C (Muffler, 1979; Reed, 1983). Many of the high temperature resources which are suitable for the generation of electricity also possess a tremendous potential for meeting the requirements of direct application projects either directly or through cogeneration. The USGS, however, choose to consider only those resources greater than 10°C above mean annual air temperature. The resource base below this arbitrary cut off temperature and down to a temperature of approximately 10°C may be as large as the entire resource base and in terms of future development may prove to be as important. For example, one of the largest single direct use projects in the world is in Lund, Sweden, where a 22°C geothermal resource is the basis for the world's largest geothermal heat pump installation. The Lund system, which is comprised of two heat pumps of 18 MW and 30 MW effect, respectively, provides approximately 40 percent of the total demand of the Lund district heating system.

In Vancouver, Washington, a 10°C resource, through the use of heat pumps, is providing the entire heating and cooling load of Clark College.

In addition to the tremendous potential which exists below 10°C above mean annual air temperature, many of the resources are co-located with population centers which increases their potential for utilization.

UTILIZATION POTENTIAL

The fact that the direct utilization of geothermal resources must occur within a relatively short distance from the reservoir, requires that factor not usually considered in a resource evaluation strategy be given significant attention. A highly desirable resource from an energy standpoint may be undevelopable unless that energy can meet existing requirements for heating and/or cooling.

In order to determine the "true" utilization potential of a geothermal resource for direct utilization, the energy offices of the states of Idaho, Montana, Oregon, and Washington, under the direction of the author, have developed a geothermal resource ranking methodology (Bloomquist, et al., 1985) which provides an estimate of the developability of the resrouce.

The analytic method is based on a weighted variable evaluation of geothermal resource favorability. This technique is a modification of a technique developed by McClain (1980), but has been improved to allow for the large uncertainties that surround geothermal resource assessment. Although some researchers have used the Monte Carlo technique to address uncertainties in the exploration programs, a simpler method of computation and interpretation to the Monte Carlo technique has been adopted here, but a technique which is well matched to the level of the data which is typically available. The technique divides the characteristics that determine direct utilization development potential into three broad areas of concern: resource, engineering, and institutional and environmental factors (Table 5).

TABLE 5
Direct Utilization Ranking Criteria

	Characteristic	Numerical Weight
I.	Resource	
	Known Temperature of Fluids	11
	Prospect Areal Extent	8
	Total Flow Rate	7
	Local Gradient	6
	Drilling Depth	7
	Estimated Pumping Depth	5
	Preferred Geothermometer Temperature	4
	Drilling Difficulty	2
	Total	50
II.	Engineering	
	Annual Heat Load/Density	22
	Distance to Heating Load	8
	Heating Degree Days	6
	Least Cost Heat Energy	8
	Resource Site Accessibility	2
	Terrain of Pipeline Corridor	2
	Trenchability of Pipeline Corridor	2
	Total	50
III.	Institutional/Environmental	
	Special Environmental Regulatory Concerns	12
	Land/Resource Management	7
	Air/Water Concerns	5
	Distance to Legally Designated Areas	3
	Owner Attitude Toward Development	3
	Total	3
	GRAND TOTAL	130

TABLE 6
Dependent Variables Used for the Correlation Procedure

Measurement Units	Dependent Variable
Degrees Centigrade	Estimated Reservoir Temperature
Faulting/Existence of Fluids	Potential for Permeability
Type/Composition of Rocks and Age	Age and Type of Volcanism
Depth in Meters	Drilling Depth
Estimated Rock Type	Drilling Difficulty
Surficial Area - Square Kilometers	Prospect Area Extent
Milliwatts Per Square Meter	Regional Heat Flow
Slope of Terrain	Terrain of Powerline Corridor
Kilometers	Distance to Powerlines
Access Road Type	Resource Site Accessibility
Number of Terrain Concerns	Terrain of Development Site
Kilometers	Distance to Heating Load
Degree of Urbanization	Heat Load Density
Private/Federal/Mixed	Land/Resource Management
Number of Special Concerns	Special Environmental Concerns
Decimal Fraction Leased	Percent Leased for Exploration
Kilometers	Distance to Legally Designated Area
Number of Pollutants Above EPA Regs	Air/Water Concerns
Positive or Negative	Owner Attitude Toward Development

The technique begins with a listing of the primary factors that are related to the developability of a resource for direct utilization. Numerical estimates are given to each variable to indicate its relative importance in the assessment. Estimates are based on a Delphi approach using "expert opinion" of geologists, engineers, and regulators. The variables and their weights are presented in Table 5.

For each of the variables, a dependent variable is selected that allows a correlation process to determine the relative score for each resource site for each of the above characteristics. A perfect score is 130. Table 6 presents the dependent variables and the measurement units used.

Based on geologic, engineering, and regulatory information, relationships between the dependent variables and the assessment criteria are established. Curves are then produced and fit by linear and non-linear procedures to determine the fractional scope of the ranking variables. This determines the points scored for any resume characteristic from the total available.

Figures 6-10 are examples of the curves utilized during the ranking procedure.

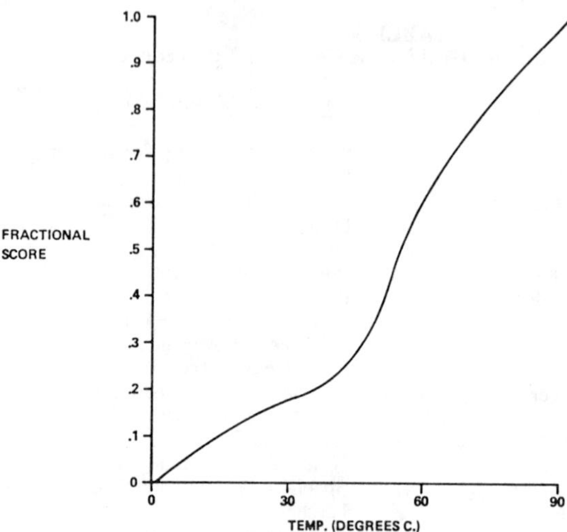

FIGURE 6
Known Temperature of Fluids

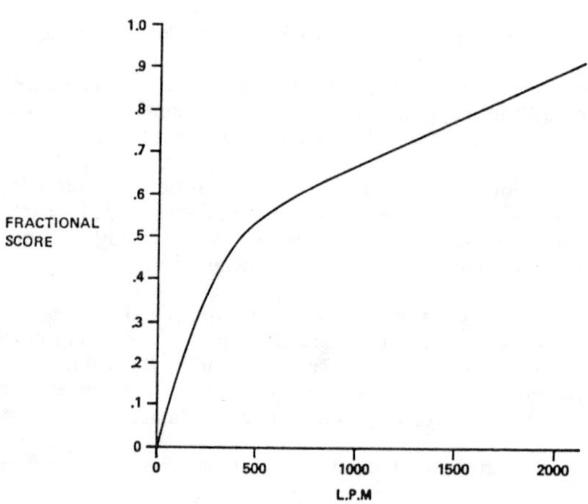

FIGURE 7
Total Flow Rate

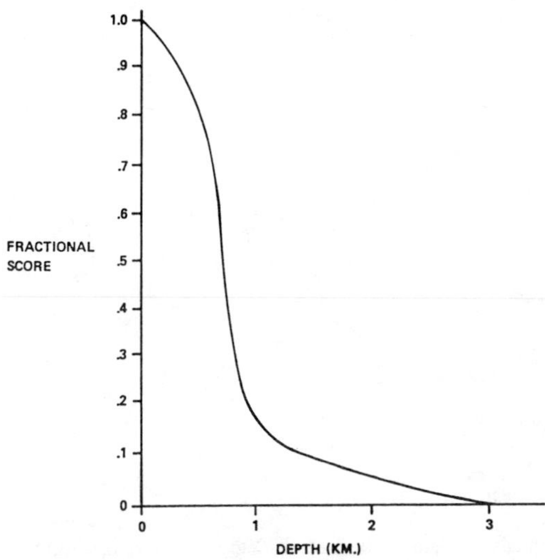

FIGURE 8
Estimated Drilling Depth

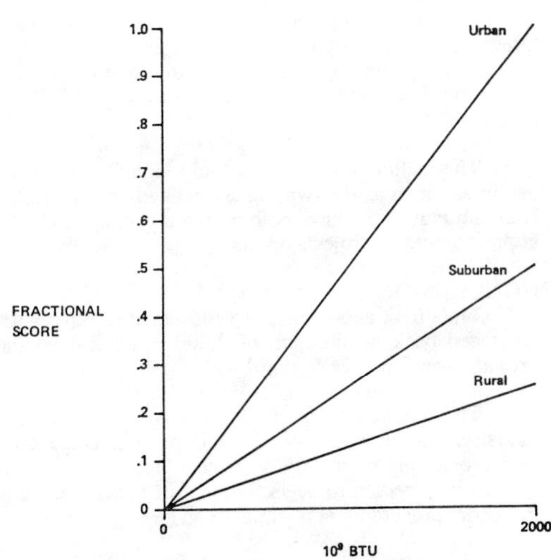

FIGURE 9
Annual Heating Load/Density

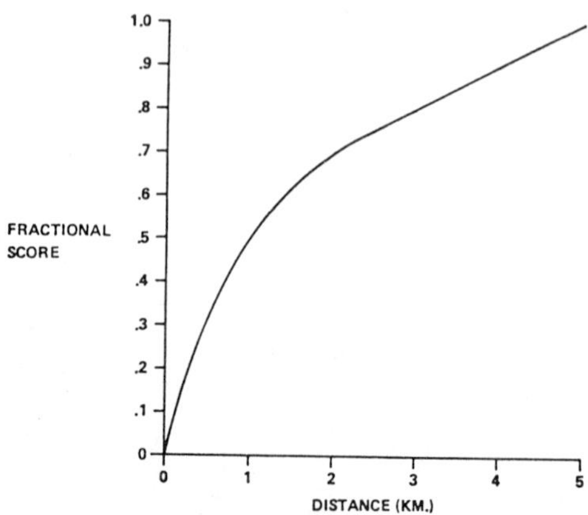

FIGURE 10
Distance to Legally-Designated Areas

Once a site has been analyzed and ranked as to degree of developability as compared to other sites under consideration, it is also possible to rapidly determine what specific site characteristics are limiting development. It is then not only possible to focus attention upon improving the developability of the highest ranked sites but also to focus attention upon sites which would be highly developable except for one or two negative factors.

In an evaluation and ranking of geothermal sites in the states of Idaho, Montana, Oregon, and Washington a total of 1,265 potential geothermal sites were identified. Of these, 145 sites were determined to have considerable direct use potential and 23 sites were determined to offer in excess of 750 MW of developable direct utilization potential.

The techniques appear to hold significant potential for further refinement and use in as much as the two highest ranked sites identified in the study (Boise, ID, and Klamath Falls, OR) have both received considerable attention by developers and have, at present, major projects on line.

CONCLUSION

The direct application of geothermal resources to meet energy requirements can be traced back a minimum of 2,000 years and geothermal direct use projects now provide over 7,000 MW world wide.

The technology for utilization is well developed and readily available. The industry has increased nearly 400 percent since the mid 1970s and continues to increase at approximately 8 percent per year. Although a majority of the future growth is expected to be in the area of district heating, aquaculture, agriculture, and industrial processing applications can be expected to increase as well.

The increase in interest in district heating and **cooling** could also bring about even wider applications of geothermal energy as absorption cooling becomes more and more efficient and cost competitive with centrifical chillers.

The future for direct use geothermal development in the United States appears to be bright and the next decade could see well in excess of 2,000 MW of additional capacity brought on line.

BIBLIOGRAPHY

Bloomquist, R.G., Black, G.L., Parker, D.S., Sifford, A., Simpson, S.J., and Street, L.V., 1985, Evaluation and ranking of geothermal resources for electrical generation or electrical offset in Idaho, Montana, Oregon, and Washington, Vol. 1, Washington State Energy Office, Olympia, Washington.

Bloomquist, R.G., 1986, A review and analysis of the adequacy of the U.S. legal, institutional, and financial framework for geothermal development, *Geothermics*, Vol. 15, No. 1, pp. 87-132.

Gudmundsson, J.S., 1985, Direct uses of geothermal energy in 1984, International Symposium on Geothermal Energy, Geothermal Resource Council, Davis, California, pp. 19-29.

Gudmundsson, J.S. and Palmason, G., 1986, The geothermal industry in Iceland, United Nations Workshop, Reykjavik, Iceland, 12 pp.

Kenkeremath, D.C., Blackett, R.E., Strape, J.V., and Beelad, G.V., 1985, The current status of geothermal direct use development in the United States, International Symposium on Geothermal Energy, Geothermal Resources Council, Davis, California, pp. 223-236.

Lienau, Paul J., 1986, Status of direct heat projects in western states, Geo-Heat Center, Quarterly Bulletin, Oregon Institute of Technology, Klamath Falls, Oregon, pp. 3-7.

Lunis, Ben C., 1987, Geothermal direct-use projects status, Rocky Mountain Section Meeting AAPG-SEPM-EMD.

McClain, David W., 1980, A site evaluation model for geothermal resource development in southwest Idaho, University of Idaho, M.S. Thesis, Moscow, Idaho, 146 pp.

Muffler, L.J.P., *editor*, 1979, Assessment of geothermal resources of the United States-1978, Geological Survey Circular 790, 163 pp.

Reed, Marshall J., *editor*, 1983, Assessment of Low-Temperature Geothermal Resources of the United States-1982, Geological Survey Circular 892, 73 pp.

ADVANCED GEOTHERMAL TECHNOLOGIES

J. T. Whetten, Associate Director,
H. D. Murphy, Program Manager,
R. J. Hanold, Project Leader,
C. W. Myers, Deputy Division Leader,
Los Alamos National Laboratory
Los Alamos, New Mexico
J. C. Dunn, Supervisor of Geothermal Research Division
Sandia National Laboratories
Albuquerque, New Mexico

ABSTRACT

Research and development in advanced technologies for geothermal energy production continue to increase the energy production options for the Nation. The high-risk investment over the past few years by the US Department of Energy in geopressured, hot dry rock, and magma energy resources is producing new means to lower production costs and to take advantage of these resources. The Nation has far larger and more regionally extensive geothermal resources than heretofore realized. At the end of a short 30-day closed-loop flow test, the manmade hot dry rock reservoir at Fenton Hill, New Mexico, was producing 10 MW thermal--and still climbing--proving the technical feasibility of this new technology. The scientific feasibility of magma energy extraction has been demonstrated, and new field tests to evaluate this technology are planned. Analysis and field tests confirm the viability of geopressured-geothermal energy and the prospect that many dry-hole or depleted petroleum wells can be turned into producing geopressured-geothermal wells. Technological advances achieved through hot dry rock, magma, geopressured, and other geothermal research are making these resources and conventional hydrothermal resources more competitive. Noteworthy among these technological advances are techniques in computer simulation of geothermal reservoirs, new means for well stimulation, new high-temperature logging tools and packers, new hard-rock penetration techniques, and new methods for mapping fracture flow paths across large underground areas in reservoirs. In addition, many of these same technological advances can be applied by the petroleum industry to help lower production costs in domestic oil and gas fields.

I. INTRODUCTION

Geothermal energy is natural heat in the earth's interior, produced largely by the slow decay of naturally occurring unstable isotopes of uranium, thorium, and potassium. Because the earth's crust is a good thermal insulator, most of this heat is stored at considerable depth below the surface. However, as is true of many insulators between a hot body and its cool surroundings, the rate of increase in temperature with depth--the geothermal gradient--is high, on a worldwide average, about 30°C per kilometer of depth. Therefore, with modern drilling equipment, it is possible almost anywhere to reach crustal rock at temperatures that are usefully high--if not for generating electricity, or, then alternatively, for space heating, food processing, and other direct uses. The reservoir of heat in the earth's crust is one of the largest energy resources that is accessible to man.

Under certain geologic circumstances, meteoric water penetrates the earth deeply enough to reach hot crustal rock. This water extracts heat from the rock, expands, and rises buoyantly where it is trapped in porous formations or natural fractures to form hydrothermal reservoirs of hot water or (rarely) of steam. This hot water or steam can be brought to the surface through drilled holes and used to generate electricity or used for a variety of other purposes.

In the United States, development of hydrothermal resources is growing, and hydrothermal energy is now used to generate 3000 MW of electricity. A comparable amount is generated in other countries. Additional details on hydrothermal resources are provided by Mock and Otte elsewhere in these proceedings. Below, we focus on the geopressured, hot dry rock, and magma resources. In our view, these advanced geothermal technologies could provide significant additional energy resources for our country and the world.

II. SIGNIFICANT ACCOMPLISHMENTS

Geopressured-Geothermal Energy

Geopressured resources are underground reservoirs of hot, pressurized brine that contain natural gas (methane) in solution. In these reservoirs pressures are essentially lithostatic rather than hydrostatic (as in conventional geothermal reservoirs); thus high brine flow rates can be achieved and hydraulic energy can be extracted from the brine at the surface. The potential for combining this hydraulic energy with the thermal energy of the brine and the chemical energy of the natural gas enhances the attractiveness of the resource. The US Department of Energy has supported research on geopressured reservoirs for over a decade to evaluate the technical problems associated with locating, assessing, and producing these resources.

The Geopressured Program has demonstrated that geopressured reservoirs can produce high-volume flows of brine saturated with natural gas over a long time period, and that the gas can be separated and sold (Ramsthaler and Plum, 1987). Solutions to the engineering problems of brine handling and brine disposal have been demonstrated. A six-month flow test of the Gladys McCall well at a flow rate of 24,000-26,000 barrels/day demonstrated that long-term production of a geopressured-geothermal system is feasible (US DOE/EG&G Idaho, Inc., 1987).

Ramsthaler and Plum (1987) state that initial geopressured-geothermal development can occcur where a deep well, initially drilled for gas production, penetrates a geopressured-geothermal reservoir. If the well was originally a dry hole or if the natural gas reservoir eventually played out, then the well could become a candidate for recompletion as a geopressured-geothermal well. Estimates by the Texas Bureau of Economic Geology indicate there are approximately 600 producing wells in Texas drilled through geopressurized-geothermal reservoirs, and the Louisiana Geological Survey has estimated there are a similar number of potential wells in Louisiana. In addition to the natural gas dissolved in the brine, geopressured-geothermal reservoirs can be associated with a gas cap above the brine reservoir. Analysis of logs from the Hulin geopressured well in Louisiana indicates the presence of enough free gas to significantly impact the economics of production from this well. Although the current best-estimate for the saturated gas content of the Hulin brines is 60 ft^3/barrel, the yield of gas per barrel of brine produced could be much higher if there is free gas above the brine reservoir.

To convert an existing deep gas well into a geopressured-geothermal well, it is necessary to recomplete the well in the geopressured brine zones. Although recompletion of a deep well is an expensive operation, the target of opportunity is a very large number of unproductive existing wells in Texas and Louisiana that have access to geopressured-brine reservoirs. If it can be demonstrated that the presence of free gas above these reservoirs can increase the gas yield to 150-200 ft^3/barrel, these wells have the potential to be economic producers at gas prices very close to today's market value (Ramsthaler and Plum, 1987). The economics should improve further if the produced brines, which can have temperatures of the order of 170^oC, are used to generate electricity.

Hot Dry Rock

About 95% of the useful heat in the earth's outer crust is in the rock itself, rather than in any fluid contained in it. Hot dry rock (HDR) technology provides a means to mine this heat in the rock by injecting cold water down one well, into the rock, through natural or manmade fractures, where the heat is conducted to the water, and then extracting the heated water using a second well (Armstead and Tester, 1987). Figure 1 illustrates the HDR concept. The US HDR resource amounts to 90 million megawatt centuries of thermal energy for just the high-grade HDR resources. Research and development programs to develop the HDR technology are well advanced in several countries--particularly in the United States, the United Kingdom, West Germany, Japan, and the Soviet Union. The US work is funded by DOE and is performed by the Los Alamos National Laboratory and by a partnership of Bechtel and Chevron, which is assessing the feasibility of using HDR technology at Roosevelt Hot Springs in Utah.

The world's first hot dry rock geothermal energy system was completed at Fenton Hill, New Mexico, in 1977; enlarged in 1979 by additional hydraulic fracturing; and then operated successfully for more than a year. Water was produced from the manmade reservoir at temperatures and thermal power rates as high as 175°C and 5 MWt. Additional information about the reservoir and reservoir testing is provided by Dash et al. (1983).

Construction of a larger, hotter, hot dry rock system was initiated at Fenton Hill in 1979 to extend HDR technology to the temperatures and rates of heat production required to support a commercial power plant. Two new wells were drilled directionally, one to a vertical depth of 4.66 km, where the rock temperature was 327°C (Figure 2). In December 1983, 21,600 m^3 of water were injected in the deepest well. Details are provided by Dash et al. (1985) and House, Keppler, and Kaieda (1985). Microearthquakes induced by the injection of water indicate seismicity occurred in a 50 x 10^6 m^3 rock volume. This rock volume is 2000 times greater than the water volume injected. Unexpectedly, the stimulated zone did not propagate into the vicinity of the upper well, and little hydraulic communication between the two wells was achieved. Consequently, in March 1985, the upper well was sidetracked at a depth of 2.9 km and directionally drilled as shown in Figure 2, through the fracture zone created from the lower well. This redrilled well provided the desired hydraulic communication.

In 1986 a closed-loop flow test of the newly completed HDR reservoir was performed to define reservoir operating characteristics so that equipment for a year-long flow test could be designed. Cold water was injected into one of the wells, and the water extracted from the other was as hot as 192°C and produced up to 10 MWt.

Work to date has shown that the HDR geothermal energy concept is technically feasible. The program goal now is to develop the technology to a level that will evaluate economic viability and environmental acceptability.

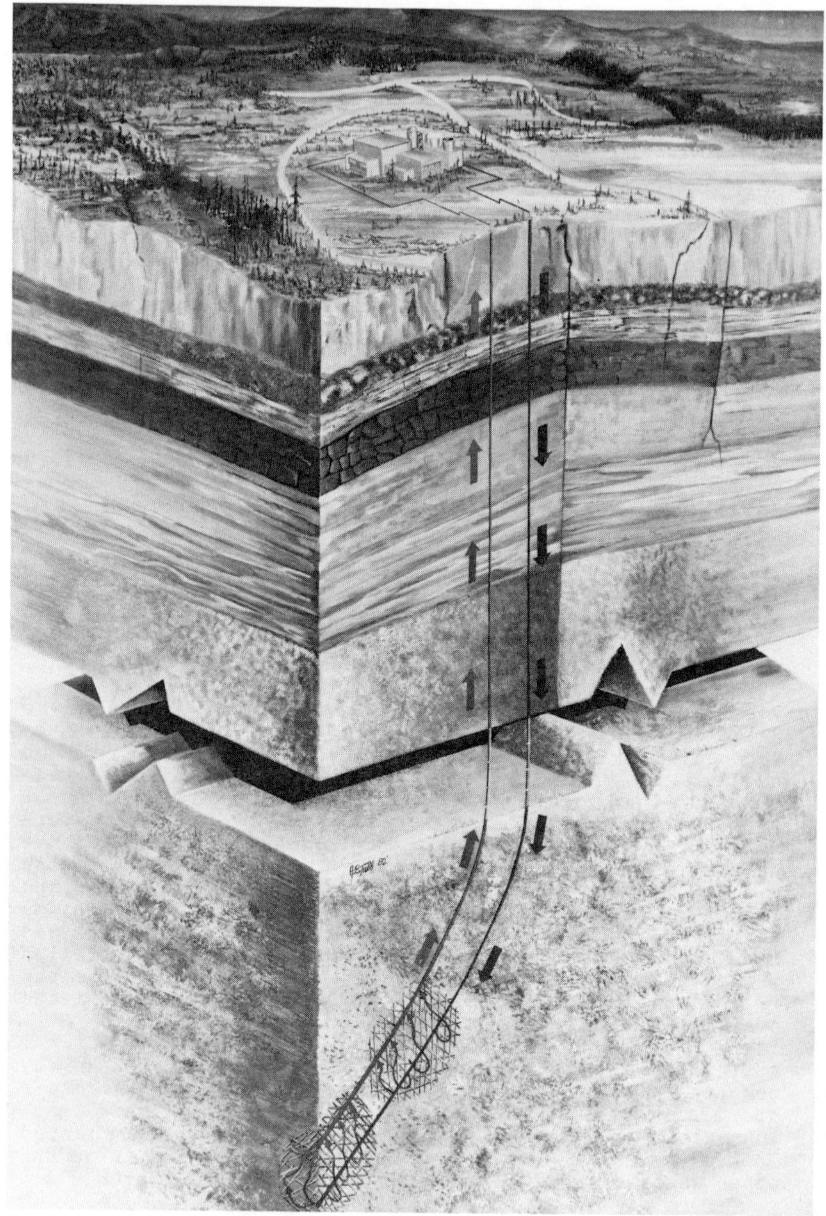

Figure 1

Hot Dry Rock Geothermal Energy Concept

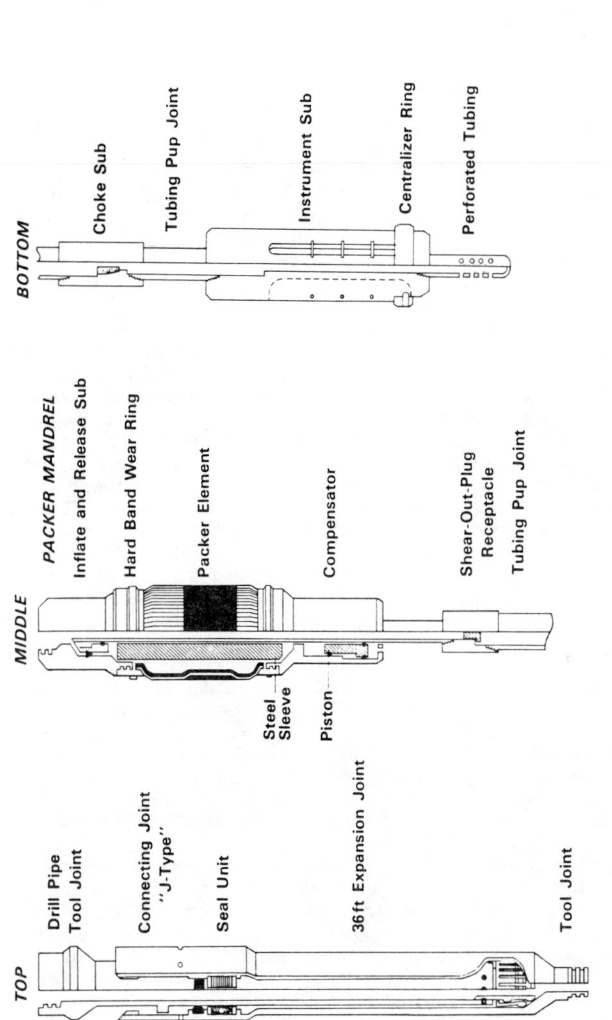

A. EXPANSION JOINT B. PACKER AND COMPENSATOR C. CHOKE AND INSTRUMENT SUB

OPEN HOLE PACKER ASSEMBLY

Figure 2

High Temperature Open-Hole Packer

Operation of the year-long flow test should suffice to observe thermal drawdown and measure long-term characteristics of the reservoir. The test will also provide operation and maintenance experience of an HDR system, thus contributing to future engineering and economic decisions.

Magma Energy

Energy contained in molten or partially molten magma represents a huge potential resource for the US. Smith and Shaw (1975, 1979) estimated this resource within the upper 10 km of the crust to be 50,000 to 500,000 quads--larger than the current estimate for fossil resources. Sponsored by the US DOE and its predecessor agency, ERDA, since 1975, researchers at Sandia National Laboratories are investigating energy extraction from silicic magma systems, which are most representative of magma bodies expected at western US sites. Unlike basaltic magma, the more viscous silicic magma will probably require direct- contact fluid circulation to achieve economic energy extraction rates. Figure 3 (Dunn, 1986) shows a conceptual representation of a single-well, open heat exchanger system. The well is cased into the plastic transition zone, and a concentric inner injection tube extends into the magma. The region surrounding the injection tube is cooled, solidified, and thermally fractured by circulation of the heat transfer fluid. Extent of the fractured zone is controlled by the rate of energy extraction. Beyond the fractured region is a transition zone that behaves like a plastic solid and does not support fracturing. Cooling in the magma zone induces large-scale natural convection that enhances heat transfer to the solidified region.

The magma energy concept was tested in the melt zone of Kilauea Iki lava lake, where an open-hole, sealed test zone was created (Dunn, 1986). During a 5-day test period, energy extraction rates were found to increase with time (indicating growth of the fractured region). Extraction rates reached more than 10 times the expected value for a closed heat exchanger in the same borehole.

The magma program became part of the Department of Energy's Geothermal Program in 1984 after demonstration that energy extraction from active magma bodies was scientifically feasible. The objective of this follow-on program is to assess the engineering feasibility of the magma energy concept and to provide the data base needed for industry to evaluate economic feasibility. Currently, a deep exploratory well is planned for Long Valley caldera in eastern California. The well will be drilled in the southern portion of the resurgent dome within the caldera. If high-temperature, near-magmatic conditions are reached, the well can be used to test newly developed drilling technology, evaluate engineering materials, and confirm heat transfer calculations.

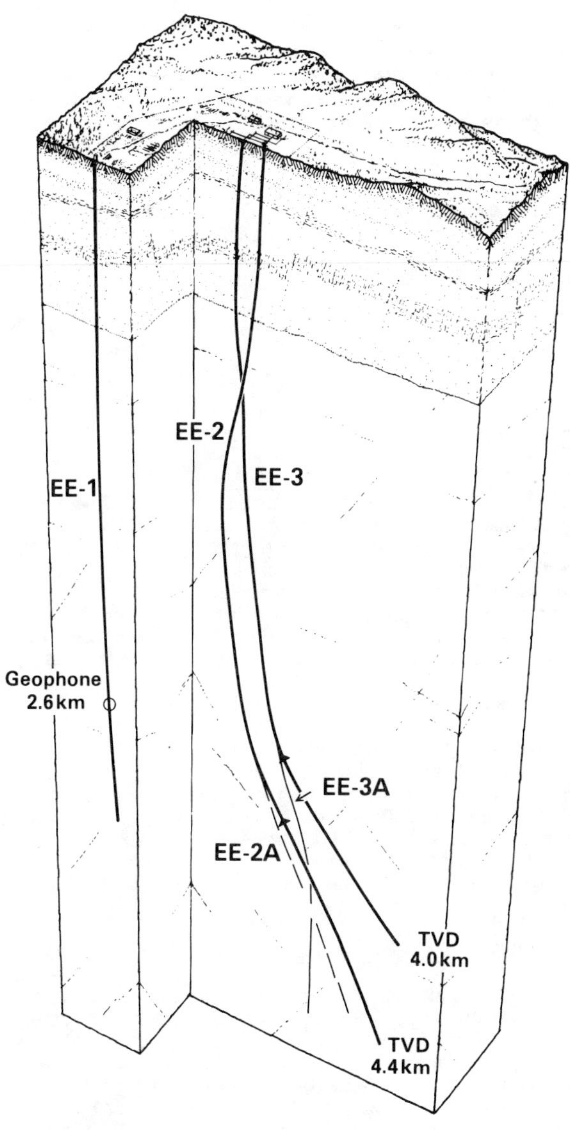

Figure 3

Perspective view of Phase II HDR boreholes and geophone emplaced for microearthquake monitoring during fracturing.

III. CURRENT PROBLEMS AND HIGH-PRIORITY RESEARCH AREAS

Regardless of the nature of the geothermal resources, whether hydrothermal, HDR, geopressured, or magma, many common problems are shared and hence form the basis for key research and development efforts. These problems and the progress toward their solution are described below.

Geothermal Reservoir Engineering

The development and application of computer models for characterizing and evaluating geothermal reservoirs represent a very significant accomplishment and a continuing technology growth area. Over the past decade, the Lawrence Berkeley Laboratory (LBL) has developed a number of sophisticated numerical tools for analyzing the behavior of geothermal reservoirs, interpreting two-phase well test data, and predicting the performance of geothermal fields under exploitation. In recent years, LBL research has focused on the formidable problems associated with fracture- and fault-dominated geothermal reservoirs.

In modeling fracture-dominated reservoirs, special attention must be directed at the coupled geological structure of the field, the dominant role of faults, the complex fluid and heat flow patterns, and the dynamic interaction between the chemical and thermodynamic fluid characteristics. Analysis of the well test data must be made with due consideration for variable fluid temperatures, pressures, and chemistry; two-phase relative permeabilities; and the heterogeneous nature of the fracture-matrix reservoir system.

LBL has completed a successful 5-year cooperative project with Mexico to study the Cerro Prieto geothermal system. This provided an opportunity to test and validate the newly developed reservoir engineering tools and computer models. LBL is currently involved in an analysis of the Ahuachapan reservoir in El Salvador, a reservoir controlled by major faults and fractured porous matrix blocks.

Well Stimulation Techniques

A common practice in the geothermal industry is to complete production wells with slotted liners throughout the production interval of the well. Although initially less expensive, slotted liner completions have the disadvantage of not allowing zonal isolation of productive intervals in the well for future clean up and stimulation treatments. The alternative procedure is to complete the well with a cemented-in liner that is explosively perforated in the production horizons and left intact through nonproductive intervals in the well. This latter completion technique allows periodic treatments to be performed in isolated well intervals without the expense of removing a slotted liner. Reluctance by the industry to accept cemented-in liner completions can be attributed, at least in part, to the questionable performance of explosive jet penetrators in providing the necessary flow communication orifices between the wellbore and the producing reservoir.

The objective of well stimulation is to initiate and maintain additional fluid production from existing wells at a lower cost than either drilling new replacement wells or redrilling existing wells. In geothermal wells, stimulation techniques must be capable of initiating and maintaining the flow of very large amounts of fluid. This necessity for high flow rates represents a significant departure from conventional oil field stimulation and requires the creation of propped fractures with very high near-wellbore permeability and/or fractures with very high flow conductivities over long intervals. The economics of well stimulation will be vastly enhanced when proven stimulation techniques can be implemented as part of the well completion (while the drilling rig is still over the hole) on all new wells exhibiting some form of flow impairment (Hanold and Morris, 1982). This will be particularly true if zone isolation can be achieved through improved well completion techniques.

Under the DOE Geothermal Well Stimulation Program, fractures were created in reservoir formations that produced hot water as a result of matrix permeability and in formations that produced hot water from naturally existing fracture systems. Overall results from this program demonstrated that stimulation is effective where formation damage or locally tight formation zones are present in the reservoir (Republic Geothermal, 1984). Formation damage by invasion of drilling mud and cement is relatively common in both fractured- and matrix-permeability-type reservoirs. Because the damage is normally confined to the near-wellbore area, fracturing or chemical stimulation can be effectively applied. For example, the two fracture treatments performed in East Mesa well 58-30 more than doubled the production rate of this previously marginal producer that contained both a formation-damaged region and a low permeability region in a matrix-type reservoir (Hanold and Morris, 1982).

In fracture-dominated reservoirs, however, the results from stimulation treatments were less consistent. Although production rate increases were always obtained, the increases were not sufficient to convert a poor producer into a commercial well. In hydraulic fracture treatments conducted at Raft River, Idaho, and Baca, New Mexico, extensive highly conductive fractures were created and propped, but they failed to establish commercial productivity from marginal reservoirs. It is suspected that these fractures may have paralleled the predominant natural fractures in the formation and failed to effectively connect them with the wellbore. Results from this well stimulation program suggest two approaches for future stimulation treatments in fracture-dominated reservoirs:

(1) In the fracture treatments performed at Raft River and Baca, large hydraulic fractures were initiated in nonproductive well intervals. A more promising approach would be to focus on stimulating existing productive fractures to take advantage of the phenomenon of "fracture compliance." Natural fractures are known to dilate during fluid injection and to constrict during production with a corresponding loss in productivity. For an elastic or compliant fracture system, it should be possible to prop fractures in the dilated state, thus retaining a higher fluid conductivity under production conditions (Republic Geothermal, 1984).

(2) New stimulation techniques capable of driving multidirectional fractures that have a high probability of intersecting nearby natural fracture systems would be a significant technological advance. The use of a propellant or gas-generating stimulation concept should be investigated for this purpose. Sandia National Laboratories has investigated high-energy gas fracturing as a technique for creating multiple fractures in a geothermal well.

Relative to other technology development work, effective well stimulation treatments continue to offer one of the greatest potential opportunities for enhancing the economics of geothermal power production.

Fracture Mapping

Determining the orientation and location of fractures along which water flows during hydraulic fracturing is of major importance in all geothermal reservoirs. A successful method developed at Los Alamos to accomplish this involves locating and analyzing microearthquakes that occur during the hydraulic fracturing operations that are carried out either to create the reservoir, as in the HDR case, or to stimulate conventional hydrothermal reservoirs. The microearthquakes occur as a direct result of fluid injections; therefore, their locations may indicate the location of flow paths. The procedure for monitoring and locating the microearthquakes has been described by House (1987), and new techniques developed by Fehler and others (1987) reveal the geometry of the fracture system along which the water flowed and microearthquakes occurred. Although this new fracture mapping technique was developed specifically for HDR reservoirs in crystalline rock, the techniques should also work in the sedimentary rocks in which the oil and gas industry conducts hydraulic fracturing to stimulate improved productivity.

Monitoring Reservoir Heat Depletion with Chemically-Reactive Tracers

Temperature-sensitive, chemically reactive tracers

have been developed at Los Alamos to map the progress of the thermal front accompanying heat extraction from HDR and those hydrothermal reservoirs that utilize reinjection of the spent, cold geothermal production fluids. When the cold front associated with the reinjected fluid reaches the production well, the temperature there will decline precipitously, signifying the end of useful heat extraction. Because of the strong temperature dependence of reaction rate with temperature, a series of reactive tracer experiments in which extent of reaction is measured provides a measure of the rate of advance of the thermal front, thus giving advance warning of the onset of severe thermal decline.

The chemical reaction kinetics for two families of reactions has been studied: the hydrolysis of organic esters and amides, and the hydrolysis of aryl halides. The esters and amides appear to be promising tracers for low-temperature reservoirs in the range of 75° - $100^{o}C$, and the aryl halides are more appropriate in the temperature range of 150° - $275^{o}C$. Preliminary adsorption studies for the aryl halides indicate a small propensity to adsorb on granitic rock, but the amount of adsorption should not adversely affect the use of the tracers. Future laboratory work is required to examine the adsorption issue more closely, as well as to develop a sensitive analytical technique for measuring the expectedly small tracer concentrations. The culmination of the reactive tracer experiment will be the field demonstration in the Fenton Hill reservoir during the upcoming long-term flow test.

Hard Rock Penetration

Drilling and well completion are difficult in most geothermal reservoirs and represent the major cost in developing geothermal resources. To address these problems, Sandia National Laboratories is conducting research and development in borehole mechanics and rock penetration mechanics. The borehole mechanics task addresses problems in lost circulation control and drilling fluids. A large, high-temperature lost circulation test facility has been constructed, and comparative data on materials performance have been generated. With Texas Tech University, Sandia has evaluated bentonite and bentonite/saponite mixtures for use as geothermal drilling fluids. Rock penetration mechanics research resulted in the introduction and acceptance of polycrystalline diamond compact bits. A joint Sandia/industry development of a computer code for analysis of drill string dynamics has recently been completed. In addition, drill strings for operation in very high temperature formations are being designed.

Borehole Logging and Well Completion Equipment

Borehole tools originally developed at Los Alamos

have been used to transmit seismic signals between wells at unprecedented rates and numbers. An acoustic source transmitter scans a section of one wellbore, while a receiver is stationed in an adjacent wellbore. The receiver consists of a piezoelectric transducer that is tuned for maximum response at the transmission frequency. The characteristics of the medium through which the acoustic vibrations pass are deduced from the character of the received signals and from their arrival times at the receiver. The distance between two boreholes can be measured with great accuracy, and the presence of fluid-filled fractures in the formation can be determined.

A high-temperature, downhole fluid sampler was developed to provide borehole fluid samples of 4 liters. This sampler was used during the Salton Sea drilling program to retrieve samples in fluids where the borehole temperature exceeded 350°C.

Developments in wellbore diagnostics at Sandia National Laboratories have included high-temperature electronic components, a wellbore navigator, and cement bond logging tools. Recently, dewared "slickline" tools with downhole memory were developed for pressure, temperature, and flow measurement. A prototype borehole radar tool with directional capability has been designed and assembled. The instrument is designed to locate producing fractures up to 100 m from the wellbore. The prototype is being evaluated and upgraded in a series of laboratory and field tests.

An open-hole packer system was designed, fabricated, and tested by Los Alamos and Baker Production, with US DOE funding. The system shown in Figure 4 has been used to isolate zones, to conduct injection tests, and to stimulate HDR reservoirs as hot as 260°C. After exposure to temperatures of 240°C, the packer has functioned at differential pressures up to 40 MPa (5500 psi). Three high-pressure, massive hydraulic fracturing operations, each injecting over 3800 m^3 of water, have been conducted using the packer system.

IV. TECHNOLOGY SPINOFFS

In the past, much of the technology needed for geothermal development came from the oil and gas well drilling industry. Recently, however, under DOE and other sponsors of geothermal development programs, numerous technology advances have evolved or been identified that could find direct application in the extraction of petroleum and natural gas resources. For example, new techniques in well stimulation described above could be used to increase production in stripper wells. The microseismic technique for mapping fracture flow paths has been identified by representatives of the oil industry as a critical area of technology. Application would be in stimulation treatments and during enhanced oil recovery

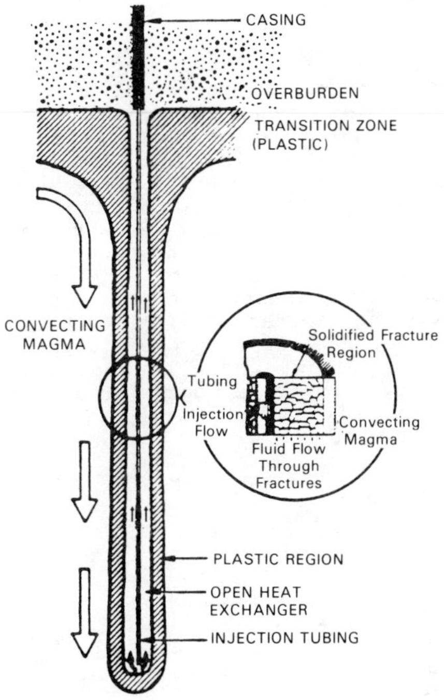

Figure 4

Conceptual representation of a single well open-heat exchanger system

reservoir treatments. New logging tools such as the fluid sampler and radar tool could find application in petroleum reservoirs where existing tools are inadequate. For example, in steam drive fields and some high-temperature development wells (e.g., 250°C wells in Texas), these tools could be useful. Diagnostics are required to evaluate the effectiveness of current steam flood and fire flood operations.

V. CONCLUSIONS

Recent advances in geothermal technology and concepts have moved geopressured, hot dry rock, and magma energy closer to the point of economic viability. These new technologies for producing geothermal energy can tap a vast geothermal energy resource within the US and elsewhere in the world. Questions about cost and technical feasibility remain. Research and development in these advanced concepts have produced numerous technological advances. These technological advances include new hardware, new methods, and new concepts for geothermal energy extraction. All contribute to enhancing the economics of geothermal production. Moreover, many of these same technologies can be applied to the petroleum industry and can provide a means for extracting additional oil from domestic reservoirs that would otherwise be considered depleted.

ACKNOWLEDGEMENTS

We thank Nola Blomker, Ada DeAguero, and Cheryl Straub for preparing this manuscript.

REFERENCES

Armstead, H.C.H., and J.W. Tester, Heat Mining, E&FN Spon, London, 1987.

Dash, Z.V., H.D. Murphy, R.L. Aamodt, R.G. Aguilar, D.W. Brown, D. A. Counce, H. N. Fisher, C.O. Grigsby, H. Keppler, A.W. Laughlin, R.M. Potter, J.W. Tester, P.E. Trujillo, and G.A. Zyvoloski, "Hot Dry Rock Geothermal Reservoir Testing: 1987 to 1980," J. Volcan. and Geothermal Res. 15, 59-99, 1983.

Dash, Z.V., D.S. Dreesen, F. Walter, and L. House, "The Massive Hydraulic Fracture of Fenton Hill HDR Well EE-3," Geothermal Resources Council Annual Meeting, Kona, HA, August 26-30, 1985.

Dunn, J.C., "Energy Extraction from Crustal Magma Bodies," ASME/JSME Thermal Engineering Joint Conference Proceedings, V. II, pp. 93-100, 1986.

Dunn, J.C., "Magma Energy For Power Generation," 11th Annual EPRI Geothermal Conference and Workshop, Oakland, CA, June 22-29, 1987.

Fehler, M., L. House, and H. Kaieda, "Determining Planes Along Which Earthquakes Occur: Method and Application to Earthquakes Accompanying Hydraulic Fracturing," J. Geophys. Res. 92, 9407-9414, 1987.

Hanold, R. J., and C. W. Morris, "Induced Fractures-Well Stimulation Through Fracturing," Proceedings of the Fractures in Geothermal Reservoirs Workshop, Circum-Pacific Energy and Mineral Resources Conference, Honolulu, Hawaii, August, 1982.

House, L., "Locating Microearthquakes Induced by Hydraulic Fracturing in Crystalline Rock," Geophys. Res. Letters 14, 919-921, 1987.

House, L., H. Keppler, and H. Kaieda, "Seismic Studies of a Massive Hydraulic Fracturing Experiment," Geothermal Resources Council Annual Meeting, Kona, HA, August 26-30, 1985.

Ramsthaler, J. H., and M. Plum, "Future for Geopressured-Geothermal Resources," Idaho National Engineering Laboratory, EG&G Idaho, Inc., 1987.

Republic Geothermal, Inc., "Geothermal Reservoir Well Stimulation Program," Final Program Summary Report, January, 1984.

Smith, R.L., and H.R. Shaw. "Igneous-Related Geothermal Systems", US Geological Survey Circular 726, 1975, pp. 58-83.

Smith, R.L., and H.R. Shaw. "Igneous-Related Geothermal Systems," US Geological Survey Circular 790, 1979, pp. 12-17.

US DOE/EG&G Idaho, Inc., "Geopressured-Geothermal Program - Annual Operating Plan," October 29, 1987.

FIGURE CAPTIONS

1. HOT DRY ROCK RESERVOIR

2. PERSPECTIVE VIEW OF HDR BOREHOLES AND GEOPHONE EN-PLACED FOR MICROEARTHQUAKE MONITORING DURING FRAC-TURING

3. A SINGLE-WELL, OPEN HEAT EXCHANGER FOR MAGMA ENERGY EXTRACTION

4. HIGH-TEMPERATURE OPEN-HOLE PACKER

ENERGY MANAGEMENT

BASELINING THE HUD HQ BUILDING FOR SHARED SAVINGS

K. Dean DeVine PE

Federal Energy Management Program

U.S. Department of Energy

On April 9, 1987, federal officials met with industry representatives at the Department of Housing and Urban Development (HUD) Headquarters building in Washington, DC, to present the results of an effort to establish a shared savings baseline for that building. The building is about 1.2 million square feet and uses about $1.8 million in electricity annually. For the first time, a sophisticated analytical tool, ASEAM-2, was being proposed for use in baselining a complex building to execute a federal shared savings contract.

Until that meeting, the federal governments efforts toward baselining for proposed shared savings contracts had consisted of either a simple application of utility records; linear regression analysis of known operating parameters; or no defined approach, ie, ask the shared savings partner to propose a baselining technique. It is noteworthy that at the time of the April meeting no federal shared savings contract had been successful in reaching an award. Each of these techniques as they were applied had serious shortcomings for a project of any complexity. However, they represented the current state of knowledge of how one might approach baselining for a federal shared savings contract.

Baselining

Before discussing these baselining approaches and the use of ASEAM-2 to baseline the HUD Headquarters building, it is useful to address how the terms baseline and baseline extension are used in this paper and in connection with the HUD project. For shared savings a baseline is an analytical method that depends on site specific data for energy use and other operative parameters during a previous period of time known as the baseline period. In general terms, a shared savings baseline is any technique that is acceptable by the contracting parties for inclusion in a shared savings contract that relates baseline energy use data to other baseline data in order to produce a reasonable representation of the real energy consumption response of the facility or components to variable conditions. It's primary use is in the development of the baseline extension. The baseline extension is that analytical part of a shared savings baseline that is used to calculate what the energy consumption would have been after the baseline period but during the contract period as though the energy conservation retrofits or procedures had not been implemented. A high quality baseline extension will account for all significant variables in order to improve the accuracy of that calculation. In practical application, the monthly energy consumption calculated by the baseline extension would be compared to the presumably lower actual metered energy consumption. The difference would be the saved energy which would have to be translated into saved dollars for contract payout. That calculation as applied to the HUD project is shown later in this paper.

Simple use of existing utility bills or meter readings both as a baseline and baseline extension has an underlying assumption that is sometimes not well understood. That assumption is that there are no significant variables which would cause future energy usage in the unmodified building to differ from past usage. That is, the baseline could reasonably be expected to extend into the future with no change. In a few limited cases, such as with pumps or lights that are on continuously for fixed periods, this may be a proper assumption. In most cases this assumption introduces an inaccuracy in the baseline extension which becomes an unquantified business risk and may, in certain cases, even be unrecognized. In those limited cases where the underlying assumption is correct, this simplest form of baseline would be the preferred approach since it is both technically sufficient and contractually easy to administer.

The use of linear regression analysis to develop a baseline extension has the potential in certain cases to be an improvement over the simple use of past utility bills. However, it too has underlying assumptions which may not be recognized. A primary assumption in the use of linear regression analysis is that all variables have a linear effect on the resultant energy consumption. In many buildings and facilities this would not be the case. For example, a central plant generally will have a part load efficiency that is different from its full load efficiency. It is by definition a nonlinear device and not accurately handled by linear analysis. On the other hand, in a specific building, a simple linear equation might be sufficient to address the relationship between the number of building occupants and electrical consumption in interior lighting. If records were already being maintained on building occupancy, a linear equation form of baseline extension would in all likelihood be the the best approach since, again, it would be both technically sufficient and contractually easy to administer.

The third approach to baselining for shared savings, that is, asking the shared savings partner to propose a baselining methodology, introduces an element of major uncertainty in the evaluation phase of a federal procurement. In addition to evaluating the efficacy of any proposed energy conservation retrofits, the proposal evaluation team would be required to evaluate any baselining techniques that might be proposed; a task it might or might not be equipped to accomplish. Evaluation of any proprietary software would be prohibitively expensive and time consuming (assuming that the source code could be disclosed to the government). One possible outcome of this approach would be that only the simpler forms of baselining could be accepted for a federal shared savings project. This could have the highly detrimental effect of limiting the types of projects undertaken to only the most simple types of systems retrofits.

In approaching the HUD shared savings project, it became evident that in order to assure that proposals could be successfully evaluated and a contract awarded, a non-proprietary baselining methodology would have to be used. Also, in order to provide an acceptable degree of accuracy in the baseline extension calculation, a more sophisticated tool than linear regression analysis would be required. For credibility, the tool would have to be based on energy calculation methodologies having national acceptance. ASEAM-2, now issued as version 2.1, met these firm requirements and was also relatively inexpensive and easy to use.

ASEAM-2.1

ASEAM-2.1, A Simplified Energy Analysis Method, Version 2.1, is a modified bin method program for doing whole building energy analysis. It runs on an IBM PC* and compatibles using nationally recognized algorithms from such sources as the American Society of Heating, Refrigerating and Air-Conditioning Engineers (ASHRAE), Illuminating Engineering Society (IES), the DOE-2 mainframe computer software developed and maintained at the Lawrence Berkeley Laboratory, and the National Bureau of Standards (NBS) life-cycle costing software. The ASEAM software was developed with DOE funding by W. S. Fleming and Associates under subcontract to the Battelle Pacific Northwest Laboratory.

ASEAM-2 accounts for those variables that are recognized as significantly affecting building energy consumption. These include the building envelope and weather effects; internal energy loads such as lighting, equipment, and people; HVAC system effects from such inputs as system type (ASEAM handles thirteen different combinations of HVAC types), setpoints, and systems efficiencies; and central plant effects from such inputs as operating schedules, plant design efficiencies and energy source types. Input of operating use profiles as well as monthly diversity factors give a wide range of flexibility in adjusting to actual on-site conditions. As an additional benefit separate from baselining, ASEAM allows for calculation of the benefits of energy conservation opportunities for building retrofit applications.

Modeling the HUD Headquarters building

The HUD HQ building has twelve floors with two floors below grade. ASEAM was originally configured to handle no more than ten zones in a single building. Initially it appeared that the HUD HQ building would have to be subdivided into as many as five smaller buildings with "null" walls connecting them in order to be simulated on ASEAM; a somewhat cumbersome approach possibly introducing some inaccuracy at the plant level. As the detailed inputs were developed it became apparent that large sections of the building had similar loads and other features that would permit them to be grouped into single zones even though they were not physically connected. As a result, all the exterior offices were grouped into six nine-story zones according to their solar orientation. The remainder of the building was divided into four zones; the building core having limited exterior exposure, the computer facility with its own dedicated HVAC system, the perimeter of the two below grade floors, and the below grade garage which has fan coil units.

All zones except the computer facility and the garage are serviced by a continuous volume reheat (CVRH) system. Cooling is provided by two 1,750 ton centrifugal chillers. Heat is supplied by a district heating system operated by the General Services Administration. All exterior zones, in addition, have perimeter fan coil units operating off of the same central plant.

Modeling the systems interaction of the HUD HQ building presented an unusual challenge. One of the constraints in the use of ASEAM was that, with one exception, no zone could have more than one HVAC system assigned to it. Other than baseboard heating, ASEAM was not designed to handle systems interactions.

In order to account for the system interaction that actually occurs in the HUD HQ building, the CVRH airflow input into ASEAM was sized to supply air to the entire building, but the CVRH system was not assigned to the peripheral zones so that ASEAM would not "see" the loads associated with those zones in the CVRH calculation. The CVRH system was assigned only to the interior zone. A heat transfer rate per square foot of interior floor space was calculated to account for the difference between the supply and return air temperatures of the air going to the peripheral zones from the CVRH system. This heat transfer rate was assigned as a miscellaneous load input to the interior zone. A heat balance was then calculated so that an offsetting heat transfer rate per square foot of peripheral floor space could be assigned to the peripheral zones. This procedure was followed for both winter and summer schedules to account for the difference in winter and summer thermostat setpoints.

Baselining for the HUD Request For Proposals (RFP)

ASEAM produces numerous loads and systems reports, but it was originally configured to produce only an annual whole building energy usage report. In preparation for the April 9 meeting with industry representatives, I had learned that a monthly energy usage report could be programmed into ASEAM with little difficulty and had asked that it be done. At the April 9 meeting, the industry representatives after seeing the good annual agreement between ASEAM with 1985 inputs and the actual annual 1985 electrical energy consumption asked if a monthly comparison for both 1985 and 1986 could be produced. The results of that effort are shown as figures 1 and 2. It should be noted that only electrical energy consumption was being considered for inclusion in a shared savings project because the building was electricity dominated (about 80%) and the accuracy of the steam metering in this case was not considered accurate enough for purposes of baselining.

The HUD HQ electrical meter readings occur on the 23rd of each month. The ASEAM monthly energy consumption calculation is through the end of each month. In order to compare the two it was necessary to export each set of data to Lotus** to produce a superimposed calendar year graph which then could be visually interpreted.

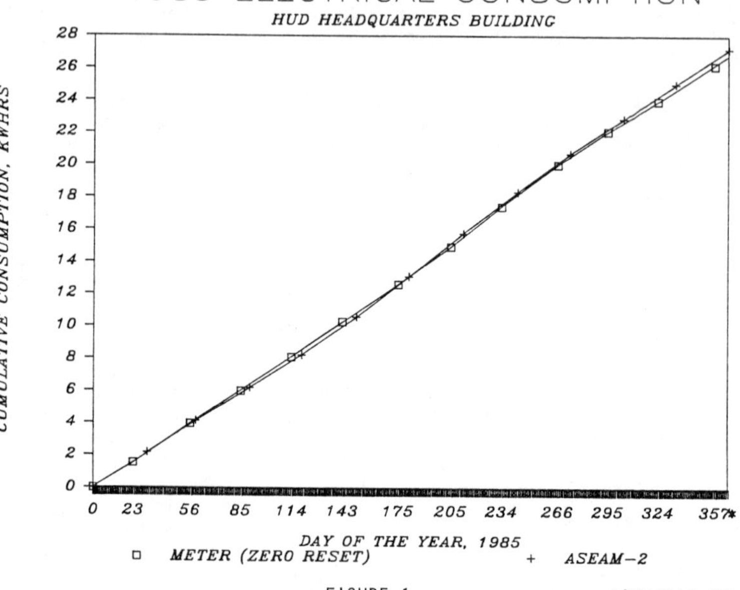

FIGURE 1

KDD 5-18-87

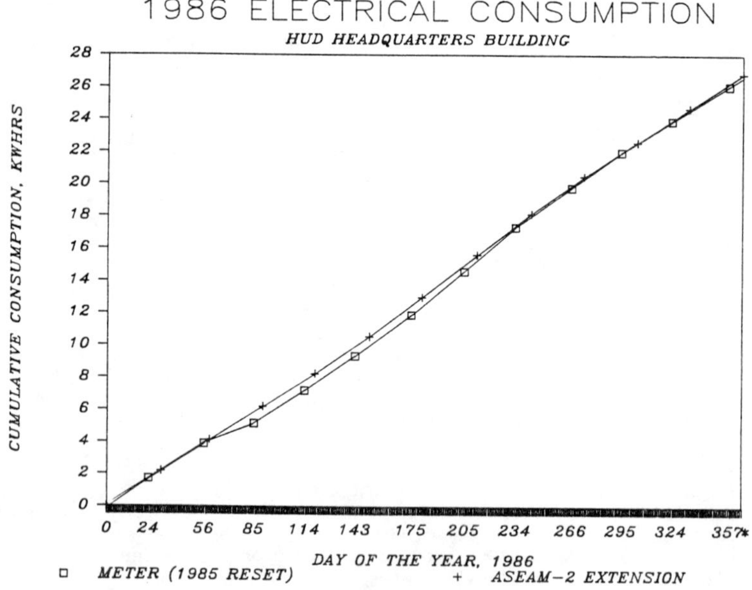

FIGURE 2

KDD 5-18-87

The primary significance of figure 1 is that by using actual 1985 weather data and operating parameters, a good month by month comparison with actual 1985 consumption was obtained giving confidence that a reasonable representation of energy flows in the building had been produced taking into account all significant variables. This is the primary purpose of a high quality baseline.

In contrast, figure 2 might best be viewed as a simulated baseline extension. It was run using only the "frozen" 1985 baseline building file with (1) the 1986 Washington weather file substituted for the 1985 Washington weather file and (2) the May 1986 introduction of motion detection lighting controls in the below grade two floors which essentially turns those lights off for twelve hours a day. There is a slight separation in the two curves beginning in March and correcting in August which may correlate with past attempts at energy conservation by operational controls. However, by the end of the year the total energy consumption was calculated within a few percent of the actual using a very inexpensive analytical tool.

Accuracy, risk and cost

It is axiomatic that you get no more accuracy than what you pay for. Improvements in baseline accuracy are justified when they are either necessary to obtain a negotiated shared savings contract (a primary requirement) or sufficiently cost effective to pay for themselves through an increased share of the savings going to the party generating the baseline, in this case the federal government. This latter situation can occur if the perception on the part of the shared savings proposer is that the inaccuracy in the baseline extension is going to be a large fraction of the projected savings and thus presents a significant business risk. The most common way for the proposer to mitigate that risk is to negotiate a higher share of the projected savings (or forgo the project).

As stated previously, ASEAM was selected for the HUD project because it appeared to be the least costly way to obtain an acceptable degree of accuracy in the baseline extension. Barring programming error, the primary source of error in using ASEAM in any specific application is likely to be either misjudgment in the engineering inputs or through misapplying the software to an application it was not designed to handle. For the HUD project we were fortunate to have a buildings operations staff that taken meter readings on primary pieces of equipment and who had access to facility construction, operational and occupancy data necessary to give a high level of assurance in the quality of the data inputs to the baseline. Nonetheless, it was recognized that a proposer will have to propose building energy conservation measures that would create significant savings in order for the baseline accuracy to be of negligible concern.

It should be noted that if the baseline accuracy is not biased, ie, the baseline error is just as likely to be high as it is low and by equal amounts, then as long as the error is small compared to the savings, the chances of a favorable effect to the proposer would offset the risk of negative effect and should not diminish chances of a successful contract negotiation. It is only when the risk of baseline error is a large enough part of the savings to potentially effect short term cash flows beyond what can be readily absorbed that it becomes a significant risk. In evaluating the HUD HQ project it is felt that the potential savings are large compared to the baseline error.

From baseline to RFP

On October 8, 1987, a second meeting was held at HUD with industry representatives; this time to review and obtain comments on a draft RFP for a shared savings project. At that meeting it was determined that, if possible, the industry representatives would want savings under each of the time of day rates, including any future rate adjustments, as well as the savings in peak demand charge accounted for separately in calculating the shared savings payout. Until that time for purposes of simplicity a composite average cost per kilowatt hour including demand charge had been considered. This average cost per kilowatt hour would have been applied to both the kilowatt hours usage calculated by the ASEAM baseline extension and to the actual metered kilowatt hours consumption to determine cost savings to HUD. But that approach would have permitted the proposer to take advantage of only gross energy savings. It would have excluded any incentive for peak load shaving, load shifting, or demand curtailment in greater proportion to average load than HUD had been able to achieve.

Following is a sample calculation of the HUD shared savings payout as included in the RFP issued in November. This sample baseline extension calculation accounts for on-peak, intermediate-peak and off-peak rates for both summer and winter, as well as summer and winter demand charges. The underlying assumption in this approach is that the energy use profile, that is, the percentage distribution between time of day rates in summer and winter would not have changed significantly even though total energy usage would be expected to respond to such variables as weather, occupancy, and equipment load. This baseline extension cost calculation is then compared to the actual utility bill to determine monthly savings.

Sample Calculation Of HUD Shared Savings Payout

Baseline Extension

If during the baseline year, the HUD electrical energy consumption and costs per kilowatt hour and demand charges were as follows:

	On-Peak	Int-Peak	Off-Peak	Total
Energy, KWH (S)	3,500,000	2,900,000	4,800,000	11,200,000
(W)	5,500,000	4,600,000	6,000,000	16,000,000
Annual KWH				27,200,000
Summer cost, $	211,750	129,978	137,424	$479,152
Winter cost, $	278,905	206,172	171,780	$656,857
Annual cost, $				$1,136,009
Rate, cents/KWH (S)	6.050	4.482	2.863	
(W)	5.071	4.482	2.863	

Key: (S)=Summer (W)=Winter

then for the baseline period, the composite rate excluding demand is:

$\frac{\$479,152}{11,200,000 \text{ KWH}}$ or 4.278 cents per KWH in the summer

$\frac{\$656,857}{16,100,000 \text{ KWH}}$ or 4.080 cents per KWH in the winter

The monthly demand charge of $15.30 per peak KW (summer) and $5.80 (winter), times the 6,286 peak KW which HUD has successfully maintained, would then be added at $95,900 (summer) and $36,354 (winter). Summer rates are defined as June through September, and winter rates as October through May. If the utility enacts a rate increase or decrease during the term of the contract, rates used to calculate shared savings payout would be changed accordingly.

Each month during the period of performance of the contract, ASEAM-2.1 would use current weather data to calculate the energy consumption that would have occurred, in kilowatt hours, as though no new energy conservation measures had been applied. The summer or winter composite rate would then be applied to determine what the energy cost would have been, and then the corresponding summer and winter demand charge would be added. This assumes that the load profile for the building would have remained relatively stable and that HUD would have continued to control demand charges through load shedding as the agency has been doing.

For example, if the ASEAM 2.1 calculation showed that the August 1988 consumption would have been 2,700,000 kilowatt-hours, then the cost to HUD would have been:

$$(2,700,000 \text{ KWH} \times \frac{\$.04278}{\text{KWH}}) + \$95,900 = \$211,406$$

<u>Actual</u> <u>Metered</u>

If the actual metered August 1988 consumption were:

650,000 KWH on-peak
560,000 KWH int-peak
850,000 KWH off-peak

and demand on June 23, 1988 had been reduced to 5,000 KW

then the actual cost calculation would be as follows:

650,000 KWH x $.06050/KWH = $39,325 on-peak charge

560,000 KWH x $.04482/KWH = $25,099 int-peak charge

850,000 KWH x $.02863/KWH = $24,336 off-peak charge

5,000 KW x $15.30/KWH = <u>$76,500</u> August demand charge

$165,260 total August 1988 time of day rate and demand charges

Savings Calculation

The savings would then be the difference between the baseline extension cost calculation and the actual cost calculation:

$211,406 - $165,260 = $46,146 August 1988 savings

Conclusion

Lack of low cost baselining techniques is a potential impediment to successful federal shared savings projects. This need for applied technology is being addressed by the Federal Energy Management Program of the Department of Energy. For large buildings having significant energy conservation potential through major retrofits of interactive systems, we hope that the HUD RFP will serve as a starting point for federal agencies to develop their own site-specific RFPs. For smaller or less complex projects where systems are not interactive or can be isolated, we expect that simpler but still inexpensive and easy to administer baselining methods can be developed.

---

* IBM is the trademark of International Business Machines, Inc.
** Lotus is the trademark of Lotus Development Corporation

A PRACTICAL APPROACH TO OFFICE LIGHTING RENOVATION

R. Arnold Tucker, P.E., C.E.M., Manager
Technical Programs, Commercial Engineering
GTE Products Corporation
Sylvania Lighting Center
Danvers, Massachusetts 01923

ABSTRACT

Lamp manufacturers share the concerns of local, state and federal energy conservation commissions and agencies, as well as electric utility companies, in their efforts to conserve electric power. Lamp manufacturers have responded by providing advanced lighting technologies and educational programs for their customers and others in the lighting industry.

It is important, however, that the need for and value of these energy-efficient lighting products be communicated to the end users. The marketplace demand for these advanced technologies must come from them.

This paper will discuss three office building lighting renovations:

- Twenty-story office building in Philadelphia, PA
- Black & Decker's Corporate Headquarters in Towson, MD
- Allentown Call-Chronicle newsroom in Allentown, PA

By using practical and innovative designs, these office buildings are using the latest advanced lighting technologies without sacrificing light output. Energy savings at each location was the measure used to calculate the return the users received from their investment in the new lighting products. Once the energy-saving benefits are understood, the price differential for value added energy-saving products is readily accepted.

INTRODUCTION

Using the standard T-12 (one and one-half inch diameter) fluorescent lighting system with standard or energy saving magnetic ballasts as the basis for a light output comparison, all energy saving T-12 fluorescent lamp/ ballast systems have reduced light output when operated in the same luminaire.

Over the past seven years, the lighting industry has introduced a family of reduced diameter fluorescent sources. The T-8 (one-inch diameter) fluorescent lamp is an energy efficient lighting system that delivers the same light output and life from the luminaire as a standard T-12 lamp/ballast combination, while reducing overall energy requirements and providing good color rendering at color temperatures of 3100, 3500, 4100K.

The first T-8 lamp was a 4-foot, 32-watt unit. Because of optical and thermal improvements when operated in a luminaire as well as improved phosphor technology, the T-8 system is able to provide the same amount of light as a 40-watt, T-12 system. The T-8 lamp uses medium bipin bases and is physically compatible with luminaires designed for 4-foot, T-12 lamps.

Lumen maintenance of the T-8 system also is increased to 90% as compared to 88% for a T-12 system because of the reduced current and use of rare earth phosphors.

Other versions of this lamp type include 2-foot, 3-foot, and 5-foot units carrying wattage ratings of 17, 25, and 40 watts, respectively.

Smallest of the T-8 lamp family, the 17-watt, 2-foot lamp has the same overall length as the commonly used 20-watt, T-12 preheat lamps, but offers some distinct advantages. It produces more light output, consumes less power and has a life rating of 20,000 hours, which is more than twice the 9000-hour life rating of the 2-foot preheat lamp.

U-shaped lamps provide added design flexibility for this family of T-8 lamps. New fixture and lighting system designs for these U-shaped lamps now are available in three wattages: 16, 24, and 31 watts. These tight-bend lamps have a leg spacing of 1 5/8 inches. Equipped with standard medium bipin bases, they are used with common U-lamp sockets and operate on the same ballasts available for comparable wattage straight T-8 lamps. These U-lamps have a rated life of 20,000 hours, excellent lumen maintenance characteristics, and are available in three color temperatures.

The 31-watt lamp has an overall length of 22 1/2 inches. Its compact size allows for the design of more efficient 2-foot by 2-foot luminaires using up to four lamps inside a modular fixture.

The 16-watt U-lamp is only 10 1/2 inches long and it will fit in a compact 1-foot by 1-foot square fixture. Two of these lamps with ballast in such a fixture consume only about 40 watts of power, but deliver approximately the same amount of light as a 150-watt incandescent lamp while lasting 20 times longer.

BALLAST COMPATIBILITY

Like all fluorescent lamps, T-8 lamps must be operated on a ballast to limit the current and provide the required starting voltage. The ballast must be designed specifically for the lamp's electrical characteristics, the type of circuit on which it is operated, and the voltage and frequency of the power supply.

Because of its 265-ma operating current, the T-8 lamp required the design of a new rapid start ballast. The magnetic rapid start ballast used in these lamps offers two primary advantages: (1) economical design and (2) long lamp life of 20,000 hours. Single and two-lamp magnetic ballasts are currently available for both 120 and 277 volt operation.

High frequency operation (20 KHz and up) improves fluorescent lamp efficacy, affording the opportunity to deliver the same light output for less power. Installations of high-frequency systems have been limited primarily by the cost and efficiency of the equipment required to convert power into higher frequencies.

Instant start circuits prove more economical at high frequency, because circuit design is simplified, with less complex ballasts and fixtures. The cathodes of T-8 lamps were designed with the knowledge that high-frequency operation would become more popular. Specific design considerations were incorporated into the lamps' cathodes to allow them to operate effectively either at high frequency or at 60 Hz. Currently there are two-lamp, three-lamp and four-lamp high frequency instant start ballasts available. With these ballasts, lamps operate in parallel, so that if one lamp fails, the others continue to operate. These high frequency electronic ballasts also are available in 120 and 277 volts.

While T-8 lamps operated instant start have reduced life ratings of 15,000 hours, they do provide the advantages mentioned above. The multiple lamp ballast designs simplify the equipment needed not only in four-lamp luminaires (by requiring just one ballast instead of two), but also in the increasingly popular three-lamp systems, which traditionally required both a single and a two-lamp ballast. Due to the increased efficiency of these systems, the shorter lamp life is more than offset by the reduction of power consumed to deliver the same light output. Also, lumen maintenance is improved to 91 percent at 40 percent of rated life when T-8 lamps are operated on the high frequency instant start systems.

CASE STUDY 1

Thirty-two-watt T-8 lamps were selected for energy-saving at the twenty-story office building on the corner of Broad and Locust Streets in downtown Philadelphia managed by Richard I. Rubin, Inc., a real estate management and development firm.

The complete renovation of the high-rise professional building included the installation of a sophisticated energy-management system. The computerized system controls interior lighting, as well as energy-conserving heating and air conditioning functions, via centralized switches.

Some 8000 32-watt T-8 lamps were installed in work areas that house lawyers, accounting firms, advertising agencies, and other clerical and professional tenants. The reduced diameter fluorescent replaced standard 40-watt lamps in all work areas throughout the building. Incandescents are used in common areas, primarily the elevator corridors.

Light levels were important in this environment. The lamps' smaller diameter meant shallower fixtures, reduced optical losses, and less heat buildup within the fixture. Special electronic ballasts also were used, boosting the expected energy savings to approximately 39 percent over standard 40-watt fluorescents. In Philadelphia, where electricity costs between 8 and 10 cents per kilowatt hour, this reduction represents a savings of over $11.00 per hour throughout the life of the lamps. (See Table I.)

TABLE I
ANALYSIS OF SAVINGS WHEN SWITCHING TO T-8 LAMPS AND ELECTRONIC BALLASTS AT BUILDING MANAGED BY RUBIN REAL ESTATE

ANNUAL SAVINGS LIGHTING		
TOTAL PRESENT LIGHTING LOAD FOR 8,000 T-12, 40-WATT FLUORESCENTS	368.00	KW
TOTAL NEW LIGHTING LOAD USING 8,000 T-8, 32-WATT FLUORESCENTS	224.00	KW
LOAD REDUCTION DUE TO LIGHTING	144.00	KW
ANNUAL LOAD REDUCTION FOR 3,000 HRS/YR	432,000	KWH
ANNUAL SAVINGS AT $.0800 PER KWH	$34,560.00	

TABLE I (cont.)

RETURN ON INVESTMENT	
TOTAL ENERGY SAVINGS FOR 2,160,000 KWH SAVED OVER LAMP LIFE	$172,800.00
LESS TOTAL INVESTMENT FOR 8,000 NEW LAMPS AT A $8.90 INVESTMENT PER LAMP	71,200.00
NET RETURN ON INVESTMENT	$101,600.00
ANNUALIZED NET RETURN FOR 5.0 YEARS	20,320.00
RETURN ON INVESTMENT	28.50%
PAY BACK PERIOD FOR PROPOSED SYSTEM	25 MONTHS

CASE STUDY 2

T-8 fluorescent lamps are being installed by Black & Decker as part of a major renovation of its corporate headquarters. The advanced fluorescent lamps will reduce electricity usage by 26 percent with a payback period of only nine months.

Renovation of the building is going forward in three phases. The first phase included relamping of 24,000 square feet on a single floor of the firm's corporate and U.S. headquarters with 1080 T-8 lamps. The drop ceilings were equipped with 360 new lay-in fixtures accepting three lamps each. They replaced the previous four-lamp, 40-watt fluorescent fixtures, and maintained previous light levels.

A second phase will install 480 fixtures and 1440 lamps in a 20,000-square-foot area on another floor of the facility, with a third phase now in the design stage. The 2520 lamps alone installed in the two initial phases will save over 604,000 kilowatt hours of energy over the life of the lamps, for over $36,000 estimated savings at Black & Decker's current average energy cost of six cents per kilowatt hour. (See Table II.)

TABLE II
ANALYSIS OF SAVINGS WHEN SWITCHING TO T-8 LAMPS AT BLACK & DECKER HEADQUARTERS

ANNUAL SAVINGS LIGHTING		
TOTAL PRESENT LIGHTING LOAD FOR 2,520 T-12, 40-WATT FLUORESCENTS	115.92	KW
TOTAL NEW LIGHTING LOAD USING 2,520 T-8 32-WATT FLUORESCENTS	85.68	KW
LOAD REDUCTION DUE TO LIGHTING	30.24	KW
ANNUAL LOAD REDUCTION FOR 3,000 HRS/YR	90,720	KWH
ANNUAL SAVINGS AT $.0600 PER KWH	$5,443.20	

TABLE II (cont.)

RETURN ON INVESTMENT	
TOTAL ENERGY SAVINGS FOR 604,739 KWH SAVED OVER LAMP LIFE	$36,284.37
LESS TOTAL INVESTMENT FOR 2,520 NEW LAMPS AT A $1.55 INVESTMENT PER LAMP	3,906.00
NET RETURN ON INVESTMENT	$32,378.37
ANNUALIZED NET RETURN FOR 6.7 YEARS	$ 4,856.73
RETURN ON INVESTMENT	124.30%
PAY BACK PERIOD FOR PROPOSED SYSTEM	9 MONTHS

The initial cost for the 32-watt T-8 lamp installation was not the lowest-cost estimate proposed, but the energy savings was maximized with this lamp. Color and light levels were other major concerns. The Black & Decker employees working at corporate headquarters perform clerical and administrative tasks, and the projected third-phase renovation will include the firm's many designers and draftsman.

CASE STUDY 3

The advanced T-8 fluorescent lamps have eliminated glare and the resulting eyestrain and fatigue from the newsroom at the Allentown Call-Chronicle in Allentown, PA.

The Call-Chronicle newsroom occupies a new wing designed for the newspaper by Breslin Ridyard Fadaro - Architects and Planners. All aspects of the lighting design, including the dispersal of natural light from outside windows, were designed specifically to accommodate the special requirements of the many video-display-terminal-equipped workstations housed in the new wing. The result is a high efficiency system consuming 25 percent less energy than standard 40-watt fluorescents, improved optical control, and superior color-rendering properties.

Glare is the primary source of complaints of eye and muscle strain among staffers working with VDT for long hours. Most complaints have been traced to screen glare and inadequate room lighting. In planning the new wing, both the architects and the Call-Chronicle's management worked to avoid the serious consequences of fatigue, such as lower productivity and moraleand higher error rates.

The indirect, "bounce" lighting system selected for the new wing eliminates screen glare and reflection and has created a virtually "complaint-free" environment for the paper's news, circulation, classified, and advertising departments, also housed in the new wing. There was no way to avoid all these problems with an old, direct lighting system. Direct lighting is still employed in the paper's executive and editorial-writing offices, and there continue to be complaints from workers in these quarters.

Indirect lighting systems are a relatively unique application for fluorescent lamps, but the features of the T-8 lamp made it the choice for the Chronicle's needs. A total of 720 four-foot T-8 lamps were installed in 1500 linear feet of fixtures. The 20,000 plus square feet of floor space in the wing, including corridors, were illuminated at 75 to 85 footcandles after installation. Ceilings are ten-foot, and rows of fixtures were installed on 8-foot centers with 20-inch stems.

Light intensity at work stations was less important, planners of the installation determined, than achieving an optimum ratio of contrast and uniformity of light falling on VDT screens. The selection of lamp was made after analysis of a series of complex comparative photometric calculations resulting in a "state of the art" installation. It is a lighting system that eliminates glare completely.

An added benefit of the "bounce" lighting system has been the flexibility of space planning the Chronicle enjoys. Under direct lighting, desks and workstations must be rigidly aligned directly beneath luminaries. The uniformity of light in the Chronicle's new wing will permit different workspace arrangement without concern for adequate light intensity.

SUMMARY

Energy conservation of office lighting can reduce operating costs without sacrificing quality of light or life. New light sources such as the T-8 fluorescent lamp with electronic ballasts increase the opportunities for retrofitting existing standard T-12 fluorescent systems to save energy while providing a good return on your lighting investment. The best way to maximize operating cost reduction while maintaining the lighting quality of the office space is to take the time to match the application to the characteristics of the T-8 lamp.

DESIGNING A COMPREHENSIVE COMMERCIAL DEMAND-SIDE MANAGEMENT PROGRAM

Jan Sayko
Northeast Utilities
Hartford, Connecticut

Skip Schick
Barakat, Howard & Chamberlin, Inc.
Oakland, California

Mike Weedall
Pacific Energy Associates
Portland, Oregon

I. INTRODUCTION

Demand-side management programs are being developed and implemented by an increasing number of electric utilities throughout the United States. Many of those programs include elements that enhance the energy efficiency characteristics of their customers. A popular end-use sector for programs being considered are commercial buildings. Not only does this sector offer a significant opportunity for load reduction or peak shaving, but also many utilities use these programs to offer additional services to their customers. Because of the resulting reduction in energy costs, some customers choose to forego fuel switching or cogeneration projects.

When a utility begins to consider a commercial sector energy efficiency program, there are four principal areas of consideration. They are the program delivery structure, the incentive design, the administration, and the quality and cost control. Unless each of these elements is carefully considered, a utility risks creating major program flaws or failure to reach participation targets. Successful commercial sector programs developed by the Bonneville Power Administration and New England Electric System stand as examples of how each of these four program planning elements can be successfully integrated. Studies of pilot programs of those two utilities identified program short-comings in one or more of those four areas, which were then corrected when their programs were implemented at full scale.

Two Northeast Utilities (NU) (a utility holding company) companies, The Connecticut Light and Power Company (CL&P) and Western Massachusetts Electric Company (WMECO), recently launched an ambitious program to assist their commercial sector customers to enhance energy efficiency. Drawing upon their own experience and that of other utilities, a comprehensive and cost-effective program design was created. This paper will explore the program Northeast Utilities created and how the four major program elements were integrated into the final program design. In this analysis, there are lessons to be considered when initiating planning of a commercial sector demand-side management program.

II. PROGRAM DELIVERY

"Program Delivery" is the overall program structure and the specific program elements that ensure the target market will be served. Specific sectors or market segments must be effectively served, while others are necessarily precluded. The existence of programs by other organizations, competition by private companies, and the regulatory climate are considerations that help to shape the final delivery structure. Specific considerations which a utility must consider are:

o What are the objectives of the utility in implementing the program; e.g., to reduce peak load, to save electric energy, to provide services to customers, to respond to a regulatory order, etc.?

o What market segments will be served by the program and who does it consist of?

o What existing programs will compete with or complement the program? What experience does the utility have in program delivery that could be structured into the new program?

o Which measures or technologies does the utility wish to have installed by customers? Is there a desire to install comprehensive packages of measures or just specific conservation measures; e.g., lighting only?

o Will the program be delivered by utility staff or by contractors? If delivered by in-house staff, are there antitrust or anticompetitive considerations?

o What budgetary and staff resources will be committed to the program?

o What skills will the delivery force need? How will training be structured?

o What elements of the program will be evaluated? How?

With these program delivery issues in focus, Northeast Utilities initiated planning and design process. The Connecticut Department of Public Utility Control ordered CL&P to expand a pilot demonstration program into a large-scale program that included working with performance contractors in the commercial sector. Because energy service companies (ESCOs) typically target only large transactions, Northeast Utilities determined that to serve the broad spectrum of customers that make up the commercial class, a more comprehensive and multifaceted program would have to be developed.

Northeast Utilities decided that a comprehensive package of services should be delivered. This strategy would provide the best level of service to NU's customers, while avoiding situations where customers would be contacted several times to install individual technologies. Northeast Utilities already had an array of specific conservation programs. For example, the Energy Saver Lighting Rebate Program provides cash incentives for the installation of approved lighting measures.

Other utility programs were reviewed to determine whether or not incentives would be required to secure adequate market penetration of comprehensive packages. The study indicated a much higher penetration rate and customer acceptance in programs that included incentives paid by the utility. Thus, paying incentives became another keystone to the program.

Northeast Utilities now turned to their own program experience. A performance contracting pilot effort in the service territory of Western Massachusetts Electric Company, produced a smaller number of transactions (where measures were actually installed in commercial sector facilities) than targeted. There were several reasons for this result: most notably, several of the energy service companies selected were not able to identify many customers that met their criteria for investment. In the few transactions that were developed, NU discovered that significant time and effort were required to actually get measures installed. Should this new program initiative achieve greater market penetration, then some mechanism would be required to expedite the process leading to measure installation.

As a result, NU decided to include technical assistance for each step of the transaction as part of their program. NU also determined that the assistance would have to come in the form of an outside contractor. Existing staff resources were already obligated to other projects, and many of the skills needed could best be provided by independent expertise. A solicitation was developed and issued to select "Contractor/ Arrangers" (C/As) who would provide those services. The C/As were selected at an early stage in program design so they could participate in the development of the program. This approach would ensure that a program was implemented that the C/As felt comfortable with and could effectively deliver.

The final cornerstone to the program delivery was the commitment and participation by the customer. A review of other utility and government programs revealed that many customers choose free or low-priced services but balk at incurring a capital investment to have measures installed. To avoid developing a program with many energy audits but few transactions, two delivery elements were included to ensure customer participation. First, NU would only pay for a portion of the energy audit at the time it was performed. The unpaid portion of the audit would then be included in the customer incentive payment calculation, made at the time measures are installed. Should the customer decide not to complete the transaction, he is liable for that portion of the audit. Similarly, if the C/A does not develop a package of measures that is cost-effective for the customer to pursue, the C/A is liable for the audit cost. By assuming a portion of the audit cost, NU offers a significant incentive, but they do so in partnership with their customer.

Next, the incentive structure developed by NU was chosen as the tool to encourage investment in a comprehensive package of measures, while also securing some customer participation. It assumes the standard investment strategy--a business should undertake financial transactions when the payback is in the 2-3 year range. Once NU removes the technical uncertainty of the investment through the involvement of the C/A, the customer should make the investment. An innovative payback methodology was structured with NU paying for the cost of all measures exceeding three years or greater payback, up to NU's avoided cost ceiling. (The incentive structure is discussed in greater detail in Section III of this paper.)

The program delivery structure was now essentially set. Northeast Utilities commercial sector energy efficiency program, originally known as Shared Energy Savings, would operate in the following manner:

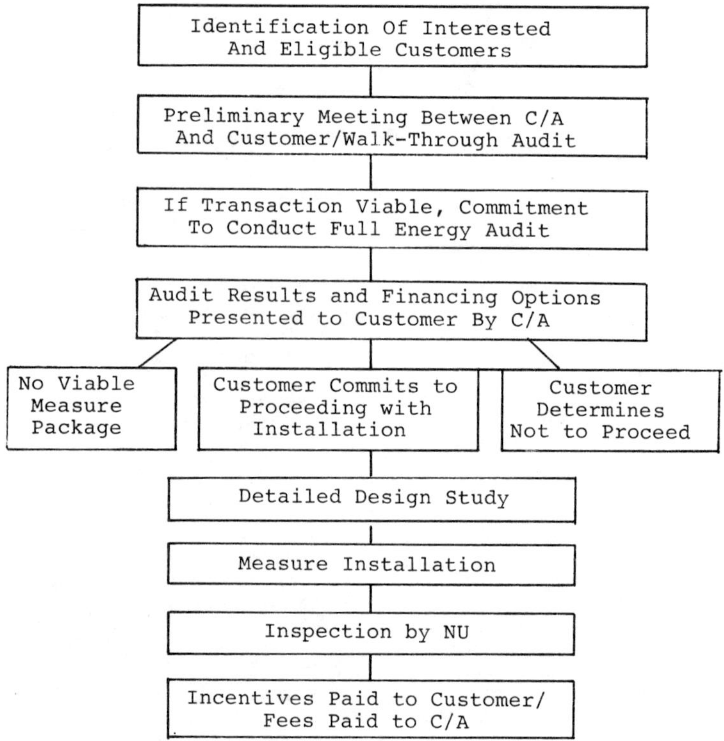

Northeast Utilities then turned to other program design issues. In the interest of program equity, NU decided that all classes and sizes of commercial sector customers should be eligible to participate. There would even be a priority to serve smaller customers who are not normally targeted by the energy services industry. A quota was assigned to each C/A targeting the number and size of customers to be served in the first year of the program. Because small transactions are likely to be more expensive to complete with C/A services, NU plans to design a specific program track for smaller customers in the future.

Next a review of existing utility and governmental programs identified some potential overlap, e.g., the federal Institutional Conservation Program. Reimbursement schedules for the utility program must consider what other programs might be contributing to the same project. However, the blending of programs is viewed as a plus, especially for organizations that can match other program dollars with utility dollars. The critical strategy was to ensure that duplicate payments are not made. Meetings with state officials introduced the program and offered the opportunity to integrate efforts.

Finally, budgets were developed. A series of analyses on typical measure packages identified probable incentive payments. Case studies were developed for the different size customers. Fees to be paid to the C/A were calculated. The budgets for administration and contractor support in the program were determined. With a specified number of dollars available for the first year activity, the utility was then able to estimate the number of transactions that could be completed in the first year. In 1988, NU projects that 18 large, 12 medium-sized, and 6 small commercial transactions will contract to have comprehensive package of measures installed. Over $800,000 is budgeted for customer incentives. Should program activity warrant, NU will seek additional funding for more transactions.

III. INCENTIVES DESIGN

There is ample evidence that financial incentives play a major role in encouraging consumer participation in demand-side management activities. The purpose of cost-effective utility incentives is to stimulate action which would otherwise not occur. In analyzing the design alternatives available to characterize and pay incentives under the Shared Energy Savings (SES) program, a number of objectives were defined. They included:

- Reaching a broad base of commercial class customers (large and small).

- Identifying a comprehensive set of measures that are cost-effective to the customer and to NU.

- Tying any financial incentive to the value of the energy savings to the utility.

- Offering no more incentive dollars than necessary to achieve the efficiency improvements.

Three basic alternatives were examined to characterize the financial incentive structure NU could employ to encourage participation in the SES program. The first was to set a fixed price that NU would be willing to pay for energy savings. The second was to set a fixed payment for specific measures. The third alternative was to calculate an appropriate incentive on an individual basis. The following paragraphs describe each alternative in more detail.

Some utilities have simply identified a fixed price per kW or kWh saved, which they are willing to pay to encourage energy efficiency. This payment is calculated for individual customers and can be based on actual or estimated energy savings. Most recently, utilities are offering rebates equivalent to the company's marginal cost to produce electricity. The attractiveness of identifying a price per kW or kWh saved is that the incentive can be based on the value of the energy savings to the utility. The drawback is that the method does not account for the value of the energy savings to the customer. As a result, the utility may pay more than necessary to encourage the efficiency improvements.

Northeast Utilities already uses fixed payments for specific measures under the Energy Saver Lighting Rebate Program. Fixed rebate amounts are specified for specific measures, such as energy-efficient lamps and ballasts. These payments are the same for all customers and are based on typical equipment costs and estimated savings. The advantage of this method is that the incentive amount can be set in advance based on the estimated value of energy savings to the utility and the customer. The problem with fixed payments for many applications (beyond lighting) is that the cost and energy savings for many measures will vary from job to job. This is especially true for large commercial and institutional buildings where a comprehensive set of measures are examined. These measures are likely to be complex and have interactive effects.

Several utilities that offer fixed payments for specific measures also offer incentives calculated on an individual basis (custom rebates) for measures where the costs and energy savings vary by application. To calculate an appropriate incentive on an individual basis, basic information about the application must be available. Central to any calculation is information on the costs and energy savings gained through a detailed audit performed on the building. With this information in hand, the incentive can be calculated and portrayed to the customer in a variety of ways. The two variations explored by NU are characterizing the incentive in terms of payback and in terms of rate of return. The main benefit of calculating incentives on an individual basis is that the approach can handle all building and measure types.

Based upon the objectives previously defined, Northeast Utilities decided to calculate an up-front incentive (rebate) on an individual basis using simple payback. Using payback, NU offers to bring a package of cost-effective measures into a payback range acceptable to the customer (two to three years). NU has decided to use a three-year payback calculation to maximize the customer's contribution to the project and thereby leverage the investment in energy efficiency. If a project has a four-year payback on all cost-effective measures, NU's incentive will equal to "one year's worth" of the energy savings. If actual program experience indicates that a higher customer incentive level is necessary to attract adequate participation, the incentive level can be adjusted.

To ensure that the Shared Energy Savings program is cost-effective to Northeast Utilities, only those measures which save electric energy at a cost equal to or below Northeast Utilities long-term marginal cost for power supply are eligible for incentives. A cost ceiling per kWh saved has been developed and is applied to each electric efficiency measure. The ceiling is applied after the costs and energy savings for each measure is identified in an energy analysis. Currently, the cost ceiling is set at four cents per lifetime kWh saved. The ceiling will be adjusted periodically to reflect changes in NU's long-term marginal cost for power. The cost ceiling assures NU that the energy savings obtained through the program "cost" no more than the marginal cost of alternative energy resources.

IV. PROGRAM ADMINISTRATION

A common misperception of program design is, once a program is designed and implemented, the "real" work is complete. The situation is analogous to many energy efficiency projects not delivering the promised levels of savings, because equipment was not maintained and operated in the proper manner. In a similar vein, effective demand-side management program depend on attention to detail during implementation and periodic reviews and evaluations.

As a utility begins to build an administrative structure, there are specific questions that must be answered. They include:

o Is the contract well written? Does it clearly cover the potential situations that may develop? How flexible is the document? Can it be revised to meet unforeseen developments?

- o What are the roles and responsibilities of all parties in the program? Does each party understand what his/her obligations are?

- o Is there a schedule for the major milestones, so that problems are identified at the earliest possible date? Have dates for program reviews been specified?

- o Has an operating guide been developed to provide clear documentation?

- o Has a tracking system been developed to collect the necessary data and provide current information on the performance of the program and its participants?

Northeast Utilities recognized the need for a strong administrative system early-on. To most effectively serve the customer and provide assistance to the Contractor/Arrangers, NU determined that their regional offices should have the lead role in program administration. While central office staff will track the overall program and provide support to the regional staff, prime administrative responsibility will reside with the regional Energy Management Service (EMS) department.

To ensure that the regional EMS staff will have the skills and knowledge necessary to accomplish this role, an implementation manual and an SES training program was developed. Further, the roles and responsibilities of each of the parties in transactions were documented. Listed below is a chart that specifies the roles of each party in the program.

NU Central Office	--Provide technical resource to regional staff --Maintain central tracking system --Disburse payments --Coordinate periodic program review and program changes --Conduct evaluations of the program
NU Regional Office	--Provide day-to-day management of program --Assist C/As in marketing the program

	--Respond to technical inquiries by customers and C/As --Review audits and installations to insure program standards met --Authorize payments
Contractor/Arrangers	--Market the program --Submit audits to NU for approval --"Package" audit results with financial options --Assist customer to complete installations --Submit installation information to NU
Customers	--Provide feasibility information to C/A --Commit to technical audits --Provide data to C/A and NU --Commit to measure installation --Participate in NU program evaluation

Contracts and reporting forms from other programs were reviewed. The experience of other utilities was analyzed to determine what contractural and reporting requirements were essential. Similarly, private contracts used by energy service companies and the needs of the C/As were evaluated. Having the C/As involved in the program design ensured that flexible and comprehensive documents were developed.

The most important elements in the NU/CA contract are:

- o Program procedures
- o Schedule milestones for program review
- o Reporting forms and payment schedules
- o Information required for data base
- o Engineering and auditing standards
- o Termination rights and procedures
- o Targeted markets to be served
- o Budget levels and payment caps

Early in the program design process an outline of the evaluation process was developed to identify the information that would have to be collected for evaluation in the administration phase. NU will select a contractor to conduct the actual evaluation. The evaluation will focus on two levels. First, technically, how well is the program operating? Are projected energy savings being realized? Are the audits being conducted according to program standards? Are there difficulties with the installation of measures?

On the second level, program delivery will be examined. How long is it taking for the average transaction to be completed? What program steps might be altered to enhance program effectiveness? How effective is the incentive structure? What energy-efficient measures are being installed?

Much of the information needed to conduct the evaluation will be tracked through the data base developed and collected as part of the administration system. Information on the data base is more fully discussed in the next section.

V. QUALITY AND COST CONTROL

Quality and cost control will be conducted to assure that all appropriate efficiency measures are identified, accurately characterized, and properly installed and maintained. NU intends to capture all the cost-effective electric conservation savings available in a building at the least cost to NU and the customer. In the SES program, it will be accomplished by focusing on two primary areas: the energy analysis conducted on each building and proper installation of approved measures.

Controlling the energy analysis is the most effective way to ensure the quality and cost of projects. NU's energy analysis standards specify auditor qualifications, analysis procedures, and requirements and measure energy saving estimating and cost estimating procedures. The standards should guarantee an accurate analysis of building energy use, measure savings, and measure costs for the full range of measures of the various buildings eligible under the program.

One challenge was identifying standards of analysis necessary for different situations. For some buildings and measures, only hand calculations are necessary. For other buildings, more sophisticated techniques detailed computer simulations capable of modeling the building's energy use on an hourly basis may be necessary. NU standards specify different levels of analysis dependent on the complexity, energy usage, or size of the building under consideration.

Electric energy conservation measures must be properly installed in a structure to produce energy savings. Quality control is provided by requiring design documents for most projects and requiring that the measures installed are those recommended in the energy analysis. The installed measures must also be consistent with the design documents and acceptable building construction practices. Measure installation inspections will be performed by qualified A&E contract support.

A review of each SES energy analysis conducted and an inspection of all measures installed will ensure NU the standards are met and the measures are installed properly. By using A&E contractors, NU will maximize its own staff resources and tap experienced professionals outside its organization.

A data base is also being constructed. It will contain critical information on each project. Elements will include measure cost and energy savings information, as well as program operational information. By collecting critical information and maintaining it in a usable format, effective evaluation will be possible. The data base will provide NU with the knowledge and feedback necessary to verify and improve planning assumptions, adjust program design features to enhance effectiveness, and assist in refining marketing targets and strategies.

VI. CONCLUSIONS

Designing a comprehensive commercial demand-side management program is a very complex undertaking. The challenge is to streamline the program design without ignoring issues critical to achieving its goals. These goals require careful consideration up front to assure that the program direction and the design decisions are appropriate.

The utility's own capabilities and the environment it is operating within must be realistically considered in devising a strategy. The four major design elements which must be addressed are: the program delivery structure, the incentive design, the program administration, and quality and cost control issues. Without adequately considering each of these areas, major design issues may be missed, resulting in an ineffective program which will require significant modifications down the road.

INDUSTRIAL EMS: ARE THEY WORKING?

Colum J. McReynolds
Energy Engineering Department
Ford Motor Company

Energy management systems in Ford date back to the early seventies, shortly after the first oil shock. The first large EMS system at Ford was in an assembly plant in New Jersey. It still appears to be one of the most successful, and after fifteen years, it is clear that the factors for its success were all there from the beginning: 1) a single strong advocate with strong management support, 2) early intense involvement at the hands-on working level by an innovative boilerhouse chief, 3) attention to detail in the early design including thoughtful choice of control points, and 4) a good plant maintenance program to ensure that mechanical equipment was in good shape to interface with computers. Our purpose today is to examine the factors for success and failure in running a large EMS, based on experience at Ford plants.

But let's step back for a moment and look at a typical Ford plant and see what these systems are attempting to control.

Ford has about 70 plants in North America and almost the same number overseas. A typical Ford plant covers about 1.5 million square feet and uses $8 million worth of energy a year. Electricity accounts for $5 million and the remaining $3 million is spent mostly on natural gas, with some coal, propane and oil. About half the electricity is used for production equipment and half for heating, ventilating, air-conditioning and lighting. By the end of the 70's, Ford had 24 energy management systems in operation with 12 others under construction or being designed.

In addition to installing EMS in many of these larger plants, Ford installed some systems in large regional parts warehouses and regional sales offices which lend themselves to smaller systems with excellent results.

Indeed, the range of building sizes in Ford Motor emphasizes what a variety of equipment comes under the umbrella title "energy management system"; even a seven-day time clock with a few simple relays has the flexibility to control hundreds of motors and accommodate changes in operating hours. They require little or no operator training, are reliable, simple to install and operate, and are suitable for small office buildings.

There has been a revolution over the last decade in energy management systems. The earlier systems were bulky, expensive and required a lot of maintenance.

However, today, microprocessor control gives us additional features at considerably lower cost: duty cycling to turn pieces of equipment off for selected periods of time to reduce peak demand and KWH; temperature setback for evening, weekend and vacation times; morning warm-up based on outside temperature; load monitoring and recording; and a lot more sophisticated graphics in full color.

Small Systems

Ford Sales Operations has had considerable success with the smaller EMS systems in District Sales Offices and warehouse buildings of 50,000 square feet area costing $10,000-$20,000. The division plant engineer used a manufacturer whose equipment and service earned the highest rating among 67 well-known EMS manufacturing firms in an annual national survey of users. In 1980, Ford installed eight of these systems in district sales offices from Boston to Dallas. All were an unqualified success, paying for themselves in a year or two. Energy consumption generally fell at least 15% and often more. The units could control up to eight separate steam, gas or electrical loads. These were programmed to turn on and off at selected times of the day including weekends and holidays. Other basic features were night-time setback, optimum start, load cycling and manual override. Outside temperatures were monitored to bring indoor temperatures to the desired level by morning. From these examples, it is clear that smaller systems have never really presented any problems; they are easy to install and maintain, and people use them readily, and results are excellent.

It appears, however, that as we go to larger and larger installations, problems arise for reasons that are not immediately clear or obvious. That is what we want to address here: why some large installations work so much better than others, and what we can do to improve our success rate. However, every successful large EMS installation of 500-1,000 points was sponsored and promoted by at least one highly-motivated individual at the local level who nurtured the system all the way through.

A few more examples of our experience at Ford may illustrate this point:

Dearborn Research and Engineering

An interesting installation is located at the Dearborn Research and Engineering Complex with about 17 scattered buildings. The facilities plant engineer in this case was faced with updating or replacing 10-year-old equipment from a well-known manufacturer whose service contracts were running to $42,000 annually for the CPU only. (In-house electricians handled the DGP's, sensors, and interconnections.) Moreover, sole-source parts replacement was increasingly expensive.

The plant engineer looked at the market for EMS systems, found nothing that precisely met his needs for the 17 scattered buildings, so he designed his own and is now patenting it. His first experimental setup was built around a computer or microprocessor and showed a 60% savings in steam. Accurate temperature control to within 0.5^{o}F was possible using DDC controls as opposed to the earlier pneumatic controls.

A second experimental setup in another building reduced heating and ventilating energy consumption by 37% and greatly improved space temperature precision. He has now converted one building to computer controls and is following that with a $5 million project for all 17 buildings with an estimated $3 million savings, a four-year program to be installed and maintained by in-house personnel. His new computer control system offers savings, simplicity, reliability and accurate control. It will be possible for a single building operator sitting at a console to pinpoint a problem anywhere in a building or group of buildings. The central monitoring, alarm and graphics makes it easy. The real-time data from the system will enable the operator to troubleshoot a problem without leaving his workstation. Once the problem has been diagnosed, data stored in the computer will show which tools and replacement parts may be needed to correct the problem.

Factors for success in this endeavor were:

- A strong technical team that knew the existing system thoroughly, including problems of the previous 10-year-old EMS.
- A strong leader who knew what could be achieved with modern systems and had strong management backing.
- Individual team members that included experienced HVAC and electronics engineers to correct problems promptly. Most problems are in the HVAC system, such as field sensors and actuators, and not in the EMS. If not fixed promptly, complaints can lead to serious acceptance problems on the shop floor.
- Enough lead time to study various systems on the market and experiment with new ideas.

It is recognized that these conditions are not available to everyone and most plants have to rely on more outside design. However, it underlines the importance of strong <u>inside</u> engineering control.

<u>Aerospace Division Experience</u>

Part of Ford's Aerospace Division engaged in microelectronics needed very accurate control of clean room temperature and humidity. The Colorado Springs plant has a 3-year-old EMS installation that was chosen for its ability to meet stringent class 10 clean room close monitoring and control of D.I. water. The facilities manager first spent a considerable amount of time and effort researching similar clean rooms in labs and universities throughout the country, mostly to determine what EMS systems were most successful for this type of close control. He ended up with a manufacturer that coincidentally ranked at the top of "middle-recognition" names in an annual trade newspaper survey of EMS ranked by user's level of acceptance based on effectiveness, freedom from problems, and quality of service. This equipment has now been in service for three years at the microelectronics plant.

The system gives particularly precise control with DDC, maintaining clean room temperature to within 1/2 ^{o}F and R.H. to $\pm$1%. The plant has obtained improved energy savings of 12%. They have upgraded the software package to generate historical data for chiller tonnage versus outside air temperature, enabling them to improve the response time for adjusting controls for rapidly changing O.A. conditions. The EMS also monitors D.I. water and compressed air alarms and calls for maintenance when required.

The key ingredients for success in this instance were: careful advance planning and research, an electronics engineer on the inside familiar with instrumentation on HVAC who followed the project from beginning to end; close teamwork with suppliers, installation crew and end-users.

Essex Engine Plant Experience

Outside Windsor, Ontario, Ford has an engine plant with 1.3 million square feet of manufacturing space plus 130,000 square feet of office space built in 1980. In 1982, the plant's electrical engineer who had some previous experience with EMS planned an energy reporting system that would rely heavily on sub-metering the energy used in individual departments of the plant.

In a large plant, nobody accepts responsibility for energy used in a department if it is not measured, no more than individual tenants in an apartment block will conserve electricity if it is not metered individually and they don't have to pay for it. It is largely human nature. The energy accounting system was designed by Essex Engine Plant's electrical engineer and installed by plant forces who got to know and understand the system as it was installed. It is a computerized, totally automated data-gathering system. At 248 selected points throughout the plant, current transformers take off readings of electricity consumption, including all 480 volt bus ducts, 13.8 KV feeders and some large individual machines.

The outputs from these points are processed through Allen-Bradley PLC-3 programmable controllers. The PLC-3 system gives printouts every 15 minutes listing electrical energy consumption by department. It includes demand, power factor and percent usage for each department. At the end of the day, it generates a summary showing high and low demand and average, enabling steps to be taken to improve demand factor. Gradually after installation, area superintendents became aware of the impact they had on total plant energy costs; as a result, by paying closer attention to prompt shutdown at end of shift, they got 10-15% in energy savings within a year. It was not all achieved overnight; during 1983 and most of 1984, the information gathered was used in department meetings to increase energy-awareness and to discuss ways for employees to conserve energy. Efforts to correlate energy use with production volume were hampered by wide swings in production volume, but eventually enough data and correlation were obtained to permit accurate energy forecasts to be made and a realistic target of 7% reduction in energy was accepted. Weekly cost meetings were held to review progress and area superintendents were held accountable for energy use in their departments. The plant energy coordinator now has several years of energy consumption data to work out a realistic budget for the plant based on history, number of shifts, production volumes and opportunities to reduce consumption. The budgets and targets are set by mutual agreement following discussions with each department.

The total cost of the Energy Report Audit System (ERAS) at Essex Engine Plant was $180,000. The rule of thumb cost is $600-$700 per point metered, including labor and material, hardware and software development. In 1983 and 1984, the estimated savings were $100,000 even though the system was only partially in operation. Savings in 1985 were $137,000. In 1986, the first year in which departmental energy budgets were implemented, the savings were $250,000 or 10% of previous year's consumption. Energy metering by department focused effort on areas where energy cost is highest and permitted more accurate assessment of potential energy saving programs.

Twin Cities Assembly Plant System

This EMS installation is notable for its fiber-optics network throughout the plant, resulting in interference-free transmission to all points. This is particularly important in an assembly plant due to the amount of signal interference generated by welding machines. Also, the Twin Cities Plant has extended EMS control beyond the usual HVAC range of equipment and is expanding control of equipment throughout the plant, initially in the paint shop for prompt shutdown of sludge pumps and washer motors. Metering of gas and electricity usage is being expanded to more points of use. Monitoring the use of eight plant traffic doors pinpointed how much time the doors were open and showed it was possible to save 77% of energy lost through open doors by using better material-handling techniques and repairing faulty doors.

Summary

To summarize the experience gained from these various installations that lead to success in large EMS installations:

- Many of the large EMS suppliers who were leaders historically in the HVAC field are meeting strong competition from many smaller companies that have become prominent over the last five or ten years. Several newer companies have proven to be more competitive, responsive to customers' needs and provide prompt service at very competitive rates. Every year, Energy Users News runs a national survey of about 1,000 users of EMS systems and what their experiences have been; the responses are divided into three categories: well-known EMS companies, medium-recognition, and lesser known manufacturers. The medium-recognition EMS manufacturers rank surprisingly high in customer satisfaction.

- A large plant installation requires an inside engineer familiar with plant operation to concentrate on detailing all points to be controlled in the plant. This should not be left to outside consultants. In most cases, it will be found that extensive maintenance work is needed on existing HVAC air houses to ensure they interface properly with the EMS; otherwise adding computerized control to the front end is useless. Sometimes, almost as much money has to be spent on refurbishing existing controls as on the EMS before the system can perform its functions. Maintenance people must be part of the team.
- Decide early if engineering or maintenance people should spearhead the endeavor. We have found that boilerhouse chiefs generally run the best EMS operations. They know how the existing operation works and can arrange to train the best maintenance people to run it. Prompt response to problems will result in better acceptance.
- It is a myth that you can put in a large EMS system and expect it to run by itself and save you energy dollars. Even the best systems seem to operate best with two people, one for each shift. Overtime control and changes in production scheduling have to be handled daily at startup. One boilerhouse chief said that if you take away the people who run it, the system will deteriorate rapidly; loads will soon be taken off EMS control and handled at the local pushbutton level; as energy management control is lost, energy savings will gradually disappear. An EMS system in a large plant can be compared to the control tower in a busy airport; it serves to keep tabs on what is happening and permits control to be exercised. Without it, you really have no control over energy use.
- Ask EMS vendors for recent successes, including names and telephone numbers of plant engineers with large systems and check them out, especially for problems, service and costs.
- Although there are numerous successful EMS installations, a national study revealed that nearly one-third of EMS users are dissatisfied with their system's performance. The main problems were expensive service contracts, over-priced spare parts, inadequately trained service people and slow response time. These problems can be overcome; forewarned is forearmed. Satisfied owners relied heavily on well-trained inside maintenance people. It helped if the same people were involved all the way from conception, design, installation and operation.

In short, EMS systems <u>do</u> work in plants where the teamwork and support prevail from the beginning to make them work.

EMS FOR COMMERCIAL HIGH RISE

LEONARD G. PETTIS

CHIEF ENGINEER - TRANSAMERICA CENTER

CUSHMAN & WAKEFIELD

Energy management systems might be considered in the following manner: Utility Cost, (Energy) controlled or handled (Management) as a group of interacting elements functioning as a complex whole (System). Experience with EMS could be likened to remote controls for the home entertainment center. The television/remote control, the vcr/remote control, the stereo/remote control the compact disc player/remote control, the tape deck/remote control and so forth are a complex group or combination of sophisticated machines each with their own local control group and each with their own separate management system.

Until recently no one has attempted to intergrade the wide variety of remote controls and combine them into one simple control that could operate any or all of these functions from one central location. Likewise, Energy Management Systems and building controls have no doubt beguiled many of us in the industry. How often have each of us experienced difficulty in programming a vcr to tape a certain program. Relating a personal experience to this end, I programmed my vcr to tape the movie Ghandi, only to find out I ended up with Pee Wee Hermans Special. The laborious task of programming EMS has no doubt created similar problems.

For years most of the major producers of EMS Systems and controls have dedicated their production to custom hardware and software, original equipment manufacturer (OEM). As a result, the industry is supplied with many smart sophisticated machines that up until now have been incapable of talking to each other. Man/Machine interface in some cases has become a significant stumbling block and has no doubt turned many people sour on the utilization of applied energy management systems.

In the beginning, EMS Systems were touted as having the capability of combining building management features of three separate systems, energy management, system monitoring , temperature control, into one compact unit. Software for containling fuel and electricity consumption while still assuring building comfort and detecting and reporting building conditions, was fed to the CPU, the central point of the system. In fact, one article mentioned the user friendly interface to be mastered by unskilled personnel in fifteen minutes.[1]

Certainly this point can be heavily contested by those who have experienced different configurations of Energy Management Systems. Case and point, Transamerica Centers EMS. To begin the discussion, it will be necessary to present an overview of the Energy Management System employed at Transamerica. Components in the system read much like the description of the hi-bred home entertainment system. Several components of different manufacturer, with different controls, none of them capable interfacing with each other. Several systems, several different managers.

In the early 1980's Transamerica purchased the Honeywell EMS System, which consisted of several components. The central processing unit the reliable Delta 1000 was coupled with a colorgraphic CRT, 5100 and finally DM2 - Datamanager. Each system requires its own dedicated data file processing unit in order to communicate with the Delta. No question, the system was highly sophisticated and infact the control room looked like a scene from Star Trek.

A close examination of the controls revealed the following: Colorgraphic CRT/keyboard, the 5100 CRT/keyboard, and finally, the DM2 CRT/keyboard. The key functions required to initiate commands of each of these three operators stations were all different, as well as the programming and data storage. Colorgraphics gave the operator a pictorial view of a configured group of points. It had a totally separate data file stored on magnetic disks that created a colored picture with the points in the mechanical system that it monitored. Graphics displays were created by key stroke cursor navigation form a predetermined equipment menu. The colorgraphics terminal retrieved a numeric address from the Delta 1000 and got back a group of points.

The daily use of this system presented some extraordinary problems. The colorgraphics terminal was not programmed to display logical grouping on the screen, the display of the physical groups was different from the one on the 5100.

----

[1]1 Power Magazine, December 1984.

The Winchester disk drives used for data file storage on the colorgraphics, were totally separate from the 5100. Consequently, both sets of files had to be exactly correlated, and those changes on the colorgraphics had to correspond to the changes made on the 5100. It is extremely doubtful that this process could be mastered in fifteen minutes.

The 5100 Consisted of a translator and MMI (Man Machine Interface), connected to the Delta. The translator functioned to put Delta field points with English language descriptors. The Man Machine Interface functioned to group various descriptors to catalogue type files for the ease of retrieval from the translator. The 5100 allowed the user to re-group points for the ease of understanding. These English language descriptors were a great aid to operators, especially compared to the more common five digit address system. However, the real design and intent with the 5100, was for Delta communications capabilities. With single Delta application it would have been adequate to program the color CRT so that it would have English language descriptors for its points as they were displayed on the screen.

The third piece of equipment in this system was the DM2. Its purpose was to periodically track the status of points throughout the facility, building data files on floppy disks. Point information was in a readable format and could be addressed for analysis programs and trend logs. DM software could request or receive data from the Delta, but it could not issue commands to the Delta, hence; the need for the 5100/or colorgraphics.

Confused? So was I. Obviously after reviewing the systems physical components, as well as its internal communication configuration, it raises the simple question, is there a better way?

Our first step in resolving this situation is often the one most overlooked. The prescription for a good engineering analysis is to first develop a strategy for the EMS System. The strategy should include the definition of a facilities control needs, i.e., what was the system required to do?

Second, was to identify the facilities limitations such as wiring and mechanical HVAC configuration.

Third, is to compare the existing system or proposed new system and determine the usefulness in its function to control the utility consumption for the complex while providing for the needs of the tenants.

Transamerica needed a system that provided start-stop, optimum start-stop, duty cycling, load shed and calculated point capability, i.e., showing the operator environmental space conditions and status of all points in the system. It should also be capable of handling card access security and back up fire life safety functions, while building data files of point history. Additionally it should have the capability of running third party software. The aforementioned list of requirements for the new system is difficult, if not impossible to fulfill especially with most EMS system producers dedicated to their own hardware and software.

Continuing with the second point in the strategy, identifying the limitations revealed the twenty-six 541 data gathering panels, installed in various locations throughout the facility, represented older technology and required field programming, consequently the addition of points in the system was limited to the physical panel and compounded by the cost of field programming. However, the system wiring was relatively new and could accommodate a newer panel with industry standard components and state of the art technology.

Analyzing the third point in the strategy, reveals there was a collection of front end equipment communicating through the Delta via limited field control panels. The question becomes, replace the entire system or salvage any of the components in the system. Cost estimates for an entirely new system from same and other manufacturers were out weighed by the costs of upgrading the existing system. In the fall of 1986 the upgrading process of The EMS System began. The governing factor and good strategy is often cost effective replacement, consequently, at this time the only consideration was to replace the Datamanager, since it had become in operable.

The Datamanager remember, was only responsible for the periodic tracking of status of points throughout the building. However, the opportunity presented itself to act directly with the designers and developers of the new system. It became clear, the other front end equipment could also be eliminated and so, the system approach phasing out the Datamanager also incorporated the capability of networking the remaining front end equipment, thus eliminating the 5100 and the colorgraphics terminal and replacing it with one PC work station.

The base component for the existing EMS system is the Honeywell Delta 1000 CPU . The strategy determined that it would not be cost effective to replace this unit; therefore, we needed to find a manufacturer who could provide us with an inexpensive user interface and replace our front end equipment.

Electronic Systems USA provided us with the PI 1000 interface for approximately five thousand dollars, ($5,000), far less than the cost of the new system. The PI 1000 interface has the capacity to be coupled with any IBM compatible PC, eliminating the requirement of being dedicated to an original equipment manufacturer. This system eliminated several pieces of front end equipment and provided for an industry standard work station capable of running off the shelf third party software, at the same time staying on line, via the PI 1000 interface through the Delta, providing the capacity to monitor the building at the same time.

The base component of the PC 1000 work station is the compact 286 desk pro. Loaded with ESUSA's software communicates with the Delta, providing the operator with English language operation, industry standard colorgraphics, multi-tasking and historical data analysis. However, it is unlikely that an unskilled individual could master this system in fifteen minutes. The systems software is user friendly. Using MS-Dos, ESUSA's PC 1000 software can be loaded easily and operated via simple instructions and help menu's provided.

The software enables the operator to address five digit function codes with English language commands. User friendly menu's in the software system enable the operator to create and custom design tables, graphs, enhance facility operation thus providing better building control. Event Activated Messages (EAM's) [Tbl. 1] give the operator an immediate message or a specific set of instructions when those pre-programmed points go into an alarm situation.

An example of the present system is at the change of each watch and EAM log on is used to notify the operator of any or all equipment on line, out of service and so forth. Tables are used and configured to group several floors or all floors in a specific building, indicating their status. Other table applications are used for CPA adjustment points. The programming is virtually unlimited with the exception of the capacity of the C drive (hard disc) of the PC.

The function of the Datamanager was replaced with PC 1000's information management software (IMS) [Tbls 2&3]. This software was configured and programmed to send all of the Datamanagers history retrieval functions directly to the C drive of the PC. Though in this case card access activity is stored on the hard drive. A user friendly menu in the IMS software enables the operator to produce any kind of trend log that is required from the information stored on the C drive. Card history, equipment information, summary status of various points in the system are just a few examples of the software's versatility.

Tbl. 1

```
15:27        042 DEG          ELECTRONIC SYSTEMS USA
             WEDNESDAY         PC-1000 WORKSTATION                         12-16-1987
                                                                       LOGGED ON: BMW
--------------------------------------------------------------------------------------



----------------------------------------------------------Hit <RETURN> to continue-
*** EQUIPMENT ON LINE:
    #2 CENT, #2&3 CHWP, #3&4 CWP, #1 SOFTENER
    #3 L.P. BOILER, #1 FEED PUMP, #1-4 AIR COMPRESSORS                        C/P
    #1&2 COOLING TOWERS, #1,2,5 AIR COMPRESSORS                               S/B
                                                                              B/B
*** EQUIPMENT OUT OF SERVICE OR OUT OF COMMISSION:
    #1 CENT, #1 CWP
    #1 L.P. BOILER BEING RETROFITTED WITH NEW BURNER, #2 FEED                 C/P
    #2 L.P. BOILER, #3 CHWP (ABSORBER)                                        S/B
    #1 C.T. MAKE-UP PUMP, #1 CONDENSATE PUMP, #3&4 AIR COMPS                  S/B
    #1 TOWER HOUSE PUMP                                                       B/B

14711   TOWER 30 EXFAN-7**SIGNON EAM**   FAIL RESPOND   15:26                 ON
```

Tbl. 2

```
15:07        042 DEG          ELECTRONIC SYSTEMS USA
             WEDNESDAY         PC-1000 WORKSTATION                         12-16-1987
                                                                       LOGGED ON: BMW
--------------------------------------------------------------------------------------



--------------------------------------------------------------------------------------
                               IMS MENU

                        1. Print History Report
                        2. Alarm Types to Be Stored
                        3. IMS Data File Statistics
                        4. IMS Data File Backup
                        5. Exit the IMS Menu

                           SELECT AN OPTION -
```

Tbl. 3

```
15:08        042 DEG          ELECTRONIC SYSTEMS USA
             WEDNESDAY         PC-1000 WORKSTATION                         12-16-1987
                                                                       LOGGED ON: BMW
--------------------------------------------------------------------------------------



--------------------------------------------------------------------------------------
                          ACCESS CONTROL MENU

                      1. Edit Access Cards
                      2. Print Card Information Logs
                      3. Allocate CPU Memory for Cards
                      4. Edit CPU Time/Day Schedules
                      5. Utility Program
                      6. Exit the Edit Menu

                          SELECT AN OPTION -
```

Transamerica's new system is customized further with the addition of a second color CRT monitor. An industry standard graphics card is installed in the 286 PC. Now the operator has the capability of monitoring a pictorial view of the facility on one screen while viewing the building system on the other screen or going off line and using third party software. The use of two monitors eliminates the need of having to toggle between screen views.

The system and its software uses standard RS232 protocol. This provides the capabilities of modem communications to remote terminals with additional expansion capacities including interfacing with a chiller optimizer and a chemical control station. Communications software that accesses at the DOS level has made it possible to run the building completely from a remote location. These powerful expansion capabilities have made viable the consideration for lighting control to be added to the energy management system.

Most of us will agree to this point, the concept of combining these functions, utilizing only one operating station has presented many problems. Advanced design of the personal computer coupled with ever growing sophisticated software has eliminated most of the previous problems. Prior discussion of the engineering strategy developed for this system included the limitation of the 541 DGP field panel. To accommodate lighting control it became necessary to upgrade or eliminate the 541 panels. It was not cost effective to add additional lighting points to these panels. Additional points would have cost an estimated three hundred fifty dollars ($350) to six hundred dollars ($600) per point. The Average cost per point approximately four hundred fifty dollars ($450) x the required 660 lighting points for the system yielded an estimated three hundred thousand dollars ($300,000) for these points to be added to the 541 panels.

At an installed cost of under two hundred thousand dollars ($200,000) Transamerica purchased new field data gathering panels compatible with the system, capable of controlling both the HVAC system and the additional lighting points required for lighting zones on all floors of the facility. Programming for these panels can be done right at the work station. This standard configuration facilitates easy addition of points and repairs should they be necessary.

Transamerica's Energy consumption bar graphs [Tbl. 4] in therms and kilowatt hours, its obvious that the need for tighter building control is required. With respect to the kilowatt hour consumption, general building analysis says that approximately two/thirds of the power consumption is related to lighting, while one/third is related to HVAC power and miscellaneous devices.

Tbl. 4

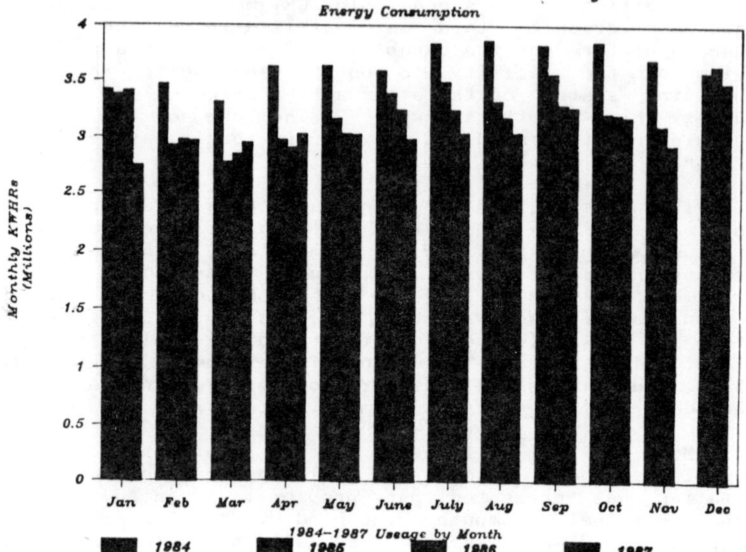
Transamerica Occidental Life
Energy Consumption
Monthly KWHRs (Millions)
4
3.5
3
2.5
2
1.5
1
0.5
0
Jan
Feb
Mar
Apr
May
June
July
Aug
Sep
Oct
Nov
Dec
1984–1987 Useage by Month
1984
1985
1986
1987

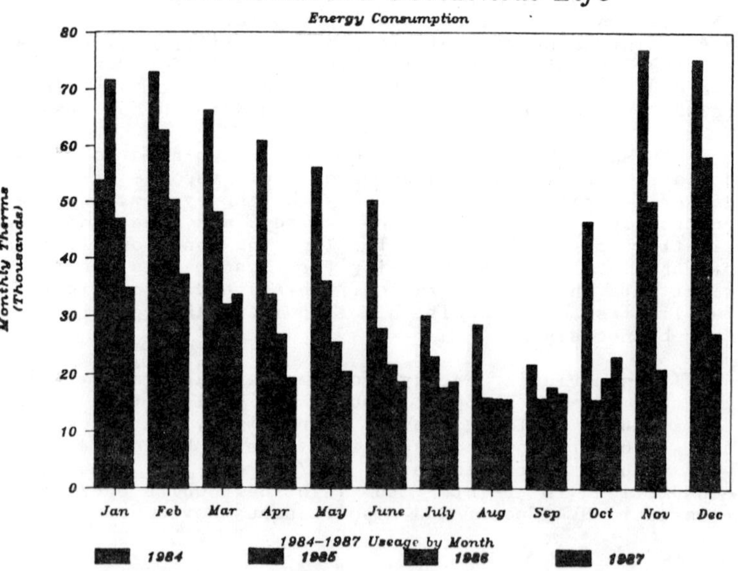
Transamerica Occidental Life
Energy Consumption
Monthly Therms (Thousands)
80
70
60
50
40
30
20
10
0
Jan
Feb
Mar
Apr
May
June
July
Aug
Sep
Oct
Nov
Dec
1984–1987 Useage by Month
1984
1985
1986
1987

MONTHLY ENERGY CONSUMPTION REPORT

BUILDING DATA			SUMMARY DATA	
NAME:	Transamerica Center		AVERAGE W/SQ.FT.	5.29681
ADDRESS:	1150 S. Olive St.		KBTU/SQ.FT-ELECTRIC	98.26138
CITY:	Los Angeles, Ca. 90015		- GAS	23.06063
NET RENT. SQ. FT:	1275234		TOTAL KBTU/SQ.FT/YR	121.32201
BEGINNING:	NOVEMBER 1986			
ENDING:	OCTOBER 1987		$/SQ.FT/YR -ELECTRIC	1.8610
		RECEIVED (month)	- GAS	0.0892
READ DATE ELECT:	4th-7th	after		
READ DATE GAS:	13th-17th	after	TOTAL $/SQ.FT/YR	1.9502

MONTH	KWHRS	KW	COST	FULL-LOAD HRS/WK	GAS	COST
NOV	2,942,600	6720	191723.62	100.77	21,154	7857.79
DEC	3,493,000	6656	226411.26	120.77	27,315	9929.01
JAN	2,751,800	6624	173428.02	95.61	34,918	12673.20
FEB	2,972,700	6528	185355.40	104.80	37,230	14710.75
MAR	2,954,200	6576	187716.70	103.39	33,792	12866.77
APR	3,034,800	6704	197373.11	104.18	27,017	10121.35
MAY	3,032,400	6784	194034.26	102.87	19,450	7833.35
JUN	2,990,300	6784	193351.14	101.44	18,777	7865.27
JUL	3,043,600	6720	200346.02	104.23	18,782	7868.07
AUG	3,044,500	6720	200484.48	104.26	15,694	6418.45
SEP	3,269,900	6720	214330.47	111.98	16,770	6712.08
OCT	3,184,600	7520	208638.79	97.46	23,178	8919.78
TOTALS	36714400		2,373,193		294,077	113775.87
AVERAGES	3,059,533	6755	197766.11	104.31	24,506	9481.32

MONTH	$/KWHR	$/MBTU	$/THERM	$/MBTU
NOV	0.06515	$19.0901	0.37146	$3.7146
DEC	0.06482	$18.9917	0.36350	$3.6350
JAN	0.06302	$18.4657	0.36294	$3.6294
FEB	0.06235	$18.2691	0.39513	$3.9513
MAR	0.06354	$18.6177	0.38076	$3.8076
APR	0.06504	$19.0556	0.37463	$3.7463
MAY	0.06399	$18.7480	0.40274	$4.0274
JUN	0.06466	$18.9450	0.41888	$4.1888
JUL	0.06583	$19.2867	0.41892	$4.1892
AUG	0.06585	$19.2943	0.40897	$4.0897
SEP	0.06555	$19.2050	0.40024	$4.0024
OCT	0.06551	$19.1957	0.38484	$3.8484
AVERAGES	0.06464	$18.9391	0.38689	$3.8689

However, in the case of Transamerica, approximately half of the power consumed is related to HVAC requirements. The facility houses a large data processing center and requires twenty-four hour a day operation.

The justification of the addition of lighting control for Transamerica's EMS system, was evaluated and determined by calculating the potential savings of reduced lighting control under the automated system. Calculating the total monthly electrical usage of approximately three million two hundred thousand (3,200,000) kilowatt hours using fifty percent or one million six hundred thousand (1,600,000) for lighting, savings were conservatively calculated by reducing the lighting hours one hour per day per month yielding an approximately one hundred fifteen thousand seven hundred eighty six (115,786) kilowatt hours per month. At an average cost of nearly seven cents per kilowatt hour an annual savings in excess of ninety thousand dollars ($90,000) per year can be realized by turning the lights off automatically one hour early. This calculates out to approximately a two year payback for the addition of the new system.

One point not previously discussed regarding the old 541 DGP field panels, is that no return air sensors were installed when the system was put in. This addition was incorporated in the cost of the new system. Consequently the new system with return air capabilities plus lighting control will render much tighter building control and energy optimization capacities for the operator.

Additional savings for the installation of the new system will also be realized because the existing maintenance cost will be reduced, industry standard components will be used and dependency upon one vendor will no longer be required.

The net result is Transamerica's EMS is now capable of controlling many complex operations, air handling fans are stopped and started on separately controlled time programs, likewise, lights are turned on and off, security card access information is retrieved stored and compiled in a Database type management system. With modem capability, the system can and does communicate with peripheral work stations. It also communicates with other manufacturers micro processing units, i.e., the chiller optimizer control and the chemical station controller. Additionally it operates third party software and produces examples such as, Transamerica's Energy Consumption Report, [Tbl. 5] a Lotus base program.

In conclusion a comprehensive engineering strategy combined with the power and versatility of the personal computer provided this facility with one fine Energy Nonmalignant System.

E.M.S. ENSURING CONTINUED PAYBACK

Richard E. Blum, Manager
Power Plant Technical Operations/Xerox Corporation
Webster, New York 14580

Xerox Corporation is a major manufacturer of duplicating and office automation equipment. Facilities located in Monroe County in upstate New York consist of approximately 6,000,000 square feet of general office, laboratory, and light manufacturing. The three main building complexes that make up this total are a 42 building campus-like facility in Webster, New York, a 30 story high-rise office building in downtown Rochester, New York, and a research and engineering facility in Henrietta, New York.

Xerox' first energy management system undertaking was a project to monitor and control all HVAC equipment on the Webster complex. This project started in 1975 and when completed in 1976 tied nearly 5000 data and control points through 130 satellite data collection panels to a mainframe computer centrally located on the site in Building 315, currently known as CMS.

Limitations inherent with that generation of system hardware made energy management programs such as the standard optimized start/stop, duty cycle, and demand forecast and load shed programs impractical and ineffective. Out of a total of 55 start/stop programs available on our system, only 20 of those could be optimized and each of those only by one space tempera-ture sensor. Twenty programs don't go far when you're controlling over 800 loads in 42 buildings with numerous occupancy schedules. An electric demand control program with a limitation of 30 sheddable loads per program was also impractical on a site fed by 3 major substations with hundreds of sheddable loads on each station. A duty cycle program that cycles equipment on and off with little regard for occupant comfort levels came under heavy criticism and was abandoned in most buildings.

In spite of all its shortfalls, our system has proven to be a valuable tool for monitoring critical HVAC functions and acquiring HVAC audit and analytical data. It also does a very effective job of starting and stopping equipment on time schedules and monitoring its operating status. CMS has become the center of the Power Plant operation on the Webster site.

In addition to ineffective energy management programs, other factors contribute to the gradual deterioration of EMS systems. The maintenance and upkeep of a system of this size and age is monumental. Five thousand sensing points plus 130 data panels, old and obsolete central hardware, and hundreds of miles of wiring need constant attention to maintain system accuracy and integrity. Often budget and manpower restraints mandate that priorities be given to other areas; therefore, needed repairs and upgrades to the EMS are not funded resulting in continued deterioration of the system and the company's investment.

Many EMS owners of large and costly systems badly in need of upgrade with an established crew dedicated to its operation and maintenance find themselves questioning the value of the system and its ability to continue paying back.

Since the installation of the original system in 1975, I've been involved in all major EMS installations in Xerox facilities in the Rochester area. These include the EMS/DDC installation at Xerox Square in 1984 and the recently completed EMS/DDC/life safety and security system in the Henrietta facility. I've had the unique opportunity of being involved in the design and selection of the system, project management, and was ultimately responsible for the day to day operation and upkeep of these systems. This opportunity has provided a first hand prospective of what makes a project successful and what is necessary to guarantee the continued payback on the original investment. Over the years I've been involved in successful EMS projects and some which were marginally successful. I also have knowledge of projects that were totally unsuccessful. I've arrived at what I believe to be the most important ingredients necessary to launch a successful project and ensure that the owner will realize his predicted savings at project completion and for many years thereafter.

STATE OF THE ART HARDWARE AND SOFTWARE

The natural tendency when in the market for a product representing a considerrable investment is to select the product having the best track record, its tried and true and you can feel comfortable that it will give you many years of reliable service.

With today's rapidly changing technology and system improvements and enhancements on the drawing board all the time, if you buy 2 or 3 year old technology you probably will not be getting the maximum benefit for your investment. Advancements in the field are continuously making EMS systems more user friendly and multifunctional with energy management software which is more effective due to adaptive and interactive programming.

PURCHASE FROM COMPANY DEDICATED TO RESEARCH AND NOTED AS A PIONEER IN TECHNOLOGICAL ADVANCEMENT

A company committed to research will ensure the system owner the latest hardware and software updates available to enhance his systems capabilities. A company who does not keep up with state of the art technology can leave you with a system which is obsolete with no available system update.

A good owner/supplier relationship is one which expresses a common interest to improve system operation, increasing its value to the owner and ensuring the maximum and continuous return on his investment. This entails keeping the owner knowledgeable of all available updates and providing him a plan for the future of his system based on projected technological evolution.

DISTRIBUTE PROCESSING PROVIDING MAXIMUM RELIABILITY AND SYSTEM UTILIZATION

When I refer to distributed processing, I mean at both ends of the system. Micro processor based direct digital field panels ensure the operation of local systems in the event of central hardware or transmission failure. Systems will start and stop, control, and energy management software will run.

At the systems front end, terminals, CRT's, PC's and printers should be provided to anyone having a legitimate use for system control and data. The more people having access to the data, the more the system will be utilized, therefore increasing the value of the system to its owner. Additionally, the more people using and reviewing the data the more likely it is the system will receive better upkeep. I believe many systems failed because of the central approach to system architecture where information and control were only available at the central location. I strongly feel that the more people having free and ready access to the system the more benefit to the owner through better system upkeep and maximum utilization.

EMS/DDC RATHER THAN EMS ALONE

Energy management systems tend to lose their importance when there isn't an energy crisis. All the thermostats have been turned up to 72 degrees, and there's plenty of gas available for our cars, boats, and recreation vehicles. To the average person an energy crisis doesn't exist.

Central monitoring systems prior to the energy crisis were installed primarily to centralize control and monitor critical functions of building operating systems. The energy management potential of these systems only evolved when shortages and costs made conservation mandatory. Installations of EMS systems were easily justified based on their potential to save energy dollars. The demand was high and dozens of systems emerged from simple time clocks to full blown computer based EMS systems.

As the cost of fuel went down and supplies went up, many of the original energy management programs were abandoned such as duty cycling, optimized start/stop, and load shed. On most of the early vintage systems these programs were only marginally effective anyway, and they did cause occupant comfort problems. Most of these systems became glorified time clocks which started and stopped and monitored the facility.

Direct digital control provides energy savings by enhancing the effectiveness of standard energy management programs. Accuracy obtained by fully adaptive P.I.D. control by its very nature provides efficient energy usage. Programs such as load reset and dead band are extremely effective energy management and control programs provided by DDC.

A properly designed DDC building control scheme takes full advantage of as many system points as possible. The effective interaction of building HVAC systems with DDC control provides optimal energy utilization. The fact that most system points are not simply monitor points but are vital inputs to the building control scheme helps to ensure their upkeep and integrity. For example, when the discharge temperature of the air handling system is determined by the average of the space temperatures, and the temperatures of the chilled and hot water supplied by the central plant are determined by the relative position of the automatic control valves, the accuracy of these inputs and outputs must be maintained or you may lose control of your building conditions.

EMS/DDC provided a necessity to maintain system accuracy and integrity and will ensure efficient energy usage while improving building conditions.

OPERATING GROUP MUST TAKE OWNERSHIP

After the contractor pulls off the job, the system warranty runs out and your engineering department considers the project complete, it is left to the operating group to successfully operate and maintain the system. They are also charged with maintaining the payback on the company's investment. The day to day decisions they make in the operation of system hardware and software determine the continued payback on the installation. It is absolutely essential that this operating group take proper ownership of the system. The ground work for this ownership may be started back at the conceptual stages of the project. It's always helpful to involve members of the operating group in the design, specifications, and selection processes. These people should become heavily involved during the project implementation so that they have a gradual introduction to the new technology and not have it dumped on them suddenly at project completion. I believe that at the end of the project your crew is more likely to accept, understand, and take ownership of the new system if they were part of the implementation team.

EMS systems were historically used not only for energy conservation but also to displace manpower, generally from the same operating group that has responsibility for its operation. This threat does not set the stage for a successful EMS project. You will probably be relying heavily on these people during the design and implementation stages of the project due to their familiarity with the building systems. They are less apt to be a willing participants in a project that ultimately threatens their job. After the job is completed and the operating group takes over the day to day operation and maintenance of the system, there may be a tendency to make the system appear less than successful.

I feel that using an EMS system as a manpower control system is only setting the system up for failure. If your operating group takes ownership of the system and doesn't feel threatened by its existence, you've gained their support for a successful installation and continued payback on your investment. This payback can be realized through energy management which is the true intent of the EMS installation.

CASE HISTORY XEROX SQUARE

In May of 1984 we started up the EMS at Xerox Square, a 30 story high-rise office building in downtown Rochester. At that time we were purchasing steam from the local utility company for approximately $20.00 per 1000 pounds. The EMS was a total direct digital retrofit replacing conventional pneumatic control systems. By the use of energy management software, such as fully adaptive optimized start/stop, load reset, zero energy band, and a totally interactive direct digital control scheme, we were able to decrease steam usage the first winter by 43.8%. This equated to a payback on the investment of less than 2 years.

The particular control strategy used in the DDC scheme was based on space temperature control with all controlled parameters reset from space conditions.

Mechanical systems in the building consist of constant volume hot and cold deck air handling systems providing the primary heating and cooling of the building. Centrifugal chillers provide the chilled water for the cold decks, and steam to hot water converters provide the hot water for the air handling unit hot decks. Separate steam to hot water converters provide the radiation hot water for the perimeter heating.

A total of 80 space sensors are strategically located within the building. Some in interior spaces and others in exterior offices in an effort to get a good representative sample of all areas fed by a single air, handling unit. All space sensors are used to control the mixed air, hot deck and cold deck temperatures of the air handling unit. A comfort range was established for the building of 69 degrees F to 76 degrees F, which provided the dead band during which no heating or cooling would take place. If any temperature within the zone was below the comfort range, hot deck temperature will reset up according to a predetermined reset schedule until that particular area was in control. If any temperature was above the comfort zone, cold deck temperature would reset down on a predetermined schedule to bring that space into the comfort zone. When all reporting temperature sensors were within the comfort zone, the dead band program would reset mixed air according to the average of all space temperatures and try to keep it in the center of the comfort zone.

Analog outputs from the DDC panels through transducers control pneumatically operated automatic valves and damper actuators on the air handling system. This control provides the ability to monitor the relative position of these devices. The position of the chilled water valves on the air handling unit cold decks provide the inputs that determine the chilled water temperature produced at the chiller. If the system detects all chilled water valves are throttled, the chilled water temperature is reset upward until it forces at least one control valve to a 90% open position. The same scheme is used to control hot water temperature from the main converter to the air handling unit hot decks. If all hot deck control valves are throttled, hot water temperature will reset down until one valve is at a 90% open position. These load reset programs have been extremely effective in improving building comfort conditions and also providing reduced energy consumption.

	May 1984	June 1984	July 1984	Aug 1984	Sept 1984	Oct 1984	Nov 1984	Dec 1984	Jan 1985	Feb 1985	Mar 1985	Apr 1985
Avg. Consumption Consumption x 1000#	1053	*	*	*	*	*	1227	2798	5774	5482	4248	2823
Consumption Last Season	1301	*	*	*	*	*	852	3473	6220	6370	4877	2956
Usage First Season with EMS	576	*	*	*	*	*	653	1532	2662	4184	2799	2242
% Reduction From Average	45.3	*	*	*	*	*	46.8	45.2	53.9	23.7	34.1	20.6
% Reduction From Last Season	55.7	*	*	*	*	*	23.4	55.9	57.2	34.3	42.6	24.1
Estimated Savings vs Last Season $20/1000#	$14,500	*	*	*	*	*	$3980	$38,820	$71,160	$43,720	$41,560	$14,280

*Steam to Facility Off During Summer Months

	1000#	% Reduction	
Total Estimated Savings vs Last Season	11,400	43.8%	$228,000

Perimeter radiation systems are also controlled from space conditions. All sensors located in exterior offices provide the inputs to this program. Radiation temperatures are scheduled according to a predetermined schedule when the average exterior temperature approaches the target temperature. A separate daytime and nighttime target temperature provide daytime comfort conditions and night setback conditions for conservation purposes.

Optimized start/stop program is used to determine the start and stop time of all building systems. The systems are automatically started in order to condition the building to within the comfort range by occupancy time. The stop time is determined by the relative position of the average space temperature within the comfort range. A temperature in the center of the range will shut down the units as much as an hour before the established time relying on flywheel effect to carry the building for the remainder of the time. Optimized start/stop also determines the time at which the perimeter radiation switches from night setback to daytime target set point.

Enthalpy optimization and duty cycle provide some additional energy savings, but programs which cycle units off and on to conserve energy usually are counterproductive when using load reset and zero energy band programs.

Xerox Square was an example of a successful EMS/DDC installation. I'm confident that this system will provide excellent control and efficient energy utilization for many years. The system just completed at the Xerox Henrietta facility was also a huge success and is expected to provide similar if not better results.

Without a doubt, an EMS system can be an excellent investment if properly designed, implemented, operated, and maintained and can provide a continuous return on your investment while providing accurate control of your facility.

11/18/87

COMMERCIAL CONSTRUCTION STANDARDS IMPLEMENTATION AND COMPLIANCE

Richard W. Dixon, P.E.
Energy Code Program
Florida Department of Community Affairs

The success of an energy efficiency building construction code is dependent upon the three major stages of its evolution. It begins with the development of the standard on which the code is based. Such standards typically are developed by national organizations and therefore reflect generalized considerations. This stage is often the most laborious to complete. It is also the most critical stage, in that the usefulness of the standard as the core elements of a building construction code are determined by the structure and concepts built into it. The next stage is the adaptation of the standard into a local building code. This stage is the responsibility of the code administrator and is characterized by compromises and modifications to the standard. Modifications are necessary to produce the local political consensus essential to the acceptance and adoption of a construction code. The final stage is the integration of the code into the design, permitting and inspection of buildings. The success of the code at this stage depends on its enforceability from the code enforcement official's perspective and in large part on the degree of voluntary compliance exhibited by design professionals.

A standard which can be developed into a successful building code has several distinguishing characteristics. These characteristics bridge the technical and political realms and provide a foundation for government regulations which can be tailored to local conditions. In order for the standards to be implemented effectively, they must provide the opportunities for addressing local technical and political issues.

Desirable characteristics of building construction standards include: 1) flexibility for adapting requirements to the local physical climate and political climate and to local construction practices; 2) flexibility in compliance options for designers and 3) clear and concise compliance criteria for both the designer and local jurisdiction building department to follow. In addition to these traits of code structure, the standard should be technically sound. It must provide solutions to conflicts between energy concerns and other building related concerns such as life safety and health. Finally, and perhaps most importantly, the standard must make realistic steps to improve the minimum acceptable energy related performance of commercial buildings. More may be gained in energy conservation with a more conservative standard than with a standard which oversteps politically acceptable bounds.

The second stage for an energy efficiency construction standard, after its development and adoption by the sponsor organization, is its integration into a code. Though politics and compromise play a major role in the development of a standard, debate at this stage focuses more on technical feasibility or appropriateness of proposed requirements. It is when the standard reaches the stage of integration into a building code, that the issues of local proprietary interest come to the foreground. Most of the time, local proprietary interests have had little input in the standard's development even though in theory national associations representing those interests have participated. The local code administrator must deal with the issues of disenfranchised constituencies such as manufacturers of technologies which are insignificant from a national perspective but very significant from a local perspective. These constituencies are often hostile because of the perception that they have been left out of the development of regulations which effect their respective industry. It is essential to the local code administrator that both the standard's structure and technical requirements be flexible enough to derive compromises which will address such local issues so that they do not become overly politicized. Many decisions are made in the development of a standard based on the geographically specific experience of committee members and on what is considered to be the national norm. Care must be taken to provide the flexibility necessary to address local issues which do not fit into these bodies of experience or expectation. Otherwise the standard will be of diminished usefulness for some locales.

The flexibility allowed by an energy efficiency construction standard in meeting its requirements is a key to its acceptance. Also if the standard is sufficiently flexible to allow a wide range of building envelope designs, it is possible to set energy conservation goals and overall compliance criteria higher in the standard. The primary means of providing flexibility within codes and standards is by moving from a prescriptive based to a performance based compliance methodology. The component performance approach of ASHRAE Standard 90 is the most widely used of its compliance procedures. This approach is basically prescriptive with minimum HVAC system efficiencies and maximum lighting budgets prescribed. However, it is hybrid in character in that a performance methodology is provided for the envelope requirements which allows tradeoffs between the efficiencies of the building envelope components. This performance approach applied to the building envelope compliance criteria, allows a limited degree of flexibility in establishing a range of acceptable building envelope designs. It is more flexible than a full prescriptive criteria but less flexible than a full compliance methodology.

The component performance approach will result in lower energy conservation goals than full performance based standards. The realistic bounds on energy performance requirements established by a standard are set by the range of building envelope designs with constituencies who support them. From the local code administrator's point of view, all energy codes must work within such a range. Full performance compliance approaches would allow for minimum code compliance with the politically determined level of least efficient building envelope design which is to be included in the code coupled with a HVAC system with efficiencies above the minimum allowable. The full performance methodology allows coupling of low end building envelope efficiencies with high end equipment efficiencies. The component performance and full prescriptive methodologies decouple equipment efficiencies from envelope and lighting efficiencies. Therefore the worst overall energy performance acceptable within such codes results from the combination of low end envelope efficiencies with low end equipment efficiencies. The difference in energy targets attainable with the full performance methodology versus the two other methodologies is significant.

The full performance compliance methodology provides the maximum flexibility to the designer. It provides the most latitude in attaining his design goals and still be in compliance with the standard's requirements. When this characteristic becomes recognized by the designer this methodology typically becomes his choice. The full compliance methodology is not without its drawbacks however. The most significant of those from the designers' and code enforcement officials' perspectives is the increased complexity.

One of the more desirable characteristics of an energy efficiency construction standard is that it be clear and concise in its requirements. These characteristics are necessary to limit the need for education of designers and code enforcement personnel. The better defined the requirements are, the easier it is to determine compliance from both a code enforcer's point of view and from the design professional's point of view. The performance approach is complex in that there is variability in requirements from one building to the next. There is no single set of prescriptive criteria which are the only set of requirements applied to all buildings. A pragmatic factor in enforcement of performance based codes is that the code official must rely more on the honesty and forthrightness of the design professionals than is the case with prescriptive codes. In reality, the system depends to a large extent on voluntary compliance by the design professionals. It relies on the design professional to define the list of building systems efficiencies which must be used in order to meet the codes performance target. The enforcement official can then use this list as a set of prescriptives to be checked for compliance during construction. Practical considerations of building department management generally result in the signed and sealed calculation of the design professional being taken at face value. Spot verification of the calculations by plans examiners is typically the best which may occur.

A judge of whether a code is effective is the balance it strikes between the strong need for flexibility and the equally strong need for conciseness and clarity. Flexibility, a strong point of full performance codes, without clarity can result in the implementation of more advanced design goals but an inability to assure compliance. Clarity, a strong point of prescriptive codes, without flexibility can result in effective policing of standards whose conservation goals do not meet the realistic potentials of today's technologies. The key to which approach results in the most realized conservation in buildings lies in the commitment of the design professionals to code compliance.

Energy efficiency codes for building construction must also solve potential conflicts with other applicable building codes and standards. From the perspective of the building community, life safety and health related codes take precedence over other codes. In order for the energy efficiency code to have credibility, it must provide solutions where conflicts between such interests occur. An example is the current concern regarding the safety and health of building occupants due to indoor air pollutants, both biological and chemical. One conflict of interests which must be resolved is the energy related impacts of the revisions to ASHRAE Standard 62. Solutions must be found which meet the health concerns addressed by proposed Standard 62 and which meet energy conservation goals if the energy code is to be implemented without serious challenge. Solutions to potential regulatory conflicts which result from opposing requirements of different standards are requisite to the viability of energy efficiency building codes. The energy efficiency code for building construction must represent a realistic advancement in energy conservation goals. The impact it makes within the design and construction industry must be gauged to match the perceived significance of the energy resources depletion issue. The code must first gain technical acceptance but, in the end, the political acceptance at the local code adoption and enforcement level will determine the success of its implementation. The construction techniques and products which must be used to meet compliance with the code must be readily available and proven technologies. The standard cannot set requirements which will result in the designer and owner having to take substantial risks with unfamiliar technologies if it is to be widely accepted. Neither can it eliminate a large segment of building construction practices. The backlash that results from a standard which takes too great a step forward will occur most dramatically upon implementation and at the local political level. Such a backlash can be so strong as to totally counter the goals and objectives the standard was developed to achieve. An effective approach to standards development which will better assist the code adoption responsibility of the local code administrator is to effect a gauged stepwise change in efficiency requirements. The combinations of construction practices and technologies existing at any time result in a range from high energy use to low energy use buildings. The changes imposed by a standard must eliminate the combinations of practices and technologies which result in relatively extremely high energy use. Elimination of combinations should be established by optimizing the cutoff between what is and is not acceptable through the analysis of how the mainstream or middle energy use level buildings will be impacted. Such a methodology bridges the unknown between the technically appropriate as established through the consensus process of the engineering community and the politically viable as determined by the construction industry at large.

The success of energy conservation construction standards in their third stage, that of the enacted building code, relies in part on the characteristics of the standard's structure and requirements discussed previously. Success in the implementation of building construction standards for commercial buildings also relies extensively on voluntary compliance with its requirements by architects, engineers and developers. Building construction standards for energy efficiency are inherently complex. Standards for commercial buildings, due to the broad range of building functions and building systems, compound that complexity. Effective policing or enforcement of such regulations is unlikely with today's methods of building construction inspection. Therefore voluntary compliance is essential to the effectiveness of these standards.

The elements of a code which will be successfully implemented are varied. They range from its structure and approach in establishing compliance criteria, to the pragmatic concerns of its enforcement and administration and to its public acceptance and social impact. The standard must first gain adoption into a local building code. Success at that stage depends on how well it can be adapted to the local circumstances. Full implementation and the end measure of the standard's effectiveness depend on the level of compliance designers and owners will commit to and the degree to which building departments can enforce its requirements.

INDOOR AIR QUALITY--EPRI HEALTH EFFECTS R&D

Cary L. Young, Project Manager
Electric Power Research Institute
Palo Alto, California

INTRODUCTION

Since the mid-1970's the Electric Power Research Institute (EPRI), on behalf of its approximately 500 member electric utilities, has been funding research to investigate the effects of air pollution on human health. This continuing effort is centered in EPRI's Environment Division, one of its six research divisions. As with most most other studies before and at this time, the principal concern in EPRI-sponsored projects was with the quality of ambient outdoor air, and particularly with the possible health risks associated with the sulfur oxides-particulate matter complex. EPRI is still actively pursuing, through community-based and other types of studies, a better understanding of such risks in order to improve the scientific database applied to regulatory and other decisions affecting the control of airborne emissions from fossil-fuel power plants. In recent years, however, concern over the quality of air in indoor environments has been added to EPRI's program of air pollution health effects research.

Initially, the interest of the electric utility industry in indoor air quality and health, reflecting the prevailing public health point of view, was limited to accounting for indoor (especially residential) exposure to certain air pollutants, so that the estimation of health effects due to outdoor combustion products from epidemiologic investigation would not be biased. This occurred because of the increasing realization (1)that there existed indoor sources for some of the same pollutants that were measured in outdoor air, as well as for other pollutants which might cause a particular health outcome under study; (2)that these sources may be unevenly distributed in a population under study; and (3)that people generally spend a majority of their time indoors, and thus indoor pollutant levels could be the predominant determinant of exposure for individual study participants. Later, when research showed that levels of many pollutants are often higher inside buildings than outside, and that reduced ventilation for energy conservation--a key part of the home weatherization programs promoted by many EPRI member companies--can cause pollutant levels to build up indoors, electric utilities, along with the scientific community, became concerned about the possible health risks independently associated with indoor exposure.

Four specific research projects are described in this paper. The first two studies are aimed, by and large, at the issue of chronic effects from low-level exposure; the latter two studies are directed more toward the issue of acute effects from periodic or episodic pollution events. Each study deals with one or more of the aspects of indoor air quality and health mentioned above.

THE SIX-CITIES STUDY

The Six-Cities Study, conducted by the Harvard School of Public Health and funded primarily by the National Institute of Environmental Health Sciences, began in 1974 as a longitudinal epidemiologic investigation of respiratory health among over 20,000 children and adults residing in six communities in the eastern and mid-western U.S. Annual physiologic and questionnaire examinations are being performed to record lung function, respiratory illness history, and respiratory symptoms such as persistent cough and wheeze. EPRI has helped support this important research since 1977.

The Harvard study was originally designed to assess the possible adverse effects of chronic exposure to ambient particles and sulfur oxides(Ref. 1). However, early on it evolved into an on-going evaluation of indoor as well as outdoor air pollution. Initial indoor-outdoor monitoring conducted by the Harvard researchers revealed that, although levels of fine particles were on average higher in the homes of cigarette smokers than in the homes of nonsmokers and increased levels of nitrogen dioxide(NO_2) occurred in homes with gas cooking stoves, a great degree of variation existed in the levels of these pollutants among homes with the same amount of smoking or the same type of stove. The investigators recognized the potential confounding effect of exposure to indoor pollutants and the need to obtain a more complete understanding of total personal exposure. In addition, they recognized the opportunity to assess the health effects that might be specifically related to certain indoor sources and other factors of the indoor environment.

Early health findings from the Six-Cities study showed that children 6 to 12 years of age living with cigarette-smoking parents had more respiratory symptoms and illness and reduced lung function when compared with those children living with nonsmokers. The findings also suggested that there was slight impairment of lung function due to the use of gas stoves for cooking(Ref. 2). Subsequent follow-up analysis with a new cohort of children indicated that symptoms were associated with passive smoking and the presence of some combustion sources in the home(unvented kerosene heaters, wood stoves and gas for cooking) and with the reporting of molds, mildew and water damage(Ref. 3).

These results have led to an attempt to quantify the relationships among symptoms and pollutant levels through an extensive indoor air pollution health study(Ref. 4). In this effort, which is now in progress and scheduled for completion in 1988, approximately 300 children in each city are enrolled in a year-long survey of respiratory symptoms and monitoring of actual pollutant levels in their homes, schools and the outdoor environment. The children participating in this study are selected in a stratified-random fashion from among the 1,000 children of the new cohort enrolled in each city for the series of annual examinations. The stratification is based on the distribution of household pollution sources in each city. Parents of the children maintain a daily log of symptom events, durations and intensities. The air monitoring component focuses on NO_2 and respirable-size particulate matter(fine particles, $PM_{2.5}$). Average air exchange rate and water vapor levels are also measured. Each home is monitored for two consecutive one-week periods in the winter and again for two consecutive weeks during the summer.

The data collected from this work will eventually be used to determine whether exposure to indoor sources increases the risk of respiratory symptoms in children. The indoor pollutant measurements have already been analyzed to identify predictors of indoor levels of NO_2 and fine particles, and methods for estimating personal exposures of children living in the monitored homes have been established.

STUDY OF 300 HOMES IN KINGSTON-HARRIMAN, TENNESSEE

As a part of the larger indoor air pollution health study carried out by the Harvard group in all six of their study communities, a special study involving supplemental indoor air quality measurements was performed in Kingston-Harriman, Tennessee, one of the six cities, by a team of investigators at the Oak Ridge National Laboratory (ORNL). The objective was to obtain much-needed additional information on residential indoor pollutant levels from a group of randomly chosen homes. A number of specific questions of interest to the several sponsors could be addressed in a cost-effective manner. The sponsors included EPRI, the Tennessee Valley Authority, and the Consumer Product Safety Commission.

As described earlier, the Harvard study focused primarily on combustion-related pollutants. Supplemental investigation carried out in Kingston-Harriman included additional pollutants, building factors(for example, the degree of weatherization), and energy use(Ref. 5). A unique aspect of the Kingston-Harriman work was the opportunity to investigate the interrelationships of woodstove and kerosene heater use, indoor air quality, and respiratory health. Since wood or kerosene is used as the primary heating fuel or as a secondary source of heating in a substantial fraction of homes in the Kingston-Harriman area, and since there are relatively few households with gas cooking stoves, the basic Harvard study design was modified so that the stratification variables resulted in the classification of 8 groups by the presence or absence of smoking, kerosene heaters, and woodstoves. Accordingly, the ORNL researchers concentrated on measuring particulate phase and vapor phase organic compounds, specifically polynuclear aromatic(PNA) species, in addition to NO2 and fine particles. PNAs, which are for the most part by-products of the pyrolytic combustion of organic fuels, are of health concern because of the potential long-term consequences of exposure to those several species known or suspected to be human carcinogens. Tobacco smoking, cooking and wood burning are important sources of PNA production indoors.

Three other indoor pollutants of interest were monitored by the ORNL group in this special study, either to answer specific local questions or to describe the distribution of levels in homes: radon, formaldehyde, and airborne microorganisms. With respect to the last of these, levels of both fungi and bacteria, generally found to be greater indoors than outdoors(Ref. 6), may turn out to be an important factor in explaining the occurrence of some childhood respiratory symptoms in view of the preliminary Harvard findings around indicators of moisture inside homes. It is known that fungal spores and aeroallergens in the indoor environment depend on conditions of high humidity or the presence of water for their successful colonization and growth.

The evaluation of any adverse health effects due to airborne microorganisms and many more detailed analyses utilizing the indoor air quality database from Kingston-Harriman are underway at present. The Harvard and ORNL scientists are collaborating to investigate relationships between various components of this multifaceted study.

STUDY OF NO2 IN NEW YORK INNER-CITY APARTMENTS

Researchers from the Columbia University School of Public Health have for the last few years been conducting, with EPRI support, an evaluation of personal and stationary monitoring devices and strategies for estimating exposure to indoor combustion emissions. The emphasis has been on inner-city apartments, many of them the homes of lower-income families, in which indoor levels of pollutants are likely to differ appreciably from those observed in single-family dwellings. A large fraction of the study participants are asthmatics, who as a class have been considered a subgroup of the population sensitive to air pollution in general and perhaps more prone to having asthmatic attacks triggered by various factors in the indoor environment. As a matter of interest, in the community from which the subjects were selected, the prevalence of asthma has been reported to be approximately four times the national average.

In the course of analyzing NO2 levels from their initial monitoring study, the Columbia group found that peak exposures exceeding the national primary standard for outdoor air were common among individuals using unvented gas cooking stoves in dwellings where air exchange rates had been minimized in the interest of energy conservation(Ref 7). Because several studies in the scientific literature have suggested that exposure to high levels of NO2, even for brief periods, can affect respiratory symptoms and lung function, a decision was made to launch a pilot study to investigate the possible respiratory health effects of such exposures in this setting. Additional funding was provided by the Environmental Protection Agency (EPA) to carry out this work.

In this acute exposure study, the person cooking the evening meal on a gas stove is monitored with a continuous NO2 monitoring instrument held at the breathing level before, throughout, and following the cooking operation. The cook and any other household members present at the time are administered lung function tests and questioned about symptoms before the stove is turned on, during a break in cooking, immediately after meal preparation, and 1 to 2 hours later. Each of sixteen study households is visited for monitoring and testing on five occasions.

The data so obtained will be used to answer certain key questions about the effects of exposure to short-term peak levels of NO2 in asthmatics and non-asthmatic individuals. Preliminary analysis of a total of 11 asthmatic adults and children who have completed the protocol suggests the existence of a possible threshold with respect to transient decline in lung function(Ref. 8). Research is continuing with the remainder of the study subjects. Current plans call for testing the same subjects in a controlled exposure chamber with levels of NO2 comparable to those measured while cooking on gas stoves in order to validate this and other findings.

TOTAL PERSONAL EXPOSURE STUDY

A new study of respiratory responses to air pollution in a single community is now underway that purposely considers total(both indoor and outdoor) exposure to NO2 and particulate matter, two pollutants with major indoor and outdoor sources. Conducted by investigators from the University of Arizona School of Medicine, this study is being coordinated between and jointly funded by EPRI and EPA. The objective is to examine relationships between day-to-day pollutant exposure and short-term changes in respiratory symptoms and lung function (Ref. 9). The study population, which includes asthmatics and other individuals who may represent a more sensitive subgroup, is drawn from several geographic clusters defined by sources and trends in outdoor air quality in the Tucson area.

Basic environmental and health status assessments in the Tucson study are household-based, and approximately 500 households are enrolled. During a two-week sampling period, which is repeated once in the opposite season, air pollutant levels inside and outside the home are intensively monitored. Each participating adult and child occupant reports his or her respiratory symptoms in a diary and performs a simple lung function test four times daily over the same periods.

The classification of homes in this multistage, nested-design study is based on information gathered from baseline exposure questionnaires and on findings from an earlier study conducted by the Arizona group suggesting what indoor and outdoor environmental factors might be important in causing the greatest number of health responses in asthmatic individuals(Ref. 10). Thus, homes are stratified by housing characteristics related to (1)the estimated NO2 levels due to the use of a gas stove and unvented gas or kerosene heaters, and (2)the levels of suspended particulate matter attributable to tobacco smoking and wood burning.

The Tucson study is perhaps unique among epidemiologic studies of air pollution currently in progress in the U.S. in that, through its strict attention to linking exposure and response in time in a fairly large number of study subjects, it aims explicitly to partition the short-term effects attributable to various indoor and outdoor exposures while retaining the ability to detect possible important air pollutant interactions. Also, when this study is completed, it will provide some of the best data available on the relative contributions of indoor and outdoor sources to total personal exposure.

CONCLUSION

This description of EPRI's major current activities in the area of indoor air quality and health effects research demonstrates the commitment of its member electric utilities to address critical questions concerning public health. EPRI will strive to continue contributing to the nation's overall effort in understanding the health risks of air pollution and looks forward to the opportunity for further cooperation with other interested funding agencies in the federal sector and elsewhere.

REFERENCES

1. Ferris, B.G., Jr., Speizer, F.E., Spengler, J.D., et al. Effects of sulfur oxides and respirable particles on human health: Methodology and demography of populations in study. Am. Rev. Resp. Dis. 1979; 120:767-779.

2. Ware, J.H., Dockery, D.W., Spiro, A., III, et al. Passive smoking, gas cooking, and respiratory health of children living in six cities. Am. Rev. Resp. Dis. 1984; 129:366-374.

3. Brunekreef, B., Dockery, D.W., Speizer, F.E., et al. An association between moisture in the home and respiratory symptoms in primary school children. Presented at American Thoracic Society Conference, New Orleans, May 1987.

4. Spengler, J.D., Ware, J.H., Speizer, F.E., et al. Harvard's indoor air quality respiratory health study. Presented at Fourth International Conference on Indoor Air Quality and Climate, West Berlin, August 1987.

5. Hawthorne, A.R., Dudney, C.S., Tyndall, R.L., et al. Case study: Multipollutant indoor air quality study of 300 homes in Kingston-Harriman, Tennessee. Presented at ASTM Symposium on Design and Protocol for Monitoring Indoor Air Quality, Cincinnati, April 1987.

6. Tyndall, R.L., Dudney, C.S., Hawthorne, A.R., et al. Microflora of the typical home. Presented at Fourth International Conference on Indoor Air Quality and Climate, West Berlin, August 1987.

7. Electric Power Research Institute. Interim report: Indoor exposure to air pollutants, Project No. 2265-1, December 1986.

8. Goldstein, I.F., Andrews, L.R., Lieber, K., et al. Acute exposure to nitrogen dioxide and pulmonary function. Presented at Fourth International Conference on Indoor Air Quality and Climate, West Berlin, August 1987.

9. Quackenboss, J.J., Lebowitz, M.D., and Hayes, C. Epidemiological study of respiratory responses to indoor/outdoor air quality. Presented at Fourth International Conference on Indoor Air Quality and Climate, West Berlin, August 1987.

10. Lebowitz, M.D., Collins, L., and Holberg, C.J. Time series analyses of respiratory responses to indoor and outdoor environmental phenomena. Environ. Res. 1987; 43:332-341.

RADON ENTRY AND CONTROL: INFLUENCE OF BUILDING FACTORS

J. P. Harper
Tennessee Valley Authority
Chattanooga, Tennessee

P. A. Joyner
Electric Power Research Institute
Palo Alto, California

N. L. Nagda
GEOMET Technologies, Inc.
Germantown, Maryland

C. S. Dudney
Oak Ridge National Laboratory
Oak Ridge, Tennessee

Introduction

Since the mid-1970's, the electric power industry has been working on ways to give customers better choices for controlling the quality of their indoor environment [1]. This research has been, in part, focused on evaluating the effects of building design and systems operations on indoor radon levels.

Building radon concentrations depend upon a variety of factors (e.g., radon availablility in the soil, interaction of building and soil, weather forces affecting radon entry and renewal, and occupant practices). Research studies, sponsored by the Electric Power Research Institute (EPRI) and the Tennessee Valley Authority (TVA), and principally conducted by GEOMET Technologies, Inc., and Oak Ridge National Laboratory, are presented to illustrate the effects of siting, building design and space conditioning operations, and air infiltration, depressurization, and weatherization processes on indoor radon levels. These studies also examine the effectiveness of different radon and radon progeny control approaches.

Site Variability

The site of the building is a primary determinant of the upper limit that indoor radon concentrations may reach, whereas building factors and weather conditions affect the rates of radon entry and removal. The variation in radon concentrations within a building is related to the proximity of the particular site to the source of radon that enters the structure. The influence of siting on indoor radon can be observed in comparisons and analyses of regional, intraregional, and local site data.

Regional Variability--A 1985 TVA study in 70 houses in the States of Alabama, Georgia, Mississippi, and Tennessee was conducted to assess the background variability of indoor radon [2]. Passive integrating (alpha track) monitors were used to obtain both quarterly and year-long measurements of indoor radon levels in the study houses [3]. All 70 houses had basements and were randomly selected in seven cities in the 4-State area to facilitate management of the year-long sampling effort. Measurements were made in both upstairs (main floor) and downstairs (basement) locations in each house. Table 1 summarizes the data by season and location for each site studied.

Table 1

INDOOR RADON LEVELS (pCi/l) IN SEVEN SITE AREAS

Site	Location	Seasonal Averages				Annual
		Summer	Fall	Winter	Spring	Average
Tupelo, MS	Main Floor	0.7	0.5	0.5	0.5	0.7
	Basement	1.5	0.8	0.9	1.1	1.0
Florence, AL	Main Floor	2.0	3.0	3.0	2.8	2.1
	Basement	2.9	3.9	3.5	2.2	3.2
Birmingham, AL	Main Floor	1.3	1.4	1.0	0.8	1.1
	Basement	1.9	2.4	1.6	1.1	1.6
Huntsville, AL	Main Floor	15.3	21.2	9.8	10.0	10.8
	Basement	18.7	23.8	19.7	12.1	16.0
Rossville, GA	Main Floor	1.8	4.7	6.4	1.9	2.6
	Basement	4.7	9.3	13.6	7.7	5.7
Chattanooga, TN	Main Floor	1.4	3.0	1.9	1.2	1.5
	Basement	1.8	3.1	2.5	2.0	2.0
Knoxville, TN	Main Floor	3.4	4.1	3.3	2.0	3.4
	Basement	4.2	5.4	5.4	3.6	4.6

Regional differences are clearly seen when comparing the annual average indoor radon levels of the lowest site (Tupelo, Mississippi) with that of the highest site (Huntsville, Alabama). A 1,400- to 1,500-percent difference between these two sites was observed in the year-long indoor radon measurements. Large variations can also be present within a State. The measurements for the three Alabama sites (Birmingham, Florence, and Huntsville) exhibit approximately a 1:2:10 ratio in radon concentrations. The two Tennessee sites (Chattanooga and Knoxville) show a 1:2.3 relationship. Such regional differences in indoor radon are usually attributed to geological variations in the distribution of radium-bearing deposits, while the broad spectrum of indoor radon levels within any region tends to be associated with variations in soil physics.

Intraregional Variation--Another EPRI- and TVA-sponsored field study in 300 homes in Roane County, Tennessee, has identified county-level clustering of indoor radon levels [4]. Average winter indoor radon levels were approximately 2.4 pCi/l. A statistical analysis done on a subset of homes examined geographical clustering around marker houses that have winter radon levels above 4.0 pCi/l [5]. The analysis indicated that houses in the geographic vicinity of a marker house have a significant probability of having radon levels similar in magnitude to those of the marker houses. To date, no geological deposit has been associated with the higher indoor radon level in the marker houses, although a higher proportion of housing with levels above 4.0 pCi/l appears north of the Tennessee River, which transverses the county. Cluster sampling approaches are used in some State radon surveys, where additional monitoring is conducted in the vicinity of a house with elevated radon levels to identify other problem situations. Thus, although a large variability in the distribution of indoor radon can be seen in an area as small as the county, the houses with elevated levels do not appear to be randomly distributed, indicating a relatively specific site-to-site variability.

Local Variability--A 1984 EPRI- and TVA-sponsored study in the cities of Oak Ridge and west Knoxville, Tennessee, suggests that even close evaluation of local geology may not adequately explain observed geographical clustering of high indoor radon levels [6]. In this field investigation involving seasonal radon measurements in 40 houses, housing sites located on a ridge transversing the area were found to have significantly higher radon levels than those located in the surrounding valley. A review of geological maps of the area could identify no radium-bearing deposit or strata in the area. Furthermore, surface gamma radiation data for the area showed lower gamma radiation rates (uR/h) on the ridge than in the valley, which seem to contradict the radon findings. Lower soil cover on the ridge was identified as a possible factor, but a specific geological cause could not be demonstrated conclusively.

Thus, although geological features or radium-bearing deposits are thought to be the primary source of indoor radon, it is difficult to identify site-specific factors that would help predict whether a particular housing site or development could pose a potential radon hazard.

Building Structure and HVAC Effects

A building's structure, HVAC, and interior zoning or partitioning provide routes for radon entry and influence its transport. The interaction of these factors in large measure determines the relative distribution of radon throughout the building.

Building Design--The relationships among different building structural types and indoor radon is not yet well understood. In general, houses with basements are believed to offer greater opportunity for radon entry than other structural types because of the relatively greater soil contact area. Detailed auditing of housing characteristics in a subset of approximately 150 houses from the previously cited 300-house study in Roane County, Tennessee, was used to categorize buildings [7]. Basement, crawlspace, and slab building type designations were made if at least 75 percent of the ground floor area was of this foundation type. Partial basements were 25 to 75 percent of ground floor area. Table 2 presents the radon distributions found for these classifications. Radon monitors were exposed 3 to 5 months each season. Winter sampling occurred between October and April, while summer sampling was between April and September. Although partial basement indoor radon levels are seen to be the highest, few of the differences seen are significant ($p<.05$). Closer inspection of the data shows that structural factors other than simple foundation types may need to be considered.

Table 2

DISTRIBUTION OF RADON LEVELS (pCi/l) AMONG BUILDING CATEGORIES AND SEASONS

Building Type	Season	Min.	Max.	Mean	SEM*
Basement	Winter	0.3	6.8	1.7	0.4
	Summer	0.2	3.6	1.1	0.2
Crawlspace	Winter	0.4	8.7	2.2	0.4
	Summer	0.1	6.4	1.0	0.2
Slab	Winter	0.6	6.4	2.2	1.4
	Summer	0.3	2.0	0.8	0.3
Partial Basement	Winter	0.5	21.6	2.9	0.5
	Summer	0.4	10.3	1.8	0.3
Other	Winter	0.4	4.1	1.5	0.3
	Summer	0.3	8.6	1.4	0.4

*Standard error of the mean.

For example, if the design of the crawlspace is considered, the location of ductwork in this area is seen to have significance. Table 3 presents a stratification of the crawlspace classification based on return duct location, which suggests that this variable can be as relevant as generic structural classification in explaining indoor radon levels. For example, the significantly lower levels ($p<.05$) in houses with return ducts in the crawlspace area are suggestive of radon transport through leaky ductwork into the house [8].

Thus, simple structural classification may not be adequate to explain indoor radon differences, but a multivariate analysis of building parameters may eventually identify critical building factors governing radon entry.

Table 3

DISTRIBUTION OF RADON LEVELS (pCi/l)
ACCORDING TO DUCT LOCATION FOR CRAWLSPACE HOUSES

Return Duct Location	Season	Min.	Max.	Mean	SEM*
Crawlspace	Winter	0.4	8.4	2.8	0.7
	Summer	0.2	6.4	1.5	0.4
Other/None	Winter	0.5	8.7	1.8	0.5
	Summer	0.1	2.1	0.7	0.1

*Standard error of the mean.

HVAC Design and Operations--Some building factors that affect radon entry and transport are the type and operation of the space conditioning system. Table 4 presents a comparison of HVAC convecting and nonconvecting systems for the aforementioned 150-house subsample. The primary difference is the apparently higher summer entry of radon for convecting systems. As with the crawlspace analysis, transport from unconditioned spaces or basements is the primary reason for this observation. Detailed tracer gas studies of air infiltration in a subset of 39 houses in the previously cited 70-house study showed a 1.8- to 4.3-fold variation in air infiltration, and crawlspaces and garages were a major source of outside air [8]. Thus, basic choices in space conditioning can potentially affect radon entry and transport.

Table 4

DISTRIBUTION OF RADON LEVELS (pCi/l)
ACCORDING TO TYPE OF HEATING, VENTILATION, AND
AIR-CONDITIONING (HVAC) SYSTEM

HVAC Type	Season	Min.	Max.	Mean	SEM*
Convecting	Winter	0.3	15.0	2.4	0.3
	Summer	0.2	10.3	1.8	0.2
Woodburning (Nonconvecting	Winter	0.3	21.6	2.4	0.9
	Summer	0.1	3.7	0.9	0.2
Mixed (Nonconvecting)	Winter	0.5	8.7	2.0	0.4
	Summer	0.2	2.2	0.7	0.1

*Standard error of the mean.

Operation of forced air space conditioning systems can also influence the potential radiological working level exposures. In an EPRI-sponsored study conducted by GEOMET Technologies, Inc., in two identical research houses in Gaithersburg, Maryland, cycling of the HVAC system was shown to affect radon progeny levels [9]. Figure 1 presents data relating equilibrium factor (i.e., the ratio of the equilibrium equivalent concentration of radon to the actual concentration) to percent running time of the circulation fan. The equilibrium factor is seen to decrease as percent running time increases. The reason for this apparent reduction in exposure is that radon progeny are removed from the atmosphere, or plated out. Increased circulation fan operation tends to equalize upstairs and downstairs radon concentrations since it primarily mixes the interior air. This property of HVAC systems could prove to be an important approach for control of radiological exposure if the ratio of suspended attached and unattached radon progeny remain relatively constant during plate out.

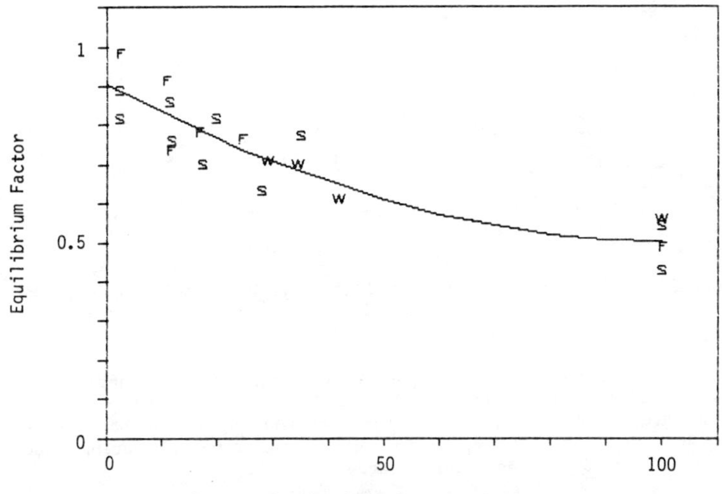

Figure 1. Effect of Circulation Fan on the Equilibrium Factor (Control House)

<u>Interior Zone Factors</u>--In Table 1, major differences in indoor radon levels are seen between the upstairs and downstairs zones. This is not too surprising considering radon enters at or below ground level. However, such differences in interior zone radon concentrations can affect our interpretation of the importance of building factors. For example, the analysis of structural classifications presented in Table 2 was made using main floor radon concentrations only, which for basement dwellings may or may not be most representative.

Other differences also exist. For example, Figure 2 shows the distribution of upstairs and downstairs equilibrium ratios from the 70-house study, estimated from alpha spectroscopic measurements and measurements using modified Lucas cells in those cases where the radon levels were greater than 3.0 pCi/l and the level of radon progeny greater than 0.015 WL [10]. The median upstairs ratio of 55 percent is higher than the downstairs ratio of 40 percent. Since radon gas entering basements from the soil can be expected to be relatively free of progeny, the equilibrium fraction might be expected to be less in the basement than in the upper levels. However, this finding has importance when evaluating the long-term effectiveness of radon progeny control strategies or the influence of circulation fan operation radon progeny levels.

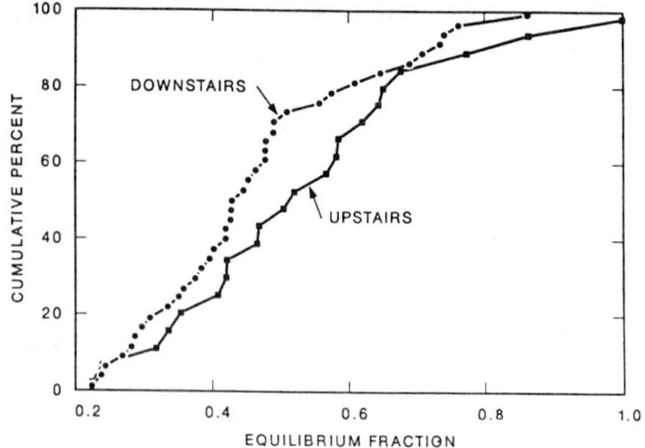

Figure 2. Downstairs and Upstairs Cumulative Distributions of Radon Progeny/Radon Equilibrium Factors for All Site Areas (Summer 1985 Data)

When appraising the influence of building and HVAC characteristics on radon or radon progeny levels, the house has to be treated as an integrated system where structural and appliance characteristics specify conditions for radon entry and transport during space conditioning and between interior zones.

Air Infiltration, Building Depressurization, and Weatherization

Weather variables are principal determinants governing air infiltration and building depressurization processes, which in turn affect radon entry and removal. Home weatherization, because it modifies the structural resistance to air infiltration as well as building pressurization relationships may similarly alter indoor radon levels. Therefore, in a given house, weather may be the major force driving indoor radon variability.

Seasonal Influences--As is seen in Table 1, season or weather conditions can have major effects on indoor radon levels. Two weather variables, temperature and windspeed, currently best explain such seasonal variations. Figure 1 shows the interrelationships between these two parameters, two important building processes (i.e., air infiltration and building depressurization) and indoor radon levels [11].

In general, as indoor/outdoor temperature differences and windspeed increase, the building becomes more depressurized. As shown in Figure 3, there is an inverse relationship between differential temperature and pressure (Pearson's correlation coefficient of -0.60). Windspeed is not as strongly correlated with differential pressure (correlation coefficient of 0.3) except during select periods, which may be explained by the variable effect wind direction has on building pressurization relationships. As the building becomes more depressurized, more air enters the structure from the outdoor atmosphere and from the soil. The correlation seen in the figure between changes in differential pressure and indoor radon, although relatively small in magnitude (-0.3), is statistically significant ($p<.05$). Both the entry of radon and its rate of removal are being affected by these weather parameters and the resultant indoor radon concentration is a function of both the source strength of radon (primarily dependent upon pressure-mediated flow) and its dilution by air infiltrating into the homes.

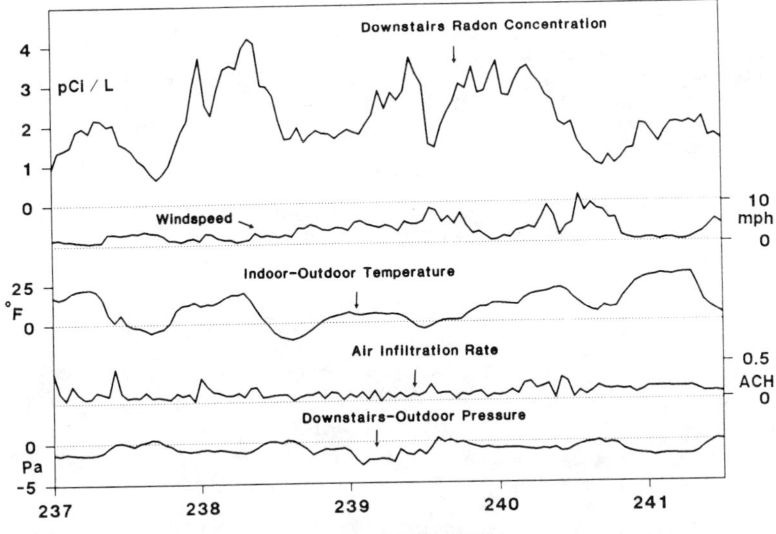

Figure 3. Windspeeds, ΔT, ΔP, Air Infiltration Rate, and Radon Concentrations in the Downstairs of the Experimental Research House in August 1986

If the rate of radon entry is relatively lower than its removal rate, then indoor radon concentration declines. The converse could also occur. This situation can lead to some counterintuitive phenomena where a building's radon levels can be seen to increase at the same time the air infiltration rate increases, which appears to occur during certain periods in the figure.

It is difficult to develop a general theory to interrelate such variables from information currently available because geophysical factors affecting radon entry and building space conditioning operation are also dependent upon local weather conditions. For example, radon entry is dependent upon soil gas transport which depends on rainfall and barometric pressure that govern soil moisture levels and gas diffusion. Likewise, weather influences building operations and occupant behavior (e.g., HVAC cycling, fenestration, ingress and egress), which independently affect the duration and degree of air transport and exchange of the structure.

Home Weatherization Effects--"Home weatherization" is commonly used to describe a set of techniques that increase the resistance of the structure to air infiltration. Common techniques include caulking and weatherstripping, addition of storm windows and doors, use of vapor barriers, sealing duct leaks, increasing crawlspace ventilation, etc. Consequently, studies on the effects of home weatherization on indoor radon levels may lead to different conclusions depending on what set of weatherization techniques are studied.

For example, in the EPRI-sponsored test house studies, a house doctor type of weatherization was done on one house. This involved principally caulking and sealing of air leaks of a house that was well insulated and had wall vapor barriers. The results of this study on air exchange rates and indoor radon levels are summarized in Table 5 [9]. Essentially, indoor radon levels were observed to increase in roughly the same proportion as air exchange decreased.

Table 5

EFFECT OF WEATHERIZATION RETROFIT ON RADON CONCENTRATIONS IN EPRI TEST HOUSES (PERIODIC FAN OPERATION)

	Control House		Weatherization Retrofit		Outdoor
	Radon (pCi/l)	Air Exchange Rate (ACH)	Radon (pCi/l)	Air Exchange Rate (ACH)	Radon (pCi/l)
Preretrofit	1.11	0.41	1.00	0.37	--
Postretrofit					
Summer	1.19	0.15	1.61	0.11	0.20
Fall	1.04	0.29	1.44	0.22	0.14
Winter	0.57	0.61	0.50	0.46	0.22

However, an analysis of the 300-house study data which was done to assess the influence on indoor radon levels of adding and weatherstripping storm windows and/or doors arrives at a different conclusion [7]. Interestingly, Table 6, which summarizes the result of this analysis, shows no significant difference ($p<.05$) between the fully weatherized and unweatherized data sets [7]. This result is different than that obtained in the test house study but is similar to results obtained in a Pacific Northwest study of conventional and model conservation home construction [12]. These apparently divergent conclusions are probably due to differences in the weatherization techniques studied and to differences in the inherent degree of weatherization in the control houses. However, future research should help elucidate an optimal set of weatherization criteria which significantly improve energy efficiency but do not result in environmental degradation.

Table 6

DISTRIBUTION OF RADON LEVELS (pCi/l) ACCORDING TO WEATHERIZATION OF DOORS AND WINDOWS

Weatherized						
Doors	Windows	Season	Min.	Max.	Mean	SEM*
Yes	Yes	Winter	0.6	7.4	2.2	0.3
		Summer	0.3	7.6	1.5	0.2
Yes	No	Winter	0.4	2.7	1.2	0.2
		Summer	0.1	3.0	1.0	0.2
No	Yes	Winter	0.3	15.0	2.5	0.5
		Summer	0.2	10.3	1.7	0.4
No	No	Winter	0.3	21.7	2.5	0.5
		Summer	0.2	6.8	1.2	0.2

*Standard error of the mean.

Radon and Radon Progeny Control

There are three generic approaches for radon and radon progeny control examined in the EPRI test house studies: heat recovery ventilation, subslab depressurization, and radon progeny removal. These approaches are applicable for most housing but their effectiveness may vary depending upon the quality of construction echniques used in the house being remediated.

Heat Recovery Ventilation--Heat recovery ventilation involves the use of a heat exchanger to recover sensible energy in the ventilator exhaust airstream into the incoming outside air. This type of system provides an energy-efficient method for increasing the air exchange rate of a house, thereby removing radon and radon progeny. The effectiveness of this technique for radon control is seen in Figure 4 [9].

Operating the air-to-air heat exchanger at the different setting reduced indoor radon concentrations consistent with the additional air exchange. The air-to-air heat exchanger had the capability to reduce indoor radon up to 50 percent. Similar reductions are observed for radon progeny. Although this form of radon control is effective for moderate indoor radon concentrations, ventilation approaches are limited by thermal comfort considerations and associated energy penalties.

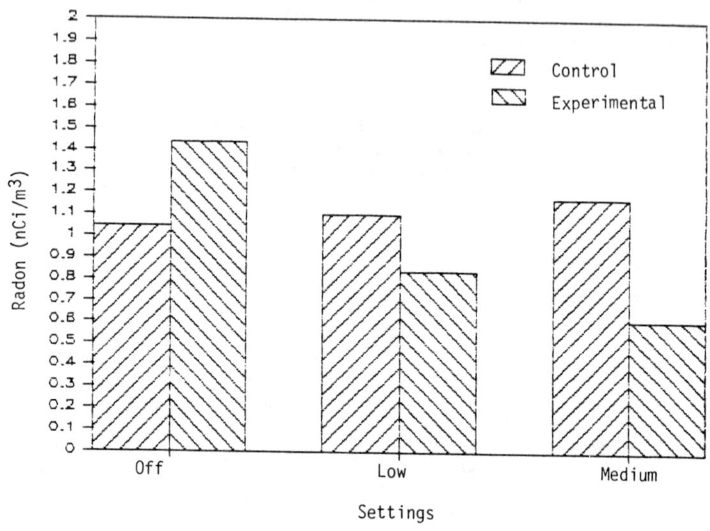

Figure 4. Effect of Heat Exchanger Settings on Indoor Radon Concentrations in Experimental House Compared to Control House

<u>Sub-Slab Depressurization</u>--One of the more effective approaches for lowering radon entry into homes is through the use of pressurization control strategies. The most effective is subslab depressurization. The subslab depressurization system has a simple design which principally consists of plastic piping which penetrates the basement slab to the aggregate layer below and a small fan.

The effectiveness of this system is clearly evident in the test sequence presented in Figure 5 [11]. The fan exhaust rate of approximately 35 cfm caused an approximately 4 Pa change in the basement/subslab differential pressure, and lowered basement radon levels from a pretest average of approximately 2.0 pCi/l to less than 0.4 pCi/l. Since the indoor radon levels during the subslab purge period were near the lower limit of detection of the analytical system, they may not be significantly different from zero and the effectiveness of this control approach is probably greater.

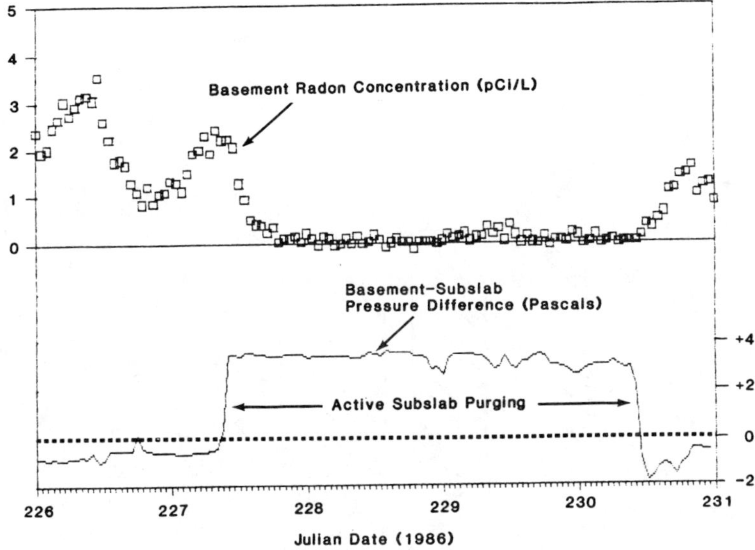

Figure 5. Radon Concentrations and Basement/Subslab Pressure Differences During Operation of the Subslab Purge System (August 1986)

Progeny Control--In a previous section, substantial reductions in radon progeny levels were observed as the circulation fan running time increased. Further experimentation was sponsored by EPRI to investigate other simple approaches for radon progeny control. The techniques investigated included: effect of standard filters in HVAC; effect of pleated filters in HVAC; use of ceiling fans; use of portable room air cleaners; and the use of an electrostatic air cleaner in HVAC. The effect of these approaches on whole house equilibrium factors is given in Figure 6.

The most effective techniques for radon progeny control involve the use of air cleaners, where equilibrium factor reductions approaching 50 percent or more were measured. However, electrostatic precipitators may generate ozone causing additional pollution. Removal by enhanced air circulation (ceiling fan use) provided equilibrium factor reductions between 13 and 37 percent. Simple filtration typically resulted in reductions that were 25 to 50 percent. Thus, even relatively simple practices for particulate removal can result in significant radon progeny reductions.

However, until more definitive data is available on changes in the levels of the unattached radon progeny associated with these control techniques, definitive radiological health benefits cannot be associated with this control alternative.

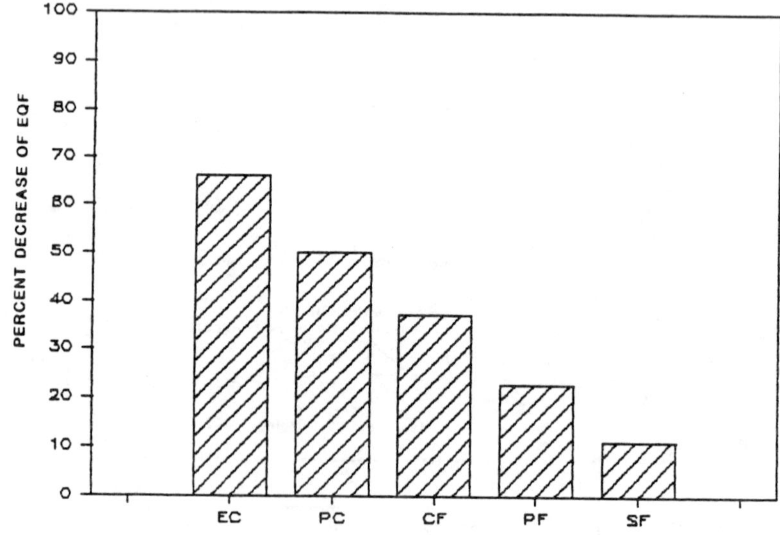

Figure 6. Effect of Radon Progeny Mitigation Techniques on the Whole House Equilibrium Factors

Summary and Discussion

As the research summarized in this paper exhibits, factors governing radon entry and control are complex and highly interrelated. As the regional and subregional analysis of indoor radon distributions suggests, indoor radon variability is large at both the regional and local levels and general rules of thumb for siting structures are not yet available. Other factors related to building design and HVAC operation are beginning to provide insight on how to reduce radon entry and transport into the house. However, the most promising area of current research is the dynamic analysis of building pressurization processes and their influence on radon entry and air infiltration. This line of research holds great potential for identifying the fundamental mechanisms that allow us not only to develop better systems for indoor radon control but also can help identify building weatherization criteria that will save energy and not increase indoor radon concentrations.

References

1. EPRI Indoor Environment - Programs and Perspectives (EU.3001.2.86), Environment Division, Energy Management and Utilization Division, Electric Power Research Institute, Palo Alto, California (1986).

2. C. S. Dudney, et. al., Indoor Air Quality in 70 Houses in the Tennessee Valley Area, Final Project Report, Oak Ridge National Laboratory (in press).

3. Alter, H. W., and Fliescher, R. L., 1981, "Passive Integrating Radon Monitor For Environmental Monitoring," Health Physics, 40, 693-702.

4. Hawthorne, A. R., Dudney, C. S., Tyndall, R. L., Vo-Dinh, T., Cohen, M. A., Spengler, J. D., and Harper, J. P., "Case Study: Multipollutant Indoor Air Quality Study of 300 Homes in Kingston/Harriman, Tennessee," Proceeding of ASTM Symposium on Design and Protocol for Monitoring Indoor Air Quality, ASTM Technical Publication (in press).

5. Dudney, C. S., Hawthorne, A. R., Bull, L. A., Cohen, M. A., Daffron, C. R., Orebaugh, C. T., and Harper, J. P., "Radon Levels in 300 Houses in Roane County, Tennessee," Proceeding 4th International Conference on Indoor Air Quality and Climate, Vol. (2), pp. 393-397, Berlin (West), August 17-21, 1987.

6. Dudney, C. S., and Hawthorne, A. R., Analysis of Indoor Air Quality Data from East Tennessee Field Studies, ORNL ITM-9588, TVA/P&E/C&EM-85/69, August 1985.

7. Harper, J. P., Dudney, C. S., Hawthorne, A. R., and Spengler, J. D., "Energy Use/Weatherization and Indoor Air Quality: Field Study Results," Proceeding 4th International Conference on Indoor Air Quality and Climate, Vol. (2), pp. 214-217, Berlin (West), August 17-21, 1987.

8. Matthews, T. G., Thompson, C. V., Monar, K. P., Dudney, C. S., Hawthorne, A. R., Harper, J. P., and Williams, A. B., "Impact of HVAC Operation and Leakage on Ventilation and Intercompartment Transport: Studies in a Research House and 39 Tennessee Valley Homes," Proceeding 4th International Conference on Indoor Air Quality and Climate, Vol. (3), pp. 209-213, Berlin (West), August 17-21, 1987.

9. Nagda, N. L., Koontz, M. D., and Rector, H. E., Energy Use, Infiltration, and Indoor Air Quality in Tight, Well-Insulated Residences, EA/EM-4117 Research Project 2034-1, Final Report, Electric Power Research Institute, Palo Alto, California, June 1985.

10. Harper, J. P., Hawthorne, A. R., and Dudney, C. S., "An Evaluation of Critical Factors Associated with Design, Protocol, Implementation, and Data Management of Large-Scale Multipollutant Indoor Air Quality Field Studies," J. Environmental Systems, Vol. 16(4), 1986-87, pp. 279-293.

11. Fortmann, R. C., Nagda, N. L., and Harper, J. P., "Radon Mitigation Through Residential Pressurization Control Strategy," Proceeding 4th International Conference on Indoor Air Quality and Climate, Vol. (2), pp. 300-304, Berlin (West), August 17-21, 1987.

12. Grimsrud, D. T., Turk, B. H., Prill, R. J., Harrison, J., and Revzan, K. L., "Effects of House Weatherization on Indoor Air Quality," Proceeding 4th International Conference on Indoor Air Quality and Climate, Vol. (2), pp. 208-213, Berlin (West), August 17-21, 1987.

ASHRAE'S RESPONSE TO THE INDOOR AIR QUALITY ISSUE

Preston McNall, Principal
Phoenix Engineers
Gaithersburg, Maryland

INTRODUCTION

The American Society of Heati ng, Refrigerating and Air-Conditioning Engineers, Inc. (ASHRAE) is a professional society of individuals from all over the world. There are no corporate members. Its main purpose is to "advance the arts and sciences of heating, refrigeration, air-conditioning and ventilation, and the allied arts and sciences, for the benefit of the general public". There are over 50,000 members, and while most are engineers associated with the design, manufacture and operation of the equipment and systems to control the interior environments of buidings, full membership status is accorded to non-engineering professionals in allied fields such as chemistry, physics, material science, environmental health, etc.

One of ASHRAE's predecessor societies, established in 1895, was the American Society of Heating and Ventilating Engineers, (ASHVE). You will notice that "ventilation" was in the title! Indeed, ventilation has been and is a major concern with ASHRAE.

Of course there are several purposes of ventilation for buildings. Most of them are listed below.

1. To establish acceptable indoor air quality.
2. To establish acceptable indoor air temperature.
3. To establish acceptable indoor humidity.
4. To establish acceptable indoor air velocity. (Items 2-4 are necessary to establish acceptable indoor thermal comfort for the occupants, and the largest quantity of ventilation is almost always needed for temperature control.)
5. To remove excess heat, humidity and contamination.
6. To provide pressure differences between building zones for various purposes.
7. To sometimes provide additional air velocity for comfort in hot environments.

ASHRAE provides many services for its members and the public, and most of those services have an air quality component. They will be covered below as they apply to indoor air quality problems. Although ASHRAE has been active and concerned with air quality for nearly 100 years, there have been a conjunction of events recently which have intensified the need for renewed concern. One of these events was the "energy crisis" of the early 1970's. This caused a stampede to reduce energy use in buildings, (and elsewhere). Actions here caused the following important changes.

1. A purposeful reduction in outdoor air use for ventilation,

which saves considerable energy.

2. Construction practices which reduce the "unwanted" leakage of outdoor air through infiltration.

These actions significantly increase the contaminant levels of any building contaminants which are internally generated. (Measurements in commercial buildings taken by the National Bureau of Standards and others have shown that this uncontrolled leakage in pre-energy efficient buildings is often enough to satisfy the air quality requirements of such buildings with <u>no</u> additional mechanical ventilation.)

3. There has been increased use of unvented combustion appliances, as well as a reluctance to use dedicated exhaust fans, to save energy, particularly in residences.

In addition to energy concerns, many new materials have rapidly found their way into buildings. Many of these can cause increased outgassing of materials not heretofore common.

1. Stuctural plastics, furniture and coatings have been introduced.
2. New machines and processes have been proliferating.
3. New cleaning and maintenance products have also been introduced and find increased use.

A third factor is significantly increased publicity about indoor air problems, and the associated technical developements. These result in:

1. Research which has identified old materials we commonly lived with as being possible health hazards.
2. Measurement advances which make possible identification of both old and new materials at extremely low levels, thereby implicating materials previously thought to be unimportant.
3. Press coverage of many cases of "sick building syndrome" and other problems like Legionnaire's disease. These increase public awareness and in many cases have caused public attention to be focused on indoor air contaminants as being health threats.

STANDARDS

ASHRAE has had a long history of developing technical consensus standards. These documents, (there are about 65 now,) cover many areas of utility to the HVAC practice. These are developed by consensus, being written by a committee of experts and users, balanced in their technologies. Each is then made available for public comment, and the conflicts resolved in so far as possible. The American National Standards Institute recognizes ASHRAE as an approved standards writing body in its areas of expertise. These standards are strictly voluntary after ASHRAE release, and have no force in law. However, legal entities, particularly building codes, can and do adopt them in whole or in part as law. In the case of several, including the ASHRAE Ventilation Standard 62, these are the only documents available which are developed by the consensus process.

For indoor air quality, ASRAE Standard 62, "Ventilation for Acceptable Air Quality" is the most important. ASHRAE assumed responsibility for that standard in 1965, employing as the reference standard the American Standards Association Standard 53.1, "Light and Ventilation", 1946. The resulting product was ASHRAE Standard 62-73, "Standards for Natural and Mechanical Ventilation". This standard found its way into practically all building codes in the US, and was also used abroad. The energy crisis was anticipated in that document by including some alternate procedures to save energy by recirculating return air through high-quality particulate and gas filters.

ASHRAE's procedures require revising, reaffirming, or withdrawing all standards on a five-year cycle, and so Standard 62 was revised during the energy crisis, and reissued as Standard 62-1981, "Ventilation for Acceptable Air Quality". It retained most of the provisions of 62-73, but updated them. It introduced a two-path approach. The ventilation rate method, in which the designer was to make sure the outdoor air was adequate, and supply quantities of it to various spaces, as noted in several pages of tables, specifying different rates for occupants in different spaces, according to their activities expected in those spaces, (offices, barrooms, etc.). It also provided for recirculating return air through filters and had several other options to save energy. In addition, an air quality approach was introduced, whereby the de -signer could use any inovative options, so long as he could provide an acceptable environment, as evidenced by a rather extensive table of contaminants with concentrations which should not be exceeded. It was realized that that option would be seldom, if ever used, since the designer cannot control what goes on in the space, let alone be responsible for it. However it was hoped that many innovations of promise might be encouraged.

Because of several questions on the ability of the current 1981 standard to provide the best state-of-the-art, and in view objections by an industry, ASHRAE decided to immediately put the standard into early revision, with a new project committee. They have been working hard at this, and the current draft has been reviewed by the public. The committee has been dealing with the comments, and approval is expected by early 1988. Until then, Standard 62-1981 is the only ASHRAE-approved ventilation standard.

The major objection with Standard 62-1981 was that the minimum outdoor air requirement was too low, at 5 cubic feet per minmute per person. This was thought to elicit complaints in use. The revision calls for 15 cfm/person. The figure on the next page summarizes the ventilation guidelines and standards as they have changed over the years. The 1836 data was developed in England by Tregold, to protect underground miners. It turns out that his number of 4 cfm/person is a good minimum for physiological needs, and comfort and health, at least chronic health were not probably considered. The later work, involving ASHVE and ASHRAE positions, have evolved from good practices, considering the very bad air quality around industrial areas in the past, as well as the

HISTORY OF RECOMMENDED VENTILATION RATES

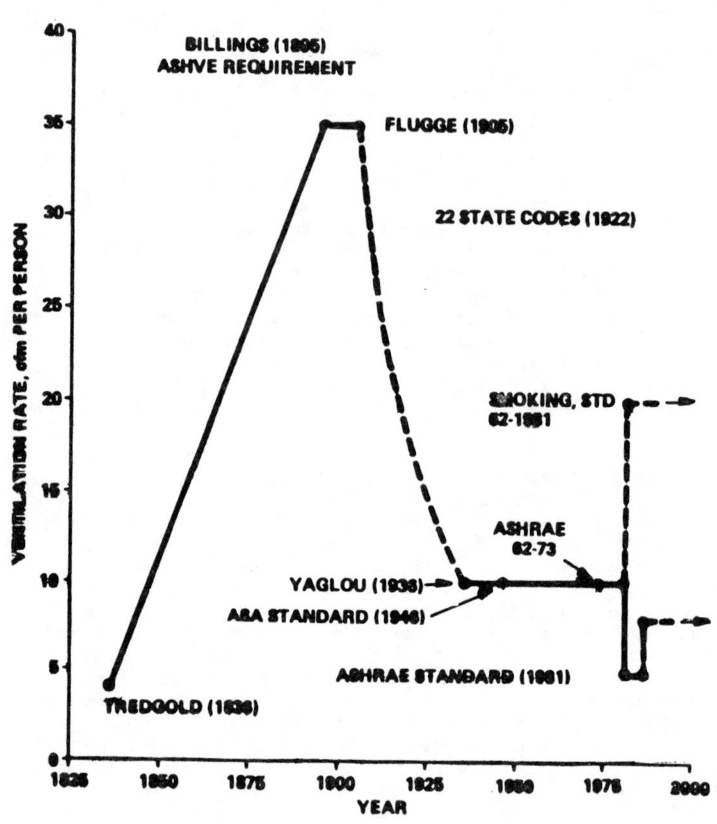

personal hygiene, and comfort expectations, which have changed considerably over time. Energy, of course, was not much of a problem in the past when the principles of heating and ventilating were being developed and applied. When Yaglou, a famous physiologist working with ASHVE in the 1930's, began to put more science and human response to odors, he came up with 10 cfm/ person as a minimum, when the environments were not unduely contaminated. It appears that 15 cfm/person may be the acceptable new minimum. Of course, more air is needed for many practical situations covered in the standard.

With the fast-moving pace of research in air quality, there will always be room for changing practices for the better.

Several other standards of ASHRAE apply to indoor air quality, and they will be mentioned briefly.

Air Cleaner Test Standard, 52-1981. This standard specifies how to properly test both low efficiency and high efficiency particulate air cleaners. It is currently being revised.

In addition to particle removal test methods, gas removal test methods are sorely needed. ASHRAE is planning to develop an appropriate standard when the necessary research is completed.

ASHRAE is also developing a standard on how to measure ventilation effectiveness. Ventilation effectiveness is a measure of how well, or poorly, the ventilation delivered to a space actually gets to the people in the occupied zone. Preliminary research indicates that even when the proper ventilation quantities are introduced into a space, often there is a considerable fraction which bypasses the space.

Also under development is a guideline spelling out how building HVAC systems should be commissioned, or set up to operate as designed. Many air quality complaints are due to inadequate operation of otherwise good systems.

ASHRAE also has a thermal comfort standard, 55. It has been shown that people often confuse being too warm with a "stuffy" feeling, or poor air quality. ASHRAE feels that without thermal comfort, no general comfort can exist.

Energy conservation is very important to ASHRAE, and its famous Standard 90 has been referenced in most energy codes in the US. It references Standard 62 in its provisions. The Standard 100 series for existing buildings also references Standard 62, in its provisions for energy saving.

RESEARCH

ASHRAE is unique in operating its own research program over the last 50 years. For the first 20 years or so it had its own lab and staff. In 1959 ASHRAE closed its laboratory and instituted a program of funding proposals from universities and other labs, so as to obtain the most appropriate staff and facilities for its changing needs. The funding for this research is from a portion of the member's dues, voluntary contributions from companies in the HVAC industry, local chapters of ASHRAE, and a portion of the profit generated from ASHRAE's annual equipment shows in connection with its Winter meetings. Currently research at the rate of about $1,000,000 per year is funded. Several years ago ASHRAE targeted 20% of its research to environmental problems. While this is not "big bucks" compared to government research, it is important to ASHRAE. ASHRAE has instituted a strategic plan, which calls for doubling its research expenditures for environmental concerns by 1990.

Currently there are some research projects which show ASHRAE's concern, and they will be mentioned. One is an extensive project to document the air quality in three different office buildings. One is a "standard" office, built according to the usual practices. Another is one in which complaints by the occupants have occurred over some years, and the third is a new office designed, constructed and furnished with features and materials which are felt to minimize indoor air quality problems. The results should be useful.

Two other projects are investigating operating problems with airto-air heat exchangers of the plate-type and enthalpy exchange type. These devices have great air quality and energy saving potential.

Two other projects are investigating the operation and leakage of special dust collectors and exhaust hoods. These devices need better application data and will be more important as partial solutions to air quality problems.

POSITION PAPERS

ASHRAE has developed several position papers on important subjects. These outline official, board of directors approved documents on various subjects for use by the public. ASHRAE has had a position paper on Indoor Air Quality since 1981, and has revised it in 1987. It states what ASHRAE is going to do about the subject, and also states recommendations which the Government and others should do to help solve this problem. Another recent paper outlines ASHRAE's position on the CFC problem, as it affects the ozone layer and the international living standard.

PROGRAMS

ASHRAE has traditionally put on two programs per year, covering all aspects of its interest. Currently ther are 350-400 separate presentations. The next meeting is in Dallas in Feb. 1988, and it has about 40 indoor air programs. About 3500 people will attend. In 1986 ASHRAE recognized the growing importance of air quality, and instituted a special Spring program devoted to air quality, called "IAQ 86". This program stressed the <u>engineering</u>

solutions to problems, rather than include only the research efforts, which most other programs stress. This sucessful program was repeated in 1987, and is planned again for 1988, to be a regular feature.

ASHRAE has a local chapter network of over 150 chapters in North-America and overseas. In the past several years, many of these chapters have organized and conducted special one-day seminars on indoor air quality. People in their local areas are attracted to these seminars, and interest in them is increasing.

PUBLICATIONS

ASHRAE publications are extensive. All program material is archived in its Transactions. Here all air quality information presented is included. A monthly magazine, the "ASHRAE Journal", includes air quality articles from all sources. The "Bible" of the industry is the Handbook, revised every four years. It includes more and more air quality information. Special Publications, covering air quality and other timely subjects are issued regularly. As previously mentioned, all of the Standards are published and are for sale to all interested parties. ASHRAE also develops special slide shows, suitable for viewing by technical and non-technical people. Recently ASHRAE has released a 40 minute air quality slide show with a sound suppliment under this program.

A NEW COMMITTEE

To better respond to environmental problems, ASHRAE established a new Standing Committee, the "Environmental Health Committee". This committee is staffed with many experts new to ASHRAE. They include medical doctors, epidemiologists, health physicists, bacteriologists, etc. These technologies will help ASHRAE broaden its research, and make its engineering applications more meaningful.

WASHINGTON FORUMS

For the past several years ASHRAE has conducted these "Washington Forums". These are one-half day programs for government officials in all interested areas of the subject matter. Their purpose is to inform the government of ASHRAE's expertise and interest in various subjects. While in the first years energy was most important, lately indoor air quality has been a major focus of these special programs.

CONCLUSIONS

As is evident, ASHRAE has long been involved in indoor air quality problems, and is increasing its efforts now and in the future. Its Standard 62 is vital to public health, as it is incorporated in almost all building codes. ASHRAE realizes that the application of its designs and products in practical ventilating systems, while not the total answer to indoor air quality problems, is a vital part of the solution. ASHRAE is committed to increase its knowledge and applications to help solve this growing international problem.

INDOOR AIR QUALITY INVESTIGATIONS IN OFFICE BUILDINGS

Kenneth M. Wallingford, CIH, Manager of Field Services
DataChem, Inc., 4388 Glendale-Milford Road
Cincinnati, Ohio 45242

ABSTRACT

Although not a "new" phenomenon, complaints regarding the quality of the indoor environment have increased substantially since the oil crises of 1974 and 1979. These oil crises understandably created a desire to conserve energy as oil became substantially more expensive. Ultimately, they led to changes in the way buildings were designed, constructed, and operated. These changes have made today's office workers totally dependent on mechanical systems for the quality and comfort of their indoor environment. A number of non-specific complaints are commonly associated with poor indoor air quality such as headache, eye, nose and throat irritation, sinus congestion, and fatigue. Generally, a similar cluster of these symptoms occur in all affected employees during working hours only to be alleviated or disappear entirely when away from the office. Thus, this is what implicates the indoor air as the suspected cause. At the present time, the largest compilation of indoor air quality investigations in office buildings are those conducted by the National Institute for Occupational Safety and Health (NIOSH) through their Health Hazard Evaluation program. In the 446 indoor air quality investigations conducted by NIOSH, problems were found to result from contaminants generated by building material sources in 3 percent, microbiological sources in 5 percent, exterior sources in 11 percent, interior sources in 17 percent, and inadequate ventilation in 52 percent. The remaining 12 percent represent those in which NIOSH investigators could not find a specific problem.

INTRODUCTION

Indoor air pollution and the compromised quality of the indoor environment is a problem that is now recognized to be of major importance to the health and well-being of the general population. It has been estimated that urban residents typically average more than 90% of their total time indoors and are, therefore, more likely to be affected by contaminated indoor air [1]. To date, much of the research regarding indoor air pollution has focused on homes and the family members. However, many of those people who work spend much of their time away from their homes but still indoors--in their offices. There has been increasing evidence that poor indoor air quality (IAQ) also affects these office workers, many of whom may actually find relief at home [2]. Although more information is becoming available concerning the office environment, the available data is still sorely limited. Currently, the largest compiled set of IAQ data available regarding the office environment is that work conducted by the National Institute for Occupational Safety and Health (NIOSH) through their Health Hazard Evaluation program [3,4]. I will discuss this NIOSH data since it provides a good overview of the IAQ problems in office buildings and provides some insight into the relationship between IAQ and energy conservation.

BACKGROUND

In the late 1970's, occupational health professionals at NIOSH began to notice an increasing number of requests for health hazard evaluation from non-industrial workers (ie. office workers) [5]. Traditionally, the industrial environment had been the only concern of the NIOSH industrial hygienists since that was where the hazardous working conditions were. This slowly changed, however, as a trend toward non-industrial problems developed. As shown in Table 1, requests for NIOSH IAQ evaluations increased dramatically since 1979 and quickly reached their saturation point in 1981 [3,4]. This represents an increase in the total number of NIOSH health hazard evaluations conducted annually from less than 1 percent in 1978 to about 20 percent at the present time and emphasizes the current importance of IAQ problems in office buildings [3,6]. This increase corresponds with an increase in the energy awareness of this country. In 1974 and again in 1979, we experienced oil crises that dramatically increased the cost of energy. What followed was a concerted effort to conserve energy use in office buildings through changes in the way these building were designed, constructed, ventilated, and operated. New building materials were used, different ventilation designs were developed, and existing systems were operated more efficiently. This all impacted on IAQ as evidenced by the fact that about half of those buildings investigated by NIOSH had IAQ problems caused or exacerbated by a conscious effort to conserve energy [2,4].

TABLE 1

NIOSH INDOOR AIR QUALITY INVESTIGATIONS BY YEAR (THROUGH DECEMBER 1986) [3,4]

Year	Number Completed	Percent
Pre-1978	6	1
1978	9	2
1979	12	3
1980	28	6
1981	82	18
1982	52	12
1983	61	14
1984	56	13
1985	81	18
1986	59	13
Total:	446	100

These 446 NIOSH IAQ investigations (Table 1) were conducted by request only [3,4]. In that respect, these studies were not conducted for research but to find a resolution to an existing IAQ problem. Other shortcomings to this NIOSH data set include the lack of a standard protocol for the conduct of all these studies, potential misclassification during retrospective review, and the lack of a deliberate follow-up mechanism to determine the efficacy of recommendations. In addition, asbestos problems are not presented since this data set only includes those cases where people were experiencing acute health effects at the time of the investigation [3,4,5,7].

A number of non-specific complaints are commonly associated with poor IAQ such as headache, eye, nose and throat irritation or dryness, sinus congestion, and fatigue. Other health effects such as skin irritation, cough, dizziness and nausea are also seen at times. Generally, a similar cluster of these symptoms occur in all affected employees. The workplace is suspected as the cause of these symptom clusters since they disappear in the evenings and weekends away from the office, only to reappear upon the return to work. At times, these symptoms are severe enough to result in missed work, reassignment, and even termination [3,4,5,7,8]. Although there are currently no conclusive data available on the subject, it seems reasonable to assume that worker satisfaction and productivity can be severely affected by this problem.

DISCUSSION

In these 446 investigations, NIOSH found a wide variety of apparent causes of IAQ problems. Although some of these IAQ problems are probably multifactorial in nature, they are simplified by the groupings of primary causes shown in Table 2. In these groupings, the primary cause of poor IAQ was found to be contamination generated by interior sources in 17 percent, exterior sources in 11 percent, building material sources in 3 percent, microbiological sources in 5 percent, and inadequate ventilation in 52 percent. The remaining 12 percent represent those investigations in which no specific problem could be found [3,4].

TABLE 2

NIOSH INDOOR AIR QUALITY INVESTIGATIONS BY PROBLEM TYPE (THROUGH DECEMBER 1986) [3,4]

Problem Type	Number Completed	Percent
Interior Sources	74	17
Exterior Sources	48	11
Building Material Sources	16	3
Microbiological Sources	24	5
Inadequate Ventilation	231	52
Unknown	53	12
Total:	446	100

Interior Sources

Contamination generated by sources inside the office space was the major problem identified in 17 percent of the NIOSH IAQ investigations [3,4]. Some examples of this type of contamination include that from wet-process copy machines such as methyl alcohol from spirit duplicators [9], butyl methacrylate from signature machines [10], and ammonia and acetic acid from blueprint copiers [4]. Other inside contaminants include tobacco smoke [4], pesticides (such as chlordane) [11], boiler additives (such as diethyl ethanolamine) [12,13], cleaning agents (such as rug shampoo) [14], combustion products (such as those from cafeterias and laboratories) [4], and cross-contamination from poorly ventilated sources that leak into other air handling zones [15]. Generally, most interior contaminants can be controlled at the source or diluted to acceptable levels using general ventilation. Sometimes, energy conservation programs cause these inside sources to become significant problems. An illustration of this occurred in a school building investigated by NIOSH where energy costs were lowered by adding insulation to the walls and roof. Additional measures such as sealing outdoor air vents, installing storm windows, and caulking around doors had also been done. This created a negative pressure inside the school building so that the flue gases from the natural gas hot water heater back-drafted and the students and staff experienced acute carbon monoxide poisoning [15,16]. Fortunately, no serious injury resulted.

Exterior Sources

Contamination from sources outside the office building were the major problem identified by NIOSH in 11 percent of their IAQ investigations [3,4]. Problems due to motor vehicle exhaust, boiler gases, and previously exhausted are are essentially caused by reentrainment [3,4,15,17,18]. This is usually the result of improperly located exhaust and intake vents or periodic changes in wind conditions [4, 15]. Other outside contaminant sources include contaminants from construction or renovation such as asphalt, solvents, and dusts [3,4,19]. Some of these construction and renovation activities are part of energy conservation programs. One interesting case of an exterior source was gasoline fumes infiltrating a building. The concentration of gasoline fumes was at explosive levels in the building's basement and was caused by a 6 million gallon gasoline leak from a ruptured underground tank at a nearby facility [5, 20,21].

Building Material Sources

Contamination from building materials and products were the major problem in 3 percent of the NIOSH IAQ investigations [3,4]. Examples of this problem include fibrous glass from the interior of lined ventilating ducts [22], various organic solvents from glues and adhesives [3,4], and acetic acid, a curing agent used in the manufacture of silicone caulking [3,4]. Perhaps the most widely known problem of this type is that of formaldehyde which can off-gas from urea-formaldehyde foam insulation (UFFI), particle board, plywood, and other composite wood products as well as many glues and adhesives [3,4]. In an investigation of a number of National Park Service buildings that had been insulated with UFFI, indoor formaldehyde levels ranging up to 0.2 ppm were measured four years after installation of the UFFI [23,24]. The air in these buildings so irritated the workers that they were moved to other facilities. The UFFI was then removed from the buildings. UFFI has also been reported by others to be the cause of many building-related problems and, as a result, is no longer widely used [25].

Interior, exterior, and building material sources are essentially chemical contaminants. Most commonly, these contaminants are measured at levels above ambient, but below any existing occupational standard.

Microbiological Sources

Although the NIOSH data indicate microbiological contamination as a problem in only 5 percent of their total number of IAQ investigations, it can result in potentially severe medical conditions such as Legionnaires' disease, Pontiac fever, hypersensitivity pneumonitis, and humidifier fever [3,4]. These respiratory problems can be caused by several different microorganisms [26,27]. In the next paper, Dr. Morey will discuss this particular problem in much greater detail.

Inadequate Ventilation

In 52 percent of the NIOSH IAQ investigations, the building ventilation was determined to be inadequate in some way [3,4]. ASHRAE Standards 62-1981, "Ventilation for Acceptable Indoor Air Quality" [28] and 55-1981, "Thermal Environmental Conditions for Human Occupancy" [29] were used in the majority of these studies as performance criteria. The most commonly identified problems of this type were: insufficient outdoor air supplied to the office space; poor air distribution and mixing which can cause statification, draftiness, and pressure differences between office spaces; temperature and humidity extremes or fluctuations (sometimes caused by poor air distribution); and poor maintenance practices [3,4]. In most cases, these ventilation problems were created or exacerbated by certain energy conservation measures which include: reducing or eliminating the introduction of outdoor air; reducing infiltration and exfiltration; lowering thermostats in winter, raising them in summer; eliminating humidification or dehumidification systems; and early shut-down and late start-up of the ventilation system (compressed cycling) [3, 4].

In this category, the single largest cause of problems was insufficient outdoor air. Of course, an easy way to conserve energy is to reduce or eliminate the supply of outdoor air. This apparently is quite common. In several cases, the building ventilation systems were not even designed to supply outdoor air. In several other cases, the supply air grilles were not only closed, but were sealed shut to prevent any leakage. Mostly though, the supply air grilles were closed allowing only the outdoor air due to leakage (5 to 10 percent) to come into the building. In these cases, infiltration helped supply some additional outdoor air; however, it seldom was enough and in some buildings, this had also been reduced through additional insulation and caulking. In addition to poor temperature control caused by poor design, temperature can also be a problem where thermostats are lowered in winter and raised in summer to conserve energy. Additionally, compressed cycling such as that adopted by many building managers does not allow sufficient purge time, prior to building occupation each morning, to sufficiently dilute many indoor air contaminants [3,4].

CONCLUSION

Although most IAQ research to date has focused on residential construction, office buildings can also have IAQ problems that can affect large numbers of people at a time. The best available data regarding office building IAQ problems is that collected and compiled by NIOSH. This NIOSH data indicate that the primary causes of IAQ problems in office buildings can be placed into three general categories (in decreasing order): inadequate ventilation, chemical contamination (mostly that which is generated within the office space), and microbial contamination. About half of these IAQ problems appear to be either caused or exacerbated by a desire to conserve energy. Although beyond the scope of this brief paper, there are ways to conserve energy while still providing acceptable indoor air quality. Those methodologies should be pursued whenever developing control strategies for any IAQ problem.

REFERENCES

1. Spengler, J.D. and Sexton, K.: Indoor Air Pollution: A Public Health Perspective. Science 221:9-17 (1983).
2. Wallingford, K.M. and Carpenter, J.: Office Ecology. Leaders 9:150-151 (1986).
3. Gorman, R.W. and Wallingford, K.M.: The NIOSH Approach to Conducting Indoor Air Quality Investigations in Office Buildings in: Proceedings of the ASTM Symposium on Design and Protocol for Monitoring Indoor Air Quality. ASTM, Philadelphia, PA (in press).
4. Wallingford, K.M.: Indoor Air Quality: The NIOSH Air Quality Investigations. Presented at the American Occupational Health Conference Postgraduate Seminar No. 4: Indoor Air Complaints: Causes and Prevention, Philadelphia, PA (1987).
5. Melius, J.M., Wallingford, K.M., Keenlyside, R.A., and Carpenter, J.: Indoor Air Quality--The NIOSH Experience. Ann. Am. Conf. Gov. Ind. Hyg. 10:3-7 (1984).
6. Flesch, J.P.: Personal Communication. NIOSH, Cincinnati, OH (1987).
7. Wallingford, K.M. and Carpernter, J.: Field Experience Overview: Investigating Sources of IAQ Problems in Office Building in: Proceedings of the ASHRAE IAQ '86 Symposium: Managing Indoor Air for Health and Energy Conservation, pp. 448-453. ASHRAE, Atlanta, GA (1986).
8. National Institute for Occupational Safety and Health: Guidance for Indoor Air Quality Investigations. NIOSH, Cincinnati, OH (1987).
9. Centers for Disease Control: Methyl Alcohol Toxicity in Teacher Aides Using Spirit Duplicators - Washington. Morbidity & Mortality Weekly Report 29:437-438 (1980).
10. National Institute for Occupational Safety and Health: Congressman Cavanaugh's Office. Health Hazard Evaluation Report No. HETA 80-067-754. NIOSH, Cincinnati, OH (1980).
11. National Institute for Occupational Safety and Health: Georgetown University. Health Hazard Evaluation Report No. HETA 83-444. NIOSH, Cincinnati, OH (1984).
12. National Institute for Occupational Safety and Health: Boehringer-Ingelheim, Ltd. Health Hazard Evaluation Report No. HETA 81-247-958. NIOSH, Cincinnati, OH (1981).

13. National Institute for Occupational Safety and Health: Cornell University. Health Hazard Evaluation Report No. HETA 83-020-1351. NIOSH, Cincinnati, OH (1983).
14. Kreiss, K., Gonzalez, M.G., Conright, K.L., and Scheere, A.R.: Respiratory Irritation Due to Carpet Shampoo: Two Outbreaks. Environ. Internat. 8:337-341 (1982).
15. Gorman, R.W.: Cross Contamination and Entrainment. Ann. Am. Conf. Gov. Ind. Hyg. 10:115-120 (1984).
16. National Institute for Occupational Safety and Health: Wappingers Falls School. Health Hazard Evaluation Report No. HETA 83-172-1409. NIOSH, Cincinnati, OH (1984).
17. National Institute for Occupational Safety and Health: Department of Justice. Health Hazard Evaluation Report No. HETA 80-024-887. NIOSH, Cincinnati, OH (1981).
18. National Institute for Occupational Safety and Health: Cincinnati Technical College. Health Evaluation Report No. HETA 82-269-1341. NIOSH, Cincinnati, OH (1983).
19. National Institute for Occupational Safety and Health: McCalls Publishing Company. Health Hazard Evaluation Report No. HETA 81-097-1021. NIOSH, Cincinnati, OH (1981).
20. National Institute for Occupational Safety and Health: Boise Medical Arts Center. Health Hazard Evaluation Report No. HETA 82-062-1077. NIOSH, Cincinnati, OH (1982).
21. Centers for Disease Control: Employee Illness for Underground Gas and Oil Contamination--Idaho. Morbidity & Mortality Weekly Report 31:451-453 (1982).
22. National Institute for Occupational Safety and Health: Ellis Hospital. Health Hazard Evaluation Report No. TA 80-080. NIOSH, Cincinnati, OH (1980).
23. National Institute for Occupational Safety and Health: National Park Service. Health Hazard Evaluation Report No. HETA 81-241-970. NIOSH, Cincinnati, OH (1981).
24. National Institute for Occupational Safety and Health: National Park Service. Health Hazard Evaluation Report No. HETA 82-337-1163. NIOSH, Cincinnati, OH (1982).
25. Gammage, R.B. and Gupta, K.C.: Formaldehyde in: Walsh, C., Dudney, P., and Copenhaver, E. eds. Indoor Air Quality, pp. 109-139. CRC Press, Boca Raton, FL (1984).
26. Morey, P.R., Hodgson, M.J., Sorenson, W.G., Kullman, G.J., Rhodes, W.W., and Visvesvara, G.S.: Environmental Studies in Moldy Office Buildings: Biological Agents, Sources and Preventive Measures. Ann. Am. Conf. Gov. Ind. Hyg. 10:21-35 (1984).
27. Hodgson, M.J. and Kreiss, K.: Building-Associated Diseases: An Update in: Proceedings of the ASHRAE IAQ '86 Symposium: Managing Indoor Air for Health and Energy Conservation, pp. 1-15. ASHRAE, Atlanta, GA (1986).
28. American Society of Heating, Refrigerating and Air-Conditioning Engineers, Inc.: ASHRAE Standard 62-1981, Ventilation for Acceptable Indoor Air Quality. ASHRAE, Atlanta, GA (1981).

29. American Society of Heating, Refrigerating and Air-Conditioning Engineers, Inc.: ASHRAE Standard 55-1981, Thermal Environmental Conditions for Human Occupancy. ASHRAE, Atlanta, GA (1981).

MICROBIOLOGICAL PROBLEMS IN OFFICE BUILDINGS RECOGNITION AND REMEDIAL ACTION

PHILIP R. MOREY
CLAYTON ENVIRONMENTAL CONSULTANTS, INC.
160 FIELDCREST AVENUE
EDISON, NEW JERSEY 08837

INTRODUCTION

When dealing with indoor air quality problems in office buildings, it is important to recognize that airborne microbial contaminants generally cause specific adverse health effects (building-related illnesses, BRI) among occupants. On the other hand, most indoor air contaminants, such as volatile organic compounds, bioeffluents, and environmental tobacco smoke are known to affect occupants by eliciting a number of annoyance and discomfort complaints, collectively known as sick building syndrome (SBS). The objective of this presentation is to provide the reader with a basis for distinguishing between BRI caused by microorganisms and the more common occurrence of SBS which is usually associated with ineffective or insufficient outdoor air ventilation.

The differences between SBI and BRI caused by microorganisms will be illustrated by case studies. Procedures for recognizing microbiological contamination in mechanical systems and in the occupied space will be discussed. Lastly, remedial actions based on elimination of water and nutrients needed for microbiological growth and on good preventive maintenance of mechanical systems will be described.

TYPES OF AIR QUALITY COMPLAINTS

The three most common types of indoor air quality complaints are SBS, BRI, and thermal discomfort. All three types of problems or any combination may exist in an office. BRI is the least common of the three.

SBS occurs when a significant number of occupants (generally more than 20 percent) offer nonspecific complaints, such as headache, fatigue, and eye, nose, and upper respiratory irritation. Relief occurs almost immediately after occupants leave the building. The source of air contaminants causing the problem is generally not recognizable. Mitigation is brought about by modifying the operation of the heating, ventilating, and air-conditioning (HVAC) system, especially by the introduction of more outdoor air. Several classes of indoor air contaminants, including volatile organic compounds, odors, bioeffluents, and environmental tobacco smoke, are thought to be important causes of SBS.

The term BRI is used to refer to disease recognizable in one or more occupants by physical signs and laboratory findings. Examples include lung cancer that may be caused by radon or asbestos and dermatitis caused by fibrous glass. Examples of BRI caused by airborne microbiological contaminants are infection (for example, legionellosis) and allergic respiratory disease (for example, humidifier fever and hypersensitivity pneumonitis).

In the case of the pneumonic form of legionellosis, the infective microorganism, Legionella pneumophila, invades or colonizes the lung of a susceptible person. On the other hand, allergic respiratory diseases are caused by a hypersensitivity response to inhaled particles that may contain viable microorganisms, nonviable spores, or nonliving components (antigens) of these organisms. An allergic respiratory illness known as humidifier fever is characterized by fever, chills, muscle aches, and fatigue without prominent pulmonary symptoms.

Hypersensitivity pneumonitis is a more severe allergic respiratory illness characterized by symptoms ranging from acute recurrent pneumonias with fever, cough, chest tightness, and muscle aches to restriction in pulmonary function and a pattern of exercise tolerance test findings compatible with interstitial lung disease. These allergic illnesses occur in indoor environments, such as offices, because some occupants are affected by microbiological antigens that may be aerosolized from HVAC system components, such as humidifiers or from office furnishings (for example, carpet and wall coverings) that have been damaged by recurrent floods or moisture. Individuals with these types of BRI usually experience relief if they leave the building for a few days.

Thermal problems in the indoor environment should not be overlooked when dealing with air quality complaints. Discomfort arising from excessive warmth and humidity in summer or a cold and dry indoor climate in winter can occur independently or in addition to SBS or BRI. Thermal environmental problems will not be discussed further in this presentation. The interested reader should refer to American Society of Heating, Refrigerating, and Air-conditioning Engineers (ASHRAE) Standard 55 for an excellent source of guidance for mitigation of this type of air quality problem(1).

CASE STUDY NO. 1 - SBS WITHOUT MICROBIOLOGICAL COMPLICATION

The facilities engineer responsible for the operation of a new 200,000 square foot office building (Building A) reported that over 50 percent of the occupants complained of "stuffy" air, especially during the winter heating season. Complaints of headache, fatigue, and eye and nose irritation were common.

Some individuals had difficulty wearing contact lenses in their offices; the same individuals had no problem with contact lenses while at home or while traveling on company business. Several office managers reported that a number of occupants left the building during their lunch breaks and momentarily felt better, until they returned to work.

A consultant hired by the owners of Building A conducted a number of environmental tests and found that while there were no Occupational Safety and Health Administration violations, a bacterium, *Staphylococcus epidermidis*, was found on desks in many offices. In the consultant's report to the owner, it was noted that similar microorganisms (*Staphylococcus aureus*) are known to cause infections in hospitals.

Did the occupants of Building A suffer from SBS or was this an example of BRI? Further discussions with Building A's facilities engineer revealed that an energy conservation plan was being used so that even the minimal outdoor air ventilation requirements [5 cubic feet per minute (cfm) of outdoor air per occupant] recommerded by ASHRAE Standard 62-1981[2] were not achieved. When this energy conservation program was relaxed so that approximately 15 cfm of outdoor air per occupant was supplied, most complaints associated with indoor air ceased. It should be noted that *Staphylococcus epidermidis* is a common skin bacterium normally shed in large numbers by humans. Its presence, therefore, on the surfaces of office desks is of no consequence. The presence of *Staphylococcus* in a surgical wound of a susceptible individual in a hospital operating room has no relevance to indoor air quality problems in office buildings.

CASE STUDY NO. 2 - BRI LIKELY DUE TO MICROORGANISMS

Building B is a 35-hear old, 10-story building with a constant air volume HVAC system including induction units for perimeter heating or cooling and separate air handling units providing conditioned air to core areas on each floor. Complaints of irritation due to environmental tobacco smoke as well as headache and fatigue were reported sporadically in zones on several floors. Occupants in zones on all floors indicated that the thermal climate indoors, especially in the summer, was unsatisfactory; during the summer months it was always excessively warm and humid.

One occupant of Building B had developed a severe, chronic cough that was exacerbated after entry into the building, especially after extended periods of absence due to travel or vacation. This individual also had consistently high titers of antibodies against *Micropolyspora faeni*, a bacterium (thermophilic actinomycete) that has been implicated as a causative agent of hypersensitivity pneumonitis in other environments [3]. Thus, in Building B, medical opinion suggested that BRI due to exposure to *Micropolyspora faeni* was a possibility.

Air sampling was conducted indoors as well as outdoors to determine if unusual numbers or kinds of microorganisms could be detected in the complainant's work area. Collection of airborne thermophilic actinomycetes revealed that only a few isolates were recovered in both the indoor and outdoor environments. Collection and rank ordering of airborne fungi showed that the complainant and nearby offices were dominated by a yeast-like fungus, Sporobolomyces, which did not occur in recoveries made outdoors. After considerable microbiological testing, the conclusion was that the source of indoor Sporobolomyces was the induction units. During the summer months, the units were moist and encrusted with dirt and debris. Because of certain constraints on this evaluation, it was not possible to determine if the affected occupant was "sensitive" to Sporobolomyces spp. and whether or not exposure to Micropolyspora faeni may have occurred in the residential environment.

Discussions with facilities engineers in Building B revealed that an energy management program had been initiated five or six years previously, and the 45 degree Fahrenheit (^{o}F) chilled water normally supplied to core air handling units was replaced with 55 ^{o}F water. The latent heat or moisture which was not adequately removed from indoor air during the summer months coincided with the onset of thermal discomfort complaints. As a result of the excessive indoor humidity, moisture condensed on the relatively cold metal surfaces of induction units (induction units are in peripheral wall locations in offices). Dirt and debris trapped for years in these units because of an inadequate preventive maintenance program together with the presence of moisture provided a niche for amplification of Sporobolomyces and other microorganisms. These microorganisms were easily aerosolized because of their location in the mechanical system.

Corrective actions for Building B involved the cleaning and disinfection of induction units and the initiation of a subsequent preventive maintenance program. It was also recommended that 45 ^{o}F chilled water be supplied to core air handling units during the summer months to ensure that adequate latent heat is removed from indoor air. A significant change in HVAC system operation and maintenance was thus required to eliminate indoor environmental conditions associated with the development of this possible case of BRI.

CASE STUDY nO. 3 - A POSSIBLE INSTANCE OF SBS AND BRI

Building C is more than 40 years old. Conditioned air is supplied to each floor by air handling units that are 15 to 20 years old. The furnishings on each floor, however, are new.

Supplemental heating and cooling as provided to peripheral zones by fan coil units located along exterior walls.

Between 30 and 40 percent of the occupants on several floors reported symptoms, such as headache and fatigue, upper respiratory and eye irritation, and annoyance from odors which were sometimes musty. The private physician of one individual who occupied a desk located in a peripheral office believed that this individual was allergic to something, possibly a mold, in the work environment. In Building C, it appeared possible that many occupants might be reporting SBS symptoms, while at the same time, one individual was being affected by a BRI (allergy).

An indoor air quality evaluation in Building C showed that the level of volatile organic compounds was high enough to possibly trigger the irritational symptoms associated with SBS. An examination of the air handling units serving the affected office showed that only the minimum amount of outdoor air possible was entering and mixing with a much greater amount of return air prior to conditioning and supply to the occupied space. It was unlikely, therefore, that the volatile organic compounds from new office furnishings were being sufficiently diluted by outdoor air.

Air sampling for mesophilic fungi was conducted in several offices including the one occupied by the individual with mold allergies. As a reference point additional collections for fungi were made outdoors. In general, levels of viable fungi recovered at indoor locations were about one order of magnitude less than outdoor collections. Recoveries were low indoors even when supply air diffusers and return registers were agitated or moved (so as to aerosolize particulate that may have settled on mechanical surfaces). When similar air sampling was carried out near the fan coil unit in the office occupied by the allergy complainant copious amounts of fungi (of a somewhat different distribution of taxa; Alternaria dominates outdoor collection; Penicillium spp. dominates air from the fan coil unit) were liberated. Examination of this unit revealed that the drain pan contained a pool of stagnant water (drain hole blocked), the porous manmade insulation on the inside surface of the housing was encrusted with dirt and debris, and considerable dirt and debris were also present beneath the unit.

It was concluded that SBS likely did exist in Building C, largely as a result of high levels of volatile organic compounds associated with inadequate outdoor air ventilation. Since definitive evidence was not available on the specific mold allergies of the occupant housed next to the contaminated fan coil unit, it is a matter of conjecture as to whether or not the complainant's problems were from microbiological contaminants or from contaminants normally associated with SBS (for example, volatile organic compounds).

Corrective actions for Building C were quite straight forward. It was recommended that the amount of outdoor air being supplied to occupied space be raised to comply with ASHRAE Standard 62. More than minimum amounts of outdoor air were recommended for those floors or zones where new office furnishings had recently been installed. A preventive maintenance program involving cleaning of fan coil units with a vacuum cleaner with a high efficiency particulate air (HEPA) filter, disinfection of drain pans, replacement of contaminated sound liners, and installation of filters was recommended to reduce the likelihood of microbiological proliferation in this component of the building's HVAC system.

REMEDIAL ACTIONS-GENERAL PRINCIPLES

Studies in these and other office buildings[3,4] show that three basic types of actions are effective in controlling microbiological contamination. Restricting the availability of both water and nutrients is the most direct method of limiting the growth of fungi, bacteria, and protozoans. Thus, moisture in the occupied space can be lowered by reducing the relative humidity (for example, in Building B) to levels below 70 percent to preclude the germination of fungal spores. In Building C mitigation by moisture control implies unplugging drain lines and removal of stagnant water from fan coil unit drain pans. Control of microbiological contamination by removal of nutrients (carbon sources) often takes the form of the installation of more efficient filters upstream of heat exchangers. Preventive maintenance is the third principle to be followed for the effective control of microbiological contamination. Although implied by moisture and substrate removal, preventive maintenance is not so easily accomplished. In mechanical systems, little thought is given to easy access into the heat exchanger section or other structural components of air handling units. Thus, proper access ports to potential niches for microbiological amplification (for example, hinged access doors near drain pans) and proper follow through with maintenance activities in well designed mechanical systems are essential aspects of mitigation.

REMEDIAL ACTIONS-WALKTHROUGH EXAMINATION

When BRI, such as hypersensitivity disorders, are thought to exist, a walkthrough examination of the occupied space and the HVAC system serving the affected area is recommended. During this examination, both the occupied space and the HVAC system are evaluated for potential reservoirs and amplification sites for microorganisms. Listed below are nine presumptive sources of microbiological contamination that can be easily recognized during a walkthrough evaluation (see also Reference 5).

(A) Cooling coil section of air handling and fan coil units - Microbiological amplification can occur on wetted surfaces of heat exchanger coils and in stagnant water in drain pans.

(B) Humidifiers with reservoirs of stagnant water - Nutrients accumulate in the reservoir, and amplification of microbial populations may occur in the reservoir itself (yeasts) or on seals and gaskets (for example, filamentous fungi).

(C) Water spray systems and air washers - Nutrients are scrubbed from the ventilation airstream and accumulate in water sumps where amplification occurs. Microbiological contaminants are aerosolized directly into the airstream.

(D) Fan coil and induction units - Amplification of microbiological populations occurs on wetted surfaces of cooling coils and drain pans, especially when preventive maintenance has been neglected.

(E) HVAC system filters - Amplification of microorganisms occurs when filters are wetted or when an excessively humid airstream is moved through the filter for an extended period of time.

(F) Sound liner in HVAC systems - Dirt and debris trapped within porosities of manmade insulation becomes a carbon source for microbial growth when wet or when humidity within the airstream is high (for example, near drain pans, cooling coil sections, and steam humidifiers).

(G) Outdoor air intake of HVAC system - Bioaerosol sources, such as cooling towers and evaporative condensers located near intakes, may contaminate HVAC systems. Wet surfaces of outdoor air intake plenums, especially in below grade locations, may be niches for microbiological amplification.

(H) Porous interior furnishings subjected to repeated water damage - Microbiological amplification occurs on carbon sources in furnishings. Antigenic materials may be released from water damaged furnishings even after drying.

(I) Relative humidity in the occupied space exceeds 70 percent - The moisture content in carbon sources (for example, organic dusts, cellulose, etc.) under these humid conditions is sufficient to support the germination of fungal spores.

SPECIFIC MITIGATION ACTIONS FOR MICROBIOLOGICAL CONTAMINATION

When presumptive sources of microbiological contamination are recognized (for example, A-I, previously listed), mitigation is often quite straightforward. Occupant complaints may be resolved, and complicated bioaerosol sampling procedures may thus be avoided. Specific corrective actions for office buildings ultimately take the form of intercepting microbiological amplification by means of moisture and nutrient control and good preventive maintenance. Space limitations do not permit a description of specific mitigations here; the reader is referred elsewhere [3,4] A brief discussion of corrective actions for Building B, However, illustrates the importance both of controlling moisture, nutrients and of preventive maintenance in mitigation activities.

As a result of a poorly conceived energy management program in Building B relative humidity during the summer months rose to the 60 to 80 percent range. Induction units, which were never designed to remove latent heat (no drain lines), became continuously wetted. Because of a poor preventive maintenance program and lack of adequate filters for these units, abundant substrate (dirt and debris) accumulated within and beneath these units. Mitigation actions for Building B involved a reduction in the availability of carbon sources in induction units by better preventive maintenance activities and improved filtration of air entering each unit. An equally important mitigation measure, reducing airborne moisture in the occupied space, can be achieved by a less restrictive energy management program for central air handling units (increase removal of latent heat by heat exchangers). It is significant to point out that unless these fundamental changes (reduction of moisture and nutrients in induction units; better preventive maintenance) are brought about in the operation of Building B's HVAC system, occupants will continue to be exposed to unusual numbers and kinds of microorganisms in their indoor work environment.

REFERENCES

(1) ASHRAE Standard 55-1981. Thermal environmental conditions for human occupancy. Atlanta.

(2) ASHRAE Standard 62-1981. Ventilation for acceptable indoor air quality. Atlanta.

(3) Morey, P.R., M.J. Hodgson, et al. 1986. Environmental Studies in Moldy Office Buildings. ASHRAE Trans. 92(1): 399-419.

(4) Morey, P.R. Experience on the contribution of structure to environmental pollution. In (R. Kundsin, ed.) Architectural Design and Indoor Microbial Pollution, Oxford University Press (in Press).

(5) ACGIH Committee on Bioaerosols 1987. Guidelines for assessment and sampling of saprophytic bioaerosols in the indoor environment. Appl. Industr. Hyg. 2: R10-R16.

GROUND SOURCE HEAT PUMP APPLICATIONS

James E. Bose
Professor and Director
Division of Engineering Technology
Oklahoma State University
Stillwater, Oklahoma 74078

During the past ten years renewed emphasis has been placed on the Closed-Loop/Ground-Source (CL/GS) heat pump to provide economic space heating, space cooling, and preheating domestic hot water. Measured performance data has shown the system to be 25% more efficient than high efficiency air source heat pumps.

Demand reductions in heating cycles are in the order of 2.5 to 3 times when compared to both air source heat pumps and electric resistant heating. During cooling cycles, demand reductions are in the order of 25% with the highest demand occurring late in the afternoon.

Installation costs have steadily decreased with a target value of $5000-6500 as the total cost of a three ton system including ground heat exchanger, heat pump, duct work, thermostat, and etc. This results from aggressive marketing programs by electric utilities and new ground heat exchanger installation equipment which automatically places and backfills multiple pipes in a single trench.

GROUND HEAT EXCHANGER TYPES

The most commonly installed ground heat exchangers include:

A. Single Loop Vertical
B. Two Pipe Horizontal
C. Four Pipe Horizontal

Figure 1, 2 and 3 are a typical layouts of these types of systems. Figure 4 are specific details describing important components and installation layout.

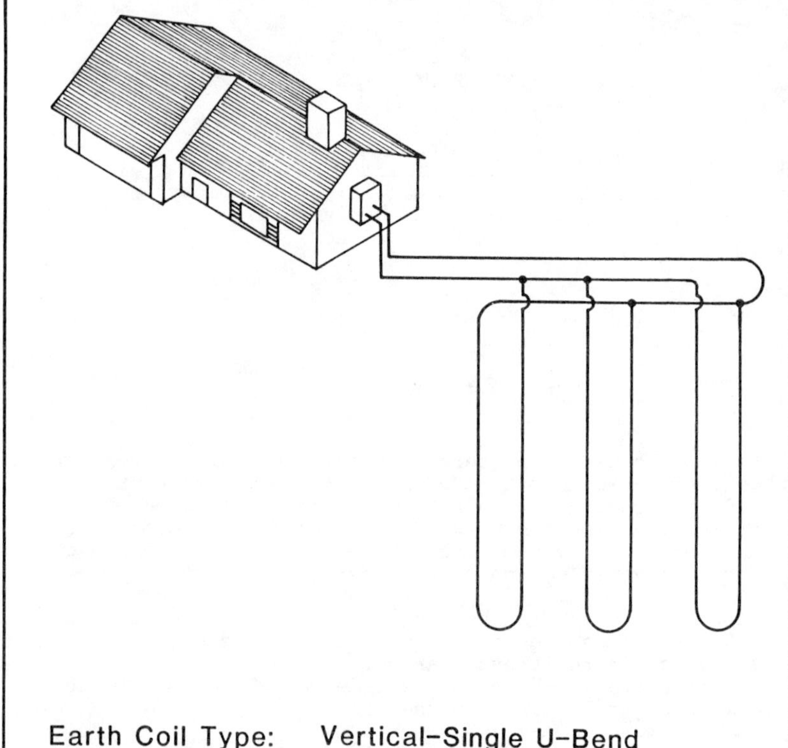

Earth Coil Type:	Vertical–Single U-Bend
Water Flow:	Parallel
Pipe Sizes:	3/4 or 1 inch loops, 1 1/2 or 2 inch headers
Bore Lengths:	175 to 225 feet/ton
Pipe Lengths:	350 to 450 feet/ton

Figure 1

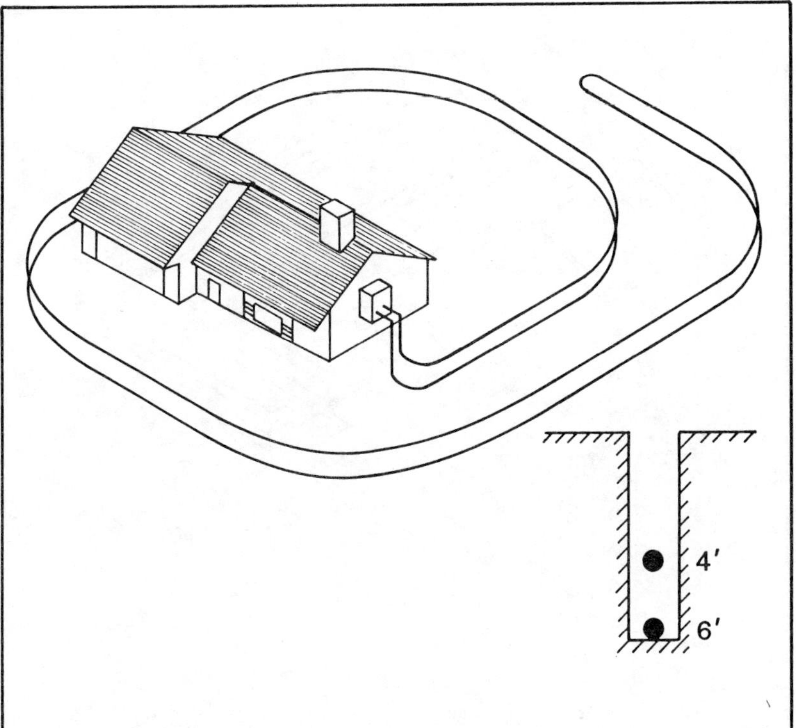

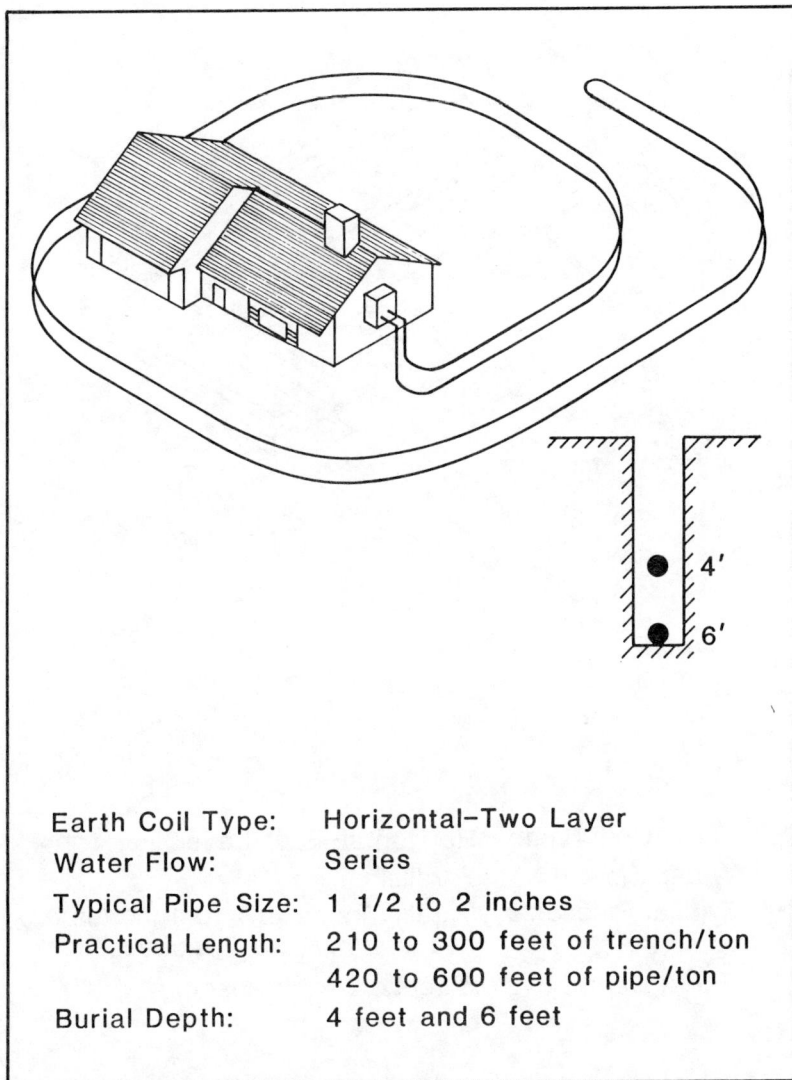

Earth Coil Type:	Horizontal–Two Layer
Water Flow:	Series
Typical Pipe Size:	1 1/2 to 2 inches
Practical Length:	210 to 300 feet of trench/ton
	420 to 600 feet of pipe/ton
Burial Depth:	4 feet and 6 feet

Figure 2

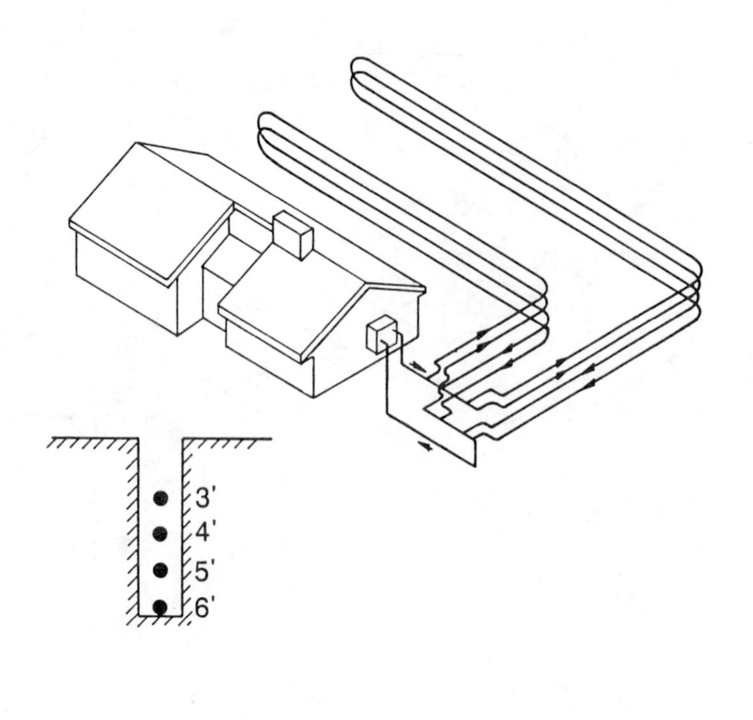

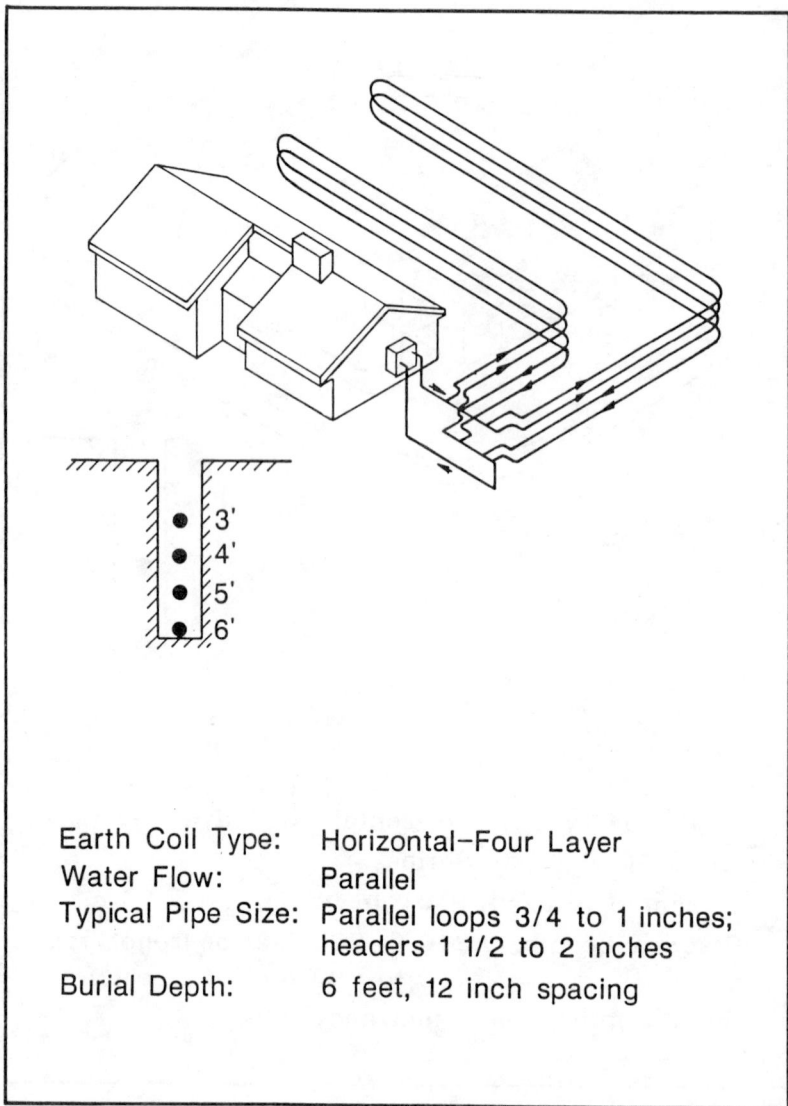

Earth Coil Type:	Horizontal-Four Layer
Water Flow:	Parallel
Typical Pipe Size:	Parallel loops 3/4 to 1 inches; headers 1 1/2 to 2 inches
Burial Depth:	6 feet, 12 inch spacing

Figure 3

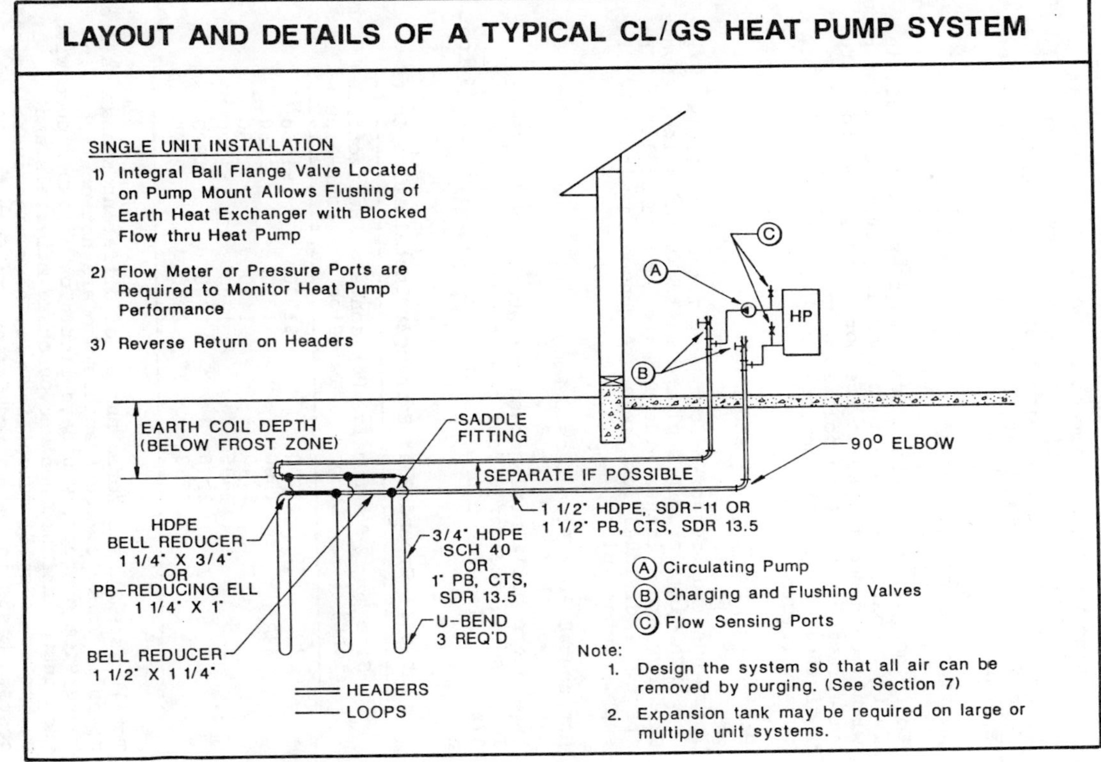
LAYOUT AND DETAILS OF A TYPICAL CL/GS HEAT PUMP SYSTEM
SINGLE UNIT INSTALLATION
1) Integral Ball Flange Valve Located on Pump Mount Allows Flushing of Earth Heat Exchanger with Blocked Flow thru Heat Pump
2) Flow Meter or Pressure Ports are Required to Monitor Heat Pump Performance
3) Reverse Return on Headers
C
A
HP
B
EARTH COIL DEPTH (BELOW FROST ZONE)
SADDLE FITTING
90° ELBOW
SEPARATE IF POSSIBLE
1 1/2" HDPE, SDR-11 OR 1 1/2" PB, CTS, SDR 13.5
HDPE BELL REDUCER 1 1/4" X 3/4" OR PB-REDUCING ELL 1 1/4" X 1"
3/4" HDPE SCH 40 OR 1" PB, CTS, SDR 13.5
U-BEND 3 REQ'D
BELL REDUCER 1 1/2" X 1 1/4"
HEADERS
LOOPS
A Circulating Pump
B Charging and Flushing Valves
C Flow Sensing Ports
Note:
1. Design the system so that all air can be removed by purging. (See Section 7)
2. Expansion tank may be required on large or multiple unit systems.

Figure 4

INSTALLATION COSTS

Installation costs will depend upon local labor costs, trenching and/or drilling conditions. Table 1 gives installation costs for the three most popular types of ground heat exchangers being installed in Oklahoma. Specific details of these three types of heat exchangers are as follows:

Vertical Closed Loop

Four inch vertical bore holes (200 feet per ton) drilled 10 feet apart. One 3/4 inch thermally fused diameter pipe with a U-shaped fitted at the bottom is pressured tested and placed in the bore hole as a heat exchanger. Individual loops are connected with 1-1/2 inch supply-return lines.

Horizontal Two Pipe Closed Loop

Three hundred feet of 6 foot deep trench per ton with two 3/4 inch diameter pipes placed at the 6 and 4 foot levels. Trenches are 6 inches wide and are located at least 7 feet apart. Individual loop legs are connected with 1-1/2 inch supply-return pipe.

Horizontal Four Pipe Closed Loop

Used where horizontal ground surface space is limited. Two hundred feet of 6 foot deep trench per ton with four 3/4 inch diameter pipes placed at the 3, 4, 5, and 6 foot depths.

Table 1: Ground Heat Exchanger Installation Costs

Size (Tons)	Vertical Loop	Horizontal Two-Pipe	Horizontal Four-Pipe
2	$1200	$1000	$1000
2.5	1500	1250	1250
3	1740	1450	1450
3.5	1995	1700	1700
4	2240	1900	1900
5	2750	2300	2300

Total system costs for a number of different scenarios are given in Table 2. Contractors who are not confident in the system concept, who have little or no experience with such installations, and who purchase materials and equipment in small quantities will have high installation costs. Costs in the United States are from $4,500 to $10,000 for a three ton (cooling capacity) system.

Financing is available from nine of 27 Rural Electric Coops (REC's) with typical interest rates of 5%. Paybacks are from 4 to 7 years.

Table 2: Representative GSHP cost in Oklahoma[a]

Installation	Responsibilities	Average cost ($)
Dealer installed (average)	All purchasing, storage, coordination, and actual installation is by a private contractor	6500
Utility assisted retrofit	Utility purchases heat pump and pipe for heat exchangers; system installed by contractor	5000
Utility assisted in new home	Same as above	4500

[a]Based on a 3 ton (cooling capacity) vertical ground heat exchanger with 600 feet of bore hole

INSTALLATION PRACTICES

A manual of accepted practices will be published during 1988 detailing methods adopted by the industry. The manual written by personnel at Oklahoma State University and supported by the National Rural Electric Cooperative Association consists of the following:

A. Introduction and Overview.
B. Economics, Marketing and Demand Reduction
C. Selecting, Sizing, and Designing the Heat Pump System.
D. Designing the Ground Heat Exchanger.
E. Pipe Joining Methods.
F. Installation of the Ground Heat Exchanger.
G. Flushing and Purging the System.
H. Heat Pump System Startup and Checkout.
I. Antifreeze Fluids and Physical Properties.
J. Trench and Pipe Spacing.
K. Specification of Polyethylene and Polybutylene Pipe.
L. Standardized Parallel System Header Design.
M. Desuperheaters for Domestic Hot Water.

The manual provides current technical information on installing closed-loop/ground-coupled heat pump systems. It summarizes acceptable practices of many successfully operating systems in the United States and Europe.

TECHNICAL ORGANIZATIONS

The International Ground Source Heat Pump Association (IGSHPA) is an organization devoted to the advancement of the ground source heat pump industry. The association is operated by Oklahoma State University and is an integral part of the University. The executive director is a member of the staff of Oklahoma State University. Charter members include Charles Machine Works (Ditch Witch), Command Aire, McElroy Manufacturing, Mississippi Power Company, National Rural Electric Cooperative Association, Oklahoma State University, Public Service Indiana and WaterFurnace International.

IGSHPA's mission is to provide programs and services for the future development of the ground source heat pump industry and the profitable marketing of the latest ground-coupled heat transfer technology. Future plans call for the development of a membership directory and buyers guide, a newsletter and various fact sheets and publications on ground source technology.

Training Programs are offered by IGSHPA and include two-day workshops on installation methods and a annual three-day workshop on design and installation. Information on these workshops is available from IGSHPA.

Membership in the IGSHPA is open to electric utilities, manufacturers, distributors, contractors, HVAC dealers and individuals. Membership information is available by writing the International Ground Source Heat Pump Association, P.O. Box 1688, Stillwater, Oklahoma 74076-1688. Phone: (405) 624-4175.

COMMERCIAL GROUND-COUPLED HEAT PUMP APPLICATIONS AND CASE STUDIES

Harry J. Braud
Professor
Agricultural Engineering Department
Louisiana State University
Baton Rouge, Louisiana

ABSTRACT

Ground loops are widely used for water-source heat pumps. Water-cooled condensing units are more efficient than air-cooled, and they can be put indoors. Indoor location makes piping for desuperheater hot water easy. Refrigeration can also be put on a ground loop. Since refrigeration equipment runs more than heat pumps, energy savings can be large for ground-coupled refrigeration. The paper presents an over view of commercial applications of ground loops for heat pumps, hot water, ice machines, and water-cooled refrigeration. The systems vary from small offices to a three-story office building with 187 tons. A chain of hamburger drive-ins uses total ground-coupling in all of its stores. A grocery store has ground-coupling for all heat pumps and refrigeration. Desuperheaters provide 80 percent of the hot water for a coin laundry in the same building. A comparison of energy costs in a bank with a ground-coupled heat pump to a similar bank building with air-conditioning and gas for heat revealed a 22 percent reduction in utility costs for the ground-coupled building. Two buildings of the Mississippi Power and Light Co. have ground-coupled heat pumps in one, and high efficiency air source heat pumps in the other. Energy savings in twenty-one months was 145,040 kWh (25 percent), and electric peak demand was reduced 42 kW (35 percent). In a retrofit application of ground-coupled heat pumps to replace air-conditioning and electric heat, energy consumption was reduced by 69 percent and peak kilowatt demand was reduced by 51 percent.

INTRODUCTION

Rising energy costs have affected all segments of the nation's economy. In the home, space heating and cooling constitute the largest energy use. Water heating is the second energy user. In businesses, such as fast food outlets, restaurants, food storage and processing, refrigeration consumes very large amounts of electric energy.

In cooling and heating processes, the natural environment (either air, water or earth) is the ultimate source or sink of the heat added to or removed from the material or process. The operating efficiency of refrigeration equipment and heat pumps is a direct function of the temperature of the environmental source or sink. Ground loops allow heat pumps to utilize the most favorable environmental temperature available, that of the earth. Reduction in equipment energy consumption can be achieved with (1) use of a thermally stable environmental source/sink such as the earth, and (2) an energy recycling system that captures waste heat or cooling effect from one device or process and uses it in another. Both of these features are inherent in a closed-loop ground-coupled heat pump system.

Consumers who are charged for electricity at a rate based on demand peaks benefit from the flat electric demand curve of the ground-coupled heat pump. This not only helps the consumer who purchases the electricity, but also benefits the utility by reducing the peak power draw on the distribution system and the generating plants.

Today, much effort is being expended in the utility industry to reduce peak demand using load control devices and time-of-day rates. These are negative actions that penalize the consumer. The utilities should promote energy conservation with something that is good for both the consumer and the utility. Ground-coupled heat pumps are good for both. Power draw is low and predictable. It is an all-electric system that can save natural gas and other fossil fuels.

Because of the large amount of pipe needed for the ground loop, ground-coupled heat pumps cost more than air source heat pumps. Cost for the ground- coupled heat pump is as much as $800 to $1,500 per ton more to install than air source systems. Despite the high cost, over 1000 homes in Louisiana have ground-coupled heat pumps. Significant energy savings have been documented in numerous residential installations with utility billing reduced as much as 20 to 50 percent compared to air-source equipment and/or gas heat.

WHY GROUND-COUPLING?

The earth contains an abundant store of heat energy that is replenished annually by the sun. A city lot 100 ft by 150 ft to a depth of 300 ft has enough energy to provide the entire annual energy needs for a household by changing its temperature only 1/6 degree Fahrenheit. It has been said that the greatest solar collector in the world is the earth beneath your feet. The enormous mass of the earth and its stable temperature make it an ideal source/sink for heat pumps. This is because the earth contains much more heat than the atmosphere. Of the thermal energy reaching the earth from the sun, 47 percent is absorbed and stored in the earth. The atmosphere, being much less dense and transparent to thermal radiation, absorbs only 19 percent (Figure 1). Heat absorbed by the earth in summer provides a free heat source the next winter. Ground-coupled heat pumps tap this free energy. They deliver what solar systems only promised. Instead of looking up to the sun, we need to look down to the earth for the free heat stored there.

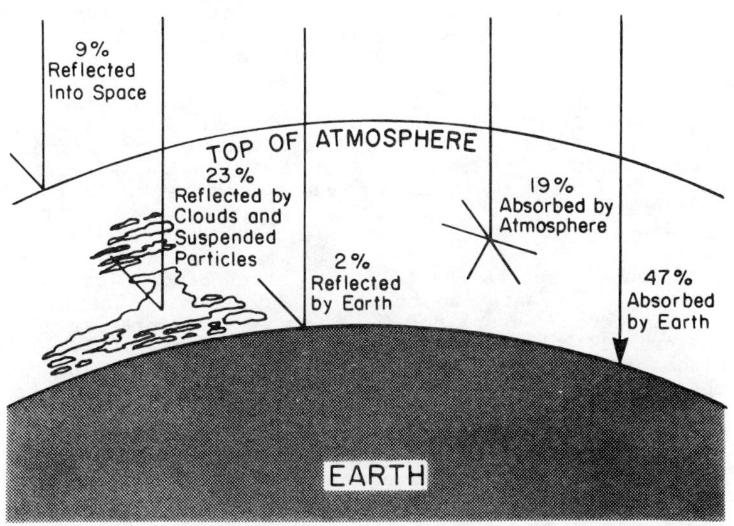

Figure 1. Distribution of solar energy to earth.

Air-source heat pumps have some drawbacks because there is less heat in the atmosphere than in the earth. Both the heating capacity and efficiency decrease as the outdoor air temperature falls. During the coldest days of the year, they must be assisted by electrical resistance heating elements. This supplemental heat increases electricity demand, thereby adding to utility load requirements. Ground-coupled heat pumps maintain full heating capacity and high performance during cold weather. They are able to deliver their rated heating capacity regardless of the outdoor air temperature because the heat pump only knows the warm earth temperature brought to the unit by the loop water circulation. Besides, water is far superior to air to deliver heat at any temperature. The thermal capacity of a cubic foot of water is 62.4 Btu for a 1°F temperature change versus 0.018 Btu for a cubic foot of air. Ground-source heat pumps do not have a defrost cycle. Defrost is the main cause of service calls in air-source heat pumps.

The economic impact of ground-coupled technology is truly unique. It is not sophisticated, high technology. It is good for local business. A new trade - ground loop contracting - is needed to provide the ground-coupling. Bore drilling gives work to small water well drillers. Pipe installation, trenching, and other loop work use small contractors and local labor. The dollars the customer invests in the ground-coupling feed the local economy instead of paying for a new large distant electric power plant. It seems reasonable to expect that this technology will now develop a momentum of its own and spread widely and rapidly into the commercial field.

Elimination of outdoor mechanical equipment is a definite advantage in both residential and commercial construction. Equipment life in the outdoor environment is short due to snow, rain, and dust. Where space is at a premium, elimination of outdoor equipment is not only a cost-saving factor but also an aesthetic one.

Ground-coupled heat pumps have been installed in several old plantation houses in Louisiana. The decision to use ground-coupling is a matter of preserving the historical value. A notable installation is the Oakley Plantation House, near St. Francisville, Louisiana, where the famous artist and painter John James Audubon lived.

> "Preserving the architectural integrity of Oakley Place Plantation, the historic home where American artist and naturalist, John James Audubon lived and painted in Louisiana, was foremost in the mind of Baton Rouge architect, James D. Dodds, AIA, when he decided to utilize earth-coupled heating and cooling to solve the humidity problem threatening first edition Audubon prints, furnishings and artifacts. By going with an in-ground closed loop system, there will be no unsightly air conditioning compressors peeking behind lush foliage, and no vents or ductwork inside to disrupt a visitor's impression of having stepped back in time. Dodds worked out a system which runs pipe from the ground coil up the gutter spouts of the three story colonial structure to the attic which houses the water source heat pump. Air conditioning and heating are then dispersed throughout Oakley by running pipes down through the chimneys in each room. Inside and out, the Twentieth Century is held at bay so that tourists will continue to view Oakley

Place much as Audubon did when he arrived there in 1821."

Along These Lines, Feb. 1986.
Dixie Electric Membership Corp.
Baton Rouge, Louisiana

COMMERCIAL APPLICATIONS

A recent development in ground loop technology is to use a ground loop for refrigerators, freezers, display cases and ice machine. These machines can even be put on the same ground loop with a heat pump. Water-cooled condensing units are more efficient than air-cooled, and they can be put indoors. Indoor location makes piping for desuperheater hot water easy. Since refrigeration equipment runs more than heat pumps, energy savings can be very large for ground-coupled refrigeration. In Louisiana, over forty office buildings are on ground loops. Systems vary from small offices to a three-story office building with 187 tons. Many commercial systems have both refrigeration and heat pumps. A chain of hamburger drive-ins, Fast-Track, uses total ground-coupling in all of its outlets. A grocery store has ground-coupling for all heat pumps and refrigeration. Desuperheaters on all units provide 80 percent of the hot water for a coin laundry in the same building. Another grocery store with 15 tons of load (11 tons in heat pumps for space conditioning plus 4 tons of refrigeration) is served by a 200 amp, 115/230 volt single phase service drop. The 6000 ft^2 building also contains a seafood market and an auto repair shop. Pool heating systems and water heating for a car wash can also be found.

GROUND-COUPLED HEAT PUMP ENERGY FLOW

Energy transfer in a ground-coupled heat pump involves four media: indoor air, the refrigerant gas, water in the loop, and the earth mass (Figure 2). Energy must pass through three heat exchangers: the indoor air-to-refrigerant coil, the refrigerant-to-water coil, and the water-to-earth pipe wall.

In the cooling mode, thermal energy flows from the indoor air to the refrigerant, to the loop water, and to the earth. Electric energy that powers the compressor enters the refrigerant gas as heat of compression and sensible heat from the motor and passes on to the earth. The total heat rejected to the earth is the sum of the heat absorbed from the indoor space plus the electric energy needed to power the compressor.

In the heating mode, the compressor heat energy goes to the indoor air along with heat absorbed from the earth. For every unit of electric energy needed to drive the heat pump compresser three to four additional units of heat energy are absorbed from the earth.

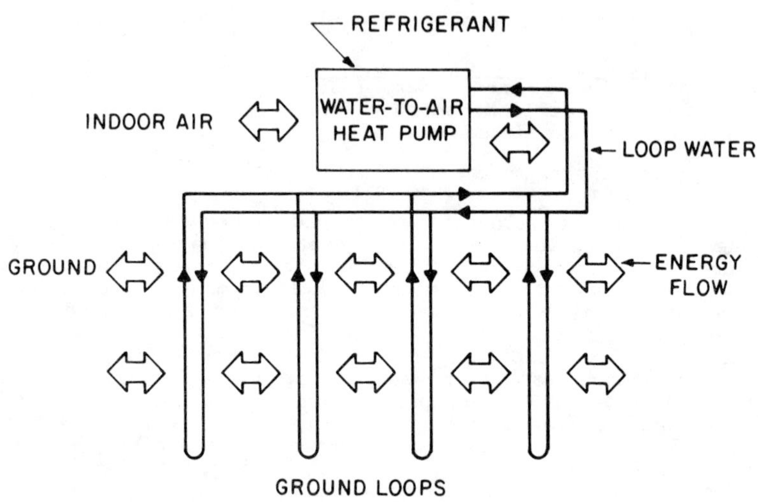

Figure 2. Ground-coupled heat pump.

A ground loop can take thermal energy rejected by one device and deliver it to another that requires heat. Energy transfer to or from the earth stabilizes loop water temperatures and satisfies energy balances. Loop length must be adequate to provide safe loop water temperatures for all units in all seasons. A loop sizing procedure for multiple units on a common ground loop was given by Braud (1986). See also Bose et al. (1985) and Partin (1981).

DESUPERHEATERS

A desuperheater coil on a water source heat pump, Figure 3, is a cost-effective device. Heat extracted from the hot compressor gas can provide most or all of the hot water in a residence. When the heat pump is in space cool mode, heat removed from indoor space goes to the hot water tank and to the earth simultaneously until the hot water tank is satisfied; then the earth heat exchanger must provide the entire heat rejection. In winter, earth source heat provides both water heating and space heat. The reduction in space heating capacity due to hot water energy is not severe with a water source heat pump drawing on earth energy. Desuperheaters can be used on both air-cooled and water-cooled refrigeration condensing units. However, water-cooled condensing units are usually located indoors, which makes hot water piping easy.

In commercial applications, heat pumps run long hours, and desuperheaters can provide very large quantities of hot water. Pierce (1983) found that a restaurant using 500 gallons of hot water per day was able to save $3,156 a year on hot water costs with desuperheaters on a total of 10 tons of refrigeration condensors. Pierce stated that desuperheaters have a fast payback, generally from 8 to 36 months in restaurants and fast food outlets. Other benefits are simple equipment with no moving parts, reduced electric demand, more efficient compressor operation and increased refrigeration capacity.

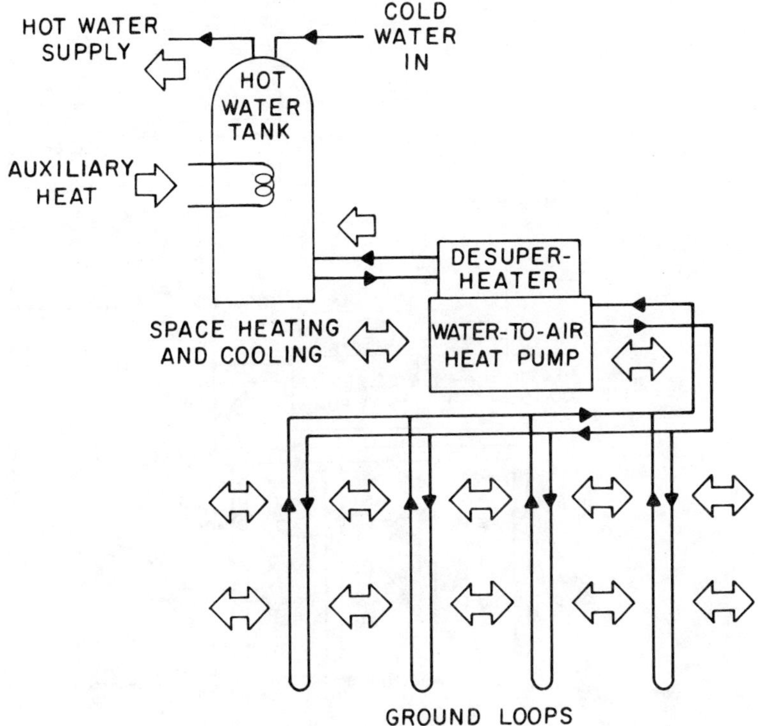

Figure 3. Ground-coupled heat pump with desuperheater.

A grocery store in Gonzales, Louisiana has desuperheaters on the ground-coupled heat pumps and refrigeration condensers. Enough hot water is produced to provide 80 percent of the hot water for a coin laundry in the same building.

A 4½ ton heat pump in a Baton Rouge office has generated enough hot water for restrooms and a small kitchen so that the electric elements have never been energized since installation in 1981. Desuperheaters on a 3½ ton heat pump in a fast food outlet produces the hot water needed for the kitchen.

HEAT PUMPS AND REFRIGERATION ON A GROUND LOOP

Ground loops offer several advantages for businesses that have large refrigeration loads as well as heat pumps. Restaurants, fast food outlets and grocery stores are examples.

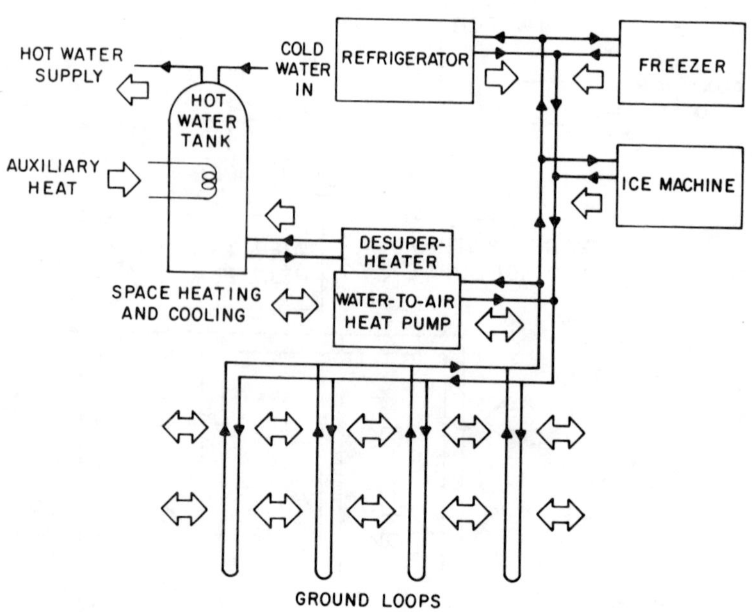

Figure 4. Ground-coupled heat pump and refrigeration.

Note: Desuperheaters for hot water can be put on refrigeration compressors.

All heating and cooling units can be put on the ground loop. Water-cooled condensing units for refrigerators and ice machines operate much more efficiently on water, and all mechanical equipment can be put indoors. Besides inherent energy recovery and transfer, a total ground loop system has very little maintenance and obvious asthetic advantage. Elimination of outdoor condensing units and cooling towers reduces land requirement. Air-cooled roof top units operate in a harsh environment and create roof leaks and noise problems.

Two grocery stores in Louisiana use the total ground-loop concept as shown in Figure 4. A 6,000 sq ft store with 11 tons of heat pumps and a 4 hp refrigeration load has a 200 amp, 115/230 volt, single phase electric service to serve the whole building that also contains an auto repair shop and a small seafood market. This is the same size electric service used for a residence.

Refrigeration heat rejection to a ground loop is always beneficial to heating devices sharing the loop. In zones of cool earth temperature, the capture of refrigeration waste heat would improve seasonal heating performance efficiency of heat pumps. Having access to earth temperatures year-round allows water-cooled refrigeration units to operate very efficiently. It would seem that in any climatic zone where annual heating energy exceeds cooling energy, refrigeration heat rejection would be highly beneficial. Loop energy transfer from cooling devices to heating devices would occur in many hours of the year. Loop length and cost could possibly be reduced for combined loads. It is interesting to note that combined heat pump/refrigeration loops are being installed in south Louisiana where earth temperature (70°F) is relatively warm and space-cooling mode dominates. The capture and recycling of refrigeration rejected heat is an energy resource that should be recognized and exploited, especially in the central and northern regions of the United States.

ECONOMICS, RESIDENTIAL

Earth-coupled water-source heat pump systems are expensive ($800 to $1,500 more per ton than conventional systems) because of the large amount of pipe needed for the ground loop. Nevertheless, long life and low maintenance and operating costs make them a good investment.

The space conditioning system is a "big ticket" item in the typical family budget. Smilie et al. (1984) compared five 3-ton space conditioning systems (Table 1). The analysis included installation costs and the operating costs derived from weather data and costs for gas and electricity. Maintenance cost was assumed to be $50/year except for air-to-air heat pumps, for which it was assumed to be $70/year. Inflation of energy and maintenance costs was estimated at 5%/year.

Low initial cost for equipment usually means high operating costs. The earth-coupled water-source heat pump system had the lowest 10-year total cost, $12,840, even in comparison to a high efficiency air-conditioner and high efficiency gas furnace, $14,082, (Table 1).

Table 1. Summary of costs of five heating and cooling systems. Three-ton capacity. Baton Rouge, LA (Smiley et al., 1984)

System	Installation Cost	Operating Cost	10-Year Total Cost
1. Air conditioner, 8.65 EER, electric heat	$2500	$1740	$19,903
2. Air conditioner, 9.15 EER, gas furnace @ 55% efficiency	2900	1294	15,836
3. Air-to-air heat pump, 9.02 EER, 3.05 COP	3300	1308	16,378
4. Air conditioner, 11.00 EER, gas furnace @ 95% efficiency	3500	1058	14,082
5. Earth-coupled water-source heat pump, 11.1 EER, 4.01 COP	4730	969	12,840

CASE STUDIES

In 1981, the author replaced a 4-ton air-conditioner and gas furnace in his home with a ground-coupled heat pump. It reduced his electric bill by 21 percent and eliminated the gas service and bill. Instead of the heating and air-conditioning consuming half the annual total utility use, the heating and cooling amounted to only 22 percent. Heat recovery from the heat pump reduced hot water energy to only 13 percent of the total, while the electric clothes dryer consumed 14 percent annually. Based on actual electric and gas rates, 1981-86, the family's utility bill has been reduced by an average of $580 per year. Cost premium for the new system was $2,200 over the replacement cost for the air-conditioner and gas furnace. In simple figures, the payback was less than four years, (Braud, 1984). In another test residence, an earth-coupled water-source heat pump reduced the overall residential electric use by 28 percent.

ENERGY SAVINGS IN COMMERCIAL BUILDINGS

In Baton Rouge, Louisiana, two bank buildings were equipped with ground-source heat pumps in one and conventional air-conditioning and gas heat in the other. The ground-coupled building was slightly larger--3,300 ft^2

vs 3,000 ft^2--than the building with the air conditioning and gas. The ground-coupled bank required 15 tons of capacity versus 11.5 tons in the other. Energy use in the ground-coupled building was 52,368 kWh less in the twenty-three-month period Aug. 1985 to June 1987 than in the building that has air-conditioning and gas, Table 2. Gas consumption in the bank with gas was 683 ccf for the billing period. Total utility billing for the ground-coupled bank was $12,233.09 versus $15,688.11 for the air-source with gas, a 22 percent difference.

Table 2. Comparison of ground-coupled heat pumps to air-conditioning and gas heat.

Baton Rouge Bank
August 1985 to June 1987

Branch	KWH	Elec. Billing	CCf	Gas Billing	Total
Jones Creek Branch A/C and Gas Heat	248,928	$15,337.61	689	$350.50	$15,688.11
Perkins Branch - Ground Coupled Heat Pump	196,560	$12,233.09	0	$0.00	$12,233.09
Difference	52,368	$3,104.52	689	$350.50	$3,455.02
Percent	21%	20%	-	-	22%

The Mississippi Power and Light Co. compared ground-coupled heat pumps to high-efficiency air-source heat pumps in two of its office buildings. The two offices each have 11,500 ft^2 of conditioned area, similar operating schedules, and the same insulation. Additional cost for the ground-coupled system over air-source was $835 per installed ton. Peak kilowatt demand was 120 in the air-source building and 78 in the ground-coupled building, Table 3. Energy use was 590,640 kWh in the air-source and 445,600 kWh in the ground-coupled, a 25 percent difference, in a 21-month period, October 1985 - June 1987. Average kilowatt demand per month was 93 in the air-source building and 65 in the ground-coupled building.

In a retrofit application, ground-coupled heat pumps reduced electric energy consumption 69 percent. The Louisiana Department of Employment Security installed 30 tons of ground-coupled heat pumps in a field office in Hammond, Louisiana to replace electric resistance heat and an air-cooled chiller. In the first seven months of operation, March - September, 1987, the ground-coupled system used 254,520 kWh less than the same 3 months in 1986, a 69 percent difference, Table 4. Peak kilowatt demand with the electric heat and air-conditioning was 125 kw versus 61 with the ground-coupled heat pumps. The utility costs were reduced by 60 percent, $21,963.81 in March - Sept. versus 1986 versus $8,612.88 in 1987. Based on these figures, the owner is expecting a 2 to 3 year payback on the cost for the entire change-out of the building's equipment. The old system required a $5,000/year maintenance contract on the pneumatic control system that is not needed with the ground-coupled heat pumps.

Table 3. Comparison of ground-coupled pumps to air-source heat pumps.

Mississippi Power & Light Co.
Jackson, MS.
October 1985 to June 1987

Office	Max KW	Average KW	Average Kwh/Month	Total Kwh
Rankin Office - Ground-Coupled Heat Pumps	78	65	21,219	445,600
Madison Office - Air-Source Heat Pumps	120	93	28,126	590,640
Difference	42	28	6,907	145,040
Percent	35%	30%	25%	25%

Table 4. Comparison of ground-coupled heat pumps to air-conditioning and electric heat.

Louisiana Department of Employment Security
Hammond, LA

System	Max Kw	Average Kw	Average Kwh/Month	Total Kwh
Ground-coupled heat pumps March 87 to Sept. 87	61	53	16,234	113,640
Air-conditioning and electric heat March 86 to Sept. 86	125	114	52,594	368,160
Difference	64	61	36,360	254,520
Percent	51%	54%	69%	69%

ADVANTAGES OF A GROUND-COUPLED HEAT PUMP SYSTEM

1. Energy savings of 20 to 50 percent over air-source equipment. Electric demand is also reduced with water-cooled condensing units for refrigeration and heat pumps.
2. Elimination of all outdoor condenser units - also cooling towers and boilers. Corrosion, dirt, vandalism, theft, high maintenance, and freeze problems are eliminated. Elimination of roof top units reduces roof maintenance, damage, noise, leaks, etc.
3. No outdoor space required. Earth bores can be put under lawns, landscape zones, driveways, and parking lots. A three story building in Baton Rouge, Louisiana has all bores underneath the building.
4. Free hot water generated with desuperheaters during the summer months, year-round with refrigeration waste heat. Hot water produced with COP advantage from earth source in the winter.
5. No depletion of ground water. Presence or quality of ground water is of no concern because heat transfer is to the earth mass.
6. No wastewater expense or disposal problem. Closed loop uses ordinary tap water for heating and cooling energy transfer to earth.
7. Elimination or reduction in electric heat strips that are required with air-source heat pumps.
8. Elimination of gas service to premises. No flue or ancillary costs for gas heat that are often hidden in the plumbing contract.
9. Long life, low maintenance system. Recent trade figures indicate that water-cooled condensers have 20+ year life expectancy. Compressor life is long because of low head pressure when operating with water.

DISADVANTAGES

1. High initial cost - $600 per ton for earth bores in Louisiana. Manifold piping, pumps, etc. will increase total cost to $800 to $1500 per ton over other types of air-conditioning systems.
2. Not all air-conditioning contractors are familiar with this technology.
3. Earth drilling is difficult in rock or other problem areas.

REFERENCES

1. Bose, J.E., J.D Parker and F.C. McQuiston. 1985. Design/data manual for closed-loop ground-coupled heat pump systems. American Society of Heating Refrigeration and Air-Conditioning Engineers. Atlanta.
2. Braud, H.J. 1986. Ground loops for heat pump and refrigeration. Building energy symposium. Mechanical Engineering Department, Texas A&M University.

3. Braud, H.J. 1984. Earth-coupled heat pumps for residential heat/cool and hot water. 7th Heat Pump Technology Conference, Oklahoma State University. 7p.
4. Partin, J.R. 1981. Closed-loop earth-coupled heat pump exchangers. Ground Water Heat Pump Journal. Water Well Journal Publishing Co., Worthington, Ohio.
5. Pierce, J.R. 1983. Refrigeration-to-water heat exchange. The Consultant. Food Service Consultants Society International. Seattle, Washington.
6. Smilie, J.L. et al. 1984. An economic comparison of the earth-coupled water-source heat pump with other methods of heating and cooling. Louisiana State University Cooperative Extension Service. 31p.

PRACTICAL DESIGN GUIDELINES FOR INDUSTRIAL HEAT PUMPS

R Gluckman, Director - Energy Division
March Consulting Group, Windsor, UK

Heat pumps for industrial heat recovery have a relatively poor reputation. Many systems have failed to achieve the savings claimed or have been very unreliable. This poor reputation combined with low oil prices in 1986/7 has led to a drop in sales. If a significant market share is to be achieved when fuel prices rise again it is vital that existing designs and applications are appraised and improved.

Much of Government sponsored research into heat pumps is aimed at new cycles and higher temperatures. In both Europe and the USA work is being undertaken to develop new fluid pairs, to use non-azeotropic refrigerant mixtures and to design various high temperature chemical heat pumps. Whilst this work is all of importance it is surprising how little effort is being spent in the refinement of existing designs. As with many other industrial and consumer products, Japanese heat pump companies are probably spending more money on improving the "state of the art" design than on R & D into new systems.

It is perfectly feasible to design and build better heat pumps providing enough effort is spent on design and that lessons are learned from a significant body of experience gained during the last 10 years. In this paper a review is made of key design requirements based on a practical assessment of industrial heat pump installations in Europe. The guidelines outlined in the paper can be used as a basis for a new design methodology for industrial heat pumps. It is recommended that this approach is developed to ensure US and European heat pumps are competitive in the 1990's.

1. Introduction

Even though the concept of heat pumping was recognised more than a century ago the technology has a long way to go before it reaches maturity. In the UK little penetration has been made into the potential commercial and industrial markets except in a few specialist areas such as swimming pool heating. A major reason for the lack of installations is related to fuel costs; even after the fuel crises of the 1970s energy prices were not high enough to encourage the technology of heat pumps to be fully developed. However, there has been another cause of disinterest - heat pumps have in many cases proved unreliable and have not met their design performance.

In 1987 we are at an interesting watershed in the history of the heat pump. We have 10 years of vigorous design activity behind us. Several thousand industrial systems (over 100 kW and up to several MW) have been installed in Europe, North America and Japan. These heat pumps can be thought of as "first generation" systems. Although in some cases they were unsuccessful in economic and engineering terms many useful lessons can be learned from this experience. If we can benefit from previous mistakes (and successes!) then it is possible to envisage a "second generation" of heat pumps that will achieve high levels of performance and reliability. If, on the other hand, we fail to use the existing base of knowledge and experience then the industrial heat pump market has little chance of development.

This paper is concerned with reviewing the practical performance of many heat pumps in Europe in order to highlight areas in which heat pump designers must take great care. The intention is not to present a rigorous design guide but to give a series of practical tips that will help the designers of second generation systems avoid the problems encountered in the last 10 years.

This paper is devoted to the analysis of closed cycle compression heat pumps. The main discussion is split into two sections, ie system design and components. Within the section on system design reference is made to the technique of "Process Integration" which is a powerful new approach to the design of energy using processes.

Ironically at the time of writing this paper fossil fuel prices have fallen very sharply and the economic case for heat pumps is weaker than at any time during the previous decade. This paper does not try to advocate the immediate up-take of industrial heat pump technology; in the short term that would only serve to encourage the poor reputation of the heat pump. We must, however, make use of the breathing space caused by low oil prices and make sure that the refrigeration industry is ready to provide reliable and economic systems in the early 1990's when fuel prices will almost certainly have risen again.

2. The Problem of First Generation Heat Pumps

With so many large heat pumps installed in industry both in Europe and the USA one would expect the relevant technologies to be well developed and well understood.

This is certainly not the case; in reality the economic and practical performance of heat pumps are not held in high regard. However, the situation can be considerably improved if sufficient attention is given to previously encountered problems. It is vital that we do not "reinvent the wheel" and that second generation heat pumps benefit from existing experience.

This paper examines some of the lessons learned during the past decade. It is possible to split the analysis into system design and component design. Details are presented in the next two sections. Before looking at specific lessons it is useful to mention some of the general reasons for the large number of problems that have been encountered.

Use of Refrigeration Rules of Thumb

It was generally assumed that heat pumps could be built with exactly the same design parameters as refrigeration plant. In fact this is not the case - great care must be taken in extrapolating refrigeration data.

Use of Fossil Fuel Rules of Thumb

In a similar way it is dangerous to design a heat pump process heater in the same way that a fossil fired heater would be designed.

General Lack of Detailed Design

Many heat pumps were installed without enough initial design work. Whilst it is often easy in hindsight to criticise the plant design it is generally accepted that a number of heat pump installations would have been much more successful if more thought had been given to the design. The heat pump is typical of many post war technologies that has suffered from an excess of enthusiasm and expectation and a great deal of attention to detail.

Poor Manufacturing Standards

In many cases too many economies were made to keep capital costs low and heat pumps consequently suffered from unnecessarily poor reliability. This is particularly true of site installation work.

System Design Problems

System Sizing

The most common problem with first generation heat pumps is oversizing. Systems have been built to meet peak process heat demand plus a contingency allowance, in the same way that boilers are designed. This is wrong for two reasons:

- heat pumps do not generally perform well at part load
- heat pumps are relatively expensive and must run for a large number of hours per year to achieve good economics.

An important rule is to make heat pumps large enough only to provide base heating load. Short peaks and spare capacity are better supplied by cheaper fossil plant. A system using a heat pump and a supplementary heat source is known as a bivalent plant. For most processes it is possible to select an optimum heat pump size by plotting the daily heat load profile and establishing the base load. In many cases a heat pump sized at 50% of the peak load will supply as much as 90% of the energy required by a process.

In a number of cases heat pumps have achieved good thermal performance in terms of COP and heating duty but have had very poor payback periods because of the low number of full load running hours.

Choice of the optimum heat pump size is always site specific and it is a complicated function of daily load profile, total annual operating hours and other factors that affect the payback period (fuel prices, capital cost, COP, etc). For average European conditions the heat pump must be 100% loaded if annual operating hours are between 4000 and 5000. Below 4000 hours the heat pump is unlikely to be economic even if it is fully loaded. If the annual usage is above 5000 hours then the load factor can fall (to about 75% for 8000 hours/year. It must be stressed again that if heat loads are highly variable (with short peaks) then a 75% load factor will only be achieved with a heat pump considerably smaller than the peak heat requirement.

Correct Choice of Thermodynamic Cycle

Many system designers are thinking of heat pumps only in terms of simple four component cycles. This is convenient for manufacturers, who can provide standard packages in a range of sizes. However, the opportunity to improve system performance is frequently being lost. Incorporation of liquid subcoolers, desuperheaters, horizontal cascade cycles and two stage systems can often give higher COP with little or no extra capital cost. Details of various alternative cycles are given in Refs 1 and 2.

As a general rule it is unlikely that a well sized industrial heat pump should ever be in the simple four component form. This is because the heat pump will always have a high load factor as described above. A more sophisticated cycle may improve the COP by 25% to 50% but will usually only have a small effect, say 10%, on the total installed capital cost. For this reason the extra sophistication is usually a good investment.

The design of any heat pump requires a different philosophy to the design of fossil fired plant. The sizing issue discussed above is a good example of the different ideas needed. When considering the thermodynamic cycle it is vital to take into account temperature differences as well as absolute temperature levels. The concept of Heating Temperature Range (HTR), the temperature range through which the heat user is heated, is very useful in order to identify applications of special cycles.

If the HTR is large then it is essential to use more sophisticated cycles than the simple four component system. A good example is the heating of boiler feed water from 10°C to 70°C. A four component system would have a COP of around 2.3 if the heat source was at 10°C. If a subcooler is included the COP rises by 50% to 3.4 and the compressor becomes 30% smaller.

Incorporation of Passive Heat Recovery

Another common system design fault is to use a heat pump when an alternative energy saving opportunity may have much better economics. The most common example of this is the omission of passive heat recovery opportunities. Although a heat pump may have an acceptable payback period it is wrong not to compare the investment with an alternative.

Passive heat recovery is always cheaper in terms of capital cost than a heat pump and, of course, has no appreciable use of energy for operation. It is vital that all opportunities for passive heat recovery are used before heat pumps are considered.

Unnecessary degrading of Waste Heat

A corollary to the omission of passive heat recovery is the degrading of waste heat down to unnecessarily low temperatures. It is wrong to degrade the heat if this can be avoided.

A common example is the use of a cooling water stream for a heat pump source. If water at 25°C is cooled to 20°C in a cooling tower it appears an obvious heat source. However, one must first examine what the cooling water is used for. In many processes water at 20°C is used to cool fluids at between 50°C and 200°C. It may be much cheaper to redesign the process cooler than to fit a heat pump to the cooling water.

Process Integration

Several of the points described above relate to whether or not a heat pump is an appropriate energy saving measure in the context of the whole process. It is wrong to identify a possible heat source/user pairing and calculate the economic feasibility of a heat pump without evaluating the complete process energy balance. A powerful technique to identify the correct way to apply heat recovery to industrial processes, Process Integration or Pinch Technology, gives very important rules about the application of heat pumps.

Process integration (P.I.) is a relatively new tool (first used during the late 1970's) that is having a major impact on the design of heat exchanger networks and on the integration of sophisticated technologies such as heat pumps or cogeneration. It is not relevant of explain the overall background to P.I. here as it is well described in the literature (Ref 3, 4). The important point to note is that P.I. acts as a very good 'filter' to ensure that heat pumps are not used inappropriately. For example, in the brewing industry many companies are considering use of an open cycle MVR system for recovering waste vapour from the evaporation coppers. P.I. can show that in many breweries this is incorrect and that passive heat recovery is more economical.

A P.I. analysis identifies a unique temperature in any industrial process called the "Pinch Temperature" (Figure 1). Knowing the pinch point can help the process designer in many ways. For heat pumps the important rule is:

- Heat pumps should only be used "across" the pinch, that is, the heat source should be below pinch temperature and the heat user should be above. (Figure 2)

FIGURE 1

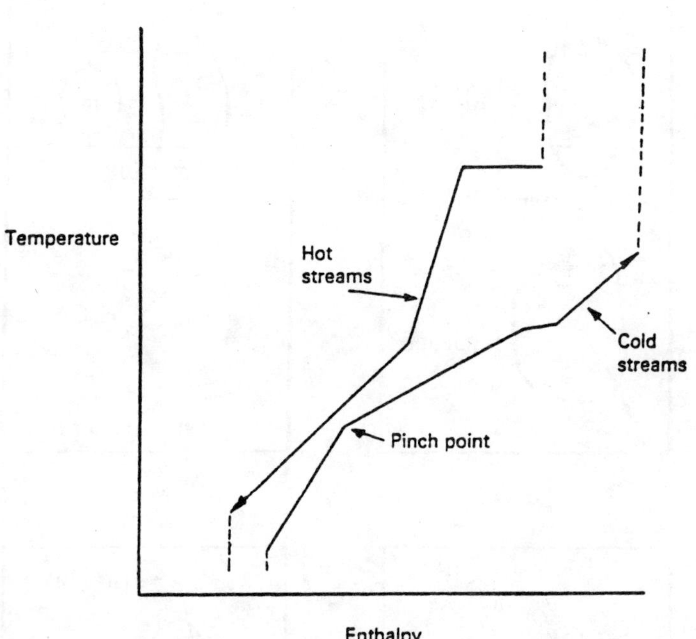

COMPOSITE CURVES FOR A PROCESS

FIGURE 2

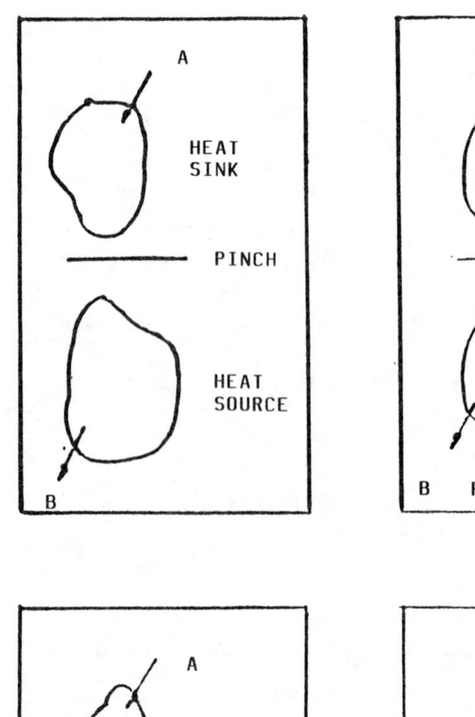

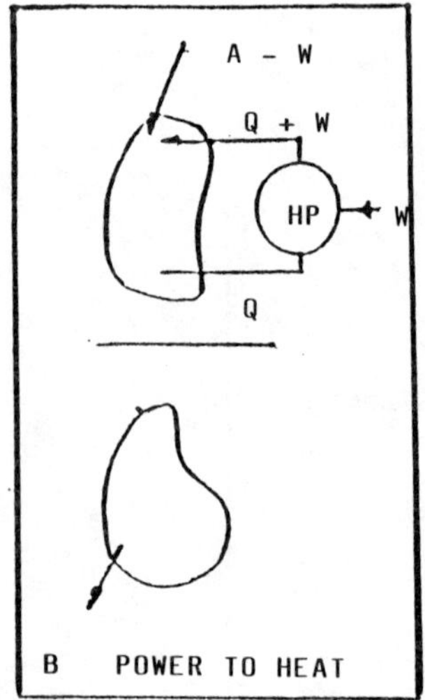

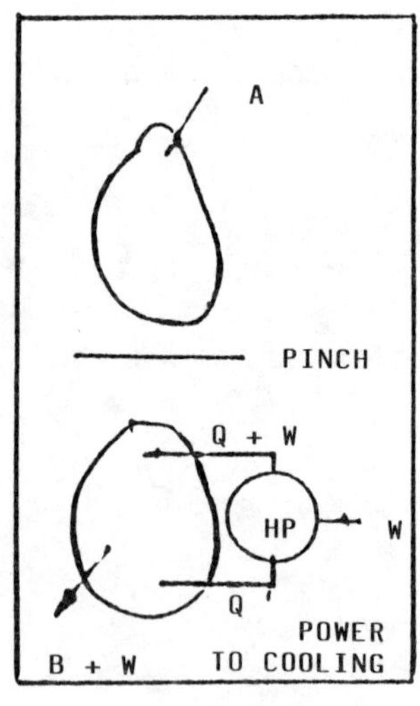

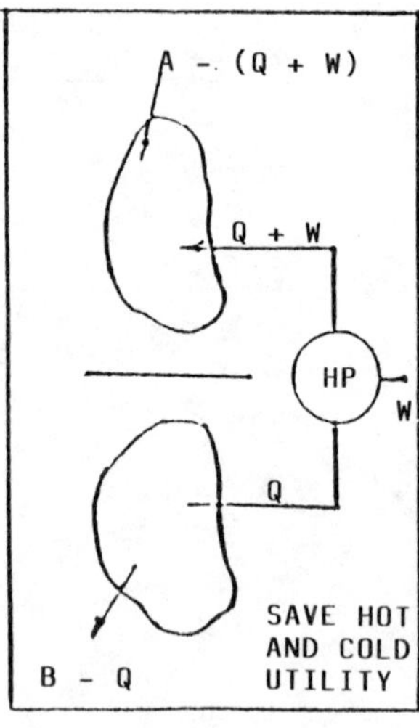

CORRECT PLACEMENT OF HEATING PUMPS

In the case of the brewery example a MVR system is completely above the pinch; therefore it is inappropriately placed. Ideally a P.I. analysis should always be used before considering a heat pump investment.

Component Design

Evaporators

Poor evaporator design has led to many problems in first generation heat pumps. The faults cause poor heat transfer coefficients and a loss of both COP and thermal capacity through low evaporating temperatures.

- **Direct expansion evaporators.** A common heat pump configuration is to use a direct expansion (DX) evaporator in conjunction with a thermostatic expansion valve. In such an arrangement refrigerant is completely evaporated in one pass through the evaporator (see Figure 3). This is different to the flooded evaporator where a mixture of liquid and vapour is present throughout the evaporator. DX evaporators suffer a number of possible problems that lead to poor heat transfer rates and disappointing heat pump performance.

  These relate to uneven distribution of liquid to the evaporator circuits, which leads to early drying out of the evaporator. This does not occur in a flooded evaporator where heat transfer is good throughout. It is recommended that flooded evaporators are used whenever possible.

- **Superheat Zone.** Many systems are operated with a high superheat at compressor suction. This can be through evaporator design or a badly set expansion valve. In these situations a significant percentage of the evaporator surface can be dry on the refrigerant side as described above. This waste of surface area leads to lower than normal evaporating temperatures. Another serious side-effect occurs with systems that have moisture in the heat source. The water vapour cannot condense in the superheat zone of the evaporator as it is too warm. This leads to particularly poor heat transfer in that part of the coil and a further loss of capacity.

- **Frost Build Up.** Most designs of air source evaporators do not minimise the losses that occur through frost build up. It is vital to stop frost forming a bridge between adjacent fins. Useful design rules are:

FIGURE 3

EVAPORATOR CONFIGURATION

a. DIRECT EXPANSION

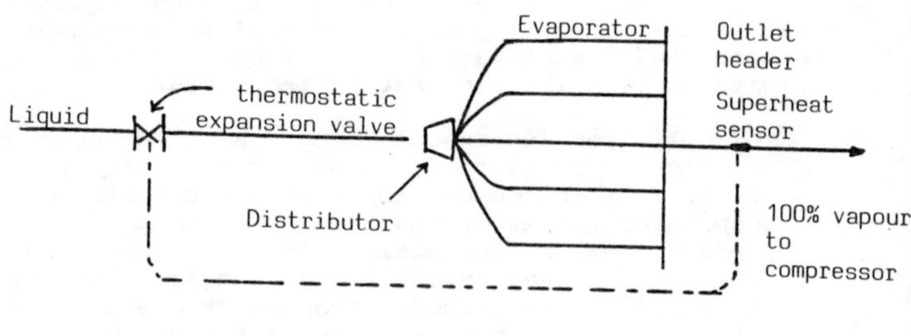

Control loop

b. FLOODED

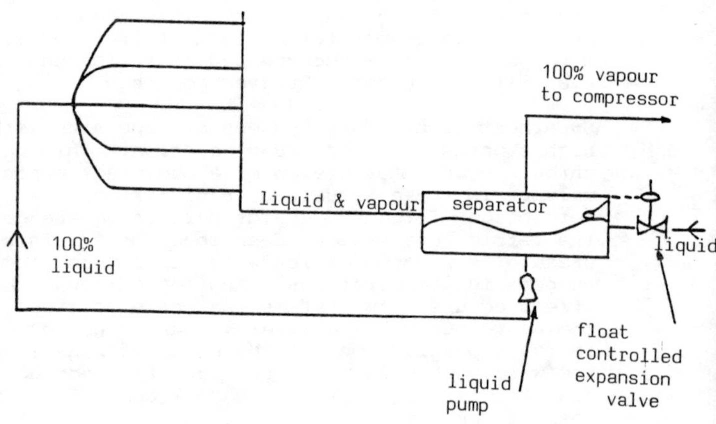

a) do not use closely spaced fins. 3 or 4 fins/inch is the minimum spacing that should be chosen. Some small sized systems have used 12 fins/inch and frost has been a tremendous difficulty.

b) use coils with relatively large face area and a high air face velocity as this encourages water droplets to be blown off before freezing occurs.

c) place coils horizontally with air blowing downwards so gravity can assist the path of water droplets off the coil.

- **Effects of Oil.** Evaporators are often designed on the assumption that the refrigerant is pure. This is not the case in most plant as oil is present as a vapour, in liquid droplets and in solution with the refrigerant. Oil can cause a reduction in evaporator capacity. The effects appear greater in many heat pump applications than in apparently similar refrigeration systems. (Ref 5)

- **Undersizing.** The COP of a heat pump is related directly to temperature lift. The temperature difference across the evaporator adds to this lift. Many heat pumps have used evaporators that have too little surface area. This undersizing is caused by use of refrigeration design rules and gives a non-optimised COP.

- **Fouling and Corrosion.** Many heat sources have dirty or corrosive constituents. Great care must be taken to select the correct materials for the evaporator. In two malt drying heat pumps plastic dipped finned coils were used as evaporators. Fouling occurred because of the close fin spacing and corrosion occurred because the plastic finish was not sound. One of the heat pumps had a new evaporator made from bare stainless steel tubes which was a much more satisfactory design. The other was actually scrapped when a leaking evaporator was added to a long list of technical problems.

<u>Compressors</u>

The compressor has seen major improvements during the last decade for heat pump applications. At first it was believed that completely standard refrigeration compressors could be used. This has been found to be wrong except for extremely robust machines that were previously overdesigned. Great care must be taken using the cheaper machines that are designed for packaged chillers and air conditioning plant. Some common faults have included:-

- Valve failure through higher than normal forces from compressed refrigerant. Valve seats, springs and plates must be carefully chosen for heat pump applications.

- Bearing failure through high side thrusts on crankshafts etc. Stronger bearings must be used.

- Shaft seal leakage.

- Failure of ancillary components such as baffles in oil separators due to higher than normal forces from compressed refrigerant.

- Failure of cylinder unloading gear.

- Frequent motor burnouts. In semi-hermetic systems this has led to great difficulty in cleaning the refrigerant pipework and heat exchangers

Compressor Efficiency

It is surprising how often a heat pump is designed without reference to compressor efficiency. Bearing in mind that the isentropic efficiency of compressors used for heat pumps varies between 40% and 80% this can lead to serious reductions in financial return. Using a low efficiency compressor has exactly the same effect on heat pump performance as the use of a low efficiency boiler has on a steam system. Boiler purchasers are unlikely to buy a 75% efficient boiler if 80% is available - they certainly will not use one at 40%!

Compressor efficiency is not necessarily related to capital cost; often a cheaper machine is more efficient than an expensive one. The manufacturer should always be requested to supply isentropic efficiency data relating to three modes of operations:-

- design point efficiency - this value allows quick comparison of performance between several machines

- off-design full load efficiency - if the heat pump is required to operate under different evaporating or condensing conditions the off-design figures are important. There is no point in buying a machine with a very high design point efficiency if the off-design values fall significantly.

- part load efficiency - most compressors have very poor part load efficiency. Ideally the heat pump should be sized in such a way that it doesn't run at part load. If this is not possible design calculations should take into account low efficiency when the compressor is unloaded.

Condensers

Of the three main components of heat pumps the condenser has caused the fewest problems. The main causes for concern have been fouling or corrosion on the heat user side and undersizing. Similar issues affect evaporators.

In some systems two condensers are used, one for heat recovery and a second unit to reject heat to the atmosphere when heat recovery is not required. The way these vessels are piped together is very important. On at least one installation the heat recovery condenser was acting as a liquid receiver!

It is necessary to consider how the condensers may effect each other. In Figure 4 we see an air cooled condenser in parallel with a water cooled heat recovery condenser. The heat pump was designed to operate with just one condenser. In heat recovery mode condensing temperature could be 60°C and in air cooled mode a typical value of 35°C was expected. The condensers were well piped, compared to the liquid receiver problem described above, having generously sized liquid line connections to the common receiver. However when the weather was cold and wet the air cooled condenser pulled the head pressure down, even though the fans were not operating; the heat recovery condenser could not deliver suitably hot water. An extra solenoid valve is required in the air cooled condenser liquid line to prevent this happening.

However, further care must be given to switching from one condenser to the other. Ideally the liquid solenoid should be operated a short time after the vapour line valves are switched to ensure that the air cooled condenser can be drained of liquid.

Engine Driven Systems

Engine driven systems are often worth considering because they improve the overall energy savings potential, particularly for applications with high temperature lift. However the engine does lead to a lot of extra design and maintenance considerations:

- **Engine Air Intake Location.** One of the classic lessons learned, and unfortunately relearned, during the last ten years has been the simple rule about engine combustion air intakes. These **MUST** be ducted from outside the engine room in a position where refrigerant cannot be ingested into the engine. The consequences of halocarbons entering an engine combustion chamber are dramatic. The refrigerant is broken down by high temperatures into highly corrosive compounds of fluorine and chlorine. Severe engine damage is inevitable.

FIGURE 4

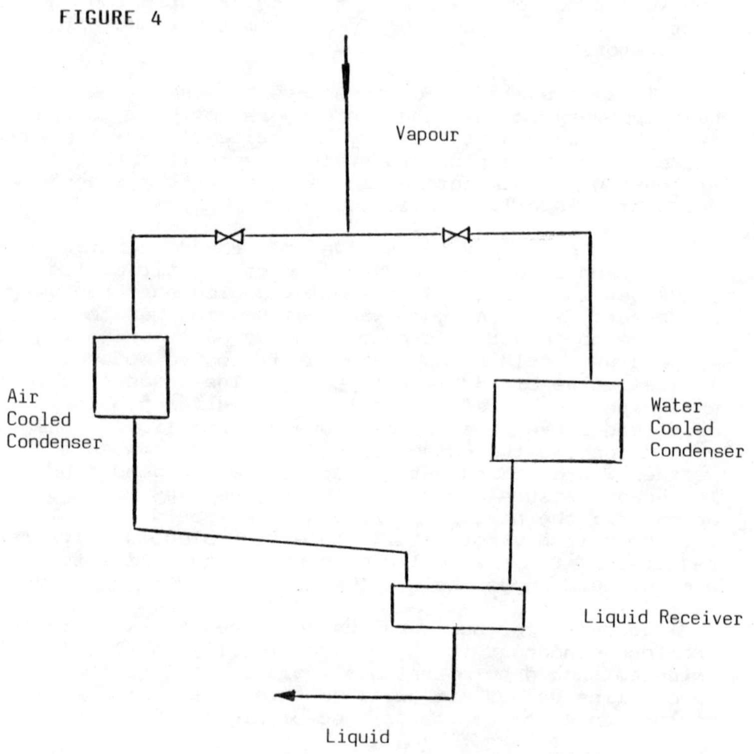

PARALLEL CONDENSER OPERATION

- **Engine Compressor Vibration.** Several large systems have suffered major problems due to the wrong type of coupling between engine and compressor. Flexible compressor and engine mountings have caused many difficulties. The engine and compressor manufacturers must carry out a rigorous vibration analysis to design the mounting and couplings. Analysis should allow for unloaded compressor cylinders, and possibly unloaded engine cylinders resulting from spark plug failure.

- **Exhaust Heat Exchanger Design.** The exhaust heat exchanger must not cause too great a back pressure otherwise engine performance is lost. Materials must be carefully selected to avoid corrosion, particularly if diesel engines are used.

- **Lubricating Oils.** These must be carefully selected in conjunction with the engine manufacturers. It is necessary to check on the rate of consumption of lube oil - on some engines a lot of oil is burned resulting in high annual maintenance costs.

Refrigerant Leakage

Many heat pumps have suffered with refrigerant leakage problems. In general the cause has been poor manufacturing standards, lack of checking and lack of attention to detail. Leakage was a major factor contributing to the downfall of the German domestic heat pump. In a recent field trial in the UK seven out of eight systems suffered from significant leaks. It should be noted that these were systems that the manufacturers knew were to be carefully tested and appraised!

Refrigerant/Oil Selection

A variety of fluids are used for heat pump applications. Certain halocarbons have been most popular ie R12, R22 and R114. Recently ammonia has been used for a number of industrial applications and R500 has been used in place of R114 for high temperature applications.

In the same way as selecting a fluid for refrigeration it is necessary to consider a number of thermodynamic and chemical properties before choosing the correct refrigerant. Other important issues such as toxicity, particularly carcinogenic properties, and cost must also be addressed. For heat pumps a major new problem has been refrigerant breakdown at high temperature. If a heat pump is to supply heat at, say, $120^{o}C$ then compressor discharge temperatures will normally be well above that figure. Many halocarbons break down at the temperatures encountered. The breakdown is considerably enhanced by the presence of lubricating oils. In high temperature applications it is necessary to use synthetic lubricating oil to avoid this problem.

Use of screw compressors is sometimes an advantage because the degree of superheat can be controlled by oil injection.

References

1. Gluckman, R. Heat pump cycles and their engineering. Part of book entitled "Heat Pumps for Buildings", ed Sherrat, published Hutchinson (1984).

2. Perry E J. Drying by cascading heat pumps, Proc 3rd Int Conf Future Energy Concepts, IEE, Conf Publ 192, IEE, London (1981)

3. Linnhoff, B et al. User guide on process integration for the efficient use of energy, IChemE, London.

4. Linnhoff, B and Vredeveld, D R. Pinch technology has come of age, Chemical Engineering Progress (July 1984).

5. McMullen, J T, Hughes, D W and Morgan, R. Influence of Lubricating oil on heat pump performance, European Commission Energy RRD Programme, Contract EEA-4-028-GB.

IMPROVED PROCESS HEAT PUMP ECONOMICS USING SEMI-OPEN CYCLES

A.P. Rossiter and R.F. Toy
TENSA Services, 17300 Saturn Lane, Suite 113
Houston, Texas 77058

ABSTRACT

For heat pumps to become widely accepted as a means of reducing process heat demands it is essential that cost competitive systems be developed and implemented. In this paper a technical and economic comparison is made between the process use of closed reverse Rankine cycle heat pumps (which are similar in concept to most domestic heat pumps) and semi-open cycle heat pumps (of which mechanical vapor recompression is an example). An example (based on a study of a liquor distillery) shows that the semi-open cycle system gives vastly superior economic performance.

INTRODUCTION

Heat pumps, used in conjunction with conventional heat exchanger networks, provide an effective means for reducing the energy usage of many industrial processes. Many different heat pump cycles have been proposed, but the ones that have thus far gained the greatest acceptance for industrial applications are based on the reverse Rankine cycle. Such systems can be used for heat pumping between process streams, between utility streams, or between a process stream and a utility stream (1). The present discussion relates specifically to process-process heat pumps.

Considerable effort has recently been invested in developing procedures, based on the principles of "pinch technology", for ensuring that industrial heat pumps are correctly placed and sized with respect to overall process temperatures and heat flows (2, 3, 4). The most detailed previous analyses of reverse Rankine cycle heat pumps have generally assumed that the cycle is closed (Figure 1). In such systems the working fluid is fully enclosed, being evaporated by accepting process heat in the heat pump evaporator, compressed, and then condensed delivering its heat at an elevated temperature to the process in the heat pump condenser. From here the working fluid recommences its cycle.

In semi-open cycle heat pumps, the working fluid is a process fluid. The most common semi-open cycle (Type 1, often known as "mechanical vapor recompression") uses a process vapor in this role (Figure 2), compressing it and then condensing it to satisfy a process heating duty at an elevated temperature. Such a system has a heat pump condenser but no evaporator. A less common type of semi-open cycle (Type 2) has the opposite configuration, i.e. an evaporator, but no condenser (Figure 3). This type of cycle can be used when a low temperature heat source is available to evaporate a process stream which is required in the vapor phase at a higher temperature.

It is important to note that semi-open cycles of these types are only feasible when the process working fluid undergoes a phase change - condensation for Type 1 systems and evaporation for Type 2 systems. A recent study of ten potential applications has shown that the economics of semi-open cycle systems, where they are feasible, are often greatly superior to those of closed cycle heat pumps (5).

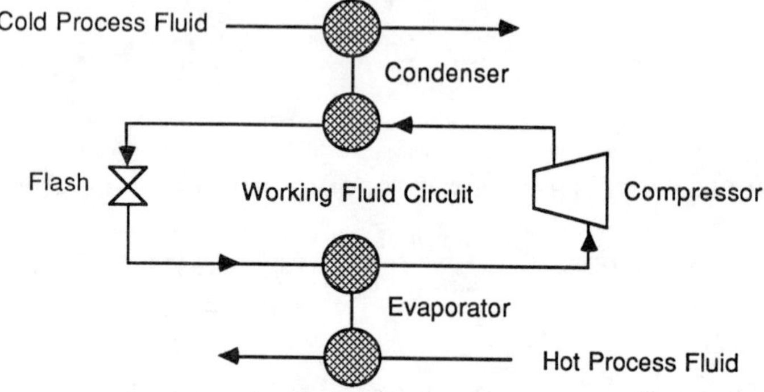

Figure 1. Closed Cycle Heat Pump

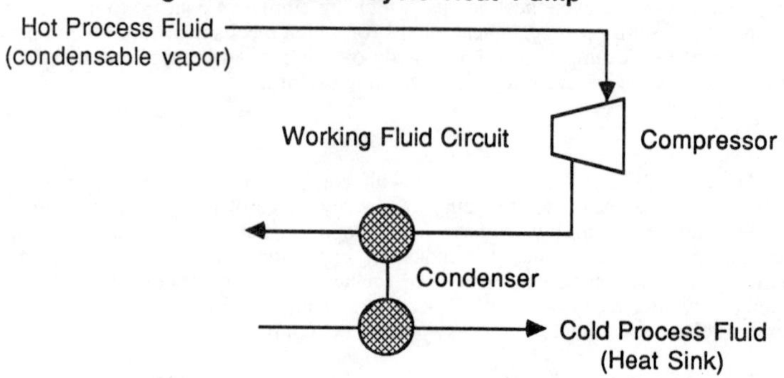

Figure 2 : Semi - Open Cycle Heat Pump - Type 1

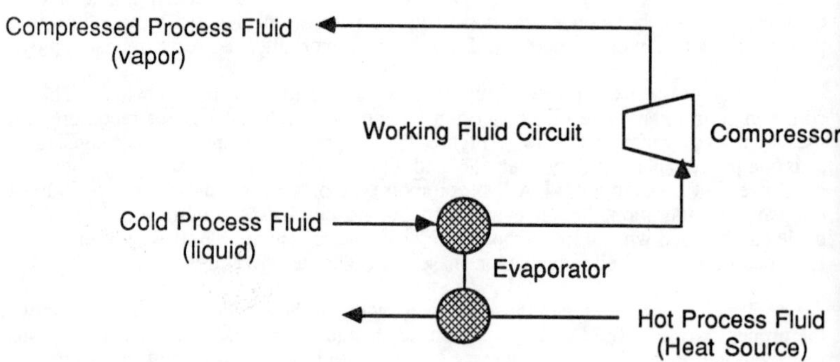

Figure 3 : Semi - Open Cycle Heat Pump - Type 2

PLACEMENT AND SIZING OF INDUSTRIAL HEAT PUMPS

Pinch technology has led to new insights into the appropriate placement and sizing of industrial heat pumps (1, 2, 3, 4). The key finding of pinch analysis is that after all viable "passive" heat integration has been implemented, most industrial processes can be divided into a "high temperature" region where the process has a net requirement Q_H for heat and a "low temperature" region where there is a net cooling requirement, Q_C (Figure 4).

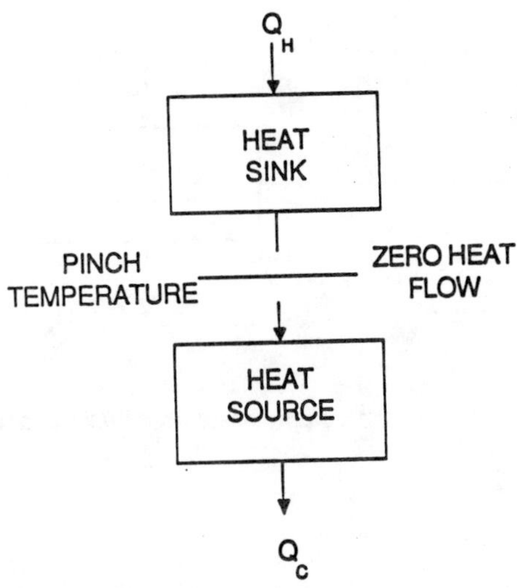

Figure 4 : The Heat Transfer Pinch

A heat pump accepts heat Q_A at some temperature T_A (see Figure 5) and, by addition of work W, delivers heat Q_D at an elevated delivery temperature T_D. T_D is higher than T_A. It follows that any heat pump which has both its heat source and its heat sink either in the "below pinch" region or in the "above pinch" region is "inappropriately placed," and cannot reduce the overall energy requirements of the process (assuming, of course, that the process is fully heat integrated). Only if the heat source is below the pinch and the heat sink above the pinch is the heat pump correctly placed and energy savings are achieved (Q_H is reduced to Q_H - Q_D, and Q_C is reduced to Q_C - Q_A).

A more detailed analysis of net process heat flows using the "grand composite curve," allows an evaluation of the amount of heat that can be beneficially elevated across the pinch by a process heat pump (2). This analysis forms the basis for a software package to facilitate the screening of industrial processes for possible heat pump use (6).

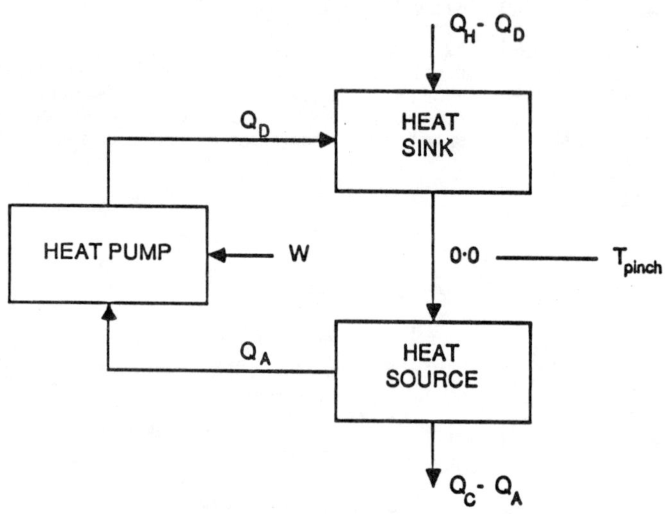

Figure 5 : Appropriate Heat Pump Integration

PROBLEM DEFINITION

In order to illustrate how semi-open cycle systems generally give rise to more favorable economics than closed cycle systems the various areas where differences occur are highlighted in the context of an example problem, namely placement of a heat pump in a liquor distillery. The semi-open cycle studied is a Type 1 system. It should be noted that similar arguments and economics would apply in circumstances where a Type 2 semi-open cycle is used, although no explicit discussion of Type 2 systems is given in the remainder of this paper. Data for this example is based on a study carried out for the Department of Energy (7).[1]

The earlier study showed that a heat pump taking heat from the Analyzer Overheads and delivering heat to the Rectifier Feed stream would be appropriately placed (i.e. elevated heat across the pinch) and would also be correctly sized (i.e. not so large that it created a new pinch). Figure 6 is a simplified diagram of this part of the process showing the location of the heat pump. In the present study, systems to implement the necessary heat pump and heat integration for a new liquor distillery, incorporating either a closed or a Type 1 semi-open cycle heat pump, are sized and costed, and compared with a "base case" in which only passive heat integration is used.

The heat pumps are modeled as reverse Carnot cycles, again to simplify the analysis, with a cycle efficiency of 65%. The heat pumps are assumed to be driven by electric motors with an electric conversion efficiency of 95%.

---

[1]The data from (7) has been modified such that the Analyzer Overheads are assumed to condense at a constant temperature of 181°F. (The original data indicates a condensing range of 199°F to 181°F). This change simplifies and clarifies the analysis presented here, but does not significantly affect the results obtained.

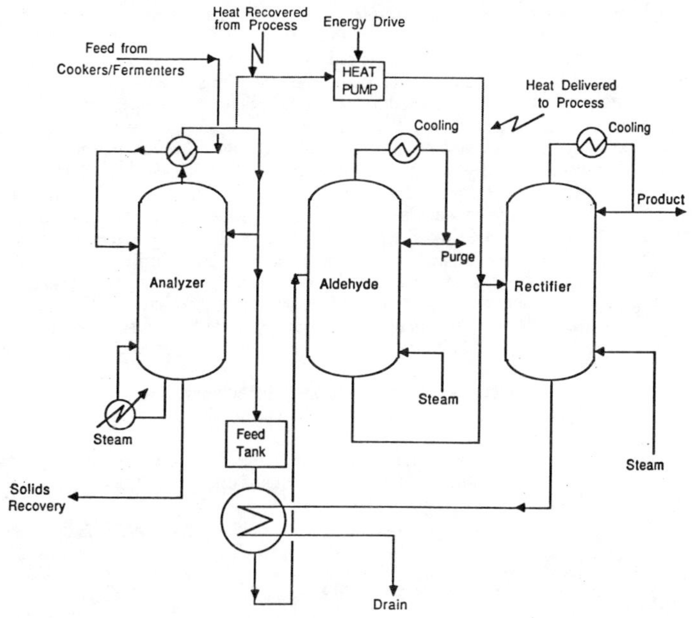

Figure 6: Heat Pump Application for Liquor Distillery

CLOSED AND SEMI-OPEN CYCLE HEAT PUMP SYSTEMS

The key differences between the systems based on closed cycle heat pumps and those based on semi-open cycle heat pumps fall into two basic categories:

- Heat Pump Cycle
- Process Heat Integration

The technical differences, and their impact on the economics of the example problem, are discussed below.

Differences in Heat Pump Cycles

A closed cycle heat pump requires both a condenser and an evaporator, whereas at Type 1 semi-open cycle has only a condenser. Thus semi-open cycles, in general, have one less item of capital equipment than closed cycles. This leads directly to a significant cost saving. Moreover, the elimination of one heat exchanger (in either type of semi-open cycle) eliminates one of the temperature driving forces in the cycle. This means that the temperature lift required in a semi-open cycle is less than that needed in a closed cycle system linking the same process heat source and sink. This, in turn, reduces the power requirement for compression, saving both capital and operating costs in the compressor.

However, there is another feature of Type 1 semi-open cycles that tends to increase their direct equipment costs, and this relates to the heat content of the liquid leaving the condenser. In the case of a closed cycle system (Figure 1), the working fluid condensate passes through a throttle valve and flashes. Consequently, the heat content in the condensate above the datum level defined by the evaporator temperature increases the amount of vapor available from the evaporator and so is effectively retained within the heat pump system. In a Type 1 semi-open cycle system, however, the condensate is a process fluid and must usually be cooled (either by process-process interchange or by an external cold utility) to its target temperature. This is invariably below the pinch as the working fluid for a Type 1 system must be a stream which, in the absence of the heat pump, would condense at or below the pinch. Consequently some of the heat that would have been retained within a closed cycle system is removed from a semi-open system and, moreover, some of this removal usually occurs below the pinch. Some relative "oversizing" of semi-open cycle systems is necessary to compensate for this and (as will be shown later) differences do occur in the heat integration of these two heat pump types as a result of these different cooling needs.

In the example under review, the calculated differences in relative sizing and cost for closed and semi-open cycle heat pumps are shown in Table 1.

Table 1: Comparison of Sizing and Direct Costs for Closed and Semi-Open Cycle Heat Pumps

		Closed Cycle	Semi-Open Cycle
Compressor:	Delivered Power (hp)	1504	1224
	Installed Cost* (M$)	599	530
Heat Transfer Area (ft^2):	Condenser+	457	703
	Evaporator	643	---
Heat Load (MM Btu/hr):	Condenser	26.08	26.08
	Evaporator	22.52	24.35**
Cost of Heat Transfer Area (M$)++		44	28
Total Cost (M$)		643	559

*Includes electric motor and starter costs.
**"Evaporator Heat Load" for semi-open cycle is taken as the amount by which the Analyzer Overheads condensing duty is reduced.
+Difference in condenser area reflects a poorer heat transfer for coefficient assumed in the semi-open cycle.
++Costed at $40/ft^2$.

Process Heat Integration

Hot and cold composite curves (8) provide a convenient means for evaluating process heating and cooling duties and for obtaining targets for heat transfer network areas (9). The hot composite curve for a process is effectively the sum of the heat loads of all "hot" streams (i.e. streams that give up heat) within the process. The cold composite curve represents the sum of the heat loads of all process cold streams (i.e. streams that require heating).

Figure 7 shows the hot and cold composite curves for the "base case" used in this study. The closest approach between the curves corresponds to the pinch point for the process. The temperature of the hot composite here is 197°F, and that of the cold composite is 192°F, giving a minimum temperature difference (ΔT_{min}) of 5°F as in the earlier study of this process (7). Figure 8 represents the process after addition of the closed cycle heat pump and Figure 9 after the addition of the semi-open cycle system.

Figure 7: Base Case Process

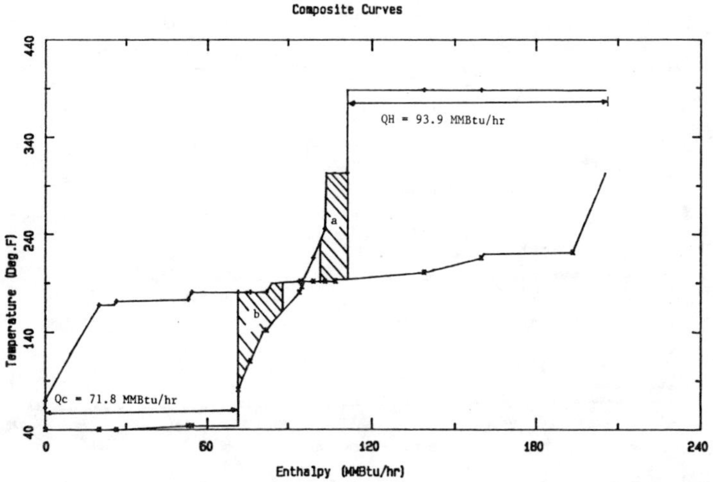

Figure 8: Process with Closed Cycle Heat Pump

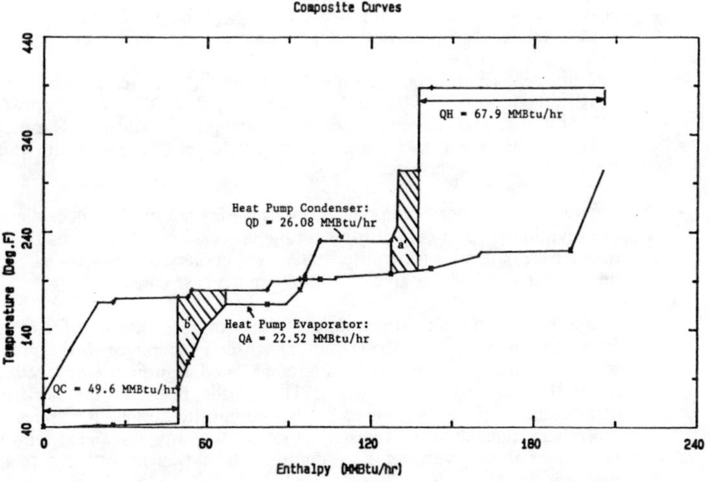

Figure 9: Process with Semi-Open Cycle Heat Pump

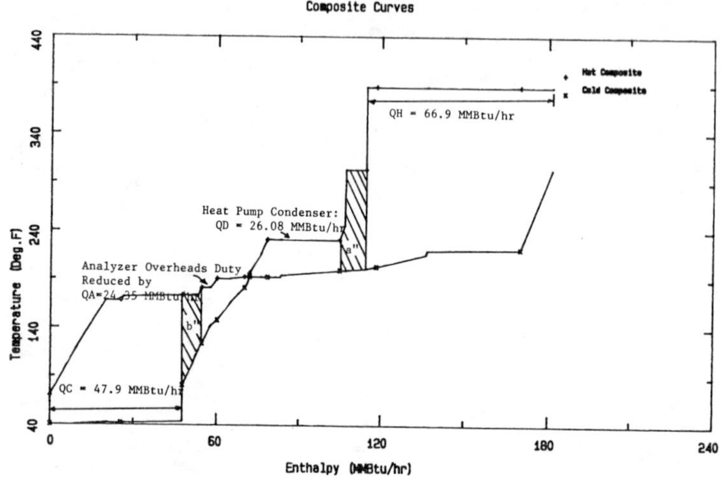

Closed Cycle System

The key points to note in comparing Figure 8 (closed cycle system) with the base case in Figure 7 are as follows:

- The heat pump evaporator and condenser appear as new process streams after the heat pump has been added. This results in an increase in the total heat available in the hot composite curve above the pinch, and an increase in the total heat accepted by the cold composite curve below the pinch.

- The net heating and cooling duties (Q_H and Q_C) are reduced from 93.9 MMBtu/hour to 67.9 MMBtu/hour and from 71.8 MMBtu/hour to 49.6 MMBtu/hour, respectively, when the heat pump is added. These load reductions are equal to the heat pump condenser and evaporator duties (Q_D and Q_A), respectively.

- The reduction in net heating and cooling duties not only reduces the cost of providing hot and cold utilities for the process but also reduces the heat transfer areas needed for utility heaters and coolers by 1649 ft^2. (Cf total utility heater and cooler area of 1024 ft^2 in the base case).

- The average available temperature driving force for the transfer of heat from the hot composite above the condenser temperature to the process streams in the cold composite (a in Figure 7 and a' in Figure 8) is reduced when the heat pump is added. This is the result of the horizontal displacement of this portion of the hot composite curve. It implies that more heat transfer area is needed to satisfy the duty associated with this portion of the curve after heat pumping than was needed before heat pumping.

- The average available temperature driving force for heat transfer from the hot composite to the cold composite curve below the evaporation temperature (b and b' in Figure 7 and Figure 8, respectively) decreases in a manner analogous to that above the condenser temperature. This also implies that additional heat transfer area is needed to satisfy the duties associated with the low temperature end of the cold composite curve when the heat pump is added.

For the example problem the overall increase in process-to-process heat transfer area (i.e. a' - a + b' - b) in going from the "base case" to the process with a closed cycle heat pump is 440 ft^2. This compares with a base case process-to-process heat transfer area of 11,820 ft^2. i.e. the increase is roughly 3.7%.

Semi-Open Cycle System

A comparison of the Type 1 semi-open cycle system (Figure 9) with the base case (Figure 7) reveals both similarities and differences to the findings for the closed system.

The key differences between Figure 7 and Figure 9 are noted below:

- The net heating and cooling requirements (Q_H and Q_C) are reduced from 93.9 MMBtu/hour to 66.9 MMBtu/hour and from 71.8 MMBtu/hour to 47.9 MMBtu/hour, respectively, when the heat pump is added. These utility usage reductions are similar to those obtained with a closed cycle system and also imply a reduction of utility heat transfer area by a total of 1901 ft^2 relative to the base case. However, whereas the reduction in Q_H and Q_C with a closed cycle system were exactly equal to the heat pump condenser and evaporator loads, Q_D and Q_A, respectively, this is not true for the semi-open cycle system. The discrepancy arises because of the heat content of the condensate leaving the condenser. This delivers roughly 0.8 MMBtu/hour above the pinch, reducing Q_H by this amount. It also delivers roughly 0.45 MMBtu/hour below the pinch, increasing Q_C by this amount.

- The condensing duty for the analyzer overheads is reduced by $Q_A = 24.35$ MMBtu/hour, due to the removal of most of this stream to provide the heat pump working fluid. A larger condensing duty (Q_D = 26.08 MMBtu/hour), together with the sensible heating duties mentioned above, is introduced at a higher temperature, leading to several changes in the shape of the hot composite curve. There is no heat pump evaporator, and there are no changes in the cold composite curve.

  This contrasts sharply with the situation obtained with a closed cycle heat pump (Figure 8), in which one stream (heat pump evaporator) is added to the cold composite, one stream (heat pump condenser) is added to the hot composite, and no streams duties are reduced or eliminated.

- The heat pump condenser displaces the high temperature portion of the hot composite curve to the right. Consequently the average available temperature driving force for the transfer of heat from the hot composite curve above the condenser to the process streams in the cold composite curve is reduced upon addition of a semi-open cycle heat pump (a" in Figure 9). This result is analogous to that obtained with a closed cycle heat pump, and indicates that the heat transfer area required to satisfy the duty associated with this part of the curve is increased by the addition of the heat pump.

- Elimination of most of the analyzer overhead condensing duty displaces the low temperature portion of the hot composite curve to the right (relative to the pinch point). This reduces the available temperature driving forces for process-process heat transfer below the analyzer condenser temperature and so increases the required heat transfer area for process-process duties (b" in Figure 9).

Although this result is superficially similar to that obtained with a closed cycle, it should be noted the reasons are different. Moreover the size of the heat load affected by the reduced driving forces is smaller in the semi-open cycle case than it is with the closed cycle (compare b' in Figure 8 with b" in Figure 9). However, the area penalty for the semi-open cycle system includes an allowance for the heat transfer area needed to cool the heat pump condensate and its overall area penalty is 980 ft^2 relative to the base case (cf 440 ft^2 for the closed cycle system).

OVERALL ECONOMICS

The total capital costs of the process using either a closed cycle or a semi-open heat pump is greater than that of the "base case" process. The overall differences in installed equipment cost are summarized in Table 2. Also shown in Table 2 are the reductions in external heating and cooling duties (relative to the base case) and the heat pump power requirements for both systems; and the monetary savings and simple payback achieved assuming typical costs for process heating and cooling and for electric power to drive the heat pump compressor.

Table 2: Comparison of Overall Economics

	Closed Cycle	Semi-Open Cycle
Incremental Capital Cost Above Base Case (M$)	594.1	521.3
Reduction in Heat Loads Relative to Base Case (MMBtu/hr):		
Heating	26.0	27.0
Cooling	22.2	23.9
Heat Pump Power (kW)	1181	961
Monetary Saving* (M$/yr)	252.1	359.4
Simple Payback* (yr)	2.36	1.45

*Assumes heat available at $3.00/MMBtu, cooling at $0.30/MMBtu and electricity at $0.045/kWh. Capital cost basis as in (7).

These results show that the semi-open system is not only less costly than the closed cycle system in terms of initial investment, but also that it yields substantially greater savings (relative to the base case). The simple payback on the semi-open cycle is 1.45 years, compared to 2.36 years for the closed cycle system. This assumes that the heat pump is installed at the same time as the process itself is installed, and these paybacks relate to the <u>incremental</u> investment required to incorporate the heat pump. The systems evaluated here have not been fully optimized and the costs quoted should be regarded as indicative only.

CONCLUSIONS

Semi-open reverse Rankine cycle heat pumps, which use a process stream as the working fluid, are sometimes a practical option for industrial process energy savings. For such systems to be possible the stream that is used as the working fluid must undergo a vapor/liquid phase change as a necessary part of the process prior to installation of the heat pump.

Semi-open reverse Rankine cycle heat pumps, where they are possible, are potentially more cost effective than closed cycle systems because:

- The capital cost of a semi-open cycle heat pump is invariably less than that of a closed cycle system for the equivalent duty;
- The power requirements of a semi-open cycle heat pump are less than those of the equivalent closed cycle system.

Both semi-open and closed cycle heat pumps reduce the heat transfer area required for utility heaters and coolers in any given process. They also generally lead to an increase in the heat transfer area needed for process-process heat integration, assuming a fixed value for the minimum temperature driving force. This area penalty is usually smaller for a closed cycle heat pump than it is for a semi-open cycle system.

In the specific example studied in this paper (a liquor distillery), a semi-open cycle system was shown to be less costly to install and capable of providing larger operating savings than a comparable closed cycle system. The system payback on the semi-open cycle system is 1.45 years.

ACKNOWLEDGEMENT

This work has been undertaken with the financial support of the Electric Power Research Institute (EPRI) (RP: 2220-3 and RP: 2783-5). However, any opinions, findings, conclusions or recommendations expressed herein are those of the authors and do not necessarily reflect the views of EPRI.

REFERENCES

1. Ranade, S.M., E. Hindmarsh and D. Boland, "Industrial Heat Pumps: New Insights on Their Integration in Total Sites," 3rd International Symposium on Large Scale Applications of Heat Pumps, BHRA, Oxford, England (March 1987).

2. Ranade, S.M., E. Hindmarsh and D. Boland, "Industrial Heat Pumps: Appropriate Placement and Sizing Using the Grand Composite," 8th Industrial Energy Technology Conference, Houston, Texas (June 1986).

3. Chappell, R.N. and S.J. Priebe, "Process Integration of Industrial Heat Pumps," 8th Industrial Energy Technology Conference, Houston, Texas (June 1986).

4. Karp, A., "Industrial Process Heat Pumps - Some Unconventional Wisdom," 9th Industrial Energy Technology Conference, Houston, Texas (September 1987).

5. Rossiter, A.P., R.V. Seetharam and S.M. Ranade, "Scope for Industrial Heat Pump Applications in the United States," In Press, Journal of Heat Recovery Systems and CHP.

6. HPSCAN (Heat Pump Screening Analysis), Software package developed by TENSA Services for the Electric Power Research Institute, Palo Alto, CA.

7. Report DE87009626 "Optimum Heat Pump Placement in Industrial Process," Prepared by TENSA Services for the U.S. Department of Energy (March 1987), Available through NTIS.

8. "User Guide on Process Integration for the Efficient Use of Energy," Institution of Chemical Engineers, Rugby, England (1982).

9. Townsend, D.W. and B. Linnhoff, "Surface Area Targets for Heat Exchanger Networks," 11th Annual Research Meeting, The Institution of Chemical Engineers, Rugby, England (1984).

THE RECOVERY OF VOLATILE ORGANIC COMPOUNDS[1]

R. N. Chappell
U.S. Department of Energy/Idaho Operations Office
785 DOE Place
Idaho Falls, ID 83402

D. S. Plaster
EG&G Idaho, Inc.
P.O. Box 1625
Idaho Falls, ID 83415-3527

VOC RECOVERY

Industry has a need to recover a wide variety of fluids from air or gas streams. These fluids are usually referred to as volatile organic compounds or VOCs. Two factors are the prime motivators for recovery of VOCs:

1. The need for clean air discharges to the atmosphere.

2. The value of the fluids.

VOCs also often represent a sizable energy expenditure in terms of their manufacture and their removal, recovery, or disposal which makes their recovery of interest to DOE.

Many of the VOCs industry would like to recover from air or gas streams are used as solvents primarily for coating and cleaning. Coating applications include the manufacture of magnetic tapes, audiotapes, videotapes, adhesive tapes, and textiles. Also included are painting, printing, and similar activities. Cleaning applications include washing circuit boards during the photochemical manufacturing process, cleaning electronic parts, cleaning mechanical parts, furniture stripping and textile cleaning. VOCs used for other purposes such as refrigerants, plastic foam manufacturing, plastics manufacturing, or fuel components also find their way into air or gas streams and their recovery is often desirable. The spectrum of opportunities for VOC recovery is very broad, covering high technology industries which can justify considerable capital outlay and technically trained personnel to operate the recovery systems to low technology industries which can afford neither.

---

[1]Work supported by the U.S. Department of Energy Assistant Secretary, Donna R. Fitzpatrick, Office of Industrial Programs, under DOE Contract No. DE-AC07-76ID01570.

In order to comply with emission standards, industry often uses incineration to destroy VOCs carried by airstreams, and incineration is a competing alternative to recovery. However, since the concentration allowed for combustible VOCs in airstreams is 25 to 50% of the lower explosion limit, combustion cannot be sustained without adding a great deal of fuel. When incineration is used for disposal of noncombustible VOCs, even more fuel or catalytic systems are needed to ensure destruction.

VOC recovery is currently done mainly by carbon bed adsorption. A carbon bed can remove many VOCs, which can then be desorbed from the carbon bed for disposal or reuse. However, carbon bed adsorption is also not entirely satisfactory. There is a potential fire hazard associated with VOCs in carbon beds. Further, if steam is used to regenerate the bed, chlorinated hydrocarbons can decompose to form hydrochloric acid, which is very corrosive. Other VOCs may decompose to the extent that the recovered solvent is no longer recyclable to the process.

Another alternative is replacement of the hazardous VOCs in the process with more benign materials which can be discharged to the atmosphere without harm. However, because the cost of these new VOCs is often high, recovery becomes necessary for economic reasons. Also, more benign VOCs need not be removed to the very low levels required with some less benign VOCs. This adds to the economic attractiveness of removing benign VOCs because removal of, say 90% is less expensive than removal of say 97% as might be required for some toxic VOCs.

3M has found the reverse Brayton cycle to be an attractive alternative for recovery of solvents from airstreams primarily because of the value of the recovered solvents and the Brayton cycle's operating flexibility. The system is inherently stable, gets down to operating temperature in minutes, and has a high turndown ratio. Also, the recovered solvents are not damaged in the recovery process which makes them readily reusable, which in turn allows product improvement through use of more expensive solvents in the tape manufacturing process. However, how far the technology will spread beyond 3M will depend primarily on the following recovery system characteristics:

1. Ease of operation and reliability

2. Operating cost

3. Capital cost

4. Lowest temperature achievable.

The first three characteristics will determine penetration into the lower technology areas. 3M is a relatively high technology company who can afford both the funds and technical manpower to obtain and maintain relatively sophisticated equipment. The VOC recovery market is like a pyramid with companies like 3M at the top and thousands of smaller less sophisticated companies at the bottom. Many other industries in the pyramid would like to recover VOCs from airstreams but they lack the funds and technical know-how. Equipment is sorely needed to fit their needs.

The last characteristic relates both to how much of any particular VOC can be recovered and the kinds of VOCs which can be recovered as well. No VOC can be completely recovered from an airstream by refrigeration, but the amount recoverable increases with lower temperatures. Of course, some VOCs require very low temperatures for acceptable recovery rates while others do not. This can be seen in Table 1 in which several VOCs are listed by the condensing temperatures required to reduce the concentrations to approximately 1000 parts per million by volume. Of course, the list of VOCs in Table 1 is by no means a complete list of fluids which industry may wish to recover from air or gas streams. It should also be noted that the dew point temperature changes with pressure of the airstream carrying the VOC. High pressure increases the dew point which means that for a given temperature, the VOC concentration by weight can be reduced to lower levels in air streams at high pressure than in those at low pressure.

TABLE 1. EXAMPLES OF FLUIDS WHICH CAN BE REMOVED WITH THE BRAYTON CYCLE SOLVENT RECOVERY HEAT PUMP

POSSIBILITIES FOR REMOVING DILUTE SOLVENT FROM NONCONDENSIBLE GAS STREAMS AT 1 ATM

Solvent	Normal Boiling Point (°F)	Condensing Temperature (°F)
R-14	-198	-297
R-22	-41	-190
Methyl Chloride	-11	-174
R-114	39	-140
R-11	75	-120
Methylene Chloride	105	-94
R-113	118	-90
THF	151	-66
MEK	175	-55
Toluene	231	-16
1,1,1 Trichloro Ethane	237	-62
MIBK	246	30
Perchloroethylene	249	-5
DMF	307	45
DMSO	372	32

Because the manufacture of VOCs and their recovery either for disposal or for recycle represents a significant energy expenditure, the problem of VOC recovery from airstreams is of interest to the Department of Energy. Heat pumps are also of interest because in certain circumstances heat pumps may offer advantages over other means of VOC removal. Depending upon the application, these potential advantages may include: (a) VOCs removed by heat pumps may be more readily recyclable, (b) heat pumps can recover latent heats of vaporization of the VOCs in the airstream and of water as well, (c) heat pumps may be more compatible with the process, and (d) heat pumps may be more cost effective.

3M HUTCHINSON, MINNESOTA INSTALLATION

In 1978 DOE initiated development of a solvent recovery heat pump using Brayton cycle technology. AiResearch of Torrance, California performed the research and development of the system, which has subsequently been purchased and installed in a 3M video tape manufacturing facility in Hutchinson, Minnesota. A measure of the success of this technology can be found in the long-range planning of 3M, who it is believed, intends widespread use of similar systems in their manufacturing facilities.

The 3M/AiResearch/DOE system is large, measuring about 30 ft by 16 ft by 14 ft and weighing approximately 20 tons. It is housed in a small building addition located adjacent to the drying oven. The capacity of the system, 8,000 cfm, is only sufficient to service part of the oven air. Figure 1 is a schematic of the heat pump configuration as installed at Hutchinson.

The solvent laden air, at approximately 45% of the Lower Explosion Limit (LEL), is first cooled by a heat pipe, which returns the heat to fresh oven make-up air. It is then compressed, and passes through a second heat pipe which recovers the heat of compression to heat the clean air returning to the oven. A water cooled heat exchanger has also been installed to provide balance if needed. Two Freon cooled heat exchangers then remove the solvent and any moisture present as well. After removal of the solvent, the clean air passes through a turbine which removes heat from the airstream in the form of work to power the compressor and reduces the temperature below -120°F. The air is then passed through a final set of heat exchangers which reheat the air returning to the oven and cool the Freon. Parallel Freon heat exchangers are used in the solvent condensers to allow defrosting for water removal. In this application the Freon is a sensible heat transfer medium and does not undergo a phase change. The system effectively removes approximately 93% of the solvent contained in the airstream. The system's operating controls are designed to allow unattended operation.

After recovery, the solvent is stored and subsequently redistilled. 3M is presently qualifying the recovered solvent for reuse in the manufacture of video tape. Recovered solvents include toluene, methyl ethyl ketone, xylene, and tetrahydrofuran.

LIMITS ON VOC RECOVERY BY REFRIGERATION

Two limitations on VOC recovery by refrigeration exist: physical and economic. The major physical limitation is the temperature to which the airstream can be reduced. Lower temperatures equate to greater VOC recovery percentages. This occurs because a VOC must reach its dew point before it will condense and dew points diminish with concentration.(1) This trend can be seen in Table 2.

As previously stated, 100% of any given compound cannot be removed by condensation. There will always be some left. However, in closed or nearly closed systems like the 3M tape drying application, the small amount of VOCs remaining after the first pass through the heat pump can be recycled to the oven with the returning air and back through the heat pump again. In the second pass and all

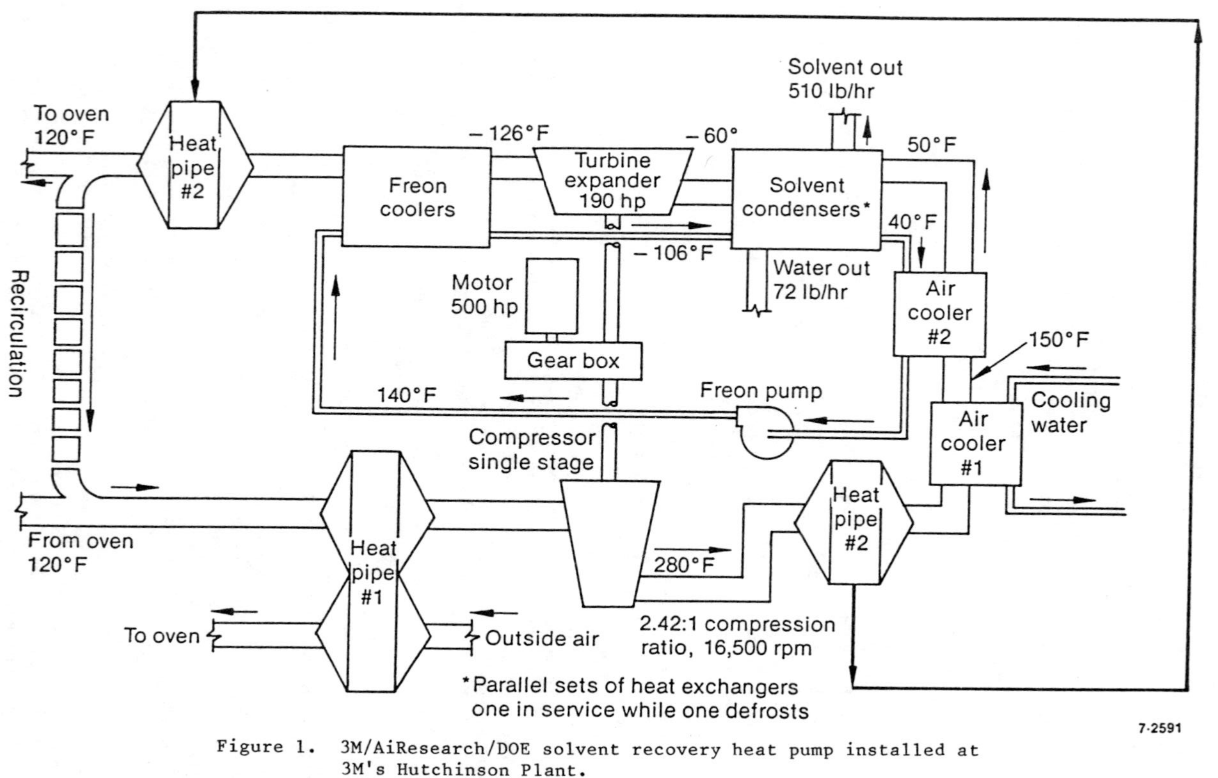

Figure 1. 3M/AiResearch/DOE solvent recovery heat pump installed at 3M's Hutchinson Plant.

TABLE 2. TEMPERATURES REQUIRED TO CONDENSE SOME COMMON SOLVENT VAPORS FROM AIR AT ATMOSPHERIC PRESSURE[1]

			Dew Point or Saturation Temperature (°F)		
Solvent	LEL (% by Volume)	Vapor Press at LEL (mm Hg)	At LEL	At 50% LEL	At 10% LEL
MIBK	1.4	10.6	87	68	30
Methanol	6.7	50.9	48	27	-14
Toluene	1.2	9.12	40	20	-17
Heptane	1.05	7.99	21	3	-32
MEK	1.9	14.4	11	-9	-48
Acetone	2.6	19.8	-6	-25	-61
THF	2.0	15.2	-9	-29	-66

subsequent passes through the heat pump, the concentration of VOCs in the airstream is returned again and again to the same level. In this way, most is recovered and very little gets into the environment even though the percentage remaining after each pass is significant.

The only physical limitation presently foreseen on the temperature to which the airstream can be reduced by the Brayton cycle is the liquefaction temperature of oxygen at -297°F. Thus refrigeration is physically capable of removing most VOCs to acceptable levels especially in closed or semiclosed systems. Of course in open systems where fresh air is brought into the oven, loaded with VOCs, passed through the heat pump, and discharged to the atmosphere, the amount of VOCs in the airstream leaving the heat pump is the amount discharged to the atmosphere. Therefore, open systems may require lower temperatures to be environmentally acceptable which will result in higher operating costs.

The second limitation, economics, depends on the cost of recovery and the value of the VOCs. The cost of recovery should include both operating and capital costs, and the value of the VOCs should include both the purchase value and the value of the avoided costs of keeping harmful quantities of the VOCs from the environment. AiResearch estimated the purchase value of the solvents in the 3M application to be \$0.28/lb in 1980.[2] Their heat pump was designed to remove about 500 lbs of solvent vapor per hour. The heat pump is driven by a 500 hp motor which at an electricity price of \$0.04/kWh yields an operating cost of \$0.03/lb of solvent. Adding to this maintenance costs of \$0.01/lb of solvent, yields an operating cost of \$0.04/lb of solvent. If the capital cost is \$600,000 installed, the simple payback is approximately seven months.

Removal of the solvents in carbon beds is reported to cost about \$0.06/lb of solvent removed,[3] including maintenance. If the installed capital costs are about \$450,000, the simple payback for the carbon bed solvent recovery system is approximately six months. Thus it can be seen that economically the Brayton cycle solvent recovery system compares favorably with recovery by carbon beds. If the improved quality of the recovered solvent, and the potential for product improvement by the use of more expensive solvents is considered, the Brayton cycle looks very attractive.

For incineration, capital cost is very low, but operating cost is high. If the VOC concentration in the airstream is 50% of the LEL (an upper limit for insurance underwriters), about 50 cu ft of natural gas per pound of typical VOC would be required to reliably sustain combustion which yields a cost of $0.15/lb of VOC. However there is no payback from recovery of the VOCs because the VOCs are destroyed. Sometimes heat is recovered from incineration of the VOCs, but in many applications incineration produces more heat than the process can profitably use.

POSSIBLE IMPROVEMENTS

The AiResearch 8,000 cfm heat pump installed in the 3M Hutchinson Facility is a second generation machine. A simpler 2,000 cfm machine(1) was installed earlier at 3M's headquarters in Minneapolis St Paul and was used on an experimental basis. 3M has a third generation machine undergoing shakedown tests in their Weatherford, Oklahoma, floppy disc manufacturing facility. DOE is not privy to design details of the first or the third generation machines. Undoubtedly later generations will also be designed and built because many configurations of the basic Brayton cycle are possible. Some of the many possible configurations will be briefly discussed here.

The 3M/AiResearch/DOE machine is a close relative to the classical regenerative Brayton refrigeration cycle(4) which is typically depicted as in Figure 2. In this classical reverse Brayton or air cycle heat pump low temperature heat flows in as shown and a higher temperature heat flows out. The corresponding temperature, entropy diagram is shown in Figure 3. Heat flows into the heat pump, heating the working fluid (which is air in these machines) over segment (4-b). The working fluid is further heated by regeneration over segment (b-1) and compressed over segment (1-2). The working fluid is cooled by discharging heat over segment (2-a). Over segment (a-3) the working fluid is further cooled by regeneration and it is finally expanded to state point (4) where it is again ready to pick up more low temperature heat.

The 3M/AiResearch/DOE machine can be represented conceptually as shown in Figure 4. The idealized temperature, entropy diagram for the 3M/AiResearch/DOE system is shown in Figure 5. The difference between this system and the classical refrigeration system (Figure 3) is readily apparent. Heat is removed from the working fluid (the air stream) over segment (b-1) in this system by evaporating the solvent in the drying oven. Heat is added to the working fluid over segment (a-3) by condensing the solvent. Regeneration occurs by transfer of heat from working fluid over segment (2-3) to working fluid over segment (4-b). Heat is pumped, then, from segment (a-3) to segment (b-1).

Comparing Figure 3 with Figure 5 shows that the heat acceptance and heat rejection segments of the classical refrigeration cycle have been switched with the regenerative segments. One result is that condensation of almost all of the solvent occurs upstream of the expander. Of course some does occur in the expander and the amount

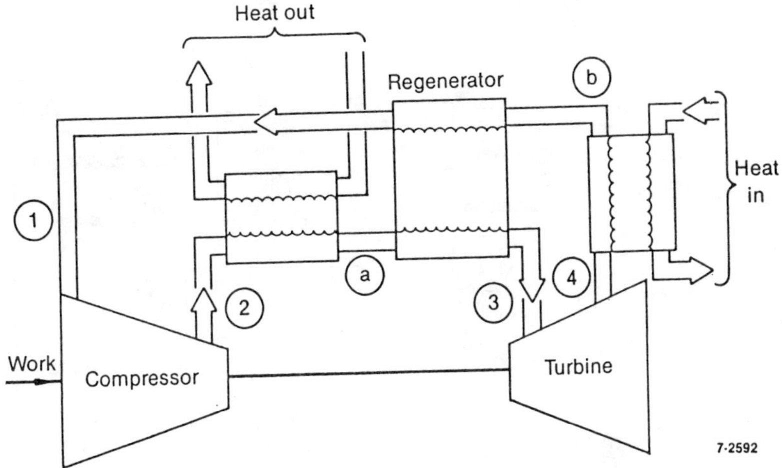

Figure 2. Classical closed Brayton or air cycle refrigerator with regeneration.(4)

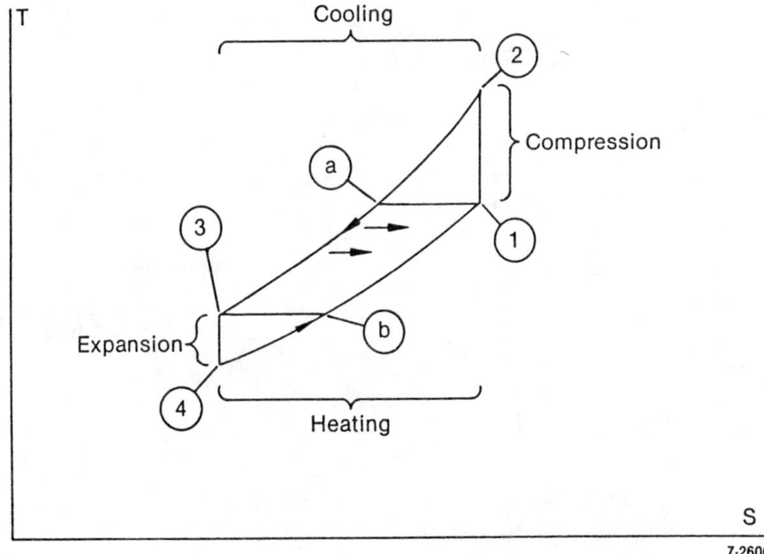

Figure 3. A temperature, entropy diagram of an idealized Brayton or air cycle refrigerator with regeneration.(4)

of solvent returning in the clean air stream is dependent on the temperature and pressure at state point (4). Removal of most of the solvent and water upstream of the expander protects it from liquid solvent, water and ice. Condensation in the expander would require a

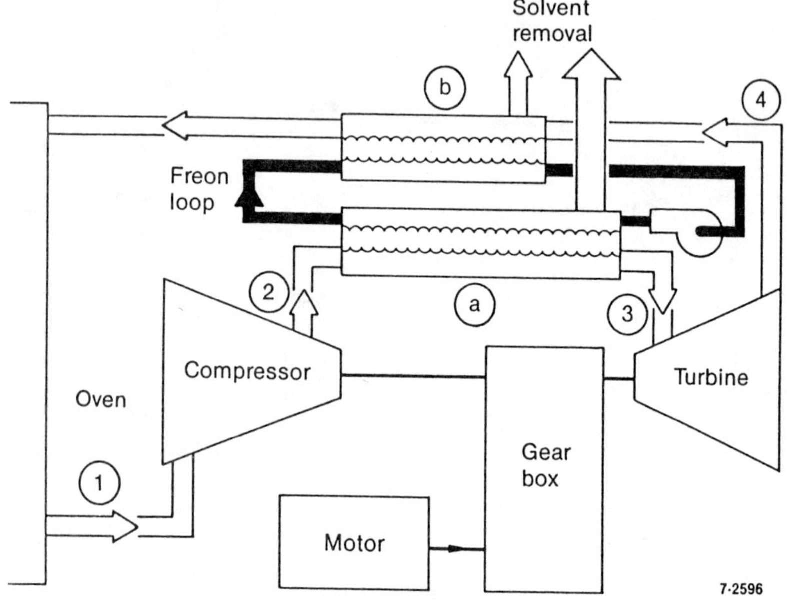

Figure 4. The 3M/AiResearch/DOE heat pump in simplified form.

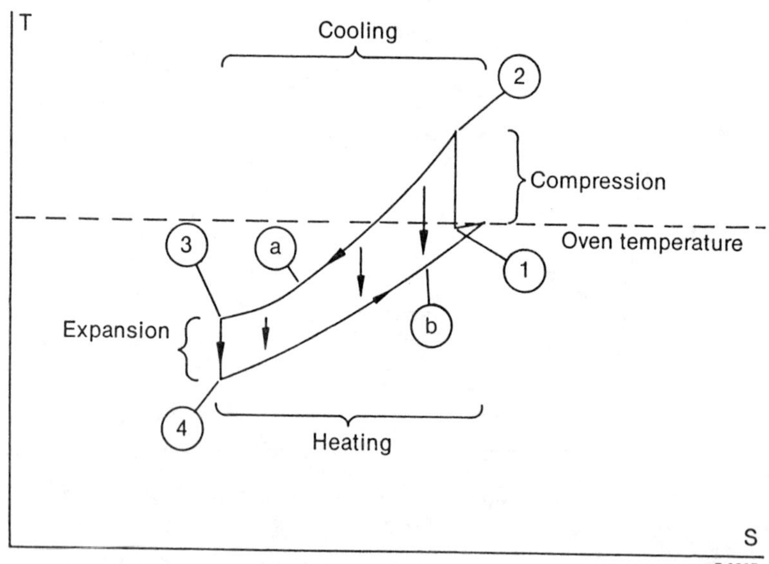

Figure 5. An idealized temperature, entropy diagram for VOC recovery heat pump.

machine capable of handling vapor, liquid, and solid phases together. Of course, solvent, water, and ice form in the AiResearch expander but only in very small quantities since most is removed in the heat exchanger upstream. Removal of solvent and water in an expander specially designed to handle all three phases may be an improvement which should be further examined.

Because of the importance of regeneration, a trade-off should be made between a lower approach temperature at the heat exchangers (and the attendant increased cost) and the external power requirement. This is shown in Figure 6 where the annualized cost represents both the operating and capital costs. Ideally from a cost standpoint, the design should correspond to the minimum of the curve. Of course some other considerations may cause the design point to shift off the minimum. Figure 7 shows the effect of increased regeneration on the temperature, entropy diagram. It is critical for VOC recovery that state point (3) remains, at the same temperature or is reduced in temperature. State point (1) must of course remain at the oven temperature. Figure 7 shows that regeneration accomplishes this, and the area encompassed by (1-2-3-4) has also been decreased which means a decrease in the power requirement.

Another power saving design feature which AiResearch used on their machine is precooling the oven air before introducing it into

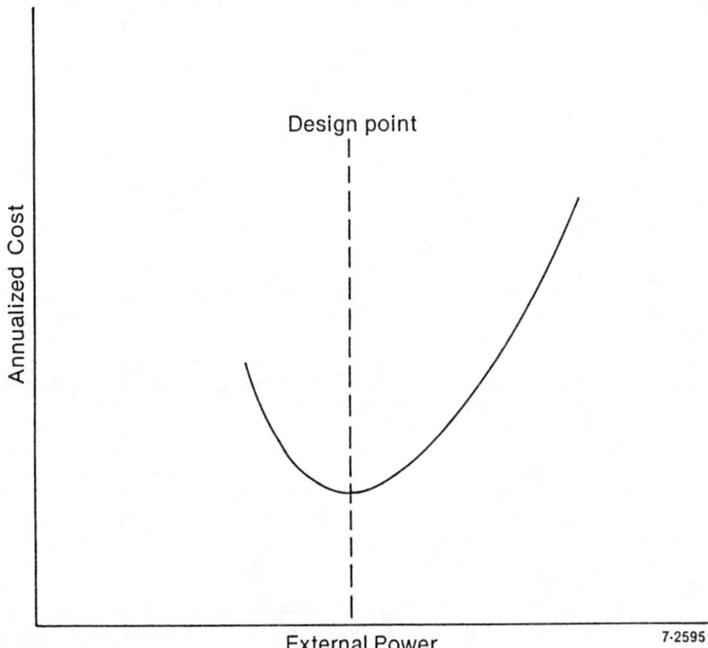

Figure 6. Hypothetical curve for optimizing the trade-off between the regenerator approach temperature and external power requirements.

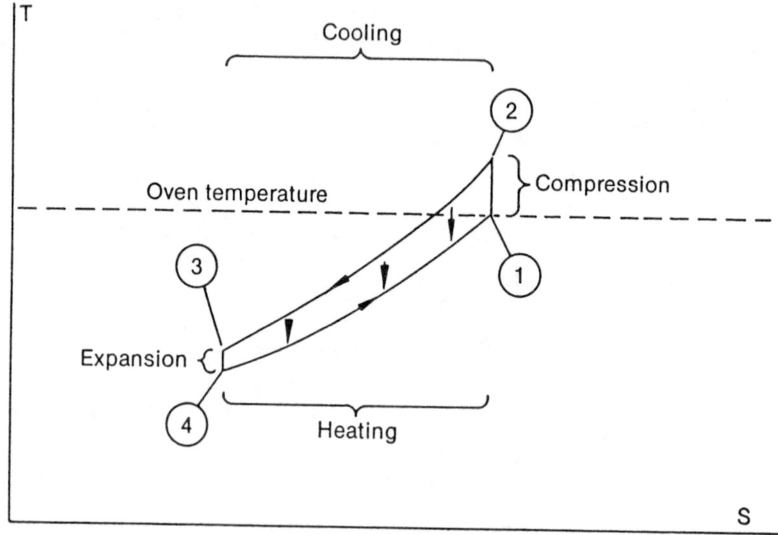

Figure 7. An idealized temperature, entropy diagram for VOC recovery heat pumps with lower regenerator approach temperatures.

the compressor. 3M has since utilized this heat (heat pipe No. 1, Figure 1) to preheat oven make-up air. This essentially represents discharging heat to the surroundings because the oven capacity at the 3M Facility is much larger than the capacity of the AiResearch machine. The effect of transferring oven heat to the surroundings from the closed cycle represented by the oven and the heat pump is shown in Figure 8. Note the reduction in power requirements as indicated by the reduction in area encompassed by the cycle. [Compare (1-2'-3-4-1) with (1-2-3-4-1).]

3M found the gear box on the machine in Figure 4 to be very expensive and was able to make a substantial reduction in capital cost of the machine installed at Weatherford by removing the gear box and introducing the power from the electric motor through an inexpensive, low speed compressor as shown in Figure 9. Also shown in Figure 9 is air to air heat exchange rather than the Freon loop. Elimination of the Freon loop would allow very low temperatures and save a little on capital cost, but some design and operational flexibility may be lost. It is believed that the third generation machine installed at 3M's Weatherford Facility retained the Freon loop, but it may be desirable to eliminate it in favor of air to air heat exchange in applications where very low temperatures are required for VOC removal.

Another possible cost reduction utilizes a high speed electric drive as shown in Figure 10. Turbocompressors are sometimes driven by high speed electric motors in which the rotors consist of permanent magnets imbedded in a nonmagnetic rotor shaft. Machines of this type may be quite inexpensive but they will be small because currently available high speed motors are limited to about 50 hp, whereas

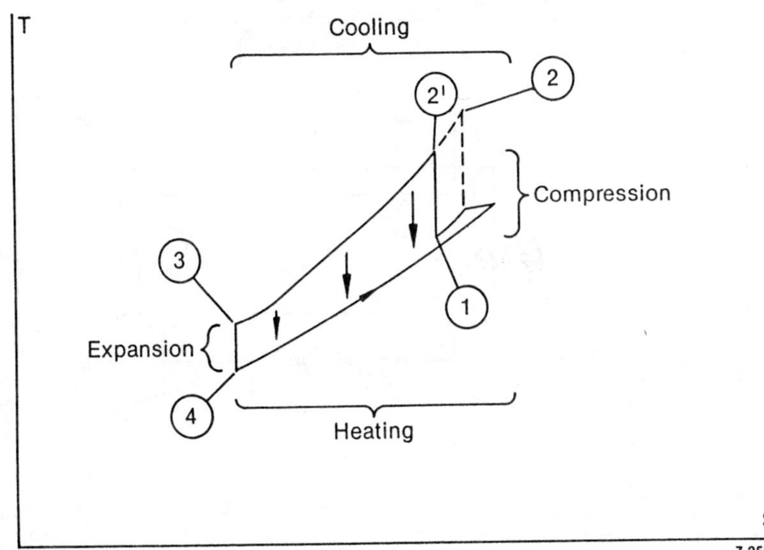

Figure 8. An idealized temperature, entropy diagram showing oven air precooling upstream of the compressor.

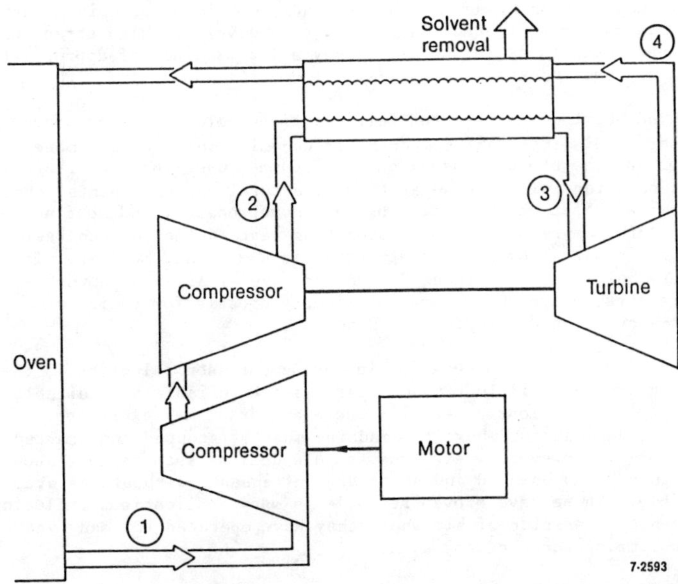

Figure 9. The 3M/NUCON heat pump installed at the 3M Weatherford Facility.

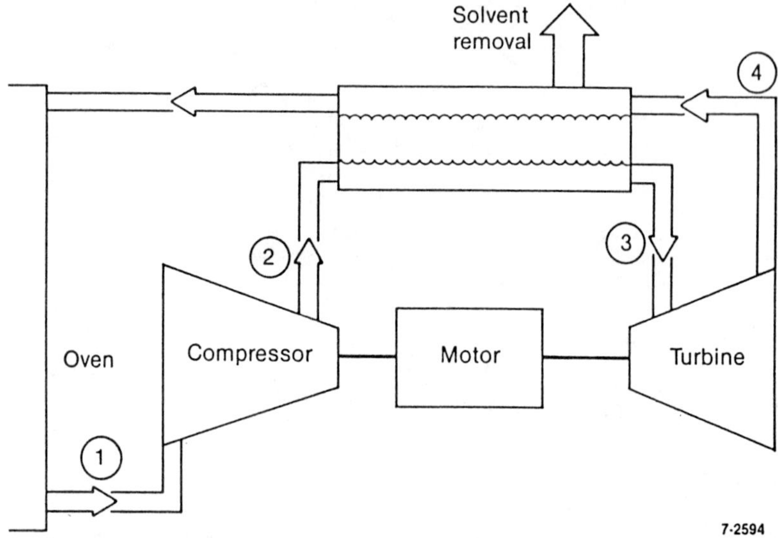

Figure 10. A high speed electric motor driven configuration with air to air heat exchange.

the 3M/AiResearch/DOE machine is driven by a 500 hp motor. However, adding heat exchange area to increase regeneration and reduce power requirements, ganging several high speed electric motor driven turbocompressors together, and the use of newly developed high strength permanent magnets(4) in the motors may allow machines of appropriate size for some industrial purposes.

The heart of any Brayton refrigeration cycle is the turbocompressor. This important component is becoming increasingly more common and therefore, less expensive. Common uses include cryogenic air separation, wellhead separation of natural gas components, cooling for aircraft air conditioning, and more recently and most ubiquitous, turbocompressors for reciprocating heat engine superchargers varying in size from large stationary diesels to automobiles. The writers believe that 3M ganged together several AiResearch turbocompressors designed for large stationary diesels for their third-generation Weatherford machine.

An important consideration in turbocompressor selection is the bearing design. Oil lubricated bearings are reliable and suitable for many applications especially where a gearbox may exert appreciable side loads or where the machine must be stopped and started frequently. However, where free spindle designs such as that shown in Figure 9 can be used and stops are infrequent, airbearings are possible. These have proven reliable in many applications including cryogenic separation of air where they have operated for many years without maintenance of any kind.

CONCLUSIONS

The 3M/AiResearch/DOE machine installed in 3M's Hutchinson Facility and its successor installed in 3M's Weatherford Facility have shown that variations on the refrigeration Brayton or air cycles are an attractive way to recover valuable solvents from airstreams. These applications represent the top and most sophisticated of the VOC recovery pyramid. To recover the larger amounts of VOCs in the lower portion of the pyramid will require less expensive and less sophisticated equipment. The many Brayton cycle configurations possible and the worldwide market potential for VOC recovery machines would indicate that companies which have this technology should explore the possibilities.

REFERENCES

1. Paper, The Air or Brayton Cycle Solvent Recovery System, by Bryce J. Fox, 3M Co., contained in Proceedings of DOE Industrial Heat Pump Workshop, October 14 and 15, 1986, CONF-8610169.

2. Topical Report - Brayton Cycle Solvent Recovery System Development Test Results (Phase III, System Test), Report Number DOE/CS/40005-T6.

The preceding references can be obtained from the National Technical Information Service, U.S. Department of Commerce, Springfield, Virginia 22161.

3. Paper, Economic Aspects of Solvent Recovery Using Active Carbon, by I. M. Yound, Sutcliffe, Speakman & Co., Ltd., contained in Solvents, the Neglected Parameter, 2nd Solvents Symposium 1977, The University of Manchester Institute of Science and Technology.

4. Fundamentals of Classical Thermodynamics, p. 315, Van Wylen, GJ and Sonntag, RE, John Wiley and Sons, 2nd corrected printing, 1968.

5. Science, Volume 223, March 2, 1984 - Powerful New Magnet Material Found by Arthur Robinson.

UTILITY MANAGEMENT/ MARKETING

TOOLS AND TECHNIQUES FOR EVALUATING DEMAND-SIDE MANAGEMENT OPTIONS

Stephen M. Barrager
Vice President
Decision Focus Incorporated

At the urging of regulators, stockholders and customers, electric utilities are offering a variety of new products. These products include conservation, direct load control, electric space heat, heat and cool storage, interruptible rates and real time pricing. Regulators are urging companies to sell conservation instead of building new plants. Utility stockholders also support many of these products as a way of avoiding new risky investments and improving the productivity of their assets. Customers are asking for many of these products hoping to reduce their energy costs and increase their competitiveness.

There are so many of these products and so many target markets that utilities need tools and techniques for choosing among them. Their decisions are confounded not only by the shear number of options but also by the technical complexity of the electric power system and energy markets.

Although the electric power system is unique in many ways, there is nothing new about the process of selecting and designing products. Product offerings in any industry have always faced at least two important economic tests:

1. The marketability test.
2. The profitability test.

These tests are applied on a daily basis in virtually every business. We are rapidly reaching the point where they can be applied effectively in the electric power industry.

The Marketability Test (the "participant" test)

In the Demand-side Management (DSM) literature, the marketability test is often called the participant test. We prefer the term marketability because it is more descriptive and more general. A DSM program has market potential if if it can provide a target customer with benefits in excess of his direct costs. This can be accomplished by lowering the cost of a necessary service like space heat. It can also be accomplished with products that increase costs, e.g., increased security lighting. There is market potential in cases like this if the customer perceives that the increase in value exceeds the estimated increase in costs. Most DSM products are marketed by demonstrating improvements in the customer's bottom line or his well being.

The Profitability Test (the "nonparticipant" test)

Generally speaking, profit is the difference between revenue and cost. A program to promote electric space heat will be profitable to nonelectric space heating customers (nonparticipants) if the change in revenues due to the program is greater than the change in costs. If, for example, a utility can sell enough electricity to heat a home for $600.00 per year and this increases utility costs (capital and operating) by only $500.00 then there is a "profit" of $100.00 per year on the transaction.

In a regulated, cost of service environment like the one we have in the electric utility industry today, this kind of profit is passed back to the customers. Most of these customers are nonparticipants and therefore the test is popularly called the nonparticipant test. In an unregulated environment, these profits would probably be shared by customers and stockholders.

Reliability

Reliability is a key determinant of the value of electrical service. DSM impacts on service reliability or quality can be included in the marketability and profitability tests by placing a price or value on unserved energy. Such economic valuations of reliability are rapidly replacing traditional reliability standards, which typically implied high reliability--no matter what the cost. Economic evaluations of reliability allow more flexibility in making tradeoffs between service quality and cost. The appropriate values for reliability are an active research topic.

What Happened to Least Cost Planning and the no Losers Test?

The marketability and profitability tests span both the least cost and no losers concepts. Any program that passes both the market and profit tests will move the whole energy delivery system to a lower cost state. This is consistent with the tenets of least cost planning. Any program that can pass these two tests can also make everyone a winner. This meets the objectives of the no loser tests. The market and profit tests have the added advantage that they are consistent with standard business practice.

TOOLS AND TECHNIQUES

The task of the DSM planner in today's utility is to assemble a portfolio of programs that pass the marketability and profitability tests. Further, in order to recruit support for DSM programs the planner must be able to demonstrate that the proposed DSM program is more profitable than alternatives. The alternatives include options like building new generation or signing long term power contracts.

In developing a resource plan that includes DSM options, at least two analytical tools are required. A demand-side screening tool and an integrated resource planning model. The steps in developing an integrated resource plan and the relationship of the tools required are sketched in Figure 1. We will briefly discuss the design and function of each kind of tool.

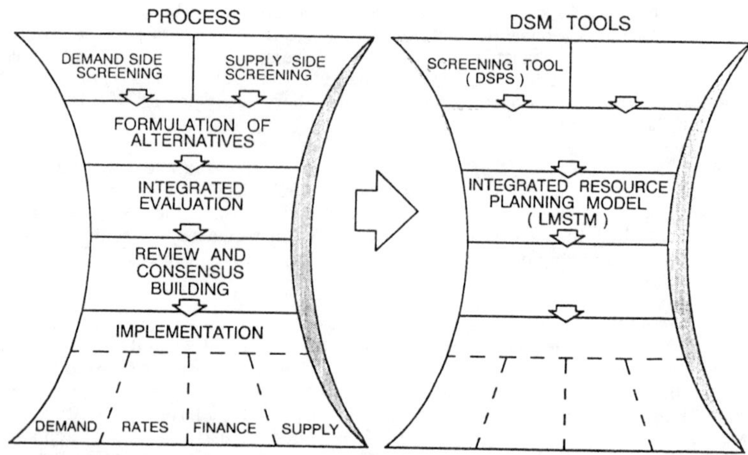

Figure 1. Integrated Resource Planning

DEMAND-SIDE SCREENING

There are literally hundreds of different DSM options that might be considered by any utility. Each option in turn can be targeted at several different market segments and each option can be promoted using one of several different rebate or rate structures. It would be hopeless to collect data and analyze all the candidates in detail. Some screening capability is needed.

A state-of-the-art DSM screening tool is currently under development in a joint project sponsored by EPRI, the National Rural Electric Cooperative Association, and Niagara Mohawk Power Company. This tool is called the Demand-side Planning Software (DSPS). The design reflects the DSM planning experience of over 30 utilities ranging in size from the largest in the country to the smallest.

The inputs to the DSPS are data items that every DSM planner is familiar with: rate schedules, fuel costs, and customer or end-use energy profiles (energy use and load shapes). In addition, there are inputs provided by generation system planners or system operators. These inputs include estimates of marginal costs (energy, generation, and transmission and distribution). Records of hourly system load shapes for the total system are also input. Depending on the availability of the required inputs, the DSPS can do economic evaluations for a single year or for up to a twenty five year horizon.

Within the DSPS, the marketability test is applied by using rates and customer energy use profiles to calculate the customer's energy costs before and after each DSM program. Usually net benefits are expressed in terms of payback period (years) or the net present value of savings. The terms in the marketability test are shown in Table 1.

TABLE 1

Elements of the Marketability Test

Rates, before and after

Customer impacts, before and after

- Load shapes
- Energy use
- Customer investments
- O&M costs

Changes in revenue needed for the profit test are calculated in the marketability test. They are equal to the changes in the participating customer's bill. The changes in cost are somewhat more complex. The DSPS uses changes in hourly load shapes and hourly marginal energy costs to estimate total energy cost changes. These are adjusted to account for transmission and distribution losses. Estimates of marginal generation, transmission and distribution costs (expressed as $/kW/year) are combined with calculations of the impact of the DSM program on system peak demand to estimate capital cost savings. The elements of the profitability calculation are shown in Table 2.

TABLE 2

Elements of the Profitability Test

- Revenues, before and after
  - Rates
  - Load shape changes
- Costs, before and after
  - Marginal costs
    - Hourly energy (corrected for T&D losses)
    - Generation
    - Transmission and distribution
  - Investments
  - Administrative costs

The DSPS has a built-in data base management system so it can store vast quantities of data: DSM options, costs, and rates schedules. Weather data can also be stored and used to correlate weather sensitive customer demands with system demands. The DSPS also has the ability to efficiently transfer demand and marginal cost data directly from detailed forecasting or production cost models. The system is designed to operate on an IBM AT microcomputer or equivalent.

When is a Screening Tool Appropriate?

Generally speaking, screening tools, whether they are simple spread sheet calculations or special purpose tools like the DSPS are always sufficient for applying the marketability test. All the value of this test is derived at the level of examining a single customer. Screening tools are also appropriate for taking a first cut at the profitability test.

More than a screening capability is needed in the following situations:

1. Where DSM programs are large enough to have a substantial impact on marginal costs. Often implementation of large DSM programs entails changing generation expansion plans. This automatically changes cost structures and the marginal costs used for screening.

2. Where the demand and supply interactions are critical. These interactions are critical for many load shifting(DLC's or storage) and demand interruption programs. For example, in order to achieve maximum savings, it may be desirable to coordinate the operation of water heater controls with system demands and generation unit availabilities. Similarly, it is often desirable to coordinate the operation of interruptible loads with the availability of alternative power supplies. These feedback effects are essentially ignored by screening tools.

3. Where impacts on system reliability may be significant. Conceptually, reliability impacts can be included in marginal cost estimates. However, in standard practice they are not. The impacts of interruptible loads, especially something like dual fuel heating which can be interrupted for weeks on end, can be significant. Credible estimates of reliability impacts require detailed simulation of the supply system operating in conjunction with the DSM programs.

4. Where interactions between several DSM programs may be important. Screening tools are appropriate for one program at a time. A typical DSM plan may incorporate ten or twenty different programs. Some may be rate oriented, like real time pricing for large industrial customers. Others may be hardware oriented, like residential heat storage. Some may combine both rates and hardware. Some may complement each other and some may compete for the same cost savings. Screening methods are incapable of testing such interactions.

Screening methods based on incremental marginal costs are a powerful member of the DSM planners tool kit. They can always be used to test marketability. However, they have limitations when it comes to determining profitability.

INTEGRATED RESOURCE PLANNING MODELS

The role of an integrated resource planning model is to apply the profitability test in the regions beyond the capabilities of screening models. With these models we can determine the most "profitable" mix of DSM and other alternative technologies. A good integrated model can quickly evaluate the tradeoffs between supply and demand options.

The LMSTM model, developed by the Electric Power Research Institute, is one tool designed explicitly for this kind of work. By examining the characteristics of this model we can see what is required to apply the profitability test in an electric power market.

LMSTM has two salient features: it is fully integrated and it is fully chronological. We will explain what we mean by each of these features.

Fully Integrated

LMSTM integrates four simulation submodels--demand, supply, finance and rates--into a single system. The structure of the model is shown in Figure 2. A fifth submodel, the Cost/Benefit module, summarizes simulation results and calculates net benefits (profit) associated with any resource strategy.

The demand submodel projects system loads and customer participation rates for any DSM program selected for testing. It can also simulate the effect of any pricing changes on the short- and long-term demand for energy and on daily load shapes.

The supply submodel projects power plant operating costs by directly simulating the effects of DSM strategies and devices on both electricity demand and generation dispatch needs. It can report on hourly operating costs, fuel use and system reliability. DSM devices are economically dispatched along with central station generators.

The finance submodel tracks the effects of alternate demand-supply strategies on utility investment and revenues. The rate submodel can calculate prices and demand charges for each customer class on the basis of demand, fixed and variable costs, and rate design. It permits the examination of different approaches to ratemaking, including time-of-use rates.

Because the demand and supply submodels are fully integrated, LMSTM has the ability to evaluate DSM options where demand and supply interactions are critical. For example, the operation of commercial cool storage units must be coordinated with at least four constantly changing factors: the demand for cooling, system-wide demand for electricity, the operating cost of available generators, and system reliability requirements. LMSTM can estimate the full potential of cool storage investments because it considers all these factors simultaneously.

Many planning models are integrated in the sense that they link more than one of the submodels, e.g., demand-supply or demand-supply-finance. Only a few planning models are fully integrated in the sense that the loop is closed by linking rates and demand.

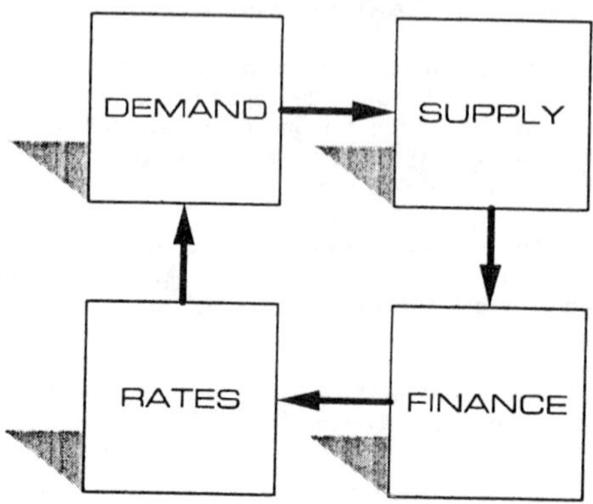

Figure 2. LMSTM Integrates Four Submodels—Demand, Supply, Financial, and Rates

Fully Chronological

Most popular production simulation methodologies (particularly those used in integrated models) are not chronological. They typically use load duration curves to represent demand for electricity over time. This aggregation simplifies calculations and works well for studying conventional thermal generation units because their potential capability is independent of system demand. In effect, conventional generating units are "on call" 24 hours a day. However, this is not true for direct load control devices or storage devices with a daily duty cycle, such as water heaters, space heaters, and air conditioning. The complex relationships between direct load control and storage capacity and total system demand over time are lost in the time shuffle implicit in a load duration curve.

The approach most suited for DSM evaluations is to dispatch central-station generation, storage, and direct load control devices on a serial, hour-by-hour basis. This method , known as chronological dispatch, most accurately represents the complex relationship between DSM device capacity and total system demand. The supply submodel of LMSTM, like the demand and rates submodels, does all simulations on an hour by hour basis, i.e., it is fully chronological.

Although the appreciation of these concepts is still quite limited, the LMSTM tool has been used by over thirty organizations to develop and test DSM programs. It has undergone over six years of continuous testing and improvement. The model is currently maintained and enhanced by a 25 member user group. We anticipate that its popularity will grow as planners learn more about incorporating DSM options into their resource plans. Whether the pressure for this will continue to come primarily from the regulators or from a more competitive market place remains to be seen. Either way the trend is clear.

SUMMARY

This brief paper offers DSM planners the following guidance:

1. A good DSM product will pass two economic tests: the marketability test and the profitability test. These tests are appropriate in either a regulated business environment or an unregulated environment. Under the umbrella of regulation they are called the participant and nonparticipant tests.

2. In order to design and evaluate DSM programs, planners need two analytical tools: a screening tool and an integrated resource planning model. A screening tool is essentially all that is needed for the marketability test and, properly applied, it can provide a good first cut on the profitability test. An integrated resource planning model, like LMSTM, is the level playing field where the ultimate profitability test is applied under a variety of scenarios and in the presence of other resource options.

3. The most realistic evaluations of DSM profitability are done with fully-integrated, fully-chronological integrated planning models.

OFF-PEAK HEATING

Henry A. Courtright, P.E.
Manager - Residential Marketing
Pennsylvania Power & Light Company

The off-peak heating market is being developed by the electric utility industry to accomplish several objectives:

1. Provide load control of present day peak demands to maintain system integrity.
2. Defer the need for future new generation by avoiding on-peak load growth.
3. Improve daily load factors.
4. Contribute to revenue growth, without peak demands, through lower-cost off-peak sales.

The availability of equipment for the off-peak heating or electric thermal storage (ETS) market has expanded to provide a storage system to meet most every heating need; whether the heat distribution system is a:

1. Zoned or individual room heating system
2. Warm air system
3. Hydronic system

ZONED OR INDIVIDUAL ROOM HEATING

CERAMIC ROOM UNITS

Ceramic room units (Figure 1) are designed for individual room control in residential and commercial applications.

How The System Works

1. Special alloy heating elements use low cost nighttime electricity to heat...
2. ...magnesite bricks which efficiently store the heat until it is needed.
3. Glass fiber and microtherm insulation keep the heat inside of the unit.
4. A quiet, low velocity fan is activated when the room thermostat calls for heat. Room temperature air is drawn into the unit and heated as it is circulated around the hot bricks.
5. A bimetallic damper mixes additional room air with the hot air inside to provide an even, comfortable flow of warm air into the room through...
6. ...the air discharge grille at the bottom of the unit.

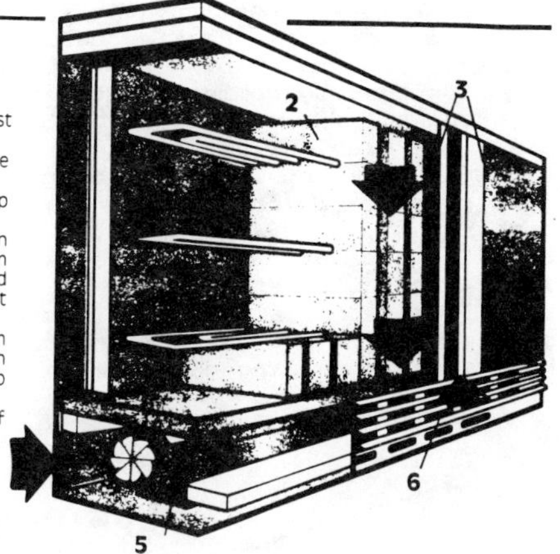

Fig. 1 - Ceramic room unit
(Courtesy: Steibel Eltron Distribution Services)

In the units, ceramic bricks are interwoven with electric heating elements and stacked in attractive, well insulated metal cabinets. The heating elements are energized with electricity during low cost nighttime hours. The ceramic room storage units produce enough heat during the nighttime to distribute to the living space during the night, and at the same time, stores enough heat in ceramic bricks to provide for the next day's entire heating requirements. During the day, the stored heat is circulated to the living space to maintain a comfortable temperature.

The storage heating unit is charged by electric heating elements surrounded by a high-density magnesite core within the well-insulated unit. On some models, when the room thermostat calls for heat, a small fan in the base of the unit circulates room air around the hot core and quietly and gently blows warm air into the room. Other models use natural convection through the heater to provide heat. Temperature control is provided by the controlled opening of a damper at the top of the ceramic room heater.

In most models, the amount of heat stored each night is automatically determined by an outdoor temperature sensor. As the outdoor temperature changes, the length of the charge period is automatically calculated to provide only the amount of heat required for the next 24-hour period.

SLAB HEATING

Radiant slab heating (Figure 2) is provided by installing electric heating cable in a bed of sand 1-3 feet under a concrete slab. This type of system is well suited for single-story commercial buildings, factories and warehouses. The cables charge the sand and earth reservoir below the slab during off-peak periods. The system is designed to maintain the slab area at a constant temperature, slightly higher than the desired space temperature. The sand bed must be insulated along the building perimeter with 2 inches of rigid closed-cell foam insulation to a depth of 4 feet. Slab heating may also be used in residential applications although it is generally coupled with a moderate amount of supplemental electric heat such as ceiling cable, baseboard or ceramic storage units.

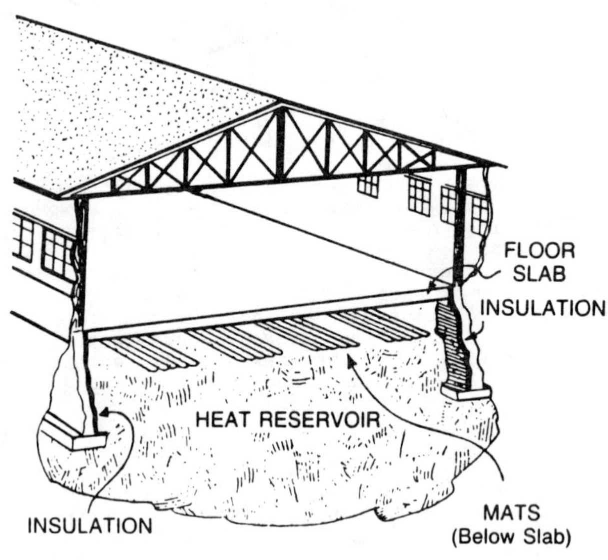

Fig. 2 - Slab Heating
(Courtesy: Smith-Gates Corporation)

WARM AIR SYSTEMS

HEAT PUMP WITH STORAGE

In the Pennsylvania Power & Light (PP&L) service area the heat pump has grown in market share of electric heating applications. However, the electric resistance supplemental heaters of the heat pump contributed to the daytime winter peak demand of the utility. To avoid the peak load of the supplemental heat and at the same time reinforce the growth of the heat pump market, PP&L engineers developed the Heat Pump Plus (Figure 3), a standard air to air heat pump with storage capabilities.

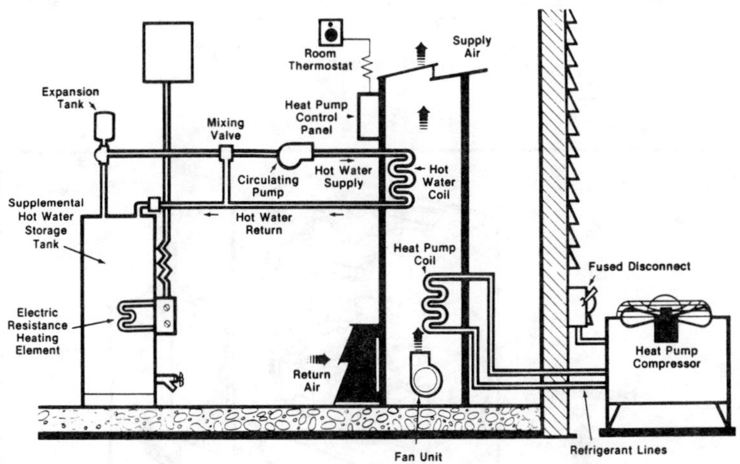

Fig. 3 - Heat Pump Plus System

The Heat Pump Plus storage system produces heat during the nighttime hours to help the heat pump satisfy the needs of the home. At the same time, it stores enough heat in the water storage tank to provide for the next day's supplemental heating requirements. When the outside temperature drops to the point at which the heat pump alone cannot maintain the home's temperature, the system uses some of the supplemental heat stored in the water. The system will assist the heat pump by circulating hot water, stored from the night before, through a heat exchanger in the supply air duct.

The same control device that regulates the hours of operation for heating the water storage also provides off-peak control for the domestic water heating tank. Several manufacturers provide UL - listed storage water heaters, ranging from 120 to 1200 gallons, to supplement the heat pump.

The Heat Pump Plus system has been applied in over 1,800 homes in the PP&L service area and several commercial installations.

CENTRAL CERAMIC FURNACE

The central storage furnace (Figure 4) uses a similiar storage principle as the ceramic room heaters but on a whole house basis. Nighttime heating is provided by the night heating elements which operate while the storage elements are recharging the storage core. The system can also provide air conditioning by installing a split system air conditioner in the cooling cabinet.

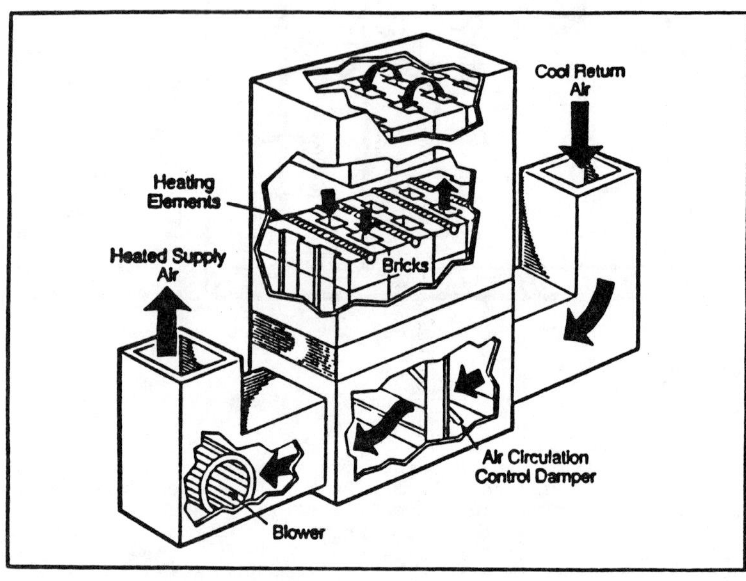

Fig. 4 - Central Ceramic Furnace
(Courtesy: Fostoria Industries)

The central furnace has also been used extensively in commercial and industrial installations to manage peak demand.

CRUSHED ROCK STORAGE HEAT PROJECT

A project administered by the Electric Power Research Institute has resulted in another warm air application of storage heat. This furnace (Figure 5) is designed to use crushed basaltic material, a rock usually used for railroad roadbed ballast. This rock is being used to lower the cost of the solid storage medium as compared to ceramic bricks. The furnace uses a variable speed charge fan to take secondary air flow through the storage bed and mixes this air with primary air in the warm air supply duct. The system uses a night heater section to warm the home while the furnace storage bed is being charged. This furnace will be commercially produced beginning in 1988.

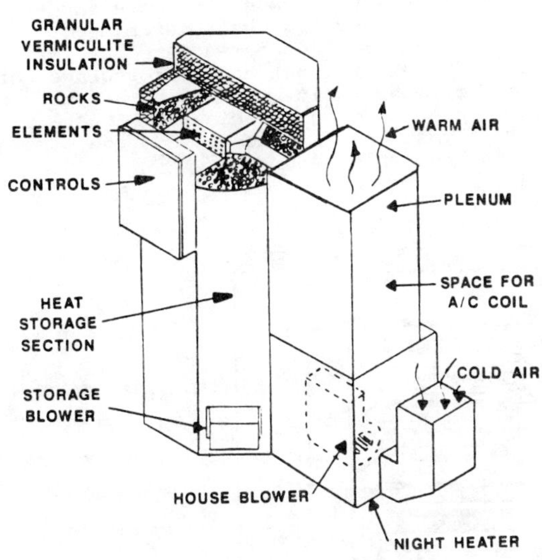

Fig. 5 - Crushed Rock Furnace
(Courtesy: Calidyne Corporation)

HYDRONIC HEATING

Although the hydronic heating market for new homes is small, it is a major replacement market particularly in the Northeast United States. In the PP&L service area nearly 60% of the existing homes have hydronic systems.

CENTRAL WATER STORAGE

Several manufacturers have developed off-peak storage heating equipment for central hydronic heating. Storage sizes for in basement applications range from 120 gallons to approximately 1200 gallons while larger storage configurations have been achieved through garage and under floor tank storage applications.

HYDRONIC WITH A SOLID STORAGE MEDIUM

Limitations on the size of central water based storage which could be installed in an existing home led PP&L to implement a demonstration program of 50 systems of a storage heat system which interfaced with hydronic distribution (Figure 6). The units, manufactured in Belgium and used in Europe, have a pig-iron central storage core which is heated up to 1,100 degrees F. with electric elements. Air is circulated through the core and transfers the heat to water through a heat exchanger. Water temperature in the heating loop is adjusted by varying the fan speed circulating air through the heat storage core. A prime advantage of the unit is field assembly of the storage core and heating cabinet, thus allowing installations in most any size home. Storage size of the system range from 180 kwh to 480 kwh.

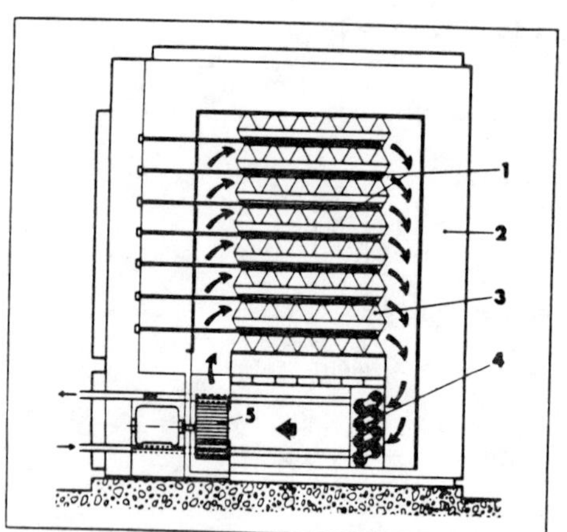

(1) ELECTRIC HEATING ELEMENTS
(2) INSULATED CABINET
(3) STORAGE CORE (CAST IRON BLOCKS)
(4) HEAT EXCHANGER
(5) VARIABLE SPEED FAN

Fig. 6 - Accubloc System
(Courtesy: ACEC Heating)

Commercial applications of the units are possible by placing multiple units on a water loop to provide the necessary storage capacity.

RATE DESIGN

Rate design for storage heating is generally on one of two concepts:

1. Different kilowatt-hour charges for on and off-peak periods.

2. Flat kwh charges coupled with an on-peak demand (kw) charge.

PP&L uses the second concept, flat kilowatt-hour charge with demand, for both its residential and commercial storage heating rates. Although this concept requires slightly more expensive metering, it does provide a better incentive to the customer to avoid the use of large loads during the on-peak period.

MARKET GROWTH

The storage heat market has grown in size during the 1980's both in terms of utilities using it as a load management strategy and in manufacturers supplying equipment to the market. This market growth should supply more price competition on installations, new equipment and improved customer understanding and acceptance of storage heating. The storage heat market taps a valuable energy resource -- available off-peak electricity -- to meet customers' needs for clean, comfortable and affordable heating.

MARKET ASSESSMENT OF A NEW ELECTRICITY DEMAND SIDE MANAGEMENT SYSTEM

by
Harvey M. Bernstein
Vice President
Applied Management Sciences
and
Dennis Van Wagenen, P.E.
Director of Load Research and Cost Allocation
Central Hudson Gas and Electric Corporation

ABSTRACT

This paper describes the application of conjoint analysis and market segmentation to analyze customer preference and potential acceptance of Demand Side Management (DSM) technology. Awad and Williams (1) showed that psychographic - based segmentation provided improved correlations with energy conservation program acceptance, compared to traditional socio-economic and demographic segmentation schemes. Gellings, Hirschberg and Williams (2) generalized the concept to a broader class of utility programs, and suggested a conceptual framework for analysis that was a motivating factor in this analysis. McKenna (3) demonstrated that the conjoint procedure could be used to define individual attribute-level preference functions for load management devices. Lewis and O'Rourke (4,5,6), using national data, have suggested a market segmentation scheme which explains and predicts customer preference and behavior relative to DSM program acceptance. This paper presents a utility-specific application of these concepts and methods for the special case of a customer programmable in-house load control device in the Central Hudson Gas & Electric Corporation (CHG&E) Service territory. The market research effort described focuses on those issues associated with DSM system features which will impact residential consumers as contrasted with features which impact utility operations. The principal emphasis of the demonstration portion of this project is to evaluate customer acceptance of the equipment under actual operational conditions and to make appropriate modifications to this initial market research and segmentation analysis based on the field test experience. Ultimately, it is intended that the market segmentation analysis will provide a means for developing a marketing strategy if CHG&E decides to expand the use of the DSM system to its full residential customer population.

The paper provides a summary of approach and methodology used in the project. Included is a methodological overview of the project, including interim results from augmented focus groups, Telephone-Mail-Telephone survey research, and the use of conjoint analysis for estimating customers relative preference functions. The paper reveals that the previously-developed methods can successfully be applied in a single-utility study, addressing a relatively complex technology. Differences between segments reported here and those previously reported are due to the unique characteristics of the CHG&E customer population studied by Applied Management Sciences and Robinson Associates (7,8,9,10).

INTRODUCTION

Central Hudson Gas and Electric Corporation, in cooperation with the New York State Energy Research and Development Authority and New York State Electric and Gas Corporation, are sponsoring a market assessment to determine how residential customers perceive and respond to alternative features that might be offered in a new electricity demand-side management (DSM) program. The assessment will help Central Hudson and the project co-sponsors better understand how to manage residential demand for electricity during periods of high electricity usage.

The assessment is being performed in three stages. First, market research has been conducted to assess Central Hudson's residential customers' attitudes and perceptions regarding alternative DSM program features. This research segments Central Hudson's residential customers according to their initial impression of alternative features that might be offered.

Among the features evaluated were several potential design features for load management control devices that might be installed in the customer's home. The results of this research on in-home devices will be used along with the research on customer perceptions regarding alternative DSM programs to define the second stage. The second stage comprises the procurement of in-home load management control devices for field testing.

Based on these and other results of the market research, CHG&E is planning to design, offer, and evaluate a 15-month Demand Side Management pilot program to a limited number of its residential customers in the third stage of the project.

The different types of DSM programs in which Central Hudson and the co-sponsors are interested are those that provide an incentive for customers voluntarily to curtail demand at time of system peak. These are: Demand Subscription Service (DSS), Time-of-Use (TOU) or Time-of-Day Rates (TOD), and Real-Time Pricing (RTP). Direct load control (DLC) programs also fit into this category; however, these programs were not of particular interest to the co-sponsors because of the involuntary nature of the curtailment action.

This paper will address the interim results of the first stage of the project, the market research stage, and touch upon future plans for stages 2 and 3, the procurement of the in-house load management control devices and the field testing and evaluation of those devices.

Exhibit 1 presents the project's overall work flowchart. It highlights the tasks that constitute the first-stage market research activities and shows how they relate to the rest of the project. The principal first-stage market research activities were a series of augmented focus groups (focus groups in which participants are asked to assist in a quantitative assessment) and a

EXHIBIT 1: OVERALL PROJECT PLAN

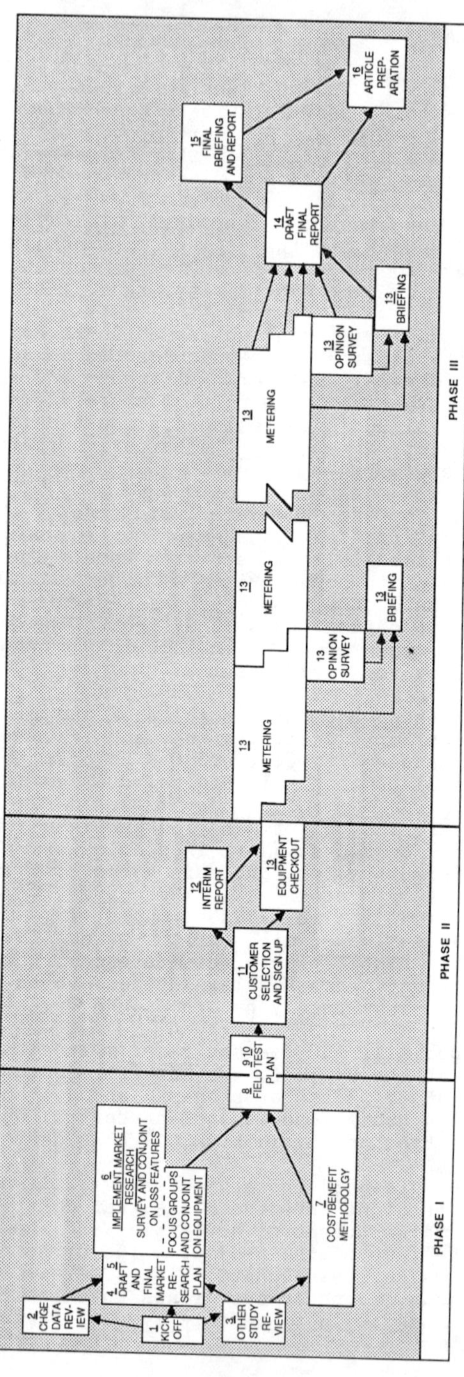

telephone-mail-telephone (TMT) survey. The following discussion pertains to the focus groups and TMT survey.

FOCUS GROUPS

The major objectives of the focus group phase of the research were to:

- determine the clarity of the demand-side management (DSM) concept to customers;
- ascertain prior awareness of DSM;
- obtain certain qualitative insights into customers reaction to the DSM concept - what they like about it, what they dislike about it, aspects/features that might motivate them to participate versus those that might deter participation;
- aid in the development of the questionnaire for the TMT survey;
- estimate customer preferences for the hardware features of a DSM control unit;
- obtain an initial understanding of whether DSM is best promoted on its own merits or in combination with other kinds of home-automation capabilities and packages.

Four focus groups consisting of a total of 34 participants were conducted on June 17 and 18, 1987. The focus groups were held in two locations, Fishkill and Newburgh, New York. The participants were residential customers of Central Hudson.

The focus groups emphasized the in-residence equipment features of the proposed DSM system and, secondarily, the potential functions of the system. The focus groups used as props one videotape which presented three DSM concepts:

(1) the Southern California Edison (SCE) Demand Subscription Service (DSS);
(2) the British Seeboard's CALMS device;
(3) the ICS Transtext system linking telephone and television.

The sessions consisted of: a) discussions among the participants on topics pertinent to DSM; and, b) a set of written tasks, the data from which were used for quantitative analysis.

The findings listed below are based upon a combination of the group discussions and the quantitative analyses of the written tasks.

Prior Awareness of DSM

Perhaps not surprisingly, most participants were unaware of load management programs. While several participants thought that they had heard the term they admitted that they really had no idea what it meant.

After exposure to the concept, many, respondents acknowledged that either they were aware of such programs in other utilities or they believed that they had heard that electricity rates were lower during certain times of the day. In either case, the notion of time-varying rates was one that was not completely foreign or novel to many participants.

For the most part, participants did find the notion of time-varying costs to be credible. This is a basic and extremely important finding, since, clearly, it is dubious that such a program would succeed if customers found their underlying rationale suspicious and lacking in credibility.

Preferences for Hardware Features

One of the goals of the four groups was to measure customer preferences for the hardware features of a DSM control unit, to ascertain the tradeoffs customers are willing to make, say, between color and location or between the kind of audio signal received and the kind of visual signal.

The two most important factors were "Number and Location of Units" and "Position of Unit." These are the two factors participants were least willing to trade off. They wanted one unit, to pick its location in the home, and they wanted it in a wall mounted position.

Home Automation

By no means was this subject explored thoroughly; time and the diversity of topics needing to be covered simply did not permit this. Our intent was merely to determine if home automation options other than DSM had much consumer appeal and whether the success of DSM would depend upon incorporating it in a much broader home automation package. In addition to DSM, the home automation options tested were:

- Appliance Operation Management
- Home Security Management
- Banking
- News
- Bill Paying
- Stock Market Information.

Interest in these options was varied. "Home security management" and "appliance operations management" did better; "stock market information" did worse. The key point, however, is that DSM attracted a high degree of interest on its own. People are interested in saving on their electric bill. Thus, we hypothesize that DSM is not a low-interest option that needs to be buttressed by other automation options such as those offered by the ICS Transtext System in order to attract a positive response from customers.

Attitudes Toward and Interest in DSM Programs

There was widespread interest in DSM generically. However interest varied dramatically across alternative program structures, with TOU rates being the most preferred by far. Interest clearly also depended on the size of the bill reduction and the number and mixture of end-uses that had to be deferred or shed in order to achieve this reduction. The perceived advantages of DSM were bill reduction and altruism. The perceived disadvantages of DSM were sacrificing some conveniences and expected conflicts among family members regarding which appliances to shed.

DSS with manual shedding (a la the SCE film) was by far the least preferred structure. Relative to other structures, it had several salient weaknesses from the customer perspective:

- utility control
- uncertainty of timing of activation periods.
- need to iteratively and manually shut off appliances in order to get below one's threshold level; uncertainty of which appliances and how many appliances to shed - removal of this uncertainty was seen as a major advantage of the CALMS unit.
- inconvenience of having to go around the house shutting off appliances
- concern over the power being cut off for up to six hours if one is not at home; fears ranged from equipment damage to meat spoilage to finding one's pets dead from heat exhaustion, et cetera; in this regard, the maximum length of the activation period was seen as very important.

A programmable automatic load shedding device substantially mitigated the last concern.

Conclusions: Focus Groups

The focus group results showed that all four groups were quite interested in lowering their utility bills, if possible. A key finding of the focus groups concerning this preliminary market segmentation was that DSM attracted a high degree of interest on its own. People in general were interested in saving on their electric bill and it was therefore, hypothesized that DSM is not a low interest option that needs to be butteressed by other automation options in order to attract a positive response from consumers. According to the focus groups, therefore, bill reduction was clearly the primary perceived advantage of DSM to the consumer. Insofar as target markets were concerned, there appeared to be little difference in interest between the higher income, higher consumption households and the lower income, lower consumption households in terms of either the desire to save money on electric bills or interest in DSM specifically.

The results of the focus groups were used (1) to refine the hardware attributes for use during the market research survey, (2) to help select the program attributes to be evaluated in the survey, and (3) to help in the development of a battery of customer psychographic questions.

MARKET RESEARCH SURVEY

The market research survey consisted of a telephone-mail-telephone survey of a sample of 400 residential customers selected according to a randomized sample design. An incentive of $5 per respondent was offered to encourage participation.

The key respondent task in this survey was a conjoint analysis* evaluation of alternative possible DSM program attributes. The results of this task were used, along with the attitude data, to generate hypotheses for examination in the field test, e.g., hypotheses relating specific psychographic orientations and preferences to the acceptance and continued use of the new DSM program, and hypotheses regarding the types of programs most likely to receive customer acceptance.

Respondent Interviews

The respondent interviews had three phases. Recruiting was accomplished through a short telephone interview designed to identify the appropriate respondent and recruit him/her for the survey. Upon recruitment, respondents were mailed a kit of interviewing materials to be used before, during, and after the final, depth interview, which was conducted by telephone. This three-phase interview procedure is termed a telephone-mail-telephone (TMT) survey and is now commonly used to collect complex data by telephone that formerly was collected by in-person interview.

The depth interview consisted of the following steps: review of DSM concept statement, evaluation of eight DSM program (conjoint analysis) profiles, and compositional preference measurement tasks for DSM program attributes and hardware features.

Segmentation

After conjoint analysis was applied to determine individual respondent preference scores for each level of each attribute, the respondents were clustered using cluster analysis. Cluster analysis, based on preference scores from the conjoint studies and more traditional demographic, psychographic and attitude data, was the principal tool for market segmentation.

---

* Conjoint analysis is a psychometric technique used to estimate customer preferences for product attributes.

CHG&E's customers were segmented three ways. One segmentation used demographic categories. The other two used categories based on customers' responses to (1) the attitude (psychographic) questions and (2) the conjoint task. Survey proportions were used to estimate the number of customers in each cluster within the sampling precision limits. Because the participants were selected according to a specific stratification plan, the results of these analyses provide inference to the residential class as a whole.

Findings: Attribute Importance Weights

As can be seen from Exhibit 2, there were six factors, ranging from two to fourteen levels, used to evaluate customer DSM program preferences. Conjoint analysis permits the researcher to determine how much importance (weight) the respondents place on any attribute relative to the others evaluated. The importance weights derived from the conjoint analysis for these six factors are provided in Exhibit 3 in the form of weighted mean scores (weighted for the sample strata) calculated across the total sample.

Frequency/Length/Certainty-Warning is, by far, the most important attribute, followed by Compliance/Penalty, Maximum Compensation, and Service Charge. Severity was a relatively unimportant factor and Method of Payment had virtually zero importance.

Preference Functions

Some customer preference functions are shown in Exhibit 4. These functions are constituted by the customer preference scores for the various factor levels. The numbers shown in these exhibits are (weighted) mean scores calculated at the total sample level and, hence, can be said to reflect what might be termed the "average" residential customer.

Preference scores can be added to determine the total preference for any DSM attribute configuration, i.e., for any DSM program that can be described by the attributes. In this way, customers' perceptions of alternative program configurations can be simulated for comparison and used in selecting a program type and configuration.

Findings: Customer Attitudinal Segmentation

The purposes of segmentation are (1) to determine the appropriate subset of the market toward which a product should be targeted to maximize effectiveness in relation to cost, and (2) to identify the optimal positioning strategy vis-a-vis this (these) target segment(s). Two objectives of this study are to reveal the extent to which Central Hudson's residential customer population comprises unique segments from a DSM marketing viewpoint and to

EXHIBIT 2: CONJOINT ANALYSIS FACTORS AND FACTOR LEVELS USED TO EVALUATE CUSTOMER DSM PROGRAM PREFERENCES

A. FREQUENCY/LENGTH/WARNING

1. Daily/1 hr./fixed
2. Daily/6 hrs./fixed
3. Daily/13 hrs./fixed
4. Daily/1 hr./5 min.
5. Daily/6 hrs./5 min.
6. Daily/6 hrs./4 hours
6. Daily/6 hrs./4 hours
7. Daily/13 hrs./5 min.
8. 1 per wk/1 hr./5 min.
9. 1 per month/1 hr./5 min.
10. 1 per wk/6 hrs./4 hours
11. 1 per wk/13 hrs/5 min.
12. 1 per month/1 hr/5 min.
13. 1 per month/6 hrs/5 min.
14. 1 per month/13 hrs/5 min.

B. COMPLIANCE/PENALTY

1. Mandatory; power shut off
2. Mandatory; with load shedder
3. Mandatory;with load shedder and override feature
4. Voluntary; 10% bill increase

C. SEVERITY

1. Less severe
2. More severe

D. METHOD OF PAYMENT

1. Bill Discount
2. Single check
3. Staggered checks

E. SERVICE CHARGE

1. None
2. $7.00 per bill

F. MAXIMUM COMPENSATION

1. 10% Reduction on bill
2. 20% Reduction on bill
3. 40% Reduction on bill
4. 50% Reduction on bill

EXHIBIT 3: MEAN ATTRIBUTE IMPORTANCE WEIGHTS FOR DSM PROGRAM ATTRIBUTES (TOTAL SAMPLE)

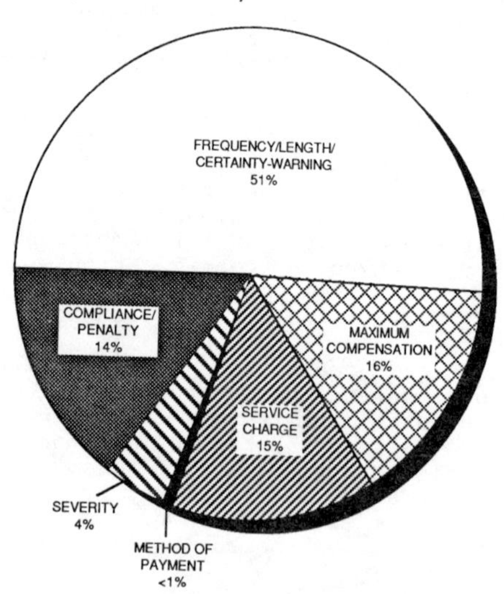

EXHIBIT 4 EXAMPLES OF MEAN PREFERENCE FUNCTIONS FOR THE DSM PROGRAM ATTRIBUTES (TOTAL SAMPLE)

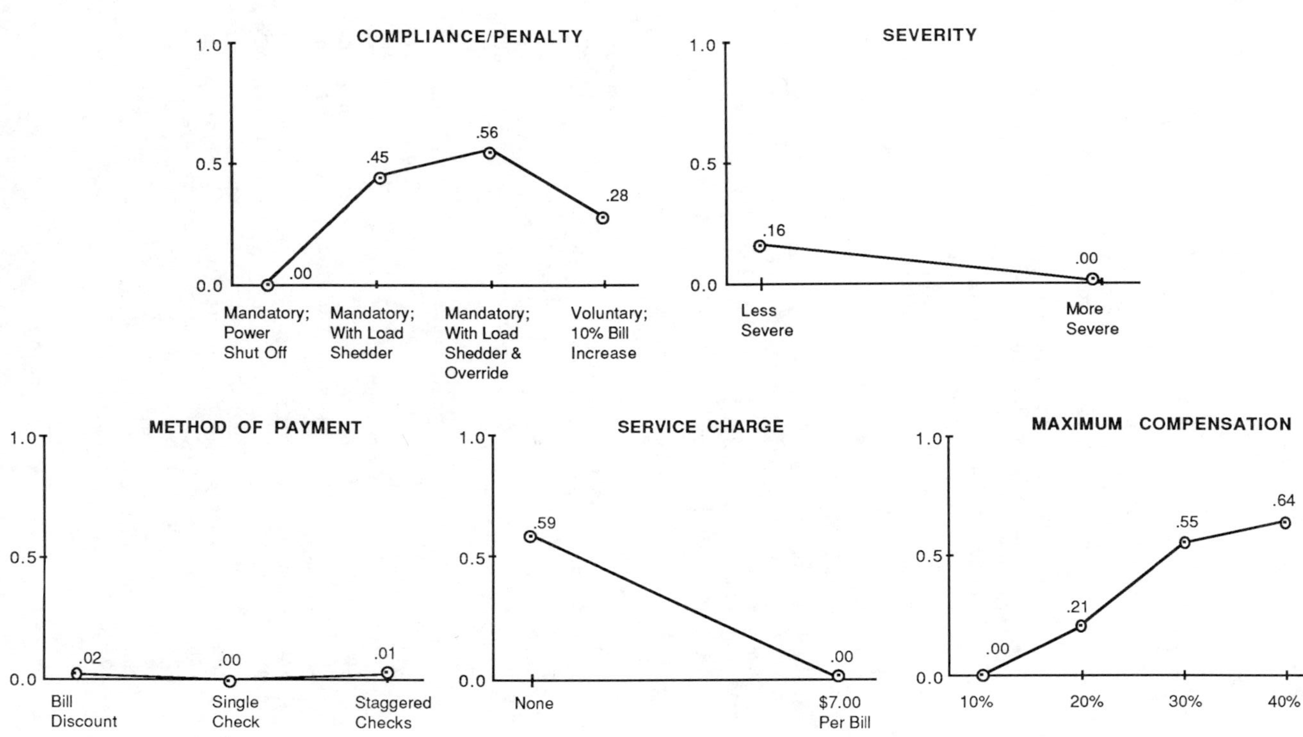

determine the predispositions of these segments toward, and their willingness to participate in, DSM programs.

The factor analysis of 63 attitude items in the study revealed thirteen key underlying dimensions, or factors. Each factor has been given a title, which reflects its component statements. The thirteen factors are:

- Conservation/Need to Preserve Resources for Future
- Willingness to Accept Restrictions
- Minimal Use of Electricity/Concern Over Cost of Electricity
- Overall Attitude Toward Electric Utilities
- Expensive Tastes/High-Tech Orientation
- Concern Over Threats to Privacy
- Schedule and Planning Orientation
- Attitude Toward Nuclear Power Plants
- Thrifty Attitude Toward Appliances
- Confident Attitude Toward Future; Risk Oriented
- Time Pressure
- Safety Orientation
- Introversion.

In this study, each factor is composed of a set of attitude statements which best describe it. These statements, along with the factor loading coefficient, measures the direction and strength of the association between the statement and the factor.

Just as each respondent could have an answer on each of the 63 attitude items, each has a score, or value, on each of the thirteen factors. These factor scores were submitted to a cluster analysis to produce the attitudinal segments (also often referred to as "psychographic segments"). The cluster analysis produced five unique attitude segments for Central Hudson's residential customers. For convenience of discussion, the contractor team has named them:

(1) <u>Thrifty, Risk Avoiders</u> - Followers of the traditional "work ethic", the Thrifty Risk Avoiders place great value on characteristics such as industriousness, prudence, thrift, hard work, simplicity, and planning. They believe in using their and the nations' resources wisely, husbanding them for future generations. They tend to be very budget-conscious and claim to have tried "to keep (their) electric bills as low as possible". This group has a high-tech orientation, an overall positive attitude toward utilities, and are concerned over keeping their electric bills prudently low. Almost half (44%) are 55 years of age or older. They are also disproportionately in the lower-income categories and widowed. Attitudinally, this segment would appear to be an attractive target for DSM programs.

(2) <u>Suspicious Emulators</u> - Members of this segment desire the good life, and tend to be extravagant and

ostentatious. For example, more so than any other segment, they tend to "like to have the latest in clothes, cars, appliances, and so on" and tend to "have expensive tastes." The attitudinal dimension that primarily differentiates this segment from the other segments, is their negative attitude toward, and mistrust of, the electric utilities. Despite their suspicions, this group may offer an opportunity for significant DSM penetration through appeals which emphasize saving on one's electric bill and thereby freeing up funds to purchase the things in life they desire.

(3) Low-Tech, Control Seekers - The primary differentiating characteristic of this segment is its strong aversion to accepting restrictions on their use of electricity without very significant compensation. A comparatively low income group, they are concerned over the high cost of electricity. They show a comparatively high sensitivity to the extent of the compensation. Demographically, this group is the least educated segment. Their appliance profile shows a low penetration of high-tech products. This group is not a particularly attractive segment for DSM programs.

(4) Comfort-Seeking Hedonists - They want it all; they want it now; and they have the income to buy much, if not most, of what they want (over half have annual incomes of $50,000 or higher). There is a world of extravagance, ostentation, and self-stratification through the pamperings of high-technology consumer products. They see little need to conserve for the future or to restrict their free use of electricity. An examination of their appliance ownership profile reveals a very definite high-tech orientation. Over half (53%) own a personal computer and over one-quarter (27%) own a programmable telephone. Demographically, they tend to be younger, highly educated, and have very high incomes. While this segment's appliance profile clearly make them a desirable target from the utilities perspective, unfortunately their attitudes and life-style are such that significant DSM penetration will be very difficult.

(5) Anti-Nuclear Conservationists - This segment is primarily differentiated by its staunch opposition to nuclear power plants and its strong advocacy of conservation. They seem quite willing to accept restrictions on their use of electricity, particularly if they are convinced that this will help alleviate the need for future nuclear power plants. In their daily activities, they tend to be spontaneous and to eschew extravagance and ostentation. They are not particularly inclined to plan ahead, or to be schedule-conscious. Theirs is not a rigorous, habit-bound, or compulsive world. Demographically, this segment is disproportionately middle-aged and lower-income, but also contains a disproportionate number of married women with above-average educations. Only one-third

have some form of air conditioning. Attitudinally, the Anti-Nuclear Conservationists are clearly an attractive target segment for DSM programs.

Exhibit 5 shows the percentage of Central Hudson residential customers in each segment.

Exhibit 6 compares these five segments on the thirteen factors discussed above. This exhibit shows the sharp attitudinal differences that discriminate these segments. Symbols such as "VP, P, A, N, and VN" are used in order to denote where each segment falls on each factor, relative to the other segments. This exhibit is a good indication of their attitudes on factors influencing DSM program design and marketing.

Findings: Customer Preferences for DSM Hardware Features

Apart from their preferences for DSM program content, customers can have preferences for the features of the equipment that goes into their house to provide information and load control services. Because some of the programs being considered by Central Hudson and the other project co-sponsors entail installing such equipment in the customer's house (referred to here as in-house hardware), the research included a separate module to identify the preferred features of this hardware.

Customers were asked to provide their preferences for alternative in-house hardware configurations using a separate hybrid conjoint analysis task. The factors and levels used in this procedure were:

- Color of consoles
- Number and location of consoles in residence
- Position of consoles
- Signal indicating need to choose appliance(s) to shut off
- Provision of additional information (such as list of appliances from which to choose, amount of current bill, etc.)

From Exhibit 7, we see that the most important factor is "Number and Location" with an importance weight of 38%. The second most important attribute is "Provision of Additional Information" with a weight of 30%. These are the factors that customers are least willing to trade off. Compared to the focus group findings, Provision of Additional Information increased substantially in importance and Position decreased substantially. Generally, however, the results presented here are quite consistent with those from the focus groups. Even the above-mentioned discrepancies are readily explainable:

EXHIBIT 5: SIZE OF ATTITUDE SEGMENTS (PERCENT OF CENTRAL HUDSON'S RESIDENTIAL CUSTOMERS)

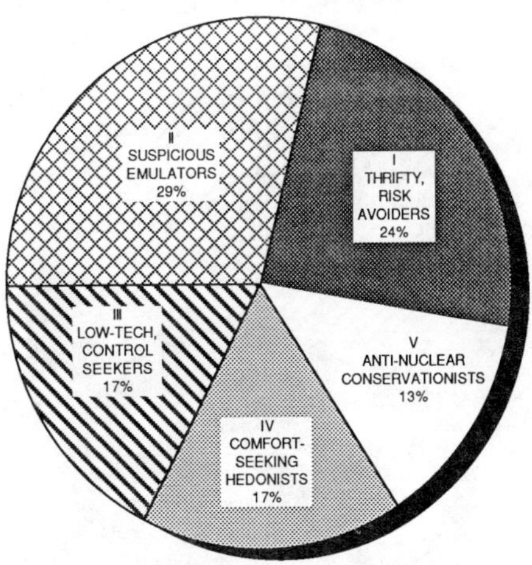

EXHIBIT 6: ATTITUDE SEGMENTS' RELATIVE POSITION ON UNDERLYING ATTITUDE FACTORS

FACTOR	I THRIFTY, RISK AVOIDERS	II SUSPICIOUS EMULATORS	III LOW-TECH, CONTROL SEEKERS	IV COMFORT SEEKING HEDONISTS	V ANTI-NUCLEAR CONSERVA-TIONISTS
1. CONSERVATION/NEED TO PRESERVE RESOURCES FOR FUTURE	P	N	A	VN	VP
2. WILLINGNESS TO ACCEPT RESTRICTIONS	P	A	VN	N	P
3. MINIMAL USE OF ELECTRICITY/ CONCERN OVER COST OF ELECTRICITY	P	N	P	N	P
4. OVERALL ATTITUDE TOWARD ELECTRIC UTILITIES	P	VN	A	A	N
5. EXPENSIVE TASTES/HIGH-TECH ORIENTATION					
a. Extravagence	N	P	VN	P	N
b. High-Tech Orientation	P	P	VN	P	A
6. CONCERN OVER THREATS TO PRIVACY	A	A	P	VN	A
7. SCHEDULE AND PLANNING ORIENTATION	P	A	A	N	N
8. ATTITUDE TOWARD NUCLEAR POWER PLANTS	P	A	A	P	VN
9. THRIFTY ATTITUDE TOWARD APPLIANCES	P	N	A	N	A
10. CONFIDENT ATTITUDE TOWARD FUTURE; RISK ORIENTED	N	A	N	P	A
11. TIME PRESSURE	A	A	A	N	A
12. SAFETY ORIENTATION	A	A	A	A	A
13. INTROVERSION	A	A	A	N	A

LEGEND:

VP Very positive toward action/attitude indicated in relation to average position
P Positive in relation to average position
A Average position on action/attitude indicated
N Negative in relation to average position
VN Very negative toward action/attitude indicated in relation to average position.

EXHIBIT 7: MEAN ATTRIBUTE IMPORTANCE WEIGHTS FOR DSM HARDWARE FEATURES (TOTAL SAMPLE)

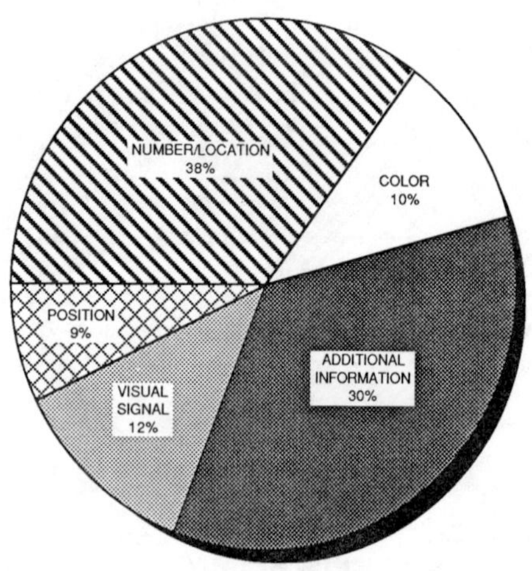

- The "Provision" factor increased in importance because the preceding tasks in the interview, particularly the DSM Program Attribute Conjoint Task, manifested the value and utility of having this capability. This "conditioning" was not present during the focus groups.
- The "Position" factor decreased because (in the interest of simplicity) respondents in the survey (unlike the participants in the group sessions) were not told to assume that the console was hard-wired in place.

Exhibit 8 presents the mean customer preference functions for in-house hardware features. As with the focus group results, customers:

- Wish to avoid a white console
- Would like a choice of colors
- Show a strong aversion to the utility choosing the room in which the console is located and to having a console in each living area of the house
- Prefer a wall-mounted to a counter/table-top console
- Want a visual signal in addition to an audio signal
- Want the console to be able to provide additional information, although preferably through a mechanism other than a synthesized voice.

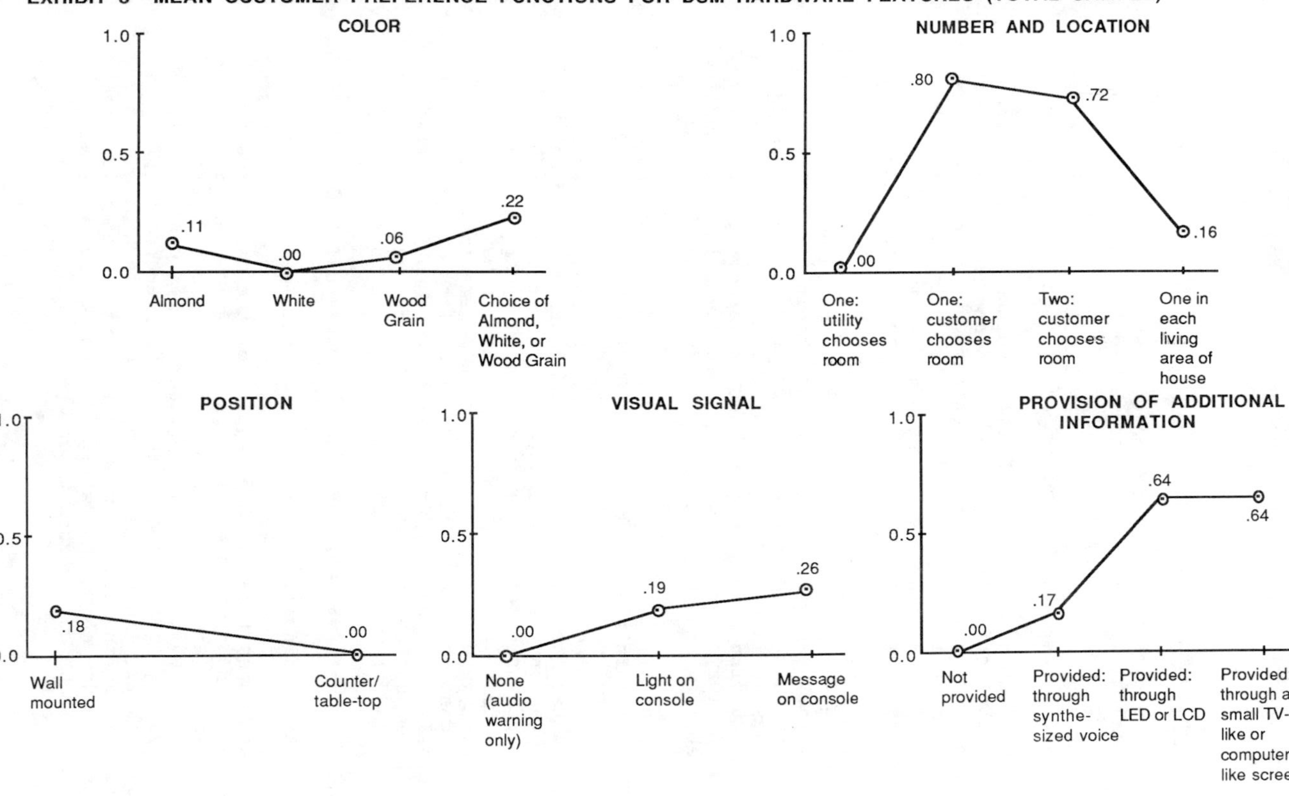

EXHIBIT 8 MEAN CUSTOMER PREFERENCE FUNCTIONS FOR DSM HARDWARE FEATURES (TOTAL SAMPLE)

As with the DSM program attribute preference sources, these hardware preference scores can be added to determine the total preference for any hypothetical console that can be formed as a combination of the attributes in the model.

Conclusions: Market Research Survey

The program-attribute conjoint analysis, although not specifically addressed to hardware-design questions, nonetheless, contributes a finding that is very relevant for the design of the hardware. The finding that respondents valued automatic load-shedding more highly than purely manual control indicates that some form of programmable load shedding is preferred to dependence on manual appliance shut-off. This preference was stated in the context of a penalty if the customer chooses not to comply manually with the utility's request for load curtailment (not to shut off one or more appliances manually). Without a penalty, this preference is likely to reverse, and exclusive manual control is likely to be the more attractive option. This reversal is expected because Central Hudson's customers have shown a general aversion to being controlled --in the absence of having an acceptable reason for it. On the other hand, the project co-sponsors must consider if they would ever offer voluntary, manual compliance without imposing a penalty for non-compliance. If a penalty would always be imposed, then a programmable load shedding capability should be included in the hardware design.

Finally, it should be noted that there was one other potentially-relevant hardware feature that was beyond the scope of the project, although other project results may help in selecting it. Neither of the conjoint tasks evaluated whether the programming feature should be operated and set by the customer or by the utility. Inasmuch as customer operation would appear to be tantamount to voluntary, manual compliance, however, if a penalty were associated with manual operation, the findings described above suggest that utility operation would be a logical choice. If a penalty were not associated with manual operation, then the utility would risk losing its benefit while the customer continues to receive his.

THE FUTURE: DESIGN, IMPLEMENT, AND EVALUATE THE DSM SYSTEM

As originally conceived, the Field Test brings together and integrates the results of the market research tasks. Specifically, the results of the market research efforts and associated findings on service and equipment attributes are integrated with data collection efforts necessary to develop input parameters for cost benefit analysis. A Field Test Plan will be prepared to provide a systematic plan for installing hardware in a sample of 200 residences and testing under actual field conditions the performance of the hardware, customer responses, and overall DSM configuration cost benefits.

The objectives of the Field Test Plan are to:

- Design field test selection procedures
- Design field test instrumentation and measurement specifications
- Design field test analysis protocols relative to:
  (1) validating or modifying conclusions on a customer attitudes and preferences of perceived value developed under the market research efforts
  (2) resolving cost benefit framework elements
  (3) recommending consumer marketing/education strategies
  (4) recommending time-phasing for introduction on DSM features by market segment.

The Field Test Plan, as shown in Exhibit 1, is the critical link between the research and experimental portions of the project, and the Plan, once finalized, will guide the subsequent experimental stages.

At this juncture of the research study, pending complete results from the market research effort, final equipment specifications for the Field Test have not been detailed. Currently, it is assumed that a programmable load shedding configuration similar to the Dencor Mini-Mizer model 44 unit will be used. The Mini-Mizer control unit contains a microelectric logic circuitry that evaluates the power consumption and makes decisions to interrupt (shed) or restore a controlled load based on a prioritized preprogrammed list established by the homeowner. Loads that can be controlled include the water heater, heating and cooling system, hot tubs, clothes dryer, etc. The customer can control the use of several appliances.

The Final Field Test Plan will provide detailed specifications for selection and recruitment of the test population and hardware installation and check-out. Further, the Field Test Plan will provide specifications for the data necessary to complete the cost benefit analysis as well as validate or reject hypotheses concerning market segmentation and penetration. The cost benefit analysis is being performed using EPRI's new integrated planning model (MIDAS) with a microcomputer pre- and post-processor to take into account the relevant data required for DSM program analysis in this project.

Because of the complexities of all of the interacting project elements and the unknown aspects of the project at the time of this writing, we reiterate the preliminary nature of this information. The information and the assumptions contained in this document should be viewed as preliminary in nature and are designed to serve as a preliminary release of project results.

BIBLIOGRAPHY

(1) Z.A. Awad and M.V. Williams, "Conservation Attitude and Intention to Engage in Electricity Conservation," presented at the annual meeting of the American Psychological Association, Toronto, Canada, 1984.

(2) Clark W. Gellings, Alan S. Hirschberg, and Michael V. Williams, "Successful Demand-Side Management: Customer Behavior Is The Key," Public Utilities Fortnightly, March 20, 1986.

(3) William F. McKenna, "Measuring Customer Preferences for Load Management Service Options," IEEE Power Engineering Society Meeting, 1985.

(4) Customer Preference and Behavior: Residential Modelling Framework, EM 5217, Electric Power Research Institute Project 2671-1, May 1987.

(5) Customer Preference and Behavior: Project Overview, Electric Power Research Institute, December 1986.

(6) EPRI Residential Preference and Behavior Workshop, Hartford, Connecticut, sponsored by the Electric Power Research Institute, Department of Energy and Northeast Utilities, October 21-22, 1987.

(7) Applied Management Sciences, Preliminary Draft Task 6 Market Research Report, November 1987.

(8) Applied Management Sciences, Review of Existing Data, Literature, and Ongoing Research on CHG&E Residential Customer Characteristics; Customer Attitudes & Perceptions About DSM Systems; Hardware & Electric Technology for DSM, May 1987.

(9) Applied Management Sciences, Task 6 Letter Report: Equipment Specifications Developed from The Focus Groups, July 23, 1987.

(10) Applied Management Sciences, Market Assessment of A New DSM System Concept: Preliminary Field Test Plan, November 1987.

ACKNOWLEDGEMENT

The authors wish to acknowledge the contributions of Dr. William F. McKenna of Robinson Associates, Inc.

HEAT PUMPS-R-US

L. G. HENISEE

DIRECTOR OF MARKETING

PHILADELPHIA ELECTRIC COMPANY

As you are aware, there are millions of shoppers in this world's largest nation of consumers. Therefore, I can probably count the number of people on both of my hands that would give up the chance to receive something for free. For example, walking down a supermarket lane, how many of you, when purchasing a buy-one-get-one-free deal, do not take both items? Or, during a happy hour, how many of you do not partake in a 2-for-1 drink special? Most Americans flock to sales at stores due to the fact that they are getting more for their dollar spent. I couldn't even imagine if we had to pay for the air we breathe. Just imagine, the dreaded Bargain Air Hunter!!

The underlying fact behind all of this is that air is free and we have every right in the world to use some of its valuable contents. One of these is heat, and many buyer-oriented Americans do not take advantage of the 2-for-1 or even 3-for-1 deal that goes on every day of the heating season. When we, as Americans, receive something for free, we always think about the strings attached. Well, this 2-for-1 free heat has nothing even close to a thread being attached. FREE is FREE.

The point is, we at Philadelphia Electric believe that the heat pump can't be beat as a revenue maker for us, and as a comfort machine for our customers. . . and we tell our customers so. With over 66,000 heat pumps installed in our service territory, we can say that Heat Pumps-R-Us.

In fact, we are proud of our long-term promotional efforts of the heat pump; we have been doing it since 1975. We do have to say that most of those sales have been in the new construction market; however, we have been promoting the add-on heat pump market with trade allies through the Electrical Association of Philadelphia. The TV, radio, cable TV, newspaper, direct mail, and bill insert advertising has all helped customers become more aware of what a heat pump is and how it can benefit them. Yes, we still have a long way to go to reach saturation of consumer awareness.

As a summer-peaking utility with a seasonal generating gap of 1,200 megawatts, Philadelphia Electric Company had to search for a way to electrically zap the gap. The heat pump was the answer to this demand management problem. By promoting the heat pump, we would acquire an electric load that was acceptable to our system both in load leveling and in profitability.

When we decided to market heat pumps in 1975, we decided that one strategy would be to find a way to ensure clean installations to provide customer comfort and no high bill complaints which we encountered a few years ago.

Working with the Refrigeration Service Engineer Society, a pilot training program was developed for heat pump technicians. That program was so successful, RSES is offering the program internationally. The industry marketing program required that participating dealers employ two trained and tested technicians. Well, over 300 technicians have been trained over the years, and we no longer require such a stringent rule. We know that jobs are being installed properly, for the most part, in the add-on and conversion market. I'll tell you a little more later about what we have done to tighten up new construction to suit the heat pump.

But first, let me tell you a little about our company so that you might better understand our marketing posture. Philadelphia Electric Company is a combination utility serving electric in the City of Philadelphia and gas and electric in five suburban counties. Philadelphia Electric Company has 1.2 million residential electric customers and 220,000 residential gas customers. Our electric revenue dominates gas revenue by a ratio of approximately 5 to 1.

To see how our heat pump marketing program relates to Philadelphia Electric Company objectives, let's look at two of our major corporate objectives.

The first one is reliable service. We will encourage the use of high efficiency appliances and equipment which benefit both the Company and the customer.

The second one is financial strength. We will vigorously sell off-peak loads which will raise the system load factor and increase Company profitability.

In the past several years, we have innovated our marketing program to include many incentives to help our Philadelphia Electric Company customers decide to buy a heat pump.

To outline our heat pump marketing efforts, let's refer to what many marketing students have branded in their minds - the "four P's" of marketing:

1. Product
2. Price
3. Promotion
4. Place

PRODUCT

What has Philadelphia Electric Company done to help improve the quality of the heat pump?

We have left it up to the manufacturers to improve the efficiency of the heat pump. However, what we have done is improve the heat pump by giving it a well-built home. Most Americans do not wish to work 10 times more than what is needed to get the job done; neither does the heat pump. There is no doubt in my mind that the heat pump will have to work many hours of overtime in a home that is leaky. Philadelphia Electric has introduced a homebuilders' program to address the problem of faulty home construction. The name of our program is "Excellence in Energy Efficiency" (EEE). This is the program that is making the new construction market prime for successful heat pump application.

In this program, we make sure that the heat pump is given its proper place in which to live. The EEE goals are to ensure customer comfort and reduce energy bills. Again, PECo customers who have EEE homes receive more for their dollar. As a result of having a more efficient heat pump and an energy-efficient home, Philadelphia Electric Company benefits by reducing high bill complaints and satisfying customers. The builder benefits by selling homes faster, and promoting customer satisfaction without substantially increasing construction costs.

The EEE program standards cover four basic areas: air infiltration, efficiencies of heating and cooling equipment, distribution system design and construction, and domestic water heating. Philadelphia Electric monitors the EEE homes to ensure that the builder is meeting these standards.

In addition, we have hired Princeton Energy Partners, originating from Princeton, New Jersey, to use the latest diagnostic tools to comb a house for major causes of heat loss in the home and to demonstrate energy-efficient construction techniques.

Another improvement to the heat pump product that is currently being tested is a device that is used in conjunction with a heat pump that uses electric backup. This device, given the name "Heat Comfort Extender", will keep the supply register temperatures at a constant temperature by bringing on the stages of backup in small increments. This is still in the beginning of its testing stages, but will definitely be a helpful device in solving comfort complaints about the heat pump.

In summary, under PRODUCT, the new approach to promoting heat pumps by focusing on its future home has so far helped give the heat pump a good name in the Philadelphia Electric territory.

PRICE

Philadelphia Electric Company has a residential electric heating rate (Rate RH) which provides an approximate 49 percent reduction (5.46¢ per kWh versus 10.67¢ per kWh) to all usage over 500 kWh per month in the eight winter months (October through May). This rate, which does not utilize a separate meter, is only available to residences heated entirely by a permanently installed electric system. As a backup source, residences may use electric, oil, or gas.

Based on energy costs in our area, we provide our sales personnel with operating costs estimates for a typical two-story 1800-square-foot home for both a new home and a home that is 10 or more years old. Remember, these estimates are based on experience and tend to be conservative (higher) for heat pumps.

ILLUSTRATION

Heating System	Equivalent Cost of No. 2 Oil		Estimated Annual Heating Cost	
	New Home	Existing	New Home	Existing
Heat Pump/Electric	71¢/gal.	72¢/gal.	$453	$707
Heat Pump/gas	66¢/gal.	67¢/gal.	$421	$658
Heat Pump/oil	74¢/gal.	75¢/gal.	$475	$736
Gas (PECo)	71¢/gal.	72¢/gal.	$451	$700
Oil	85¢/gal.	84¢/gal.	$542	$829

As you can see, our pricing is competitive in both the add-on and new construction markets. However, unlike the days when oil and gas were more expensive, we now have to sell the quality benefits of the heat pump. That is the challenge we give to our sales force - sell up. Sell the "quality comfort machine." As a combination company, you can also see that we are indeed interested in the figures that show gas backup as the lowest heating cost. That offers a great marketing opportunity.

Because our Rate RH is a single meter rate, we need enough heating usage to justify any reduction in base load revenue (over 500 kWh in the eight heating months). Therefore, we require that there be a two-stage heating thermostat that can be set to turn off the heat pump above 20 F outdoor temperature. We do not allow a cut-off of the heat pump at the "economic balance point." However, an outdoor thermostat that controls the backup system is allowed, which means that it keeps it off above the balance point.

Also available under Philadelphia Electric Company's tariff is a commercial heating rate for customers that permanently install heat pumps or electric radiant heat. The rate is the same as our residential heating rate (5.46¢ per kWh) during the eight heating months with no demand charge.

To summarize PRICE, Philadelphia Electric Company has committed itself to provide the customer with not only the most efficient system, but also a cost-competitive product, with staying power.

PROMOTION

The third "P" of marketing - PROMOTION - has been approached in a variety of ways over the years. We have tried network TV, cable, radio, all forms of print, direct mail, bill inserts, and customer seminars. We have learned that our customers do not want us to use humor. They have told us through research and pre-testing that they view our company as just about the most credible source of information on technology and want us to give them the facts, in a straightforward way, especially when the price tag is around $3,000.

Well, here is where we are right now. Our goals are to achieve 70 percent penetration of electric heating in new construction, with 80 percent heat pumps. We currently have 93 percent PECo fuels heating penetration, 63 percent penetration electric heating, with 90 percent heat pumps. Our current strategies include:

- To sell heat pumps in conjunction with the Excellence in Energy Efficiency program to builders.

- To sell customers on upgrading to a heat pump in the central air conditioning replacement market, and to sell customers on adding a heat pump to a current fossil fuel heating system.

The current programs include these items of promotion in the add-on market:

- 330 sixty second radio spots on eight stations for six weeks.

- A $275 rebate offer ($175 PECo, $50 dealers, $50 manufacturers).

- Bill inserts sent to 800,000 customers in September bills.

- Telemarketing of all customer inquiries with the goal of producing very qualified leads for the dealers.

Right now, the only promotion we have for the new construction market is the residential consumer awareness of the heat pump from the add-on media campaign and the individual sales efforts by the representatives who are selling heat pumps with the Triple E program.

Costs of this promotion? $235,750

Estimated first-year revenue from sales? $165,000 add-on. The 9,830 heat pumps connected in new construction in 1986 produced a revenue of over $3.9 million.

PLACE

As far as PLACE objectives are concerned, we use the demographic and psychographic data produced by market research to target where the product message should be placed to get the best results. In other words, we target direct mail, bill inserts, radio, and newsprint to best reach the market to stimulate interest in a heat pump. Television, of course, is more general but can be controlled to some extent by the selection of time of day and programming. We look at how the demographics are changing for heat pump buyers to determine the PLACE objectives. By the way, who buys a heat pump in your service territory? It used to be an upper-middle-class male, 45 to 54 years old, making in excess of $50,000. Now, it is a double-income male-female buying decision (with the male still having the edge in the decision), 30 years old and over, with a combined income of over $45,000.

That is an overview of heat pump marketing at Philadelphia Electric Company. Our strategies for the future include shifting our focus to thermal storage and other heat pump applications, and putting more money into the new construction market, maybe even paying to have heat pumps installed in sample houses. You can see that we intend to keep up the momentum so that maybe, in the not too distant future, you - our peers - will point to Philadelphia Electric Company as a company with the best track record in heat pump sales and say that PECo-R-Heat Pumps.

ELECTRIC ALTERNATIVES TO PACKAGED COGENERATION SYSTEMS

Morton H. Blatt
Electric Power Research Institute
Palo Alto, California

The economics of packaged cogeneration systems were characterized for selected building applications and a range of electric-to-gas price differences. (Table 1 shows the applications studied and Table 2 shows the electricity and gas prices used.) We found that analyses made by developers and promoters of cogeneration systems generally considered low-cost, low-efficiency electric options as the baseline. The analyses made on this basis showed attractive economics for cogeneration systems for high electric-to-gas price differences in many of the applications studied. The favorable applications were situations where the cogenerator was sized for baseload electrical and thermal energy requirements, i.e., where the cogeneration system could be used continuously throughout the year.

The same situations that make cogeneration attractive--high utilization rates and high electric-to-gas price differences--make high-efficiency electric alternatives attractive. Furthermore, the use of high-efficiency electric alternatives as the baseline in a cogeneration feasibility analysis frequently results in a lower rate-of-return than when the cogenerator is compared to conventional electric equipment. This is so because the thermal energy of the cogenerator displaces less electrical energy and, therefore, has less value when the high efficiency alternative is used as the baseline.

For example, if a cogeneration system is designed for installation in an office building with a computer center, represented by the load shape in Figure 1, the cogenerator would be sized to provide the baseload electrical power (200 kW) needed for the computer, lights and HVAC system, and the baseload thermal energy needed to drive an absorption chiller to cool the computer room (in the core of the

Table 1

COGENERATION APPLICATIONS STUDIED

Application	Capacity (kW)	Thermal Energy Use	Developer/ Manufacturer
Computer Center Office Building	200	Absorption Chiller	Caterpillar
Fast Food	70	Absorption Chiller	Waukesha
Hospital	500	Absorption Chiller Space Heating Water Heating	Martin
Supermarket	82	Absorption Chiller	Foster-Miller
Health Club	60	Water Heating	Thermo Electron

Table 2

ELECTRICITY AND GAS PRICES USED IN THE STUDY

Electricity Prices

	Energy Charge	Demand Charge
High Rate Case	10¢/kWh	$ 8/kW
Medium Rate Case	8¢/kWh	$10/kW
Low Rate Case	4¢/kWh	--

Gas Prices

45¢/therm

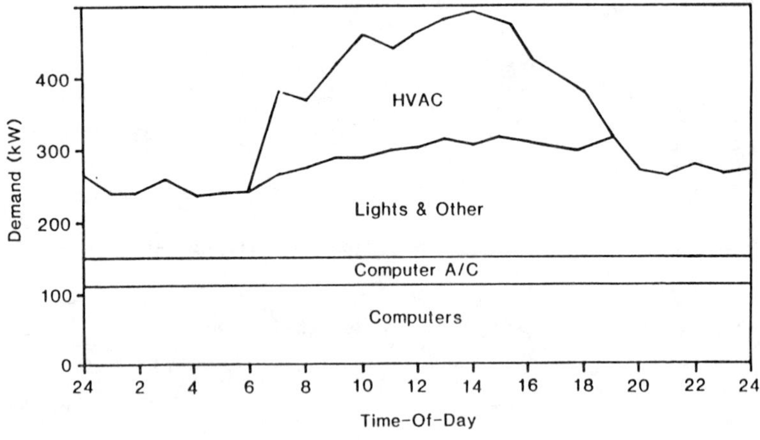

Figure 1. Computer Center/Office Building

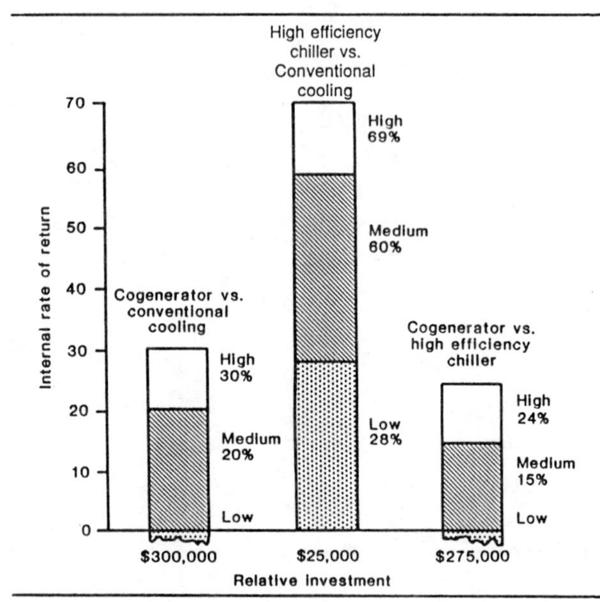

Figure 2. Internal Rate of Return of Cogeneration and Electrical Cooling in an Office Building with a Computer Center

building) year-round. The thermal energy would displace the electrical energy that would normally be used to drive a rooftop air conditioning unit dedicated to the computer.

The cogeneration economic comparison (shown in Figure 2) uses this relatively inefficient system as the baseline. As can be seen, the cogeneration system has a fairly high rate of return (30% for the high-rate case) compared to the baseline air conditioner with an EER of 10. If we substitute a high efficiency electrical chiller with an EER of 20.5--for the rooftop air conditioner--the chiller will have a rate of return of almost 70% (for the high rate case), compared to the rooftop air conditioner. The rate of return for an investment of $25,000 is clearly better than the rate of return for the cogenerator and is a much lower risk investment than the cogenerator.

If we now look at a high-efficiency chiller as the baseline in the cogeneration comparison (the left-most bar in Figure 2), the cogenerator rate of return has been reduced to 24%. This reduction in rate of return may be significant enough to convince the customer not to cogenerate--and to install the lower-risk, higher rate of return high-efficiency electrical equipment.

Other cases studied included hospitals, health clubs, fast food restaurants, and supermarkets. These cases are cited in the presentation and have been documented in a report being prepared by the Electric Power Research Institute (RP2034-9) that should be available shortly after the time this is published.

A brochure on electric alternatives to cogeneration was printed in January 1987. This brochure describes other examples and a wide range of other electrical equipment that should be considered by electric utilities and their customers as alternatives to cogeneration. This equipment includes the high efficiency centrifugal chillers cited in this paper as well as; state-of-the-art multiplex unequal commercial refrigeration systems, chiller heat recovery system including heat recovery heat pumps, heat pump water heaters, and thermal storage systems.

Additional work on electric alternatives is being performed by EPRI. This work includes expanding the analysis cited here to include; current tax laws, packaged cogenerator installed costs and operating based on recent field experience with these units, additional building types such as hotels, and additional electric equipment such as heat recovery heat pumps and thermal storage. Ongoing work also includes; demonstrating the performance of a state-of-the-art refrigeration system in an operating supermarket in Menlo Park, California; developing a screening tool for comparing cogeneration and electric alternatives in commercial buildings; and preparing a handbook with examples and worksheets--for analyzing cogeneration and electric alternatives.

EXPERIENCES WITH SMALL COGENERATION SYSTEMS

Hans Gransell
Electric Power Research Institute
Palo Alto, California

ABSTRACT

The installation of small cogeneration systems has expanded in the commercial and industrial customer sectors. As a result, EPRI recently conducted a survey to examine the availability and performance of existing small-scale (less than 2 MWe) cogeneration systems. Data were collected from 23 sites for survey purposes; during the final analysis period, data from a prior survey of Southern California Edison and San Diego Gas and Electric customers were included, bringing the total sample size to 54 sites. This paper briefly discusses the survey method used and evaluates the findings of this 1986 EPRI research project.

BACKGROUND

Cogeneration has become a viable, potentially cost-effective energy service option for electricity users due to changes in the economics of power generation and passage of the Public Utility Regulatory Policies Act of 1978 (PURPA). From 1980 through 1986, applicants to the Federal Energy Regulatory Commission (FERC) who wanted to qualify as cogenerators or small power producers under PURPA's guidelines could have potentially contributed over 46,000 MW. Approximately 20,000 to 26,000 MW, or about half of this proposed capacity, is projected to materialize. Projections of installed U.S. cogeneration capacity in the year 2000 range from 30,000 to 50,000 MW (1).

An expanding market for cogeneration will be the commercial customer sector. Packaged cogeneration systems, which reduce the installed costs of cogeneration for small facilities, are now making cogeneration an economically attractive option for many commercial facilities. In recent years, many packaged cogeneration systems have been installed, and projections indicate numbers will increase as these systems are further modified for these customers' unique needs. As customer and utility interest in these systems has increased, questions regarding the availability, performance, and costs of these packaged systems have also increased. Therefore, EPRI decided to specifically investigate cogeneration systems smaller than 2 MWe, focusing primarily on availability, but also on efficiency, installation requirements, and maintenance cost. This information will help utilities understand the potential impact of interconnecting a large number of these systems to their grids, and determine actual system performance and cost, as well as provide objective information to their customers. The survey was conducted by Science Applications International Corporation in Los Altos, California (2).

METHODOLOGY

The objective of this study was to provide an estimate of the availability and performance of small-scale (less than 2 MWe) cogeneration systems based on sample data from actual operating systems. An additional aim was to identify factors influencing system reliability, performance, and cost, including technical and economic factors. To accomplish this, data was collected from 23 sites.

The sites were chosen to include the six factors (listed below) which field experience has showen to be important. Within each factor, the range of characteristics included is defined.

- Operating mode--Continuously operated systems and cycled systems.
- Maintenance contracts--Installations with and without maintenance contracts.
- Ownership--Cogeneration systems owned by end-users, utilities, and third parties.
- Engine speed--Engines operating at high and low speeds.
- Emission controls--Engines with and without catalytic converters.
- Absorption chillers--Cogeneration systems with and without absorption chillers.

DATA COLLECTION METHODS

Data were collected from 23 packaged small-scale cogeneration installations that were fully operational following an equipment break-in period. Data on system outages and their causes was taken from site maintenance logs, inspection and test reports, or work orders. If no such documentation existed or the information from these sources was insufficient, failure information was obtained by interviewing maintenance personnel. Where available, electric utility records were obtained to verify the data.

Members of the survey team visited as many installations as possible to obtain first-hand data. In some instances, when the cogeneration system was maintained under contract, team members contacted the maintenance contractor and visited his field office. If necessary, the records made by maintenance personnel during their regularly scheduled inspections were examined.

Team members also obtained data, where available, on the characteristics of the installation, its maintenance procedures and costs, operating performance and costs, and installation costs.

The process of calculating the availability of each system had several steps. For each site where written documentation was available, the following information was identified for each system outage:

- the date of the outage,
- the duration of the event,
- the engine age at time of event,
- the system that initiated the outage, and
- a description of the event.

If no documentation existed or data from the sources listed earlier were insufficient, information obtained from maintenance personnel was used to estimate these items.

Economic shutdowns were not classified as failures. If the cogenerator was shut down for economic reasons, it was assumed that iy was not originally supposed to be operating during that period.

Once the characterization of the outages had been completed, then the overall system availability was calculated as:

$$\text{Availability} = \frac{\text{Operation time}}{8760 - \text{economic shutdown time}}$$

Normally, availability is defined as:

$$\text{Availability} = 1 - \frac{\text{unplanned outages}}{8760} - \frac{\text{planned outages}}{8760}$$

When the traditional formula to determine availability is used, the calculated value reflects the system's overall availability. This formula can incorporate both planned and unplanned outages into the calculation process.

The formula used in this survey simplifies the traditional formula. It does not differentiate between planned and unplanned outages, such as the fact that planned maintenance work can also be done during unplanned shutdowns. Also, a single subsystem was assigned the responsibility for each outage, even if more than one contributed to the outage.

In order to expand the database, fieldwork results from this survey were combined with the results of a recently completed study of Southern California Edison and San Diego Gas and Electric cogeneration customers. When data from the latter study was added, a sample size of 54 sites was available for analysis.

RESULTS

AVAILABILITY

A summary of the site characteristics represented in the survey sample is shown in Table 1.

TABLE 1

SUMMARY OF SITE CHARACTERISTICS REPRESENTED IN THE COGENERATION DATABASE

Site Characteristics	Number of Sites
Engine type	
Reciprocating engines	46
Gas turbines	8
Engine speed	
1800 rpm	29
1200 rpm	12
Others	13
Turbocharged	
Yes	20
No	34
Emissions control	
Lean burn	1
Catalytic converter	6
Water injection	6
Absorption chiller	
Yes	20
No	34
Packaged system	
Yes	36
No	18
Ownership	
Self	33
Third party	15
Others	6

The average availability for all sites over their years of operation was calculated to be 81.8%. In order to chart availability trends over the years of operation, Table 2 categorizes the data by year.

TABLE 2

AVERAGE COGENERATION SYSTEM AVAILABILITY BY OPERATING YEAR

Year of Operation	Sample Size	Average Availability (%)
1	49	80.1
2	40	83.2
3	21	83.2
4	9	97.3
5	8	98.6
6	7	98.0

(Data from 5 of the 54 units was unavailable.)

As Table 2 illustrates, availability increases with operating time. One reason is, of course, that these systems have been "debugged." Another reason is that during the most recent years, cogeneration system designs have included reciprocating engines, which exhibit a lower availability level.

Because of the relatively small data base, survey results should not be generally applied to other small-scale cogeneration sites. In addition, there are some important differences in specific site characteristics and their resulting availability levels.

As Table 3 indicates, cogeneration systems based on gas turbines had a higher availability than reciprocating engines. Also, a maintenance contract increased availability levels from 70% to 87%. There were also significant differences in availability due to the use of absorption chillers, turbocharged engines, and emission controls.

For each site with sufficient data, a single subsystem was assigned as the reason for each outage. These data were then compiled for all outages and sites (see Table 4). Based on this data, the primary cause of failure was the engine system, at 21.4% of the total outages categorized. Control system problems caused 20.4% of the outages and the cooling system caused 16.3%.

TABLE 3

AVAILABILITY FOR COGENERATION SITES WITH SPECIFIC CHARACTERISTICS

Site Characteristic	Site Characteristic Value	Sample Size	Average Availability (%)
All sites		54	81.8
Maintenance contract	Yes	38	87.0
	No	16	69.8
Absorption chiller	Yes	20	78.2
	No	34	84.0
Turbocharged	Yes	20	86.3
	No	34	77.8
Emissions control	Yes	13	69.8
	No	39	85.1
Engine type	Gas turbine	8	88.4
	Reciprocating	46	80.6

TABLE 4

SUMMARY OF OUTAGES BY SUBSYSTEM

Outages by Subsystem	Percentage of Total Number of Shutdowns
Engine/turbocharger	21.4
Control system	20.4
Cooling	16.3
Generator	12.3
Lube oil	7.1
Heat recovery	6.1
Starting	6.1
Emissions control	5.1
Others	6.2

Survey results indicate that many of the outages were caused by poor design of the packaged systems. For instance, diesel engines were not properly redesigned when converted to natural gas. The control systems were often too complex, causing reduced system reliability. Some cooling water pumps were not designed for continuous operation.

COGENERATION SYSTEM COST AND PERFORMANCE

Data on cogeneration system performance and operating costs from this study and from the Southern California Edison study were entered into a database. Average values for cost and performance variables are shown in Table 5.

TABLE 5

AVERAGE VALUES OF COST AND PERFORMANCE

Variable	Sample Size	Average Value
Electric efficiency	31	0.254
Thermal efficiency	13	0.327
Total efficiency	15	0.607
Installed cost	33	$1436/kWh
Maintenance cost	37	$0.0191/kWh
Payback period	23	5.8 years

Average values for different site characteristics are presented in Table 6.

TABLE 6

IMPACT OF SITE CHARACTERISTICS
ON COST AND PERFORMANCE VARIABLES

Site Characteristics	Site Characteristic	Cost or Performance	Average Value of Cost or Performance Value	Sample Size
Engine type	Reciprocating	Inst. cost	$1438/kW	32
	Gas turbine	Inst. cost	$1357/kW	1
	Reciprocating	Main. cost	2.05¢/kWh	32
	Gas turbine	Main. cost	1.04¢/kWh	5
	Reciprocating	Elec. effic.	0.258	27
		Therm. effic.	0.336	12
	Gas Turbine	Elec. effic.	0.225	4
		Therm. effic.	0.212	1
Absorption Chiller	Yes	Inst. Cost	$1812/kW	12
	No		$1221/kW	21
Emissions Control	Yes	Inst. Cost	$1382/kW	26
	No		$1797/kW	6
Turbocharger	Yes	Inst. Cost	$1585/kW	10
	No		$1372/kW	22
RPM	1200	Inst. Cost	$1596/kW	9
	1800	Inst. Cost	$1273/kW	20

Average thermal efficiencies represented in Table 6 are relatively low. This may be due to the fact that the cogeneration systems are characterized as electric load following and therefore, don't always have the capability to use all the thermal energy.

CONCLUSIONS

Since the survey database is rather small it is important to exercise caution when applying these results to other sites. These results do, however, indicate the availability, efficiencies and installation costs. Today, these small cogeneration systems are competitive compared to electric tariffs in some areas, with an average payback period of 5.8 years. The payback period is longer than the owners prefer but is still often acceptable.

To consider the small cogeneration systems as a reliable supply alternative, the reciprocating engines must be improved, so that availability levels increase and maintenance costs decrease.

Collecting field data from these sites is necessary when evaluating the technology. EPRI plans to continue this work by updating the survey and to expand the database.

REFERENCES

1. Cogeneration and Electric Utilities: Status and Prospects. EPRI RP1276-23. Report in print.

2. Small Cogeneration System Performance. EPRI RP1276-27. Report in print.

INNOVATIVE USES OF ELECTRICITY
ELECTROTECHNOLOGY DEVELOPMENT FOR THE METALS INDUSTRY

Joseph E. Goodwill
Director
Center for Metals Production

Introduction

The Center for Metals Production was established in 1984 by the Electric Power Research Institute (EPRI) for the purpose of helping the Metals Industry. This segment of the economy represents about 5% of all purchased electricity in the United States, and is even more significant in that metals plants are often the single largest load of individual utilities.

During the early 1980's the state of the metals industries was not good. These companies were particularly hard hit by the slowing economy, the strong dollar and the flood of imports. At the same time the industry was facing rising environmental concerns about some production processes, such as electric furnace dust and foundry cupola sludges; and questions were also being raised about electrical system disturbances such as flicker and harmonics possibly due to electric furnace operations.

Also at that time the Electric Power Research Institute felt that not only had the metals industry been forced to make drastic restructuring cuts in R&D staff and spending, but that advances in areas such as lasers, arc furnaces, plasma, solid state devices and electronic controls had been made that could help make U.S. metals manufacturers more competitive.

Establishment of CMP

Initially some technology developments were being organized by the Palo Alto, California staff of EPRI. But a closer feel of the metals market was needed. Therefore, the Center for Metals Production was established at Mellon Institute of Carnegie Mellon University. With the help of the American Iron and Steel Institute, several technical programs were initially undertaken. These were in the areas of electric furnace arc stability and in electric arc furnace dust treatment.

CMP Approach

The project approach followed by the Center is to initially perform a scoping study to look at the extent or scope of the problem or opportunity and to identify possible courses of action. This is followed by development of specific projects with industry cofunding. For example, in the Arc Stability Project, we had 20 companies contribute $20,000 each to the project with matching funds from EPRI. For the Electric Arc Furnace Dust Project a total of 23 companies contributed $30,000 each to support two projects. The Center provides project management at its expense. After completion of projects an extensive Tech Transfer or Communications program is implemented to bring word of new developments to U.S. industry. Included in this program are reports, videos, newsletters, and shorter bulletins or Tech Commentaries.

Generally, the approach we take is opportunity or problem oriented. However, for this talk, I would like to review electrotechnologies for metals production. The specific topics of interest are: arc melting, induction melting and holding, induction heating, resistance melting and holding, resistance heating, plasma, lasers, power electronics, and electrolytic reduction. The title of this section is innovative uses. In our sense of the word, innovative means opportunities for further usage exist, rather than, that the specific technologies are not now being used at all.

Arc Melting

Arc melting using alternating current furnaces is a major well-established technology. In conjunction with the U.S. Department of Energy, we have just taken a indepth look at the future of electric steelmaking until the year 2000. The study indicated a reasonable possibility that electric steelmaking could substantially increase its market share. This should occur as a result of favorable economics. High capital cost blast furnace, coke oven, and basic oxygen furnaces will be vulnerable to replacement by low capital cost electric furnaces using abundant scrap. However, some technical improvements may be needed to help this develop. For example, not much sheet steel is now being made in electric furnaces because of concerns about residual elements from scrap and nitrogen pickup from arcs. CMP is now developing projects in both these areas. The upgrading of steel scrap is a topic of broad concern. We have a growing supply of scrap in this country as we move to more recycling and less landfilling. However, the scrap is of lower quality as more combinations of materials are used such as zinc, tin and plastic coated steels, and more high alloy steels are used containing materials detrimental to the steelmaking process such as copper.

The electric arc furnace also has some rivals in development such as the coal based Energy Optimization Furnace and other fossil fuel based systems. Therefore, work has to be done to continue the improvements that have been made in arc furnaces through the years.

Also of mention are the ladle furnaces which resemble small electric furnaces. These units are finding greater use in the steel industry as they offer the ability to much more closely control the composition and temperature of molten steel. Furnaces operating on direct current are also finding some application as they offer smoother operation with better electrical characteristics, reduced electrode consumption and slightly improved power consumption.

Induction Melting

Induction melting is in widespread use in the iron foundry industry where it has about 40% of the market. The remainder is mostly cupola melting. Cupolas are large shafts where coke and iron scrap are fed into the top and air blown up from the bottom. EPRI has completed a development program (I will talk about later) involving a plasma torch assisted cupola. Cupolas require extensive investment in air pollution control devices. You then have a problem as to what to do with the sludges or dust collected. Closing landfills in the Northeast have in particular presented an opportunity for induction melting as the cost of disposing of cupola waste increases. In addition to eliminating pollution problems the workplace environment improves, operating flexibility is enhanced and productivity benefits.

Other opportunities opening up for induction are in ladle refining for foundries and small steel mills. The development of nonmetallic ladles allows heating as well as melting to be done outside the furnace in a special ladle which improves quality and productivity. Induction can also be used to heat tundishes which feed continuous casters.

Aluminum foundries have mainly used gas melting. However, the much lower yield losses experienced with induction melting has resulted in a number of new facilities choosing induction furnace equipment. One of the drawbacks to induction melting of aluminum has been the buildup of deposits of dross or oxides in the furnace that reduce efficiency. There are a number of ways to minimize this problem and we now have underway a project to document and detail how this is done.

The use of induction as a bulk melter for the steel industry is another interesting use of this technology. Allegheny Ludlum Steel has been doing this since 1979 using three 65 ton coreless furnaces to supply molten metal for finishing in basic oxygen furnaces. An induction heated melter/mixer is in operation at ISCOR in South Africa. As blast furnaces reach an age where they must be extensively rebuilt or replaced, this may be an attractive lower cost alternative.

Induction Heating

Induction has a place in heating materials prior to rolling. Some steel mills such as Nucor and Washington Steel are now doing this routinely. However, at the present time, the currently low price of natural gas has made this the usual choice for new installations. Electric induction heating does offer the user greatly reduced scale losses and better surfaces. However, the higher energy and capital costs are difficult to overcome when considering heating a cold billet or slab to rolling temperature of about 2300°F. Induction can be the economical choice in the new trend of rolling steel directly, that is, not allowing the material to cool to room temperature for inspection, conditioning and transportation to the rolling mill. In newly designed steel mills the continuous caster is placed close to the rolling mill. Ideally the slab or billet can go directly to the rolling mill without cooling to room temperature. Generally some additional heat is required, usually in the coolest areas such as slab or billet edges. This heat can often be most economically supplied by induction. We believe the induction role can be significant in making practical the new thin slab and strip casting technologies now being developed. Another induction heating technology being developed that should be significant to the metals industry is traverse flux. The EPRI Center for Materials Production is developing a project in this area.

Resistance Melting

Resistance melting and holding is a simple technology often overlooked. It is a low capital cost way to obtain heat. While no stirring action is generated such as with induction, this often an advantage for some processes such as melting aluminum.

Resistance Heating

Resistance heating also has its place in metals production. The Center for Metals Production is working to make practical ladle preheating using this technology. Ladles for handling molten metals at up to 2900°F require drying and preheating to cure ladle refractories and to avoid freezing of the metal in the ladle. This is generally done with gas, but the thermal efficiency is quite low, only 5 to 25%, because of the heat carry off of the exhaust gases even with recuperators. Electrical resistance units have been used on a limited basis and generate thermal efficiencies of up to 80%. However, they have not entered into widespread use because of durability problems. We currently have a project addressing both design and operating practice which is quite encouraging.

Plasma

Plasma torches offer an attractive energy source for metals production in that a high temperature inert gas reactive zone is established. Temperatures can be in the area of 10,000^{o}F. vs. 5,000^{o}F in an arc furnace. However, the limited power size torches available and the cost of capital equipment has worked against widespread use.

The use of supplemental plasma torches in a cupola now being installed by General Motors will allow the use of fine materials such as uncompacted turnings which would ordinarily be blown out of cupolas. EPRI sponsored tests at the Westinghouse Waltz Mill, PA, facility indicate ore can also be readily reduced in such a unit.

The treatment of waste material such as electric furnace dust with plasma has also been successfully demonstrated in a CMP collaborative project. The technical feasibility but not necessarily the economics of plasma specialty steel melting, ore reduction, tundish heating and carbon steel scrap melting has also been demonstrated.

Lasers

High energy lasers have been investigated by CMP to see if any spin-off from the Strategic Defense Initiative would benefit the metals area. Opportunities do exist in surface cleaning and modification. For example, laser treatment could do away with the need for acid pickling with the resulting waste disposal problems. However, it appears for the next few years applications will be limited to special applications such as surface enhancement of electrical steels or of steel rolls. An interesting project we are participating in is the development of a system using a laser to develop a vapor plume from molten metal that can then be analyzed by spectrographic means. This has the potential of speeding up many metal production processes.

Power Electronics

Power Electronics is a term that includes all the advances in solid state devices that have already had extensive applications in the communications area. Thyristors, solid state rectifiers, gate turn off devices, etc. make practical things such as adjustable speed AC motors at a small fraction of the cost of the DC motors normally used. Our Center is working with the new Power Electronics Applications Center established by EPRI to further implement these technologies.

Electrolytic Reduction

Electrolysis of metal solutions to refine or form solid metals is well known. Electrorefining of copper has been practiced for many years. Electrowinning of copper from ores is now coming into common use in the domestic industry and is helping to make domestic producers competitive with overseas producers. We have been looking into direct metal forming of mill shapes from solution using electrolysis. If we could eventually plate out parts of the shape and properties necessary, a tremendous quantity of capital and energy could be saved.

Summary

In summary, The Center for Metals Production is doing considerable work in bringing technology to industry. Much of it evolutionary rather than revolutionary, however, in my opinion, our work and that of many others is going to make the metals industry of the year 2000 a greatly changed industry but one still supplying materials that are an important component of most manufactured goods.

THE RHODE ISLAND FOUNDATION AND CENTER FOR THIN FILM AND INTERFACE RESEARCH

Michael P. Lauro, Director of R&D
Tanury Industries
Lincoln, Rhode Island

The Committee on Science, Engineering and Public Policy of the National Academies of Science and Engineering and the Institute of Medicine identified the field of Thin Films and Interfaces as a "high leverage research opportunity that is ripe for discovery." The estimated commercial market for Thin Films and Interface applications is two billion dollars annually with an expected annual compound growth rate of 10%.

In an effort to advance the state-of-the-art in Thin Film Technology, Tanury Industries has established a Foundation as a Research & Development Joint Venture by implementing a unique methodology for funding such projects. This methodology has been used successfully by Tanury Industries during the past two years for funding basic, applied and developmental research in the field of Thin Films at Brown University. The structure avoids many of the downside risks of funding industry/university collaborations and presents a more structured, applied and "deliverable" oriented process. We believe that our methodology, expertise, and successful record can benefit each member organization of the Joint Venture.

The scope of each basic, applied and developmental research project will be controlled by individual member(s) funding each project. Funding for projects will be sent to a cooperative Thin Film Research Center, organized by Brown Unviersity and the University of Rhode Island. The cooperative Thin Film Research Center represents the first center of its kind in the country devoted entirely to the field of thin films and interfaces and has the endorsement of the National Science Foundation and the Rhode Island Department of Economic Development. The Center will be located at the two universities.

The Joint Venture represents a proposed structure for the Industry Membership described in the Prospectus for the Rhode Island Center for Thin Film and Interface Research. The organization will be structured in this manner and will realize a greater return on its membership's R&D investments by means of exclusive licensing, non-exclusive licensing, cost sharing, laboratory participation, information control, and research agenda control. The proposal is directed to achieving commercially viable technology that will generate acceptable returns on investment while allowing the technological benefits of such partnerships to develop at a time when emerging technology is vital to our respective businesses.

The goals and objectives of the Industry Foundation are as follows:

Goals

- Establish an R&D Joint Venture whose purpose will be to increase the level of industry sponsorship, industry participation and commercially viable technology in the field of Thin Films and Interfaces.

- Use the money raised by the Joint Venture to fund the first University Cooperative Research Center in the United States devoted entirely to the field of thin films and interfaces.

- Encourage the growth of the University Cooperative Thin Film Research Center which will be located at each university under the direction of Brown University and the University of Rhode Island.

Objectives

- Organize a consortium of companies as an R&D Joint Venture to fund and monitor basic, applied and developmental research on thin films and interfaces beginning in 1987.

- Raise $500,000 from the Joint Venture in the first year of operation and $1,000,000 each year after to fund ongoing activities of the Center.

- Provide the Joint Venture partners funding the Center exclusive licensing, non-exclusive licensing, cost sharing opportunities, information control, research agenda control, and active laboratory participation during the activities of research projects.

- Provide to the Joint Venture a unique methodology for contracting R&D from a corps of University experts dedicated to accomplishing the research and development.

- Structure the reporting requirements of funded research agenda's and project workscopes in a manner that generates commercially viable technology transfer based upon an acceptable return on investment.

- Provide the University Thin Film Center access to an industry sponsored Joint Venture which is dedicated to funding the advancement of thin films and interfaces.

- Provide the Joint Venture a range of membership classifications which are both flexible and economical.

FOUNDATION MANAGEMENT

In view of the role of Tanury Industries in establishing the Industry Joint Venture, Tanury will serve as Managing Venturer. As part of its duty as Managing Venturer, the Executive Director of the Industry Joint Venture will be selected from its staff by Tanury Industries.

Responsibilities of the Executive Director of the Industry Joint Venture

1. Advise and consult with coventurers and act as an administrator in accordance with coventurer direction to insure that the marketability, profitability and return on investment of basic and applied and developmental research projects are addressed in the planning process and achieved.

2. Provide continuous liaison between the Industry Joint Venture and the Center.

3. Provide consulting services to coventurers requesting such services in the area of contract negotiations with the Center including drafting research agendas and project workscopes for applied and basic research, negotiation of property rights with research administrators and monitoring reporting requirements and transfer of technology.

4. Develop with coventurers a data base information file of risk management techniques for emerging technologies.

5. Advise and consult with coventurers to expedite technology transfer at the point when technology is ready for prototype development and commercialization.

6. Oversee the operation and management of the Industry Joint Venture.

7. Preside over the Industry Advisory Board.

INTRODUCTION TO THE THIN FILM AND INTERFACE RESEARCH CENTER

For over thirty years, Brown University and the University of Rhode Island have operated thin film and interface laboratories in which their faculty, post doctoral scientists and students conducted thin film research in many areas including microelectronics, epitaxial growth, photovoltaics, corrosion and wear protection, amorphous materials, optical coatings, synthetic diamond coatings, sputtering, evaporation, chemical vapor deposition (CVD), chemical vapor transport (CVT), chemical spray pyrolysis (CSP), composites, laser induced fluorescence, ceramics, metallographic analysis, electron tunneling microscopy, and continuous load lock coating systems. As a result at both Universities there are highly qualified experts in deposition and characterization of semiconductor, insulator, polymer, metal, carbon and ceramic coatings and the interfaces between these coatings and the substrates on which they have been deposited.

Brown and URI have decided to combine their expertise and resources in this field to establish a Center devoted to research on Thin Films and Interfaces. The Universities intend to structure the Center for implementing a specific methodology for performing basic and applied research.

This methodology has been successfully used by both Universities, on a small scale, in their independent relationships with industry during the past few years. The operating structure proposed herein expands on their success by establishing a system of industry-university cooperation which generates a synergistic effect in the course of the collaboration.

Funding for research will come mainly from industrial companies which will be organized into an Industry Joint Venture (the Joint Venture). Companies interested in becoming coventurers will be offered three types of participation: subscriber, affiliate, and contractor. Each type of participation is described in this manuscript. The research projects, which will be organized and conducted by the Center, will be selected in the course of consultations between the Center and the coventurers. The Executive Director of the Industry Joint Venture will preside over the Center's Industry Advisory Board, will provide consulting services to coventurers and will serve as the liaison between the coventurers and the Center for expediting communication, transfer of technology, identification of patentable material, etc. The Executive Director will also be responsible for the operation and management of the Industry Joint Venture. The Industry Advisory Board will identify research activities of common interest to a number of coventurers and facilitate pooling financial resources to explore them at the Center.

Representative of industry, who have expressed an interest in supporting this venture and of the Universities, which will establish the Center, believe that the cooperation between representatives of the academic and industrial worlds which will result from implementation of their plan will advance the science and technology of thin films to the benefit of all cooperating parties.

This portion of the manuscript summarizes the goals and objectives of the Center, the planning stages, and the organization structure. It contains a policy statement and also provides descriptive examples of basic and applied projects which the Center is prepared to undertake. The research projects to be finally implemented will be selected by agreement between the Center's Administration and the Industry Advisory Board.

The Goals and Objectives of the Thin Film Research Center are as follows:

<u>Goals</u>

- Establish an Industry-University Cooperative Research Center utilizing facilities, equipment and personnel from Brown and URI, which will increase the level of fundamental engineering and scientific research in the field of thin films and interfaces.

- Organize the Thin Film and Interface Research Center using a methodology that encourages academic excellence, self-sufficiency, industry collaboration and technology transfer.

- Encourage the growth and participation by Industry in the Center.

Objectives

- Structure the operating policy of the Center in a manner that encourages industrial funding support and participation in basic and applied research projects involving thin films and interfaces.

- Establish a flexible work plan for the Center to permit faculty, principal investigators, technicians, graduate students, and undergraduates to work on basic and applied research projects in an effective manner.

PLANNING ACTIVITIES

In 1986 the Division of Engineering at Brown and the College of Engineering at URI began to explore the feasibility of establishing a Rhode Island Thin Film and Interface Research Center as an Industry-University (IU) cooperative research venture. The idea was endorsed by a number of companies under the leadership of Tanury Industries of Lincoln, Rhode Island.

This favorable response from industry led the Universities to submit a proposal to NSF for financial support of a planning conference which NSF agreed to do. Forty-five companies manufacturing thin film products sent representatives to the conference which was held in Providence, September 27 through 29, 1987. At the conclusion of the conference, twelve attendees said that they would recommend affiliation with the Center to their managements; another eight indicated that they were inclined to do likewise but they needed additional information. These initial successes have resulted in the preparation of a proposal for submission to NSF and to the emerging industrial participants in the venture.

Intra-University Discussions

The administrations of Brown and URI have provided a wide range of inputs into the planning of this Industry-University Cooperative Research Center. A draft proposal was widely circulated to the interested faculty members and to appropriate members of the two University administrations. The Center and its organization have been endorsed by the Deans of Engineering, Deans of Research, the University Patent Officers, and the two University Presidents, Dr. Howard Swearer of Brown, and Dr. Edward Eddy of URI.

Background Meetings

In the early stages of the effort to explore feasibility of the Center, meetings were held with representatives of ten companies engaged in thin film activities to determine the level of industry interest in such a Center, what industry expected from the proposed Center, and which administrative structure and methodology would be most attractive and responsive to industry's needs. The response to these overtures was overwhelmingly favorable. Those contacted expressed strong interest in a broad research agenda spanning the range from fundamental to developmental research. They liked the concept of an industry organization to support research on thin films at the Center.

At the recommendation of these industrial organizations, discussions were held with personnel from existing NSF-IU centers and Industry organizations to determine the most practical approach to establishing a successful collaboration. In particular, Mr. Malcolm McLaren of the Center for Ceramic Research at Rutgers University in New Jersey was most cooperative in sharing detailed information about the structure of the Rutgers Center, how it operates and how it is coupled to its industrial sponsors.

The Planning Conference

These discussions led to the NSF sponsored two-day planning conference held in September, 1987, at the Omni Biltmore Hotel in Providence, RI. Its purpose was to introduce the proposed Thin Film and Interface Research Center to a larger group of potential industrial participants. As we have already noted, forty-five companies responded favorably to an invitation to participate in the planning of the Center.

The Planning Conference Schedule

The first day of the two-day conference included a description of the NSF-Industry-University Center Program by Dr. Alexander Schwarzkopf of NSF, of the Center proposal by the proposed directors, Prof. Joseph J. Loferski of Brown and Prof. Shashanka S. Mitra of the University of Rhode Island, and of the role that industrial organizations will play by Mr. Michael Lauro of Tanury Industries. This introduction was followed by descriptions of research proposed by eighteen faculty members of the two Universities. The conference organized itself into workshops at which the University Faculty and Industry representatives identified research topics of greatest interest to the potential industry coventurers.

Level and Sources of Funding

The principal funding for the Center will be provided by the industry coventurers. Funding from the NSF will supplement the industrial support during the start-up years. The State of Rhode Island will provide funds for the purchase, maintenance and operation of the major pieces of diagnostic equipment. The State Government through its RIPSAT program may also enter into partnerships with industrial organizations which want to support research at the Center.

Industrial organizations wishing to become coventurers in research at the Center will be offered three levels of participation as described below. The fees of subscriber and affiliate coventurers will be pooled with the NSF contribution to fund research projects selected by negotiation between the Industry Advisory Board, the Administration of the Center and the faculty researchers. It is expected that at least $300,000 will be provided by the industrial coventurers during the first year and that this amount will increase steadily until it approaches $2 million within five years.

Industry Coventurer Participation

Industrial organizations will be offered three types of participation in the Industry Joint Venture with different levels of financial commitment and different benefits and privileges, as described below.

Type of Participation	Financial Commitment
1. Subscriber	$10,000/yr./min. 2 yr. commitment
2. Affiliate	$25,000/yr./min. 2 yr. commitment*
3. Contractor	About $70,000 for a 6 mo. contract* (maximum 2 yr. commitment)

*These figures do not include capital equipment costs. They will cover direct and indirect costs associated with each project funded by the Center by the Industry Joint Venture. The maximum 2 yr. commitment for contractor participation is recommended, although contracts requiring additional time and funds will be considered.

Coventurer Description

1. Subscriber A Subscriber has the opportunity to track technological developments occurring at the University Center for Thin Film and Interface Research through the following mechanisms.

- Attendance at semi-annual symposia and research seminars.
- Participation in educational programs on specific thin film and interface topics, designed jointly with the participating industries.
- Organized visits to any of the Center laboratories on request.
- Collaborative use of specialized laboratory equipment and expertise.
- Information about ongoing federally funded thin film and interface research projects at the Center and access to the resulting reports.
- A continuously updated listing of researchers at the Center as well as their fields of expertise, topics under investigation, techniques used, processes examined, and properties measured.
- Help in the negotiation of contracts with the Thin Film and Interface Research Center.
- Abstracts of research agendas proposed to the Center and to federal agencies in support of the research agendas.
- Information about graduating students participating in Center research including their thesis abstracts.
- Reprints of Center publications.
- Annual CTFIR summary reports.

2. Affiliate An Affiliate member has a seat on the Industry Advisory Board. Affiliate members actively participate in defining the Center's annual research agenda based upon the collective needs of the membership. A workscope and budget, supplemented with performance milestones will be drafted for the various research projects submitted by the Center. In making the agenda recommendations, the board will use the following criteria:

- Faculty interests
- Industry need
- Product and market relevance
- Scientific and technical merit
- Investigator qualifications
- Center facilities available
- Potential for contract level funding from industry or other sources
- Potential for developing business ventures between the Center, Universities, and/or individual co-venturers.

Affiliate contributed funds together with funds contributed by Subscribers are intended to support the preparation of full scale - applied and developmental research programs. Industrial organizations wishing to become Affiliates may do so at any time and will be entitled to participate in benefits from previously conducted research only if they become Affiliates prior to disclosure of any discovery or potential invention generated by such research.

In addition to receiving the benefits described in the Subscriber description, Affiliates receive:

- A non-exclusive, non-transferable royalty free license to the technology to those Affiliates who elect to fund the securing of patent protection of the technology.

- Indirect cost rate (15%). Contributions to the funding of research by NSF and the Universities (through a reduction in indirect cost rates)

- Highest priority of use of Center personnel, facilities and equipment

- Access and use of Center-University libraries

- Quarterly Affiliates Newsletter

- Data base/literature search access

- One hour per month free consulting service from participating Center Investigators

- Quarterly research agenda report (one page)
- Option to participate in Affiliate Enhancement Program

Through the Affiliate Enhancement Program, an affiliate or group of affiliates may elect to increase funding of research in an area of particular interest or commercial relevance to the affiliate(s) participating in the Program. Thus, the Affiliate Enhancement Program affords affiliates a level of participation similar to Contractors in terms of information and research agenda control but with the benefits of Affiliate Status, particularly reduced indirect costs and highest priority of use of Center personnel and equipment.

3. Contractor A Contractor funds a project of applied, developmental or commercial relevance to the Contractor or its market. Contractors may negotiate their respective contracts and workscopes directly with the Center. The research agenda and workscope will remain proprietary, subject to publication policy 10 section 4.4, and will be implemented with the assistance of the Executive and Deputy Directors of the Center. Contractors also have the option to implement their respective research agendas and workscopes with the assistance of the Executive Director of the Joint Venture upon payment of an additional fee to the Joint Venture. Separate non-disclosure agreements will be required for any Center personnel associated with a Contractor.

Contractors receive the following benefits:

- Right to an Exclusive royalty bearing license with option to sublicense
- Information control and research agenda control
- Monthly reports
- Project research calendar not to exceed twenty-four months
- Indirect cost rate of 50%
- Priority of use of Center personnel, facilities and equipment over contracts negotiated outside the Center directly with the individual Universities
- No user fee for Center facilities and equipment

Proposed Research Applications

Coatings and Interfaces for Microelectronics

Wear and Corrosion Resistant Materials

TV Pickup Tubes

Biocompatible Materials

Tribology

Synthetic Diamond Coatings

Refractory and Hard Coatings

Continuous Thin Film Coating Systems

Amorphous Materials

Superconducting Thin Films

Laser Induced Fluorescence

Thin Film Oxides and Nitrides

Ceramics

Inorganic Compound Semiconductors

Metallographic Analysis

Electron Tunneling Microscopy

Epitaxial Growth Techniques

Optical and Magnetic Storage Media

Polymer, Metal, Carbon and Ceramic Interfaces

High Performance Plastics, Composites and Adhesives

Optical Materials and Coatings

Infrared Sensors

Chemical Vapor Deposition

Chemical Spray Pyrolysis

Decorative Coatings

Multi-Element Thin Films

Thin Film Integrated Circuits

Physical Vapor Deposition

Fiber Reinforced Composites

Petroleum Refining

Semiconductor Films

Holography

EMI-RFI Shielding Films

Microwave Integrated Circuits

Solar Cells

Solid State Power Generation

MATERIALS PROPERTIES INFLUENCED BY COATINGS

MECHANICAL	CHEMICAL	ELECTROMAGNETIC
Wear	Corrosion	Superconductivity
Friction	Oxidation	Semiconductor doping
Hardness	Electrochemistry	Photoconductivity
Adhesion	Catalysis	Resistivity
Fatigue		Magnetic Properties
Toughness		Reflectivity
Ductility		Dielectric constant
Erosion		

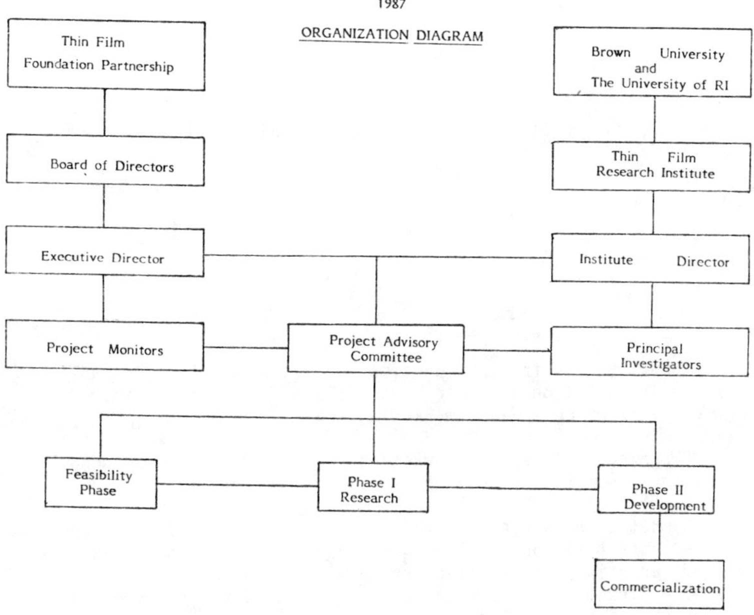

Inquiries of the Thin Film Foundation and Research Center can be directed to the following people:

Dr. Joseph Loferski
Brown University Box D
Division of Engineering
Providence, RI 02912
401-863-2652

Mr. Michael P. Lauro
Director of R&D
Tanury Industries, Inc.
6 New England Way
401-333-9400

Dr. Shashanka S. Mitra
University of Rhode Island
Dept. of Electrical Engineering
Kelly Hall
Kingston, RI 02881
401-792-5849

SYSTEM:GT TM, GEOTHERMAL HEATING COOLING AND HOT WATER HEATING

Michael C. Lyle

Public Service Company of Indiana, Inc.

Plainfield, Indiana

Thank you for the introduction. I also have the opportunity to make an introduction this morning. It's my privilege to introduce a new Public Service Indiana marketing program.

"Warning" - this is a marketing talk. And as such, depending on where your from, it could be hazardous to your health.

Competition is keen in Indiana - and unfortunately it doesn't end on the basketball court. The "gas house" gang has done an excellent job of marketing, and has made serious inroads into our share of the new home market - and it doesn't stop there. I would suspect this may be the case elsewhere besides Indiana.

There's nothing fun about getting beat at your own game - but it does make you knuckle down and ask some of the real basic questions. Hard questions. Like what is really best for our customers - and our Company? What is the best heating, cooling and hot water heating system for someone building a new home?

As we were searching for answers last fall - Oklahoma State University, in the name of Dr. Jim Bose, paid us a visit in Indianapolis. He had with him, a task force representing many of the key players in the water source heat pump technology.

They made us stop - look - and listen to this technology. and we learned it's hightech - it's environmentally sound - and absolutely will outperform any other viable heating, cooling and hot water heating system, offering customers significantly lower utility bills - in Indiana, as much as 30% lower than gas.

Having no outdoor unit gives this technology esthetic advantages from both the appearance and noise aspects. That's important and will only get more important.

The indoor compressor greatly enhances reliability and serviceability. If esthetics are important, then consider how important better reliability and serviceability are.

But most important of all, the air temperature at the register during the heating season is several degrees warmer than those produced by our old friend, the air-to-air heat pump. It's more comfortable.

If you think about the problems we are having now - and consider that here is a proven technology that:
-- Operates cheaper than anything
-- Offers better esthetics
-- Better reliability
-- Better serviceability
-- And is more comfortable
Well, I would be sick if the "gas house" gang had it to offer customers.

It is the best heating, cooling and hot water heating system available. Down the road we must be able to offer customers the best product - or we won't get the business.

The other reason why this is the best product for our customers - is because it's the best for us.

The water source heat pump represents a better annual load factor to the utility than other electric or fossil fuel systems.

It's a smart selling opportunity!

As the Oklahoma State task force demonstrated, the technology is in place - it is proven reliable. The benefits to both the customer and the electric utility are real. It's truly a win-win situation/

But the technology needs a champion in the marketplace. This champion must consolidate the fragmented marketing efforts that exist. It must lend creditability to the technology. And it must assist, encourage and/or participate in seeing that the necessary
- Manufacturer
- Distributor
- Dealer
- Loop Contractor
infracture is expanded and strengthened.

This champion is most likely the electric utility. The OSU task force asked us to accept the charter of developing such a marketing program.

We accepted the challenge - and gave our creatives the following direction.

In Indiana we did not feel that using "heat pump" nomenclature was necessarily a plus. And, the concept of "electric heat", at least in PSI land and mainly due to our Marble Hill nuclear problem, carries the stigma or perception of being expensive.

We also felt it a problem that this technology had so many "handles"; water source, earth coupled, ground coupled, earth loop, ground loop, etc., etc.

But we felt there was still some magic in the word Geothermal.

With that as a starting point, I would now like to introduce to you the result - System:GT.

(Multi-Media Presentation - 7 Minutes)

The acceptance and interest in System:GT is exciting and encouraging. Our HVAC dealers and builders are very receptive and our sister utilities and rural electric cooperatives in Indiana have been very supportive of our effort.

I think all of us see this as a new opportunity to take advantage of the power of joint advertising. Joint utility advertising, as you well know, is very difficult to pull off with our existing products and programs. But we're on the threshold with this technology and it offers us a tremendous opportunity to start off together.

In Indiana we're working closely to jointly advertise System:GT to increase our customer's awareness of geothermal heating, cooling and hot water heating.

In addition to an advertising and promotional program, at PSI System:GT is a full fledged marketing program, with both a lead generation and a lead qualification procedure.

Since November 1986, we have pilot marketed System:GT in 4 of our 33 districts. On June 1, 1987 we rolled the program out to the rest of our company.

We are now playing a much bigger role in the sales process. We're no longer turning leads over to dealers who in turn install gas furnaces. A PSI representative is the first person and the last person our customers sees. We feel this is awfully important.

Through our pilot effort, the customer's interest in geothermal heating, cooling and hot water heating is well documented. We have realized a consistent 5% response to direct mailers. For every 1000 letters mailed, we're getting 50 responses. If you are experienced in direct mail or solo marketing, you realize how unusually high of a response this is.

As was mentioned in the multi-media presentation, System:GT is supported by highway billboards and radio and newspaper advertising with TV support on the drawing board. All advertising carries a 1-800-622-HEAT customer response number. I would like to play one of the 30-second radio spots for you now.

(Radio Spot)

When a customer responds to:
- A direct mailer or bill stuffer
- A radio or TV spot
- A newspaper ad
- A highway billboard advertisement
- Or just word of mouth

they are sent a letter along with an informational piece explaining System:GT.

The letter tells the customer they will be contacted by a PSI sales representative.

The sales rep contacts the customer by phone and pre-qualfies or screens the lead.

- Does he or she want information only
- Does the customer have a need
  - --Is he/she building
  - --Or considering building in the future
  - --Or about to replace an aging system
- Is System:GT right for the customer?
- Does the customer know it's a $3500 to $8500 investment?

If a lead is still viable, an appointment is made. Our sales rep visits the customer's home and makes a formal "sales presentation" utilizing our sales packet.

- A site survey is filled out to capture the geography of the property.
- Information is collected so the sales rep can return to the office and do a heat loss on the home so the unit can be properly sized - not over sized, properly sized.

This fully qualified lead and the information is given to participating dealers in that district on a rotating basis.

I say participating dealers because we have taken another step with System:GT.

HVAC Dealers are invited to a meeting, shown the multi-media presentation and given a questionnaire. To participate in the program and be eligible to receive qualified leads, they must provide us several pieces of information about this dealership.

They must also sign the questionnaire indicating their interest and willingness to follow the "Participating Dealer Guidelines and Standards", of the program.

Once a dealer is given a qualified lead he is expected to quote a price and close the sale with the customer. In many cases this will be a joint call between our sales rep and the HVAC dealer.

In all cases, we follow up with the customer. If the HVAC dealer sold them gas after they were a fully qualified geothermal lead -- we have a serious talk. If it happens again, he is off the team and is no longer provided leads.

Our Sales Reps also follow-up an installation and complete a post installation checklist, which includes making sure the customer is satisfied.

It's working well for us. At least in Indiana we are making great strides at consolidating the marketing of this technology - we are developing a lot of awareness and interest in geothermal.

A bigger market is spawning more competition among manufacturers, dealers and installers. The laws of economics should bring the price down. If it doesn't, electric utilities may have to get more involved - I know many, many I.O.U.'s and Rural Electric are seriously looking at ways to bring the initial cost of geothermal down to parity with AAHP's or gas/heat/electric air combos.

Once the market is established, this technology could easily become the flagship product of our industry in the new home market or the replacement market.

If so - everyone will win - our customers - our trade allies - and our companies.

THE UTILITIES ROLE IN CONCEPTUAL BUILDING DESIGN

Kyle E. Wilcutt, P.E.
Southern Company Services, Inc.
Atlanta, Georgia

My message for the utility industry and the building design community is an old story that needs retelling. The continued growth of many cities like Atlanta is evidence of the need to address this issue as long as we have a viable economic system and utilities have the legal responsibility to provide for growth. Today I want to share my vision for a more complete building design process.

The utility role that I want to address is a utility marketing role. Most utilities are talking the demand-side management process, but how many marketing and sales organizations are meaningfully involved with the supply side planners of their companies? Are the marketing programs of utilities really a part of their companies' load shape objectives? Are the marketing organizations of utilities including a concern for the load shape of new buildings and the effect on their companies' electric system 15 years from now?

Demand-Side Management Options

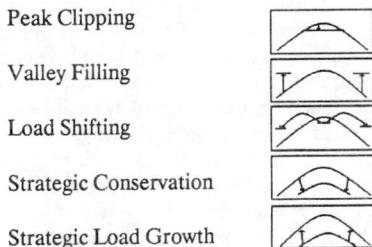

Peak Clipping

Valley Filling

Load Shifting

Strategic Conservation

Strategic Load Growth

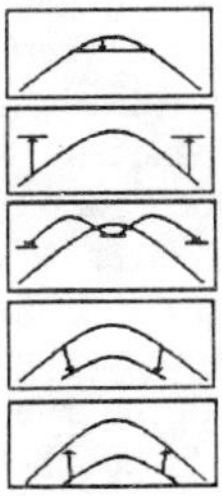

Figure 1

Demand-side management programs are one of the most important roles that utility marketing people should play. However, I believe a commitment to marketing programs is difficult to attain due in part to the ease with which they can be stopped. Meaningful marketing contributions to load shape goals will require a long term commitment to well defined goals that are pursued with the same focus on accomplishment that has been given to completing power plants. A marketing program designed to meet demand-side load shaping goals cannot be a year to year effort. The marketing effort that I believe should be common place is one that will make significant impact on commercial building load shapes. When utility marketing offers services that have tangible value to the conceptual design community - the architects, developers and owners of proposed new buildings - the marketing programs will make significant contributions.

What commitment does a utility make to a new building compared to the building designers? How much involvement do most utility marketing organizations have in the conceptual design of commercial buildings? How long will the utility be responsible for providing the energy needs of each new building? These are a few of the issues related to the utilities role.

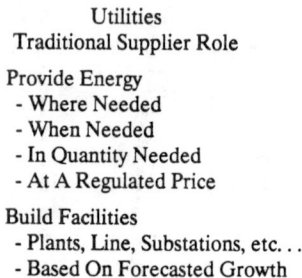

Utilities
Traditional Supplier Role

Provide Energy
- Where Needed
- When Needed
- In Quantity Needed
- At A Regulated Price

Build Facilities
- Plants, Line, Substations, etc...
- Based On Forecasted Growth

Figure 2

The historical role of utilities has been straight-forward and easily understood. As a monopoly, it really was pretty simple. Provide the customer with energy - when, where and in the quantities desired at a price that reflected the cost of providing the service. When and where are not too difficult to determine but utilities must decide how much before the customers even know they want new buildings. Forecasting new construction becomes the real issue. It really was not that difficult to forecast before 1968. Until that time the utilities load growth was almost a straight line and the more capacity they built the lower the cost per unit of energy became. Lower unit cost encouraged the supply side planners to add capacity. About 1968, the pendulum changed directions. The nice comfortable environment where all utilities had to do was to show up with the product at the right place, at the right time and the right amount became unknown territory. The pleasures of deficit financing to enjoy the benefits of lower unit cost came to an end and the financial nightmare began.

During the late 50's and 60's utilities engaged in a significant sales campaign to capitalize on the lower unit costs and offset the peaks created by air conditioning. But, selling the off peak capacity game gave way to conservation at all costs in the 70's. Many of the architects, developers, engineers and contractors had become accustomed to someone from the utilities being available and interested in their next building to sell heating. But now, the utility sales engineers were no longer there and the message from the industry became confusing at best.

Figure 3

Today, utilities need more than a sales plan. Now 15 or so years later utilities have a new story to tell and a new audience to hear the message. The new message is more than load management - it is marketing. I believe load management has a reaction connotation and what is needed is the development of an active marketing role in conceptual building design and development. Too often in the past, utilities have arrived too late with too little to be a real factor in getting consideration of new or more advantageous systems that had tangible benefits for the customer. In general there was a sales mentality. One marketing textbook says that the sales mentality means that you're focusing on your own needs. You are saying - "what's in it for me" - you are preoccupied with yourself -- what's good for me. This sales mentality was part of the driving force behind the utilities electric heating sales effort but marketing is the answer today.

The change to a marketing mentality is difficult, but it is the mentality that all businesses need and the utilities must have. All of the participants in the conceptual

Sales vs. Marketing Orientation

Selling	Marketing
Focuses On The Needs Of The Seller Preoccupied With The Seller's Need To Convert His Product Into Cash	Focuses On The Needs Of The Buyer; Preoccupied With How To Generate Customer Satisfaction At A Profit

Figure 4

building design need a marketing attitude if utilities are going to be able to be a part and the long range view is to be given serious consideration.

The marketing mentality means being preoccupied with how to generate customer satisfaction. But all importantly, at a profit. Businesses want customers to like what they do. But they must make a profit to survive. Customers understand the profit motive but they are not going to make business decisions; they are naturally concerned for their interests.

To have a marketing philosophy, businesses must have marketing research. They need to sincerely want to know: What does the customer want? What is he saying? How does he want to live? What price is he willing to pay? With these answers then a market plan and programs can be developed.

Figure 5

Most utility programs of the past have not been based on marketing research. But, many companies are now trying to incorporate the customers' wants and needs into programs and action plans. The long lead times required for facilities construction should lead utilities to longer range marketing programs than most other businesses. The long range view focuses on the marketing perspective. I believe the marketing programs should include comprehensive energy analysis services for the conceptual design community to assure the building process is really a marketing effort to meet customers' needs.

If the marketing perspective is adopted by everyone and the utility is involved in the building process from the concept of a building, to its completion and operation, the customers' needs will be satisfied. But the other parties - architects, contractors, developers, engineers, and facility managers will also have their needs met. But what about the customers' needs. In general customers think that businesses should want to satisfy their needs and wants. The customer is always right and to have a marketing perspective will mean that business must move toward the customer and increase the areas of mutual benefit. Better decision making for the mutual benefit of all can be the result of consideration of comprehensive energy studies during conceptual design.

The Marketing Perspective

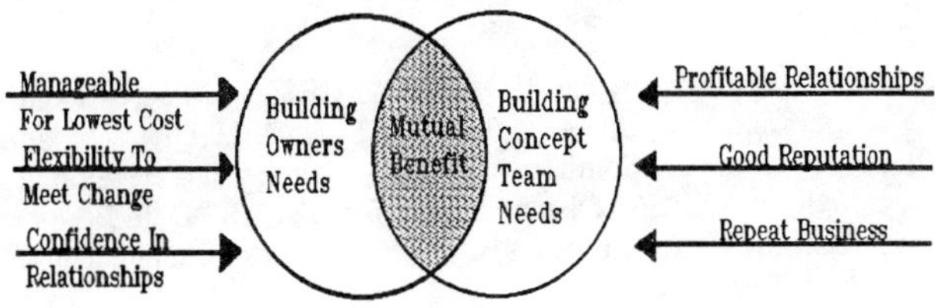

Figure 6

Alternative Systems Analysis

AXCESS

Micro Version 8.1

On
Personal Computer
With
Panel Displayed
Data Entry

Figure 7

The electric utility industry has developed AXCESS and micro-AXCESS for PC's with the cooperation of engineering firms like Syska & Hennessy of New York City and others. My company, Southern Company Services, has developed an exciting program called the AXCESS Display System for AXCESS Data Base development. These programs are designed for all of the concept design team. These easy to use analysis tools are ready.

In my opinion, this hourly energy analysis computer program for alternative systems comparison is the best that is available. Energy analysis services should be a part of meaningful marketing programs designed to accomplish load shape change in the commercial market. However, even with the new Micro Personal Computer Version of AXCESS and the user friendly panel input for data base development it is still just a "tool". For years, energy analysis has been like a hammer without a house to build in many utility companies. It was a nice thing to do but there was no commitment to provide the service.

My vision is for energy analysis services to be provided by utilities during conceptual building design. I envision the utilities of the United States becoming a viable contributor in the conceptual design of buildings and their energy using systems. Not to design systems, but to provide comprehensive comparisons of alternatives.

As mentioned earlier, during the 60's many utilities worked closely with some of the design team usually with the consulting engineers. They provided energy analysis services to gain the acceptance that electric heating in commercial buildings still enjoys.

At the New York meeting of ASHRAE, I attended a forum of consulting engineers. The subject was "What Do Consultants Expect From Energy Analysis Programs". The discussion that followed focused more on why consultants don't perform more energy analyses. The impressions that I gained from that meeting have been verified in numerous discussions with consultants since that time.

The following observations are not intended as criticism and of course may not be accurate for all consultants, architects and developers, but in general I believe;

1. Consulting engineers do not routinely perform alternative energy analysis studies as a part of their contracts.

2. Most consultants are willing to do analyses but few architects, developers and owners are willing to pay to evaluate new options.

3. Consultants may be hesitant to take the risks involved in new designs or newly developed system concepts and equipment.

4. Consultants are understandably comfortable with recommending systems with proven complaint free and litigation free history.

5. Consultants are typically contractors to the architects and developers.

6. Consultants depend on manufacturers for design assistance.

7. Consultants respond positively to professional utility engineers who provide valuable services.

Furthermore I believe architects and developers:

1. Are inclined to focus on the architectural aspects of buildings and to consider the possible energy effects as a secondary issue.

2. View engineers and contractors more as suppliers of services than as concept design participants.

3. Do not usually want the utilities involvement during the concept design phase of projects.

With these observations assumed to be at least close to typical, what are the possibilities for utilities to develop programs that offer an active and responsible role in the conceptual design process?

I expect some utilities can show that they are already active in the conceptual design process with some individual architects and developers. However, most utilities typically work more closely with the consultants based on plans after the conceptual design phase is completed.

Utilities must sell themselves into the conceptual design process. Their programs must include long range commitment to providing alternative energy analyses for the concept design team. Why should the utility want to do this?

These questions may shed some light:

1. Who has the most to gain from the energy using devices in buildings?

2. Who has the longest commitment to the energy using devices?

3. Who has the most to lose if the systems installed in buildings contribute to increasing the capital cost of providing the energy?

4. Who has the resources and knowledge of rate options that affect the economics of energy using systems?

The answers are obvious. The utility is the only player that must be fully committed to the building for life.

During conceptual design, there should be a complete analysis of how systems interact and how they create the total energy bill. Energy using systems and building operations should be analyzed during conceptual design. Options should be considered before they are eliminated by other decisions.

In the typical building development process, the owners determine their needs and wants. They vocalize this to someone, usually an architect or a contractor. Their needs and wants are translated into a concept plan to meet those needs and wants. The concept plan will become a building design and building systems will be added, but where is the utility in the process? When should the utility/customer relationship begin?

The utility/customer relationship typically begins when the service is connected and it continues for the life of the building. The architect or engineer may or may not even know the building owners in 15 years. But, what about his utility? The customer doesn't have an option with the utility company. Not only does he not have an option, he gets a bill every month. He gets the bill and he wants answers. Such as: "Why is this bill so high? Can I do anything about this bill? Is the rate right? How many rate options do you have? How do I know that I am on the correct rate? How can I control my bill?

These questions are basically management type questions and the occasion for the questions happens because the building owner needs to manage the energy using systems.

When the building is completed and the bills begin to arrive, it is the utilities job to answer the customers' questions. Sales representatives are dispatched to talk to the customers about questions like these.

I make a presentation called "Your Power Bill and How You Control It". It was developed to help customers understand the fact that they can manage utility energy use. The water heating system, lighting, cooling and heating, are all Systems that are essentially employees. Employees come to work on time, work overtime, or do very little depending mostly on how well they are managed. But the energy using systems will work overtime. They will provide their full capacity all of the time. They are great employees but they do not work for free. They may be working and the management doesn't even know it. The question is - how can they manage Systems without understanding the cause and effect relationships?

Managing Systems use is really no different than managing employees. With employees, the building owners are probably trying to get them to work more. But managing energy using Systems usually means getting them to work less and still get the job done. When the local utility sales representative answers the owner's call and reviews the billing, he needs information about the Building Systems. He will in most cases have general information but few facts - except the weather, billing periods and the rate schedule. To answer the customers questions, the utility needs to be involved in the building's development.

In some instances, of course, utilities have been involved in the early stages of the development and they have been heard. This is generally due to the efforts of some individuals who have done a good job of proving themselves to individual owners, architects, developers, engineers, etc. But, it is not typical that utilities become a part of the concept phase.

It is more typical that the utility sales representative discovers a planned new building when it is out for construction bids. He then obtains information on the systems designed for the building. If he determines that there could be customer benefits derived from changes, he will begin a sales effort to get one or more of the systems modified or changed. If this effort involves the suggestion of a fuel switch, the situation becomes more complex. The Systems consultants have in most cases completed their designs and are satisfied with the decisions they have made. They have the confidence of the architect and the owner and a major part of their investment in the job has been made.

When the sales representative calls on the Systems consultant to discuss the changes he wants to be considered, the situation is difficult at best. If the sales representative's suggestions have merit, the consultant is in the position of having the professional decisions that have already been made called into question. If he rejects the suggestions and the architect or owner is informed the situation probably becomes adversarial. Then if the added complication of fuel switching is at issue all of the design team can be subjected to hearing the arguments of both sides. The situation becomes so complex that the issue of what is best for the customer can be lost in the process of challenges to decisions that have been made. The whole process is expensive for all of the parties and in the final analysis -- nobody "wins".

If utilities are going to be able to apply their knowledge to the mutual benefit of all, they must be more involved earlier in the building process. The problem is not should the utility be involved, it's simply a matter of when. They can be involved during conceptual design and make a real contribution. They should provide all of the information they have or can develop to the conceptual design team - the owners and designers - before the design decisions are made - not after. When this happens, then utilities will play a meaningful role in the building process. They will understand the building systems and be able to provide meaningful answers when something is not right with the bill.

My vision for this process is really straightforward. The utilities should want to have and to be given the opportunity to present their story to the conceptual design team. If more than one fuel supplier is proposed then both should present their proposals using information supplied to them by the concept design team. The owner should be part of the process since he must "live with" the decisions that are made. The Systems designs could then be completed without the possibility of a redesign or major change being called for by the owner or architect. The utilities routine facilities design would also be more effectively coordinated and utility services provided in a timely cost-effective manner.

The advantages of this cooperative approach would accrue to everyone:

1. Most importantly, the owner could be assured that the available utility programs, rates and suggested Systems options had been considered by his architect and Systems consultants.

2. The architect could be better informed about Systems options that his consultants may have inadvertently overlooked.

3. The Systems consultants could be assured that they were not going to be "second guessed" by the local utility representative.

4. The utility representative would have his opportunity to present System alternatives and other options without creating adversarial relationships.

5. The consideration of Systems that contribute to the load shape goals of the utility can result in lower design costs, equipment costs, operating costs and Building Systems that capitalize on utility programs that may not be known by the present design team.

I believe most utilities will develop programs that include the cost of comprehensive energy analysis and alternative studies if the concept design team wants this to be part of their role. The utilities would be assuming a needed initial building cost to assure the consideration of new technology in buildings, of alternative control strategies, of even old technologies that have been on the shelf. This can be a valuable and well accepted service that accrues benefits to all of the utility's rate payers through better use of capital investment.

Let me leave you with this summary of the discussion today.

(1) Utility construction is based on a forecast of what they think their customers are going to do.

(2) Utilities and customers have a common need to control the growth in demand and the cost of electricity.

(3) The utilities have in the past and will always have the need to encourage customers to modify their use patterns.

4) A customer's long range ability to take advantage of change and to control costs will be affected by the design of their energy using Systems.

(5) Utilities and customers are unavoidably locked together for the life of a building and should both benefit from a meaningful relationship beginning as early as possible.

(6) Utilities could benefit all concerned by providing valuable energy analysis services and energy use consulting during the conceptual design phase of buildings.

The question for utilities is: Do utilities want to be part of the process? If so, how can they become a part without creating problems with the present players - architects, developers, engineers, and contractors? I believe the answer is yes, and it can be done by providing a valuable, professional, consistent, and reliable service with no apology. Ask for the order and deliver.

The question for the present conceptual building design team is: If the utilities want to be part of the team, will their involvement be encouraged? I hope the answer is positive and that they will encourage the utilities by providing positive suggestions that will be mutually beneficial for all.

DEVELOPING AN INTEGRATED VALUE-BASED PLANNING PROCESS*

John Chamberlin
Barakat, Howard & Chamberlin, Inc.

Phillip Hanser
Electric Power Research Institute

Long regarded as a "natural monopoly," the electric utility industry is seeing the painful signs of vigorous competition: loss of profitable sales as large customers begin generating their own power; defection of customers from one service area to another; and more vocal demands for concessions by remaining customers. As in several other traditionally regulated industries, growing competition has resulted from price changes, introduction of new technologies, and changes in the regulatory framework. On the horizon looms the threat that the deregulated transmission of electricity will open markets to all bidders--as has recently occurred in the natural gas industry.

These changes encourage a reconsideration of the planning process used to identify and evaluate the nature, packaging, and delivery of the services offered by utilities. The new planning process will have to begin with the value customers place on the services and products they consume, and then examine the service options and products lines that arise from those customer preferences. These new services must consider the utility's costs and profitability, all the while realizing that such offerings take place in a regulated environment. Finally, the process must integrate into a single framework the values of the customer, the objectives of the utility, and the concerns of the utility's regulator.

The planning process actually used by utilities has changed over the past several decades in response to changing technology, costs, and market conditions. Traditionally, utilities have been concerned primarily with identifying the least-cost new resource required to meet a growing demand. By the late 1970s, instability in costs and customer dissatisfaction with rising prices led many utilities to consider variations both in the planning

---

*This paper describes work performed under contract for the Electric Power Research Institute. Views expressed are the authors' alone.

approach and in the nature of the product offered. The traditional planning method was expanded to consider measures that affect customer usage. While utilities were still generally perceived to sell kWhs, demand-side management (DSM) programs had begun to modify the product through variations in reliability, risk, and convenience.

In part to increase customer participation in these DSM programs, utilities began to pursue a research agenda aimed at understanding their customers' needs and preferences. By the early 1980s, a considerable body of research was developing on the preferences of customers for electric service. It became clear that customers differ in the value they place on different aspects or dimensions of service. Some customers highly value reductions in risk, for example, while others place highest value on convenience. Likewise, it became clear that utilities could "unbundle" services in a variety of ways and improve the overall satisfaction customers obtain from their products.

Growing competition during this period has increased the need for the development of multiple service options and product lines. Market niches have been created in which third parties are meeting unsatisfied needs of customers. The current regulatory process is approving such activities for third parties, creating increased pressure to allow utilities to compete.

These pressures have encouraged many utilities to reconsider the nature, packaging, and delivery of their product. Utility customers do not seek kWhs and kWs; rather, they purchase warmth, hot water, motor power, and other basic services. Delivery and packaging greatly influence whether and how customers will purchase any product. In the case of electricity, the packaging and delivery include convenience, safety, and reliability factors, as well as the manner in which customers obtain the service.

Research at EPRI has resulted in the realization that utilities must expand their single product service and develop integrated product lines of service options, providing for each different type of customer those services most highly valued. Such an approach must have at its core the objective of maximizing the net benefit of service both to customers and to the utility.

While there is growing regulatory support for a mandated least-cost planning (LCP) process, the process itself can be enhanced; since customers clearly value other dimensions of service, the LCP process must also reflect other service attributes. That is, changes in customer value must be included as well as changes in cost. For example, a high-efficiency fluorescent lamp program reduces both kWh usage and costs. If the quality of the resulting light also differs, this change in value must be incorporated into the analysis. If induction heat treatment of steel increases usage and costs, it also decreases the customer's use of other materials; therefore consideration must also be given to impacts on the customer's overall production costs (i.e., use of nonelectric resources).

As competition grows, these kinds of considerations become critical. They are part of the customer's decision-making process, whether or not the utility includes them in its analysis.

The concept of "integrated value-based planning" (IVP) is gaining acceptance as a means of fulfilling these needs. The idea itself is simple enough: utilities should offer products and services that maximize both the value received by customers and the net revenues resulting from these sales. In practice, the process advocates a fundamental change in the way utilities plan and operate their systems.

THE INTEGRATED VALUE-BASED PLANNING PROCESS

A fully integrated value-based planning process must reflect four major elements:

- It must identify the basic values of service sought by customers.
- It must consider the opportunities, constraints, and rewards to utilities to develop new service options.
- It must consider the regulatory environment in which utilities operate.
- It must determine the combination of product lines and service options that maximizes the net benefit to both customers and utilities.

CUSTOMER VALUES

Understanding customer values requires assessing the following questions:

- What do customers want from the utility? In other words, what attributes of the product (electricity) are valued by the consumer?
- What are the customers' tradeoffs between these attributes? What value does a customer put on getting a little more of one, if it means getting a little less of another?

In addressing these issues, it is important to understand that customers do not value electricity itself. They value activities or work that can be accomplished with electricity--for example, lighting a home, cooling the air in a building, or automating a manufacturing facility. Given this orientation, customers' use of electricity for these purposes is based on certain features of the product or service they receive. The attributes of electricity most frequently mentioned by residential customers, for example, are appearance, safety, lack of utility control, comfort, convenience, economy, and "caring for me."

UNDERSTANDING THE UTILITY'S VALUES

The utility's organization, technology, and financial goals must also be incorporated into its planning process. As with any competitive business, the utility cannot simply seek to maximize the value of service to customers; rather, it must take its financial goals and other constraints into account in seeking to increase the net benefit both to customers and to itself.

TECHNOLOGY. While some product lines and service options can be offered with existing technology, many others require new hardware. In either case, numerous technological questions arise: How can power quality be varied among customers on the same system? Is it feasible to vary frequency, for example? What kind of system is best suited to offering prepaid service to customers? What would be the impact of large-scale distributed generation on a utility system? A utility may also wish to consider the provision of end-use services-- for example, providing hot water directly to customers. How would the necessary devices interface with the utility's system? How could they be metered?

ORGANIZATION. Most utilities today are organized according to the traditional planning function. It is likely that an IVP utility would look quite different, probably with far more decentralized authority and responsibility, more emphasis on customer account representatives, and more focus upon market research. In addition to these changes, widespread contractual agreements involving customers, other utilities, and power pools limit the ability of utilities to benefit from operational changes.

FINANCIAL ANALYSIS. The need to incorporate some measure of value into the investment planning process is clear. How to implement this, however, is much less apparent. Not only is it difficult to assign a dollars-and-cents value to customers' preferences for various levels of convenience, risk, and appearance, but these preferences themselves are interdependent. For example, the value a customer places upon reliability is in part a function of his or her value of other dimensions as well. Many of these changes will influence costs and revenues directly, and will also have major effects upon financial risk, the competitiveness of the business, and the utilities' cost of acquiring money.

UNDERSTANDING THE REGULATORY FRAMEWORK

Any effort by utilities to adapt their planning methods and product must consider the regulatory environment. For utilities to develop an effective IVP process, regulators must be convinced that customers will benefit from the changes. While the eventual response of regulators to these changes is not yet known, their interest in the increasingly competitive market and in the actions required by utilities is great.

In the newly competitive environment, a focus upon cost alone may not provide desirable results. It protects neither the utility nor its customers, and is likely to increase, not decrease, the costs of service in the long run. Instead, a regulatory process such as IVP, which focuses attention upon the value customers place on various dimensions of service in addition to cost, may generate superior results for three reasons: First, cost alone as a selection criterion results in the consideration of programs that are not always beneficial to customers. Second, competitors can and do fill value niches when utilities do not, with consequently decreased revenues and increased average rates as sales are lost Third, the current narrow product definitions result in lost opportunities to serve all customers.

DEVELOPING SERVICE OPTIONS

The idea that utilities can develop a spectrum of new "products" is central to the IVP process. This does not mean that utilities must diversify into soap and hamburgers. Rather, it means that they can provide alternative energy services that provide increased value to specific types of customers.

Utilities can also vary their existing characteristics of service. Early discussions of value-based planning focused on the ability of a utility to vary the reliability of service to individual customers. Alternatively, residential customers could have specific end uses served at reduced reliability (e.g., through an air conditioner cycling program), or could receive a general class of reliability of service (e.g., by choosing to be placed in the first rotating outage block). The heart of the process involves tailoring service to customer preferences.

How can the results of an IVP analysis result in the development of a new set of products? What are the attributes of these products/services from the utility's point of view? A number of service characteristics can be varied for particular types of customers. Some examples include variations in product reliability, time of use, assurance, and time patterns in customer costs. Incentive, end-use sales, and on-site generation offer further opportunities for customer satisfaction. While the potential to develop new product lines or service options is very large, not all customers will value these options. The appropriate direction is clearly to develop options tailored to individual market segments, by emphasizing the attributes of service most highly valued in each segment.

SUMMARY

The growing competition in electric utility markets has created the need to consider an expanded set of product attributes in planning and evaluating services. Developing such a process requires a greater understanding of the all three of the primary parties involved: the customers, the regulators, and the utilities themselves. While developing a useful framework will not be easy, there are significant opportunities for utilities to progress in their ability to identify and put into place product lines and service options that are valued by customers.

INTEGRATED RESOURCE PLANNING AT PUGET POWER: PROCESS AND RESULTS

Eric Hirst
Oak Ridge National Laboratory
Oak Ridge, Tennessee 37831

Corey Knutsen
Puget Sound Power & Light Company
Bellevue, Washington 98009

1. INTRODUCTION

Puget Power (1987a) is a medium-sized utility, serving 650,000 customers in western Washington. Electricity sales totaled 15,000 GWh and peak demand was 3500 MW in 1986. Because of rapid expansion in the Puget Sound economy during the 1960s and 1970s, Puget Power participated in construction of several large coal and nuclear power plants during the 1970s. These new facilities were needed to meet the expected rapidly growing loads; even with the plants then under construction, the Pacific Northwest region (and the Puget Sound area in particular) were forecast to be deficit in the early 1980s.

The coal plants were completed and began operating in the early 1980s; the nuclear plants were cancelled at about the same time. Puget Power's cost of providing electricity to its customers increased dramatically between the mid-1970s and the mid-1980s as a result of high inflation, rising fuel costs, and the introduction of these new, higher cost power plants. The combination of higher electricity prices and a serious recession in the region greatly reduced load growth. Forecasts of power deficits became forecasts and the reality of a large regional surplus starting in the early 1980s.

In addition to these sharp changes in electricity prices, economic growth, and load growth; competition became important in the mid-1980s. While electricity prices were increasing, natural gas prices were declining. Thus, the gas companies attracted much of the new-home construction market for space- and water-heating that had traditionally gone to electricity; the gas companies were also encouraging people to switch their water-heating energy source from electricity to gas.

Puget Power responded to these changes and challenges by establishing a Demand and Resource Evaluation program (DARE) in early 1986. DARE had two primary objectives: (1) enhancement of the internal planning process and (2) development of a long-term plan. The overall goals of the plan and process were to keep energy-service costs low, improve customer service, increase flexibility for Puget Power and the Washington Utilities and Transportation Commission (WUTC), and reduce controversies over future resource acquisitions (Hirst 1987).

This paper discusses the planning process and initial plan. Section 2 traces DARE's activities from inception through completion of the plan in November 1987. Sections 3 and 4 discuss future load growth and resource options. Section 5 summarizes results obtained with DARE's analysis and Section 6 interprets these results.

2. DARE PROCESS AND ACTIVITIES

OVERVIEW

Conceptually, the DARE process begins with suggestions and questions that lead to assessment of Puget Power's markets and options for meeting customer needs (upper left part of Fig. 1). These assessments are then converted into inputs to an integrated analytical process (center of Fig. 1). This analysis combines individual options into broader strategies and analyzes the strategies using Puget Power's corporate models, an integrated planning model, and/or a screening model developed by the WUTC.

The strategies are also reviewed for customer and political acceptance, environmental effects, and other factors generally not included in planning models. A critical element of the process is called "make sense of it all," which involves staff and management review of results, a combination of analysis and numbers with judgment and experience. Communication at and among various levels within the Company is very important.

The key output from DARE is a plan, which identifies the steps to take over the next few years to enhance understanding of the costs, benefits, and risks associated with customer programs and with resources that are attractive candidates for acquisition. Finally, feedback and monitoring of post-DARE activities provide important information, needed to modify plans for future customer programs and for resource acquisitions.

The actual DARE process (described in Hirst and Knutsen 1987) was much more complicated, iterative, and dynamic than suggested here. Many of the steps that logically follow in sequential order actually occurred simultaneously and repeatedly as we improved the process and analyses. Nevertheless, it was helpful to have an image of the desired process to keep us on target.

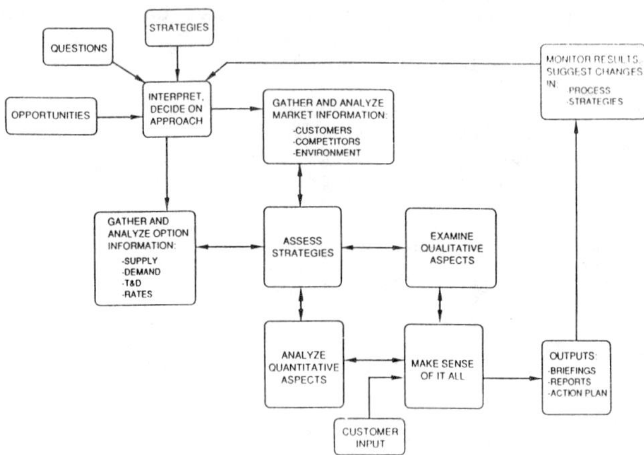

Fig. 1. Diagram of Puget Power's DARE program.

DARE ACTIVITIES

The CEO announced DARE and appointed a full-time manager for the project in February 1986. The DARE manager reported directly to the CEO. All other staff came from existing departments.

During spring 1986, meetings were held among directors and staff of various departments to plan this new activity (Fig. 2). The culmination of these discussions was a two-day meeting in April, attended by about 25 people from several departments.

The major outcome of the April meeting was formation of ten ad hoc task forces, staffed by people at the planning meeting. These task forces studied a variety of issues and presented reports on their topics at a two-day meeting in July, attended by about 40 staff.

The July 1986 meeting led to the formation of working groups (comprised primarily of those who participated in the initial task forces) to deal with the DARE activities identified by the earlier task forces:

- Define the analytical methods to use in DARE,
- Review integrated planning models and, if appropriate, select one for use in DARE,
- Select and install end-use forecasting models for the residential and commercial sectors,
- Develop a range of long-term load forecasts,
- Define the reference (base) case for the models,
- Collect base case data and run models,
- Complete cost methodology to screen resources on the basis of levelized cost per kWh,

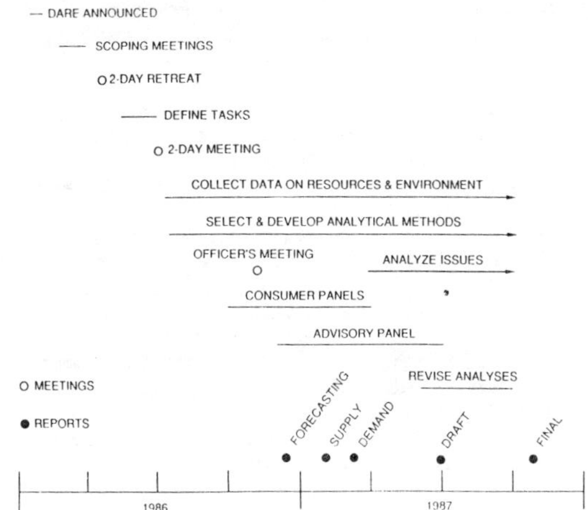

Fig. 2. Timeline showing key activities and events of DARE.

Examine importance of load shapes,
Prepare data on T&D loss-reduction options,
Prepare data on supply options,
Prepare data on demand options,
Analyze and segment markets for electricity services,
Maintain awareness of external environment
Assemble data on competition,
Develop a public involvement program,
Develop a plan to communicate DARE results,
Develop strategies for market segments and programs,
Conduct quantitative analyses,
Conduct qualitative analyses,
Conduct uncertainty analyses,
Review results, and
Prepare final report for Puget Power and the WUTC.

In May 1986, the WUTC directed the Company to conduct a least-cost planning study. In July, the Commission sent a letter outlining the requirements of the study and directing the Company to submit a report in July 1987.

Data collection and analytical activities were emphasized during early phases of DARE. Collection and assessment of information covered demand, supply, and T&D resources. A broad array of demand-side programs was considered, including efficiency (conservation), market-share retention, and sales promotion. Information on Puget Power's market segments was obtained from customer data bases, program operations, surveys, and field staff; and from external sources. The supply options encompassed a variety of sources from which the Company could purchase power (other utilities within the region, independent power producers, and utilities outside the region). In addition, several possibilities for Company-owned generation were examined.

DARE's analytical efforts followed three paths. The first used existing inhouse (corporate) models. The second approach used a new, microcomputer-based integrated planning model. After reviewing several screening models, Puget Power agreed with the Electric Power Research Institute to be a test case for their new Multiobjective Integrated Decision Analysis System (MIDAS) model, developed by Temple, Barker & Sloane (1987). The third approach involved use of a screening model developed by the WUTC (1987).

Extensive public-involvement activities started in fall 1986. Puget Power asked its 1986/87 Consumer Panels to review demand and supply issues for DARE. The Company also established an Advisory Panel, made up of representatives from several regional organizations.

Many meetings were held among staff and directors from the Power Planning, Customer Programs, T&D Engineering, Rates, and Financial Planning departments during the first several months of DARE. Initially these meetings focused on definition of the key issues to include in DARE and how they could be addressed. After much discussion, the group agreed to focus on three strategic issues within which specific questions could be organized (Table 1). After model results became available in Spring 1987, discussions dealt with review and interpretation of analytical results, their relevance to the key issues, and suggestions for additional analysis.

Table 1. Key issues addressed in DARE

Key issues
Effects of alternative load growth paths
Number of customers
Electricity use per customer, by end-use
Overall load growth
Suitable mix of resources to fill gap between load growth and existing supply resources
Definition and provision of improved customer service, appropriate responses to competition

Staff in these departments devoted considerable time between fall 1986 and spring 1987 to making MIDAS operational, and to coordinating inputs and outputs among the corporate models and between MIDAS and the corporate models. MIDAS was used to address issues related to conservation, sales promotion, and alternative supply resources (purchase power, combined-cycle combustion turbines, and coal plants). These alternatives were tested under different assumptions about load growth. The WUTC model was used to evaluate alternative resource portfolios under a variety of assumptions.

A draft DARE report was completed in May 1987. This draft was extensively reviewed by people within Puget Power. A second draft, completed in June, was distributed to the DARE advisory panel as well as internally. The final report was published and submitted to the WUTC in November (Puget Power 1987b).

3. FUTURE ELECTRICITY DEMAND AND MARKETS

Between 1960 and 1975, demand for electricity in Puget Power's service area grew at an average rate of almost 9%/year; during the following decade (1975 through 1985), demand grew at less than half that rate (Fig. 3). The rapid increase in electricity use during the 1960s and early 1970s was a consequence of economic growth (reflected in increases in the number of customers served by Puget Power) and declining real electricity prices. Growth slowed after the mid-1970s because of slower economic growth and increasing electricity prices. In addition, natural gas prices began to fall relative to electricity prices in 1982 (Fig. 4), increasing the competition from gas.

The implications for future load growth of changes in the Puget Sound economy, shifts in the mix of economic activities, improvements in end-use energy efficiency, and competition are unclear. Therefore, alternative load forecasts were developed for DARE. The medium forecast shows electricity sales increasing at 2.0%/year between 1988 and 2007. Residential sales grow more slowly, while commercial and industrial sales increase more rapidly in this forecast. Generally, electricity use per customer is forecast to decline, more than offset by growth in the number of customers.

The high and low load forecasts (which differ primarily in economic growth, and therefore, in customer growth) show growth rates in electricity use of 3.5 and 0.5%/year, respectively. Consumption in the year 2007 ranges from 17,000 to 30,000 GWh between these two forecasts.

Other forecasts were developed to assess the effects of increased fuel switching (e.g., greater competition from natural gas), because half of Puget Power's sales are subject to direct competition from other fuels (Fig. 5). These forecasts used the same customer growth as the high, medium, and low forecasts but included greater declines in per customer electricity use.

Tracking changes in the number of customers and in usage per customer separately is important because these factors have different effects. For example, the demand for generation resources is related to the product of these two factors, while demand for distribution facilities depends primarily on the number of customers.

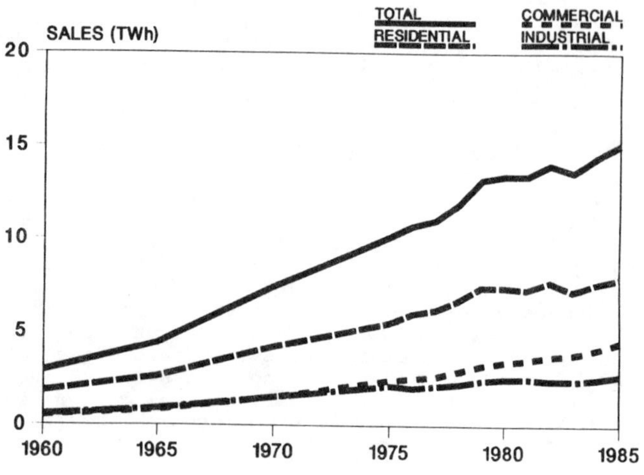

Fig. 3. Electricity sales by class, 1960 - 1985.

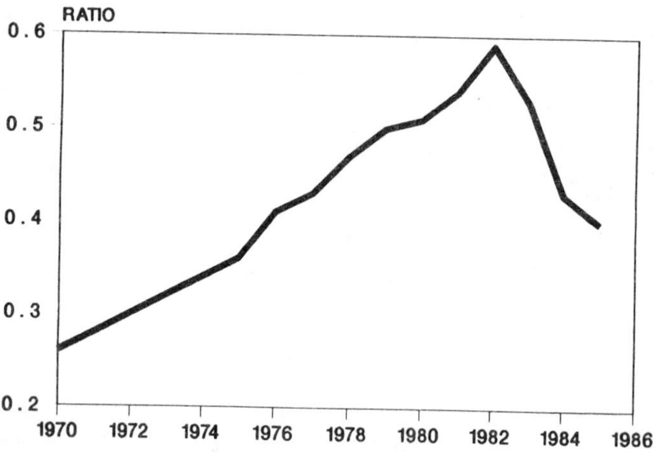

Fig. 4. Ratio of natural gas-to-electricity prices for Puget Power customers, 1970 - 1985.

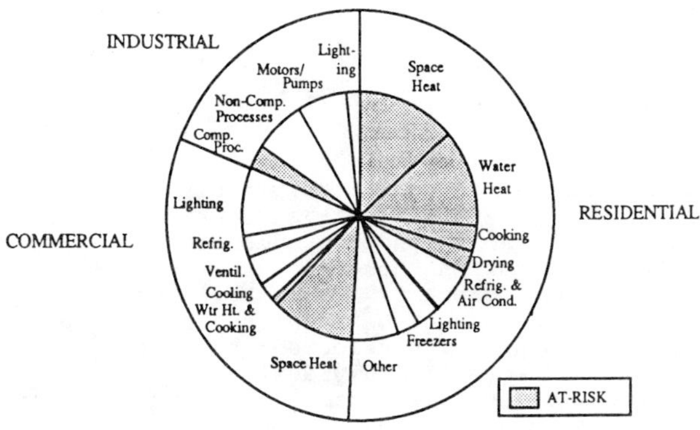

Fig. 5. Distribution of electricity consumption by end use and customer class, showing those susceptible to fuel conversion.

4. RESOURCE OPTIONS

Because loads are forecast to grow and because Puget Power's supply resources will decline over time, the Company needs additional demand and supply resources to meet customer needs. The gap between demand and existing supplies is likely to be between 5,000 and 18,000 GWh in 2007.

Several conservation programs for all end-use sectors were considered. The programs were aggregated into two levels for DARE analysis. The moderate level included all the conservation resources that could be obtained at a cost of 5 ¢/kWh or less and the high level included all resources up to 9 ¢/kWh. Because more conservation resources are available under high than under low load growth (primarily because of new construction), the amount of conservation that Puget Power can purchase varies both with incentive level and with load growth.

The supply resources were also combined into generic categories: purchase power (from other utilities within the Pacific Northwest, utilities elsewhere, independent power producers), combined-cycle combustion turbines (low capital cost, short leadtime, volatile operating cost), and coal plants (high capital cost, long leadtime, stable operating cost).

These resources were examined with MIDAS (using the corporate models to check MIDAS results) and also with the WUTC screening model. Because the two approaches were developed and implemented sequentially during only a few months, the assumptions used in the two approaches are not fully consistent.

5. RESULTS

MIDAS

MIDAS was used to assess the likely effects on utility revenue requirements and electricity prices of the resources discussed above. An 18 endpoint decision tree was constructed that tested these resource options against the high and low load forecasts (Table 2). These resources represent stylized scenarios in which the maximum amount of a particular resource was selected; this was done to emphasize the effects of individual resources. In addition, the effects of alternative load growth paths on electricity prices were assessed.

MIDAS results suggest that construction of capital-intensive, long leadtime power plants (represented by coal plants) is likely to raise rates and increase revenue requirements, relative to a reference case that relies entirely on power purchases for incremental supplies (Table 2). Construction of inexpensive, short-leadtime plants (represented by combined-cycle combustion turbines), on the other hand, might lower revenue requirements slightly if fuel supplies (gas and oil) can be obtained at modest cost. If, on the other hand, fuel prices increase rapidly, combustion turbines will increase both rates and revenue requirements, although not as much as coal plants would.

Both the high and low conservation programs result in lower revenue requirements and slightly higher electricity prices than the purchase-only case. If load grows rapidly, the high conservation program yields a lower revenue requirement than does the moderate program; if loads grow slowly, the reverse is true. This comparison suggests that conservation is a valuable resource, and that the amount purchased should depend on load growth.

Comparison of revenue requirements and average rates across these cases shows only small differences. For example, levelized rates differ by 0.2 ¢/kWh across the cases, excluding coal. This finding is similar to that observed in the Michigan Electricity Options Study (Michigan Department of Commerce 1987).

Time permitted only limited sensitivity analysis. We examined the effects on revenues and rates of deferring conservation programs for five years (i.e., to wait until the regional surplus was ending and purchase-power prices were increasing). We also examined the effects of a sudden increase in gas and oil prices in 1991 (primarily for the impact on combustion turbines) and the effects of more rapid increases in the price of purchased power.

Table 2. Effects of alternative resource strategies on revenue requirements and on electricity prices[a]

	Present value of revenue requirements (million-$)	Levelized prices (¢/kWh)
	High load growth	
Purchase	10,090	5.8
Coal	12,000	6.8
Combustion turbines		
High fuel prices	10,400	6.0
Low fuel prices	10,030	5.8
Conservation		
High	9,690	6.0
Moderate	9,760	5.9
	Low load growth	
Purchase	7,260	5.6
Coal	7,740	6.0
Combustion turbine		
High fuel prices	7,370	5.7
Low fuel prices	7,300	5.6
Conservation		
High	7,060	5.9
Moderate	7,040	5.7

[a]These calculations use an 11% discount rate over the 1987 -2007 period.

MIDAS was also used to address the first of the three issues discussed above (Table 1): effects of alternative load growth paths. Results showed that levelized electricity prices were 5.8, 5.6, and 5.6 ¢/kWh, for the high, medium, and low load forecasts, respectively. Electricity prices are lowest for the medium load growth case until 1993, after which prices are lowest for the low load growth case. The shift occurs because of the assumed increase in the cost of purchase power as the regional surplus disappears. These results show two things. First, there is little effect on retail electricity prices of differences in overall load growth for the next two decades; on a year-to-year basis, prices differ by less than 1 ¢/kWh across the different load forecasts. Second, prices are slightly lower if loads grow more slowly.

The effect of increased competition on electricity prices was also examined. Here, too, the effects are small. Higher competition increases the levelized price of electricity, relative to the medium growth case, by about 0.1 ¢/kWh over the next 20 years. Prices are higher with increased competition until 2005, after which prices are lower with increased competition.

WUTC SCREENING MODEL

The WUTC screening model estimates the average incremental cost of providing new resources to meet the gap between growing demand and diminishing supplies. Unlike MIDAS, it does not simulate the operation of power plants, nor does it produce financial statements. The WUTC model was used to identify "least-cost" portfolios of resources based on the levelized cost of each resource and various input assumptions.

Because this screening model is easy to use, we tested various assumptions concerning growth rates in future loads, inflation (and related financial parameters), coal prices, natural-gas prices, and purchase-power prices. A total of 36 cases were examined, which yielded four patterns of resource selection:

Pattern 1 - occurs with low to moderate increases in prices for natural gas and purchase-power. Purchase power and conservation dominate resource selection until the late 1990s (i.e., until additional conservation and purchase power are no longer available). Combined-cycle combustion turbines and PURPA facilities dominate during subsequent years.

Pattern 2 - occurs with low to moderate increases in coal prices and high increases in gas prices. Until the late 1990s, purchase power and conservation dominate (as in pattern 1) with the addition of PURPA facilities. Subsequently coal plants dominate.

Pattern 3 - occurs with high increases in purchase-power prices. Purchase power dominates only until the early 1990s, and conservation continues to play an important role until the late 1990s (as in previous cases). PURPA resources are used more heavily during the 1990s than in the previous patterns and combustion turbines dominate in the long run.

Pattern 4 - occurs with high increases in prices for coal, gas, and purchase power. All available conservation and PURPA resources are used. Near-term deficits are filled with purchase power and long-term deficits are filled with combustion turbines, supplemented with coal plants.

These patterns show that conservation and purchases dominate until the mid-1990s, when the limits of availability for these resources are reached. PURPA qualifying facilities are important resources during this time under some conditions. In the long-run, combustion turbines generally dominate, although if natural gas prices increase rapidly coal dominates. Conservation and PURPA continue to provide some resources in the long-term.

The WUTC screening model computes annual and levelized incremental cost (the average cost over all the resources added to fill the supply/demand deficit). Avoided cost increases with inflation and with load growth, although these two factors have only minor effects on the portfolio of resources selected. The 20-year levelized cost (typical of what might be offered to a cogenerator) ranges from 20 to 100 mills/kWh, with about two-thirds of the cases falling between 32 and 65 mills/kWh (Fig. 6).

6. DISCUSSION

INTERPRETATION OF RESULTS

The MIDAS and WUTC models examine demand and resource issues in different ways although their results lead to similar conclusions. Both models suggest that conservation and power purchases will be important resources for Puget Power, especially during the next decade or so. PURPA facilities may also be important during this period. Combustion turbines offer another attractive option beginning in the late 1990s, especially if a long-term, reasonable-cost supply of natural gas can be obtained. Finally, under the assumptions used here, large central-station power plants (e.g., coal plants) are generally not attractive.

Although the range in estimates of future load growth is large, the effects of this range on electricity prices over the next two decades is small. On average, the difference in price between the high and low forecasts is only 0.2 ¢/kWh, although the difference in the year 2007 is almost 2 ¢/kWh. The range in the average cost of incremental resources, however, is much larger - as much as 3 ¢/kWh.

Increased competition that reduces per customer electricity use has only a small effect on prices. This suggests that aggressive, undifferentiated sales promotion is not a good strategy to pursue. Rather, Puget Power is examining individual end uses to determine appropriate customer programs for each one. For example, the Company has implemented programs to retain existing market shares for residential water heating because of the substantial difference between marginal cost and marginal revenue for this end use.

ADDITIONAL ANALYSIS

Although substantial progress was made during the first cycle of DARE, much remains to be done. Fortunately, the large and enduring regional power surplus provides time to conduct additional analysis on resources that appear to be attractive for Puget Power's customers. Additional data collection and analyses are needed to:

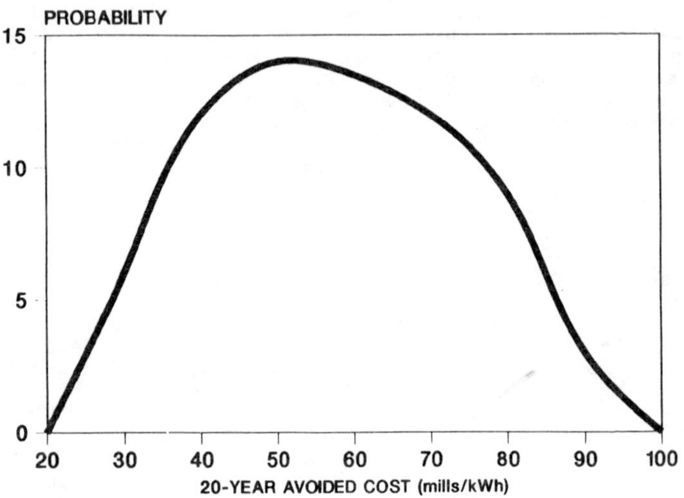

Fig. 6. Distribution of 20-year levelized costs for incremental resources obtained by Puget Power.

Examine alternative rate options that better align revenues with costs and provide more choice to customers,

Analyze loss reduction opportunities in the transmission and distribution system,

Use MIDAS and the WUTC screening model to more fully explore resource options and the uncertainties that surround them, and

Use results from a marginal cost-of-service analysis of end use/customer class/rate schedule combinations to help identify appropriate customer-service programs for each segment.

DARE set in motion a new planning process for Puget Power, one that encompasses the talents and experience of many people (both inside and outside the Company). This process will continue its emphasis on keeping energy-service costs low, improving customer service, increasing flexibility for Puget Power and the WUTC, and reducing controversies about future resource acquisitions.

REFERENCES

E. Hirst 1987, **The Key Elements of Integrated Resource Planning for Electric Utilities**, Oak Ridge National Laboratory, Oak Ridge, TN, October.

E. Hirst and C. Knutsen 1987, **Developing an Integrated Planning Process: An Electric Utility Case Study**, Oak Ridge National Laboratory, Oak Ridge, TN, November.

Michigan Department of Commerce 1987, **Electricity Options for the State of Michigan: Results from the Michigan Electricity Options Study**, Lansing, MI, September.

Puget Sound Power & Light Company 1987a, **Puget Power Annual Report 1986**, Bellevue, WA.

Puget Sound Power & Light Company 1987b, **Securing Future Opportunities: The Demand and Resource Evaluation Project**, Bellevue, WA, November.

Temple, Barker & Sloane, Inc. and M.S. Gerber & Associates, Inc. 1987, **MIDAS Overview**, prepared for the Electric Power Research Institute, Palo Alto, CA, June.

Washington Utilities and Transportation Commission 1987b, **Least-Cost Planning and Avoided Costs: Evaluating Resources for an Uncertain Future**, Olympia, WA, June.

ADJUSTABLE SPEED DRIVES: UTILITY APPLICATIONS AND TECHNOLOGY ADVANCES

by

J. A. OLIVER
BECHTEL POWER CORPORATION

BACKGROUND

The EPRI project RP14644-3 "Retrofitting Large Power Plant motors for Adjustable Speed", "Opportunities, Techniques and Cost", with Bechtel Power Corporation as contractor was in effect during a time that has seen the development of a power adjustable speed drive technology for large squirrel cage motors in the United States. In fact, EPRI, with Ralph Ferraro, at first Project Manager and later as Program Manager, took the initiative to influence this development to some considerable extent. EPRI recognized there was a need for converting large power plant induction motors to adjustable speed for fuel conservation. When this project started, only the synchronous motor ASD was available which required a new synchronous motor to replace the existing squirrel cage motor.

By pointing out to U.S. manufactures that there was a large induction motor ASD technology available in Japan, EPRI, in effect, challenged US manufactures to show the world what they could do.

Ross Hill Controls simultaneously invented a a-c induction motor version of their d-c drill rig drive, provided it with superb packing including water-cooling of the thyristors and a rugged housing and offered the package to U.S. utilities at a very attractive price.

Ross Hill Controls initiative has caused several manufactures to offer somewhat similar technology, but at this time only General Electric has been successful sharing this utility retrofit market.

1. INTRODUCTION

The U.S. utility industry is interested in advancing the state of the art in power electronics because improved conversion equipment will soon be needed in new electricity based industrial process applications such as induction heating and melting, plasma fire cupolas and microwave heating, drying and curing end users. A ready made market for state of the art power electronics in ratings of over 1000 kW is in power plant applications to convert existing power plant squirrel cage induction motors to adjustable speed operation. In 1982 EPRI contracted Bechtel Power Corporation to study the use of power electronics ASDs in such applications. Some of the questions that were addressed during the investigation are as follows:

- o What type of power plant equipment can benefit from ASDs.
- o How do the economics work.
- o What power electronic equipment is available that is tried and proven.
- o How reliable is the equipment.
- o What are the spare requirements.
- o What are the interface issues between ASD and motor, and between ASD and power system.

This paper reports on utility applications and ASD technology advances discovered by EPRI with Bechtel Power Corporation as contractor.

2.1 ANALYSIS

To determine the type of power plant equipment that can benefit from conversion to adjustable speed operation, over 200 motors rated 1000 HP and larger were evaluated in 60 generating units. A computerized screening technique was developed that determines the horsepower requirements for fixed speed operation and for adjustable speed operation. With adjustable speed operation, control valves or vanes are positioned full open or in many cases completely removed. This technique considers the fan or pump curve, affinity laws, system resistance and tested horsepower v flow to determine kW savings obtained from eliminating valve or vane loss. Then, tested heat rate v load, fuel cost and hourly load duration curve are used to convert kW savings to fuel cost savings. The fuel cost savings is then evaluated over the remaining lifetime of the plant and compared to the cost of the ASD equipment over the same period. (See Figure 1 Flow Chart)

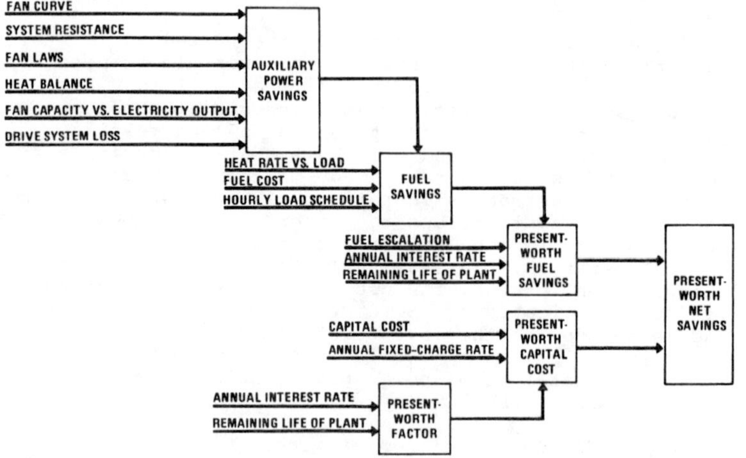

Figure 1 Flow Chart for Computer Program for Economic Evaluation

This survey showed the following power plant motors would provide excellent economic benefits with conversion to ASD speed control.

- o Induced Draft Fans
- o Forced Draft Fans
- o Boiler Feed Pumps
- o Condensate Pumps
- o Recirculating Gas Fans
- o Primary Air Fans

There are several key determinants for producing satisfactory fuel cost savings:

2.2 FUEL COST

Units burning higher priced gas and oil are more likely to produce paybacks of 2 years or less than are units that consume lower priced coal.

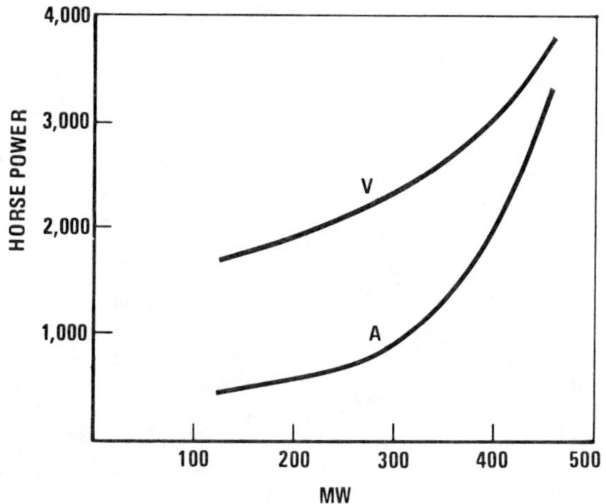

Figure 2 Motor Horsepower for 45ØØ HP IDFAN
V = Vane Control A = ASD Control

2.3 LOAD DURATION CURVE

The curves in Figure 2 show how horsepower changes with output with fixed speed and adjustable speed operation. For most boiler auxiliaries, reduced unit load means more vane or valve throttling. Thus, with more operation at low power output, large savings occur. Figure 3 shows a load curve of the type used in the study. Coal fired units with deep load cycling generally show good paybacks.

2.4 HEAT RATE

Applying ASDs to large power plant motors improves heat rate which is important to many utilities. Heat rate, the Btu of fuel per kW hour of generation, worsens with reduced load. This adds to the fuel cost required in throttling situations. Heat rate v load is shown in Figure 4.

2.5 DISPLACED GENERATION

With the availability of economical hydro or coal fueled generation during off peak hours it is often desirable to reduce minimum load on gas an oil fired units and replace the difference with cheaper power. ASDs can reduce minimum load in boiler fed pump applications by allowing sliding throttle operation of boiler and turbine. Fuel cost savings derived from displacing high fuel cost generation with lower fuel cost generation may be several times the control valve or inlet vane power savings.

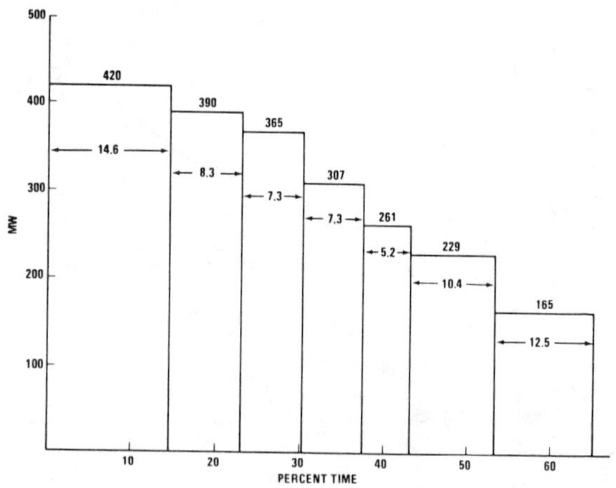

Figure 3 Hourly Load Curve

2.6 INCREASED CAPACITY

Eliminating fan power or pump power throttling at full load which occurs with oversized fans or pumps results in additional generating capacity. It is possible to realize this extra output on some units by installing ASDs.

Other units with inadequate fans for hot summer conditions can obtain additional fan capacity by overspeeding existing fans with ASDs.

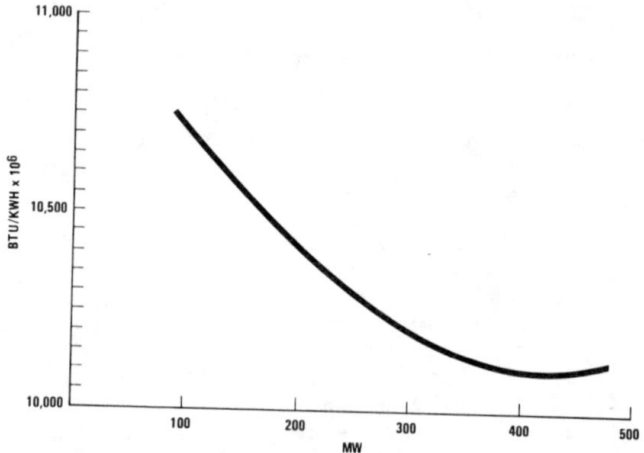

Figure 4 Heat Rate V. Load

When considered from a system wide perspective, retrofitting with ASDs along with planned consumer conservation practices can defer the addition of new generating capacity.

3. COMMERCIALLY AVAILABLE EQUIPMENT

The present trend in large adjustable speed drives is to one of the configurations that use 12 pulse rectifiers to eliminate the 5th and 7th harmonics to the power system. The input transformers provide the necessary phase shift between the rectifiers, provide electrical isolation between the ASD and the power system and a means of grounding the ASD system.

With the 12-pulse system, the rectifier dc outputs are added in series to provide sufficient input voltage to the inverter so that an output transfer is not needed. The concept of single inverter and no output transformer has resulted in a 25 percent drop in ASD costs in the period of the study. The ASD of figure 5a employs three modes of inverter operations.

startup - source side converter commutation

low speed range - dc link commutation

high speed range - load commutation

This system of Figure 5a builds on the experience of the synchronous motor-load commutated inverter system. With the d-c link inductors it has the short circuit proof characteristic of the current source inverter. The output filter smooths the wave shapes of currents and voltage to the motor and provides kVAR for motor excitation.

The ASD of Figure 5b uses the gate turn off thyristor (GTO) and operates in a current source, pulse width modulation mode.

Other systems that are available from Westinghouse, GEC Automation Projects, Toshiba and Hitachi for large induction motors are shown in Figures 6a, 6b and 6c. The system of 6a is a large voltage source inverter which produces excellent current and voltage wave shapes, but is has a cost penalty in terms of inverter sections and output transformers. The system of Figure 6b is a large current source inverter which also carries a cost penalty in inverter sections. The system of Figure 6c is a large voltage source GTO-PWM inverter with input transformers with 12-pulse rectifier, and dc link capacitor.

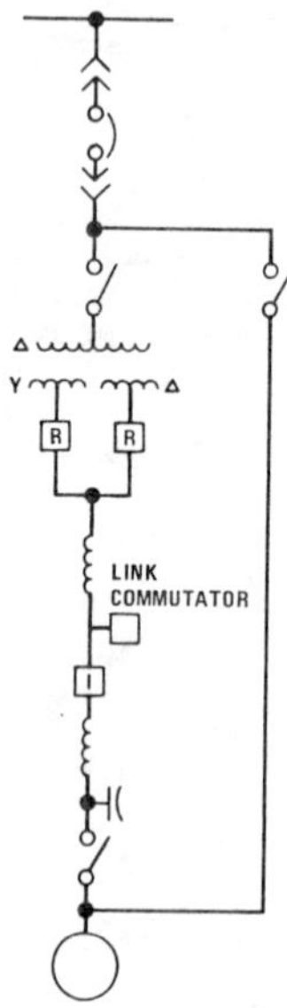

Figure 5A
DC Link Commutated
Modified LCI Type ASD

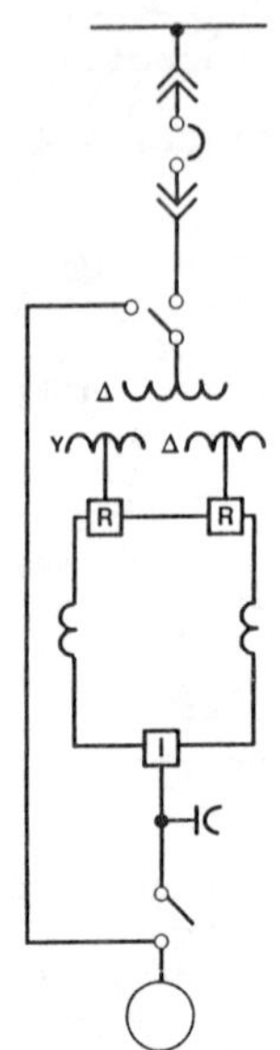

Figure 5B
Current Source
GTO-PWM Type ASD

4. FACTORS AFFECTING COST

As can be seen from the circuitry of Figure 5a and 5b and Figure 6a, 6b and 6c, the number of inverter sections, input transformers, output transformers, dc link inductors and filters all affect equipment cost. There are additional factors of analog or digital control, diagnostics capability, dynamic braking requirements, cooling system, packaging, redundancy of components, acceleration rate and isolation and bypass switches.

Isolation and bypass switches are useful in power plant retrofits because they allow the control dampers, valves or vanes to be used as a backup control system in case of any ASD problems.

Dynamic braking is an important consideration for ID fan retrofits for boiler implosion control. Acceleration rate and deceleration rate affects the current carrying capacity of the thyristers.

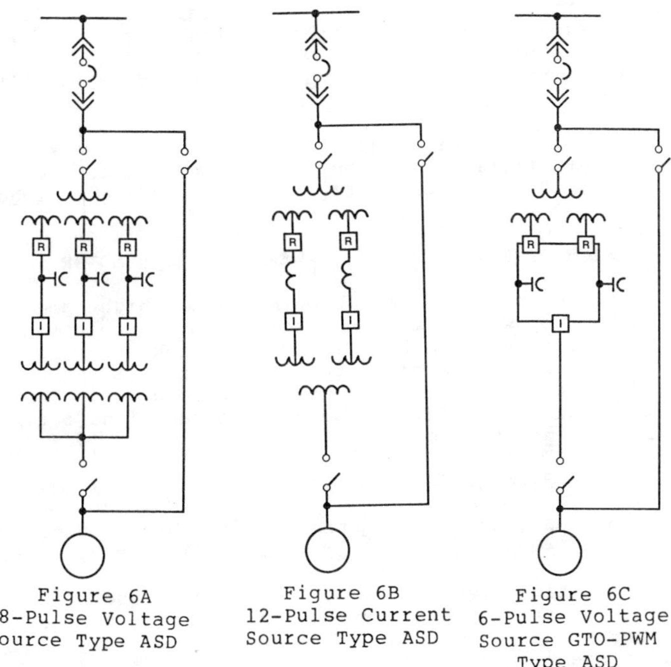

Figure 6A
18-Pulse Voltage Source Type ASD

Figure 6B
12-Pulse Current Source Type ASD

Figure 6C
6-Pulse Voltage Source GTO-PWM Type ASD

5. COOLING SYSTEM AND PACKAGING

Opportunities for reducing the overall installed cost are abundant in the method of packaging of the equipment by the manufacturer. By water cooling the rectifier and inverter thyristors, large air conditioning or air handling units can be eliminated. Integrating capacitor and bypass switching units into the basic rectifier and inverter cabinet line up with internal bus connections eliminate cable and conduit runs which are expensive in large horsepower ratings.

6. ADVANTAGE OF INDUCTION MOTORS IN POWER PLANTS

Squirrel cage induction motors have been used for most power plant drive motors applications for many years in the US. They have been used because of the inherent reliability of their simple design. The squirrel cage induction motor has no insulated windings in the rotor, does not require an excitation system and has no slip rings and carbon brushes.

The EPRI sponsored Field Test Program has served demonstrate that induction motors can be converted to adjustable speed operation with commercially available power electronics. Also, the squirrel cage induction motor can be used in new power plants in speed control applications, thus retaining the inherent reliability and cost advantages.

Economic studies and field applications have shown that retrofitting large pumps and fans can have a pay back period of 3 months to 5 years depending on load curve and fuel costs.

7. HIGH SPEED, HIGH HORSEPOWER INDUCTION MOTOR

Prototype tests have been made on a high speed, high horsepower induction motors. This development points out that the high speed induction motor is just as feasible as the high speed synchronous motor when each is powered by an adjustable speed drive. The adjustable speed drive provides two functions for either high speed motor:

- Synchronous starting
- Adjustable frequency, adjustable voltage power supply for high speed operation to 7,200 rpms.

The high speed electric motor can be used to replace steam turbine drives in power plants in cases where the steam turbine has proven to be a high maintenance cost item.

8. SLIDING PRESSURE OPERATION WITH ADJUSTABLE SPEED BOILER FEED PUMP

A problem facing many utilities is that of reducing minimum load during off peak periods or operation. One approach is sliding pressure operation of the generating unit which reduces boiler pressure and temperature during these periods of low load. Minimum load may be reduced by 25-30% resulting not only in fuel cost savings but also reduced stress on boiler and turbine components.

When the ASD is applied to boiler feed pumps, it provides means to reduce pump speed for reduced output pressure without excessive power loss in regulating valves.

9. FIELD TEST PROGRAM

To verify the benefits of using adjustable speed drives for large power plant motors, EPRI contracted with Bechtel Power Corporation to develop a field test program to demonstrate the economics, reliability, costs and improved operating performance of power plant equipment when equipped with adjustable speed drives. This program is discussed in a companion paper.

10. CONCLUSION

This electric utility industry sponsored study and field test program has served to identify existing power electronic ASD technology for converting induction motors to adjustable speed. The program has identified the types of power plant motors suitable for conversion and has developed the method of calculation of the economics. Most importantly, this effort has provided a catalyst for the early introduction of large power electronics motor speed control systems into power plants to demonstrate the benefits of ASDs for utilities and their industrial customers.

POWER ELECTRONICS : FROM DEVICES TO CIRCUITS TO OPPORTUNITIES

D.M.Divan
Department of Electrical & Computer Engineering
University of Wisconsin
1415 Johnson Drive
Madison, WI 53706

Introduction

The ready availability of energy in its electrical form has become one of the basic tenets of the industrial infrastructure in the modern world. This results from the relative ease of distribution, coupled with the ability to generate power at locations which may be far removed from the point of consumption. It also permits integration of a wide variety of sources such as small wind or photovoltaic systems, medium sized diesel generating or industrial cogeneration units and large hydroelectric, thermal or nuclear power stations, into one standard electrical network with well defined voltage and frequency levels.

Given the diverse types of industrial loads, a fundamental problem that is frequently encountered is a mismatch between the supply characteristics and the load requirements. For example, electroplating processes require direct current (dc) power, while certain induction heating loads may need single phase ac power at 500 kHz. Critical computer type loads require uninterrupted and clean 60 hertz ac power of a quality and integrity that is difficult for most utilities to guarantee. Various motor loads such as position servo drives in robotic applications, fan and pump drives in industrial and utility applications and traction drives in transportation have to be supplied with three phase ac power of variable frequency and variable voltage. This highlights the need for power conversion apparatus which accepts electrical energy from the available supply and converts it in a controlled manner into another form which is more compatible with the load or process.

In the past such power converters have often relied on the principles of electromechanical energy conversion. AC to DC power conversion was typically accomplished by a motor-generator set. An induction motor operating off the ac supply is coupled to a field excited dc generator, which can produce a variable dc output voltage . In order to convert this dc power into variable frequency ac power, an addtional dc motor-ac alternator set is required. Although functionally adequate, such arrangements are bulky, expensive, inefficient and exhibit extremely poor speed of response. Modern technology makes it possible to process power directly in its electrical form using electronic devices to realize multiple benefits of low cost, low volume, high efficency, low maintenance, long equipmrent life and maximum adaptability and controllability.

Although the history of electronic power conversion dates back to the 1920s and the mercury arc rectifier, power electronics did not become a commercially viable technology until the invention of the silicon controlled rectifier or thyristor in the late 1950s. Tremendous strides have been made since and a wide variety of power semiconductor devices are presently available to cover a power spectrum ranging from 1 watt to 100 megawatts for applications including computer power supplies, adjustable speed drives and high voltage transmission systems.

The Need for Power Electronics

The ability to control electrical power efficiently and economically are applied first to industrial processes where less efficient techniques had previously been used. Important examples include the fixed speed variable throttle pumps and fixed speed fans and blowers with their variable speed conterparts. Most of these applications realized significant efficiency improvements and relied mainly on energy savings for a payback of additional capital investment required. The energy crisis in the seventies strongly reinforced the value of energy efficiency and provided a tremendous boost to the power electronics industry.

In the recent years, the oil glut has driven down energy prices and with it the nations interest in energy conversion and power electronics. However, technological developments in the last decade in power electronics, microprocessors and integrated circuits have created another window of opportunity for the power electronics industry. Dramatic reductions in the size of computers and other electronic equipment have demanded concomitant improvements in power supply technology. Futher, intense international competitition has spurred strong interest in advanced manufacturing automation techniques and improvements in industrial productivity. Power electronics plays a dominant role in virtually all these applications supplying the muscle that interfaces the controller with process.

Principles of Power Conversion

In order to better understand the principles involved in electronic power conversion, let us examine a simple power converter application. A 100 Volt dc battery is to supply a load of 10 ohms resistance with variable power. If the load is connected directly across the battery , a current of 10 amperes flows in the load, corresponding to a power level of 1 kilowatt. One approach to controlling the power delivered to the load is the connection of another resistance in series with the load. This effectively controlls the load current and thus the power transferred to it. To realize variable power flow to the load, the series resistance has to be varied over an appropriate range. This arrangement is shown in Figure 1. The case for R_S=0 corresponds to

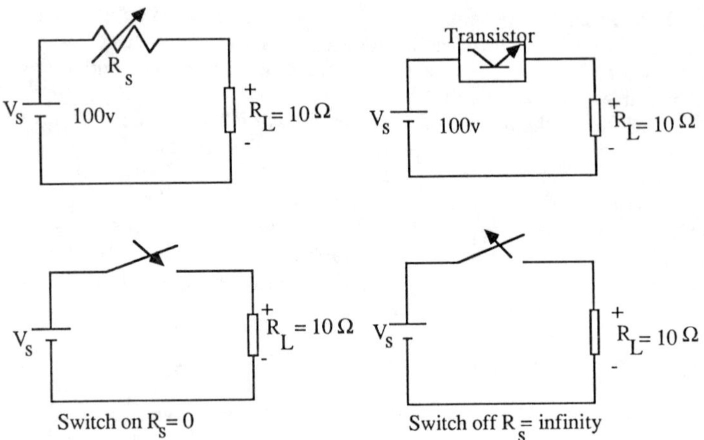

Figure 1 Electronic Device used as a switch

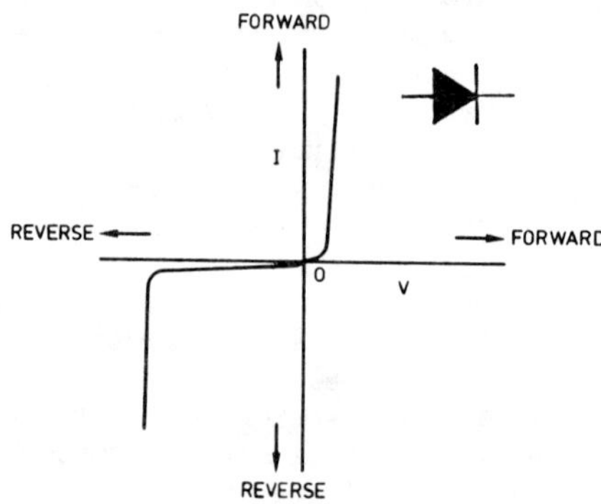

Figure 2 Typical Static Voltage-Current characteristic of a Silicon Diode

maximum power transfer, while an infinite value for R_S yields no power to the load. An electronic device such as the transistor can realize the equivalent of an infinitely variable resistance, thus accomplishing the desired control function . However, as in the case of the series resistance above, the device also dissipates a substantial amount of power, which represents a loss in the system efficiency. As one of the primary goals in power processing is high efficiency, this is not a desirable approach.

An alternate strategy uses the device as a switch, i.e. with only two states corresponding to fully conducting or on, and fully blocking or off as shown in Figure 1b. With the switch on, energy is transferred to the load at the rate of 1kW. On the other hand, no power transfer occurs while the switch is off. The average power into the load can thus be controlled by varying the proportion of time for which the device is on or off. It can also be observed that the switch in the on state has zero resistance, while the off state switch has zero current through it. Both conditions correspond to zero power dissipation in the device, raising the possibility of power converters with close to 100% efficiency.

It is important to note that it is the average power transfer which is being controlled, and that large variations exist in the instantaneous power flow. For the control technique to be effective, it is imperative that this pulsed power be smoothed or filtered before it is applied to the process. This filtering function can be provided by the process itself, or by passive non-dissipative electrical components such as inductors and capacitors. The size of this filter is inversely related to the frequency of the pulse power seen by the load. Thus, higher switching rates for the device result in smaller filter components and lower volume. This correlation between component size and frequency is of primary importance as it drives the continuing search for higher and higher converter switching frequencies.

Four basic types of power converters can be identified.These are

AC-DC DC-DC DC-AC AC-AC

It is possible to realize all four converter types with switches and passive filter elements, using techniques similar to above. The switches are normally semiconductor devices which have been designed to handle the high voltages and currents dictated by load and supply constraints. A power converter consists of one or more of these switches interconnected with appropriate filter elements in a specified circuit arrangement. This power circuit is often referred to as converter topology. Different converter topologies are required to implement the various conversion functions.

If the existence of ideal switches with bidirectional voltage blocking and current conduction capabilities, infinite speed and zero losses could be postulated, a minimum number of converter circuits would be required to handle the entire range of power conversion applications. Unfortunately, power semiconductor devices are far from ideal and almost invariably limit converter performance achievable. Moreover device characteristics often dictate the choice of circuit as well as the control technique used. In the next section we will examine various power converters with particular reference to the topology and method by which control is accomplished.

Power Devices and Converter Circuits

Power semiconductor devices can be divided into three groups based on the terminal properties of the device. The simplest device is the uncontrolled rectifier or the diode. This is a two terminal device which does not conduct current when there is a reverse voltage or reverse bias across the device, and which conducts current with a low voltage drop when it is forward biased. Figure 2 shows the circuit symbol and the current voltage characteristics of the diode. The conduction state of the diode is dependant solely on terminal conditions and cannot otherwise be controlled.

Almost all other devices are three terminal devices. Two of these terminals constitute a high power switch, much as in the case of a diode, while the third terminal, often called a gate or base, is a control input which influences the conduction state of the device. Applying an appropriate low power control signal at the gate terminal puts the device into its conducting state, thus turning it on. All these devices with the exception of the thyristor may also be turned off and put into the blocking state through gate control. The thyristor, as a result of a regenerative turn-on mechanism continues in its conducting state even after the gate current is removed. Thyristor turn-off can only be accomplished by external action which impresses a reverse voltage or bias across the device and forces device current to zero. Other devices including the bipolar junction transistor (BJT), the power MOSFET, the gate turn-off thyristor (GTO), and the insulated gate bipolar transistor (IGBT) may all be turned on and off via gate action.

At a glance it may seem that lack of gate turn -off capability makes the thyristor the least desirable of the many devices available. However, it is the only device capable of operating at power levels of over a few megawatts. Further, it has the simplest gate control circuit and is fairly economical as a result of mature technology. Thyristors, manufactured since the late 1950s, were the first semiconductors to gain commercial acceptance. This was due to their ruggedness, high surge current capability, high power gain, high efficiency and ease of control. Over two decades from 1960 to 1980, the thyristor completely dominated the field for power conversion for applications in the 1 kW - 10 MW power range . The last few years have seen an emergence of various gate turn-off devices and a slow decline in the application of thyristors.

Most thyristor converters depend on the ac power line for device commutation and as such are used mainly in ac/dc and ac/ac conversion applications. The ac/dc converter, also called the controlled rectifier bridge, has been the workhorse of industry for over two decades. Figure 3a shows a circuit schematic of a single phase thyristor bridge. Devices T_1T_4 and T_2T_3 are gated on alternately such that segments of ac line voltage are impressed across the load. Figure 3b shows the output voltage of the converter, V_o. The average value of V_o constitutes a net dc output voltage. Further, controlling the instant of thyristor gating, denoted by α, yields control of V_o. Filtering of the oscillatory content in V_o is provided by the inductance of the load.

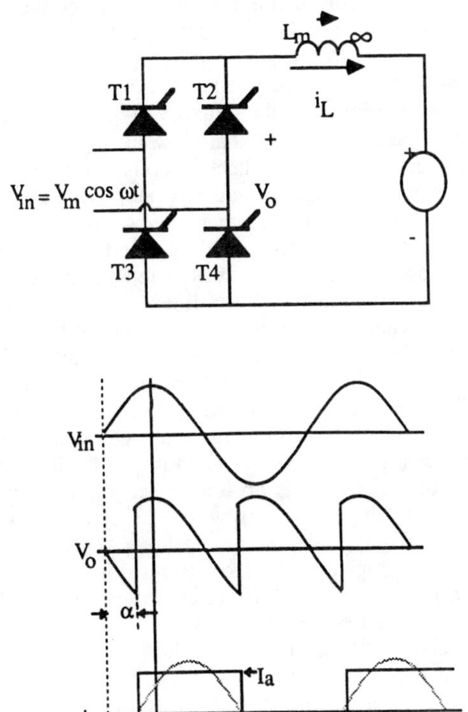

Figure 3 Single phase thyristor fully-controlled rectifier bridge

a) Circuit

b) Waveforms

A preferred embodiment of this circuit is the three phase controlled rectifier bridge shown in figure 4. The operating mechanism and control principles are very similar to the single phase case. The output voltage consists of segments of the ac line to line voltage impressed across the load. Figure 4b shows the waveforms of the output voltage V_o,while Figures 3b and 4b depict the shapes of currents that flow in the ac line. Unlike for conventional loads such as motors or heating coils, the current waveforms are not sinusoidal and contain higher frequency harmonics as well. The high frequency current components enter the power supply network and can potentially cause various problems including interference with sensitive electronic and computer equipment, excitation system resonances and overload of components connected to the line. It is recognized that such harmonic related disturbances caused by the switching inherent in power converter loads is a growing concern. A national effort is presently underway to develop guidelines for their mitigation and control.

For most dc/dc and dc/ac conversion, natural commutation is not possible and thyristor turn off requires auxilliary commutation or turn-off circuits. With the recent proliferation of gate turn off devices suitable for a wide power range, that approach is no longer economically viable and is rarely used in industry today. Circuits with gate control devices realize substantial benefits. High power commutation circuit components are replaced by lower power gate drive circuits resulting in lower cost and efficiency. Further these circuits are also easier to manufacture, control nad to protect under certain fault conditions.

The ability to convert an available dc voltage to a desired ac voltage is also of fundamental importance to the control of industrial processes. The induction motor has been the workhorse of industry because of low cost and low maintenance requirements. For variable speed applications, the dc motor, although more expensive, has been the preferred choice in the past. This is because a simple and inexpensive ac/dc power converter adequately handles the control requirements. In order to vary the speed of the induction motor, it is necessary to obtain independent control of both the output voltage and frequency, implying a more expensive power converter. With rapidly decreasing power semiconductor prices, the last five years have finally seen variable speed ac motor drives become a competitive technology. Other applications of ac output power conversion that have mushroomed include uninterruptible power supplies, power line conditioners cogeneration-utility interfaces and induction heating.

The most popular dc/ac power inverter topology is shown in Figure 5. A dc source, V_d, is connected to the load through four gate controlled devices labelled Th_1 - Th_4 . If switch pairs Th_1 $Th_4$and Th_2 Th_3 are switched alternately, it can be seen that positive and negative voltages are sequentially impressed across the load. As the switching rate of the devices can be controlled, the resultant load voltage is an alternating or ac square wave at the desired frequency. In this mode of operation, the output voltage can be controlled by varying the dc bus (V_d) using an ac/dc or dc/dc

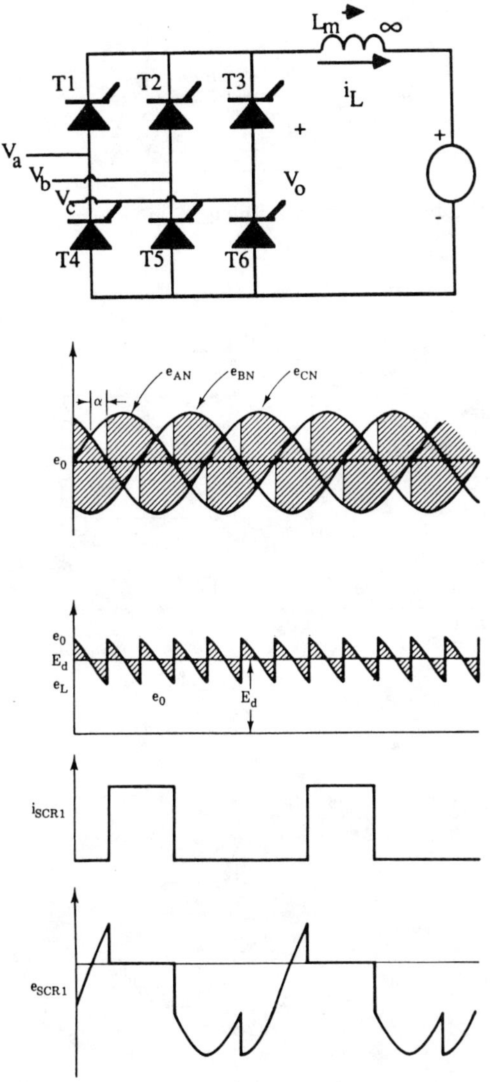

Figure 4 Three phase thyristor fully-controlled rectifier bridge
a) Circuit
b) Waveforms

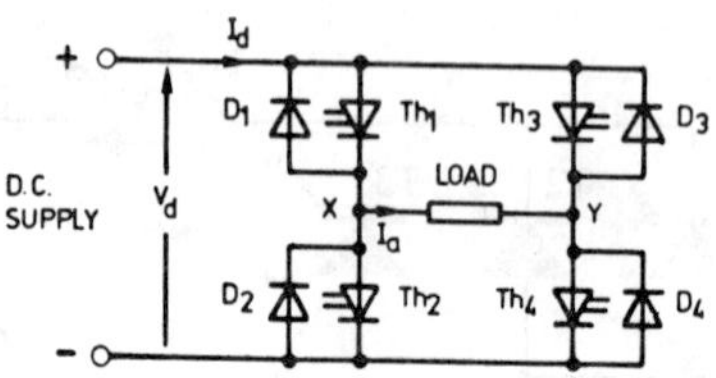

Figure 5 Single phase Voltage Source Inverter

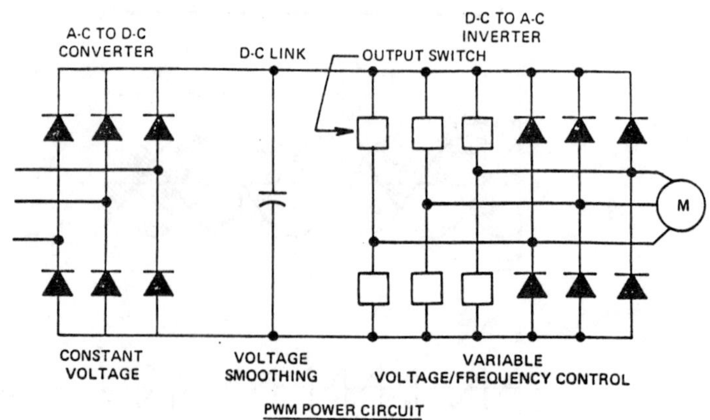

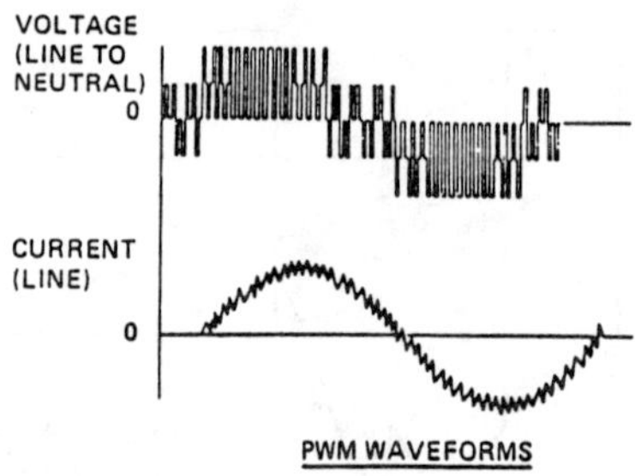

Figure 6 Three phase PWM-Voltage Source Inverter and waveforms

converter. Such an inverter system is often referred to as a variable voltage inverter (VVI). A three phase version of the VVI is also easily realized with six switches, one switch pair for each phase. As in the single phase case, each switch pair is gated alternately to synthesize a square wave at a desired frequency. Each square wave is phase shifted by 120 degrees to realize a three phase output. Voltage control still requires variation of the dc bus V_S .

The requirement for two independent power stages for voltage and frequency control can be avoided by the use of a pulse width modulation strategy. This technique typically trades off a higher inverter swithcing frequency for voltage control capability. Let us assume that the single phase inverter in Figure 5 switches at a high frequency, say 2 kHz, while it synthesizes a lower frequency say 50 hertz. If Th_1Th_4 are kept on for a longer time as opposed to Th_2Th_3, an average positive voltage is generated across the load. Varying the duty cycle so that Th_2Th_3 are on longer, yields a negative voltage across the load. Controlling the duty cycle so as to alternately obtain positive and negative voltage across the load, thus accomplishes the objective of synthesizing a low frequency ac voltage. The higher switching frequency also implies smaller filters for smoothing the high frequency content in the output waveform. To obtain a sinusoidal filtered output voltage, the duty cycle thus needs to be controlled or modulated in a sinusoidal manner at the desired low frequency. As a result of this duty cycle modulation, indivudual pulses on the inverter outputs have varying widths, giving it the name of 'pulse width modulation'.

The pulse width modulated voltage source inverter (PWM-VSI) can realize voltage and frequency control in one power stage. Consequently, it can be implemented using a simple uncontrolled ac/dc converter front end followed by a voltage source inverter for the desired dc/ac conversion function, Figure 6. The low cost, simple power structure and modest control requirements have made the circuit the most popular inverter configuration in industry. The circuit has been implemented using MOSFETs, bipolar junction transisitors (BJTs) and GTO thyristors in power ratings ranging from a few watts to more than a megawatt. PWM inverters are extensively used in a wide variety of applications including spindle drives, fan and pump drives, traction drives, position servos, uninterruptible power supply systems, active power filters and photovoltaic-utility interface systems. However for applications rated in excess of a megawatt, the thyristor is still frequently the only suitable device.

Applications and Opportunities

Application opportunities for power electronics in industry are virtually unlimited. It has been predicted that by the year 2000, upto 60% of the electrical power produced in the US will flow through a silicon power device. As power electronics technology matures, costs decrease and performance improves opening up new application areas where the technology can be beneficially applied. Potential candidates for the technology include utility and heavy industry, transportation, industrial manufacturing as well as the commercial and domestic sectors.

Applications of power electronics technology which are representative of the state of the art today include high voltage dc transmission and static var compensation at the 100 MVA power level for utility applications and variable speed drives for pumping and blower applications rated in the 500 - 25,000 HP range. As may be anticipated, for systems rated above 1000HP, thyristor converters are typically used. For the ac/dc converter front end, natural commutation is the invariable choice. For ac drive applications, a load commutated inverter with a synchronous machine load is often the economical choice. For systems requiring low frequency output, a cycloconverter which directly converts ac/ac is often used. In the past, smaller systems have used a force commutated current source inverter(CSI) with an induction machine load. Voltage source inverters using GTO thyristors are gradually replacing the CSI systems today.

Of even greater interest are new applications in this power range which are becoming increasingly viable. Interfacing renewable energy sources such as wind or photovoltaic energy to the utility often requires a power converter interface. Utilities are also examining the possibility of replacing mechanical switchgear with static switchgear for transformer switching. The use of active compensators for harmonic and reactive compensation of utility systems is also being investigated. Distribution of power at 500 Hz in large industrial plants is an idea that is receiving a great deal of attention. The use of batteries, fuel cells and superconducting magnetic energy systems (SMES) for energy storage and load levelling are making the transition from experimental to operational systems.

The industrial sector is also gradually increasing its use of power electronics systems. Adjustable speed drives have moved from traditional tension control and low performance servo systems to encompass a wide variety of spindle drives and multiple axis position and velocity servos ranging from fractional horsepower to 500 HP for use in industrial robots and machines. The extensive use of microprocessors, modern control techniques and new developments in power devices and circuits have substantially enhanced the level of performance attainable. Figure 7 shows a multiple axis servo controller used in rotating shear applications at power levels upto 300 HP. Also of importance is the role of power conversion in induction heating and other metal fabrication and processing technology. The state of the art includes a 200 KW 250 KHz induction heating system using power MOSFETs as made by Inductoheat. Other emerging technologies include magnetic bearings and precision welding and cutting using plasmas, lasers and unconventional electrodes.

The transportation industry is also poised for a major infusion of power electronics technology. The all electric fly by wire aircraft is already a reality. All electric and hybrid electric automobiles have been undergoing tests for the last few years. Extensive use of smart power integrated circuits in automobiles will all but eliminate miles of wiring and will dramatically impact cost of the car. AC motor drives are replacing dc motor drives in diesel-electric and all electric locomotives. Magnetically levitated trains offering the potential of speeds upto 400 Km/hr have been undergoing extensive testing in Japan and Germany.

Figure 7 Multiple-Axis position servo controller
(Courtesy : UNICO Inc.,Franksville,WI)

The impact of power electronics also extends to the computer industry as well as to the commercial and consumer sectors. Power supplies for the computer and electronics instrumentation industries comprise the largest dollar value for power electronics industry. As computers shrink in size due to rapid developments in VLSI technology, the power supply becomes an increasingly important component in terms of cost and size. Substantial efforts are currently underway to improve power density of converters by raising the switching frequency to several megahertz. The computer industry also sustains the uninterruptible power supply (UPS) and the power line conditioner (PLC) industry.

Looking at the consumer market, power electronics continues to make inroads into the heating, ventilation and airconditioning (HVAC) market. Major manufacturers are looking into incorporating ac motor drives into washers and refrigerators. Variable speed has already appeared in drills, blenders, fans and an assortment of kitchen and shop appliances. The smart house has received considerable attention with computer control and activation of lights, appliances and security systems. Power electronics already plays an important part in audio and video equipment, a role that will also dramatically increase in the years ahead.

Conclusions

This paper has reviewed some of the progress that has been made in recent years in power electronics technology. Basic principles involved in power conversion were discussion including power device characteristics and power circuit topologies. Application areas and new opportunities were also highlighted and it was seen that power electronics will be increasingly used in the years ahead.

Acknowledgements

The author would like to thank M.Kheraluwala & Giri Venkataramanan for assistance in preparing the manuscript.

Further Reading

1) B. Pelly, "Thyristor Phase-Controlled Converters and Cycloconverters", John Wiley & Sons, 1971.

2) P. Wood, "Switching Power Converters",Van Nostrand, 1981.

ELECTRIC ADJUSTABLE SPEED DRIVE APPLICATIONS

David L. Seitzinger, P.E.

Project Manager

CRS Sirrine, Inc.

INTRODUCTION

Electric adjustable speed drives (ASD) are an electrotechnology that is currently available for application on existing and new equipment drive applications. Sometimes called variable frequency drives (VFD), they are installed in the power circuit to a standard electric motor and connected with a process control loop to provide varying speed control so that the motor and driven equipment can exactly match the requirements of the process. Historically, when speed control systems could be justified, this function has been performed by eddy current, fluid couplings, and steam turbine drives. The ASD has significant cost and efficiency advantages over these systems, especially in the lower horsepower ranges while providing the equivalent speed control functions.

Prior to ASD's, most systems using pumps and fans could not justify variable speed devices. The systems were designed with constant speed motors and driven equipment and control of the process was accomplished by varying the resistance of the system using a throttling device at the inlet or discharge of the driven equipment. The advent of the ASD allows a re-examination of 95% of the processes in this country that have been designed to operate with constant speed motors. The load matching ability of the ASD changes control of the process true variation of the system to variation of the driven equipment rather than the system resulting in lower energy consumption. An operating process with constant speed motor consumes energy to overcome four components; process work, throttling losses, pump losses, and motor losses. The application of an ASD is used to recover the throttling losses, which are at their maximum during off design operating conditions.

This paper is an overview of the ASD electrotechnology, including operation, application, and justification. An understanding of these topics is crucial to the correct application of ASDs. The number of potential applications may be high but the actual justification requires significant analysis of the process operation to insure a cost effective installation. (Figure 1 and 2)

FIGURE NO. 1

APPLICATION OF HIGH EFFICIENCY MOTORS
AND
ELECTRONIC ADJUSTABLE SPEED DRIVES

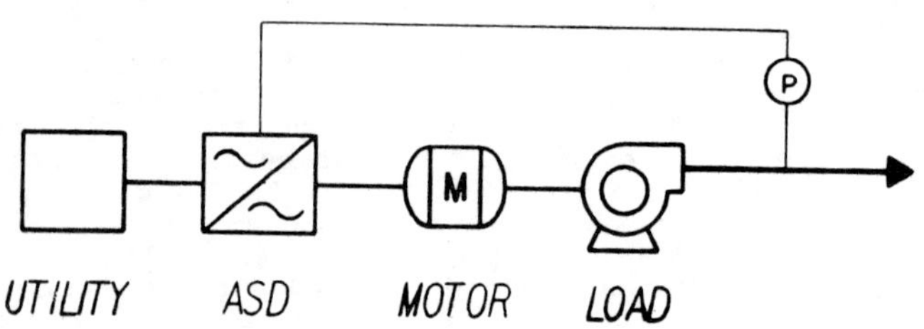

FIGURE NO. 2

TYPICAL CONSTANT SPEED SYSTEM
AND
ENERGY CONSUMPTION

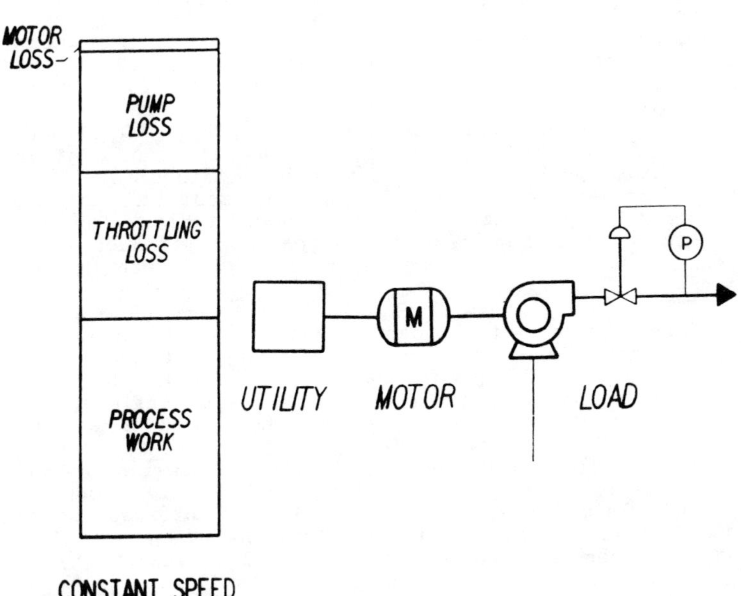

Operation

During the 1970's and 1980's, the development of power electronic devices that can handle high voltages and currents much the same way transistors handle low voltages and currents has allowed for the rapid development of electric adjustable speed drives to control motors. These drives, first applied in the textile industry, in the late 1970's, are now available for general application from many suppliers in sizes that range from fractional horsepower up to 20,000 HP.

The electric ASD has three major components, a converter, a filter and an inverter. The converter takes the incoming AC power and changes it to DC, where the voltage is varied to meet established set points for control. The power is then filtered to control harmonics. Finally, the power is converted back to AC at a reduced voltage and frequency. This is accomplished using devices known as silicon control rectifiers (SCR) and gate turnoff thyristors (GTO) and power transistors in circuitry that modifies the AC waveform at a constant volts to hertz ratio. The net effect is the motor speed varies with frequency at constant motor torque characteristics. (Figure Nos. 3 and 4)

ASD's offer significant flexibility of speed and speed controls. Operating speed ranges are from 0 to 100%; however, speed control accuracy and ASD efficiency decay below 50% speed. ASD efficiencies range from 95% at full speed to the low 80's at 50% speed on the average. ASD's offer other speed control features that can be specified into the design of the unit. Automatic soft starting and accelerating to preset minimum speed levels as well as pre-programmed speed changes for specific operational sequences are all features that add to the operational flexibility of ASD's.

Two important operating considerations are power system disturbances and heat dissipation. The ASDs with the electronic switching operation generate harmonic voltages and currents that can effect the motor but primarily manifest themselves in disturbances in other parts of the power system, whether it be a hum in the intercom system to erratic operation of a flame management system. These disturbances can be minimized by using isolation transformers in the feed to the

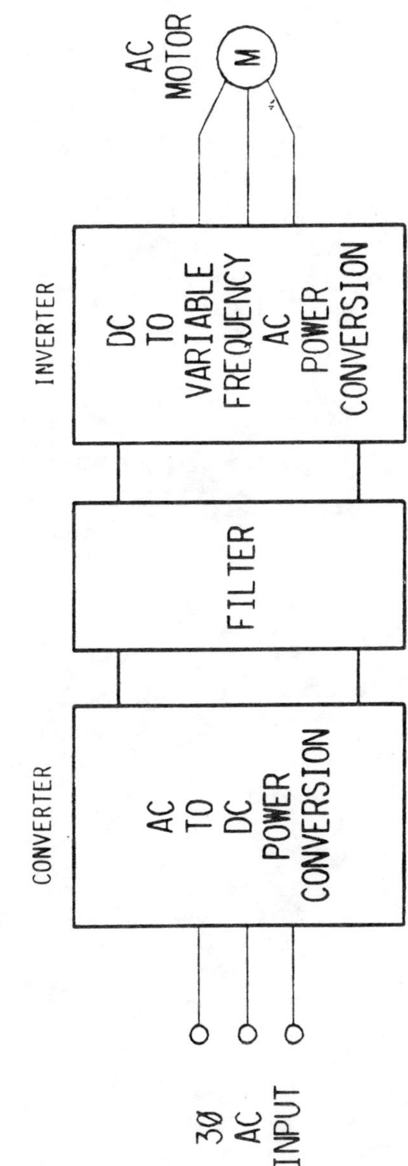

INVERTER POWER CIRCUIT

FIGURE NO. 4

HOW ASDs CHANGE MOTOR SPEED

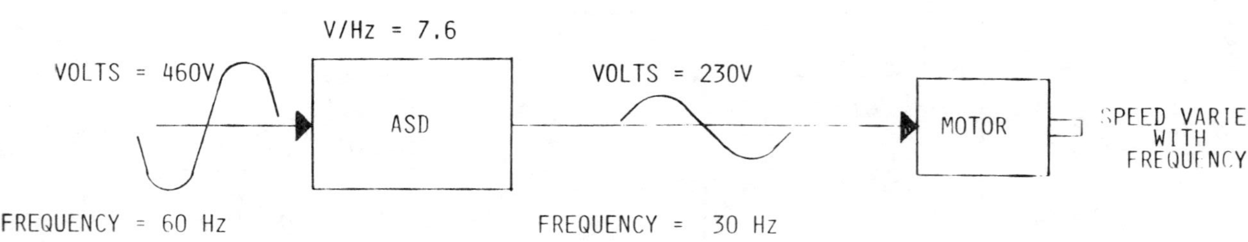

NET EFFECT ASD REDUCES SPEED WITH CONSTANT
MOTOR TORQUE CHARACTERISTICS

drive or in the feed to sensitive circuits and specifying drive harmonic levels. The dissipation of heat from the ASD requires consideration especially if installing the ASD in an existing air conditioned space. ASD efficiency ranges from 80 to 95% of the total energy passing through the unit. This is rejected heat can be quite high on units in the hundreds and thousands of horsepower.

Applications

There are three types of ASDs, voltage source, current source and pulse width modulated (PWM). Each has distinct characteristics or limitations. The voltage source is strictly for multiple motor applications in which a group of motors are required to run at the same speeds, such as a production line operation. The current source, both six (6) pulse and twelve (12) pulse, are for single motor applications and some multi-motor applications in any horsepower sizes. The current source is primarily for horsepowers greater than 20 and particularly the twelve (12) pulse variety are only cost effective at sizes over 2000 HP. PWM can be applied in any motor configuration. They are normally more efficient than the other sizes, but are currently limited to 200 HP based on the electronic device type and configuration used to make up the drive.

FIGURE NO. 5

ASD TYPES AND APPLICATIONS

- o VOLTAGE SOURCE (MULTI-MOTOR APPLICATIONS)
- o CURRENT SOURCE (SINGLE MOTOR APPLICATIONS)
- o PULSE WIDTH MODULATED (ANY MOTOR ARRANGEMENT SIZE LIMITED TO 200 HP)
- o MOTORS: SYNCHRONOUS AND INDUCTION
- o DRIVEN EQUIPMENT: FANS, PUMPS, AND COMPRESSORS

The best potential ASD applications are in systems that have continuously varying loads and cycling loads. Under these conditions, the system is spending a large portion of its operational time at off design conditions where throttling losses are high. Consideration should also be given in new installations that are projected to be operating at or near full load to using an ASD in lieu of a throttling device based not on operating energy savings but on a first cost comparison.

FIGURE NO. 6

GUIDELINES FOR POTENTIAL APPLICATION

TYPES OF OPERATION	EXISTING	NEW
Continuous Full Load	No	Yes
Continuous Varying Load	Yes	Yes
Cycling Load	Yes	Yes
Intermittent	No	No

ASDS can be configured in different arrangements depending on the driven equipment operation and reliability requirements. A single ASD can drive three motors at the same speed or any combination at the same speed if its power rating is equal to the sum of the motor sizes. A single ASD can be installed to serve several motors of equivalent power rating, if only one will be operating at any given time. A single ASD with dual channels can be purchased to provide maximum reliability for protection against power electronic device failure if no other means of operation is provided for a critical piece of driven equipment. (Figure 7)

ASDs range from simple wall mounted cabinets for 0 to 49 HP models up to free standing cabinets eight feet high and twelve feet long for 1000 HP sizes. The cabinets are provided in standard NEMA enclosure ratings. The cabinets can be located adjacent to the motors or in a motor control center or relay roomes far removed from the motor. Adequate cooling must be provided to remove the heat generated by the ASD operation. Smaller drives have their own convective heat sinks. Drives in the horsepower range of 1000 and above have forced convective cooling and/or water cooled components.

FIGURE NO. 7

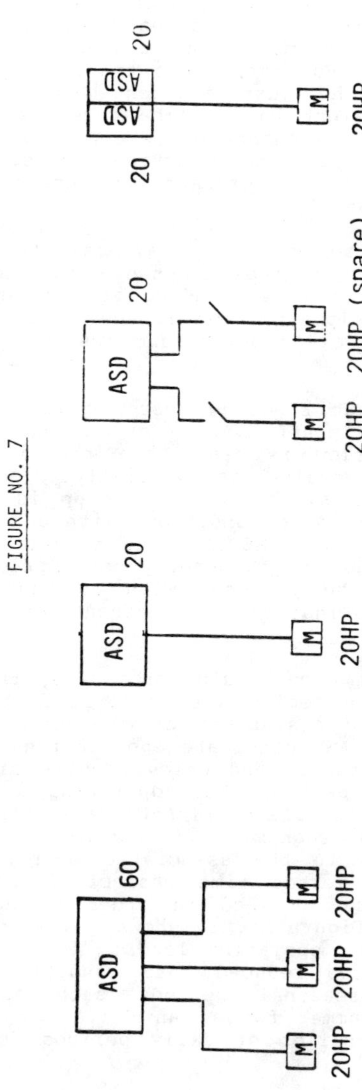

ASD AND MOTOR CONFIGURATIONS

Justification

An ASD installation, whether new of retrofit, is justified based on improved product control and/or on energy savings. The justification based on improved product control is normally the easiest way to cost justify the drive. However, it is the most specific to an application. The justification based on energy savings is the easiest to describe generically and is almost always a component of every justification. Therefore, the following section describes the methodology to use to prepare an energy savings justification for an ASD.

The principle behind energy savings with an ASD is complex because it requires a change to the process operation and a good understanding of load duty cycle for the driven equipment, performance requirements of the system, and specific performance capability of the driven equipment.

In many constant speed process applications, flow is controlled by a control valve or damper. When the required process flow is less than the design flow rate, the control valve is partially closed. The result is that the system pressure drop is increased over the fully-open-valve condition, with an associated wastage of energy. If an ASD is used to vary the speed of the driven equipment, the energy consumption is only that required by the process, with no wastage other than that of the individual component efficiencies. (Figure No. 8)

The analysis of a particular process application of an ASD installation begins with precise definition of the application and assessment of the need for speed control. The best ASD candidate applications are those which operate constantly and which require significant throttling a large part of their operating hours. (The indefinite adjectives "significant" and "large" are required since the economics of any ASD applications are very sensitive to the associated energy costs.) Data on the load versus time characteristics of the application must be obtained in order to define its load/duty cycle. Figure No. 10 shows a load duty cycle with three different operating loads: full (design or rated) load and two reduced load conditions. These might represent seasonal periods such as winter, spring/fall, and summer for a fan drive for a process and heating steam boiler or daily periods for a pump

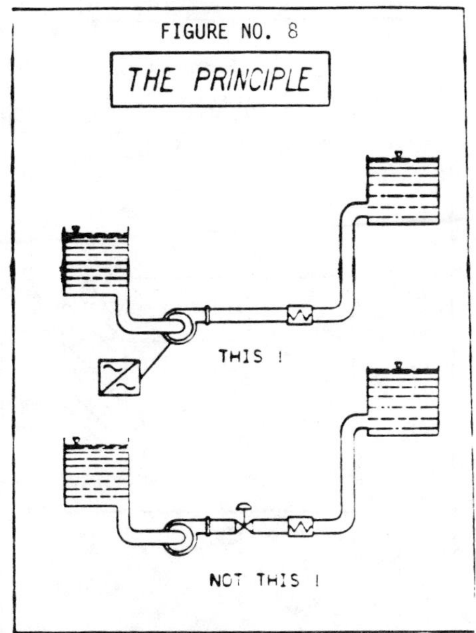
FIGURE NO. 8
THE PRINCIPLE
THIS !
NOT THIS !

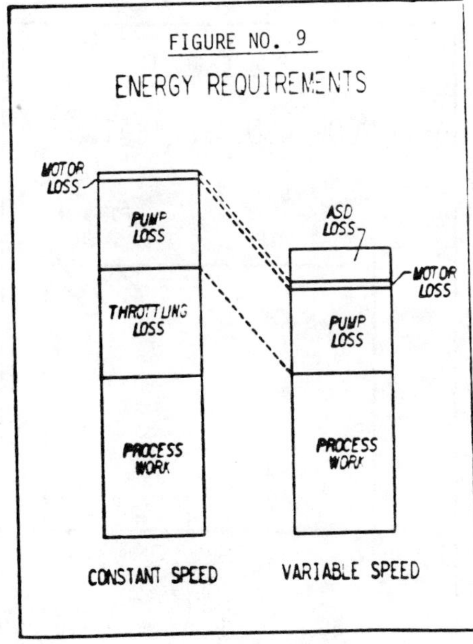
FIGURE NO. 9
ENERGY REQUIREMENTS
MOTOR LOSS
PUMP LOSS
THROTTLING LOSS
PROCESS WORK
ASD LOSS
MOTOR LOSS
PUMP LOSS
PROCESS WORK
CONSTANT SPEED
VARIABLE SPEED

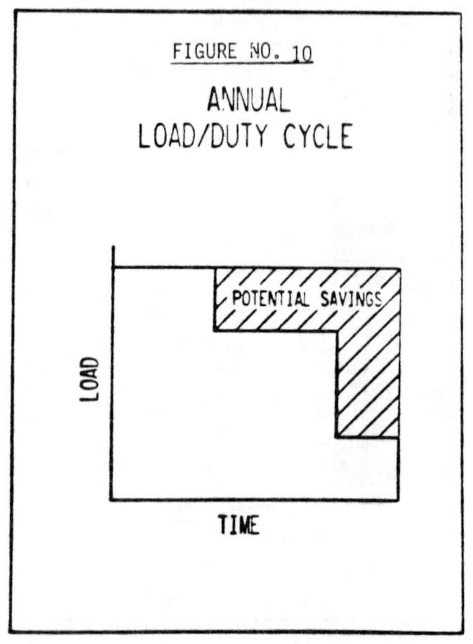
FIGURE NO. 10
ANNUAL
LOAD/DUTY CYCLE
POTENTIAL SAVINGS
LOAD
TIME

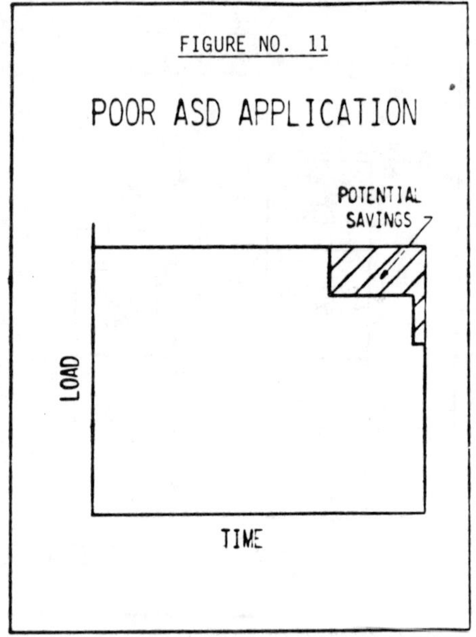
FIGURE NO. 11
POOR ASD APPLICATION
POTENTIAL
SAVINGS
LOAD
TIME

supplying cooling water to production lines for that operate at different shifts. To illustrate further, Figure Nos. 11 and 12 show hypothetical load/duty cycles which typically result in, respectively, a poor ASD application and a good ASD application, in terms of energy savings.

The next step in the analysis technique is to develop or obtain the head flow characteristics of the system under investigation. Figure No. 13 shows a typical pumping system configuration in which both static head, represented by the elevation difference between "A" and "B", and frictional losses are present. For an existing installation, this characteristic curve may be available from the design engineer's files or be derived by analyzing historical operating records, while for a new installation appropriate calculations of system resistance must be made to develop the curve.

The final technical information is the characteristic curve of the driven equipment. This is available from the original design data, the manufacturer, or can be developed from field test data. This data correlates head flow efficiency and horsepower requirements for the driven equipment. Superimposing the equipment curve over the systems curve establishes the operating condition points for each load duty cycle point for both constant and variable speed operation. (Figure 14 and 15) The actual horsepowers and operating conditions at each point are established using the affinity laws governing centrifugal pumps and fans that express relationships between speed and performance parameters.

In analyzing any process for ASD application, the constant and variable speed operating points for each operating mode/must be determined as described above. The energy savings between the constant speed and variable speed operating are determined by first establishing the shaft horse power for each operating condition. Significant savings are realized because horsepower is related to the cube of speed. This means that a 10% reduction in speed results in a 27% reduction in horsepower.

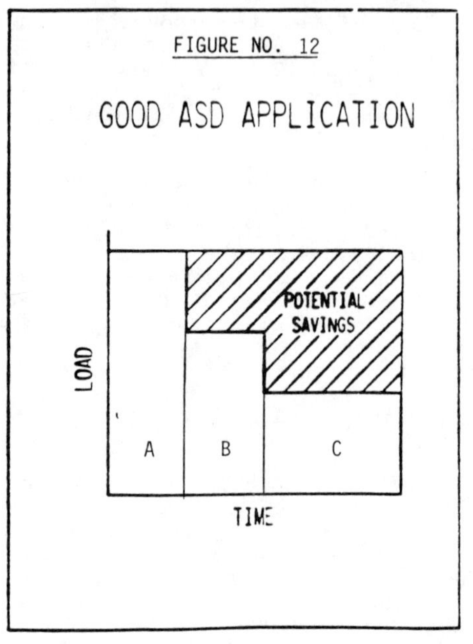

FIGURE NO. 12

GOOD ASD APPLICATION

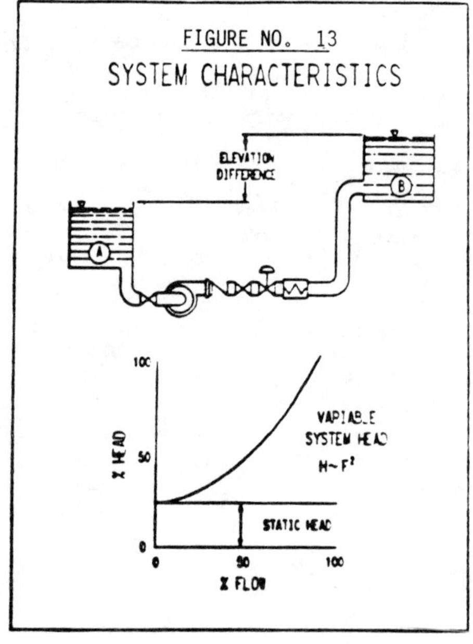

FIGURE NO. 13

SYSTEM CHARACTERISTICS

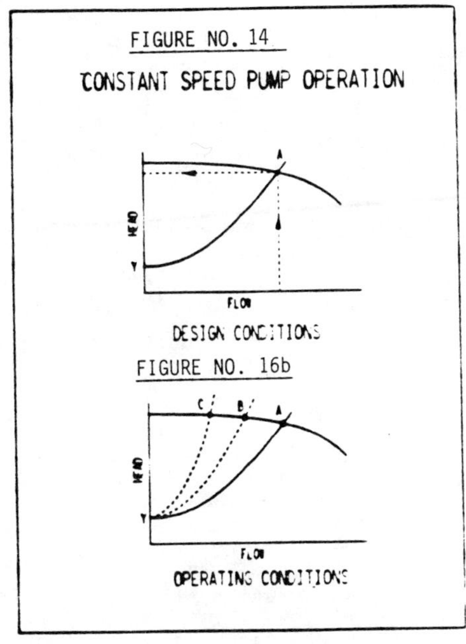
FIGURE NO. 14
CONSTANT SPEED PUMP OPERATION
A
HEAD
Y
FLOW
DESIGN CONDITIONS
FIGURE NO. 16b
C
B
A
HEAD
Y
FLOW
OPERATING CONDITIONS

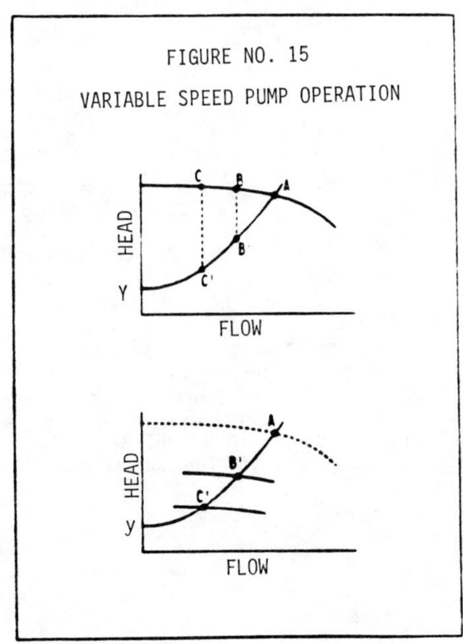
FIGURE NO. 15
VARIABLE SPEED PUMP OPERATION
C
B
A
HEAD
B'
C'
Y
FLOW
A
B'
C'
HEAD
y
FLOW

The calculation of energy required at the constant and variable speed operating points is the next step in this procedure. Using the shaft horsepower for each selected point, the energy consumption for constant speed operation is:

$$E_{CS} = \frac{HP \times 0.746 \times 8760 \times LDC}{e_M}$$

Where: E_{CS} = kilowatt-hours of energy for constant speed operation at the selected point

HP = Shaft Horsepower at the selected point

LDC = Load/duty cycle for the selected point (product of % time at that point and % of year process operates)

E_M = Motor efficiency at selected point

For variable speed operation, the energy consumption is:

$$E_{VS} = \frac{HP \times 0.746 \times 8760 \times LDC}{e_M \times e_D}$$

Where: E_{VS} = Kilowatt-hours of energy for variable speed operation at the selected point

HP = Shaft Horsepower at the reduced speed point

e_D = ASD efficiency

LDC and e_M as above

The annual energy consumption in each case is calculated by summing the energy required for each load duty cycle point for the year. The difference between the two is the energy savings resulting from variable speed operation; using applicable energy cost, and/or motor equipment costs and installation costs, a simple payback can be derived.

The above procedure can, in general, be applied to any process application with a centrifugal pump or fan. However, the procedure becomes more complex for some applications such as compressor processes, and should be undertaken only by people knowledgeable in the specific equipment operation and analysis.

Adjustable speed drives offer several benefits that enhance the overall operation that are often hard to quantify at the time of justification.

- Better process control
- Lower equipment operating speeds
- Reduced equipment and system stresses
- Soft starting and lower inrush currents
- Lower noise levels

Summary

Electrical adjustable speed drives are a relatively new electrotechnology based on power electronic devices. They can be easily retrofit into existing motor applications to effectively control the speed of driven process equipment. They are justified based on energy savings on process that operate at continuous varying loadings. Their development will continue to improve as the field of power electronic devices matures.

ASD FIELD TESTS: LESSONS LEARNED

J. A. OLIVER
BECHTEL POWER CORPORATION

NORWALK, CALIFORNIA

INTRODUCTION

In December 1984, Sierra Pacific Power Company started up a 2000 HP adjustable speed drive on the 1750 HP 2A boiler feed pump motor at its Ft. Churchill Plant in Yearington, Nevada. This ASD is configured as a 12 pulse input, 12 pulse output current source system as shown in the 1-line diagram of Figure 1.

A year later in January 1985, Gulf States Utilities Inc. started up a 2250 HP ASD on its 1A boiler feed pump at Willow Glen Plant at St. Gabriel, LA. This ASD is a six pulse input, six pulse output, modified load commuted inverter as shown in Figure 3. This modified LCI system operates in the LCI mode from 50% to 100% speed and operates with a dc link commutation circuit at lower speeds.

Both of these ASDs were evaluated under the EPRI field test program of EPRI contract RP 1966-6, "Retrofitting Large Power Plant Motors for Adjustable Speed: Field Test Program." The Field Test Program is the latest work in the four year program of studying the retrofitting of existing fixed speed induction motors in power plants to adjustable speed with power electronics.

FIELD TEST PROGRAM

The field test program includes five power plant retrofit projects:

- o Sierra Pacific Power Co.
  1-2000 HP Boiler Feed Pump current source
  ASD at Ft. Churchill Plant, Unit 2

- Gulf States Utilities
  1-2250 HP Boiler Feed Pump modified LCI
  ASD at Willow Glen Plant, Unit 1

- Iowa Public Service Co.
  2-6300 HP Boiler Feed Pump Modified LCI
  ASDs at George Neal Plant, Unit 2

- Oklahoma Gas & Electric Co.
  2-5500 HP FD Fan current source, GTO-PWM
  ASDs at Seminole Plant, Unit 1

- Sierra Pacific Power Co.
  1-2000 HP Boiler Feed Pump, current source GTO-PWM
  ASD at Tracy Plant, Unit 3

These five field test projects use the existing power plant squirrel cage induction motors. The power electronics equipment has been added to control feedwater flow or air flow directly by motor speed, thus eliminating the control valve or inlet vanes and the power losses associated with these devices.

This paper describes tests made on the first two field test projects both of which were boiler feed pump motors, but each with a different ASD technology Reports on the later projects will be made after testing in 1987. In conducting these tests EPRI was interested in determining the following information:

- Power measurement to the ASD and to the motor
- Measurement of voltage and current harmonics
- Additional motor losses from harmonics
- Vibration from mechanical resonance in system
- ASD efficiency
- Verification of calculated fuel cost savings.

Following is a description of each project, a summary of the test method and test results, a schematic of the ASD technology and a discussion of what has been learned to date.

SIERRA PACIFIC POWER CO.
FORT CHURCHILL PLANT
UNIT 2, 2A BOILER FEED PUMP

PURPOSE OF PROJECT

The purpose of converting the 2A Boiler Feed Pump to Adjustable speed was as follows:

- o Reduce minimum load on the unit by 2MW and replace the 2MW by lower cost power.
- o Eliminate the control valve at the feed pump discharge thereby eliminating the power loss in the valve and valve associated maintenance cost.
- o Convert the low load operation of the unit to sliding throttle.
- o Extend the MW output of the unit for operation with one pump.
- o Extend the feed water and flue gas low range controls.

DESCRIPTION OF APPLICATION

The 2000 HP ASD was connected in line with the existing 2A Boiler Feed Pump Motor. A manual electrical by-pass circuit was provided to allow operation of the motor without the ASD in event of serious long term ASD outage. The common control valve for the 2A and 2B Boiler Feed Pumps was relocated to the discharge of the 2B pump. With this arrangement, the 2A pump with ASD control is used for normal unit operation which is a minimum load, spinning reserve mode. The 2A pump is used for loads up to 90MW. Above 90MW, the 2B pump is operated with the control valve wide open and the 2A pump is backed off and is used for control.

ASD TECHNOLOGY

The ASD used for this project is a current source type with input and output transformers to control harmonics to the 4 kV bus and to the motor. The ASD requires no input filters or output filters. Solid state, digital microprocessor type control and diagnostics are used. The power circuit for this ASD is shown in Figure 1.

OPERATING EXPERIENCE

The ASD has been in service since December 1984. There have been no operating problems with either the ASD or the control system until the summer of 1987. The ASD is used to control boiler drum level and has been operating on automatic control since December 1984, except for planed unit outages.

The generating unit output was reduced by 2MW as planned. At normal minimum load operation boiler pressure is held at 700 psi, down from the designed 1750 psi. Dollar savings have been estimated at $1.6 million per year by Sierra Pacific Power. Half of this is from savings of generating the 2MW elsewhere and half from better operating efficiency at 700 psi.

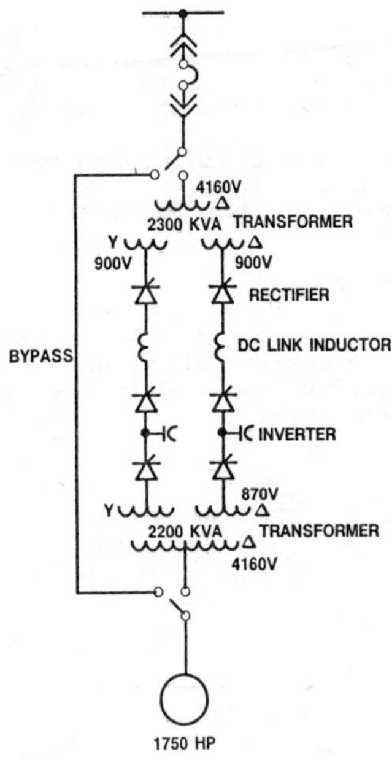

Figure 1
12-PULSE CURRENT SOURCE ASD
FT. CHURCHILL PLANT, UNIT 2

FIELD MEASUREMENTS

As part of the detailed engineering work of this project, a coast-down test was conducted on the motor and pump or fan. The vibration amplitude and frequency were recorded as the motor and driven equipment coasted down after being tripped at full speed. The data was evaluated to determine if there were any serious mechanical resonances in the system that are a function of speed. If a serious resonance frequency existed that is excited at a particular rotating speed, operation at that speed would be avoided. The vibration measurements were taken with a real-time spectrum analyzer.

For electrical measurements to verify performance, volts, amps and watts at the input and output of the power converter were needed. When using conventional meters, it is difficult to know if the readings are correct because the operator of the metering equipment has no way of knowing of the provisions, if any, that the meter manufacturer has made in his equipment for distorted current and voltage wave forms.

To solve this metering problem, the same apparatus that was used for the vibration measurements was used to record electrical quantities. This equipment is as follows and it was connected as shown schematically in Figure 2:

HP5423A Structural Dynamics Analyzer
HP54470B Digital Filter
HP54410A Analog/Digital Converter
HP7275A Plotter
Oscilloscope
Cassette Data Recorder

These devices operate at a low signal level in the range of a few volts. A current shunt was used in the CT circuit and a voltage divider was used in the PT circuit to obtain the proper voltage levels.

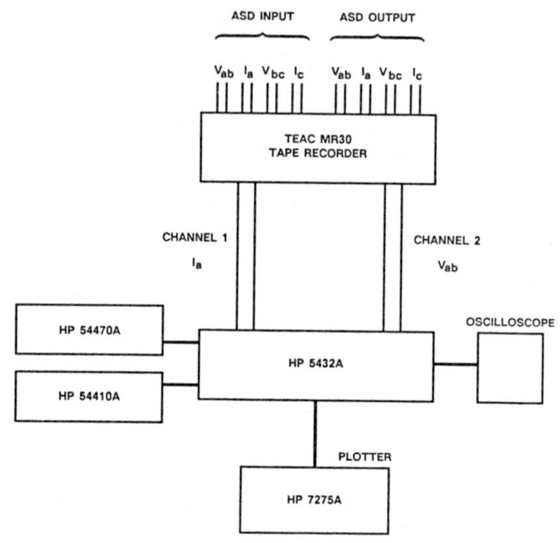

Figure 2
EQUIPMENT FOR MEASURING
ASD INPUT AND OUTPUT ELECTRICAL QUANTITIES

POWER MEASUREMENT

The two wattmeter method was used to measure power. With the motor operating at constant load, first one set of readings was taken at the 4 kV switchgear for the input to the ASD, the voltage between Phases A and B and current in Phase A. Then another set taken of voltage between Phase B and C along with the current in Phase C. Then, another set of similar readings were taken at the output of the ASD at a point in the circuit past any output transformer or filter.

The analysis of the field measurements taken at Sierra Pacific Power are shown in Table I.

TABLE I

FT. CHURCHILL, UNIT 2 1750 HP BOILER FEED PUMP - FIELD RESULTS

Unit	Motor			% Extra	Harmonics*				ASD
				Motor	Input		Output		
MW	HP	FREQ.	RPM	Loss	THD-V	THD-I	THD-V	THD-I	Eff
90	1857	60.2	3576	.7	2.4	10.7	10.6	9.3	.91
75	1380	55.8	3315	.9	2.3	11.0	16.4	9.6	.91
50	1058	52.5	3119	1.0	2.1	11.4	16.0	9.4	.91
25	769	50.3	2989	1.1	1.86	11.9	16.7	9.5	.89
12	204	31.7	1883	1.7	1.0	10.9	24.6	8.6	.82

* THD refers to total harmonic distortion, -V for voltage and -I for current.

GULF STATES UTILITIES
WILLOW GLEN PLANT
UNIT 1, 1A BOILER FEED PUMP

UNIT DESCRIPTION

Willow Glen Unit 1 is a 145MW unit located on the Mississippi River south of Baton Rouge, LA. It is designed for gas or oil firing.

PURPOSE OF PROJECT

Gulf States Utilities decided to convert one of the 2-2250 HP Boiler Feed Pumps at Willow Glen, Unit 1 to adjustable speed operation for the following reasons:

- o improve unit heat rate by eliminating the power loss in feed pump control valve.
- o eliminate control valve maintenance by relocating control valve to the 2B pump.
- o obtain experience with large adjustable speed drives for consideration in other generating units.

DESCRIPTION OF APPLICATION

After observing the ASD in operation at Sierra Pacific Power Company at Ft. Churchill Unit 2, GSU purchased a 2250 HP ASD for Willow Glen, Unit 1. They relocated the control valve to the discharge of the 1B pump. Since they already operated the unit in a sliding throttle mode, there were no sliding throttle considerations. Fuel cost savings of $130,000 per year were estimated by GSU.

DESCRIPTION OF TECHNOLOGY

GSU selected the transformerless six pulse input, six pulse output modified load commutated inverter type ASD as shown in Figure 3. For this type of ASD, the rectifier and inverter are identical, each using a three-phase thyrister bridge. The rectifier is line commutated and the inverter is load commutated. A three-phase line-to-line connected capacitor is connected to the motor terminals. This provides magnetizing current for the induction motor. With the capacitor, the motor is capable of providing a voltage source to commutate the inverter. The capacitor is not capable of providing this function as the frequency drops below 50% of rated frequency. Below 50% frequency a dc link commutation circuit diverts current from the inverter and allows it to commutate.

Both rectifier and inverter bridges are water cooled. The combination of water-cooled thyristers and transformerless design allowed a compact ASD design which was attractive to GSU since they were doing their own design work at the power plant.

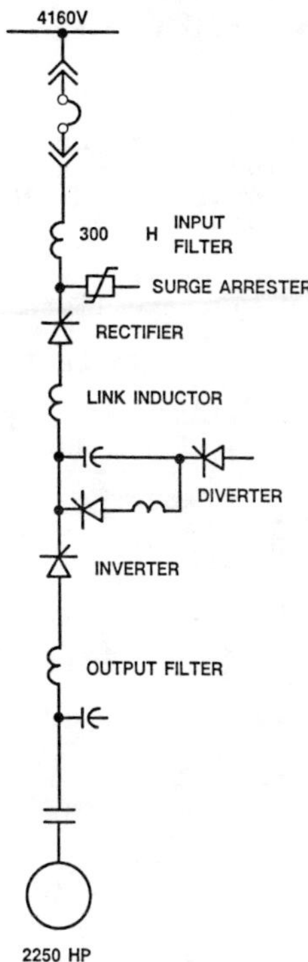

Figure 3
6-PULSE MODIFIED LOAD-COMMUTATED ASD
WILLOW GLEN PLANT, UNIT 1

OPERATING EXPERIENCE

The Willow Glen Plant, Unit 1, Boiler Feed Pump ASD has been in service since January 1986. They have experienced three failures of capacitors in the output filter which shut down the ASD. All capacitors were replaced and GSU has used a fan to cool the capacitors on hot days. No further failures have resulted and the ASD has performed well otherwise.

Testing onsite revealed that the current wave shapes were distorted as the frequency was reduced to 35 hz. This apparently was caused by an increase in the fifth harmonic component of current as the output capacitor and motor winding inductance became resonant around 35 hz. This condition did not affect the operation of the ASD or the motor.

Since the completion of the EPRI-Bechtel testing at Willow Glen, the manufacturer of this ASD has determined that the lack of an input transformer causes a neutral shift on the motor six times per cycle which results in increased levels of voltage to ground on the motor. This has resulted in some motor failure and needs to be considered when applying ASDs to motors rated 2300 volts and higher in retrofit applications.

The test results of measurements taken at Willow Glen Plant in February 1986 are listed in Table II.

TABLE II

WILLOW GLEN PLANT UNIT 2 BOILER FEED PUMP - FIELD RESULTS

Unit	Motor			% Extra	Harmonics*				
				Motor	Input		Output		ASD
MW	HP	FREQ.	RPM	Loss	THD-V	THD-I	THD-V	THD-I	Eff
115	2099	58	3451	.6	2.05	24.8	7.8	14.46	.92
80	1313	50	2915	1.5	1.49	25.7	10.32	25.6	.92
40	821	44	2618	2.6	.99	26.6	12.06	38.1	.91
15	361	35	2083	7.3	.70	35.3	16.88	67.1	.91

IOWA PUBLIC SERVICE COMPANY
GEORGE NEAL PLANT,
UNIT 2 BOILER FEED PUMPS

PURPOSE OF PROJECT

IPS decided to convert the 2-7000 HP boiler feed pumps on Unit 2 to adjustable speed operation for the following reasons:

- change the unit to sliding throttle operation to improve part load efficiency of the unit.
- improved part load efficiency of the unit will result in more operating hours for the unit in the MAPP power pool and increase revenues for IPS.

DESCRIPTION OF APPLICATION

Each 7000 HP boiler feed pump on Neal No. 2 is driven by 2-3500 HP, 3600 rpm motors connected in tandem. A by-pass switch arrangement is provided so that the motors can be returned to original constant speed operation if there is serious ASD trouble. Prior to the installation of the ASDs, pump flow was controlled by a control valve. The control valve for each pump has been retained and becomes an integral part of the ASD control scheme. With the ASD controlling motor speed, constant boiler drum level is maintained by control valve position and superheater spray pressure is held constant by pump speed. Pump maximum flow and minimum flow limits under adjustable speed operation are monitored by the plant computer system.

DESCRIPTION OF TECHNOLOGY

Each ASD is a modified LCI type unit and is comprised of a three winding input transformer to provide for the 12 pulse input rectifier, a dc link inductor, a GTO link commutator circuit, and a six pulse inverter with output L-C filter. The power circuit for these ASDs are shown in Figure 4.

Operation of these ASDs commenced in November 1987.

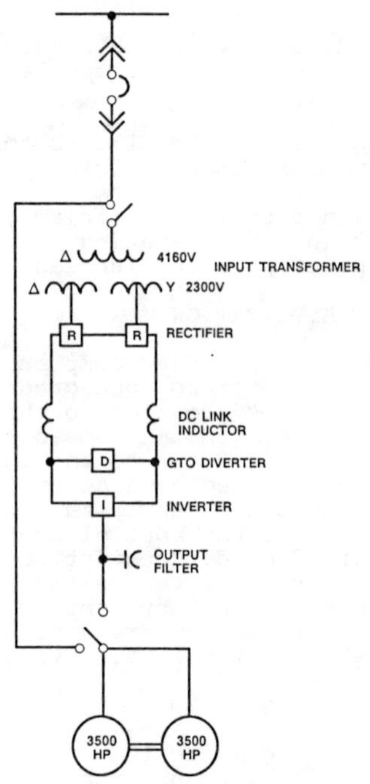

Figure 4

IOWA PUBLIC SERVICE CO.
GEORGE NEAL PLANT UNIT 2
BOILER FEEDPUMP ASD
MODIFIED LCI TYPE INVERTER

OKLAHOMA GAS & ELECTRIC COMPANY
SEMINOLE PLANT
UNIT 1, FD FANS

PURPOSE OF PROJECT

Oklahoma Gas & Electric Company's decision to install a 5500 Hp ASD on each of the 2-4000 HP FD Fans at Seminole Plant, Unit 1 is based on the following benefits:

- o Annual fuel cost savings of $530,000 for improved operational efficiency at part load.
- o Increased fan flow and unit output during peak demand periods during summer months.
- o Evaluation of operating experience with ASDs for further use in power plants at OG&E.

DESCRIPTION OF APPLICATION

The ASDs were being furnished in a factory prefabricated house complete with air conditioning. The redundant 30 ton air conditioners are provided with economizer cooling units that allow the use of filtered outside air during much of the year when the outside air temperature is below 85°F.

The ADS house is located near the fan motors so that additional cable, conduit and tray are minimal. The existing motor cable is terminated in a new splice box near the motor. From the splice box, cables are extended to the isolation switches, the transformers and to the ASDs. The control system modification consists of using the existing vane control signal to control motor speed.

TECHNOLOGY DESCRIPTION

Each current source GTO-PWM ASD has a 12 pulse input type rectifier with isolation transformer, a dc link inductor, a six pulse GTO-PWM inverter and an output capacitor filter. This system has the advantage of good input and output voltage and current harmonics. It has no resonance between the output filter and the motor. Control and diagnostics are by digital microprocessor type technology. A telephone modem is furnished with allows evaluation of the onsite operation of the ASD at the manufacturers factory by engineering specialists. The power circuit for these ASDs is shown in Figure 5.

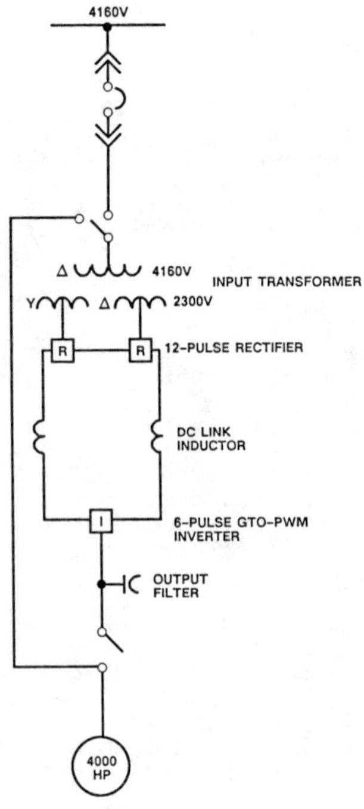

Figure 5
OKLAHOMA GAS & ELECTRIC CO.
5500HP FD FAN ASD

SIERRA PACIFIC POWER COMPANY
TRACY PLANT,
UNIT 3, 3A BOILER FEED PUMP

PURPOSE OF PROJECT

Tracy Unit 3 is a duplicate unit to the 110MW Units 1 and 2 at Ft. Churchill. Based on the excellent results obtained with the ASD installation on the 2A Boiler Feed Pump at Ft. Churchill, Sierra Pacific Power decided to convert the 3A Boiler Feed Pump at Tracy Unit 3 to adjustable speed. Operating benefits are expected to be very similar to those realized at Ft. Churchill.

DESCRIPTION OF TECHNOLOGY

EPRI included this project in its field test program because of the current-source, gate-turn-off (GTO) thyrister type inverter. The current source GTO inverter has the ability to eliminate the 5th and 7th harmonics to the motor at all frequencies. At Tracy, the ASD is comprised of a 4000/4000V input transformer, a six pulse rectifier, a dc link inductor, a six pulse GTO-PWM inverter, an output capacitor filter and a by-pass switch arrangement. The circuit arrangement is in Figure 6.

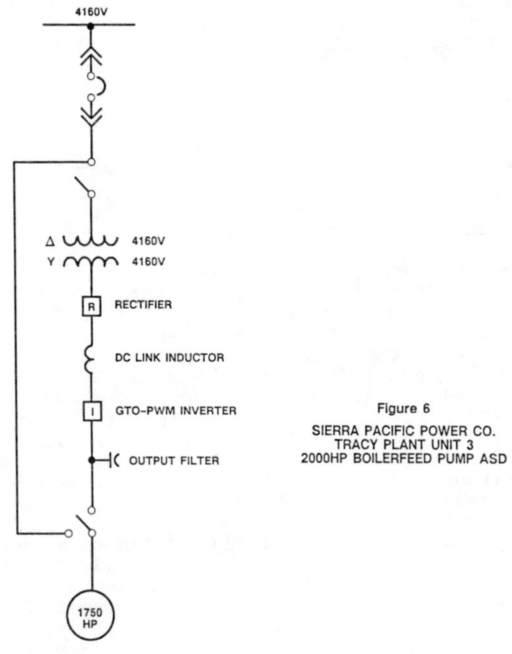

Figure 6

SIERRA PACIFIC POWER CO.
TRACY PLANT UNIT 3
2000HP BOILERFEED PUMP ASD

LESSONS LEARNED

EPRI has provided a strong leadership role in the development of a sophisticated power electronics based technology for converting fixed-speed squirrel cage induction motors in power plants to adjustable speed operation. Although a number of inverter technologies have been found to exist commercially for large motors, three have survived the rigors of competitive bidding and are being tested in this EPRI study. They are as follows:

Current - source
Modified load commutated (modified LCI)
Current - source GTO-PWM

Of these three, the latter two are still being successfully sold for large motors (2000 HP and larger). The current source system has been shown to have a number of excellent features at Sierra Pacific Power, Ft. Churchill Plant on the Unit 2 boiler feed pump. It has good harmonic control when used in a 12 pulse input, 12 pulse output configuration, it has no output filter capacitor requirement and can be used in a full regenerative braking mode. It is, however, too costly for large motors.

The modified LCI inverter has provided an economic ASD system that has shown the utility industry how to reduce fuel costs in many motor applications with electronic speed control. The modified LCI system has the simplicity afforded by a rectifier and inverter using the same components. The dc link diverter circuit provides for inverter commutation when the output filter capacitor can no longer provide excitation to the induction motor to allow LCI operation. This system has been packaged with water cooling of the power electronics to simplify the overall cooling system. Water cooling is important for many power plant applications where the air is contaminated with coal or ash dust.

The modified LCI system has been offered in a six pulse input, six pulse output arrangement without an input transformer and with an output filter capacitor of about the motor KVA rating. Experience has shown that there are problems with this concept. First, without the input transformer excessive line-to-ground voltages can develop. Motor winding failures have occurred in form wound stator coils which are generally used in motors rated 2300 volts and higher. Motors rated 575 volts and lower use a random would insulation system which has more voltage margin and ASDs without input transformers have been widely successful on the lower voltage motors.

The input transformer eliminates this overvoltage problem. Once a decision has been made to use an input transformer, the rectifier should be configured in a 12 pulse arrangement to eliminate the powerful 5th and 7th harmonics to the auxiliary busses.

The second problem that has surfaced with the modified LCI system is not as serious as the first but bears reporting. The output capacitor filter can provide a resonant circuit with the motor's leakage reactance. Resonance has been observed with the fifth harmonic current in measurements at Willow Glen Plant. While this condition caused no problems at Willow Glen there have been other instances reported of motor frame vibration and rotor fan blade fatigue that may be related to high 5th or 7th harmonic currents in the motor windings.

Another version of the modified LCI system is being readied for test at Iowa Public Service, Neal Unit 2 on 2-7000 HP boiler feed pumps. This system with input transformers and 12 pulse rectifiers has a GTO diverter circuit. This installation uses a river water heat exchanger for cooling the ventilation air with redundancy in blowers and in heat exchangers. The housing for this system is noteworthy. It consists of a system of factory made steel-faced and steel-backed polyurethane insulated panels which are assembled into an interlocking engineered structure. The housing has advantages over some of the housings supplied by ASD manufacturers in that it can be designed for site specific conditions. The panels provide for easy assembly in locations not accessible to the factory designed house. This housing warrants further consideration by utilities for large ASD installations requiring either an outdoor house or an indoor dust proof housing.

Both the modified LCI and current source GTO-PWM technologies use inductors in the dc link. This makes both of these systems current source type system rather than voltage source system. The advantage of the current source system seems to be that the large dc link inductor limits fault current to the inverter and misfiring of inverter power devices does not result in shutdown. The voltage source system which is widely used in ASDs rated 5 HP to 200 HP is available in large ASDs manufactured by two Japanese companies. They have not been competitive in price in the U.S. It is not apparent that the voltage source inverter has an advantage for large motor ASDs other than the capability being able to be used on any motor without regard to matching ASD to motor reactance.

The current source GTO-PWM inverters being demonstrated in this EPRI field test program represent a high degree of technology. The pulse width modulation technology along with a smaller output filter allows wave shaping at all inverter outputs giving the effect of a 12 pulse or 18 pulse inverter with a single three-phase bridge. With the smaller output filter, the frequency for resonance between the motor winding inductance and the capacitance of the filter is increased to about 173 hz, but resonance is eliminated by omission of existing frequence with PWM control.

The complex PWM operating system requires the use of microprocessor control to change the pulse width patterns with frequency. At full speed, the output is a filtered square wave without PWM wave shaping.

CONCLUSIONS

This study has provided means to test large ASDs for converting fixed speed power plant squirrel cage induction motors to adjustable speed operation.

The results of the Sierra Pacific Power CO., Ft. Churchill Plant installation have been impressive in terms of reliability, controlability and fuel cost savings. The Willow Glen installation, although marred by several capacitor failures, has also been successful, recognizing that the fuel cost savings expectations were not nearly as great as those anticipated at Ft. Churchill.

The remaining installations will go into service in 1987 when field measurements will be resumed.

This test program is bringing to the attention, observation and analysis of EPRI members the remarkable advances being made in power electronics control of large induction motors in power plant applications. Different housings, different cooling systems, different rectifier arrangements and different inverter technologies are being studied in this program.

ASD APPLICATIONS ACCEPTANCE: A SIM²PLE ACTION PLAN

Albert B. Giesecke
Charles S. See, Jr.
Applications, Sales and Marketing, Inc.

ASD is an acronym for adjustable speed drive. The term ASD could be applied to a broad spectrum of products including mechanical adjustable pitch belt drives, hydraulic adjustable clutches, eddy current clutches, rotating and static DC drives and rotating and static adjustable frequency AC drives. For purposes of this paper, the term ASD will be used to define static, adjustable frequency, variable speed AC drives.

The basic definition of an ASD is fairly common. In general terms an ASD rectifies AC power to constant or adjustable voltage DC and then converts (or inverts, if you will) the DC voltage to an adjustable frequency, adjustable voltage AC output. There are numerous methodologies for accomplishing this rectification - inversion process. The most common types are variable voltage source inverters (VVSI), current source inverters (CSI) and pulse width modulated inverters (PWM).

Certain ASD types are more applicable than others to specific applications. It is not uncommon to read a given manufacturer's literature stating that an ASD is a good match for a specific application and that another adjustable speed product type is a better selection for another application. Reading between the lines, the message is that the specific ASD type supplied by that specific manufacturer may not be a good selection for that specific application.

It is also common to read literature and reports which promote comparisons between specific and general drive types. These comparisons generally conclude that one methodology is better than another.

In reality ASDs have been in the marketplace for better than 20 years. Many major suppliers have, at one time or another, offered one of or all of the basic ASD types as a commercial product.

The bottom line is that it is not what an ASD is as much as what it is capable of doing that is key to gaining improved ASD applications acceptance. The purpose of this paper is to describe an action plan to support an increase in the acceptance of ASD products.

SIM²PLE Defined

SIM²PLE is an acronym ASM created to focus our efforts to establish needs and values as part of an assessment process. The letters in SIM²PLE have different meanings and different applications for a given project. SIM²PLE was first applied to describe a manufacturing need to produce a world class ASD product.

In the context of this paper SIM²PLE defines a framework for focusing potential benefits available from applying an ASD as part of an operating system. In the context of ASD applications acceptance, the letters in SIM²PLE are applied as follows:

"S" Take a "s"ystems perspective to review the opportunity.

"I" An ASD must be "i"ntegrated into the system. There is an impact, not only on the process, but as importantly on the equipment and installation to which and with which the ASD is applied. Recognizing and addressing integration issues is an important element in assuring the ultimate success of the application.

"M" Develop a "m"ethodology which considers the existing operating practice as well as the operation potential when quantifying the benefits.

"M" Consider the available "m"arket options. Each option has relative merits and drawbacks. Give the ASD Vendor the opportunity to demonstrate the application benefits available from their 'best' hardware offering.

"P" Consider the "p"eople factor. People do things for their own reasons. It is the users needs and values that will ultimately dictate whether the project is implemented.

"L" "L"everage the benefits. Determine what else is impacted by the application. Quantifying benefits versus an existing operating method can result in an understatement of benefits. Similarily, indirect system benefits could outweigh apparent direct benefits.

"E" "E"ducate the user in the application potential offered by integrating the ASD into the system. As stated in the preface, it is more important to understand what an ASD can do than what it is.

With SIM²PLE defined, the balance of this paper will be devoted to demonstrating, by example, the application of a SIM²PLE action plan. An example which provides a broad spectrum of application benefits is the City of Chicago Retrofit Project.

The City of Chicago Retrofit Project

Project Background

In early 1986, ASM developed the opportunity, as part of an Electric Power Research Institute (EPRI) contract, to identify and develop industrial user candidates to participate in an ASD retrofit demonstration project. As conservation benefits of ASD applications are well known, EPRI directed ASM to focus on locating candidate applications where benefits could be quantified for more reasons than energy conservation alone.

Based on a prior working relationship with the City of Chicago Water System Design Engineering Staff, ASM was aware that there was an opportunity at Water Pumping Operations. It was also known that past attempts to implement an ASD retrofit project at water pumping had been unsuccessful.

Water Pumping Operations System Background

The City of Chicago Water Pumping Operation consists of eleven pumping stations. Each station has four to seven pumping units ranging in capacity from 25 to 85 MGD. Of the eleven stations six utilize electric motor driven pumps and five utilize steam turbine driven pumps. There are a total 52 pumping units, 27 electric motor and 25 steam turbine driven. Installation dates range from 1920 to 1981. The average age of the pumping units is 37 years.

The water pumping system is essentially open loop. System pressure is established based on demand and number of pumps in operation. System pressure is monitored at telemetering points by Water Distribution and pumps are added or deleted by Water Pumping Operations based on requests from Water Distribution. Pumping Operations monitors station discharge pressure at each unit. In general, the pump head capacity curves reflect a design condition of approximately 40 to 50 feet above the normal system head requirement at the pump design flow condition.

The only real constraint on the operating system is the requirement to maintain a minimum pressure to preclude water supply contamination. There is essentially no storage in the system. As such the ability to maintain pumping capability is the single most important issue to the City.

Of the six electric pumping stations, three control discharge pressure by throttling and three operate unthrottled. All five steam stations maintain discharge pressure by adjustable speed operation.

The steam stations are designed to start and operate totally independent of external power or fuel supply. The six electric stations rely on multiple incoming power lines, generally supplied from separate substations and separate distribution systems.

The steam stations run on natural gas. Fuel to water efficiency cycle is between 10 to 15 percent. The electric pumping station wire to water efficiency is between 80 and 90 percent depending on the pumping unit considered.

The pumping system includes 43,800 horsepower of electric motor driven pumps and 67,360 horsepower of steam turbine driven pumps, or approximately 83 megawatts of equivalent electric load. The total 1986 expenditure for energy was approximetely $16,000,000.

It should be noted that a significant percentage of overall water use is by non-metered customers. As such, it is impossible to calculate leakage impact. In addition, water demand based on over pressure supply impacts water processing costs, but not necessarily water operation revenues.

Applying SIM²PLE Principles

"S" Take a Systems Perspective

To maximize the opportunity to establish and quantify the systems benefits potential of the retrofit work two project activities were described and two separate memorandum of understandings were developed. The first memorandum addressed the retrofit opportunity as it applied specifically to the 68th Street Electric Pumping Station. The second memorandum was designed to consider the retrofit opportunity as it applied to the overall water pumping system.

The site specific study allowed for a detailed analysis of the constant speed pumping operation. Two operating modes could be considered. The first would reflect how the system was being controlled and the second how the system could be controlled with the addition of ASDs. The site specific study also allowed for a detailed analysis of ASD compatibility with the existing motors.

The systems study presented the opportunity to identify benefits directly related to the system. As stated in the background, considerable water demand is realized from non-metered loads. In these cases, water flow delivered due to system over pressure conditions represents increased cost for both filtration and sanitation. The over pressure contribution to water loss due to leakage impacts filtration costs only.

The systems study allowed the investigators to quantify the potential cost benefit of converting the steam stations. In addition, it presented an opportunity to address issues related to power supply availability, flexibility and reliability. As such, it was from a systems perspective that the load growth opportunity associated with the steam pumping stations became practical.

There are other systems oriented benefits associated with the ASD retrofit opportunity. Some of these items will be addressed later. It is apparent, however, that "S" deserves its position as the first element in the "SIM²PLE" action plan.

"I" Consider the Integration Issues

There is more than enough experience and documentation to support a statement that the integration of an ASD into an operating system requires careful thought. When that integration process involves an existing operating system where average equipment age is almost 37 years the "I" in SIM²PLE takes on added meaning. As with the "S", the discussion of "I" issues will spill over into other aspects of the basic principles being described. Some general integration issues to address include:

- The impact of the non-sinusoidal waveform output on the driven equipment (motor, pump and coupling) and on the installation in general.

- The effect of harmonics generated by the ASD to the incoming bus, other in-plant loads connected to that bus and potentially to loads external to the installation site.

- The desired level of plant control required and the methodology for reliably establishing and maintaining that level of control.

- The contribution that the ASD makes on overall system reliability.

- The impact of the ASD application on equipment life.

- The level of modification required to existing equipment and to existing operating procedures.

- The level of coordination required between and among ASDs when multiple ASDs are utilized.

In the case of 68th Street these issues have visible application. Operating parameters which impact the ASD application at 68th Street include:

- Motor installation dates range from 1947 to 1961. The impact of common mode voltages and harmonic heating contribution must be carefully considered. It is mandated that existing machine operating performance capability be evaluated. All reasonable attempts should be made to secure basic motor physical and equivalent circuit design information to assist the ASD Vendor in evaluating and addressing basic integration issues.

- The City is currently installing an electronic control and monitoring system to allow for remote station operation. The impact of the ASD on, compatibility with and applicability to the control system are all issues for consideration.

- Issues associated with impact on equipment life and level of modification required tend to be hardware specific. The relative merits of specific hardware options could be addressed by preparing an applications oriented specification document. An applications oriented document would afford the ASD vendors an opportunity to present their "optimum" hardware solution.

- o One of the five pumps at 68th Street was supplied by a different manufacturer and has significantly different performance characteristics. Of the four apparently duplicate pumps, date of supply, hours in service and general use patterns have caused each pump to have varying performance capabilities. As such, the overall performance and capability of the station at various load levels is pump specific. Pump repair could result in a reduction of the differences between the four pumps. The optimum performance of the station will, in all probability, remain pump specific. The ultimate application of ASDs in the pumping system will, therefore, need to address these performance capability differences and preferences.

The "I" in the SIM²PLE action plan is described to define data acquisition needs and address compatibility issues. With the development of an applications oriented specification the ASD vendor can then present their "best" hardware solution.

"M" Establish a Methodology

The problem with considering methodology, as a separate element in an action plan, is that each element represents a basic methodology, in and of itself. The basis for developing an overall methodology for improved ASD application acceptance is to focus the work based on the benefits of what an ASD can do and not on what it is.

There were two elements to the overall methodology proposed for and being implemented for the Chicago Retrofit project. Those two elements are described by the two separate memorandum documents.

In the first memorandum, the 68th Street document, the goal was to address the basic applicability, compatibility and merits of an ASD application as they applied to a specific pumping station. The second memorandum document considered the application benefits of ASDs across the entire pumping system.

The two memorandum documents provided an opportunity to develop an applications methodology which describe benefits of ASD application based on the way the system could be operated as opposed to the quantifications of benefits based on how the system is being operated. Two examples of the potential offered by this approach are demonstrated by reviewing the operation of a throttled and unthrottled pumping station.

At the electric pumping stations three stations can be operated utilizing throttle valves to control pressure. The pump head capacity curves indicate that, at rated capacity, considerable throttling is necessary to meet system resistance requirements. The pumps can be operated at above capacity conditions and throttling requirements reduced. The impact of this operating practice is two-fold. First, energy consumption is minimized, per million gallons of water delivered. Second, pump wear and, as such, pump performance degradation is accelerated. (At 68th Street efficiencies are generally 4 to 10% below acceptance test levels).

When traditional conservation justification methodology is applied at a throttled electric pumping station, the apparent savings, versus historical energy usage, appeared to be relatively low. Average pumping rates tended to cluster evaluation points above the rated operating points of the pumps.

An obvious goal at Pumping Operations is the control of operating costs. As such the discharge pressure at the station is allowed to vary, within a set tolerance, to minimize energy use and reduce throttling requirements.

To address this apparent dilemma a savings potential table was developed. The purpose of the table was to describe the benefits of various ASD application alternatives along the idealized system resistance curve. The development of a savings potential table provided three benefits. First, it quantified the regions where the traditional conservation benefit calculations were made. Second, it demonstrated the relative merits of different application configuration solutions. Third, it exposed the full potential of economic opportunity for the ASD application at the station.

The problem of quantifying ASD benefits by traditional cost payback calculations is even more graphically demonstrated in the case of the unthrottled electric pumping stations. Like the throttled pump case, there is significant head capacity margin at the pump design point. In this case, the pumps run at runout loads at all times. The station operating curve is portrayed by several short islands.

Each island represents an operation range from maximum allowable pressure and minimum unthrottled flow to minimum allowable pressure at maximum unthrottled flow. The islands repeat for multiple pumps until maximum station capacity is realized. As pumps are generally 25 to 50 MGD in design capacity, and as operating ranges at runout are 30 or 60 to 70 MGD, the addition of a new pump at a station results in a large change in pressure and flow. The islands cluster above the pump design operating flow point and, as such, the apparent cost payback is minimum.

In this case, the cost savings potential curve has an added dimension. In addition to demonstrating energy savings along the system resistance curve the savings table also quantify potential water flow savings along the curve. These water flow savings translate into reduced filtration and treatment costs.

The first "M" in SIM²PLE defines the need to establish an assessment methodology. In the process of developing the assessment methodology it is critical to consider not only how a system does operate, but as importantly what is the ASD enhanced system operation potential. Unless systems operating potential and practice are carefully reviewed, it may be possible to bypass an excellent ASD application candidate.

"M" Considering Market Availability

It is not always the obvious ASD hardware option that affords the "best" value. In today's market there are generally a number of options available for any given application. Each option has relative merits and drawbacks. Different manufacturers have different philosophies and different reasons for choosing a given product selection. The important thing to consider when reviewing market availability is that...

"Different Equals Different,
Different Does Not Equal Wrong."

The case offered by the 68th Street retrofit is a classic example of an application with many options.

The motors at 68th Street are synchronous type. The first thought would be to apply a load commutated inverter (LCI). As an LCI drive utilizes the motor counter EMF to commutate the converter SCRs, LCI inverters tend to be simple in design and offer fairly high efficiency.

The motors are 1.0 power factor and probably relatively high reactance design. They also have brush type excitation. Conventional LCI motor requirements call for 0.85 to 0.90 leading power factor and a motor reactance of 15% or less.

The motors are 1500 HP, 2300 volt. A first thought would be to apply a 6 pulse 2300 volt inverter. 1500 HP is well within the range of capability of a small 6 pulse 2300 volt bridge and 6 pulse inverters are generally cost effective. The motors are, however, 26 to 40 years old. The motors were not designed for harmonic or common mode voltage impact. A 6 pulse inverter tends to produce an output with relatively high harmonic contribution.

The ASD vendors have expressed confidence that the motors can be applied to LCI or modified LCI type drives. Different manufacturers have recommended different application solutions to deal with the harmonic contribution impact. The motors are conservatively rated and direct application of an LCI drive may even be practical.

There are, however, other application options. Some options include applying a 12 pulse single power device type bridge configuration with input and output transformers. The purpose would be to reduce harmonic impact and eliminate the need to series power devices to meet the motor rated voltage requirement. Another option would be to consider the motor as an induction type design and utilize an induction motor class drive. In this case the need to modify or de-rate the motor to meet LCI requirements is minimized.

The eventual application of ASDs across the overall water system introduces another dimension in the review process. On an overall systems basis, issues of parts commonality, spares, maintenance and training become important considerations.

As the goal of a SIM²PLE action plan is to enhance applications acceptance, it is important to collect information and provide specification flexibility to allow the ASD vendor to support that goal. The second "M" in a SIM²PLE action plan, therefore, plays an important role in insuring the long term success of the ASD application.

"P" Address The People Factor

Forget technical issues here. The "P" in SIM²PLE could be the most important element in the action plan. Recognize first and foremost that...

"People do things for their own reasons."

Unless the action plan addresses the needs and values of each party participating in the program; the technical merits of an ASD application are mute. If the goal is to improve ASD application acceptance, the first responsibility is to attempt to understand the needs and values of each project participant, individually and collectively. A primary reason for the continued progress on the City of Chicago Project is that each project participant can see the project implementation as a "win" situation.

"L" Leverage the Benefits

The "win" factors in the Chicago Project become increasingly apparent when the "L" in SIM²PLE is reviewed. "L" stands for leverage. Leverage can mean different things to different projects. In the case of Chicago leverage has a special dimension. To consider leverage at work it is convenient to again consider the Chicago Project as two separate tasks.

From a technology standpoint, a 68th Street Project goal was to establish the applicability of an ASD to the existing motors. In process, the project supported the development of a methodology to review and collect information to allow for the retrofit of the other electric motor driven pumps. The project also provided a structure for establishing and quantifying the ASD Retrofit benefits at other units. In addition, the project provided a forum for ASD Vendors to present hardware alternatives, to demonstrate capabilities and develop understandings.

To Chicago, 68th Street was an opportunity to review and become comfortable with a new technology. To the utility and engineer, 68th Street was an opportunity to develop relationships and build confidence. In all, 68th Street represented an opportunity to demonstrate, on a small scale, what a potential system-wide ASD retrofit implementation plan can offer to Chicago.

The overall system analysis presented an opportunity to consider issues that are not readily apparent from a station review. Some of these issues included the ability...

- To better control and therefore reliably reduce system pressure.
- To demonstrate a plan to enhance system reliability.
- To consider more cost effective power supply and pump drive alternatives at the steam stations.
- To explore the load growth potential available to the utility.
- To reduce filtration and purification costs by better controlling water utilization rates and reducing leakage losses.
- To preserve a natural resource, lake water, and therefore, make more water available from Chicago to existing and potentially new water system customers.
- To modernize the water system.

- o To stablize and perhaps reduce user water rates.
- o To provide equipment suppliers with a significant market opportunity.
- o To create new jobs for engineers, constructors, contractors and suppliers.

When the "L" is considered, it is clear that a SIM²PLE action plan can offer more than an opportunity to quantify conservation benefits for an ASD. As such "L" becomes an integral element in a SIM²PLE action plan to improve ASD applications acceptance.

"E" Educate the User

The action plan is complete when the "E" is added. "E" serves to identify the need to "e"ducate the user and to provide the user with an understanding of the SIM²PLE plan. "E" provides the user a working knowledge of the value available from the ASD application.

CONCLUSION

Seven letters provide seven keys to improved ASD applications acceptance. Seven letters help focus the needs for and value of an ASD application. SIM²PLE...

"S" Take a "S"ystems Perspective

"I" Define the "I"ntegration Issues

"M" Establish"M"ethodology to describe the benefits

"M" Consider the "M"arket alternatives

"P" Address the "P"eople Factor

"L" "L"everage the benefits

"E" "E"ducate the user

These seven principles are a framework for SIM²PLE actions. From the smallest to the largest product, whether it is a single custom or a high volume institutional application, the basic logic remains the same. If the goal is to improve ASD applications acceptance, consider a SIM²PLE action plan.

SIM²PLE is a registered service mark of Applications, Sales and Marketing, Inc.

THE EPRI/PEAC POWER QUALITY PROGRAM

Earle Wright, Power Quality Program Manager
Power Electronics Applications Center
Knoxville, Tennessee

Sensitive electronic equipment is pervading our lives, from our homes to commercial businesses, industry, government, and utilities. This feat of science and engineering carries with it both the well recognized benefits, and some not so well recognized problems. The benefits include being able to perform a host of feats never before imagined through a computer driven environment that generates a seemingly endless flow of improvements and advances in the way we live. The bad news is that we have created a vast array of electric loads that are highly sensitive to the quality of the electricity being supplied, unlike the industrial loads that brought this country into prominence in the first half of this century. The microelectronics revolution that gave us computers and other solid-state systems has also given us a new challenge--power quality.

From the customer's point of view, the most urgent issues related to the quality of power are how to prevent the loss of valuable computer data and the expense of shutting down process control or manufacturing lines because of power disturbances. The reason why today's complaints about the quality of power cannot be handled so simply is that they seem to reflect both a multitude of different causes and a variety of specific sensitivities in the customer equipment most affected.

Recognizing the challenges imposed by the need for improved power quality, the Electric Power Research Institute (EPRI) and the Power Electronics Applications Center (PEAC) have established a power quality program to help quantify the costs and benefits associated with the power quality issue through laboratory research and field measurement and to effect power quality solutions through education and assistance in the development of nationally-recognized guidelines and recommended practices.

Program Activities

Power Quality issues are complex and involve utility supply and end-use loads as well as perceptions of needs and obligations. The power quality program has been designed to accomplish the following objectives:

* determine the effects of power disturbances on power electronics systems and related technologies;

* assess the effects of present and future power electronics systems on the quality of power;

* develop and implement a power quality training program to teach detection, analysis, and mitigation of power quality problems;

* provide facilities for undergraduate training and graduate-level research in power quality issues and problems;

* assess the costs of poor power quality as manifested in lost productivity and shortened equipment lifetimes; and

* assist in the development of power quality guidelines and recommended practices that may be beneficial to traditional standards-making organizations.

Researching Power Quality Problems

The need to develop a quantitative understanding of the impact of disturbances on electronic equipment and the effect electronic equipment may have on utility-supplied power provides a major focus for PEAC in developing a power quality laboratory at its facilities in Knoxville, Tennessee. The laboratory contains advanced data acquisition and analysis equipment that is intended to shed new light on power quality issues and provide the information that will ultimately lead to the recommended practices of the future.

The power quality program will establish sensitivity thresholds for various classes of commercially available and prototype power electronics equipment through extensive laboratory testing. One arrangement of the laboratory equipment will allow the operator to assess the susceptibility of a system under test to a series of voltage disturbances. Using this arrangement the line and load parameters of interest (usually voltage and current) are sampled through the proper signal conditioning and interface equipment. The conditioned signals are then digitized at high speed and the resulting digital data are bused to hard disk storage where they may be recalled for analysis and hard copy output.

System control via the IEEE-488 bus is provided to the disturbance simulation equipment, the line monitoring equipment, the load monitoring equipment, and in some cases the load. Analysis capability is effected through several software packages and includes Fast Fourier analysis.

In this test, a low-amplitude, short-duration voltage disturbance is applied to the system. During the test, high-speed data acquisition equipment automatically records the results. In subsequent test runs, the amplitude and duration of the voltage disturbance is increased until performance degradation occurs. By repeating this test for a variety of systems from various manufacturers, it will be possible to construct an amplitude-duration sensitivity figure of merit for each major equipment class. A variety of equipment will be tested including adjustable speed drives, uninterruptible power supplies, active power conditioning systems, computers, home appliances, and office and industrial equipment.

As a complement to the disturbance sensitivity work, systems will also be tested for their impacts on utility-supplied power. Many modern electronics systems do not provide a linear load. Rather, they operate by drawing current in pulses. As a result, they inject harmonic currents back into the utility power system creating harmonic voltages, another type of power disturbance. The data taken from these tests will be used for quantifying harmonic pollution and will also be available to allow equipment designers to modify their designs to reduce the types of disturbances generated. To quantify further system interactions, tests will be conducted in which harmonic polluters will be operated in parallel with sensitive equipment.

While controlled laboratory testing is the best way to achieve a quantitative, reproducible data set, it is not practical or cost-effective to test large industrial and utility size equipment in the laboratory. Thus, PEAC will conduct numerous field tests in cooperation with industry. The data collection and analysis equipment has been designed for portability. In some cases, field sensors and data acquisition equipment will be installed at the industrial site, and data will be transmitted via telephone lines for analysis in the laboratory.

Training Power Quality Engineers

Power quality issues are relatively new, and many of the approaches to disturbance detection, analysis, and mitigation are only now being developed. Therefore, the laboratory will support not only research but also training in an effort to disseminate knowledge through courses offered both on-site at PEAC and regionally throughout the United States.

The overall objective of the power quality training program is to train field service engineers, customer service representatives, and utility instructors in the techniques of conducting site surveys, power monitoring, and disturbance mitigation. Several courses, aimed at different audiences, are in development. The first course will provide hands-on training to utility field service personnel, whose jobs are to assist customers in identifying the causes of disturbances that may be affecting their equipment. As presently formulated, this course will

* identify and define terms used to describe the quality of power,

* provide instruction on the methods for monitoring sites and locating the sources of disturbances,

* explain the various techniques and equipment used to mitigate or correct power quality problems, and

* provide available information on suppliers of power quality monitoring and mitigation equipment.

The student who completes the first course will be able to assist customers in isolating the causes of equipment problems and arriving at solutions to those problems. This course is considered to be a prerequisite to other courses.

The second course is intended to educate utility training personnel so that they may teach the first course within their utility, thereby allowing the power quality program to reach more students. Both of these courses will be offered regionally to enable more students to attend.

The third course is offered at the PEAC'S Knoxville, Tennessee laboratory for the student seeking advanced power quality training. Hands-on training is emphasized, using the laboratory's instrumentation. The graduate of this advanced course should be an expert in handling power quality issues.

In addition to these training programs, the power quality program will provide facilities and support of undergraduate course work and graduate-level research in power quality in conjunction with the PEAC Chief Scientist, the Condra Chair of Excellence Professor in Power Electronics, and through a special collaborative arrangement with the University of Tennessee. As part of their education, students will assist in conducting many of the laboratory experiments mentioned above and will have the opportunity to conduct in-depth front-line research in quantifying the impacts of various power disturbances.

Quantifying the Cost of Poor Power Quality

A primary difficulty in attacking power quality problems is the present lack of adequate quantification of the costs associated with poor power quality. Poor power quality often manifests itself in ways that are subtle and difficult to quantify economically. The problems fall into two general categories: lost productivity and hardware damage.

Lost productivity is caused largely by errors introduced in office and industrial computer equipment. In the office environment, these errors may show up as random, garbled, or lost data that yield inaccurate results. In the industrial environment, the effect may be damaged machinery, damaged products, and/or lower yields, all of which increase production costs and decrease profits. Although some hardware damage is visibly obvious, such as damage caused to a computer by a momentary over-voltage, some is subtle and not easily recognized. Damage to a utility transformer or a refrigerator motor due to overheating that results in a burned-out coil after 8 years instead of perhaps 12 is much more difficult to trace to poor power quality.

A major goal of the power quality program is to begin documenting and quantifying these effects. This is a difficult but necessary task for improving industrial productivity and reducing maintenance costs. To meet the challenge, PEAC will take a dual approach.

In cooperation with industry and electric utilities, PEAC will set up a data base to record power quality effects and their related causes. As more and more data are collected and analyzed, it will be possible to develop a relationship between costs and disturbance types.

Also in cooperation with industry and electric utilities, PEAC will study long-term effects of transformer and capacitor heating as a function of harmonic current injection. Using this information, along with models of dielectric (insulation) aging rates as a function of temperature, it should be possible to make quantitative life-degradation estimates.

Information from the data base and laboratory experiments should make it possible for the first time to determine quantitatively the best long-term tradeoffs among possible power quality solutions, such as adding protective equipment, installing utility-side filters, and/or imposing more stringent standards.

Publishing Power Quality Information

After conducting laboratory research and collecting field data, PEAC will produce several publications about power quality in an effort to transfer information and technology advancements from the laboratory to the appropriate audiences. These publications will discuss power quality terms and definitions as well as sources of power disturbances, their propagation, impacts, and mitigation. Other publications will deal with power quality guidelines and recommended practices. These guidelines will incorporate new findings resulting from work in the laboratory, from field measurements, and from new products and methods that evolve during the course of the program.

Program Benefits

The electric utility, the customer, and the public will realize many benefits from the research conducted under the power quality program. Some of these benefits will be

* information that helps minimize the cost while maximizing the value of maintaining an adequate quality of power,

* trained utility personnel who are better able to help industrial customers make the correct decisions relating to power quality issues,

* future electronics engineers who are attuned to the importance of power quality issues,

* information useful for standards-making bodies in formulating guidelines and recommended practices that lead to the optimum economic solutions to power quality problems, and

* advanced equipment designs that produce fewer power quality problems and are less sensitive to power quality disturbances.

The coming decade will bring more advances in power electronics technology. PEAC through the power quality program will deliver valuable benefits to electric utilities and end-users. By promoting cooperation and providing technology transfer, PEAC will make available extensive information, which will enable consumers and utilities to arrive at better solutions to real-world power quality challenges, resulting in higher productivity for U.S. industry.

POWER QUALITY: END USER IMPACTS

J. CHARLES SMITH

McGRAW-EDISON POWER SYSTEMS

CANONSBURG, PA

1.0 INTRODUCTION

The increasing application of microprocessors and sensitive digital circuitry in residential, commercial, and industrial products has led to a growing awareness and concern over the quality of electrical power which is being supplied to the consumer. The increasing application of solid state switching devices has increased the concern because of their associated injection of harmonic currents into the power system. The problems and solutions are viewed from different perspectives by the three parties involved: the utility, the customer, and the equipment supplier (Figure 1.1) The power quality problem as discussed in this paper will deal with the continuity of service as well as concerns for transient and steady state aspects of waveshape distortion, as they impact the end user.

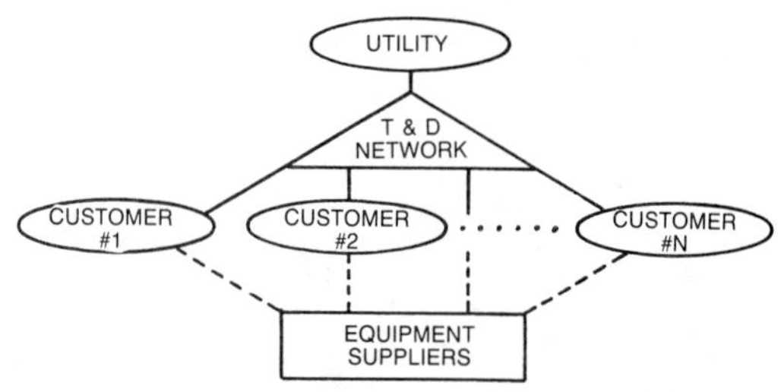

Figure 1.1
Utility - Customer - Supplier Interactions

Both the utility and the customer are responsible for generating disturbances through normal operation of production and protective equipment. Because the utility serves as the interconnection between all of the points in the system, including different customers, it is even possible for one customer to generate a disturbance which causes another customer's problem. In the remainder of this paper, we will examine the origins of the power quality problem in terms of the types and sources of disturbances, their impacts on customers, and associated remedies.

2.0 CATEGORIES OF POWER QUALITY PROBLEMS

There are an abundance of terms used to describe the various disturbances which are associated with operation of electrical systems. Some of these terms have standard definitions, while others do not. In order not to add any additional confusion to the situation, we will try to use terminology which has some general acceptance in the industry. A definition of terms is summarized in Figure 2.1.

Figure 2.1
Categories of Disturbances

Type of Disturbance	Range of Magnitudes	Duration
Fast Voltage Fluctuations (Transients, Impulses, Spikes, Noise, Notches, Glitches)	up to 6 pu	< 0.5 cycles
Short Duration Voltage Variations (Sags, Surges)	0 - 1.76 pu	0.5-30 cycles
Long Duration Voltage Variations (Overvoltages, Undervoltages, Brownout)	0.8 - 1.2 pu	> 30 cycles
Power Interruptions (Momentary, Temporary, Permanent)	0	milliseconds to hours
Harmonic Distortion	up to 1 pu	seconds to steady state

3.0 FAST VOLTAGE FLUCTUATIONS

Transient disturbances or fast voltage fluctuations can occur at customer locations due to events on the utility distribution system or to events within the customer premises. These disturbances are of very short duration and can be very high magnitude. Durations range from a fraction of a microsecond to several milliseconds. Figure 3.1 summarizes some of the important events which can cause transient disturbances affecting customer equipment. Some of these are described in more detail below.

Figure 3.1

Typical Sources of Transient Disturbances

Disturbances Initiated on the Distribution System	Disturbances Initiated on Customer Premises
Lightning Impulses	Lightning Impulses
Feeder Energizing/Reclosing	Capacitor Energizing
Transformer Energizing	Power Electronics Switching
Capacitor Energizing	Motor Interruption

3.1 Lightning Transients

Lightning surges can occur as a result of a direct lightning stroke to a conductor or as a result of a lightning stroke to a ground conductor or pole. The resulting surge on the distribution lines will be of relatively short duration (30-200 usec) with very fast rise times (1-10 usec). Due to the fast rise times, these surges can be coupled to secondary circuits by the capacitance ratio of step down transformers, rather than the turns ratio. In pu terms, the transient magnitudes on the secondary can be many times higher than the transient magnitude on the transformer primary. The transients must then be limited by surge protection equipment on the transformer secondary or within the customer premises.

3.2 Capacitor Energizing Transients

Capacitor energizing operations on the utility system are an important source of transient disturbances to customers because these energizing operations can occur quite frequently (one or more times per day). One situation of particular importance associated with capacitor energizing transients occurs when a customer installs his own capacitor banks for power factor correction. The customer capacitors on the secondary usually have much lower kVAr ratings than the utility capacitors on the primary.

The resonant circuit formed by these capacitors and the step down transformer reactance can cause significant magnification of the transient oscillations caused by capacitor switching on the utility primary. While the primary oscillation will have a transient magnitude less than 2.0 pu, the magnified transients on the secondary can have magnitudes of 3-4 pu with significant energy content.

Substation
13 kV
1200 kVAR
Feeder
Cap.
3 kVAR Cap.
for Dispersed
Generator

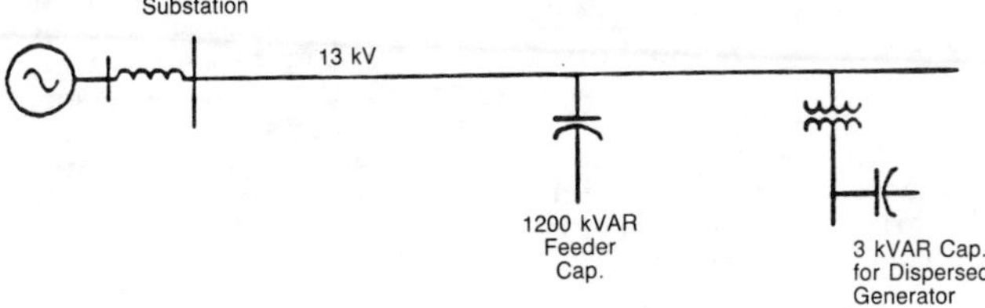

Figure 3.2

Example Circuit Illustrating Concern for Capacitor Switching Transient

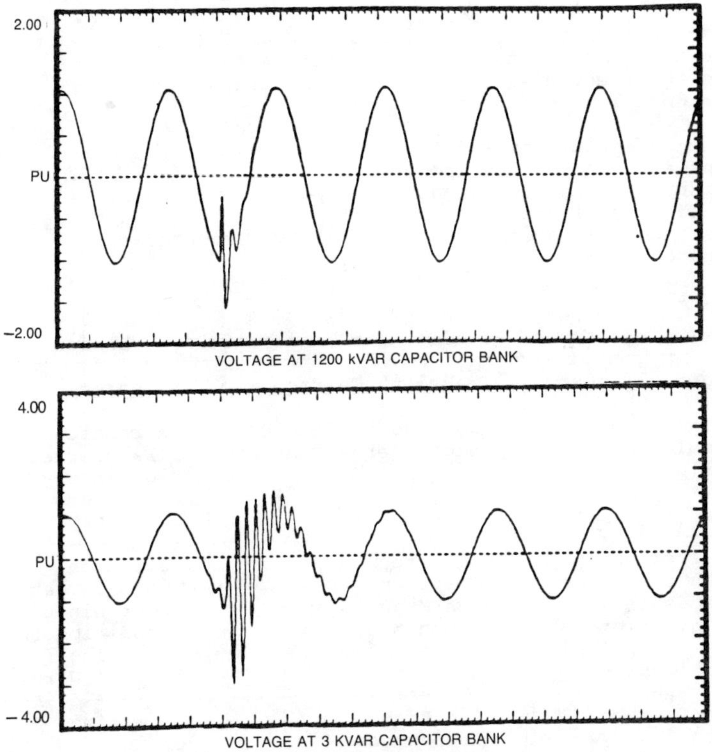

2.00
PU
−2.00
VOLTAGE AT 1200 kVAR CAPACITOR BANK
4.00
PU
− 4.00
VOLTAGE AT 3 KVAR CAPACITOR BANK

Figure 3.3

Capacitor Energizing Waveforms Illustrating Magnification Phenomena

3.3 Power Electronics Switching Operations

The use of power converters for motor speed controls, dc loads, power supplies, UPS systems, and other applications has increased the power ratings of these devices and the number of them on the system. Besides creating harmonic distortion by switching the ac current waveform, they also create high frequency transients (notches) whenever the current flow from one of the ac lines must be switched to another line. During this period (commutation), there is a short circuit on the system resulting in a notch in the voltage waveform. The notch characteristics are dependent on the magnitude of the current being commutated and the short circuit reactance of the ac supply to the converter.

3.4 Impacts of Transient Disturbances

Transient disturbances can cause a number of important problems with customer equipment. The important characteristics of transient disturbances are:

- the magnitude of the transient overvoltages
- the energy content of the transients
- the frequency components of the transients
- normal mode or common mode

These characteristics determine the potential impact of the transients and the equipment protection requirements. A summary of important impacts and possible remedies is provided in Figure 3.4, while Figure 3.5 and Figure 3.6 show some generally accepted power quality parameters for computer loads.

Figure 3.4
Impacts and Remedies for Transient Disturbances

Potential Impact	Transient Charact.	Remedies
Equipment Insulation Failure	High Magnitude and/or High Energy Content	Ferroresonant Transformer High Energy Varistors Surge Capacitors
Interference with Data Processing, Acquisition, and Control Applications	High Frequency Components High Magnitudes Common Mode and Normal Mode	Isolation Transformers Power Line Conditioners Grounding Neutral Wires
Interference with Communication Lines	High Frequency Components	Shielding Grounding Neutral Wires

Parameters*	Range or Maximum
1) Voltage regulation, steady state	+5, −10 to +10%, −15% (ANSI C84.1−1970 is +6, −13%
2) Voltage disturbances	
Momentary undervoltage	−25 to −30% for less than 0.5 s with −100% acceptable for 4 to 20 ms
Transient overvoltage	+150 to 200% for less than 0.2 ms
3) Voltage harmonic distortion †	3−5% (with linear load)
4) Noise	No standard
5) Frequency variation	60 Hz ± 0.5 Hz to ± 1 Hz
6) Frequency rate of change	1 Hz/s (slew rate)
7) 3ϕ, Phase voltage unbalance ‡	2.5 to 5%
8) 3ϕ Load unbalance §	5 to 20% maximum for any one phase
9) Power factor	0.8 to 0.9
10) Load demand	0.75 to 0.85 (of connected load)

*Parameters 1), 2), 5), and 6) depend on the power source, while parameters 3), 4), and 7) are the product of an interaction of source and load, and parameters 8), 9), and 10) depend on the computer load alone.

† Computed as the sum of all harmonic voltages added vectorially.

‡ Computed as follows:

$$\% \text{ phase voltage unbalance} = \frac{3(V_{max} - V_{min})}{V_a + V_b + V_c} \cdot 100$$

§ Computed as difference from average single-phase load.

Figure 3.5
ANSI/IEEE — Std 446-1987
Typical Range of Input Power Quality and Load Parameters of Major Computer Manufacturers

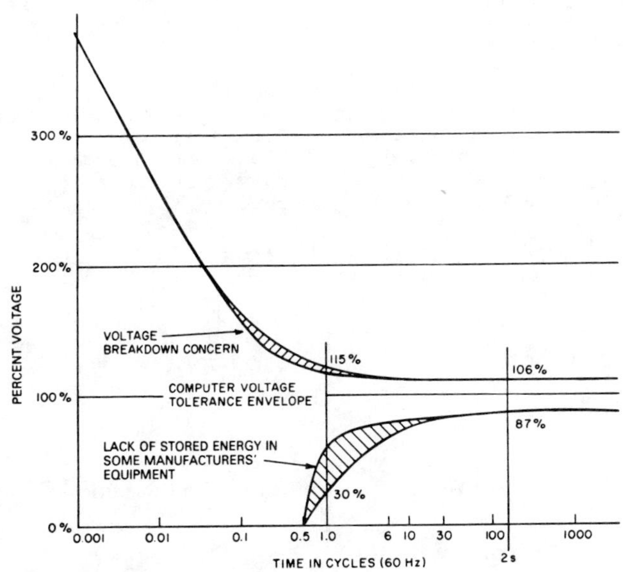

Figure 3.6
ANSI/IEEE — Std 446-1987
Typical Design Goals of Power-Conscious Computer Manufacturers

4.0 SHORT DURATION VOLTAGE VARIATIONS

Undervoltages or overvoltages which last from one half cycle to approximately 30 cycles are often referred to as sags or surges (although the term surge is also used to refer to fast transient voltages or currents). The associated voltages can range from 0% voltage during fault conditions to 173% voltage on ungrounded systems during a single line-to-ground fault.

4.1 Sources of Short Duration Voltage Variations

The most important cause of short duration disturbances to the fundamental frequency voltage magnitude is a fault condition on the utility distribution system. A system fault will generally last from 3 to 30 cycles (depending on the fault location, the fault current magnitude, and the protection equipment) before a switching device clears it. A voltage drop occurs on the faulted phase(s) during the period of the fault. For a single line-to-ground fault, a voltage increase may occur on the unfaulted phases. This voltage increase is a function of the system grounding (X0/X1 ratio); the voltage can be as high as 173% for an ungrounded system.

It is also possible to have a self-clearing fault which can last for as little as one half cycle. In this case, the fault clears itself before a switching operation occurs on the utility system.

Short duration overvoltages can also be associated with ferroresonance during fuse operations on transformers or dynamic overvoltages during transformer energizing operations. These conditions are less common but significant overvoltages lasting many cycles can be associated with them when they occur.

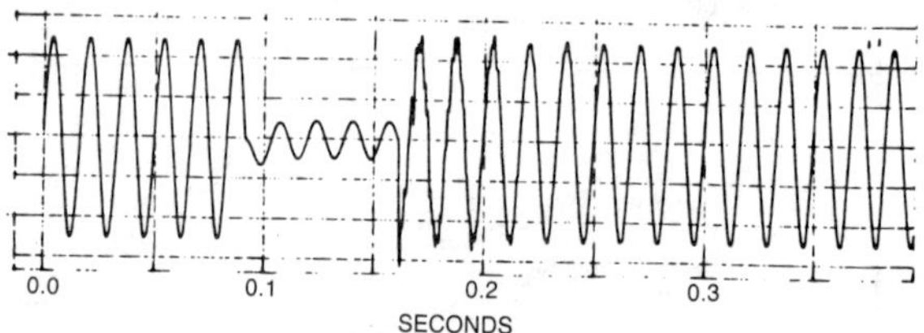

Figure 4.1
Faulted Phase Voltage During a Remote Fault Condition

4.2 Impacts of Short Duration Voltage Variations

Both undervoltage and overvoltage conditions can have important consequences for customer equipment. Undervoltages can result in increased currents and overheating of motors, lights dimming, and computers malfunctioning. Overvoltages can cause increased equipment stress which can result in misoperation or damage.

Solutions to the short duration voltage variation problem can take the form of devices added by the customer to protect his equipment and/or system design and equipment changes implemented by the utility to decrease the frequency of occurrence.

4.3 Correction of Voltage Variations at the Customer Site

A range of voltage regulation equipment is available to provide a constant voltage magnitude at critical loads during short duration variations in the supply voltage. A few of the important categories of these devices are described here.

Equipment Power Supplies. Improved power supplies can provide the capability for equipment to ride through short duration undervoltage conditions. Larger capacitors in the output circuit can increase the ride through time for loss of voltage from 1/4 cycle to approximately two cycles (longer for low power devices). For low power devices such as radios and clocks, a battery backup in the power supply can provide the capability to ride through much longer duration undervoltage conditions.

Voltage Regulators. Fast responding voltage regulators can typically control the output voltage to within +/- 2% when the input voltage varies within +/- 15%. Often the output voltage can be controlled to within 10% of nominal for input swings as large as 65%. The major classifications of voltage regulators and their characteristics are discussed in Section 8.

Line Conditioners. Very accurate voltage regulation can be provided by the linear amplifier type of line conditioners. Slightly less accurate regulation at a lower cost is provided by the ferroresonant type of conditioners.

Motor-Generator Sets. Motor-generator sets are generally employed to provide complete isolation between two systems or as frequency changers. They can also provide the capability to ride through complete loss of voltage for 0.3-0.5 seconds. Longer ride through capability is associated with less severe voltage reductions.

Uninterruptible Power Supplies (UPS). UPS systems are designed to provide uninterruptible power for much longer durations than the short duration disturbances being discussed here. With the battery backup capability, they can easily ride through short duration outages or undervoltages.

4.4 Solving Voltage Variation Problems on the Utility System

As discussed above, the most important cause of short duration disturbances is the occurrence of system faults. Therefore, anything the utility can do to minimize the number and duration of system faults will reduce the impact of these short duration disturbances. Techniques available include:

- Underground systems instead of overhead.
- Tree trimming policies, animal guards.
- Minimizing system ground impedance.
- Shielding conductors.
- Coordination practices and switching procedures.

The short duration variations and interruptions will occur on any electrical system. The need for improved voltage control is dependent on the sensitivity of the load equipment to the voltage variations, the frequency of occurence for the voltage variations, and the cost of improving the situation.

5.0 LONG DURATION VOLTAGE VARIATIONS

Voltage variations which last longer than 30 cycles (1/2 second) are classified as long duration for our purposes. These variations are generally in the range of -20% to +10% and are not the result of system faults. They are caused by load variations on the system and system switching operations. A few important specific causes are described below. The impacts of these voltage variations are the same as were discussed for short duration voltage variations.

5.1 Motor Starting

Large motors can cause significant voltage dips on the system when they are started, depending on the motor starting technique employed. A motor will typically from 6 to 10 times its full load current during starting. This current magnitude then decreases over a period ranging from 1 second to 1 minute (depending on the inertia of the motor and the load) until the motor reaches full speed. The resulting voltage dip during the motor starting period will depend on the ratio of the motor size to the system short circuit capacity where it is connected.

5.2 Switching System Loads and Capacitor Banks

Energizing a load on the system will result in a sustained voltage drop on the system until voltage regulation equipment or other devices compensate for the change. Similarly, deenergizing a load will result in a sustained overvoltage on the system. Shunt capacitor switching has the opposite effect - energizing a capacitor increases the system voltage, while deenergizing a capacitor decreases the system voltage.

If the load or capacitor bank is large enough relative to the system capacity, distribution system voltage regulators or transformer load tap changers will respond in 10's of seconds to bring the voltage back within allowable tolerances. In the longer term, system generators will respond to control the overall system voltage.

5.3 Voltage Flicker

Loads which can exhibit continuous, rapid variations in the load current magnitude can cause voltage variations referred to as flicker. Flicker normally refers to voltage variations which exhibit frequencies in the range of 1/2 to 30 Hz. Fluctuations which are in this frequency range can cause perceptible flicker of lighting for magnitude changes as small as 1%. Arc furnaces are the most important system load which can cause voltage flicker problems.

5.4 Intentional Voltage Reductions

Many utilities have voltage reduction procedures identified to help reduce load during severe peak load conditions. The system voltage may be intentionally reduced in steps from 3% to 8%, depending on the severity of the overload condition.

5.5 Solving Voltage Variation Problems

The same voltage regulation equipment described in the previous section for short duration voltage changes is also applicable for longer duration voltage variations. In particular, various types of tap changers, ferroresonant regulators, line power conditioners, motor-generator sets, and uninterruptible power supplies can be used to maintain a constant voltage at critical loads during long duration swings in the supply voltage.

If voltage flicker is a problem for a critical load, it may be necessary to provide a dedicated feed so that it is not on the same circuit with an arc furnace or other varying load. The utility can also control voltage changes using fast switching compensation, such as a static var system.

6.0 POWER INTERRUPTIONS

Power interruptions involve the complete loss of voltage to the load for at least 0.5 seconds. The interruptions can be classified as momentary interruptions (less than 2 seconds), temporary interruptions (2 seconds to 2 minutes), or outages (longer than 2 minutes).

Momentary and temporary power interruptions occur when a system fault is successfully cleared by an interrupting device and then the circuit is reenergized. Reclosing controls on substation breakers, reclosers, and sectionalizers accomplish this task. The duration of the interruption will depend on the fault location on the system and the settings of protection equipment used for interruption and reclosing.

Most temporary faults will result in total interruption periods of less than two seconds when an instantaneous reclose setting is used for the interrupting device. If the fault does not clear during the first interruption and several reclosing operations are allowed, the interruption can last for up to two minutes with several attempts at reenergizing within that period.

If the fault is not temporary in nature, the interruption can last for hours until a line crew repairs the problem or the circuit is reconfigured to supply power to affected loads.

6.1 Impacts of Power Interruptions

The complete loss of voltage to a load obviously has very important consequences. The need for uninterruptible supply from UPS systems or backup generators depends on the critical nature of the load. Some important loads which could justify either backup generators or at least UPS systems include critical industrial processes, computer installations, and medical facilities.

6.2 Solutions to the Interruption Problem

Backup supplies for outage contingencies take the form of UPS systems or backup generators. UPS systems are typically capable of providing uninterrupted supply for at least 15-30 minutes. This covers all momentary and temporary interruptions and provides sufficient time for an orderly shut down in the event of a permanent outage. A UPS system can be used in conjunction with a switching scheme involving multiple feeds from the utility to provide an even higher level of reliability.

If backup power is needed beyond the capability of a UPS system and multiple feeds are not realistic or adequate, then backup generators are required. Diesel generators are typically used in these applications.

The utility determines the duration of interruptions through protective device coordination practices on the circuits supplying the customers. Fuses, sectionalizers, reclosers, and relays are coordinated so that the minimum number of customers experience an outage when there is a permanent fault, and so that virtually all temporary faults are cleared without the occurence of an outage.

7.0 HARMONIC DISTORTION

Harmonic distortion, like transient surges, can come from either the utility supply or from the customer's own equipment. Harmonics are generated by devices and loads on the system that have nonlinear voltage/current characteristics. These devices fall into three major categories:

1. Power Electronics. This category of harmonic sources is one of the main reasons for the increasing concern for harmonic distortion on the power system. The applications for power electronic type devices (rectifiers, variable speed drives, UPS systems, cycloconverters, inverters, etc.) are continually growing. Besides being the most important sources of harmonics on the system, this equipment can also be the most sensitive to harmonic distortion in the voltage waveform.

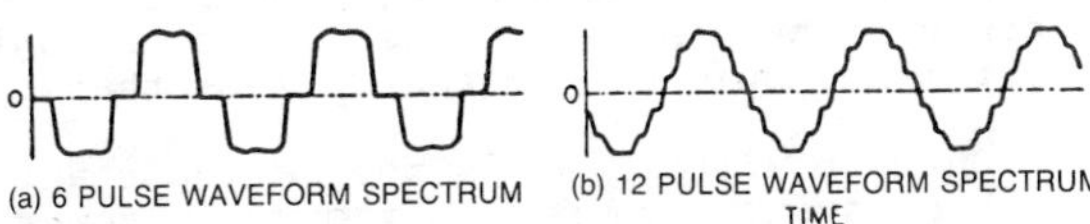

Figure 7.1 Converter Current Waveforms

2. Ferromagnetic Devices. Transformers are the most important devices in this category. Transformers generate harmonics as a result of the nonlinear magnetizing characteristic. The level of harmonic generation increases substantially as the applied voltage increases above the transformer rating.

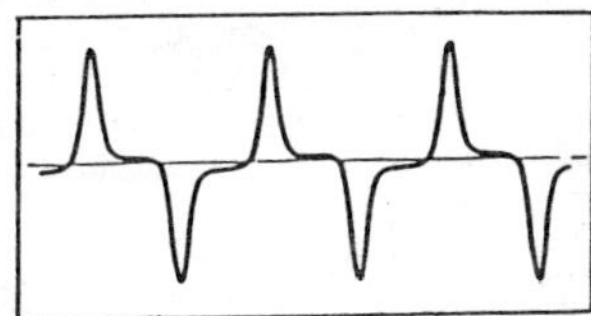

Figure 7.2 Typical Transformer Magnetizing Current

3. Arcing Devices. Arcing devices generate harmonics due to the nonlinear characteristics of the arc itself. Arc furnaces are large harmonic sources in this category. However, fluorescent lighting has basically the same characteristic and is much more prevalent as a power system load.

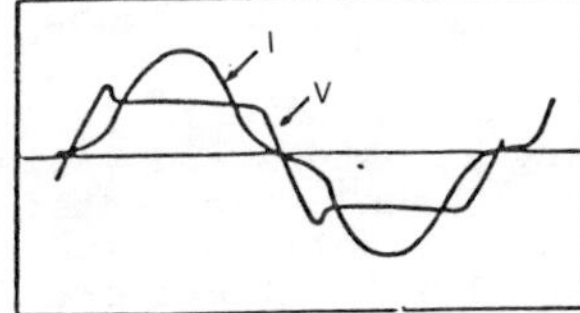

Figure 7.3 Arc Furnace Voltage and Current

The seriousness of the harmonic problem is determined by the response of the utility system to the harmonics injected, which is dominated by capacitor banks.

7.2 Effects of Harmonic Distortion

Concerns for harmonic distortion can be divided into concerns associated with voltage distortion and concerns associated with current distortion.

The one thing that all the loads on a power system have in common is the voltage. When the voltage is distorted, everyone is affected. Equipment which can be adversely affected by significant levels of voltage distortion include electronic controls, capacitors, and motors. Electronic controls are potentially the most sensitive since many controls rely on a clean sinusoidal waveform for synchronization or control purposes. Capacitor banks are affected by the peak of the voltage waveform - insulation can be degraded if the harmonic distortion is excessive. Motors and transformers experience increased heating in the presence of harmonics. Overall, the harmonic voltage distortion should be limited to less than approximately 5%.

Current distortion is not as important in terms of its impact on system loads. In fact, the power system generally has the capability to absorb significant amounts of harmonic current without creating unacceptable voltage distortion levels. However, current harmonics themselves are a concern for communication interference and because they result in increased losses in the lines and transformers on the system. In some cases, current harmonics can also result in improper relay response. There is also a concern for metering accuracy in the presence of harmonics. Watthour meters accurately register the direction of power flow at harmonic frequencies but they have a magnitude error which increases with frequency. The response of demand meters and VAr meters is even less accurate in the presence of harmonics.

8.0 PROTECTIVE AND CONDITIONING EQUIPMENT

There are a wide variety of devices available to help protect sensitive loads from disturbances and interruptions on the power system. Selecting the proper load protection equipment is not a simple task because the cost of the equipment must be weighed against its benefits and a variety of the available approaches overlap to some degree in their capabilities. The various types of equipment available to protect sensitive loads are described briefly in the following sections.

8.1 Arresters and Varistors

Secondary arresters and varistors are used to limit the magnitude of voltage transients. Gap type secondary arresters will typically operate at relatively high voltages (approximately 1 kv). Therefore, all of the equipment being protected must be able to withstand transient surges of this magnitude. The advantage of the gap type arresters (especially expulsion arresters) is that they can withstand higher energy duties than most varistors and, therefore, will not fail for most transients which can occur on the secondary.

Varistors can be obtained with much lower protective levels (on the order of 2.0 pu based on the normal peak voltage). However, high magnitude transients associated with lightning surges or capacitor switching can easily exceed the energy capability (20-300 joules) of these devices. Once the varistors fail due to a high magnitude surge, there is no overvoltage protection left for the equipment being protected. However, high energy varistors are now available for industrial applications where lower transient protective levels are required.

8.2 Isolation Transformers

Isolation transformers are used to attenuate the passage of noise and transients from the primary winding to the secondary winding. The most important function is the reduction of common mode noise. This is accomplished by the fact that the common mode noise does not result in a differential voltage input to the transformer primary and, therefore, does not get transformed to the secondary. However, stray capacitances in the transformer must also be taken into account and a Faraday shield between the primary and secondary windings is often required to provide sufficient common mode noise rejection (80 dB or more).

8.3 Line Voltage Regulators

Line voltage regulators are used to maintain a constant output voltage to the load in the presence of variations in the the supply voltage. There are many different ways of accomplishing this and there are also many variations within the basic techniques. We will only give an overview of the basic techniques which are used for voltage regulation - see Figure 8.1.

Figure 8.1
Types of Voltage Regulators

Type of Regulator	Typical Response Time
Motor Actuated	Seconds
Saturable Reactor	5-10 cycles
Ferroresonant	1.5 cycles
Electronic Tap Switching	0.5 cycles

8.4 Power Line Conditioners

Power line conditioners combine the functions of the isolation transformer and the voltage regulator, providing both regulation and noise rejection. The most accurate and sophisticated type of line conditioner uses a complex linear amplifier in a feedback arrangement to cancel out the effects of voltage variations and normal mode noise. The power transformer supplying the line conditioner is used as the isolation transformer to provide common mode noise rejection.

A lower cost alternative type of line conditioner uses the ferroresonant principle. It combines the ferroresonant regulator with the characteristics of a good isolation transformer. Normal mode noise is reduced by the saturated operation of the transformer (on the order of 60 dB reduction) and common mode noise is reduced by adding appropriate shielding (60-120 dB reduction can be attained depending on design).

8.5 Motor-Generator Sets

Motor-generator sets consist of a motor driving an ac generator or alternator so that the load is completely isolated from the power line. They have been widely used to supply 415 Hz power for many mainframe computer applications. However, there is currently a substantial shift to solid state inverters for this purpose. Motor-generator sets shield the load from transients and from voltage variations at least up to +/- 20%. The output voltage can be maintained within +/- 1% for these conditions. The M-G set can also bridge short term sags and interruptions due to the rotational momemtum of the rotating elements. By adding an inertial flywheel to the set, the allowable duration of an interruption to the supply voltage can be increased to seconds.

8.6 Uninterruptible Power Supplies (UPS)

If continuous operation in the presence of interruptions lasting longer than approximately 1/2 second is required, then a UPS system should be used. The basic UPS system consists of a rectifier/battery charger which takes ac line power and rectifies it to dc, an inverter which takes the dc voltage and converts it back to ac for the load, and a battery bank which takes the place of the ac supply in the event of an interruption or voltage sag. A properly designed UPS system will protect a load from virtually all types of power line disturbances. When an interruption occurs, the size of the battery bank determines the length of time the inverter will supply normal power to the load. In a typical application, this time is on the order of 15-20 minutes. An alarm is used to initiate an orderly shut down within five minutes of the allowable duration. If more extended protection is required, a backup generator would typically be used.

9.0 SUMMARY

The topic of power quality obviously encompasses a wide range of engineering disciplines and also has significant political implications. Assuring adequate power quality for customer loads requires cooperation and understanding between the utility, the customers, and equipment suppliers. Some of the potential problems can be solved through the distribution system design process. Others must be solved at the customer location with appropriate protective equipment or through the design of the load equipment itself. In either case, an understanding of the potential problems, their causes, and the possible solutions is required of all the parties involved.

10.0 BIBLIOGRAPHY

1. "Quality of Power in the Electronics Age", EPRI Journal, November, 1985.

2. Dugan, R. C., and McGranaghan, M. F., "Electric Power System Harmonics Design Guide". McGraw-Edison Power Systems, 87011, September, 1987.

3. Gulachenski, E. M.,and Symanski, D. P., "Distribution Circuit Power Quality Considerations For Supply to Large Digital Computer Loads". IEEE Transactions on Power Apparatus and Systems, Vol. PAS-100, No. 12, December, 1981.

4. Skabinski, G., "Uninterruptable Power Supplies and Power Conditioning to Protect Computers". Presented to EEI T&D Committee, New Orleans, LA, January, 1987.

5. Key, Thomas S., "Diagnosing Power Quality Related Computer Problems". IEEE Transactions on Industrial Applications, IA-15, No. 4, July/August, 1979.

6. Martzloff, Francois D.,and Gruz, Thomas M., "Power Quality Site Surveys: Facts, Fiction, and Fallacies." IEEE Industrial and Commercial Power Systems Conference, Nashville, TN, May, 1987.

7. Clemmensen, Jane M., and Ferraro, Ralph J., "The Emerging Problem of Electric Power Quality". Public Utilities Fortnightly, November 28, 1985.

8. Clemmensen, J. M., and Samotyj, M. J., "Electric Utility Options In Power Quality Assurance". Public Utilities Fortnightly, June 11, 1987.

9. "Emergency and Standby Power Systems". ANSI/IEEE Standard 446-1987.

10 "IEEE Guide for Harmonic Control and Reactive Compensation of Static Power Circuits". IEEE Standard 519-1981.

11. "IEEE Guide for Surge Voltages in Low-Voltage AC Power Circuits". ANSI/IEEE C62.41-1980.

12. "Guideline on Electrical Power for ADP Installations". FIPS Publication 94, National Bureau of Standards, September, 1983.

ENERGY TECHNOLOGY DEVELOPMENTS

UPDATE '88

UPDATE ON THE CURRENT REGULATORY ENVIRONMENT FOR NATURAL GAS TRANSPORTATION

by Robert R. Nordhaus, Partner
Van Ness, Feldman, Sutcliffe & Curtis
Washington, D.C.

I. Summary of Federal Natural Gas Regulation

This outline provides an overview of federal and state regulation of natural gas sales and transportation, describes recent regulatory intitiatives of the Federal Energy Regulatory Commission ("FERC" or "Commission"), and analyzes the options available to end-users when purchasing natural gas.

A. Regulatory framework

The gas supply options available to an end-user of natural gas are largely determined by federal and state regulatory constraints applicable to sellers and transporters of natural gas. The transportation and sale of natural gas may be regulated at the federal level, the state level, or both. This discussion will cover the federal statutory provisions governing transportation and sale of natural gas, an explanation of what gas is subject to federal regulation and what gas is deregulated, and a brief discussion of the division of labor between federal and state regulation.

---

*/ Benjamin L. Israel, Associate, Van Ness, Feldman, Sutcliffe & Curtis, assisted in the preparation of these materials.

1. Natural Gas Act (1938)

The Natural Gas Act ("NGA") provides the Commission with jurisdiction over the sale for resale and the transportation of natural gas in interstate commerce. "Sale for resale" refers to the wholesale sale of natural gas. A direct sale of natural gas to its ultimate consumer is not subject to the Commission's NGA sales jurisdiction. Nonetheless, the transportation of such gas in interstate commerce remains subject to the Commission's NGA transportation jurisdiction.

The United States Supreme Court, in 1954, interpreted the NGA to require the Commission to regulate sales for resale in interstate commerce by producers as well as by pipelines. However, this FERC jurisdiction over producers has been drastically curtailed by the Natural Gas Policy Act of 1978 ("NGPA"), discussed below.

Local distribution of gas is specifically excluded from FERC jurisdiction under the NGA, as are so-called "Hinshaw pipelines." (A pipeline is a Hinshaw pipeline if it receives natural gas within a state for ultimate consumption within that state, and if its rates, services and facilities are regulated by a state commission.)

a. NGA Rate and certificate authority

Under the NGA, the FERC's principal regulatory powers are to regulate rates for jurisdictional transportation and sales services (NGA §§ 4 and 5) and to regulate commencement and abandonment of these services (NGA § 7).

1) Certification and abandonment requirements under NGA § 7

Section 7(c) of the NGA requires that a certificate of public convenience and necessity be issued by the Commission prior to: (1) any transportation or sale of natural gas subject to the jurisdiction of the Commission, (2) the construction or extension of any facilities for the transportation or sale of natural gas, or (3) the acquisition or operation of facilities for the transportation or sale of natural gas. In issuing a certificate, the Commission is required to find that the proposed service or facilities are permitted by the "public convenience and necessity." In making that finding, the Commission must consider a wide range of factors, including environmental and antitrust impacts, gas supply, markets, and public need. Under NGA § 7(c), the applicant must be able and willing to provide the service to be certificated. (However, under NGA § 7(a), unwilling interstate pipelines may be compelled to render sales service to local distribution companies.) In addition, pipelines and producers must obtain Commission abandonment authorization pursuant to NGA § 7(b) prior to terminating jurisdictional services, even when the underlying contract has expired or is otherwise no longer in effect.

2) Rate regulation under NGA §§ 4 and 5

Under NGA § 4 all rates for jurisdictional sales and transportation service must be filed with FERC, must be just and reasonable, and may not be unduly discriminatory or preferential. FERC may suspend any change in rates for up to 5 months, and may require rate increases to be collected subject to refund. NGA § 5 permits the Commission on its own motion or upon complaint to conduct a hearing to determine whether rates are unjust, unreasonable, unduly discriminatory or preferential, and to order a prospective change in any such rate.

2. Natural Gas Policy Act of 1978

The NGPA created a complicated regulatory scheme which provided for an initial expansion of federal pricing authority to all producer sales of natural gas, regardless of whether the gas was sold in interstate commerce or in intrastate commerce, and for gradual deregulation of most of such sales over the course of a decade. However, a significant percentage of producer sales remains subject to ceiling price regulation under the NGPA and to certificate and abandonment regulation under § 7 of the NGA. Ceiling prices vary for the gas remaining subject to regulation, but for most of that gas the ceiling price is well in excess of current market prices, and thus does not constrain the operation of the market. Nonetheless, NGA certification and abandonment requirements still apply and (absent FERC authorization) impede producers from selling this gas as they wish.

a. Deregulation of certain natural gas

Producer sales of deregulated gas are exempted from the Commission's NGA jurisdiction. This means that it is unnecessary for the producer to obtain a certificate under NGA § 7(c) in order to sell the gas in interstate commerce. Further, there is no need to seek abandonment authorization under NGA § 7(b) prior to terminating such producer sales. (Similar rules apply to natural gas marketers who are not pipelines or local distribution companies.) However, a subsequent sale by a pipeline or local distribution company of such gas for resale in interstate commerce is subject to the Commission's NGA jurisdiction, though a pipeline's or distributor's sale of such gas to an end-user will not be subject to NGA jurisdiction.)

b. Non-jurisdictional transportation under NGPA § 311

NGPA § 311(a) permits the Commision to authorize certain transportation of natural gas that, prior to enactment of the NGPA, would have required NGA § 7(c) certificate authorization. Under this section, the Commission may authorize interstate pipelines to transport natural gas "on behalf of" any intrastate pipeline or any local distribution company, and it may authorize intrastate pipelines to transport natural gas "on behalf of" any interstate pipeline or any local distribution company served by an interstate pipeline.

Under NGPA §§ 311(a)(1) and (2), the transportation arrangements must be performed "on behalf of" the appropriate entity. The Commission has said that any "nexus" between the transporter and the entity on whose behalf the transportation will be undertaken will suffice, including a showing that such entity has title to the gas at the time it is transported.

c. Blanket transportation authorization.

Under NGA § 7(c), the FERC ordinarily grants a certificate of public convenience and necessity to an individual pipeline, authorizing the pipeline to transport a specific amount of gas, for a specified term, to an identified customer, to be picked up and delivered at identified points. However, FERC can also provide a pipeline a "blanket" transportation certificate under NGA § 7(c), under which the pipeline is given considerable flexibility in providing transportation without FERC approval, so long as it complies with certain generally applicable conditions to providing transportation. The Commission can also give interstate and dntrastate pipelines blanket authorization (similar to a blanket certificate) under NGPA § 311(a), thereby permitting the pipeline to engage in interstate transportation without prior FERC approval.

3. Division of labor between federal and state regulation

State agencies have authority to regulate (1) retail (i.e., end-user) sales of natural gas, (2) transportation and sales by local distribution companies, and (3) transportation and wholesale sales by intrastate pipelines of gas produced and consumed in the same state.

B. FERC's attempt to make gas markets more competitive in the 1980s

With the enactment of the NGPA, interstate pipelines utilized the Act's pricing provisions to try to shore up lagging gas reserves. However, the recession of the early 1980's and the subsequent drop in oil prices reduced demand for natural gas. The net result of these converging factors was to convert the gas supply shortage in 1977-78 into a surplus which still exists today. Initially, high-priced gas contracts entered into under the NGPA with contractual take-or-pay provisions requiring pipelines to purchase minimum amounts of gas from producers, even when cheaper supplies were available elsewhere, maintained an artificially high price of natural gas in the interstate market. In response to this and in an effort to increase competition in the natural gas markets, the FERC embarked upon a number of regulatory initiatives.

FERC initially tried a piecemeal approach in which it set up a blanket certificate program under NGA § 7 for certain transportation of gas, special marketing programs which enabled new direct sales between producers and eligible end-users, and Order No. 380, which eliminated variable costs from pipelines' minimum bills. However, in May of 1985 both special marketing programs and Commission orders issued under the blanket certificate program were overturned by the United States Court of Appeals for the District of Columbia in Maryland Peoples Counsel v. FERC, 761 F.2d 768, and 761 F.2d 780 (1985). Only Order No. 380 survived.

1. Order No. 380

Order No. 380 made interstate pipelines' "minimum bills" inoperative to the extent that such provisions enabled pipelines to recover variable costs for gas not purchased by their customers. Order No. 380-C affirmed application of Order No. 380 to "minimum take" provisions.

a. Background

Minimum bills require a customer to pay the pipeline for a minimum volume of gas whether or not the gas is actually taken. Minimum take provisions require customers to physically take the specified amount of gas.

A pipeline's bill reflects both variable and fixed costs. Variable costs are recovered in a "commodity charge," which is levied upon each unit of gas sold, and includes the cost of providing service, and a portion of the pipeline's fixed costs. The remaining fixed costs are recovered in a pipeline's "demand charge," which is a fixed sum assessed in proportion to the customer's peak day demand or the customer's maximum contract volume.

FERC objected to permitting recovery of variable costs in minimum commodity bills because such recovery permitted the collection of costs not incurred, restrained competition, and insulated pipelines and producers from market risk, thereby inhibiting price decreases.

b. Provisions of Order No. 380

Order No. 380 did three things. First, it provided that "currently existing sales tariffs shall be inoperative to the extent they provide for recovery of purchased gas costs for gas not taken by the buyer." Second, it stipulated that "no tariffs filed in the future may provide for recovery of any variable costs associated with gas not taken by the buyer." Finally, it requires purchased gas costs to be stated separately on pipeline sales tariff sheets. (Order No. 380 was largely affirmed by the D.C. Circuit in Wisconsin Gas Co. v. FERC, 770 F.2d 1144 (1985).)

2. Order No. 436

a. Open access transportation

In Order No. 436, promulgated in October, 1985, the Commission established a streamlined transportation program that permitted interstate pipelines and intrastate pipelines to transport natural gas for others without receiving prior FERC approval if they were willing to comply with standard "open access" conditions prescribed in the Order. Any interstate pipeline wishing to enter into new "self-implementing" transportation arrangements outside the traditional NGA § 7 procedures, including transportation under NGPA § 311(a)(1), was to (1) provide non-discriminatory access to such transportation, (2) charge volumetric, downwardly flexible cost-of-service based rates for such service, and (3) give its customers the option to (i) reduce their firm sales contract entitlements, and/or (ii) convert such firm sales service to firm transportation service upon payment of a reservation fee. Intrastate piplines wishing to transport under NGPA § 311(a)(2) were to provide non-discriminatory access to such transportation but were not to be subject to the rate provisions or contract demand reduction and conversion requirements just decribed. Existing blanket transportation transactions were permitted to continue for various periods without complying with all of the open access conditons.

b. Take-or-pay

Order No. 436 reaffirmed of FERC's existing policy providing for case-by-case review of the prudency of payments made in settlement of producer take-or-pay claims. The FERC also issued a new policy that provided for expedited processing of producer abandonment and certificate requests in connection with take-or-pay controversies involving gas for which producers' sales are still subject to NGA jurisdiction.

c. Optional expedited certification

Order No. 436 also provided for a new optional procedure for obtaining expedited FERC certificate authorization and conditional pre-granted abandonment for new service.

d. Associated Gas Distributors v. FERC

The United States Court of Appeals for the District of Columbia reversed and remanded Order No. 436 in its opinion in Associated Gas Distributors v. FERC ("AGD"), issued June 23, 1987. While the court as a general matter upheld the substance of Order No. 436 and the procedures the Commission employed in adopting it, the court vacated the Order because FERC failed to meaningfully address pipeline take-or-pay problems and because it found the contract reduction option "irrational."

3. FERC reaction to the AGD decision: Order No. 500

Within two months of the D.C. Circuit's remand of Order No. 436 in the AGD case, the Commission issued Order No. 500 as an interim rule and statement of Commisison policy. (Order No. 500 is discussed below.) However, during the period between the remand of Order No. 436 and the effective date of Order No. 500, FERC granted blanket certificates which permitted a number of interstate pipelines to transport gas without complying in full with Order No. 436's conditions.

a. Order No. 500

Order No. 500 readopted the regulations originally adopted by Order No. 436 with the following modifications:

(i) An open access pipeline may condition access to transportation upon a producer's agreement to credit volumes transported against that pipeline's take-or-pay liability under certain purchase contracts. Under this crediting mechanism, an open access pipeline may refuse to transport gas unless the producer files an offer of credit with the pipeline under which the producer agrees to credit volumes transported against take-or-pay liability accrued by the pipeline in the period beginning the later of January 1, 1986, or the date upon which the pipeline became an open access transporter.

(ii) As an alternative to the standard method of passing through take-or-pay settlement costs as part of sales service commodity rates, open access pipelines may: (i) agree to absorb between 25 to 50 percent of take-or-pay costs, (ii) pass through a like percentage as a fixed charge to sales customers on the basis of cumulative purchase deficiencies, and (iii) recover the remainder of take-or-pay costs through volumetric commodity and throughput surcharges which may be billed to interruptable sales customers in addition to firm sales customers.

(iii) An open access pipeline may charge sales service customers a gas inventory fee designed to prevent the accrual of future take-or-pay liability.

(iv) The contract demand reduction option was removed from the Commission's regulations while it compiled a record to determine whether to reinstate this option in the final rule. The Commission reserved the right in individual cases to order a pipeline to reduce its contract demand levels.

b. Order No. 500-B

On October 16, 1987, FERC issued Order No. 500-B which: (1) granted a stay from November 1, 1987, to January 1, 1988, of take-or-pay crediting and contract demand conversion requirements of Order No. 500; (2) revised the take-or-pay crediting mechanism to require an open access pipeline to transport all tendered volumes if offers of credit are received from the owners of 85 percent or greater of the volumes to be transported; and (3) modified certain other aspects of the take-or-pay crediting mechanism by removing Order No. 500's requirement that a producer's offer to provide take-or-pay credits be in the form of an "irrevocable" affadavit, and by explaining that upon the receipt of such an offer a pipeline must transport gas tendered for shipment. The effect of the stay until January 1, 1988 is that transportation service initiated after September 15, 1987 is subject to Order No. 500 immediately, and transportation service initiated before September 15, 1987 is grandfathered through January 1, 1988, affording the industry enough time to arrange for transportation service in accordance with these orders.

c. Implications of Order Nos. 500 and 500-B

It is possible that the result of Order Nos. 500 and 500-B will be that producers will be unwilling to sell gas subject to the take-or-pay crediting mechaism if the gas is to be transported over an Order No. 436 pipeline. Prices for gas not subject to take-or-pay crediting are likely to increase.

Compounding the problems that could result from the take-or-pay crediting mechanism, the Commission has imposed a one-year limit on transaction-specific NGA § 7(c) transportation certificates it has granted to non-Order No. 436 pipelines. New transportation service over these pipelines therefore can only be obtained for one year, making it difficult for an end-user to contract for a long-term supply of gas if it must transport that gas on a non-Order 436 pipeline.

4. Order No. 451

Order No. 451, issued in June, 1986, established a new alternative maximum lawful price for producer sales of all vintages of "old" gas subject to NGPA §§ 104 and 106. (This is gas that was committed or dedicated to interstate commerce as of November, 1978.) The new ceiling price was equal to the highest price applicable to NGPA § 104 gas -- currently about $2.69 per MMBtu. This ceiling price is about 60% above current natural gas spot prices and, as a result, prices for this gas are market constrained rather than being constrained by regulation. Order No. 451 also contained a good faith negotiation procedure which was designed to ensure that Order No. 451 would not cause gas to be repriced above market levels.

5. Producer abandonment policy

The determination of the "public interst" for purposes of granting abandonment of producer sales pursuant to NGA § 7(b) has undergone considerable change in recent years as the Commission has sought to reconcile jurisdictional service obligations with the operation of free market forces in the natural gas industry. Traditionally, the Commission applied a comparative needs test, which contained a presumption against abandonment, by weighing the needs of the servicing pipeline and its customers against those of the alternative pipeline and its customers.

In recent years, the Commission in a series of rulemakings and orders has tried to liberlize its producer abandonment policy applicable to producer sales of regulated natural gas. It has attempted to redefine the "public interest" standard by assessing the beneficial effects on the market overall (such a increasing competition and lowering prices), and balancing those benefits against any adverse effect to the purchaser (and its customers) to whom the gas was presently dedicated. The Commission's objectives in liberalizing abandonment were to: (1) allow purchasers to decrease gas costs by displacing high-cost gas; (2) encourage producers to reduce gas prices to avoid being shut-in; (3) permit pipelines to buy increased volumes of low-cost gas from producers; and (4) provide producers and pipelines with incentives to renegotiate take-or-pay clauses in problem contracts. The Commission's new policy in this area has met with mixed success in the courts. In 1987, the D.C. Circuit in Consolidated Edison Co. of N.Y. v. FERC, 823 F.2d 630, generally upheld the goals of Felmont, but (as in the AGD decision) reversed and remanded the order to the Commission for its failure to adequately address the take-or-pay problem.

II. Options Available to an End-User Purchasing Natural Gas

As a consequence of changes in FERC regulatory policy, end-users of natural gas now have greater commercial latitude in structuring their own gas acquisition arrangements. In traditional gas supply arrangements, an end-user paid a price for gas delivered to its facility and relied on others to purchase, transport and deliver the gas, and guarantee against interruption of service. In contrast, in a direct purchase arrangement or any other type of arrangement short of purchasing from a local distribution company ("LDC"), the end-user is responsible for putting together parts or all of its own supply chain, and is responsible for protecting itself in the event that one of the links of the chain fails. An analysis of the regulatory considerations in assembling a complete natural gas supply chain is provided below.

A. Gas supply options

1. Direct purchase from producers

End-users can purchase their gas supply directly from natural gas producers. Producer sales of deregulated gas are not subject to the regulatory constraints of NGA §§ 4, 5 and 7. Nonetheless, the transportation of deregulated gas in interstate commerce is not exempt from federal regulation, and requires FERC authorization under NGA § 7(c) or NGPA § 311. Order No. 436 provides blanket authorization for such transportation by certain pipelines.

Producer sales of gas which was not deregulated under the NGPA are subject to a maximum lawful price at which it may be sold. The sale of regulated gas also remains subject to NGA § 7(c) certification, and once certificated that sale may not be terminated without abandonment authorization under NGA § 7(b). FERC has issued blanket sales certificates which permit many producers to commence and terminate sales without prior regulatory approval.

2. Use of brokers

A natural gas broker merely brings together willing sellers and buyers and charges a fee or commission for arranging the deal. Generally, brokers are not subject to regulation, but the underlying sale and transportation arrangements may be subject to the same regulatory constraints that would apply if a broker were not used.

3. Direct purchase from a marketer

A natural gas marketer actually purchases and takes title to natural gas and is a principle in the purchase. The marketer is a "middleman" that matches packages of gas acquired from producers with the needs of LDCs and end-users. For the most part, marketer sales are subject to the same regulatory constraints as apply to producer sales.

4. Purchase from pipeline

Another option is for an end-user to purchaser its natural gas supply from a pipeline. As in a direct producer sale, a pipeline sale of deregulated gas is not subject to federal rate regulation, but the transportation by the pipeline is subject to FERC authorization under NGA § 7(c), NGPA § 311, or Order No. 436. In addition, authorization may be required for any construction or modification of pipeline facilities.

5. Problems in making direct long-term purchases

In addition to market risks of long-term supply arrangements, there are regulatory uncertainties which must be considered prior to making a long-term purchase agreement. The ground rules of regulated sales may change and long term transportation authorization may be unavailable or be withdrawn. Without reasonable assurance of transportation, an end-user could be liable for a gas supply which it cannot transport.

B. Pipeline transportation

An end-user arranging for pipeline transportation must first identify the interstate or intrastate pipelines that are interconnected with the LDC that serves the end-user, or those pipelines which are in close proximity to the end-user's facilities. Once a pipeline or pipelines are identified, an end-user must ascertain whether the pipeline is an Order No. 436 transporter. If the pipeline is not an Order No. 436 transporter, the end-user must inquire as to whether the pipeline is willing to offer end-user transportation and to apply for a NGA § 7(c) certificater from the FERC. Finally, an end-user must determine the availability of pipeline capacity, either for firm or interruptible service, and the rate charged for such service.

1. Open access interstate pipelines

An open access pipeline under Order No. 436 must transport gas on behalf of any party wishing to ship gas if that party is willing to pay the pipeline's rate and comply with certain operating conditions, which under FERC's regulations may include natural gas quality standards and requirements with regard to the financial viability of the shipping party. Pipeline capacity is allocated on a "first come, first served" basis, with existing transportation authorized under NGA § 7 and LDCs converting sales service to transportation service being first in line.

Pipelines with excess capacity and pipelines in competitive markets have engaged in transportation rate discounting. Therefore, an end-user dealing with an open access pipeline should ascertain whether the pipeline's other transportation customers are receiving discount transportation and should request that it be granted any discount available. At the same time, some open access transporters have been authorized to charge balancing penalties for under- and over-deliveries by parties shipping gas. These penalties are designed to discourage parties shipping gas from abusing their transportation entitlement by using a pipeline for storage or as a bank from which to borrow gas. In addition, in some instances the FERC has considered authorizing a "use it or lose it" provision for interruptable transportation customers to prevent parties shipping gas from reserving capacity that they do not presently intend to use. An end user arranging for transportation should therefore be aware of these discount and penalty provisions and their potential impact on the economies of a direct purchase arrangement.

2. Non-open access interstate pipelines

If an interstate pipeline has not become an open access transporter under Order No. 436, each individual transportation transaction must be certificated by the FERC on a case-by-case basis pursuant to NGA § 7(c). The process of getting an individual transportation arrangement certificated takes at least several months, and may take several years if the pipeline's certificate application is contested. In addition, FERC generally does not authorize these arrangements for a period longer than one year. An end-user attempting to obtain transportation service from a non-open access pipeline should remember two things: (1) except for certain limited instances, the pipeline is under no legal obligation to offer transportation service; but (2) it may nonetheless be in the interest of the pipeline to offer such service. (The pipeline may be facing declining market sales or seasonally sensitive sales, or the pipeline may be transporting gas which it released as part of a limited-term abandonment program and therefore will receive take-or-pay credit for gas sold under such a program.)

3. Intrastate pipelines

An end-user may need to use an intrastate pipeline as a link in the chain of its interstate transportation arrangement. To transport gas on behalf of an end-user under such an arrangement, an intrastate pipeline must have or obtain Order No. 436 blanket transportation authorization pursuant to NGA § 311, or specific NGA § 7(c) prior approval from FERC.

C. LDC services

LDCs are the last link in the supply chain from the wellhead to the end-user's facility. The gas acquired in a direct purchase must go through the LDC's facilities or else go through alternate facilities constructed to transport the gas from the pipeline to the end-user. As noted at the begining of this outline, LDCs are regulated by state public service commissions ("PSCs") and therefore the policies governing industrial and commercial sales and transportation service vary from state to state. An end-user's first step in dealing with its LDC is to ascertain whether transportation service is offered and, if so, at what rate.

1. Transportation service

An end-user's purchase from an alternative supplier threatens a LDC with loss of sales revenues. Therefore, LDCs have developed several strategies to maintain their system capacity. First, for customers with alternate fuel capabilty, some LDCs have been authorized by their PSCs to offer flexible sales rates that may be discounted to equal the cost of the alternate fuel. Second and more significant to an end-user with its own supply, many LDCs now offer transportation service over their systems -- some PSCs have enacted mandatory carriage regulations requiring that transportation service be offered.

2. Transportation rates

LDCs generally prefer rates that leave them indifferent as to whether they provide sales or transportation service. Generally, such rates enable LDCs to recover the same margin without regard to which service they provide.

3. Backup sales service

To retain the option of returning to its LDC for backup sales service, an end-user may pay a standby or reservation fee to its LDC. Some LDCs provide such backup service as part of their transportation service. Also, some LDCs offer storage service that can be used to protect against supply interruption. For an end-user without alternate fuel capability or with directly purchased gas of low reliability, these options may be worth considering and must be factored into the cost of the direct purchase arrangement to get an accurate picture of the cost savings actually achieved.

D. The bypass option

If the LDC refuses to offer transportation service, or if the LDC's transportation rates are so high that they destroy the economies that would otherwise be realized by means of a direct purchase agreement, an end-user might consider a bypass arrangement. This involves the construction of a tap and meter on the pipeline that is transporting the end-user's gas and a pipeline segment extending from the tap to the end-user's facility. However, a bypass arrangement, even if physically feasible, may be costly and time-consuming.

1. Viability

The viability of a bypass arrangement depends on several variables, including the cost of constructing a pipeline and appurtenant facilties, and the fact that interstate pipelines, regardless of their open access availability, are under no legal obligation to construct the tap and meter necessary to interconnect with the pipeline segment originating at the end user's facility.

2. Federal and state regulation

Depending upon the type of FERC authorization pursuant to which a pipeline proposes to transport gas for an end-user, the construction and operation of the interconnecting facilities may require FERC authorization. A non-Order No. 436 pipeline may apply to the FERC for a certificate to construct and operate bypass facilities under NGA § 7(c), but if the pipeline's application is contested it could take years to obtain a final, non-appealable FERC order authorizing the bypass facilities. Even if prior FERC approval is not required to construct the facilities, the environmental compliance requirements of the Commission's regulations remain applicable, as do other federal and state environmental laws.

While a PSC does not have jurisdiction to regulate the activities of an interstate pipeline and may not reach beyond the borders of its state to regulate the sale of gas occurring in another state, a PSC may nonetheless have statutory jurisdiction over the intrastate transportation of natural gas. Some states have hinted that they would use such authority to regulate the construction and operation of bypass facilities. Even if a PSC does not prohibit bypass, it may authorize the LDC to charge an exit fee to end-users leaving its system and a standby fee for end-users that might wish to return to the system.

DEVELOPMENT OF A GAS FIRED VACUUM FURNACE FOR ION NITRIDING.

Klaus H. Hemsath, Indugas, Inc., Toledo, Ohio
Shery K. Panahe, Southern California Gas Company, Los Angeles
Stephen J. Sikirica, Gas Research Institute, Chicago

1. INTRODUCTION.

Vacuum furnaces for industrial heat treating processes are normally heated by electric energy. These furnaces are considered high performance, high technology equipment and are increasingly used to produce high quality heat treated parts. They are used for high temperature heat processing and they are finding increasing application in industries with critical performance specifications such as the aircraft industry. Gas heated vacuum furnaces previously were not available. By combining a novel gas heating system with a new vacuum door design it became possible to concept a gas fired vacuum furnace which combines the best performance features of existing electric vacuum furnaces with those of a gas heated system. The resulting combination of performance features of the new, gas fired vacuum furnace is unique. Temperature uniformity of the load is improved; heating and cooling rates are significantly accelerated; and overall cycle times are shortened. Test results confirm that the performance of the gas heated vacuum furnace exceeds those of comparable electrically heated furnaces.

Design limitations still exist in the availability of high temperature construction materials. As a result gas fired vacuum furnaces are currently limited as far as maximum component temperatures are concerned. Presently suitable materials limit the proposed vacuum furnace design to maximum process temperatures of 1750 degrees F. As advances in the development of metallic and ceramic materials continue, the range of viable process temperatures will be extended to higher values. Tests were carried out at a maximum process temperature of 1250 degrees F because the initial application of the new furnace design was targeted for ion nitriding processing which requires process temperatures between 750 and 1050 degrees F.

2. OBJECTIVE.

The objective of the equipment and process development program was the development of a high performance gas fired vacuum furnace for intermediate temperatures. The furnace specifications called for a design capable of at least duplicating and preferably improving the performance of similar, presently available vacuum heat treating equipment in terms of initial equipment costs, in energy and overall operating costs, and in heat processing performance.

It was decided to especially target improvement of three performance features: temperature uniformity of the load, heating rates, and cooling rates. These performance characteristics affect product quality, furnace productivity and heat treating costs.

Other desirable improvements were related to furnace appearance and furnace emissions. The gas fired vacuum furnace was to exhibit low surface temperatures and emit flue gases only at the furnace exhaust. Operational features were to be improved to facilitate easy control and permit utilization of the most sophisticated digital control equipment.

3. FURNACE CONCEPT.

Vacuum furnaces are heated almost exclusively by electric energy. Materials shortcomings and design problems have prevented the utilization of gas heating. By applying a novel convection heating concept natural gas can be used for the heating of vacuum furnaces.

The design concept is based on heating a thin walled vessel from the outside. This vacuum vessel must be strong enough to withstand the stresses imposed by atmospheric pressure on the hot vacuum vessel and must permit the heating of a load placed into the interior by conducting heat through the vessel wall. The selected design is based on heat resistant alloys such as 300 series or 800 series stainless steels. In the future it may become possible to utilize other materials like ceramics or refractories.

A heat treating furnace must repeatedly heat a substantial mass of metallic parts to the final heat treat temperature, hold this temperature for a predetermined time, and cool the entire mass down to a temperature at which surface oxidation will not occur when the part is exposed to an ambient atmosphere.

All furnace parts are, therefore, repeatedly subjected to thermal cycling, and thermal fatigue problems must be foremost on the designer's mind. From a process point of view, heating rates, cooling rates and ultimate temperature uniformity in the heated load are of utmost concern for the furnace designer.

Fast heating and cooling rates can increase productivity. Heat treating processes are either directed at achieving an equilibrium stage at a selected part temperature or are aimed at achieving a percentage transformation of a certain metallurgical modification by subjecting a part to a tightly specified time-at-temperature history. In this latter case transformation kinetics must be reliably duplicated. Repeatability of heat treatments can be rather difficult because transformation rates are very responsive to temperature level and accelerate at higher temperatures. Heat treating processes producing critical parts for e.g. aircraft are, therefore, trending toward tighter and tighter temperature specifications and related documentation to improve part quality and reliability.

Predictable and repeatable heat transfer from the hot combustion gases to the vacuum vessel and from the inside of the vacuum vessel to the load are of utmost importance for a high performance heat treat furnace. The proposed design must be under complete control of the furnace operator or the process control system during each process step.

Upon review of the side elevation of the furnace shown in figure 1, the vacuum vessel, or muffle, can be seen as the central furnace portion (part 6 in figure 1). The next

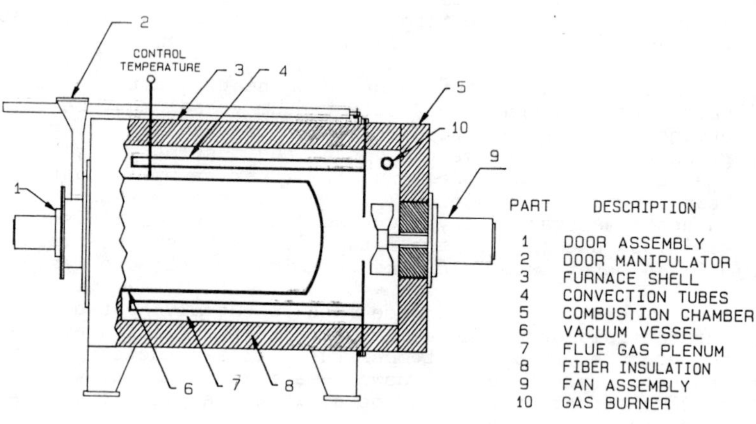

FIGURE 1: FURNACE SCHEMATIC - GAS FIRED VACUUM FURNACE

prominent module is a recirculation fan, part 9. This fan pressurizes spent combustion gases and mixes them with fresh combustion products from a high velocity gas burner, part 10. The gases enter convection tubes, part 4, and are discharged toward the outside surface of the vacuum vessel, part 6, where they impinge and heat the vessel wall.

The vacuum vessel is kept vacuum tight by a vacuum door, part 1, which rides on a door mechanism, part 2. The functions of the important modules of the furnace assembly are explained further in the following sections.

4. CONVECTION HEATING BY JET IMPINGEMENT.

The major contributions of the heating system to furnace performance are made in several areas:

Fast Heating: Cycle times are in its most simple form dependent on three cycle segments: heating to process temperature; maintaining process temperature; and cooling or quenching. Jet impingement allows one to create exceptionally high local heat fluxes and the vacuum vessel can be heated to high temperatures in a very short time. Heat from the vessel wall is transferred by convection or by radiation. To accelerate heating rates at low temperatures it is advantageous to refill the vacuum vessel with an inert gas (nitrogen) and transfer heat from the vessel wall to the parts by convection. At higher temperatures this convection assistance is no longer necessary and heat can be transferred by radiation even under vacuum.

Maintaining Process Temperatures: Close control of process temperatures and exceptional temperature uniformity will assure that heat treat processes can deliver consistent high quality in repeated cycles. Temperature uniformity assures uniformity of heat treat results within the same load and permits performance to tight quality specifications. Temperature uniformity of a furnace is determined by a special test. In this test a frame with the outside dimensions of a representative load is instrumented with thermocouples and the temperature uniformity of the furnace is determined from readings of these thermocouples.

Fast Cooling: After completion of the heat processing cycle the furnace must first be cooled before it can be opened. Surface temperatures of all parts must be reduced to low temperatures to prevent surface oxidation. Parts can either be quenched or fast cooled to reduce the duration of this cycle segment. Forced cooling of the vacuum vessel exterior with cold air accelerates the cooling segment appreciably.

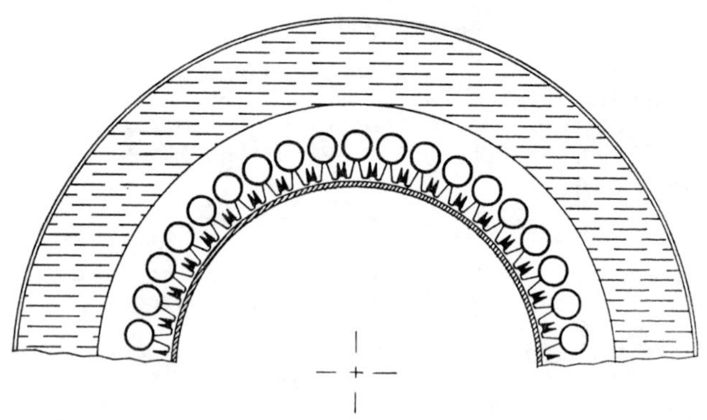

CONVECTION HEATING BY JET IMPINGEMENT

FIGURE 2

In figure 2 the selected concept is depicted. It consists of heating and cooling the furnace shell by a multitude of perpendicularly impinging jets. Each of these jets heats and cools a relatively small area of less than ten square inches. A multitude of jets are used to uniformly heat the entire surface of the vacuum vessel. This is accomplished by supplying an array of tubes with pressurized gases and discharging these gases with high velocities. The impingement points are selected such as to create a uniform pattern on the outside of the vacuum vessel.

5. THE RECIRCULATION LOOP AND ITS FUNCTION.

To obtain the high heat fluxes on the outside of the vacuum vessel and to simultaneously induce high temperature uniformity, a large number of closely spaced jets are needed. Heat fluxes increase with higher velocities and with enlarged mass flows. To maintain uniform heat fluxes under a variety of thermal load conditions a recirculating mass flow system was considered mandatory.

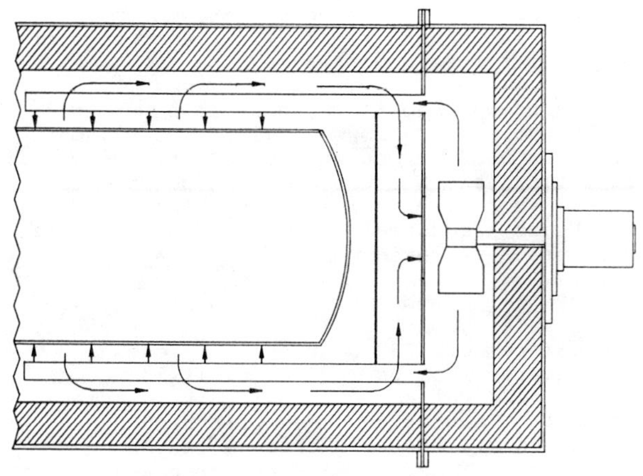

THE RECIRCULATION LOOP AND ITS FUNCTION
FIGURE 3

In figure 3 the recirculation system is shown. A high temperature fan pressurizes and mixes cooled, previously impinged gases with fresh, high temperature gases delivered by gas fired burners. Combustion gases and recirculation gases are well mixed in the combustion chamber before they enter and pressurize the gas distribution manifold. The gases are distributed uniformly along the furnace and are discharged as a multitude of identical, circular jets.

These jets create very high local and average heat fluxes. Average heat transfer coefficients have been measured at values between 25 and 35 Btu/hr-sqft-F. These high heat fluxes can be achieved with moderate fan pressures (1 to 2 inches W.C.). Achievable pressures are, however, limited due to the strength limitations that high temperatures impose on allowable creep stresses in the fan blades. For the described furnace a paddle wheel fan was used with a mass flow rating of 2000 CFM at 2 inches W.C. Limited availability of recirculation fans suitable for high temperature service is the major obstacle in expanding the temperature capability of the described vacuum furnace concept to temperatures above 1750 degrees F.

6. THE COMBUSTION SYSTEM.

The gas burners must supply hot combustion gases over a wide range of input conditions. The major requirements on the combustion system are:

<u>Wide turndown range:</u> Turndown of a burner is defined as the ratio of maximum to minimum gas input. A burner which can operate not only under stoichiometric conditions (the point of highest gas temperature and highest thermal efficiency) but also under excess air conditions has normally an even wider operating range in terms of variations in input of available heat.

<u>Fast Mixing:</u> Combustion gases discharged by a burner firing under stoichiometric conditions can reach temperatures of 3250 degrees F. These high temperatures must be reduced by mixing colder recirculated furnace gases with fresh combustion products. Combustion gases with high burner exit velocities mix fast and produce reduced gas temperatures. Reduced gas temperatures result in lowered specifications for maximum use temperatures of the refractories in the combustion chamber. Reduced combustion gas temperatures will also facilitate temperature uniformity of pressurized recirculation gases in the distributor manifold.

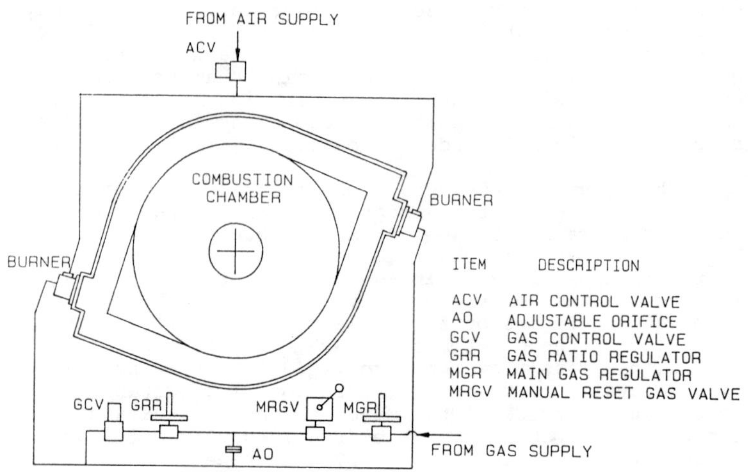

THE COMBUSTION SYSTEM

FIGURE 4

In figure 4 the combustion system is shown in more detail. Two burners fire into a tangential track. Controls consist of an air control valve and a gas control valve. The furnace can be controlled in both the stoichiometric mode and the excess air mode. The mode is selected by either the operator or the cycle control program. At high heat demand the stoichiometric mode is selected, at low heat demand the excess air mode may be preferred. The bypass with adjustable gas orifice allows one to start up the furnace with minimum gas flow but with full airflow. Further details on combustion system design can be found in reference [1].

7. THE INTERNAL CONVECTION SYSTEM.

The present furnace design assures uniform furnace wall temperatures and that every heat treated part will eventually reach the controlled process temperature. Furthermore, the temperature uniformity of all heated parts will be very good provided that sufficient time is allowed for the heating process to occur. In practical heating operations the heating time needs to be kept at a minimum. To accelerate the heating process, especially at lower process temperatures, an internal fan must be added.

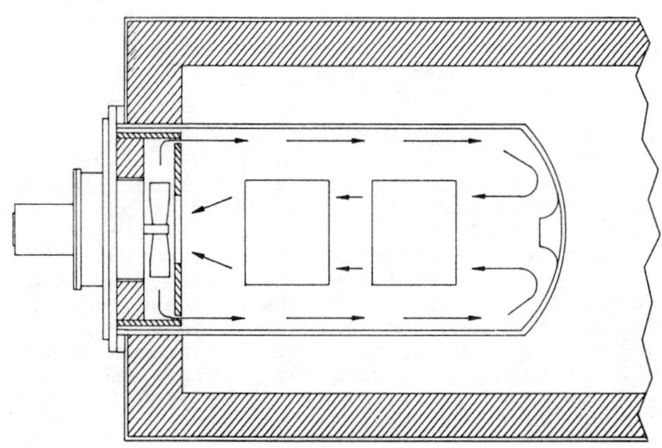

THE INTERNAL CONVECTION SYSTEM

FIGURE 5

The internal fan is shown in figure 5. This figure also shows some further design details of the vacuum door. The fan creates a suction at the center opening of the door, pressurizes the gases, and discharges them through an annular opening located at the perimeter of the door. As a result, a strong internal recirculation flow is set up inside the vacuum vessel. To create a convective flow the presence of a heat transfer medium, a gas, is required. To prevent oxidation of the heat treated parts the furnace is first evacuated and then refilled with either an inert nitrogen atmosphere, an atmosphere containing hydrogen, or any other atmosphere that will serve the particular heat treat application.

In this application the furnace vessel functions not only as the vacuum pressure barrier but also becomes a heat exchanger. The entire vessel wall participates in transferring heat on both sides of the thin walled vacuum vessel. As a result high convective heat transfer coefficients can be induced on both sides resulting in unusually high overall coefficients. Heating and cooling rates with this type of system can approach rather high values, and will approach performance values previously reserved for specially designed convection furnaces.

The internal gas flow patterns have been designed such that the gases flowing along the vessel wall are reversed at the far end of the vessel and form an annular jet with high turbulence. This jet impinges on the load and penetrates it. Convective heat transfer in a properly fixtured load will be elevated resulting in high heating rates even at low process temperatures, fast cooling at cycle completion, and creation of very uniform load temperatures.

8. THE VACUUM DOOR WITH DOOR MANIPULATOR.

The vacuum door is one of the major sub-assemblies of the vacuum furnace. It assures vacuum integrity but it also serves several other functions. It is used to provide openings for thermocouples and other instrumentation, it provides a vacuum duct connection to the vacuum pump, and it houses the internal convection fan. The size and location of the fan housing requires that the vacuum door is retracted in a straight motion parallel to the axis of the vacuum vessel. Conventional vacuum door designs and conventional hinges could, therefore, not be used for this design. Instead a different approach was used.

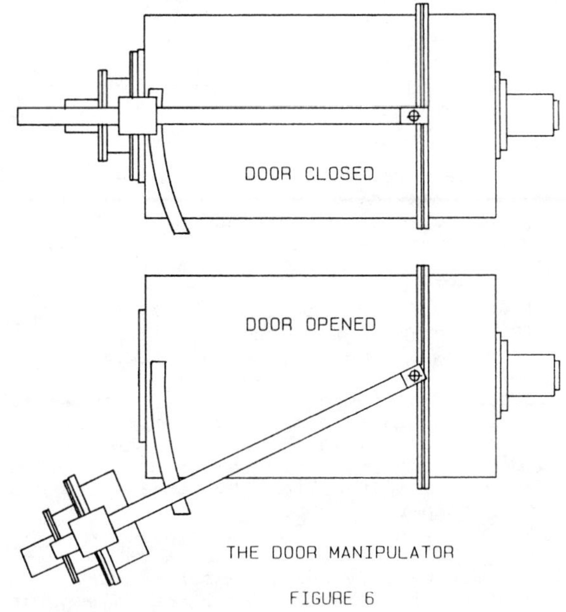

THE DOOR MANIPULATOR

FIGURE 6

The movements of the vacuum door are illustrated in figure 6. The vacuum door is first retracted parallel and concentric to the vacuum vessel. After the door has cleared the outer opening of the vacuum vessel it is further retracted. The motion is facilitated by a trolley which rides on an overhead beam which can be rotated. The rotating motion is facilitated by rolls affixed to the beam and riding on a short circular track. This motion clears the vacuum door sideways from the vacuum vessel opening and provides clear access to its inside by all types of conventional material handling equipment.

The vacuum door also contains the elastic vacuum seal which assures that very high vacuum levels can be achieved in this gas heated vacuum furnace. To protect the seal material the mating surfaces are water cooled and their temperatures under test conditions were very close to the water temperature.

9. TEST RESULTS

After the design had been completed the furnace was built, installed and tested. The initial tests were directed at determining temperature uniformity, vacuum integrity, ease of operation, controlability, and general performance.

To determine temperature uniformity a test frame was installed and instrumented. Thermocouple locations on the test frame were selected in conformance with AMS 2750 [2]. Temperatures were determined under three sets of test conditions:

At 1000 deg F with air atmosphere,
At 1000 deg F under vacuum (0.01 Torr.)
At 1250 deg F under vacuum (0.01 Torr.)

The least degree of temperature uniformity was achieved at 1000 deg F with the furnace under an air atmosphere, the best temperature uniformity was reached at the highest temperature under vacuum. Minimum temperature uniformity was +/- 7.5 degrees F, best uniformity was +/- 3.5 degrees F around the median temperature.

Vacuum integrity was excellent. Leak rates were determined at levels below 0.001 Torr per hour. Controlability of the furnace was excellent. Temperatures could be controlled to the accuracy of the control instrument (1 degree F digital). Programmable heat up and cooling could be adjusted over a wide range.

Start up of the gas burners was simple. Burners were ignited under full air flow and with minimum gas flow resulting in excess air conditions. This start up procedure provided an extra measure of convenience and safety. The gas flow at start up was set to prevent the formation of an ignitable mixture inside the furnace proper. As a result ignition can occur only inside the burner but not outside the burner. Light off with this procedure will not create any noise. Light off was by spark ignition and always occurred immediately once the correct gas flows to the burners had been adjusted. Conventional purging procedures were adhered to and added a redundant safety measure. Furnace and burner design complemented each other resulting in no perceptible burner noise at all tested operating conditions.

The furnace operated under considerable backpressure of exhaust gases, but no leaks or hot spots were observed. Wall temperatures were such that walls could be touched at furnace temperatures of 1250 degrees F. The flue gases were under backpressure created by the gas burners and were exhausted through a small diameter flue gas pipe.

The overall impression of the furnace in operation was that of a vacuum furnace. No combustion noise, no thermal furnace radiation, no exhaust gas leaks, no visible flame, and no hot spots could be detected. Consumption of cooling water was low and water temperature rise was small.

10. MAJOR RESULTS.

The tests confirmed that the selected design approaches were sound and appropriate. The temperature uniformity achieved with this furnace is unusual for an industrial heat treat furnace and will open up new possibilities for precision heat treating. Vacuum integrity was excellent as tested. In addition a visual inspection of some of the vacuum vessel welds was performed at the conclusion of the tests and did not show any incipient or existing weld cracks.

Inspection of the refractories in the high temperature combustion chamber did not show any deterioration, shrinking or surface decay.

The operation of the furnace was without any problems. The general appearance of the furnace is that of a vacuum furnace. All negative features of certain gas fired equipment have been eliminated. The furnace is clean, has low wall temperatures, and exhaust gases are totally contained, and are kept away from the operator's environment.

Initial tests confirm that a novel furnace type has been designed which will open up new opportunities for the application of natural gas in high technology heat treating.

11. THE ION NITRIDING PROCESS.

After completion of the development phase comprising vacuum furnace design and testing of its heating system, additional tests must be run to confirm the suitability of this furnace design for selected heat treating processes. One of the most promising applications for this new furnace concept appears to be in ion nitriding. Ion nitriding is a case hardening process that is performed under moderate vacuum at temperatures between 750 and 1050 degrees F.

A reaction gas is ionized under the influence of an electric potential and reacts with the metal surface of the heat treated part. At higher temperatures the nitrogen diffuses from the surface into the inner layers of the treated part. Ion nitriding has many unusual features which make it ideally suited for many difficult surface hardening operations. Very long and very heavy parts can be surface hardened with relative ease. But ion nitriding is even better suited for mass production. Parts can be heated free of distortion and do not require a subsequent quenching operation to develop excellent surface hardness. The part can, therefore, be finish machined to close tolerances prior to heat treatment! Combining distortion free heating with exceptional temperature uniformity will result in parts with uniform case depth and consistent, high quality layer hardness. This case hardening process combined with the new high performance vacuum furnace can, therefore, produce heat treated parts which, after case hardening, are ready for assembly. No further machining and no further inspection appears to be necessary after the process has been observed long enough to assure repeatable, documented operation under automated cycle control.

In addition to exceptional parts quality some other benefits will be realized when using this new furnace for ion nitriding. The features of the convection heating system will assure very fast heat up times. The benefits will be twofold. Overall process times will be shortened and an attendant increase in furnace productivity will become possible when compared to conventional ion nitriders. One particular feature of conventional ion nitriders, their propensity to generate high energy electrical arcs on the surface of the treated parts, will most likely be eliminated. Heating of the load will not be performed by ion plasma discharge heating but will be achieved by convective heating. Plasma discharge heating will not be used at all during the most critical portion of the cycle, the surface cleaning segment. As a result the chance of surface defects due to cratering will most likely be eliminated with this new heating approach.

Overall energy consumption will be significantly reduced. The gas fired ion nitrider operates with an insulated furnace wall while conventional ion nitriders loose heat continuously to the water cooled furnace walls. Gas heating will occur at very high (60% +) thermal efficiencies resulting in appreciable savings in energy costs.

Cooling at the completion of the heat treating cycle provides additional advantages. The parts will be force cooled and conventional cooling in vacuum furnaces will be substantially accelerated. It is expected that reductions in cycle times of up to 25 % will become possible through combined reductions in heating cycle times and cooling cycle times.

12. SUMMARY.

A gas fired vacuum furnace has been designed, built and tested. Performance was superior when compared to conventional vacuum furnaces. Several novel design concepts had to be developed. These concepts, which relate to the heating system, the vacuum door design, and the internal convection flow design, have been made part of three patent applications. The patent applications have been filed.

PROGRESS TOWARDS A COST EFFECTIVE, THIN WALLED RBT

ROBERT E. RICHARDS - 3M

DOUGLAS W. BODKINS - COLUMBIA GAS SYSTEM

DR. JANE S. COPES - 3M

INTRODUCTION

The development of higher temperature radiant tubes for indirect heating with gas, at temperatures above 2000°F has become a major focus of gas utilities and their research organizations. Ceramic matrix composites appear to offer a promising route towards achieving the desired goals for temperature, thermal transfer and operational latitude.

A program for the development of a cost-effective silicon carbide composite radiant burner tube (RBT) has been under-way for over five years. These efforts were led by a team consisting of Amercom, Chatsworth, California; Columbia Gas System, and Industrial Furnace Services, Inc. (IFSI), Streetsboro, Ohio. The subsequent extension of these efforts to include processing and commercialization came when 3M Company joined the team effort in 1986.

The roles of the team are explained as follows:

AMERCOM

- Developed first full-sized composite tubes
- Continues to supply test materials for program

COLUMBIA GAS SYSTEM

- Evaluates tube performance
- Coordinated furnace/component evaluations

IFSI

- Builds, sells, services furnaces using RBT's

3M

- Manufactures Nextel^R 312 fiber used as tube preform and fiber reinforcement
- Characterizes materials, established process development plan

SPONSORS:

Columbia Gas System
Consolidated Natural Gas Service Company
Southern California Gas Company

This program is a direct extension of the efforts started during the 1960's and continuing today to develop the components and the designs for high temperature gas-fired furnaces for the thermal processing industry. (High temperature controlled atmosphere heating)

BACKGROUND

Silicon carbide has been identified as a candidate radiant tube material and evaluation of tubes in furnace test programs are already underway [1,2]. The high emissivity, thermal conductivity and thermal shock resistance of silicon carbide make it an attractive choice to develop into a manufacturable tube product [3]. Early processing routes included extruding and sintering either crystalline or powdered mixtures of SiC and bonding aids. Tubes of these types are in operation in temperature ranges from 1800°F to 2100°F, but because of material limitations have not been successfully applied at higher temperatures (2200°F+) [3,4].

Both greater thermal stability and thinner walled tube constructions are needed. Tubes of CVD silicon carbide were identified as potentially having these desired properties [4,5]. Evaluations were started by Holcroft and Company, Livonia, Michigan and Columbia Gas System. Monolithic CVD tubes had the thin walls and the requested thermal properties, but proved too fragile for the vibration and thermal excursions experienced. Nextel 312 fiber reinforced CVD silicon carbide tubes from Amercom appeared to offer the most promising combination of properties. In 1984, a program for the development of large size (8 inch by 78 inch) tubes was undertaken with the sponsorship of the three gas companies named earlier. While the process has proven difficult and, at a one at a time basis is also expensive, tubes have reached a limited field test status in an aluminum melter located at Arrow Aluminum, in Avon Lake, Ohio.

3M Company became keenly interested in the project and entered the program in 1986, by assuming responsibility for developing testing for tubes, characterization for the material and support for field testing. Limited tube availability from Amercom has thwarted much of the expected roll-out of furnace testing in environments other than the aluminum melter. This report will summarize the findings to this date based on testing at Columbia Gas System, IFSI, 3M and the aluminum melter at Arrow Aluminum in Avon Lake, Ohio.

TUBE PERFORMANCE SUMMARY

PHASE I - FIRST FULL SIZE TUBES

During Phase I (1984-85) four tubes were produced at Amercom; using a standard heavy braid for the Nextel fiber wall, and Amercom's CVD process for SiC. Tube #1 was evaluated at Columbia Gas System laboratory, and performed very well in exhaustive thermal stress tests using a test procedure developed by John Bjerklie of Consolidated Gas and Doug Bodkins of Columbia. The test was called the "3G" Test. Over the months of testing approximately 900 hours of on-off furnace operations experience was gained on tube #1. In order to reduce permeability of the thin walls, an experimental coating was applied to tube #2. That coating is believed to have caused the early failure of #2 in the Gas Company thermal test. After being tested in the Columbia Gas test, tube #3 was installed into the #2 slot of the aluminum melter and survived 4 months before a large splash of molten aluminum created a hole and caused the tube to fail. Tube #4 which also completed a portion the Gas Company "3G" test series, was installed at Arrow. Four conclusions were drawn from this phase.

(1) The thin walled tubes showed promise as productivity in the melter was increased with the thin walled tubes in only 2 of the 4 tube locations.

(2) Small gaps or holes in the CVD layer, make the tube leaky, and a change in the fiber preform was desired.

(3) The accelerated 3G testing showed promise of predicting which tubes could survive the longer lifetimes needed.

(4) 3G testing was detrimental to tube life[6], and would be used only for laboratory evaluations, not as a release means for future tubes.

PHASE II

Phase II - (1985-86) concentrated on developing options for a gas tight tube construction. Amercom produced tube #7 by using Nextel AF-40 cloth, seaming the wrapped cloth into a tube with sewing thread, then CVD coating the SiC. The resultant tube passed the 3G test, had one tenth the leakage rates of the braided constructions; and, based on Amercom's assessment would cost only one-half of the Phase I braided construction. Agreement was reached to pursue the cloth wrapped construction. During Phase II, tubes #8 and #9 were made. Tubes #8 and #9 were made like the Phase I (braid), as controls. Both appeared much more uniform in construction. It was decided to field test these without the 3G pre-exposure. These were both installed in the furnace at Arrow without being tested at Columbia. Tube #8 survived for 15 months, when a severe circumferential crack was observed. However it was not replaced until eighteen months. Tube #9 survived for 11 months, although a crack had occurred earlier. One interesting additional benefit was recognized when tube #8 was installed without shutting the furnace down.

Because the tube weighs only 10 pounds, IFSI devised a method of the hot exchange and was able to reload the tube "on the fly" with minimum difficulty. From Phase II, these additional results were obtained.

(1) The thin-walled tubes are susceptible to damage from heavy accumulation of splashed metal, and/or dross.

(2) Lifetimes of over one year are possible with the braided construction.

(3) The cloth tube is a better leak tight construction, but problems with the fabrication techniques need resolving.

(4) Thermal stress and residual stress measurements are variable and confusing.

(5) Mechanical testing of the tubes was started, and 3M has begun to characterize the material both as received and after thermal aging [7].

(6) The recommendation to follow-up this Phase II series with a larger test series of cloth wrapped tubes was agreed upon.

PHASE III

By mid 1986 an extension of the test program was agreed upon. 3M had joined the team effort and assumed responsibility for:

- tube procurement and testing
- laboratory evaluations of both initial and field tested materials
- coordinating field tests with Columbia Gas System
- establishing a comparison of laboratory,"3G" and field test data

The test program plans called for using ten cloth wrapped tubes plus a series of thirty small diameter tubes to study the material responses to both different thermal and furnace environments. Tube procurement became a major stumbling block after successive attempts to fabricate the cloth wrapped tube failed, due to problems with the seams, the CVD coating and unusually poor material properties.

After a searching review of the processing data, Amercom began a run of eight tubes to more methodically compare the cloth construction with an imporoved triaxial braid. That series was funded by 3M.

The eight tubes, four of each construction were produced at Amercom during mid 1987. To date, the testing and evaluations show the following results.

(1) The triaxial braided construction can be produced and repeated more easily than the cloth wrapped type.

(2) Procedures for the braiding and CVD processing are documented and being applied to help reduce variability.

(3) The triaxial tube is not gas tight and cannot be recommended in other controlled atmosphere environments; improvement is needed.

(4) Seam problems and residual stress anamolies persisted with the cloth construction tubes.

(5) Initial strengths of the tubes are more than adequate.

(6) Variability in the response of the material to thermal aging and cycling needs to be further understood.

EXPECTED TUBE REQUIREMENTS (2,3,4.)

SIZE RANGES	diameter	up to 8 inches
	length	up to 100 inches
	wall thickness	up to 3/8" inches
	straightness	less than 1/2" bow
TEMPERATURE LIMITATIONS	working temp	up to 2500°F
	maximum limit	up to 2800°F
	thermal shock resistance	forced air cooling or furnace cycle
THERMAL PROPERTIES	conductivity	above 75BTU/Hr/Ft^2/In-°F
	diffusivity	10,000 BTU/Hr/Ft^2
PERMEABILITY	thru/wall	none at 2 psig
STRENGTH	at temperature	sufficient to retain structure
USEFUL LIFE	average	2+ years

FIGURE 1

TUBE PROPERTIES (PHASE II)

(COMPARISON OF PREFORM TYPES)

	AF 40 CLOTH	TRIAXIAL BRAID
Straightness	± 1/4"	± 1/4
Wall Thickness	0.08"	0.18"
Burst Strength (RT)	6,000 PSI (MOR)	4,500 PSI (MOR)
Residual Stress	high tensile and variable	variable
Leakage @ 0.01" H_2O	0.3 CFH/FT^2	6.0 CFH/Ft^2
Tube Life	untested	~one year

FIGURE 2

SUMMARY

This program has been augmented by testing of the composite materials at 3M, and other complimentary programs at Amercom. From the coordination of the team efforts by the three sponsoring Gas Companies an extension of this testing effort is being focused towards the development of improved processing, both for the preforms and the CVD operation. 3M has initiated commercialization of the product under the trade name Siconex™ Fiber Reinforced Ceramic.

The Siconex tube is now viewed as a potential solution to the next higher temperature niche for controlled atmosphere heating.

To conclude, we are focused on reaching the tube requirements outlined in Figure 1.

Our status is shown in Figure 2. We expect that the effort to improve the processing, the gas tightness and to extend tube life will enhance the program prospects even further. This should enable the thin walled radiant tube to be used in operations requiring work temperatures far above 1800°F, and tube temperatures above 2100°F.

REFERENCES

1. Taus, W.J. Bodkins, D., Price, D., Bjerklie, J., Watkins, L., "APPLICATION OF HIGH TEMPERATURE RADIANT TUBES", 12th ENERGY TECHNOLOGY CONFERENCE, March 25-27, 1985.

2. Liang, W.W. and Schreiner, M.E., "ADVANCED MATERIALS DEVELOPMENT FOR RADIANT TUBE APPLICATIONS"; 1986 INDUSTRIAL COMBUSTION TECHNOLOGY SYMPOSIUM, April, 1986.

3. Jayaraman, V., "CERAMIC RADIANT TUBE HEATED ALUMINUM MELTER," DIE CASTING TECHNOLOGY. YESTERDAY'S ART, TODAYS SCIENCE , CONFERENCE PROCEEDINGS, MINNEAPOLIS, MN, October 31 - November 3, 1983.

4. Jayaraman, V., CERAMIC RADIANT TUBES, COMMUNICATION TO 3M, 1985.

5. Federer, J.I., "CORROSION OF MATERIALS BY HIGH-TEMPERATURE INDUSTRIAL COMBUSTION ENVIRONMENTS - A SUMMARY," ORNL-TM9903, February, 1986.

6. Bodkins, D., "RADIANT TUBE TESTING, COLUMBIA GAS ACTIVITIES," REPORT #2 - 10, 1985, PRIVATE COMMUNICATION.

7. Copes, J.S., Richards, R.E., "MECHANICAL PROPERTIES OF OXIDE FIBER-REINFORCED SIC CERAMIC COMPOSITES" PRESENTED AT 88TH ANNUAL MEETING, AMERICAN CERAMIC SOCIETY, May, 1986 (No. 56-C-86).

ACKNOWLEDGEMENTS:

AMERCOM - Large tube prototypes

COLUMBIA GAS SYSTEM - Testing of tubes, sponsor

IFSI - Prototype Aluminum Melter

3M - Material evaluation, process development

Southern California Gas Company - Sponsor

Consolidated Gas Service System - Sponsor

NATURAL GAS USAGE IN MUNICIPAL WASTE DISPOSAL

DAVID G. LINZ
MANAGER, ENVIRONMENT AND SAFETY RESEARCH
GAS RESEARCH INSTITUTE
CHICAGO, ILLINOIS

ABSTRACT

The thermal treatment or destruction of wastes is not a new technology. There are new pressures, however, which are acting to greatly expand the use of this technology and make it a significant combustion source over the next few years. The primary technical considerations associated with these operations that may limit this expansion are combustion efficiency, air emissions, and process residues (ash). Natural gas, because of its unique combustion properties, has several advantages as a supplemental fuel used in conjunction with other lower grade fuels such as municipal solid waste.

The potential benefits that might be achieved from the strategic firing of natural gas are improved combustion efficiency, reduced emissions, lower cost alternatives to other pollution control techniques, and new gas loads. The key goals for GRI and the natural gas industry are to evaluate gas cofiring concepts and demonstrate that the firing of gas with wastes can result in these benefits either in emissions reduction or other operational performance measurements.

This paper will provide a brief background of MSW combustion technology; identify technical, regulatory, and market factors which can potentially influence the use of gas; propose technical concepts which merit further investigation and/or R&D; and provide a brief description of GRI research in this area.

MSW COMBUSTION EQUIPMENT

There are three major classes of equipment used for the combustion of municipal solid waste. These are illustrated in Figures 1 through 3. The first class is the mass burn systems which handle unprocessed municipal solid wastes. Modern mass burn designs feed the MSW onto a reciprocating grate that "walks" the solids into a utility boiler class furnace. The solids burn on the bed of the grate and generate hot flue gas that moves into the boiler furnace. These units are generally the largest units manufactured and are installed on a municipal or regional basis.

The second class of units which burn refuse derived fuels (RDF) are also generally large utility boiler class furnaces for municipal and regional application. In contrast to mass burn units, however, in RDF units, the waste is first processed by metals removal and size reduction. Then the RDF can be thrown into the boiler furnace through the use of a spreader and the RDF falls onto a traveling grate.

The final major class of units represents the smaller institutional/township applications. These units are similar to mass burn units in that the waste is not processed but are unique in the fact that the MSW is introduced into an oxygen deficient zone. The remainder of the air needed to complete combustion is added downstream in a second chamber. This two stage arrangement is sometimes referred to as a starved air unit and is used to incinerate refuse from hospitals or other institutional or industrial generators.

TECHNICAL, REGULATORY, AND MARKET FACTORS

State-of-the-art waste combustion technology is significantly improved in comparison to past practice. Further improvements are driven by the need to increase efficiency and lower costs, and the need to comply with escalating regulatory requirements for air emissions. The regulatory requirements are expected to have even greater impact on waste combustion practice over the next few years and will, therefore, be discussed first.

The U.S. EPA has recently completed an extensive review of municipal waste incineration, including the evaluation of emissions performance, risks and current best combustion practice. A report to Congress was prepared which summarized these results. The agency has recently indicated the intent to regulate these sources. The regulatory strategy proposed is to develop New Source Performance Standards (NSPS) for new units and to define emission limits for existing units. The states will then be required to develop plans for meeting these limits for existing units based on guidance issued by the EPA.

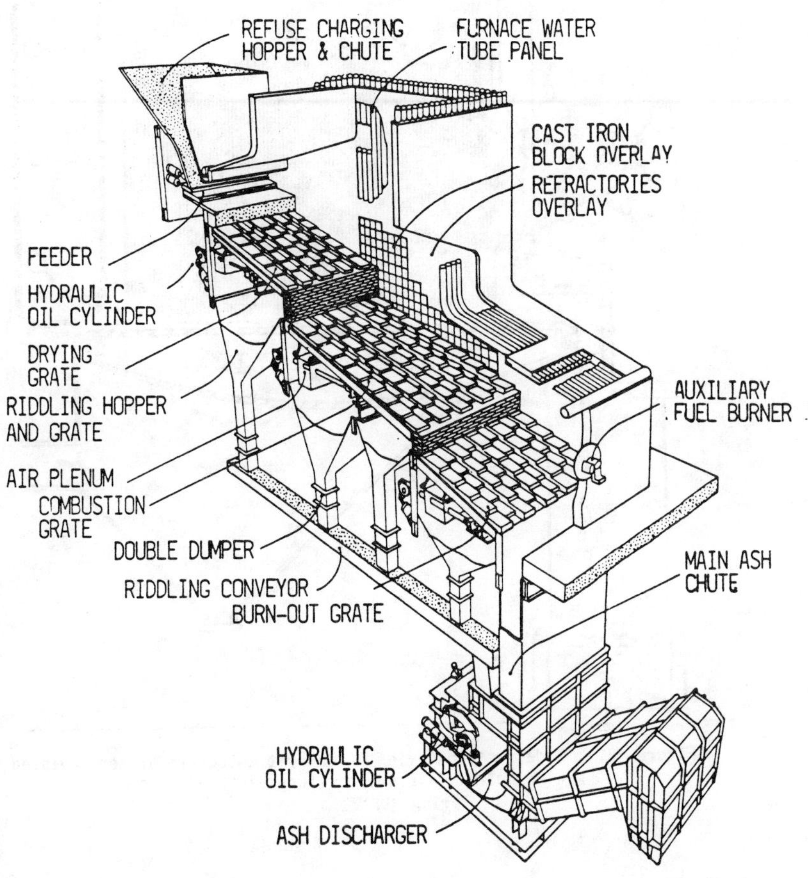

Figure 1. Cross sectional schematic of combustion zone on a Riley-Takuma mass burn plant.

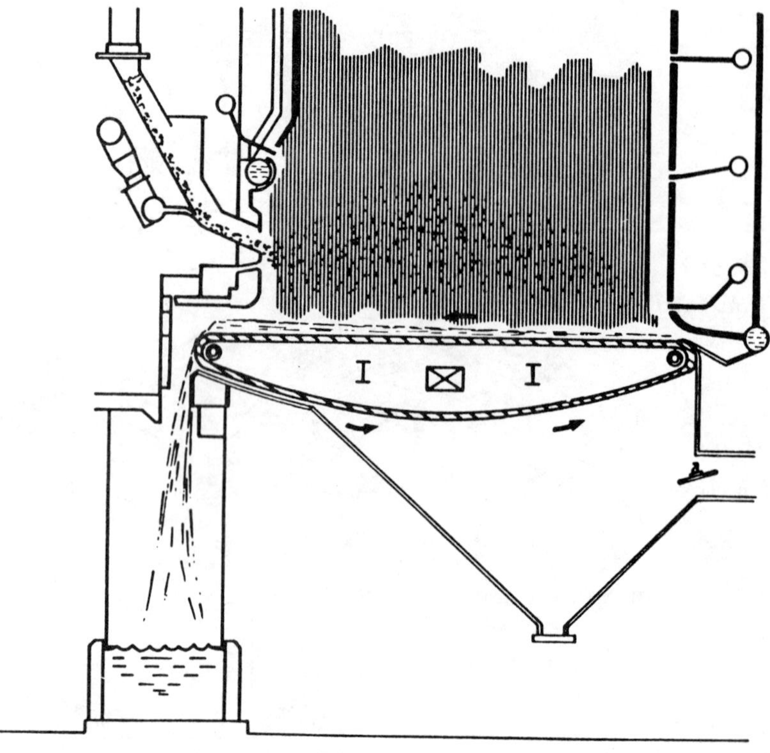

Figure 2. Side sectional view of Detroit Rotograte Stoker equipped with Detroit air swept refuse distributor spouts (used for firing RDF).

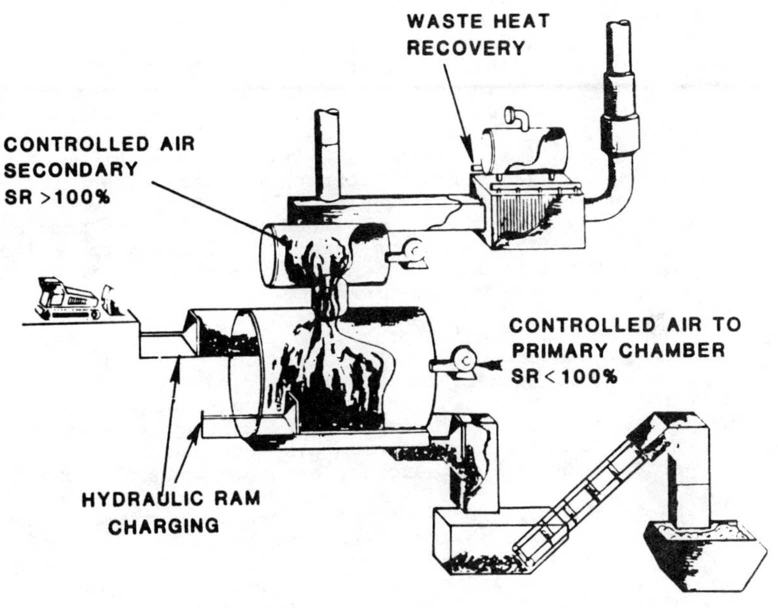

Figure 3. Components of typical starved-air modular combustor.

The risk analysis performed by the EPA showed the possible health effects of chlorinated dioxin and furan emissions to be the dominant factor in the risk calculation. It is therefore expected that emission limits will be established for chlorinated dioxin and furan based on the lowest achievable levels in modern units utilizing best available control technology (BACT). Proposed guidelines for both new and existing units are scheduled to be published in November 1989. Until then, interim guidance has been issued to the EPA regions for permitting new units. The interim guidance calls for the twofold control strategy based on the results of the report to Congress. First, BACT is defined as dry scrubbers (spray dryers) in combination with either fabric filters or electrostatic precipitators (ESP). Second, best combustion practice as defined in the report must be followed (See Table 1). The agency is planning to revise the interim guidance by the end of 1988 to reflect results from ongoing research and field tests.

The "best combustion practice" guidelines contain several provisions with implications for gas usage. Auxiliary fuel burners are required as part of the design. These must be fired at startup to achieve minimum temperature conditions prior to introduction of waste. Firing is also required to maintain some minimum temperature and prevent excessive carbon monoxide levels.

Another conclusion from the report to Congress is that the existing units, although representing only 20 percent of the capacity in the year 2000, have a risk comparable to all of the new units expected to come on-line between now and then. This, of course, is the reason that regulation of existing as well as new units is being recommended. EPA has initiated a study to define retrofit options for these existing units. The other major conclusion is that refuse derived fuel (RDF) combustors have been found to have relatively higher dioxin emissions than the other combustion designs, although the data base is somewhat limited for these units. This result has led to a major EPA research activity (conducted jointly with Environment Canada) to evaluate emissions from modern RDF units.

Although EPA plans are now fairly well defined, changes in these plans and schedules could be forced by litigation or by legislation in Congress. There is currently some objection to the EPA approach on the basis that it will take too long to implement and does not clearly define control approaches for specific "hazardous air pollutants."

In addition to the emissions of concern cited in the EPA report (metals, particulate matter, acid gases, trace organics) NO_x emissions are also important in California today. It is likely that NO_x emissions will eventually be important in the rest of the country. One result of

TABLE 1. GOOD COMBUSTION PRACTICES FOR MINIMIZING TRACE ORGANIC EMISSIONS FROM RDF COMBUSTORS

Element	Component	Recommmendations
Design	Temperature at fully mixed height	1800°F at fully mixed height
	Underfire air control	As required to provide uniform bed burning stoichiometry
	Overfire air capacity (not necessary operation)	40% of total air
	Overfire air injector design	That required for penetration and coverage of furnace cross-section
	Auxiliary fuel capacity	That required to meet start-up temperature and 1800°F criteria under part-load operations
Operation/ Control	Excess air	3-9% oxygen in flue gas (dry basis)
	Turndown restrictions	80-110% of design - lower limit may be extended with verification tests
	Start-up procedures	On auxiliary fuel to design temperature
	Use of auxiliary fuel	On prolonged high CO or low furnace temperature
Verification	Oxygen in flue gas	3-9% dry basis
	CO in flue gas	50 ppm on 4 hour average - corrected to 12% CO_2
	Furnace temperature	Minimum of 1800°F (mean) at fully mixed height
	Adequate air distribution	Verification Tests

the actions recommended by the EPA to improve combustion will be to increase NO_x emissions. NO_x control technologies for MSW incinerators which are compatible with controls for trace organics are not well established.

One final environmental issue with MSW incineration is ash disposal. Toxic metals such as lead, cadmium and arsenic can be concentrated on the fine fly ash particles. If dry scrubbers and fabric filters are relied upon to remove trace organics, then the toxic organics will be captured on the particles and become part of the fly ash waste disposal problem.

The key technical issue relevant to this discussion is the operation of thermal destruction equipment in such a fashion that organics are completely destroyed in the furnace and no toxic organics are formed subsequently and emitted from the stack. This must be done in a way that will not increase other pollutants of concern such as particulate matter, NO_x, toxic metals and acid gases. Despite the significant amount of attention that has been paid to the subject of dioxin, there is still a lack of detailed understanding of dioxin formation and destruction, and the failure modes which contribute to dixoin emissions.

The most plausible theory today suggests that the presence of a uniform, high temperature, oxygen rich zone is the basic design requirement which will destroy organics in general and dioxin specifically. Establishing this zone and maintaining it under all operating conditions may be difficult in waste combustion because of the variability of the fuel (i.e., the waste). Supplemental firing can play a role in meeting these design requirements.

Supplemental firing has been employed in Europe and, in fact, is required in West Germany as part of the permit conditions. Discussions with all of the major designers and manufacturers in Europe and the U.S. has confirmed, however, that this practice has not been optimized or even well characterized from a performance point of view. No data exists on auxiliary burner mixing, temperature or CO profiles, or emissions performance either as a function of the burner design and operation or with and without the burner firing.

In order for supplemental gas firing to be successful for organic emission control technology, the above factors must be well understood. In addition, the technology of natural gas injection into a large furnace to achieve the desired mixing is not now available. Sophisticated temperature and other important parameter monitoring and control schemes must be defined and developed. This applies to both mass burn and RDF type firing. RDF firing differs from mass burn in that the fuel is more fine and more uniform and is fed into the furnace using a spreader stoker. This practice results in the elutriation of some portion of the fuel and burning or partial burning in suspension (up to 30 percent) rather than on the grate. There are some dioxin formation theories which suggest that this is could contribute to the elevated dioxin emissions experienced with RDF boilers.

The "good combustion" practice that has been used to date has generally increased combustion temperatures and improved mixing. This, plus the high excess air used, has tended to increase NO_x emissions from large mass burn and RDF facilities. To date only flue gas recirculation, ammonia injection, and selective catalytic reduction have been considered for NO_x control. Ammonia injection is installed and operating on one plant and is currently being installed on another in Southern California. Although significant NO_x reductions have been reported, there is still a strong majority opinion in the industry that this is not an attractive option and that a combustion based technology would be preferable.

Natural gas reburn has not yet been evaluated for waste combustion applications. However, small air starved units are essentially air staged combustion devices and do have relatively lower NO_x emissions. Also, fuel staging is a recognized means of achieving NO_x reductions, and there are no obvious fundamental restrictions to its use in MSW combustion systems. Even lower levels of NO_x should be achievable with natural gas reburn. This process is totally consistent with good combustion practice for trace organic control and, in fact, is superior to the "good combustion" conditions cited above in that reduced emissions of organics and NO_x can be simultaneously achieved.

NATURAL GAS FIRING CONCEPTS

This section presents a discussion of the gas firing concepts which are considered to be promising. In municipal waste combustion, the key issue continues to be dioxin despite controversy over the health effects and claims by various sources that the problem is solved. The primary opportunity for gas is firing to control trace organics. It is now clear that auxiliary burners will be required at least for startup and possibly for low temperature or high CO transients. There is some sentiment within the manufacturing community that if these systems can be improved such that improved temperature control during normal operations and improved dioxin destruction under all operating conditions can be achieved, then there will be great incentive to incorporate such a scheme into the design. Although the specific limits have not been quantified, it is thought that up to 10 percent of the thermal load could be fired as gas without significant redesign of the furnace. If this additional thermal load is considered in the initial design, then gas firing will not displace waste firing.

For all types of municipal solid waste combustion systems, supplemental gas firing would be almost an "afterburner" designed to achieved sufficient temperature and mixing to destroy any organics which may escape the primary combustion zone immediately above the grate. With adequate monitoring and control, the natural gas injection could be modulated in such a manner to damp out spatial and temporal variations in the furnace that allow the trace amounts of unburned hydrocarbons to escape the furnace. Also, the monitoring and control would allow the minimum amount of gas to be used to accomplish the objectives, thus providing an optimized design.

For RDF units, gas firing may be particularly useful for dioxin control since the lower furnace velocities can be reduced which in turn will result in less particle carryover. The carryover of unburned particles has recently been identified as a major pathway for escape of dioxin precursors and is particularly important for RDF spreader stoker systems. Also, the afterburning effect may be used to enhance the burnout of those particles that are entrained.

Gas cofiring may also have particular applications to existing units, for which large reductions of dioxin emissions will most likely be required. These may be achieved by the addition of scrubbers and high performance particulate control equipment; however, this is very costly and may not be possible because of space or other limitations. Gas cofiring is significantly less costly than retrofitting scrubbers.

For gas to have a major role in the retrofit of existing municipal waste combustion systems, it is likely to have to be part of a multi-pollutant control scheme. For example, most older units do not have scrubbers, although they do have particulate control equipment. The new regulations for existing facilities will likely require tighter control on particulate matter and control of trace organics and acid gases for the first time. Thus gas cofiring for trace organic control must be combined with other control schemes for acid gas and particulate matter to have general applicability. As already stated, acid gas scrubbers are expensive and difficult to retrofit. One possibility is to combine gas cofiring with in-furnace or duct injection of sorbents to control acid gases. This is a similar approach to that currently being demonstrated by GRI for combined NO_x/SO_x control using gas reburning/sorbent injection in coal-fired utility boilers. Then, combined with improved particulate control, a multi-pollutant retrofittable control scheme would have general applicability for the existing MSW combustion system and would employ gas cofiring.

For units to be built in California, another concern is NO_x emissions. Several manufacturers have expressed a reluctance to compete in the California market because of the NO_x control requirements. There is considerable interest on the part of manufacturers in GRI's gas reburn process for NO_x control. Expanding on a comment above, if auxiliary burners will be required in any event, then a system which can be used to start the unit, stabilize temperature, improve organic destruction, and reduce NO_x will be very attractive for California and elsewhere.

Two other concepts not involving emission control also could utilize gas in conjunction with MSW combustion. Ash disposal was mentioned in the previous section as a regulatory concern. Firing of the ash to destroy organic residues or to melt the ash could lead to a product which is not hazardous and is potentially suitable for recycle. A second concept involves separate firing of gas to superheat the steam generated in the municipal waste boiler furnace. This will result in significant increases in the steam temperature that would be achievable and thereby improve the thermal cycle and electric generation efficiency. There will also be improvements of the waste boiler performance because of the lower operating temperatures.

GRI R&D PROGRAM

The concepts identified in the previous section include cofiring gas to reduce dioxin emissions in RDF boilers, cofiring gas as an alternative control technology for trace organics such as dioxin and any other potentially designated pollutants in existing units, and gas reburn for combined NO_x and organic control in mass burn and possibly RDF units. The technical issues which must be addressed for these applications include 1) characterization of the in-furnace conditions in a modern mass burn unit, 2) development of the gas reburn process for the conditions present in modern waste combustors, and 3) development of the technology for injecting and mixing gas and potentially sorbents in a cofiring application and controlling the process. Three projects have been defined to address these technical issues, each involving significant industry support.

The first project is being conducted by a team of Institute of Gas Technology and Riley Stoker. The first task is to perform in-furnace measurements in an operating mass burn incinerator to characterize the gas composition and temperature conditions. The next task involves laboratory furnace tests to define the conditions necessary for gas reburn. The remaining task is to design and test at the pilot-scale a gas reburn system. Following successful completion of this work, a field test of the gas reburn process will be conducted.

The second project is being conducted with Energy and Environmental Research Corporation and is cofunded by Northern States Power (NSP). The project will include analysis of an RDF boiler owned and operated by NSP followed by design and testing of a gas cofiring system in the RDF boiler. The purpose of this work is to demonstrate the feasibility of a gas fired system to improve combustion and achieve dioxin destruction in an RDF fired boiler.

The third project will be conducted and cofunded by a project team which includes an MSW equipment manufacturing partner. Negotiations with the manufacturing partner are in progress. In this project the characteristics in an operating mass burn furnace will be mapped to provide data to locate the burners to be used to test a novel gas-firing system. Using a special design burner to create the proper atmosphere above the grate in strategic locations, the initial test will evaluate the feasibility of achieving both reduced NO_x and reduced organic emissions. This initial feasibility test will be followed by a field test of an improved prototype also conducted at full scale in an operating incinerator.

Other planned work includes evaluation of ash treatment, separate gas-fired steam superheating (cofunded with New York State Energy Research and Development Authority), and gas cofiring with sorbent injection for combined organic and acid gas control. This last activity will be pursued through laboratory, pilot, and full-scale testing.

POTENTIAL ENERGY SAVINGS FROM AQUIFER THERMAL ENERGY STORAGE

M. R. Anderson, R. O. Weijo, and J. L. Smoot
Pacific Northwest Laboratory[a]
Richland, Washington 99352

INTRODUCTION

Aquifer thermal energy storage (ATES) is a technology that allows energy to be stored in aquifers and retrieved when needed. With this technology, energy is transferred to and from an aquifer through a network of wells. The aquifer operates as a containment vessel that permits very little loss of stored energy. From 50% to 90% of the energy transferred to the aquifer can be recovered for use in space heating and cooling or as process heat (Allen, Kannberg, and Raymond 1984).

This paper summarizes a study conducted for the U.S. Department of Energy's ATES Program. Pacific Northwest Laboratory conducted the study to estimate the overall potential energy savings from ATES utilization in the U.S. This estimate included the potential short- and long-term savings from both heating and cooling applications of ATES. The results can be used in determining the direction of research conducted on ATES, specifically whether the primary focus of research should be on heat or chill storage, and which end markets are the primary users and sources of heat or chill ATES.

ESTIMATION MODEL

An aggregate-level model was used for this analysis because the focus was on deriving national estimates of potential energy savings. This model considers two key factors that affect the application of ATES systems for

---

(a)Operated for the U.S. Department of Energy by Battelle Memorial Institute under Contract DE-AC06-76RLO 1830.

heating and cooling: the proportion of the U.S. with suitable underground aquifers and the economic feasibility of ATES systems. The model performs the following calculation:

Total National Heat or Chill Energy Use	x	Proportion of U.S. Land Area Suitable for ATES	x	Proportion of Geographic Units Economically Suitable for ATES	=	Potential Energy Savings from Heat or Chill ATES

The first factor, the availability of suitable aquifers, requires that natural conditions at each aquifer site be evaluated so that the aquifer's suitability for ATES development can be accurately determined. These conditions include the aquifer's productivity and the presence or absence of primary and secondary porosity.

To determine the proportion of aquifers suitable for ATES, a random sample of geographic units was selected nationally and then analyzed. The geographic units chosen were zip codes. Zip code areas were chosen over other geographic areas (such as metropolitan statistical areas and counties) primarily because the zip code areas were considered sufficiently small for ATES land area requirements. Current ATES systems are restricted to relatively small serviceable areas because of the energy lost when it is distributed over large areas from a single source. A second important advantage in using zip code areas is that detailed secondary information can be obtained. Commercial market research firms can offer very detailed demographic and economic information on zip code areas because this type of data is used by the private sector for market planning.

The second factor affecting the potential of ATES is economic feasibility. Most of the costs associated with developing ATES systems are fixed costs. Generally, high, fixed-cost systems can be cost competitive only by using the economies-of-scale associated with high energy consumption.

If the economic feasibility analysis for this study had been site-specific, a variety of cost factors would have been considered. These factors would have included the purchase price for thermal energy, exploration and well drilling costs, capital equipment costs, operation and maintenance costs, and interest rates available for loans. Technical characteristics of the aquifer and its supply and distribution system also would have been considered as influences on ATES system economics.

For this study, an aggregate-level analysis was conducted based on the findings of Reilly, Brown, and Huber (1981) and Brown (1983), who developed estimates of aquifer system size requirements for heat and chill sources, respectively. Those studies found that significant economies-of-scale are available for point-demand systems of approximately 10 MW or larger.

In the present analysis, the proportion of total zip code areas that use heat or chill beyond a certain cost-effective energy consumption level (expressed in MW) was determined. To determine that proportion, a representative sample of U.S. zip codes was selected; the total heat and chill energy consumption of those zip codes areas for commercial and residential space heating/cooling and industrial process heat was then determined. Each zip code area was then evaluated to ascertain whether heat or chill energy consumption was above or below the cost-effective energy consumption level established in this study (i.e., 10 MW). The proportion of those falling above the minimum range was computed and used to estimate the total number of U.S. zip code areas that could cost-effectively use ATES systems.

To evaluate the sensitivity of required system size on ATES energy savings, a range of system sizes was studied. Studying a range was felt to be necessary because of the many situation-specific factors that influence when an ATES system will become cost-effective. Energy savings could then be calculated over a complete range of cut-offs, thereby providing a "what if" analysis. Also, short- and long-term energy-savings scenarios could then be developed. Instead of providing only one short-term and one long-term estimate of energy savings, the megawatt sliding scale was used. This scale provides a more complete range of short- and long-term energy-savings estimates for various sizes of ATES systems.

Total U.S. energy savings from ATES can be calculated from the following formula, which is derived from the model presented above:

$$\text{Total Potential Energy Savings} = \left(\begin{array}{l}\text{Proportion of Zips Both Geo-}\\ \text{logically/Economically Suit-}\\ \text{able for Heat Storage}\end{array} \times \begin{array}{l}\text{Total Space and Process}\\ \text{Heating in the U.S.}\end{array}\right) + \left(\begin{array}{l}\text{Proportion of Zips Both Geo-}\\ \text{logically/Economically Suit-}\\ \text{able for Chill Storage}\end{array} \times \begin{array}{l}\text{Total Space Cooling}\\ \text{in the U.S.}\end{array}\right)$$

EVALUATION OF LAND AREA SUITABLE FOR ATES

To determine the proportion of the U.S. land area suitable for ATES applications, a simple random sample of zip codes was selected. A normal random number generator was used to draw 50 zip codes from a complete data base of 40,000 U.S. zip codes.

Table 1 shows the results of the evaluation of the 50 zip code areas. Of the 50 sites, 14 (28%) were found to be unsuitable for any form of ATES. Twenty-two sites (44%) were found to be suitable for both large- and small-scale ATES. Fourteen sites (28%) were found suitable for only small-scale ATES; of these, four (29%) were suitable for only chill and low-heat storage because of insufficient overburden for high heat conditions.

ESTIMATION OF ENERGY USE IN SELECTED ZIP CODES

The formulas used to estimate the total energy use within a zip code are displayed in Figure 1. These formulas show the three important components in the estimates:

1. energy use by residents - To estimate energy use by residents, a regional estimate was developed of average per person energy use for heat and chill (Table 2). Residential energy use in each zip code area was obtained by multiplying the average energy use per person by the number of individuals who live in that area.

2. energy use by employees - The basic method for estimating energy use by employees was similar to that described above. A regional estimate of average per employee energy use was developed for heat and chill (Table 3). Employee energy use in each zip code area was then the product of average energy use per employee and the number of individuals who work in that zip code area.

3. industrial process energy use - The estimate of industrial process heat was determined from a list of individual Standard Industrial Classification (SIC) codes within each zip code. Industrial process energy consumption was calculated as the proportion of firms from an SIC code (on a national basis) located within a zip code multiplied by that SIC code's total national consumption of process heat. Table 4 includes industrial process sources and uses of heat by SIC code.

TABLE 1. Suitability of 50 Potential ATES Sites

Unsuitable	Small-Scale Only[(a)]	Large- and Small-Scale[(b)]
14/50 (28%)	14/50 (28%)	22/50 (44%)

(a) A small-scale ATES site can support a <10-MW peak demand.

(b) Large-scale aquifers can also be used for small-scale applications of ATES.

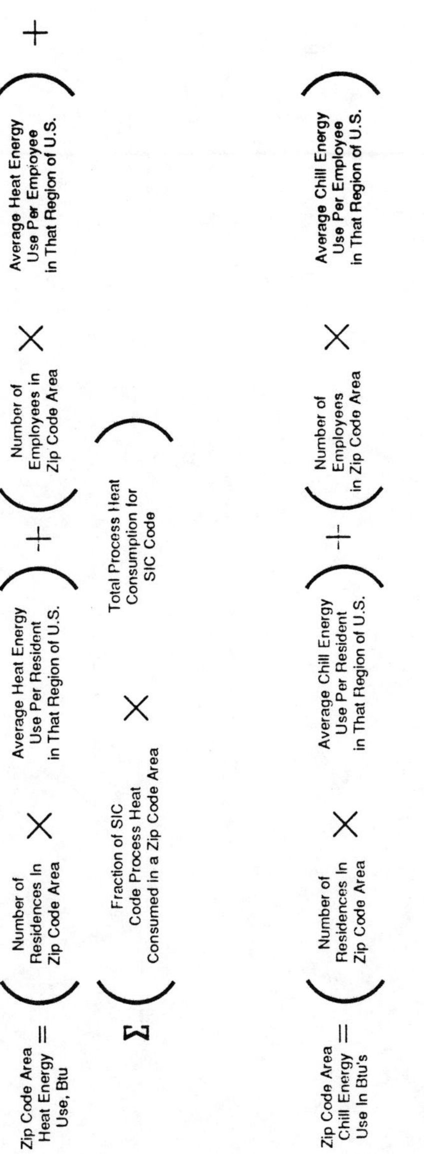

FIGURE 1. Model to Estimate the Total Heat and Cool Energy Use

TABLE 2. Average Annual Energy Use (MMBtu) Per Resident

Area	Heat					Chill	
	Electricity	Gas	Oil/ Kerosene	LPG	Total	Electricity	Total
Northeast	1.84	16.81	18.71	0.44	37.80	0.32	0.32
North Central	1.96	31.84	2.20	2.04	38.03	0.84	0.84
South	3.40	13.03	1.99	1.27	19.69	2.86	2.86
West	2.44	17.87	0.86	0.58	21.74	0.53	0.53

TABLE 3. Average Annual Energy Use (MMBtu) Per Employee (U.S. Department of Energy 1983)

Area	Heat					Chill				
	Electricity	Gas	Oil	Steam	Total	Electricity	Gas	Oil	Steam	Total
Northeast	3.71	17.65	12.31	5.14	38.81	5.09	1.11	--	--	6.20
North Central	3.46	42.04	1.33	6.38	53.21	8.49	4.18	--	--	12.67
South	5.22	18.8	4.04	1.28	29.35	10.93	1.95	--	--	12.88
West	5.23	24.29	0.91	2.58	33.01	6.15	2.22	--	--	8.37

TABLE 4. Industrial Process Sources and Uses of Heat by SIC Code

Industry Description	SIC Code	Waste Energy Available for Storage, trillion Btu	Industry Demand for 80°F to 400°F Heat, trillion Btu
Food	20		
	2011	48.8	36.6
	2026	21.4	7.9
	2033	16.5	16.4
	2046	37.2	23.1
	2051	7.1	1.8
	2062	29.2	26.3
	2063	53.2	34.7
	2075	36.2	40.9
	2082	41.9	23.9
Textiles	22		
	2221	34.5	22.5
	2262	46.8	32.0
Lumber	24		
	2411	0.1	--
	2421	144.7	148.4
	2499	4.1	1.8
Pulp/paper	26		
	2611	152.9	115.2
	2621	533.0	419.1
	2631	477.8	342.7
	2653	2.5	3.5
	2661	18.2	14.9
Chemicals	28		
	2812	249.0	151.2
	2813	87.0	34.8
	2816	24.5	12.0
	2819	98.3	105.1
	2821	42.9	11.2
	2822	29.0	8.7
	2823	25.4	25.4
	2824	148.9	32.0
	2834	6.2	4.4
	2865	137.6	94.0
	2869	239.1	46.8
	2873	247.2	25.7
	2874	62.7	22.6
	2899	3.1	1.6
Petroleum	29		
	2911	1880.1	2.3
	2951	7.2	--
Rubber	30		
	3011	9.3	25.5
	3069	30.1	39.4
	3079	35.6	--

TABLE 4. (contd)

Industry Description	SIC Code	Waste Energy Available for Storage, trillion Btu	Industry Demand for 80°F to 400°F Heat, trillion Btu
Stone, clay and glass	32		
	2311	13.7	--
	3221	55.9	--
	3229	14.4	--
	3241	179.1	--
	3251	32.9	--
	3273	1.2	--
	3274	27.2	--
	3275	27.3	--
	3296	32.1	7.5
Primary metals	33		
	3321	789.1	62.5
	3313	16.5	--
	3321	117.7	--
	3331	46.5	1.1
	3334	89.6	--
	3341	5.9	--
	3353	21.8	--
	3362	32.8	--
Machinery	35		
	3523	30.7	--
	3531	32.3	--
	3711	44.4	--
	3714	74.2	--
Instruments	38		
	3861	4.0	--

POTENTIAL ENERGY SAVINGS FROM ATES

Calculating the total energy-savings potential from ATES applications was the primary goal of this study. That value is the product of 1) the proportion of the U.S. with suitable aquifers, 2) the proportion of economically feasible ATES locations, and 3) the total U.S. space heating or cooling energy and process heat consumption.

Figure 2 shows the total energy savings for heat ATES systems in the U.S. for the different megawatt ranges. As illustrated, the potential energy savings ranges from 14.88% to 2.38% of total energy consumption. Because the cost-effective limits of ATES do not include the <10-MW range, the most optimistic long-term savings possible are approximately 10%, or about 8 quad of the total

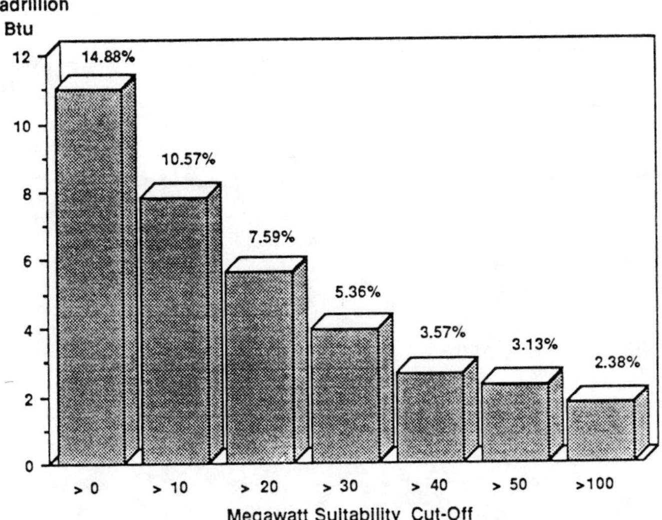

FIGURE 2. Potential Energy Savings From ATES

U.S. energy consumption. Approximately 3% to 5% (or about 3 to 4 quad) of energy is estimated as the short-term savings possible from ATES.

Table 5 displays the proportion of various-sized heat ATES systems that are economically feasible at different residential and employment population densities. These data suggest that the most lucrative markets for heat ATES systems are those with employment population densities greater than 2000 employees per square mile. This includes about 1500 zip codes, or approximately 4% of those in the U.S.

In the past, ATES systems have been viewed as a means of supplying either cost-effective heat or chill energy to end users. However, another major finding of this study was that chill storage did not display any market potential above the 10-MW level, which is typically viewed as the minimum for a cost-effective ATES heat or chill system. The implication of this finding is that large chill ATES systems will not significantly impact the U.S. energy consumption. However, this study did not address the application of chill ATES to specific sites that are uniquely suited for small-scale ATES systems. Therefore, the markets for chill ATES systems most likely would be large, single-site commercial or industrial buildings (e.g., wine cooling).

TABLE 5. Proportion of Economically Feasible Heat ATES Systems at Different Megawatt Sizes and Residential Population Densities

			Residential Density	
			>6500	<6500
Employment Density	>6500	> 10 MW	77%	73%
		> 20 MW	57%	57%
		> 30 MW	37%	43%
		> 40 MW	20%	30%
		> 50 MW	17%	17%
		>100 MW	7%	10%
	<6500 and >2000	> 10 MW	80%	77%
		> 20 MW	50%	60%
		> 30 MW	33%	47%
		> 40 MW	33%	33%
		> 50 MW	30%	33%
		>100 MW	27%	30%
	<2000	> 10 MW	53%	10%
		> 20 MW	37%	3%
		> 30 MW	27%	3%
		> 40 MW	7%	3%
		> 50 MW	7%	3%
		>100 MW	7%	3%

Currently, the reasonably acceptable levels for short-range heat ATES application estimates are those found above 30 to 40 MW because these levels have the most attractive short-term economies-of-scale. The energy savings from these levels are approximately 3 to 4 quad of energy, or about 3% to 5% of the total energy consumed in the nation.

CHARACTERIZATION OF END-USE SECTORS

Further analysis was conducted to characterize which end-use sectors will achieve the largest energy savings in the short term. This analysis assumed that larger-sized ATES systems will be economically feasible in the short term. Results from this analysis are intended to impact research and development by directing expenditures to those sectors that offer the greatest short-term energy savings.

The individual sector contributions were calculated by adding together the specific end-use sector consumptions for zip code areas whose total heat energy consumption fell within the various megawatt ranges being studied (i.e., >10 and ≤20; >20 and ≤30; >30 and ≤40; >40 and ≤50; >50 and ≤100; and >100 MW). The totals of each sector within the megawatt ranges were then converted to proportions. The findings from this analysis are summarized in Figure 3, which indicates that the industrial sector is the primary consumer of energy in larger-sized ATES systems.

Additional analysis was conducted to determine the number of industrial energy users included in zip code areas that can support larger-sized ATES systems. This analysis indicated that an average of 9.97 high energy consuming plants are located in zip code areas that consume greater than 50 MW of heat energy.

The results of this analysis indicate that the industrial sector should receive the most research and development attention because it is both the largest source and the largest user of waste heat in larger-sized ATES systems. Further, this sector is attractive because of the smaller number of hookups required for industrial users.

SOURCES OF ENERGY FOR ATES

One significant issue related to ATES is the availability of sources of waste heat to operate such a system. An important question is whether sufficient waste heat is already available from existing industrial processes to meet energy user needs or whether supplemental sources, such as cogeneration or refuse burning, must be added to an ATES system to meet those needs.

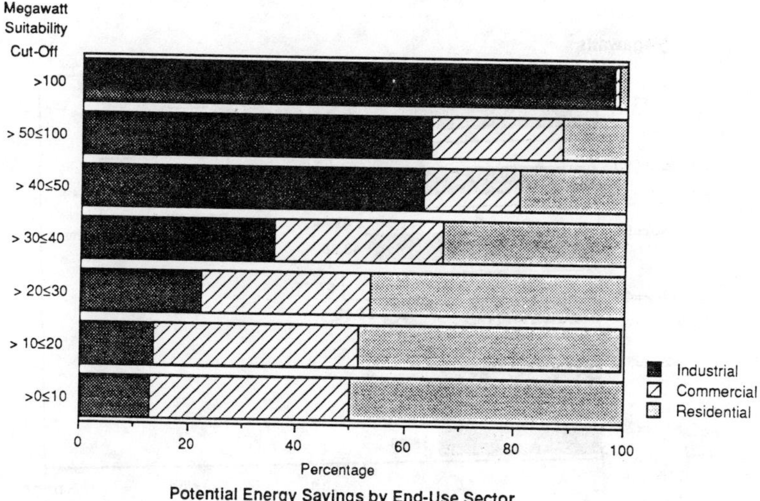

FIGURE 3. Heat Energy Savings by End Use

The availability of waste energy can be calculated using a method similar to that used to estimate the consumption of process heat. Industrial process waste heat was estimated from a list of individual SIC codes within each zip code area. Waste industrial process energy was calculated as the proportion of firms from an SIC code (on a national basis) located within a zip code area multiplied by that SIC code's yearly total national waste process heat. The waste energy values listed in Table 4 were summed to find the total energy available for storage in each zip code area.

The next part of the estimate was to sum separately the total consumption and waste for each of the zip code areas whose consumption falls into the following categories: >10 and ≤20; >20 and ≤30; >30 and ≤40; >40 and ≤50; >50 and ≤100; and >100 MW. The total consumption and waste values were then averaged for each group whose consumption values fell into one of the ranges. The waste heat averages for each range were then adjusted by multiplying the values by 66% (Reilly, Brown, and Huber 1981). The averages were adjusted to account for the energy lost in the transfer to an ATES system and from storage. With this adjustment, the average consumption can be compared to the adjusted waste energy available for each of the ranges.

The results, illustrated in Figure 4, show that most of the ranges have an average waste supply of heat energy that exceeds the average consumption of heat energy.

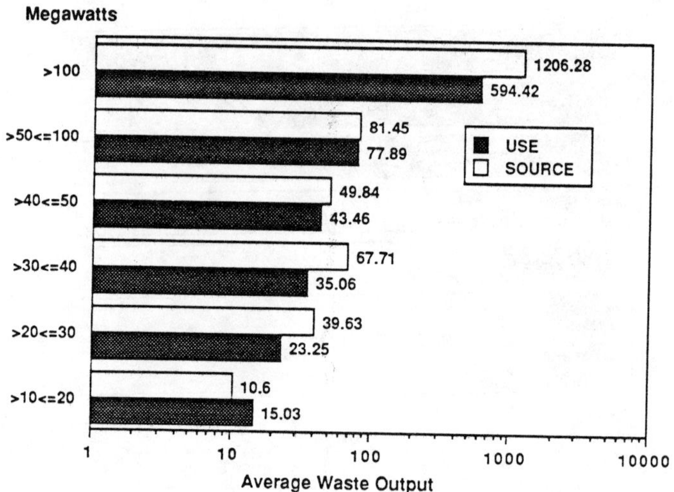

FIGURE 4. Source and Use of ATES

This demonstrates that ATES can virtually be run on waste energy that is already available in a proximity suitable for ATES applications. Only the 10- to 20-MW range failed to demonstrate the ability to supply its total consumption requirements. This implies that savings from ATES systems can legitimately be termed "energy savings" because additional sources of heat are not required.

CONCLUSIONS AND RECOMMENDATIONS

The study demonstrated that the potential energy savings for ATES are concentrated in heat applications. The estimated long-term potential energy savings for heat ATES applications were from 10.57% to 2.38% of total national energy consumption. The most attainable short-term savings were in the above 30- to 40-MW market, which translates into 3 quads of energy or approximately 3.5% of total national energy consumption.

Chill storage did not display significant energy savings with the model used. However, this finding does not indicate that chill-based ATES systems should be abandoned as a means of decreasing national energy consumption. Instead, it suggests that chill ATES should be considered for specialized markets that are not sensitive to economies-of-scale due to consumption.

The evaluation of end-use sectors determined that the industrial end users can achieve the highest potential energy savings for the large consumption markets (e.g., >50 MW). This indicates that the industrial sector is the most logical choice for further research and development, given the assumption that economic feasibility is tied directly to consumption.

The availability of waste process heat indicates that, for the markets characterized by consumption above 20 MW, sufficient excess waste heat already exists to operate heat-based ATES systems. This suggests that potential energy savings can be considered "real savings" because generally no additional sources of waste heat are needed to match energy consumption demands in a zip code area.

This study addressed the potential energy savings on an aggregate level for the U.S. However, it did not try to address the potential penetration of ATES. Penetration deals with such factors as how political and environmental issues affect the use of ATES. Further study is needed to determine the influence of these factors on market penetration.

REFERENCES

Allen, R. D., L. D. Kannberg, and J. R. Raymond. 1984. Seasonal Thermal Storage. PNL-5067, Pacific Northwest Laboratory, Richland, Washington.

Brown, D. R. 1983. Aquifer Thermal Energy Storage Costs with a Seasonal Chill Source. PNL-4587, Pacific Northwest Laboratory, Richland, Washington.

Reilly, R. W., D. R. Brown, and H. D. Huber. 1981. Aquifer Thermal Energy Storage Costs with a Seasonal Heat Source. PNL-4135, Pacific Northwest Laboratory, Richland, Washington.

U.S. Department of Energy. 1983. Nonresidential Buildings Energy Consumption Survey: Commercial Buildings Consumption and Expenditures. DOE/EIA-0318(83), Energy Information Administration, U.S. Department of Energy, Washington, D.C.

FIELD EXPERIENCE WITH AQUIFER THERMAL ENERGY STORAGE

Landis D. Kannberg
Pacific Northwest Laboratory[a]
Richland, Washington 99352

ABSTRACT

Aquifer thermal energy storage (ATES) has the potential to provide storage for large-scale building heating and cooling at many sites in the U.S. However, implementation requires careful attention to site geohydraulic and geochemical characteristics. Field tests in the U.S. have shown that over 60% of the heat injected at temperatures over 100°C can be recovered on a seasonal cycle. Similarly, aquifer storage of chilled ground water can provide building cooling with annual cooling electrical energy reductions of over 50% and a reduction in summer peak cooling electrical usage by as much as a factor of 20.

A number of projects have been built and operated around the world. China has installed numerous ATES systems in many major cities. Shanghai alone has 32 chill ATES systems for cooling textile mills and at least 10 cinemas that use ATES chill systems, as well as other locations. Installations in Europe and Scandinavia are almost exclusively low-temperature heat storage systems that use heat pumps. Two high-temperature systems (over 100°C) are in operation or undergoing preliminary testing: one in Denmark, the other in France.

Heat ATES often requires water treatment to prevent precipitation of calcium and magnesium carbonates. At some sites, consideration of other geochemical and microbiological issues (such as iron bacteria) must be resolved.

(a)Operated for the U.S. Department of Energy by Battelle Memorial Institute under Contract DE-AC06-76RLO 1830.

Progress is being made around the world to address these challenges.

INTRODUCTION

Since 1975, the United States has been actively investigating the potential for utilization of aquifers for seasonal storage of heat and chill energy.

Studies of seasonal thermal energy storage (STES) were initiated because of its promise as a means of reducing consumption of energy and especially premium fuels such as oil and natural gas. While that promise still exists, the need for rapid development and implementation of STES technologies has abated during the last several years, as premium fuel costs have remained stable or fallen.

The scope of U.S. studies, principally sponsored by the U.S. Department of Energy, has included literature review, numerical modeling of hydrothermal and geochemical processes, laboratory investigation of geochemical phenomena, and field testing. While recent efforts have concentrated on relatively high-temperature storage (up to 150°C) and on storage of winter-chilled water, earlier studies included a number of field tests at lower temperatures. Technical features of ATES will be discussed, followed by results of recent testing at the St. Paul field test facility (FTF). Discussion will then focus on field experience for lower-temperature ATES, chill ATES, foreign ATES systems, and economic factors affecting ATES. The focus of these discussions will be field results.

ATES TECHNICAL FEATURES

Aquifers are porous, permeable geologic zones containing water. Aquifer thermal energy storage (ATES) typically involves pumping ground water from an aquifer at a source well(s) for heating or cooling with waste energy and injecting the water into the aquifer for storage. The stored energy is recovered from the storage well(s) by pumping, circulating it through heating or cooling equipment, and returning to the source well(s) to complete the cycle.

Aquifers potentially suitable for ATES underlie approximately 60% of the U.S. including many metropolitan areas. However, the existence of an aquifer does not guarantee that an effective, efficient storage system can be constructed and operated. The suitability of the aquifer depends upon a number of geohydrologic factors including:

- aquifer factors
  - permeability profiles (vertical and horizontal)
  - porosity
  - thickness (especially of high permeability zones)

- regional flow
- thermal conductivity (a secondary issue)
- specific heat (thermal capacity, a secondary issue)
- physical boundaries to the aquifer (confined or unconfined)
- discovery pressure

• aquiclude/aquitard factors[a]
  - permeability
  - boundaries
  - thermal conductivity (a secondary issue)
  - specific heat (a secondary issue)

The most desirable features for an ATES system depend on the application. For example, if you intend to store heated water at temperatures over 100°C, the discovery pressure must be greater than 1 atm, meaning that a water table aquifer cannot be used. The properties listed above affect not only the system design and performance (storage efficiency, pumping requirements, number and location of wells, etc.) but also regulatory and institutional issues. It should be apparent that the development of an ATES system requires characterization of the site's geologic and geohydrologic conditions and careful attention to their impact on the design and performance of the ATES system. Legal statutes will normally regulate the use of ground water; however, additional attention should be paid to existing and planned use of the target ATES aquifer to prevent seriously impacting others as well as to protect the ATES investment. No legal groundwork has been laid concerning protection of an ATES energy inventory because no commercial heated ATES system currently operates in the U.S.; although at least two chill ATES systems are in operation.

ATES systems are rate limited as opposed to capacity limited. Hence, ATES is different from most other storage technologies. This offers distinct advantages, as well as certain disadvantages. The store can be overcharged if surplus energy is available. However, the store charge or discharge rate cannot be increased beyond a limiting value. Furthermore, the cost of the ATES system is directly related to fluid flow rates, which determine the number and size of the wells, pumps, and well spacing. In many ways these factors favor integration with buffer storage units and/or heat pumps to compensate for storage system limitations. It should be noted that the storage efficiency will improve with subsequent cycles as the aquifer is thermally conditioned.

The use of ground water for heating and cooling applications has been investigated and implemented to varying degrees for a number of years. Such utilization

---

(a)Aquicludes and aquitards hydraulically confine an aquifer due to their low hydraulic conductivity.

has, for the most part, involved modest temperature changes such as those associated with ground-water heat pumps and ground-water source air conditioners. The water chemistry issues associated with these applications have been characterized to a degree sufficient for most low-temperature applications. ATES systems can involve ground-water heating, injection, and storage at higher temperatures. Substantial changes in water chemistry are often associated with heating ground water, principally precipitation of calcium and magnesium carbonates from the ground water in heat exchangers, on piping, on well screens, and in the aquifer. Once in storage, the chemically-treated ground water will react with minerals comprising the aquifer to restore chemical equilibrium at the temperature in the storage zone. The importance of precipitation and dissolution of carbonates and silicates increase with the temperature change of the water for ATES systems. An example of this is shown in Figure 1, which shows the amount of calcium carbonate ($CaCO_3$) that precipitates from the ground water at the St. Paul FTF site upon heating to various temperatures.

Design of appropriate measures for dealing with water chemistry issues requires accurate estimation of the ground-water chemical behavior. Water treatment will be required at most ATES sites where temperatures are altered significantly (over 50°C, 120°F). While suitable water treatment techniques are readily available, the long-term requirements and impacts associated with various treatment methods are not well known. Their characterization is one objective of current field and laboratory research.

HIGH-TEMPERATURE ATES TESTING AT ST. PAUL

The St. Paul FTF was designed to inject and recover heat at a rate of 5 MW (thermal), using a well doublet spaced at 255 m (840 ft), operating at 18.9 liters/sec (300 gpm) injection rate and maximum water temperature of 150°C (302°F). Steam from the campus district heating plant (coal-fired) is used to supply heat for storage in the ground water. The first phase of testing at the St. Paul FTF consisted of four short-term test cycles of heated water injection-storage-recovery, which were completed in December 1983. The second testing phase included two long-term test cycles, both comprising 60 days each of injection, storage, and recovery.

The short-term test cycles involved relatively small fluid volumes injected and stored for relatively short time periods. When approximately equal injection, storage, and recovery periods were employed, and when the geohydraulic and heat transfer characteristics of the aquifer were considered, full seasonal storage efficiencies between 60% and 70% are expected.

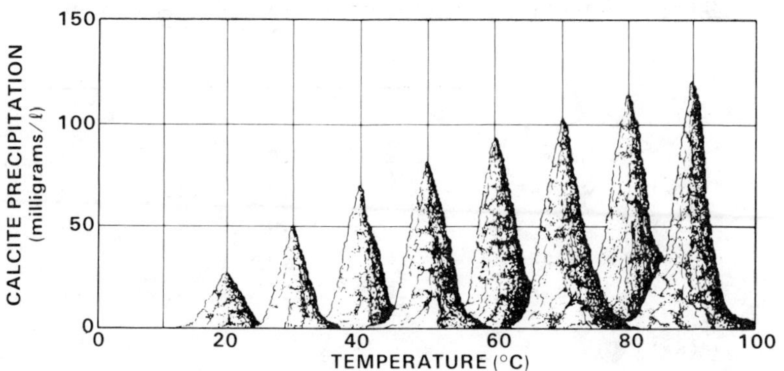

FIGURE 1. Calcite Precipitation as a Function of Temperature at the St. Paul Field Test Facility

Dealing with the large amount of $CaCO_3$ precipitation was a major issue of the short-term cycle tests. Rather crude temporary precipitation reactor beds of crushed limestone were installed downstream of the heat exchangers to reduce precipitate in the injection stream. However, this method required frequent changes of the reactor bed limestone and cleaning of the heat exchanger. A sodium ion exchange water softening system was installed prior to the initiation of the first long-term test cycle. After initial problems, the water softening system effectively provided soft water to the heat exchanger, thus eliminating further $CaCO_3$ precipitation problems.

The first long-term test cycle was initiated on November 14, 1984, and proceeded until January 22, 1985. Storage was maintained until April 2, when withdrawal began. Withdrawal was complete May 31, 1985. The second long-term test cycle was initiated on October 2, 1986 and completed April 4, 1987. Unlike earlier cycles, there were no significant water treatment related problems encountered during operation. Pertinent data resulting from the short-term and long-term test cycles are given in Tables 1 and 2 (Hoyer and Splettstoesser 1987). Figure 2 illustrates the injection and withdrawal temperatures for the latest long-term test cycles and is generally representative of that expected for candidate ATES sites using similar operating conditions.

The performance of the St. Paul FTF during the short-term and first two long-term test cycles is encouraging. Reasonably high storage efficiencies (approximately 65%) are being achieved for relatively high fluid injection temperatures. A third test cycle is scheduled to evaluate storage and geochemical behavior in a more restricted portion of the aquifer. Plans call for the stored heat to be used to heat a local building.

TABLE 1. Summary of Short-Term Cycles, University of Minnesota Field Test Facility

	Cycle 1	Cycle 2	Cycle 3	Cycle 4
Duration (days)				
Injection, pumping	5.2	8.0	7.7	7.7
Injection, total	17	10.0	10.4	12.0
Storage	13	90.0	9.7	10.1
Recovery, pumping	5.2	8.0	7.7	7.7
Recovery, total	5.2	8.0	8.0	7.7
Temperature (average °C)				
Source water	11.0	20.5	36.1	52.6
Injected water	89.4	97.4	106.1	114.8
Recovered water	59.2	55.2	81.1	89.1
Flow rate (average ℓ/sec)[(a)]				
Injection	18.4	17.6	18.3	17.9
Recovery	18.1	17.8	17.3	17.8
Volume (10^4 m^3)[(b)]				
Injection	0.83	1.22	1.22	1.19
Recovery	0.81	1.23	1.18	1.19
Energy (GWh)[(c)]				
Added	0.770	1.084	0.989	0.867
Recovered (above source temperature)	0.453	0.495	0.617	0.503
Energy recovery factor[(d)]				
Using source[(e)] temperature	0.59	0.46	0.62	0.58
Using ambient[(f)] temperature	0.59	0.52	0.71	0.75

(a) Multiply ℓ/sec by 15.85 to obtain gal/min (i.e., 18 ℓ/sec = 285 gal/min)

(b) Multiply m^3 by 264.2 to obtain gal (10^4 m^3 = 2.6 x 10^6 gal)

(c) Multiply GWh by 3412 to obtain million Btu (i.e., 1 GWh = 3.412 x 10^9 Btu)

(d) Recovered energy divided by injected energy.

(e) Energy recovery factor computed using actual source temperature. Source temperature increases because of "storage" in the zone around the source well between subsequent cycles.

(f) Energy recovery factor computed using the normal groundwater temperature at the site, 11.1°C, as the reference temperature for both injected and recovered energy.

TABLE 2. Summary of Long-Term Cycles, University of Minnesota Field Test Facility

	Cycle 1	Cycle 2
Duration (days)		
Injection, pumping	59.1	59.3
Injection, total	74.7	65.0
Storage	64.0	59.1
Recovery, pumping	58.0	59.7
Recovery, total	58.8	59.8
Temperature (average °C)		
Source water	19.7	33.1
Injected water	108.5	117.7
Recovered water	74.7	85.1
Flow rate (average ℓ/sec)[(a)]		
Injection	18.0	18.3
Recovery	18.4	17.9
Volume (10^4 m^3)[(b)]		
Injection	9.21	9.37
Recovery	9.22	9.21
Energy (GWh)[(c)]		
Added	9.47	9.05
Recovered (above source temperature)	5.86	5.46
Energy recovery factor[(d)]		
Using source[(e)] temperature	0.62	0.60
Using ambient[(f)] temperature	0.65	0.68

(a) Multiply ℓ/sec by 15.85 to obtain gal/min (i.e., 18 ℓ/sec = 285 gal/min)

(b) Multiply m^3 by 264.2 to obtain gal (10^4 m^3 = 2.6 x 10^6 gal)

(c) Multiply GWh by 3412 to obtain million Btu (i.e., 1 GWh = 3.412 x 10^9 Btu)

(d) Recovered energy divided by injected energy.

(e) Energy recovery factor computed using actual source temperature. Source temperature increases because of "storage" in the zone around the source well between subsequent cycles.

(f) Energy recovery factor computed using the normal groundwater temperature at the site, 11.1°C, as the reference temperature for both injected and recovered energy.

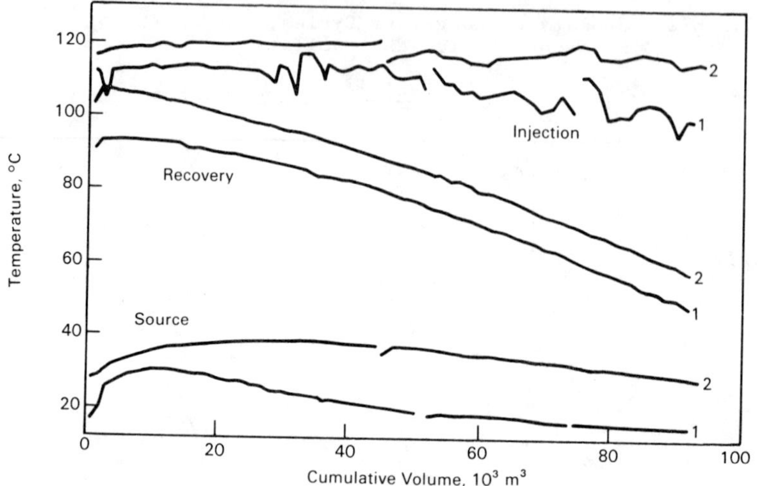

FIGURE 2. Temperatures of Source, Injected, Recovered, and Returned Water for Long-Term Cycles 1 and 2

LOW-TEMPERATURE HEAT ATES

Low-temperature ATES has advantages in terms of higher storage efficiencies and greater flexibility for integration with other sources, such as solar. Furthermore, the technical demands and problems associated with lower-temperature ATES are less challenging, specifically in geochemical and water treatment issues. It is likely that high-temperature ATES applications will involve higher quality energy sources and will be used where either process heat or domestic hot water requirements encourage storage at higher temperatures (up to 150°C).

The temperature of operation is a significant issue when dealing with storage, especially solar-collected heat or at sites where high-temperature waste heat is not available. For solar systems, the cost of collectors decreases as design temperature is reduced (Kannberg 1986). With ATES, the temperature of the recovered fluid declines steadily with time during energy recovery. Design of solar/ATES systems must take this into account by either overcharging the aquifer, employing supplemental fuel consumption, or integrating with heat pumps. The use of heat pumps significantly increases the flexibility of the entire solar/ATES or waste heat/ATES system. Design criteria can be relaxed because the system need not be designed for extreme annual conditions (such as minimum solar collection or waste heat supply, maximum annual load, or minimum storage efficiencies). An optimum can be defined based on relative costs of solar collection or waste heat supply, storage, and supplemental energy. Of course the optimization of these factors is site-specific because of local solar, waste heat, geotechnical, and economic conditions.

CHILL ATES

The primary function of chill ATES is to store winter chill in an aquifer for meeting summer air conditioning requirements. Two operating systems of this nature are installed in the U.S. A chill ATES system has been in operation at the Student Recreation Center of the University of Alabama, in Tuscaloosa, Alabama, since 1984. The U.S. Department of Energy is supporting extensive monitoring of this system by the University. The system is shown schematically in Figure 3. The system was originally designed to meet the 148-ton cooling load by using six wells, three for supply of water (warm wells) and three for storage of chilled water (cold wells). If geohydraulic conditions had been good, the site would have been overdesigned. However, the presence of a strong geohydraulic gradient and high hydraulic conductivity in the aquifer combined to substantially reduce potential system performance. Even under the most adverse conditions, the system was able to reduce annual cooling electrical energy consumption by 50% and summer peak electrical demand for cooling from 147 kW to 8 kW (Raymond and Kannberg 1986). The major electrical energy consumer in the system is the cooling tower blower. Cooling ponds are now being considered to reduce this energy expense.

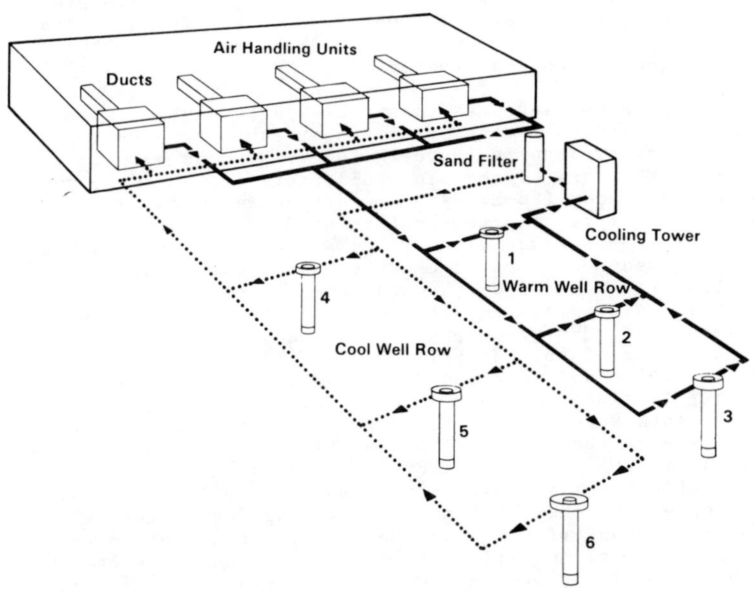

FIGURE 3. Student Recreation Center Chill ATES System

Despite the satisfactory energy performance of the system, modifications have been made to use only four of the existing wells (two each for warm and cold wells) and to use the recovered water for either irrigation or pumping to waste as opposed to reinjection in the source well. These changes have been undertaken to control regional flow. Unfortunately, the exceptionally warm winter of 1986-1987 reduced the amount of chill that could be stored, reducing the system's effectiveness in the summer of 1987.

A second system, similar to the one at Tuscaloosa, has been installed at a new U.S. Postal Service mail processing center in Melville, New York, on Long Island. This system will serve, in conjunction with two 100-ton chillers, a cooling load of 385 tons. The system was placed in operation in the fall of 1987.

Economic studies indicate that chill ATES will rarely benefit from economies-of-scale associated with large loads (over 10 MWt). This is because such cooling loads are not as prevalent as large heating loads. Nonetheless, the technology could provide cost-effective chill storage to reduce summer electric peak loads and annual electrical consumption.

FOREIGN ATES SYSTEMS

A number of European and Scandinavian countries have installed ATES systems. Most of these systems have stored low-temperature (nominally 30 to 40°C) heat for use with heat pumps. However, two high-temperature (over 90°C) systems have been constructed.

The Netherlands has constructed a low-temperature heat ATES system for use with a heat pump for a building in the town of Bunnik (Bredero Energy Systems 1986). In this system, heat from solar collectors (285 MWh/yr) and a computer room (96 MWh/yr) are either injected into a shallow aquifer at a temperature of 30°C for storage (316 MWh/yr) or used directly in a heat pump (55 MWh/yr). A gas-fired heat pump is used to increase the 305 MWh/yr of heat recovered from the aquifer at a temperature from 26°C to 14°C to 576 MWh/yr. A gas-fired boiler augments this with 85 MWh/yr to provide the annual building heating requirement of 661 MWh/yr. The ATES portion uses a single well doublet and is assumed to have an energy recovery factor (defined in Table 1) of 0.80. By design, one-third more water is recovered than injected to achieve this energy recovery. Although this system became operational in the spring of 1985, limited information is available. Early reports from small-scale initial tests indicate that there was some minor clogging of the well due to leakage of air into the mains, precipitation of iron in water, and filtration of iron in one portion of the well. There was no clogging of the heat exchanger. From early results it was also determined that buoyancy-driven circulation in the well and aquifer resulted in loss of all injected soft water. There was no scaling with calcite when using the original (unsoftened) ground water and, therefore, the clogging risk determined by geochemical equilibrium calculations, was overestimated for this system. Precautions will be taken in the future to prevent air leakage in the circulating system and the well will be blocked with a packer to retard buoyancy-driven circulations. Measurements of the chemical and hydraulic behavior and energy performance at this site will continue until the end of 1989.

Sweden has installed four ATES systems, has two under construction, is designing two more, and has field tests underway at yet another (Kannberg 1986). All of the systems involve low-temperature storage in conjunction with heat pumps. Information is only available for a few of the sites.

At an ATES site in Klippan, energy is extracted from a lake at 15 to 20°C and used to heat ground water, which is then injected into a water table aquifer for storage. Information from a year ago indicates that the injection wells clogged during operation of this system. Although a temporary solution was used to inject the water, a permanent solution has not been obtained.

At Kristianstad, Sweden, an ATES system was designed for low-temperature heating and cooling in conjunction with a heat pump. Little information is available at this site; however, it is known that the system requires more cooling than heating. This has resulted in breakthrough of heated water into the cold storage well reducing the cold recovery temperature.

At Falun, Sweden, pumping was conducted from a line of wells to draw nearby warm lake water into the ground water. By continued pumping, it was reasoned that the warm ground water would be recovered in winter for heating applications. Actual pumping temperatures when the warm ground-water plume reached the pumping wells (1985) were far less than expected, possibly as a result of flooding at the site in 1984. There is some suspicion that iron is precipitating in the piping as well.

A low-temperature heat pump/ATES heating and cooling system has been designed for installation at Brunnsviken, Sweden. While little information is currently available on this project, it is planned that this system will provide 2100 MWh/yr of heating and 2600 MWh/yr of direct ground-water cooling. The waste cooling heat from the administration and computer buildings will be a source of very low-temperature (15°C) heat for storage in the aquifer.

A high-temperature (100°C) ATES site in Denmark has been studied since 1975 when geohydraulic and heat transport investigations began (Kannberg 1986). The first low-temperature energy test occurred with injection at about 35°C. The energy recovery was 55% of that injected. The first high-temperature cycle began in 1983 and provided nearly 9.2 MWh to the local district heating system. Operations at the site continue through the present but not without difficulties. Early operations at the site were plagued by flow of heated water up the outside of the injection well casing to the surface, breaching the confining layer. A second injection well was necessary to correct this problem. As with most high-temperature ATES systems, water treatment to control precipitation of calcium carbonate was necessary. The treatment method involved mixing acid with the source ground water, followed by vacuum degassing to remove CO_2. Vacuum leaks that introduced oxygen into the system, and poor acid control enhanced corrosion in the system, making system piping and water treatment control system changes necessary.

A unique ATES concept is being tested near Lausanne, Switzerland (Kannberg 1986). The SPEOS concept involves solar-heated ground water injection into an aquifer at one elevation through perforated radial spokes from a large diameter center well. Source water for heating and injection is obtained from a similar but deeper radial spoke arrangement using the same center well. During recovery the process is reversed with water withdrawn from the upper radial spokes and reinjected, after cooling in a heat exchanger, in the lower radial spokes. In this manner the system works somewhat like a stratified tank. Work on the project began in 1979, with the heat source being solar energy. Problems related to scaling due to precipitation of calcium carbonate required strong acid treatment. Additionally, regional ground-water flow at the site is quite significant and limited measures have been undertaken to control this flow. Two test cycles have been conducted. Injection temperatures have ranged from 30 to 80°C and recovery ranged from 52°C to 19°C. The recovery factors for the two cycles were 0.41 and 0.42, respectively (using the natural ground-water temperature of 12°C). Over 1300 MWh were injected on the last cycle with 643 MWh recovered. A third cycle is being conducted, although results have not yet been reported.

Perhaps the most aggressive ATES project is being conducted by the French (Housse and Despois 1985). A 20-MW, very high-temperature (180°C) ATES system has been installed near Thoiry, France, approximately 90 km southwest of Paris. The system will take heat from a nearby waste incineration plant during the summer to charge the store. The aquifer is located at a depth of approximately 1500 m (over 8 times deeper than the aquifer used in the St. Paul tests). The project has made use of French directional drilling technology, practiced in the petroleum industry. A single injection well is surrounded by three peripheral source wells. On-site water treatment tests were conducted followed by plant design. Water treatment is required not only to control calcium carbonate scaling but also for silica scaling, an issue not yet demonstrated to be a problem at lower-temperature ATES sites. At last word, preliminary testing was being conducted in the late spring of 1987. It was anticipated that the system would be operational for summer heat charging in the summer of 1987. This project is part of an ambitious French program to use waste heat and electricity from French nuclear plants and other sources to displace oil consumed for winter heating of buildings. At 20 MWt, the system has nearly four times the power rating of the St. Paul field test facility, known to be the largest in the world to date.

The only known countries investigating or using chill ATES are the Republic of China, Canada, and United States. Chill ATES has been practiced in China for nearly 20 years and now is used in many large cities for both chill storage and low-temperature heat storage (Sun 1986). Although most of the applications have been in sand and gravel aquifers, some systems have used limestone karst aquifers. At good sites, recovery efficiencies up to 75% have been obtained. ATES is often combined with other purposes such as control of subsidence and salt water intrusion.

Chill ATES began in China inadvertently. The water table was being drawn down dramatically in Shanghai during the summer as water was extracted for cooling textile mills. Subsidence had begun to be a problem. To correct this problem, cold river water was injected into the aquifer during the winter to artificially recharge the aquifer. The Chinese discovered that the recovered water was substantially cooler than normal. Chill ATES has been implemented at a large number of sites in China as a result of this experience for the sole purpose of providing reduced temperature ground water for industrial cooling. In Shanghai alone, over 32 textile factories use ATES, primarily for cooling. It is estimated that they save nearly 81,000 tons of coal that would normally be required for running absorption cooling systems. Water warmed during cooling operations is reinjected and used for heating in the winter, saving another 10,000 tons of coal. Also in Shanghai, chill ATES is used for air conditioning at least 10 cinemas and the airport lounge.

In Canada, two government office buildings have been equipped with ATES systems. One of these, in Scarborough, near Toronto, is connected to a solar collection system to provide both heating and cooling. A second chill ATES system has been installed at the Atmospheric Environment Service building in Downsview, Ontario. The aquifer used at Scarborough is 50-m deep and 10-m thick. Four wells have been drilled and completed for both injection and pumping. To date the system has only been used for cooling but operators have found the system very flexible and use for both heating and cooling is planned. The project at Downsview has proceeded through site characterization and the installation of six wells. Problems with completion of these wells has delayed the project.

In addition to the projects described above ATES is under investigation in Japan, Finland, England, and Italy.

ATES ECONOMICS

Generally, significant economies-of-scale are available for ATES systems. In fact, fairly large systems are often required for cost-effectiveness. For point demand heat systems, costs are fairly constant for peak demands (at 25% load factor) of 8 MW to 10 MW. Costs rise quickly for systems with peak demands less than 3 MW. Distributed demand systems (such as residential loads) require at least this size because of the necessity to include distribution piping networks. Lengthy transmission distances can quickly result in prohibitive costs, especially for smaller (less than 5 MW) ATES systems, because of piping costs and transmission losses.

Studies of hypothetical ATES/district heating systems indicate that significant ATES factors affecting cost of delivered energy are the cost of charging energy, ATES capital cost, charging temperature, system size, transmission distance, and storage efficiency (Reilly, Brown and Huber 1981). ATES systems are capital-intensive, making the cost of financing important. Thus, groups such as municipalities (having access to relatively cheap financing) are good candidates for early commercialization. Unfortunately, such groups and their financial sources tend to be risk-averse, increasing the need for state and federal research and development agencies to fund demonstration facilities.

REFERENCES

Bredero Energy Systems. 1986. Office Building at Bunnik: Aquifer Storage of Solar Energy. Bredero Energy Systems, Bunnik, The Netherlands.

Housse, B. A., and J. Despois. 1985. "Prototype de Stockage Souterrain de Chaleur a Haute Temperature a Thiverval-Grignon (France)." In Proceedings of the III International Conference on Energy Storage for Building Heating and Cooling, pp. 71-74. Public Works Canada, Ottawa, Canada.

Hoyer, M. C., and J. F. Splettstoesser. 1987. "Results of Short- and Long-Term Aquifer Thermal Energy Storage Experimental Cycles." In Proceedings of the 22nd Intersociety Energy Conversion Engineering Conference, pp. 1283-1287. American Aeronautics and Astronautics, New York, New York.

Kannberg, L. D., 1986. "Aquifer Thermal Energy Storage in the United States." In Proceedings of the 1986 Annual Meeting of the American Solar Energy Society, Inc., pp. 522-525. American Solar Energy Society, Boulder, Colorado.

Raymond, J. R., and L. D. Kannberg. 1986. Underground Energy Storage Program 1985 Annual Summary. PNL-5925, Pacific Northwest Laboratory, Richland, Washington.

Reilly, R. W., D. R. Brown and H. D. Huber. 1981. Aquifer Thermal Energy Storage Costs with a Seasonal Heat Source. PNL-4135, Pacific Northwest Laboratory, Richland, Washington.

Sun, Y. September, 1986. "Aquifer Energy Storage Applications in China." STES Newsletter. C. F. Tsang, ed., Vol. VIII, No. 4.

COMPARISON OF U. S. AND INTERNATIONAL PROGRESS IN NUCLEAR POWER GENERATION

Dr. Peter Murray, Director, Nuclear Programs

Westinghouse Electric Corporation
Washington, D. C. 20006

INTRODUCTION

Four decades of effort have now been devoted worldwide to the development of nuclear power. Much has been done, much has been achieved and many lessons have been learned. More than 400 nuclear power plants [1] are now in operation in 26 countries supplying 16% of the world's electricity demand and 4500 reactor years of experience have been accumulated. In some countries, notably France, nuclear power has become the most important source of electricity. The progress of nuclear power from technical concept to commercial reality has been characterized by many successes and also some failures. The successful results are seldom publicized and it is the purpose of this paper to outline the status of nuclear power, compare the position in the U. S. with that overseas and finally to describe the programs proceeding in the U. S. in anticipation of the return of nuclear power orders and new starts in the 1990's.

STATUS OF NUCLEAR POWER

The status and future prospects for nuclear power have been reviewed extensively by J. S. Moore(2). The major points are:

o Nuclear power now supplies 16% of the world's electricity as shown in the data compiled by the International Atomic Energy Agency in Table 1. France produces over 70% of its electrical energy from nuclear power Belgium and Taiwan 60% Switzerland and Sweden 42% . . . and the United States 18.4%. There are 307

TABLE 1

NUCLEAR POWER REACTORS IN OPERATION, UNDER CONSTRUCTION AND PLANNED AT THE END OF 1986

COUNTRY	IN OPERATION		UNDER CONSTRUCTION		PLANNED		NUCLEAR ELECTRICITY SUPPLIED IN 1986	
	UNITS	MWe	UNITS	MWe	UNITS	MWe	TWh	% of Total
BELGIUM	8	5,486	-	-	-	-	37.1	67.0
BULGARIA	4	1,632	4	3,862	2	1,906	11.2	30.0
CANADA	18	11,249	5	4,361	-	-	67.2	14.7
CZECHOSLOVAKIA	7	2,799	9	5,508	6	5,484	16.2	21.0
FINLAND	4	2,310	-	-	-	-	18.0	38.4
FRANCE	49	44,693	14	17,809	1	1,450	241.4	69.8
GERMANY DR	5	1,694	6	3,432	4	1,632	12.2	11.6
GERMANY FR	21	18,947	4	4,052	10	12,621	112.1	29.4
HUNGARY	3	1,235	1	410	5	4,750	7.0	18.3
ITALY	3	1,273	3	1,999	2	1,900	8.2	4.5
JAPAN	35	25,821	10	8,431	7	6,785	166.5	24.7
KOREA RP	7	5,380	2	1,800	2	1,800	26.6	43.6
SPAIN	8	5,599	2	1,920	4	3,780	35.9	29.4
SWEDEN	12	9,455	-	-	-	-	67.0	50.3
SWITZERLAND	5	2,932	-	-	2	2,140	21.3	39.2
TAIWAN	6	4,918	-	-	4	4,120	25.8	43.8
UK	38	10,222	4	2,520	1	1,175	51.8	18.4
USA	99	84,592	21	23,301	-	-	414.0	16.6
USSR	50	27,657	33	30,660	36	36,163	148.0	10.6

Source: International Atomic Energy Agency Power Reactor Information System,

nuclear power plants operating outside the Soviet Bloc today. Those 307 plants have provided about 4,000 reactor years of operating experience and are operating safely and economically. 134 of these plants are based on Westinghouse pressurized water reactor technology and over 50 are based on the boiling water reactor technology developed by General Electric.

o Nuclear power is the second largest source of electricity in the U. S. Only coal provides more. Today, 108 nuclear plants are operating in the U. S. -- and these plants now generate more electricity than the U. S. was using in total as recently as 1953. By the early 1990's, 127 nuclear plants will be generating 20% of our electricity. Nearly all of the continental U. S. is served by nuclear power -- either directly by a local plant . . . or indirectly through utility power purchases and wheeling. In four States (Vermont, Maine, Connecticut and South Carolina) nuclear power provides more than 50% of the total electricity generated. Six other States produce more than 30% of their electricity from nuclear plants.

o Since the oil embargo of 1973, the amount of electricity produced by nuclear power has quadrupled. As a result, the use of oil for electrical generation has dropped dramatically. In the past decade, nuclear power has saved U. S. consumers between $35 billion and $56 billion, when compared to the cost of the same amount of electricity generated by coal or oil.

o Nuclear power has in addition enabled countries without the indigenous natural resources of the U. S. to generate economical electricity. Nuclear power is now the largest and most economical single source of electricity in Japan, where 35 nuclear plants provide 29% of its electrical energy. By the year 2030,(3) Japan is planning to achieve 60% of its electricity production by nuclear power with 100 additional plants. Side by side with the commitment to nuclear power plants, is the resolve to have an independent nuclear fuel cycle established in Japan early next century.

o Korea and Taiwan now obtain a considerable proportion of their electricity from nuclear power. Because they lack substantial supplies of indigenous fossil fuels, nuclear power is an essential requirement for economic growth in both countries. For example, Korea's analyses indicate that electricity produced by nuclear power is as much as 40 percent cheaper than energy produced by imported coal. With eight plants in operation and four more either in construction or on the drawing board, Korea gets 54% of its electricity from nuclear power. And, Taiwan's six nuclear plants produce 60% of its electricity.

In Europe, France produces over 70% of its electricity from 49 nuclear plants and another 14 are under construction. All of these plants were built by Framatome. Nuclear power from French plants also provides energy for much of the continent. In 1986, Electricite de France, the French utility, exported 25 billion kilowatt-hours of electricity throughout the continent and to the United Kingdom. Switzerland imported 9.5 billion kilowatt hours; Italy -- 6.3 billion, the U.K. -- 4.4 billion, the Benelux countries -- 2.2 billion, Germany -- 2 billion, and Spain -- approximately 1 billion.

In 1987, the United Kingdom decided to continue its nuclear power program by adopting Westinghouse pressurized water reactor technology. This decision was based on the results of an exhaustive evaluation of PWR technology. After a four year inquiry and another two years of evaluation, Sir Frank Layfield, in charge of the inquiry, recommended approval of the project. A major factor in the decision was the large amount of worldwide experience which exists with the mainstream PWR. Initial construction work for the Sizewell B nuclear plant has already begun. The four loop 1150 MWe Sizewell B is based on the Standardized Nuclear Unit Project System (SNUPPS) Callaway design, modified to U.K. licensing requirements. Present studies indicate that a PWR plant such as Sizewell B typically would save U.K. consumers £40M ($60M equivalent) per year compared with the U.K. Advanced Gas Cooled Reactor and £100M ($150M equivalent) per year compared with a new coal plant. Sizewell B is designed as a standard reference plant, and the U.K. Central Electricity Generating Board plans to build a series of five or six identical units for entry into service up to the year 2000. In September 1987 CEGB made a formal application to build the second PWR at Hinckley Point in Southwest England.

CHERNOBYL

The British decisions are particularly significant in the post-Chernobyl environment. Chernobyl reinforced public fears; we cannot minimize the importance of those fears, nor can we minimize the importance of the accident itself. Chernobyl was an appalling accident. It was also an anomaly caused by a technology that developed in relative isolation.

The Chernobyl reactor's RBMK technology is fundamentally different from the reactor technology adopted by the rest of the world. After an extensive analysis, the U. S. Nuclear Regulatory Commission saw no need to make design or operating changes in U. S. plants. The decision of the British to build the Sizewell B plant, of the Koreans to build their 11th and 12th plants with Combustion Engineering units and of the Japanese to proceed with their expanded nuclear program reinforced the NRC's evaluation. Those decisions clearly demonstrated that U.S. light water reactor technology continues to have the confidence of the developed and developing world. Furthermore, the international adoption of U. S. light water reactor technology provides a growing reservoir of data, development and experience. As an example, more than twenty nations have active technology transfer arrangements during the steady refinement and growing reliability of PWR technology and an increasing number of nations are recognizing the great benefits from these arrangements.

As regards power generation costs, data for the U. S. for 1986 has been assembled and analyzed by the Utility Data Institute (4) for 389 coal fired plants, 135 gas fired plants, 74 oil fired plants and 61 nuclear power plants. These plants generated 98% of all steam-electric generation in 1986. Nuclear plants produced 19% of the electricity at an average cost of $19.05 per net megawatt hour of electricity. Corresponding rates for other fuels were coal ($21.64 per mwhr), gas ($30.43 per mwhr) and oil ($33.99 per mwhr). The top 20 plants (least expensive) included 11 nuclear plants, eight coal fired plants and one gas fired plant.

THREE MILE ISLAND

Chernobyl brought little information that was relevant to U. S. technology. In contrast, the enormous amount that we learned from the Three Mile Island accident nearly a decade ago changed the direction of the U. S. nuclear industry. Three Mile Island brought about the most rigorous self-examination that any industry has ever undertaken. Before TMI, the industry worked hard to make the technology failsafe, but the baseline assumption was faulty. It was assumed that the worst case accident -- the design basis accident -- would be based on a single equipment failure and also that operators would be unlikely to intervene incorrectly in plant operation. Three Mile Island clearly demonstrated the fallacy of those assumptions.

The industry learned the need to refocus the design efforts. Redundancy, separation, and diversity became the guidelines. Plants were designed for safety in the event of multiple equipment failures, and those plants which were under construction or in operation were backfitted.

The design efforts were also focused on the plant operators. The man-machine connection was enhanced and made smooth and direct. Control rooms were redesigned to enable plant operators to see -- at a glance -- what is going on within the plant. Then we made it easier for operators to interpret and act on that information. Operating procedures were studied and made clearer and easier to follow. Training also was emphasized to ensure that operators can respond quickly, decisively, and correctly to all kinds of situations.

The formation of the Institute of Nuclear Power Operations and the many initiatives on self improvement by INPO, EPRI and the Nuclear Management and Resources Council (NUMARC) were the main driving forces for these successful developments. Innovations[5] developed by these groups have resulted in a decrease of more than 47% in unplanned reactor shutdowns between 1980 and 1986, a decrease in the forced outage rate by more than 26% between 1982 and 1985, and a reduction of 60% in the volume of low level radioactive waste generated.

PRESENT NUCLEAR DEVELOPMENTS IN THE U.S.

Efforts underway in the industry with the support of the Department of Energy (DOE) to extend the life of existing nuclear power plants beyond their current arbitrary regulatory limit of 40 years are very important.

Plant Life Extension Studies - the process of prolonging the useful life of a power plant is relatively new and spurred by the fact that most of the nuclear plants will reach the end of their 40 year life between the year 2000 and 2010. For older plants, plant life extension is the most economical alternative available for maintaining the capacity currently produced by these plants. Studies indicate that nuclear power plants are following the same pattern as fossil plants - on the average they reach peak availability between 15 and 20 years into their lifetimes and then they begin a slow downhill slide with availability declining in a predictable pattern. The decline in availability is a source of concern and expense to utility owners. Early implementation of plant life extension programs woven into the plant's regular schedule can prolong the availability peak by as much as 5 to 10 years. Plant life extension programs are structured in three phases:

* Phase 1 involves preliminary engineering to determine if life extension is feasible for a particular plant.

* Phase 2 involves detailed engineering work and application to the NRC for a 20 year license extension.

* In Phase 3, plans made during the first two phases are implemented during scheduled outages over a period of 10 to 15 years.

As examples, a model PLEX project is underway on VEPCO's SURRY 1 plant as a cooperative project funded by EPRI, DOE, VEPCO and the Westinghouse owner's group. Westinghouse is also performing a PLEX evaluation on Kansai Electric's Mihama plant involving three major components - the reactor vessel, the reactor internals and the steam generators.

Utilities are also planning for new generation capacity that will be needed in the 1990's and beyond and it is generally agreed that certainty is needed to revitalize the nuclear option; certainty with respect to reasonable costs; certainty with respect to reasonable schedules; assurance that significant changes will not be required by the NRC during construction; and assurance that when construction is completed the plant can be placed into operation without undue delay. To meet these conditions there must be initiatives in three areas -- design, construction and licensing. The development activities of the industry are directed toward making the improvements needed in these areas. These industry initiatives are advancing the technology in a logical extrapolation of the current broad base of light water design, construction, licensing and operating experience. The DOE reactor development program properly emphasizes the needs in each of these three areas and acts as a catalyst to support industry initiatives.

STANDARDIZATION AND CERTIFICATION

The nuclear industry has learned by experience that nuclear power plants can be built in a cost effective manner and we can anticipate that past errors will be avoided so that nuclear power plants ordered in the future will be built at lower cost than those completed recently. Standardization of nuclear power plant designs will play a major role in this and will provide further benefits and cost reductions.[6] However, standardizing nuclear power plant designs of itself is not enough. To provide the assurances that significant changes will not be required by the NRC during construction, there must be a certification of pre-approval of an essentially complete standardized design by the Nuclear Regulatory Commission (NRC). NRC strongly supports the concepts of standardization and certification and the EPRI and DOE programs are very important in order to clear the way for certification of standard designs by the 1990's. There is a wealth of design, construction, operating, maintenance, and regulatory experience residing with the utilities, NSSS vendors, architect-engineers, and the NRC. It is imperative, therefore, that we build on this experience in developing improved designs for the future and that is exactly the objective of the EPRI/DOE/Industry program. In the past, the differing requirements of the various utilities posed an obstacle to standardization. The EPRI requirements program[7] is generating detailed requirements for LWR's which take into account and balance the differing requirements. The DOE is providing valuable support in the review of the document to ensure general industry acceptance, in certain areas of design verification, and as a catalyst for obtaining NRC review and approval. Standardized ALWR designs being developed are being reviewed against these requirements as they are being generated. The results of NRC reviews and approvals will also be taken into consideration in the requirements documents.

ADVANCED LIGHT WATER REACTORS

Both major U. S. vendors (Westinghouse and General Electric) have undertaken large design and development programs jointly with the Japanese on the APWR and ABWR respectively. The incentives for undertaking these programs were to remain competitive in the international markets. The lack of new orders in the U. S. also precluded the reactor manufacturers from undertaking such projects alone.

The Westinghouse APWR program has been described by J. L. Gallagher[8] and is a major cooperative effort with the Mitsubishi Company of Japan, and a consortium of five Japanese utilities. The $150 million total development costs are being shared by Japanese utilities, the Japanese Government (MITI), and Westinghouse. Westinghouse and the Japanese partners are committed to completing this advanced design and Kansai Electric Power Company has announced its intent to build the first APWR plant.

The General Electric Advanced Boiling Water Reactor has been developed with a substantial cooperative program with Toshiba, Hitachi and Tokyo Electric Power Company. In May 1987, Tokyo Electric Power Company selected General Electric and its partners to supply two ABWR's (Kashiwasaki - Kariwa Units 6 and 7). The plants, each of 1356 MWe, are scheduled for operation in 1996 and 1998 and General Electric will supply the nuclear systems, the initial fuel and the turbine generators.

SMALLER REACTOR DESIGNS

One important thrust of new development activities is the widespread interest in small plants incorporating passive, rather than active, safety features. While large nuclear units (1000 MWe or greater) are generally considered to enjoy an economy-of-scale advantage over smaller units (600 MWe or less), there are market situations where smaller units may be preferred. The small plant may be the best choice for applications on a relatively small grid or when load growth rate is expected to be low on a large grid. Also, the small plant has advantages in terms of lower total capital requirements and potentially shorter lead times relative to larger units. Both PWR's(9) and BWR's(10) are being developed for small plant application and the characteristics of the conceptual designs are shown in Tables 2 and 3.

As described by J. L. Gallagher(9) the starting point for developing the AP-600 advanced 600 MWe PWR design was the experience gained through design, construction, operation, and maintenance of PWR plants of this size over the past twenty years. Plants of the 600 MWe class of PWR plants are in operation in Korea and Yugoslavia. From this proven plant design basis, specific design improvements are being pursued to respond to utility and industry objectives for increased safety and operational margins, reduced plant capital and operating costs, simplified plant systems and components, and increased certainty of meeting construction schedules and costs.

An important requirement established from the outset was to eliminate the need for a prototype plant. Accordingly, the AP-600 design, uses many proven plant design features. The reactor core is a low power density design using standard fuel. The reactor vessel and internals, as well as the steam generator, are also standard designs.

TABLE 2

MAJOR AP-600 FEATURES

- o Low Power Density Core
  - Reduced fuel cycle costs with radial neutron reflector
- o Reduced Reactor Vessel Neutron Fluence
- o Improved Loop Geometry
  - Long radius pipe bends reduce hydraulic resistance, eliminate many pipe spool welds, and reduce inservice inspection requirements, costs, and complexity of loop piping.
- o Proven Canned Motor Pumps
  - Coupled to steam generator channel head in inverted position
  - Eliminates separate pump supports
  - Simplifies auxiliary fluid systems
  - Reduces potential for small-break LOCA events
  - Improves reliability
- o Passive Primary Side Protection System (PSSS)
  - Provides functions of RCS inventory control, emergency heat removal, safety injection, and containment spray systems
- o Passive Containment Cooling - Ultimate Heat Sink (UHS)
  - Provides protected, redundant means of moving heat from steel containment shell within the shield building
  - In conjunction with PSSS removes core decay heat for an unlimited time period and ensures containment integrity following any design basis event
- o Design capable of modularization

TABLE 3

MAJOR SBWR FEATURES

- Low Power Density Core and Natural Circulation
  - Reduces fuel cycle costs and reduces number of operational transients
- Isolation Condenser
  - Eliminates conventional BWR safety relief valves by controlling reactor pressure automatically
- Gravity Driven Core Cooling System
  - Passive safety system
  - Eliminates need for pumps and diesels
- Passive Containment Cooling System
  - Provides 72 hr passive containment cooling capability
  - Eliminates containment venting to maintain integrity
- Simplified Control and Electrical System
- Simplified Power Generation Systems
- Key Safety Functions Maintained
  - Reactor plant protection maintained under transient and accident conditions for 72 hr.
- Design Capable of Modularization

The areas in which the design has been significantly modified are the primary loop which uses reactor coolant pumps which are integral with the steam generator, and the plant safeguard features which incorporate passive systems which are particularly suited to plants of this small size. Plant layout is also being largely modified from existing designs due to the use of passive safeguard systems and simplified systems and due to the fact that the AP-600 is being designed to accommodate a high degree of shop fabrication by the application of modular technology with Burns and Roe and Avondale Shipyard being involved in the conceptual design efforts.

In the small, simplified boiling water reactor (SBWR), the important new features are designing the reactor to have strong natural circulation, incorporating an isolation condenser to automatically control the reactor pressure, a gravity driven cooling system which acts as a passive safety system to inject water into the reactor from the suppression pool and a passive containment cooling system which is capable of cooling the pool for three days without the need for active pumps and standby diesels.

Beyond these conceptual design efforts, there are two broad areas of effort which will be needed to bring these plant designs, both PWR and BWR, to a point where plant construction could reasonably be undertaken. These two areas are detailed design development and design certification. Once the current conceptual studies are successful in establishing an attractive set of plant design features, the detailed design efforts and design certification could begin in the 1989 time frame.

CONCLUSIONS

Worldwide, nuclear power is established and growing as a major energy source with light water reactor technology and plant designs, developed mainly by the U.S., being the principal choice. Forecasters of energy development and growth have become very cautious in recent years; however, the assessment of national plans and intentions to either proceed with ongoing nuclear power programs or to go nuclear provides grounds for an optimistic view on the worldwide future of nuclear power. Currently, the International Atomic Energy Agency[11] expects a total of 480 plants with 350,000 MWe capacity to be in operation by 1990, corresponding to a 25% increase in nuclear capacity with a further 50 plants under construction.

In the U. S., most of the current forecasts of load growth fall within the range of 2 to 3% per year and at that rate, electrical loads could increase by as much as 50% from today's demand level by the year 2000. That allows 12 years to build the capacity that will be needed. Clearly the time for action is now but it is difficult to predict when new starts will arise since many factors, which are mainly institutional have to be resolved.

As examples, Congress and the NRC must continue the efforts towards reducing regulatory uncertainty and taking positive action on standardization and one step licensing. These institutional developments are needed as part of the equation. On the other hand, as outlined, the U. S. nuclear industry has taken positive actions in successful competing in international markets, in setting up arrangements for joint development projects with Japan on light water reactors and in actively pursuing key design and development objectives on design verification and also on small reactors in the domestic program. With these developments, the U. S. industry is well positioned to meet the needs of the 1990s when they arise.

REFERENCES

1. International Atomic Energy Agency Bulletin Vol. 29 No. 3 1987 pp/ 24 and 25.

2. J. S. Moore "The Future of Nuclear Power" ASME/AICHE National Heat Transfer Conference, August 1987.

3. Japan's Nuclear Energy Vision, M. M. Hecht, Fusion Vol. 9, No. 1 page 19, Jan./Feb. 1987.

4. Utility Data Institute, 1986 Production Costs - Operating Steam Electric Plants October 1987.

5. U.S.C.E.A. Press Release "Nuclear Industry Cites Improvements" October 20, 1987.

6. Standardization of Nuclear Power Plants in the U.S., Report by the Study Group on the Practical Application of Standardization Nuclear Power Plants in the U. S., Atomic Industrial Forum, Nov. 1986.

7. K. Stahlkopf, Nuclear Engineering International, June 1987 p. 58.

8. J. L. Gallagher, The Pressurized Water Reactor Reliable Power for Today and Tommorrow, Sixth Pacific Nuclear Basin Conference Bejing, PRC, Sept. 1987.

9. J. L. Gallagher, Testimony to the House Science, Space and Technology Committee, Subcommittee on Energy Research and Development, March 18, 1987.

10. Small/Simplified Boiling Water Reactor, Nuclear Engineering International, June 1987, p. 57.

11. International Atomic Energy Agency Bulletin, Vol. 29., No. 3, 1987, Nuclear Power Development: History and Outlook by N. L. Char and B. J. Czik.

RADIOACTIVE WASTE MANAGEMENT UPDATE

Colin A. Heath
Vice President, Government Programs
NUS Corporation
Gaithersburg, Maryland

The use and control of the nuclear fission process and associated radioactive materials has resulted in significant benefits including the generation of large quantities of electricity, applications for both diagnosis and therapy in nuclear medicine, advanced geophysics techniques used in mineral exploration and specialized manufacturing process control techniques. In addition, for the last 43 years, the United States has used nuclear weapons to bring about the ending of a major World War and as the central element of our National defense.

Our enjoyment of these benefits and the dependence of our National defense has, however, been clouded by the realization that the fission process produces wastes that must be treated with the utmost care and which, if not carefully managed and isolated permanently from our environment, could cause major and significant harm to ours and future generations. Some critics have even asserted that we should not have used the fission process as we have until a complete capability for safe disposal of these radioactive wastes was demonstrated and in place (ref. 1). It is, at once, the curse and the blessing of those responsible for management of radioactive wastes that the consequence of high levels of exposure include deaths of individuals and that radiation, by the nature of its imperception by the regular senses, is a source of dread and concern to the average person. The curse is the fact that public concerns over radioactivity are especially acute to the point that gaining public acceptance of almost any facility to store, process, or isolate radioactive materials at times seems unattainable. The blessing is that, since the toxicity and hazards of radioactive wastes were recognized at the very onset of nuclear programs, steps to control these wastes and isolate them from the human environment have always been taken.

It must be admitted that mistakes have been made and that significant remedial programs have been and will be required to restore some radioactive waste disposal areas. However, it is also true that no widespread catastrophic effects have resulted from our management of radioactive wastes nor did they need to occur before a strong commitment was made to safe management and disposal. Consequently, we are able to identify both the complete inventory of radioactive wastes in the United States today and their condition. Furthermore, active programs for safe and environmentally acceptable management and disposal of all radioactive wastes in our country are currently underway with specifically identified financing for their completion.

WHAT ARE RADIOACTIVE WASTES?

Radioactive wastes in their purest form are radioactive elements formed from the fission of atoms or by activation in a nuclear reactor or accelerator. They seldom, however, exist in their purest form since they are found as a constituent of irradiated fuel elements and other reactor components or as a contaminant of materials and equipment that have been used in their handling. Consequently, radioactive wastes are generally categorized by the level and type of radioactivity contained in the waste materials.

Although the focus of this conference is energy technology, it is necessary to consider also wastes from production of nuclear weapons, from applications of nuclear medicine, and from industrial process control in describing the management of radioactive wastes. This is because the strategy for disposal of radioactive wastes has always and should continue to be based upon comingling and colocation of wastes of a similar nature, regardless of their source.

The U.S. Department of Energy maintains a complete data base on the inventories of radioactive wastes in the U.S. at its Oak Ridge National Laboratory. Figures 1 and 2, taken from the annual summary report on this data base (Ref. 2), illustrate the volumes and radioactivity of various categories of waste. In these figures, Spent Fuel and about 57 percent of commercial Low Level Waste are seen to come from power reactors used for electricity generation. Notice that while the volume of existing radioactive wastes is primarily from sources other than energy generation (about 17 percent by volume is from power reactors), radioactive waste contained in spent reactor fuel accounts for more than 90 percent of the radioactivity.

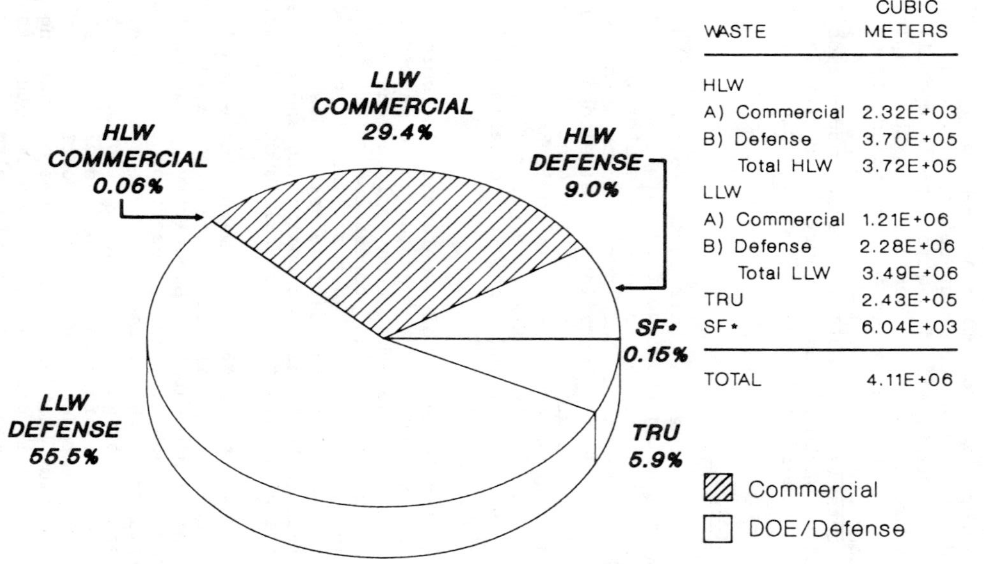

*Includes spacing between fuel assembly rods.
DOE/Defense spent fuel to be reprocessed is not shown.

Fig. 1. Volumes of commercial and DOE/defense wastes and spent fuel accumulated through 1986.

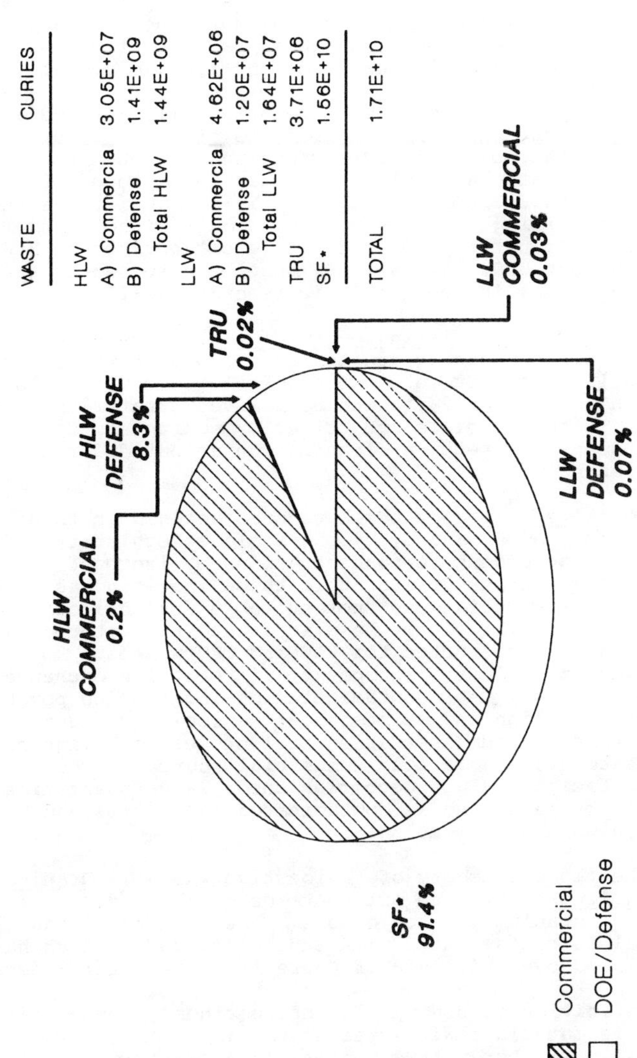

*DOE/Defense spent fuel to be repocessed is not shown.

Fig. 2. Radioactivities of commercial and DOE/defense wastes and spent fuel accumulated through 1986.

CATEGORIES OF RADIOACTIVE WASTE

Radioactive wastes are categorized by the level and duration of their radioactivity. This categorization is used to identify the wastes according to their relative hazard and to prescribe acceptable practices for their handling, storage, transportation and final disposal.

High level wastes (HLW) were originally defined as the contents of the waste stream from the first stage of solvent extraction in fuel reprocessing. Since it has become apparent that nuclear fuel may be disposed of directly without reprocessing, HLW is now defined as those wastes containing the highest levels of radioactivity.* If spent fuel is not reprocessed, it is categorized as HLW. Under current U.S. law, all HLW must be disposed by the U.S. Government in deep geologic repositories.

Transuranic-contaminated (TRU) wastes are classified as materials containing greater than 100 nanocuries per gram (0.1 curies per metric ton) of elements with mass number higher than 92, having half lives greater than 20 years. These materials are primarily equipment, filters, and personnel protective clothing contaminated during fuel reprocessing.

Low level wastes (LLW) have been defined in three categories, A, B, and C, by the Nuclear Regulatory Commission according to concentrations by isotope. Wastes with concentrations greater than those specified as category C are defined as "not suitable for shallow land disposal" and will likely be placed into repositories specifically constructed for HLW and TRU wastes. Low level wastes include: equipment, filters, ion exchange resins, and equipment contaminated during routine power reactor operation and maintenance; medical equipment used for storage and administration of isotopes for diagnosis and treatment; and various industrial sources. When nuclear facilities are decommissioned, large quantities of LLW will be generated as contaminated facilities and equipment are disassembled.

The final category of radioactive waste is Uranium Mill Tailings. Uranium ore contains on the order of five pounds of uranium per ton of ore. The residue of sand-like material is contaminated with radium and radon which has accumulated over billions of years from the natural decay

---

*The definition of HLW by the International Atomic Energy Agency is materials with greater than:

1 curie per metric ton of alpha emitters
100 curies per metric ton of beta or gamma emitters
10^6 curies per metric ton of tritium

of the uranium. This material exists in large tailings piles at both active and inactive uranium mills.

HIGH LEVEL WASTE MANAGEMENT AND DISPOSAL

All currently existing high level waste is located in temporary storage facilities pending final disposal. No permanent disposal sites have been developed in the United States or anywhere in the world.

As previously discussed, the dominant component of HLW in the United States is spent fuel discharged from operating power reactors. At the end of 1986, 13,500 metric tons of spent fuel was stored in fuel storage pools of 105 reactors at 67 locations throughout the U.S. (Ref. 2). Another 547 tons are stored at the West Valley, New York, and Morris, Illinois, reprocessing plants. DOE projects that the total inventory will grow to 40,000 tons by the year 2000 and about 78,000 tons by 2020 even if no new nuclear plants are ordered.

2300 cubic meters of liquid HLW are stored in tanks at the site of the West Valley reprocessing facility in New York state. An additional 370,000 cubic meters of HLW from defense materials production programs are stored in tanks in DOE facilities at Savannah River, South Carolina, Hanford, Washington, and Idaho Falls, Idaho.

The U.S. program for development of final disposal of spent fuel is spelled out in the Nuclear Waste Policy Act (NWPA) of 1982. In this legislation, Congress specified that the U.S. Department of Energy will take title to spent fuel at the utility sites and ship it to government facilities for permanent disposal. A fee of one mill per kilowatt-hour of electricity generated and sold by nuclear power plants has been assessed against the utilities to finance the DOE program. By the end of 1987, $2.7 billion had been collected from the utilities through this fee and another $1.3 billion is owed. $1.54 billion has been spent by DOE on the civilian waste management program to date. A waste management trust fund established to handle proceeds from this fee and which accumulates interest from treasury bills has a current balance, including receivables, of approximately $2.9 billion. This fund is only available to DOE as Congress appropriates funds each year so that Congress continues to exercise strong oversight and control of the program.

As originally passed, the NWPA specified a schedule in which the site for the first geologic repository for disposal of HLW would be designated by March 31, 1987. This schedule supported a deadline that DOE would begin to accept spent fuel for permanent disposal in a licensed repository by January 31, 1998. Unfortunately, in the five years since passage of the Act, DOE has been unable to meet the milestones of the specified schedule and in 1986 announced that the earliest possible date for repository operation would be 2003.

The process of site selection and characterization specified in the NWPA has proven extremely difficult to implement. The Act specified that affected states and Indian tribes be heavily involved in a process of consultation and cooperation in the siting studies but these entities have consistently complained that DOE has not afforded them a proper and meaningful role in the process. Consequently, the required steps of development of siting criteria, preparation of environmental assessments of alternate sites, and designation of three sites for detailed characterization have been protracted and drawn out in a climate of confrontation.

In May of 1986, President Reagan formally approved the designation of sites at Hanford, Washington, Yucca Mountain in Nye County, Nevada, and in Deaf Smith County, Texas, for detailed characterization. Concurrently, DOE announced that the consideration of sites in the North-Central and Eastern regions of the U.S. for a second repository location was being suspended; ostensibly because the need for a second repository could be delayed as a result of a reassessment of future waste generation.

Since May of 1986, the program has been stalled by Congressional restrictions on proceeding with exploratory shafts at any site, by consideration of over 40 lawsuits brought by states and tribes over the perceived inadequacy of DOE's compliance with the NWPA, and by considerable modifications within DOE's programs to comply fully with NRC requirements for quality assurance and detailed site characterization planning.

DOE has also proposed a revision to the original program by introducing a Monitored Retrievable Storage (MRS) facility for the initial receipt and packaging of spent fuel prior to disposal. In 1985, DOE announced that the preferred site for such a facility was in Oak Ridge, Tennessee, prompting an immediate court challenge by the State that it has been improperly excluded from the process of site selection. This court suit was only decided in DOE's favor by the U.S. Supreme Court in mid-1987 allowing DOE's proposal for the MRS to be presented to the Congress.

The loud objections by the affected states and Indian tribes over DOE's stewardship of the program and DOE's actions in proposing to modify the scope and schedule of the NWPA have prompted the Congress to take steps to modify and redirect the program. At the time of the writing of this paper, final legislation has not actually been passed.

However, enough actions have been taken that it seems likely that amendments will have been made to the Nuclear Waste Policy Act by the time of this conference.

The most sweeping changes have been promoted by Senator Bennett Johnston, who succeeded in persuading the Senate to change the nuclear waste program through amendments to the Energy and Water Appropriations bill for FY 1988. Under the terms of the Johnston amendments, the previous requirement for simultaneous characterization of three potential repository sites, including construction of exploratory shafts and underground facilities at each, has been dropped. Instead, DOE is instructed to select a single site for detailed characterization by January 1, 1989, and to proceed with characterization of that site only. Additionally, the investigation of potential sites for a second repository is to be terminated with consideration of the possible need deferred until 2007. The authorization of a monitored retrievable storage facility in Oak Ridge, Tennessee, is specifically rejected and provisions made for the need for the MRS to be studied by an independent panel.

Perhaps the most significant of the Johnston amendments is a provision to provide large payments to the state in which a repository might be constructed. The host state is to receive $50 million per year in unrestricted funds throughout the period of site investigation and repository construction. When waste receipts begin, this amount increases to $100 million per year.

In order for the Johnston amendments to become law, agreement will have to be reached in a conference committee with the House of Representatives. Several issues need to be resolved. The first is that many members of both the House and Senate do not believe that significant changes to legislation should be made as part of an appropriations bill since the responsible authorizing committees in each house tend to be bypassed. Key committees of the House of Representatives had voted to support legislation for a moratorium on the program to allow a reevaluation and reassessment by an external review committee for one to two years before any further work would be done. It has been reported that Congressman Udall of the House Interior Committee would participate as a member of the conference committee in an effort to negotiate a compromise on new directions for the program that will be acceptable to both House and Senate.

In the meantime, DOE has been proceeding with its baseline program until Congress orders redirection. Work on preparation of detailed site characterization plans for each of the three preferred sites is proceeding with draft plans to be issued for all three in January 1988. DOE then intends to allow until January 1989 for review of these plans and discussions with the states. DOE has also restarted its review of comments on the area report for second repository siting in a perfunctory fashion pending Congressional redirection.

As for the utilities, they now realize that the prospect for the Federal government to follow through on its obligation to begin shipping significant quantities of spent fuel from their sites in 1998 is growing exceedingly dim. Newly constructed plants are being provided with very large spent fuel storage pools; some large enough to accommodate discharges for the life of the plant. Older plants are expanding the storage capacity of their pools as much as they can. Several are turning to the use of auxiliary casks for dry storage of fuel at the reactor sites.

The remaining HLW at the various DOE facilities and at the West Valley plant will eventually be consigned to the same disposal site as the commercial spent fuel. DOE is proceeding with a program to solidify the high activity sludges, that precipitate when these wastes are neutralized, into a borosilicate glass that will be molded into 2-foot diameter cylinders 20 feet long. The salt cake that results from evaporation of the supernatant will be treated and disposed of as low level waste. Construction of facilities for solidification of these wastes is currently underway at both West Valley and Savannah River. The final treatment of Hanford wastes has not yet been formally decided but vitrification to glass seems likely there also. The HLW at the Idaho facility is currently stored in the form of a dry calcine which can be readily vitrified at some future date.

TRANSURANIC WASTE MANAGEMENT AND DISPOSAL

The status of programs for final disposal of TRU wastes appears more encouraging. Almost all of these wastes are under DOE control having been generated during the production of weapons materials. Because weapons production facilities are viewed as vital to national security, DOE has been exempted from external oversight and control by the Nuclear Regulatory Commission for this waste. Furthermore, states in which management of transuranic wastes is undertaken and in which disposal is planned have benefitted economically from the existence of large DOE facilities and have, therefore, tended to be more willing to participate in programs for waste disposal from these operations.

Before 1970, transuranic wastes were buried with low level wastes in shallow pits and trenches at both DOE and commerical burial sites. Whether or not this material may need to be recovered and treated has not received much attention. In 1970, the AEC decided that all wastes with TRU levels greater than 10 nanocuries per gram should be stored retrievably pending a decision as to their disposition. In 1983, the NRC and EPA agreed that TRU waste should be defined as material with TRU levels greater than 100 nanocuries per gram. DOE anticipates that approximately 47% of the retrievably stored wastes will be classified as LLW. (Ref. 2) The total volume of DOE retrievably-stored TRU waste is 51,000 cubic meters located at six DOE locations. Sixty percent of this material is at the Idaho National Engineering Laboratory.

Under Congressional direction to provide "a research and development facility to demonstrate the safe disposal of radioactive wastes from defense activities," DOE is completing construction of the Waste Isolation Pilot Plant at a depth of 2200 feet in a salt bed near Carlsbad, New Mexico. This facility will begin operation in 1988 and will accept transuranic wastes from all six DOE locations.

When WIPP begins operations it will be the first deep geologic disposal facility for radioactive waste operational in the world. The experience gained in siting and constructing the WIPP facility should be very valuable in the siting of future facilities. It may also allow the public to understand better what these facilities are and hopefully gain confidence that safe permanent disposal of radioactive wastes can be achieved.

LOW LEVEL WASTE MANAGEMENT AND DISPOAL

Disposal of low level wastes for many years has been by shallow-land burial in which materials are placed in trenches 20 to 30 feet deep and covered by a few feet of soil. A small quantity was disposed of at sea prior to 1970 by the U.S. and some European nations have continued disposal at sea to the present time.

Six commercial shallow-land disposal have been operated in the U.S. but three of these proved to be unsuitable and operations were terminated between 1975 and 1978.

In the late 1970's, the governors of the three states with continuing operations grew concerned that they were unfairly taking all the nation's wastes and exerted pressure by first banning shipments and then imposing ceilings on amounts to be received. In 1980, Congress specified that after January 1, 1986, any interstate compact approved by Congress could prohibit access to its LLW disposal facility. This specification failed to produce any real progress toward developing new sites, so in 1985 a second law was passed which imposed deadlines for development of new facilities and surcharges on waste disposal for those states that failed to meet these deadlines.

The mandatory schedule imposed is shown in the following table:

Table 1: State Deadlines for Establishment of LLW Facilities

July 1, 1986:	Ratify compact or certify intent to develop independent facility
January 1, 1988:	Identify host state for new facility and develop siting plan
January 1, 1990:	Submit license application for new facility
January 1, 1993:	Begin operation of disposal facility

Figure 3 is taken from a recent DOE report to the Congress concerning the LLW program (Ref. 3). It illustrates the state compacts that have been formed and the progress being made toward identifying new disposal facilities. Since this figure was prepared, California has moved toward joining with Arizona and South Dakota and to provide the first disposal facility, the Midwest region has named Michigan as the host state, and the Northeast and Central regions are working to meet the deadline for naming a host state. Failure to meet the deadline by either regional compacts or individual states will lead to significant surcharges on waste from their regions when disposed of at existing sites.

In the meantime, the volumes of LLW being shipped to the three existing sites are dropping and falling well below limits set in the 1985 legislation. This could well be due to more vigorous steps being taken to reduce waste volumes due to the increasing costs of waste disposal. Before the application of any surcharges, disposal prices at Barnwell in 1987 were reported to be $33.32 per cubic foot. It could also be affected by new restrictions on the acceptance of RCRA-defined hazardous wastes mixed with radioactive materials. It seems clear that more emphasis on volume reduction and stabilization of low level wastes will occur as costs of disposal increase and more controls are applied to hazardous wastes.

Another factor that will lead to increased disposal costs is actions being taken by several individual states

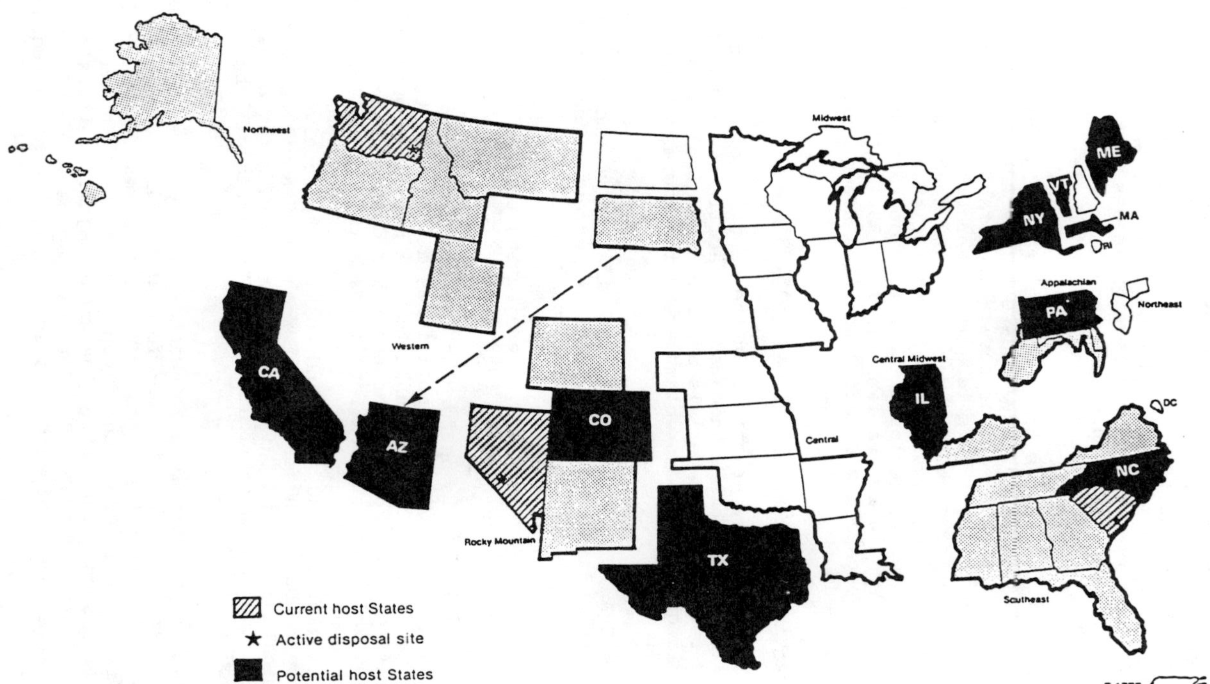

Figure 3. Current host States and potential host States for low-level radioactive waste disposal facilities.

and compacts to prohibit shallow-land burial as previously practiced. This practice is now prohibited by the Appalachian and Central Midwest compacts and by the states of Maine, Massachusetts, New York, and Texas. Alternate practices may require deeper disposal depths, specialized engineered barriers, or even above grade designs such as the tumulus, pioneered in France. Each of these approaches will be more expensive than shallow-land burial.

Most of the states and compacts are moving to meet the requirements of the Low Level Waste Policy Act Amendments of 1985 and the prospect for several new facilities being in operation in the 1990's is quite favorable. There will undoubtedly be setbacks and reversals and deadlines will be missed but in general the safe controlled disposal of low level wastes in regional facilities operated by states or compacts should be available in the 1990's. In the meantime, the capacity of existing sites seems adequate to meet the needs.

MILL TAILINGS AND DECOMMISSIONING WASTES

Although early practices in the handling of uranium mill tailings and the abandonment of facilities that handled radioactive materials are now recognized to have been inadequate, these problems are being addressed and resolved.

The EPA issued new regulations in 1986 to control the management and control of tailings at currently operating uranium mills. Mill tailings at inactive mill sites are being stabilized and controlled to EPA requirements under an active DOE program. DOE is projecting that all required actions can be completed by 1993 (Ref. 2).

Similarly DOE is performing remedial action activities at sites formerly used for activities of the Manhattan Project and the AEC now thought to have been inadequately decommissioned at the time of their abandonment and for 320 radioactively-contaminated facilities still controlled by DOE but considered surplus. Both of these programs are proceeding at a steady rate and continue to receive priority in DOE's budget. Most of the wastes will be contaminated soil and building rubble but in a few cases, mill tailings and a small amount of TRU wastes will be involved.

The projected volumes of wastes for these two DOE programs are significant. DOE forecasts 850,000 cubic meters of LLW from the formerly utilized sites program, which is close to the planned capacity of the existing Barnwell disposal facility. The great majority of wastes from this program are in New York, New Jersey, and Missouri so the development of planned disposal facilities in these states or their associated compacts by 1993 will be very timely. Similarly 800,000 cubic meters of LLW will be generated from DOE's surplus facilities program. This quantity is also significant compared to the 100,000 cubic meters per year generated by ongoing DOE defense activities and the 2.3 million cubic meters already disposed of at DOE LLW facilities.

Finally, we must be aware of the wastes that will arise when operating nuclear reactors are decommissioned. DOE projects that decommissioning of a 1000 MW nuclear power plant will generate 15,000 to 16,000 cubic meters of LLW. (Ref. 2) For the number of reactors now in operation or under construction we will therefore eventually produce somewhere between 1.5 and 2 million cubic meters of LLW. This represents the capacity of two to three sites equivalent to the Barnwell facility. Given the progress being made by state compacts in developing new disposal facilities, the accommodation of decommissioning wastes forty or more years from now should not be a problem.

CONCLUSION

The requirements for adequate and safe disposal of radioactive wastes are now well understood and are being aggressively pursued despite some obvious mistakes made during early stages of the development and use of radioactive materials. Although many politically difficult siting decisions still remain to be made, the required technology appears to be well understood and reliable and adequate methods of paying the required costs are in place. Radioactive waste management is a very demanding task and the consequences of failure are high. However, the total system of proper waste management and disposal is being developed and appears to be adequate to meet the need.

REFERENCES

1. L. Carter, Nuclear Imperatives and the Public Trust, Resources for the Future, Washington, D.C., 1987

2. U.S. Department of Energy, Integrated Data Base for 1987: Spent Fuel and Radioactive Waste Inventories, Projections, and Charateristics, DOE/RW-0006, Rev. 3 (September 1987)

3. U.S. Department of Energy, 1986 Annual Report on Low-Level Radioactive Waste Management Progress, DOE/NE-0081, (June 1987)

FUEL CELLS: THEIR PLACE IN THE EVOLVING NATURAL GAS INDUSTRY

William D. Travers
Manager, Energy Technology Development
American Gas Association

I will begin by saying that the natural gas industry is in an evolutionary process unlike that of any other time in its history, including the tremendous discovery and growth eras of the fifties and sixties. I will also say, that I know of no one who can accurately predict the part fuel cells will play in that gas evolutionary process. As I move on in this presentation, I will explore some "what ifs", with you, which should at least disclose how I have come to a renewed interest in fuel cells.

Selecting a title for a talk, before you have your major thoughts on paper, can be a trap. I knew I wasn't going to just sit down and pound out my ideas from the top of the head, because fuel cells hadn't occupied that particular place of high interest in a fairly long time. As a matter of fact, if not for the efforts of a quietly friendly, and very persistent chap, who shall remain nameless, I wouldn't be talking to you today. Though I have done a lot of digging and probing, you could do well without my talk, but if you're interested in the future of fuel cells, you can't do without the kind of activity the gentleman I speak of, is performing. I plan to pursue the importance of his kind of activity a bit further on.

It has been my good fortune to spend some thirty years of my gas and electric utility career rubbing shoulders with a wonderful array of technically astute people. A few have been awesome in the breadth of their knowledge, and the quality and quantity of their production. For the most part, these people, from various industries, were busy making a living by encouraging the manufacture, establishing tests and demonstrations, and by engaging in hard sell of that merchandise which brought forward important technologies perceived at the time, to be ahead of their time. They were largely successful because they held a deep and abiding belief that what they were doing was good, and correct for their customers and companies, both of whom were often at the same time resistant to those efforts.

History is rich with the stories of products and inventions we wouldn't consider doing without today, and the trials of bringing them to that status of essentiality.

At one time, violent market rejection existed for such technologies as automatic water heaters...they were thought to be dangerous and expensive, and other than Saturday night, who needs hot water? Home refrigeration had a very difficult time in retiring the iceman, fluorescent lighting was bad for your eyes, made you look like a corpse, and raised hell with utility coffers with its greater efficiency. Believers got out and sold lots of it, evolution took care of the color problems and strobe effects, and sales volume took care of the utility coffers. The list of those technologies foisted off on an innocent public is long; made long, by my friends and their progenitors.

Through all of this period of technology discovery, through the various consumer addictions, and long before (149 years to be precise), there has existed a tantalizingly, wonderful, and proven concept that could seemingly improve all of our lives. That concept is a compounding of materials and static parts, resulting in a device which can silently produce direct current electricity from hydrogen and oxygen, while remaining environmentally benign. The device is so compact and environmentally acceptable, while exhibiting astounding load tracking capabilities, high efficiency potentials, and expand in place features, it may be sited very near the load it will supply. As that load may grow, so can the device.

After 149 years and all of the other technology, why is it that so many people wouldn't have any idea of what I am talking about? Many don't, you know. I recently tested my supposition, asking friends: "What is a Fuel Cell?" She said: "Isn't it one of those round things where they keep the gasoline for the gas stations?"--He said to her: "Boy, are you stupid, haven't you ever watched a space launch?" I thought he had it, but then he said, "it's on the first stage of the booster rocket."

Well, after all it's not color television, maybe everybody doesn't have to know what fuel cells are, but all of my technical cronies do. I recently talked to eight of them, and asked them what they thought about the future of Fuel Cells. I couldn't bore you with all of their responses, because some of them won't quit responding. Talk about touching a hot button. The comments ranged widely from, (1) "I stopped believing in Fuel Cells about six months after I learned the truth about the tooth fairy." (This guy made me feel that I too had never seen a space launch)... (2) "I think they just might make it. Are you aware of the GRI phos/acid tests, and the new company that's trying to get started selling the 200 kw units? They are pricey, but if they make it on the first go-a-round, they might break through the price barrier. A whole lot of people are watching." (3) ..."I think the phos/acid Fuel Cell might find a niche if they can get the price down and prolong the stack life, but the real winner will be the molten carbonate cells. They are coming on slower, but in the long run, they're going to be a lot less trouble."

This is one of the people who won't stop responding, and I am pleased that he won't. Even though this fellow isn't directly involved, he digs and reads a lot and is willing to share what he learns. He is a "sub-awesome, but you had better believe what he says, kind of a guy." He is also the guy who told me that heat pumps were going to make it. This, some few years ago, after their second dismal failure in the marketplace, and with largely only village idiots out there to install and service them. Wonderful as that theoretical COP of 6 to 1 sounded, I didn't think they had a prayer. The same folks who had been given the government money to produce a heat pump winner, and Betty Furness to tell me, "you can be sure", did much to produce my faint heart. Truth is, heat pumps are here, and here to stay, and they get better, and more idiot-proof, at the regular intervals competition dictates.

In August of this year, I asked myself, do I really think Fuel Cells have a prayer of making it in the marketplace? My response was disturbingly slow in coming, but it was finally, yes I do. Coming to that position took some time because I know well that turbines have once again slipped in to dampen that inventive spirit which long ago might have produced an immediate and intelligent response from my friends. Do you know what a Fuel Cell is? "Of course we do, why do you ask?"

Wheels and turbines in falling water combined with our infatuation with steam, the power and production made possible by strung wire, and our natural use of coal, initially, the only abundant fuel we knew, have provided the might and the good life for our country. Turbines have always obviated any need for that wonder of wonders, the Fuel Cell...until now.

Most of my work for the A.G.A. is in Executive Branch Relations and what I have found among those loyal government employees working in the Energy Vineyard, is a genuine lack of communication between the various divisions. For instance, some areas are still in a mind lock from the "Sky is Falling/Chicken Little" years of the Carter presidency. Other areas are out front making things happen, and work diligently to stay abreast of what is really going on in the world of energy availability and use.

My eyes were opened with the realization that while working down here, I was going to have to deal with folks who actually still believed that oil and gas were almost the same thing, and that we were just plain running out of both.

I innocently thought that when important people in our nation's largest industries had extricated themselves from that debilitating mental trap with the realization we are a country rich with economically available natural gas, all of the other bright minds would get on the right track. I am continually astonished to find some otherwise intelligent people still derailed in this regard, particularly so, when they have their own unbiased resources at hand to become better informed.

Because I personally believe that <u>rapid</u> development of the fuel cell is so closely tied to the availability of natural gas, I am going to take just a few minutes to state, who is stating what, about natural gas supplies.

As most of you are well aware, there were very real gas <u>supply</u> shortages in the 1970's , and that those shortages were compounded by some very cold back-to-back winters which exacerbated the demands on storage wells, and the in-ground pipe capacity. The North East was particularly hard pressed during this period. Several of the States mandated moritoriums on new gas sales which lasted several years.

Few people in that period of time realized that our country wasn't really running out of natural gas, but that the folks who made their living drilling for natural gas had quite some time before stopped drilling. They weren't' being mean about it; they had just calculated that with the price they were allowed to charge for the gas they found, they were going broke. Many of the drilling rigs which should have been punching holes in the good old U.S.A., were in fact, probing the desert sands of far off lands.

By the late 1970's, as foreign oil prices began to soar and we began an awareness of the environmental problems of other fuel options, it was finally recognized that there was a genuine other option, natural gas, and that what we had experienced in the earlier 70's was not a gas resource problem, but that it was an economic problem, coupled with some in-ground plumbing trouble in the North East. As I said before, there are still people working in Washington, and not all with the Federal Government, who have yet to realize or perhaps admit, what truly happened with the gas business.

Well the drill rigs returned, and those remaining here came out of mothballs when their owners found out the Federal Government was finally going to allow them a sensible profit from the fruit of their labors. And as they say, the rest is history in the making.

A.G.A. does not of itself predict how much gas there actually exists in the lower 48 states, Alaska, or the rest of the world for that matter, as a lot of other people are busy much of their time doing precisely that work. A.G.A. does generate data on annual gas production, in addition to making estimates of future usage and production.

We do gather data on total gas resources available from sources such as, the Potential Gas Agency, of the Colorado School of Mines, and the Gas Research Institute (GRI).

The Potential Gas Agency, in 1986, estimated the total gas potential in the lower 48 states at some 619.8 trillion cubic feet (tcf), with an additional 118.8 tcf in Alaska. That adds to 738.6 tcf of natural gas underlying lands beneath the flag of the United States. At the present time, our national use of natural gas is something in the magnitude of 17 tcf/yr. If our use grew to 20 tcf, a distinct possibility, a brilliant mind could quickly calculate a minimum 37 year supply of natural gas.

GRI, in January 1987, made a baseline projection of natural gas remaining in the lower 48 states alone. Their estimate, 801 tcf.

The U.S. Geological Survey, in 1981, estimated a total resource in the lower 48 states and Alaska as 973.0 tcf.

If I haven't sold you yet, that the natural gas industry is not going to hell in a hand basket, I promise to stop with this excerpt from the March 1987 "Energy Security Report" to the President of the United States; "If unconventional gas supplies (such as gas shales, tight sands, and gas hydrates) are included in the total, the Nation's supplies of natural gas may support 200 years of consumption at current rates.

As I immediately break my promise, I would invite those who may still be a bit depressed over the Nation's gas resources to investigate the work of Dr. Thomas Gold, Cornell University, and his fascinating theories, (perhaps by now, more than theories) regarding abiogenic gas.

I titled my presentation, "Fuel Cells: Their Place In The Evolving Natural Gas Industry". When I speak of my belief that a rapid, and rapid is a key word, development of the fuel cell is tightly tied to the health of the natural gas industry, the title could have been "Natural Gas: Its Place In the Evolving Fuel Cell Industry", and of course I should also set about explaining myself.

If you set aside my obvious bias for natural gas, I believe you will still agree that it is a wonder fuel. Other than running it through some scrubbers, and this is not always necessary, and adding an odorant, you use it just about as it comes from the ground. The United States can boast of its one million mile gas pipeline system, which carries this clean burning energy to 3.8 million commercial customers, and 189 thousand industrial customers, all of whom could be later fuel cell prospects. These customers are familiar with using natural gas, fully realize that they don't have to store it, nor do they tie up cash and credit in maintaining a supply. Unlike almost any other commodity today, they pay for it after they have used it.

I don't profess to know all about methanol, but I know it has some potential problems in storage and transport because it tends to be corrosive. Combustion can take place without visible flame. These are certainly not problems that are insurmountable. What really gives me pause however, is the fact that you have to throw away half of your beginning energy just to produce the stuff, and that may be just untenable in the future. Some would say that I'm being overly kind, when I state the energy loss at 50%.

Someday, and perhaps that is today, the United States must seriously address its most abundant resource, coal. Methanol may be the way to move coal energy to market, I don't know. I believe I do know that fuel cells have enough problems of their own getting on line with a long-life, economically acceptable product, let alone trying to package it with a fuel which might be unfamiliar, troublesome and expensive. Energy discovery, conversions, development, and husbanding will employ most of our Nation's best minds in the future.

If my son were young enough to be just starting to look at college, I would try to steer him into chemistry. Putting "agent orange", and some of the pesticides behind us, I believe the chemistry people will bring "The Better Things Through Chemistry", in the future, more so than the wonders they brought us in the past.

A few areas I said I would talk about, and haven't as yet, could begin with what I said about my persistent friend who refocused my attention on fuel cells. He even patiently listened to my story of how I at one time had owned my own fuel cell, and lost it by placing it on a table during a talk I was giving very early in my career. The talk was about the wonders to come from natural gas through fuel cells, thermionics, and magnetohydrodynamics. The fuel cell was an extremely well built cigarette lighter fueled with alcohol. I have often wondered what they would be producing today, if those people on Long Island, who made the product, had stuck with their concepts.

I don't wish to digress beyond my point, which is that my determined friend must be multiplied 1,000 times before fuel cells can become the market success they must in order to keep the concept alive. Of the eight friends I called, only five were optimistic that the fuel cell is ready for center stage now. All of them must believe it can find a place in the near tomorrow, if not today. Only people like my friend can make that happen.

The optimistic people who would push the fuel cell into its rightful place, much as those who brought us automatic water heating, home refrigeration, and fluorescent lighting, to again name only a few of our essential products which weren't always thus, cannot do it alone. They must have hardware that is not five years down the road. They must have something to sell that won't get them thrown out in the middle of their sales presentation. It needn't be perfect, that can, and will come later, but it must show promise, and it must be <u>now</u>.

I recall as a young lighting systems designer, walking around for the better part of two years with a plastic mock-up of a new square fluorescent tube which the General Electric Company threatened to make. It was a square/oblong room, lighting designer's dream come true. When it finally did come true, it really wasn't very good, and it was too expensive to sell. The moral of that quaint rememberance is that you can't sell holograms, and ectoplasm.

What if the GRI program had with its initiation, sufficient funding, and commitment to keep those 40 kw fuel cells running for ten years no matter what the consequences, even if they had to be eviscerated and replumbed every six months just to keep them running. Missouri folks aren't the only ones who have got to be showed. This is not a criticism of the program; I know, with few qualifications, it could only be called a success.

The heat pump failed several times before the believers brought us all to their state of confidence. The turbine generator failed miserably in the 1960's. It is extremely difficult to come back from laughing stock to success. Given their druthers, the people who market heat pumps and turbine generators would eliminate those sad days from their history.

With that thought in mind, I am sobered to think how much is riding on the bold stance of the new company born of International Fuel Cells. I won't even ponder "what ifs". Everyone who is watching, and there are many, wish them the greatest of success.

I would say one last thing before I step away from this subject. Thinking again of past successes, I am reminded that success came to be through team work. I believe heat pumps became successful when associations of fellow sufferers came into being. The same can be said for good lighting, electric heating, and countless other products. I can recommend to you that if you have an interest in fuel cells, and you must or you wouldn't be here, you might look into membership in the Fuel Cell Association.

When discussing associations the old saying goes, "Does Macy's tell Gimble's?" The answer, of course, is no they didn't, and now Gimbles is out of business.Even Macy's laments that.

FUTURE ROLE OF FUEL CELLS IN TRANSPORTATION

S. Romano, Program Manager
Georgetown University, Washington, D.C.

INTRODUCTION

Experiences of the past fifteen years indicate that we must ultimately replace the petroleum fueled internal combustion engines used for transportation with alternative systems. The two predominant drivers for this necessity are air quality and the finite supply of petroleum. The air pollution problem is dramatically brought out on a summer's day in Los Angeles, California where the concentration of pollutants is visible. Gasoline powered vehicles discharge 450 tons of nitrogen oxides and 4765 tons of carbon monoxide per day into the air in the L.A. basin[1]. The increased usage of the automobile and its concentration in urban areas has partially neutralized the progress auto manufacturers have made in cleaning up the internal combustion engine.

As to the finite supply of petroleum, a recent status report[2] made the point that neither the U.S. nor the world will run out of petroleum for a long time, however, world demand and limited worldwide oil production can strain the availability of supply and create major problems. In fact a difference of + or - 5% in the demand/supply differential can cause a swing from long lines at retail stations with high prices, to a petroleum glut. We have all experienced these extremes. One of the most pressing economic problems we are faced with today is the trade deficit which is partially due to the requirements for large amounts of imported oil. In addition increases in the price of imported oil, due to the demand/supply imbalance produce a negative impact on the U.S. gross national product. These economic problems leave us little choice but to reduce our dependence on petroleum. Since 1979 there has been a major switch by most energy consumers away from petroleum to alternative fuels. However, the transportation industry is still almost totally dependant on petroleum and uses over 63% of the total consumed in this country. And despite the improvements in fuel economy and the increase in sales of small cars, the use by the transportation sector is increasing. It is obvious then, that something must be done in transportation to reverse the trend. The electric vehicle (EV) has been proposed as a means to accomplish this. But it can only succeed if we have a major replacement of the internal combustion engine (ICE) powered vehicle with the EV. To accomplish this the EV must be on a par with the ICE vehicle in terms of user acceptance. The key factor in market acceptance that has prevented the EV from competing with the ICE is its inability to provide unlimited range by rapid replenishment of the energy source. The battery electric vehicle, as presently configured cannot meet this criterion.

THE ELECTRIC VEHICLE DILEMMA

While it is not certain that the electric vehicle predates other automobile types, it clearly outsold the ICE in 1915[3] when more than 4,000 electrics were sold versus less than 1,000 ICE automobiles. Today very few EV are being sold. Initially it was the potential for unlimited range and reasonable cost that caused the ICE to replace the Electric for transportation. The fact that the electric motor is a preferred source of motive power is apparent when it is realized that the ICE has not been successful in replacing the electric motor in industry where a ready, continuous supply of energy is available. At the onset the ICE was high in cost, unreliable, awkward, noisy and messy to deal with. These characteristics did not hinder its development because its potential was recognized. The force that was responsible for the development of the ICE into the remarkable, affordable machine we have today was market demand.

It has been recognized for some time that the electric vehicle is the most promising candidate for a non-polluting, non-petroleum based alternative to the gasoline or diesel powered automobile. However, the difficulties arise in making the transition. The question is how do we effect the major replacement of the ICE vehicle that is required to make a significant difference in petroleum usage and air quality in urban areas? The efforts on battery powered EV's that have been directed towards this objective since the first oil crisis in the 1970's have been successful in producing improvements in batteries, motors, motor controllers, both ac and dc and integrated drive trains but have not come close to producing the unlimited range capability necessary for direct competition with the ICE vehicle. Dual powered battery/ICE (hybrid) vehicles, capable in some cases of unlimited range through liquid refueling have also been developed and tested. Tests have shown that the overall efficiency of these systems, in terms of miles per gallon of gasoline, is much greater than the straight ICE vehicle[4]. However, life cycle cost studies in most cases show that the battery/ICE hybrid cannot be justified on an economic basis until the cost of gasoline exceeds $2.18 a gallon[5]. With these systems the dependence on petroleum and the air pollution problems, while reduced, are not eliminated.

A number of battery EV have been evaluated in limited fleet service and demonstrated that battery electric vehicles can replace ICE vehicles for this specialized service. The Electric Vehicle Development Corporation (EVDC) is presently developing a van for urban fleet use and intends to market it aggressively. The present expectation is that using the advanced lead acid batteries developed in the past few years, a range of 60 miles is possible. Market studies, figure 1, have shown that this performance will potentially meet the needs of 3 million light duty commercial vehicles. If the improved batteries listed become available and there is no requirement for any of these vehicles to be used beyond the maximum range shown, then the market is 8 million vehicles. With over 150 million vehicles operating on our roads and highways this represents only a small percentage of the vehicles creating our pollution and dependence problems. However, if this program is successful in meeting only a portion of this market (and indications are that it can be) then it will have the effect of stimulating industry to invest in the research and development necessary to produce the ultimate EV which must provide the flexibility of extended range required by the general public (which is what they now have in their ICE powered automobiles). Extended range through rapid refueling (energy recovery) cannot be achieved by battery power alone.

THE FUEL CELL

The fuel cell (FC) is a device which produces electricity by catalytically reacting hydrogen and oxygen to form water. If the fuel is a hydrogen rich liquid such as methanol, then a fuel cell powered EV has the key characteristic to enable it to compete with the ICE for transportation and at a significant reduction in the key emissions responsible for pollution. Figure 2, is a comparison of these

FIGURE 1

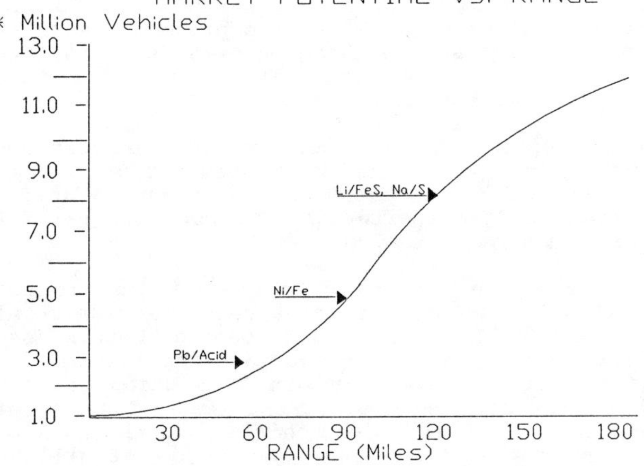

* Light Duty Commercial Vehicles

Source: Electric Vehicle Development Corporation

FIGURE 2

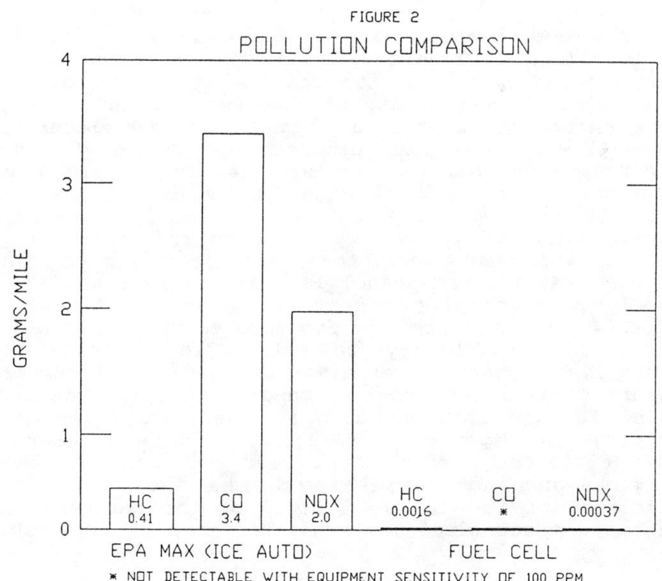

* NOT DETECTABLE WITH EQUIPMENT SENSITIVITY OF 100 PPM

emissions using the Environmental Protection Agency (EPA) maximum allowables for autos and those produced by a fuel cell operating under utility power plant conditions[6].

Unfortunately, the fuel cell powered EV is not "just around the corner". There are problems, such as high cost, the size and weight of present systems, the ability to be mobile, an infrastructure for the fuel and others that need to be addressed before it can meet our transportation needs and replace the ICE. These problems are not impossible to overcome and indications are that they can be solved in a systematic way. A start has been made with the U.S. Department of Energy and Department of Transportation (DOT/DOE) program for a fuel cell-battery powered bus[7].

The use of fuel cells for transportation is not new. In 1960 Allis-Chalmers converted an agricultural tractor to fuel cell power. In 1965 General Motors used a 32 kw fuel cell in a van to evaluate the possibility of its use on the highway and in 1970 Union Carbide produced a fuel cell powered automobile. The use of pure hydrogen as fuel in these vehicles and the lack of strong incentives at that time (the supply of oil was not considered a problem and the impact of emissions standards were not yet fully realized) probably contributed to the lack of follow through. The situation has changed and today the fuel cell is perhaps our best prospect for an ICE alternative. What is needed is a strategy for the evolutionary conversion of our gasoline powered vehicles to electric vehicles.

The operation of a fuel cell is shown in its simplest form in figure 3. Here the energy source is shown as hydrogen. Air is used to supply the oxygen. The chemical combination of the two element produce water, nitrogen (contained in the air) and electrons, (the flow of which produces electricity). The temperature of the reaction for most fuel cells under consideration for vehicle use is low enough so that oxides of nitrogen are not a problem. To meet the requirement for rapid replenishment of the energy source, a liquid fuel that can be reformed into hydrogen is used. Methanol is one such fuel and it is readily produced from the abundant supply of methane and coal, and can also be produced from biomass which makes its availability unlimited. In addition the automotive industry "perceives fuel methanol as the primary candidate to replace gasoline"[8]. The methanol fueled ICE is therefore also a candidate system for reducing our dependency on petroleum but it is much less efficient and its performance on reducing emissions can not compete with the fuel cell. The efficiency of the ICE is limited by the carnot cycle and has a theoretical maximum efficiency of 40% - 50%.

FIGURE 3

FUEL CELL OPERATION

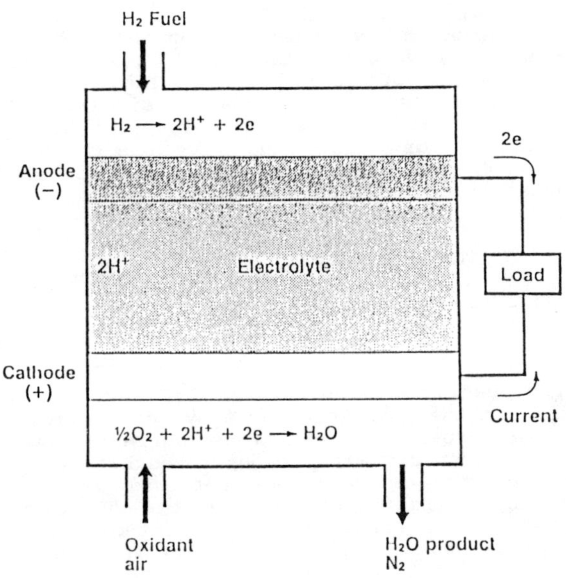

FIGURE 4

POWER SYSTEM EFFICIENCY COMPARISON

EFFICIENCY BASED ON LOWER HEATING VALUE

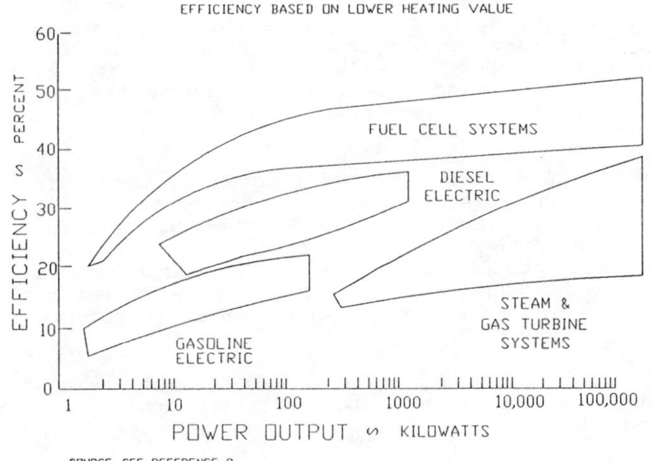

SOURCE: SEE REFERENCE 9

The theoretical efficiency of the fuel cell is 80% - 90%. Figure 4 is a comparison of the efficiencies of various electrical power generating systems[9].

The "DOT Fuel Cell Powered Bus Feasibility Study"[10] which recommended a phased program be undertaken to develop a fuel cell bus contains an excellent review of fuel cells. The final report outlines fuel cell developments since 1960 and discusses the candidate systems for use in transit buses. The report lists the five basic fuel cells under development today and their applicability to transportation. The list, ranked in order of the state of development, is as follows:

- Phosphoric acid
- Alkaline
- Ion exchange membrane
- Molten carbonate
- Solid oxide

The advantages and disadvantages for each system are discussed and the phosphoric acid system was identified as "the only fuel cell technology currently available in full scale stacks with demonstrated high efficiency performance when operated on reformed fuels". This availability dictated its use as the first step in accomplishing the essential system integration needed for a vehicle powered by a fuel cell. The ion exchange membrane fuel cell, also referred to as a proton exchange membrane (PEM) and the improved phosphoric acid systems were identified as the most likely candidates for improved vehicle systems for the future. The system recommended, for the initial step in the introduction of fuel cells in transportation, is a hybrid system utilizing a battery as the supplementary power source. The reasons for the use of batteries is the inability of current FC systems to respond to the severe cyclic load requirements of the city bus (stop and go) and the power density of current phosphoric acid fuel cells is not adequate to provide the peak power required for acceleration without excessive weight and size penalties.

The DOT/DOE Fuel Cell bus program is continuing and the next phase is designed to prove the feasibility of the concept by laboratory testing the fuel cell in a proof of concept system which includes the entire fuel cell battery propulsion system. If feasibility is confirmed subsequent phases call for a test bed bus development and eventually operational testing in limited fleet quantities.

The fuel cell bus program should demonstrate what the fuel cell can do in a transportation application. The transit bus has been selected as the first application of the fuel cell because its large size permits accommodation of the first generation fuel cell designs which presently exist. Also the centralized maintenance and fueling available avoid the necessity of establishing a widespread support infrastructure. Another factor is the long life service of transit buses which allows the amortization of higher acquisition costs over a reasonable time period. In addition, since transit buses operate mostly in urban areas, the quiet operation and the low pollution of the FC bus will be very noticeable. The successful demonstration of these buses in fleet service will provide the stimulus needed for accelerating the development of the improved fuel cell systems which are presently under consideration for use in the private automobile.

GEORGETOWN UNIVERSITY INTEREST[11]

Georgetown's interest in transportation energy usage is part of a larger concern for the cost and the continuing availability of energy sources to keep the University operating. The global energy crunch initiated by the OPEC oil supply and price crisis of 1973 forced society to acknowledge that the world's economy is dependent upon a finite supply of fluid fossil fuel. The spiraling increase in oil prices following the initial conflict and the subsequent inflation of fuel costs caused economic shocks of major magnitude.

Georgetown University, like other academic institutions throughout the country was faced with high fuel costs as well as inflated prices for many other related goods and services. Georgetown responded to these new challenges with an innovative energy management and investment program that served as a model for institutions throughout the world.

The initial thrust of Georgetown's energy program was the implementation of a wide range of conservation measures which resulted in a significant reduction in energy consumption. The next stage of the program involved the development of a plan for cogeneration, an integrated campus-wide energy system. The plan, known as the National Exemplar Integrated Socio Energy System (NEISES) is designed to demonstrate a cost-efficient, environmentally sound system for producing power to operate the University.

The program has progressed more slowly than first expected, perhaps because of the recent abundant supply and the temporary reduction in crude oil prices and the competitive pricing of natural gas. The accomplishments thus far have included the installation and operation in 1979 of a 10 MW coal fired atmospheric fluidized bed steam generation system, which was the first successful industrial application of its type in the country and which later included cogeneration capability. Also implemented was a 300 KW solar photovoltaic system integrally mounted on the roof of the University's Intercultural Center. The solar panels cover more than 36,000 square feet of roof surface and its KW output provides a substantial portion of the building's electrical energy requirements. This project was the first and largest roof-mounted photovoltaic system developed. It established performance criteria for such systems and was a major step in the commercialization process.

The current phase in the plan is the construction of a gas turbine cogeneration system which will produce from 60 to 80 MW of electrical power with a majority of it for sale to others. The NEISES program also planned the use of an alternative power source for the small transit buses used in the Georgetown University Transportation Society (GUTS) bus system which is operated for students and faculty in the greater Washington D.C. area. The feasibility study sponsored by the Department of Transportation recommended a fuel cell/battery powered electric drive system for the buses. The University had oversight responsibility for the study and coordinated efforts of the advisory committee.

In the following phases Georgetown University will provide technical support and contract management services to the Department of Energy for the development and test of the fuel cell bus. In addition, Georgetown will monitor the state of development of fuel cells and assure that the advances in the technology and the progress made in the bus program have widespread dissemination in the industry. It is intended that this technology transfer activity will serve to keep interest in the development of the fuel cell as an alternative power system at a high level and to stimulate continued development by industry.

REFERENCES

1. Southern California Air Quality Management District, "1983 Emissions Inventory".

2. E.E. Eklund, "Status of Commercialization of Alternative Fuels for Highway Use," Proceedings of the Fourteenth Energy Technology Conference, Washington, D.C., April 1987.

3. L.G. O'Connell, "The Future of Electricity for Automobiles, Advanced Electric Concepts," DE81 028235, EVC Symposium VI, Baltimore, MD, October 1981.

4. M.C. Trummel, et al, "Performance Testing and System Characterization," DOE Hybrid Test Vehicle Phase III: Final Report, JPL, Pasadena, CA, December 1984.

5. Minicars, Inc. Near Term Hybrid Passenger Vehicle Development Program, Phase I, Final Report to JPL, Pasadena, CA, October 1979.

6. D.K. Lynn, et al, "Simulated Performance of Solid Polymer Fuel-Cell Powered Vehicles", SAE830351, Society of Automotive Engineers, Warrendale, PA, 1983.

7. "Program Plan for Research and Development of a Fuel Cell/Battery Powered Bus System," January 7, 1987, U.S. Department of Energy and Department of Transportation.

8. E.E. Eklund, "Status of Commercialization of Alternative Fuels for Highway Use," Proceedings of the Fourteenth Energy Conference, Washington, D.C., April 1987.

9. T.G. Benjamin and E.H. Camara, "The Fuel Cell: Key to Practically Unlimited Energy," Foot Prints, Vol. 48, No. 2, Foot Mineral Co. Exton, PA, 1985.

10. H.S. Murray, et al, "DOT Fuel Cell Powered Bus Feasibility Study," Final Report, Los Alamos National Laboratory, December 1986.

11. Georgetown University, "Campus Plan 1983 - 2000 A.D and Beyond," Washington, D.C., 1983.

High TC Materials in the Electric Network Why or Why Not?

Kenneth W. Klein
Director, Office of Energy Storage and Distribution
U.S. Department of Energy

The new high temperature superconducting ceramics could revolutionize the design of some electrical power systems if major obstacles are cleared. The obstacles include improving the critical current density with applied magnetic fields, improving mechanical properties and chemical stability. For over a decade, the Office of Energy Storage and Distribution (OESD) has supported three applications of superconducting materials: superconducting generator; superconducting transmission cable; and superconducting magnetic energy storage (SMES). The future prospects for these and other power system applications depend, first and foremost, on the material properties of the superconductor. For most power applications, the critical current density is the crucial property. An understanding of the properties of the high temperature materials will suggest which applications may be the easiest to realize and which may have the greatest potential. This desired understanding can help formulate research goals and priorities.

BACKGROUND

The scientific discovery of a new class of materials that is superconducting above the boiling point of nitrogen, 77K, may revolutionize many technologies and create new applications rivaling those of the transistor and the laser. This new temperature range has the benefit of using liquid nitrogen for cooling rather than liquid helium required until now. The advantages of cooling with liquid nitrogen rather than liquid helium are -- cheaper coolant, higher electrical insulating strength, and reduced complexity of equipment. In addition to the scientific excitement of this development, the possibilities for practical applications of superconductivity clearly need to be re-examined, if only because of the vastly greater ease in cooling to 77K compared to the liquid helium temperature range (4K) used in all previous applications of superconductivity.

Researchers in the United States have played a pivotal role in the discovery of the new ceramic oxide superconductors. The response of the U.S. research community since the initial discovery has been exemplary. Our nation's scientist are leading the way in the search for a fundamental understanding of the ceramic superconductor and in pushing the limits even higher with new modifications or new materials. Potential applications are almost limitless. They range from faster supercomputers to more efficient power transmission to magnets that confine fusion reactions. The international race for commercialization is on.

The knowledge that some materials are superconducting occurred in 1911 when the phenomena was discovered in the element mercury at about 4 kelvin. A significant development took place in the 1960's when the type II A-15 superconducting compounds like niobium tin, niobium titanium, and niobium germanium were developed for temperatures near 20 kelvin. This brought forth the development of high intensity magnets, leading to many products including nuclear magnetic imaging for medical diagnostics. Since then the progress has been steady, but slow until 1987. In only a few months, the transition temperature of the new ceramic class of materials has soared to 98 K. Higher temperatures have been announced, but either they have been transient, non-stable events, or they have not been reproducible. However, it does indicate that there is a possibility for even more dramatic temperature ranges available for the future.

KEY TECHNICAL ISSUES

Materials in their superconducting state offer a means to circulate direct electric currents (DC) with no resistive loss. Materials in their superconducting state also offer a means to convey low-frequency alternating currents (i.e., AC at 60 Hz) with unusually small losses. The absence or significant reduction of losses prompts universal interest in superconductors as energy savers.

Materials become superconducting only in certain circumstances, which differ for each material. Superconducting materials only remain superconducting as long as they are kept below a certain temperature, do not experience too large a magnetic field and as long as the current passing through them is not excessive. There are thus three important numbers associated with each superconductor, the critical temperature (Tc) the critical field, (Hc) and the critical current, (Jc). Each represents a maximum value above which superconductivity does not survive.

There are two basic methods of determining if a material is, in fact, superconducting. One method is to measure the electrical resistance of the material as the temperature is lowered. Even non-superconducting materials will exhibit a lowering of resistance as the temperature is decreased. However, only a superconductor will have its resistance drop dramatically to zero at some transition or critical temperature.

The second method is the Meissner Effect. This effect shows that a superconductor (below the critical temperature) will expel a magnetic field by an internally induced electric current. However, if the external magnetic field exceeds the critical value, the material reverts to a non-superconducting state.

There are significant limitations to the ceramic superconducting material. So far the critical current density is too low to be used in all power system applications. Presently, the critical current density for bulk high temperature superconducting material is about 1000 amps per square centimeter at zero magnetic field. This compares to a critical current density of 1,000,000 amps per square centimeter for the widely used metallic superconductors. For many power system applications, current densities as much as 1000 times the present laboratory levels of the bulk high temperature ceramics are needed. While IBM has announced higher levels for a single crystal, making miles of the material into wire or tape may be much more difficult. The critical current density of the new superconductors is the single most important factor if the material is to be fabricated into conductors for use in power system devices.

Beyond the three critical properties of temperature, magnetic field and current density, mechanical properties such as durability must be understood and characterized, since the material properties deteriorate when exposed to air and water over time. Fabrication and processing techniques and suitable protective coatings must be developed.

The emphasis of basic research in this field is now twofold. First is to develop an understanding of superconductivity in these new materials and characterizing the effects that the new arrangement of atoms (crystal structure) will have on the development of technological applications; and second, the search continues for even higher critical temperatures (currently at 98 K), and there is every reason for continued optimism in this direction.

NEW APPLICATIONS

Superconductors have potential applications in electric utilities, electronics, transportation, industry, instrumentation and research.

Of the many potential applications for superconductors only a very limited number has reached the marketplace in any form. The most widespread use is for superconducting magnets for research devices. The use of superconductors in this application has brought the capability for performing experiments in large magnetic fields within the economic realm affordable by most laboratories.

Superconducting magnets have also been applied successfully to the technology of particle accelerators along with superconducting radio-frequency cavities. In the area of electronic devices, superconductors have been successfully developed for information storage applications. While no commercial or large scale power system applications have occurred, several demonstration projects such as the Japanese levitated train and the Los Alamos designed magnetic energy storage system for the Bonneville power line have been carried out.

DEPARMENT OF ENERGY (DOE) ACTIVITIES

In the rapidly developing field of superconductivity research, it is essential that the U.S. maintain its competitive advantage by encouraging and facilitating the free flow of information and scientific data within the U.S. research community. To this end, DOE has responded to the recent developments in superconductivity by establishing a national database of information which the scientific and commercial community can draw upon. DOE is beginning to take an aggressive role in the formation of a consortium of national laboratories, universities and industry to share information.

The White House Office of Science and Technology Policy is coordinating research activities with other agencies through its Committee on Materials (COMAT) and the Federal Coordinating Council for Science, Engineering and Technology (FCCSET). The Department of Energy is also coordinating with other federal agencies, the scientific community, and industry.

The Department of Energy's research programs are designed to 1) enhance the understanding of the properties of materials and the phenomenon of superconductivity; 2) apply the technology of superconductivity to the Department's programs in fusion; accelerator physics; and electrical energy transmission, generation and storage; 3) involve industry to the maximum extent possible; and 4) assess the feasibility of potential applications.

The DOE has established three Superconductivity Research Centers, and a computer database. The Center for Superconductivity Applications will be at the Argonne National Laboratory and the Lawrence Berkeley Laboratory will be the Center for Thin Film Applications. The Center for Basic Scientific Information will be at the Ames Laboratory; and the Computer Data Base on Superconductivity will be at the DOE Office of Scientific & Technology Information.

PRESENT POWER SYSTEM APPLICATIONS

The Office of Energy Storage and Distribution (OESD) has been supporting research and development efforts on superconductivity for 15 years. The research covers a broad spectrum of the R&D cycle. It has focused on developing an understanding, and advancing the knowledge of superconducting material properties, and applying the expertise to potential applications in the U.S. electric network. The three technologies that have been supported are: superconducting generator; superconducting transmission cable; and superconducting magnetic energy storage (SMES).

Transmission and distribution losses now run about ten percent nationwide (not twenty percent, as has been widely reported). About four percent occurs over long distance bulk power lines, the rest of the losses occur in the lower voltage lines serving residential and commercial customers. The idea that superconductors are loss-less in a misconception. They still require cooling. They will have lower losses, but also will help improve overall electric system reliability and stability.

Superconducting electric power transmission can eliminate much of the power loss associated with the electrical resistance of conventional transmission lines with potentially large economic benefits. Underground superconducting cables would be less susceptible to the vagaries of weather, for instance, and in a small space have many times the power carrying capacity of ambient underground cables.

Superconducting magnetic energy storage would permit more efficient use of our nation's generating capacity by storing energy during periods of low demand to use during periods of peak load. The application of superconducting generators can improve the generating efficiency itself. In terms of actual resource conservation, it is possible that the new superconductors may have their largest impact in the electric power arena. In each application, the savings is due largely to the improved efficiency and the reduction in cost of refrigeration. It is important to remember that in all these devices for power systems, the cost of the superconductor is very small, compared to the total system cost.

SUPERCONDUCTING GENERATOR

The research on the superconducting generator has been conducted at Massachusetts Institute of Technology. Today's generators are very large and very efficient. A typical modern generator must be assembled in a huge factory, tested, and then disassembled for shipment. At the power plant site, it is then reassembled and retested. To have a superconducting generator that is much smaller has been a dream of utility designers for years. This would greatly simplify all aspects of a new power plant.

In this DOE-sponsored research program a 10 MVA machine was fabricated using niobium titanium as the superconductor. The experimental test protocol to allow the connection to the local electric utility system has been completed and unit testing is underway. The smallness of this device gives hope for scaled up units to also be much smaller in the future.

Superconductors capable of operating at liquid nitrogen temperatures can have many advantages in electric machinery. However, they must be fabricated into windings with appropriate cross sections carrying sufficiently high current densities in reasonable magnetic fields while sustaining the resulting mechanical forces. For a brittle ceramic material, this is a real challenge.

The potential impacts of the new high temperature superconductors are the reduction in refrigeration, and simpler thermal isolation systems. This will lead to smaller less expensive, more reliable and efficient designs. Some studies also show that the reduced unit impedence will lead to greater system stability.

SUPERCONDUCTING TRANSMISSION SYSTEM

Possibly a better way of describing this transmission system is that it is designed as an underground transmission cable. This would take the place of aerial lines where required.

The DOE-sponsored research at Brookhaven National Laboratory has been completed. This helium temperature cable is the world's largest and longest superconducting transmission cable with the capacity of 1000 MVA. This is sufficient to carry the entire load of the largest modern generating plants. The present superconductor is niobium tin.

To match the conductor and electrical insulation expansion ratios, a special synthetic tape was developed. This not only has exceptional low temperature characterization but is also found to be superior to modern ambient cable insulating materials. It is directly applicable to ambient cables and this technology is being transferred to the private sector for application on ambient cables.

The key technical issues are fabricating a superconductor with sufficient current carrying capacity and low AC losses, and able to be bonded to a metal substrate, in the form of a flexible tape. The potential impacts of the high temperature superconductor are a reduction of life cycle costs, and an improvement in refrigeration efficiency.

SUPERCONDUCTING MAGNETIC ENERGY STORAGE (SMES)

With this device, off peak power can be stored for use during peak times. Thus, use of generating and transmission facilities can be greatly improved.

The DOE-sponsored research program at Los Alamos National Laboratory has completed a field test on a small prototype tested in the Bonneville Power Administration system. The SMES concept was proven even though the prototype was too small to indicate scale-up design parameters.

A 1985 study for OESD has showed that a coil with a diameter of 1,100 yards could handle the power from a 1,000 megawatt, 5,000 megawatt-hour superconducting magnetic energy storage plant. This device might reduce the peak load sufficiently to save the cost of building some new power plants. This application woud require the new high temperature superconductor to have much higher current densities in a high magnetic field environment.

FUTURE APPLICATIONS

There are two broad classes of power system applications to which high temperature superconducting material may have significant advantages. These are large electric and storage equipment; and electronics.

The large electric and storage equipment area includes the three technologies in which OESD has had considerable experience (i.e., superconducting generator, superconducting transmission cable, and superconducting magnetic energy storage) and several which could prove to be just as important to the nation in the future: electric motors of very high efficiency; AC to DC converters and inverters; magnetic separation of particulates, and metals; and levitating/friction-free moving parts. The electronics area could include: smart control systems for electric and storage systems; higher speed real-time system information gathering and analysis; computers; and power system protection and control devices.

Before the recent discoveries, the DOE superconductivity applications research was being phased out. The market wasn't ready, and the product was not sufficiently competitive to allow its entry into the commercial arena. In order to determine the best future action, key scientists from the national laboratories, federal agencies, and other selected groups were asked to assess potential high temperature superconductivity applications, to quantify system benefits and to determine material requirements for power system applications. The following bulk material requirements were determined in this assessment:

Material Requirements for Bulk
High Temperature Superconducting Materials

	Current Density (KA/sq cm)			
Application	Operating (Jop) (Present Design)	Minimum Operating (Jop)	Estimated Minimum(Jc)	Operating Magnetic Field (Tesla)
1.Generator	30	30	45	2
2.Magnetic Storage	600	200	250	5
3.A.C. Transmission Cable	230	190	380	<1

Material Requirements for Bulk
High Temperature Superconducting Materials
(continued)

Application	Current Density (KA/sq cm)			
	Operating (Jop) (Present Design)	Minimum Operating (Jop)	Estimated Minimum(Jc)	Operating Magnetic Field (Tesla)
4. Transformer	40	40	50	0.3
5. Motors	<10	5	50	2-3
6. Magnetic Separation	<10	5	50	2-5

Note: Strain Tolerance for all applications: 0.2%

R&D PROGRAM PRIORITIES

From the above table, it is obvious that the most important task for the research scientists is to increase the current density at liquid nitrogen temperatures. Increasing the critical current density is presently of greater importance than higher transition temperatures.

The following indicates the near term research priorities for the OESD program, in order of importance:

1. To conduct focused research to increase the critical current density in wires and tapes, with special emphasis on the chemical and anisotropy issues.

2. To conduct a more-in-depth technical assessment and market analysis to identify the most promising designs and applications using the high temperature materials as a base, and to consider the most appropriate sized devices.

3. To assess the cooling approach, especially at the conductor surface, and to develop new electrical stability criteria.

4. To devise processing and fabrication techniques, to include working samples of wires and tapes.

5. To characterize the mechanical behavior required for each application.

6. To develop techniques to assure the adhesion of the high temperature superconductors to various mechanical and electrical stabilizers.

MAJOR CHALLENGES

Presently, basic research is dynamic, exciting, highly competitive, and, most importantly, productive. There is a need to gain a fundamental understanding of the mechanism of superconductivity in the ceramic oxides. Continued emphasis must be placed on pushing towards new limits of superconducting material parameters, especially the critical current density, and mechanical properties.

Technology implementation is difficult due to the lack of knowledge about designing, processing, and manufacturing superconducting materials. This offers its own set of challenges which require more research.

A major challenge is to produce a flexible wire, tape in bulk quantities possessing adequate characteristics for critical field and critical current density while meeting the thermal and mechanical requirements of the various applications.

Due to the competitive environment, the R&D program will require parallel efforts of research, design, development, manufacturing, and prototype testing, in order to keep pace and in some cases lead the scientific discoveries.

There is a need for a concerted national effort of our industries, universities, and national laboratories to market and successfully commercialize superconducting applications. There is great excitement, but at the same time there is a realistic concern of whether this material will be able to meet the challenging problems facing us in applying the material to real power systems.

A PLANNING ASSESSMENT ON THE ROLE OF SUPERCONDUCTORS IN THE ELECTRIC UTILITY INDUSTRY

Dr. Kirby C. Holte, Program Manager
Advanced Electrical and Communications Systems
Southern California Edison Company

Mr. Steven E. Mavis, Planning Engineer
Electric System Planning
Southern California Edison Company

In 1987, US electric utilities generated approximately 2650 billion kilowatt hours of which 214 billion kilowatt hours never reached the customer [1]. The 214 billion kilowatt hours, approximately 8 percent of the power generated, was lost to heat in transformers, transmission lines and distribution lines. Another 50 to 70 billion kilowatt hours of electrical losses occurred in power plant generators and motors resulting in a net electrical loss of 10 to 11 percent. We can assume that electrical losses for customer owned transformers and motors are of the same order of magnitude, thus total losses are approximately 20 percent.

Superconductors, with essentially zero losses for direct current and small losses for alternating current applications, offer the potential for system loss reduction while providing a wide range of new capabilities and options available to the electric utility planner. This paper reviews the current state of the art for superconducting cables and generators and suggests areas where electric utilities may benefit from new advancements with high temperature materials.

Although first discovered in 1911, commercial application of superconductors has only occurred during the past decade. The largest current markets for superconductive materials are Magnetic Resonance Imaging devices for medical diagnosis. This markets is, however, vary small compared to the potential applications by electric utilities and their customers.

Superconducting Cables - Past and Present

Research in the 1960's led the National Science Foundation, in 1971, to recommend the construction of a

1000 MVA superconducting cable and cable test facility at the Brookhaven National Laboratory [2]. Research for the cables commenced in 1972 and the facility was energized in October of 1982.

The Brookhaven installation consists of two 115 meter helium cooled coaxial cables operated at 80 kilovolts line to neutral and 333 MVA (138 kilovolt, 1000 MVA three phase equivalent) [3,4]. Each single phase cable consists of concentric inner (2.95 cm diameter) and outer (5.36 cm diameter) niobium-tin superconductors operating at a maximum surface current density of 500 Amperes per square centimeter. AC losses at rated current (4160 Amperes and nominal operating temperature (7.5 K) were 0.32 Watts per meter (per phase). Each cable has a nominal shunt capacitance of 326 pF per meter and nominal series inductance of 0.185 uH per meter. The calculated surge impedance is 24 Ohms and the propagation constant is 0.17 degrees per kilometer.

The Brookhaven project successfully demonstrated that a superconducting cable could be constructed and operated under conditions similar to those found in an electric utility. Extensive testing of the cables, refrigeration systems, terminations and controls between 1982 and 1985 confirmed technical feasibility and reliability [5]. It also demonstrated that a superconducting cable could be designed to operate at its surge impedance loading thus allowing underground transmission lines exceeding 200 kilometers without compensation. This latter point suggests that superconductor cables could be a direct replacement for long distance overhead transmission lines.

AC losses for the Brookhaven cable were comparable to conventional transmission lines. Using the Brookhaven design but assuming a 160 kilometer (100 mile), 1000 MVA double circuit configuration, current and voltage dependent losses are 64 and 48 kilowatts respectively. Heat-in losses for the double circuit is 144 kilowatts yielding a total of 256 Watts of heat to be removed by the refrigeration system. If the refrigeration system has an overall cooling efficiency of 225 Watts per Watt, total losses are 57.6 megawatts for a system efficiency of 94.2 percent [4]. For comparison, a single circuit overhead 500 kV transmission line operating at 1000 MVA would have losses ranging between 70 and 150 megawatts depending on the conductors used.

The Philadelphia Electric Company has compared the construction and operating costs of superconductor cables to conventional underground and overhead systems for a 10,000 MVA, 105 kilometer transmission corridor [6]. Fifteen underground and one combination overhead/underground lines were compared with the three flexible 230 kilovolt superconducting cables circuits, rated at 5000 MVA per circuit, showing the lowest overall cost for the underground alternatives. This configuration allows two circuits to carry full rated capacity during an outage of the third circuit. Cost comparisons were based on total system costs including substations, compensation circuits and capitalized losses. When viewed from total system costs, the liquid helium cooled superconducting AC cable was approximately seven percent less expensive than gas insulated rigid cables and 24 percent less expensive than high pressure oil filled cables. The superconducting cable was approximately twice the cost of 500 kilovolt overhead circuits.

Superconducting Cables - Lessons Learned

Past experimental and economic studies, although confined to helium cooled niobium superconductors, provide a number of lessons learned which appear to be applicable to the new high temperature ceramic superconductors.

Lesson 1: Superconductive cables are most cost effective when used for moderate to long distance (beyond 250 kilometers) direct current transmission lines through environmentally sensitive or high right-of-way cost corridors.

AC losses for superconductor cables, while lower than those in a typical conventional cable, remain significant; thus the full benefit of superconductors can only be achieved with direct current systems. Consider, for example, the Pacific Northwest - Southwest intertie, an overhead 1360 kilometer (845 miles), 500 kilovolt, bipolar DC line linking Southern California with the Pacific Northwest. The line is currently rated at 2000 MW but is being upgraded to 3100 MW. At rated current (3100 Amperes, line losses through the 38 Ohm line resistance are 365 megawatts or 12 percent of rated power. A bipolar dc line rated at 400 kilovolts and 3875 Amperes would reduce line losses to near zero and lower the cost of the converter terminals.

Lesson 2: There is no magnetic or electric field external to the superconductor cables.

Three phase superconducting AC cable circuits are constructed as three single phase coaxial cables in a common cryogenic enclosure to minimize losses. The outer conductor carries the full return current thus constraining the magnetic and electric fields to the cable itself. This effectively eliminates negative and zero sequence coupling between conductors as well as any potential concern relative to biological effects associated with transmission lines.

Lesson 3: AC superconductor cables, when optimized for least cost, have electrical properties similar to those of overhead transmission lines.

Superconductor cables can be operated at high current densities thus providing a rated capacity at or near surge impedance loading, without shunt or series compensation, for cables up to 300 kilometers in length. Surge impedance loading for the 230 kilovolt cable used in the Philadelphia Electric study is approximately 4700 megawatts (Zc = 11.2 Ohms) with a thermal limit of approximately 5000 megawatts (steady state). Surge impedance loading of the circuit yields a flat voltage profile at a total phase shift (delta) of 32 degrees. An equivalent overhead system (with equal phase shift and voltage profile) would require five 500 kilovolt circuits. Conventional oil filled or solid dielectric underground cables are limited to 20 to 40 kilometers without compensation. AC superconductor cables are thus most cost effective for long distances (over 100 kilometers) and high capacities (over 2000 MVA) and are the only practical AC alternative for overhead lines at this distance.

Lesson 4: Additional research is required to reduce AC losses and improve thermal stability of the cable during transient overcurrent conditions.

AC losses remain high in the Brookhaven cable to justify superconductors strictly on the basis of loss reduction. The most promising approach to net loss reduction may be the use of high temperature superconductors. Assuming conductors can be fabricated with current and voltage dependent losses equivalent to those of helium cooled niobium superconductors, net losses become a function of heat leak into the enclosure and the efficiency of the refrigeration. Operation at liquid nitrogen temperatures results in a small reduction in heat leak and approximately a 25 to 1 increase in refrigeration efficiency. Net efficiency could potentially be improved from approximately 95 percent for the helium cooled system to 99.5 percent for a nitrogen cooled system.

Superconducting Generators - Past and Present

U.S. design and analysis work on superconductor generators was begun in the 1960's culminating with the construction and testing of a 20 MVA generator by General Electric [7,8]. A 120 MVA superconductor rotor was tested in West Germany and 3, 6, 30 and 50 MVA generators were constructed in Japan. An EPRI sponsored program to develop a 300 MVA superconducting generator was terminated in 1983 due to a declining market in the United States for large generators. More recently, the Ministry of International Trade and Industry (MITI) in Japan announced plans to design and build a 250 MVA superconductor generator [9].

These generators all used helium cooled niobium superconductors for the DC rotor windings and conventional copper or aluminum conductors for the AC stator windings. AC rotor losses are thus vary small except during transient conditions. A 0.5 percent improvement in net efficiency for commercial size (600 to 1200 MVA) generators has been postulated.

The superconductor generator will be approximately 40 percent smaller than a conventional generator of equal voltage and MVA ratings [10]. It's short circuit ratio will be larger and reactance smaller than conventional generators thus leading to improved steady state and transient stability. In addition, larger air gaps allowed in a superconductor generator (due to higher rotor field strengths) has led to conceptual designs of 230 and 500 kilovolt stator voltages thus eliminating the need for step up transformers between the generator and the line.

Superconducting Generators - Lessons Learned

Lesson 1: Reduced synchronous reactance can significantly increase the benefit to cost ratio for superconducting generators.

A superconductor rotor can produce high magnetic fields in the air gap while maintaining low rotor losses. This allows designers to increase air gap clearances thus reducing reactance by 50 percent or more. Reduced generator reactance will, in turn, allow increased loading of transmission lines within safe steady state and transient stability limits. System studies are required to verify potential savings; however, a 10 percent (or more) increase in line loading seems reasonable.

Lesson 2: Superconducting generators will be physically smaller and lighter than conventional generators.

Generators with superconducting rotors can potentially achieve a 40 percent weight and size reduction relative to conventional 300 MVA and above synchronous generators. Although difficult to quantify, cost savings in material and tooling could potentially offset the added costs for refrigeration, etc. Reduction in weight and physical size will allow fabrication and transport of larger generators (eg 2000 MVA) if required in the future.

Lesson 3: Losses can be reduced from 30 to 70 percent in a superconducting generator.

Experience to date suggests that use of a superconducting direct current rotor in large machines (300 MVA and above) could reduce electrical losses by up to 50 percent. Use of a superconducting stator would improve efficiency; however, the gains will not be as great due to AC losses. Overall efficiency could potentially increase from approximately 99 percent to between 99.3 and 99.7 percent.

Lesson 4: Additional research is required to understand the effect of reduced rotor mass on system damping, subsynchronous resonance, quenching of the superconductor rotor during transients, etc.

Although several experimental superconducting rotors have been built, none have been operated under conditions representative of those of an actual electric utility system. The potential benefits of this technology must therefor be considered as speculative. MITI in Japan and EPRI in the United States have proposed RD&D projects leading to demonstration of a superconducting generator in an electric utility system.

High Temperature Superconductors - Current Status

The discovery of a new class of superconductors by Mueller and Bednorz in 1986 and the subsequent demonstration of superconductivity at liquid nitrogen temperatures has dramatically altered our outlook for the role of superconductors for electronics and power apparatus. These ceramic materials may have their greatest impact in power equipment where the low efficiency of helium refrigeration, 200 to 250 Watts/Watt removed as compared to 8 to 10 Watts/Watt removed for nitrogen refrigeration, has prevented economic operation with niobium based superconductors.

On the plus side, thin films and tapes from the high temperature superconductor (htsc) have been produced and several firms expect to have htsc wire samples available for testing in 1988. The basic materials (Barium, Yttrium, Copper and Oxygen) are abundant and relatively inexpensive. Critical temperatures of 94 to 98 K are easily achieved and critical magnetic fields are at least as high as those reported for niobium superconductors. There have been a large number of laboratories reporting superconductivity at temperatures in excess of 200 K; however, these experiments are not easily replicated and there is some doubt if the observation was actually superconductivity or an artifact of the measurement system. More recently, there have been reports of stable and repeatable superconductivity at 130 K.

On the negative side, critical current densities for the bulk htsc materials have been extremely low, generally less than 1000 Amperes per square centimeter. Reports of up to 100,000 Amperes per square centimeter by IBM for thin film htsc materials are encouraging but the IBM thin film technology is not directly applicable to power cables, generators and other power apparatus.

Power apparatus will require superconducting wire and tapes with current densities of 10,000 to 1 million Amperes per square centimeter. Cables and generators could be designed with nitrogen cooling and 94 K htsc wires or tapes however the refrigeration system may be complex due to requirements to operate close to the liquid nitrogen temperature of 77 K. An increase in critical temperature to 130 K would allow less complex refrigeration and provide a greater temperature margin during transient conditions.

The Electric Utility - Losses

Loss reduction remains as one of the major motivations for use of superconductors within the electric utility industry. As previously noted, U.S. utilities had approximately 214 billion kilowatt hours of losses within the transmission and distribution system. Although 8 percent loss is relatively low, it becomes meaningful when translated into $15 billion per year at 7 cents per kilowatt hour.

The breakdown of losses between transmission and distribution and between lines and transformers is not available on a National basis; however, the breakdown for Southern California Edison (Table 1) is probably representative.

Table 1
Transmission and Distribution
Average Transformer and Line Losses* (1978)

Generator to EHV step up Transformers......	0.34 %
EHV Transmission Lines**..................	0.68 %
EHV to 220 and 115 kV step down Transformers	0.43 %
220 and 115 kV Transmission Lines..........	0.96 %
220 kV to EHV step up Transformers.........	0.40 %
220 kV to 66 kV step down Transformers.....	0.51 %
66 kV Transmission Lines..................	0.76 %
66 kV to 220 kV step up Transformers.......	0.60 %
66 kv to 4, 12 or 16 kV step down Transformers	0.81 %
4, 12, 16 kV Distribution Lines............	3.60 %
Distribution Transformers..................	2.63 %
Secondary 120/240 Volt Circuits...........	0.40 %

* Losses = 100*(Pin - Pout)/Pin
** Excludes interconnections with other utilities

Losses associated with long distance EHV transmission lines are directly proportional to distance. Typical line resistances for a 500 kilovolt line range from .015 to .03 Ohms per mile. Losses for a 300 mile line with an average loading of 500 amps (430 MVA) are 3.375 to 6.75 megawatts (.8 to 1.6 percent). If loading on these lines were increased to 800 amps, losses would increase to a range of 8.65 to 17.28 megawatts (2 to 4 percent).

Economic Value of Losses

If current research and development efforts result in superconducting cables, generators, transformers and motors which are technically comparable to their non-superconducting (conventional) counterparts, the decision to choose superconducting over conventional equipment becomes one of engineering economics. In practice, the superconducting and non-superconducting technologies are not fully comparable and any meaningful analysis should look at total system costs. In this discussion, however, we will ignore all factors other than the cost of the cables and the cost of losses.

The assumptions used in an engineering economic analysis may change considerably from utility to utility and from month to month. The following methodology is, however, universally applied by all utilities with possible minor variations dictated by individual circumstances. The following example, based on present worth [11] illustrates typical assumptions and procedures.

This example compares flexible superconducting cables to a 230 kilovolt gas insulated transmission line. The required line capacity is 2000 megawatts and the line length is 50 miles. Technical performance for superconducting and conventional gas insulated cables are assumed to be comparable and both meet project reliability and operating criteria. Three 230 kilovolt, 2,928 Ampere superconducting circuits will be compared to three 230 kilovolt, 3,070 Ampere gas insulated circuits in order to provide full capacity with one circuit out of service. No compensation is required and the total cable losses, at a rated power of 2000 megawatts, are assumed to be 2.42 megawatts for the superconducting and 30.35 megawatts for the gas insulated cables. Cost and financial assumptions are shown in Table 2. Computations for the present worth for the two projects are shown in Table 3.

Present worth cost of the superconducting cable in this highly simplified example is lower that that of the gas insulated transmission line. Furthermore, this cost advantage increases as we increase the average loading. The example, however, is only intended to show the relative value of loss reduction in the calculation of cost and the reader is advised to make a much more thorough cost analysis for the intended application.

Table 2
Cost and Financial Assumptions for
Engineering Economic Comparison of Conventional
and Superconducting Cables

Installed Cost - Superconductor [12]	$600,000,000
Installed Cost - Gas Insulated [13]	$550,000,000
Project Life	30 years
Project Start Date	1990
Levelized Annual Fixed Rate Charge	18.5%
Annual O&M (as % of installed cost)	2%
Cost of Money	14%
Annual Escalation Rate, 1988-1990 Transmission	5%
Total Escalation 1988 - 1990 Transmission	15.8%
Levelized Annual Capacity Cost*	$93/kW-yr
Annual Energy Costs (1990)	$40.4/kw-hr
Annual Escalation Rate, 1990-2019 Energy	8.1%
Average Cable Loading (% utilization)	70%
Capacity Loss - Superconducting Cables	2.42 MW
Capacity Loss - Gas Insulated Cables	30.35 MW
Energy Loss - Superconducting Cables	18,088 MW-hr/yr
Energy Loss - Gas Insulated Cables	186,106 MW-hr/yr

* Based on the installed cost of a combustion turbine

Table 3
Present Worth Comparison of
Superconducting and Gas Insulated Cables
(dollars X1000)

	Superconductor	Gas Insulated
1987 Capital Cost (1)	$600,000	$550,000
1990 Capital Cost (2)	$695,000	$637,000
1990 PW of Capital and O&M (3)	$998,000	$915,000
Cost - Lost Capacity (K$/yr) (4)	$225	$2,823
1990 PW Cost - Lost Capacity (5)	$1,600	$19,800
1990 PW Cost - Energy Loss (6)	$10,800	$112,000
1990 PW - Project (3+5+6)	$1,010,400	$1,046,800

Summary

Materials research in industrial and university laboratories rarely attract the attention of corporately boards of directors much less receive front page coverage in the world press. The laboratory demonstration of superconductivity at liquid nitrogen temperatures was not only the rare exception; it stands alone as the only scientific discovery to mobilize hundreds of research laboratories within days of the discovery becoming widely known in the science community.

Clearly, the role of high temperature superconductors in the electric utility industry depends on progress in developing reliable and low cost conductors capable of handling the required current densities while maintaining acceptable low AC losses. Assuming this can be done, the next hurdle will come in designing the power cables, generators, motors, transformers, energy storage devices etc. meeting present and future utility technical and cost requirements. This done, electric utilities will have the data required to fully assess the role of superconductors within their system. None of this is, however, likely to occur unless the electric utility industry takes an active role in the necessary research and development leading up to commercial products.

The role of superconducting cables, generators, and motors depends more on the future structure of the electric utility industry than specific comparisons with today's systems and technology. The trend in electric system planning is clearly toward strengthening of interconnection and bulk power sales between utilities separated by hundreds of miles. Efficiency will continue to increase in importance as will the trend toward compaction of power plants and transmission for reduced land use.

Fifteen years of research and development with helium cooled superconducting generators, cables and energy storage devices has verified technical feasibility and provided many of the answers needed to assess the potential of this technology within the utility.

References

1 "Annual Industrial Forecast", Electrical World, (September, 1987), 37.

2 E.B. Forsyth, "Underground power transmission by superconducting cable," BNL50325, (March 1972).

3 E.B. Forsyth, "The 60 Hz Performance of Superconducting Power Transmission Cables Rated for 333 MVA per Phase," IEEE Transactions on Power Apparatus and Systems, Vol. PAS-103, No. 8, (1984), 2023.

4 E.B. Forsyth, R.A. Thomas, "Operational Test Results of a Prototype Superconducting Power Transmission System and Their Extrapolation to the Performance of a Large System," IEEE Transactions on Power Delivery, Vol. PWRD-1, No. 1, (1986), 10.

5 E.B. Forsyth, R.A. Thomas, "Performance summary of the Brookhaven superconducting power transmission system," Cryogenics, Vol. 26 (November, 1986), 599.

6 Evaluation of the Economical and Technical Viability of Various Underground Transmission Systems for Long Feeds to Urban Load Areas, by the Philadelphia Electric Company, Department of Energy Report HCP/T-2055/1 (1977).

7 T.A. Keim, T.E. Laskaris, J.A. Fealey, P.A. Rios, "Design and Manufacture of a 20 MVA Superconducting Generator," IEEE Transactions on Power Apparatus and Systems, Vol. PAS-104, No. 6 (1985), 1475.

8 J.A. Fealey, W.D. Jones, T.A. Keim, T.E. Laskaris, "Comprehensive Test and Evaluation of a 20 MVA Superconducting Generator," IEEE Transactions on Power Apparatus and Systems, Vol. PAS-104, No. 6 (1985), 1484.

9 "Feasibility Study on Superconducting Generator and Related Technologies," Ministry of International Trade and Industry, (March, 1987).

10 "High-Voltage Stator Winding Development," Electric Power Research Institute, prepared by the General Electric Company, Report EPRI EL-3391, (April, 1984).

11 E.L. Grant, W.G. Ireson, Principles of Engineering Economics, 5th edition, The Ronald Press Co. (1970)

12 R.A. Thomas, E.B. Forsyth, "Preliminary Economic Analysis of High Tc Superconducting Power Transmission System," BNL 39973, (July 1987).

13 "Villa Park-Lewis-Barre 220kV T/L Project, Lewis-Barre Segment (Phase II) Underground Study Area, Supplemental Report," prepared by the Southern California Edison Company, (1987).

SCIENCE AND TECHNOLOGY OF THE NEW SUPERCONDUCTORS

Mario Rabinowitz
Electric Power Research Institute
Palo Alto, CA 94303

ABSTRACT

Higher temperature superconductivity has the potential of leading to practical applications that may dramatically change the electrical and electronics industries. However, before this can happen, we must increase the critical current density, and decrease the ac power loss as discussed in this paper.

Electrons are paired in the new Perovskite superconductors just as one might expect. However, it is not likely that they are paired by the same mechanism as in the metallic sueprconductors. Although the pairing mechanism ultimately limits the transition temperature, it is possible to calculate an upper limit for the transition temperature without knowledge of the electron pairing mechanism or its strength.

I. ELECTRON PAIRING MECHANISIMS

Spin one-half particles such as electrons, that obey Fermi-Dirac statistics exhibit frictional or viscous flow because there are available states into which the particles may be scattered such that momentum in the flow direction may be lost. Momentum is always conserved, but momentum transferred to the lattice ions does not contribute to the flow momentum or electron current. Since the lower energy states can be completely filled for integer-spin particles which obey Bose-Einstein statistics, they cannot lose energy in collisions since lower energy states are not available. They thus can exhibit frictionless or viscous-free flow or current.

According to the BCS theory (1), in a superconductor carrying no current the paired electrons have equal and opposite momenta, and opposite spin. The rule of opposite momenta gives a tautological explanation of why the electron pairs move through the superconductor without friction. When one electron of a pair undergoes a diffuse scattering collision (which normally results in electrical resistance), the other electron must scatter in the opposite direction to maintain opposite momentum. The result is that the center of mass motion (associated with a current) remains unchanged, i.e., undisturbed. The net spin 0 (singlet state) of the two Fermions (electrons) form a Boson to produce superconductivity just as a pair of He^3 atoms at low temperature form a Boson of net spin 1 (triplet state) to produce superfluidity. In both cases, particles that could not otherwise exhibit frictionless flow because they individually obey Fermi-Dirac statistics, pair-up to obey Bose-Einstein statistics which allows a condensation in phase space and collective motion without friction.

Although the BCS theory uses phonons (lattice vibrations) to produce electron pairs, this is not an essential ingredient of the theory. Eliashberg generallized the BCS theory for stronger coupling mechanisms many years ago. Recently, Marsiglio and Carbotte (2) have examined the Eliashberg generalization with respect to the new higher temperature Perovskite superconductors.

Unless the phonons have unusually high frequency (high Debye temperature, T_d) the transition temperature, T_c, is probably limited to no more than 50K. ($Y_1Ba_2Cu_3O_{7-y}$ has a $T_c \geq 94K$.) Metallic hydrogen (which could only be produced at very high pressure) might be expected to be superconducting at room temperature with phonon coupling of electrons because it would have a very high T_d. But this is an exception.

From both flux quantization and tunnelling measurements, we know that the electrons are paired in the new superconductors. We do not know what the pairing mechanism is, though it is not likely phonons alone could do it. Nevertheless, as we'll see in the next section, we can calculate an upper limit for T_c.

II. HIGHEST POSSIBLE TRANSITION TEMPERATURE (on earth)

The coherence length as a concept can be looked at in three different ways in simple physical terms (3). The simplest way is to think of coherence length as the rms distance between an electron pair as the electrons oscillate 180° out of phase about their center of mass (1).

The second meaning is related to the fact that the superconducting electrons are in a more ordered (more coherent) state than the normal electrons. Pippard identified the change in density, n_s, of superconducting electrons with this order. Pippard called the distance over which n_s cannot change rapidly with position, the coherence length ξ. In the metallic superconductors $\xi \sim 10^3 - 10^4 Å$, so that there were a large number, N, of electron pairs within a volume ξ^3:

$$N \sim 10^{22} \text{electrons/cm}^3 (5 \times 10^{-5} \text{cm})^3 \sim 10^9. \quad (1)$$

Figure 1 shows the structure of the Perovskite superconductor. In the 1-2-3 Perovskite, ξ varies between about 5 to 20Å. So there are very few electron pairs within a coherence volume. This raises serious questions about the second meaning of coherence. Nevertheless, a simple lower limit for ξ suggests itself:

$$n_s \xi^3 \geqslant 1, \text{ or} \quad (2)$$

$$\xi \geqslant n_s^{-1/3}. \quad (3)$$

That is, there has to be at least one electron pair within a coherence length. So ξ cannot be less than given by Eq. 3. In a neutron star, where the density is very high, n_s is very high, and hence ξ may be a small fraction of an Å. In the 1-2-3, ξ can't be smaller than about 5 Å. Now we can use this lower limit of ξ in connection with the next meaning of ξ.

The third physical meaning of ξ relates to the flux quantum or fluxoid

$$\phi_o = \frac{h}{2e} = 2.07 \times 10^{-15} \text{ Weber}, \quad (4)$$

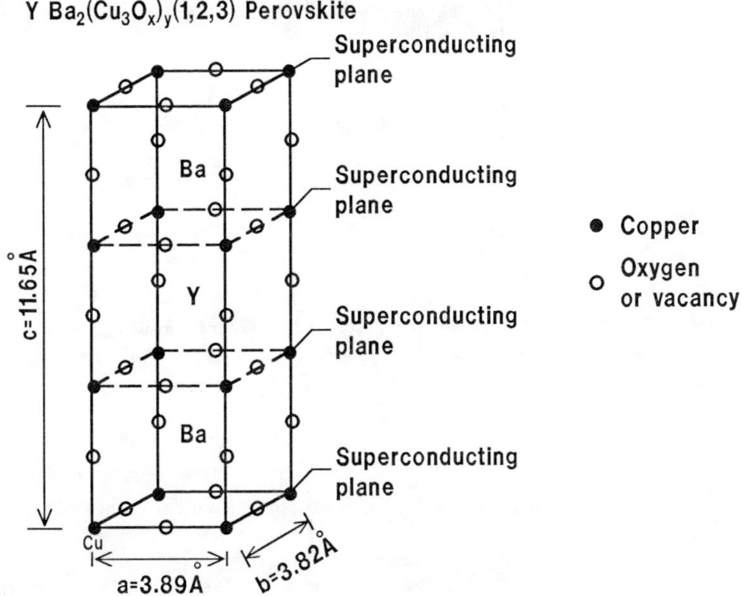

Figure 1. Crystaline Structure of Yttrium-Barrium-Copper Oxide With a Superconducting Transition Onset Temperature of 98K.

where h is Planck's constant, and e is the charge of an electron. In the mixed state, the superconductor is threaded with a lattice of fluxoids. The density of superconducting electrons goes to zero only at the center of each fluxoid. However, to a first approximation, the core of each fluxoid may be thought of as equivalent to a cylinder of normal material of radius $2^{1/2}\xi$. Thus we have

$$B_{c2} \doteq \frac{\phi_o}{2\pi\xi^2} . \tag{5}$$

When a magnetic field is applied to a conductor, the force on the magnetic moment of the electrons tends to align the spins of all the electrons opposite to the applied field (called Pauli paramagnetism). This acts to break up the Cooper electron pairs which have anti-parallel spins. As a result, an important mechanism for transition to the normal state is the paramagnetic limit when a large enough field is applied.

In 1962, Clogston calculated the paramagnetic limit for H_{c2} (4). He thus established a simple linear relationship between H_{c2} and T_c as given by Eq. 6.

$$H_{c2} = 1.4 \times 10^6 \, T_c \text{ A/m.} \tag{6}$$

For $YBa_2Cu_3O_{7-y}$ with $T_c = 94K$, Eq. 6 predicts $H_{c2} = 1.7 \times 10^6$ Oe which is close to the value projected from experimental measurements. This gives reason to expect that this equation is applicable to the Perovskite superconductors.

We are now in a position to tackle this problem from the other end. Having established an upper limit on H_{c2} from another consideration which resulted in Eq. 5, then we can use Eq. 6 to put an upper limit on T_c.

Combining Eqs. 4, 5, and 6 we have for an upper limit on the transition temperature

$$T_c \leqslant \frac{\phi_o}{1.4 \times 10^6 (2\pi\xi^2)\mu} = \frac{h}{5.6 \times 10^6 \pi e \xi^2 \mu} = \frac{hn^{2/3}}{5.6 \times 10^6 \pi e \mu} \tag{7}$$

where μ is the permeability of the material. For $\xi \sim 5\text{Å}$, or $n_s \sim 10^{22}$, Eq. 20 gives as an upper limit:

$$T_c \leqslant 750K = 477^0C. \tag{8}$$

The actual transition temperature may be considerably less than this. It would be quite surprising if a higher T_c were found for the state of matter as exists on the earth. Because of the much higher n_s that is possible on a neutron star, T_c could be considerably higher there.

Figure 2 shows a time history of transition temperatures. A linear extrapolation would have led to the expectation that the present T_c>94K would have been achieved in about another 300 years.

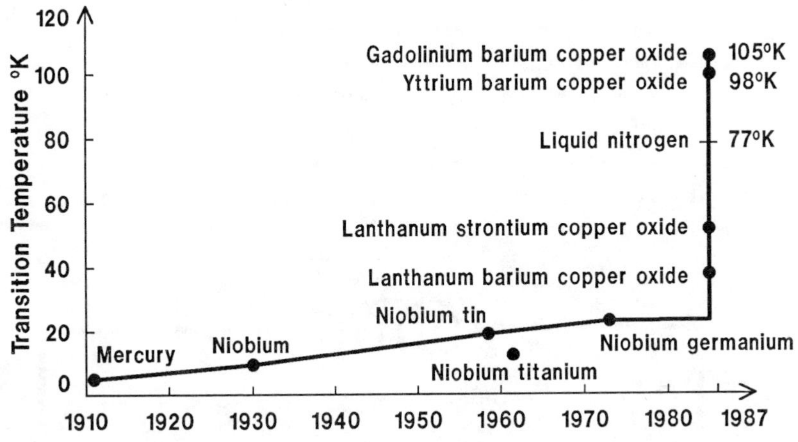

Figure 2. Transition Temperatures and Their Year of Discovery

III. AC POWER LOSS

A. Introduction

A superconductor may be thought of as composed of two variable interpenetrating fluids -- one of normal electrons and the other fluid of superconducting electron pairs. As the transition temperature is approached the electrons all become normal. As the temperature approaches 0 K, all the free electrons become superconducting. This is shown schematically in the parallel circuit diagram of Figure 3. The top branch which has only inductance represents the superconducting electrons. The bottom branch which has both inductance and resistance represents the normal electrons. For dc, the current divides inversely proportional to the resistance of each branch. Thus the current goes solely through the superconducting branch without power loss, since there is no current in the normal (resistive) branch.

For ac, the current divides inversely proportional to the impedance of each branch. Since the superconducting branch has inductive reactance, current flows in both branches with power loss in the resistive branch. This loss is fundamental and always present regardless of the magnitude of the current or magnetic field. Fortunately, it is a relatively small loss which is generally negligible. Let us look at the hysteresis loss mechanism which is generally not negligible.

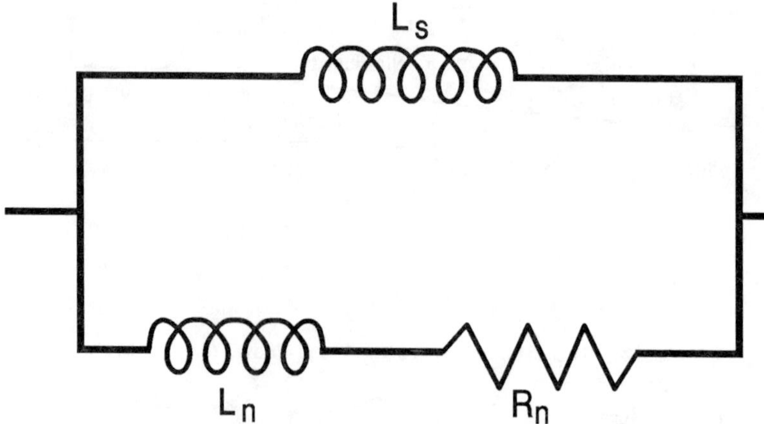

Figure 3. AC Superconductivity.

B. Hysteresis Power Loss

At low frequencies, such as 60 Hz, a hysteretic power loss has been the dominant loss mechanism. As the magnetic field increases, magnetic flux penetrates into the superconductor. When the field reverses, magnetic flux first leaves the superconductor near its surface so that when the field goes to zero there is still flux inside the superconductor. This magnetic hysteresis results in an energy loss each cycle.

Let us consider the one-dimensional case relevant to a transmission line where the flux due to the self-magnetic field, penetrates into the superconductor a distance δ which is small compared to the superconductor's thickness a.

$$J_c = \nabla X \frac{B}{\mu_o}$$
$$= \frac{-1}{\mu_o}\frac{\partial B}{\partial x}$$
$$= \frac{B}{\mu_o(\delta - x)}, \qquad (9)$$

where J_c is the critical current density and B is the magnetic flux density at any point x in the superconductor.

The flux inside the superconductor is

$$\phi = (\frac{1}{2} B_s) \; z \; \delta$$
$$= \frac{1}{2} Bsz \; (\frac{B_s}{\mu_o J_c})$$
$$= \frac{1}{2} \mu_o H_s{}^2 z \; J_c^{-1} \qquad (10)$$

where H_s is the magnetic field tangential to the surface of the superconductor.

The area of the hysteresis loop

$$W = \frac{4}{3} H_m \phi_m , \qquad (11)$$

is the energy loss per cycle per length of the superconductor in terms of the maximum flux ϕ_m that penetrates into the superconductor and the maximum self magnetic field H_m.

The power loss is the frequency, f, times the energy loss, and substituting Eq. 9 into Eq. 10 we obtain the hysteretic power loss per unit surface area of the superconductor

$$P/A = \frac{2}{3} \mu_o H_m^3 f J_c{}^{-1}, \delta << a \qquad (12)$$

The derivation of Eq.11 has neglected the decrease of J_c as H increases, and the effect of a potential surface barrier to the entry of flux.

When there is a large penetration of the field into the superconductor, $\delta \sim a$, the functional dependence changes, as is the case for superconducting electromagnets. Then the hysteresis power loss is proportional to $a^2 H_m J_c$.

Let us see what power loss Eq. 12 predicts for an ac transmission line with H_m=1000 Oe = 7.96 X10^4A/m. For the metallic superconductors $J_c \sim 10^6 A/cm^2 = 10^{10} A/m^2$, Eq. 12 predicts a power loss of

$$P/A = 250\ \mu W/cm^2 .$$

Thanks to the achievement of a surface barrier, a power loss of only $\sim 10 \mu W/cm^2$ was achieved for metallic superconductors such as Nb_3Ge and Nb_3Sn. For the ceramic Perovskite-like superconductors at 77K in polycrystalline form $J_c \sim 10^3 - 10^4 A/cm^2$, and Eq. 10 predicts a power loss of

$$P/A \sim 25\text{-}250\ mW/cm^2 .$$

If a surface barrier can be achieved to give us a similar reduction of power loss as in the metallic superconductors, we may be able to achieve

$$P/A \sim 1\text{-}10\ mW/cm^2.$$

Thanks to the increased refrigeration efficiency at 77K, the overall loss related to $1mW/cm^2$ at 77K is approximately equivalent to the overall loss related to $10\mu W/cm^2$ at 4.2K. However, I don't think we can tolerate an ac loss of more than $10mW/cm^2$.

IV. APPLICATIONS

A. Underground Superconducting Power Transmission.

Because of both increasing environmental concerns and lack of right-of-ways in high-population density areas, an increasing percentage of transmission lines will be underground. In the past, underground superconducting transmission lines (STL) could compete economically with conventional underground lines only at very high power ratings in excess of 3 GVA. (VA equals Watts when the voltage and current are in phase. In this case, 3 GVA equals 3 billion Watts.) The advent of the new higher-temperature superconductors opens up the possibility of competing at the 1-GVA power level at which most underground transmission lines operate.

Because of the large surface to volume ratio, the refrigeration requirements (and hence capital and operating costs) of a transmission line are most sensitive to operating temperature. Thus, the superconducting transmission line is a major recipient of the benefits presently afforded by the new superconductors.

Low-temperature (4 K-10 K) STL using niobium (Nb), niobium-tin (Nb_3S_n), and niobium-germanium (Nb_3Ge) for ac, and niobium-titanium (NbTi) for dc demonstrated technical viability (5). With these materials, the superconductor problem was much less difficult to solve than the electrical insulation problem because of the presence of the liquid helium (LHe) cryogen in the initial dielectric designs. A novel solution to this problem was found which excludes the cryogen from the high-electric field regions by using bulk extruded dielectric (6).

With the new superconductors, the dielectrics problem in STL may now be easier either because of the new bulk dielectric approach or because the dielectric strength of the expected cryogen, liquid nitrogen (LN_2, 77 K) has both a higher dielectric strength and a higher dielectric constant than LHe. However, the problem related to superconducting properties may be relatively more difficult than in the past. The new ceramic superconductors such as Yttrium-Barium-Copper-oxide are much more complex in structure, anisotropic, presently have orders of magnitude lower bulk current density capability ($10^3 A/cm^2$) than the old superconductors, and their ac power loss has not been determined.

B. Superconducting Power Generators And Motors.

Although quite different in their function, generators and electric motors are essentially the same machine operated in inverse modes. A generator converts mechanical energy to electrical, and when the process is reversed it functions as a motor. The high-magnetic flux density produced by a superconducting rotor field winding permits a great reduction of iron in both the rotor and the stator. This introduces degrees of freedom not previously possible in generator or motor design.

Voltage is induced and power is produced as the magnetic field lines of a rotating rotor periodically cut the stator windings. Elimination of iron in the stator (armature) allows an increased density of turns to be cut by the rotating field. This also reduces insulation requirements, both changes making for better use of space and materials. When grounded iron is removed from these windings, less insulation is needed between adjacent bars. Full interphase insulation is still needed between end winding groups, but the reorganized windings and insulation (made possible by the absence of the stator's iron teeth) permit reduced insulation stress, and, in turn, higher voltage operation. As yet, the ac superconducting power losses in a high-magnetic field are too large to replace the copper in the stator coils with superconductor.

Beginning in the 1960s, superconductors were discovered that are capable of high current densities in the presence of very high magnetic fields. It was soon realized that the use of such superconductors in the dc field winding (rotor) of ac electrical machines could, in principle, result in large improvements in efficiency, weight, and size with concomitant cost savings. The substantial reduction of losses by a factor of 800 in the rotor, translates to an overall reduction in losses of about 50%, or an improvement in efficiency to about 99.5% (7).

There are currently two major obstacles to the use of the new higher T_c superconductors in any electromagnet-based applications: low critical current density, and brittleness. These are particularly exacerbated in generators and motors because of physical limitations on rotor size and because in addition to very high magnetic forces on the wires there is also a very large centrifugal force. The magnetic field produced by an electromagnet is a function of the number of ampere-turns per unit length of the magnet. Although the critical magnetic field (H_{c2}~10^6 Oe) of the new higher T_c materials is almost an order of magnitude higher than the old superconductors, their current carrying capacity (critical current density) in wire form appears to be considerably less in a high magnetic field than not only the old superconductors, but even copper.

Thus an electromagnet using the new materials would be bulkier and more costly than its conventional counterpart, even without taking into account its refrigeration requirements. Also, for applications requiring a precise magnetic field and/or rapid changes in the field, the superconductor must be fabricated as very fine filaments inside a matrix of a good normal conductor such as copper or aluminum. (This is so that if superconductivity is lost locally at a spot, the entire superconductor does not quench because a good parallel electrical and thermal path is provided by the matrix.) The brittleness of the new materials makes this an extremely difficult production requirement.

Much more effort has been devoted to developing superconducting generators than motors primarily because generator power ratings are much larger. Nevertheless a relatively small (compared to generators, but large compared with motors) 2.24-MW superconducting homopolar motor has been constructed. This 3000-hp motor was built in the United States for shipboard propulsion by the U.S. Navy.

V. CONCLUSION.

In 1981 French scientists synthesized the Perovskite ceramic materials that led to the 1986-87 discoveries of high temperature superconductivity (8). They were searching for conducting ceramics as possible substitutes for noble metals such as platinum and palladium for high temperature electrode applications. They were not looking for a new class of superconducting materials.

At present, the new materials appear to allow us to do the same old things the classical superconductors could do, but more easily. Just as the superconductivity application of these new materials was not anticipated when they were first discovered in 1981, similarly these materials may lead to totally new and as yet completely unexpected superconducting devices in the future.

REFERENCES

1. J. Bardeen, L.N. Cooper, and J.R. Schrieffer, "Theory of Superconductivity." Phys. Rev. 108, 1175 (1957).

2. F. Marsiglio and J.P. Corbette, "Eliashberg Theory and The High T_c Oxides." Solid State Commun. 63, 419 (1987).

3. I am indebted to Chao-Yuan Huang for a valuable discussion in which we had similar views regarding the material in Section II.

4. A.M. Clogston, "Upper Limit For The Critical Field In Hard Superconductors." Phys. Rev. Let. 9, 266 (1962).

5. M. Rabinowitz, "Advanced Electric Power Trawnsmission", Encyclopedia of Science and Technology, 1981 Yearbook", pp. 12-21, McGraw-Hill.

6. G. Bahder, M. Rabinowitz and M. Sosnowski, "Bulk Solid Dielectric For Cryogenic Cables," Cryogenics 22, 95 (1983 U.S. Patents #4,241,233 (1980); #4,315,098 (1982); #4,394,534 (1983); and #4,397,807 (1983).

7. M. Rabinowitz, "Cryogenic Power Generation." Cryogenics, 17, 319 (1977).

8. L. Er-Rakho, C. Michel, J. Provost, and B. Raveau, "A Series of Oxygen-Defect Perovskites Containing Cu^{II} and Cu^{III}: The Oxides $La_{3-x}Ln_xBa_3[Cu^{II}{}_{5-2y}Cu^{III}{}_{1+2}]O_{14+y}$," J. Solid State Chem. 37, 151 (1981).

INDUSTRY-LABORATORY SYNERGY: TECHNOLOGY TRANSFER AT THE FRONTIERS OF PHYSICS

William Marcuse
Head, Office of Research and Technology Applications
Brookhaven National Laboratory
Upton, New York

Following the end of World War II, a great debate ensued concerning the future of nuclear weapons and research. The outcome of this debate was the formation of the Atomic Energy Commission (AEC).[1] This new civilian agency was endowed with the responsibility both for weapons development and peaceful uses of the atom, including "...conducting, assisting and fostering research and development in order to encourage maximum scientific and industrial progress."[2] From its inception, the AEC, and its successor agencies, the Energy Research and Development Administration and the Department of Energy have had the responsibility for supporting continuing research at the frontiers of physics.

To carry out its research mission, large pioneering research facilities such as reactors and accelerators were required. These were very expensive and the specialized scientific talent and resources needed to design, construct, commission and operate them were scarce. The cost of reproducing such facilities at a number of university centers was prohibitive. Moreover, the facilities that already existed were a legacy from the Manhattan Project and were located at laboratories associated with weapons development. These were difficult to access because of security and classification requirements. The new Agency solved this problem by proposing to nine major Eastern research universities that they contract with the AEC to operate a Laboratory where these specialized research facilities would be funded by the government. The nine Universities formed a non-profit corporation, Associated Universities Incorporated which contracted with the AEC to operate

Brookhaven, a new Laboratory located in central Long Island on the site of a former military post.

User Facilities

Brookhaven's primary mission since its inception has been the design, construction, commissioning and operation of large complex research facilities for scientific studies, and to carry out both basic and applied research in energy-related life and physical sciences. In the early days Brookhaven accelerators were the world's largest. Consequently, high energy physics has always been a major research activity at the Laboratory. Among the renowned research machines created at Brookhaven were the BGR (Brookhaven Graphite Reactor), and the AGS (Alternating Gradient Synchrotron). The BGR was the world's first reactor designed specifically for research purposes and was a pioneer for all that have followed. The AGS was for several years the world's largest accelerator and was a tool that led to several Nobel prizes confirming physical theories of matter and the universe.

The Department of Energy and its predecessor agencies have provided many user facilities over the past forty years. Not only have others been created at Brookhaven, but many have been established at other Department of Energy Laboratories. Today, there are over 250 identified designated user facilities or other user resources available at 9 multiprogram, 12 major single program, and 14 other Department of Energy Laboratories.[3] These are used by tens of thousands of researchers to perform thousands of experiments every year. Although university and research laboratory users predominate, in recent years industrial users have multiplied, especially as facilities that lend themselves to applied research become more common.

These facilities are provided for the use of all qualified scientists from any institution. The key considerations are:

- that the proposed research is suitable for the facility,
- that the proposed research is of interest to DOE programmatic goals,
- that the proposed research is of a quality level acceptable to scientific peers, and
- that the results of the proposed research be published.

The prospective user is required to submit a research proposal. This is reviewed by a committee associated with, but not necessarily drawn from the staff, of the facility. After the proposals are reviewed, the Laboratory Director makes the decision based upon the committee's recommendations.

Some of these facilities are classified as designated user facilities. These were constructed by DOE to serve the in-house staff and users from the outside scientific community. The instruments, equipment and personnel are maintained to assist in-house and visiting users in performing experiments at the facility. The facility is expensive and is one that will not be reproduced in large numbers within the United States. Funding for constructing and commissioning the facilities, and to provide support services and routine operation, maintenance and repair is supplied by the government.

DOE has the following stated policy for user facilities:

- o DOE laboratories represent valuable, often unique, resources for university and industrial scientists in many important resource fields,
- o DOE policy is to make its laboratories and facilities available to qualified scientists who can make the best use of these capabilities,
- o class waivers have been created to govern patent rights.

Another set of user facilities are designated other user resources. Although these exist primarily to serve the needs of in-house laboratory staff in the attainment of Department research objectives, they will be made available to outside qualified users where it is in the national interest. A designated user facility consists of instruments, equipment, laboratories, special facilities, or collections of expertise that are not available elsewhere on an independent, convenient and timely basis and at a reasonable charge. Their use is subject to scheduling considerations and the primacy of their use for DOE research programs.

These facilities, both designated and other user, will be made available at no cost to users performing nonproprietary research related to DOE's mission where all results are published. Use of the facilities by industrial researchers for proprietary research is relatively new. In these cases use of the facilities requires that the government be reimbursed for the full cost of the amount of use. Schedules of costs have been generated for many facilities. Additional industrial users have resulted from recent technology transfer initiatives. These industrial users wish to use facilities other than those designated as user facilities, including unique expertise, under the work-for-others arrangements with the Department. They are willing to pay full cost recovery for proprietary, and sometimes even nonproprietary, use of the facility.

A prospective user should contact the user facility by mail or phone for availability and access requirements. A user proposal may then be submitted, and once approved, user agreements will be formulated specifying operating procedures, time allotted, user fees (if applicable), collaborative arrangements, and proprietary provisions (if any).

Use of DOE facilities by private sector organizations for proprietary research is forbidden if equivalent commercial facilities are available. Where the DOE facility is unique, class waivers relating to patent rights have recently been formulated by DOE. These allow individuals and organizations performing research at DOE user facilities to elect to retain title to patents on inventions made under the user agreement. The Government retains the right of free use, to publish the results and to compel licensing if the owner refuses to do so. The waivers also apply to users who are paying full cost recovery and where the work is outside DOE's programmatic mission responsibilities. Under these conditions, the sponsor retains the right to acquire ownership of patents covering the inventions including some of those made by the operator of the DOE facility. The sponsor may also mark and remove any proprietary data generated in the course of the experimental work.[4]

It is likely that any American industrial user who identifies a collection of instruments, equipment, special facilities and staff at a DOE Laboratory that is not available in the private sector will be able to make arrangements to use it. This is in keeping with the recent legislation encouraging the use of government facilities and research results by the private sector to increase national competitiveness, industrial productivity and to improve the balance of trade. THe critical test is that a similar commercial capability is not available on an independent, convenient and timely basis, and at a reasonable charge.

Technology Transfer at the Frontier

The newest designated user facility at Brookhaven is the National Synchrotron Light Source (NSLS). It is the beneficiary of over thirty years and hundreds of millions of dollars of accelerator research, design, construction, commissioning and operation at Brookhaven and other Department of Energy Laboratories. Over the past thirty years many small accelerators have been built at DOE Laboratories. Large accelerators have been built at Fermi, Stanford, Berkeley, Argonne, Oak Ridge, Los Alamos, Bates and Princeton. Presently, there are plans to construct the multi-billion dollar Superconducting Super Collider (SSC), the world's largest proton accelerator, two light sources larger that the NSLS, first at Lawrence Berkeley Laboratory, and then an even larger one at Argonne National Laboratory, and the world's most powerful heavy ion collider at Brookhaven.

However, the NSLS, an electron synchrotron accelerator, represents the culmination of this immense thirty years of effort that has provided America with the world's greatest concentration of accelerator technology in the form of scientists, designers, operators, metrology, infrastructure and know-how. Up to now the primary application for accelerators has been the expansion of man's knowledge base - basic research. This does not mean that there has been no contribution to the applied world and improved quality of life and industrial productivity. In fact the spinoffs have been many. Accelerators have been the source of many of the radioisotopes and their generators, so important in radiodiagnostic and radiotherapeutic medicine. Accelerators themselves are being applied to medical applications. Advances in magnet, cryogenic, vacuum, and material technologies have had immense impacts on applied fields; for example, magnetic resonance imaging and levitating trains. Instrumentation , electronics and computer requirements to handle the huge quantities of data have been important in leading to applied developments in electronics, control systems and supercomputers. However, the NSLS has the potential of providing the technology that will maintain (perhaps regain) America's leadership in the semiconductor world of the future.

The NSLS has two electron storage rings. There are a total of 44 beam ports emanating from these rings, each port capable of supporting one to four experiments on individual beam lines. There were fifty-one operational beam lines at the end of 1987. The number of beam lines will continue to increase and level off at about eighty-five once the facility is fully occupied. Demand for the use of NSLS services is impressive. The current configuration supports about fifty-seven beam lines accommodating about 850 scientists representing over one hundred and forty university, industry or government laboratory research activities. Beam lines are constructed by participating research teams (PRTs) that often have mixed university, laboratory and industry participation. Forty universities, fourteen government institutions and eleven industrial concerns are members of PRTs. The beam lines are available 25 percent of the time to scientists not affiliated with PRT members. About 20 percent of the universities and 10 percent of the government laboratories are foreign.

The remainder of this paper is devoted to describing a transfer of accelerator technology in the form of a commercial electron synchrotron. Memory capacity of high density semiconductors has been doubling every 6-9 months for the past ten years. While this rate cannot continue indefinitely, there is still room for at least a dozen doublings raising densities of mass produced chips from 256 thousand bits per chip to one billion bits. Since memory density is inversely related to the resolution of reproduction, this means improving resolution from about 1.5 microns at present to 0.25 microns or better. The current production technology is optical lithography. The limit of optical lithography is on the horizon, perhaps 4 to 6 doublings. Beyond that other technologies will have to be introduced.[5] It seems clear that the technology of choice will be x-ray lithography using a synchrotron source.[6]

In 1983, the Germans recognized that x-ray lithography using a synchrotron source would most likely be the dominant semiconductor technology a decade hence. A consortium was formed that included Siemens, Phillips, Scanditronics, Oxford Instruments and other European companies. Its purpose was to develop a compact synchrotron source and the associated process technology. It was heavily funded by the German government and located at the Frauenhaufer Institute, home of the Berlin Electric Synchrotron. A joint venture, Cosy Microtech, was formed to manufacture and market the commercial synchrotron when it was developed.

Two years later the Japanese recognized that they would have to develop a synchrotron if they were to maintain their position as the world's leading semiconductor producer that they had just wrested from the United States. As in West Germany, substantial government funding was provided to a consortium of Japanese companies. Since not only the synchrotron but the accompanying process technology must be developed, there are at least thirteen cooperative efforts in Japan, including four that are developing synchrotrons.

As soon as the NSLS was available at Brookhaven, IBM made arrangements to use a beam line to perform proprietary research using x-rays from the Brookhaven synchrotron as a source. They soon showed that pattern resolutions up to 0.1 micron were possible. At this time there was no evidence that other American semiconductor users, semiconductor manufacturers, or semiconductor equipment vendors were investigating this technology.

Although x-ray radiation is essential for the production of very high density chips, several other technologies must also be mastered to produce billion bit chips commercially. Development of these ancillary technologies awaits the availability of a source. Successful commissioning of an x-ray synchrotron source is the initial goal of the Germans and the Japanese and must be the first milestone in any American effort. Fortunately thirty-five years of effort and immense amounts of money spent by DOE (formerly ERDA and AEC) on particle accelerators provides the United States with a knowledge and personnel base that far surpasses that in other parts of the world. Thus, in early 1986, it appeared that a U.S. effort would have a high degree of likelihood of recapturing the world lead in the commercial production of billion bit chips; but only if started immediately and if traditional institutional barriers to integrating national laboratory, university and industry work could be overcome.

At this point the Brookhaven Office of Research and Technology Applications was curious as to why the rest of the semiconductor industry was not involved with x-ray lithography development.

Historically, IBM's primary interest in process technology has been directed at their being smart consumers. Traditionally, they have not been in the business of producing and selling process equipment. At about this same time it became clear that both the German and the Japanese efforts were stalling because the base of accelerator technology in both countries was small. The ORTA decided that American industry must be alerted to the great window of opportunity that appeared to exist and be given the opportunity to exploit the years of effort and taxpayer money that had gone into American accelerator programs.

The ORTA along with the National Synchrotron Light Source convened a series of three workshops at Brookhaven. The first of these, held in March, 1986, brought some eighteen industrial companies together with scientists from six national laboratories and four universities.[7] The purpose of this workshop were:

- to inform industry that, as a legacy of thirty-five years of accelerator research, the technology base for a synchrotron source existed at Department of Energy Laboratories;
- to notify industry that this technology base was available if they desired to commercialize it;
- and to inform industry of the efforts underway in Europe and Japan to perfect this technology.

Those attending the workshop concluded that there was a window of opportunity and American industry should take advantage of it.

Following the initial workshop, a steering committee was formed composed of the senior industry people who attended the workshop. It was hoped that they might be able to infiltrate to higher levels of management. A plan was developed that proposed two more workshops, one in the summer to examine straw man designs and generate parameters for a commercial synchrotron and a second in the fall to generate rough costs and schedules for a synchrotron program.

Visits were made to some of the major industrial companies. Others, that had not attended the March workshop were contacted, informed and invited to participate. One of the BNL technology proponents spent several months at BESSY in Berlin and came back well informed on the status of the German effort. A key event was a Symposium held at the National Academy of Science in June, 1986, to hear the report of their Panel on Materials Science on Advanced Processing of Electronic Materials in the United States and Japan.[8]

The second workshop was held at the end of August. Three straw man designs were presented. Design parameters were generated and agreed upon by the technical people present. Over twenty industrial firms were represented at this workshop. The recommendations of this workshop were:[9]

"1) Establish a plan to build, at the earliest possible date, a prototype synchrotron source. This machine should be located within an IC processing environment so that other manufacturing associated technologies can be developed.

"2) Establish a parallel research and development plan on critical technologies which could improve the cost effectiveness of the synchrotron source. These include, in particular:

a) Superconducting magnets
b) Low energy injection options.

"3) Distribute a small number of second generation prototype synchrotrons to other IC manufacturing centers to expedite the commercialization of the synchrotrons as well as other technological components."

The third workshop met in November, 1986, and consisted of six panels.[10] Each addressed a specific activity required for the development of processing technologies for commercial x-ray lithography. Each panel developed a plan for its piece of the program, a schedule for undertaking the work and an estimated cost for completion. The program was estimated to take six years and cost almost $400 million. Only about $60 million of this was required for the synchrotron with the prototype available in 24-30 months.

Brookhaven was provided with $750,000 in the Spring of 1987 to perform a preconstruction planning study. As part of that study a technology transfer workshop was convened in July, 1987 to receive industry's views on the best means of transferring accelerator technology during the construction of the prototype. The workshop recommendations were:[11]

- Brookhaven will supply preliminary specifications and design information to preselected qualified companies;
- companies will prepare a proposal to perform Title II detailed design and Title III construction of the prototype machine;
- the Laboratory will transfer its know-how in commissioning and operating accelerators by actively assisting the industrial partner in bringing the machine on line and up to satisfactory operating levels.

The Government has recognized the need to take action.[12] It is assisting the industry in the near term through a consortium called Sematech.[13] For the farther out billion bit technology, a million dollars has been directed to initiating a synchrotron based capability.[14] Congressional committees are authorizing additional funding for both SEMATECH and the X-ray Lithography Synchrotron (XLS). At the time this paper is written, in December, 1987, the Congress has appropriated $37 million for x-ray lithography in FY 1988. The initial government support is directed primarily to designing and emplacing a conventional ring and developing a superconducting compact ring. For the effort to succeed industry must commit itself to developing the ancillary process technologies. Although the first hurdle has been surmounted, it is clear that there are still some major hurdles to overcome if the U.S. is to have this technology in place in time to beat the foreign competition and assist in restoring our balance of payments equilibrium and world technology leadership.

Outlook

In one industry after another American industry finds it difficult to effectively compete with foreign companies. One reason for this is the targeting of product areas by foreign government/industry consortia. This is the mechanism that was used by the Japanese to slowly erase the American lead in the semiconductor industry.[15] Starting several years ago, the Japanese government sponsored and supported a cooperative effort of Japanese chip manufacturers to target the semiconductor market, at that time dominated by American companies and technology. By 1985, they had effectively attained dominance over large portions of the market. As a result the American semiconductor industry has been in crisis for over a year.[16] American industry has finally responded to this with the formation of Sematech, an industry consortium seeking government assistance to develop the next generation process technology.[17] Sematech's goal is to cooperatively develop a prototype manufacturing facility that will permit U.S. industry access to advanced technology so as to be able to effectively compete with Japanese manufacturers.

Synchrotron technology appears to be the lowest cost production technology for the chip generation following that targeted by Sematech. The industry can scarcely afford Sematech, no less a more advanced effort with a longer wait for returns. Thus the reluctance of industry to commit financial resources to a synchrotron based x-ray lithography effort is understandable. Moreover, even if industry had the resources and the willingness to commit them, there is no model that indicates how it would proceed in this cooperative effort with government as a partner.

In short, a tradition of uncertainty and apprehension permeates relations between industry and government and a tradition of go-it-alone competitiveness exists among industrial equipment suppliers and their customers, the semiconductor manufacturers. We need to be able to surmount these difficulties by developing cooperative institutions that marry government, government laboratories, universities and industrial participants into effective partnerships for transferring technology.

A year ago American industry either did not recognize or had rejected the technology that would permit them to compete in the computer chip markets a decade and more hence. So far as is known, only IBM was actively pursuing the technology. Unless an American firm becomes an equipment vendor, American manufacturers will be dependent upon foreign suppliers of processing equipment. IBM has recently contracted with an English company to supply them with an experimental compact synchrotron.

Today, the rest of the industry (equipment suppliers as well as chip producers), the Congress, the Executive Department, and the Departments of Energy and Defense know that the technology base exists at U.S. laboratories. They recognize that transferring it to industry will permit the U.S. to compete in this arena. A program has been advanced by scientists at Brookhaven and technologists from industry that can provide American industry with the capability to recapture world electronic markets.[18] This foresight to identify and foster this program is a direct result of the establishment of the Stevenson-Wydler Act and subsequent emphasis on transferring technology from Federal Laboratories to industry. However, political considerations with respect to the location of the project and the availability of funding may prevent America profiting from our technological legacy.

Having reached this point, American industry may still stumble and fail to capitalize on this opportunity. If failure results, it will be due to a combination of institutional factors that have plagued the American system for the past two decades. These are the following:

- government has created and owns the technology base and user facilities resident in Federal Laboratories. Effective transfer of public intellectual property from Federal Laboratories to the commercial sector has been a major concern of Congress since 1980. Federal Laboratories must find a way to interact more effectively with industry and to increase the rate at which public intellectual property is transferred;

- the scale is beyond that of individual companies and requires cooperation and collaboration among competing equipment manufacturers both with each other and with their customers. It also requires cooperation among their highly competitive customers, the fragmented and competitive semiconductor manufacturers. Recent softening of antitrust interpretation is a step in the right direction;

- the scope of the effort in cost, time-horizon and risk is greater than can be carried by any industrial entity. Government support is necessary but will be hard to come by, both because of overhanging budget deficits and a prevailing philosophy that believes industry should do it alone. This flawed policy must be changed and recent legislative initiatives such as SEMATECH indicate that the Congress has grasped the significance of this problem;

- even if government support is forthcoming, there is no precedent in the United States for the use by industry of government money without government control. A successful program requires that the management be performed by managers with a profit motivation, not by researchers at Government Laboratories or program managers in Washington offices. New institutional arrangements must be explored. Recent attempts by the Department of Energy to encourage cooperative efforts among national laboratory, university and industrial partners is a step in the right direction. Collaborative arrangements between the public sector and the private sector to transfer public sector technology to the private sector will produce handsome rewards;

- this program may be a real turning point in American industrial history. If it fails, the trend of industrial decline that has become increasingly pronounced in the last two decades will be reinforced. Successful program management will reestablish American leadership in an important industrial sector, and will supply a model for maintaining that leadership in other industrial sectors.

Endnotes

1. Section 291 of Atomic Energy Act of 1946.

2. Sections 2011 and 2013 of the Atomic Energy Act of 1954.

3. Directory of Federal Laboratories and Technology Resources, 1986-87, PB86-100013 National Technical Information Service, U.S. Department of Commerce, Springfield, VA, 1986.

4. A more detailed description of how the facilities and how to use them as well as descriptions of many of them can be found in User's Guide to DOE Facilities, U.S. Department of Energy. Washington, D.C. 1984.

5. Ruddell, Richard L., "The Time Has Come for X-Ray Lithography.", SPIE Vol. 537 Electron Beam, X-Ray, and Ion Beam Techniques for Submicrometer Lithographies IV, 1985.

6. Wilson, Alan D., "X-Ray Lithography: Can It Be Justified.", SPIE Vol.537 Electron-Beam, X-Ray, and Ion-Beam Techniques for Submicrometer Lithographies IV , 1985.

7. Marcuse, W., G. Williams, F. Cerrina. B. Craft, and J. Murphy, eds., Proceedings of Workshop on Compact Storage Ring Technology: Applications to Lithography, BNL 52005, Brookhaven National Laboratory, Upton, NY 1986.

8. Panel on Material Science, Advanced Processing of Electronic Materials in the United States and Japan, National Academy of Science, National Academy Press, Washington, D.C.,1986.

9. Barton, M., B. Craft and G. Williams, eds. Report of the Second Workshop on Synchrotron Radiation Sources for X-Ray Lithography, BNL 38769, Brookhaven National Laboratory, Upton, NY 1986.

10. Godel, J.B., W. Marcuse. And G.P. Williams, eds., Report of the Third Workshop: Program for X-ray Lithography Development, BNL 52046, Brookhaven National Laboratory, Upton, NY 1986.

11. Marcuse, William, Report of the Workshop on Transferring X-Ray Lithography Synchrotron (XLS) Technology to Industry, BNL 52096, Brookhaven National Laboratory, Upton, NY, 1987.

12. Robertson, J., "DOD Task Force Urges $1.7B for Five-Year Semiconductor Thrust.", Electronic News, Dec. 8, 1986.

13. Sanger, D.E., "Chip Makers in Accord on Plan for Consortium.", New York Times, March 5, 1987.

14. Lane, E., "Lab Wins $1 Million to Help Develop Faster Computers.", Newsday, March 23, 1987.

15. Robinson, A.L., "U.S. Electronics Needs New Strategy.", Science, Vol. 232, June 20, 1986.

16. Bairstow, J., "Can the U.S. Semiconductor Industry be Saved.", High Technology, May 1987.

17. Sanger, D.E., "Chip Makers in Accord on Plan for Consortium.", New York Times, March 5, 1987.

18. Godel, J.B., W. Marcuse. And G.P. Williams, eds., Report of the Third Workshop: Program for X-ray Lithography Development, BNL 52046, Brookhaven National Laboratory, Upton, NY 1986.

NOVEL APPROACHES: LICENSING AND INDUSTRIAL CONSORTIA

Warren D. Siemens and E. Jonathan Soderstrom
Oak Ridge National Laboratory*
Martin Marietta Energy Systems, Inc.
Oak Ridge, Tennessee 37831

ABSTRACT

In 1984, the U.S. Department of Energy and Martin Marietta Energy Systems, Inc., began implementing an experimental program to enhance the flow of technologies from a national laboratory to the private sector. Energy Systems has been able to pursue an aggressive licensing program in accordance with accepted commercial practices. Our approach includes negotiation flexibility which recognizes the unique circumstances of each technology, client, and market. A licensing strategy, developed for each technology, aims at maximizing its commercial potential. The license may include various terms and conditions, up to and including exclusive arrangements.

The ability to offer attractive licensing arrangements is generating increasing interest by industry in working with the scientists and the facilities in Oak Ridge. The number of R&D agreements with industry is dramatically increasing. In order to facilitate and accommodate the demand for interaction with our people and facilities, we are experimenting with the establishment of industrially funded and

* Operated by Martin Marietta Energy Systems, Inc., under Contract No. DE-AC05-84OR21400 with the U.S. Department of Energy.

managed R&D consortia. A variety of different initiatives are being organized. The different objectives of these consortia dictate different organizational arrangements unique to the circumstance.

Cooperative ventures with industry will help the federal laboratories to become more fully integrated into the nation's economy. Better integration of this vast technical resource will help the nation to achieve the goal of enhanced economic productivity through technological innovation, in a highly competitive global economy.

INTRODUCTION

At the same time that the United States is enjoying a period of relative economic stability, our nation faces a serious challenge to its future competitiveness. Our competitive preeminence in world commerce has eroded over the past decade. We are being challenged in the trading arena by our European trading partners and emerging nations of industrial significance in Asia and Latin America. Sustaining our competitiveness over the long term is all important in maintaining our standard of living, advancing our foreign policy aims, and our national security.

Fueled by research and development (R&D), technological innovation is vital to our future because it is the key to productivity advances. Over the past 50 years, it has been the most important generator of productivity growth, far surpassing the contributions of capital, labor, or economies of scale. The United States must advance and apply technology toward the goals of enhancing our economic vitality, maintaining our national strength, and improving our general well-being. We must use it to improve our industrial productivity and competitiveness. Successfully directed to this purpose, new technology can provide us with our greatest comparative advantage and ensure our industrial leadership in an increasingly competitive world.

An analysis by the President's Commission on Industrial Competitiveness (1985) recently revealed that our national investment in total R&D (as a percentage of GNP) is on a level commensurate with other nations, and that the portion funded by the federal government is about 50%. But, it also pointed out that of this amount, more than 50% is directed toward defense-related purposes. Such countries as West Germany and Japan, on the other hand, devote the vast majority of their government-supported R&D toward civilian purposes. Thus, there will need to be an increased U.S. effort to develop technologies to restore global market competitiveness and redress the international trade imbalance.

The extent to which we approach effective R&D parity with our trading partners depends heavily on our ability to derive commercial benefits from federally-funded R&D programs. Over one-third of the R&D supported by the government is being conducted in the more than 700 federal laboratories employing about one-sixth of our nation's scientists and engineers.

To optimize application of U.S. R&D, industry must more fully utilize the research results and research capabilities of these federal laboratories. One way to achieve this goal is to create a framework of incentives for private sector firms to invest in the commercial development of federally-developed technologies, and to make government-developed technologies readily available to the commercial sector under licensing terms that are attractive to them. Another way is through increased R&D cooperation between federal laboratories and specific industries. Oak Ridge National Laboratory (ORNL) has been moving in this direction in recent years by increasing our emphasis on technology transfer through such mechanisms as granting of exclusive licenses on inventions waived by the U.S. Department of Energy (DOE) and conducting collaborative R&D with industry.

LICENSING OF INTELLECTUAL PROPERTY

In 1984, the DOE and Martin Marietta Energy Systems, Inc. began implementing an experimental program to enhance the flow of technologies from a national laboratory to the private sector. Four primary measures, which form the basis for such a program, were proposed by Martin Marietta to:

1. Broaden the scope of existing technology transfer functions to include all operating facilities under the management contract and establish a central function, headed at the executive level, that would not just permit but would cause increased levels of technology transfer.

2. Put the title to all intellectual property of commercial value in the contractor's name under the terms of an advanced blanket waiver.

3. Develop and implement an array of financial rewards and recognition for the inventors.

4. Create supporting mechanisms to cause and encourage new business formation based on Oak Ridge-developed technologies.

These measures were to form the basis for a system of incentives that will reward the various organizational participants in the technology transfer process. All but the second of these has been implemented with the approval of DOE. Though the blanket patent waiver initially requested has yet to be granted, Martin Marietta has received title on several specifically requested pieces of intellectual property. Prior to licensing these inventions, however, Energy Systems developed various specimen licensing agreements which were approved by DOE for use in our licensing activities.

Energy Systems has used the waived inventions to pursue an aggressive licensing program in accordance with accepted commercial practices. Our approach includes negotiation flexibility which recognizes the unique circumstances of each technology, client, and market. Specimen licensing agreements approved by DOE, are used as the basis for negotiations. The license may include various kinds of protection, up to and including exclusive agreements. In those technologies where significant additional development is necessary to take the product emanating from the laboratory to the production line of a private concern, it was considered essential to issue exclusive licenses in the field-of-use to which the licensee would subscribe. This degree of exclusivity provides the necessary incentive for a firm to invest in commercializing the technology.

As would be expected, Energy Systems would agree to extend to the licensees any improvements or modifications that we may develop during the life of the agreement and are waived by DOE so as to assure licensees the greatest possible benefit from the use of the federally-sponsored invention and to provide licensees with the most up-to-date inventions available from the Laboratory. In exclusive licensing arrangements, it would be expected that the licensee would agree to a reciprocation with regard to improvements and modifications of the basic technology they develop in their field-of-use. This would allow Energy Systems to provide other licensees the right to use such modifications in non-competing fields-of-use. It is hoped that this approach will spur additional developments in the technology.

We also include provisions for policing the license agreement in order to provide a measure of protection for the licensees' investment. In addition, by combining the patenting actions with commercial licensing activities, the types of intellectual property protection needed in the commercial sector become better understood. The probable end-result is improved patent protection for commercial needs.

In addition to moving more inventions out of the government facilities and into commercial practice, we believe our approach preserves certain, traditionally important national objectives. This approach preserves for the government a royalty-free, paid-up, non-exclusive license to the invention. What this translates into is contractual freedom for any firm to use the invention for government purposes without a license from Martin Marietta Energy Systems. In addition, no royalties are assessed to commercial product licensees on sales of the invention for government use. In fact our license agreements require proof that the firm actually reduced the price charged for government sales by at least the amount of the royalty due on a commercial sale.

Our licensing policy requires an active plan for commercial exploitation of the invention by the licensees. This plan typically includes technical goals and milestones for developing a commercial product, planned levels of investment for the invention, and a timeframe for introducing the product onto the market. It also provides contractual "strings" such that, if the licensee does not aggressively pursue the invention, the license may be terminated by Energy Systems freeing us to pursue other clients.

Importantly, our licensing policy requires, at a minimum, that products sold on the U.S. market be substantially produced in the U.S. This enables all firms wishing to pursue U.S. markets to compete on a level playing field with similar costs of capital, labor, and the like. Since American workers make up the primary labor force manufacturing the products based on the technology, U.S. taxpayers, the original investors, are the big winners through the gencration of additional jobs and tax revenues from increased domestic economic activity.

Experience confirms our belief that we can accelerate the rate of successful transfers of technologies from the Martin Marietta Energy Systems facilities to industry. This conviction is based on a number of considerations.

First of all, the contractor is provided an incentive to establish technology transfer programs that may lead to commercialization of the research, by receiving substantial rights to intellectual property. Royalty proceeds provide the means to reward inventors, to cover the cost of producing sample materials or prototype instruments required to demonstrate the technology to potential licensees, and to establish the other initiatives necessary to enhance commercial interest in the technology; all at no cost to the government or the performing contractor.

Secondly, commercialization of technologies developed at government laboratories is best facilitated by the originating organization because it is in the best position to assess the technology's stage of development and commercial potential for various applications. Laboratory inventors are often in contact with their commercial counterparts who follow developments in the technology area. These interactions are a fruitful source of information on the technology's potential commercial applications. Martin Marietta's licensing policy provides incentives for increased inventor contacts with companies wishing to commercialize the technology. These contacts should increase both the number of companies interested in pursuing government ideas and the number of patents on government-sponsored R&D which become the basis for commercial products.

INDUSTRIAL R&D CONSORTIA

In many cases, industrial firms are first attracted to a laboratory by interest in inventions which require additional development before becoming marketable products. Because of its unique understanding of the development, the federal laboratory where the technology originated may be viewed as the best place to conduct the follow-on work. In such situations, industrial firms may wish to enter into cooperative arrangements to further develop the invention. Increased emphasis in the U.S. on the development of technologies to restore global competitiveness and redress the trade imbalance has led Energy Systems and DOE to explore means to expand its horizons through the formation of unique partnerships between national laboratories and industry.

Herman Postma, Director of ORNL and Vice President of Energy Systems, has recently stated in the Oak Ridge National Laboratory Review that the value to the Laboratory of such collaborative R&D with industry is three-fold. First of all, it permits a cost-effective use of funds and facilities in the development of new technology for both industry and government. Secondly, it helps ORNL focus on national issues and scientific priorities. Finally, it allows ORNL to interact with some of the best minds in the country. We benefit from exposure to fresh points of view, new insights, and provocative questions. Such collaborations can also help make us preeminent in certain areas of expertise, enabling us to attract other high-quality researchers.

In addition to promoting one-on-one interactions with industry, we have created various mechanisms to bring several companies together on a technology application in collaboration with a national laboratory. These mechanisms are most appropriate in cases where: the companies can identify generic technology developments critical to their international competitiveness; the risks and resources are too great for a single company to undertake by itself; and the national laboratory has strong capabilities which supplement or complement those of industry.

We have been assisting in the initiation of industrial R&D consortia to expedite the commercialization of R&D results in areas of national importance. This mechanism, in time, will contribute significantly to our nation's economy and international competitiveness. These include:

Tennessee Center for Research and Development

In 1985, the Tennessee Center for Research and Development (TCRD), a not-for-profit corporation, was established on the Technology Corridor between Oak Ridge and Knoxville for the express purpose of creating economic value from the strong science and technology bases that exist in the region at such institutions as the Oak Ridge National Laboratory, University of Tennessee, and the Tennessee Valley Authority. Energy Systems was instrumental in getting TCRD initiated and currently participates on its board of directors. The purpose of the Center is to bridge the gap between R&D and commercialization by supporting market-driven applications development. It allows R&D organizations in the Oak Ridge-Knoxville region to "mature" their technologies beyond what may be appropriate to their respective missions. TCRD's activities may be funded by a variety of sources, including federal and state agencies, industry associations, individual companies, and private investors. It draws on the R&D resources and capabilities of the organizations in the region to accomplish its objectives through various consulting and contractual agreements.

(1) Power Electronics Applications Center. One of the first major achievements of TCRD was the establishment of the Power Electronics Applications Center. Developing the proposal for the Center provided the first opportunity for the three organizations, Energy Systems, TVA, and the University of Tennessee, to aggressively work together on initiating a regional activity. The purpose of the Center is to regain the competitive position of the power electronics industry in this country through the development, demonstration and transfer of power electronics technologies for U. S. companies. Initial, multi-year funding of $6M was provided by the Electric Power Research Institute. However, R&D partnerships are currently being formed and funded by interested U. S. companies to conduct specific power electronics developments for such applications as adjustable speed drives, power line conditioners and uninterruptable power supplies. The objective is to develop high voltage and high current electronic devices and systems which provide more efficient electricity end-use management. Development areas include devices and components, circuits and controls, industrial electrotechnology systems, power conversion and conditioning systems, and power quality. As industries become more productive users of electricity, their product costs become more competitive and they become healthier electric utility customers, which has a moderating effect on electricity rates. Thus, all economic sectors ultimately benefit from advances in power electronics.

(2) Thermomechanical Model Software Development Center. The Thermomechanical Model Software Development Center is another R&D center initiated by Energy Systems under the umbrella of TCRD. Thirteen sponsoring companies are funding the development of a user friendly and intelligent software system for more easily accessing a highly complex set of finite element analysis models. These models, which analyze thermomechanical stresses in refractory systems, such as furnace linings, were developed by MIT for ORNL over an eight year period. In their current configuration they are too complex for industrial design

engineers to use, requiring persons with considerable background and experience in thermomechanical modeling, thermomechanical behavior, mechanics, and finite element analysis.

In addition, preparation of the input files requires considerable time, and interpretation of the results requires considerable background and experience with the model. The consortium development will allow design engineers to input the necessary design parameters and interpret the analysis results without being an expert in these complex models. Such a system will be valuable to those concerned with refractory behavior in coal gasification systems as well as in other systems which include high-temperature refractory applications, such as blast furnaces in the steel industry. This industrial consortium effort is augmenting a national laboratory technology to significantly increase its commercial attractiveness and utility.

Ceramics Advanced Manufacturing Development and Engineering Center

The Ceramics Advanced Manufacturing Development and Engineering Center (CAMDEC) is a newly formed technology center initiated by Energy Systems but sponsored and managed by U. S. companies to develop advanced ceramic processing and manufacturing technologies. It will develop the technologies needed to reliably produce advanced ceramic parts, by characterizing and controlling each step of the production process. Energy Systems views industrial consortia such as CAMDEC as a new and exciting mechanism for transferring its technology to industry and as a means for contributing to the improvement of our Nation's international competitiveness.

The systematic investigation of process technologies addresses the current technology gap that exists between R&D and commercialization. Our foreign competitors, particularly in Japan, know how to bridge this gap and are again demonstrating this ability in the field of advanced ceramics. Unless U. S. companies can more quickly transform their excellent research and development base into commercial processing, they will lose, to foreign competitors, the emerging and potentially large markets requiring advanced ceramic parts.

To determine more specifically what needs to be done, CAMDEC conducted a comprehensive survey in the fall of 1986. Seventy out of eighty-three companies contacted answered a lengthy questionnaire - an exceptional response rate. According to the survey results, the most critical requirements for U. S. industry's commercialization of advanced ceramics are to:

- control defect size, concentration, and distribution in finished ceramic products
- develop cost-effective, highly reliable mass production processes
- develop new composite materials
- increase the understanding of ceramic characteristics by designers and users
- improve forming technologies
- develop in-line sensors and in-process nondestructive evaluation

The concept of CAMDEC and its Technology Plan were developed with the assistance of an Advisory Board of key executives from six companies: Allied Signal, Boeing, Dow Chemical, GTE Products, Norton, and Standard Oil. The Board, which met in September 1986 for an intensive review of the initial plan, concluded that it was headed in the right direction but was not bold and aggressive enough to meet the challenge. These executives recommended that the CAMDEC staff visit each company for input to the Technology Plan, to better understand industry's processing needs. The visits produced a revised plan which was presented to the Advisory Board in February 1987. It was approved after careful review, and the Board recommended that CAMDEC launch its membership campaign.

A primary feature of this consortium is its proximity and accessibility to the technologies, capabilities, and facilities of ORNL and its new $20 million High Temperature Materials Laboratory (HTML). Energy Systems has developed, with DOE's approval, all the necessary policies and procedures to permit ready access to its facilities by U. S. industry. CAMDEC or its members will thus be able to access them in a variety of ways, subject to the approvals appropriate to each facility. Agreements will allow use of any of the User Facilities at ORNL, such as the HTML, in either of two ways: (1) if the work is conducted in a non-proprietary mode where the user is willing to publish the results, the research may be conducted at no cost; (2) if, on the other hand, the work is conducted in a proprietary mode, the user must pay full cost. In either case, the rights to any intellectual property are waived to the user. In certain cases, CAMDEC may contract with ORNL to conduct its R&D or alternatively, it may use ORNL scientists and engineers on their own time as consultants. DOE has approved a policy which permits Energy Systems' employees to engage in outside activities, such as consulting, provided there is no conflict of interest.

Advanced Processing Science Center

Energy Systems has also proposed the establishment of the Advanced Processing Science Center (APSC) industrial consortium for semiconductor R&D closely modeled after CAMDEC. The laboratory/industry consortium would be organized and funded jointly by DOE and industry. The proposed center would focus on (1) advanced processing technology and (2) new materials development. Development would occur in three phases.

In the first year start-up phase, the APSC would access the resources existing in the Surface Modification and Characterization Collaborative Research Center at ORNL. Phase II, expected to extend from years 2-4, would be an evolutionary period during which separated space and facilities are to be developed in Oak Ridge for the APSC, with continued access to the Center and other ORNL facilities. Focused, collaborative R&D projects would be initiated at this stage. Phase III would be the stable state, with core support from ORNL and full-scale collaborative programs, also involving universities, in operation.

Among the advantages offered by the APSC arrangement are that it: (1) provides a multidisciplinary approach to a multifaceted problem; (2) expands the mission of the laboratory to an explicit focus on industrial competitiveness; (3) establishes a "MITI laboratory"-like entity (Japan's Ministry of International Trade and Industry charged with forging cooperative relations between the Japanese government, universities and industry on targeted technology areas) within the U.S. system; and (4) provides an educational center in this vital field.

CONCLUSION

The need to improve technology transfer from the public- to the private-sector has been underscored numerous times by recent acts of Congress and Presidential directives. In spite of these mandates, the effectiveness of these programs has been uneven. Industry has often cited, as a primary reason for not adopting such developments, its inability to secure assurances for a reasonable return on its investments in new, government-sponsored technology. The recent changes in federal patent policy will contribute a significant measure of certainty to this issue.

In addition, the rewards and incentives provided by our technology program have encouraged researchers to become more aggressive in promoting the transfer of their technologies to the private sector. In the same manner, the protection available through patent licenses should provide companies with motivation to become more interested in commercializing the results of federally-funded research. As we have already begun to see, these incentives collectively provide a synergism of interest that helps promote closer linkages between government laboratories and industry. Such linkages are essential if the results of federally-sponsored R&D are to be applied in the commercial, as well as the government, sector of the economy. Only when these developments are exploited in the commercial sector can the United States be certain that it is also receiving the maximum utilization of national scientific and technical resource that the federal laboratories embody.

Cooperative efforts, such as those outlined above, provide industry with a financially leveraged investment, not only through cost sharing, but, perhaps more importantly, through cost avoidance achieved by accessing existing facilities, equipment, and trained people in Oak Ridge. We believe that we can forge such relationships in such a way as to satisfy the goals and objectives of both our industrial partners and the federal government. Experience with government laboratories in other countries, particularly Harwell in England and Karlsruhle in West Germany, has shown that such cooperation can be beneficial for both the laboratory and industry.

Industry and laboratory interactions, from the beginning, will make possible future, additional joint technology development ventures. Collaboration between industry and government scientists permits cross-fertilization which result in the generation of new ideas and technologies that enhance the productivity of both organizations. Most importantly, these cooperative ventures with industry will help the federal laboratories to become more fully integrated into the nation's economy. Better integration of this vast technical resource will help the nation to achieve the goal of enhanced economic productivity through technological innovation, in a highly competitive global economy.

INNOVATIVE ARRANGEMENTS FOR INDUSTRY/DOE LABORATORY COLLABORATION IN HIGH TEMPERATURE SUPERCONDUCTIVITY

James M. Williams
Deputy Director, Office of Industrial Applications
Los Alamos National Laboratory
Los Alamos, New Mexico

BACKGROUND

The scientific discovery of a new class of materials that are superconducting (able to conduct electricity without energy loss) above the boiling point of nitrogen offers the possibility of revolutionizing many technologies and creating many new applications. These applications could rival, in variety and number, those created by the transistor and the laser.

The race to commercialize this technology is on. The United States must quickly exploit its lead or watch the commercialization of superconductors follow the same path as that of microchips and VCRs. As Frank Press, president of the National Academy of Sciences, recently stated, "superconductivity has become the test case of whether the United States has a technological future." To really excel then, we must explore new partnerships among universities, national laboratories, and industry, making optimum use of the capabilities of all.

President Reagan indicated his support for creative, new collaborative efforts and a fast-paced program at a federal conference on commercial applications of superconductivity, held in Washington, D.C., in July 1987. He clearly expects a strong national laboratory role because he stated earlier that "one focus of the ...quest for excellence... would be to free federal laboratories, including defense labs, to aid in making American products and technology better and more competitive."

Secretary of Energy Herrington has not only strengthened his department's initiatives in basic research in superconductivity, but, on July 30, 1987, asked Los Alamos National Laboratory to "explore private sector interest in the establishment of cooperative research programs to develop enabling technologies for commercial application of superconductivity." He further stated that this "effort could lead to a pilot program which, if successful, will be expanded to other Department of Energy (DOE) laboratories."

ASSESSMENT OF INDUSTRIAL INTEREST IN HIGH TEMPERATURE SUPERCONDUCTIVITY (HTS)

This report represents an early assessment of industry interest in R & D collaborations with the DOE laboratories in high temperature superconductivity. They are based on a sampling of companies who have expressed interest.

To be successful, collaborative arrangements with the purpose of serving industrial interests, must contain an effective mechanism for assuring the research and development agenda focuses on industry needs. In order to do this, we must first, determine industry needs, then see how DOE laboratories (as a network) can satisfy these needs; second, we must recognize that effective mechanisms to satisfy these needs are not now in place and that DOE and the laboratories must be willing to change how they do business; and third, find an early demonstration that we can work effectively with industry; superconductivity applications is an excellent test. The key conclusions of our assessment are that:

> There is only one reason for industry interest in collaboration with DOE labs: self-interest in attaining their business objectives.
>
> Industry collaboration must be developed. It will take significant time and commitment from industry, labs and DOE to develop this relationship.
>
> If we are to aggressively pursue solutions to industrial competitiveness, innovative new institutional arrangements are needed.

Industry interest in R & D partnerships varies across a spectrum of company purposes and characteristics. Our preliminary findings on how companies would like to work with DOE laboratories are summarized below.

LARGE COMPANIES

Most large companies which have extensive, in-house R & D capability and are not interested in substantive collaboration with government laboratories. They may, when socially or politically motivated, contribute funds to universities or other research institutions, but it is usually viewed as an philanthropic venture. The R & D in federal labs, when focussed on engineering and technology development with commercial potential, is viewed by major companies as a potential threat to their market position. Federally funded R & D helps these companies' smaller competitors and increases the likelihood that their products will be obsoleted before they have exploited them fully. Even if institutional changes could be made to make substantial proprietary R & D possible in the federal laboratories, these companies are very skeptical of the notion that a federal laboratory could effectively partition R & D activities to assure each company's proprietary interests are protected. They are, however, interested in maintaining a window on federally funded high temperature superconductor research and development and, in some cases, believe they can leverage their own corporate R & D by working with the national laboratories.

MID-SIZED COMPANIES

These firms are difficult to characterize other than to say that their common features are: annual revenues of $50 to $500 million dollars, they have limited or no R & D budgets and their future is perceived to depend on innovative new products and capabilities. Mid-sized companies probably benefit most from having free access to the technologies emerging from the federal laboratories and to laboratory experts and facilities. They cannot afford the investment on their own. They would like to have exclusive use of technology developed at public expense. Many of them have developed aggressive strategies for ferreting out good ideas and exploiting them without further involvement with the laboratories. Probably the biggest limitation on this process as an effective technology transfer mechanism is the lack of resources committed to filling development gaps in this part of the innovation cycle.

SMALL COMPANIES

Small companies and entrepreneurs who are developing new products usually look at the laboratories as a source of funds to do R & D they need. When this is done, it allows them to control the use of the development as long as there are not too many strings attached (patents, licenses, etc.). Federal labs in general are not funded to do this kind of work, but the Small Business Innovative Research (SBIR) program is an effective mechanism for small business to accomplish R & D. Small companies may benefit most from partnerships in vertically integrated consortia.

All industries appear to agree on two key roles of the DOE laboratories. The first is the accomplishment of basic research in HTS. The second is the role of providing well characterized materials to industrial researchers, performing measurements and diagnostics for industry and acting as an impartial technical referee in evaluating technical concepts and results.

INSTITUTIONAL MODELS FOR INDUSTRIAL INVOLVEMENT

A number of institutional models for industrial involvement with federal laboratories exist. The efficacy of these models must be tested against the primary criterion of how successful they have been in or could be in assisting U.S. industrial competitiveness. This value judgement is best made by U.S. industry.

Examples of candidate existing models are: NASA's Technology Development Centers, National Science Foundation Engineering Research Centers, the Solar Energy Research Institute and the Sandia National Laboratory Combustion Center. In general, these models do not appear to meet our primary criteria. Thus, new mechanisms are being explored in our discussions with industry. The approaches to developing new models for industrial partnerships are discussed below. These approaches take two general organizational forms. The first form is privately organized entities whose purpose is to combine industry resources to interact with the DOE laboratories. The second form is publicly organized entities whose purpose is to provide an efficient mechanism for industry access to laboratory generated technology. Either or both may be needed. Some companies feel no formal organizations are needed.

Industry Organized Approaches

Vertically Integrated Consortia: The concept of vertically integrated consortia is to form industry partnerships of companies which are not competitors but have a mutual interest in one another's business success. For example, an electric utility, an architect engineering firm, a large power equipment manufacturer, a wire manufacturer, and a material production company could form an R & D partnership. By pooling their R & D dollars, they could diversify their financial risk in developing technologies which would enable their whole industry to compete. The R & D partnership could use DOE laboratory capabilities to develop the enabling technologies which will emerge from high temperature superconductivity research. By sharing the risk of development in a consortium or partnership, it should be possible to enter into long term R & D collaborations necessary to successful applications of high temperature superconductors.

Horizontally Integrated Consortia: This concept is best described by the MCC model for computer research and development. Such a consortium has as partners companies who are willing to share funding and people to jointly perform R & D of mutual interest to each partner. This type of consortium is made up of companies who are competitors in the market place, but who see a strong common interest in collaborating in research. In the case of MCC, the common interest was to counter the common Japanese threat in the microelectronics business.

Unlike the vertically integrated consortia, the horizontally integrated consortia has the disadvantage that the partners are not likely to collaborate on R & D that is close to the commercial market place. Apparently MCC ran into this problem even on research which was far removed from early application.

Regional Entrepreneurial Partnerships: Entrepreneurial spin-offs from federal laboratories has been one of the most effective mechanisms for creating new businesses and the jobs that go with them. The potential for U.S. small business to prosper by exploiting high-technology spin-offs has not been fully exploited by U.S. companies. We are constantly facing competition from foreign entities who are aggressively exploiting these opportunities.

The concept of the Regional Entrepreneurial Partnership is to establish regional networks of entrepreneurs, venture capitalists, business support groups, and universities which could work in partnership with national laboratories in various regions of the country. The primary purpose of such partnerships would be to stimulate entrepreneurial activity, to enhance the conditions under which effective access to federal laboratories could be assured, to support small business start-ups and to develop strong, new, high-tech based industries. A key element in this approach would be obtaining the mutual commitment of all members of the partnership to assure that entrepreneurs are developed and supported in establishing viable small businesses based on high-technology products.

DOE LABORATORY ORGANIZED APPROACHES

Exploratory R & D Centers: The concept of Exploratory R & D Centers at appropriate DOE national laboratories is to set up technology partnerships with industry to identify and exploit the most promising enabling technologies, and potential applications of high-temperature superconductors. Prerequisites for creating such centers would include: (1.) demonstrated expertise in superconductivity research and other relevant technologies and (2.) a proven record of performance in exploratory R & D (including people and facilities, the ability to field R & D teams, and to coordinate R & D goals). Industry would be encouraged to participate at the inception, first by providing program guidance and later through cooperative R & D and as a funding source. The centers would perform R & D in:

> Generic, enabling technologies that are pervasive to many potential applications. These efforts are most appropriately funded by the federal government.
>
> More specific enabling technologies that should be cost shared between government and industry, either through industry consortia or individual companies.
>
> Very specific enabling technologies or help with occasional advanced development with full cost recovery from industry. (Naturally, this would result in exclusive intellectual property rights for industry.)

The Exploratory R & D Centers would offer great opportunities to private industry, especially for small and medium-sized companies. The laboratories would provide staff with deep scientific foundations in the physics of superconductivity and other related technologies They also have many of the facilities required for the synthesis, processing, and characterization of the new superconductors. This would allow industry to collaborate with laboratory researchers or try out some of their own ideas without major capital investments and in an environment that is very knowledgeable of what other scientific research is going on in the world. It would also provide almost immediate response, which is crucial in this fast moving field.

These benefits may also be very attractive to some large companies which have traditionally not been involved in superconductivity research or applications. Large companies such as AT & T and IBM may also benefit from scientific collaboration in basic research. They most certainly could contribute in helping to guide the development of generic, enabling technologies. Regardless of size and specific interest of private industry, this initiative would help U.S. industry to capitalize on our scientific lead in superconductivity.

The Adjunct Organization: The concept of an adjunct organization is to establish an effective mechanism for industry to gain access to DOE laboratory science and technology, while not interfering with the primary mission of each laboratory. One of the main features of an adjunct organization is the ownership of intellectual property. The intellectual property developed in the adjunct organization belongs to and can be exploited by the adjunct organization separately from federal government rules, regulations and policies. Such an arrangement has many advantages for both industry and the laboratories:

> Ability to contract with industry outside of government control.
>
> Separation of proprietary technology development from laboratory development.
>
> Alternative technical challenge for Laboratory employees to consult and work part-time on industry problems without conflicting with laboratory responsibilities.
>
> Avoids problems of access to sensitive technologies.
>
> Provides working environment for industry and laboratory engineers and scientists to work together on problems of interest to commercial industry.

<u>Laboratory-Industrial Affiliates/Consortia:</u> This approach is typically organized by a laboratory or university and has the main feature of assisting a large number of industrial affiliates to gain effective access to specific areas of laboratory technology. In one form, there are classes of membership with varying membership costs. For example, if a company wants a window on certain technologies being developed in the laboratory, that company can subscribe to a menu of laboratory provided services such as a news letter, prepublications access to selected technologies, participation in educational seminars, state of the art workshops, and some limited amount of free consulting. If the company wants a more substantial involvement, a second class of membership allows them to participate on a collaborative basis with laboratory researchers and appropriate other industry researchers in a jointly-funded and managed research program. In the most fully developed version of this relationship, the laboratory will work with individual companies or will work to arrange R & D partnerships with a small number of companies interested in diversifying both financial and technical risk in the conduct of product/process development to meet specific industry requirements.

<u>Ad Hoc Arrangements:</u> There is a body of opinion that believes a centrally organized approach to exploiting the DOE laboratories' R & D capability is undesirable compared to the ad hoc arrangements that evolve from normal initiatives that drive normal interactions between individuals and institutions. This approach depends upon the competitive spirit of individual companies and laboratories and their ability to initiate and carry through individually tailored arrangements to transfer technology to the private sector.

Although current mechanisms for technology transfer are improving, they continue to be basically an ad hoc process and variable from one laboratory to another. Also, our track record in terms of significant commercialization payoffs has been quite unwarrantable to date, especially when viewed in the light of the right national need to improve industrial competitiveness.

Finally, our policy for assuring fairness in access to laboratory R & D has been to deal with companies and individual entrepreneurs on a first-come, first-serve basis as long as the effort required does not conflict with our ability to carry out the laboratory's mission. Up until recently, this was accomplished with relatively few problems of fair access. This situation is not likely to persist in view of the strong national desire to assure industry has effective, expeditious access to the technical base in the federal laboratories. This further underlines the need for more formal arrangements such as those suggested in this paper.

RECENT DEVELOPMENTS IN INDUSTRIAL ENERGY TECHNOLOGY IN WESTERN EUROPE

JEAN-LOUIS POIRIER, VICE PRESIDENT
HAGLER, BAILLY & COMPANY
901 D ST., SW, #700, WASH., DC 20024

Europe continues to develop very actively new industrial energy technologies, in most cases heavily aided by strong governmental support. In 1986, the governments of France, West Germany, Sweden and United Kingdom spent together $59 million to promote industrial energy conservation, 2.8 times more than the United States, on a GNP-adjusted basis. European government assistance is very diversified and comes at all stages of technology R&D and commercialization, including cost-sharing of new product development; demonstration grants; targeted investment grants to stimulate demand for specific new products; and free prefeasibility studies to convince users to purchase new products.

It is therefore not a surprise if Europe has come up with a lot of innovative industrial energy technologies in the last 10 years. Most of these technologies can be of double interest to the United States -- to both U.S. energy users who can adopt them often very easily and to U.S. manufacturers looking for new licenses.

Recognizing this, Hagler, Bailly -- a management consulting firm based in Washington, D.C. -- has for several years monitored energy technology developments in key Western European countries such as France, the United Kingdom, Sweden and West Germany. Our firm also follows R&D programs sponsored by the European Economic Community (EEC) in Brussels, Belgium. In many fields, including energy R&D, the EEC is the largest single R&D sponsor in the free world.

In this presentation, we discuss a few interesting European technologies promoted in the last 2-3 years and falling in five generic fields: Burners; Industrial heating; Heat recovery; Waste-to-energy; and Expert Systems for Energy Management.

BURNERS

One success of British industrial energy R&D is the development by British Gas of a compact regenerative ceramic burner (RCB) which can recover heat from contaminated gas streams at temperatures up to 2550 degrees F. A

RCB burner can exhibit fuel savings of 55-60 percent over conventional burner technology and 20-30 percent more than regular recuperative burners. Furthermore, RCBs can be retrofitted to existing furnaces, ovens or kilns, without major structural changes. In virtually all applications, waste gas temperatures can be reduced to about 300-400 degrees F.

A RCB system includes two burners, each fired alternatively and each connected to a packed bed of ceramic material acting as a heat exchanger. Each packed bed is in turn heated by the hot flue gases and cooled by the combustion air. The flow direction is switched by a reversal valve connected to the cold ends of each packed bed. The combined use of high surface area packings, high heat transfer coefficients, and short reversal periods (2 to 5 minutes) provides a compact and effective design. The beds are made up of alumina balls that can easily be removed for cleaning.

Between 1450 and 2500 degrees F, the RCB transfers 90 percent of the flue gas heat to the incoming combustion air, thereby offering a 80 percent gross thermal efficiency. This generally results in paybacks of less than one year. Now licensed by British Gas to Hotwork Development and eight other U.K. manufacturers, RCBs are available in sizes from 300 kW to 2.1 MW. RCBs are also commercialized in the rest of Europe. In France, for example, over 10 RCB installations exist, and the technology is promoted by both Hotwork and a French company, Stein-Heurtey.

Another interesting U.K. burner technology was developed by Spectus, Ltd. The Spectus burner is a recirculation axial flow tip shut-off burner particularly efficient for oil-fired industrial or utility boilers but also an efficient warm-up gun for coal-fired cycling boilers. Two reasons for this:

- First, as an axial air flow burner, the Spectus burner gives superior mixing, achieves more complete combustion, and can operate with far less than 3 percent excess air. This minimizes CO or SO3 emissions, and yields less than 0.1 percent of unburnt fuel carryover.

- Second, the Spectus burner is designed to allow the continuous recirculation of heated oil through the tip at a temperature high enough (135 degrees F) to avoid coking. This feature not only minimizes burner maintenance, it increases start-up reliability, and, most importantly, allows to use residual oil as a start-up fuel, a very significant cost saving. The Spectus burner can burn number 6 oil with only 0.4 percent excess oxygen. On a utility burner, such performance means a payback of less than 1.5 years in three cases out of four.

Sold over a thousand times to the Central Generating Electricity Board (CGEB), the Spectus burner has become CGEB's benchmark. In the U.S., the demand for Spectus burners could exceed 1,500 burners over the next ten years.

INDUSTRIAL HEATING

Very innovative industrial heating technologies have been recently developed in Europe, including new immersed burners, rapid furnaces, and plasma technology.

The immersed burner technology, developed by the French nationalized gas utility, Gaz DE France, has opened the road to no less than eight licenses over the last 4 years. GdF's immersed burner can be used in any industrial heating liquid applications such as concentration operations in the chemicals industry; bleaching operations in the textile industry; applications in milk processing plants, breweries and slaughterhouses; and, perhaps, most appropriately, surface treatment, degreasing, and phosphatation operations in the chemical industries.

With GdF's immersed burners, liquids arc heated either by pulverizing the liquids through the combustion gases or by letting the gases bubble through the liquids. Bubbles multiply the exchange surface considerably, up to an impressive 333 square feet per cubic foot. With exhaust temperatures kept below 100 degrees Fahrenheit, the heating efficiency comes very close to 100 percent. There are over 70 existing immersed burner installations in France, representing a total heating capacity well in excess of 20 MW. The cost of an immersed burner is around $25 per kW, installed.

A second interesting industrial heating technology is a new aluminum melting process developed jointly by GdF and Secoflam, a French furnace company. The new process shows a 40 percent savings against the best existing melting aluminum furnaces. The super furnace includes a smart and compact design which eliminates the need for separating the melting stage from the temperature stabilization stage. The GdF/Secoflam is also equipped with a special GdF patented burner and a unique preheating heat exchanger. Tests have shown a 72 percent efficiency, almost equal to that of induction furnace. The bottom line: a consumption of 600 kWh per melted ton versus 1000 kWh per ton for the best furnaces currently commercialized, or 2000-3000 kWh for most operating furnaces.

Europe is actively pursuing the use of plasma torches where high local temperatures are required. In this field, the French Aerospatiale company has developed a prominent technology with very successful results in three different blast furnace applications, at Cockerill-Sambre; SFPO (Boulogne-sur-Mer); and Uckange.

Ten months of tests at SFPO showed that the 1.5 MW Aerospatiale torch could achieve a blast temperature of 3100 degrees F. This is an increase of 250 degrees F in average blast temperature and this led to coke savings of 140 lb per ton of manganese-iron. SFPO tests also showed a tuyere life exceeding one year; a 85 percent plasma generator efficiency; and a 72 percent system efficiency. Finally, electrode life exceeded 1000 hours, much better than expected. Following such good results, SFPO ordered six more plasma torches.

But, no doubt, the most ambitious tests are taking place at the Uckange works where six plasma torches with a total power output of 10 MW have been installed. Start-up took place this summer and full results will be available by mid-1988. Here again, the blast temperature should reach 3100 degrees F, but the plasma torches are also used to boost coal injection at a rate of 440 pounds per ton of hot metal (thm), thereby resulting in coke savings of 120 pound per thm. Lower consumption of coke has always been particularly attractive to Europeans, since it is a generally imported commodity traded in dollars.

Aerospatiale is now marketing 5 MW torches. In addition, the company has developed, with the help of the French Energy Conservation agency, a unique tool: a 2 MW "transportable" plasma torch which fits on four trailers and can be tested on various blast furnaces in Europe. In addition, Aerospatiale is considering other plasma torch applications such as: cement kiln retrofits; heavy-petroleum cracking units; replacement of oxygen burners in fusion arc furnaces; synthesis of acetylene; synthesis of titane bioxide; and metal coatings facilities.

HEAT RECOVERY

In Europe, recent developments in industrial heat recovery include new types of heat exchangers, new heat pump designs and the increasing use of the so-called pinch technology.

Heat Exchangers

Over the last 3-4 years, numerous new types of heat exchangers have appeared in France, under the impulsion of the French Energy Conservation Agency (AFME) which funded the creation of a unique R&D center, called GRETH and based in Grenoble.

One major innovation is the use of plastics, as shown in three examples. First, the French company Ciat has manufactured for two years a "plate-and-film" heat exchanger equipped with a special turbulator grid in plastic that creates a heat exchange film in what is otherwise a rather conventional plate heat exchanger. The result is a substantial increase in heat transfer.

Second, Ecopol has developed a plastic-based flue gas waste heat recovery in medium temperature applications. Designed like an organ, it is an assembly of several hundred plastic tubes, one inch in diameter and 80-micron thick. This intricate curtain hangs in the waste heat exhaust stream. One remarkable application was demonstrated in a printing shop which rejected up to 2.1 million cubic feet per hour of air polluted with toluene solvent.

Third, the French Kestner company is marketing an evaporator which uses plastic films as heat exchange surfaces. The film has a thickness of 100 micrometers and offers the same heat exchange characteristics as an iron surface that is ten times thicker... at a price at least ten times cheaper.

Compactness in heat exchangers is critical. The more compact a heat exchanger is, the cheaper and the more suitable it is for retrofit applications, which can account for up to 90 percent of the market. The best prize for compactness goes to the Packinox, an extremely compact high-load plate heat exchanger with stainless steel plates assembled by a specially patented technique. The Packinox was first demonstrated in Elf's refinery in Donges in France.

Although the unit weights 47 tons and handles 71 tons/hour of petroleum gases, its footprint is 81 square feet only. This translates in a 3-year payback. Following that success, Shell ordered 8 units for its French refineries, where it expects to cut its energy reforming costs by 10 percent. NAT -- a joint venture of Elf, Bertin and the French Institute of Petroleum -- is targeting a worldwide market of 500 cracking units for the Packinox. Packinox can also be used in the chemicals or food industries, whenever the heat exchange surface exceeds 9000 square feet with a pressure differential between the two fluids below 20 bars. Two sales are in process in the United States.

Heat Pumps

Europe has always been fascinated by heat pumps. A recent survey conducted by Hagler, Bailly identified not less than 57 commercial installations, demonstration projects or R&D initiatives in non-conventional (i.e., non-mechanical vapor recompression) industrial heat pump applications. To be more specific, we found 20 industrial closed-cycle compression heat pumps projects; 18 absorption heat pump initiatives; 11 hybrid-cycle heat pump applications pursued; and 7 chemical heat pump cycles under tests.

In our opinion, the most interesting applications involve full-scale industrial applications of absorption heat pumps in West Germany, the Netherlands, and Sweden and cascading hybrid cycles in Sweden, Italy and France.

Industrial Absorption Heat Pumps

Several large-scale "heat transformers" using a water/BrLi technology have been installed with success in the last two years.

In West Germany, the ECOFLOW technology promoted by GEA is successfully demonstrated in two applications that show the suitability of the technology in sizes between 2.5 MW and 10 MW. The first project, located in a brewery near Stuttgart, transforms 5 tons per hour of humid air (at 212 degrees Fahrenheit) into 2.2 tons per hour of high quality steam (at 277 degrees Fahrenheit) and cooling water (at 88 degrees Fahrenheit). At a temperature lift of 65 degrees F, the transformer is 50 percent efficient. This unit, in operation for over 18 months, saves 10 billion Btu per year, and has an estimated payback of 4 years.

A second ECOFLOW heat transformer started last summer in a Degussa chemical plant in West Germany. The unit transforms waste steam (at 212 degrees F) into higher quality steam (266 degrees Fahrenheit) and cooling water (at 104 degrees F). The expected efficiency of the transformer is 48 percent. Operating 8000 hours per year, the heat pump should produce 31,600 tons of steam or 81 billion Btu per year, resulting in a 4-year estimated payback. This second project cost $3.5 million, 40 percent of which was funded by the European Community.

At Delfzijl, in the Netherlands, a 6.4 MW heat transformer went on line in October 1985 in an ethylene amino production plant belonging to Delamine B.V.

The demonstration unit, built by Hitachi Zosen, cost nearly $2 million and was partly funded by NEOM, the Dutch Energy Development Company. The heat source is industrial waste steam (at 212 degrees F) which is used to produce higher temperature steam at 302 degrees F. The flow rate of the heat source is 22 tons per hour, or 14 MW. The heat sink flow rate is 10.5 tons per hours, or 7 MW. The efficiency of the transformer is therefore around 50 percent. With annual energy savings of 222 billion Btu, the project has a payback of 2 years.

Finally, another large installation, in operation since November 1984, is a 7 MW absorption heat pump installed at Trollhatan, in Sweden. The unit, manufactured by Sanyo, recuperates waste heat at 104 degrees F from the Kema Nord electrochemical company to heat a district heating loop from 135 degrees F to 167 degrees F. The flow rate of the heat source is 6.5 tons per hour and the temperature lift ranges between 50 degrees F and 63 degrees F. This project has the particularity to be thoroughly metered. With temperatures measured within +/- 0.06 degree F and flows measured +/- 0.25 percent, the average heat balance error is 2 percent with +/-2 percent hourly variations. The COP of the Trollhatan unit varies between 1.3 and 1.8 with a mean value of 1.6. Very flexible, the unit can handle load variations from 0 percent to 100 percent without complications. The heat pump is very reliable with a near 100 percent availability.

Cascading Hybrid Heat Pump Cycles

Cascaded hybrid cycles combine a closed-cycle compression heat pump with a mechanical vapor recompression stage. These cascaded cycles have now been demonstrated and commercialized in Europe for the last 3-4 years.

For example, a 11.5-MW cascaded hybrid cycle was successfully installed at the Hallsta Paperbruck pulp and paper mill in Sweden. The unit, manufactured by ASEA-Stal, demonstrates a new application: waste heat recovery from moist air in paper machines. A news print machine will typically discharge between 10 MW and 30 MW in moist air with a dew point around 115-125 degrees F. A heat pump can recover at least half of this energy to produce steam and preheat the pulp.

In the ASEA-Stal cycle, humid air (at around 120 degrees F) ends up producing low pressure steam (at 275 degrees F and 32 psi). The first stage is a compression heat pump using R114 as a working fluid. The second stage increases the steam pressure from 17 psi to 36 psi and the temperature from 220 degrees F to 275 degrees F. The overall lift temperature is 160 degrees F. Sixty percent of the 12-MW output comes from the waste heat recuperated; 28 percent from the first stage compressor; and 12 percent from the second stage steam compressor. The overall COP of the ASEA cycle is 2.4 but ASEA claims that the COP could be increased to 3, depending on the site conditions.

The total cost of the project was SEK 21 million, that is the equivalent of $3 million. The project was supported by a loan from the Swedish National Energy Administration (STEV) of SEK 6 million (or $750,000). In addition, the Swedish Board for Technical Development (STU) provided some financial aid for the project prefeasibility study.

The French Electric utility -- Electricite DE France -- has developed a similar cycle, based on a prototype that includes two compressors of 75 kW and 64 kW. Tests started in July 1986 and continued through early 1987. EdF reached its target of 250-300 kWh per ton of water evaporated -- versus 1,000-1,200 kWh/ton for conventional paper drying machines. EdF found that its new cycle could also apply in the food industry, including concentration of pomades, waste heat recovery on vats, and milk processing. Consequently, EdF is contemplating a demonstration of its new cycle in a food application.

A Belgian engineering company -- Martel Catala -- is pursuing the same idea as EdF, but its cycle -- called ECONERGIE -- includes a heat pipe heat exchanger. ECONERGIE, developed for a milk spray drying application, reaches condenser temperatures ranging between 302 degrees F and 338 degrees F.

Another interesting cascading application started in 1985 at an Italian polypropylene plant belonging to Himont SpA. The unit is a UNITOP heat pump cycle designed by Sulzer around two UNITURBO 22 BX refrigerant compressors. In the Himont cycle, 1.6 MW of cooling water (at 138 degrees F) is used to produce 2.5 MW of low pressure steam at 255 degrees F and 32 psi. The temperature lift is 147 degrees Fahrenheit and the COP is 2.7. Following the success of this application, a second UNITOP installation was ordered by a Norwegian firm (Protan A/S) to use desalination water (at 45 degrees F) to produce industrial steam; the heating capacity of that second order is 6.8 MW.

Pinch Technology

Pinch technology is another subject strongly promoted in Western Europe. Developed in Britain, largely by a team led by Professor Bodo Linhoff, first at Imperial Chemical industries (ICI) and now at the University of Manchester (UMIST), pinch technology has evolved from a novel energy conservation tool into a powerful design system that enables the user to realize the full potential of a process, in terms of reduced energy consumption, cost savings and process improvements, through the correct placement of unit operations and utilities. The analytical methods have been applied, mostly in Europe, in both new and retrofit process applications in a variety of fields, including petrochemicals, chemicals, petroleum refining, pulp and paper, food processing, and textiles.

In Europe, several groups are now refining the use of pinch technology, including:

- Imperial Chemical Industries which is offering its TENSA Services (United Kingdom)
- The Energy Process Integration Services Consultancy, within the U.K. Harwell Laboratories which is promoting ICI's approach.
- The University of Manchester (UMIST) Research Consortium -- headed by professor Bodo Linhoff.

- Linnhoff March Consultants (United Kingdom) with their TARGET I, Target II, Target III or SUPERTARGET, and BABYTARGET computerized programs.
- Trondheim University (Norway) with Professor Per A. Loeken's INTERHEAT model.
- Goeteborg University (Sweden) with Dr. Sunden's OPTIMUS model.
- Ecole Central DE Paris (France) with Professor Depeyre's programs (OPTNET and OPT2PH).
- ETH-Zurich (Switzerland) with Dr. Rippin's HENSYN model.

In most cases, the pinch technology has been made user-friendly by embodying the approach in a PC-based computer program which can quickly determine a plant's "pinch point" and from there define what are the plant's minimum heating and cooling needs. With this knowledge, pinch technology can help maximize heat recovery, decide which type of heat exchanger to use, where to place a heat pump or a cogeneration cycle, and how to minimize plant capital costs. For new projects, pinch technology can result in savings of 20-30 percent. Pinch technology can also help assess the validity and attractiveness of various retrofit design options, with savings as high as 60 percent and payback times as short as a few months.

A Hagler, Bailly survey showed that pinch technology had been used in the last 4-5 years to evaluate about 200 energy conservation investments or process improvements in a wide variety of European plants. Over 80 percent of the cases involved potential process retrofits, and some form of implementation took place in 60-70 cases. European companies that have used the pinch technology include: BASF, Shell, Proctor and Gamble, British Petroleum, Unilever, ELF, and Norsk Hydro. Furthermore, pinch technology has been supported by European government agencies such as the U.K. Department of Energy and the Swedish National Technical Board. In the U. K., the government funded several case studies and prefeasibility assessments in the textile, food, and beverage processing industries.

Pinch technology has now started to be promoted in the United States by companies such as Linhoff-March and Union Carbide (which developed the ADVENT system based on ICI's approach).

WASTE-TO-ENERGY

Interesting innovative small-scale waste-to-energy technologies have been developed in Europe, including an oscillating incineration technology developed in France and a new small-scale gasification pursued in Sweden.

The French Laurent-Bouillet incineration technology is particularly well adapted to incineration applications in the 2 to 5 tons/hour size range. Oscillating instead of rotating, the unit is uniquely designed around a conical/cylindrical combustion chamber which is a perfect hybrid of a grid stoker and a rotating oven. The special shape of the chamber allows the natural separation of the drying and the igniting stages. The chamber is also wrapped in a high-efficiency heat exchanger which feeds a waste heat recovery boiler. As a result, the Laurent-Bouillet installation can handle waste with heat content as low as 1,800 Btu/lb. The technology has been installed in over 10 installations in various European countries.

In Sweden, Waste Gas Energy (WGE) AB, owned by VBB Stockholm and Elajo Oskarshamn, has developed a small-scale technology for the gasification of municipal solid waste (MSW) which offers two key advantages: low rates of dioxine emissions and extensive binding of heavy metals in the ash. WGE's technology includes two steps: first the gasification of the municipal waste and second the combustion of the gases under controlled conditions. The gasification step eliminates the need for flue gas cleaning equipment which can be exorbitantly expensive for small scale MSW.

Tests were run on a 2 MW prototype fed with a fuel mix of 40 percent wood chips and 60 percent of densified refuse-derived fuel. Measured Nox levels were between 166 and 207 ppm and SO2 levels between 11 and 31 ppm. Dioxine emissions were measured to be 3.3 ng/nm3 in average. Large quantities of heavy metals were found bound to the ash, with the exception of cadmium and zinc. System efficiency from fuel to steam reached 60 percent. The total investment cost for the gasifier prototype was approximately SEK 1 million ($120,000) for a gas output of 3 MW. This project was funded in part by the National Energy Administration of Sweden. WGE AB is planning on further research -- in particular, to improve the burner geometry, and the furnace design and volume. WGE AB should be offering its system worldwide fairly soon.

ENERGY MANAGEMENT EXPERT SYSTEMS

Energy management expert systems are actively promoted in several energy intensive industries, such as steel mills, refineries and pulp and paper mills.

In the United Kingdom, the ETSU arm of the U.K. Department of Energy sponsored the development of the LINKman process control expert system which has been very satisfactorily used in forging operations. Still in the U.K., British Steel, with the help of the European Community, has developed several expert models which have satisfactorily been tested for two years. One of BSC's expert system is designed to automate the operation of a continuous basic oxygen steelmaking unit; this new system is built upon advanced on-line blowing control using "fuzzy logic" -- a theory allowing to express imprecise and qualitative information from operators in exact form. BSC is also developing the SESAME expert system to manage the whole maintenance of the Ravenscraig steel complex and a new expert system to monitor blast furnace operations and correct unstable furnace conditions.

In France, the steel company Solmer recently developed ESOPE -- a completely integrated system that can manage all the utility flows in an iron and steel complex. First presented in Paris at the 1987 MEI Symposium, ESOPE was found impressive by most attendees. Also in France, a consortium of industrial companies (including Elf Aquitaine) has developed the SECI-Manager, a unique computer-driven utility manager that can operate large energy complexes, such as pulp and paper mills, sugar beet processing plants, refineries, power plants, and building central heating plants.

SAMPLE REFERENCES

Regenerative Ceramic Burner -- Mr. G. Dickinson, Hotwork Development Ltd; Bretton Street; Saville Town; Dewsbury; W. Yorkshire WF12 9DB; U.K.

Spectus Ltd -- Mr. Huw Morgan; 56 Suttons Park Avenue; Suttons Industrial Park; Reading, Berks. RG6 1AZ; United Kingdom.

Gaz DE France -- Mr. Denantes; Direction des Etudes et Techniques Nouvelles; Courcellor 2; 35, rue d'Alsace; 92531 Levallois-Perret Cedex; France.

CIAT -- Mr. Gardiol; 30, rue du Rhone; 01350 Culoz; France.

Packinox -- Mr. Schwall; NAT; 70 rue Napoleon Bonaparte; 92500 Rueil Malmaison.

Heat Transformer in a Brewery; Stuuttgarter Hofbrau AG; Postfach 11 88; 7000 Stuttgart 1, Federal Republic of Germany.

Steam Production by a Heat Transformer in the Degussa Plant -- Mr. Serchis; Directorate XVII; European Community; 200 rue DE la Loi; Brussels; Belgium.

Heat Transformer in Ethylene Amino Plant -- Mr. Bouma, NEOM, Postbus 17; 6130 AA sittard; Swentibolstraat 21; 6137 AE Sittard; Netherlands.

Hybrid Cycle in Hallsta Pappersbruck -- Mr. Sandberg Edvard; Holmens Bruck AB; S-601 88 Norrkoping; Sweden.

The Himont Hybrid Cycle in Ferrara, Italy -- Mr. P. Punchera; PB-Verfahrens- und Kaltetechnik; Gebruder Sulzer Aktiengesellschaft; SULZER Brothers Limited; CH-8401 Winterthur; Switzerland.

Pinch Technology -- Dr. Ewan McDonald; Energy and Process Integration Service; Building 151; Harwell Laboratory; Oxfordshire OX 11 ORA; U.K.

Laurent Bouilllet -- Tour Europe; Cedex 07; 92080 Paris La Defense.

Waste Gas Energy AB -- Mr. Jan-Eric Svensson; Forradsgatan 6-8; Box 904; 572 29 Oskarshamn; Sweden.

LINKman -- Mr. D.W. Haspel; SIRA Ltd; South Hill; Chislehurst; Kent BR7 5EH; U.K.

BSC Expert systems -- Messrs. Anderson and TAYLOR OF BSC Teeside Laboratories and Mr. Mc. Queen of BSC Ravenscraig Works, United Kingdom.

ESOPE -- Messrs Constant and Saby at SOLMER, France.

SECI-Manager -- M. Coeytaux of the Serete, France. Tel: 45-70-50-00.

AN APPROACH TO MONITORING HVAC TECHNOLOGY DEVELOPMENTS IN JAPAN

Paul M. Lewis
W. Bradford Ashton
Sean C. McDonald

Battelle Northwest Laboratories

This paper presents a discussion of methods to periodically monitor Japanese advanced technology developments for equipment and components in the heating ventilating and air conditioning (HVAC) industry. The emphasis in the approach recommended is on evaluation of foreign literature - both technical and trade publications - because of both the increasing availability of these materials and the usefulness of information they present. Although not a comprehensive nor completely detailed source of information, HVAC technology literature is an important component of "scanning the business/technical environmental" for many purposes. Moreover, despite obstacles in obtaining and translating some important literature, this paper shows that useful knowledge can be obtained from many foreign literature sources for relatively modest costs.

1.0 INTRODUCTION

The HVAC industry is a small but important part of equipment manufacturing in the U.S. The value of shipments and total employment figures indicate that penetration of U.S. markets by foreign equipment would cause severe losses to the domestic economy. This is particularly important since the equipment components and manufacturing technology and general engineering knowledge for the HVAC industry is applicable in several other product areas.

1.1 THE U.S. DOMESTIC HVAC EQUIPMENT MANUFACTURING INDUSTRY

Table 1 presents summary economic data for U.S. companies primarily engaged in the manufacture of HVAC equipment.[a] According to the latest Census of Manufactures, a total of 865 firms were engaged in the manufacture of HVAC equipment with a work force of 125,500 employees. The total value of factory shipments, as noted in the table, includes some non-HVAC equipment.

(a) HVAC equipment represents greatest portion of the company shipments.

Table 1. Characteristics of HVAC Equipment Manufactures (1982)[a]

SIC Code	Industry Definition	Number of Companies	Number of Employees	Value of Shipments (Millions)
3585	Refrigeration and Heating Equipment	865	125,500	$12,390.3

Source: U.S. Department of Commerce, Bureau of the Census, 1982 Census of Manufactures: Industry Series, Service Industry Machines and Machine Shops, MC82-1-35G.

Data is available for just the value HVAC equipment (see Table 2). According to the Annual Survey of Manufactures, shipments have risen steadily from $11.0 billion in 1982 to $14.5 billion in 1985. Data for 1986 is incomplete although certain sectors of the HVAC equipment industry have continued to show growth.[b]

Table 2. HVAC Equipment Industry (3585) Value of Shipments (Millions of Dollars)

SIC	1982	1983	1984	1985
3585	11,035.6	12,063.8	14,439.8	14,508.8

Source: U.S. Department of Commerce, Bureau of the Census, Annual Survey of Manufactures, Value of Product Shipments, 1985, M85(AS)-2.

1.2 GENERAL TRADE POSITION

The U.S. Heating, Ventilation, and Air-conditioning (HVAC) equipment manufacturing industry (SIC 3585) is still a net export industry (see Figure 1). However, exports of HVAC equipment peaked in 1981 at around $2 billion. Since 1983, exports have remained relatively flat hovering near $1.5 billion per year.

Meanwhile, imports have risen dramatically since 1982. While less than $300 million in 1982, imports of HVAC equipment reached nearly $1 billion in 1986 -- an increase of over 300 percent. As a result, the U.S. trade surplus in HVAC equipment fell from over 1.7 billion in 1981 to less $300 million in 1986.

(a)Manufacture of HVAC equipment is primary business.
(b)See U.S. Department of Commerce, Bureau of the Census, Current Industrial Reports, Air-Conditioning and Refrigeration Equipment, 1986, MA35M(86)-1.

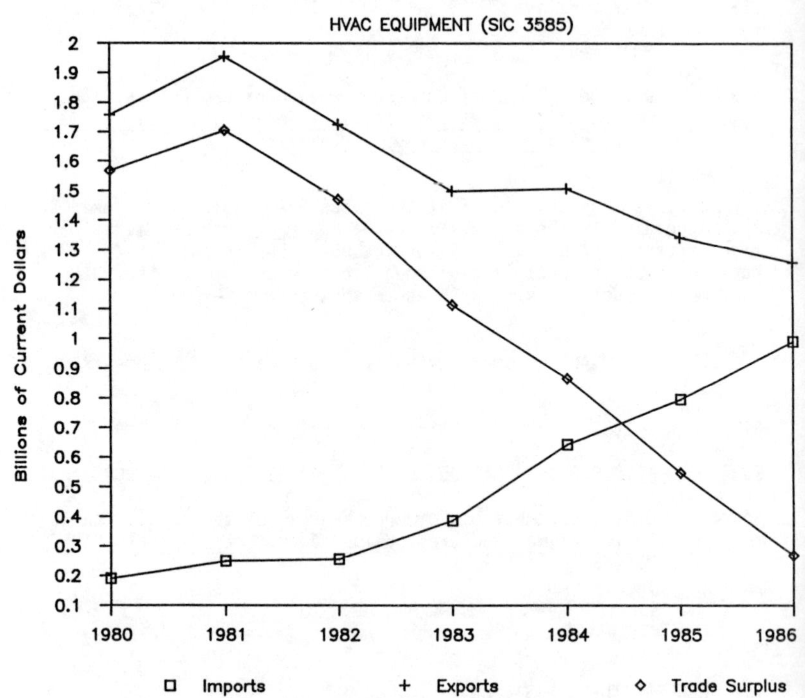

Source: U.S. Department of Commerce

This trade information can be combined with the domestic production data to gauge the size of the domestic market. As can be seen from Table 3, both domestic production and consumption of HVAC equipment has been growing since 1982. However, growth in consumption has out-paced domestic production. As a result, imports have taken an increasing share of the domestic market.

Table 3. U.S. Domestic Market for HVAC Equipment (Millions of Dollars)

	1982	1983	1984	1985	1986
Domestic Production	11,035.6	12,063.8	14,439.8	14,508.8	- -
(less) Exports	1,726.0	1,499.3	1,507.9	1,342.1	1,257.1
(plus) Imports	255.1	386.0	642.5	795.6	990.2
Apparent Consumption	9,564.7	10,950.5	13,574.4	13,962.3	- -
Imports as % of of Consumption	2.7	3.5	4.7	5.7	- -
Exports as % of Production	15.6	12.4	10.4	9.2	- -

Source: U.S. Department of Commerce, Bureau of the Census, Annual Survey of Manufactures, Value of Product Shipments, 1985, M85(AS)-2, Current Industrial Report, and official trade statistics.

Also, U.S. exports of HVAC equipment have been declining both in monetary terms and as a proportion of domestic production. While exports accounted for over 15 percent of total domestic production in 1982, by 1985 exports were only about 9 percent of the value of domestic production. The value of U.S. exports of HVAC equipment have declined each year straight through 1986.

Table 4 shows the overall trade balance by five-digit SIC code to better understand the character of import penetration. Those sectors of the HVAC equipment manufacturing industry which were in a net import position in 1986 were: Compressors and Compressor Units (SIC 35854), Refrigeration Condensing Units (SIC 35855), and Room Air Conditioners and Humidifiers (SIC 35856). Together these three industry groups accounted for 98 percent of the total of almost $1 billion of all imported HVAC equipment.

Table 4. 1986 Trade by Five-Digit SIC Code[a]
(Millions of Dollars)

SIC #	Description	Imports	Exports	Net Exports
35854	Compressors and Compressor Units	437.0	109.7	(327.3)
35855	Refrigeration Condensing Units	448.8	26.9	(421.9)
35856	Room Air Conditioners and Humidifiers	85.4	23.2	(62.2)
Sub-total	35854, 35855, and 35856	971.2	159.8	(811.4)
Others	All Other Five-digit 3585 Groups	19.0	1,097.4	1,078.5
All 3585	Refrigeration and Heating Equipment	990.2	1,257.1	266.9

Source: U.S. Department of Commerce, Official Trade Statistics.

1.3 THE ROLE OF TECHNOLOGY IN TRADE POSITION

While this imbalance in favor of imports can be due to both economic or technological factors, the role of improved foreign technology, particularly in advanced compressors, is an increasingly important area of concern, according to many industry sources. Several advanced compressor designs under active development in Japan, e.g. the scroll compressor, have a number of inherent performance advantages which will make them attractive once they can be manufactured cost-effectively.

It is now clear that important technical advances in HVAC equipment are being made in Japan. Particularly in areas of heat pumps and compressors, new efficient systems are nearing widespread introduction into U.S. markets. Because the Japanese are at the leading edge of advances in these systems, it is important for the U.S. equipment industry to remain abreast of new Japanese developments and of research trends which could lead to even more improved systems in the future. This paper presents methods to accomplish this end.

(a) Totals may not sum due to independent rounding.

2.0 A FRAMEWORK FOR MONITORING FOREIGN TECHNOLOGY

This section presents a general framework for monitoring foreign technology advances. Many sources of information exist regarding foreign science and technology activities and developments. The problem for U.S. information users is to identify the most valuable sources and to use them cost-effectively. This can be understood more readily with a framework for organizing the types, sources and uses of information on foreign activities.

As one element for such a framework, Table 5 summarizes the key types of foreign technology information useful to U.S. users. The topics are grouped according to information content (technology, institutions, product news, business news and government policies) to allow further comparisons of information types regarding uses and costs of the material. These topics would be of varying degrees of interest to different types of users, so those individuals most likely to benefit from the information are shown in parentheses.

Table 5 also shows the key applications for each type of information. Of course, these are not unique applications, but rather indicate the major uses. Often combining more than one type of information for an application produces very useful insights.

Table 6 summarizes the major sources of foreign technology information for monitoring overseas technology developments. These sources are grouped into four major categories to indicate generic types of sources which differ in terms of cost of use, information content provided and overall value to various users.

2.1 THE ROLE OF TECHNICAL PUBLICATIONS

This paper will focus more specifically on the publications category as an effective information source to monitor foreign technology. Table 7 presents more detail on the categories of publications available for review. Several characteristics of each form are summarized. As indicated, each type is likely to contain information of interest to only selected types of information users.

Unfortunately, even when a user is matched with the best types of literature, barriers to effective use remain. The key barriers to effective use of these sources are search effort, availability, timeliness, content limitations and foreign language translation.

2.2 RECOMMENDATIONS FOR FOREIGN LITERATURE MONITORING

To overcome the barriers to using foreign literature effectively, several suggestions are provided below:

1. Search Effort - Use of computerized library data bases or literature abstracting services can be helpful in identifying the most pertinent literature. It may be necessary to use personal contacts for obscure or company-generated material.

Table 5. Types and Applications of Foreign Technology Information

1. **Technology Development Activities and Programs:** Basic and Applied Research, System Development, and Demonstration Projects (R&D staff, product planners/developers)

   Key applications: understanding technical objectives, project activities and R&D progress.

2. **Institutional Information:** Personnel, Organizations and Budgets for Technological Activities. (R&D and technical staff, executives)

   Key applications: identifying key researchers and their work, understanding R&D projects.

3. **New Product Descriptions:** Features, Components, and Performance Data. (marketers, planners)

   Key applications: understanding product features, costs and performance.

4. **Industry Economic Performance and Trends:** Production, imports, exports (Strategic planners, executives)

   Key applications: understanding industry economic health and outlook.

5. **Business or Industry News:** (industry executives, planners)

   Key applications: keeping up to date on news regarding specific firms, personnel, or business decisions and agreements.

6. **Government Policy:** Regulations, Standards, Incentives (industry planners, executives)

   Key applications: monitoring government political activities affecting technology.

Table 6. Sources of Information for International Research Monitoring

PUBLICATIONS

1. Literature (foreign and English language)

    - Journals
    - Trade Publications
    - Newspapers
    - Computerized Data Bases
    - Company In-House Publications
    - Government Publications
    - Translation and Abstracting Services

2. Information Exchange Agreements

3. Trip Reports

4. Patents

DIRECT OBSERVATION

5. Site Visits

    - Foreign Installations and Companies

PERSONAL CONTACTS

6. Attendance at Open Conferences

7. Attendance at Industry/Government Meetings

8. Personal Technical Contacts

    - Short Term Interviews
    - Long Term Relationships

ORGANIZATIONAL CONTACTS

9. Membership in Foreign Industry Associations

10. Membership in International Organizations

11. Business contacts through Joint Ventures, Mergers, Licensing Agreements, Branch Offices, Sales Representatives

Table 7. Types of Publications

1. Referred Research Journals

   - Long, detailed reports.
   - Long lead time.
   - Basic and applied research

2. Symposium Reports

   - Detailed reports.
   - Shorter lead time.
   - Basic and applied research.

3. In-house or Company Journals

   - New product announcements just before commercialization-fairly detailed.
   - Articles on wide variety of subjects.

4. Technical Journals

   - Shorter technical reports.
   - Shorter lead time.

5. Association Journals

   - Technical reports, but low technical level.
   - Association news.
   - Production data.
   - Government policy, regulation and standards.

6. Trade Journals

   - Technical Reports
   - Industry News

7. Newspapers

   - New products.
   - Production data.
   - Business news

8. Patents

   - New inventions
   - Business technological capabilities and trends.

9. Government Publications

   - Production data.
   - Government policy, regulation and standards.

2. Document/Publications Availability - Use of personal contacts to identify and obtain copies is an obvious approach when documents are not readily available.

3. Timeliness of Publications - The most reliable way to overcome this obstacle is to rely directly on personal contacts for current information.

4. Content Limitations - Failure of the content of literature to provide desired information is often difficult to overcome. However, two general avenues may be helpful. First, cross-checking multiple literature sources covering the same general topic may reveal missing information when a collection of materials is viewed in total. Second, personal contacts may provide the missing material upon direct inquiry with a specific request.

5. Language Translation - Translation services can be expensive and time consuming. To overcome this barrier, we recommend developing a "preliminary or survey translation" and discuss how this would be implemented in the next section of this paper. This is basically a "quick and dirty" translation to determine the "high points" of the document's contents. More detailed translations can then be targeted to the most valuable documents.

In the remainder of this paper, we concentrate on using methods for efficiently obtaining desired information on Japan from Japanese publications. Because of the wide variety of information sources and the difficulties of Japanese language translation, several suggestions to target the particular information needed and to complete "quick" translations are given. Examples are presented for the case of HVAC technology literature.

3.0 AN APPROACH TO SURVEYING HVAC LITERATURE

Japanese literature on HVAC technology is voluminous; only a small part of it may be of interest to any one company or reader. In order to contain costs, one needs a method to limit the search to material that is of interest. The search can be limited to particular types of subject matter, or to particular types of publications, both of which are discussed below[a].

3.1 TYPES OF SUBJECT MATTER AND INFORMATION

The subject matter of a literature search can be limited to particular technologies (compressors, scroll compressors, heat

---

(a) Information in this section was obtained primarily from HVAC Literature in Japan: A Critical Review (forthcoming), prepared for the U.S. Department of Energy by G.J. Hane, Pacific Northwest Laboratory, Richland, Washington.

exchangers, etc.). In addition, the search can be limited to types of information from those in Table 5: 1) research, 2) technology development and demonstrations, 3) new applications for existing technologies, 4) new product announcements, 5) market and industry trends, and 6) industry news. Each of these kinds of information is discussed below:

3.1.1 Research

Many Japanese manufacturers consider themselves to be the technological equals of their American counterparts, and as such are placing more and more emphasis on basic research, in a concerted attempt to become the world's technological leaders.

3.1.2 Technology Development

Technology development can be distinguished generally from research in that it is applied work that is closer to commercialization. The focus for this type of work is generally considered to be too narrow to be of interest in a symposium or research journal. This category includes demonstrations.

3.1.3 New Applications for Existing Technologies

One example of a new application for an existing technology is the use of remote controls, a technology that reached maturity in the consumer electronics industry before it was introduced into the HVAC industry. This category includes reports on demonstrations.

3.1.4 New Product Announcements

In addition to advertising, most association journals contain articles on new products. Some weekly newspapers introduce new products and recent patent applications in regular features. These articles often include information on features and components and contain quantified data on efficiency and performance.

3.1.5 Market and Industry Trends

Some publications regularly report production, import, and export data, collected by industry associations or by the government. In addition, unusual successes or even failures often appear as news articles in journals and newspapers.

3.1.6 Industry News

This category includes news on company reorganizations, acquisitions, mergers, joint ventures, international developments, symposium announcements, industry associations, and government regulations.

3.2 TYPES OF LITERATURE

The types of information described above can be contained in various types of literature as shown in Table 7: 1) refereed research journals, 2) symposium proceedings, 3) in-house journals, 4) technical journals, 5) association publications, 6) trade journals, 7) newspapers, 8) patents, and 9) government publications. Some overlap exists among these categories. In particular, major associations publish several types of publications; in order to provide a coherent indication of the activities of these associations, association publications of all types are discussed in Section 3.2.5, "Association Publications."

3.2.1 Refereed Research Journals

Because they are refereed, the articles in research journals are generally of high quality, and contain considerable technical detail. However, the articles are often published about two years after the completion of the research project.

3.2.2 Symposium Proceedings

Research results generally appear sooner in symposium proceedings than in refereed research journals. However, the technical detail is also usually less.

- Kuki Chowa - Reito Rengo Koenkai (Air Conditioning and Refrigeration Federation Symposium) is the transactions of a symposium, held each April, under the sponsorship of a federation of associations, including Nihon Reito Kyokai (the Japan Association of Refrigeration), Kuki Chowa Eisei Kogakkai (The Society of Heating, Air Conditioning and Sanitary Engineers of Japan), and Nihon Kikai Gakkai (The Japan Society of Mechanical Engineers). New concepts and technologies are introduced here twelve to eighteen months before they appear in research journals. Usually about two thirds of the papers are from industry and one third are from universities.

In addition to this symposium sponsored by a federation of associations, many associations sponsor their own annual symposia and publish their symposium proceedings. These symposium proceedings are discussed in Section 3.2.5, "Association Publications."

3.2.3 In-House Journals and Reports

All major HVAC manufacturers -- Hitachi, Mitsubishi, Toshiba, etc. -- publish their own in-house journals. In-house journals and reports contain a wealth of information. Unfortunately, outsiders cannot subscribe to these publications. If copies of the publications are obtained through personal connections, translating articles, quoting them, and citing them may be problematic.

The major Japanese HVAC manufacturers are large conglomerates, and as such HVAC equipment is only one of a large number of products produced by the conglomerate and written about in its journal. Thus, one potential disadvantage with monitoring in-house publications is that they only rarely include articles on HVAC equipment.

Like the in-house publications of manufacturers, many reports from Japan's national laboratories are not formally made public, and usually must be obtained through personal connections.

3.2.4 Technical Journals

A technical journal is a journal that reviews and explains the state of the art or presents detailed technical information on installation and maintenance, without presenting new information. Several technical journals are published by associations, and are discussed below.

3.2.5 Association Publications

A selection of Japan's major HVAC industry associations, and their various publications, is as follows.

- Hito Ponpu Gijutsu Kaihatsu Senta (Heat Pump Technology Center of Japan). Established in 1986, the principal task of this center is to promote the use of heat pumps in the industry by sponsoring demonstrations and reporting the results. Its reports are a good source for reviewing commercial industrial heat pump applications in Japan. The Center's regular publication is Hito Ponpu Gijutsu Kaihatsu Senta Kaiho (Bulletin of the Heat Pump Technology Center of Japan).

- Kuki Chowa Eisei Kogakkai (The Society of Heating, Air Conditioning and Sanitary Engineers of Japan). Established in 1963, one of the primary activities of this society is to develop and disseminate the industry standards known as HASS. Where applicable, these standards are also influential in determining some of the general industrial standards known as the Japan Industrial Standards (JIS), which are set by MITI.

  This organization has the responsibility of disseminating information about HASS, which it does in its publication Kuki Chowa - Eisei Kogaku (Air Conditioning and Sanitary Engineering. This journal focusses on new technologies, and the articles are typically quite detailed. Each issue has a special theme. This society also has an information exchange agreement with the American Society of Heating, Refrigeration and Air-Conditioning Engineers (ASHREA). Much of the information on the American industry published in this journal is obtained through this agreement.

  This society publishes a refereed research journal, Kuki Chowa - Eisei Kogakkai Ronbunshu (Transactions of the Society of Heating, Air Conditioning and Sanitary Engineers of Japan). The articles typically describe fundamental research. Coverage is broad, spanning both HVAC and sanitary engineering. Each article has two referees, with a third in cases of dispute.

- Nihon Kikai Gakkai (Japan Society of Mechanical Engineers). This society publishes the most prestigious research journal in the general field of mechanical engineering. It has three series: Series A (solid mechanics, materials), Series B (fluid engineering, heat transfer, combustion, thermophysical properties), and Series C (vibration, control engineering, tribology). Few HVAC related articles appear in any one issue of this journal; articles that do appear usually appear in Series B.

  Two committees of the JSME cover technical areas that are relevant to HVAC technologies. The Thermal Applied Energy Committee meets each November; at these meetings approximately fifty papers on fundamental research are presented. The relevance of these papers to HVAC varies from year to year. A second, smaller committee, the Environmental Committee, meets each December, at which time ten to twenty papers are presented, some of which may be related to HVAC.

- Nihon Reito Kucho Kogyo Kai (Japan Refrigeration and Air Conditioning Industry Association). Founded in 1929, this association currently has 120 member companies. Activities of this association include 1) representing the views of the industry to the government, 2) disseminating information about the national JIS standards and the international ISO standards, 3) testing products to certify their efficiency, and 4) collecting industry data.

  This association publishes Reito to Kucho (Refrigeration and Air Conditioning), a journal of industry sales statistics and industry news. Although the journal is short, much of the data it presents are collected by the association and are particularly valuable.

  A more detailed summary of annual sales is presented in its annual publication, HVAC&R, which uses English as well as Japanese table headings.

- Nihon Reito Kucho Setsubi Kogyo Rengo Kai (Japan Association of Refrigeration and Air Conditioning Contractors). Founded in 1972, the purpose of this association is to provide the HVAC contracting industry with information about new technological developments and practices. In addition to its journal, the association also publishes handbooks describing equipment practices and regulations. The Industrial Machinery Division of MITI provides the association with money derived from taxes on bicycle racing. These funds, approximately $100,000 per year, are used for surveys and commissioned research projects. The project for 1987 was to develop an expert system for HVAC design. The association also provides the industry with information concerning government policy and regulations.

- Nihon Reito Kyokai (Japan Association of Refrigeration). This association publishes manuals and technical reference texts for engineers that describe equipment operation and new technologies. The Association, which was founded in 1926, occasionally commissions and publishes special studies by experts. All of these publications are good resources for technical details of practices and developments in the refrigeration industry in Japan. The association has an information exchange arrangement with ASHRAE.

  This association publishes a refereed research journal, Nihon Reito Kyokai Ronbunshu (Transactions of the Japan Association of Refrigeration). In addition to five or six articles on research results, each issue also usually contains one or more articles describing current research.

  This association publishes the transactions of its annual symposium, Nihon Reito Kyokai Gakujutsu Koenkai (Symposium of the Japan Refrigeration Association). Held each November, this symposium is usually designed around a theme. Past themes have included Energy Conservation and Refrigerated Food Storage (1982), Energy Conservation and Air Conditioning (1983), and New Applications for Heat Pumps (1984). About one third of the papers presented at this symposium and published in this transactions are also published in the Kuki Chowa - Reito Rengo Koenkai (The Air Conditioning and Refrigeration Federation Symposium), mentioned above.

  This association also publishes Reito (Refrigeration), which typically contains a large number of short articles, most of which describe demonstrations and review the state of the art, rather than introduce new technology developments. For example, the October 1987 issue contained nine articles reviewing the state of the art in reciprocating, rotary, and scroll compressors.

- Sho Enerugi Senta (The Energy Conservation Center). This organization was established by the Ministry of International Trade and Industry (MITI) in order to disseminate information about energy conservation. Thus, the coverage of its publication, Sho Enerugi (Energy Conservation), is broader than the HVAC&R industry. Discussions of energy policy appear with only minimal delay.

3.2.6 Newspapers

Three newspapers focus on Japan's HVAC industry.

- JARN: Japan Air Conditioning and Refrigeration News. This is the only English language publication devoted to Japan's HVAC industry. This monthly newspaper emphasizes new product developments, market trends, and general industry news. It relies primarily on articles contributed by outside writers. This organization publishes an English language annual, Japan

HVAC&R Directory, which lists the names, addresses, capitalization, and products of HVAC&R companies in Japan. Every few years it publishes Refrigeration and air Conditioning Equipment in Japan, which is a good source of product information.

- Nihon Reito Reibo Shinbun (Japan Refrigeration and Air Conditioning News). Coverage of this weekly newspaper is divided approximately evenly between refrigeration and air conditioning. Articles announcing new products and describing general industry news are well represented. Circulation is approximately 34,000.

- Kucho Taimusu (Air Conditioning News). This weekly newspaper focusses on the air conditioning industry, and so its articles on air conditioning are more detailed than the articles on air conditioning in Nihon Reito Reibo Shinbun (Japan Refrigeration and Air Conditioning News). Circulation is the largest in the industry in Japan, approximately 50,000.

- Occasionally HVAC news is published in general economic newspapers such as the Nihon Keizai Shinbun (Japan Economic Journal) and the Nikkei Sangyo Shinbun (Nikkei Industrial Journal).

3.2.7 Patents

Patents can help forecast future technological and commercial trends. The Japanese have been accused of flooding patent offices with pseudo patents. Such patents might not reflect solid technological breakthroughs, but, properly interpreted, they could be indicators of future commercial plans.

3.3 TRANSLATION AND/OR SUMMARY

After the scope of the literature search is limited by subject matter and by the type of literature, several alternative methods exist for providing the desired information in English. The cost for full translations by independent translators is approximately twelve cents per English word.

Pacific Northwest Laboratory is currently using a different approach in monitoring Japanese HVAC literature for the U.S. Department of Energy. The first step of this approach is to do a quick, rough, unverified translation. The translation might be of the abstract alone, of the first section of an article, or of the complete article. If the article is a highly technical research report in a field in which the translator has had no previous experience, these drafts may even contain a few blanks to indicate that the translator was unable to translate a word or phrase.

The second step is to have people who are familiar with the area 1) read the drafts, 2) select articles of interest, and, if appropriate, 3) suggest probable additions or corrections in the translation.

The third step is to summarize articles of interest and to distribute the summaries to a wider audience. At this stage, summaries are preferred to complete translations, because 1) with a large number of articles available on a wide variety of topics, most readers would prefer to be able to read a short summary than a long article, 2) sometimes the most difficult passages to translate are actually unimportant, and can properly be omitted in a summery, 3) getting the grammatical details of a full translation exactly right is a major expense in translation, and 4) a summary with proper reference to the original author avoids some of the requirements of obtaining permission from the original author.

As a possible fourth step, after reading a summary, a reader who is interested in obtaining a full translation may continue to pursue that course.

Translations are facilitated if the translator has read articles in English on similar topics, has discussed similar topics with knowledgeable persons, and is able to ask questions of knowledgeable persons concerning specific passages being translated. Costs can be further reduced as a translator specializes and accumulates experience in a particular field. Given these facilitating factors, it is unnecessary to search for a someone with a masters degree in mechanical engineering, who also has a masters degree in Japanese, who is willing to work as a translator, for a low fee per word.

4.0 CONCLUSIONS

The Japanese have been monitoring American literature assiduously for over a century. Every Japanese schoolchild studies English beginning in middle school. Many American books, including technical books, are translated into Japanese and sell well in Japan almost as soon as they appear in the United States. Virtually every major Japanese company has an office in the United States. One American observer states, "In some companies I have worked for (in Japan) you may find between 20 and 40 percent of all engineers at any given time will be abroad for periods of a couple years -- working for foreign companies, attending foreign universities, doing independent studies about foreign technologies."[a] American industry feels threatened by Japanese competition, but compared to Japanese industry, American industry is doing little to learn from or about its foreign counterpart.

One way to learn from Japan is to monitor Japanese literature. Based on the fact that virtually every American HVAC manufacturer reads the English language JARN: Japan Air Conditioning and Refrigeration News, one can conclude that American HVAC manufacturers would like to know more about Japan's industry if the information were less expensive and more readily available. This article has presented one potential means of providing that service.

(a) "Nipponese Know-How," p. 297, Science News, November 6, 1982.

REFERENCES

"America Starts Looking Over Japan's Shoulder." February 13, 1984. Business Week. p. 136.

Chandler, Clay. September 8, 1987. "U.S. Industry Cool to Tracking Japan's High-Tech Publications." Washington Post.

Congressional Research Service. 1984. The Availability of Japanese Scientific and Technical Information in the United States. U.S. Government Printing Office, Washington, D.C.

Farnsworth, Clyde H. September 6, 1986. "Fishing for Japan's Technology Data." The New York Times.

Gibson, W. David. June 12, 1985. "Tracking Technology Around the Globe." Chemical Week. 136(24):34.

Hane, G.J. October 1987. "Japan Trip Report". U.S. Department of Energy. Washington, D. C.

Hane, G.J. November 1987. HVAC Literature in Japan: A Critical Review. draft report. Pacific Northwest Laboratory. Richland WA.

Hane, G.J. and R.A. Hutchinmson. September 1987. Stirling Engine Research at National and University Laboratories in Japan. PNL-6078. Pacific Northwest Laboratory. Richland, WA.

Hane, G.J., et. al. September 1984. Assessment of Technical Strengths and Information Flow of Energy Conservation Research in Japan. Vol. 1, Executive Summary. PNL-5244, Pacific Northwest Laboratory. Richland, WA.

Hane, G.J. et. al. April 1985. Assessment of Technical Strengths and Information Flow of Energy Conservation Research in Japan. Vol. 2, Background Document, PNL 5244 Vol. 2. Pacific Northwest Laboratory. Richland WA.

Hane, G.J., et al. April 1985. Long-term Research in Japan: Amorphous Metals,Metal Oxide Varistors, High-Power Semi-Conductors and Superconducting Generators. PNL-5376. Pacific Northwest Laboratory. Richland, WA.

Howard, C.D. July 1987. IRM National Reference Series: Japan. An Evaluation Energy Conservation Research and Development. PNL-6237. Pacific Northwest Laboratory. Richland, WA.

Hutchinson, R.A., et. al. 1985. "Information Flow From Japan to U.S. Researchers in Applied and Basic Energy Fields". Journal of Technology Transfer. 10(1):1-10.

"Nipponese Know-How". November 6, 1982. Science News. p.297.
Peters, E.B. February 1975. "International Scientific and Technical Meetings: Why Go? Who Profits?" R&D Management. 5(2):139.

Ronstadt, Robert and Robert J. Kramer. Jan.-Feb. 1985. "Getting The Most Out of Innovation Abroad". Harvard Business Review.

Van Wyk, Rias J. 1984. "Panoramic Scanning and The Technological Environment" Technovation. 2(1):101-120.

INTERNATIONAL FOSSIL ENERGY R&D COLLABORATION

Miles A. Greenbaum
International Programs Manager
U.S. Department of Energy
Office of Fossil Energy

I am pleased to speak to you today to describe the U.S. Department of Energy's Fossil Energy International Program, to provide you with several case examples illustrating just how the U.S. benefits from international research and development (R&D) collaboration projects, and to emphasize the increasing contribution of this program to both U.S. energy and trade security.

International cooperation in energy R&D between the United States and other countries predates the energy crises of the 1970's and the establishment of the U.S. Department of Energy (DOE). As world energy awareness intensified during the 1970's, the DOE was created and became the agency responsible for the majority of international energy activities of interest to the U.S. Within the DOE, the Office of Fossil Energy (FE) is the principal coordinator of fossil energy international activities.

As stated in current policy of the DOE, U.S. national energy policy encourages effective international collaboration in research and development focusing on opportunities to enhance the competitiveness of U.S. technology and industry, and improve long-term national energy security. Furthermore, the U.S. Government is actively seeking to facilitate the long-term reduction of U.S. and international dependence on oil by supporting research which could lead to the development and substitution of other energy forms.

The FE International Program consists of bilateral and multilateral research and information projects established by agreements between the U.S. and foreign countries to improve technologies for producing and using fossil fuels. The program is established within the guidelines of Administration policy and U.S. DOE policy to support longer range, higher risk research with potential for many benefits to the U.S. In support of this policy, therefore, the program goes further than transferring U.S. technology to our bilateral and multilateral partners in that it derives reciprocal benefits for the U.S. in return for any information or technology transferred to these partners. The program is based on the concept of "quid pro quo"--both in terms of direct and indirect benefits--rather than unilateral technology transfer.

To date, there are 46 active bilateral fossil energy agreements underway between the U.S. and 15 foreign countries. The foreign countries involved are Brazil, Canada, Finland, India, Israel, Italy, Japan, Korea, Mexico, Norway, the People's Republic of China (PRC), Spain, the United Kingdom (UK), Venezuela, and Yugoslavia.

In addition, there are eight active multilateral projects--seven under the auspices of the International Energy Agency (IEA), and one with the joint United Nations Institute for Training and Research (UNITAR)/United Nations Development Programme (UNDP) Information Center--with participation varying from three to more than a dozen countries over time. The 21 countries participating in these multilateral projects include Australia, Austria, Belgium, Canada, Denmark, Egypt, the Federal Republic of Germany (FRG), Finland, Ireland, Italy, Japan, Netherlands, New Zealand, Norway, Portugal, Spain, Sweden, Switzerland, Turkey, the UK, and the U.S.

At present there are also eight new, planned bilateral projects between the U.S. and Canada, the FRG, France, Mexico, and the PRC.

International projects involve most of the FE program offices. These offices work with international counterparts to expand, enhance, and leverage their own domestic programs. A majority of these projects are task-shared; that is, each party incurs all the costs associated with carrying out the tasks of the project for which it is responsible. Many of these tasks reflect basic elements of the FE domestic research program and thus incur no additional funding other than that already allocated through the budgetary program. FE also participates in cost-shared agreements in which each party contributes an agreed-upon share of the total costs of a cooperative project.

In evaluating potential collaborative energy R&D activities, it must be evident that an identifiable and equitable value will be realized by either the public or private sectors of the U.S. Key factors related to program rationale are the matching of U.S. domestic program goals and objectives with those of the other parties, and the anticipated receipt of data of at least equal value from the joint effort. In keeping with Administration and DOE policy guidelines, several criteria are considered in the evaluation process:

- Projects should respond to identified U.S. technology needs and should be selected in accordance with individual DOE/FE program goals.
- Projects should merit investment of U.S. funds; however, budgetary constraints may inhibit funding.
- International collaborative projects should not transfer technology to foreign countries without commensurate benefits accruing to the U.S.
- Projects/agreements should be actively pursued which could improve the export potential of U.S. technologies.

In terms of determining quid pro quo, it is important to consider both direct and indirect benefits accrued to the U.S. Several examples of direct benefits and collaborative projects in progress or completed include the following:

Benefit: Supplementing the domestic budget by participating in a project that may be outside the budgetary scope of a domestic venture.

Projects: Two active bilateral implementing agreements with Venezuela--1) a project to evaluate past and ongoing enhanced oil recovery (EOR) projects in the U.S. and Venezuela, and 2) a cooperative effort to develop improved enhanced oil recovery thermal process technology.

In conducting the first project, Venezuela provides EOR data which is used in U.S. modeling activities. Venezuela has also provided assistance with the actual modeling projects and documentation of the modeling. This support has made it possible for the United States to receive the results of EOR activities while contributing only a share of the labor and funding.

With respect to the second agreement, Venezuelan research in both the areas of heavy oil and thermal recovery technology is much more advanced than that of the United States. However, the U.S. can contribute valuable information from other pertinent research and testing projects. Thus, the U.S. can greatly benefit in this cooperative venture for little investment.

Benefit: Participating in foreign demonstration projects which exceed the level of our own government's research and development objectives.

Project: A recently signed bilateral agreement with PAMA (Energy Resources Development) Ltd., a private research facility under contract to the Ministry of Energy and Infrastructure of Israel, to develop a fast-heating rate oil shale retorting process.

The U.S. research effort, which has been examining the effects of shale matrix and kerogen chemical composition has resulted in very limited and unsatisfactory test data. This project gives DOE the opportunity to accelerate access to needed fast-heatup systems test data through use of PAMA's newly modified research unit at relatively low cost. In addition, as DOE data to date has been from laboratory scale retorts, this opportunity to obtain data from PAMA's large-scale research reactors is unique.

Benefit: Developing and pilot-testing new technologies at a fraction of the total cost.

Projects: An active multilateral project utilizing the refurbished, pressurized fluid-bed combustor located at Grimethorpe, UK to install, test, and evaluate a coal-water mixture feed system and test and evaluate an in-bed tube bundle supplied by the U.S. manufacturer Foster Wheeler, at no cost to the project. The memorandum of agreement for the project exists between the United Kingdom's National Coal Board and Central Electricity Generating Board, and the U.S.'s Electric Power Research Institute (EPRI) and the DOE.

Another example in this category is a completed bilateral project with the Federal Republic of Germany in research and development for the conversion of methanol to gasoline/olefins in a fluidized bed reactor. The project involved the design, construction, testing, and evaluation of a plant converting approximately 100 barrels of methanol per day.

This precommercial demonstration accelerated the testing of a promising approach to making conventional transport fuels from methanol--which can be produced from coal--and thus provided a licensable technology for an alternative energy supply. DOE incurred only one-third of the total development costs as a result of this collaborative project, and the U.S. can receive a return of twice the DOE investment through licensing and royalties.

Benefit: Expanding the natural resource base available for research through the testing and application of technologies to natural resources unavailable in the U.S. Similarly, there are benefits from the use of facilities that would otherwise be unavailable.

Projects: An ongoing bilateral agreement with Brazil to evaluate the applicability of underground coal gasification (UCG) to the Triunfo coal deposits in Rio Grande do Sul for producing synthetic gas and other fuels for import substitution.

Through the opportunity provided by the project for the DOE to increase its knowledge base in translating technology to a broad set of resource conditions, the U.S. will have the capability to more efficiently utilize our vast coal resource by increased underground coal gasification technology development. The United States will also benefit from increased market opportunities for U.S. industry as a result of maintaining its leadership role in world-wide UCG technology.

A current bilateral memorandum of understanding with Canada to conduct a program of cooperation in R&D activities in the field of tar sands and heavy oil extraction, processing, and related technologies utilizing Canada's vast 1 to 2 trillion barrels of tar sand bitumen resource and advanced 200,000 barrels per day production capability.

The major benefit for U.S. research is to gain freer access to Canadian state-of-the-art research and test results. This strongly complements the U.S. domestic research program. Specific benefits to date include in situ pilot test design and operational counsel provided by Canadian personnel to DOE researchers, and a methodology for tar sand characterization.

Benefit: Expanding the intellectual resource base without the additional cost of hiring staff. All projects, whether they are information exchange or joint project research, benefit in this way.

Projects: A bilateral memorandum of understanding with Italy to sustain active, cooperative fossil energy R&D efforts through the exchange of scientific and technical data and information; exchange of scientists, engineers, and other specialists; and joint planning for the conduct of research projects.
Through this base agreement, more than a dozen projects have been or will be undertaken utilizing this form of collaborative exchange. Identified areas of common interest to Italy and the United States include:

- advanced environmental control technology
- coal water mixtures
- structure and reactivity of coal

- fluidized bed combustion
- coal logistics study
- combustion study
- coal preparation
- coal liquefaction
- gasification
- enhanced oil recovery
- fuel cells
- magnetohydrodynamics

These coal-related projects will enhance the probability of increased coal and coal technology exportation from the United States to Italy. In addition, this R&D collaboration advances the commercialization opportunities of clean coal technologies.

The direct benefits of international cooperative research and development activities reside in the technical program areas under which they are conducted. Indirect benefits follow as a consequence of improved knowledge of national needs, intents, and capabilities by one R&D partner with respect to another; the opening up of personal and institutional lines of communication leading to increased technical access in both the original and related program areas; and increased confidence, arising from successful cooperation, leading to areas of mutual support which extend beyond R&D--such as new export/import trade relationships, political support in international forums, and other high-value outputs. Specifically, indirect benefits include the following:

- Better understanding of the infrastructure of the international community and the subsequent opening of trade markets and increased purchase of U.S. export fuel (coal), equipment, technology (through licenses), and services.

- Cooperation in the development of international consensus on technical issues (e.g., appropriate near-term responses to global concerns about acid deposition, nuclear waste disposal, and other energy-related technical/environmental matters).

- Sharing of experience and technical information outside of specific R&D projects through cooperation in broad technical assessments of the status of specific emerging technologies and/or the evaluation of measures to enhance shared national objectives (e.g., increased use of coal in the industrial sector).

- The availability of additional communication links, which can be activated in periods of international stress, to transmit information on U.S. objectives and interests, and to receive information on how U.S. actions are perceived and what primary motivating factors are influencing the actions of others (e.g., the experiences of the oil disruptions of the seventies and the European decision to increase natural gas purchases from the Soviets).

- The possible facilitation of extensions of R&D cooperation beyond the sphere of energy (e.g., U.S. initiatives in international cooperation in R&D for space defense).

- The possible facilitation of extensions of R&D cooperation in non-R&D, but energy-related actions (e.g., parallel programs of other countries to develop national versions of the U.S. Strategic Petroleum Reserve).

In many cases, the above indirect benefits, if achieved, enhance the posture of the U.S. private sector. In others, they support U.S Administration policy and strategic objectives.

The United States now faces stiff competition in almost every high-technology sector from governments and companies in both developed and developing countries. All U.S. Government policies must contribute to increased U.S. competitiveness, not only from an economic standpoint, but on the grounds of national security as well. Export competitiveness is essential to the health of the U.S. domestic economy. The U.S. quest for competitiveness in the international arena of fossil fuels can lead to more jobs, the strengthening of national security, and a reduction in the trade deficit. By adhering to a policy that both fosters the competitiveness of U.S. industry in the international fossil energy marketplace and insures its investment through a quid pro quo reciprocity arrangement, the U.S. DOE/FE not only enhances the value of its international collaborative R&D program, but also plays a significant role in the recapturing of our country's world leadership position.

POWER QUALITY MEASUREMENTS: BRINGING ORDER OUT OF CHAOS

François D. Martzloff
National Bureau of Standards
Gaithersburg, MD. 20899

ABSTRACT - The quality of the power supplied to sensitive electronic equipment is an important issue. Quantifying this quality, however, is difficult under the present state of nonexistent or uncoordinated standards concerning two related questions: (1) what levels of power quality are required for what types of loads, and (2) what measurement techniques are required to determine reliably the level of disturbances that reduce quality. Development of standards by the consensus process and voluntary compliance, although a slow process, is a mechanism for reaching technically sound and cost-effective solutions. Several standards projects are in progress, but need an industry-wide support to become the generally accepted basis for valid and useful measurements of power quality.

INTRODUCTION

The issue of Power Quality has gained increased recognition as the result of two unrelated but parallel developments: (1) an increase in the sophistication of electronic systems, sometimes resulting in an unintentional increase in their sensitivity to power supply disturbances, and (2) an increase in the number and power rating of power conversion equipment, generally resulting in the distortion of the power system voltage. Improvements in the situation described as "poor power quality" can be achieved by reducing the sensitivity of equipment to power line disturbances, or by limiting the injection of disturbances -- or better yet, by reducing both in a coordinated approach. While these remedies might seem obvious in principle, their implementation (enforcement) appears more difficult. Voluntary standards provide a guide for such an implementation. To that end, three types of standards are necessary. The first concerns measurements, to obtain correct and universally acceptable data. The second concerns equipment performance, to define both its tolerance to disturbances and its limits on emission of disturbances. The third concerns acceptable disturbance levels on the utility supply, to promote compatibility of equipment with the utility supply. These standards are developed by reconciling purely technical objectives with economic reality. For a standard to be effective and acceptable, both aspects must have an accurate basis. This paper gives emphasis to the technical aspects of the measurements, specifically field measurements of power quality.

THE GOAL: MATCHING EQUIPMENT CAPABILITY WITH POWER QUALITY

To achieve a satisfactory operational environment regarding power quality, a coordinated approach is needed to match the characteristics of equipment with those of the power supply. The concept of matching is important: it implies actions on both sides of the issues, not unilateral demands for corrective action based on a posture that the other party is the offender. Three approaches will lead to this matching, separately or in combination:

1. Increasing equipment tolerance for disturbances,
2. Controlling the emission of disturbances by equipment, (utility equipment as well as end-user equipment)
3. Providing interface devices when necessary.

Each of these three approaches requires accurate information on power supply disturbances for any action to be effective. Action can be preventive, when a potential problem is identified before new equipment is installed. Action can be curative, when a problem arises after new equipment is installed. The problem can appear in two forms: (1) the new equipment is sensitive to disturbances already present in the system (the equipment is the *victim*); (2) the new equipment creates a disturbance that affects equipment already in service (the new equipment is the *offender*).

These two terms used to label the situation reveal the adversarial postures that can exist. In an ideal world, one would consider total system goals to optimize economical and technical solutions, rather than point fingers. In the real world, cooperation can lead to a mutually satisfactory solution between the *source* and the *receiver* of disturbances (note the neutral words) in contrast with the other labels.

The first step towards recognizing the need for improving the power quality situation is to determine the level of disturbances occurring in the system. The parameters characterizing a power supply are: frequency, voltage amplitude, waveform, and symmetry. Therefore, the nature of disturbances may be classified by their effect on these four parameters. The severity of disturbances is associated with their amplitude, their duration, and the probability of occurring at a given site over a time period.

The level of disturbances is determined by measurements conducted at the site of an existing installation or at a future installation of potentially sensitive equipment. These measurements are described as "site surveys." If the tolerance of the equipment for disturbances is defined (a need that is not always recognized) and the level of disturbances determined by the site survey is excessive, then the three matching actions mentioned above come into play. Any one of the three, or a combination, can be the most effective solution. Knowledge of the situation will point toward a solution, rather than reliance on a common misconception that providing a simple interface (line conditioning) will solve all problems. This misconception is nurtured by frequent observations that many problems have in fact been solved by simply inserting a line conditioner. However, one should not yield to the temptation of making a general rule from these isolated success stories, and ignore other, more effective or more economical approaches achieving inherent compatibility.

Because this additional line conditioning equipment may require significant capital investment, the choice of corrective measures is made by economic trade-off. However, if technical inputs to this trade-off are incorrect because erroneous conclusions result from a faulty site survey, the whole process is worthless or misleading. For this reason, a good understanding of the merits and limitations of site surveys is essential for reconciling expectations with reality before specifying expensive line conditioning equipment. In their review of power quality site surveys, Martzloff and Gruzs [1] discussed how one should deal, not with fiction or fallacies, but with facts.

In an attempt to clarify the issues, this paper first presents a review of the origins and definitions of disturbances. Next, the development of monitoring instruments during the last 25 years is described. Finally, an appeal is made for improving measurement methods to provide more consistent reporting of power disturbances recorded in future surveys.

CLASSIFICATION AND ORIGIN OF POWER LINE DISTURBANCES

The four power system parameters identified above -- frequency, amplitude, waveform, and symmetry -- can serve as frame of reference to classify the disturbances according to their impact on these four parameters.

Frequency disturbances are associated with power system faults. Interconnection of the utility grid ensures frequency stability, except when a fault occurs that isolates the local system from the grid, leaving local generation more sensitive to load variations. Transient frequency disturbances, just before an outage, occur in a system containing large rotating machines: should the system trip out, the machines will maintain some voltage, with decaying amplitude and frequency, while they coast to a final stop.

Amplitude variations can occur in several forms; their description is inextricably associated with their duration. They range from extremely brief durations to steady-state conditions, making the description and definition difficult, even controversial at times. Their causes and effects need close examination to understand the mechanisms and to define an appropriate solution.

Waveform variations occur when nonlinear loads draw a current which is not sinusoidal. One could also describe an amplitude variation as momentary waveform variation, but the intended meaning of the term is a steady variation of the waveform, or lasting at least over several cycles. This type of disturbance is also described as harmonic distortion because it is easy to analyze as the superposition of harmonics to the fundamental frequency of the power system.

Dissymmetry, also called unbalance, occurs when unequal single-phase loads are connected to a three-phase system and cause a loss of symmetry. This type of disturbance primarily concerns rotating machines, and as such is not receiving broad attention. It is important however, for machine designers and users. The percentage by which one phase voltage differs from the average of all three is the usual description of this type of disturbance.

The origin of disturbances can be described as external to the particular power system, or as internal. In a typical situation, the boundary of a power system is defined as the watthour meter, and reference is made to the utility side of the meter (external source), or to the user side of the meter (internal source). A different approach is to describe the origin in technical terms, such as lightning, load switching, power system fault, and nonlinear loads. Depending on local conditions, one can be more important than the others, but all need to be recognized. The mechanism involved in generating the disturbance also determines whether the occurrence will be random or permanent, unpredictable or easy to define.

Lightning surges are the result of direct strikes to the power system conductors as well as the result of indirect effects. Indirect effects include induction of overvoltages in loops formed by conductors and ground potential rises resulting from lightning current in the soil. A lightning strike to thc power system can activate a surge arrester, producing a severe reduction or a complete loss of the power system voltage for one half-cycle. A flashover of line insulators can cause a breaker to trip, with reclosing delayed by several cycles, causing a momentary power outage. Thus, lightning can be the obvious cause of overvoltages near its point of impact, but also a less obvious cause of voltage loss at a considerable distance from its point of impact. Clearly, the occurrence of this type of disturbance is unpredictable at the microscopic level. At the macroscopic level, it is related to geography, seasons, and local system configuration.

Load switching is a major cause of disturbances. Switching large loads on or off can produce long-duration voltage changes beyond the immediate transient response of the circuit. Whether the switching is done by the utility or by the user is immaterial from the technical point of view, although the responsibility may be the subject of a contractual dispute. The occurrence of these disturbances is somewhat predictable, but not necessarily under controlled conditions. The introduction of power conversion equipment and voltage regulators operating by switching on and off at high frequency has created a new type of load switching disturbance. These disturbances occur steadily, although their amplitude and harmonic content will vary for a given regulator as the load conditions vary.

Power system faults occur on both sides of the meter, resulting from equipment failure or external causes (vehicle collisions, storms, human errors). These disturbances can range from a momentary voltage reduction to a complete loss of power lasting for minutes, hours, or days. Their accidental origin makes them unpredictable, although the configuration of a power system and its environment can make it more or less prone to this type of disturbance.

Nonlinear loads draw non-sinusoidal currents from the power system, even if the power system voltage is a perfect sine wave. These currents produce non-sinusoidal voltage drops in the system source impedance which distort the sine wave produced by the power plant generator. A typical nonlinear load is a dc power supply with capacitor-input filter, such as used in most computers, drawing current only at the peaks of the voltage sine wave.

Characterizing these four types of disturbances and disturbance mechanisms involves detection (measurement) of their occurrence and description of the results of these measurements. What might appear a simple process is in fact made difficult by deficiencies in defining disturbances observed when making site survey measurements.

DEFICIENCIES IN DEFINITIONS

One difficulty in coordinating efforts for improving power quality is that terms used to describe power disturbances are poorly defined. An effort is being made by standards writing organizations to resolve this problem, as described later in this paper, but consensus has yet to be reached. The following two examples of this lack of consensus illustrate the point; resolving them is beyond the scope of this paper.

What is a surge? The accepted meaning of surge, in the context of power systems, is a short-duration overvoltage, typically less than a few milliseconds. These surges are caused by lightning, power system switching, or faults. Protection against them is obtained by protective devices called *surge arresters* (formerly called lightning arresters) for utility systems, and *surge suppressors*, or spike suppressors for end-user systems. This first meaning of the word 'surge' is not that established by manufacturers and users of disturbance monitors and line conditioners. The unfortunate second meaning, a consequence of nonexistent standards on the subject, is a momentary overvoltage at the fundamental frequency, with a duration of typically a few cycles. What the designers and users of surge arresters or suppressors calls 'surge' is called 'impulse' or 'spike' by the monitoring instrument community. Figure 1 shows graphic descriptions of the confusion created by the dual meaning of the word 'surge.'

What is an outage? Most users agree that it means a loss of line voltage. The duration of this event, however, is quite different when 'outage' is cited by computer users (as short as one half-cycle), or by power engineers (seconds, perhaps minutes). Furthermore, some users and manufacturers of line conditioners do not make a clear distinction between complete loss of line voltage (zero voltage condition), severe undervoltages ('deep sags'), or the single-phasing of polyphase power systems. Part of the problem may be that the definition of 'outage' has regulatory implications for evaluating the performance of public utility companies.

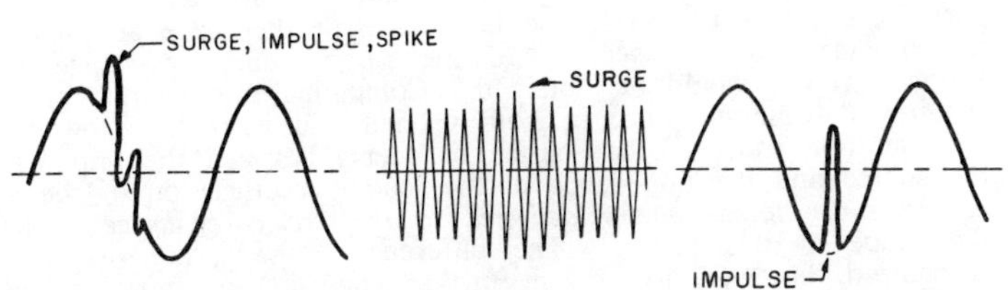

Figure 1 - Graphic illustration of different meaning of 'surges' and other disturbances

As another example of definitions deficiencies, standards dictionaries do not define the term 'sag'. It is accepted as meaning a momentary voltage reduction at the ac power frequency. However, there is no consensus on the details (threshold, duration, etc.) of what characterizes a sag.

With the present definition deficiencies, manufacturers and users of disturbance monitors are left without guidance and consequently define terms independently from each other, hence the confusion. In fact, the development and widespread use of disturbance monitors should motivate a more coordinated and rational approach toward resolving these deficiencies. Progress in technology of monitoring instruments during the last two decades is remarkable and worthy of a brief review.

DISTURBANCE MONITORS DEVELOPMENT HISTORY

Historically, the first (unintended) disturbance monitors were the actual load equipment. Only later, when confronted with unexplained failures or upsets, did the users start monitoring the quality of their power systems. Electric utilities have been monitoring the parameters of their systems, but the precise characterization of microsecond-duration surges in the early 1960s required special oscilloscopes. For the next 15 years, oscilloscopes or simple peak-detectors were the basic instruments for monitoring transient overvoltages. Starting in the 1970s, commercially-produced digitizers became available. Since then, technology has made continuing progress as experience has accumulated.

Early site surveys were limited to voltage measurements. This limited interest reflected concerns for damage to sensitive electronic components connected across the line. Ignoring the importance of the source impedance led to some performance standards [2] that do not specify the current-handling requirements for surge protective devices. With the introduction and widespread application of new clamping protective devices (silicon avalanche diodes or metal oxide varistors), the surge current diverted through these devices became a very important factor for proper device selection. Therefore, the need emerged for characterizing current surges as well as voltage surges, but few surveys to date have addressed this need. This need offers a challenge and an opportunity to designers of monitoring instruments.

This challenge has also produced attempts to measure 'energy' with an instrument which is actually only a voltmeter. By assigning parametric values to the source impedance of the surge and integrating the product (volts · seconds) of the surge, some knowledge of the energy involved would be obtained. Computing true energy, of course, requires the measurement of both voltage and current. However, the real question concerns the sharing of energy between the impedance of the source and the impedance of the load. A discussion of the *energy in the surge* versus *energy delivered to the protective device* is beyond the scope of this paper. The difference between the two must be recognized, however, to prevent further confusion as future monitoring instruments include an 'energy' parameter in their readouts.

With the present development of sophisticated multi-channel digitizing instruments, future surveys should monitor both voltage and current. Note, however, that the current of interest is that which the surge source would force through a surge protective device. The amplitude as well as the waveform of the surges needs to be characterized for the correct application of surge protective devices. Peak-reading monitors provide useful information on surge activity at a given site, but assessment of the surge severity level for the proper sizing of protective devices also requires waveform and source impedance information.

One difficulty facing users of monitoring instruments in this fast-paced technology is that manufacturers are steadily improving their instruments. These improved features respond to specific wishes of the users or result from their own product research and development, a desirable situation. On the negative side, however, data collected by different instruments become equipment-dependent. Comparison of survey results by third parties is then difficult in the absence of details on the instrument characteristics and methods of measurement.

TYPES OF MONITORS

The instruments used in past surveys reflect technology progress as well as logistics constraints, resulting in a diversity of approaches. Until recently, all monitoring instruments were just special voltmeters. Some of the monitors recorded a single parameter, such as the value of voltage peaks, or the occurrence of voltage peaks above a preset threshold. Other monitors combined time with voltage measurements, to characterize the voltage waveforms. The following list shows the evolution of simple surge monitors into complex disturbance monitors.

Threshold counters - The surge is applied to a calibrated voltage divider, triggering a counter each time it exceeds a preset threshold. The early types had analog circuitry; more recent types have digital conversion of signals.

Digital peak recorders - The surge is converted to a digital value and recorded in a buffer memory for later playback. In the early types of recorders, only the peak was recorded. In later types, the duration of the surge was also recorded, opening the way to the more complex digital waveform recorders now available.

Oscilloscope with camera - The surge triggers a single sweep on the cathode ray tube of the oscilloscope, and is recorded as it occurs by an automatic shutterless camera.

Screen storage oscilloscope - The surge is displayed and stored on the cathode ray tube, and a camera is used for permanent recording after the surge has occurred. The writing speed capability of these oscilloscopes was a limitation in the late 1960s.

Digital storage oscilloscope - The surge is digitized and stored in a shift register for subsequent playback and display whenever it exceeds a preset threshold. An important feature is the capability of displaying events occurring before the beginning of the surge.

Digital waveform recorder - With the advent of compact, portable instruments, a revolution has taken place in the field of disturbance recorders. The earlier surge waveform recorders were large and difficult to transport to field sites [3], [4]. New microprocessor-based instruments have introduced a portable storage and computing power which has made waveform analysis and graphic display possible. In these instruments, voltage and current signals are digitized and stored, allowing reports of many different parameters of the disturbance. The range of parameters which can be monitored is expanded, long trends can be detected, harmonic analysis can be performed, and the types of possible measurements are limited only by the creativity of the instrument designers and the curiosity of the users.

Although some site surveys might aim at high accuracy, the real world experiences an infinite variety of disturbances, making it difficult to fit them into simple, orderly categories. Any attempt to describe these disturbances in fine detail restricts general usefulness of the data and can lead to illusions on applicable accuracy. Some simple (and inexpensive) instruments are useful indicators of frequent disturbances. Other instruments, more complex (and more expensive), provide comprehensive data on disturbances. A general observation from many surveys conducted by different researchers is that results vary widely from site to site. Thus, there is a practical limit to the detail that a survey can yield, and unrealistic expectations of precise information should be avoided. What is really needed is a more uniform and compatible recording and reporting of the data.

COMPARISONS AMONG SITE SURVEY REPORTS

Relative occurrence of different types of disturbances. Two site surveys have been widely cited. One was performed in the early 1970s by Allen and Segall [5], the other in the late 1970s by Goldstein and Speranza [6]. Each of these surveys presented results by describing various kinds of disturbances (overvoltages, sags, etc.) and cited the percentages of each type of disturbance in the total of all the observed disturbances. The findings did not at first appear to agree, raising questions on the likelihood of a change in power systems between the first and second survey. However, a detailed comparison of these two surveys [1], revealed that the disagreement was rooted in a difference of the thresholds built into the monitors, rather than a change in the behavior of power systems.

Differences in surge amplitudes. Amplitudes of surges reported in several surveys vary over a wide range. Comparisons are difficult because the reports do not present the data in a uniform format. Attempting to get a quantitative comparison of the amplitudes reported seems a futile exercise, because of the following reasons:

1. Looking at the 'maximum values' cited in the reports, one finds that in some surveys this maximum is actually a value known only as being above the range of the instrument, while for others it is the measured value.

2. Because the threshold of the recorder varies among surveys, and the frequency of occurrences increases dramatically with a lower threshold, the labels of average, median, most frequent, typical, etc., are not meaningful for comparing amplitudes.

Differences in surge waveforms. What a 'typical' surge might be has been the subject of many discussions. Several surveys confirm the finding of ringing waves, as opposed to the traditional unidirectional impulses. However, wide differences still exist among the reports. The following examples illustrate this point.

Martzloff-Hahn [7] were among the first to report ring waves, recorded by 1960 vintage oscilloscopes. Their findings were incorporated into the data that resulted in the selection of a 100 kHz ring wave for the UL Standard *Ground Fault Circuit Interrupters* [8] and the IEEE *Guide on Surge Voltages* [9].

Odenberg and Braskich [10] used different instruments recording only two points of the waveform: (1) the peak amplitude and time to peak, and (2) the time to 50% of the peak amplitude. As such, this description is not a complete waveform. Furthermore, they reported that 90% of their 250,000 recordings show the 50% point occurred between 900 and 1100 microseconds. This finding is unique among all the surveys.

Wernstrom et al. [11] report ring waves of 500 kHz, bursts of fast transients lasting a few microseconds, and even some unidirectional isolated impulses.

Goedbloed [12] is more concerned with interference than damage; his report gives emphasis to amplitude, rate of rise, and 'energy', rather than to waveform.

With the advent of portable monitors capable of presenting the digitized data with graphic details as well as summaries, an explosion in the volume of data can expected. Just the detail and weight of the information being collected might swamp the researchers, unless data reduction procedures are implemented. However, whenever data reductions are performed by different persons, there is a high probability that criteria for reduction will be different, making comparisons difficult, even impossible. Thus, this increased sophistication of available instrumentation makes coordination even more imperative. The added availability of harmonic analysis by portable monitors will also lead to an expansion of data supporting standards on harmonic control [13].

Agreement and disagreement on rate of occurrence versus levels. Several survey authors have attempted to fit a classic statistical distribution or a simple relationship between the rate of occurrence of surges and their amplitude. The motivation for such a simplified presentation might be rooted in a belief that nature obeys simple mathematical laws. The reality, however, is that so many different mechanisms contribute to the generation of surges that a simple relationship is unlikely. Notwithstanding this rationale, a remarkable finding emerges from plotting the results of all the surveys on the same graph. Figure 2 shows the relative distributions of the findings, normalized for voltage level and frequency of occurrence for each survey report. The *slope* of the lines is what can be compared, not the absolute rate of occurrence. It is remarkable that slopes are similar among the surveys, although the absolute frequency of occurrence is site-dependent.

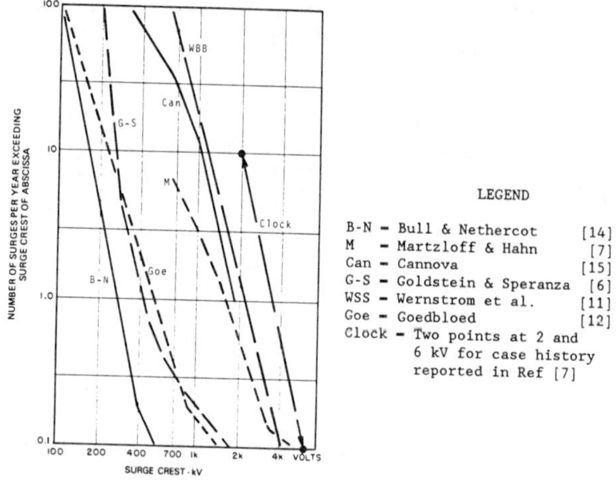

Figure 2 - Rate of surge occurrence as a function of peak voltage

WORKING TOWARD MORE CONSISTENT SURVEYS

The ambiguities plaguing the field of site surveys have become apparent to many interested researchers, resulting in the formation by IEEE of a new Working Group on Monitoring Electrical Quality. The scope of a Recommended Practice being prepared by this group reads:

> This Recommended Practice concerns the application of instruments used for monitoring electrical disturbances on power systems. The scope includes the definition of disturbance terms, the calibration and connection of the instruments, and the interpretation and reporting of the results. It does not include specific design aspects of the instruments.
>
> The disturbances of interest are those conducted on ac power lines for single or polyphase systems with direct operating voltage connections to the instruments not exceeding 1000 V RMS. Depending on the design of the instruments, the duration of the recorded disturbances may range from nanoseconds to many seconds, or more.
>
> While the prime interest is focused on monitoring low-voltage ac power systems (50, 60 or 400 Hz), suitable interfaces may allow monitoring systems of higher voltage; dc systems may also be monitored with these instruments. It is also recognized that available instruments may be capable of monitoring other parameters such as radiated EMI or environmental conditions; however, the scope of this document is limited to conducted electrical parameters (voltage, current, and derived parameters).

EXPECTATIONS VERSUS REALITY ON POWER QUALITY

Improved credibility of power quality data offers an opportunity to revisit existing standards or develop new standards dealing with power quality. Three areas would benefit from this review:

1. **More realistic definitions of the limits of system voltages.** The limits currently defined are relatively small percentages (5 to 15%) of nominal values. Many anecdotal stories have been told on momentary overvoltages exceeding the limits of the only standard addressing these limits, ANSI C84.1 [16]. Until well documented, these stories can only remain anecdotal. However, ignoring them can lead to misapplication of surge protective devices by attempting to suppress surges at a level too close to the momentary overvoltages that do occur.

2. **Improved consensus on the characteristics of surges.** The IEEE Guide on Surge Voltages [9], dating back to 1980, attempted to simplify the situation by describing the surge environment with only two waveforms and an upper practical limit. Unfortunately, this Guide was misconstrued by some users as a mandatory standard. A revision is underway, proposing two additional waveforms and presenting the information in a manner that should discourage the misguided use of the document as a performance standard.

3. **Improved Consensus on harmonic control.** Harmonic causes and effects have been the subject of many studies and technical papers, but no performance standard exists to settle potential disputes between sources and receivers of harmonic distortion. The prevailing document is a Guide [13]; significant improvements are expected from a revision currently being conducted.

CONCLUSIONS

Power quality measurements, typically performed by site surveys, have evolved from the simple monitoring of surge voltages to the sophisticated analysis of many criteria of power quality. There is still room for improvement in the procedures -- an improvement that can be guided by voluntary standards. Detailed observation of the issues lead to the following conclusions:

1. **Considerable progress** has been made in the recording capability of monitoring instruments as the result of progress in the hardware and software used in digitizing systems. Improvements include multi-channel synchronized recording of different parameters, fast data acquisition, automated data reduction, and improved resolution.

2. **Improvements in consistency** must be made, commensurate with the steady progress and expanded capability of instruments. This greater consistency is needed in the definitions of the disturbance parameters and the methods of application of the monitoring instruments.

3. **Site-to-site variations** in the occurrence of disturbances prevent making precise predictions for a specific site from an overall data base.

4. **Differences among results** indicated by a cursory comparison can be resolved by a closer examination of the conditions under which the surveys were conducted. However, some differences are less likely to be explained if raw data have been processed and the initial parameter measurements are no longer available for review.

5. **A new IEEE Working Group** on Monitoring Electrical Quality has been formed with a broad scope that encompasses this process of improving consistency in definitions and interpretation of power disturbances. In addition, the IEEE Working Group on Surge Characterization is also attempting to obtain a broader data base for the revision of the *Guide on Surge Voltages*.

6. **Improved cooperation**, promoted by the process of voluntary standards development and the exchange of ideas made possible by forums such as the Energy Technology Conference, will avoid some of the difficulties on sharing the data pool recited in this paper. This paper is presented in support of this effort and to promote greater participation among interested workers and users.

REFERENCES

1. Martzloff, F.D., and Gruzs, T.M., "Power Quality Site Surveys: Facts, Fiction, and Fallacies," *Conference Record*, IEEE Industrial & Commercial Power Systems Conference, May 4-7, 1987.

2. *Interface Standard for Shipboard Systems*, DOD-STD-1399, Sec. 300, 1978.

3. Allen, G.W., "Design of Power-Line Monitoring Equipment," *IEEE Transactions on Power Apparatus and Systems*, Vol. PAS-90, No.6, Nov/Dec 1971.

4. Key, T.S, "Diagnosing Power Quality-Related Computer Problems," *IEEE Transactions on Industry Applications*, Vol. IA-15, No. 4, July/August 1979.

5. Allen, G.W., and Segall, D., "Monitoring of Computer Installation for Power Line Disturbances," *IEEE PES Winter Meeting, Conference Paper C74199-6*, January 1974.

6. Goldstein, M., and Speranza, P.D., "The Quality of U.S. Commercial AC Power," *Proceedings of INTELEC Conference*, 82CH1818-4, 1982.

7. Martzloff, F.D., and Hahn, G.J., "Surge Voltages in Residential and Industrial Power Circuits," *IEEE Transactions on Power Apparatus & Systems*, Vol. PAS-89, No. 6, July/August 1970.

8. *UL Standard for Safety 943, Ground Fault Circuit Interrupters*, Underwriters Laboratories, 1976.

9. *Guide on Surge Voltages in Low-Voltage AC Power Circuits*, ANSI/IEEE C62.41-1980.

10. Odenberg, R., and Braskich, B., "Measurements of Voltage and Current Surges on the AC Power Line in Computer and Industrial Environments," *IEEE Transactions on Power Apparatus and Systems,* Vol. PAS-104, No. 10, October 1985.

11. Wernstrom, H., Broms, M., and Boberg, S., *Transient Overvoltages on AC Power Supply Systems in Swedish Industry, Report FOA E 30002-E2,* Foorsvarets Forskningsanstalt, Huvudavdelning 3, Sweden, 1984.

12. Goedbloed, J.J., "Transients in Low-Voltage Supply Networks," *IEEE Transactions on EMC*, May 1987.

13. *IEEE Guide for Harmonic Control and Reactive Compensation of Static Power Converters* ANSI/IEEE Std 519-1981.

14. Bull, J.H. and Nethercot, M.A., "The Frequency of Occurrence and Magnitude of Short Duration Transients in Low-Voltage Supply Mains," *Radio Electronic Engineer,* September 1964.

15. Cannova, S.F., "Short-time Voltage Transients in Shipboard Electrical Systems," *Conference Record,* IEEE-IAS 1972 Annual Meeting, CHO685-8-IA.

16. *American National Standard for Electric Power Systems and Equipment - Voltage Ratings (60 Hz),* ANSI C84.1-1982.

AUTHOR INDEX